McCUTCHEON
ON
INHERITANCE TAX

McCUTCHEON
ON
INHERITANCE TAX

Sixth Edition by

Withers LLP

Aparna Nathan LL.B (Hon.)   and   Marika Lemos M.A.
LL.M (LSE, London)   (Cantab.), LLM (Lond)
Barrister of the   Barrister of the
Middle Temple   Middle Temple

Both at Gray's Inn Tax Chambers, London

SWEET & MAXWELL   THOMSON REUTERS

2013

First Edition 1980
Second Edition 1984
Third Edition 1988
Fourth Edition 2004
Fifth Edition 2009
Sixth Edition 2013

Published in 2013 by
Thomson Reuters (Legal) Limited
(Registered in England & Wales,
Company No 1679046. Registered Office and address
for service: 100 Avenue Road, London, NW3 3PF)
trading Sweet & Maxwell. For further information on
our products and services, visit *www.sweetandmaxwell.co.uk*
Computerset by Interactive Sciences Ltd, Gloucester
Printed and bound in Great Britain by
TJ International, Padstow, Cornwall

No natural forests were destroyed to make this product;
only farmed timber was used and replanted.

A C.I.P. Catalogue record for this book is available from the British Library

ISBN 978-0-41402-502-8

Withers LLP wish to acknowledge the contribution of the following, together with their secretaries and other support, in the production of the Sixth Edition of this book.

Murray Hallam	Lucy Johnson
Dora Clarke	Caroline Moss
Imogen Davies	Robin Waghorn
Tim George	Matthew Woods
Christopher Groves	

Together with

Sophie Carter	Lauren Peaty
Claire Harris	Robert Posgate
Paul Fairbairn	James Radcliffe
Christopher King	Venetia Taylor
Robert McLean	Caroline Thompson
Chris Munday	Moire Trustram Eve
Filippo Noseda	

PREFACE TO THE SIXTH EDITION

It is now three years since the last edition of McCutcheon. There have been no major changes equivalent to the revised taxation of trusts that took place in 2006. Changes, however, have been made and the tax has continued to evolve. Two wholly new chapters on the Human Rights Act and on new anti-avoidance measures have been added. Despite what is said in the draft GAAR, or perhaps because of it, the barriers between tax evasion, tax avoidance and basic tax planning are now less clear cut than they were. Measures to tax the ownership and transfer of wealth are more commonly proposed in the UK than elsewhere even if not implemented. Rumours of the amelioration or indeed abandonment of the tax have dissipated, but the need to understand the tax, its development and ramifications remains constant. Aparna Nathan and Marika Lemos, both of Gray's Inn Tax Chambers, have revised the Special Trust Section and added the two new chapters. The remaining chapters had been brought up to date by Withers LLP, with some editorial contributions, in particular to the chapter on Partnerships, by Marika Lemos. As in previous editions, Chapter 1, the overview, has been retained essentially in its original form as composed by Barry McCutcheon QC, as it sets out the framework for the tax. It is a tribute to his perspicacity that it remains relevant more than 30 years on from the first publication of the book.

Sweet & Maxwell have updated the index.

The law is stated as at April 5, 2012, but, where possible, later developments have been incorporated.

Withers LLP
Marika Lemos
Aparna Nathan

PREFACE TO THE FOURTH EDITION

There have been many developments since the last edition of this book 16 years ago. We have taken the opportunity of incorporating these developments to review the book generally. The result is that the book has been extensively rewritten and reorganised. Perhaps three developments are particularly worth mentioning. First, a new section of the book is devoted to the international dimension which includes material not readily available elsewhere on such matters of interest to the international estate planner as forced heirship regimes, both in Europe and the Islamic world, community property regimes and key international tax planning considerations. The discussion of double tax treaties has also been expanded. Secondly, the rewriting of the provisions dealing with reservation of benefit provisions includes, in keeping with the policy of considering other relevant tax developments, a supplementary discussion of the preowned assets regime introduced by the Finance Act 2004. Finally, the chapter on business relief and agricultural relief, beside putting the many case law developments into perspective, has been extensively reorganised with a view to fostering a systematic approach in this complicated and often misunderstood area.

Finally, two comments on presentation. First, as a general rule, discussion of planning points is now generally highlighted by a separate, flagged heading. Secondly, as per previous editions, the authors have themselves prepared the index with a view to allowing readers to locate material in the book as easily as possible.

The law is stated as at August 31, 2004.

November 2004

Barry McCutcheon
Withers

APPROACH AND STRUCTURE

The underlying purpose of this book has always been to foster in readers a genuine understanding of how inheritance tax works and that remains the underlying goal of this edition. But, how best to do this?

The first edition was written in response to the introduction by the Finance Act 1975 of capital transfer tax, the predecessor to inheritance tax. Capital transfer tax replaced estate duty, and the temptation was to examine capital transfer tax with the same eyes as had been engaged in peering into the murky depths of its venerable predecessor.

The first edition recognised that, while all the estate duty learning had not been rendered irrelevant overnight, it was vital to recognise that capital transfer tax was a self-contained tax with an unusually coherent structure which needed to be understood on its own terms and that seeing it through estate duty eyes could be at best misleading and at worst counterproductive. Accordingly, the first edition emphasised the architecture of capital transfer tax with a view to encouraging readers to accept that the estate duty era was indeed a thing of the past and enabling them to develop a comprehensive approach to advising on transactions with capital transfer tax implications. It did so, in one respect, in a rather unusual way—its structure reflected the structure of the tax. Accordingly, rather than dealing with the categories of property or circumstances which readers were likely to encounter in everyday practice, it concerned itself with how the tax was designed to operate. It was, if you like, "organic" before that approach became fashionable.

Capital transfer tax lent itself to this approach because, at least in its original form, with its unusually coherent conceptual structure it was a "designer tax". Based upon the fundamental premise that all gifts of property, whether made during lifetime or on death, should be cumulated together and progressive rates of tax applied to the ever-increasing cumulative total it was, in every sense, a cradle to grave tax with the passing of a taxpayer's property on death being merely the last of his gifts. As an intellectual bonus, the tax included a special regime for taxing property held on discretionary ("relevant property") trusts, which property would otherwise have been outside the scope of a tax aimed at individuals.

Changes to the legislation over the years derogated from the conceptual coherence of the tax, but until the Finance Act 1986 the basic edifice remained intact. It would be easy to think that that Act, by introducing the potentially exempt transfer regime and the reservation of benefit rules—and changing the name of the tax to "inheritance tax"—so distorted the tax as to alter it beyond recognition. This, however, was not the case. The basic structure of the tax remained intact, but its centre of gravity shifted so that the emphasis changed to making potentially exempt transfers that were not caught by the reservation of benefit rules. In taking account of the changes introduced by the 1986 Act, the third edition therefore retained its original structure.

Choosing an approach

By the time it came to write the fourth edition, it was appropriate to ask whether it is worth retaining the original approach. The advantage of that approach is that it aims to ensure that the reader understands how the tax actually works so that he develops an underlying confidence in his ability to diagnose and solve problems. The disadvantage is that sometimes it does not always allow readers to find the answer to the precise problem with which they think they are confronted as quickly as they might like.

The authors' experience has been that the original approach continues to recommend itself and it has therefore been followed in this sixth edition. Readers have found this approach helpful in the past, should do so in the future and, indeed, have come to expect it from *McCutcheon*. Experience has shown that inheritance tax often gives rise to subtle points which may elude superficial analysis. This is particularly true where inheritance tax is being considered as a derivative issue arising as the result of, e.g., capital gains tax planning. There is simply no diagnostic substitute for a thorough grounding in the architecture of the tax and this is perhaps further substantiated by the interaction between inheritance tax and the new pre-owned assets regime. So far as accessing immediate problems is concerned, this is made easy with a comprehensive index specifically designed to aid the reader in his search by characterising topics in as many different ways as possible.

It is perhaps worth noting in this context that, since the third edition, private client work has experienced significant growth, increased prestige and accompanying profability, not least because of the substantial increase in privately held wealth. This development has not been without its downside—private client work has never been so perilous. Private client practitioners now find themselves faced with a range of more complicated and challenging issues than was hitherto the case and will therefore be called upon to develop the theoretical tools needed to advise confidently on inheritance tax. We hope that *McCutcheon* continues to be of assistance in this regard.

Using this book

The book can be used at two levels. First, as an explanation of the tax generally and as a guide to analysing such transactions as real life may present. Secondly, as a commentary on specific issues.

So far as the former is concerned, the structure of the book is informed by and follows that of the tax. Thus, in the same way that the tax has two sets of charging provisions, so the first two parts of the book deal with these provisions in turn. Part 1 is concerned with how the tax conceptually attacks property generally, whether settled or non-settled. The book refers to the provisions dealing which such property as "the main charging provisions". Part 2 addresses the treatment of a special subset of settled property, that held on relevant property trusts, referring to the provisions dealing which such property as "the special charging provisions".

Considerable emphasis is thus placed on appreciating the conceptual hierarchy of the tax, with introductory chapters concerning structure being included in both Parts 1 and 2. *Readers are strongly recommended initially to read these chapters by way of introduction to the tax* (they are not very long).

Part 3 then deals with various considerations which are common to both Parts 1 and 2. Lastly, Part 4 addresses the international dimension which is of increased importance for private client practitioners and which, again, impacts on both Parts 1 and 2.

The book continues to be intended primarily to be of assistance to practitioners, and should serve as a reference work on most points. Readers' criticism, suggestions and comments generally, whether as to technical or stylistic matters, will be gratefully received.

The Inheritance Tax Manual

The authors' policy towards referring to HMRC's Inheritance Tax Manual (IHTM) is to refer readers to relevant passages selectively, where they think it particularly helpful to do so, but not exhaustively on the basis that the Manual is readily available to readers to consult.

INTRODUCTION

Most countries impose some kind of wealth tax, usually in the form of a death duty levied on property inherited or on the value of a deceased's estate on death. The United Kingdom introduced estate duty in 1894 as a tax on property in a deceased's estate at death, whether that property passed under a will, on intestacy or otherwise. Over its long life estate duty was then extended from this relatively narrow fiscal base to catch gifts made in the period before death. By the time it was replaced by capital transfer tax, it had been extended to embrace gifts made by the deceased in the seven years before his death. By the 1970s estate duty was widely criticised as a voluntary tax—voluntary in the sense that it could be avoided by the simple expedient of giving away property and living for seven years or, alternatively, by taking advantage of the numerous loopholes afforded by the legislation. Its replacement by an inheritance tax was considered by the then Conservative Government in 1972 but, in the event, it was the Labour Government's return to office in 1974 which saw the duty replaced by capital transfer tax. The main purpose of this new tax was, in the words of the then Chancellor Denis Healey, "to make the estate duty not a voluntary tax, but a compulsory tax, as it was always intended to be".

Capital transfer tax was in many ways a brilliantly simple tax in conception since it was based upon the fundamental premise that all gifts of property, whether made *inter vivos* or on death, should be cumulated together and progressive rates of tax applied to the ever-increasing cumulative total. In every sense, therefore, it was a cradle to grave tax with the passing of a taxpayer's property on death being merely the final gift.

The advent of Conservative Governments since 1979 resulted in a steady erosion in some of the basic principles of capital transfer tax. Ten-year cumulation (introduced in 1981) removed the old concept of a cradle to grave tax, whilst the Finance Act 1986 effected fundamental reforms. Donors could, under the new potentially exempt transfer regime, once again escape tax by making gifts which they survived by seven years, cumulation was reduced to a seven-year period and provisions, modelled on the old estate duty, were introduced to deal with gifts subject to a reservation. The Chancellor, Nigel Lawson, also seized the opportunity to re-christen the tax "inheritance tax", which change took effect from July 25, 1986. The current position is that the old capital transfer tax legislation (consolidated as the Capital Transfer Act 1984) *may* now be cited as the Inheritance Tax Act 1984. All references to capital transfer tax take effect as references to inheritance tax; as all references to estate duty became references to capital transfer tax in 1974, they, in turn, are now references to inheritance tax. Accordingly, the legislative basis of inheritance tax is the 1984 Act together with various changes effected in subsequent Finance Acts.

Capital transfer tax, in its original form, was characterised by an unusually coherent conceptual structure, and the main thrust of the first edition of this book was to identify and stress that structure, both with a view to encouraging readers to accept that the estate duty era was indeed a thing of the past and enabling them to develop a comprehensive approach to advising on transactions with capital transfer tax implications.

Changes to the legislation over the years have derogated from the conceptual coherence of the tax, but until 1986 the basic edifice remained intact. It would be easy to think that, by introducing the potentially exempt transfer regime and the reservation of benefit rules (and changing the name of the tax to "inheritance tax"), the Finance Act 1986 so reformed the tax that its original structure was altered beyond recognition. This, however, is not the case. The basic structure of the tax remains intact. What has happened is that there has been engrafted onto it new rules of such practical import that the centre of gravity of the structure has shifted. Now the whole emphasis is on making potentially exempt transfers that are not caught by the reservation of benefit rules.

As with the tax, the basic structure of the book remains intact, reflecting the fact that, on one system of classification, the various provisions in the legislation can be regarded as falling into three broad categories. First, there are the provisions which govern the majority of occasions on which a charge may arise. These provisions are referred to in this book as the "main charging provisions". Under them tax is charged on "chargeable transfers," an ominous term, which can apply both to lifetime and death transfers of settled and non-settled property. Secondly, there are provisions under which tax is charged on property which is held on relevant property trusts, which were principally discretionary trusts but have by the Finance Act 2006 been extended with a few exceptions to all trusts. The main charging provisions have no impact on such property. Instead, the treatment of such property is regulated by a separate code, especially designed to deal with such property. The book refers to this code as the "special charging provisions". Finally, there is a host of supporting provisions dealing with a wide range of matters affecting the way tax is calculated and collected under the main and special charging provisions.

The book generally reflects this structure. It begins by considering, in Part I, the main charging provisions. Part II then deals with the special charging provisions, while Part III examines the various supporting provisions that are relevant to both sets of charging provisions. Considerable emphasis is thus still placed on appreciating the conceptual hierarchy of the tax. Special attention is given, however, to the new potentially exempt transfer regime and the reservation of benefit rules, separate chapters being devoted to both.

Inheritance Tax has always had specific provisions to counter tax planning opportunities as well as being subject to the Ramsey doctrine and its developments. It is, however, one of the taxes that is intended to be included under a "General Anti-Abuse Rule" (GAAR) announced in the June 2010 budget and the subject of a Consultation that ended in September 2012. The Government's response to the Consultation was published in December 2012. The GAAR will apply to abusive arrangements entered into on or after Royal Assent to the Finance Bill 2013. For a full discussion of the GAAR, see Chapter 30.

The book continues to be intended primarily to be of assistance to practitioners and should serve as a reference work on most points. It is, however, designed to be read rather than merely referred to, the emphasis being throughout the statutory provisions. Readers' criticisms, suggestions and comments generally, whether as to technical or stylistic matters, will be gratefully received. References to "the legislation", "the Act" and "the 1984 Act" are references to the Inheritance Tax Act 1984, unless otherwise indicated.

CONTENTS

PART 1

THE MAIN CHARGING PROVISIONS

PART 2

THE SPECIAL CHARGING PROVISIONS

PART 3

SPECIAL SUBJECTS

PART 4

THE INTERNATIONAL DIMENSION

ACKNOWLEDGMENTS

Parts of this book were first published as follows:

"Capital transfer tax: The deemed domicile rules", *Accountancy*, August 1980.
"Finance Bill notes", *British Tax Review*, No.3, 1978.
"Loans by trustees", *British Tax Review*, No.4, 1979.
"Loans by trustees", *British Tax Review*, No.6, 1979.
"Resettlements: a muddle" and "Finance Bill notes", *British Tax Review*, No.3, 1980.
"Partnerships and capital transfer tax", *British Tax Review*, No.5, 1980.
"Control and capital transfer tax", *The Law Society Gazette*, March 5, 1980.
"CTT associated operations provisions", *The Law Society Gazette*, June 4, 1980.
"CTT: annuities under trusts", *New Law Journal*, June 21, 1978.
"CTT treatment of free loans", *New Law Journal*, March 20, 1980.
"CTT and CGT treatment of reversionary interests", *New Law Journal*, April 10, 1980.
"The new CTT Convention with the US", *New Law Journal*, September 11, 1980.
"Interest in possession: special CTT provisions", *New Law Journal*, September 18, 1980.
"Payment of CTT by instalments", *Taxation*, September 15, 1979.
"CTT relief for woodlands", *Taxation*, September 22/29, 1979.
"Residence of trustees", *Tolley's Practical Tax*, August 13, 1980.
"CTT Convention with Ireland", *Tolley's Practical Tax*, September 24, 1980.
"CTT related property rules", *Tolley's Practical Tax*, November 5, 1980.
"Posthumous Variations", *Taxation*, September 23, 1988.
"The Implications of *Eversden*", *Taxation*, September 11, 2003.
"Pre-Owned Assets—Some Introductory Comments", *Taxation*, September 2004.

Parts of this book were also first published in:

Capital Taxes—A Quarterly Commentary, 1984–1988.
Capital Taxes and Estate Planning Quarterly, 1989–1992.
Private Client Business, 1992–2004.

The Publishers would like to record their grateful thanks to the following for permission to reprint extracts from the cases indicated:

Butterworths: *Thomas v IRC* [1981] S.T.C. 282.
The Incorporated Council of Law Reporting: *Pearson v IRC* [1979] 2 W.L.R. 353; [1981] A.C. 753.
Inglewood v IRC [1983] 1 W.L.R. 866.

TABLE OF CASES

TABLE OF STATUTES

xliii

lii

lix

TABLE OF STATUTORY INSTRUMENTS

PART ONE

THE MAIN CHARGING PROVISIONS

CHAPTER 1

OVERVIEW

I. INTRODUCTION

Inheritance tax is an intensely technical tax, with an unusually coherent structure. **1–01**
Failure to understand exactly how the tax works makes advising with confidence
impossible and may sooner or later lead to a seriously botched analysis. The purpose
of this chapter is to orient readers as to the shape and structure of the tax while at the
same time introducing them to the structure and approach of this book. From a
technical standpoint, IHT is something of an acquired taste, but once the intellectual
taste buds are engaged, working with it can be (so far as these things go) interesting and
enjoyable.

In the following discussion, with a view to making the reader's introductory ride a
little less bumpy than it might otherwise be, only a general picture is presented and
references to statutory provisions are kept to a minimum. We want you to get a feel for
the tax; there will be plenty of time later for detailed analysis.

Before addressing the structure of the tax, it will be useful to consider the goal which **1–02**
the tax is designed to achieve. The broad goal is to tax any reduction in the value of
an individual's estate, be it during his lifetime or on his death. It is therefore apposite
that the basic building block in the IHT legislation is called a "transfer of value". Such
transfers will normally take the form of gifts, but the tax caters for other means of
transmitting wealth. Even if the tax caught all such transmissions it would still have
been deficient, because it would not have extended to property held in trust. Although
such property is not owned by individuals, they might have certain rights of enjoyment
in respect of it, e.g. they might be entitled to the income from it. Or, where such
property was held upon discretionary trusts, so that they had no right to enjoy it, the
property might be applied for their benefit. This was not an academic consideration: a
vast amount of wealth is held in trust. The architect of the tax thus had to cater not just

for property owned by individuals, but also for property which was enjoyed or capable of being applied for their benefit by reason of being held in trust.

1–03 The legislation seeks to achieve its goal by establishing two separate charging codes. In this book these are called "the main charging provisions"—dealt with in Part 1—and "the special charging provisions"—dealt with in Part 2 ("Settled Property"). (Various special subjects are considered in Part 3 and the international dimension is covered in Part 4.)

The special charging provisions are confined to dealing with one kind of property, namely that held, with a few exceptions, on trust ("relevant property"). The main charging provisions deal with all other kinds of property, i.e. all property comprised in an individual's free estate and certain limited settled property principally that in which an individual has an interest in possession. For this purpose an individual has an interest in possession in settled property if he has a present right to enjoy that property, e.g. because he is entitled to the income from it.

1–04 It might be thought that a more logical approach would have been to have three codes, with a separate code to deal with settled property in which an individual had an interest in possession. Rather than two codes with an overlap legislation the legislation previously subsumed into an individual's free estate all settled property in which he had an interest in possession. It did this by providing in s.49(1) that such an individual is to be treated as owning the property in which his interest in possession subsists.

This was the main deeming provision in the legislation and was regarded as a cornerstone of IHT. Post-Finance Act 2006, that has now changed.

1–05 Although the legislation now establishes separate freestanding codes for dealing with relevant property and all other property, it also contains provisions which apply to both codes, e.g. provisions concerning valuation, tax collection, the nature and availability of certain reliefs, etc. Most of these provisions, which are considered in Part 3, are framed by reference to terminology used in the main charging provisions. The legislation ensures that they also apply to the special charging provisions by including a special linking provision, discussed below.

Excluded property

1–06 A good indication of the technical nature of the tax is to be found in the rules concerning excluded property. "Excluded property" is a term used by the draftsman to refer to a ragbag of various kinds of property which, for one reason or another, are intended to qualify for favoured treatment. For example, the territorial limits of IHT are established by providing that certain kinds of property situated outside the United Kingdom, e.g. that owned by an individual not domiciled in the United Kingdom for IHT purposes, are "excluded property".

The mechanism of excluded property is not confined to limiting the territorial scope of the tax: other forms of property not situated outside the United Kingdom are also in the ragbag regardless of where they are situated. Assume, for example, a pre-Finance Act 2006 settlement under which the trust fund is held for A for life, remainder to B. A is elderly, and therefore his life interest has little actual value, while B's reversion is valuable. For IHT purposes, however, A is treated by s.49(1) as owning the trust fund. It would therefore not be fair also to leave B's reversion within the charge to tax, and the legislation accordingly provides that B's interest is excluded property.

The fact that property is excluded property is, of course, not in itself sufficient to secure favoured treatment for that property—the legislation must also provide for the treatment which is given to that property. The way in which this treatment is given demonstrates the technical nature of the tax, because the method by which relief is given varies according to the means by which a charge would otherwise be imposed, with the various rules by which favoured treatment is conferred operating as a series of cut-outs at critical IHT junctions. By way of illustrating how IHT works the discussion below indicates the place on the IHT circuit board of each of these cut-outs.

II. THE MAIN CHARGING PROVISIONS

Under the main charging provisions a charge to tax is imposed when an individual **1–07** makes a "chargeable transfer", with the "value transferred" by such a transfer being the amount on which tax is charged. A "chargeable transfer" is in turn defined as being "any transfer of value which is made by an individual but is not . . . an exempt transfer".

There are thus three fundamental concepts—"chargeable transfer", "transfer of value" and "exempt transfer". Of these, "transfer of value" is perhaps the most important in the sense that, in the absence of a transfer of value there is nothing on which the main charging provisions can fasten.

Transfers of value generally

Transfers of value come in two forms—actual and notional. These are not terms used **1–08** in the legislation, but are used throughout this book.

As is discussed below, a great deal may turn on whether a transfer of value is an actual transfer of value or a notional one. Some reliefs and exemptions available to actual transfers of value are not available to notional transfers of value, and different rules apply for determining the value transferred by actual transfers of value and notional transfers of value. Furthermore, though there is only one kind of actual transfer of value, there are three distinct kinds of notional transfers, with separate rules for each.

Actual transfers of value

Section 3(1) effectively defines an actual transfer of value and the value transferred **1–09** by it by providing:

> " . . . a transfer of value is a disposition made by a person (the transferor) as a result of which the value of his estate immediately after the disposition is less than it would be but for the disposition; and the amount by which it is less is the value transferred by the disposition."

An actual transfer of value is thus an estate-diminishing disposition.

The consequential loss rule

Note that the value transferred is not the value of the property disposed of; rather, it **1–10** is the loss in value to the transferor's estate occasioned by the disposition. This is known as "the consequential loss rule". It means that where, e.g. A owns 51 of the 100 shares in A Ltd and gives away 2 of them the value transferred is equal to the difference between a controlling 51 per cent holding a non-controlling 49 per cent holding, not the value of the gifted two shares.

Excluded property

1–11   We are now in a position to understand the first way in which the legislation provides favoured treatment to excluded property: s.3(2) provides that for purposes of s.3(1) (which, as we have seen, defines a transfer of value as an estate-diminishing disposition) no account is taken of the value of excluded property which ceases to form part of a person's estate as a result of a disposition. The basic effect of s.3(1) is thus to prevent a disposition of excluded property from diminishing the value of a person's estate and so from being an actual transfer of value.

1–12   It is worth noting that the draftsman's choice of terminology could easily lead one to assume that excluded property is somehow outside the scope of IHT because it is excluded from a person's estate. Far from it; indeed, the fact that in determining whether a disposition has diminished the value of a person's estate no account is taken of excluded property which has ceased to be comprised in his estate shows that the position is just the opposite—somewhat bewilderingly, and subject to one exception noted below, excluded property is included in a person's estate.

Note also that s.3(2) will not automatically prevent a disposition of excluded property from being an actual transfer of value. This follows from that fact that under s.3(2) in determining whether a person's estate has been diminished only the value of excluded property leaving his estate is ignored; account must still be taken of the value of excluded property which remains comprised in his estate. Returning to the example of A and the gift of two of his 51 shares, even if all the shares were excluded property, the diminution in the value of his estate occasioned by the gift would not be expunged by s.3(2), because that diminution would exceed the value of the two gifted shares.

Dispositions: actual and deemed

1–13   "Disposition" is not defined, save that it includes a disposition effected by associated operations.[1] The legislation recognises that certain events which would not constitute a disposition as a matter of general law could present opportunities for the avoidance of tax and provides that in three cases events are to be treated as dispositions, as follows.

First, an omission to exercise a right is in some cases treated as a disposition.[2] Secondly, an alteration in a close company's shares or loan capital or in any rights attaching to that capital is treated as having been effected by a disposition made at the time of the alteration by the participators of the company.[3] Last, certain transactions

[1] IHTA 1984 s.272; see Ch.9.
[2] IHTA 1984 s.3(3); see paras 2–20 and following.
[3] IHTA 1984 s.98(1); see para.2–18.

involving back-to-back life policies are treated as having been made by a transfer of value made by a disposition.[4]

Reliefs: qualitative and quantitative

The legislation then goes on to provide two kinds of relief, qualitative and quantitative. Both kinds of relief apply to any actual transfer of value, regardless of whether it was made by an actual disposition or a deemed disposition.   **1–14**

So far as qualitative reliefs are concerned, the legislation provides that certain dispositions are not transfers of value at all notwithstanding the fact that they diminish the value of the disponer's estate. For example, a person may simply make a bad bargain and the legislation provides that if that is genuinely all that has happened then his, e.g., sale at an undervalue will not be a transfer of value.   **1–15**

So far as quantitative reliefs are concerned, the legislation provides that the value transferred by certain transfers of value falls to be reduced by a specified percentage—up to 100 per cent—if the property which is the subject matter of the transfer meets certain requirements. It is to be noted that the favoured treatment given by s.3(2) to excluded property is not a quantitative relief, because such reliefs operate only to reduce the value transferred by a transfer of value, and that value is computed only after applying s.3(2).   **1–16**

Exemptions

Where no qualitative relief is available or, in the case of a quantitative relief, the relief does not reduce the value transferred to nil, there will be a transfer of value. The next issue is the extent, if any, to which that transfer of value is an exempt transfer. Two basic kinds of exempt transfers exist—actually exempt transfers and potentially exempt transfers. If a transfer of value is actually exempt, that is the end of the matter, i.e. it is not a chargeable transfer. If, on the other hand, a transfer of value is potentially exempt, in which case it is commonly called a "PET", it is assumed to be exempt and no tax is due at the time it is made, but if the transferor dies within seven years of making the transfer, the exemption is lost, and the transfer becomes chargeable. The use of the term "potentially exempt transfer" is thus something of a misnomer—such transfers are provisionally exempt but potentially chargeable.   **1–17**

Grossing-up

The consequential loss rule mentioned above has a special, rather notorious feature, namely that where the transferor bears the tax on an actual transfer of value which is a chargeable transfer the value transferred by that transfer has to be grossed-up to reflect the fact that the transferor is effectively making a gift of the tax. This follows from the fact that in determining the amount by which the value of the transferor's estate has been diminished by a chargeable transfer regard must be had to whether or   **1–18**

---

[4] IHTA 1984 s.263; see para.2–25.

not the IHT on that transfer is to be borne by the transferor himself. The reason for this lies in two provisions relating to the method by which a person's estate is valued for these purposes. As we have seen, the value transferred by an actual chargeable transfer is the loss to the transferor's estate. It therefore follows that the value transferred is found by comparing the value of the transferor's estate before the transfer with the value of his estate thereafter, the difference between the two figures being the value transferred by the transfer. The plot thickens when the tax on that transfer is to be borne by the transferor. This is because, by s.5(3):

"In determining the value of a person's estate at any time his liabilities at that time shall be taken into account, except as otherwise provided by this Act".

And, by s.5(4):

"The liabilities to be taken into account in determining the value of the transferor's estate immediately after a transfer of value include his liability for tax on the value transferred . . ."

This means that if the transferor bears the tax the value of his estate is diminished both by:

(1) the gift he made to the transferee; and
(2) his liability for the tax on that gift.

He must therefore pay, as it were, two rounds of IHT—one on the diminution occasioned by the gift, and one on the diminution occasioned by his liability to the tax on that gift.

1–19   That, however, is not the end of it. Since his liability to pay the tax on that liability will also diminish the value of his estate, he will therefore also have to pay tax on that diminution, and so on. This is a special feature of the consequential loss rule. Lest the faint-hearted take fright, two things should be pointed out in connection with this process. First, grossing-up is not a never-ending process; since each liability is but a fraction of its predecessor, an amount will eventually be reached which is too small to tax. Secondly, and more importantly, in practice it is seldom necessary to go through the grossing-up process, either because the transfer is a PET or because recourse is had to a simple formula[5] from which it is quite simple to determine the grossed-up amount of a given sum.

Notional transfers of value

1–20   The legislation provides that on the happening of three events IHT is to be charged as if a person had made a transfer of value. In this book such a person is described as having made a notional transfer of value.

Linking provision

1–21   Before considering what kind of events give rise to a notional transfer of value it will be helpful to consider a slightly obscure point which highlights the technical nature of

[5] See para.6–30.

the tax. As was noted, actual transfers are defined as estate-diminishing dispositions, while notional transfers arise by reference to certain events on the happening of which the legislation specifies that IHT is to be charged as if a transfer of value had been made. In order to keep the drafting simple, various provisions intended to apply both to actual and notional transfers of value simply refer to transfers of value, without referring expressly to the aforesaid events. But, on a close analysis such provisions would, in the absence of a linking provision, apply only to actual transfers, not to the aforesaid events on the happening of which IHT is chargeable as if a transfer of value had been made, because such events are not, in terms, transfers of value. Accordingly, s.2(4) bridges the gap by providing that references to "transfer of value" include such events, with "transferor" falling to be construed accordingly.

Death

Probably the most important event is a person's death, at which time he is treated as if he had made a transfer of value immediately before he died of all the property to which he was then beneficially entitled.[6] Note in this connection that in two cases he will be deemed to be beneficially entitled to property which he does not actually own as a matter of general law.   **1–22**

First, if he had an interest in possession in settled property that property is included in his estate.[7] This follows from the s.49(1) rule that a person with an interest in possession is treated as owning the property in which his interest subsists. The fact that the person's life terminates on his death is not relevant, because under s.4(1) the relevant time is immediately before he died, and at that time he will still have been entitled to his interest and so treated as owning the trust property. Secondly, if during his lifetime he gave away property that property may nevertheless be regarded as comprised in his estate immediately before he died if that property is caught by the reservation of benefit anti-avoidance rules.[8]   **1–23**

Settled property

The second event on the occurrence of which a person makes a notional transfer of value is where a person has a qualifying interest in possession[9] in settled property and during his life that interest comes to an end or is deemed to have done so. In such a case tax is chargeable under s.52(1) as if he had made a transfer of value. Given the changes introduced by the Finance Act 2006 what previously had universal application is now limited to certain specific cases.   **1–24**

The value transferred

Section 52(1) also provides that the value transferred by a s.52(1) transfer is the value of the property in which the terminated interest subsisted. Note the difference in   **1–25**

---

[6] IHTA 1984 s.4(1); see para.8–02.
[7] Unless the settled property is excluded property; see para.32–49.
[8] See Ch.7.
[9] See para.11–50.

9

the way the value transferred by such a notional transfer and the value transferred by an actual transfer is computed. As discussed above, where an actual transfer is concerned the consequential loss rule applies. Where, on the other hand, there is a s.52(1) notional transfer, regard is had only to the value of the property in which the interest subsisted. Assume B owns 49 of the 100 shares in B Ltd outright, and that he has an interest in possession in two shares subject to which his son is entitled to the shares. For IHT purposes he is thus treated as owning 51 shares. If he gives to his son two of his 49 shares he will make an actual transfer of value and the consequential loss rule will apply. But if the trustees terminate B's interest in possession, so that the son becomes entitled to the two shares held in trust, the consequential loss rule will not apply; instead the charge will be on the value of the two shares held in trust, valued in isolation from the 49 shares owned by B.

Dispositions of interests in possession

1–26   At this juncture it may be useful to consider another example of the interlacing of the various IHT provisions. As was just noted, the termination of an interest in possession is the occasion of a notional transfer. It may have occurred to the reader that such a termination might also give rise to an actual transfer of value. Assume, for example, a trust under which D is entitled to a life interest, remainder to E. D surrenders his life interest, with the result that E becomes absolutely entitled to the trust fund. The surrender is clearly a disposition by D; it also clearly results in the termination of his life interest.

1–27   The draftsman anticipated the difficulties that might be caused by a person disposing of an interest in possession and provided in s.51(1)(a) that such a disposition is not a transfer of value. Section 51(1)(a) is thus another example of an estate-diminishing disposition which is relieved from being an actual transfer of value. Such a disposition is dealt with exclusively under s.52(1).

Close companies

1–28   In the absence of express provision to the contrary it would be possible for an individual to make tax-free gifts indirectly by arranging for a company which he controlled to make the gifts. These gifts would constitute transfers of value by the company but, as was mentioned above, only an individual can make a chargeable transfer and so, in the absence of provision to the contrary, no IHT would be due. The legislation accordingly provides that where a close company makes a transfer of value that transfer falls to be treated as having been made by the participators in the company.[10]

Excluded property

1–29   It will be helpful at this stage to consider how the legislation ensures that notional transfers do not occur in respect of excluded property. First, so far as the transfer

---

[10] See paras 2–76 and following.

treated as having been made by a person immediately before he dies is concerned, s.5(1) provides that immediately before a person's death his estate does not include excluded property. Accordingly, any such property which he then owns, including any settled excluded property in which he has an interest in possession, will not be included in the notional transfer of value of his estate which he is treated as making immediately before he dies. (Note that s.5(1) confirms that excluded property is—except immediately before his death—included in a person's estate.) Secondly, with regard to the s.52 lifetime termination of an interest in possession, s.53(2) provides that IHT is not charged under s.52 if the settled property in which the interest subsists is excluded property. Given the s.2(4) linking provision discussed above, the strict effect of s.53(2) is to prevent any transfer of value from arising. Last, so far as close companies are concerned, the legislation does not provide favoured treatment where shares held by a participator are excluded property, but it does achieve a similar result by providing relief for participators domiciled outside the United Kingdom.

Reliefs: qualitative and quantitative

As with actual transfers of value, both qualitative and quantitative reliefs are **1–30** available to notional transfers of value, but the position is rather more complicated in so far as qualitative reliefs are concerned because the legislation does not provide any qualitative relief that applies to all three kinds of notional transfers. This is not surprising since the three kinds of notional transfers vary considerably from each other. The approach of the legislation is to adapt certain of the qualitative reliefs available to prevent estate-diminishing dispositions from being actual transfers of value so that they apply, in suitably modified form, to prevent certain events from giving rise to notional transfers of value.

The quantitative reliefs, on the other hand, apply to notional transfers in the same **1–31** way as to actual transfers. This follows from the fact that those reliefs are given to the value transferred by a transfer of value. Although the calculation of the quantum of that value may vary according to whether a transfer of value is actual or notional, once the value transferred is calculated the quantitative reliefs fasten on it regardless of how it was generated.

Exemptions

The legislation both follows and departs from the treatment given to the exemptions **1–32** available to actual transfers of value.

It follows that treatment in that where no qualitative relief is available or, in the case of a quantitative relief, the relief is not wholly available, there will be a notional transfer of value. The next issue is the extent, if any, to which that transfer of value is an exempt transfer. Again, two basic kinds of exempt transfers exist—actually exempt notional transfers and potentially exempt notional transfers. If a transfer is actually exempt, that is the end of the matter, i.e. it is not a chargeable transfer. If, on the other hand, a transfer is potentially exempt no tax is due at the time it is made, but if the transferor dies within seven years of making the transfer, IHT becomes chargeable.

IHT departs from that treatment in two ways: first, only certain of the exemptions available to actual transfers of value are available to each of the kinds of notional transfers of value; secondly, not all kinds of notional transfers of value are capable of being PETs.

Grossing-up

1–33   Since the consequential loss rule does not apply to notional transfers, there is generally no need to gross-up such transfers. Thus, where a notional transfer of value is concerned, the last step involved in determining how much value transferred is chargeable is to apply such exemptions as may be available. Assume, for example, that X makes a notional transfer of value of £200,000 of which, under his annual exemption, £3,000 is exempt. The result is that he has made a chargeable transfer of £197,000.

III. THE SPECIAL CHARGING PROVISIONS

1–34   The special charging provisions are concerned with relevant property which was previously restricted to discretionary trusts. The provisions recognise that certain kinds of such property deserve favoured treatment. There are therefore two separate sets of provisions—one to deal with property accorded favoured treatment, another to deal with property not accorded such treatment.

The legislation establishes a single, separate code for dealing with relevant property and a series of mini-codes for dealing with each kind of favoured property. The code regulating the treatment of relevant property has a number of features in common with each of these mini-codes, which in turn share a number of common features. The somewhat complicated position is thus:

- some rules apply only to relevant property;
- some rules apply only to favoured property; and
- some rules apply only to certain kinds of favoured property.

Relevant property

1–35   The basic approach was originally to tax relevant property once a generation by imposing a charge at such intervals and at such a rate of tax that the net result would be the same as if the property had been comprised in an individual's estate. As a back-up, a charge was also imposed if property ceased to be held upon discretionary trusts. The result was two kinds of charge—a periodic charge and an exit charge.

The periodic charge

1–36   The periodic charge has since the inception of the tax been imposed on each tenth anniversary of the creation of the settlement in question. On each such anniversary the value of all the property then held upon discretionary trusts is brought into charge. In determining the rate of tax account is taken of how long the property has been relevant property. The rate of tax is such that it no longer achieves a generational tax.

The exit charge

In the absence of an exit charge it would be a simple matter to avoid the periodic charge. Exit charges are broadly imposed where the value which would be otherwise subjected to the periodic charge ceases to be so chargeable. Exit charges take two forms. The primary exit charge is imposed on property which ceases to be held on ordinary, i.e. non-favoured, relevant property trusts. This could happen by reason of property being distributed outright to beneficiaries or becoming held upon favoured trusts. The secondary exit charge is imposed where relevant property is devalued. Again, in determining the rate of tax account is taken of how long the property then held has been relevant property. **1–37**

Excluded property

Favoured treatment is conferred on relevant property which is excluded property by providing that such settled property is not relevant property. **1–38**

Qualitative reliefs

Various reliefs are available to prevent exit charges from arising on certain occasions on which they would otherwise do so. For example, relevant property which becomes held for charitable purposes only is not subject to an exit charge and, since excluded property is not relevant property, provision is also included to prevent an exit charge being imposed where trustees who hold relevant property replace it with excluded property. **1–39**

Quantitative reliefs

Quantitative reliefs such as business relief are available to both the periodic charge and exit charges. **1–40**

Favoured property

The legislation singles out for favoured treatment the following kinds of property: **1–41**

- property held for a limited time for charitable purposes only;
- property held indefinitely for charitable purposes only;
- property held upon bereaved minors trusts;
- property held upon age 18 to 25 trusts;
- property held by trustees of superannuation funds;

- property held upon certain trusts for employees;
- property held upon protective trusts;
- property held upon trusts for disabled persons;
- property comprised in a trade or professional compensation fund; and
- property forming part of a premiums trust fund or ancillary trust fund of a corporate member of Lloyd's underwriters.

The previous favoured treatment for accumulation and maintenance trusts with effect from April 2006 has been removed.

1–42　　The special charging provisions have the following main features in relation to favoured property:

1. *Exemption from periodic charge*: the periodic charge is not imposed on favoured property.
2. *Exit charges*: the legislation divides favoured property into two categories—that on which an exit charge may be imposed, and that on which it may not. The exit charges imposed on favoured property are largely identical to those imposed on relevant property. Certain reliefs available to relevant property are also available to favoured property.
3. *Rate of tax*: the rate at which an exit charge is imposed on favoured property is determined in a much simpler way than that prescribed where an exit charge is imposed on relevant property. The rate is found by multiplying one or more percentages, ranging from 0.25 per cent down to 0.05 per cent, by a specified number of quarters geared to take account, broadly speaking, of the period during which the property in question has been held as relevant property.

Excluded property

1–43　　Anomalously, charges can be imposed on favoured property even though it is excluded property.[11]

Linking provision

1–44　　It will be helpful at this point to mention s.2(3) which provides that, broadly speaking, references in the legislation to chargeable transfers are construed as references to occasions on which tax is charged upon relevant property. This allows all the provisions framed by reference to chargeable transfers to apply to charges imposed under the special charging provisions.

IV. COMMON PROVISIONS AND SPECIAL SUBJECTS

1–45　　The legislation contains many provisions which apply to the main and special charging provisions alike, e.g. business and agricultural relief, valuation rules, the associated operations provisions and various administrative provisions. These are

[11] See para.10–24.

covered in Part 3, which also considers other matters—e.g. partnerships and heritage property—which were thought best dealt with separately from the main and special charging provisions.

V. THE INTERNATIONAL DIMENSION

The international dimension is considered in Part 4. All taxes have territorial limits. **1–46** The basic posture of IHT is not to impose tax on foreign situs property which is either:

(a) beneficially owned by an individual not domiciled in the United Kingdom for IHT purposes; or
(b) comprised in a settlement made by an individual who was not domiciled in the United Kingdom for IHT purposes when he made the settlement.

Such property is generally but not always treated as excluded property.[12]

Deemed domicile rules

There are special rules for determining where an individual is domiciled for IHT **1–47** purposes. Under these rules longstanding residents are treated as domiciled in the United Kingdom, as are recent émigrés from the United Kingdom. The special rules apply for most, but not all, IHT purposes.[13]

Double tax treaties

It may be that, notwithstanding the territorial limits of IHT, the same assets fall to **1–48** be subjected both to IHT and tax imposed by one or more foreign jurisdictions. In that case relief may be afforded from double taxation, either under one or more double tax treaties or, in the absence of treaties, by the United Kingdom unilaterally.[14]

Planning

Wealthy individuals increasingly have connections with more than one jurisdiction. **1–49** This makes estate planning challenging, interesting and perilous. Compared to information on more or less conventional estate planning, information on multi-jurisdictional planning is hard to come by. Part 4 therefore focuses on this aspect of planning with a view to providing readers with information that might not be otherwise available to them.[15]

---

[12] See Ch.32.
[13] See para.32–25.
[14] See Ch.33.
[15] See Ch.34.

CHAPTER 2

TRANSFERS OF VALUE

I. INTRODUCTION

2–01   The discussion of the main charging provisions starts by considering what constitutes a "transfer of value." Such transfers are the main concepts on which the
legislation is built. This follows from the fact that under the main charging provisions
a charge to tax can arise only if there has been what is known as a "chargeable
transfer",[1] and such a transfer is defined as "a transfer of value which is made by an
individual but is not . . . an exempt transfer".[2] It follows from this that in applying the
main charging provisions one is concerned with two primary questions—first, has there
been a transfer of value; secondly, if there has been such a transfer, is it exempt? This
chapter is accordingly concerned with transfers of value, the next chapter, with exempt

[1] IHTA 1984 ss.1 and 2(1).
[2] IHTA 1984 s.3(1).

16

transfers. The following chapter then goes on to consider the position with regard to PETs, which, as has already been explained, though not exempt transfers as such when made, are treated as exempt for the time being.[3]

Actual and notional transfers

Transfers of value fall into two categories, actual and notional. The distinction is an important one, and the key to understanding the structure of the main charging provisions lies in grasping this distinction from the outset and bearing it firmly in mind. This is because different consequences often follow according to which category a transfer falls into, namely: **2–02**

(1) certain reliefs are available to actual transfers only;
(2) certain exemptions are available mainly to actual transfers only;
(3) the PET regime applies mainly to actual transfers only; and
(4) the principles for determining the amount on which tax is charged may differ according to whether a transfer is actual or notional.

ACTUAL TRANSFERS

II. DEFINITION

The definition of an actual transfer of value is found in s.3(1), which provides that a transfer of value is: **2–03**

"... a disposition made by a person ... as a result of which the value of his estate immediately after the disposition is less than it would be but for the disposition."

It follows from this definition that an actual transfer of value is comprised of two essential ingredients:

(1) a disposition by a person; and
(2) a consequential diminution in the value of that person's estate.

This in turn, raises three questions:

- What is the meaning of "estate"?
- What is the meaning of "disposition"?
- When does a disposition diminish the value of a person's estate?

III. MEANING OF "ESTATE"

The meaning of "estate" is discussed in Chapter 25. Basically, a person's estate is "the aggregate of all the property to which he is beneficially entitled."[4] Property, in **2–04**

---

[3] See para.5–20, and *Private Client Business* (1993), p.138 and (1994), p.6 for a consideration of whether it is possible to have a chargeable transfer of a nil amount.
[4] IHTA 1984 s.5(1).

turn, is widely defined; it includes rights and interests of every description.[5] The result of these definitions is that, subject to a few exceptions discussed at paras 25–11 and following, a person's estate is comprised of virtually anything which he owns beneficially including property to which a deceased was entitled under a statutory right created by the intestacy rules, but where the Grant of Letters of Administration had not been obtained at the time of the beneficiary's death.[6] Does a person's estate at death include property which he has gifted by a *donatio mortis causa?* As such gifts are revocable during the lifetime of the donor and are only perfected by his death it is thought that the relevant transfer of value must occur on death.[7] Lifetime exemptions and reliefs will not therefore be available and although the personal representatives will be liable to pay IHT in respect of such gifts the ultimate burden of tax will fall on the donee.[8]

Immediately before a person's death his estate does not include "excluded property",[9] but at all other times it does include such property. Precisely what constitutes "excluded property", and the effects of property being excluded property are all discussed below.[10] What is important at this stage is not to be misled by the term "excluded property". A common error is to assume that excluded property is "excluded" from a person's estate, or from the scope of the tax altogether. This is not the case. Excluded property is always *included* in a person's estate, except, as we have noted, just before he dies.

The meaning of "estate" is thus relatively simple and is unlikely to cause problems either in principle or in practice. A slightly more difficult question, and one which it will be convenient to consider here is: who has an estate for these purposes? The importance of this question derives in part from the definition of an actual transfer of value. As we have seen, for there to be an actual transfer of value a person must make a disposition, and that disposition must diminish his estate. If he has no estate to diminish then, by definition, he cannot make a transfer of value; therefore no charge to tax can arise under the main charging provisions.

As we have seen, a person's estate is the aggregate of all the property to which he is beneficially entitled. It follows from this definition that any person who is beneficially entitled to property has an estate for these purposes. The question thus arises: is there a kind of person who as a matter of general law is precluded from being beneficially entitled to property to which he holds the legal title?

Persons fall into three basic categories for this purpose—individuals, companies and trustees. There has never been any doubt as to the position of the individual. It is clear that as a matter of general law a company[11] is beneficially entitled to assets to which it is legally entitled as a company (and not, e.g., as a trustee). It follows, therefore, that a company has an estate for these purposes. Any possibility of successfully arguing to the contrary has been eliminated by s.95(1) which, by expressly referring to "the estate of a company", puts the matter beyond doubt. A company, like an individual, has an estate, and consequently can make an actual transfer of value (but, as was mentioned above at para.1–07, only an *individual* can make a chargeable transfer). This is subject to the qualification that in *Von Ernst Et Cie SA v IRC*[12] the Court of Appeal held that a company[13] with exclusively charitable objects could not be an object for whose

---

[5] IHTA 1984 s.272. The words in square brackets were introduced by FA 2002 s.119 in order to reverse the decision in *Melville v IRC* [2001] S.T.C. 1271; see para.25–12.

[6] *Daffodil v IRC* [2002] S.T.C. (S.C.D.) 224.

[7] See para.7–05.

[8] IHTA 1984 s.211.

[9] IHTA 1984 s.5(1).

[10] See Ch.31.

[11] Not the shareholders of the company: *Short v Treasury Commissioners* [1948] A.C. 534.

[12] *Von Ernst Et Cie SA v IRC* [1981] W.L.R. 468; [1980] S.T.C. 111; see paras 32–32 and 32–35.

[13] And an unincorporated association.

benefit settled property or income from it could be applied or which might become beneficially entitled to an interest in possession. It appears to follow from this that such a company[14] does not have an estate for IHT purposes.

The position of trustees is different. It is a well-established principle of English law that trustees are not beneficially entitled to property to which they hold the legal title as trustees, and there is nothing in the legislation which can be taken as derogating from that principle. On the contrary, the special charging provisions are predicated upon the assumption that trustees do not have an estate, and if they were to do so the same transaction would often give rise to a charge to tax under both the main and the special charging provisions. This plainly cannot have been intended. Indeed, the legislation expressly acknowledges that trustees are not beneficially entitled to settled property which they hold on trust.[15] This means that trustees, unlike individuals and companies, cannot make an actual transfer of value.

IV. MEANING OF "DISPOSITION"

There is no statutory definition of "disposition". Section 272 does provide that the term "disposition" includes a disposition effected by associated operations; however, this only indicates one way in which a disposition can be made—it still leaves open the question of what constitutes a disposition in the first place. The legislation also provides that in certain circumstances a person is to be *treated* as having made a disposition whether or not he made a disposition under the general law. Dispositions can thus be actual and notional. What amounts to an actual disposition is a question of general law; what amounts to a notional disposition is determined by the legislation. **2–05**

Actual dispositions

Precisely what the term "disposition" means as a matter of general law is not entirely clear. There is little relevant case law and although the estate duty legislation used the term, the litigation concerning its meaning dealt with particular estate duty provisions. What is clear is that, as was said in *Ward v IRC*,[16] "disposition" is not a technical word, but an ordinary English word of very wide meaning. **2–06**

Lack of relevant authority notwithstanding, it seems that virtually any act by which a person intentionally divests himself of his beneficial ownership of property should constitute a disposition. Thus, for instance, a sale or a gift will constitute a disposition; but as will be seen, even the making of a loan or the incurring of a liability may do so.

The CGT legislation may also provide some guidance here, because an act that constitutes a disposition will often also amount to a disposal for CGT. Under the CGT legislation a disposal can be actual or notional, and among the circumstances in which a person is treated as having disposed of property are those in which he receives a capital sum by way of compensation for the loss or destruction of an asset.[17] Whether

---

[14] *Von Ernst Et Cie SA v IRC* [1981] W.L.R. 468; [1980] S.T.C. 111.
[15] IHTA 1984 s.52(3).
[16] *Ward v IRC* [1956] A.C. 391.
[17] TCGA 1992 s.22.

the destruction or loss of property will amount to a disposition is not clear.[18] In so far as the CGT legislation makes specific provision to deal with loss or destruction it assumes that such loss or destruction would not constitute a disposal—or, presumably, a disposition—under the general law. But this is by no means conclusive. Capital gains tax and IHT are very different taxes: one taxes the gains made on the realisation of assets, the other the diminution in an individual's estate. The loss or destruction of an asset does not normally involve the realisation of that asset—but it will diminish the value of the owner's estate. Normally, of course, "disposition" connotes a transfer *to* someone, but it seems clear that for IHT purposes there need not be a disposition to someone, only a disposition *by* someone. If a person intentionally divests himself of the beneficial ownership of property by destroying it then that should amount to a disposition. Accidental loss or destruction, on the other hand, should not do so.[19]

Difficulties may occur when considering informal transfers of value such as arise by the operation of the equitable doctrines of proprietary estoppel or constructive or resulting trusts. Although it is usually clear that a disposition of some sort has taken place, it is not at all certain as to exactly how much value has been transferred or when the disposition effectively happened, given the very nature of these equitable principles and the fact that in most cases the court is asked to confirm or otherwise an already existing state of affairs. In such cases, it is necessary to consider each stage of the "transfer" carefully so as to determine exactly when a disposition occurred and what are the IHT consequences (and indeed the CGT consequences as well).[20]

Free loans

2–07   The term "free loan" is used in this context as a matter of convenience to describe an interest free loan repayable on demand. At one time special provisions applied to loans that were repayable on demand, but these provisions are no longer in force.[21] The authors' view is that whether or not a free loan constitutes a disposition (for a full analysis, see para.12–35), so long as it is genuinely repayable on demand, the making of it should not diminish the value of the lender's estate. The authors recognise as a general point that the question of whether a loan arrangement gives rise to a transfer of value, and the extent of any such transfer, is one of fact and degree and depends on the circumstances of the case. Factors to be considered include whether the loan is repayable on demand or on short or fixed notice, whether the loan carries interest and at what rate, and whether the loan is secured. Whether a limitation period exists may also be relevant. In IHTM14317, HMRC say that the grant of an interest free loan repayable on demand is not a transfer of value because the value of the loan is equal to the amount of it, but they say that it is a gift because there is a "clear intention to confer bounty: the property disposed of is the interest foregone".[22]

---

[18] In *Re Leven* [1954] 1 W.L.R. 1228; [1954] T.R. 325, Wynn-Parry J. held that the primary meaning of "disposition," at least in relation to property, is to deal with the property in one of a number of ways, the property remaining in existence. It was held that the fact that A extinguishes B's liability to make annual payments to C does not constitute the disposition by A of an annuity to B within the meaning of FA 1940 s.44. See *Private Client Business* (1993), p.334 for a discussion of whether the destruction of an asset can be a disposition for IHT purposes.

[19] Even if it does, the disposer may be able to rely on s.10 for relief: see paras 2–41 and following.

[20] For a detailed analysis of this point, please see "The inheritance tax and capital gains tax consequences of informal transfers of rights in land", B.T.R. 2006, 4, pp.458–481.

[21] See para.2–24.

[22] HMRC also say in IHTM14317 that the grant of such a loan is not, in itself, a gift with reservation of benefit but refer to IHTM14401 with regard to the provision relating to loans to settlements in FA 1986 Sch.20 para.5.

The authors' view is that a loan that is for a fixed term at less than commercial interest will, usually, diminish the value of the lender's estate unless it is to a company in which he owns all the shares, although the facts and circumstances of the case must be taken into account and the factors mentioned above will be relevant in assessing whether there is a transfer of value and the extent of it. In the event that a loan not repayable on demand does constitute a transfer of value it may still be possible to establish that the transfer is within one or more of the exemptions specified in ss.18–29. Section 29 includes certain provisions which are designed to ensure that those exemptions apply to loans as they do to other transfers of value.

Gifts made under a power of attorney

Careful consideration needs to be given to the position where a gift is proposed to be made, or is purported to have been made, under a general power of attorney or an enduring or lasting power of attorney.   **2–08**

Gifts made under a general power of attorney

An attorney under a general power may only make gifts out of the donor's estate to the extent that it is necessary to do so to implement the purpose for which the power was granted. He may not make gifts to himself unless the power expressly authorises him to do so. A general power under s.10 of the Powers of Attorney Act 1971 would not generally be considered to be sufficient to enable the attorney to make gifts. Thus, the terms of any general power under which an attorney purports to be making a gift out of the donor's estate must be checked so as to ensure that the attorney has the requisite authority. Otherwise such gifts are likely to be voidable unless subsequently ratified by the donor.   **2–09**

In *McDowall's Executors v Inland Revenue Commissioners*,[23] the Special Commissioners held that the powers of an attorney must be strictly construed. Mr McDowall's attorney had made gifts out of excess income and in line with the donor's established pattern of giving. However, there was no express power to make gifts out of Mr McDowall's estate in the power of attorney and no such power could be imported into the document.[24] Therefore any gifts which had been made by the attorney were ultra vires and would have been recoverable by Mr McDowall (if he had regained capacity)[25] immediately before his death. The right to recover the gifts therefore formed an asset of Mr McDowall's estate as at the date of his death.

Gifts made under an enduring power of attorney or a lasting power of attorney

Following the coming into force of certain parts of the Mental Capacity Act 2005, there is a dual system in place, whereby enduring powers of attorney made before October 1, 2007 remain valid and can be used to make gifts, whilst from October 1,   **2–10**

---

[23] *McDowall's Executors v Inland Revenue Commissioners* [2004] S.T.C. (S.C.D.) 22.

[24] A provision allowing the attorney "to buy lease sell and otherwise deal with any interest in any property both heritable and moveable" was not sufficient to allow gifts to be made.

[25] *McDowall* was a Scottish case and the general power remained valid under Scottish law despite the donor's intervening incapacity.

2007, only lasting powers of attorney can be created. The system of making gifts under both systems is similar subject to the differences noted below.

As regards enduring powers of attorney, two categories of gift are permitted by virtue of Sch.4 of the Mental Capacity Act 2005. The first is to provide for "the needs" of persons for whom the donor might be expected to provide[26]; the second, to make gifts of a seasonal nature or on anniversaries (such as birthdays, wedding anniversaries) and gifts to charity, provided that "the value of each gift is not unreasonable having regard to all the circumstances and in particular the size of the donor's estate".[27] Lasting powers of attorney also enable the attorney to make gifts of both a seasonal nature and to charity provided such gifts are not unreasonable (as with enduring powers of attorney),[28] but there is no express power to provide for the needs of another person.[29]

Gifts can be made to the attorney himself.[30] Of course, if the enduring power or lasting power contains restrictions or conditions which negate the statutory power, then the enduring power or lasting power must be operated subject to those restraints or conditions. Where the statutory power is applicable the attorney may exercise it without the need to obtain the Court of Protection's consent to the making of the gift. It should be noted that it is not possible to widen the statutory gift making power in the enduring power or lasting power itself.

Guidance which used to be issued by the Office of the Public Guardian made it clear that an application to the Court of Protection was necessary where the purpose of a gift is for IHT planning.[31] The Mental Capacity Act Code of Conduct provides that the attorney "can apply to the Court of Protection for permission to make gifts that are not included in the LPA". An order can be made after the gifts are made to validate them.

There is still scope for debate about the appropriate size of lifetime gifts out of a donor's estate authorised under the statutory power and what may be considered reasonable in all the circumstances of the particular case (taking into account the overall size of the estate, the amount of excess income, etc.).[32]

Practitioners should therefore give very careful thought before advising attorney clients upon the making of tax motivated gifts out of a donor's estate by the attorney and ensure that any proposed gifts fall within the statutory power or have the prior authority of the Court of Protection. HMRC Form IHT400 asks if any gifts were made under a power of attorney.

Joint bank accounts

2–11   Joint bank accounts raise a number of issues.[33] Whether a payment into a joint account by one of the joint account holders, or a payment out of a joint account, or the

---

[26] Mental Capacity Act 2005 Sch.4 para.3(2).

[27] Mental Capacity Act 2005 Sch.4 para.3(3).

[28] Mental Capacity Act 2005 s.12(2).

[29] See *Re Strange* Unreported May 21, 2012 (Court of Protection) for a case where an LPA which contained guidance asking attorneys "to provide for the financial needs of my husband in the same manner that I might have been expected to do if I had capacity to do so" was found not to have contravened Mental Capacity Act 2005 s.12 as any spouse would have specific maintenance obligations under National Assistance Act 1948 s.24(1)(b) and the Social Security Administration Act 1992 s.105(3).

[30] Mental Capacity Act 2005 Sch.4 para.3(2).

[31] The power to make such an application is contained in Mental Capacity Act 2005 s.23(4). The guidance was "Lasting Powers of Attorney: A guide for people taking on the role of Property and Affairs Attorney under a Lasting Power of Attorney" (2007), p.31. This guidance is no longer available from the Office of the Public Guardian.

[32] See a two part article in Private Client Business (2000), pp.175 and 254.

[33] See also para.25–60, below.

change of a sole name account into a joint account, amounts to a disposition depends on the type of account. In *Young v Sealey*[34] and *O'Neill v IRC*[35] it was held that no immediate gift was intended when the sole name account became a joint account; the gift took place only on death.[36] Where the purpose of a joint account is just administrative, e.g. to enable someone to pay bills on behalf of an elderly relative, there may have been no donative intention at all, and hence no disposition.

Where the funds in the account derive from one person, unless the relationship between the parties concerned is such that a presumption of advancement arises,[37] there is a rebuttable presumption that the joint holders hold the account for the original depositor alone. This presumption is, however, easily rebuttable upon proof of an intention on the part of the original depositor that the joint holder was to take beneficially.[38]

Where there was no donative intention, the joint holder may take legal title by survivorship on the other's death (by virtue of what effectively is a contract with the bank), but the bank will hold it as resulting trustee for the estate. At the other extreme, a joint account may be treated as a trust account, with an agreement between the parties as to how deposits and withdrawals should be treated and accounts being kept of who owns the funds.[39]

Whether or not there was a disposition when the account was opened or deposits into it were made, for IHT it will normally have been a non-event. Megarry J. suggested in *Re Figgis* that:

> "It may be that the correct analysis is that there is an immediate gift of a fluctuating and defeasible asset consisting of the chose in action for the time being constituting the balance in the account".[40]

This analysis was followed in the *Sillars* case,[41] the result being that the whole balance was liable to IHT in the original depositor's estate under s.5(2) on the basis that the original depositor had a general power enabling him or her to dispose of the balance as they thought fit.

Assume that M opens a deposit account in the names of herself and her daughters S and D with an initial sum of £40,000. Although S and D's estates are clearly increased by the power to draw the money out at any time, M's estate has not been reduced because she could herself draw out the money. The IHTM confirms HMRC's view that each party to a joint current account is treated as beneficially entitled to that proportion of the account which represents his or her payments in, with withdrawals by each party being treated as withdrawals from his or her own payments in.[42] Therefore, if M retains the right to withdraw the whole of the money, there will not be a transfer of value when the account is opened. Joint accounts were further considered in the case of *Taylor v*

---

[34] *Young v Sealey* [1949] 1 Ch. 278.

[35] *O'Neill v IRC* [1998] S.T.C. (S.C.D.) 110.

[36] See *Drakeford v Cotton* [2012] EWCA 1414 (Ch) for a case where the presumption that a joint bank account was held on resulting trust for a mother's estate was rebutted with evidence that she had intended her daughter to inherit the account by survivorship. The presumption of advancement did not apply as when the accounts were established the mother did not intend to give her daughter a beneficial interest.

[37] Under Equality Act 2010 s.199, the presumption of advancement is due to be abolished (although the abolition will not affect anything done before the section commences); however this provision is not yet in force.

[38] See, e.g., *Jose Manuel Pitta de Lacerda Arosa v Coutts and Co* (2002) 1 All E.R. (Comm) 241.

[39] See the discussion in *Sillars v IRC* [2004] S.T.C. (S.C.D.) 180; see paras 25–08 and 25–60. For recent examples where there was no rebuttal of the presumption of resulting trust, see *Re Northall (Deceased)* [2010] EWHC 1448 (Ch) and *Musson and Wonfor v Bonner* [2010] W.T.L.R. 1369.

[40] *Re Figgis* [1969] 1 Ch. 123 at 149.

[41] *Sillars v IRC* [2004] S.T.C. (S.C.D.) 180 at 184.

[42] HMRC Manuals IHTM15042.

Revenue and Customs Commissioners[43] where it was held that, inter alia, as the deceased had paid in all of the money into two joint accounts, and could dispose of the whole balance for the time being in the accounts, she was to be treated as beneficially entitled to the whole of the money in the accounts at the time of her death and IHT levied accordingly.

In the above example, the £40,000 forms part of M's estate for IHT purposes. Arguably it also forms part of S and D's estates. However, in practice it is understood that even though a joint account holder may have an unrestricted right to withdraw any part of the credit balance, HMRC will not use this right of withdrawal to claim tax on a share of the account greater than that resulting from the application of general equitable principles.[44]

On this analysis, when someone withdraws more than his or her "share" of the balance there will be a disposition by the original depositor provided, of course, that there was a donative intention originally[45]; if there was no such intention then the recipient of the withdrawal will hold it as constructive trustee for the original depositor and there will effectively have been no disposition.

For an example of a joint bank account found to be held on the terms of an express trust, see *Smith v Revenue and Customs Commissioners*.[46]

Waivers generally

2–12   Whether a waiver constitutes a disposition depends on the nature of that which is waived. If, for instance, a stepson waives all gifts which may be made to him during life or on death by his hated stepfather, the waiver will not constitute a disposition. The stepson had no right to the gifts; consequently he had nothing to dispose of. In such circumstances the waiver operates only as an avoidance, not as a disposition.[47] If, on the other hand, the stepson owns shares in a company and he waives his rights to a dividend in respect of those shares, that waiver may constitute a disposition.

As a matter of company law,[48] a shareholder has a right to a final dividend once it has been declared, and can, if necessary, sue for it. A person who waives a right to a final dividend therefore disposes of a right whose value will normally be that of the dividend itself. The position where no dividend or an interim dividend only has been declared is slightly different. In such a case, the waiver should not of itself diminish the value of his estate.[49] This view is based on the assumption that any such waiver will bind only the person who made it, and not, for example, a subsequent purchaser of the shares. If this assumption is correct, the market value of the shares will be unaffected by the waiver, and therefore the waiver will not have diminished the value of the estate of the person who made it. Consequently, he will not have made a transfer of value. Once the dividend is paid, the question will arise as to whether, by failing to rescind his waiver, the individual in question made a notional disposition under s.3(3) of an amount equal to the dividend in question. This, in turn, raises the difficult question as

---

[43] *Taylor v Revenue and Customs Commissioners* [2008] S.T.C. (S.C.D.) 1159.
[44] HMRC Manuals IHTM15042.
[45] See *KO Pflum v Revenue and Customs Commissioners* [2012] UKFTT 365 (TC) for a case where, in the context of the income tax liability on withdrawals from an offshore joint bank account by one party, which account was funded by the foreign earnings of the other party, the First Tier Tribunal said that "the essence of joint ownership of a bank account where withdrawals can be made without restriction by either party is that the sums belong to the party who withdraws them".
[46] *Smith v Revenue and Customs Commissioners* [2009] UKVAT SpC 00742.
[47] *Re Paradise Motors Co Ltd* [1968] 1 W.L.R. 1125.
[48] See also *British Tax Review* (1977), p.28 and *Potel v IRC* [1971] 2 All E.R. 504.
[49] See para.2–71.

to what constitutes a "right" for the purposes of s.3(3). In the circumstances, it is thought that the failure to rescind the waiver would not amount to the deliberate omission to exercise a right, and that therefore no disposition would be made under s.3(3).[50]

The alternative, if unlikely, possibility is that the waiver is to be regarded as binding a purchaser, in which case the waiver may diminish the value of the estate of the person who made the waiver. The amount of the diminution, if any, will depend on such factors as the likelihood of the company making a profit, and the likelihood of it declaring a dividend if it does so.

Where a person waives remuneration, the position would appear to depend on whether he waives the remuneration before or after he becomes entitled to it. If he waives it before he becomes entitled to it, the waiver should not constitute a disposition because he had nothing to dispose of. If, on the other hand, a person waives remuneration after becoming entitled to it, he will dispose of his right to remuneration in question, with the result that he makes a transfer of the right, the value of which will normally be the amount of the remuneration in question. There are, however, special relieving provisions which apply both to waivers of dividends and waivers of remuneration.[51]

Waivers of loans

HMRC take the view that loans can only be waived by deed. See the following item **2–13** that appeared in the Law Society Gazette, December 18, 1991, p.40:

"Inheritance Tax: execution of documents
The purpose of this article is to serve as a reminder that the Revenue will not accept the validity of certain transactions (which may be carried out for tax planning purposes) unless the transactions are evidenced by deed. It is not intended to be a general guide to the execution of documents by deed, but it is the case that if there is no consideration to support a contractual arrangement, then execution by deed can become vital.

Loans

It has recently been brought to the attention of the Revenue Law Committee that the Capital Taxes Office will not accept that a loan made between individuals has been waived by the lender, so the estate of the lender is reduced, for inheritance tax purposes, by the amount of the loan realised—unless the waiver was effected by deed.
Letters and circumstantial evidence clearly indicating an intention to absolve the beneficiary of the loan from any liability to repay will be insufficient.
The Revenue has quoted in support of its contention that a waiver is ineffective unless made by deed (*Pinnell* (1602) 5 Co. Rep. 117a, and *Edwards v Walters* (1896) 2 Ch. 157, CA).

Importance of deeds

In the Revenue Law Committee's view, although the Revenue's contention is not unassailable, unless and until the contention is confirmed or rejected by judicial authority, it must be prudent to advise all clients that any inheritance tax planning strategy involving the making of a loan, and subsequent waiver, should be effected by deed in order to ensure the estate of the lender is reduced accordingly.

---

[50] For a fuller discussion, see paras 2–20–2–23.
[51] See paras 2–70 and 2–71.

For alterations of dispositions taking effect on death, s.142 of the Inheritance Tax Act 1984 does not require execution of a deed, but simply 'an instrument in writing', though in practice as a prudent precaution, a deed is normally used.

Clearly it is not necessary to effect every single transaction carried out as part of an estate planning exercise by deed (loans can be repaid and a gift made by exchange of cheques), but members should be aware of the danger of a transaction being defeated by the Revenue unless it has been evidenced by a duly executed deed."

Parents often make a loan to their children supported by a promissory note which states that the loan is repayable on demand (to safeguard any diminution in the parent's estate). The parent then uses his or her annual exemption to make loan reductions, supported by a letter to the child informing him or her by how much the loan has been reduced. On the death of the parent, the personal representatives are usually told by HMRC that the annual write-offs are invalid because the release of debt must be made by deed or supported by consideration.

However, personal representatives should refer HMRC to ss.62 and 89 of the Bills of Exchange Act 1882 which provides that, if the lender has unconditionally renounced in writing his right to repayment, the effect is to discharge the obligation on the borrower (or promissory) notwithstanding the absence of consideration. Section 89 provides that the rule applies to promissory notes as well as to bills of exchange. In addition, para.23–009 of *Chitty on Contracts* (28th edn) states that: "The release of . . . a promissory note need not be effected by deed nor is any consideration required for such discharge".[52] However, HMRC appears still to require loans to be waived by deed.[53]

The writing off or waiver of all or part of a loan could constitute a transfer of value if the loan has value at that time.

Timing: generally

2–14   A related question which it will be convenient to consider here is the time when a disposition is made. This can be important. It will often determine who is accountable for tax and how much tax is payable. Problems may arise, for instance, because of an ambiguity as to the order in which the gifts were made. Given the cumulative nature of the tax, later gifts may be subject to a higher rate of tax than earlier ones. If it is a condition of the gifts that the donee bears the tax there may be a dispute between donees as to which gift was made first. In addition, if a gift was made on or within seven years of the transferor's death it may be subject to a supplementary charge. Conversely, if a transferor survives a gift by seven years it will cease to form part of his cumulative total. The importance of ascertaining the date on which a gift was made is well illustrated by the estate duty case of *Re Owen*.[54]

The taxpayer drew three cheques on May 21, 1941, which were respectively presented for payment on June 4, 5 and July 2, 1941. The taxpayer died on June 1, 1944. The question was whether he died within three years of making the gifts; if he did, estate duty was payable on the gifts. Romer J. held that the gifts were not completed until the cheques had been honoured. The case has been authority for this proposition ever since, and was applied in *Parkside Leasing v Smith*.[55] It has two

---

[52] See *Private Client Business* (2002), p.199.
[53] HMRC Manuals IHTM19110.
[54] *Re Owen* [1949] 1 All E.R. 901. See also *Bromley v Brunton* (1868) L.R. 6 Eq. 275 and *Re Swinburne* [1926] Ch. 38.
[55] *Parkside Leasing v Smith* [1985] 1 W.L.R. 310.

important consequences. First, it means that as a general rule a gift by cheque is completed when the cheque is honoured. Secondly, the fact that a gift by cheque is not completed until the cheque is honoured means that the gift will be completed in the place where the cheque is honoured, and this can be crucial where a gift is made by a foreign domiciliary. Assume, for example, that Pierre, a French domiciliary who has a current account with a Parisian bank, wishes to make a cash gift to his daughter Marie, who is a student in London. She maintains bank accounts in Paris and London. The correct procedure will be for the cheque to be presented for payment at her Paris bank. If this is done, the gift will be completed in France, with the result that Pierre will have made a gift of excluded property.[56] If, on the other hand, the cheque is presented for payment at Marie's London bank, the gift will have been completed in London, with the result that it is not a gift of excluded property.

This proposition was applied in *Curnock v IRC*.[57] A cheque drawn for £6,000 to utilise X's IHT annual exemptions was paid into the bank before, but did not clear until after, X's death.[58] The Special Commissioner held that there was no completed gift until the cheque cleared, so the sum of £6,000 was an asset of X's estate at his death. Cheques should thus normally be encashed promptly. If this is not possible, then it may be necessary to use a banker's draft, or, in extreme cases, to make a cash gift.

The general rule, of which *Re Owen* is just one example, is that all the requirements relating to the kind of gift in question must have been satisfied before the gift is regarded as having been completed. Exceptionally, it will suffice that the donor has done everything in his power to effect the gift. The leading case in this area is *Re Rose*.[59] The taxpayer had executed transfer forms of shares in an unlimited company in accordance with the company's articles of association. Under those articles the directors had a discretion to refuse to register the transfer. The transfer was in fact registered by the directors three months after the deceased made it. The question was when in law the transfer had been made: under the estate duty legislation then in force no duty was payable if the taxpayer died more than five years after the transfer. The timing of events was such that the taxpayer had died more than five years after he presented the completed transfer forms for the directors' approval, but less than five years after the directors registered the transfer.

The Court of Appeal held that the transferor had done everything in his power to effect the transfer, and that therefore the transfer had been made at the earlier time. Consequently no duty was payable. This approach was confirmed in the decision in *Pennington v Waine*[60] where it was stated that the test of whether a gift is completely constituted is whether it would be unconscionable, in the eyes of equity, for the donor to change his mind. In *Pennington v Waine* the donor had executed a transfer by way of gift of private company shares and sent it to a partner in the company's auditors, and the donee had been told of the gift and been asked to become a director of the company (which he could not be without holding at least one share). It was held to be an effective gift despite the fact that the transfer had not been registered, was in breach of a pre-emption provision in the company's articles of association, and was not in the possession of the donee. The position in *Re Rose* might well have been different if the taxpayer had himself seen to the registration rather than acting as agent for the transferee; in that case, the transfer would probably have remained imperfect until the

---

[56] See para.31–45.

[57] *Curnock v IRC* [2003] S.T.C. (S.C.D.) 283.

[58] See also *T Choithram International SA v Pagarani* [2001] 2 All E.R. 492 where the Privy Council held that, notwithstanding that a gift to a charitable trust had not immediately vested in all the trustees, it was valid at the date the donor (who was also one of the charity trustees) declared that he was making the gift even though the subject matter of the gift was not vested in all the trustees prior to the donor's death.

[59] *Re Rose* [1952] Ch. 499.

[60] *Pennington v Waine* [2002] W.T.L.R. 387.

registration was completed, because the transferor could still have asked for the share transfers to be returned to him or not to be registered.[61]

The cases of *Re Rose* and *Pennington v Waine*, it should be stressed, are in any event unusual since they involved a form of property, private company shares, which could not be transferred without the assistance of a third party. Hence, it was possible for the court to conclude in that case that the donor had done everything in his power to effect the transfer even though legal title to the shares had not been transferred.

In *Zeital v Kaye*,[62] a case concerning the transfer of an equitable interest in a share, the Court of Appeal took a stricter approach than that taken in *Pennington v Waine* as to what a donor had to do to effect an assignment of an equitable interest in a share (which was the interest which the donor had in the share). It was found that the donor had not done all in his power to transfer the share when he gave the intended donee a stock transfer form which did not have the name of the donee filled in. In *Shah v Shah*[63] the Court of Appeal found that a person intending to make a gift of shares which would be imperfect (for example, because of the lack of a share certificate) could first declare a trust of the shares and then give the donee the means to perfect the gift.[64]

The courts have also considered the question of when a disposition has been made for purposes of stamp duty. Formerly stamp duty was payable on an ad valorem basis on any written instrument under which property is transferred or vested in the transferee. A settlor could thus avoid duty by first making a declaration of trust and only later signing a document recording that declaration: as the trust was effected by the initial declaration no duty was payable on the instrument, which merely recorded the previous transfer.

The use of a slightly more complicated version of this technique was considered by the House of Lords in *Grey v IRC*.[65] The taxpayer first created six small settlements for various beneficiaries. He then settled on the trustees of those settlements shares to be held on trust for himself.[66] The settlor then *orally* directed the trustees to hold those shares on trusts of the six small settlements. The trustees later executed six documents, which they intended to be regarded as merely confirming the settlor's oral direction and accepting the new trusts.

The issue was thus whether the settlor's oral direction was a disposition of the shares, in which case no duty was payable, or whether the disposition was made only when the trustees executed the documents, in which case duty was payable. The House of Lords held that the oral direction given by the settlor *was* a disposition, but that it had not satisfied the requirements of s.53(1)(c) of the Law of Property Act 1925 which requires that the disposition of an equitable interest must be in writing. Consequently, although the settlor's oral direction was a disposition, it was an ineffective disposition[67] which subsequently became effective on the execution by the trustees of the written documents. Those documents therefore transferred the settlor's interest in the shares, and duty was payable accordingly.

Two propositions thus emerge from the case: first, both an oral direction and a written declaration of trust are capable of being dispositions; secondly, it does not

---

[61] See *Macedo v Stroud* [1922] 2 A.C. 330.

[62] *Zeital v Kaye* [2010] EWCA Civ 159.

[63] *Shah v Shah* [2010] EWCA Civ 1408.

[64] For discussion of these points see William McCormick QC, "How difficult is it to gift a share? *Shah v Shah* [2010] EWCA Civ 1408" in *Trusts & Trustees* (Oxford: Oxford University Press, 2011), Vol.17, No.5, pp.438–440.

[65] *Grey v IRC* [1960] A.C. 1.

[66] As the beneficial interest in the shares remained his, stamp duty of just 10s. was payable on the transfer to the trustees of the legal estate in the shares.

[67] See *Vandervell v IRC* [1967] 2 A.C. 291 for the inapplicability of s.53(1)(c) where the intended disposition is of both the legal and the equitable interest.

suffice that an act amounts to a disposition—it must also be effective to affect the property in question.

Timing: transfers by instalments

Section 262 applies when:

(1) a person makes a disposition for a partial consideration with the result that there is an actual transfer of value of the amount foregone (as, e.g., in the case of a sale at an undervalue or at an overvalue); and

(2) more than one year after that disposition and in pursuance thereof he makes payments (sale at overvalue) or transfers assets (sale at undervalue).

In such circumstances the actual transfer of value occasioned by the initial disposition is effectively ignored. Instead, tax is charged as if each instalment made by the disponer was a separate disposition. The gift element of each instalment is found by multiplying the amount of each instalment by a fraction:

$$\frac{\text{the value transferred by the actual transfer before any grossing-up}}{\text{the total value of the payments or assets involved}}$$

EXAMPLE: On April 1, 2002, X buys from Y for £30,000 assets worth only £10,000. X pays two-fifths of the purchase price on June 1, 2002, and the remainder on October 1, 2003. Under s.262, the initial gift of £20,000 is ignored. Instead, when X transfers two-fifths of the price (£12,000) on June 1 he is charged as though he has made a gift of

$$£12,000 \times \frac{£20,000}{£30,000} = £8,000$$

The gift element of the October transfer will be calculated in the same way, i.e.,

$$£18,000 \times \frac{£20,000}{£30,000} = £12,000$$

If X died before making the second instalment, his liability to Y for the purpose of computing the value of X's estate on his death would be that element of the outstanding instalment which reflects the consideration provided by Y,[68] i.e. £18,000 less two-thirds of £18,000 (gift element) = £6,000 outstanding liability to be brought into account in valuing X's estate.

Section 262 thus spreads the transfer over the period during which the instalments are made. The spreading effect may mean that even though the initial transfer was not made within seven years of the transferor's death some of the later instalments will nevertheless be chargeable at the death rates. Even if this is not the case, tax may still be chargeable on the instalments at a higher rate than would have been charged on the initial disposition if the transferor makes other chargeable transfers between the instalments. Each instalment therefore will be considered separately and consequently if they are made over a period of years certain exemptions (discussed in Chapter 3)

---

[68] IHTA 1984 s.175.

might cover the whole gift, whereas they probably would not do so if there was only a single disposition.

Incurring a liability

2–16 A person who incurs a liability may be considered as making a disposition when he does so. This is because he disposes of his right to deal freely on the due date with the property which is the subject matter of the liability in question. Whether or not that disposition constitutes a transfer of value will depend on the circumstances in which that liability is incurred.

Where a person incurs a liability unilaterally, e.g. where without consideration X enters into a covenant to pay Y £200 annually for the next seven years, then as a matter of general law he will have made a disposition, and that disposition will diminish the value of his estate by his liability, discounted to take into account the fact that that liability falls to be discharged over seven years, to make those annual payments in the future. Under the legislation, however, his estate will have suffered no such diminution. This follows from the fact that although in valuing a person's estate at any time his liabilities at that time are to be taken into account, only those liabilities which he incurred for a consideration in money or money's worth[69] are to be taken into account.[70] Therefore a person who unilaterally incurs a liability does not diminish the value of his estate by doing so. Consequently he does not make a transfer of value.

He will, however, make a transfer of value each time he subsequently discharges the obligation he has incurred. This follows from the fact that, as we have just seen, his liability to discharge that obligation will *not* be taken into account in valuing his estate. Consequently each time he discharges his obligation, e.g. each time X pays Y £200, he will be regarded as making a transfer of value and tax will be chargeable accordingly.

If, on the other hand, a person incurs a liability for a full consideration in money or money's worth, then, although he will make a disposition both on incurring and on discharging that liability, neither disposition will diminish his estate; consequently neither disposition will constitute a transfer of value. He will not diminish the value of his estate on incurring the liability for he incurred the liability for full consideration: he will not diminish the value of his estate on discharging the liability for the discharge will merely eliminate a liability which has already been taken into consideration in valuing his estate.

If X's estate consists of non-appreciating assets whose value is £100, and he undertakes for a full consideration, e.g. £20, to pay Y £25 in one year's time then on incurring that liability X's estate suffers no diminution in value, because the value of the obligation (£25), discounted to £20 because of the delay in payment, is offset by the consideration (£20) moving from Y. In one year's time X's assets will be worth, say, £125. In determining the value of X's estate, his liability to pay Y £25 must be taken into account: therefore the value of X's estate for these purposes is £100, not £125. When X pays Y the £25 X therefore does not diminish the value of his estate—before he made the payment his estate was worth £100, and after he makes the payment his estate, now free of his liability to X, is still worth £100. Consequently he has not made a transfer of value.

---

[69] Or which are imposed by law; IHTA 1984 s.5(5).

[70] IHTA 1984 ss.5(3) and 5(5). In *Curnock v IRC* [2003] S.T.C. (S.C.D.) 283, cheques drawn by the deceased but not cleared prior to death constituted a failed gift and not a debt on the deceased's estate. The cheque could not be considered an allowable liability of the deceased as it was not in respect of a liability incurred for consideration in money or money's worth; see para.2–14.

Where a person incurs a liability for less than a full consideration in money or money's worth, then, as in the cases considered above, he makes a disposition both on incurring and on discharging that obligation. Since the liability is incurred for a consideration in money or money's worth, albeit for less than a full one, that liability will be taken into account in valuing his estate; consequently he will have made a transfer of value on incurring that liability, the value transferred being the difference between the discounted value of the liability and the consideration received.

The way in which tax will be charged will depend upon whether s.262 applies. If the liability falls to be discharged within one year of the date on which it is incurred s.262 will not apply and tax will be charged only when the liability is incurred. There will be no transfer of value when the liability is discharged since at that stage, the liability having been incurred for a consideration in money or money's worth, the *full* amount of the liability will be taken into account in valuing the transferor's estate (notwithstanding the fact that the consideration actually received was less than full): therefore the value of the transferor's estate will be the same before and after he discharges that liability. Where the liability falls to be discharged more than one year after it is incurred s.262 will apply, with the result that the transfer of value initially made when the liability was incurred will be ignored, tax instead being charged when the liability is discharged.

Notional dispositions

The legislation includes anti-avoidance provisions under which a person is treated as having made a disposition whether or not he made a disposition under the general law. These provisions are aimed at two kinds of mischief. **2–17**

The first kind of mischief occurs in two situations, i.e. (i) when certain alterations are made in the structure of a close company, and (ii) when a person omits to exercise a right. On both these occasions the value of a person's estate may be diminished but no disposition will have been made under the general law. Therefore, but for the anti-avoidance provisions, such an alteration or omission would be outside the tax altogether, since one of the two essential ingredients in an actual transfer of value, a disposition, would be missing. The anti-avoidance provisions remedy this potential deficiency by providing that such an alteration or omission results in a notional disposition. The presence of such a disposition will not, of course, of itself result in a charge to tax; it merely gives the tax an event upon which to fasten. If there has also been a diminution in the value of the disponer's estate both the essential ingredients in an actual transfer of value will be present and the taxpayer may have made a chargeable transfer.

The second kind of mischief involves back-to-back life assurance policies. The problem occasioned by these policies is not so much that they do not constitute dispositions, but rather that their nature is such that—but for the anti-avoidance provisions—the amount by which the disponer's estate would be diminished by his taking out such policies would not accurately reflect the true financial state of affairs. The legislation solves this problem by specifying the amounts by which a disponer's estate is diminished as a result of his taking out such policies. The fact that the legislation deals with both types of mischief by providing for a notional disposition is significant not only from the standpoint of anti-avoidance. It also means that certain reliefs and exemptions are available to the taxpayer which might not have been available to him if a different approach had been adopted. The legislation could have dealt with the above transactions by simply providing that they should be treated as notional transfers of value rather than as notional dispositions. Had this approach been adopted,[71] various reliefs and exemptions which apply to actual transfers of value but not to notional transfers would not have been available to the taxpayer. As matters stand, however, those reliefs and exemptions are available. This follows from the fact that although under the anti-avoidance provisions the dispositions may be notional, the transfers of value which they occasion, being estate-diminishing dispositions, are actual. Consequentially the reliefs and exemptions are available.

Close company alterations

2–18   Section 98(1) is designed to charge a person who reduces the value of his shares in or debentures of a company by altering the company's structure. To achieve this, s.98(1) provides that, where there is an alteration[72] in a close company's unquoted share or loan capital or in any rights attaching to that capital, that alteration is treated as having been effected[73] by a disposition made at the time of the alteration by the participators of that company.[74] The result is that in the event of such an alteration *all* the participators in the company are treated as making a disposition, not just those participators who voted for the alteration. Those participators whose estates have been diminished in value by that disposition will therefore have made an actual transfer of value. Such a transfer cannot be a PET: see para.5–13.

Assume a father, F, and his sons, X and Y, are the participators in Family Business Ltd, a close company. F owns 75 per cent of the shares, X and Y 12.5 per cent each. F wishes to transfer his shares to his sons. If he simply transfers his shares to his sons outright he will have made an actual disposition which diminishes the value of his estate, and tax will be chargeable accordingly. Alternatively, F could retain his shares but restructure the voting rights in the company so that the value in his shares passed to his sons. He could do this by arranging that his shares are stripped of their rights and that those rights become attached to the shares held by his sons. The transfer would have been effected by F voting on the resolution to alter the rights attaching to the company's shares. This would not amount to a disposition under the general law and F would thus have managed to transfer the value in his shares to his sons without making a transfer of value. As a result of s.98(1), however, F will have made a disposition, and, given the diminution in the value of his estate, an actual transfer of value.

The definition of "close company" for these purposes is basically the same as that for corporation tax,[75] save that it extends to a non-resident company which, if it were resident in the United Kingdom, would be a close company for corporation tax purposes. The definition of "participator" also differs slightly from the corporation tax definition: any person who is a participator for corporation tax purposes[76]—or who would be if the company was resident in the United Kingdom—is also a participator for these purposes, save that a person who would be a participator by reason only of being a loan creditor is not a participator for these purposes.[77]

---

[71] See FA 1975 s.41 for a case in which it was adopted but not implemented (s.41 was repealed by IHTA 1984 s.77 and Sch.9).

[72] "Alteration" includes "extinguishment"; cf. *Re Saltdean Estate Co* [1968] 1 W.L.R. 1844.

[73] The legislation thus does not provide that the alteration is itself a notional disposition, but rather that the alteration is made by a notional disposition.

[74] Whether or not it would be treated that way apart from the section, e.g. under s.3(3) (omission to exercise a right); see para.2–20.

[75] IHTA 1984 s.102(1); see Corporation Tax Act 2010 s.439.

[76] See Corporation Tax Act 2010 s.454.

[77] IHTA 1984 s.102(1).

It is important to realise that under s.98(1) the participators are *not* treated as having made a transfer of value. They are treated only as having made a disposition; whether or not they have made a transfer of value will depend on a number of considerations, the first of which is whether their estates have been diminished in value by the disposition. It may be that the estates of some are diminished in value, and the estates of others increased—indeed, as has been seen, that is one reason why such an operation would be undertaken, i.e. to avoid tax by diluting the value of some of the shares and increasing the value of others. In deciding whether there has been a diminution the alteration is not to be taken as having affected the value of the shares or debentures immediately before the alteration.[78] This is apparently intended to preclude any argument that the diminution is attributable to the imminence of the alteration rather than the alteration itself.

Even if there has been a diminution it may be possible to rely on s.10(1),[79] which provides that a disposition is not a transfer of value—notwithstanding the fact that it diminishes the disponer's estate—provided, inter alia, that the disponer can show that it was not intended to confer any gratuitous benefit on any person. It is quite possible that an alteration caught by s.98(1) may in reality have been procured against the wishes of one of the participators, but under s.98(1) he is still treated as having made a notional disposition as a result of the alteration. It would be unfair if he could not rely on s.10(1).

Assume A, B, C and D each have a 25 per cent shareholding in X Ltd; A, B and C vote to pass a special resolution as a result of which the rights attaching to D's shareholding are adversely altered, while the rights attaching to others' shareholdings are enhanced. D votes against the resolution. A, B, C and D will all have made a notional disposition, yet only D's estate will have been diminished as a result of the alteration. D will clearly not have intended to benefit A, B and C gratuitously, and in fairness he should be able to rely on s.10(1), provided, of course, that his dissent was genuine, and not merely part of a concerted attempt to disguise the true character of a transaction, the underlying intention of which was to avoid tax.

It is worth stressing that s.98(1) refers both to an alteration in a close company's unquoted share or loan capital and to an alteration in the *rights* attaching thereto. In the field of company law the courts have drawn a distinction between a person's rights and the *enjoyment* of those rights. In the leading case, *White v Bristol Aeroplane Co*,[80] preference shareholders objected to a proposed bonus issue of preference and ordinary shares to the existing shareholders on the ground that the issue would affect the voting rights attached to the dissentients' shares and that under the company's articles such an alteration could not be effected without the preference shareholders' consent, which had not been obtained. The Court of Appeal held that the rights themselves were to be distinguished from the enjoyment of those rights, and that the proposed issue would not affect the preference shareholders' rights, since those rights would be the same after the issue as before—only the enjoyment of the rights would be affected.

This distinction has since been both approved and applied in various cases.[81] But, since s.98(1) also applies to alterations in the capital itself, alterations such as bonus issues will constitute notional dispositions even though such alterations do not affect the rights attaching to the share or loan capital in question. In the event of such an alteration the question will thus arise—in the same way as it does when there is an alteration in the rights attaching to such capital—as to whether the alteration has diminished the value of any participator's estate. Normally, of course, a rights issue or

---

[78] IHTA 1984 s.98(1).
[79] This section is discussed in detail below at paras 2–41–2–53.
[80] *White v Bristol Aeroplane Co* [1953] Ch. 65.
[81] See, e.g., *Re John Smith's Tadcaster Brewery Co Ltd* [1953] Ch. 308.

a bonus issue, the most common ways in which a company's capital is altered, will not of itself result in any such diminution.

Deferred share schemes

2–19   One of the estate planning devices that became fashionable after the introduction of capital transfer tax was deferred share schemes. These took a number of forms but typically involved the bonus issue of a new class of shares (the deferred shares) which initially had limited rights and so, it was thought, a low value. These rights ripened over a period of years until they ranked pari passu with the existing share capital. The owner of the deferred shares gifted them at an early stage, when they were worth relatively little. The subsequent increase in value occurred, it was thought, as the result of the efflux of time, not as the result of any alteration in the rights attaching to the shares nor as the result of any alteration in the share capital of the company.

HMRC initially accepted this view but published the following revised view in *The Law Society Gazette* of September 11, 1991:

> "Following recent legal advice, the Inland Revenue's interpretation of s.98 of the I.H.T.A. 1984 has changed.
>
> Until now the Capital Taxes Offices have taken the view that when deferred shares come to rank equally with another class of shares there would be no alteration in the rights of the shares within the meaning of s.98(1)(b). But there would be an alteration in the company's share capital within the meaning of s.98(1)(a).
>
> The Board of Inland Revenue has now been advised that an alteration of rights, within the meaning of s.98(1)(b), occurs when deferred shares come to rank equally with another class of shares. Accordingly, claims for inheritance tax will be raised where deferred shares, issued after August 5, 1991, subsequently come to rank equally, or become merged, with shares of another class."

It subsequently emerged that HMRC would not raise claims in relation to deferred shares issued before August 6, 1991, under either s.98(1)(a) or s.98(1)(b).

HMRC's interpretation is not thought to be well founded; even if it is, any charge can only arise at the time when the deferred shares acquire enhanced rights; if at that time the donor has died no problems will arise because a deceased person cannot make a chargeable transfer for IHT purposes.

Deliberate omission to exercise a right

2–20   Normally some kind of positive action is necessary for there to be a disposition, and thus special provision had to be made to deal with a person who diminishes the value of his estate by failing to act. Section 3(3) accordingly provides that where the value of one person's estate is diminished and the value of another person's estate (or, the value of settled property in which there is no subsisting interest in possession) is increased by the first person's omission to exercise a right, the first person is treated as having made a disposition at the time, or at the latest time, when he could have exercised the right, unless he can show that the omission was not deliberate.

If this section is to apply, three requirements must be satisfied. First, there must be an omission to exercise a right, and not merely, e.g. a failure to take up an opportunity. Secondly, the value of the estate of the person who omitted to exercise the right must be diminished by that omission. Thirdly, the value of some other person's estate or, broadly speaking, the value of a discretionary trust fund, must be increased as a consequence of that omission. This third requirement is to the taxpayer's advantage, because it means that in order for s.3(3) to apply someone must have benefited from the omission. Note, however, that *any* increase in the value of another's estate (or of a discretionary trust) suffices: the increase need not be equal to the diminution in the estate of the person who omitted to exercise the right, it need only have been caused by that omission.

Perhaps the most obvious instance of a person omitting to exercise a right is when a person fails to exercise an option. Assume X has a house worth £100,000. He sells Y on arm's length terms an option to buy the house any time within the next five years for £100,000. If at the end of five years the house is worth £150,000 and Y has still not exercised the option, he has made a gift of £50,000 to X.

A landlord's deliberate failure to exercise his right to increase a tenant's rent under a rent review clause would be within s.3(3), as would a person's deliberately failing to take up a rights issue. The deliberate non-exercise of voting rights, e.g. in a company, could be within the section, provided, of course, that the requisite decrease and increase were consequential on that non-exercise.

Agreements to bear tax

A UK domiciled and resident settlor is, in certain circumstances, subject to CGT on **2–21** gains realised by trustees of a non-UK resident settlement which he has created.[82] The Taxation of Chargeable Gains Act 1992 Sch.5 para.6 gives such a settlor a right to recover from the trustees any tax that he has paid. In relation to this statutory right Statement of Practice SP 5/92 provides that:

(i) it does not create an interest in the trust for the settlor under the income tax deeming provisions of ICTA 1988 Pt XV[83];
(ii) neither the right nor any payment made brings the settlor within the transfer of assets provisions in ICTA 1988 ss.739–740[84] and does not involve a capital payment for the purposes of the Taxation of Chargeable Gains Act 1992 s.97; and
(iii) the statutory right is not regarded as a reservation of benefit for IHT purposes and nor is a provision in the trust deed requiring the trustees to recognise the settlor's right to reimbursement or to reimburse the settlor.

However, if the settlor fails to exercise his right "the failure to exercise this right may give rise to an inheritance tax claim under IHTA 1984 s.3(3) in which case the usual rules for lifetime transfers would apply".[85] In an ICAEW Guidance Note on December 14, 1992,[86] HMRC commented that the duration of the right is governed by the normal six year limitation period which will therefore fix the moment when there is a diminution in the value of the settlor's estate (unless, of course, he had earlier surrendered the right).

The ability to enforce this right is a matter of uncertainty: is it enforceable in a foreign court? Can trustees be forced to pay a reimbursement in a case where the settlor is excluded from all benefit in his trust (bearing in mind that the trustees themselves are

---

[82] See TCGA 1992 s.86 and Sch.5, as amended by FA 1998.
[83] ICTA 1988 Pt XV is now found in ITTOIA 2005 Pt 5 Ch.5.
[84] ICTA 1988 ss.739–740 is now found in ITA 2007 Pt 13 Ch.2.
[85] See SP 5/92 para.9.
[86] ICAEW memo Tax 20/92.

not liable for the CGT)? The question of when HMRC will accept that the settlor has done everything in his power to enforce payment has been considered in correspondence reported in *Taxation Practitioner* for July 1998. If it can be shown that he has taken all reasonable steps to enforce his right to reimbursement it cannot be said that the omission was deliberate.[87]

Definition of "right"

2–22   As was mentioned above, s.3(3) applies only where a person has failed to exercise a *right*. The term "right" is not defined by the legislation, and therefore regard must be had to its meaning as a matter of general law.[88]

Precisely what constitutes a right is, however, still far from clear and raises questions which are among the most difficult—and intriguing—in the whole field of jurisprudence. Readers interested in this topic should refer to Hohfeld's seminal work *Fundamental Legal Conceptions*. Hohfeld considered that jural relations fell into finite ascertainable categories, and that rights were to be distinguished from privileges, powers and immunities. In Hohfeld's view, a person with a right is in a position to oblige another to behave in a particular way; in effect, he can say to the other person, "you must". A person with a privilege is free to do something in relation to another; in effect, he can say to the other person, "I may". Where a person has a power, he has the ability to alter another's legal position; he can say, in effect, "I can". A person with an immunity is in a position to prevent his own legal position from being altered by another; he can say, as it were, "you cannot".

It remains to be seen to what extent the courts will be influenced by such theoretical niceties. It does seem clear that some limit must be placed on the meaning of the term "right", and it would be surprising if this was not in time the subject of litigation. This has already happened in relation to the CGT legislation.

A "right" may be used in both a colloquial and legal sense. In its wider (colloquial) sense a right is not an asset for CGT purposes: it must be legally enforceable and capable of being turned into money. Thus in *Kirby v Thorn EMI Plc*,[89] HMRC argued, at first instance, that the right to engage in commercial activity was an asset for CGT purposes with the result that if the taxpayers agreed to restrict their commercial activities in return for a capital payment, that sum would be brought into charge to tax. This argument was rejected on the basis that freedom to indulge in commercial activity was not a legal right constituting an asset for CGT purposes. On appeal, HMRC produced an alternative argument that by restricting their activity the taxpayers had derived a capital sum from the firm's goodwill and that therefore the payment in question was chargeable to CGT. In this argument they were successful.[90]

Trusts of pension policies

2–23   Pension policies confer two basic interlinked benefits—death benefits and lifetime benefits. To the extent that lifetime benefits are enjoyed, death benefits are reduced or eliminated.

---

[87] See also a series of articles in Personal Tax Planning Review [1997/8] 6(3), p.237; [1999] 7(1), pp.71, 75 and 77.

[88] See para.25–02.

[89] *Kirby v Thorn EMI Plc* [1986] S.T.C. 200.

[90] *Kirby v Thorn EMI Plc* [1987] S.T.C. 621.

Many individuals with pension policies arrange their affairs so that although they continue to enjoy the possibility of enjoying lifetime benefits under the policy the death benefit under the policy is held on trust for, e.g. their surviving spouse or civil partner and children. The attractions of such arrangements are discussed at para.2–63. In such circumstances the question arises as to the IHT position where the individual does not exercise his right to enjoy all the lifetime benefits available to him.

The kind of lifetime benefits capable of being enjoyed depends on the policy. The most straightforward option is for the policyholder to apply the sums standing to the credit of the policy to purchase an annuity, also referred to as a scheme pension or secured income, to provide himself with a pension. Such a purchase will completely cancel the death benefit. Other more sophisticated options such as "drawdown pensions", available under personal pension plans but not retirement annuity contracts, leave a portion of the death benefit intact. The position with regard to annuities is simpler and we will consider it first.

1. *Annuities.* Assume that some years ago Simon, when he was in excellent health, purchased a pension policy which he settled on trusts under which the trustees held the lifetime benefits on trust absolutely for Simon and the death benefit on discretionary trusts in favour of his widow and their children. Under the policy Simon was entitled to draw a pension at the earliest at age 60 and at the latest at age 75. When he reached 60 he continued to enjoy good health, kept working and chose not to draw any benefits from the policy. He died when he was 64, at which time he had still not enjoyed any benefits under the policy.

Under HMRC's former policy[91] (if, at the time he deferred the date for taking retirement benefits, Simon was aware that he was suffering from a terminal illness[92] or was in such poor health as to be uninsurable), and then, with effect from April 6, 2006, under legislation,[93] Simon was prima facie treated by s.3(3) as having omitted, immediately before he died, to exercise his right to enjoy lifetime benefits and this omission was treated as both diminishing the value of his estate and increasing the value of the death benefit held on the discretionary trusts for his widow and children. Immediately before he died Simon was therefore treated as having made a notional disposition under s.3(3). Depending on the facts of the case, s.10 (dispositions not intended to confer any gratuitous benefit) could prevent the s.3(3) disposition from being a transfer of value on the basis that Simon's failure to take benefits was not intended gratuitously to benefit anyone.

A change in policy occurred when s.12(2ZA) was inserted (by the Finance Act 2011 with effect in relation to dispositions made on or after April 6, 2011) into the IHTA, specifically disapplying s.3(3) where a member of a registered pension scheme, a s.615(3) scheme or a qualifying non-UK pension scheme omits to exercise pension rights. Section 12 subss.(2A)–(2E) were repealed from that date.

Where s.3(3) applies (e.g. in the case of an unregistered pension scheme) and s.10 relief is not available, the s.18 exemption will be available if the only person who can enjoy the death benefit at the time of the s.3(3) disposition is the spouse or civil partner. Where neither s.10 relief nor the s.18 exemption is available, any charge to IHT will

---

[91] *Inland Revenue Tax Bulletin*, February 1992, issue 2, p.12. See further HMRC correspondence with the Association of British Insurers, June 5, 1991; ICAEW, TR 854, December 2, 1991; Association of British Insurers Guidance Note of June 10, 1999.

[92] In *Fryer v Revenue and Customs Commissioners* [2010] UKFTT 87 (TC), the First Tier Tax Tribunal found that there had been a relevant transfer of value where the deceased was diagnosed with cancer shortly before her retirement date and she omitted to take any benefits up to her death two years after retirement. Her executors argued that the exemption under s.10 applied but the Tribunal rejected this on the basis that the transfer did confer a gratuitous benefit and was not at arm's length.

[93] IHTA s.12(2A)–(2G).

be on the diminution in the value of the individual's estate that has been occasioned by the s.3(3) notional disposition.

2. *Drawdown pensions.* Income drawdown plans are unsecured plans where the pensioner has chosen to defer buying an annuity and leaves the fund invested whilst drawing a tax free lump sum and income from the fund. There is no minimum limit that may be withdrawn but there is a maximum limit based on the single life annuity that the pensioner could have purchased. Previously there was a differentiation of treatment where the pensioner reached the age of 75 but the rules since April 6, 2011 have abolished this age restriction.

A drawdown pension has the effect of being an omission to exercise a pension right (the right to purchase an annuity) within the meaning of s.12(2ZA) of the Inheritance Tax Act 1984 which states that s.3(3) of that Act does not apply to such an omission if the person was a member of a registered pension scheme, a qualifying non-UK pension scheme or a s.615(3) scheme. Therefore there is no disposition and no charge to IHT.

For a more detailed discussion of the IHT treatment of pension funds, and specifically the IHT treatment of death benefits post A-Day, please see Chapter 23.

Free loans

2–24   The legislation in this area has had a chequered, if short, history. It was originally provided in the Finance Act 1975 s.41 that a person who allowed another person the use of property for less than a full consideration was treated as making a transfer of value of the consideration foregone. This provision was not to come into effect until after April 5, 1976. Long engagements can be disastrous, however, and s.41 never did come into effect. Instead, it was replaced by the Finance Act 1976 s.115, under which certain loans repayable on demand were treated as notional dispositions. Section 106 of the Finance Act 1981 subsequently provided that s.115 was to cease to have effect as from April 6, 1981, presumably because such loans were either expressly relieved from being chargeable by provisions in the Finance Act 1976 accompanying s.115 or fell within the normal expenditure out of income exemption, with the result that in practice few loans expressed to be repayable on demand were subject to tax anyway. Thus, as from April 6, 1981 a free loan which is repayable on demand will not constitute a notional disposition, and thus will not be subject to tax. It is important to note that certain loans which are not repayable on demand can give rise to a charge, though on the basis that they constitute actual dispositions rather than notional ones. The position regarding loans generally is discussed in detail at para.2–07.

Back-to-back policies

2–25   It will be helpful to begin this discussion by considering briefly how estate duty was avoided through the use of:

(1) insurance policies in general; and
(2) back-to-back policies in particular.

In that way, the provisions relating to back-to-back policies, the purpose of which is not immediately apparent on a first reading, will be more likely to make sense.

Generally speaking, insurance policies were used to avoid estate duty in the following manner. Assume that X, a wealthy person, wished to leave £500,000 to his son free of tax. To do so, he first entered into an annuity contract with an insurance company, under which he paid the company the £500,000; in return the company agreed to pay X an annuity of an appropriate amount for the rest of his life. X then took out an insurance policy on his life. Under this policy, on X's death a lump sum of, e.g., £475,000 was to be paid to X's son. X used the annuity payments to fund the premiums on the life policy. Such an arrangement had the following effects:

(1) Income tax. Before he purchased the annuity X had only the income from the £500,000. By purchasing the annuity he converted the entire £500,000 into an entitlement to income. For purposes of income tax, however, only the income element in each annuity payment was treated as income; no income tax was charged on the capital element in each annuity payment.
(2) Estate duty. For estate duty purposes, on the other hand, the *whole* of each annuity payment, not just the income element, was treated as income. This meant that the premiums paid by X on the life policy were not subject to estate duty, because they are paid entirely out of X's normal income expenditure, and therefore were exempt. When he died no duty was payable on the annuity since at that stage, because the annuity lasted only as long as X remained alive, it was worthless. Nor was any duty payable on the proceeds of the life policy, because the proceeds had belonged to the son from the time the policy was effected.
(3) Capital gains tax. There was no charge to CGT on the vesting of the benefit of the life policy in X's son,[94] nor was there any charge to CGT when the insurance company paid the £475,000 to the son.

The end result was that X managed to transfer virtually the whole of the £500,000 free of all tax. The price he had to pay to do this, £25,000, was minute compared to the estate duty which he avoided. This result was achieved by means of a relatively simple fiscal alchemy: first X converted his capital into income by purchasing the annuity; then, with the purchase of the life policy and the subsequent payment of the proceeds thereunder, the income was converted back into capital in his son's hands. The essence of the matter was that a large capital sum subject to estate duty was converted through the insurance policies into a slightly smaller sum which was not subject to estate duty.

Back-to-back policies were simply a more refined version of this arrangement. The refinement was that both the annuity and the life policy were issued by the same insurance company. In the estate duty era this refinement was attractive to insurance companies and taxpayers alike. Since the insurance company was handling both ends of the transaction, it enjoyed built-in protection against the risk of X's living to a ripe old age (in the case of the annuity) or of dying prematurely (in the case of the life policy), because each risk offset the other. If X lived longer than expected, the payment of the lump sum was deferred; if, on the other hand, he died prematurely, the company was relieved of its obligation to payments under the annuity contract. In addition, subject to its liability to make annuity payments to X, the insurance company had the use of X's capital until he died. Therefore it required only comparatively small premiums from X, the life policy in fact being funded partly by the premiums paid by X and partly by the interest on X's capital, only part of which, given the company's secure position, was needed to cover the company's risk in respect of the annuity. X, who did not have to apply the entire annuity to funding the premiums, was thus able

---

[94] TCGA 1992 s.210.

to pass the capital to his son at a smaller total cost to himself. Only HMRC lost out.

Inheritance tax provisions generally

2–26   In the absence of special provisions, the above mentioned methods of avoiding estate duty would also have been effective to avoid IHT. The legislation accordingly includes special provisions which nullify the effectiveness of these methods of avoiding tax. These special provisions fall into two categories: those affecting insurance policies and annuity contracts generally, and those affecting back-to-back arrangements in particular. Although, strictly speaking, only the provisions relating to back-to-back arrangements are the subject of this discussion, these provisions are best understood against the background of the general provisions, which will therefore be considered first.

There are two general provisions. First, by s.21(3), the capital element in a purchased life annuity never constitutes income for purposes of the normal expenditure out of income exemption. Consequently a person who purchases a life annuity with a capital sum no longer has the best of both worlds. He still does not have to pay income tax on the capital element in the annuity payments, but the capital element does not constitute income in his hands for the purposes of the normal income expenditure exemption. Therefore, if he uses the annuity to fund the premiums of a life policy on behalf of someone else he will not be able to rely on the normal income expenditure exemption in so far as the capital element is used to fund the premiums. There will therefore be a chargeable transfer in respect of the capital element unless he can rely on some other relieving or exempting provision.

Secondly, s.167(1) makes special provision to bring into account the true diminution occasioned in the value of the taxpayer's estate by his transferring the benefit of the policy and/or the annuity to someone else. In the event of such a transfer, the value of the policy or the annuity is taken to be the greater of:

(1) the market value of the policy or the annuity contract[95]; or
(2) the total of the premiums[96] or other consideration which have been paid before the transfer of the benefit of the policy or the annuity contract.[97]

The reason the legislation provides these alternatives is that in the few years immediately after the policy is taken out its surrender value, which, assuming the insured is in good health, will be its market value, will probably be small. This is because during those years the premiums will be used by the insurance company to defray its heavy initial costs (commissions, etc.), and therefore under the terms of the policy the company will normally be obliged to pay out only a nominal sum on the surrender of the policy. During that period the value to be brought into account will thus usually be the premiums or other consideration paid by the transferor, because that will represent the true amount by which his estate has been diminished by the transfer. As the policy

---

[95] IHTA 1984 s.160.

[96] Where a premium is paid net after deduction of tax under ICTA 1988 s.266(5), only the net amount of the premium is brought into account. Where the premium is paid without any such deduction, the gross amount falls to be taken into account. Since IHTA 1984 s.167(1) refers to "premiums" the amount to be brought into account is thought to be the amount of the premium disregarding any life assurance relief that may be available; cf. para.3–16.

[97] Any sum which, at any time before the transfer of value, had been paid under, or in consideration for the surrender of any right conferred by the policy or contract is deducted: IHTA 1984 s.167(1)(b). And see subss.(3) and (4) for the treatment of term policies and unit-linked policies; discussed at paras 25–74 and 25–75.

matures, the market value of the policy will represent the loss to his estate, and therefore that value will be brought into account.

The result of the legislation is thus as follows: **2–27**

(1) As a matter of general principle, if a person pays a premium on behalf of another he will be charged on the premium unless one of the relieving or exempting provisions applies.

(2) Under s.21(2), if the premium is being paid out of an annuity the normal income expenditure exemption will not be available in respect of the capital element of the annuity.

(3) If a person pays premiums on a policy under which he is the beneficiary there is no charge on those payments, because they do not diminish the value of his estate. If he transfers the benefit of the policy,[98] then, subject to any relieving or exempting provisions, on making that transfer he will as a result of s.167(1), be charged on the greater of:

    (a) the market value of the policy; or

    (b) the premiums he has paid up to that time.

Special provisions affecting back-to-back policies

Although the above mentioned provisions are sufficient to frustrate the first method **2–28** of avoiding tax that was outlined above, they would not have nullified the effectiveness of back-to-back policies. If, for example, X, after purchasing a life policy and an annuity contract from the same company under a back-to-back arrangement, vested the benefit of the policy in his son and used the annuity to fund the premiums on the policy, the result would have been as follows. To begin with, the purchase of the annuity would not have resulted in a charge, because, given X's right under the annuity contract, the purchase of the annuity would not have diminished the value of his estate, and consequently no charge would have arisen at that stage. If X immediately vested the benefit of the policy in his son then, as we have seen, the figure to be taken into account under the normal rules would have been the amount of the premiums paid by X at that stage, nil. When X subsequently paid the premiums on his son's behalf the charge to tax, if any, would have been minimal, since the premiums, being small, would have been paid wholly or mainly out of the income element of the annuity, topped up, perhaps, by X's annual exemption.

Section 263 accordingly contains special provisions to nullify the effectiveness of such transactions. The section applies where three conditions are satisfied, namely that:

(1) a policy of life insurance is issued in respect of an insurance made on or after March 27, 1974, or is on or after that date varied or substituted for an earlier policy;

(2) at the time the insurance is made or at any earlier or later date an annuity on the life of the insured is purchased; and

(3) the benefit of the policy is vested in a person other than the person who purchased the annuity.

---

[98] Or an annuity contract.

This is subject to the qualification that the section does not apply if the taxpayer can show that the purchase of the annuity and the making of the policy were not associated operations. The possibility of a taxpayer bringing himself within this qualification is discussed below.

Where s.263 applies, the person who entered into the arrangements is treated as having made a transfer of value by a disposition made at the time the benefit of the policy was vested in the transferee, and the value transferred by the transfer is the lesser of:

(1) the aggregate of
   (a) the value of the consideration given for the annuity, and
   (b) any premium paid or other consideration given under the policy on or before the transfer; and
(2) the value of the greatest benefit capable of being conferred at any time by the policy.[99]

The reason the charge is imposed both on the value of the consideration given for the annuity *and* on the value of any premiums paid under the policy rather than, as in the case under the normal rules, merely on the premiums paid under the policy, is that, given the fact that the annuity and the policy are associated operations, the consideration given for the annuity is in reality also given for the policy. The result is that, as under the general rules, the true cost to the transferor of vesting the benefit of the life policy in the transferee is brought into account, and he will be charged on all the sums he has paid out under the arrangement with the insurance company unless the value of the benefit he would have received under the life policy is less, in which case that lesser sum will be brought into account.

In addition, *no* part of any premium paid at any time by the transferor on the life insurance policy will be regarded as part of his normal expenditure.[100] This is the case regardless of:

(1) when the payments are made; and
(2) whether the payments under the annuity contract are used to pay the premiums or whether the premiums are paid out of other income.

Once the benefit of the policy has vested in the transferee the transferor may thus be charged in full on any premiums he pays—rather than, as under the normal rules, on only the capital element of any premium he pays.

2–29   Given the above anti-avoidance provisions, it is important to consider the circumstances in which a person may be able to show that the purchase of a life annuity and the making of a life policy were not associated operations. The practice under estate duty, which is thought to continue, was that HMRC did not regard such transactions as associated provided that the issue of the annuity and the issue of the policy were not linked to one another. This is made clear in Revenue Statement of Practice E4 which states:

---

[99] IHTA 1984 s.263(2). This may present problems when the policy is such that the benefits payable under it fluctuate with the fortunes of the insurance company, e.g. in the case of a "with profits" policy. By s.263(3), s.263(1) and (2) apply with the necessary modifications where a contract for an annuity payable on a person's death is after March 26, 1974 made, varied, substituted for or replaced by a policy or annuity contract to which s.263(1) applies as those subsections apply where a policy is issued, varied or substituted as mentioned in s.263(1).

[100] IHTA 1984 s.21(2); see para.3–14.

"Life assurance policies and annuities are regarded as not being affected by the associated operations rule if, first, the policy was issued on full medical evidence of the assured's health and, second, it would have been issued on the same terms if the annuity had not been bought."[101]

The issue of whether the purchase of a life assurance policy and an annuity were associated operations was considered in the case of *Smith v Revenue and Customs Commissioners*,[102] which was appealed from the Special Commissioners to the Chancery Division of the High Court. In this case, HMRC conceded that the provisions of Statement of Practice E4 were binding on it for the purposes of the claim to inheritance tax. The life company stated (and it was accepted by all) that it would have issued the policy on the same terms had the annuity not been bought and so the case hinged on whether the policy was issued on full medical evidence of the assured's health. In respect of one of the life's insured, the policyholder was only required to complete a standard medical questionnaire; she did not have to undergo a medical examination. Lightman J. held that when construing Statement of Practice E4, its evident objective of "providing an effective means of protecting the Revenue from efforts made to avoid payment of inheritance tax" must be borne in mind. This requires the provision to the insurer of full medical evidence of the assured's health. In this case, the answers to a standard questionnaire did not constitute full medical evidence, as although it was sufficient for the purpose of protecting the insurance company for its purposes, it was not sufficient for protecting HMRC.[103] Lightman J. held that there was no one rule as to what full medical evidence constituted and it would rely on the facts in each case. He noted that:

"I suspect in the great majority of cases a report from the applicant's medical practitioner familiar with his health record will be called for. On occasion there may be need for a specialist. There may be exceptional cases when medical evidence can be dispensed with. I have no doubt that the Revenue, the Commissioners and the court can determine without appreciable difficulty in any particular case what is called for and whether what is provided to the insurance company is sufficient."[104]

Although it will obviously be easier to demonstrate that the purchase of a life annuity and the making of a life policy are not associated operations if more than one insurance company is involved, the fact that both the annuity and the policy have been purchased from one company need not be fatal: it will just make the taxpayer's burden more difficult to discharge. If he can discharge that burden, and to do this, the taxpayer would be advised to have a full medical check up and provide full medical evidence to the insurance company as per Lightman J. above, the purchase of an annuity to be applied in funding the premiums of a life policy may still be an attractive proposition. The annuity will receive favourable income tax and CGT treatment when it is used to fund the premium; the interest element will be eligible for the normal expenditure out of income exemption, and the rest of the premium may be covered by the annual exemption. On the annuitant's death there will be no charge to tax, because at that stage the purchased life annuity will be worthless.

Availability of reliefs and exemptions

It was pointed out previously that the true function of s.263 is not so much to **2–30** establish that a disposition has taken place, but to fix the true value of that which has

---

[101] Statement of Practice E4, Yellow Book Vol.3, p.16272.
[102] *Smith v Revenue and Customs Commissioners* [2008] S.T.C. 1649.
[103] *Smith v Revenue and Customs Commissioners* [2008] S.T.C. 1649 at 22–23.
[104] *Smith v Revenue and Customs Commissioners* [2008] S.T.C. 1669.

been disposed of. As we have seen, s.263 achieves this end by providing that on the vesting of the benefit of the policy in a person other than the person who purchased the annuity a transfer of value is to be treated as having been made; the value transferred by that transfer is then fixed by s.263. At first glance s.263 therefore seems to provide for a notional rather than for an actual transfer of value. In the authors' view, however, the fact that s.263 provides that the transfer is to be treated as having been made by a *disposition* clearly establishes that under s.263 the transferor makes an actual, not a notional, transfer of value. Therefore the reliefs and exemptions which apply to actual transfers of value should be available and the transfer is capable of being a PET.

Value transferred

2–31   Normally when there is an actual transfer the value transferred is the amount by which the transferor's estate has been diminished by that transfer. This is not the case under s.263, however, since s.263 specifies what amount is to be taken as the value transferred by the transfer in question. This is important, because it appears to mean that, given the fact that the legislation stipulates the amount to be taken into account, there will be no grossing-up, in contrast to the normal position where there is an actual transfer, even if the transferor pays the tax.

V. DIMINUTION

2–32   As was noted previously, for there to be an actual transfer of value two ingredients must be present. First, a person must have made a disposition, be it actual or notional; secondly, that disposition must have diminished the value of his estate. Whether a disposition causes such a diminution is a matter of valuation. In practice it will normally be clear whether or not there has been a diminution, with disputes being relegated to questions of quantum.

The consequential loss rule

2–33   It should be obvious that not every disposition will diminish the value of a person's estate. If a person disposes of something but receives something of equal value to his estate in return that disposition will not have diminished the value of his estate. If A sells his house to B for £200,000, and that is what the house is worth to A, the value of A's estate is the same after the sale as it was before it. Thus, a sale at market value will not normally result in an actual transfer of value. But this is by no means an inflexible rule since the item disposed of may be worth more to the disponer than its market value.

Assume X owns 51 per cent of the 100 shares in X Ltd, a private company with assets of £100,000. As X's holding is a controlling one it will be valued on an assets basis and will therefore be worth, say, £51,000. Each share, in turn, will be worth £1,000 to X. Now assume that X decides to sell two shares to Y. Those two shares, although they form part of a majority holding, in themselves constitute only a minority holding. Consequently their market value will not be £2,000, but much less than that, say £800. Therefore even if X receives market value for the two shares his estate will nevertheless have been diminished by £1,200 in respect of those two shares.

44

In fact this diminution of £1,200 is merely the tip of a diminution of iceberg proportions. The sale will have diminished the value of X's estate not merely by £1,200, but by a much larger sum, namely £20,400. This is because after the sale X will have only 49 of the shares in X Ltd. He will thus have lost control of the company, and his remaining shareholding will therefore be valued on a minority basis. On a minority basis his holding will not be worth £49,000 but (say) only half that, £19,600 (49 × £400).

The sale to Y will thus have seriously diminished the value of X's estate. Before the sale the value of his shareholdings was £51,000; after it, £19,600, a difference of £31,400. Against this drop can be set the £800 received from Y, but this will reduce only slightly the overall diminution to £30,600. Thus, while every disposition will not necessarily diminish a person's estate, every disposition for which he does not receive in return something equal in value *to him* will normally do so.

Discharge of a liability

The discharge of a liability will not diminish the value of a person's estate, provided **2–34** that the liability was imposed by law or incurred for a consideration in money or money's worth. This follows from the fact that, by s.5, such liabilities are taken into account in valuing a person's estate, so that the value of his estate will be the same before and after he discharges such a liability.

Assume A has £100 in the bank, £10 of which was lent to him by B. As A is under a liability incurred for money or money's worth to repay £10 the value of A's estate is £90. When A repays B the £10 he will not make a transfer of value since the value of his estate will be £90 both before and after that payment.

It will be noted that in order for a liability to be taken into account in valuing a **2–35** person's estate it suffices that it was incurred for a consideration in money or money's worth, i.e. *any such consideration suffices*. An example of a liability imposed by law is a liability under a court order, such as one made in pursuance of divorce proceedings. If under such an order a husband is ordered, e.g. to transfer the matrimonial home to his former wife, his doing so will not diminish the value of his estate. This will be so even if the order is a consent order, because the liability to make that transfer arises under the court order, and the mere giving of consent cannot of itself amount to a disposition.

Excluded property

In one very important case a disposition will not normally diminish the value of a **2–36** person's estate even though he receives nothing in return and that disposition is not made to discharge a liability imposed by law or incurred for a consideration in money or money's worth. This will happen if the disposition is of excluded property. This follows from s.3(2) which provides that "no account shall be taken of the value of excluded property which ceases to form part of a person's estate as a result of a disposition." The result is that a disposition of excluded property will not normally diminish the value of the disponer's estate, since the value of the excluded property which has ceased to form part of his estate will be ignored in computing the value of his estate after the disposition. Consequently the value of the disponer's estate will remain the same after the disposition as it was before it.

45

Assume R (who is a foreign domiciliary) owns a villa in Spain, worth £50,000, which is excluded property. The value of R's estate, including the villa, is £450,000. R gives the villa to his son as a birthday present. Before the gift the value of R's estate was £450,000, after the gift £400,000. But since the villa is excluded property no account will be taken of the £50,000 in value which has gone out of R's estate. Consequently his estate will have suffered no diminution, and therefore he will not have made an actual transfer of value.

2–37   Exceptionally, a disposition of excluded property can result in a diminution in the value of the disponer's estate. This follows from the fact that although no account is taken of the value of excluded property which *ceases* to form part of a person's estate, account is taken of the value of property which *continues* to form part of a person's estate. Therefore if a disposition of excluded property diminishes the value of any of the property remaining in the disponer's estate that diminution will have to be brought into account, and this will be so even if the property remaining in the estate whose value is diminished is itself excluded property.

Consider the previous example of X and X Ltd, X owning 51 shares worth £51,000, two of which he sells to Y for £800, but assuming this time that all the shares are excluded property. As the shares are excluded property, no account will be taken of the value of the two shares that X sells to Y, and therefore the value of X's estate will not be diminished by the market value (£800) of the two shares. But the more damaging diminution in the value of X's estate, deriving from the reduction of his controlling shareholding to a minority shareholding, will still have to be brought into account, because the drop in value of the 49 shares which continue to form part of his estate must be taken into account even though they are excluded property. Before the sale X's shareholding was worth £51,000, after it, £19,600 (49 × £400 per share), a prima facie diminution of £31,400. Part of this diminution—£800—is attributable to the value of excluded property which ceased to form part of X's estate, the two shares, and therefore will be left out of account. And, of course, the £800 cash paid by Y falls to be brought into account even though it was paid to X in respect of that same excluded property. The final result will thus be that the sale of the two shares will result in a diminution of £29,800 (£31,400 − (£800 + £800)) even though both the two shares sold and the shares which continue to form part of X's estate are all excluded property. This result is all the more surprising when it is recalled that in the original example, where the shares were not excluded property, the diminution was only slightly greater —£30,600. The only difference where the shares are excluded property is that the value of the two shares sold—£800—is left out of account, with the result that the diminution is £29,800. Whether HMRC would actually take this point remains to be seen.

It is not clear why the legislation provides that no account is to be taken of the value of excluded property which ceases to form part of a person's estate with the result that the above trap awaits the unwary. It seems strange that if X gives away all his shares at once he suffers no diminution in the value of his estate, and thus no tax, while if he merely reduces his holding to a minority he loses virtually all the protection which the excluded property provisions are presumably intended to afford him. This is especially perplexing since the favourable treatment extended to excluded property in relation to notional transfers and discretionary trusts is virtually[105] trap-free.

What is more, if the above analysis is correct and a disposition of excluded property can diminish the value of a person's estate, the territorial scope of IHT would appear to be extended in a quite unjustified and presumably unintended way. Assume, for example, that X in the above example is a German domiciliary who has lived his whole life in Germany and that X Ltd is a German company. If the above analysis is correct,

---

[105] See para.10–23.

he would, notwithstanding the fact that he lacks any connection with the United Kingdom, be liable to UK tax in respect of the diminution occasioned in the value of his estate by the sale of two shares. To what extent HMRC seek to apply s.3(2) literally, and to what extent such an application can be resisted along the lines just mentioned, remains to be seen. Happily, there are some indications that in applying the legislation the courts will have regard to the overall scheme of the legislation and endeavour to achieve consistent rather than punctilious interpretations.[106]

As first glance the position where a loan is made of excluded property also gives cause for concern. When a person loans property the property lent does not cease to form part of his estate. But under the excluded property provisions, as we have just seen, only the value of excluded property which ceases to form part of a person's estate is left out of account in computing the diminution in that person's estate. This suggests that a loan of excluded property will diminish the value of a person's estate where an outright gift would not.

This, in fact, is not the case. As we have seen, when a person makes a loan something does cease to form part of his estate, namely the right to use the property lent. Presumably a right to use excluded property is itself excluded property. Therefore no charge to tax will normally arise on a loan of excluded property since the value of that which is disposed and on which any charge will therefore be based, the value of the right to use the property lent, will be left out of account in determining any diminution in value in the lender's estate occasioned by that loan.

The fact that excluded property is comprised in a person's estate, except immediately before he dies, means that a person will not diminish the value of his estate by purchasing property that is in his hands excluded property.

Purchased interests and "deemed" diminutions

Note that special anti-avoidance rules apply in two cases where a person purchases an interest under a settlement: **2–38**

(1) by s.49(2), discussed at para.25–49, where a person becomes entitled to an interest in possession in settled property as a result of a disposition for a consideration in money or money's worth, any question whether and to what extent the giving of the consideration is a transfer of value or a chargeable transfer is determined without regard to s.4(1); and

(2) by s.55(1), discussed at para.25–15, where a person entitled to any interest (whether it is an interest in possession or otherwise) in settled property acquires a reversionary interest which is expectant (whether immediately or not) on that interest, the reversionary interest does not form part of his estate.

The effect of those rules is to occasion a diminution in a person's estate which, in the absence of these rules, would not have occurred.

VI. RELIEFS

Normally a person who makes a disposition that diminishes the value of his estate will have made an actual transfer of value. Exceptionally, this will not be the case. This **2–39**

---

[106] See *Von Ernst Et Cie SA v IRC* [1980] 1 W.L.R 468; [1980] S.T.C. 111.

is because the legislation provides by way of relief that dispositions which satisfy certain conditions are not transfers of value even though they diminished the value of the estate of the person who made them.

Before considering these reliefs, it will be helpful to note how they fit into the overall framework. To begin with, these reliefs apply to actual transfers only, never to notional ones. This follows from the fact that these reliefs apply only to dispositions which would otherwise be transfers of value. As will be seen, a disposition is not essential to the making of a notional transfer, and there is no case in which a disposition itself constitutes a notional transfer. Consequently these reliefs do not apply to notional transfers, only to actual ones.[107]

Secondly, there is a fundamental difference between these reliefs and the exemptions considered in Chapter 3 below. Where one of these reliefs applies, it operates to prevent a disposition from being a transfer of value in the first place, and that is the reason why there is no charge to tax. Where, on the other hand, one of the exemptions applies, there has been a transfer of value, and the exemption operates to prevent that transfer of value from being a chargeable one.

This difference between reliefs and exemptions is important from a planning stand-point, since many of the exemptions are quantitatively limited, and once that limit is passed the exemption ceases to be available. Wherever possible recourse should thus first be had so any available reliefs, the exemptions, some of which may be quickly exhausted, being relied upon only as a last resort.

Disposal of an interest in possession

2–40 By s.51(1)(a), where a person beneficially entitled to an interest in possession in settled property disposes of his interest, the disposal is not an actual transfer of value, but is instead deemed to be the termination of the interest in question, with the result that the disponer may have made a notional transfer of value under s.52(1). This is discussed in detail below at paras 2–124 and following. What is important to grasp at this point is that whatever effects such a disposal may have so far as notional transfers are concerned, such a disposal will never constitute an actual transfer of value.

Essentially commercial transactions

2–41 The broad effect of s.10(1) is to relieve from being a transfer of value a disposition which, although it diminishes the value of the disponer's estate, is nevertheless essentially commercial in nature. Assume that X, thinking his house is worth £200,000, sells it for that price when it is in fact worth £250,000. Although by making the sale X has diminished the value of his estate by £50,000, he has not done so intentionally. He has simply made what for him was a bad bargain. Such transactions occur constantly, and are not intended to be chargeable. Hence this relief.

The relief afforded by s.10(1) is of considerable importance, and it will be helpful to begin by citing the section in its entirety. It provides that:

---

[107] See also para.3–01. Some reliefs are adapted to apply to notional transfers, see ss.51(2), 52(3) and 65(6).

"A disposition is not a transfer of value if it is shown that it was not intended, and was not made in a transaction intended, to confer any gratuitous benefit on any person and either

    (a) that it was made in a transaction at arm's length between persons not connected with each other, or

    (b) that it was such as might be expected to be made in a transaction at arm's length between persons not connected with each other:

but this subsection does not apply to a sale of shares or debentures not quoted on a recognised stock exchange unless it is shown that the sale was at a price freely negotiated at the time of the sale or at a price such as might be expected to have been freely negotiated at the time of the sale. In this subsection 'transaction' includes a series of transactions and any associated operations."

It will be noted that s.10(1) lays down both an objective and a subjective test. It should also be noted that in no circumstances does s.10(1) apply to a disposition by which a reversionary interest is acquired by a person in the circumstances mentioned in s.55(1), that is to say by a person already entitled to an interest in settled property on which that reversionary interest is expectant. The reason for this is discussed at para.25–15.

Objective test: arm's length transaction

The primary objective test, which applies in all cases, is that either: **2–42**

    (1) the disposition was made in an arm's length transaction between unconnected persons; or

    (2) where the disposition is between connected persons, that the disposition was such as might be expected to be made in an arm's length transaction between unconnected persons.

The second limb of this test is particularly important, since s.10(1) will frequently be relied upon to prevent a charge arising in consequence of a depreciatory transaction between connected persons. Assume, for instance, that X owns a large house, the value of which he wishes to depreciate in order to reduce the tax that will be payable on his death, at which time the house will pass under X's will to his son. To this end, X might grant a lease of one wing of the house to his son at a rack rent, thereby reducing the value of the freehold by an amount greatly in excess of the capitalised value of the rent. Since the lessee is a connected person, the question arises as to whether the grant of a lease is a disposition "such as might be expected to be made" in an arm's length transaction between unconnected persons.

The answer to this will depend on precisely what test s.10(1) posits. If the proper test is "could a person in X's position be expected to enter into such a transaction with an unconnected person in the first place?", X might be unable to avail himself of the s.10(1) relief. This follows from the fact that normally a freeholder would not grant a lease which so depreciated the value of his freehold. If, on the other hand, the correct test is, "assuming a person might enter into such a transaction, are the terms in fact arrived at equivalent to those that one might expect to find in an arm's length transaction between unconnected persons?", the transaction would pass the objective test, the lease having been granted at a rack rent. Strictly speaking, it is the disposition rather than the terms of the disposition which must be such as might be expected to be made in an arm's length transaction between unconnected persons, but in practice it appears that, at least in some cases, HMRC may also have regard to the terms of the transaction.

Divorce settlements made under court orders

2–43   In practice most divorce settlements are within the s.18 exemption or the relief given for family maintenance dispositions (see paras 2–55 and following) and therefore the question of the availability of s.10 relief does not arise in practice. But s.10 may be relevant in relation to financial arrangements where neither that exemption nor that relief is available. In the past HMRC accepted that, so long as the parties were independently and competently advised such that there was strong evidence of negotiation between them any disposition made by either of them was either made in an arm's length transaction between unconnected parties or such as might be expected to be made in an arm's length transaction between unconnected persons.

FA 2010 introduced a new s.5(1B) to the IHTA, which affects interest in possession trusts established (as settlements created on divorce can be) in reliance on s.10. The changes were introduced to counter an IHT scheme designed to avoid the immediate entry charge on setting up interest in possession trusts by qualifying as a commercial transaction falling within s.10, and taking advantage of the fact that, after FA 2006, a non-qualifying interest in possession is not chargeable to IHT as part of a person's estate. By FA 2010 s.53, an interest in possession falls within s.5(1B) if the person was domiciled in the UK on becoming beneficially entitled to the interest and he became so entitled by virtue of a disposition which was prevented from being a transfer of value by IHTA 1984 s.10. A s.5(1B) interest forms part of the estate of the person entitled to it; where the interest comes to an end during that person's life there is a 20 per cent tax charge (it is an immediately chargeable transfer and not a PET), and where it comes to an end on his death there is a 40 per cent tax charge. In addition, the trust is subject to the relevant property regime. Although it appears that the provisions introduced by FA 2010 were intended to be targeted specifically at the scheme, the provisions actually have wider application and, for example, affect trusts created on divorce where it is often agreed that one spouse should have an interest in possession in a settlement owning the matrimonial home, terminating either on her death or on her children attaining the age of 18. At the time of writing STEP has taken the issue up with HMRC and a response is awaited.

With regard to CGT, HMRC traditionally took the view that the transfer by one spouse or civil partner to the other of assets as part of a divorce settlement, was invariably for money or money's worth because the assets in such cases were understood to be transferred in return for the surrender by the transferee of rights over other property, which he or she would otherwise have been able to exercise to obtain alternative financial provision. As a consequence the assignment of the assets was potentially within the charge to CGT.

The "no gain, no loss" CGT provisions in the Taxation of Chargeable Gains Act 1992 s.58, cannot apply in such cases if the transfer occurs in a tax year after factual separation took place since the couple are no longer living together. In addition HMRC applied s.165(7) of the Taxation of Chargeable Gains Act 1992 to deny the application of holdover relief on transfers of business assets between spouses or civil partners under a court order made under the Matrimonial Causes Act 1973, on the grounds that the recipient spouse or civil partner gave actual consideration (in the form of surrendered rights which he or she could otherwise have exercised to obtain alternative financial provision) for the transfer.

Legal advice received by HMRC has meant that it has had to revise its view of the relevant matrimonial legislation and the nature of court orders following proceedings under it. This follows observations by Coleridge J. in *G v G*[108] that the wife gave no consideration for the transfer of shares to her. Accordingly holdover relief should be available and no liability to CGT should arise on the husband as a result of the transfer. The view taken by HMRC that a wife to whom assets were transferred might have given consideration for those assets in that she might be surrendering rights which she would otherwise be able to exercise to obtain alternative financial provision was criticised as being based on the misconception that each party had "rights". In fact neither party was giving up a claim for maintenance as a "quid pro quo"; the court was exercising the statutory powers vested in it by legislation and the court may choose to exercise those powers or not. The parties to the divorce may suggest how those powers may be exercised but that is all.[109]

The advice received by HMRC was that where there is recourse to the courts and a court makes an order:

(1) for ancillary relief under the Matrimonial Causes Act 1973 (or for financial provision under the Family Law (Scotland) Act 1985) which results in a transfer of assets from one spouse or civil partner to another; or

(2) formally ratifying an agreement reached by the divorcing parties that deals with the transfer of assets,[110]

the spouse or civil partner to whom the assets are transferred does not give money or money's worth, in the form of surrendered rights, for their transfer. A court order made in these circumstances reflects the exercise by the court of its independent statutory jurisdiction. The transfer of ownership is not therefore the consequence of any party to the proceedings agreeing to surrender alternative rights that they might have.

HMRC now accepts that with effect from July 31, 2002 (the date of the decision in *G v G*), it will not restrict the availability of holdover relief in circumstances where the transfer is the subject of a court order or where there is a court order ratifying an agreement reached between the parties. However, except in exceptional circumstances (e.g. where the parties can demonstrate that there was a substantial gratuitous element in the transfer) HMRC intends to continue to apply its practice of restricting holdover relief where there is no recourse to the courts.[111] The position, however, may not be settled. A more recent decision in the Court of Appeal, in the bankruptcy case of *Haines v Hill*,[112] confirmed that a spouse did provide consideration within financial remedy proceedings for the transfer of property following a court order and threw doubt on the interpretation arising from the case of *G v G*.

For s.10 relief (disposition not intended to confer gratuitous benefit), if each party to a divorce is independently and competently advised such that there is strong evidence of negotiation[113] between the parties, HMRC seem to accept that the transaction is such as would have been negotiated between unconnected parties and allow relief in cases not falling within s.11 despite the fact that making CGT holdover relief available would appear to undermine the argument in favour of s.10 applying in such cases.[114]

---

[108] *G v G* [2002] 2 F.L.R. 1143.

[109] Coleridge J. also commented that his view applied equally to a consent order: [2002] 2 F.L.R. 1143 at 1159.

[110] CG67192 also refers to property adjustment orders under the Civil Partnership Act 2004.

[111] *Tax Bulletin*, August 2003, (6): i.e. a court order will be required to secure CGT holdover relief. See also CG67190–CG67192.

[112] *Haines v Hill* [2007] EWCA Civ 1284.

[113] HMRC Manuals IHTM04165.

[114] HMRC Manuals IHTM04173.

Although *G v G* has clearly been of assistance to some taxpayers so far as CGT is concerned, it does raise the question in relation to s.10 as to whether, where the disposition is made pursuant to a court order, any "transaction" at all is involved for purposes of s.10, be it one actually made between the parties or a notional one of a kind such as they might have been expected to have made had they not been connected. It remains to be seen whether HMRC take this point.

Meaning of "transaction"

2–44   It is important to note that for purposes of s.10(1), "transaction" includes "a series of transactions and any associated operations". This rather ominous provision is open to three interpretations. It could mean:

(1) "transaction" includes a series of transactions plus any associated operations; or
(2) "transaction" includes
  (a) a series of transactions, and also includes
  (b) any associated operations; or
(3) "transaction" includes
  (a) a series of transactions, and
  (b) any associated operations, and
  (c) a series of transactions plus any associated operations.

The point is not an entirely academic one.[115] If the first, and narrowest interpretation is correct, associated operations become relevant only if there is also a series of transactions, and vice versa. If, on the other hand, either of the other two interpretations is correct, any associated operation and any transaction in a series of transactions is relevant. This could be important since, by s.268(2), the grant of a lease for full consideration in money or money's worth is not associated with any operation effected more than three years after the grant. By contrast, no time limits apply in determining whether a transaction is part of a series of transactions. The question may thus arise as to whether a transaction which is part of a series of transactions is to be brought into account in the absence of any associated operations. It is thought that it would be optimistic indeed to assume that such a transaction would not be brought into account: the third, and normally least helpful, of the above-mentioned interpretations would appear to be the correct one particularly in light of the decision in *Macpherson v IRC*.[116]

The onus is on HMRC to establish the presence of any associated operations or transactions forming part of a series of transactions. Precisely what constitutes an associated operation is discussed at paras 9–05 and following. The term "series of transactions" is not defined by the legislation, and appears to have been added to the legislation almost as an afterthought. Its significance lies primarily in the fact that, as was mentioned above, no time limits apply in determining what transactions are to be brought into account in deciding whether the conditions necessary for s.10(1) relief are satisfied. However, only "relevant" associated operations should be brought into

---

[115] Matters are not made any easier by the provision in s.272 that "disposition" includes a disposition effected by associated operations.
[116] *Macpherson v IRC* [1988] S.T.C. 362, discussed at paras 9–18 and 15–15.

account, i.e. relevant in the context of being part of a scheme intended to confer gratuitous benefit.[117]

The stamp duty legislation uses the words "larger transaction or series of transactions," and in *Att Gen v Cohen*[118] these words were given a restrictive interpretation, Green L.J. holding that transactions formed part of a series only if they were integrally related; the fact that they were concerned with the same property was not sufficient. It is not clear to what extent this will also be the case for IHT. Given the wide definition of associated operations, to assign too narrow a meaning to "series of transactions" would be to render the words otiose. Nevertheless, it would seem arguable that transactions form part of a "series" only if they are directed towards achieving a single specific objective, or are otherwise dependent on each other; it is understood that this view is that taken by HMRC.[119] This does not rob the term of all significance, since, given the time limits which operate with regard to associated operations under s.268(3), a transaction may in certain circumstances constitute a transaction in a series of transactions without being an associated operation.

Connected persons

By s.270, the definition of connected persons is the same as that for CGT under s.286 **2–45** of the Taxation of Chargeable Gains Act 1992 except that for IHT purposes "relative" includes uncle, aunt, nephew and niece and "settlement", "settlor" and "trustee" have the meaning given them under ss.43–45 of the 1984 Act, as discussed in Chapter 11. The result is that an individual is connected with:

(1) his spouse or civil partner;
(2) his relatives, i.e. brother, sister, ancestor, lineal descendants, uncles, aunts, nephews and nieces;
(3) his relatives' spouses or civil partners;
(4) his spouse's or civil partner's relatives and their spouses or civil partners; and
(5) his partners   except in relation to acquisition or disposal of
      his partner's spouse   partnership assets pursuant to bona fide commer-
      his partner's relatives   cial acquisitions.

In addition, there are special rules for settlements and companies. A trustee of a settlement is connected with:

(1) any individual who is a settlor in relation to a settlement;
(2) any person who is connected with such a settlor; and
(3) a body corporate during a year of assessment which at any time during that year is an IHT close company[120] whose participators include the trustees of the settlement.

A company is connected with another person if:

---

[117] Per Lord Jauncey at p.369 of his judgment, the order in which transactions take place can affect whether the associated operation is "relevant" or not, i.e. it may contribute nothing to the gratuitous benefit.

[118] *Att Gen v Cohen* [1937] 1 K.B. 478.

[119] See also "The legal effect of transactions infected by 'an understanding'", *British Tax Review* (1979), p.301.

[120] See para.2–102.

(1) he controls the company; or

(2) he and persons connected with him together control the company.

A company is connected with another company if:

(1) the same person controls both companies; or

(2) a person controls one company and persons connected with him control the other company; or

(3) a group of two or more persons controls each company, and the group either
  (a) consists of the same persons, or
  (b) could be regarded as consisting of the same persons by treating (in one or more cases) a member of either group as replaced by a person with whom he is connected.

For the purposes of the company provisions:

(1) any two or more persons acting together to secure or exercise control of a company shall be treated in relation to that company as connected
  (a) with one another, and
  (b) with any person acting on the directions of any of them to secure or exercise control of the company[121];
  and

(2) "control" is construed in accordance with Corporation Tax Act 2010 ss.450 and 451.

In each of the above cases, the provision that A is connected with B is taken, not surprisingly, to mean that B is connected with A.[122] There is no general provision, however, that says that where A is connected with B, and B is connected with C, A is connected with C, or that C is connected with A. The only such "link-up" provisions are those expressly stated above in the provisions dealing with settlements and companies.

Unquoted securities: freely negotiated price

2–46 Where the disposition or transaction involves a sale of unquoted shares or unquoted debentures, s.10(1) does not apply unless a second objective requirement is satisfied, namely that the sale was either:

(1) at a price freely negotiated at the time of the sale; or

(2) where the price was not freely negotiated, at a price such as might be expected to have been freely negotiated at the time of the sale.[123]

It will be noted that this requirement becomes relevant only if there has been a "sale". It has been held that in the absence of express statutory provision "sale" means a transfer for a consideration in money, not a transfer for a consideration in money's

---

[121] TCGA 1992 s.286(7).
[122] TCGA 1992 s.286(1).
[123] IHTA 1984 s.10(2).

worth.[124] The exchange of shares for some other property should thus not constitute a sale for these purposes; it is understood that HMRC do not dispute this.

It will be noted that it is insufficient that the price of the shares is equal to their market value. What matters is that the price is a freely negotiated one. Evidence of bargaining, separate advisers, etc. may therefore be crucial. In some cases, the price will not be freely negotiated, notably where the sale is governed by pre-emption rights in the articles of the company concerned. In such circumstances, it will be necessary to show that, assuming free negotiations had been possible, as good a price as that in fact obtained would have been obtained. This may be difficult to establish where the pre-emption clause is stringent.

Subjective test: absence of gratuitous intent

Beside satisfying the above requirements, the taxpayer must also show in all cases that the disposition: **2–47**

(1) was not intended to confer any gratuitous benefit on any person; and
(2) was not made in a transaction intended to confer any gratuitous benefit on any person.

The accepted judicial definition of "intention" was given by Asquith L.J. in *Cunliffe v Goodman*[125] (a landlord and tenant case) in which he said:

> "An 'intention' to my mind connotes a state of affairs which the party 'intending'—I will call him X—does more than merely contemplate: it connotes a state of affairs which, on the contrary, he decides, so far as in him lies, to bring about, and which, in point of possibility, he has a reasonable prospect of being able to bring about, by his own act of volition.
>
> X cannot, with any due regard to the English language be said to 'intend' a result which is wholly beyond the control of his will. He cannot 'intend' that it shall be a fine day tomorrow: at most he can hope or desire or pray that it will. Nor, short of this, can X be said to intend a particular result if its occurrence, though it may be not wholly uninfluenced by X's will, is dependent on so many other influences, accidents and cross-currents of circumstances that, not merely is it quite likely not to be achieved at all, but, if it is achieved, X's volition will have been no more than a minor agency collaborating with, or not thwarted by, the factors which predominately determine its occurrence. If there is a sufficiently formidable succession of fences to be surmounted before the result at which X aims can be achieved, it may well be unmeaning to say that X 'intended' that result."

As with the arm's length transaction test, a question arises as to precisely what the subjective test involves. HMRC might well argue that certain dispositions confer a gratuitous benefit by their very nature, and that no person would enter into such a transaction in the first place unless he was donatively disposed. The taxpayer, on the other hand, will contend that the proper approach is to assume that such a transaction could be entered into without any gratuitous intent, the test being whether the terms of the transaction disclose such an intent. This, of course, is the same approach that the authors thought appropriate in applying the arm's length test, however they are less sure that it applies here, where the hypothetical element is lacking. Here the taxpayer must show that the *disposition* was not intended to confer any such benefit, not that it

---

[124] See *Coats (J and P) v IRC* [1897] 1 Q.B. 778; *Kirkness v Hudson (John) Co Ltd* [1955] A.C. 696; *Robshaw v Mayer* [1957] Ch. 125; *Littlewoods Mail Order Stores Ltd v IRC* [1963] A.C. 135.
[125] *Cunliffe v Goodman* [1950] 2 K.B. 237 at 253.

was made in a transaction such as might be expected to be entered into by a person without such an intent.

The test is thus a stringent one, and it is worth stressing that it must be shown that there was no intent to confer *any* gratuitous benefit on *any* person. The slightest benefit thus suffices to infringe the requirement. It is important to note that it is insufficient to show that the disposition was itself uninfected by any donative intent. It is also necessary to show that the disposition was not made in a transaction intended to confer any gratuitous benefit on any person, and for this purpose "transaction" has the wide, if somewhat unclear, meaning discussed above.[126] It should also be noted, particularly where there are a series of transactions, that it appears that it is not only necessary that the transferor had no donative intent, but that there was no donative intent on the part of any of the persons involved in the series of transactions. It is thought that the making of a will may be an associated operation,[127] but even if this is correct, the subjective test should still not be infringed. This is because, in the authors' view, the words "gratuitous benefit" in s.10(1) imply an element of choice, and benefits conferred by a testator cannot be regarded as gratuitous: his assets must pass under his will or under the law of intestacy; he cannot, though the actions of some suggest they may think otherwise, take his assets with him.

IRC v Spencer-Nairn

2–48   The uncertainties thrown up by s.10 have long been a source of concern and accordingly the decision in *IRC v Spencer-Nairn*[128] is welcome as providing guidance on the meaning of the section in the context of transfers between connected persons.

The taxpayer owned a large estate in Scotland. He had little experience of farming and estate management and therefore relied heavily on the family's adviser, a chartered accountant and actuary. In 1975 one of the farms was leased to a Jersey resident company at a rent which was largely absorbed in the costs of repairs and maintenance. Furthermore, the Jersey company almost immediately demanded that the piggery buildings on the farm should be replaced at the taxpayer's expense. The adviser obtained a professional report which estimated the cost in the region of £80,000. As the taxpayer could not afford this the adviser recommended that the farm should be sold. The adviser handled all matters connected with the sale and eventually it was sold for £101,350 to a second Jersey company. The farm was never advertised and the taxpayer accepted this offer on the recommendation of his adviser: interestingly, neither the taxpayer nor the adviser were aware at the time that the company was a "connected person".

For CGT purposes the Lands Tribunal for Scotland determined the market value of the farm at £199,000 on the basis that, contrary to the adviser's view, the taxpayer was not liable to pay for the improvements demanded by the tenant. In due course (not entirely surprisingly) HMRC raised a CTT assessment on the basis of a transfer of value of £94,000. It was generally accepted that the taxpayer did not have a gratuitous intention: but HMRC argued that the transfer was not such as the taxpayer would have made in an arm's length transaction with an unconnected person.

For s.10 to be relevant the transferor must have made a transfer of value (that is, he must have entered into a disposition as a result of which his estate has been diminished) and, once that is shown, the taxpayer is then forced into the position of having to show

---

[126] At para.2–44; see *Macpherson v IRC* [1989] A.C. 159, discussed at paras 9–18 and 15–15.
[127] See para.9–05.
[128] *IRC v Spencer-Nairn* [1991] S.T.C. 60.

56

that he did not intend to make any gift and that what he did would satisfy the test of an objective commercial arrangement. It is understood that HMRC had taken a restricted view (some would say a minimalistic view) of the section. In effect they argued that if there was a substantial fall in the transferor's estate that is the end of the matter. In *Spencer-Nairn* the Lord President dismissed arguments of this nature in a summary fashion:

> "The fact that the transaction was for less than the open market value cannot be conclusive of the issues at this stage, otherwise the section would be deprived of its content. The gratuitous element in the transaction becomes therefore no more than a factor, which must be weighed in the balance with all the other facts and circumstances to see whether the onus which is on the transferor has been discharged."[129]

The case is a curiosity in that a substantially higher value had been determined by the Lands Tribunal, largely because of the view it took of the relevant Scottish agricultural holdings legislation. It had concluded that under the legislation the landlord was not obliged to erect the new piggery buildings. Clearly, had this burden rested on the landlord the actual sale price which he received would not have been unreasonable. The difficulty of ascertaining any sort of market value for an asset, such as the lease in this case, is all too apparent in a situation where the farm was really only of interest to the sitting tenant and he, on being approached on behalf of the landlord, expressed no interest in acquiring the freehold.

In applying the test in s.10 it was accepted by HMRC that the vendor had no intention of conferring a gratuitous benefit on anyone. Thus there was no need to discuss the meaning of "intention" as set out in *Cunliffe v Goodman*,[130] nor was that case referred to in the judgment. Both the Special Commissioners and the Court of Session accepted that the test as to whether or not the transferor had an intention to confer gratuitous benefit on any person was a subjective one, though this seems at odds with *Cunliffe*.[131] The sole question for the court was whether the sale achieved was such as would have been made with a third party at arm's length. When the court came to apply this test, although it was basically drafted in objective terms, they found it necessary to incorporate subjective ingredients. The hypothetical vendor must be assumed to have held the belief of the landlord that the value of the property was diminished by his obligation to rebuild the piggeries. A wholly reasonable (albeit mistaken) belief will presumably be relevant. The *Spencer-Nairn* case is unusual in that the parties did not know that they were connected: in a sense therefore they were negotiating as if they were third parties on the open market. The Lord President commented that in the circumstances:

> "A good way of testing the question whether the sale was such as might be expected to be made in a transaction between persons not connected with each other is to see what persons who were unaware that they were connected with each other actually did".[132]

For the purposes of the second limb of s.10 there can be a sale at arm's length even though the price realised is not approximately the same as the "market value" and in considering what amounts to an "arm's length" sale features of the actual sale (such as the reasonably held beliefs of the vendor) must be taken into account. Accordingly

---

[129] *IRC v Spencer-Nairn* [1991] S.T.C. 60 at 67.
[130] *Cunliffe v Goodman* [1950] 2 K.B. 237 at 253.
[131] *IRC v Spencer-Nairn* [1991] S.T.C. 60 at 67.
[132] *IRC v Spencer-Nairn* [1991] S.T.C. 60 at 71.

this limb of the s.10 test is not wholly objective in contrast to that for the first limb of the test.[133]

Postlethwaite's Executors v Revenue and Customs Commissioners

2–49   The Special Commissioners considered the further application of s.10 in the case of *Postlethwaite's Executors v Revenue and Customs Commissioners*[134] which involved the payment of £700,000 by the directors of a close company to a Funded Unapproved Retirement Benefit Scheme (FURBS) for the benefit of the sole beneficial shareholder of the Company. The shareholder died before he could start drawing his pension and the funds became held on discretioanry trusts for a class of beneficiaries including, inter alia, his wife. HMRC contended that this payment represented an intention to confer a gratuitous benefit on the shareholder and his family and so was a transfer of value and accordingly taxable. The taxpayers appealed.

The Special Commissioners held that s.13(1) (see para.2–68, below) did not apply to the payment, as the funds in the FURBS were allocated solely to the shareholder's Accumulated Fund and was not held as a common fund for anyone else employed by the company, such as the directors. Moreover, there was no intention that any of the directors would be admitted to the FURBS.

It therefore fell to the Special Commissioners to determine whether s.10 was relevant to the transfer or not. It was common ground between the parties that the relevant intention was that of the Company (though it would be imputed to the shareholder and taxed in his hands under s.94(1)). It was found that although the Company had followed the wishes of the shareholder, there was no question that the powers of the board had been usurped and that the intentions were necessarily the same. It was found that whilst working for the Company, the shareholder had been paid under £120,000 but had earned fees for the Company of £950,000. It was therefore not unreasonable that they make such a payment for his benefit. The Special Commissioners held that although there were no prior legal obligations for making the payment and that it was substantially, if not entirely, in consideration of past services, this "did not mean that it was made with the intention of conferring a gratuitous benefit".[135] Interestingly, the Special Commissioners decided that the natural meaning of gratuitous benefit is not limited to dispositions otherwise than for full consideration under a legal obligation. The fact of past consideration may be sufficient to negate an intention to confer a gratuitous benefit provided that the past consideration is commensurate with the benefit conferred.[136]

HMRC argued that, given that the shareholder had died and so the sum had became payable to his wife then this was sufficient to introduce an intention to confer a gratuitous benefit on the spouse and would only be relieved if covered by s.12 (see below, paras 2–62 and following). This was given short shrift by the Special Commissioners, being described as "more in keeping with Victorian times than with modern family law and pension legislation".[137] The taxpayers' appeal was therefore allowed.

This case further developed the concept of intention to confer a gratuitous benefit and helpfully sets out that there need not be any binding legal obligation before it can

---

[133] Compare a similar conclusion reached by the Court of Appeal in *Walton's Executors v IRC* in the context of applying the market value rule at s.160 to agricultural tenancies: see para.25–46, below.
[134] *Postlethwaite's Executors v Revenue and Customs Commissioners* [2007] S.T.C. (S.C.D.) 83.
[135] *Postlethwaite's Executors v Revenue and Customs Commissioners* [2007] S.T.C. (S.C.D.) 83 at 86.
[136] *Postlethwaite's Executors v Revenue and Customs Commissioners* [2007] S.T.C. (S.C.D.) 83 at 90.
[137] *Postlethwaite's Executors v Revenue and Customs Commissioners* [2007] S.T.C. (S.C.D.) 83 at 90.

be found that there is no gratuitous intent in any transfer made. Even within a close company and without a binding legal obligation it is possible to make reasonable payments to a participator in the company in recognition of past services without there being any intention to confer a gratuitous benefit, thereby making for an objective test in considering both the services previously performed and the remuneration received as payment for such past consideration.

Employee Benefit Trusts

For several years, HMRC have taken issue with employee benefit trusts and have **2–50** attacked them from several angles.[138] One angle of attack in relation to employee benefit trusts established by close companies has been HMRC's argument[139] that although s.10 provides that no charge arises if there is no intention to confer a gratuitous benefit, this is unlikely to be satisfied in the context of an employee benefit trust as the trust is likely to confer a gratuitous benefit on the participators. Section 10 was one of the provisions relied upon to effect the transfer to the employee benefit trust without it being a transfer of value. HMRC have maintained that there is both a subjective test and an objective test in s.10 and that both tests must be met to satisfy s.10. HMRC maintain that the subjective test requires that there must not be the slightest possibility of gratuitous intent at the date the contribution is made. They maintain that the objective test requires that the transaction must either have been made at arm's length between persons not connected with each other (as defined in s.270) or was such as might be expected to be made in a transaction at arm's length between persons not connected with each other. HMRC maintain that

> "given that the potential beneficiaries under an Employee Benefit Trust normally include the participators themselves, the employees or former employees, and/or the wives, husbands, civil partners, widows, widowers, surviving civil partners and children and step children under the age of 18 of such employees and former employees, it will normally be difficult to show that the conditions of s10 are met."[140]

This analysis has been criticised on the grounds that it is the overall commerciality of the arrangements which is relevant, and if it can be shown the motivation behind the creation of the EBT was "a genuine desire to remunerate the employees and officers of the close company establishing it", there is no reason why s.10 should not apply.[141] Nevertheless, where an employee benefit trust is established by a close company, where

---

[138] This culminated in the introduction of the "disguised remuneration" rules in Pt 7A of ITEPA 2003 (introduced by FA 2011) which has had a significant impact in relation to employee benefit trusts. From April 6, 2011, where a trustee earmarks, pays, transfers or makes available a sum or asset for a current, former or prospective employee, or a person chosen by that employee, which is, in essence, a means of providing reward or recognition in connection with employment, that step may be subject to income tax (under the PAYE system) and NICs.

[139] See Revenue and Customs Brief 18/11, *http://www.hmrc.gov.uk/briefs/inheritance-tax/brief1811.htm* [Accessed 30 October 2012].

[140] Revenue and Customs Brief 18/11, *http://www.hmrc.gov.uk/briefs/inheritance-tax/brief1811.htm* [Accessed October 4, 2012].

[141] See I. Maston, "Gifts with strings attached" (2009) *Taxation*, Vol.164, 4225. The author notes that similar issues were examined in the case of *Postlethwaite's Executors* (SpC 571) in the context of the transfer of funds to a FURBS where the transfer was for the benefit of the company's sole beneficial shareholder. In that case the Special Commissioners noted that the directors would not have considered themselves to be conferring bounty on him, as whatever they gave to the FURBS reduced the value of his shares. In fact the article was written in response to an earlier version of Revenue and Customs Brief 18/11, namely Revenue and Customs Brief 49/09 which was updated by Revenue and Customs Brief 18/11.

practicable it may be wise to consider the exclusion of the participators if the intention is to rely on s.10 (although employee benefit trusts will more usually rely on the relief under s.13).

Application in practice

2–51   Section 10(1) will apply to relieve a number of estate-diminishing dispositions from being transfers of value. The most obvious case will be where property is unwittingly sold for less than its true value. An intentional sale at an undervalue in extenuating circumstances should also qualify, as should, e.g., an ex gratia payment in connection with an out of court settlement.

One situation in which s.10(1) may prove particularly useful is where a person has an interest in possession in some shares and at the same time is also the beneficial owner of some more of the same kind of shares. As will be seen below, under s.49(1) he will be treated as the beneficial owner of the shares in which his interest in possession subsists, with the result that he will be regarded as the beneficial owner of all the shares. This may have adverse valuation consequences. Assume, for example, that A has a life interest in 30 per cent of the shares in B Ltd, and that he also owns 25 per cent of the shares outright. He will be treated as owning 55 per cent of the shares. Assume also that for commercial reasons he sells his 25 per cent holding at market value to a third party. Since the sale is of a minority interest he will receive a price based on a minority value only. The shares, however, will have been valued on a majority basis. Consequently, the value of his estate will have been diminished by the sale even though the sale was for market value, and thus A will have prima facie made a transfer of value. In the circumstances, however, he should be able to rely on s.10(1) with the result that he will not have made a transfer of value after all, and no tax will be chargeable.

Section 10(1) should also be available where A sells all or part of his holding to avoid the IHT that will be charged on him because of the above adverse valuation. Assume the facts are those above, but A sells his 25 per cent holding to his son. So long as the sale satisfies the three requirements of s.10(1), which it should do provided the shares are sold for a "freely negotiated" price, s.10(1) should operate to prevent the disproportionate diminution in the value of A's estate occasioned by the sale resulting in A making a transfer of value, in which case A will have escaped from some of the adverse consequences of having the beneficial ownership of the 30 per cent holding attributed to him.

Accident insurance schemes: payments to employees

2–52   HMRC issued the following self-explanatory statement on January 6, 1976:

> "The Board of Inland Revenue understand that there is uncertainty about the capital transfer tax position of payments by an employer to an employee or his dependants following a claim by the employer under the terms of an accident insurance policy effected by the employer under the terms of which the benefits are payable to him absolutely.
>
> Time Board wish to make it clear that s.20(4) of the Finance Act 1975[142] provides that there will not be a 'transfer of value' where the employer and employee are at arm's length and not connected with each other and where there is no intention to confer a gratuitous

---

[142] The forerunner to s.10.

benefit. Where the employer and employee are connected there will be no liability if the payment was such as might reasonably be expected between non-connected persons.

In many cases the payment will be covered by the exemption in para.9 of Sch.6 to the Finance Act 1975 as being allowable as a deduction in computing the taxable profits of a trade, profession or vocation, so that no question of a capital transfer tax liability can arise. If a payment not covered by para.9 of Sch.6 is allowable for income tax or corporation tax purposes. *e.g.* under the provisions of s.72 or s.304 of the Income and Corporation Taxes Act 1970,[143] the Board will accept that this of itself establishes that the requirements of s.20(4) are met."

Paragraph 9 of Sch.6 to the Finance Act 1975 has since been replaced by s.12(1).[144]

HMRC "clearances"

There is no statutory clearance procedure under s.10, but in practice it is possible to write to HMRC, setting out the details of a proposed transaction and asking for confirmation that s.10(1) applies to relieve the transaction from being a transfer of value. A confirmatory reply, though not binding on HMRC, will obviously be of great comfort.

2–53

Grant of a tenancy of agricultural property

Section 16(1) provides that a person who grants a tenancy of agricultural property in the United Kingdom, the Channel Islands or the Isle of Man for use for agricultural purposes does not make a transfer of value so long as he grants the tenancy for full consideration in money or money's worth. For these purposes "agricultural property" has the meaning given to it for the purposes of agricultural relief.[145]

It is important to note that the tenancy of the property must be:

2–54

(1) "for use for agricultural purposes"; and
(2) "for full consideration in money or money's worth".

Given the first requirement, a tenancy agreement should expressly provide that the tenancy of the property is "for use for agricultural purposes". The term "agricultural purposes" is not defined; presumably it will be given a fairly wide meaning. The meaning of "full consideration in money or money's worth" is not entirely clear. In particular, is the only relevant consideration the amount of the rent initially chargeable, or do the terms of the lease generally, including rent revision clauses, fall to be taken into account? HMRC's views are summarised in *The Law Society Gazette*, 1984, p.2361. Shortly stated, HMRC take the view that, in purely rental terms, "full consideration" means:

> " . . . the rent which would be expected to be achieved on the grant in the open market by a willing lessor to an *unconnected* incoming tenant of a new tenancy of the particular land being considered".

---

[143] ICTA 1970 s.304 is now ICTA 1988 s.75; ICTA 1970 s.72 became ICTA 1988 s.25 but has since been repealed.
[144] See para.2–62.
[145] See paras 26–115–26–133.

It should be noted that HMRC expressed the view that rents fixed by reference to the new rent that would be charged to a sitting tenant (the so-called "arbitration" rent) would be unlikely to constitute "full consideration" within s.16(1).

"Consideration" for the grant of a tenancy need not be limited to the reservation of a rent; for example, if the grant of the tenancy was connected with the formation of a partnership with onerous obligations for the "partner/tenants", those obligations might constitute additional consideration for the grant of the tenancy.

Section 16(1) contains no tapering relief for tenancies granted for, say, 90 per cent of "full consideration". If full consideration is given for the grant, there is no transfer of value; anything less than full consideration is a transfer of value. This treatment is harsh, because the transfer of value occasioned by the grant of an agricultural tenancy arises from the diminution in the value of the freehold interest retained by the grantor; that diminution is principally a reflection of the security of tenure afforded to the agricultural tenant. This security of tenure will exist whether the tenancy has been granted for full consideration or not.

Family maintenance dispositions

2–55   Under s.11 a number of dispositions which diminish the value of a person's estate which are made by way of maintaining others who, broadly speaking, form part of the disponer's family are relieved from being transfers of value. These dispositions fall into three categories:

    (1) dispositions for a party to a marriage or civil partnership;
    (2) dispositions for children; and
    (3) dispositions for dependent relatives.

2–56   Before considering s.11 in detail, it is worth noting that: (a) it is relevant only to transfers between parties to a marriage or civil partnership when the s.18 exemption is not available, e.g. post decree absolute or dissolution transfers; and (b) where payments are made under a court order, s.11 relief will not normally be needed. This is because, as was discussed at para.2–34, when a court order is made the value of the estate of the person who is liable to make payments under the order is diminished, but, since the making of the order does not constitute a disposition by him, the making of the order does not constitute a transfer of value. When the person against whom the order is made later makes payments in accordance with the order, he does not make a transfer of value, since, although the payments constitute dispositions, they are made to discharge a pre-existing liability imposed by law, and therefore do not diminish the value of his estate; see also para.2–43. Thus, where payments are made under a court order, there is both a disposition and a diminution, but the diminution is not occasioned by the disposition, and consequently there is normally no transfer of value. Section 11 will therefore be needed only in the rare case where the value of the disponer's estate is diminished by a sum in excess of the liability imposed by the court order.

It should be noted that s.11(1) will not apply on death as it refers only to "dispositions". Also s.11 will only cover dispositions that qualify as "maintenance"[146] of the

---

[146] See para.2–57.

other party to the marriage or civil partnership. However, payments in excess of this are likely to be covered by s.10.[147]

Dispositions for a party to a marriage or civil partnership

By s.11(1)(a), a disposition is not a transfer of value if it is made by one party to a **2–57** marriage or civil partnership in favour of the other party for the latter's maintenance. This provision uses two terms "party to a marriage or civil partnership" and "maintenance", which are used elsewhere in s.11 and which bear some scrutiny.

"Party to a marriage or civil partnership" Here, two points are worth making. First, it suffices that the parties involved are married or in a civil partnership; they need not be living together as man and wife or as civil partners during the year of assessment in question. For this purpose, a marriage ceases only on the grant of a decree absolute[148] and a civil partnership only ceases on its final dissolution. Secondly, and more importantly, persons who in consequence of a dissolution or annulment are no longer married or in a civil partnership can still be "parties to a marriage or civil partnership" for purposes of s.11. This is because for this purpose "marriage" or "civil partnership" includes a former marriage or civil partnership where the disposition in question:

(1) is made on the dissolution or annulment of a marriage or civil partnership; or
(2) varies a disposition made on the dissolution or annulment of a marriage or civil partnership.[149]

This is important, since it means that relief may be available under s.11(1)(a) in circumstances where the s.18 exemption is unavailable. If, on obtaining a divorce from his wife (or on the dissolution of a civil partnership), Y covenants to make maintenance payments to her, the s.18 exemption will not be available, but s.11 will apply, since at the time of the disposition[150] X and Y are still parties to a marriage even though they are no longer spouses. Care must be taken, or course, to ensure that the original disposition is made on the occasion of the dissolution or annulment of the marriage; otherwise the relief will not be available (where time has run out it may still be possible to rely on s.10(1)).

If X later agrees to increase the payments, the increased payments will also qualify for relief since they will be variations of the original disposition. The position is less favourable if Y volunteers to accept a lesser sum, e.g. because she has remarried. In that case, she will have released her right to the maintenance foregone, and thus will herself have prima facie made a transfer of value. Whether that disposition can be said to be made for X's maintenance seems doubtful, though in certain circumstances this may be established, e.g. where the variation is occasioned by X's remarriage. Difficulties in this area can be avoided by ensuring that the initial agreement is given effect under a court order made under s.23 of the Matrimonial Causes Act 1973; such an order can be varied by order made under s.31 of the Act.

Where dispositions are made between spouses or civil partners of a continuing marriage or civil partnership the s.18 exemption will normally suffice to prevent a

---

[147] See HMRC Manuals IHTM04161–04181.
[148] See *Fender v St. John-Mildmay* [1938] A.C. 1.
[149] IHTA 1984 s.11(6).
[150] The payments will themselves be part of the disposition X makes on entering into the covenant: this follows from the fact that by s.272 "disposition" includes a disposition effected by associated operations.

charge arising. This is subject to one qualification, namely that, as will be seen at para.3–35, where the transferor spouse or civil partner is a UK domiciliary and the transferee spouse or civil partner is not, the s.18 exemption applies only to the first £55,000 transferred.[151] In such a case, recourse may, in appropriate circumstances, be had to the s.11(1)(a) relief before relying on the s.18 exemption.

HMRC accept that in appropriate circumstances "party to a marriage or civil partnership" may include a widow/widower.[152] "Spouse" or "civil partner" for the purposes of s.18 does not include a common law spouse or civil partner,[153] and such spouse or civil partner will presumably not be a "party to a marriage or civil partnership".

"*Maintenance*" This term is not defined, and there is not a great deal to be gleaned from the family law cases on its meaning. The best guide appears to be the Matrimonial Causes Act 1973, which distinguishes between "financial provision orders" and "property adjustment orders". "Financial provision orders" are orders for:

(1) periodical payments (secured and unsecured); and
(2) orders for lump sum payments.

"Property adjustment orders" are mainly concerned with the transfer of property such as the matrimonial home; it is thought that such a transfer could not be said to be for maintenance, and thus would not qualify for relief under s.11. Periodical payments, on the other hand, will normally be for maintenance. The payment of a lump sum would not normally be regarded as being made to maintain a person, but, exceptionally, may be regarded as doing so either retrospectively or prospectively. Under s.23(3)(a) of the 1973 Act, the court has power to order the payment of a lump sum to enable the recipient to meet "any liabilities or expenses reasonably incurred by himself or herself or any child of the family before applying for . . . " such an order. If the court orders such a payment there will, of course, be no need to rely on s.11. In the absence of a court order, it may be possible to contend on the basis of s.23(3)(a) that the voluntary payment of a lump sum by way of providing for such "retrospective" maintenance also qualifies as maintenance under s.11. If this is the case, there seems to be no reason why the voluntary payment of a lump sum which constitutes provision for future maintenance should not also constitute a payment by way of maintenance for these purposes. Indeed, on this reasoning, the transfer of the matrimonial home may constitute a payment by way of maintenance.

Dispositions for children

2–58   These fall into three sub-categories, namely:

(1) dispositions made by one party to a marriage or civil partnership in favour of a child of either party;

---

[151] On Budget Day 2012 (March 21, 2012) it was announced that the capping of IHT spouse relief to £55,000 in respect of transfers between spouses and civil partners where the transferor is domiciled in the UK and his spouse or civil partner is not, would be revised inasmuch as non-domiciled spouses and civil partners would have the option of electing to be UK domiciled for IHT purposes. For those who do not elect, the cap would increase to the nil rate band, currently £325,000. At the time of writing draft legislation is awaited.
[152] Private Client Business (1997), p.278.
[153] *Holland v IRC* [2003] S.T.C. (S.C.D.) 43.

(2) dispositions made by any person in favour of a child not in his parent's care; and

(3) dispositions made in favour of the disponer's illegitimate child.

In all cases the disposition must satisfy at least two tests. First, it must be for the maintenance, education or training of the child in question. The meaning of "maintenance" was discussed above; neither "education" nor "training" is defined. Their ordinary meaning is wide; it is thought, for instance, that the education or training need not be at an establishment, and that private tuition would constitute either "education" or "training" or both.[154] Secondly, certain age limits must be observed. In all cases, the disposition cannot be for a period ending later than the end of the year of assessment in which a child attains 18. This is subject to the extremely important qualification that a disposition in favour of a child who has attained 18 will not be disqualified so long as the child has not ceased to undergo full-time education or training.[155] Whether a person who returns to school after having left it has ceased to undergo full-time education or training will probably depend on such factors as the length of time he was away from school and his age on leaving and returning to school. A gap of more than three years would almost certainly preclude the relief being available. Summer vacations, on the other hand, would obviously be ignored.

The particulars relevant to each sub-category of dispositions are as follows:

1. *Dispositions made by one party to a marriage or civil partnership in favour of a child of either party.* "Child" for these purposes does not include an illegitimate child, but does include a stepchild and an adopted child. It is important to note that it suffices that the child is the child of *either* party to the marriage or civil partnership in question. The meaning of "party to a marriage or civil partnership" for these purposes was discussed above; its effect here, as above, is that dispositions made on the dissolution or annulment of a marriage or civil partnership and dispositions varying such dispositions can qualify for relief.

2. *Dispositions made in favour of a child not in his parent's care.* Under this head the disponer must be someone other than the child's parent, and the child must not be in the care of any of his parents. "Child" for this purpose is defined as under the previous sub-category; "parent", in turn includes a step-parent or an adoptive parent. Under this head, the age limit is more stringent; dispositions to a child who has attained 18 will qualify for relief after the end of the year of assessment in which he attained that age only if besides not having ceased to undergo full-time education or training the child was in the disponer's care for "substantial" periods before attaining 18.

3. *Dispositions made in favour of the disponer's illegitimate child.* Under this head the child must be the child of the person making the disposition.

Dispositions for dependent relatives

By s.11(3), a disposition made in favour of a dependent relative is not a transfer of value if it is a reasonable provision for his care or maintenance. For this purpose, by s.11(6), "dependent relative" means either: **2–59**

(1) any relative of the disponer or of the disponer's spouse or civil partner who cannot maintain himself or herself because of infirmity or old age; or

---

[154] cf. *Heaslip v Hasemer* (1927) 138 L.T. 207.
[155] IHTA 1984 ss.11(1)(b), (2), (4) and (6).

65

(2) the disponer's mother or mother-in-law provided she is "on her own", i.e. she is

    (a) widowed, or

    (b) living apart from her husband, or

    (c) in consequence of dissolution or annulment of marriage or civil partnership, a single woman.

"Relative" is defined elsewhere in the legislation (see s.270) but that definition does not apply in this context. HMRC will probably reject only the most fanciful interpretations of the term. So far as the meaning of "spouse" or "civil partner" is concerned, it is understood that in practice HMRC concede that in this context "spouse" or "civil partner" includes a deceased spouse or "civil partner". "Dependent relative" is defined as in s.226(6) of the Taxation of Chargeable Gains Act 1992, which exempted from CGT the disposal of a house provided rent-free for a dependent relative. The relief was generally withdrawn for disposals after April 5, 1988, but it may be that the provision of such a house could constitute reasonable provision for the care of such a person for IHT purposes.

This relief is useful in the case of handicapped persons and widows. It will be noted that it also applies to a woman who, although divorced from her husband, is still living with him. In contrast to the relief confined to children, only *reasonable* provision is allowed, but that provision may be for care or maintenance. In *McKelvey v HMRC*[156] which related to the provisions of IHTA 1984 s.11(3), the Special Commissioner (having decided that the case concerned "care" not "maintenance") found that the reasonableness of the provision had to be considered in light of the circumstances as they were reasonably believed to be at the time of the gift, and not as they later turned out to be. However, he also found that an objective standard must be applied in considering whether provision was reasonable.

It will also be noted that, unlike a widow, a widower will be a qualifying recipient only if he is unable to maintain himself because of old age or infirmity. This appears to be male chauvinism in reverse: the relief afforded to children is not limited to dispositions for female children; why should a widower who requires reasonable provision for his care or maintenance be treated differently from a widow who does so?

The relief has been extended by extra statutory concession F12, which provides that:

> "A disposition by a child in favour of his unmarried mother (so far as it represents a reasonable provision for her care or maintenance) qualifies for exemption under IHTA 1984 s.11(3) if the mother is incapacitated by old age or infirmity from maintaining herself. By concession such a disposition is also treated as exempt if the mother (although not so incapacitated) is genuinely financially dependent on the child making the disposition."

The effect of this extension is not clear. As has been noted, relief under s.11(3) is available to a mother "on her own" (the reference to an "unmarried mother", read literally, suggests that the extension applies only to dispositions by bastards) *or* to an elderly or infirm relative incapable of maintaining himself. Why, then, does the concession, which appears to ease the condition governing dispositions to the aged or infirm, start with a reference to "unmarried mothers"? Presumably the relief is now available to any disposition which is reasonable provision for the care and maintenance

---

[156] *McKelvey v Revenue and Customs Commissioners* [2008] W.T.L.R. 1407.

of any relative of the disponer or of the disponer's spouse or civil partner who is "genuinely financially dependent" on the person making the disposition.

Partial relief

Where a disposition satisfies the requirements of s.11 to a limited extent only, the qualifying part is treated by s.11(5) as one disposition, and the non-qualifying part as another, with the result that relief will be available to the qualifying part. **2–60**

Posthumous rearrangements

The reliefs given to variations, disclaimers, orders under the Inheritance (Provision for Family and Dependants) Act 1975 and renunciations of legitim are considered in detail in Chapter 8. **2–61**

Dispositions allowable for income or corporation tax

Section 12(1) provides that a disposition is not a transfer of value if it is allowable in computing the disponer's profits or gains for the purposes of income tax or corporation tax, or if it would be allowable if the disponer's profits or gains were sufficient and fell to be so computed. Thus, a disposition which is allowable as a deduction from trading income or as a management expense of an investment company will not constitute a transfer of value. Non-allowable expenditure, on the other hand, does not qualify for this relief. Where a disposition qualifies only partially for this relief the qualifying and non-qualifying parts are by s.12(5) treated as separate dispositions, with the result that the relief will apply to the qualifying part. **2–62**

The costs incurred by a close company in establishing and running an employee share ownership plan which satisfies the requirements laid down in the Finance Act 1989 ss.67–74 and Sch.5 will fall within s.12(1) as a disposition allowable in computing the company's profits or gains for corporation tax purposes.

Employee benefit trusts

As mentioned in para.2–50, for several years HMRC have taken issue with employee benefit trusts and have attacked them from several angles.[157] HMRC maintain[158] that the relieving effect of s.12 cannot be given provisionally while waiting to see whether the contribution will become allowable for corporation tax purposes. They maintain **2–63**

[157] This culminated in the introduction of the "disguised remuneration" rules in Pt 7A of ITEPA 2003 (introduced by FA 2011) which has had a significant impact in relation to employee benefit trusts. From April 6, 2011, where a trustee earmarks, pays, transfers or makes available a sum or asset for a current, former or prospective employee, or a person chosen by that employee, which is, in essence, a means of providing reward or recognition in connection with employment, that step may be subject to income tax (under the PAYE system) and NICs.

[158] In Revenue and Customs Brief 18/11, *http://www.hmrc.gov.uk/briefs/inheritance-tax/brief1811.htm* [Accessed October 4, 2012].

that s.12 is only available to the extent that a deduction is allowable to the company for the tax year in which the contribution is made. HMRC provide several reasons why a deduction in the corporation tax accounts can be permanently disallowed[159] or the timing of a deduction can be deferred to a later period[160] and say that if expenditure is not allowable for any of these reasons then s.12 does not apply.

HMRC's analysis of s.12 has been criticised on the grounds that it imposes a timing restriction on the relieving effect of s.12 which is not in the legislation itself.[161]

Retirement annuities

2–64   One final point needs to be made about the application of s.12(1). A self-employed individual and, from July 1, 1988, an individual in employment, may contribute to a retirement scheme so as to provide a pension for himself, on retirement, a pension in the event of his death either before or after retirement for his surviving spouse or civil partner, and a lump sum benefit payable if he dies before retiring. Prior to April 6, 1980, any such lump sum death benefit arising under a retirement scheme approved under ss.226 or 226A of the Taxes Act 1970 had to be payable to the individual's personal representatives with the result that those benefits formed part of his estate. As from April 6, 1980, there is no longer any such restriction on the destination of such lump sum death benefits.[162] This means that where a registered pension scheme provides for benefits on death to be paid to a person other than the individual contributing to the scheme, each contribution paid toward the scheme will diminish the value of the contributor's estate. If contributions are not made by an employer, such contributions are not relieved by s.12(2) from being transfers of value. This means that the contributor will have to rely on the various exemptions that may be available to him, e.g. the normal expenditure of income exemption, to prevent a charge from arising in respect of his contributions to the scheme. Had s.12(1) relief been available, on the other hand, he would have been able to use those exemptions to shield other gifts from a charge. Please see Chapter 23 for a further discussion regarding contributions to pension schemes.

Planning

2–65   An individual should consider settling into trust the lump sum death benefit payable under his retirement annuity contract or personal pension arrangement. Since under English law[163] it is not possible to assign only part of a chose in action this is normally

---

[159] Namely by capital expenditure disallowed by Corporation Tax Act 2009 s.53 and expenditure not wholly and exclusively incurred under Corporation Tax Act 2009 s.54. See Revenue and Customs Brief 18/11, *http://www.hmrc.gov.uk/briefs/inheritance-tax/brief1811.htm* [Accessed October 4, 2012].

[160] Namely by the following: generally accepted accounting practice (UITF32) which capitalises Employee Benefit Trust contributions by showing them as an asset on the company's balance sheet until and to the extent that the assets transferred to the intermediary vest unconditionally in identified beneficiaries; expenditure subject to FA 1989 s.43 and post-November 27, 2002 expenditure subject to FA 2003 Sch.24 and CTA 2009 s.1290(2)(3). See Revenue and Customs Brief 18/11, *http://www.hmrc.gov.uk/briefs/inheritance-tax/brief1811.htm* [Accessed October 4, 2012].

[161] See I. Maston, "Gifts with strings attached" (2009) *Taxation*, Vol.164, 4225. In fact the article was written in response to an earlier version of Revenue and Customs Brief 18/11, namely Revenue and Customs Brief 49/09 which was updated by Revenue and Customs Brief 18/11.

[162] FA 1980 s.33.

[163] The authors are advised that under Scottish law it may be possible to assign part of a chose in action and that it may therefore be possible to settle the death benefit on trust without settling the policy.

done by the individual transferring his contract to trustees upon trust to hold the pension rights for the individual absolutely and the right to the lump sum death benefit upon discretionary trusts for him and his family. HMRC consider that in the normal case although there may technically be a transfer of value, the value in question will be nominal, on the basis that the individual is expected to survive and draw his pension. Furthermore, the omission by him subsequently to draw his pension should not normally result in his making a notional disposition under s.3(3). For a full discussion, see para.23–17.

Once the contract is held in trust the lump sum death benefit will be subject to the special charging provisions governing the treatment of discretionary trusts but so long as the settlor is alive and able to draw his pension the value of the death benefit will be nominal. See Chapter 23 for a more detailed discussion of the IHT treatment of pension benefits. After the individual dies the death benefit will become valuable, but HMRC practice is, under certain circumstances, to grant exemption on any payment made by the trustees of the death benefit to a beneficiary within two years of the settlor's death. Once the two years is past the special charging provisions apply in the usual way.

Contributions to pension schemes[164]

2–66

Prior to the Finance Act 2004, there were eight different sets of rules for pension schemes. With effect from April 6, 2006 ("A-Day"), the Finance Act 2004 introduced one single regime based on a "Lifetime Allowance" for the amount of pension savings that can benefit from tax relief. The intention was to simplify the UK pensions system. On A-Day, all approved UK pension schemes became registered pension schemes under the new regime. Pension trustees were given the opportunity to opt out of the new regime and become an unregistered scheme, but this came at a 40 per cent tax charge and also meant that funds withdrawn from the scheme after A-Day are liable to both income tax and national insurance contributions.

The term "pension scheme" is defined by reference to the types of benefit that are payable by the scheme, and there is no restriction on the type of entity which may be a pension scheme. Three types of schemes are specifically defined: public service pension schemes, occupational pension schemes and recognised overseas pension schemes. Any new pension schemes set up post A-Day can be registered and the act of registration confers tax advantages on a pension scheme with assets held within a registered pension scheme not being subject to capital gains tax or income tax. However, pension trustees cannot reclaim the notional 10 per cent tax credit in UK dividends and so there is not a total exemption from income tax. The new regime allows only authorised payments to be made to members, such payments being defined to include pensions, lump sums, recognised transfers (to another recognised scheme), scheme administration member payments and payments made under a pension sharing order or provision.[165] A key concept in the legislation is the "Lifetime Allowance". Although a detailed discussion of the "Lifetime Allowance" is outside the scope of this book, a charge to tax will arise where an individual's total pension savings exceed a threshold and any such savings are brought into payment (though transitional rules offered protection, in the form of either Primary Protection or Enhanced Protection). The "Lifetime Allowance" for 2008/9 is £1.65 million and this will increase to £1.75

---

[164] See also IHTA 1984 s.28, discussed at para.3–68.
[165] The definitions of these terms being found in FA 2004 ss.164 and following.

million for 2009/10 and then to £1.8 million for 2010/11 but reduces to £1.5 million from 2012/2013.

Current position

2–67 From A-Day, under s.12(2), a disposition made by any person is not a transfer of value if it is a contribution under a registered pension scheme[166] or any pension fund to which the Taxes Act 1988 s.615(3) applies (pension funds for overseas employer) in respect of an employee of the person making the disposition. Such relief given by s.12(2) operates without prejudice to that given by s.12(1). Contributions by close companies to pension schemes will often be deductible for tax purposes, and where that is the case s.12(1) will suffice to provide relief. This may be important in relation to contributions conferring benefits on widowers, as such contributions will not come within s.12(2).

Previously, and prior to the changes introduced from A-Day by the Finance Act 2004, relief was conferred on three kinds of dispositions by s.12(2)(a)–(c)[167]: contributions to "strict" approved pension schemes, contributions to "discretionary" approved schemes and contributions to approved personal pension arrangements. The requirements for each scheme differed considerably. As the majority of such schemes have become registered pension schemes from A-Day the IHT position of employers contribution to pension funds has become considerably simpler.

Dispositions to "employee" trusts by close companies

2–68 Certain trusts receive favourable treatment. Among these are trusts which fall within s.86, referred to here for the sake of convenience as "employee" trusts.[168]

Section 13 provides that a disposition of property made to trustees by a close company whereby the property is to be held on trusts coming within s.86(1) is not a transfer of value if the persons for whose benefit the trusts permit the property to be applied include all or most of either:

(1) the persons employed by or holding office with the company; or
(2) the persons employed by or holding office with the company or any one or more subsidiaries of the company.

At first glance it would appear that, under s.13(1)(b), it suffices that the property can be applied for the benefit of the persons employed by the company making the disposition or (to the exclusion of such employees) for the benefit of the employees of a subsidiary, but it is thought that, strictly speaking, this is incorrect, and that it is not possible for the trust to permit the property to be applied only for the employees of a subsidiary. If that were the case, (1) would be otiose.

HMRC were disposed to interpret s.13(1)(b) liberally. In Statement of Practice E11, they confirm:

---

[166] Namely a scheme which has been registered under the procedure set out in FA 2004 Pt 4 Ch.2 ss.153–159.
[167] These sections were repealed by the FA 2004.
[168] These trusts are discussed in detail in Ch.24.

"The Board regard [the section] as requiring that where the trust is to benefit employees of a subsidiary of the company making the provision those eligible to benefit must include all or most of the employees and officers of the subsidiary and the employees and officers of the holding company taken as a single class. So it would be possible to exclude all of the officers and employees of the holding company without losing the exemption if they comprised only a minority of the combined class. But the exemption would not be available for a contribution to a fund for the sole benefit of the employees of a small subsidiary. This is because it would otherwise have been easy to create such a situation artificially in order to benefit a favoured group of a company's officeholders or employees."

Participator prohibition

The relief under s.13 is subject to one overriding qualification intended to guarantee **2–69** that it applies only to dispositions to genuine employee trusts and not to dispositions to trusts benefiting participators and/or persons connected with participators.[169] By s.13(2), the relief is not available if the trusts permit any of the subject-matter to be applied *at any time* for the benefit of:

(1) a participator in the company making the disposition;
(2) any other person who is a participator in any close company that has made a disposition whereby property became comprised in the settlement in question and which was relieved by s.13(1) from being a transfer of value;
(3) any other person who has been a participator in any such company as is mentioned in (1) or (2) at any time after, or during the 10 years before, the disposition made by that company; or
(4) any person connected with any of the above participators.

It will be noted that this prohibition against participators benefiting will be infringed if the trusts permit such a benefit to be conferred "at any time". It will thus be necessary to frame the trust instrument so as to exclude the possibility of such a benefit being conferred. The simplest way of doing this is to incorporate verbatim the restrictions imposed by s.13(2) into the trust instrument, but such a precaution may be unnecessarily drastic.

By s.13(4), in determining whether the s.86 trusts permit the subject-matter of the disposition to be applied in any of the prohibited ways, no account is taken of any power to make a payment which is the income of any person for any of the purposes of income tax, or which would be the income of a non-resident if he were resident. This is important since it means that participators and persons connected with them can be given benefits so long as they are restricted to income benefits. In drafting the trust instrument, it will thus be necessary to exclude only participators and those connected with them from non-income benefits. In this connection, HMRC are understood not to regard improved working conditions and other facilities which derive from the establishment of an employee's trust as infringing the prohibition against other than income benefits, provided that the benefits are enjoyed by the employees generally.

Further, in determining whether the trusts of a profit sharing scheme approved under the Taxes Act 1988 Sch.9 permit property to be applied as mentioned above, no

---

[169] HMRC state in Revenue and Customs Brief 18/11 that s.13 does not apply where the contributions by a close company are made to an employee benefit trust that does not satisfy IHTA s.86 and where the participators in the company and any person connected with them are not excluded from benefit under the terms of the employee benefit trust (such that s.13(2) applies to disapply s.13(1)).

account is taken of any power to appropriate shares under the scheme,[170] and in determining whether the trusts of an employee share incentive plan approved under the Income Tax (Earnings and Pensions) Act 2003 Sch.2 permit property to be so applied, no account is taken of any power to appropriate shares to, or acquire shares on behalf of, individuals under the plan.[171] Therefore, a disposition by a close company in favour of a share incentive plan may have the benefit of this relief despite the presence of participators amongst the beneficiaries of the scheme or plan.

Section 13(5) provides that, for these purposes, "close company" and "participator" have the meanings given them in Pt IV of the Act,[172] except that the meaning of participator is both widened and narrowed. It is widened to include, in the case of a company which is an open company, a person who would be a participator if the company were a close company. It is narrowed to exclude any participator who:

(1) is not beneficially entitled to, or to rights entitling him to acquire, 5 per cent or more of, or of any class of the shares comprised in, its issued share capital; and

(2) on a winding-up of the company would not be entitled to 5 per cent or more of its assets.[173]

Waiver or repayment of remuneration

2–70   An individual may sometimes waive remuneration to which he is entitled, usually because his marginal rate of tax is such that the gain in public relations outweighs the loss of income. In the absence of provision to the contrary, such a waiver could constitute a transfer of value. Section 14 therefore provides that where a person waives or repays any remuneration that would otherwise be earnings or treated as such and would constitute employment income[174] under the Income Tax (Earnings and Pensions) Act 2003, that waiver or repayment is not a transfer of value. This is subject to the qualification that, if, apart from the waiver or repayment, the remuneration in question would have been allowable as a deduction in computing the payer's profits or gains (or losses) for purposes of income or corporation tax the relief is available only if no such deduction is allowed. There is no time limit on the waiver or repayment.

It will be noted that the relief applies only if the waiver or repayment is of "remuneration" which would otherwise have been assessable to income tax under the Income Tax (Earnings and Pensions) Act 2003. The main charge under the Income Tax (Earnings and Pensions) Act 2003 is on the earnings from an office or employment, and such earnings will clearly constitute "remuneration" for purposes of s.14. The charge under the Income Tax (Earnings and Pensions) Act 2003 also extends to other income in the form of certain pensions, annuities, stipends, social security benefits and other specific items. None of these other than pensions would appear to constitute "remuneration" in the ordinary sense of the word. So far as pensions are concerned, HMRC have taken the view that as a matter of general principle a pension will not constitute "remuneration" for the purposes of s.14.[175]

---

[170] IHTA 1984 s.13(4)(b).

[171] IHTA 1984 s.13(4)(c).

[172] See para.2–74.

[173] IHTA 1984 s.13(3).

[174] See ITEPA 2003 s.7(2)(a) and (b). For waivers or repayments prior to the tax year 2003/04 (or April 5, 2003, in relation to corporation tax), the income needed to be assessable under the old Sch.E of ICTA 1988.

[175] See *Inheritance Tax Manual*, 04210, although note that this section of the manual refers to ICTA 1988 s.833(4)(a) which was repealed by ITEPA 2003 s.722 Sch.6 paras 1 and 108.

Further, HMRC take the view that certain foreign earnings (previously remuneration) attract a 100 per cent deduction for the purposes of the Income Tax (Earnings and Pensions) Act 2003 (or the old Sch.E charge) if the duties are performed or the earnings received outside the United Kingdom. Though the earnings are not in fact chargeable, they may be assessable and so fall within the ambit of s.14.[176]

Waiver of a dividend

By s.15, a person who waives any dividend on shares of a company within 12 months before any right to that dividend has accrued does not by reason of that waiver make a transfer of value. It will be noted that the waiver must be made no more than 12 months before any right to the dividend has accrued. To waive dividends for future years there must be an agreement to waive followed by annual waivers, although it should be noted that if the agreement to waive is entered into as part of a genuine commercial arrangement which is not intended to confer gratuitous benefit, relief should be available under s.10. Under English company law a right to a final dividend accrues when the dividend is declared by the company in general meeting.[177] The right to an interim dividend does not accrue until the time the dividend is actually paid; this is because the declaration of an interim dividend can always be rescinded by the directors before that time.[178]

This relief is restricted to a waiver of dividends on shares and does not extend to a waiver of rent, or interest on loans and debentures. The section refers to waivers by persons and so covers the waiver by a close company which would otherwise be attributed to its participators by s.94 (see paras 2–73 and following).

2–71

NOTIONAL TRANSFERS

VII. DEFINITION

The legislation provides that in four cases a person who has not made an actual transfer of value is nevertheless to be treated as having made a transfer of value. The legislation achieves this effect by a two-step process. First, it provides that on the happening of certain events which do not in themselves constitute a transfer of value by the individual in question tax is to be charged as if that individual had made a transfer of value. Arguably, in itself this might prove insufficient to justify a charge. This follows from the fact that under the main charging provisions tax is charged on chargeable transfers, and s.2(1) defines a chargeable transfer to be "a transfer of value which is made by an individual but is not (by virtue of Part II of this Act or any other enactment) an exempt transfer" not as "any transfer of value or any event on the happening of which tax is chargeable as if a transfer of value had been made . . . " Accordingly, s.3(4), a seemingly innocuous provision (which, as will be seen below, is also vital in the context of exempt transfers), provides that:

2–72

> "Except as otherwise provided, references in this Act to a transfer of value made, or made by any person, include references to events on the happening of which tax is chargeable as if a transfer of value had been made, or, as the case may be, had been made by that person; and 'transferor' shall be construed accordingly."

[176] ITEPA 2003 s.722 Sch.6 paras 1 and 108.
[177] See *Bond v Barrow Hæmatite Steel Co* [1902] 1 Ch. 353.
[178] See *Lagunas Co Ltd v Schroeder & Co and Schmidt* (1901) 85 L.T. 22.

Any doubt as to the chargeability of notional transfers is thus removed, and the alignment of actual and notional transfers, at least for charging purposes, is complete. It is also to be noted that s.3(4) applies only in respect of events "on the happening of which tax is chargeable". This is important, since it means that if the legislation provides by way of relief that no tax is to be charged on the happening of such an event, the event is not an event which comes within the terms of s.3(4), and consequently will not, strictly speaking, constitute a transfer of value at all.

Transfers of value thus fall into two categories, actual and notional. A person makes an actual transfer of value when he makes a disposition which diminishes the value of his estate, unless, of course, one of the reliefs discussed above applies. He makes a notional transfer when circumstances are such that under the legislation he is treated as having made a transfer of value. The reason the legislation normally provides for notional transfers is that circumstances may arise in which the value of a person's estate is diminished even though he has made neither an actual nor a notional disposition. In the absence of special provisions, such diminutions would go untaxed.

There are three cases in which a person who does not make a disposition may make a notional transfer, which are as follows:

(1) when a close company in which he is a participator makes a transfer of value;
(2) when he is beneficially entitled to an interest in possession in settled property and that interest comes to an end during his life; or
(3) when he dies.

The first two cases are considered in this chapter. The third, the notional transfer made on death, is discussed in Chapter 8. There is a fourth case in which a person who has made a disposition is regarded as having made a transfer of value, i.e. where he acquires a settlement power. This is discussed at the end of this chapter.

What is important to bear in mind at this point is that different consequences follow according to whether a transfer is actual or notional. First, none of the reliefs discussed above, e.g. those available to essentially commercial transactions, family maintenance dispositions, etc. apply to notional transfers, because those reliefs provide only that certain dispositions are not transfers of value. The existence of a notional transfer, on the other hand, is predicated on the happening of an event, not on the making of a disposition. Therefore the reliefs that apply to dispositions which, apart from the existence of those reliefs, would constitute actual transfers of value do not apply to notional transfers. Exceptionally, some of the above-mentioned reliefs have been modified to apply to what would otherwise constitute notional transfers. These modifications are discussed below. Secondly, certain exemptions apply to actual transfers only, not to notional ones. Thirdly, there are special rules for determining the value transferred by each kind of notional transfer. These rules, which for the sake of convenience are discussed in this chapter, override the consequential loss provisions discussed above.

Finally, a notional transfer of value, other than the transfer deemed to occur on the lifetime termination of an interest in possession, cannot be a PET.[179]

VIII. TRANSFERS BY CLOSE COMPANIES

2–73   Close companies have in the past been used to avoid tax, and there are a number of provisions in the UK tax code designed to prevent such avoidance. Not surprisingly,

---

[179] IHTA 1984 s.3A(6); see paras 5–12 and 5–13.

close companies could also have been used in two ways to avoid IHT had the legislation not included provisions to prevent such avoidance.

First, the share or loan capital of a close company or the rights attaching thereto could have been altered so that value passed out of one person's shares into those of another. This would have diminished the value of the first person's estate, but he would not have made a transfer of value since as a matter of general law such an alteration would not amount to a disposition. Section 98(1) therefore provides that such an alteration is to be treated as a disposition made by the participators in the company. The result is that any participator whose estate is diminished in value by such an alteration will have made a transfer of value.[180]

The second way in which a close company could have been used to avoid tax was even simpler; the company could have made gifts to the persons whom the individuals controlling the company intended to benefit, e.g. by a sale at an undervalue of the company's assets. Such a sale would have diminished the value of the shares in the company, but the owners of the shares could not have been charged on that diminution since the only disposition made would have been made by the company, not by them. The disposition by the company, having diminished the value of the company's estate, would clearly have constituted an actual transfer of value by the company. But this would have been insufficient to give rise to a charge, because although a company can make a transfer of value, it cannot make a chargeable transfer. That dubious distinction is reserved for individuals.

The possibility of such schemes occurred to the framers of the tax rather late in the day. Provision was hastily made by s.94 to counteract them by attributing the value transferred by a transfer of value made by a close company to the individual participators of that company and treating them as having made transfers of value of the amounts attributed to them. The result is that the legislation looks through the company and treats the transfer made by the company as having been made by the individuals standing behind that company. As will be seen below, this transfer cannot be a PET.[181]

While this was an effective way of preventing close companies being used to avoid tax, it had an unfortunate element of overkill in it, because (a) it overlooked the fact that such gifts were often already dealt with under the existing income and corporation tax legislation so that the imposition of an additional charge was therefore inequitable, and (b) it meant that tax became chargeable on a large number of corporate transactions which were never intended to be caught at all. Subsequent statutory enactments introduced a number of provisions designed to remedy these deficiencies and the amended legislation is much more consistent with the tax code in general. Even so, the provisions relating to close companies remain among the least satisfactory in the code. The reader should accordingly prepare himself for some testing moments.

Definitions

Before examining how the provisions operate, it will be useful to consider the **2–74** definition of "close company" and "participator".

By s.102(1), a close company for these purposes is a company which comes within the Corporation Tax Acts definition, or which would come within that definition, non-resident companies not being close companies for corporation tax purposes, if it were resident in the United Kingdom. A company is a close company for corporation tax

---

[180] See para.2–18.
[181] See para.5–13.

purposes if, basically, it is under the control[182] of five or fewer participators, or of participators, however many, who are directors (including persons who are de facto directors). Additionally, a company is also a close company if, on a notional winding up, five or fewer participators would be entitled to receive more than half of any distributions.[183] Many private companies in the United Kingdom are close companies, while most public companies are not. The fact that a non-resident company can be a close company is important, and in the following discussion such a company will be referred to as a non-resident close company, while a company which is a close company for both IHT and corporation tax purposes will be referred to as a resident close company.

"Participator" for these purposes means any person who is, or who would be if the company were resident in the United Kingdom, a participator within the corporation tax definition in Corporation Tax Act 2010 s.454, other than a person who would be such a participator by reason only of being a loan creditor.[184] When determining, however, whether or not a company is a close company, because of the interaction of the IHT and the corporation tax legislation, a participator will include a loan creditor of the company, but only for the purposes of determining the status of the company.[185] The definition of "participator" for corporation tax purposes is extremely wide and includes virtually anyone with a tangible interest in a company.[186] The best example of a participator is a shareholder.

It should be noted that under the corporation tax definition of "participator" it is possible for one close company, Company B, to be a participator in another close company, Company A. In that case the value transferred by the transferor company is apportioned through the participator company to the individual participators in the participator company. Thus, if Company A makes a transfer of value, the value transferred by that transfer will first be apportioned to Company B, and then sub-apportioned to the individual participators in Company B.

As a practical matter, Shares and Assets Valuation Division will determine what is a "close company" and who is a "participator".[187]

Transfer of value

2–75   The first requirement that must be satisfied if an apportionment is to be made under s.94 is that the close company in question must make a transfer of value. In deciding whether it has done so, the normal rules apply. The effect of those rules is that although

[182] For the meaning of "control", the reader is referred to Corporation Tax Act 2010 s.450 and the cases of *R. (on the application of Newfields Developments) v Inland Revenue Commissioners* [2001] 1 W.L.R. 1111 and *Gascoines Group Ltd v HM Inspector of Taxes* [2004] S.T.C. 844. The cases demonstrate how widely "control" can be interpreted. It might be necessary, e.g. to attribute to an individual the rights and powers of persons over whom he might in "real life" have little or no power or control.
[183] Corporation Tax Act 2010 s.439. There are a number of exceptions to these rules to be found in ss.442–447.
[184] IHTA 1984 s.102(1).
[185] IHTA 1984 s.102(1) provides (broadly speaking) that "close company" is as defined in the Corporation Tax Acts ("close company" is defined in Corporation Tax Act 2010 s.439) and "participator" is as defined in Corporation Tax Act 2010 s.454, but excluding a mere loan creditor. However, since Corporation Tax Act 2010 s.439 is not read into IHTA 1984 s.102, the references to "participator" in Corporation Tax Act 2010 s.439 are not subject to the qualification in IHTA 1984 s.102. Therefore a loan creditor may be a participator for the purposes of determining whether a company is a close company for the purposes of IHTA 1984 Pt IV, even if that will only have IHT implications for other participators (i.e. participators who are not mere loan creditors).
[186] Corporation Tax Act 2010 s.454.
[187] See HMRC Manuals IHTM14851.

a transfer of value made by a close company may constitute a notional transfer by the participators in that company, a close company itself can make actual transfers of value only, never notional ones. This is because the provisions relating to notional transfers are such that a close company is incapable of making one. First, if a close company is itself a participator in a close company which makes a transfer of value, then, as we have just seen, the value transferred by that transfer is attributed through the participator company to the individuals standing behind it, and they, not that company, are treated as having made that transfer. Secondly, if a close company has an interest in possession in settled property, then, as will be seen below, the participators of that company are treated as being beneficially entitled to that interest[188] and consequently on the coming to an end of that interest it is they, not the company, who will be treated as having made a transfer of value. Finally, a company never dies,[189] and therefore it cannot make a notional transfer on death. Accordingly, only the rules relating to actual transfers need to be considered. In applying those rules, the following points should be borne in mind.

Excluded property

A close company may own excluded property, either in the form of a reversionary   2–76
interest, or if the company is domiciled and ordinarily resident outside the United Kingdom, in the form of exempt government securities. A disposition by the company of such property will not normally result in a transfer of value.[190]

Free loans

A free loan by a close company in respect of which there is an immediate right to   2–77
repayment should not have any adverse IHT consequences.[191] A free loan in respect of which there is no immediate right to repayment, on the other hand, may constitute a transfer of value by the company. In that case the value transferred by that loan may be apportioned under s.94.

Reliefs

Many of the reliefs discussed previously[192] will be available in respect of disposi-   2–78
tions by close companies. The reliefs relating to essentially commercial transactions, dispositions allowable for income or corporation tax, retirement benefit schemes, and

[188] IHTA 1984 s.101(1). See para.2–97.
[189] It just gets struck off the register.
[199] See para.2–80. See *Foster's Inheritance Tax*, para.F1.23 for the view that a transfer of exempt government securities by a company resident abroad qualifies as excluded property.
[191] See paras 2–07 and 2–24.
[192] See paras 2–39 and following.

"employee" trusts will in practice relieve many dispositions which would otherwise constitute transfers of value.

Availability of agricultural and business relief

2–79   The way s.94 works does not sit easily with the rules regulating the availability of agricultural relief and business relief. Two points arise.

The first point concerns the availability of agricultural relief and business relief when the company makes a transfer of value. Those reliefs operate by reducing the value transferred by a transfer of value. The problem is that under s.94 there are two transfers of value—that made by the company and that deemed to have been made by the participators. What falls to be apportioned among the participators is the value transferred by the transfer of value made by the company. It therefore seems clear that, in determining the amount of the value transferred, account is taken of the availability of any agricultural relief or business relief to the transfer of value made by the company. In making this determination regard is had to the circumstances of the company, e.g. whether it owned the asset transferred for two years, not the circumstances of the participators. If the relief is available in respect of the company's transfer then that will reduce or eliminate (depending on the extent to which relief is available) the value transferred by the transfer made by the company and therefore the amount which falls to be apportioned among the participators.

If after giving relief some value transferred remains that value falls to be apportioned among the participators who are treated as if they had made a transfer of value of the amount so apportioned. The legislation does not refer to the value transferred by this notional transfer made by the participators, but it is clear that the value transferred is taken to be the apportioned amount as is discussed in paras 2–82 and following. In previous editions of this work it was stated that in the authors' view no agricultural relief or business relief can be available in respect of the value transferred by that transfer because in their view no part of that value transferred is "attributable to" the agricultural value of agricultural property or the value of relevant business property as is required by those reliefs. Rather, it simply arises as a result of the operation of s.94.

The alternative view is that the value transferred by the participator's transfer is "attributable to", e.g., his shares in the company (assuming he is a participator by reason only of being a shareholder). This view leads to the conclusion that relief may be due in respect of the participator's transfer in place of, or even in addition to, the company's transfer.[193] Some support for this view can be found in Sales J.'s decision

---

[193] For an argument that "a natural and harmonious approach to the legislation requires BPR to be considered in relation to the deemed transfer of value by the participators, rather than the actual transfers made by the company" see I. Maston, "The availability of business property relief in relation to a close company's transfer to an EBT", *Private Client Business* (2010), 4, 223–228. Note that HMRC recognises that where a close company makes a transfer of value to an employee benefit trust, an IHT charge under s.94 can be avoided if the disposition is eligible for business relief, provided that the company's business does not consist wholly or mainly of making or holding investments, the property has been held for the requisite period of time and the property transferred is not an excepted asset. However, HMRC does not set out an analysis of whether the business relief is applied to the value transferred by the company rather than the value transferred by the participators (see Employee Benefit Trust (EBT), Settlement Opportunity, Frequently Asked Questions, August 2012: *http://www.hmrc.gov.uk/specialist/ebt-faqs.pdf* [Accessed October 30, 2012].

in *Revenue and Customs Commissioners v Trustees of the Nelson Dance Family Settlement*.[194]

Clawback of agricultural relief and business relief

The second difficult point concerns the rules governing relief clawback. The legisla-   **2–80**
tion makes provision to claw back both agricultural relief and business relief on
lifetime transfers of value in certain cases; see paras 26–101–26–112 and
26–157–26–166. This occurs where, e.g., the transferor dies within seven years of
making a lifetime chargeable transfer or a PET and the transferee no longer owns the
property that was the subject-matter of the transfer. These provisions do not sit easily
with s.94, because they are triggered by the transferor's death within seven years of the
transfer and are clearly framed by reference to the transfer of value he made. Where
s.94 is concerned, on the other hand, there is (as explained above) in the authors' view
an element of asymmetry: for purposes of giving the relief the company is the
transferor, while for clawback purposes the participator is the transferor. There are thus
two possibilities. The first is that, given this asymmetry, the clawback rules can never
operate, because no relief was ever given in respect of the transfer made by the
participator and the company never made a chargeable transfer or a failed PET. The
second, more equitable, approach is to apply the clawback rules on the basis that the
transferor participator was the company so that if, e.g., the person to whom the
company made the transfer no longer owns the property transferred when the transferor
participator dies the relief falls to be clawed back. It is open to question, however,
whether the legislation will bear such a reading. What is clear is that even if the relief
is clawed back, such a clawback will leave the transferor participator's IHT cumulative
total unaffected. This is because the transfer made by the participator transferor will be
prevented from being a PET[195] and so will necessarily be an immediately chargeable
transfer and although the cumulative total of the transferor of a failed PET falls to be
adjusted that anomalously is not the case where the transfer was an immediately
chargeable transfer.[196]

Group relief and advance corporation tax

Special provision is made for the surrender of group relief and advance corporation   **2–81**
tax ("ACT"). Although the latter was abolished on April 6, 1999, the regulations
permitted carry forward of unused ACT so it may still be in point for some companies.
By s.94(3), in determining whether a disposition made by a close company is a transfer
of value, no account is taken of the company's surrendering either any relief under
s.402 of the Taxes Act 1988 (group relief) or the benefit of any ACT paid by it under
s.240 of the Taxes Act 1988.[197] Such surrenders will therefore not result in a transfer
of value even though they may diminish the value of the estate of the company which

---

[194] See [2009] S.T.C. 802 at [28], in which he sets out passages from the skeleton argument on behalf of
the taxpayer, and in respect of which he also records that no good reply was given by counsel for HMRC.
See, in particular, the passage concerning unquoted shares in a company.
[195] See para.5–13.
[196] IHTA 1984 ss.113A(2) and 124A(2); see paras 26–101–26–112, and 26–157–26–166.
[197] This section was repealed by FA 1998 Sch.3 para.13 for accounting periods of the surrendering
company beginning after April 5, 1999.

79

made them. The legislation thus acknowledges that such standard corporate transactions are outside its province.

Apportionment

2–82   Once a close company makes a transfer of value, the value transferred by that transfer is apportioned among the participators in the company. In certain circumstances, even though the company makes a transfer, no apportionment is made, since the legislation recognises that in certain circumstances an apportionment would be inappropriate. It will be useful to examine when this happens before considering the method by which an apportionment is in fact effected.

The cases in which no apportionment is made are as follows:

(1) *Excluded property alignment.* By s.94(2)(b), no apportionment is made to an individual domiciled outside the United Kingdom of so much of the value transferred as is attributable to the value of any property situated outside the United Kingdom. The purpose of this provision is to align the provisions relating to close companies with those relating to excluded property. Where an individual who is not domiciled and not deemed domiciled in the United Kingdom is beneficially entitled to property situated outside the United Kingdom that property is excluded property in his hands.[198] Normally, as was seen previously, a disposition of excluded property does not constitute an actual transfer of value. Therefore such an individual could dispose of such property without making such a transfer. The position is different, however, where a close company is beneficially entitled to property situated abroad, since, even if the close company is domiciled abroad, the property will not be excluded property in its hands because s.6(1) only applies to individuals.[199] A disposition of that property by the company may thus result in a transfer of value. Yet if the individual himself had disposed of the property he would not have made such a transfer. Therefore no apportionment is made to him, and this is so even though the company is itself resident and/or domiciled in the United Kingdom.

In the above circumstances, if the company were resident abroad but made a transfer of exempt government securities, there would be no question of a transfer of value as those assets are categorised as excluded property in their own right.[200]

(2) *Payments brought into account for purposes of income or corporation tax.* By s.94(2)(a), no apportionment is made of so much of the value transferred as is attributable to (i) any payment, or (ii) any transfer of assets which falls to be taken into account in computing the recipient's profits or gains or losses for purposes of income or corporation tax or would fall to be so taken into account but for Corporation Tax Act 2009 s.1285 (exemption for UK company distributions). Section 1285 was repealed for company distributions paid after June 30, 2009. In the context of a dividend which falls within one of the exempt categories within Corporation Tax Act 2009 Pt 9A, assuming that the effect of that Part is that the dividend does not "fall to be taken into account in computing [the recipient's] profits or gains", it would seem that there is no

---

[198] IHTA 1984 s.6(1).
[199] Unless the property is a reversionary interest in settled property situated abroad; see para.2–76.
[200] IHTA 1984 s.6(2) and see HMRC Manuals IHTM14854.

exclusion from being taken into account in an apportionment under s.94. However, HMRC Statement of Practice E15 provides that a dividend paid by a subsidiary company to its parent is not a transfer of value.

Whether or not a payment or a transfer of assets falls to be taken into account in computing a person's profits, gains or losses for purposes of income tax or corporation tax will depend on the law relating to such payments or transfers, and that law is outside the scope of this book. One example of such a payment is a dividend paid by a UK company to an individual resident in the United Kingdom, which, given the income tax liability attaching to it, might not increase the value of his estate by the full amount of the dividend and could in any event affect the value of other participators' estates. Another is a payment made in respect of expenses to a director or higher-paid employee, wherever the company may be resident,[201] which might give rise to similar problems. An example of a transfer of assets that would be so taken into account is a sale of an asset at an undervalue by a company resident in the United Kingdom to a participator in that company.

Two particular kinds of disposition are noteworthy in this context. First, as was mentioned above, a loan by a close company in respect of which there is no immediate right of return may constitute a transfer of value. If such a loan does constitute a transfer of value, the question arises as to whether that loan comes within s.94(2)(a) with the result that the value transferred by that loan is non-apportionable. If the loan is a "payment" or a "transfer of assets",[202] it will not be apportionable if it falls to be taken into account in computing the borrower's profits or gains for income tax. Free loans often have income tax consequences, notably under Corporation Tax 2010 s.455 and ss.173–175 of the Income Tax (Earnings and Pensions) Act 2003. However, in the authors' view, the sums lent do not fall to be taken into account under those provisions so as to prevent an apportionment under s.94(1). Under s.455 the loan has consequences only for the lender, not for the borrower. Under the Income Tax (Earnings and Pensions) Act 2003 the amount to be brought into account by the borrower is the official rate of interest deemed to have been foregone by the lender, not the sum lent. This means that if a close company makes a free loan in respect of which there is no immediate right of repayment the value transferred by that loan will be apportionable. Accordingly, loans by close companies should always be loans in respect of which there is an immediate right of repayment.[203]

It is to be stressed that what matters is the *recipient's* income or corporation tax position. The fact that the transferor company must also pay corporation tax, e.g. under the rule in *Sharkey v Wernher*,[204] or its CGT statutory equivalent, s.17 of the Taxation of Chargeable Gains Act 1992, is irrelevant. Where the transferor company can claim a deduction, on the other hand, there may not be, as a result of s.12(1), a transfer of value to begin with; see para.2–62. It is also to be noted that the reference to "profits or gains or losses" in s.94(2)(a) should mean that no account is taken of any chargeable gain (or allowable capital loss) made by the transferee, see Income Tax Act 2007 s.989, so that a sale by the transferee of an asset at an overvalue will not qualify for relief under s.94(2)(a); this seems anomalous, since if the transferee were to sell trading stock at an overvalue, relief would be available.

The provision by a close company of a benefit-in-kind, e.g. of facilities, services, or entertainment may have tax consequences under Pt 3 of the Income Tax (Earnings and Pensions) Act 2003 or Corporation Tax Act 2010 s.1064, but in the authors' view such

---

[201] ITEPA 2003 ss.70–72.
[202] See para.10–22.
[203] See paras 2–07 and 2–24.
[204] *Sharkey v Wernher* [1956] A.C. 58.

provision will not constitute either a "payment" or a "transfer of assets". Consequently if the provision of such benefits constitutes a transfer of value the value transferred will be apportionable. Normally, however, the company should be able to claim a deduction for such expenditure, except perhaps, where entertainment is concerned,[205] and therefore the relief under s.12(1) for dispositions allowable for corporation tax will apply, with the result that there is no transfer of value in the first place.[206]

2–83 Finally, it is important to bear in mind that although the definition of a close company extends to a non-resident company, only a resident company can be a close company for corporation tax purposes. This means that the value transferred by a payment or a transfer of assets by or to a non-resident close company may be apportionable where an identical payment or transfer by or to that company would not be apportionable if that company were resident in the United Kingdom. If, for example, a UK resident shareholder sells an asset at an overvalue to a company resident in the United Kingdom, he will be assessable to UK income tax on the excess amount which will therefore not be apportionable under s.94. But if the sale is to a non-resident company, he will not be liable to UK income tax on the excess, which accordingly will be apportionable.

This, of course, is consistent with the purposes of s.94(2)(a), which is to take out of charge transactions brought into charge for the purposes of income or corporation tax. Transactions not brought into charge for the purposes of those taxes therefore remain subject to apportionment under s.94(1).

Method of apportionment

2–84 The apportionment of the value transferred by the company is made according to the participators' respective rights and interests in the company immediately before the transfer.[207] "Rights and interests" for this purpose include, but are not limited to, the participators' rights and interests in the assets of the company that are available for distribution among the participators in the event of a winding-up or in any other circumstances.[208] The value transferred is thus apportioned to the participators according, as it were, to their respective stakes in the company.

Preference shares and minority participators

2–85 In determining the participators' rights and interests two factors are left out of account.

(1) *Preference shares.* By s.96, where part of a close company's share capital consists of preference shares, and a transfer of value made by the company has only a "small" effect on the value of those preference shares compared with its effect on the value of other parts of the company's share capital, the preference shares are left out of account in determining the participators' respective rights and interests. "Preference shares" for this purpose mean shares which:

(a) carry rights in respect of dividends and capital which are comparable with those general for fixed-dividend shares listed in the Official List of the Stock Exchange; and

---

[205] Corporation Tax Act 2009 s.1298. The company might be able to rely on IHTA 1984 s.10(1).
[206] Assuming the company is resident in the United Kingdom.
[207] IHTA 1984 s.94(2).
[208] IHTA 1984 s.102(2).

(b) do not carry any right to dividends other than dividends at a fixed rate per cent of the nominal value of the shares.[209]

The effect of s.96 is that when a close company makes a transfer which has a comparatively small effect on the value of the preference shares in that company the value transferred is apportioned as if the preference shares did not exist. This will generally be fair, since normally the preference shareholders will not, as preference shareholders, have had any say with regard to the transfer.

"Small" is not defined. It also appears in the CGT legislation in a provision[210] which gives Inspectors of Taxes a discretion to defer payment of CGT on certain distributions made in respect of shares if "satisfied" that the amount of the distribution is small compared with the value of the shares in question. In practice HMRC has regarded "small" as meaning 5 per cent or less for this purpose,[211] and will probably adopt a similar standard in applying s.96. Fortunately, the IHT relief, unlike that under the CGT legislation, does not depend on the exercise of any discretion by HMRC. "Small" must be a question of fact in every case, and circumstances may well arise in which the HMRC view proves unduly parsimonious.[212]

It will be noted that the effect of s.96 differs from the effect of the provisions under which no apportionment is made, e.g. where the payment falls to be taken into account for income tax. Under those provisions the whole or part of the value transferred is not apportioned at all. Section 96, on the other hand, is concerned with the method of apportionment, not with the amount to be apportioned. Moreover, while the former provisions operate to the advantage of all the participators in the company, s.96 gives relief to the preference shareholders at the expense, as it were, of the other partici-pators, to whom the whole of the value transferred, including the portion that would otherwise be apportioned to the preference shareholders, falls to be apportioned.

Finally, s.96 does not operate just to relieve the preference shareholders in the transferor company. It also applies to the preference shareholders of any other close company whose shares are affected by that transfer, provided, of course, that the effect is only "small". Section 96 thus contemplates the situation in which one of the participators in the transferor company is itself a close company. In that case the value of the participator company's shares in the transferor company may be decreased by the transfer; this, in turn, would affect the value of the shares in the participator company itself. In such circumstances the rights and interests of the preference shareholders in the participator company will be left out of account when the sub-apportionment is made.[213]

(2) *Minority participators—group transfers*. Where one company within a group disposes of an asset to another member of the group there is no charge to corporation tax. Instead, the acquiring company inherits the base cost of the disposing company, and the charge to tax is deferred until the asset leaves the group. Such a transfer could have adverse IHT consequences, however, because the disposal might constitute a transfer of value if the transferor company did not receive full consideration for the assets, as is often the case. This would depend to some extent on whether the disposal was made from parent to subsidiary, or vice versa.

If the disposal is from parent to subsidiary, the parent company may not make a transfer of value, because its estate may not suffer any diminution in value. This follows from the fact that even though the parent will no longer own the asset, the parent's shares in the subsidiary will register an increase in value which reflects the

[209] IHTA 1984 s.96; Corporation Tax Act 2010 s.1023(5).
[210] TCGA 1992 s.122(2).
[211] RI 34 (now obsolete) and RI 164.
[212] Support for this view is found in IHTA 1984 s.202(2), which specifies 5% as the relevant test.
[213] IHTA 1984 s.96.

increase in the value of the subsidiary's estate. If the parent owns 100 per cent of the subsidiary, the disposal will not affect the value of the parent's estate. Should the parent company enjoy less than full ownership of the subsidiary, e.g. where the subsidiary is only 75 per cent owned, then, of course, only 75 per cent of the value of the asset will be reflected in its shares, and the parent will have made a transfer of value.

If the disposal is from subsidiary to parent the position is less happy. When the subsidiary disposes of the asset to the parent, there will not be any corresponding increase in the value of the subsidiary's share in the parent, since, by definition, the subsidiary will own no shares in its parent. Consequently the subsidiary will have made a transfer of value.

Given the above, it is not difficult to envisage situations in which inter-group transfers could prejudice the position of minority participators. Assume the following group structure:

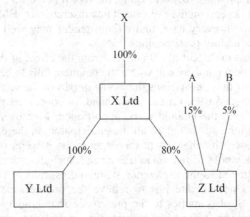

Z Ltd transfers an asset worth £50,000 to Y Ltd for £30,000, the price which Z Ltd originally paid to acquire the asset. Z Ltd will thus have made a transfer of value of £20,000. Of this 80 per cent will be apportioned to X Ltd, but, as will be seen below,[214] this will be cancelled out by the increase in value of X Ltd's shares in Y Ltd resulting from Y Ltd's acquisition of the asset. A and B, on the other hand, will be unable to claim such a set-off, and therefore, in the absence of provision to the contrary, would have made notional transfers of the values apportioned to them.

The legislation accordingly provides a measure of relief to "minority participators" where a close company which is a member of a group disposes of an asset to another member of that group. For this purpose a "minority participator" is a participator of the transferor company who is not, and who is not connected with, a participator of the "principal company" of the group,[215] (see below) or of any of the principal company's participators. The principal company of a group is the company of which all the other members are 75 per cent subsidiaries[216] (see below).

By s.97(1), if the disposal is (i) within s.171(1) of the Taxation of Chargeable Gains Act 1992 (transfers within a group: general provisions) or an election has been made[217] to bring it within s.171 and (ii) a transfer of value, then if the transfer has only a "small" effect on the rights and interests of the "minority participators" their rights and interests are left out of account in determining the respective rights and interests of the participators in that company for the purposes of s.94.

---

[214] See para.2–05.
[215] IHTA 1984 s.97(2)(b).
[216] IHTA 1984 s.97(2)(a).
[217] Such elections only being possible in relation to events after March 31, 2000.

"Small" is again undefined, and the 5 per cent standard can again be expected to be adopted by HMRC, and disputed by the taxpayer. It will be noted that the effect under s.97(1), is the same as that under s.96, namely that the value transferred which would otherwise be apportioned to the minority participators who qualify for the relief is apportioned to the other participators, with the result that relief is given to the minority participators at the expense of the participators.

The above is subject to one qualification, namely that the transferor company cannot be the "principal company" (as defined below) of the group. If it is the principal company, the relief under s.97(1) does not apply.[218]

The following definitions apply in relation to s.97(1):

(1) *Group*: two companies are members of a group if one is the 75 per cent subsidiary of the other. Any other company which is either a 75 per cent subsidiary of one of those two companies, or of which one of those two companies is itself a subsidiary is also a member of the same group.[219] Section 170(6) of the Taxation of Chargeable Gains Act 1992 provides that a company cannot be a member of more than one group and sets out rules for determining to which group a company belongs in these circumstances. It should also be noted a group cannot include (other than as the principal) a company which is not an effective 51 per cent subsidiary of the principal company.[220]

(2) *75 per cent subsidiary*: a company is a 75 per cent subsidiary of another company if and so long as at least 75 per cent of its ordinary share capital is owned directly or indirectly by that other company.[221] "Ordinary share capital" means all the issued share capital of the company other than capital the holders of which have a right to a dividend at a fixed rate but have no other right to share in the company's profits.[222]

(3) *Principal company*: the "principal company" is the member of the group of which all the other members are 75 per cent subsidiaries.[223]

(4) *Minority participator*: a "minority participator" is a participator of the transferor company who is not, and is not a person connected with, a participator of the principal company of the group or of any of the principal company's participators.[224]

The notional transfer

Under s.94(1), tax is charged on the amount apportioned to an individual participator as if he

> " . . . had made a transfer of value of such amount as after deduction of tax (if any) would be equal to the amount so apportioned, less the amount (if any) by which the value of his estate is more than it would be but for the company's transfer; but for this purpose his estate shall be treated as not including any rights or interests in the company."

2–86

The reader should not be dismayed if he finds this incomprehensible. It *is*, at least at first reading, incomprehensible. Basically, s.94(1) contemplates two operations. First,

---

[218] IHTA 1984 s.97(1).
[219] IHTA 1984 s.97(2).
[220] The principal company must be entitled to more than 50% of the profits and 50% of the assets available on a winding up (see TCGA 1992 s.170).
[221] Corporation Tax 2010 s.1154(3).
[222] Corporation Tax Act 2010 s.1119.
[223] TCGA 1992 s.170 incorporated by reference in IHTA 1984 s.97(2)(a).
[224] IHTA 1984 s.97(2)(b).

any increase in the value of the participator's estate occasioned by the company's transfer is set off against the amount apportioned to him. Secondly, the resulting sum is grossed up to find the value transferred by the transfer of value which he is treated as making. Each of these operations will be considered in turn, and then the reason why s.94(1) is drafted as it is will be briefly discussed.

Set-off

2–87 In computing the amount of the transfer of value which he is treated as making under s.94(1), a participator is entitled to set off against the amount apportioned to him under s.94(2) any increase in the value of his estate which has occurred as a consequence of the company's transfer. If the increase suffices to cancel the amount apportioned to him then he will not have made a transfer of value at all. If the increase is less than the amount apportioned to him, he will have made a transfer of value, but only of what remains of the apportioned amount after the set-off.

Section 94(1) provides that in determining whether and to what extent a participator's estate has been increased in value by the company's transfer "his estate shall be treated as not including any rights or interests in the company". This is intended to help the participator by preventing a charge from arising which in fairness ought not to arise, e.g. where A Ltd, which is wholly owned by A, transfers an asset to him. In the absence of this provision the diminution occasioned in the value of A's shares would have cancelled out the increase in the value of his estate resulting from the acquisition of the asset, with the result that A would have been deprived of the set-off to which in fairness he ought to have been entitled. Section 94(1) accordingly provides that in determining the amount available for set-off the participator's rights and interests in the transferor company are to be left out of account.

Group transactions

2–88 Group transactions can be complicated and special provision was needed to prevent tax being charged in situations where the value of estates of individuals owning shares in various companies in a group remained unchanged even though a company within the group had made a transfer of value.

Assume the following group structure:

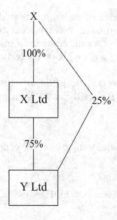

If X Ltd sells an asset to Y Ltd for £10,000 less than that asset is worth, the value of X's estate remains unchanged, since directly or indirectly he owns both companies, and their aggregate assets are the same after the transfer as before. Nevertheless, in the absence of provision to the contrary, this seemingly innocuous transaction would give rise to a charge. As X Ltd owns only 75 per cent of the shares in Y Ltd, only 75 per cent of the value of the asset would be reflected in X Ltd's shareholding in Y Ltd. Therefore 25 per cent of the £10,000 would be apportioned to X. As the value of X's estate would not be *increased* by the transfer, he would have made a transfer of value of £2,500 (25 per cent of £10,000), even though the value of his estate in fact remained unchanged.

Section 95 attempts to deal with this anomaly by providing that the increase in the value of Y Ltd's estate is to be set off against the £2,500 apportioned to X, with the result that X does not make a transfer of value after all. Section 95 provides that in determining the amount to be set off the increase occasioned in the value of any close company's estate by the transfer is to be apportioned to the participators in that company according to their respective rights and interests.

The increase in the value of the transferee company's (Y Ltd's) estate is taken to be "such part of the value transferred as accounts for the increase". This means that what is set off is not the increase itself, but an appropriate part of the value transferred by the transferor company. This is intended to deal with the situation where the increase and the value transferred differ, either because the transfer occasions a disproportionately large diminution in the value of the transferor company's estate or a disproportionately large increase in the value of the transferee company's estate.

Unfortunately, the legislation is still far from adequate to deal with group transactions. Consider an even simpler situation involving nothing more than a sale by a subsidiary to a parent at less than market value, e.g. at book value, as follows:

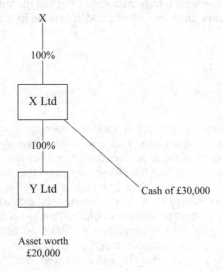

Besides the shares in Y Ltd, X Ltd's estate consists of £30,000 in cash; Y Ltd's estate consists solely of an asset worth £20,000. Y Ltd sells the asset to X Ltd for £10,000. Y Ltd has thus made a transfer of value of £10,000. That £10,000 will be apportioned through X Ltd to X, who will have made a transfer of value of £10,000 unless he can effect a set-off. To do so he will have to show either:

(1) an increase in the value of his estate; or

87

(2) an increase in the value of X Ltd's estate.

His own estate consists of shares in X Ltd; therefore he must show an increase in the value of X Ltd's estate. But the value of X Ltd's estate has remained unchanged. Before the sale X Ltd's estate was worth £50,000 (£30,000 in cash, £20,000 in shares). After the sale X Ltd's estate is still worth £50,000 (£20,000 in cash, an asset worth £20,000 and shares worth £10,000).

Fortunately, HMRC have shown that they are disposed to have regard to the spirit of the legislation rather than to the letter thereof and they will not regard s.94 as applying in the circumstances just outlined or in similar circumstances where a dividend is paid by subsidiary to parent company.[225] Nevertheless, it is clear that s.94(1) has gone only part of the way to curing the basic deficiency in s.95, the requirement that only increases in the value of the participator's estate can be taken into account by way of set-off. What the legislation should provide for is a comparison between the value of the participator's estate before and after the company's transfer.

Grossing up

2–89   On a first reading, s.94(1) appears to provide that the value transferred by the notional transfer made by a participator under s.94 is the amount apportioned to him grossed-up, less any set-off. This, however, would have the peculiar result that even if the amount to be set off was exactly equal to the apportioned amount the participator would still have made a transfer of value since the apportioned amount grossed-up would exceed the amount to be set off. Fortunately, the wording of s.94 admits to an alternative and more reasonable interpretation, namely that the amount to be grossed up is the apportioned amount *after* any set-off. HMRC are understood to accept that this is the correct view.

Exemptions

2–90   At first glance the correct procedure in applying exemptions to the notional transfer made under s.94(1) is to apply any available exemptions against the grossed-up equivalent of what remains of the apportioned amount after set-off. This follows from the fact that s.94 appears to say that the grossed-up amount is the value transferred by the transfer. If this was correct, then, if X Ltd made a transfer of value of £100,000, of which £10,000 was apportioned to X, whose estate was increased by £4,500 by the company's transfer, the correct procedure would be first to set off the £4,500 against the £10,000, then to gross up the remaining £5,500, and only then to apply any available exemptions, e.g. the annual exemption. But, in the authors' view, this is incorrect. Section 94(1) provides that the value transferred is "such amount as *after deduction of tax* (if any) would be equal to the value so apportioned". As was noted above, tax can be charged only on a chargeable transfer, and a chargeable transfer is any transfer of value other than an exempt transfer. Therefore before the amount of tax due can be determined any available exemption must be applied against what remains

---

[225] See Statement of Practice E15.

of the apportioned amount after any set-off. Such part, if any, of the apportioned amount as is not exempt is then grossed up.[226]

The correct, and simplest, approach is thus:

(1) to regard the apportioned amount after set-off as the value transferred by the notional transfer made under s.94(1); and

(2) to regard the legislation as requiring that amount to be grossed up for the purpose of charging tax.

The provision that the value transferred by the notional transfer of value is determined by reference to such tax as may be chargeable is a contradiction in terms and is best regarded as an unsuccessful (if ingenious) attempt by the draftsman to accomplish a conceptually simple but technically difficult drafting exercise, namely to provide that where a person makes a notional transfer under s.94 the value transferred by that transfer is the apportioned amount less any set-off, and that such part of that value as is not exempt is then to be grossed up for the purpose of charging tax.

Annual exemption

As will be seen in Chapter 3, certain exemptions normally apply only to actual **2–91** transfers of value. One such exemption is the annual exemption. In the absence of special provision that exemption would therefore not be available to notional transfers made under s.94. Fortunately, there is such a provision and so the exemption is available; see s.94(5). The exemptions, for small gifts, normal expenditure out of income and gifts in consideration of marriage or civil partnership are not available because they cannot apply to deemed transfers.[227]

Cumulation

If the notional transfer made under s.94 is a chargeable transfer[228] the value **2–92** transferred by that transfer is brought into the transferor's cumulative total in the usual way. This is subject to one qualification, namely that by s.94(4) a participator to whom not more than 5 per cent of the value transferred by the company is apportioned need not bring into his cumulative total the *tax* chargeable on the notional transfer.[229] Happily, it is HMRC's official practice to go one step further and to leave the entire value transferred by such a chargeable transfer out of the transferor's cumulative total.

If a person to whom apportionments have been made dies within seven years of the **2–93** transfer, and if the transfer of value by the company was reduced by the application of

---

[226] That this is the correct view is supported by the wording in s.94(5) (discussed below), which provides that references in s.19 to transfers of value made and the values transferred by them include references to apportionments made to a person under s.94 and the amounts for the tax on which (if charged) he would be liable.

[227] IHTA 1984 ss.20, 21 and 22. See also HMRC Manuals IHTM14853.

[228] As was mentioned, such a transfer cannot be a PET; see para.5–13.

[229] In fact, the legislation provides that he need not bring into account the tax chargeable "in determining with respect to any time after the company's transfer what previous *transfers of value* have been made" by him. This, however, does not make sense, for that tax would not be brought into account in that way in any event; the tax chargeable is only significant in relation to the *chargeable transfers* he has previously made. HMRC are understood to accept that the correct view is that stated in the text.

either business relief or agricultural relief, the author's view is that the "clawback" provisions in ss.113A and 124A will not apply. Even if they do apply, the cumulative total of any participator should be unaffected: see para.2–75.

Liability for tax[230]

2–94   When a notional transfer is made under s.94, tax is charged on the basis of each individual participator's cumulative total. It is the company itself, however, which is primarily liable for the tax on each participator's transfers. In so far as the tax remains unpaid after it ought to have been paid both the persons to whom apportionments have been made[231] and any other individuals whose estates have been increased by the transfer are liable. This is subject to the following qualifications:

(1) a person to whom no more than 5 per cent of the value transferred is apportioned is not liable for any of the tax;

(2) the other persons to whom an apportionment has been made are liable only for so much of the tax due from the company as corresponds to the part of the value transferred which was apportioned to them; and

(3) any individual, whether a participator or not, whose estate was increased in value by the company's transfer is liable only up to the amount of that increase.[232]

As a practical matter, the question of liability will be determined by Shares and Assets Valuation Division.

IX. TERMINATION OF AN INTEREST IN POSSESSION

2–95   The second case in which a person makes a notional transfer of value occurs where he is beneficially entitled to "qualifying interest in possession" (being a pre-March 22, 2006 interest in possession or, in the case of an interest in possession which arose after March 22, 2006, an immediate post-death interest, a disabled person's interest within s.89B(1)(c) or (d), or a transitional serial interest[233] in settled property as considered in Chapter 11) and *during his life* that interest comes to an end.[234] By s.52(1), tax is charged as if at that time he had made a transfer of value and the value transferred had been equal to the value of the property in which his interest subsisted. There is no charge to tax however if the person became beneficially entitled to the interest in possession before March 22, 2006, the interest came to an end on or after that date and immediately before the disposal of the interest, s.71A or s.71D applies to the property

---

[230] See also para.29–64 and, for accountability, see para.29–09.

[231] Whether or not they made a transfer of value.

[232] IHTA 1984 s.202. See also HMRC Manuals IHTM30124.

[233] IHTA 1984 s.51(1) and IHTA 1984 s.51(1A).

[234] An interest in possession that is included as part of a person's estate by virtue of IHTA s.5(1B) (see para.2–43) is treated as a qualifying interest in possession for the purposes of IHTA ss.51 (disposal of interest in possession—see s.51(1A)), s.52 (charge on the termination of interest in possession—see s.52(2A) and (3A)), s.100 (alteration of capital, etc. where participators are trustees—see s.100(1A)) and s.101 (companies' interests in settled property—see s.101(1A)). It should be noted, however, that a transfer of value under s.52 is not a PET where the s.52 charge arises in respect of an interest that is treated as part of a person's estate under s.5(1B).

in which the interest subsists.[235] Please see Chapter 12 for further details. The trustees carry primary liability for any tax due; the transferor is not liable at all.[236]

It is important to understand the place of s.52(1) within the legislation as a whole. Under the legislation settled property falls into two categories: settled property in which there is a qualifying interest in possession, and settled property in which there is no such interest. Settled property in which there is no such interest falls to be charged, if at all, under the special charging provisions, which are considered in Chapters 13–16. Settled property in which there is a qualifying interest in possession, on the other hand, is brought into charge under the main charging provisions. This is done in two ways. First, if the interest comes to an end during the life of the person entitled to it then it is brought into charge under s.52(1). Secondly, if a person dies beneficially entitled to a qualifying interest in possession that interest is brought into charge on his death under s.4(1); this is discussed below.

Precisely what constitutes (a) settled property, (b) an interest in possession, and (c) a qualifying interest in possession[237] in such property are technical matters which, together with the legislation's treatment of settled property generally, are dealt with in Chapters 11 and 12. In practice it will normally be clear whether one is dealing with settled property in which there is an interest in possession and whether that interest is a qualifying one, and what follows assumes that one is dealing with such property. The points of difficulty arise when such an interest comes to an end within the meaning of s.52(1) and the resulting consequences.

Although the charge to tax under s.52(1) does not depend on it, it will be helpful to note that under s.49(1) a person entitled to a qualifying interest in possession in settled property is treated as being beneficially entitled to the property in which his interest subsists. Assume A has a qualifying interest in possession in a trust fund worth £100,000. The market value of his interest is, say, £25,000. A is treated as owning the trust fund with the result that he owns property worth £100,000, not merely an interest worth £25,000. This is the case whether his interest is for life, a year, or even just a day. **2–96**

It is also helpful to bear in mind from the outset that s.52(1) specifies not only the occasion of this kind of notional transfer, the coming to an end of a qualifying interest in possession, but also the value transferred, which is stated by s.52(1) to be the value of the property in which that interest subsisted. This means that tax is charged not merely on the value of the interest (£25,000 in the above example) but on the value of the property (£100,000) in which that interest subsisted.[238] **2–97**

The occasion of the transfer

Under s.52(1), a person makes a notional transfer when he is beneficially entitled to a qualifying interest in possession and during his life that interest comes to an end. This can happen in any one of three ways. His interest: **2–98**

---

[235] IHTA 1984 s.51(1B).

[236] See paras 25–80 and following.

[237] One small word of warning: it is possible for an interest to be an "intermediate interest," i.e. an interest which is neither "interest in possession" nor a "reversionary interest". Such interests are discussed at para.11–65. The following discussion does not apply to intermediate interests, only to interests in possession.

[238] See also para.25–05.

(1) can *actually* come to an end; or

(2) can be *treated* as coming to an end; or

(3) can be *deemed* to come to an end.

Actual termination

2–99   A person's interest will actually come to an end during his life if that interest terminates as a matter of general law while he is still alive. Thus, if a person's interest is a revocable one, it will come to an end on the exercise by the trustees or other appropriate person of their power of revocation. If his interest is defeasible, it will come to an end on the occasion of that defeasance. For example, if a person has a right to the income of a capital fund for 10 years or until he marries, which ever comes earlier, his interest will terminate at the end of 10 years unless he marries before then, in which case it will come to an end on his marrying.

It may be that he has an interest *pur autre vie*, i.e. his interest is defined in terms of the life of someone else. Thus, A may be entitled to a qualifying interest in possession in Blackacre for as long as B lives. On B's death A's interest will come to an end, and tax will be charged accordingly. The coming to an end of a qualifying interest in possession on the death of the person who is beneficially entitled to that interest will, of course, not be a notional transfer under s.52(1), since, by definition, his interest will not have come to an end during his life.[239] Section 52(1) will apply only on the coming to an end of a qualifying interest in possession on a person's death if the deceased is someone other than the person beneficially entitled to the interest, i.e. in the case of an interest *pur autre vie*.

The actual termination of a qualifying interest in possession may result in the settled property in which that interest subsisted becoming settled property in which there is no such interest. This would be the case, for example, where property was held on trusts such that A had a qualifying interest in possession in the property until she married, the property thereafter to be held on discretionary trusts. On A's marriage there would be a notional transfer under s.52(1), and the trust property would become settled property in which there was no subsisting interest in possession. The main charging provisions would then cease to apply to the trust property, which would then be subject to the special charging provisions discussed in Chapters 13–16.

Notional termination

2–100   A person's interest will be *treated* as coming to an end during his life for the purposes of s.52(1) in three situations.

Disposal of interest in possession

2–101   The first situation in which a person's qualifying interest in possession will be treated as coming to an end is where he disposes of that interest.

[239] But tax may be charged under IHTA 1984 s.4(1).

Section 51(1)(a) provides that such a disposal is not in itself a transfer of value, even if it diminishes the disponer's estate.[240] Instead, s.51(1)(b) provides that such a disposal is treated as the coming to an end of the disponer's interest.

This is important. It means that the various reliefs discussed above at paras 2–39 and following, which apply to dispositions which would otherwise constitute actual transfers of value, e.g. the reliefs afforded to essentially commercial transactions, etc. do not apply to such a disposal, because such a disposal is not in itself a transfer of value of either the disposer's interest or of the property in which that interest subsists.[241] Rather, it is treated as the coming to an end of the disponer's interest, and it is that coming to an end which constitutes the transfer of value in question.

HMRC consider that a release of a qualifying interest in possession does not constitute a disposal for purposes of s.51.[242]

HMRC confirm, as would be expected, that a *revocable* mandate given by a beneficiary to pay income due in respect of his beneficial interest to another merely confers a running right to receive such income as and when it arises until the mandate is revoked; it neither disposes of nor determines the beneficial interest itself.[243]

Disposal of rights in close company

The second situation in which a person's qualifying interest in possession will be treated as coming to an end arises where he is a participator in a company which has a qualifying interest in possession in settled property and he disposes of some or all of the rights by virtue of which he is a participator. The reason is that s.101 provides that where a close company has a qualifying interest in possession in settled property the participators in that company are treated as the persons entitled to that interest according to their respective rights and interests in that company: see para.12–43. Thus, if a shareholder in such a company disposes of his shares and thereby ceases to be a participator he will no longer be deemed by s.101 to have a qualifying interest in possession in the property in which the company's interest subsisted. This can have some anomalous results, as *Powell-Cotton v IRC*[244] shows.

2–102

Mr Powell-Cotton owned 8,993 of the 46,000 issued shares in a close company which had an interest in settled property. He transferred 2,999 of his shares to a charity. This had two effects. First, he clearly made a transfer of value of his shares and the Revenue accepted that the whole of the value transferred by that transfer was attributable to property—the shares—given to the charity notwithstanding the amount of the value transferred exceeded the value of the 2,999 shares.[245] Secondly, part of his deemed interest in possession in the settled property in which the company had an interest in possession came to an end because, given his reduced shareholding, he was no longer deemed by s.101 to own as much of the company's interest as he did before the gift.

Vinelott J. accepted HMRC's argument that none of the value transferred by transfer of value occasioned by the deemed termination of part of Mr Powell-Cotton's interest qualified for the charity exemption, because the notional transfer he made was prevented from doing so by what is now s.56(3)(a), which provides that the exemption is

[240] See para.2–40.

[241] But in relation to family maintenance dispositions, see para.2–109 below.

[242] It is treated as a termination of the qualifying interest in possession and brought into charge by IHTA 1984 s.52(1); see HMRC Manuals IHTM14391.

[243] HMRC Manuals IHTM04085.

[244] *Powell-Cotton v IRC* [1992] S.T.C. 625.

[245] Since the participators rather than the company were treated by s.101 as owning the interest in possession, such part of the value of the company as was attributable to the interest would have been ignored for IHT purposes: see para.12–43.

93

available only if the settlement in which the interest in possession subsisted comes to an end, and that was not the case.

It is hard to fault the reasoning of Vinelott J., but the denial by the legislation of the exemption seems anomalous. This is especially so given that what is now s.56(3)(a) originated in 1976 as part of a raft of anti-avoidance provisions and arguably merits review in the light of *Powell-Cotton*. As it stands, the case bears testimony both to the hazards of deeming provisions and HMRC's jealous guarding of the charities exemption.

Close company makes a transfer of value

2–103   The third case where a person's qualifying interest in possession is treated as coming to an end occurs, by virtue of s.101(2) where a person has a qualifying interest in possession in settled property by virtue of which the trustees of the settlement are participators in a close company, e.g. where trustees hold shares in a close company. If that company makes a transfer of value and any part of the value transferred by that transfer is apportioned to the trustees under s.94(1)[246] an appropriate part of that person's interest is treated by s.99(2)(a) as coming to an end.

Assume A has a qualifying interest in possession in a trust fund worth £100,000. The fund consists of a 60 per cent shareholding in X Ltd worth £40,000 and other assets worth £60,000. X Ltd makes a transfer of value of £10,000: 60 per cent of this, £6,000, will be apportioned so the trustees under s.94(1). The effect of s.99(2)(a) is to apportion this amount through the trust to A, who is treated as having made a transfer of value of £6,000.

This is achieved in a rather roundabout way. Section 99(2)(a) provides that a part of A's qualifying interest in possession

"corresponding to such part of the property as is of a value equal to the part so apportioned . . . shall be treated as having come to an end".

The part of the settled property in relation to which the trustees are participators which is equal in value to £6,000 is six-fortieths of the shareholding. Therefore six-fortieths of A's interest in the settled property is treated as having come to an end. As the value transferred by that notional transfer is equal to the value of the property in which A's interest subsisted the value transferred is six-fortieths of £40,000 which equals £6,000.[247]

2–104   The above is subject to the obvious qualification that if the value of the settled property is increased by the company's transfer the amount by which it is increased is deducted from the amount apportioned through to A.[248] This gives rise to one slight difficulty. It is not clear whether this offset applies only if the value of the settled property which the trustees hold as participators is increased, or whether it suffices that the value of the trust property increases as a whole, i.e. is it necessary that the company's transfer be made to the trustees in their capacity as participators, or does it suffice that it is made to them simply as trustees?

The opening words of s.99(1) are:

"Subsection (1) of s.94 above shall not apply in relation to a person who is a participator in his capacity as trustee of a settlement . . . ";

[246] See paras 2–69 and following.
[247] It will be noted that this is not grossed up.
[248] IHTA 1984 ss.99(2)(a) and (3). In determining the amount of any such increase the value of any rights or interests in the company are left out of account.

and as a matter of statutory construction they must be regarded as establishing the context in which the remainder of the paragraph is intended to operate. It is on this basis that six-fortieths of A's interest in the shares rather than six-hundredths of his interest in the trust fund generally was said to come to an end in the above example, though whichever approach is adopted the result is the same, namely that A has made a transfer of £6,000. On the other hand, it is clearly arguable that the intention of the legislation is to bring into charge any diminution in the value of A's interest as a whole which results from the company's transfer, and that therefore what matters is that value accrues to the trustees, not the capacity in which they are acting when that accrual takes place. This argument notwithstanding it will clearly be prudent to ensure that transfers by a company are made to the trustees in their capacity as participators rather than simply to them as trustees.

HMRC confirm in Statement of Practice E5:

> "... that the general intention of IHTA s101 is to treat the participators as beneficial owners for all the purposes of that Act. Consequently, the conditions of IHTA ss.52(2), 53(2) are regarded as satisfied where it is the company that in fact becomes entitled to the property or disposes of the interest."

Thus, where a qualifying interest in possession terminates and a close company in which the individual entitled to that interest is a participator becomes entitled to the property in question, that individual's interest will be regarded as having been enlarged to an appropriate extent, and no charge will arise under s.52(1) in respect of that part of the property to which he is regarded as having become absolutely entitled.

Deemed termination

2–105   A person's interest will be deemed to come to an end in two situations. The first is where trustees of settled property in which there is a qualifying interest in possession enter into certain transactions which depreciate the value of that property. As the trustees have no estate[249] they cannot make a transfer of value; even if they could, not being individuals, that transfer would not be a chargeable one. Therefore, they could enter into such transactions with impunity. This could be useful to a person who had an interest in possession in the trust property since any charge to tax in respect of his interest would be on the depreciated value of that property. Provision is therefore made to counteract such transactions.

By s.52(3), where a transaction is made between the trustees of settled property and a person who is, or is connected with:

(1) the person beneficially entitled to a qualifying interest in possession in that property; or
(2) a person beneficially entitled to any other interest in that property or to any interest in any other property comprised in the settlement; or
(3) a person for whose benefit any of the settled property may be applied,

then, if that transaction results in the value of the property being reduced, a corresponding part of the qualifying interest in possession is deemed to come to an end.

The result is that in the event of the trustees entering into a "proscribed" transaction any person beneficially entitled to a qualifying interest in possession in the trust property is treated as having made a transfer of value of an amount equal to a

---

[249] See para.2–04.

corresponding part of his interest. If he has an interest in all of the property whose value is depreciated, the entire depreciation is attributed to him; if his interest is in only half of the property, only half of the depreciation is attributed to him, and so on.

Assume A has a life interest in Blackacre, and that Blackacre is worth £100,000. The trustees grant a lease to A's son at a peppercorn rent with the result that Blackacre's value on the open market is reduced by 80 per cent to £20,000; 80 per cent of A's interest will be deemed to come to an end. A will thus have made a notional transfer under s.52(1), and the value transferred by that transfer will be £80,000.[250]

The above is subject to one qualification, namely that the interest in question shall not be deemed to come to an end if the transaction entered into by the trustees would not be a transfer of value if the trustees were beneficially entitled to the settled property.[251] This means that if the trustees can show that, for example the transaction was an essentially commercial one under s.10(1), the interest in question will not be deemed to have come to an end. In the event that s.10(1) cannot be relied upon all is not necessarily lost because one of the reliefs considered below at paras 2–107 and following may still apply.

In the relatively rare case where trustees of an interest in possession settlement exercise their power to augment out of capital the income of a beneficiary not entitled to an interest in possession in that capital, HMRC regard the case as involving a distribution of capital and not the reduction of its value, so that s.52(1), not s.52(3), applies.[252]

2–106   The second situation in which a person's interest may be deemed to come to an end occurs when an individual is beneficially entitled to a qualifying interest in possession in settled property consisting of unquoted shares or unquoted securities in a close company in which the trustees are participators. If an alteration in the company's share or loan capital or of any rights attaching to the shares in or debentures of the company would otherwise be treated as a disposition made by the trustee-participators under s.98 then, by s.100, the part of that individual's qualifying interest in possession which is proportional to the decrease in the trust property's value caused by the alteration is deemed to come to an end. Thus, if the alteration decreased the value of the shares held on trust by 30 per cent then, assuming the shares were the only trust assets, 30 per cent of the interest in possession would be deemed to come to an end, and tax would be charged on the value of 30 per cent, of the property in which that interest subsisted.

This is necessary since it would be useless merely to attribute that disposition to the trustees who, as was noted previously, can make neither transfers of value nor chargeable transfers. There is, however, an anomaly here. It will be recalled that circumstances may arise in which an alteration is made in, e.g. the rights attaching to a close company's shares, against the will of one of its shareholders.[253] Under s.98(1) he will be treated as having made a disposition as a result of that alteration. If the alteration diminishes the value of his shares—probably the reason he objected to it—then prima facie he will have made an actual transfer of value notwithstanding the fact that the diminution was engineered against his wishes. In the circumstances, however, he may be able to rely on s.10(1), in which case he will not have made a transfer of value at all.

This is not the case where an individual's qualifying interest in possession is deemed to come to an end as a result of a notional disposition under s.98 being indirectly attributed to him under s.100. This is because there is no provision to the effect that "all is forgiven" if it is shown that were that individual entitled to the property beneficially

---

[250] For the position where the trustees make a loan, see para.15–05.
[251] See *Macpherson v IRC* [1989] A.C. 159, discussed at paras 9–18 and 15–15.
[252] See Statement of Practice E6.
[253] See para.2–18.

the notional disposition would not constitute a transfer of value. Consequently no recourse can be had to a relief such as s.10(1) and there will have been a notional transfer notwithstanding the fact that the alteration was effected against the wishes of the trustees and the beneficiary under the trust. This contrasts with the first situation in which a person's interest is deemed to come to an end, i.e. where the trustees enter into depreciatory transactions with certain persons associated with the trust. There, it will be recalled, the interest in question is not deemed to come to an end if the trustees can show that the transaction would not have been a transfer of value if they had been beneficially entitled to the trust property. The omission from s.100 of a similar qualification may be a drafting oversight. In practice, HMRC may be persuaded to extend concessionary reliefs where the trustees take no part in the alteration and no beneficiary under the trust benefits from the alteration.

Reliefs

The legislation provides three kinds of relief which prevent a charge to tax arising **2–107** under s.52(1). Although the end result is normally the same, namely that no tax is charged, a distinction should be drawn as to how the three reliefs achieve this end. Under the first kind of relief it is provided that in four cases there is no termination of a qualifying interest in possession to begin with, and therefore there is no notional transfer under s.52(1) at all. Under the second kind of relief, in six cases there is a coming to an end, but, as tax is not chargeable, s.3(4)[254] does not operate, and no transfer of value is made. Under the third kind of relief, in one case tax is simply not charged. Normally the fact that the reliefs operate differently will not be important. Exceptionally, it may be of consequence in relation to the associated operations provisions discussed in Chapter 9. The reliefs are as shown in the following table.

No termination	No transfer of value	No tax charged
1. Family maintenance dispositions	1. Excluded property	1. Trustees' annuities
2. Variations	2. Surviving spouse exemption	
3. Disclaimers	3. Acquisition of property	
4. Surviving spouse or civil partner election	4. Settlor's spouse or civil partner entitled	
	5. Settlor's widow or widower entitled	
	6. Court orders	

No termination

The legislation provides that in four cases a person beneficially entitled to a **2–108** qualifying interest in possession in settled property can dispose of his interest without that interest coming to an end under s.52(1).

(1) *Family maintenance dispositions.* First, relief is given to disposals which are **2–109** "family maintenance dispositions" within the meaning of s.11, as discussed at paras

---

[254] See para.3–01.

2–55 and following. Such a disposal does not result in the coming to an end of the disponer's qualifying interest in possession even though in the absence of this relief it would be treated as so doing.[255]

The relief is an adaptation of the relief given under s.11 dispositions for family maintenance which, in so far as they diminish the value of the disponer's estate, would otherwise constitute actual transfers of value. Since that relief applies only to *dispositions* which constitute transfers of value, it would be ineffective to relieve a transfer of value caused not by a disposition, but by the coming to an end of a qualifying interest in possession. Hence this adaptation.

It will be noted that the relief applies only where the qualifying interest in possession is *disposed* of; it is insufficient that, e.g. the interest is released[256] or simply terminates at the end of a designated period with the result that a person within the s.11 criteria becomes entitled to the property in which the interest subsisted or where an individual with a qualifying interest in possession requests the trustees of the settlement to advance capital for the education of his children as no relief will be available in respect of any termination in his interest which the trustees' compliance with his request occasions, since the termination will not have arisen in consequence of his disposing of his interest.

In the event that only part of the disposal is within s.11, the relief applies only to that part.[257]

2–110   (2) *Variations*. Relief is provided in certain circumstances where a person assigns or surrenders a qualifying interest in possession in settled property within two years of the death of the person in whose free estate that property had been comprised immediately before the latter died.[258] This is discussed at paras 8–115 and following.

2–111   (3) *Disclaimers*. Where a person becomes entitled to a qualifying interest in possession in settled property but disclaims that interest, he is treated by s.93 as never having been entitled to the interest in the first place. Consequently there is no coming to an end of any interest in possession on his making the disclaimer. This matter is fully discussed at paras 8–186 and 8–187.

2–112   (4) *Surviving spouse or civil partner election*. Under the Administration of Estates Act 1925, as amended by s.28 of the Administration of Justice Act 1977, when an intestate leaves a spouse or civil partner and issue, part of the intestate's estate, including, inter alia, a life interest (being an immediate post-death interest) in half his residuary estate, devolves on the surviving spouse or civil partner.[259] Under s.47A of that Act, the surviving spouse or civil partner can elect within 12 months of the grant of representation[260] to have the deceased's personal representatives redeem this qualifying life interest by payment of its capital value.[261] In the absence of provision to the

---

[255] IHTA 1984 s.51(2).

[256] HMRC Manuals IHTM16180.

[257] IHTA 1984 s.11(5).

[258] IHTA 1984 ss.17(a) and 142. By s.142(7), in relation to Scotland, property which is subject to a proper life rent is for this purpose deemed to be held in trust for the life-renter. This extension of s.142(4) brings s.142(4) into line with the extension of the definition of "settled property" to include property subject to a proper life rent: see para.11–03.

[259] The Law Commission recommended changes to the intestacy rules in a report published on December 14, 2011 (*Intestacy And Family Provision Claims On Death* (HMSO, 2011) (Law Com. No.331)). It recommended that if the deceased left a spouse and issue, the surviving spouse should receive the deceased's personal chattels, a statutory legacy of £250,000 and half of any balance of the estate outright (the issue would receive half of any balance of the estate on the statutory trusts).

[260] The court may extend this period. See AEA 1925 s.47A(5).

[261] The Intestate Succession (Interest and Capitalisation) Order 1977 (SI 1977/1491) art.3.

contrary, such a redemption would result in that interest coming to an end. Section 17(c) accordingly provides that such an election is not a transfer of value. Instead, on making such an election the surviving spouse or civil partner is treated as if, rather than being entitled to the qualifying life interest, he or she had been entitled to a sum equal to the capital value mentioned in s.47A. The effect is therefore that he or she is treated as never having had an interest in possession in the first place; consequently on making the s.47A election there is no coming to an end of any interest.

No transfer of value

The legislation provides that in six cases no tax is chargeable on the termination of a person's qualifying interest in possession, with the result that, as was mentioned above at para.2–72, the termination is not the occasion of a transfer of value. The six cases are as follows. **2–113**

(1) *Excluded property.* The first kind of relief under this head relates to excluded property. If the settled property in which the interest subsists is excluded property then, by s.53(1), no tax is chargeable under s.52 even though that interest comes to an end during the life of the person then beneficially entitled to it. The general rule is that settled property is excluded property if (a) it is situated outside the United Kingdom and (b) at the time the settlor made the settlement he was domiciled outside the United Kingdom.[262] **2–114**

(2) *Surviving spouse exemption.* Under estate duty where the first spouse to die gave a life interest in property to the surviving spouse that interest was exempt from duty when the survivor died, duty already having been paid on the property on the first death. The legislation honours the estate duty exemption in relation to the charge under s.52(1) by providing in para.2 of Sch.6 that where a person died before November 13, 1974, leaving his surviving spouse a qualifying interest in possession in property, no IHT is chargeable on the termination of the surviving spouse's interest if that value would have qualified for the surviving spouse exemption under s.5(2) of the Finance Act 1894. **2–115**

The reference in para.2 to a "surviving spouse" suggests on a first reading that no relief is available in respect of a former marriage, but it is understood that HMRC do not apply para.2 in this way.

It is to be noted that para.2 applies only where the first spouse died before November 13, 1974. If the first spouse died on or after that date para.2 does not apply, and tax is charged in the usual way. This is because after November 12 the estate duty "surviving spouse exemption" was abolished, exemption from estate duty in respect of deaths between November 13, 1974 and December 12, 1975, being given instead on the death of the first spouse rather than on the death of the survivor.

A similar relief is given under para.2 of Sch.6 where a charge arises on the death of the surviving spouse possessed of a qualifying interest in possession in respect of which the spouse would have benefited from exemption from estate duty. It might therefore be thought that there is nothing to be gained from taking advantage of the relief afforded to a lifetime termination of the qualifying interest in possession, but this is not necessarily the case because the mechanism for providing the relief on death differs from that given to the lifetime termination of such an interest. Where relief is given on death, it is given by leaving out of account the value of the property in which

---

[262] IHTA 1984 s.48(3). For a full discussion see Ch.32.

the qualifying interest in possession subsists, and this means that that property may still be taken into account in valuing other property comprised in the deceased's estate.[263]

Assume A, a widow, owns 45 shares in B Ltd, an investment company with 100 issued ordinary shares and also has a qualifying interest in possession in 10 shares in B Ltd, with remainder over to her son, in circumstances such that the estate duty surviving spouse exemption is available. If immediately before A's death she still has a qualifying interest in possession in the 10 shares, no charge will arise in respect of those shares, but they will be taken into account in valuing the 45 shares, which will accordingly be valued on a majority rather than minority basis. If, on the other hand, A were to surrender her interest during her lifetime, there will still be no charge on the 10 shares, but on her death the 45 shares will be valued on a minority basis.

A similar valuation consideration arises in relation to lifetime transfers. Assume A in the above example is prepared to surrender her qualifying interest in possession to her son and that she also wants to give him the 45 shares. The 10 shares will be taken into account in determining the value of the 45 shares. Accordingly, in order to secure a minority valuation on the 10 shares she should first surrender her interest and only subsequently give her son the 10 shares.[264]

In the examples just given, no business relief is available because B Ltd is an investment company. If 100 per cent business relief is available the impact of the property held in trust on the valuation of the property held in the deceased's free estate will be unimportant.

2–116   (3) *Reversion to settlor.* There is a reversion to the settlor during his life. Relief is available where on the termination of a pre-March 22, 2006 interest in possession the trust assets revert to the original settlor. In that case, by s.53(3), no tax is chargeable under s.52 notwithstanding that termination. If the effect of the entitlement is that the person whose qualifying interest in possession terminated becomes entitled to only part of the property or to an interest in possession in only part of the property the relief is restricted accordingly. Without this relief there might be a charge (i) when the settlor settled the property, (ii) when the property reverted to him, and yet again (iii) when he died (or disposed of the property before dying). This relief eliminates the middle charge. In the case of a life interest arising on or after March 22, 2006 and which is subject to the relevant property regime (and so not a qualifying interest in possession), s.53(3) does not apply.[265]

2–117   The relief is not available if the settlor or his spouse or civil partner acquired the reversion for a consideration in money or money's worth.[266] Section 53(6) provides that a person is for this purpose treated as acquiring an interest for a consideration in money or money's worth if he becomes entitled to it as a result of transactions which include a disposition for such a consideration, whether to him or another, of that interest or of other property. This qualification is designed to prevent tax being avoided in the following way. Assume that elderly A has a life interest in £100,000, and that on his death B is to become absolutely entitled to that sum. But for the above qualification, the tax that would otherwise have been payable on A's death could have been avoided by the settlor purchasing B's reversion for £100,000, with the result that on A's death

[263] See para.8–22.
[264] See also para.6–16.
[265] See *Farm Tax Brief*, October 2006, pp.4–5.
[266] IHTA 1984 ss.53(5)(a) and 54(3). This would include an acquisition by a close company in which he was a participator or by trustees of a settlement in which he had an interest in possession. See HMRC Manuals IHTM04353.

no charge would have arisen (thanks to the reverter to settlor relief) and the £100,000 would have reached B free of tax.

This is, in fact, a rather draconian qualification, and if there is a reversion to a settlor or a settlor's spouse or civil partner who acquired his reversionary interest for a consideration in money or money's worth the consequences can be dire indeed.

Assume A's estate consists of Blackacre, worth £100,000, and £50,000 in cash in the bank. As matters stand, if A were to die HMRC would charge tax on £150,000, the value of A's estate. Assume A settles Blackacre on B for life, remainder to C, whom he ultimately wishes to benefit. Before the settlement A's estate was worth £150,000, after it, £50,000. He has therefore made a transfer of value of £100,000. Now consider two alternative scenarios.

First, C assigns his interest to A. This will not constitute a transfer of value by C since his interest, being a reversionary interest, is excluded property,[267] and therefore his estate will suffer no diminution in value.[268] If B then assigns his qualifying interest in possession to A, no tax will be chargeable since he will be covered by the reverter to settlor relief. A will again own Blackacre, his estate will again be worth £150,000, and everyone concerned will be back in their starting positions without any charge other than that imposed on A when he created the settlement.

If, on the other hand, C *sells* his reversionary interest to A, the situation changes dramatically. Assume the sale is for market value, say £50,000. The purchase by A will not constitute a transfer of value by him since his estate, swollen by the reversion worth £50,000, is not diminished by the disposition of the purchase price to C. C's position is as above: he has disposed of excluded property, and, in any event, the value of his estate also remains the same before and after the sale. A's overall position at this stage remains the same as when C assigned the reversion in that if A had died before buying the reversion tax would have been charged on the £50,000 in the bank. If he dies after acquiring the reversion he will still be assessed on £50,000, since the reversion, having been acquired for a consideration in money or money's worth, will not be excluded property in his hands.[269]

Now assume that B's interest comes to an end, e.g. because he assigns it to A. So far as Blackacre is concerned, A will be back in his original position, i.e. he will own Blackacre outright, since on B's assignment of his interest to A, B's interest and the reversion A acquired from C will merge in A's hands to give A outright ownership of Blackacre as a whole. The reversionary interest acquired from C will thus have ceased to exist.

But A's starting position is not the same as far as his bank balance is concerned. **2–118** Indeed, he no longer has a bank balance, having paid the £50,000 to C to purchase the reversion, which has since ceased to exist. If A dies, HMRC would therefore stand to tax him on only £100,000, not on £150,000. The legislation remedies this by withholding the reverter to settlor relief from B, so that tax is charged under s.52(1) on £100,000 on the termination of his qualifying interest in possession, not merely on the £50,000 missing from A's estate.

Section 53(5)(b) provides that the relief is also not available when its application **2–119** depends on a reversionary interest having been transferred into a settlement on or after March 10, 1981. The avoidance technique which this restriction is designed to counteract is best explained by way of an example. Assume that A has settled property on his wife for life, remainder to his son, and that his wife wishes to release her qualifying

---

[267] IHTA 1984 s.48(1).
[268] IHTA 1984 s.3(2); see para.2–36.
[269] IHTA 1984 s.48(1)(a).

interest in possession in order that the son may become absolutely entitled. As matters stand, if she simply releases her interest she will make a notional transfer under s.52(1). Assume, however, that first the son settles his reversionary interest on his father for a short period, remainder to himself absolutely, and that his mother then releases her interest. On releasing her interest she will make a notional transfer under s.52(1), but that transfer will be within the s.18 exemption. At the end of the month the father's interest will terminate, but, on the basis that the son is the settlor of the father's interest, s.53(3) operates to prevent any charge from arising. The efficacy of this type of planning was confirmed in *IRC v Fitzwilliam*.[270]

In determining the availability of this relief the identity of the settlor is crucial and has been the subject of complicated judicial analysis. Particular problems may arise where there is more than one settlor of a settlement.[271]

2–120   (4) *Settlor's spouse or civil partner becomes beneficially entitled.* Section 53(4) provides that if a qualifying interest in possession comes to an end and on the same occasion the settlor's spouse or civil partner becomes beneficially entitled to the property in which that interest subsisted then, subject to two qualifications, no tax is chargeable under s.52, provided that the settlor's spouse or civil partner is a UK domiciliary at that time. It is understood that HMRC accept that, given s.49(1), this relief is available if the spouse or civil partner becomes entitled to a qualifying interest in possession in the property. In determining whether the spouse or civil partner is a UK domiciliary the deemed domicile rules[272] apply. This may work to the taxpayer's advantage, for it may result in the spouse or civil partner being a UK domiciliary for IHT purposes even though he or she is not a UK domiciliary as a matter of general law. The qualifications are that the relief is not available, in the same way as under the reverter to settlor relief,[273] if (a) before the spouse or civil partner became beneficially entitled to the property either the spouse or civil partner or the settlor acquired a reversionary interest in that property for a consideration in money or money's worth, or (b) the reversionary interest was transferred into a settlement on or after March 10, 1981.[274]

This relief should not be confused with the exemption given to transfers between spouses or civil partners. The situation envisaged here is that A settled property on B, remainder to A's wife. B's interest terminates while B is still alive, A's spouse becoming beneficially entitled to the property. B, not A, has thus, in effect, made a notional transfer to A's wife. That being the case, the s.18 exemption would not apply, and, but for this relief, B would be chargeable. As with the relief given under s.52(3), difficulties may arise if there is more than one settlor.[275]

2–121   (5) *Settlor's widow/widower/surviving civil partner becomes entitled.* Under the legislation a widow/widower/surviving civil partner is not a spouse or civil partner, and therefore, in the absence of special provision, the relief just considered where the settlor's spouse or civil partner becomes beneficially entitled to property would not apply when the settlor's widow/widower/surviving civil partner became so entitled. Fortunately, s.53(4) provides that for purposes of that relief a widow/widower/surviving civil partner is still regarded as a spouse or civil partner when the settlor died less than two years before the interest came to an end and HMRC's view is that a person

---

[270] *IRC v Fitzwilliam* [1993] S.T.C. 502; see para.11–42.
[271] See paras 15–42 and following.
[272] IHTA 1984 s.267.
[273] IHTA 1984 s.49(2).
[274] See para.2–116.
[275] See paras 15–42 and following.

continues to be the widow/widower/surviving civil partner of the settlor notwithstanding subsequent remarriage.[276]

It is understood that HMRC accept that, given s.49(1), this relief is available if the widow/widower/surviving civil partner becomes entitled to a qualifying interest in possession in the property. As with the relief given under s.52(3), difficulties may arise if there is more than one settlor.[277]

2–122 (6) *Court orders.* Under the Inheritance (Provision for Family and Dependants) Act 1975 the court has power to order financial provision where the dispositions of the estate of a person who died domiciled in England and Wales[278] do not make reasonable provision for his family and dependants. By s.146(6), where an order under[279] the Act provides for property to be settled, or for a variation of a settlement, s.52(1) does not apply if, were it to apply, a charge to tax would arise by virtue of its operation. Thus, although there is a termination of an interest, there is not a notional transfer.[280] This relief is most likely to be of assistance where the court varies a marriage settlement or a settlement made in anticipation of, or during the subsistence of, a civil partnership, as it may do under s.2 of the Act.

No tax charged: trustees' annuities

2–123 Section 90 makes special provision for trustees who are entitled to an interest in possession (e.g. an annuity) by way of remuneration. So long as such an interest represents no more than a reasonable amount of remuneration, no tax is charged under s.52(1) when that interest comes to an end.

The value transferred

2–124 As was noted previously, there are special rules for determining the value transferred by a notional transfer made under s.52(1). These rules override the consequential loss provisions, which apply only to actual transfers. In addition, there are three reliefs, which apply only to transfers involving a qualifying interest in possession, and which operate to reduce the value of the property by reference to which the value transferred is computed. These are discussed below.

The basic rule

2–125 The basic rule is that when a person makes a notional transfer under s.52(1), the value transferred by that transfer is treated as being equal to the value of the property

---

[276] HMRC Manuals IHTM04360.

[277] See paras 11–43 and following.

[278] In a report published on December 14, 2011 (*Intestacy And Family Provision Claims On Death* (HMSO, 2011) (Law Com. No.331)) the Law Commission recommended that a family provision claim should be possible if either the deceased was domiciled in England and Wales or English succession law applies to any part of the estate, including (for these purposes) assets passing by survivorship, assets subject to a statutory nomination and assets that were the subject of a deathbed gift (*donatio mortis causa*). This would mean that a claim could be made where the deceased is not domiciled in the UK.

[279] See also IHTA 1984 s.146(8).

[280] Note that s.146(6) does not negative a subsequent charge, e.g. on termination of a life interest created or substituted by the order; HMRC Manuals IHTM35208.

in which his interest subsisted. It is important to note that the value transferred is not the amount by which the value of his estate has been diminished as a result of the transfer, so there is no question of grossing-up. Nor is it the value of the interest which has come to an end. Instead, the value transferred is the value of the property in which that interest subsisted and that property is to be valued in isolation without reference to any similar property in the person's estate or to any related property under s.161.[281] For the position where the transferor bears the tax, see paras 6–33 and following.

The procedure, therefore, is to ascertain the value of the property in which the interest subsisted. Any available reliefs and exemptions are then set against the value. What is left constitutes the value transferred by the chargeable transfer which that transfer comprises.

The property in which the interest subsisted

2–126 Normally it will not be difficult to determine the value of the property in which the interest subsisted. If the qualifying interest in possession subsists in the whole of the property, e.g. where an individual was entitled to the whole of the income from a trust fund, then the value of the whole of the property will be brought into account. If the interest subsisted in part of the property, only the value of the part will be brought into account.[282]

In three cases, the position is more complicated. First, it may be that two or more persons not entitled to any income at all from the property are entitled to use the property; this is discussed at para.12–42. Secondly, a lease may be treated as an interest in possession; this is discussed at para.32–59. Thirdly, a person may be entitled to a specified amount from property whatever income that property may yield, e.g. where X is entitled to the first £1,000 a year which accrues to the trust fund. This is discussed below.

Specified amounts

2–127 By s.50(2), where a person is entitled to a specified amount (such as an annuity) for any period his qualifying interest in possession is taken to subsist in the part of the property that produces that amount in that period. It may be that his entitlement is defined negatively, i.e. that he is entitled to the whole or part of the income less a specified amount. In that case his interest is taken to subsist in the whole or part of that property less so much of the property as it takes to produce the specified amount during any period.

A person will be entitled to a "specified amount" for these purposes even though the amount to which he is entitled may vary from period to period. A person who is entitled, e.g. to "such sum as after deduction of income tax at the basic rate for the time

---

[281] HMRC Manuals IHTM16103—refers to valuation of a share which seems apposite. Note that settled property is valued in isolation but the *rate* of business relief or agricultural relief is still determined by reference to that property and any other property held by the transferor.

[282] The part will be valued on a pro rata basis, IHTA 1984 s.52(4)(a). It may be that the trust instrument is so drafted that instead of being entitled to the income from part of the property the beneficiary is entitled to a part of the income from the property, e.g. where he is entitled to one-third of the income (versus where he is entitled to the income from one-third of the property). In that case, by s.50(1), his interest is taken to subsist in a part of the property which bears the same relation to the whole of the property as the part of the income to which he is entitled bears to the whole of the income from the property.

being in force equals £1,000", is entitled to a specified amount for these purposes because the amount to which he is entitled is ascertainable at any time. A person who is entitled only to "such sum as the trustees in their absolute discretion think fit", on the other hand, is not entitled to any ascertainable amount whatsoever.[283]

Section 50(2) refers to "any period" during which the person is entitled to a specified amount. But which period is the appropriate one to take into account in a given case is far from clear. Assume that five years after A becomes entitled to £1,000 a year from a trust fund worth £40,000 his qualifying interest in possession comes to an end. During the first two years the trust's investments reap a bumper harvest and the £1,000 paid to A represents only a small part of the trust income with the result that for those two years A's interest is taken to subsist in only a small part of the fund, say £4,000. In the next two years the yield on the investments falls off drastically, and there is just enough income to pay A his £1,000. In those two years A's interest is thus taken to subsist in the whole of the £40,000. In the last year disaster strikes and the trust receives no income at all. During that year A's interest is worthless.

The question thus arises, which period should be brought into account in determining the property in which A's qualifying interest in possession is to be taken to subsist? A, no doubt, would claim that the proper period is the last year, and that therefore no tax is chargeable. This view is supported by the fact that under the terms of the settlement A's entitlement is an annual one, so the argument is fair if it ends in that year, but that is hardly likely to be conclusive.

HMRC, on the other hand, would probably seek also to bring into account the two preceding years, for during those years A's qualifying interest in possession subsisted in the whole of the £40,000. A, in turn, would argue that if the appropriate period is not the last year the whole history of his entitlement should be taken into account with the result that the value of the property in which his interest subsisted was only £17,600 (£4,000 + £4,000 + £40,000 + £40,000 + 0 divided by 5).

It is obviously impossible to predict what "any period" will be taken to mean, either by HMRC, or by the courts. HMRC practice under estate duty where settled property consisted of investments with varying dividends was to take into account the income in the year before death. Whether this or any other approach operates to the taxpayer's advantage will depend, of course, on the facts of his case.

A more beguiling question is whether fluctuations in the income yield of trust property will result in transfers of value or capital distributions. Assume A is entitled to £1,000 a year for life (and A and B's interests are qualifying interests in possession) from a trust fund worth £20,000, the remaining income to be held on trust for B for life, remainder to C. In year 1 the total income arising under the trust is £2,000; A and B thus each have qualifying interests in possession in half the trust fund. In year 2 the total income is £4,000 with the result that A now has an interest in only one-quarter of the trust fund, while B's interest is in the remaining three-quarters of the fund. Does this mean that half of A's interest has come to an end with the result that he has made a notional transfer under s.52(1) of £5,000?

Now assume that in year 3 the total income drops back to £2,000, with the result that A and B again each have an interest in half the fund. Does this mean that one-third of B's interest has come to an end so that it is his turn to have made a transfer under s.52(1) of £5,000?

The answer to both questions may be that s.50(2) is merely a measuring section to be invoked as and when a notional transfer occurs.

It is clear that charges were not intended to arise in such circumstances. But precisely how they are to be obviated in practice is less clear. The solution may have to be sought (if not found) to those enigmatic words "any period". If read as meaning "any period

---

[283] Such a person would not have an interest in possession to begin with; see paras 12–20–12–35.

during which the property that produces the amount to which the annuitant is entitled remains unchanged", then at least charges which would on a strict reading of the legislation appear to arise merely as a result of changes in income yield would be avoided.

Statutory yields

2–128　　The purpose of the statutory yield provisions can best be explained by an example. Assume A is entitled to a specified amount of income from, e.g. half of a trust fund. A intends to give his interest to his son in the near future. In the absence of provision to the contrary (and subject to what was just said about the meaning of "any period") it would not be difficult for A to make the gift largely tax-free. The trustees would simply invest that part of the fund in high-yield investments with the result that a relatively small part of the trust fund provided his share of the income. His interest would therefore be taken to subsist in at best a small part of the trust fund, and little if any tax would be chargeable on his interest coming to an end. Once the gift had been made the trustees would switch back into low-yield investments.

By s.50(2) where a person is entitled to a specified amount, the part of the property which yields that amount is taken to be *at least* what it would be if that part produced income at such "higher rate" as may be prescribed by statutory instrument.[284] Thus, if the property produces income at a rate in excess of the "higher rate", the actual yield will be ignored, and instead the person in question will be regarded as having an interest in that part of the property which, if it produced income as the "higher rate", would yield the specified amount. If, on the other hand, the property produces income at less than the "higher rate", it is the property which in fact yields the specified amount that is brought into account.

The operative statutory instrument is the Capital Transfer Tax (Settled Property Income Yield) Order 1980,[285] which applies as from August 1, 1980. Under this Order, the higher rate is that shown in the FT Actuaries Share Indices for British Government Stocks ("Irredeemables") on a day to day basis.

Where a person is entitled to the whole of the income less a specified amount, the part which yields the specified amount is taken to be at most what it would be if it produced income at the "lower rate". It is thus not possible to avoid tax by investing in property with a very low yield so that the person entitled to the "remainder" of the income is regarded as having an interest in only a very small part of the trust fund. If in fact the property produces income at more than the "lower rate" yield it is that higher yield which is brought into account. Under the 1980 Order art.3 the "lower rate" is the current gross dividend yield on the FT Actuaries All-Share Index, taken, as above, from day to day.

Quantitative reliefs

2–129　　Certain reliefs are available which have the effect of reducing the amount on which tax is charged on the coming to an end of a qualifying interest in possession. These reliefs fall into two categories. First, there are two reliefs which apply only to

---

[284] This is subject to the qualification that the value to be taken as the value of part of a property shall not exceed the value of the whole of the property: IHTA 1984 s.50(3).
[285] SI 1980/1000.

qualifying interests in possession. These reliefs operate to reduce the value of the property by reference to which the value transferred is ascertained. Secondly, there are other reliefs which apply to transfers of property generally, and which operate to reduce the value transferred by a given transfer. Only the reliefs which are peculiar to interests in possession are considered here; the reliefs available to transfers generally are dealt with in Chapter 14.

The two reliefs peculiar to qualifying interests in possession are:

(1) dispositions for a consideration (s.52(2)); and
(2) enlargement of an interest (s.53(2)).

Each will be considered in turn. But before doing so, it will be useful to consider the interaction of these reliefs, the reliefs available to transfers generally, and exemptions. It may be that the same transfer qualifies both for one of the reliefs available only to qualifying interests in possession and for one of the reliefs available to transfers generally, e.g. business relief. In that case the relief peculiar to qualifying interests in possession is applied first. This follows from the fact that those reliefs operate to reduce the value of the property in which the interest subsists, and that value must be determined before the value transferred, to which the general reliefs apply, can be ascertained. Any exemptions that may be available are brought into account last of all.

The best way to understand the two reliefs is to regard them as intended to ensure that when a person's qualifying interest in possession comes to an end he is charged only to the extent that the value of his estate is reduced. What must be borne in mind here is the cardinal rule that a person entitled to a qualifying interest in possession is treated as being beneficially entitled to the property in which his interest subsists. The reliefs are framed with reference to the value of that property, not with reference to the value of the interest in question.

Dispositions for a consideration

As was noted previously, a person's qualifying interest in possession will come to an **2–130** end when he disposes of it.[286] If this happens and the disposal is for a consideration in money or money's worth, then, by s.52(2), the value of the property in which the interest subsisted is treated as reduced by the amount of the consideration received.

Assume A is entitled to a life interest in settled property worth £100,000 and the market value of A's interest is £25,000. He sells his interest for £25,000. He will have made a notional transfer of value under s.52(1), and the value transferred will be £75,000, the value of the property in which his interest subsists (£100,000) as reduced by the consideration he received (£25,000).

Unfortunately, A cannot rely on the relief afforded to essentially commercial transactions under s.10(1),[287] because it relieves only dispositions coming within its aegis which would otherwise constitute transfers of value. The disposal of a qualifying interest in possession, however, does not of itself constitute a transfer of value.[288]

---

[286] See para.2–95.
[287] See paras 2–41–2–53.
[288] IHTA 1984 s.51(1)(a).

Instead it constitutes the notional coming to an end of that interest, and it is that notional termination which constitutes the notional transfer under s.52(1).[289]

2–131   *Interests left out of account.* In determining the amount of the consideration paid for the interest the value of two kinds of interest received as consideration by the disponer must be left out of account, namely (i) a reversionary interest in the property, and (ii) any interest in other property comprised in the same settlement.[290]

2–132   *A reversionary interest in the property.* This is an anti-avoidance provision. Assume that property worth £100,000 is settled on the following terms (when A and B's interests are qualifying interests in possession): A for life, B for life, remainder to C and that B's reversion is worth £30,000. A is treated as being beneficially entitled to the property itself. This means that he is treated as owning not only his own interest, but those of B and C as well, if A were to die, then on the present facts HMRC would stand to collect tax on £100,000. Now assume two alternative transactions.

First, A gives one-quarter of his interest to B. This will result in A making a notional transfer of £25,000, and tax will be charged accordingly. After the transfer A's estate will be worth £75,000. HMRC therefore still expect to collect tax on £100,000, on £25,000 now and on £75,000 later.

If, on the other hand, A gives one-quarter of his interest to B in exchange for, e.g., half of B's interest, then, in the absence of provision to the contrary, the position would be quite different. The value transferred by A would be reduced by the consideration—half of B's reversion, worth £15,000—he received from B. A would therefore have made a notional transfer of only £10,000 (£25,000 − £15,000). This would not trouble HMRC if after the transfer A's estate was worth £90,000 (£75,000 left + £15,000 received from B), because they would still collect tax from A on £100,000 eventually—on £10,000 now, on £90,000 later.

But that, in fact, would not be the case. This is because the reversion A acquired from B would not increase the value of A's estate. This follows from the fact that A, by virtue of being treated as owning the property in which his interest subsists, was already treated as owning the half of the reversion he acquired from B. After the transfer A's estate would therefore be worth only £75,000, not £90,000, with the result that, in the absence of provision to the contrary, A would have succeeded in making a tax-free gift of £15,000 to B.

Section 52(2) accordingly provides that the value of the reversionary interest (£15,000) acquired from B is to be left out of account in determining the amount of consideration received by A. The result is that A will have made a notional transfer of £25,000, and HMRC will still charge tax on the entire £100,000—£25,000 now, and £75,000 later.

2–133   *Any interest in other property comprised in the same settlement.* The authors, despite their best efforts, have not succeeded in discerning the purpose of this qualification. It does not appear to be an anti-avoidance provision, because the transactions it contemplates will not result in anyone gaining an IHT advantage.[291] One explanation is

---

[289] Nor, for the same reason, can the disponer rely on any of the other reliefs available only to actual transfers of value, such as s.11, etc.

[290] IHTA 1984 s.52(2).

[291] If the interest in question is an interest in possession, there will be a charge under s.52(1) on its coming to an end; if it is a reversionary interest, it will not be excluded property in the hands of the person acquiring it. If it is an intermediate interest it will increase the value of the estate of the person acquiring it.

that the draftsman did not include this provision with anything specific in mind, but merely as a long-stop against the infamous ingenuity of tax advisers.

Enlargement of an interest

If the person whose qualifying interest in possession comes to an end becomes on the **2–134** same occasion beneficially entitled to the property in which the interest subsists, or to another interest in that property, then, by s.53(2), tax is chargeable only on the difference, if any, between the value of the property in which his interest subsisted and the value of the property to which he has become entitled.[292] The consequences of this provision can best be explained by two examples.

First, assume A has a qualifying interest in possession in a trust fund of £50,000, and that the trustees have power to advance capital to him. If the trustees advance £50,000 to A, his qualifying interest in possession in that £50,000 will have come to an end. But there will be no charge to tax under s.52(1) because the value of the property to which A becomes entitled (£50,000) is the same as the value of the property in which his interest ceased to subsist. The fact that there is no charge to tax in such circumstances makes perfectly good sense, since both before and after A's qualifying interest in possession comes to an end his estate is worth exactly the same.

Next, assume A is entitled to a qualifying interest in possession in settled property worth £200,000, and that on A's death B is to become absolutely entitled to that property. The market value of A's interest is, say, £80,000, though A's interest is in effect worth £200,000 since he is treated as owning the property in which his interest subsists. Now assume two alternative transactions.

If B assigns his reversion to A, B will not make a transfer of value since his reversion is excluded property.[293] A's interest will come to an end, but A will not be charged under s.52(1), because there will be no difference between the value of the property in which his interest subsists and the value of the property to which he became entitled as a result of B's assignment. Before the assignment he was treated as owning the property; after the assignment he in fact owns it. The value of his estate remains unchanged, and therefore no tax is chargeable.

If, on the other hand, A and B decide to partition the property, e.g. on an actuarial basis with the result that, say, A assigns to B three-fifths of his qualifying interest in possession in return for B assigning two-fifths of his reversion to A, the position will be different. As in the first transaction, all of A's interest comes to an end, because he ceases to be entitled to three-fifths of it, and the remaining two-fifths merges with the reversion acquired from B so that he becomes absolutely entitled to two-fifths of the fund, i.e. to £80,000.

In "real life", of course, the value of A's estate has remained unchanged. Before the partition he had a qualifying interest in possession worth £80,000; after the transfer he is absolutely entitled to £80,000. But what matters for IHT is that before the partition A was treated as owning property worth £200,000; after the partition, property worth only £80,000. Therefore, tax is chargeable on the difference between the two values—£120,000. No relief is available in respect of the consideration received from B, because that consideration was a reversionary interest and therefore left out of account.[294]

---

[292] IHTA 1984 s.53(2) read in conjunction with s.52(4)(b).
[293] IHTA 1984 ss.24(3) and 3(2).
[294] IHTA 1984 s.52(2).

As noted above at para.2–99, HMRC have confirmed, in Statement of Practice E5:

"... that the general intention of I.H.T.A. 1984 s.101 is to treat the participators as beneficial owners for all the purposes of that Act. Consequently, the conditions of I.H.T.A. s.52(2), s.53(2) are regarded as satisfied where it is the company that in fact becomes entitled to the property or disposes of the interest."

Thus, where a qualifying interest in possession terminates and a close company in which the individual entitled to that interest is a participator becomes entitled to the property in question, that individual's interest will be regarded as having been enlarged to an appropriate extent, and no charge will arise under s.52(1) in respect of that part of the property to which he is regarded as having become absolutely entitled.

Annual and marriage or civil partnership gift exemptions

2–135   As will be seen in Chapter 3, certain exemptions normally apply only to actual transfers of value. The annual exemption and the exemption given to marriage or civil partnership gifts both fall into this category. The legislation expressly provides, however, that these two exemptions are available.[295]

Quick succession relief

2–136   A person entitled to a qualifying interest in possession in settled property may be taxed quickly after he becomes so entitled, e.g. because the interest itself is of a short duration, or because he disposes of it soon after acquiring it.[296] If the property was taxed when he became entitled to his interest tax will within a short period be charged twice in respect of the same property. This would be a bit hard, especially since the broad policy of the legislation is to tax property once a generation. The legislation therefore provides relief in so far as the two charges arise within five years of each other. The relief, which takes the form of a tax credit, is discussed in detail at paras 8–32 and following.

X. DEATH

2–137   The third case in which a person makes a notional transfer is when he dies. This, of course, will be the last transfer he ever makes, and, coming as it does at the end of his IHT history, it will also be subject to the highest rates of tax he will ever pay. The basic provision relating to death is straightforward. By s.4(1), when a person dies he is treated: (i) as if he had made a transfer of value immediately before he died; and (ii) as if the value transferred by that transfer had been equal to the value of his estate at that time. What is likely to be in issue, therefore, is the amount on which tax is to be

---

[295] IHTA 1984 ss.57 and 94(5); see paras 3–05 and 3–23.
[296] Or, alas, because he dies. As was noted previously, IHTA 1984 s.52(1) does not apply on death, but quick succession relief may be available on a death; see paras 8–32 and following.

charged, not whether a charge has arisen in the first place. As was mentioned earlier, the rules governing the notional transfer made on death are discussed in Chapter 8.

XI. PURCHASED SETTLEMENT POWERS

The draftsman foresaw that by excluding settlement powers from the property **2–138** comprised in a person's estate[297] he had created a potential device for tax savings because it opened the door to a person making IHT-free gifts by purchasing a non-asset for IHT purposes. Assume X wishes to benefit Y. Y could create a settlement under which Y had a settlement power. X would then purchase the power from Y for an arm's length price, contending that, e.g. s.10[298] prevented him from making a transfer of value.

The Finance Act 2002 accordingly introduced a new s.55A which addresses the situation where, after April 16, 2002,[299] a person makes a disposition by which he acquires a settlement power for money or money's worth. He is for this purpose regarded as acquiring such a power if he becomes entitled to the power or:

(a) to exercise, or to secure or prevent the exercise of it (whether directly or indirectly); or

(b) to restrict, or secure a restriction on the exercise of it (whether directly or indirectly),

as a result of transactions which include a disposition (whether by him or another) of a settlement power or of any power of a kind described in (a) or (b) above which is exercisable in relation to a settlement power.[300]

Where the person acquires the settlement power as aforesaid:

(a) s.10(1) does not apply to the disposition;

(b) the person is taken to make a transfer of value;

(c) the value transferred is determined without bringing into account the value of anything which the person acquires by the disposition; and

(d) the s.18 exemption and the exemptions for transfers to charities, political parties, housing associations, for national purposes and to maintenance funds for historic buildings do not apply in relation to that transfer.[301]

---

[297] See para.25–12.
[298] See paras 2–41–2–53.
[299] FA 2002 s.119(6).
[300] IHTA 1984 s.55A(2).
[301] IHTA 1984 s.55A(1).

CHAPTER 3

EXEMPT TRANSFERS

I. INTRODUCTION

3–01   The legislation provides that certain transfers of value are exempt transfers, with the result that, although they remain transfers of value, they do not constitute chargeable transfers. The availability of an exemption may also prevent the reservation of benefit rules from applying.[1] The exemptions fall into four general categories, three of which, exemptions that apply to actual transfers only, exemptions that apply both to actual and notional transfers, and exemptions for transfers of shares to employee trusts, are considered in this chapter. The fourth category, exemptions for national heritage transfers, which comprises conditionally exempt transfers and transfers to maintenance funds for historical buildings, is a topic in itself, and is dealt with separately in Chapter 21. Partly exempt transfers, also a subject in their own right, are discussed in Chapter 8. Potentially exempt transfers are the subject of Chapter 5. For the sake of convenience, one other topic, voidable transfers, is dealt with in this chapter.

Manner in which exemptions are generally given

3–02   HMRC regard the exemptions as cumulative, and HMRC practice is to bring the exemptions into account in the way that is most advantageous to the taxpayer. Thus, if on day one a taxpayer makes a transfer of value to charity and on day two makes a

[1] See para.7–36.

transfer of value equal in amount to the annual exemption to trustees of a relevant property trust, HMRC will not regard the annual exemption as having been applied against the first transfer to charity so as to leave the second transfer unprotected by the annual exemption. It may be that in theory this practice is unjustified,[2] but it is sensible and in any event unlikely to be called into question.

Interaction with PETs

Because a PET is defined (inter alia) as being a transfer of value "which apart from this section would be a chargeable transfer . . . ",[3] HMRC generally take the view that the relevant exemptions must be deducted first and only if any value remains will the PET regime come into play; see para.5–40, etc. The impact of the annual exemption on a PET is considered at paras 5–06 and following.

3–03

II. EXEMPTIONS THAT GENERALLY APPLY TO ACTUAL TRANSFERS ONLY

As was mentioned at para.2–72, s.3(4) operates to align the treatment afforded to actual and notional transfers of value by providing that:

3–04

> "Except as otherwise provided, references in this Act to a transfer of value made, or made by any person, include references to events on the happening of which tax is chargeable as if a transfer of value had been made, or, as the case may be, had been made by that person; and 'transferor' shall be construed accordingly."

It follows from this that, in the absence of provision to the contrary, any provision to the effect that a transfer of value was exempt would apply equally to actual and notional transfers. It is therefore important to note that s.3(4) is expressed not to apply to certain of the exemptions so that this application is limited to actual transfers.[4] In some cases, s.3(4) is expressed not to apply subject to certain qualifications.[5]

These qualifications are discussed below; subject to them, the exemptions that apply only to actual transfers of value are the:

- annual exemption;
- small gifts exemption;
- normal expenditure out of income exemption; and
- marriage gifts exemption.

Each will be considered in turn. As will be seen below, these exemptions are available only so long as certain conditions discussed below are not infringed.

Annual exemption

By s.19, transfers of value made by a transferor in any tax year (April 6–April 5)[6] are exempt provided that they do not, taken together, exceed £3,000.[7] The annual exemption is available to notional transfers in two ways.

3–05

---

[2] See *British Tax Review* (1977), p.20.
[3] IHTA 1984 s.3A(1)(b).
[4] IHTA 1984 ss.20(3) and 21(5).
[5] IHTA 1984 ss.19(5) and 22(6).
[6] IHTA 1984 s.19(4).
[7] IHTA 1984 s.19(1).

First, the exemption applies to apportionments made to a person under s.94(1).[8] Secondly, and more importantly, the exemption applies to transfers made on the termination of an interest in possession under s.52(1).[9] It is essential to note that where a notional transfer is made on the coming to an end of an interest in settled property the exemption will be available only if the transferor gives the trustees notice of the availability of the exemption:

(1) within a prescribed time limit; and
(2) on a prescribed form.

The time limit is the end of the period of six months beginning with the date of the transfer.[10] The prescribed form used to be CAP 222 but that form no longer exists; in the absence of any form it is thought that a simple written notice to the trustees suffices. The exemption is then given except to the extent specified in the notice. There is no provision allowing HMRC to extend the time limit and they are known to refuse to allow the exemption to be applied in the absence of strict compliance with the above procedure. The appropriate notice procedure should be followed even if the transfer is a PET in order to ensure that the exemption will be available should the transferor die within seven years. The following three points should be noted about the annual exemption generally.

Grossing-up

3–06   The £3,000 is taken off the value transferred by the transfer (or transfers) in question before any grossing-up. Thus, if X makes a transfer of value of £10,000 on which he pays the tax, the £3,000 exemption will operate to reduce the £10,000 to £7,000, and only the £7,000 will be grossed-up.

Attribution of exemption

3–07   It may be that a transferor in the same year makes more than one transfer and that while no one transfer exceeds £3,000, the aggregate value transferred by the transfers in question is more than £3,000. In such a case the position varies according to whether the transfers were made on the same day or on different days.

    If the transfers were made on the same day the exemption is attributed to the transfers in proportion to the value transferred by them. Assume that on the same day X makes transfers of £4,000 and £8,000:

$$\text{Total value transferred} = £12,000$$

$$\frac{£4,000}{£12,000} \times £3,000 = £1,000$$

$$\frac{£8,000}{£12,000} \times £3,000 = £2,000$$

[8] IHTA 1984 ss.19(5) and 94(5).
[9] IHTA 1984 ss.19(5) and 57.
[10] IHTA 1984 s.57(3) and (4).

Thus, £1,000 of the £4,000 transfer will be exempt, and £2,000 of the £8,000 transfer will be exempt.[11]

If the transfers are not made on the same day the exemption is given on a first come, first served basis. This rule does not apply if the transfer is a failed PET; see para.5–06. Thus, if the above transfers of £4,000 and £8,000 were made on successive days, £3,000 of the £4,000 transfer would be exempt, while no part of the £8,000 transfer would be so.[12]

Shortfall

It may be that a person does not use the whole of his exemption in a given year. In that case he may carry the unused portion forward to the next following year *but no further*.[13] Assume that in 2008–2009 X made transfers totalling £1,300 with the result that £1,700 of his annual exemption went unused. In 2009–2010 he made transfers totalling £3,200: his exemption for 2009–2010 would have exempted the first £3,000, and the £1,700 carried forward from the previous year (2008–2009) would have exempted the remaining £200. In 2010–2011 X made transfers totalling £3,400: his £3,000 for 2010–2011 would have exempted the first £3,000 but he would have made a chargeable transfer of the remaining £400, notwithstanding the fact that he still had £1,500 unused from 2008–2009. The rule is thus that one must first use the amount appropriate to a given year; if that is exhausted—but only if that is exhausted—any unused amount carried forward from the previous year may be used.   **3–08**

Small gifts exemption

By s.20(1), a transfer of value made by outright gift to any one person in a given tax year[14] is exempt so long as it does not exceed £250. Thus, a taxpayer can give £250 to as many different people as he likes, and each of the transfers will be covered by this exemption. Once a gift exceeds £250, however, no part of it is covered by this exemption. Though simple, this exemption is noteworthy in three respects.   **3–09**

No carry forward

As is the case with all exemptions, the small gifts exemption applies before any grossing-up; but in contrast to the annual exemption, any shortfall cannot be carried forward.   **3–10**

Multiple use

Both the annual exemption and the small gifts exemption are available in any given year, with the result that every tax year a person can give at least: **3–11**

[11] IHTA 1984 s.19(3)(b).
[12] IHTA 1984 s.19(3)(a).
[13] IHTA 1984 s.19(2).
[14] IHTA 1984 s.20(2).

(1) £3,000 free of tax to one person; and

(2) £250 free of tax to as many different other people as he likes.

Outright gifts only

3–12   The exemption applies only to outright gifts made to any one person. For this purpose a loan (whether made by an actual or a notional disposition) is treated as an outright gift.[15] The position with regard to gifts to unincorporated associations and to trustees is not clear. The law on gifts to unincorporated associations has long been in a muddle, and it is unclear whether such a gift takes effect in law as a gift to the members of the association or as an accretion to the funds of the association.[16] If the former is the correct view a gift to an incorporated association may qualify for this exemption.

Before Finance Act 2006 there was an argument that gifts to a settlement in which there was an interest in possession took effect as a gift to the person entitled to that interest and therefore the exemption should be available. Since a gift can no longer be made to trustees outside the relevant property regime (except in certain very limited circumstances such as the creation of a trust for a disabled person under s.89), this argument has no relevance to gifts made after March 21, 2006.

In practice, HMRC only allows gifts to trustees where the trust property is held on trust for a beneficiary absolutely.

Normal expenditure out of income

3–13   Section 21 provides that a transfer of value is an exempt transfer to the extent that it is shown that:

(1) the transfer was made as part of the transferor's normal expenditure;

(2) the transfer was (taking one year with another) made out of the transferor's income; and

(3) the transferor, after allowing for all transfers of value forming part of his normal expenditure, was left with sufficient income to maintain his usual standard of living.

There is no quantitative limit on this exemption, with the result that it may be very useful to wealthy individuals with income to spare.

Normal expenditure

3–14   The transfer must be made as part of the transferor's normal expenditure. In *Bennett v IRC*,[17] Mrs B was life tenant of a trust fund, the main asset of which was shares in the family company. Until 1987 the income produced was small albeit adequate for Mrs

---

[15] IHTA 1984 s.29(3).

[16] See *Leahy v Att Gen for New South Wales* [1959] A.C. 457; *Re Recher's Will Trusts* [1972] Ch. 526; *Re Grant's Will Trust* [1980] 1 W.L.R. 360.

[17] *Bennett v IRC* [1995] S.T.C. 54.

B's modest needs. In that year, however, as the result of a takeover the trust acquired shares in another company together with a substantial cash sum which resulted in the trust income increasing enormously. Mrs B's modest lifestyle did not change and in 1989 she signed a document directing her trustees to distribute equally between her three sons "all or any of the income arising in each accounting year as is surplus to my financial requirements of which you are already aware". This direction could have been revoked at any time: what Mrs B intended to give away was income after it had arisen—she did not purport to assign her life interest in whole or in part.

In February 1989 payments of £9,300 per son were made and in the following year £60,000 per son. Mrs B then died unexpectedly in February 1990 and the sons contended that the payments fell under s.21: HMRC viewed them as failed PETs and hence as chargeable transfers.

Lightman J. upheld the taxpayers' arguments and the case (which was not appealed) is an important authority on the ambit of s.21. At first glance it might seem a surprising result since only two payments were made, one of £27,900 and one of £180,000. So far as the size of the two payments is concerned, although the trustees adopted a conservative approach and only distributed a fraction of the total trust income, Lightman J. was satisfied that Mrs B's direction was to distribute all the surplus income. He therefore held that this satisfied the requirement that there must be "normal expenditure", i.e. expenditure which at the time it took place accorded with the settled pattern adopted by the transferor. So far as requirement for a "settled pattern" is concerned, he commented as follows:

> "The existence of the settled pattern may be established in two ways. First, an examination of the expenditure by the transferor over a period of time may throw into relief a pattern, *e.g.* a payment each year of 10 per cent of all income to charity or members of the individual's family or a payment of a fixed sum or a sum rising with inflation as a pension to a former employee. Second, the individual may be shown to have assumed a commitment, or adopted a firm resolution, regarding his future expenditure and thereafter complied with it. The commitment may be legal (*e.g.* a deed of covenant), religious, (*e.g.* a vow to give all earnings beyond the sum needed for subsistence to those in need) or moral (*e.g.* to support aged parents or invalid relatives). The commitment or resolution need have none of these characteristics, but nonetheless be likewise effective as establishing a pattern, *e.g.* to pay the annual premiums on a life insurance qualifying policy gifted to a third party or to give a predetermined part of his income to his children."[18]

So far as the requirement that the expenditure should be "normal" is concerned, he commented:

> " . . . there is no fixed minimum period during which the expenditure shall have occurred. All that is necessary is that on the totality of the evidence the pattern of actual or intended regular payments shall have been established and that the term in question conforms with that pattern. If the prior commitment or resolution can be shown, a single payment implementing the commitment or resolution may be sufficient. On the other hand, if no such commitment or resolution can be shown, a series of payments may be required before the existence of the necessary pattern will emerge. The pattern need not be immutable; it must, however, be established that the pattern was intended to remain in place for more than a nominal period and indeed for a sufficient period (barring unforeseen circumstances) in order for any payment fairly to be regarded as a regular feature of the transferor's annual expenditure. Thus a 'deathbed' resolution to make periodic payments 'for life' and a payment made in accordance with such a determination will not suffice."[19]

---

[18] *Bennett v IRC* [1995] S.T.C. 54 at 58.
[19] *Bennett v IRC* [1995] S.T.C. 54.

Since the days of estate duty[20] HMRC have regarded "normal" as meaning "typical" or "habitual" and the (IHTM14243) confirms the position originally set out in a letter to *The Law Society Gazette* on June 9, 1976, that:

> " . . . 'Normal' is considered to mean in this context 'typical' or 'habitual'—but typical of the transferor and conforming with his or her habits and patterns of expenditure, not those of the average or reasonable man. Thus an isolated gift by a miser does not satisfy the test because it would have been a normal gift if made by an ordinarily generous person of similar means . . . It is considered that [*Bennett v I.R.C.*] substantially confirms the office practice on [s.21] . . . "

Occasionally, the first of a series of payments will be regarded by HMRC as part of normal expenditure ab initio. HMRC agree that where the transferor gives away a life policy requiring regular premiums which he is paying the first of the premiums qualifies as normal expenditure.[21] Under estate duty, it sufficed that there was a clear intention to make regular payments, e.g. as with insurance premiums, and thus the first payment under a deed of covenant will also qualify,[22] as might also a payment made under a banker's order or any other payment made in circumstances where there is evidence of an intention to make regular payments over a period of time.

In one case a premium on a life policy will not be regarded as part of normal expenditure. By s.21(2), a payment of a premium of a policy of insurance on the transferor's life, or a gift of money or money's worth applied, directly or indirectly, in payment of such a premium is not regarded for the purposes of the section as part of his normal expenditure if, when the insurance was made, or at any earlier or later time, an annuity was purchased on his life. Section 21(2) does not apply if it is shown that the purchase of the annuity and the making of any variation of the insurance were not associated operations.[23]

The normal expenditure exemption applies to transfers made by way of free loans provided that that kind of transfer was a normal one on the part of the transferor.[24]

Out of income

3–15 The transfer must be made, taking one year with another, out of the transferor's income. The legislation does not define "income". It therefore is to be construed according to its ordinary meaning.

Income must be construed as net income after payment of income tax. HMRC consider[25] that "income" must be interpreted in accordance with "normal accountancy rules" and that this does not necessarily coincide with income tax for income tax purposes. In line with this it seems reasonable to expect that sums remaining after CGT has been levied will not count as income. HMRC consider[26] that part surrenders from an insurance policy (such as sums paid under the chargeable event regime, within the 5 per cent annual limit) are capital and therefore do not count as income for these purposes.

A transfer by a Lloyd's Name to special reserve will reduce disposable income, but it is understood that HMRC take the view that since a transfer to general reserve is not

---

[20] *Att Gen for Northern Ireland v Heron* [1959] T.R. 1 (N.I.).
[21] HMRC Manuals IHTM14241.
[22] HMRC Manuals IHTM14241.
[23] See paras 2–28 and following.
[24] IHTA 1984 s.29(4).
[25] HMRC Manuals IHTM14250.
[26] HMRC Manuals IHTM14250.

taken into account for income tax purposes the deduction by the underwriting agents from the profits of a particular account will not be regarded as reducing available income if it can be shown that the transfer was in fact to be borne out of capital.

The following points should also be borne in mind:

(1) Gifts-in-kind. A gift-in-kind will normally be made out of a person's assets, not out of his income. A gift-in-kind purchased out of income may qualify, however. This is important because given the consequential loss provisions under which only the second-hand value of the gift will be brought into account it will normally be advantageous to purchase that which is to be given rather than to provide the funds with which to purchase it.[27]

(2) Taking one year with another. This phrase must not be overlooked. Gifts made in a particularly good year, e.g. where there has been a windfall, will not be made out of income for these purposes if they do not adhere generally to the pattern of gifts in normal years. In the same way, losses brought forward may increase disposable income, but gifts made out of the increase may not come within this exemption.

(3) Section 21 contains limiting wording. A transfer of value is exempt if, *or to the extent that*, it is shown to be made as part of one's normal expenditure. As a result, limited exemption may be given during a particular accounting period even if, taken all together, gifts made by the transferor would fail the test. Where the transferor has committed himself to making regular payments (such as those under deed of covenant or in payment of life policy premiums), early payments can be considered to satisfy the test even when later payments would not because, for example, the transferor had then taken on additional regular commitments requiring him to have recourse to capital.[28]

(4) Free loans. The same qualification that applied to para.3–14 above applies here, e.g. this exemption applies to free loans only if that kind of transfer was a normal one on the part of the transferor.[29]

(5) Purchased life annuities. By s.21(3), the part of a purchased life annuity treated as the capital element contained in the annuity is not regarded as part of the transferor's income.

In *Nadin v IRC*[30] Mrs Nadin, as executor of her great aunt Miss Perry, tried to claim normal expenditure out of income exemption in relation to a series of payments of varying amounts on diverse dates made to her and two other members of her family by Miss Perry in the years before her death. The Special Commissioner held the exemption was not available, not least because the payments were not made out of income. In particular, in the tax year before her death Miss Perry gave a total of £261,770 to Mrs Nadin, while her gross income was only £18,625. The case adds little to *Bennett*, serving merely to emphasise that the payments must be out of income.

Uneroded estate

The last test that must be satisfied is commonly thought to be that the transferor must **3–16** have been able to maintain his usual standard of living without dipping into his capital.

---

[27] It is to be noted that s.272 provides that a disposition includes a disposition effected by associated operations but it is thought that the HMRC would be unlikely to invoke the associated operations provisions to counteract this technique.

[28] HMRC Manuals IHTM14251.

[29] IHTA 1984 s.29(4).

[30] *Nadin v IRC* [1997] S.T.C. (S.C.D.) 107.

In fact, the test is more subtle: the transferor must be left with sufficient income to maintain his usual standard of living after allowing for all transfers of value forming part of his normal expenditure, but disregarding any other gifts that he may have made. That he has in fact dipped into his capital is thus irrelevant: what matters is whether his normal expenditure on gifts would on its own have caused him to do so.[31] The standard of living is that of the individual transferor, not of the man on the Clapham omnibus, and the time his standard of living falls to be determined is the time he made the gift in question.[32] Where a premium on a life policy is paid net after deduction of tax under the Taxes Act 1988 s.266 only the net amount of the premium is brought into account. Where the premium is paid without any such deduction, the gross amount is brought into account; see the Inland Revenue (as it then was) press release of January 17, 1979.

Quantum

3–17   In the *Bennett* case,[33] Lightman J. commented that

> " . . . the amount of the expenditure need not be fixed in amount nor need the individual recipient be the same. As regards quantum it is sufficient that a formula or standard has been adopted by application of which the payment (which may be of a fluctuating amount) can be quantified *e.g.* 10 per cent of any earnings whatever they may be or the costs of a sick or elderly dependant's residence at a nursing home. As regards the payees, it is sufficient that their general character or the qualification for benefit is established, *e.g.* members of the family or needy friends".[34]

He concluded that there was no requirement for the expenditure to be reasonable or such that an ordinary person might have incurred in similar circumstances although he suggested that this characteristic might be relevant in deciding whether the necessary pattern had been established. The objective behind the expenditure (e.g. tax saving) was irrelevant.

The judgment gives scope for flexibility in satisfying the requirements of s.21: for instance (assuming that the payments do not depress the taxpayer's usual standard of living)—

(a) Adam resolves to distribute £20,000 out of his income each year amongst his needy relatives. In year 1 Bert receives the entire sum; in year 2 it is split between Celia and Daphne. The requirements of s.21 appear to be satisfied.

(b) Edward signs a "letter of intent" in which he undertakes to pay 10 per cent of his income to a local hospice. In year 1 his income is £50,000 but in year 2 it falls to £10,000. Section 21 should be satisfied in respect of the payments of £5,000 and £1,000.

(c) Frank covenants to pay £10,000 to his sister each year and dies after the first payment. His death was: (i) wholly unexpected; (ii) envisaged as likely since he had just been diagnosed as suffering from leukaemia. From the remarks of Lightman J. quoted above, s.21 may apply in (i) given that there is a legal commitment to make the payments but not in (ii).

[31] HMRC Manuals IHTM14251.
[32] HMRC Manuals IHTM14251.
[33] See para.3–14.
[34] *Bennett v IRC* [1995] S.T.C. 54 at 59.

The implications of the *Bennett* case should be remembered when completing Form IHT 400 after a death. In reviewing lifetime gifts made by the deceased it is important to check whether there is evidence of a settled pattern falling within the tests set out above.

Planning

When advising clients in relation to the regular expenditure out of income exemp-   **3–18**
tion, the most important factors to bear in mind, as highlighted by the *Bennett* and *Nadin* cases are:

(1) evidence of a discernible pattern; and
(2) evidence of normal expenditure.

The simplest thing is for the donor to write a letter setting out his or her intention to make regular payments of surplus income to the recipient, which should obviously be kept by the recipient, or alternatively signed by the recipient and returned to the donor by way of acknowledgement.

When claiming the exemption on death the following information must be provided   **3–19**
on HMRC Form IHT 403 in such a way that a regular pattern of gifts can be discerned:

(1) the date of the gift;
(2) the name of the recipient and the donor's relationship to the recipient;
(3) a description of the assets given away;
(4) the value at the date of the gift;
(5) the amount and type of exemption claimed; and
(6) the net value of the gift after the exemption.

On Form IHT 403 information must be given for each of the years in which gifts were made about the donor's income, the tax paid on the income and the donor's expenditure (the amount the donor spent to maintain his usual standard of living).[35]

Before March 2008 HMRC said[36] that if a donor relied on the exemption to avoid   **3–20**
a lifetime charge to IHT (for example, where a gift is made into a relevant property trust), it need not be reported.[37] However, in light of regulations[38] which excuse transferors and trustees from delivering an account to HMRC in respect of certain immediately chargeable lifetime transfers made on or after April 6, 2007, HMRC

[35] Note that HMRC propose to redesign certain IHT forms in summer 2008, including Form D3a (the working draft of the new form reporting normal expenditure out of income on death is called "IHT402").
[36] The following question was put by STEP/CIOT to HMRC in November 2006 in a list of questions about Finance Act 2006 Sch.20: "It is understood that additions to a trust which fall within the normal expenditure out of income exemption will not need to be reported as and when they are made as, following the normal rules, it is not necessary to report exempt transactions? Please confirm." HMRC responded: "We can confirm this".
[37] There is no question, and there never has been, of having to report to HMRC a transfer which would otherwise be a potentially exempt transfer at the time the transfer is made.
[38] The Inheritance Tax (Delivery of Accounts) (Excepted Transfers and Excepted Terminations) Regulations 2008.

issued guidance[39] which changed the rules about reporting gifts made in reliance on the normal expenditure exemption. Like the regulations, the guidance applies to transfers made on or after April 6, 2007. The guidance says that where the normal expenditure exemption is in point a transfer of value remains a chargeable transfer unless and until it is shown to be exempt. The guidance states that:

(1) Where denial of the exemption would not breach the limits for a cash transfer there is no need for an account to be delivered. HMRC will consider whether the exemption is due if and when the matter is material when a later transfer is made or on death. The "limits for a cash transfer" are set out in the regulations and apply if the asset transferred is cash or quoted shares. The limits are that the value transferred, together with the transferor's chargeable transfers made in the last seven years, does not exceed the nil rate band for the year in which the transfer was made. (There is a more complicated test if the asset given away is not cash or quoted shares (e.g. land), which is based on a proportion of the nil rate band.)

(2) Where denial of the exemption, either in respect of a single gift (whether it is the first of a planned series of gifts or a gift within a series) or cumulatively taking into account earlier transfers, would mean that there is a liability to IHT, an account should be delivered so that the availability of the exemption can be agreed.[40]

A Form IHT100 should be submitted within 12 months of the end of month in which the transfer was made. HMRC have said verbally that reference to the normal expenditure exemption should be made in the box on p.4 of Form IHT100 and have suggested that a schedule be attached containing the information which would be requested if the issue were being addressed on death.

It is assumed that it is not necessary to report normal expenditure transfers made before April 6, 2007, but it may be necessary in practice in order to demonstrate a pattern of gifts.

Gifts made in consideration of marriage

3–21   This is an extremely useful exemption, the full value of which is not always appreciated. Its basic effect is fairly simple, however it is somewhat labyrinthine in its construction, different rules applying according to:

(1) the identity of the donor; and
(2) whether the gift is an outright gift or a gift settling property.

The general (if oversimplified) rule is that:

(a) each parent of a party to the marriage can give £5,000 tax-free;
(b) each grandparent or remoter ancestor, and each party to the marriage can give £2,500 tax-free; and
(c) anyone else can give £1,000 tax-free.

[39] HMRC Manual IHTM06106.
[40] Note that these requirements are those of the guidance not the Regulations.

The exemption is also available to notional transfers made under s.52(1) on the termination of an interest in possession.[41]

Giving notice

Again, as set out at para.3–05 above in relation to the annual exemption, it is **3–22** essential to note that where a notional transfer is made on the coming to an end of an interest in settled property the exemption will be available only if the transferor gives the trustees notice of the availability of the exemption:

(1) within a prescribed time limit; and
(2) on a prescribed form.[42]

The prescribed form used to be CAP 222 but that form no longer exists; in the absence of any form it is thought that a simple written notice to the trustees suffices.

In consideration of marriage

The factor complicating the rules under s.22 is that in order to be exempt the transfer **3–23** must be "in consideration of marriage". (For this purpose, in relation to transfers made on the termination of an interest in possession, references in the legislation to transfers of value made by gifts in consideration of marriage are references to the termination of such interests in consideration of marriage.) Here regard must be had both to the decided cases and the express provisions. The effect of the decided cases appears to be that to be made "in consideration of marriage" a gift must:

(1) be made on the occasion of the marriage, i.e. before the marriage or con-temporaneously therewith;
(2) be conditioned only to take effect on the marriage taking place; and
(3) (where the gift is made by way of settlement) be made by a person for the purpose of, or with a view to, encouraging or facilitating the marriage.[43]

"Marriage" is thought to mean a legally recognised marriage. For the impact of the Civil Partnership Act 2004 and the Gender Recognition Act 2004, see paras 3–31 and 3–32.

Section 22 adds to this by providing that to be "in consideration of marriage or civil **3–24** partnership" the gift must be made to certain persons in certain ways. First, in the case of an outright gift, the gift must be made to a party to the marriage or civil partnership. Thus, all references to outright gifts should be read as "outright gifts to a party to the marriage",[44] or, in the case of a notional transfer made under s.52(1), to cases where

---

[41] IHTA 1984 ss.22(6) and 57.
[42] IHTA 1984 s.57(3) and (4); see para.3–05.
[43] See *Att Gen v Jacobs-Smith* [1985] 2 Q.B. 341; *Rennell v IRC* [1946] A.C. 173; *Re Park (No.2)* [1972] Ch. 385.
[44] A free loan is for this purpose treated as an outright gift; IHTA 1984 s.29(3).

the property ceases to be settled property on the termination of the interest in possession in question.[45]

Qualifying categories

3–25   Secondly, in the case of a gift settling property the persons who are or may become entitled to any benefit under the gift must fall within one of six categories. Section 57(2) provides that for this purpose references to cases where property is settled by gift are in the case of a notional transfer made under s.52(1) references to cases where the property remains settled property after the termination of the interest in possession in question. The six categories set out in s.22(4) are as follows:

(1) The parties to the marriage or civil partnership, any child of the family of the parties to the marriage or civil partnership or the spouse or civil partner of any such issue. For purposes of s.22(4) "child of the family" in relation to parties to a marriage or civil partnership means a child of one or both of them.[46]

(2) Persons becoming entitled on the failure of:
   (a) the trusts for any such child where the terms of those trusts are such that the trust property would vest indefeasibly[47]
      (i) on the attainment by such child of some specified age, or
      (ii) on the attainment by such child of some specified age or the earlier happening of some event; or
   (b) any limitation in tail.[48]

   A normal contingent remainder for persons outside the marriage on the failure of children attaining 18 or marrying under that age will thus be acceptable, and this is so even if that remainder is to vest on the failure of a particular child rather than on the failure of all children. It may be that the remainder takes effect only after the failure of some other acceptable trust, e.g. where there is a second class of beneficiaries such as the issue of a subsequent marriage.[49] This would not infringe the requirement, but it is important to note that the contingency must be the failure, not merely the determination of the prior trusts. Moreover, the remainder must vest indefeasibly, i.e. the vesting of a limited interest will not suffice.

(3) A subsequent spouse or civil partner of a party to the marriage or civil partnership, or any child of the family of the parties to any such subsequent marriage or civil partnership, or a spouse or civil partner of any such child.

(4) Persons becoming entitled under trusts subsisting under English or Northern Irish law such as those protective trusts specified in s.33(1) of the Trustee Act 1925 or s.34(1) of the Trustee Act (Northern Ireland) 1958, so long as the principal beneficiary is a person falling within (1) or (3) above. Persons becoming entitled under such trusts where those trusts are modified by the enlargement (as respects any period during which there is no such child as mentioned in (1) and (3) in existence) of the class of potential beneficiaries specified in s.33(1)(ii) and s.34(1)(b) are also acceptable.

(5) Persons becoming entitled under equivalent protective trusts subsisting under Scots law.

---

[45] IHTA 1984 ss.22(6) and 57.
[46] IHTA 1984 s.224A.
[47] Subject only to any power of appointment to a person falling within (1) or (3) in the text above.
[48] IHTA 1984 s.224A.
[49] e.g. under (3) in the text above.

(6) The trustees of the settlement, in so far as a reasonable amount of remuneration is concerned.

Quantitative limits

As was noted above, a transfer of value made by a gift in consideration of marriage **3–26** or civil partnership is only exempt up to a certain limit, depending on the identity of the donor. The limits are as follows:

(1) £5,000 limit: a transfer of value made in consideration of marriage or civil partnership by a parent of a child who is a party to a marriage is exempt up to £5,000 if it is
   (a) an outright gift, or
   (b) a gift settling property.[50]
   "Child" in the context of the limit to which a transfer is exempt includes an illegitimate child, an adopted child, and a stepchild.[51]
(2) £2,500 limit: a transfer made in consideration of marriage or civil partnership is exempt up to £2,500 if it is
   (a) an outright gift from one party to a marriage or civil partnership,[52] or
   (b) an outright gift by a grandparent or remoter ancestor of either party to a marriage or civil partnership,[53] or
   (c) a gift settling property from one party to a marriage or civil partnership[54] or a grandparent or remoter ancestor of either party to a marriage or civil partnership.[55]
(3) £1,000 limit: a transfer of value made by anyone else in consideration of marriage or civil partnership is exempt up to £1,000 if it is an outright gift or a gift settling property.[56]

If a person makes more than one gift in consideration of marriage or civil partnership and the total of gifts made by him exceeds the authorised limit, the excess is attributed to the transfers made by him in proportion to the values transferred by them.

Planning

A good deal can thus be transferred under this exemption on the occasion of a **3–27** marriage or civil partnership. Were four parents and eight grandparents to take maximum advantage of this exemption, £40,000 free of tax could be transferred to the lucky couple. It may well be that one spouse or civil partner, for example, the wife, lacks the resources to take full advantage of the £5,000 exemption. If her husband provides her with the necessary funds, which she then passes on to the child who is to be married, it is unlikely that HMRC will attempt to invoke the associated operations

---

[50] IHTA 1984 s.22(1) and (2).
[51] IHTA 1984 s.22(1) and (2).
[52] IHTA 1984 s.22(1) and (2).
[53] IHTA 1984 s.22(1) and (2).
[54] IHTA 1984 s.22(1) and (2).
[55] IHTA 1984 s.22(1) and (2).
[56] IHTA 1984 s.22(1).

provisions.[57] It is important to note, however, that where the intention is to pass on assets which in the husband's hands qualify for business relief such a "channelling operation" may be inadvisable, since business relief will not be available to any gift made by the wife in the following two years.[58]

The fact that the parties to the marriage or civil partnership can make exempt gifts may also prove helpful in relation to premarital gifts such as an engagement ring. Where, on the other hand, property is purchased in joint names during the engagement and the parties' respective contributions are unequal, the exemption may be insufficient to cover the transfer made by the person who provided the greater contribution.[59] Where the transferor spouse or civil partner is a UK domiciliary but the transferee spouse or civil partner is not, the exemption will help to preserve the limited spouse exemption under s.18.[60]

III. EXEMPTIONS THAT APPLY TO BOTH ACTUAL AND NOTIONAL TRANSFERS[61]

3–28   As was mentioned above, the exemptions given by Ch.1 of Pt II which do not fall within ss.19–22, 27 and 28 apply equally to actual and notional transfers. Five exemptions fall within this category, as follows:

(1) s.18 exemption;
(2) charities exemption;
(3) political parties exemption;
(4) gifts for national purpose exemption; and
(5) gifts for public benefit exemption.

Each will be considered in turn. As will be seen below, these exemptions are available only so long as certain conditions are not infringed.[62]

Section 18 exemption

3–29   Transfers of value between spouses and civil partners should nearly always be exempt. This follows from s.18(1), which provides that a transfer of value is an exempt transfer to the extent that either:

(1) the value transferred by the transfer is attributable to property which becomes comprised in the estate of the transferor's spouse or civil partner; or
(2) the estate of the transferor's spouse or civil partner is increased.

---

[57] See para.9–06.
[58] See para.26–59.
[59] Difficulties may arise if one party incurs expenditure for the other.
[60] See para.3–35.
[61] See *British Tax Review* (1979), p.72.
[62] See paras 3–47 and following.

One cannot help but think that something has gone slightly wrong in the drafting of (1), because it is difficult to see how a person's estate can be increased except where property becomes comprised in it. Presumably what the draftsman intended to cover is the case where the *value* of the spouse or civil partner's estate is increased notwithstanding the fact that no property becomes comprised in it, e.g. where a husband releases a debt owed to him by his wife.[63] It is thought that this is the way HMRC apply the exemption in practice, and some justification for this can be found in s.29(2), which, by providing that where the transfer in question is made by a loan, the borrower's estate is increased by an amount equal to the value transferred by the transfer, implies that the relevant increase is an increase in value, not in property.

The wording of s.18(1) can be contrasted with that in ss.3(3) and 94(1), which both refer to an increase in the value of a person's estate, but it is thought that in practice nothing turns on this.

The use of the words "attributable to" means that problems should not arise where **3–30** a gift diminishes the value of the transferor spouse or civil partner's estate more than it increases the value of the estate of the transferee spouse or civil partner; see para.3–39.

Thus, the circumstances in which a transfer between spouses or civil partners is not exempt should be rare, and will probably occur only where the transferor spouse or civil partner omitted to exercise a right in circumstances where s.3(3) (omission to exercise a right, see paras 2–20 and following) applied with the result that the transferor spouse or civil partner's estate was decreased:

(1) without any property becoming comprised in the transferee spouse or civil partner's estate; and
(2) by an amount greater than any increase in the value of the estate of the transferee spouse or civil partner.

"Spouse" is not defined by the legislation. As a matter of general law, it means **3–31** anyone to whom a person is legally married. In *Holland v IRC*[64] the spouse exemption was not available in relation to a couple living together as husband and wife who were not legally married to one another. A marriage ceases only on the grant of a decree absolute.[65] The fact that the parties live apart or that they have separated is irrelevant. The s.18 exemption will apply to transfers made in connection with divorce proceedings until pronouncement of decree absolute, but not thereafter. In relation to transfers made on or following a divorce being made absolute, it may well be that no transfer of value arises in the first place, because the disposition takes place under a court order,[66] or is relieved under s.11 (family maintenance dispositions, see paras 2–55 and following) or s.10(1) (essentially commercial transactions, see paras 2–41 and following).

The Tax and Civil Partnership Regulations, SI 2005/3229 amended the tax legisla- **3–32** tion so that all references to "spouse" now read "spouse or civil partner".

The Civil Partnership Act 2004, which received Royal Assent on November 18, 2004, defines a "civil partnership" as a relationship between two people of the same

---

[63] A similar problem arises in relation to IHTA 1984 s.3A(2)(b); see para.5–23.
[64] *Holland v IRC* [2003] S.T.C. (S.C.D.) 43.
[65] *Fender v St John Mildmay* [1938] A.C. 1.
[66] See para.2–54.

sex that is registered under the Act.[67] Note that cohabiting heterosexual couples are not included on the basis that they have the option to marry. A civil partnership ceases to exist only following formal dissolution under the provisions of this Act. The availability of the s.18 exemption on dissolution of a civil partnership is as on a divorce.

A widow/widower or surviving civil partner is not a spouse or civil partner, but the s.18 exemption still applies to transfers made on death since, as was noted above, on a person's death he is treated under s.4(1) as having made a transfer of value immediately before he died, and at that stage his spouse or civil partner is still a spouse or civil partner and not a widow/widower/surviving civil partner.

3–33   The Gender Recognition Act 2004 received Royal Assent on July 1, 2004. Under the provisions of this Act it is now possible for transsexuals legally to be recognised in their acquired gender. Those who acquire a "gender recognition certificate" will be able to marry someone of the opposite gender or enter into a civil partnership with someone of the same gender. It follows that the parties to such a marriage will be entitled to the benefit of the s.18 exemption. Equally if, as a result of gender reassignment, one party to an existing marriage changes their gender such that the parties are then in a same sex partnership, that marriage can be voided. If it is, then any prior IHT planning using the s.18 exemption will become ineffective unless the parties have the type of relationship capable of registration under the Civil Partnership Act.[68] Similar provisions apply for voiding a civil partnership if one of the parties changes their gender.

Purchased reversions

3–34   By s.56(2), the s.18 exemption does not apply in relation to settled property in which a spouse or civil partner has acquired a reversionary interest for a consideration in money or money's worth when that property becomes the property of that spouse or civil partner on the termination of the interest on which that reversion is expectant. The purpose of this provision is best illustrated by an example. Assume that elderly A has a life interest in £100,000, and that on his death B is to become absolutely entitled to that sum. But for s.56(2), the tax that would otherwise have been payable on A's death could have been avoided by A's spouse or civil partner purchasing B's interest for £100,000, with the result that on A's death, thanks to the s.18 exemption, no charge would have arisen, and £100,000 would have reached B free of tax. Alternatively, the exemption could have been exploited more actively. Assume that H and his wife W each have substantial estates, and that between them they wish to make a gift of £200,000 free of tax to their son, S. In the absence of s.56(2) they could have done this in two simple steps. First, H would have settled £200,000 on himself for, say, a week, remainder to his son S. Given the fact that under s.50(2) H would have still been treated as being beneficially entitled to the entire £200,000, this step would have had no adverse effects. Secondly, S would have sold his interest to his mother for its market

---

[67] Civil Partnership Act 2004 s.1.

[68] The Gender Recognition Act 2004 is silent on the issue of taxation but ss.9 and 11 would seem to indicate that those holding a gender recognition certificate will be able to take advantage of the tax saving provisions currently available to spouses because such a certificate is to be recognised "for all purposes" and such a person is to be able to marry.

value of £200,000. This purchase would not have been a transfer of value by W, and the son would have received £200,000 free of tax. On the expiry of the father's interest, the mother would have become absolutely entitled to the trust fund with the result that, thanks again to the s.18 exemption, no charge would have arisen, so that the net result was that between them the parents had transferred £200,000 free of tax to their son. Section 56(2) stops this. It is to be noted that, by s.56(5), for purposes of s.56(2) a person is treated as acquiring an interest for a consideration in money or money's worth if he becomes entitled to it as a result of transactions which include a disposition for such a consideration, whether to him or another, of that interest or of other property.

A second avoidance technique, since rendered ineffective, involved the purchase by one spouse or civil partner from the other of a reversionary interest in circumstances where that purchase constituted a gift of the purchase price; this is discussed at para.32–59.

Note also that the anti-avoidance provisions introduced by Finance Act 2012 s.210 may also apply in the case of purchased reversions (discussed further in para.5–18). A reversionary interest will not be excluded property where arrangements have been entered into in the course of which a UK domiciliary acquires or becomes able to acquire an interest in settled property, consideration is given, and there is a non-domiciled settlor or a corporate, non-close company, settlor.

Foreign domiciliaries

There is a ceiling on the exemption where immediately before the transfer the **3–35** transferor spouse or civil partner is a UK domiciliary but the transferee spouse or civil partner is not. In that case the exemption is limited by s.18(2) to the first £55,000 transferred. The purpose of this limitation is to prevent a UK domiciled spouse or civil partner from transferring his property to his foreign domiciled spouse or civil partner, in whose hands the property would be (or could be made into) excluded property with the result that the transferee spouse or civil partner could then gift the property without making a transfer of value, thereby avoiding IHT altogether.

This limit, which is cumulative, not annual, applies before any grossing-up.

In some cases, the effect of a double taxation agreement may be to override this £55,000 limitation.[69]

A measure was announced in the 2012 Budget proposing to increase the limit to match the nil rate band (currently £325,000). The measure will also offer non-domiciled spouses and civil partners the option of electing to be UK domiciled for inheritance tax purposes. At the time of writing, draft legislation on this issue is awaited. The European Commission published a memo on October 24, 2012 stating that the difference in tax treatment of transfers between domiciled and non-domiciled spouses is discriminatory and contrary to EU rules (TFEU art.18). The Commission has therefore asked the UK to review the matter. If there is no satisfactory response within two months, the Commission may decide to refer the matter to the ECJ.[70]

Sometimes the domicile limitation may not be a matter for concern, for two reasons. First, until January 1, 1974, a wife automatically took her husband's domicile on marriage, although, following the coming into force on that date of the Domicile and

---

[69] See e.g. art.8 of the United States–United Kingdom Treaty, discussed at para.33–150.
[70] IN/2012/2111.

Matrimonial Proceedings Act 1973, she can now acquire a separate domicile.[71] Secondly, the deemed domicile rules[72] apply so that a spouse who is not a UK domiciliary under the general law may still be domiciled here for IHT purposes.

Capital gains tax

3–36   The basic CGT rule is that any disposal in a year of assessment between a husband and wife or civil partners living together in that year takes place on a no-gain, no-loss basis.[73] The residence and domicile of the parties is irrelevant.

Holdover relief trap

3–37   Note that the availability of the s.18 exemption can have an adverse CGT effect. Assume X settled shares in circumstances such that CGT holdover relief was claimed under either s.165 or s.260 of the Taxation of Chargeable Gains Act 1992 and that X is entitled to a life interest, followed by a life interest for his widow or surviving civil partner, with remainders over to their children. X and his wife or civil partner are both domiciled in the United Kingdom. The s.18 exemption will thus be available to prevent any charge to IHT arising on X's death.

From a CGT standpoint, on the other hand, the position is much less helpful if the trustees still own the shares. X's death will give rise to a deemed market value disposal and reacquisition by the trustees under s.72(1)(a) of the 1992 Act and although s.72(1)(b) might seem to operate to prevent any gain arising on that disposal from being a chargeable gain, s.74(2) will prevent s.72(1)(b) from applying in respect of the gain that was held over on the transfer by X of the shares to the settlement.[74] This gain will thus prima facie be clawed back into charge. It is in theory open to the trustees to claim holdover relief to hold over this gain once again, but since the s.18 exemption prevents the s.72(1) deemed disposal from being a chargeable transfer, no such claim will be capable of being made under s.260(2)(a); rather the only possible claim will be under the more restrictive s.165.

Charities exemption

3–38   A transfer of value is exempt to the extent that the value transferred by it is attributable to property which is given to a charity.

By s.23(6), property is "given to a charity" for these purposes if it either:

(1) becomes the property of a charity; or
(2) is held on trust for charitable purposes only.

In *Guild v IRC*,[75] a testator left his residuary estate to the Town Council of North Berwick, "for use in connection with the Sports Centre in North Berwick or some

[71] Or, if she marries on or after that date, maintains her domicile: see para.32–09.
[72] See paras 32–14 and following.
[73] TCGA 1992 s.58(1); see s.58(2) for exceptions to this rule.
[74] The position would remain the same even if the shares had fallen in value.
[75] *Guild v IRC* [1992] S.T.C. 162.

similar purpose in connection with sport". At his death the Town Council had ceased to exist and the executor presented a cy-près scheme which was approved by the court. HMRC considered that the gift was not exempt under s.23(6) which required the bequest to be "held on trust for charitable purposes only".

The House of Lords held, first, that the bequest in favour of the Sports Centre in North Berwick was charitable within s.1 of the Recreational Charities Act 1957 in that it served "the interest of social welfare". Secondly, their Lordships adopted a benign approach to the second branch of the bequest ("for some similar purpose in connection with sport") inferring that the intention of the settlor was that any other purpose to which the Town Council might apply the bequest (or any part of it) must display the same characteristics as those exhibited in the first limb. As a result the IHT (and CTT) exemption applied.

It is important to note that in applying the IHT charity exemption it is necessary to look at the terms of the original will and not at the cy-près scheme approved by the court. Section 23(6), which limits the exemption to bequests for charitable purposes only, is not intended to be affected by a wrong decision by the court nor, indeed, a misapplication of funds by the trustees.

Where the transfer is made by a free loan:

(1) the value transferred is treated as being attributable to the property lent; and
(2) the property is treated as having been given to the borrower (unless the loan involves use for purposes other than charitable purposes).[76]

Meaning of "attributable to"[77]

Prior to April 15, 1976, there was some doubt as to the proper meaning of the words **3–39** "attributable to". Where, e.g., a person who owned 51 of the 100 issued shares in a company gave two of those shares to a charity,[78] it was not clear whether the whole of the value transferred was attributable to the shares given to the charity or whether only a proportionate part of the value transferred was so attributable, so that only a small part of the transfer was exempt. Originally HMRC took the former view but on April 15, 1976, issued the following self-explanatory press release:

> "1. Finance Act 1975, Sch.6, paras.10, 11 exempt from CTT certain gifts to charities and political parties to the extent that the value transferred is attributable to property given to a charity etc. Finance Act 1975, Sch.6, para.12, 13 exempt in similar terms gifts for national purposes and for the public benefit.
>
> 2. Where the value transferred (i.e., the loss to transferor's estate as a result of the disposition) exceeds the value of the gift in the hands of a charity etc. the Board of Inland Revenue have hitherto taken the view that the transfer is exempt only to the extent of the value of the property in the hands of the transferee. The Board wish it to be know that they are now advised that the exemption extends to the whole value transferred."

Meaning of "charity" and "charitable"

For the purposes of inheritance and other taxes, para.1 Sch.6 Finance Act 2010 now **3–40** defines a charity as: (a) a body established for charitable purposes only, and (b) one that

---

[76] IHTA 1984 s.29(5).
[77] See also *Powell-Cotton v IRC* [1992] S.T.C. 625, discussed at para.2–102.
[78] The two shares given to the charity would now be related property; see para.25–65.

meets the jurisdiction, registration and management conditions, these latter conditions being set out in paras 2, 3 and 4 respectively of Sch.6. The jurisdiction condition is the most important change in the law brought in by the 2010 Act, as it allows, for the first time, charities established outside the United Kingdom to qualify for the exemption (see further below at para.3–42). The registration condition requires the charity to comply with the UK registration requirements, or such foreign registration requirements as apply in its jurisdiction. The management condition requires the managing body of the charity to be "fit and proper persons".

3–41   With regard to the definition of "charitable purpose", para.1 of Sch.6 refers to s.2 Charities Act 2011. Until April 1, 2008 the meaning of "charitable purposes" had been for the most part determined in line with case law which was summarised in *Special Commissioners of income tax v Pemsel*.[79] In *Pemsel* "charity" was defined as comprising the following four heads:

(1) The relief of poverty.
(2) The advancement of education.
(3) The advancement of religion.
(4) Other purposes beneficial to the community, not falling under the preceding heads.

In addition there was a general requirement that charities must be for the benefit of the public at large or a sufficient section of the public. It was presumed that charities falling under the first three heads would meet this condition.

From April 1, 2008, the definition of "charitable purposes" has been set out in statute, now Ch.1 of the Charities Act 2011. First, to qualify, a "charitable purpose" must come within one of the following 13 heads:

(1) Prevention or relief of poverty.
(2) The advancement of education.
(3) The advancement of religion.
(4) The advancement of health or the saving of lives.
(5) The advancement of citizenship or community development.
(6) The advancement of the arts, culture, heritage or science.
(7) The advancement of amateur sport.
(8) The advancement of human rights, conflict resolution or reconciliation or the promotion of religious or racial harmony or equality or diversity.
(9) The advancement of environmental protection or improvement.
(10) The relief of those in need by reason of youth, age, ill-health, disability, financial hardship or other disadvantage.
(11) The advancement of animal welfare.
(12) The promotion of the efficiency of the Armed Forces of the Crown or of the efficiency of the Police, Fire and Rescue Services or Ambulance Services.
(13) Purposes not falling under the preceding heads, but recognised under existing charity law and any other purposes that may reasonably be regarded as analogous to, or within the spirit of, any charitable purpose falling under any of the heads.

Section 5 of the Act sets out requirements for recreational charities to qualify. Regulated sports clubs cannot qualify.

---

[79] *Special Commissioners of Income Tax v Pemsel* [1891] A.C. 531.

In the second stage of the test to qualify as a "charitable purpose", a statutory public benefit test must be satisfied. The test applies equally to all 13 heads.

In the leading case of *Dreyfus (Camille and Henry) Foundation v IRC*[80] the House **3–42** of Lords held that a body of persons established outside the United Kingdom for purposes which were charitable under the general law of England was not a charity for purposes of the pre-Finance Act 2010 definition of charity (s.506(1) of the Taxes Act 1988). Applying this case to the s.23 exemption, it was clear that in general a transfer to a foreign charity was not exempt, since such a charity was not established in the United Kingdom for charitable purposes only within the meaning of s.506(1).

However, following the ECJ decision in *Persche v Finanzamt Lüdenscheid* (C-318/07) [2009] P.T.S.R. 915; [2009] All E.R. (EC) 673, the law has been amended to allow charities established in the EU, Norway and Iceland to qualify for the inheritance tax exemption (and other charity tax exemptions, including Gift Aid). As noted above, under FA 2010 s.30 and Sch.6, a charity must meet the "jurisdiction condition" to qualify for relief. The "jurisdiction condition" is that the charity is subject to the control of the UK courts or to the courts of certain other jurisdictions which are, at present, defined as the member states of the EU, Iceland and Norway.

The Finance Act 2010 Sch.6 Pt 2 (Commencement) Order 2012 (SI 2012/736) and the Finance Act 2010 Sch.6 Pt 1 (Further Consequential and Incidental Provisions etc) Order 2012 (SI 2012/735) together have the effect that from April 1, 2012, the new definition applies to IHT. HMRC announced on March 24, 2010 that claims for tax relief on gifts to charities made between January 27, 2009 (the date of the *Persche* decision) and the date the new rules came into force would be considered on a case by case basis. The changes mean that where payments are made by trustees in exercise of their discretion to non-UK based organisations which qualify as "charities" for the purposes of Sch.6, these will qualify for exemption from inheritance tax and there will be no exit charge.

Reduced Charitable Rate

Charitable giving has been encouraged further by the Finance Act 2012, through the **3–43** application of a reduced rate of IHT to the chargeable estate of an individual who leaves at least 10 per cent of his net estate to charity on death. Should the 10 per cent bar be reached, IHT will be charged to the estate at a rate of 36 per cent, applying to deaths on or after April 6, 2012.

The reduced rate has been introduced by s.209 of the Finance Act 2012, with the detailed workings of the reduced rate set out in Sch.33 of the Act, which in turn is inserted into IHTA 1984 at Sch.1A, with consequential amendments made to IHTA 1984 ss.7, 33, 78 and 128 (as set out in Sch.1A).

Baseline amount

In calculating the "baseline amount", by reference to which the 10 per cent is **3–44** calculated, the following property is excluded:

- property passing by an exempt transfer;

[80] *Dreyfus (Camille and Henry) Foundation v IRC* [1956] A.C. 39.

- property passing within the nil rate band; and
- the relievable value of relievable property.

Therefore to donate the "baseline amount", it is important to draft a gift of 10 per cent of the total net value or as a share of residue and not as a gift of 10 per cent of the total estate.

General Component

3–45   The free estate of the deceased, labelled the "general component" by the Finance Act 2012, may be viewed in isolation from settled property in which the deceased has a qualifying interest in possession, property in which the deceased has reserved some benefit and jointly held property. Therefore, if at least 10 per cent of the free estate passes to charity, the chargeable part of the free estate will benefit from the lower rate. The other components of the estate will only benefit from the lower rate if the baseline amount is donated to charity from each of them. It is possible, however, to take two or more components together.[81]

Benefit of reduced rate

3–46   It is estimated that where a testator's will already provides for charitable gifts of at least 4 per cent of his net estate, it would be to the benefit of chargeable beneficiaries to increase the charitable gifts to the baseline amount to gain the benefit of the reduced rate.

Wording of legacy

3–47   HMRC have provided example wording for a 10 per cent legacy to charity under a will.

Opting out

3–48   IHTA 1984 Sch.1A para.8 allows an election to be made to treat the amount donated as if it is less than 10 per cent of the baseline amount. Where such an election is made, the component concerned is subject to IHT at the full rate.

This may be attractive in circumstances where the administrative costs, for instance the valuation of assets, outweigh the benefit of the reduced rate of taxation. For instance if land is specifically bequeathed to charity it would not ordinarily need to be valued; however, to qualify for the reduced rate, the value must be ascertained and the

---

[81] Further discussion of the components can be found at IHTM45003–45007.

cost of doing so could outweigh the benefit of the reduced rate. An election must be made by an appropriate person and within statutory time limits.[82]

Deed of Variation

The new provisions will also apply to charitable legacies made by a Deed of **3–49** Variation. The reduced rate will only apply if it is shown that the charity has been notified that the devolution of the estate has been varied in its favour.[83]

Calculator

HMRC have produced a useful online calculator to work out whether a component **3–50** of an estate qualifies for the reduced rate. It is found at *http://www.hmrc.gov.uk/tools/ iht-reduced-rate/calculator.htm*.

Grossing-up

An example of the reduced charitable rate (for the general component) and grossing- **3–51** up (in relation to other components not reduced) can be found in the IHT Manual.[84]

Political parties exemption

A transfer of value is exempt to the extent that the value transferred by it is **3–52** attributable[85] to property which becomes the property of a qualifying political party.[86] Where the transfer is made by a free loan:

(1) the value transferred is treated as being attributable to the property lent; and
(2) the property is treated as becoming the property of the borrower (unless the loan involves use for purposes other than those of the party).[87]

A party qualifies if, at the last general election preceding the transfer in question:

(a) two members of that party were elected to the House of Commons; or
(b) one member of that party was elected to the House of Commons and at least 150,000 votes were given to candidates who were members of that party.

The last general election was held in 2010; the qualifying parties as a result of that election are:

[82] See IHTM45042 and IHTM45043.
[83] *http://www.hm-treasury.gov.uk/d/reduced_iht_charities.pdf* [Accessed October 4, 2012].
[84] See IHTM45030.
[85] For the meaning of "attributable to", see para.3–39.
[86] IHTA 1984 s.24(1).
[87] IHTA 1984 s.29(5).

- Labour;
- Conservative;
- Liberal Democrats;
- Scottish National Party;
- Democratic Unionist;
- Plaid Cymru;
- Sinn Féin;
- Social Democratic & Labour; and
- Green Party.

Gifts for national purposes exemption

3–53   By s.25(1) and Sch.3, a transfer of value is exempt (without limit) to the extent that the value transferred by it is attributable[88] to property which becomes the property of the following bodies, institutions or organisations.

1. The National Gallery.
2. The British Museum.
3. The National Museums of Scotland (from October 1, 1985. Previously the Royal Scottish Museum).
4. The National Museum of Wales.
5. The Ulster Museum.
6. Any other similar national institution which exists wholly or mainly for the purposes of preserving for the public benefit a collection of scientific, historic or artistic interest and which is approved for the purposes of this paragraph by the Board. Approval has, to date, been given to:
   6.1   British Library,
   6.2   British Museum (Natural History) (before September 1, 1992),
   6.3   Fleet Air Arm Museum,
   6.4   Geological Museum,
   6.5   Imperial War Museum,
   6.6   Lambeth Palace Library,
   6.7   London Museum,
   6.8   National Army Museum,
   6.9   National Galleries of Scotland,
   6.10 National Library of Scotland,
   6.11 National Library of Wales,
   6.12 National Maritime Museum,
   6.13 National Museums and Galleries on Merseyside,
   6.14 National Museum of Antiquities, Scotland (before October 1, 1985),
   6.15 National Portrait Gallery,
   6.16 National Postal Museum,
   6.17 National History Museum,
   6.18 Portsmouth Royal Naval Museum,
   6.19 RAF Museum,
   6.20 Royal Botanic Gardens, Kew,
   6.21 Royal Marines Museum,
   6.22 Science Museum,

---

[88] For the meaning of "attributable to", see para.3–39.

6.23 Submarine Museum,

6.24 Tate Gallery,

6.25 Tower Armouries,

6.26 Ulster Folk Museum,

6.27 Victoria and Albert Museum,

6.28 Wallace Collection.

7. Any museum or art gallery in the United Kingdom which exists wholly or mainly for that purpose and is maintained by a Local Authority[89] or University in the United Kingdom.

8. Any library the main function of which is to serve the needs of teaching and research at a University in the United Kingdom.

9. The Historic Buildings and Monuments Commission for England.

10. The National Trust for Places of Historic Interest or Natural Beauty.

11. The National Trust for Scotland for Places of Historic Interest or Natural Beauty.

12. The National Art Collections Fund.

13. The Trustees of the National Heritage Memorial Fund.

14. The Friends of the National Libraries.

15. The Historic Churches Preservation Trust.

16. The Nature Conservancy Council (before April 1, 1991).

17. Nature Conservancy Council for England (from April 1, 1991).

18. Nature Conservancy Council for Scotland (from April 1, 1991).

19. Countryside Council for Wales (from April 1, 1991).

20. Any Local Authority.

21. Any government department (including the National Debt Commissioners and a Northern Ireland department).

22. Any University or University College in the United Kingdom.

23. A health service body, within the meaning of s.519A of the Taxes Act 1988 (added to the list with effect from September 17, 1990).

Where the transfer is made by a free loan:

(1) the value transferred is treated as being attributable to the property lent; and

(2) the property is treated as having become the property of the borrower (unless the loan involves use for purposes other than those of the qualifying body),[90]

with the result that the exemption effectively applies to free loans as it does to outright gifts.

Gifts for public benefit exemption

The Finance Act 1998 s.143 abolished in relation to transfers made after March 16, **3–54** 1998, the exemption for transfers to approved non-profit making bodies that was

---

[89] IHTA 1984 s.272.

[90] IHTA 1984 s.29(5).

previously contained in s.26. For a discussion of this exemption, see paras 3–37 and following of the third edition of this book.

IV. QUALIFICATIONS

3–55   Various provisions limit the availability of the above exemptions in a number of ways designed to prevent their being abused. The qualifications fall into two categories: first, there are certain blanket qualifications which affect all the exemptions available under ss.18 and 23–25 to actual and notional transfers; secondly, there are qualifications which affect only the exemptions available under ss.23–25, but which do not affect the s.18 exemption. None of the qualifications apply to free loans.[91] As will be seen, the provisions frequently refer to property which is "given" to a person or a body; they also provide that for these purposes property is so given if it becomes the property of, or is held on trust for that person or body, and "donor" is construed accordingly.[92]

Blanket qualifications

3–56   There are two blanket conditions.

Intervening interest or period

3–57   None of the above exemptions apply in relation to property if the disposition by which it is given takes effect on the termination after the transfer in question of any interest or period.[93] Thus, a transfer of property, e.g. to trustees to hold the property on trust for X for life, then for a charity will not be exempt. Strictly speaking, the gift in remainder to the charity "takes effect" immediately on the making of the settlement, but it is thought that in this context "takes effect" will be read as meaning "takes effect in possession"; otherwise the provision would be robbed of any effect.[94] This qualification does not apply to the s.18 exemption where property is given to a spouse or civil partner only if he survives the transferor spouse or civil partner for a specified period.[95]

Conditional gifts

3–58   None of the above exemptions apply in relation to property if the disposition by which it is given depends on a condition which is not satisfied within 12 months after the transfer.[96] It follows from this wording that there may be a "wait and see" period

---

[91] IHTA 1984 s.29(5).
[92] IHTA 1984 ss.18(3) and (4), 23(2), (4) and (6), 24(3) and (4), and 25(2).
[93] IHTA 1984 ss.18(3)(a), 23(2)(a), 24(3), and 25(2).
[94] Compare *Bickersteth v Shanu* [1936] A.C. 290; *Re McGeorge, Ratcliffe v McGeorge* [1963] Ch. 544.
[95] IHTA 1984 s.18(3).
[96] IHTA 1984 ss.18(3)(b), 23(2)(b), 24(3), and 25(2).

before it can be determined if the transfer is exempt.[97] If by its very terms a condition cannot be satisfied within a year, e.g. where a gift which does not carry the intermediate income is made to a widow or surviving civil partner conditional on her surviving 18 months, this condition will be infringed from the outset but this can normally be corrected in a deed of variation.[98]

Qualifications to sections 23–25

By ss.24(3), and 25(2), the exemptions given in ss.23–25 are not available in relation **3–59** to any property in the following cases.

Defeasible gifts

No exemption is available if the disposition by which the property is given is **3–60** defeasible.[99]

Less than complete gifts—property generally

No exemption is available if the property is itself an interest in another property, and **3–61** that interest is less than the donor's interest or the property is given for a limited period.[100]

Less than complete gifts—settled property

No exemption will be available if the property is an interest in settled property and **3–62** the settlement does not come to an end in relation to that settled property on the making of the transfer.[101] This prevents a person with a life interest in a continuing settlement who is near the end of his days from avoiding tax by assigning his interest to an exempt body. The exemptions will be available, however, where on the assignment the assignee becomes absolutely entitled to property in which the interest subsists.

Interest reserved—land or building

No s.23(4) exemption will be available if the property is land or a building and is **3–63** given subject to an interest reserved or created by the donor which entitles him, his

---

[97] See *Bailhache Labesse Trustees Ltd v The Commissioners for HMRC* [2008] S.T.C. (S.C.D.) 869; the point was addressed in this case, in which appointments were made after the death of the life tenant for the benefit of certain charities. It was held that the appointments could not be construed as bringing the ultimate defeasible gift to charity within the requirements of s.23(2)(b) by completing the appointment within 12 months of the death of the life tenant.

[98] See paras 8–63 and following. It may be possible to extend the 12 month period by leaving property on discretionary trusts and making distributions within two years of the deceased's death; see paras 8–189 and following.

[99] IHTA 1984 ss.23(2), 24(3), and 25(2).

[100] IHTA 1984 ss.23(2), 24(3), and 25(2), except that this qualification does not prevent s.25 from applying in relation to property consisting of the benefit of an agreement restricting the use of land.

[101] IHTA 1984 s.56(3)(a). See *Powell-Cotton v IRC* [1992] S.T.C. 625, discussed at para.2–102.

spouse or a person connected with him to possession of, or to occupy, the whole or any part of the land or building rent free or at a rent less than might be expected to be obtained in an arm's length transaction between unconnected persons.[102] The "reservation" of a lease at a rack rent is, however, permissible and may materially affect the value of the property transferred.

Interest reserved—other property

3–64   No exemption is available if the property is not land or a building and is given subject to an interest reserved or created by the donor other than:

    (1) an interest created by him for full consideration in money or money's worth; or

    (2) an interest which does not substantially affect the enjoyment of the property or body to whom it is given.[103]

Non-charitable, etc. purposes

3–65   No exemption is available if the property or any part of it may become applicable for purposes other than charitable purposes or those of a body mentioned in ss.24 or 25 above.[104]

Defeasibility and timing

3–66   For the above purposes, any disposition which has not been defeated 12 months after the transfer in question and which is not defeasible after that time shall be treated as being indefeasible, whether or not it was capable of being defeated before that time. In addition, any question as to whether any interest is less than the donor's is decided as at a time 12 months after the transfer in question.[105]

Purchased reversions

3–67   By s.56(3)(a), ss.23–27 do not apply in relation to any property if:

    (1) immediately before the time when it becomes the property of the exempt body it is settled property; and

    (2) at or before that time an interest under the settlement is or has been acquired for a consideration in money or money's worth by that or another exempt body (disregarding any acquisition from an exempt body within ss.23–25).

---

[102] IHTA 1984 ss.23(2), 24(3), and 25(2).
[103] IHTA 1984 ss.23(2), 24(3), and 25(2).
[104] IHTA 1984 s.23(2) and (3).
[105] IHTA 1984 ss.23(2), 24(3), and 25(2).

This is an anti-avoidance provision the purpose of which is best shown by an example. Assume A wishes to transfer £100,000 to his son B. But for s.56(3)(a) and before the introduction of the Finance Act 2006, A could have done so without paying any tax by first settling the £100,000 on himself for a short period, with remainder to his son, who, in turn, would have sold his reversion to an exempt body such as a charity for, say, £99,500. Before March 21, 2006, the creation of the settlement would not have had any adverse effects since, thanks to s.49(1), the value of A's estate would have been unaffected by the creation of the settlement. Nor would the sale by B have had any consequences, both because B's reversion would have been excluded property and because the sale to the charity would have been on a commercial footing. On the termination of A's interest:

(1) no charge would have arisen since the notional transfer made at that stage under s.52(1) would have been exempt under s.23; and
(2) the charity would have become entitled to the £100,000.

The net result of the operation would thus have been that, by using the charity as a middleman, A managed to pass £99,500 free of IHT to his son.

Section 56(3) puts a stop to this by providing that, as was noted above, none of the exemptions in ss.23–27 apply to the transfer as a consequence of which the property becomes vested in the charity, with the result that in the above example tax would be chargeable on the £100,000 on the termination of A's interest. Section 53(5) provides that a person is for this purpose treated as acquiring an interest for a consideration in money or money's worth if he becomes entitled to it as a result of transactions which include a disposition for such a consideration, whether to him or another, of that interest or of other property.

A second avoidance technique, since rendered ineffective, involved the purchase from a charity or an exempt body of a reversionary interest under a settlement by a person already entitled to an interest under that settlement in circumstances where the purchase price constituted a gift.[106]

V. TRANSFERS OF SHARES TO EMPLOYEE TRUSTS

By s.28, a transfer of value made by an individual is exempt to the extent that the **3–68** value transferred is attributable to shares or securities in a company which become comprised in a settlement which satisfies the following conditions:

(1) the trusts of the settlement must be "employee" trusts within s.86(1)[107];
(2) the trustees at the time of the transfer or within one year thereafter must hold more than half of the ordinary shares in the company in question[108];
(3) the trustees at the time of the transfer or within one year thereafter must have a majority of the votes on all questions affecting the company as a whole[109];
(4) the persons for whose benefit the trusts permit the trust property to be applied must include all or most of the company's employees[110];
(5) the trust must not permit any of the trust property to be applied at any time for the benefit of:

[106] This is discussed at para.32–65.
[107] IHTA 1984 s.28(1); see paras 24–07 and following for a discussion of s.86.
[108] IHTA 1984 s.28(2)(a)(i).
[109] IHTA 1984 s.28(2)(a)(ii).
[110] IHTA 1984 s.28(1)(b).

(a) a participator in the company in question; or

(b) any other person who is a participator in any close company that has made a disposition whereby property has become comprised in the settlement in question and which was relieved from being a transfer of value by s.13[111]; or

(c) any other person who at any time after the transfer in question or during the 10 years before that transfer has been a participator in either the company in question or a participator in a close company that has made a disposition of the kind just mentioned; or

(d) any person connected with any of the above participators.[112]

This exemption may be particularly helpful where no one in a testator's family is willing or able to run the business after the testator's death.

3–69   The prohibition against participators and/or persons connected with them benefiting is intended to guarantee that only transfers to genuine employees' trusts secure the exemption. It will be noted that the prohibition against participators benefiting will be infringed if the trusts permit such a benefit to be conferred "at any time". It will thus be necessary to draft the trust instrument so as to exclude the possibility of such a benefit being conferred. The simplest way of doing this is to incorporate the restrictions mentioned above into the trust instrument verbatim, but such a precaution may be unnecessarily drastic. By s.28(6), in determining whether the s.86 trusts permit any of the trust property to be applied for the benefit of any of the prohibited persons, no account is taken of any power to make a payment which is the income of any person for any of the purposes of income tax, or which would be the income of a non-resident if he were resident. This is important since it means that participators and persons connected with them can be given benefits so long as they are restricted to income benefits. In drafting the trust instrument it will thus be necessary to exclude partici-pators and those connected with them only from non-income benefits. In this connec-tion it is helpful to note that in relation to s.90(2) of the Finance Act 1976, which s.28 effectively replaces, HMRC were understood to regard improved working conditions and other facilities which derive from the establishment of an employees' trust as not infringing the prohibition against other than income benefits, provided that the benefits are enjoyed by the employees generally.[113]

3–70   For these purposes "close company" and "participator" have the meanings given them in s.102[114] except that the meaning of participator is both widened and narrowed. It is widened to include, in the case of a company which is an open company, a person who would be a participator if the company were a close company.[115] It is narrowed to exclude any participator who:

(1) is not beneficially entitled to, or to rights entitling him to acquire, 5 per cent or more of, or of any class of the shares comprised in, the issued share capital; and

(2) on a winding up of the company would not be entitled to 5 per cent or more of its assets.[116]

---

[111] See paras 2–103 and following.

[112] IHTA 1984 s.28(4).

[113] The HMRC Manual is currently being re-written and the website refers to the HMRC Brief 18/11 published on April 4, 2011. No guidance on the above prohibition is given.

[114] See para.2–18.

[115] IHTA 1984 s.28(7).

[116] IHTA 1984 s.28(5).

"Ordinary shares" means shares which carry either:

(a) a right to dividends which is not restricted to dividends at a fixed rate; or

(b) a right to conversion into shares carrying such a right.[117]

Deferred shares and participating preference shares are thus within the definition.

VI. VOIDABLE TRANSFERS

Even if an individual makes a chargeable transfer, it may transpire that the transfer, **3–71** or part of it, is subsequently rendered void, e.g. under ss.423–425 of the Insolvency Act 1986. By s.150, provided the transfer has been set aside as voidable or otherwise defeasible by virtue of any enactment or rule of law, it will be possible in such a case to reclaim any tax[118] paid on the transfer, plus interest from the date of the claim at the rate applicable under s.233. Such interest does not constitute income for any tax purposes. If tax on the avoided transfer was outstanding, liability for that tax will be cancelled. In addition, any chargeable transfer made subsequently will be determined as if the avoided transfer was void ab initio. No specific time limit is specified for the claim, and therefore the general six-year rule in s.241 applies.

---

[117] IHTA 1984 s.28(7).
[118] "Tax" includes interest on tax: IHTA 1984 s.150(2).

THE NIL RATE BAND

I. INTRODUCTION

Background

4–01 IHT became a two rate tax two years after it replaced Capital Transfer Tax with the introduction of a nil rate band, with a flat rate of 40 per cent applying thereafter, in relation to chargeable transfers occurring on or after March 15, 1988.[1] The nil rate band was £110,000 in 1988–89 and this has increased gradually each tax year to its current rate of £325,000 for transfers made from April 6, 2009–April 5, 2015.[2]

This chapter outlines the effect of the nil rate band in the computation of IHT for chargeable transfers made during lifetime (considered in more detail in Chapters 5 and 6) and on death (discussed in Chapter 8). It also considers the new rules introduced in Finance Act 2008 regarding the transferability of the nil rate band between spouses and civil partners. Finally, there is a discussion of the various planning techniques designed to utilise the nil rate band.

Rates

The rates of the nil rate band are set out in Sch.1 to the Act. Since 1982 the rates of **4–02** tax have been linked to the Retail Prices Index by what is now s.8. Section 8 provides that, if in the future the Retail Prices Index for the month of September is higher than it was in the previous September, new rates will apply in line with this percentage increase as from the following April 6 unless Parliament determines otherwise; if the result is not a multiple of £1,000 the amount is rounded up to the nearest such multiple. The procedure by which the new rates are brought into effect is that the Treasury makes an order by statutory instrument specifying the new amounts. However, under s.208 of the Finance Act 2012 the nil rate band will rise in line with the Consumer Prices Index as from April 6, 2015, although Parliament retains the discretion to set a different amount from the one indicated by automatic indexation. Regard is currently had to the General Index of Retail Prices (for all items) published by the Statistics Board, but under the amended s.8 of the Inheritance Tax Act 1984, this will be the all items consumer prices index published by the Statistics Board from April 6, 2015 onwards.

Current HMRC practice has generally been to announce the new nil rate band and any changes in rate in the Budget prior to the start of the new tax year, although the rates for the 2008–2009, 2009–2010 and 2010–2011 tax years were announced further in advance.[3] The nil rate band has been incrementally increasing with the effect of gradually reducing the effective rate of IHT, while the 40 per cent rate above the nil rate threshold has not been changed since 1988. In the 2007 Pre-Budget Report the Chancellor announced that in determining the nil rate band for future years the government will take account of house price inflation in addition to the Retail Prices Index.[4] This would presumably require an amendment to s.8 to reflect this since, as it stands at present, there must be an increase in the Retail Prices Index (as opposed to any other index) or the Consumer Prices Index, after 2015, to allow the nil rate band to be adjusted. There has as yet been no amendment made to s.8.

[1] FA 1988 s.136.
[2] FA 2006 s.155.
[3] For 2008–09 the increased nil rate band figure was announced on Budget Day, March 22, 2006 and implemented by FA 2006 s.155. The increased nil rate bands for 2009–2010 and 2010–2011 were also implemented in advance (by FA 2006 s.155 and FA 2007 s.4 respectively).
[4] Paragraph 5.78, 2007 Pre-Budget Report.

II. OVERVIEW

Lifetime chargeable transfers

4–03   In calculating the IHT due on chargeable transfers, the available nil rate band must be ascertained. As explained further in Pt VI of Chapter 6, in calculating the IHT due on lifetime gifts the total value of chargeable transfers[5] made by the transferor in the seven-year period ending with the date of the last transfer is deducted from the current value of the nil rate band. In this way the nil rate band is "refreshed" every seven years and this gives scope for planning tax efficient lifetime gifts, which is considered in detail in para.4–24 below. IHT is charged at 20 per cent on the excess of the value transferred over the available nil rate band.

Assume, for example, that A, who has made no gifts in the predeceasing seven years, made a gift to a discretionary settlement of £100,000 in January 2004 and a further gift of £250,000 to the same settlement in December 2007. The first £6,000 of the January 2004 gift is exempted by A's 2002–03 and 2003–04 annual exemptions and the remainder is taken out of charge by A's 2003–04 fully available nil rate band (£255,000), so no IHT is payable. The first £6,000 of the 2007 gift is exempted by A's 2005–06 and 2006–07 annual exemptions, and £206,000 is charged at a nil rate by A's available nil rate band (£300,000 for 2007–08 less the 2004 chargeable transfer of £94,000), leaving IHT of £7,600 payable (20 per cent on the balance of £38,000).

Transfers on death

4–04   On death, the deceased's nil rate band is calculated by taking into account chargeable transfers made by him in the seven years immediately preceding his death. This will include PETs[6] made during this period, which have become chargeable by reason of his death within seven years of making them. Lifetime gifts will use up the nil rate band first, with any balance being applied to the chargeable transfer on death and any excess taxed at 40 per cent.

For example, if B died in December 2007 having made a chargeable transfer of £50,000 in June 2005 and a PET of £150,000 in January 2007, the available nil rate band to set off against the chargeable value of his death estate will be £103,000. The £50,000 chargeable transfer is set against the nil rate band of £300,000 first. The chargeable value of the PET is £147,000 after deducting the annual exemption for 2006–07, which is set against the remaining nil rate band.

If B had instead made two lifetime chargeable transfers of £200,000 in September 2006 and of £200,000 in July 2007, the first transfer would have been covered by his 2006–07 nil rate band. For the July 2007 transfer, the first £100,000 of this would have been covered by his nil rate band while the remaining £100,000 would have been chargeable to IHT at 20 per cent, leaving £20,000 IHT payable. On B's death there is

---

[5] See Ch.6.
[6] See Ch.5.

no available nil rate band to set against his death estate and in addition a further £20,000 IHT would be payable in respect of the July 2007 transfer.

Relevant property trusts

The nil rate band also has a role to play in calculating the IHT 10-year anniversary and exit charges applicable to relevant property trusts, which are considered in detail in Chapters 14 and 15. **4–05**

THE TRANSFERABLE NIL RATE BAND BETWEEN SPOUSES AND CIVIL PARTNERS

III. INTRODUCTION

In the Pre-Budget Report on October 9, 2007 the Chancellor announced a proposal to enable spouses and civil partners to transfer their unused nil rate bands to the survivor to be set against the survivor's estate on the second death, at the rates prevailing at that time. Given the numerous and complex tax planning mechanisms used in recent years to ensure that the nil rate band of both spouses and civil partners is fully utilised (considered further in para.4–25 below), this was a welcome proposal. **4–06**

The rules concerning the transferable the nil rate band have been implemented in the Finance Act 2008 and are discussed below.

IV. OUTLINE

The rules are contained in ss.8A–8C. Section 8A provides that where an individual dies, leaving a surviving spouse or civil partner and there is some unused nil rate band on the death of the deceased, a claim can be made when the survivor dies for their nil rate band to be increased by the proportion of the nil rate band unused on the first death. Section 8A sets out a number of formulae for calculating the unused nil rate band and the increased nil rate band available on the survivor's death. **4–07**

The nil rate band can only be transferred where the survivor's death occurs on or after October 9, 2007. For spouses the first death can have occurred any time before or after October 9, 2007, regardless of whether the first death occurred under the IHT, Capital Transfer Tax or Estate Duty regimes.[7] Where the first death occurred before July 25, 1986, Sch.4 paras 10 and 11 of Finance Act 2008 address which amounts should be treated as the nil rate band.

The term spouse refers only to the parties of a legal marriage.[8] For civil partners, the first death must have occurred on or after December 5, 2005.[9] The rules do not apply

---

[7] HMRC Manuals IHTM43001.

[8] HMRC Manuals IHTM43003; *Holland (Executor of Holland, Deceased) v IRC* [2003] SpC 350. It should be noted that a marriage ceremony conducted abroad must meet the legal requirements of the relevant country for the purposes of these new rules.

[9] HMRC Manuals IHTM43001. Partners in a legal relationship registered under the law of another country will be recognised as having formed a civil partnership provided the requirements of the Civil Partnership Act 2005 are met.

where a marriage or civil partnership has come to an end by divorce or dissolution of the civil partnership.[10]

Calculating the unused nil rate band on the first death

4–08   Section 8A(2) sets out the following formula for calculating the unused nil rate band on the first death:

$$M > VT$$

M = the maximum value which could be transferred on death at the nil rate, less any lifetime chargeable transfers made by the deceased.

VT = the value of the chargeable transfer made on death. This therefore includes the value of non-exempt or relievable legacies under the will or intestacy, assets passing by survivorship which are not otherwise exempt, gifts with reservation which became chargeable on death and any settled property forming part of the deceased's estate. It does not matter if the deceased's estate is less than the applicable nil rate band at the date of the first death.

Assume, for example, that C died in January 2005 when the nil rate band was £263,000, leaving an estate of £300,000, half of which is to go to his wife and half to his son. In the seven years before death he only made a PET of £50,000 in January 2004 against which the 2003–04 annual exemption of £3,000 was used.

Lifetime chargeable transfer	£47,000
Chargeable estate	£150,000
Gift to wife is exempt	

M is £216,000 (£263,000 (the nil rate band in force on the first death) − £47,000 (the January 2004 PET which has become chargeable is £150,000)), so the unused nil rate band is therefore £66,000.

VT is £150,000 (the chargeable gift from the estate to C's son).

It should be noted that even if IHT had become payable in respect of the PET owing to an earlier chargeable lifetime transfer in the seven years before the date of the PET using up a proportion of the nil rate band, this does not necessarily mean that there will be no unused nil rate band on the first death.[11]

Calculating the transferable nil rate band available on the second death

4–09   The transferable nil rate band available on the survivor's death is increased by a percentage based on the unused proportion of the nil rate band on the first death. This is calculated using the following formula set out in s.8A(4):

[10] HMRC Manuals IHTM43005.
[11] HMRC Manuals IHTM43024.

$$\frac{E}{NRBMD} \times 100$$

E = the amount by which M exceeds VT.

NRBMD = the nil rate band in force on the first death.

The percentage is taken to four decimal places.[12]

Continuing the example of C in para.4–08 above, E is £66,000 and NRBMD is £263,000. The percentage to apply is therefore 25.095 per cent. If C's wife died in May 2008, her personal representatives could make a claim for the nil rate band on her death to be increased by this percentage to £390,296 (£312,000 (nil rate band in 2008–09) + [312,000 × 25.095%]).

Calculating the transferable nil rate band where there has been more than one marriage or civil partnership

If the survivor has been married more than once, or been in more than one civil **4–10** partnership, the amount of the unused nil rate band at each previous death can be transferred to the survivor's nil rate band subject to a maximum of 100 per cent of the nil rate band at the survivor's death.[13]

Assume, for example, that following the death of D's first wife, 20 per cent of her nil rate band was unused. D remarried and his second wife died leaving 50 per cent of her nil rate band unused. On D's death in September 2008 his personal representatives can make a claim for his nil rate band to be increased to £530,400 (£312,000 + [£312,000 × 20%] + [£312,000 × 50%]). However, if the percentage of the nil rate band unused on the death of D's second wife had instead been 90 per cent, the transferable nil rate band available on D's death would be limited to 100 per cent, giving a total of £624,000 (£312,000 + [£312,000 × 100%]).

The guidance published by HMRC also addresses the situation where the personal representatives of the deceased's spouse or civil partner were entitled to claim a transferable nil rate band from an earlier death (which must have occurred on or after October 9, 2007) (the "first death") as a result of that spouse's or civil partner's previous marriage or civil partnership.[14] In order to calculate the unused nil rate band on the death of the deceased's spouse or civil partner (the "second death"), the nil rate band (M in the formula in para.4–08) will include the transferred nil rate band from the first death, less lifetime chargeable transfers made by the spouse. However, NRBMD (see para.4–09) will instead be the nil rate band in force on the second death.

Assume, for example, that E's first wife had survived an earlier marriage. On the death of her first husband, 50 per cent of his nil rate band was unused and on her death in July 2007 her personal representatives made a claim for this to be transferred to her nil rate band. As a result the increased nil rate band available on her death is £450,000 (£300,000 + [£300,000 × 50%]). Her chargeable estate on death was £300,000, leaving an unused nil rate band of £150,000 (£450,000 – £300,000). Using the formula in para.4–09 above to calculate the nil rate band available for transfer on her death, E will

[12] HMRC Manuals IHTM43020.
[13] IHTA 1984 s.8A(5).
[14] HMRC Manuals IHTM43032.

be £150,000 and NRBMD will be £300,000. The percentage to apply is therefore 50 per cent. If X subsequently died in May 2010, the increased nil rate band available on his death will be £487,500 (£325,000 + [£325,000 × 50%]).

Again, in each case the nil rate band cannot be increased by more than 100 per cent,[15] so taking the above example of E, if the chargeable estate on the second death had instead been only £75,000, leaving an unused nil rate band of £375,000, the percentage would have been 125 per cent ([375,000 ÷ 300,000] × 100), restricted to 100 per cent on E's death, giving an increased nil rate band of £650,000 (£325,000 + [£325,000 × 100%]).

Effect of claiming the transferable nil rate band

4–11 The transferable nil rate band can only be set against the death estate of the surviving spouse or civil partner. This means that, as normal, it will be applied first against lifetime transfers made by the survivor, which have become chargeable or on which additional IHT has become payable by reason of death within seven years of the transfer. However, it cannot be set against chargeable lifetime transfers made by the survivor during his/her lifetime, which give rise to an immediate IHT liability.

Claim for transferring the unused nil rate band

4–12 On the death of the surviving spouse, the personal representatives of that spouse must make a formal claim on form IHT404, which is one of the supplementary pages to the form IHT400 (inheritance tax account). Guidance published by HMRC sets out a list of documents, which should accompany the claim:

(1) a copy of the grant of representation (or if none, a copy of the death certificate);
(2) a copy of the will left by the spouse or civil partner, if applicable; and
(3) any deed of variation or similar document executed in respect of the estate.[16]

A provisional claim can also be made if the time limit for making the claim is close to expiry. If the personal representatives do not make any claim within the relevant time period, trustees or the donee of a gift may make a claim instead (on form IHT216).[17]

In the guidance HMRC accept that where the first death occurred many years ago there may be limited evidence to support the claim, but they will only accept the claim if the documents produced show that the claim is valid. However, where the first death occurred on or after October 9, 2007, HMRC advises that, in addition to the documents listed in (1)–(3) above, the following information should be kept (but may not need to be provided to HMRC), perhaps in a bundle with the survivor's will,[18] to help identify how much of the nil rate band was unused at the first death:

[15] HMRC Manuals IHTM43032.
[16] HMRC Manuals IHTM43006.
[17] HMRC Manuals IHTM43006.
[18] *Taxation*, July 3, 2008, 17.

(1) a copy of form IHT200/400, IHT205 (excepted estates) or full written details of the assets in the estate and their values;

(2) death certificate;

(3) marriage/civil partnership certificate;

(4) a copy of the grant of representation;

(5) if there was no will, a note of how the estate passed;

(6) valuations of any assets that passed under will or intestacy to someone other than the survivor and of any other assets that passed, e.g. assets held in trust, details of PETs; and

(7) evidence to support relief claimed, such as agricultural or business relief, where the relevant assets passed to someone other than the survivor.[19]

The time limit for making the claim is no later than either:

(1) 24 months after the end of the month of the second death; or, if later,

(2) 3 months beginning with the date on which the personal representatives first act as such.

Nevertheless, HMRC have discretion to extend the time limit. Examples of circumstances in which they would admit a late claim include a dispute which prevents identifying the personal representatives within the period under (2) above, an event beyond the claimant's control, e.g. serious illness.[20]

However, if the personal representatives make no such claim within the above periods, once these periods have expired any other person liable for tax on the survivor's death, such as the trustees of a settlement or the donee of a gift, may make a claim.[21] The time limit for such a claim is at the discretion of HMRC.

Claim for transferring the nil rate band where there has been a second marriage or civil partnership and no claim on the earlier death

As illustrated in para.4–10 above, where the surviving spouse or civil partner had survived an earlier marriage or civil partnership and there was unused nil rate band on the first death available for transfer on the death of the surviving spouse or civil partner, this can increase the transferable nil rate band available on the survivor's death. **4–13**

Nevertheless, it is possible that on the death of the surviving spouse or civil partner no claim may have been made in relation to that earlier death, e.g. as the transferable nil rate band was not required because the value of the chargeable estate on death was below the single nil rate band. However, this would have the result of reducing the transferable nil rate band available on the survivor's death. This is addressed by s.8B(2), which allows the surviving spouse or civil partner's personal representatives to make a claim in relation to an earlier death provided it will not affect the tax chargeable on that earlier death and that earlier death occurred on or after October 9, 2007. Again, the transferable nil rate band available on the surviving spouse or civil partner's death will be limited to 100 per cent.[22]

For example, assume that F's wife had been married before and on her first husband's death 50 per cent of his nil rate band was unused. On her death in May 2008,

[19] HMRC Manuals IHTM43012.
[20] HMRC Manuals IHTM43009.
[21] IHTA 1984 s.8B(1)(b).
[22] HMRC Manuals IHTM43035.

the increased nil rate band available on her death would have been £468,000 (£312,000 + [£312,000 × 50%]). However, as the value of her chargeable estate was £234,000, her personal representatives did not claim the transferable nil rate band. Her unused (single) nil rate band was therefore 25 per cent ([78,000 ÷ 312,000] × 100). If a claim had been made to transfer the unused nil rate band from her first husband's death, her unused nil rate band would instead have been 75 per cent ([(468,000 − 234,000) ÷ 312,000] × 100). By making a claim in accordance with s.8B(2) on F's death in December 2010, his personal representatives are able to increase his available nil rate from £406,250 (£325,000 + [£325,000 × 25%]) to £568,750 (£325,000 + [£325,000 × 75%]).

V. MISCELLANEOUS POINTS

Commorientes

4–14   Where spouses or civil partners die at the same time and it is presumed that the younger died last,[23] any unused nil rate band on the death of the elder is transferable. In addition, under s.4(2) assets passing to the estate of the younger spouse or civil partner from the elder's estate are left out of account in calculating the charge to IHT.

The nil rate band can similarly be transferred where a couple die intestate, although in this case the presumption that the elder died first does not apply.[24]

Domicile

4–15   On the death of a non-UK domiciled spouse or civil partner, the unused nil rate band is calculated by reference only to UK situate assets, which will represent VT in the formula in para.4–08 above.[25] In this case the chargeable estate is calculated after deducting the s.18 exemption of £55,000, to the extent this is available.

HMRC guidance also states that if the survivor dies in the United Kingdom, his or her personal representatives can claim any unused nil rate band available on the death of their spouse or civil partner where that person died abroad with no UK assets.[26] This will therefore be of advantage where a non-domiciled survivor has substantial UK assets, reducing the IHT liability on their UK death estate significantly.

Double taxation relief/successive charges relief

4–16   If a double taxation agreement provides that an asset is not subject to tax, this may result in unused nil rate band on the first death. However, if the agreement or successive charges relief merely reduces an IHT liability to nil, this does not mean that there is

---

[23] Law of Property Act 1925 s.184. See paras 8–06 and 8–07.
[24] Intestates' Estates Act 1952 s.1(4). See paras 8–06 and 8–07. See also HMRC guidance on the transferable nil rate band published on February 4, 2009, HMRC Manuals IHTM43040.
[25] HMRC Manuals IHTM43042.
[26] HMRC Manuals IHTM43042.

unused nil rate band. Instead, as there is a liability to IHT, the nil rate band will still be fully used.

Conditionally exempt property and woodlands—outline

Section 8(C) provides how the transferable nil rate band interacts with the IHT **4–17** charges arising on chargeable events under s.32 and s.32A in the case of conditionally exempt property,[27] and on the disposal of woodlands under s.126,[28] where the chargeable values have to be included in the person's death estate.

Conditionally exempt property and woodlands—chargeable event or disposal before the second death

If the chargeable event or disposal occurs before the surviving spouse or civil partner **4–18** dies, s.8C(2) provides that the revised percentage of nil rate band available to transfer to the surviving spouse or civil partner's estate is calculated by reducing the original percentage (see para.4–08) proportionately to reflect the chargeable event as follows:

$$\frac{E}{NRBMD} - \frac{TA}{NRBME} \times 100$$

E and NRBMD = as outlined above in para.4–09.

TA = the chargeable value under s.32, s.32A or s.126, as applicable.

NRBME = the nil rate band in force at the date of the chargeable event or disposal.

Where there is more than one chargeable event before the surviving spouse or civil partner's death, s.8C(3) provides that the above calculation should be carried out in respect of each event, with the transferable nil rate band reduced by each fraction.[29]

Conditionally exempt property and woodlands—chargeable event or disposal after the second death

If the chargeable event or disposal occurs after the surviving spouse or civil partner's **4–19** death, when the unused nil rate band from the first death has already been transferred to their estate, s.8C(4) and s.8C(5) reduce the available nil rate band[30] on the first death

---

[27] See paras 27–37 and following.
[28] See paras 26–194 and following.
[29] HMRC Manuals IHTM43045.
[30] This will include any transferable nil rate band claimed by the personal representatives on the first death if the deceased had survived an earlier marriage or civil partnership and there was unused nil rate band from that earlier death—IHTA 1984 s.8C(5).

by the transferred nil rate band actually used (and set against the chargeable estate) on the survivor's death. As this reduction is the amount of the transferred nil rate band required to keep the survivor's estate free of tax, the chargeable value of the survivor's death estate will be required.[31]

Legitim

4–20   Legitim is a right under Scottish succession law which enables the children of a deceased Scottish domiciled person to claim entitlement to one-third of that deceased's moveable estate in preference to the terms of his or her will.

Section 147(10) enables HMRC to amend the transferable nil rate band claimed on the survivor's death where a claim for legitim is subsequently made in respect of the other spouse's earlier death, thereby using up part of the nil rate band available on that earlier death.[32]

Alternative Secured Pension (ASP)

4–21   The introduction of transferable nil rate bands also applies to a surviving spouse or civil partner with inherited ASP funds. Please see para.23–17 for further details.

VI. IMPLICATIONS FOR TAX PLANNING

Advantages

4–22   Until now the principal manner of making use of the nil rate band on the first death has been to include a nil rate band legacy or nil rate band discretionary trust in the will.[33] For many couples whose principal asset was the family home, this has often meant entering into complex and costly tax planning arrangements, which were not always successful.[34] The transferable nil rate band therefore means that drafting wills will now be much simpler for many couples. It will also remove concerns regarding access to funds for those spouses or civil partners, who felt uncomfortable about losing control over that part of their deceased spouse or civil partner's estate held in a nil rate band discretionary trust.

The transferable nil rate band also benefits those couples who may not have sought previous professional advice regarding including a nil rate band legacy or trust in their

---

[31] HMRC Manuals IHTM43046.
[32] HMRC Manuals IHTM43041.
[33] See para.4–25.
[34] See para.4–26.

wills and, in the absence of a deed of variation executed within two years of death, would otherwise have wasted a nil rate band.

Before October 9, 2007 it was often sensible for couples to equalise their estates with a view to maximising use of the nil rate band on both deaths. With the introduction of the transferable nil rate band this is no longer such a priority from an IHT perspective as any unused nil rate band on the first death can now be transferred to the surviving spouse or civil partner's estate. Nevertheless it may still be advisable to equalise estates during lifetime to enable the spouse or civil partner with fewer assets to make their own PETs and lifetime chargeable transfers in order to utilise their annual exemptions and nil rate band while they are alive.[35] However, it must be borne in mind that if the lifetime gifts become chargeable on the first death, this will reduce the nil rate band available to transfer to the surviving spouse or civil partner's estate. Given that the transferable nil rate band is calculated on the basis of the nil rate band in force on the second death, it may be preferred to use as little of the nil rate band as possible on the first death in order to benefit from the increase in the nil rate band between both deaths.[36] This will involve considering carefully, for example, which spouse or civil partner should make lifetime gifts, taking into account factors such as their likelihood of surviving seven years and availability of annual exemptions.

Implications for will drafting

Where the nil rate band has been unused on the first death, often no special **4–23** provisions will need to be included in the survivor's will to enable that unused nil rate band to be transferred on their death—it will simply be a matter for the survivor's personal representatives to make a claim under s.8A.

Where it is desirable to include a nil rate band legacy or discretionary trust, care will need to be taken with wills of spouses and civil partners to ensure that the wording will cover the transferable nil rate band, e.g. leaving a sum "that is equal to an amount that will not give rise to an IHT charge".[37] Existing wills will need to be reviewed, and if necessary and appropriate amended by codicil or by making a new will, to ensure that the nil rate band amount includes any unused nil rate band transferable from an earlier death.

The interpretation of wording in existing nil rate band legacies and discretionary trusts will become particularly relevant where the surviving spouse or civil partner's available nil rate band passes to non-exempt beneficiaries but the residuary estate passes to an exempt beneficiary such as a charity. If the nil rate band legacy is interpreted as including the transferable nil rate band from an earlier death, this will reduce the amount passing to charity and increase the amount passing to the non-exempt beneficiaries. At the time of writing it is not clear whether the personal representatives in this situation would have discretion not to make a claim under s.8A. However, it appears more likely that making the claim is merely an administrative function, which the personal representatives must carry out if the wording of the legacy is capable of referring to the transferable nil rate band.

---

[35] See para.4–24.

[36] *Trusts & Estates Journal* (2008), 22 1 (1), January 1, 2008 and 22 4 (1), April 1, 2008; see also HMRC Manuals IHTM43065.

[37] HMRC guidance on the transferable nil rate band published on February 4, 2009, HMRC Manuals IHTM43065.

A more detailed discussion of the effect of the transferable nil rate band on nil rate band legacies under wills is contained in para.4–27 below.

TAX PLANNING USING THE NIL RATE BAND

VII. NIL RATE BAND TRUSTS CREATED DURING LIFETIME

4–24   Since the nil rate band is "refreshed" every seven years during lifetime, it can be used for making tax efficient gifts into trust during lifetime.[38] As a result of the Finance Act 2006, transfers in excess of the available nil rate band into most lifetime trusts[39] will attract an immediate 20 per cent IHT charge. By transferring an amount equal to the available nil rate band, an upfront IHT charge is avoided, so this offers a useful tool for winding down the value of an individual's estate and also for transferring assets that are likely to increase substantially in the future. In addition, the use of trusts facilitates succession planning.

If an individual started giving an amount equivalent to the nil rate band at the age of 50, by the time they were 71 they could have given in the region of £975,000 (based on current rates—the actual sum would be higher given the trend for the nil rate band to increase each tax year). If both spouses or civil partners give an amount equal to the nil rate band into trust every seven years in this manner, the value removed from their combined estates is doubled. If one spouse or civil partner has insufficient assets to give a sum equal to the nil rate band, the wealthier spouse or civil partner could consider transferring sufficient funds to them. However, this would have to be a genuine gift with no obligation for the donee spouse or civil partner to make further gifts as otherwise HMRC could challenge the gift on the basis that the donee spouse or civil partner was a mere conduit.

Obviously if the settlor fails to survive seven years, there will be no nil rate band available for reducing the value of his death estate. If he is married or in a civil partnership, this means there will be no unused nil rate band available for transferring to the survivor's estate.

If a couple wish to gift an amount equal to a single nil rate band between them, it may be sensible for the spouse or civil partner with the longer life expectancy to make the gift provided, of course, that he or she has not previously used up the nil rate band in the last seven years.

A tax planning technique designed to take advantage of the fact that each relevant property trust benefits from its own nil rate band[40] is for a settlor (with no history of previous chargeable transfers[41]) to set up a number of trusts on different dates on the same or similar terms with the nil rate band amount spread across each trust. Each trust's nil rate band will then be more likely to cover the growth in the trust fund, thereby minimising the periodic IHT charges and in particular the first ten year

---

[38] Care should be taken where the settlor has made PETs prior to transferring assets to relevant property trusts. If these become chargeable by reason of his death within 7 years, thereby using up part or all of his nil rate band, this will affect the settlor's cumulative total of chargeable transfers used to calculate the trust's available nil rate band. Consequently this will increase the IHT charges applicable throughout the lifetime of the trust.

[39] Apart from certain limited categories of trusts for disabled persons—see Ch.21.

[40] See Ch.14.

[41] In this regard a PET made by the settlor in the last seven years could undo the tax planning if it becomes chargeable—see fn.34.

anniversary charge. In *CIR v Rysaffe Trustee Co (Channel Islands) Ltd*[42] five discretionary settlements were created by the same settlor, each on the same terms and with a minimal amount of £10. The Court of Appeal upheld the decision of Park J. in the High Court that the associated operations rule in s.268 did not apply and that five settlements rather than one had been created.

This planning works particularly well when each trust is set up with a nominal sum and property qualifying for business or agricultural relief is subsequently added.[43] Even if the relief is subsequently withdrawn, this does not affect the settlor's cumulative total for the purposes of calculating each trust's available nil rate band.

VIII. TAX EFFICIENT WILL DRAFTING

The position before the introduction of the transferable nil rate band

Before the rules concerning the transferable nil rate band came into effect, it was **4–25** important for wills of spouses and civil partners to contain a nil rate band outright legacy or discretionary trust in favour of children or other non-exempt beneficiaries in order to ensure that the nil rate band was used on the first death. In the case of a nil rate band discretionary trust the survivor was typically included within the class of beneficiaries for flexibility. Where the estate did not contain sufficient assets to satisfy the nil rate band legacy with cash or other liquid assets, and the principal asset consisted of the family home, complex arrangements were used which are considered in more detail in para.4–26 below.

Debt/charge schemes

These schemes have been used in the past to enable the nil rate band legacy to be **4–26** satisfied using the deceased's share of the family home where the survivor wishes to continue living there. In both cases where the home is jointly owned it must be held as a tenancy in common as if the family home was held as joint tenants it would pass to the survivor by right of survivorship and not under the will.

These schemes addressed concerns that the survivor would otherwise be treated as having an interest in possession in the deceased's share of the property by virtue of occupying the property,[44] thereby rendering the nil rate band legacy ineffective.

Under the debt scheme the nil rate band legacy is satisfied by a debt from the surviving spouse or civil partner (where residue has passed to outright to him/her) or the trustees of the residuary estate (where the residue has been left on trust for the survivor). The debt is usually expressed as being repayable on demand to avoid the risk of the survivor having an interest in possession in it. However, in the recent case of *Phizackerley (Personal Representatives of Phizackerley, Deceased) v Revenue and Customs Commissioners*[45] a debt scheme failed. In this case the deceased had left a nil rate band discretionary trust in favour of her husband and children under her will with the residue passing to her husband outright. Her half share of the house was assented

---

[42] *CIR v Rysaffe Trustee Co (Channel Islands) Ltd* [2003] S.T.C. 536.
[43] See Ch.26.
[44] SP 10/79.
[45] *Phizackerley (Personal Representatives of Phizackerley, Deceased) v Revenue and Customs Commissioners* [2007] SpC 591.

to her husband subject to a debt from him in favour of the nil rate band trustees. On the husband's death the debt was held not to be deductible under Finance Act 1986 s.103 as the deceased's share of the family home had derived from him. Although the home had been held jointly (initially as joint tenants and then as tenants in common), the court found that the husband must have funded the purchase price and paid for the £30,000 mortgage as the deceased did not work.[46] Consequently the debt scheme should not be used where the survivor has made substantial lifetime gifts to the deceased spouse or civil partner. However, the risk should be avoided if the residuary estate is held on trust for the survivor as in this case the debt is incurred by the trustees of the residuary estate. It would therefore be advisable for the survivor not to be a trustee of the residuary estate.

Under the charge scheme an equitable charge is imposed by the executors over the deceased's interest in the family home and this is transferred to the nil rate band trustees in satisfaction of the nil rate band legacy. The charge is only enforceable against the interest in the property, not against the survivor (if they take the residue outright) or against the trustees of the residuary estate (where the residuary estate is held on trust). The Finance Act 1986 s.103 problem does not apply as the charge is imposed by the executors.

For both schemes ideally the executors and the nil rate band trustees should not be the same persons and in particular for the debt scheme it is advisable for the survivor not to be one of the nil rate band trustees where there could be a potential Finance Act 1986 s.103 problem.

On the surviving spouse or civil partner's death the debt or charge is set against the share of the property held by the residuary trustees (where the residue was held on trust after the first death) or held by the survivor's estate (where the residue passed to the survivor outright) together with any additional interest if it was interest-bearing or value if it was index-linked.

However, while HMRC have accepted that the debt/charge schemes are in principle effective for IHT purposes, they can challenge the schemes on the basis that they are a sham. Consequently, in order to be effective, the schemes must be properly documented, the nil rate band trustees must meet regularly to consider whether to enforce the charge or demand repayment of the debt or charge interest and they must record their decisions.[47] As the surviving spouse or civil partner will usually be one of the beneficiaries of the nil rate band trust, the trustees will be entitled to consider the survivor's interests. Having a professional trustee as one of the nil rate band trustees strengthens the position that the scheme has been properly implemented.

HMRC have also challenged the effectiveness of the schemes by arguing that the surviving spouse or civil partner has an interest in possession in the nil rate band trust. In order to counter such an argument it is advisable for the trustees to be able to establish that they are receiving some return from the loan, for example in the form of interest[48] or that it is repayable on demand[49] in order to show that the survivor does not have such enjoyment of the property as to amount to an interest in possession.

[46] In this case James Kessler QC, acting for the couple's daughter, argued that the husband's gift of a half share in the house did not constitute a transfer of value as it was a disposition for family maintenance under IHTA 1984 s.11. However, this argument was rejected by the Special Commissioner, Dr John Avery Jones, on the basis that the ordinary meaning of maintenance had a "flavour of meeting recurring expenses", but that it was "wide enough to cover the transfer of a house or part interest in a house if, and only if, it relieved the recipient from income expenditure, for example on rent". In this case the husband had put the property into joint names (the home was initially held as joint tenants and then as tenants in common in equal shares) to give his wife security of joint ownership.

[47] For more information about this and debt/charge schemes generally see *Journal of International Trust and Corporate Planning* [2006] 135, September 1, 2006.

[48] See also *Taxation*, December 4, 2003, 235; *Taxation*, August 25, 2005, 572.

[49] See *Tolley's Practical Tax Newsletter*, 23 TTN 26, 201, December 20, 2002.

However, following the changes introduced by the Finance Act 2006, if the surviving spouse or civil partner's interest in the home is not an IPDI,[50] the IHT advantages of the nil rate band trust will still be available as the trust will continue to be a relevant property trust.

Nevertheless now that it will be possible to transfer any unused nil rate band from the first death to the surviving spouse or civil partner's estate, these schemes are less likely to be used in the future. However, they will still be relevant where it is desirable to include a nil rate band discretionary trust and there are insufficient assets in the estate to fund the trust, particularly where there is an enhanced nil rate band, e.g. in the case of second marriages where there is an unused nil rate band transferred from an earlier death.

The implications of the transferable nil rate band

With the introduction of the transferable nil rate band, will drafting for many couples **4–27** should become more straightforward. Many may decide not to include nil rate band legacies or discretionary trusts in their wills. Where a will provides for a nil rate band trust to be implemented, on the death of the testator the executors may consider appointing the funds instead to the testator's surviving spouse or civil partner between three months[51] and two years of death,[52] thereby taking advantage of the s.18 exemption and preserving the transferable nil rate band for the second death. If the surviving spouse or civil partner has sufficient resources of their own, gifts to children can be made of the residuary estate (either by the survivor if the residue passed outright or by the trustees if the residue is held on an IPDI for the survivor) free of IHT provided the survivor lives for another seven years while the NRB will have been preserved for the survivor's death.

Nevertheless, the inclusion of nil rate band legacies and discretionary trusts may still be desired for a variety of reasons. They offer flexibility and address concerns a spouse or civil partner may have over giving up control of his or her estate to the survivor, especially if they do not wish everything to pass to the survivor, e.g. for succession or creditor protection reasons.

The use of a nil rate band legacy or discretionary trust also offers the option of benefiting other beneficiaries in addition to the surviving spouse or civil partner, to whom the bulk of the estate may pass, as well as the opportunity to pass assets that are likely to increase substantially in value in the future, thereby potentially exceeding the nil rate band available on the second death. Nevertheless, as referred to in para.4–22 above, since the nil rate band may increase substantially in the future,[53] it may be preferred to delay using up the nil rate band on the first death in order to benefit from the increased rates on the second death.

Where there are children from previous marriages or civil partnerships and on the first death the estate passes to the survivor on an IPDI with the remainder to children of that marriage, failure to include a nil rate band legacy or discretionary trust can mean that in certain circumstances the children of the first to die could lose out on some of the nil rate band that would otherwise have been available on that first death, leaving them with a higher IHT liability in respect of the trust assets passing to them on the

---

[50] For this to be the case, the survivor's interest in the trust would have to be appointed within three months of the first death or after two years of that death to avoid the interest being read back into the deceased's will, thereby constituting an IPDI.

[51] To avoid the *Frankland* trap—see para.8–193.

[52] See para.4–28.

[53] See paras 4–02 and 4–03.

survivor's death. This could happen, for example, where the transferable nil rate band is apportioned between the survivor's free death estate passing to beneficiaries other than the children of the first marriage and the assets held on the IPDI which do pass to the children of the first marriage. Including a nil rate band legacy or trust can therefore ensure equality of treatment in such circumstances.

Furthermore, where the nil rate band on the first death is largely unused and the survivor remarries or enters into a new civil partnership, one nil rate band may be lost if that survivor predeceases the second spouse or civil partner, leaving their entire estate to him/her. This is because the transferable nil rate band is limited to 100 per cent. To avoid this, it will be important to include a nil rate band legacy or discretionary trust in the survivor's will, making sure that this includes the transferable nil rate band from the first death.

It should be recognised that transferring the nil rate band to the surviving spouse is only attractive if it is accepted that the value of the assets that are then passed to the surviving spouse, rather than under a nil rate band legacy, will appreciate in capital value at a lower rate than the rate of increase in the nil rate band, as decided by the Treasury from time to time. Therefore it may be advisable to pass property that is expected to appreciate significantly under the nil rate band rather than to a surviving spouse. In addition, no allowance is made under the Act for a future decrease in the amount of the nil rate band and while this may not currently be in the contemplation of any major political party it is not hard to envisage circumstances where one government could raise the amount of the nil rate band substantially and a successive one then reduce it.

For this reason, it may always be preferable to include a flexible nil rate band trust that can be appointed to the surviving spouse if necessary, when drafting a will.

In the case of nil rate band trusts in wills, it is preferable for only a single nil rate band to pass into these given that the relevant property exit charges can be avoided in the first ten years of the nil rate band's trust on this basis.

Where it is advisable to include a nil rate band legacy or discretionary trust in wills and there are insufficient liquid assets in the estate, the debt/charge schemes discussed in para.4–26 above will continue to be relevant.

IX. POSTHUMOUS ARRANGEMENTS INVOLVING THE NIL RATE BAND

Use of deeds of variation to insert a nil rate band legacy

4–28   If a nil rate band legacy or discretionary trust has not been included in the deceased's will, a deed of variation can be executed within two years of death to insert such a legacy[54] if it is desired to make use of the nil rate band. Provided the conditions of s.142 are satisfied, it will be read back into the will. Please see para.8–142 for further details as to the conditions that need to be met under s.142 within a two year period after a death in order to alter the dispositions taking effect on that death.

In the past deeds of variation have been used in order to use the nil rate band on the first death in circumstances where it would otherwise have been wasted, e.g. where the entire estate passed to exempt beneficiaries. With the introduction of the transferable nil rate band, this will no longer be such a concern for persons who are married or in a civil partnership. However, there may be situations in which it is advisable to use the nil rate band on the first death (or the intermediate death in the event of a second

[54] See paras 8–115 and following.

160

marriage).[55] Where no nil rate band legacy is included in the will, a deed of variation will be a useful tool in this regard. Nevertheless, deeds of variation should not be relied upon in case the IHT benefits of this tool are withdrawn in the future.[56]

Use of sections 142 and 144 to preserve the nil rate band for the second death

A married couple or persons in a civil partnership may have existing wills which **4–29** already provide for a nil rate band legacy to come into effect on the first death, or alternatively they may wish to include such a legacy for flexibility.

On the first death it may instead be decided to preserve the deceased's nil rate band so that it can be transferred to the surviving spouse or civil partner's estate on his or her death. In the case of a nil rate band legacy, this can be disclaimed[57] or varied[58] under s.142 so that the fund instead passes to the survivor free of IHT under the s.18 exemption. In the case of a nil rate band discretionary trust, the trustees can appoint the fund to the survivor between three months[59] and two years of the deceased's death so that it is read back into the will under s.144[60] and is covered by the s.18 exemption.

---

[55] See para.4–27.
[56] See para.8–123.
[57] The effect of disclaiming a legacy is that it passes with the residuary estate (in the case of persons who are married or in a civil partnership, the survivor will typically be entitled to residue). See paras 8–176 and following.
[58] See paras 8–115 and following.
[59] See fn.51 above.
[60] See paras 8–189 and following.

CHAPTER 5

POTENTIALLY EXEMPT TRANSFERS

I. INTRODUCTION

5–01   The introduction into the IHT code of the PET regime by the Finance Act 1986 was one of the most significant developments since the inception of the legislation. PETs offer many taxpayers the greatest planning opportunities although the Finance Act 2006 has, to a large extent, limited the availability of making PETs into trusts. The rules governing them, the effects of some of which are quite subtle, accordingly deserve careful study. This chapter concentrates on the definition of a PET and the immediate IHT consequences that flow from making a PET. What happens when a PET fails is discussed in the next chapter.

Advantages of making a PET

5–02   The following are the main advantages of making a PET:

(1) A PET is assumed to be an exempt transfer when it is made,[1] so that any charge to tax that might have arisen is displaced.

(2) If the transferor survives the making of the PET by seven years, the PET becomes a fully fledged exempt transfer.[2]

(3) If the transferor does not survive the making of the PET by seven years, the exemption which was provisionally given to the transfer is lost retrospectively

---

[1] IHTA 1984 s.3A(5).
[2] IHTA 1984 s.3A(4).

and the transfer becomes chargeable.[3] PETs might thus have been more accurately called "potentially chargeable transfers".

(4) The fact that the transferor of a PET dies within seven years of making the PET does not alter the date on which the transfer was made or the value transferred by that transfer.[4] A PET thus has an inherent estate freezing quality. Assume, for example, that on January 1, 2008 X gives Y property worth £300,000, thereby making a transfer of value of £300,000, which transfer is a PET. Five-and-a-half years later, by which time the value of the gifted property has risen to £650,000, X dies. The effect of his dying within seven years of making the PET will be that the original transfer is treated as chargeable at the time X died, and the amount to be brought into charge will prima facie be £300,000. The fact that the gifted property has increased in value is irrelevant for this purpose. It might be, of course, that the property fell in value, e.g to £200,000. This, too, would be irrelevant, unless certain revaluation reliefs[5] were available. The possibility of retrospectively losing such agricultural or business relief as was available when the PET was originally made would also have to be considered.[6]

(5) The rate at which tax is charged on a failed PET depends on how long the transferor survived the making of the PET, because IHT is charged on a failed PET at the appropriate percentage of the rates in force when the transferor died.[7] This is discussed in detail in the next chapter, but it may be helpful to note the appropriate percentages now:

Years between transfer and death	Appropriate percentage
3 or less than 3	100
more than 3, up to 4	80
more than 4, up to 5	60
more than 5, up to 6	40
more than 6, up to 7	20

This taper relief affects only the rate at which tax is charged, not the value transferred by the PET. In the previous example, for instance, tax would be charged on £300,000 at 40 per cent of the rates in force on X's death (ignoring any available nil-rate band).

(6) No account needs to be delivered in respect of a PET.[8]

(7) Tax on a failed PET is due six months after the end of the month in which the transferor's death occurs.[9] Thus, in addition to their built in estate freezing quality, PETs also offer a cash flow advantage. When a person makes a transfer which is chargeable at the time it is made, tax is due, broadly speaking, six months after the end of the month in which that transfer is made.[10]

Actual and deemed PETs

As a preliminary point, it should be mentioned that there are two kinds of PETs— **5–03** actual and deemed. There is an actual PET when a person makes a transfer of value (be

---

[3] IHTA 1984 s.3A(4).
[4] IHTA 1984 s.3A(4).
[5] See paras 25–109 and following for revaluation reliefs.
[6] See paras 26–157 and following.
[7] Unless those rates have increased since the PET was made; IHTA 1984 Sch.2 para.1A.
[8] See para.29–07.
[9] IHTA 1984 s.226(3A).
[10] See para.29–95.

it actual or notional) which satisfies certain requirements discussed below. There is a deemed PET when an event occurs on the happening of which the legislation specifies that a taxpayer is to be treated as though he had made a PET. The two cases in which this happens are discussed below at paras 5–37 and following.

How PETs fit into the legislation

5–04   Prior to the introduction of the PET regime, an advisor had to ask two basic questions in relation to the main set of charging provisions. First, had a taxpayer made a transfer of value? Secondly, if he had, was that transfer wholly or partly exempt? Since PETs were introduced[11] a third question must be asked, i.e. if the transfer in question is not exempt,[12] is it potentially exempt? If it is not, then it will be chargeable at the time it is made. If, on the other hand, it is potentially exempt, then the consequences are as stated above, i.e. it is assumed to be exempt when it is made, the final position depending on whether the transferor survives the making of the PET by seven years.

Relevance of annual and conditional exemptions

5–05   The general rule that an exempt transfer is not a PET is subject to two qualifications designed to assist taxpayers. Normally, of course, it is to a taxpayer's advantage for a transfer of value to be exempt, because in that case no charge can arise in respect of it, regardless of when the transferor dies. But, in two cases, the availability of an exemption could be counterproductive.

Annual exemption

5–06   If a taxpayer makes two transfers, one of which is capable of being a PET and one of which is not, then it will be to his advantage to apply the annual exemption (so far as he is able to do so) against the one that is not. In that way the transfer that is capable of being a PET will—assuming the requirements discussed below are satisfied—shelter under the PET regime, while the charge that would otherwise be imposed on the other transfer will be reduced or eliminated. The legislation accordingly endeavours to provide that the annual exemption is disregarded in determining whether a transfer of value is a PET at the time that it is made.[13] Whether, strictly speaking, it succeeds in this endeavour is far from clear. Although s.19(3A)(a) provides that a transfer of value which is potentially exempt is to be left out of account for the purposes of ss.19(1)–(3) (the provisions governing the annual exemption) this does not solve the problem. Since a transfer of value can be potentially exempt only if it is not an exempt transfer it remains arguable that s.19 will already, by definition, have been taken into account so that it makes no sense to say that that section shall be left out of account in relation to

---

[11] i.e. as from March 18, 1986.
[12] For this purpose, the annual exemption is disregarded, see para.5–06.
[13] The application of the annual exemption if a PET becomes chargeable is considered at paras 6–24 and following.

a transfer of value which is a PET. Despite this legislative nonsense there is no doubt in practice that the annual exemption is left out of account in determining whether a transfer is potentially exempt.

Conditional exemption

In the same way that it may be helpful to a taxpayer to ignore the annual exemption in determining whether a transfer is a PET, so it may also be helpful to him to ignore the possibility of a transfer of heritage property qualifying for conditional exemption under s.30. Accordingly, that possibility is disregarded in determining whether the transfer is a PET.[14] **5–07**

It is therefore not possible to claim conditional exemption at the time of making a lifetime gift of qualifying heritage property. If, however, the transfer of such property becomes chargeable as a result of the donor's death within seven years, conditional exemption may then be claimed retrospectively. Assume, for instance, that Adam gives his stately home to his son Bertram. The inter vivos transfer will be a PET, but if Adam dies within seven years of the gift conditional exemption may then be claimed. The requirements relating to this exemption must be satisfied at the time *when the claim is made*, not at the time of the initial gift of the property to Bertram.[15] **5–08**

Unfortunately, the ability to claim conditional exemption for heritage property retrospectively on a PET that has failed does not apply to supporting property which otherwise would have been put into a maintenance fund. The owner of heritage property is therefore faced with a dilemma: should he make a lifetime gift of the heritage property together with supporting property in the knowledge that if he does not survive for seven years it will not be possible to elect that the supporting property shall be treated as comprised in a maintenance fund? **5–09**

II. DEFINITION OF A PET

The basic requirements to be satisfied if a transfer of value is to be a PET are set out in s.3A (as amended) of the Act, as follows: **5–10**

> "(1) Any reference in this Act to a potentially exempt transfer is a reference to a transfer of value—
>   (a) which is made by an individual on or after 18 March 1986 but before 22 March 2006; and
>   (b) which, apart from this section, would be a chargeable transfer (or to the extent to which, apart from this section it would be such a transfer); and

[14] See IHTA 1984 s.30(3A)–(3C) inserted by FA 1986 s.101(3) and Sch.19 para.7 with respect to transfers of value made after March 17, 1986.
[15] See para.27–24.

(c) to the extent that it constitutes a gift to another individual or a gift into an accumulation and maintenance trust or a disabled trust.

(1A) Any reference in this Act to a potentially exempt transfer is also a reference to a transfer of value—

(a) which is made by an individual on or after 22 March 2006,

(b) which, apart from this section, would be a chargeable transfer (or to the extent to which, apart from this section, it would be such a transfer), and

(c) to the extent that it constitutes—

(i) a gift to another individual,

(ii) a gift into a disabled trust, or

(iii) a gift into a bereaved minor's trust on the coming to an end of an immediate post-death interest.

(1B) Subsections 1 and (1A) above have effect subject to any provision of this Act which provides that a disposition (or transfer of value) of a particular description is not a potentially exempt transfer.

(2) Subject to subsection (6) below, a transfer of value falls within subsection (1)(c) or (1A)(c)(i) above, as a gift to another individual,—

(a) to the extent that the value transferred is attributable to property which, by virtue of the transfer, becomes comprised in the estate of that other individual, or

(b) so far as that value is not attributable to property which becomes comprised in the estate of another person, to the extent that, by virtue of the transfer, the estate of that other individual is increased,

(3) Subject to subsection (6) below, a transfer of value falls within subsection (1)(c) above, as a gift into an accumulation and maintenance trust or a disabled trust, to the extent that the value transferred is attributable to property to which, by virtue of the transfer, becomes settled property to which section 71 or 89 [of this Act] applies.

(3A) Subject to subsection (6) below, a transfer of value falls within subsection (1A)(c)(ii) above to the extent that the value transferred is attributable to property to which, by virtue of the transfer, becomes settled property to which section 89 [of this Act] applies.

(3B) A transfer of value falls within subsection (1A)(c)(iii) above to the extent that the value transferred is attributable to settled property (whenever settled) that becomes property to which section 71A [of this Act] applies in the following circumstances—

(a) under the settlement, a person ('L') is beneficially entitled to an interest in possession in the settled property,

(b) the interest in possession is an immediate post-death interest,

(c) on or after 22 March 2006, but during L's life, the interest in possession comes to an end,

(d) L is beneficially entitled to the interest in possession immediately before it comes to an end, and

(e) On the interest in possession coming to an end, the property—

(i) continues to be held on the trusts of the settlement, and

(ii) becomes property to which section 71A [of this Act] applies . . .

(6) Where, under any provision of this Act other than section 52, tax is in any circumstances to be charged as if a transfer of value had been made, that transfer shall be taken to be a transfer which is not a potentially exempt transfer.

(6A) The reference in subsection (6) above to any provision of this Act does not include section 52 below except where the transfer of value treated as made by that section is one treated as made on the coming to an end of an interest which falls within section 5(1B) below.

(7) In the application of this section to an event on the happening of which tax is chargeable under section 52 below, the reference in subsection (1)(a) or (1A) (a) above to the individual by whom the transfer of value is made is a reference to the person who, by virtue of section 3(4) above, is treated as the transferor."

5–11 To be a PET, a transfer of value must thus satisfy four requirements. First, it must be made by an individual. Secondly, it must not be expressly prevented by any provision in the legislation from being a PET. There are, at present, five such provisions. Next, it must be made to a qualifying recipient. Finally, it must constitute a "gift" to the recipient within the meaning of the legislation.

Prohibited transfers

The legislation expressly prohibits certain kinds of transfers of value from being PETs. The transfers falling into this category effectively fall into two groups—those relating to close companies, and those relating to timber.

5–12

Close company transfers

The legislation provides that two kinds of transfers involving close companies are prevented from being PETs. It is not clear why such transfers should have been singled out for such treatment. The prohibitions, which may represent an excess of caution by the draftsman, are as follows:

5–13

(1) *Close company transfers*: a transfer of value by a close company which is treated by s.94(1) as having been made by a participator therein[16] cannot be a PET.[17]

(2) *Close company alterations*: the legislation makes specific provision to cover the case where there is either:

(a) an alteration in so much of a close company's share or loan capital as does not consist of shares or securities quoted on a recognised stock exchange; or

(b) an alteration in any rights attaching to shares in or debentures of a close company which are not so quoted such that a participator in that company is treated by s.98(1) as having made a disposition.[18] If that disposition is a transfer of value, s.98(3) provides that it cannot be a PET.

The fact that a transfer of value arising as the result of an alteration of the share capital of a company cannot be a PET raises an interesting question. As will be seen in the discussion of the reservation of benefit rules[19] it is thought that a person who controls a company and who wishes to give away shares in that company without diluting his voting power can, without infringing those rules:

(1) arrange for the company's share capital to be reorganised into voting and non-voting shares; and

(2) give away the non-voting shares.

While it is thought that this would be fine as far as those rules are concerned, it remains to be seen whether HMRC would attempt to argue that the combination of the reorganisation and the gift amounted to an alteration of the company's share capital by means of associated operations, with the result that the transfer of the non-voting shares

---

[16] See para.2–73.
[17] IHTA 1984 s.3A(6).
[18] See paras 2–18 and following.
[19] See paras 7–132 and following.

was prohibited from being a PET. The authors' view is that such an argument is wrong, but HMRC have, to their knowledge, not yet expressed a view on the point.

Timber clawback

5–14   Under the estate duty regime, duty was not charged on the value of timber, trees, wood or underwood growing on land comprised in an estate at death. Instead the tax was deferred until such time as the woodlands were sold and was then levied at the death estate rate on the net proceeds of sale (subject to the proviso that the sum liable to duty could not exceed the value of the timber at the date of the death). Pending sale, duty was therefore held in suspense and this deferral period ceased only on the happening of a later death when the woodlands again became subject to duty. The introduction of a charge on lifetime gifts with the advent of Capital Transfer Tax (CTT) resulted in this deferral period terminating immediately after the first transfer of value occurring after March 12, 1975, the value transferred by which was determined by reference to the land in question (subject only to an exclusion if that transfer was to the transferor's spouse and therefore exempt from CTT: see Finance Act 1975 s.49(4)). In such cases the deferred estate duty charge was superseded by a charge to CTT on the transfer of value.

5–15   With the introduction of the PET regime it was realised (during the passage of Finance Act 1986 through Parliament) that a transfer of value of woodlands subject to estate duty deferral to another individual would, prima facie, be a PET but that the transfer would have the effect of ending the deferral period, thereby cancelling any charge to estate duty without a compensating charge to IHT. Schedule 19 para.46 was therefore inserted into Finance Act 1986. It provides that transfers of value made on or after July 1, 1986 which fall within Finance Act 1975 s.49(4) and thereby bring to an end the estate duty deferral period cannot be PETs. Accordingly, such transfers are immediately chargeable to IHT at the transferor's rates (with the possibility of a supplementary charge should he die within the following seven years).

5–16   Assume, for instance, that on his death in May 1973 Claude left his landed estate to his son Charles. That estate included woodlands valued, in 1973, at £4,000. Consider the tax position in the following three alternative situations:

(1) If Charles sells the timber in 1989 for £16,000 the net proceeds of sale would be subject to an estate duty charge levied at Claude's estate rate but duty will be limited by reference to the value of the timber in 1973 (i.e. it will be charged on £4,000).

(2) If Charles retains the timber until his death in 1989 when it passes to his daughter, this transfer of value will end the estate duty deferral period so that the potential charge to duty will be removed. The transfer to his daughter will be subject to an IHT charge unless the woodlands deferral election under s.125(2) is claimed.[20]

(3) If Charles makes an inter vivos gift of an estate including the woodlands in August 1989 to his daughter such a gift will not be a PET because of para.46. Accordingly, it will terminate the estate duty deferral period and will result in an immediate IHT charge levied according to Charles' rates. From the wording of para.46 it is not clear whether part of this transfer can be potentially exempt

[20] See paras 26–197 and following.

or whether the entire value transferred is subject to an immediate charge. Undoubtedly, the value of the timber will attract such a charge and likewise it would seem that the value of the land on which the timber is growing will fall outside the definition of a PET. But what is the position if the transfer of value made by Charles includes other property, e.g. other parts of a landed estate which are not afforested? There is a real danger that none of the value transferred will be a PET because para.46 is not limited to that part of any transfer of value comprising the woodlands. Accordingly, it is important that, whenever practicable, two or more transfers are made so ensuring that the transfer which does not include the woodlands will be a PET.

Qualifying recipient

The second requirement is that the transfer must be made to one of the following: **5–17**

(1) *An individual*: following the Finance Act 2006, gifts must be made either to an individual outright, to a bare trust, to a disabled trust or, in certain circumstances, to a bereaved minor's trust (see further below) in order to qualify as a PET. Gifts to any other form of trust, including to a trust in which an individual has a pre-March 22, 2006 interest in possession, or to a trust subject has a transitional serial interest, will constitute lifetime chargeable transfers. It should be noted that, although s.3A(3) refers to transfers which become settled property to which s.71 applies qualifying as PETs, it is no longer possible since March 22, 2006 to settle property to which s.71 applies. Consequently, the reference in s.3A(3) to s.71 applies only to gifts made before March 22, 2006.

(2) *Bare trusts:* HMRC agrees,[21] having previously indicated that they thought otherwise, that the transfer of assets to bare trusts, including bare trusts where the recipient beneficiary is a minor, would constitute a PET and not a lifetime chargeable transfer. HMRC also agrees that it is not necessary to exclude s.31 of the Trustee Act 1925 to qualify as a bare trust.

(3) *Trustees of a disabled trust:* a disabled trust is a trust which satisfies the conditions laid down by s.89.[22]

(4) *A gift into a bereaved minor's trust on the coming to an end of an immediate post-death interest:* a bereaved minor's trust is a trust which satisfies the conditions laid down by s.71A (broadly, a trust for the testator's children to take capital at 18). In effect, this allows an Immediate Post-Death Interest[23] to be terminated during the life tenant's lifetime and for the property to be retained in trust provided the trust qualifies as a bereaved minor's trust.[24]

It follows from the foregoing that transfers to the majority of trusts, whether or not life interest trusts, or to a company, will not be PETs even though, in the case of a

[21] HMRC Inheritance Tax Manual, para.16068.
[22] See paras 21–01 and following.
[23] Defined in IHTA 1984 s.49A, see para.11–51.
[24] See paras 19–03 and following.

transfer to a company, the transfer increases the value of the estate of the individuals who own shares in the company.[25]

Termination of a qualifying interest in possession

5–18   Five points need to be borne in mind where the occasion of the transfer of value is the termination of a qualifying interest in possession. A qualifying interest in possession is an interest in possession that subsisted on March 22, 2006, a transitional serial interest, or an Immediate Post-Death Interest. First, such a transfer can be a PET provided the transfer constitutes a gift to a qualifying recipient.[26] Thus, if A, a life tenant with a qualifying interest in possession, surrenders his qualifying interest so that the trust fund passes to his daughter, B, absolutely, A will have made a PET.[27] Between March 22, 2006 and October 5, 2008, it was also possible to make a PET by creating an inter vivos transitional serial interest: see paras 11–56 and following. Secondly, if on the termination of the qualifying interest in possession the trust fund is then held otherwise than absolutely or on bare trusts, e.g. on wide discretionary trusts, not only will the transfer not be a PET, so that A will have made an immediate transfer of value, but, in addition, special anti-avoidance rules discussed below[28] may apply.

Thirdly, if the interest in possession is terminated but the life tenant continues to benefit from the property, a gift with reservation will arise (see further para.7–99 below).

Fourthly, if the interest in possession was created by a disposition to which s.10 applied (dispositions not intended to confer gratuitous benefit), and the disposition creating the interest was made after December 9, 2009, then the termination of the interest will not be a PET but the interest is nonetheless within the life tenant's estate.[29] Whilst this provision was intended to block one particular scheme, it has a wider effect and in particular is causing difficulty with settlements created on divorce, where it is often agreed that one spouse should have an interest in possession in a settlement owning the matrimonial home, terminating either on her death or on her children attaining the age of 18. At the time of writing STEP has taken the issue up with HMRC and a response is awaited.

Fifthly, an additional anti-avoidance provision has been included in Finance (No.4) Bill 2012 at cl.208. The clause amends IHTA s.48 and adds new ss.74A–74C. The provisions affect only arrangements entered into on or after June 20, 2012, and only arrangements either made in respect of excluded property settlements or settlements made by a person who is neither an individual nor a close company. They apply where:

(a) one of more persons enter into arrangements;
(b) in the course of the arrangements a person domiciled in the UK (the "taxpayer") acquires or becomes able to acquire an interest in settled property;
(c) consideration is given by a person who entered into the arrangements (not necessarily for the acquisition of the interest);
(d) the estate of the taxpayer is reduced; and

---

[25] See para.5–23.
[26] IHTA 1984 s.3A(6), as amended by F(No.2)A 1987 s.96(1) and (2)(c) with respect to transfers of value made after March 16, 1987.
[27] So far as that portion of the fund which passed to B is concerned.
[28] See paras 5–27 and following.
[29] IHTA ss.3A(6A) and 5(1B).

(e) either the settlement had a non-domiciled settlor and the property concerned is non-UK situs at the time of the arrangements (together "condition A"), or the settlor was neither an individual nor a close company and condition A is not met.

If these conditions are fulfilled then if the taxpayer had a qualifying interest in possession, and if it was reduced in value because of the arrangements, then the interest in possession is deemed to come to an end to the extent of the reduction in value, and this event is deemed not to be a PET but a chargeable transfer. Further, the interest in settled property acquired by the taxpayer referred to in (b) above loses its status as excluded property.

The provisions also apply where the taxpayer does not have a qualifying interest in possession but his estate is nonetheless reduced.

It appears that the provisions were aimed at a particular tax avoidance scheme which involved the purchase by a UK domiciliary of a right to income in an excluded property settlement, with the use of a call option; but the scheme was, it seems, not much used.

Concerns were expressed when the first draft of the clause was published that it could impact on deeds of variation of the estate of a non-domiciliary entered into by a UK domiciliary. However, the requirement of consideration to be given by a person entering into the arrangements (which was one of the amendments, published on July 20, 2012, to the draft clause) would appear to obviate this in view of the necessity to avoid any consideration being given for the variation to meet the requirements of IHTA s.142.

A possible scheme?

It may be possible to make a PET to trustees of a discretionary trust notwithstanding the foregoing rules. Assume that Daniel wishes to settle property on discretionary trusts in favour of his family by means of a PET. He settles the property on discretionary trusts the terms of which are such that he reserves a benefit which is so substantial that the transfer to the trustees scarcely reduces the value of his estate, so that little or no charge to tax arises when he makes the settlement. Later matters are arranged so that the reserved benefit is released, with the result that there is at that stage deemed to be a PET of the settled property, which at that time becomes held on discretionary trusts for the family of Daniel. It remains to be seen whether HMRC would attempt to argue that the initial transfer and the subsequent release of the reservation are associated operations. HMRC have, to the authors' knowledge, not expressed a view on this point.

Qualifying gift

The third requirement is the trickiest. The transfer must constitute a gift, within the meaning of the legislation, to a qualifying recipient. The notion of a "gift" was largely unknown in the Capital Transfer Tax legislation, which based the charge to tax on the concept of a transfer of value. The Finance Act 1986 incorporated the requirement of a gift into the PET regime and into the reservation of benefit rules. In the latter case the result is to create some uncertainty: in s.3A, however, a gift is sufficiently explained in the subsections to remove any major definitional problems. These provisions define a gift in terms of certain lifetime transfers of value. Accordingly, there is no need to investigate the general legal meaning of the term.

The legislation distinguishes between gifts made to individuals and gifts made to trustees of qualifying trusts, such as disabled trusts. The rules concerning gifts to individuals are considered first.

Gifts to individuals

5–21   The rules governing gifts to individuals are laid down in s.3A(2)(a) and (b), which draw a distinction between, in effect, direct and indirect gifts.

Direct gifts to individuals

5–22   The first transfer of value which falls within the PET definition is a gift by one individual to another individual. Under s.3A(2)(a) such a gift is a PET to the extent that the value transferred is attributable to property which by virtue of the transfer becomes comprised in the estate of that other individual. This will include a direct gift between individuals (e.g. A gives to B £100,000). More problematic is the situation where the transfer of value results in a greater diminution in A's estate than gain to B's estate. This will occur, for instance, where A transfers a small number of shares in a private company thereby losing control of that company. HMRC had previously indicated[30] that in such cases the entire diminution in A's estate constitutes a PET and the wording of the legislation arguably supports this interpretation since the value transferred out of A's estate is "attributable to" the shares which have passed into B's estate even though the diminution in A's estate exceeds the value of the gifted share.[31] However, the current entry in the Manual states that any case where the diminution in the value of the donor's estate exceeds the increase in the transferee's estate should be referred to the Technical Group.[32] The possibility that HMRC may argue that the difference between the two is an immediately chargeable transfer should therefore be borne in mind in planning. Assume that X owns 60 of the 100 shares in X Ltd and that none of the shares qualify for agricultural or business relief. He wishes to give half the shares to his son and to settle the other half on trust. The first gift will result in his losing control of the company, and so will diminish the value of his estate more than the second gift. On the basis of HMRC's previously stated view, since the gift to the son would have been a PET, he should make that gift first, so as to shelter under the PET regime as much as possible of the total value transferred by the two gifts.[33] At present, he will need to be advised of the risk of HMRC taking the view that a majority of the value lost on the transfer to the son is not a PET.

Indirect gifts to individuals

5–23   A transfer of value is also regarded as a gift to another individual if the value transferred, so far as it is not attributable to property which becomes comprised in his

---

[30] Paragraph C.34 of the (now superseded) Advanced Instruction Manual. HMRC take a similar view of the words "attributable to" in the context of the s.18 exemption and charities exemption; see para.3–30.
[31] Paragraph C.34 of the (now superseded) Advanced Instruction Manual.
[32] HMRC Manuals IHTM4066.
[33] See para.6–71.

estate, nonetheless increases his estate (see s.3A(2)(b)). Strictly speaking, it is difficult to see how a person's estate can be increased except where property becomes comprised in it. Presumably what the draftsman intended to cover is where the *value* of a person's estate is increased notwithstanding the fact that no property becomes comprised in it, e.g. where A releases B's debt of £10,000. It appears that this is how HMRC apply s.3A(2)(b) in practice.[34] Even then, there can be problems. Assume that Jack pays the school fees for his infant grandson Jude or alternatively that Simon buys a holiday for his Uncle Albert. In both cases a transfer of value is made but in neither case does property become comprised in the estate of another by virtue of that transfer, nor does that transfer increase the value of the transferee's estate. Accordingly both Jack and Simon have made immediately chargeable transfers of value. (Such problems will be avoided if a direct gift is made to the intended donees or if the gift qualifies for the normal expenditure out of income exemption.) There may also be other problems with s.3A(2)(b). Indirect gifts of the kind contemplated by it only qualify as PETs "so far as the value transferred is not attributable to property which becomes comprised in the estate of another person". This prohibition will catch transfers which increase the estate of a company—hence the words "another person" are employed rather than "another individual". Assume, for instance, that A gives £100,000 to B Limited, a company which is wholly owned by B. This gift is not a PET because the value transferred (£100,000) becomes comprised in the estate of another person (B Ltd). If the opening words of s.3A(2)(b) quoted above had been omitted from the subsection the gift would have fallen within the definition of an indirect gift to another individual to the extent that the value of B's shares was increased by A's gift to B Ltd.

The restrictive words limiting the ambit of indirect gifts may apply in other situations and, if read literally, constitute an important limitation on the definition of a PET. Assume, for instance, that Claude pays Debussy's wine bill by handing over a cheque for £100,000 to Chinns Up Vintners Ltd. This is not a direct gift to Debussy nor does it appear to be an indirect gift within s.3A(2)(b) since the value transferred by Claude (£100,000) is attributable to property which becomes comprised in the estate of another person (Chinns Up Vintners Ltd). Whilst it is strongly arguable that in such a case the creditor's estate has not been increased, as the payment of the debt has merely substituted one form of property (cash) for another (the right to call in the debt), nonetheless property—£100,000—has become comprised in the creditor's estate, thus giving rise to the operation of the opening words of the subsection. **5–24**

Quantum limitation

So far as the *quantum* of the gift is concerned, the value transferred by an indirect gift will be within the PET regime to the extent only that the other individual's estate is increased. Accordingly, if the diminution in value in the transferor's estate exceeds that increase the excess will be excluded from the definition. **5–25**

Gifts to trustees

Gifts into bare trusts, disabled trusts, and, in certain circumstances, bereaved minors' trusts can be PETs.[35] The definition of a gift to such trusts is, however, limited to **5–26**

---

[34] The s.18 exemption contains similar wording (see para.3–29), and no difficulties have been known to arise in respect of that wording. See HMRC Manuals IHTM4058–4060.

[35] See Chs 19 and 21.

property "which becomes settled property"[36]: hence indirect gifts to these trusts do not qualify. Assume, for instance, that B settles an insurance policy, taken out on his own life, on disabled trusts for the benefit of his disabled daughter. This transfer is potentially exempt. He subsequently pays annual premiums on that policy directly to the Life Office concerned. Although those payments are transfers of value (assuming they are not covered by the normal expenditure out of income exemption), they do not become settled property and therefore are not PETs. To avoid this problem the settlor should transfer the premium moneys to the trustees each year so that they can discharge the obligation to the insurance company. See further paras 5–44–5–46 below as to the payment of premiums in respect of policies held in pre-March 22, 2006 interest in possession trusts, and in converted accumulation and maintenance trusts.

III. ANTI-AVOIDANCE

5–27   From March 22, 2006, a gift into settlement cannot be a PET unless it is held on:

(1) bare trusts;
(2) disabled trusts; or
(3) bereaved minor's trusts and the gift is made on the coming to an end of an immediate post-death interest.

Therefore the inter vivos creation of other types of trust may lead to an immediate IHT charge. In order to protect this charge, special anti-avoidance rules operate if property, having been first settled by a PET on interest in possession trusts, provided such trusts were established before March 22, 2006 or are transitional serial interests, subsequently becomes held on trusts lacking such an interest. The mischief which these rules are designed to prevent may be illustrated by the following example. If X wished to settle £330,000 on discretionary trusts for his family and descendants there would be an immediate IHT charge on at least £330,000 if such trusts were created. To avoid this, X decided, prior to March 22, 2006, to settle the money on trusts under which his three sons, A, B and C each took revocable life interests in one-third of the trust fund. X would thus have made a PET of £330,000. If in, say, four years, the trustees revoked each son's interest and appointed his share of the trust fund on the discretionary trusts which X wanted to create all along, each of the sons would make a chargeable transfer, but it would be within their respective nil rate bands, with the result that if they survived the transfers by seven years the chargeable transfers they made when their respective interests in possession terminated would have had no ill IHT effects. The anti-avoidance rules are designed to render such an arrangement ineffective.

When the rules apply

5–28   The anti-avoidance rules[37] are designed to render such an arrangement ineffective. They apply if the following conditions are satisfied:

---

[36] See IHTA 1984 s.3A(3A) and (3B).

[37] IHTA 1984 ss.54A and 54B inserted by F(No.2)A 1987 s.96 and Sch.7 with respect to transfers of value made and other events occurring after March 16, 1987.

(1) the original settlement contained a qualifying interest in possession, i.e. an interest in possession that existed before March 22, 2006, a transitional serial interest or a disabled person's trust, and was created by a PET;

(2) within seven years of the creation of that settlement a qualifying interest in possession terminates[38] (either during the life or on the death of the relevant beneficiary) whereupon property becomes held on trusts without an interest in possession; and

(3) when the interest in possession terminates the settlor is still alive.

Even if these requirements are satisfied, the rules will still not apply if within six months of the ending of the relevant interest in possession the property becomes either:

(a) held on disabled trusts; or

(b) property to which an individual is beneficially entitled.[39]

The legislation thus gives taxpayers a period of grace: if, for example, trustees revoke a beneficiary's life interest and appoint the property in which it subsisted on discretionary trusts, they can escape from anti-avoidance provisions by appointing, within six months of the revocation, that, e.g. the property in question be held on disabled trusts. Note that the six-month let-out applies only if the whole of the property in question becomes held in the manner stipulated by the legislation.

The alternative calculations

When the anti-avoidance rules apply, the IHT on the termination of the relevant interest in possession is the greater amount produced by two alternative calculations.   5–29

The first calculation

Under the first calculation the tax is computed in the ordinary way, i.e. by reference   5–30
to the circumstances of the beneficiary whose interest terminates. If this occurs on his death, his death estate rate will be relevant.

The second calculation

The second calculation proceeds on the assumption that the relevant beneficiary's   5–31
cumulative total at the time when his interest ended was equal to that of the settlor at

---

[38] The interest which terminates (called "the relevant interest") need not have been the original interest in possession when the settlement was created: hence the rules may apply when there is a succession of short-lived interests in possession provided that all of the interests existed pre-March 22, 2006 or are TSIs.

[39] IHTA 1984 s.54A(2)(d)(i).

the time when the settlement was created. IHT is then charged at 50 per cent of the full rates, and this is so even if the interest ended on the death of the beneficiary.[40]

EXAMPLE

5–32   Assume, for instance, that A, with a cumulative total of £300,000, settles property worth £90,000 on disabled trusts for B for life, and that B's interest determines after one year whereupon the property becomes held on discretionary trusts. B has a nil cumulative total. Under the first calculation, the value of the settlement at the termination of B's interest in possession will fall within his nil rate band so that no IHT is due. The second calculation, however, involves attributing a cumulative total of £300,000 to B with the result that tax will be due.

Previous application of the rules

5–33   If there has been a chargeable transfer within the previous seven years which was also subject to these special rules, whether in respect of the same settlement or another settlement made by the same settlor, the amount of that chargeable transfer is added to the cumulative total of the settlor (and hence to that of the beneficiary under the second calculation).[41] If, in the example considered in para.5–32, B's interest in possession terminated in one-third of the fund in year one, in a further one-third in year two and in the remainder in year three, B's cumulative total in year two would be £330,000 (i.e. £300,000 plus £30,000 from year one) and in year three £360,000.

Simultaneous terminations

5–34   What is not provided for, however, is the simultaneous termination of a number of interests in possession. Thus had A created three concurrent life interests in his £90,000 fund which then determined at the same moment, tax on each transfer would be calculated by taking the settlor's cumulative total to be only £300,000.

No switching

5–35   It is important to realise that once the IHT calculation has been made, using whichever method produces the greater amount of tax, it is not possible to switch to the alternative calculation if subsequent events would result in that calculation yielding more tax. This position could arise in the event of either the relevant beneficiary or the settlor dying within seven years of the termination of the interest in possession. Thus, if tax had been arrived at by the first calculation (i.e. on the basis of the beneficiary's own cumulative total, see para.5–30) the death of that beneficiary within seven years will result in a recalculation of IHT in the usual way. By contrast, if the second calculation had been employed (see para.5–31) the subsequent death of the beneficiary

[40] IHTA 1984 s.54A(5) and (6).
[41] IHTA s.54B(4)–(7).

176

will be irrelevant, but the death of the settlor may result in an extra tax charge because his cumulative total at the time of creation of the settlement will be increased by any PETs made before that date which have become chargeable as a result of his death. Notice, however, that the death of the settlor does not result in a switch to full rates from the lifetime rates.[42]

When the rules do not apply

The special anti-avoidance rules do not apply in the following cases: **5–36**

(1) once an interest in possession in the property has lasted for at least seven years;

(2) if the original interest in possession was not created by a PET—as, for example, if the first beneficiary was the settlor's spouse or the interest in possession is over relevant property; or

(3) if the original settlement was an accumulation and maintenance trust, followed by an interest in possession trust that then determined in favour of discretionary trusts.

IV. DEEMED PETs

The Finance Act 1986 provides that in two cases a person is deemed to have made **5–37** a PET. Note that in these cases the various requirements as to a qualifying recipient and a qualifying gift are irrelevant. If the circumstances in question arise, then a PET is deemed to have been made, and that is the end of the matter. In a similar manner, Finance Act 2006 deems two further cases to be PETs, albeit that the recipient would not be a qualifying recipient.

Cessation of reservation

The first case in which a person is deemed to make a PET occurs where property **5–38** which is subject to a reservation in respect of a person under the reservation of benefit rules ceases to be such property in relation to him within seven years of his death. Assume, for example, that A gives his house to B but continues, with B's consent, to live in it rent-free. If, two years later, A ceases to live in the house, he will at that time make a PET under the Finance Act 1986 s.102(4).[43] Although s.102(4) seems straightforward enough, its effect is in two cases uncertain and considered further at paras 5–40 and 5–41 below.

It should be noted that s.102(4) may, after March 22, 2006, apply in situations where **5–39** formerly it would not have done. Following the introduction of Finance Act 1986 s.102ZA, the termination of an interest in possession will, from March 22, 2006, be treated, for the reservation rules, as if the life tenant had made a gift. Therefore, if the

---

[42] See para.5–31.

[43] Strictly, whether he makes a PET will depend on when he dies, but the assumption in practice is that he made a PET when he ceased to reserve a benefit.

former life tenant may benefit from the assets previously subject to the interest in possession, the reservation rules can apply. A PET will be made should the life tenant cease to have a reservation of benefit as at the date the reservation was released.

Valuation uncertainty

5–40   Section 102(4), which will also apply to the release of reservations following the termination of interests in possession referred to in para.5–39 above, provides that the deemed PET is to be regarded as having been made by a disposition, but it does not state what property is to be regarded as having been disposed of, still less what the value transferred by the deemed PET is to be taken as having been. This will not give rise to difficulties in a straightforward case where, had the property actually been disposed of, the disponor's estate would have been diminished by an amount equal to the value of the property in question. Where, on the other hand, the diminution occasioned in the value of the disponor's estate would have exceeded the value of the property had the disponor actually disposed of the property, it appears that a charge can be imposed only on the value of the property in respect of which the individual has ceased to reserve a benefit, not on the amount of the diminution. Assuming the deemed PET is valued on the basis of the actual property in question, there may be a death bed advantage in releasing the property subject to a reservation where that otherwise would obtain a high value by being aggregated with other property in the ownership of the taxpayer (e.g. a private company shareholding).

Excluded property

5–41   As was explained at para.2–36, a disposition of excluded property does not normally give rise to a charge to IHT, because the legislation provides that no account is taken of the value of excluded property which ceases to form part of a person's estate.[44] Thus, a gift of excluded property does not normally diminish the value of a person's estate and so does not normally constitute a transfer of value. Further, HMRC now accept that ceasing to reserve a benefit in excluded property does not constitute a PET under FA 1986 s.102(4), as the excluded property rules take precedence over s.102(4) so that there is no potential charge.[45] See further para.7–11 below.

Discharge of non-deductible liability

5–42   The second case in which a person is deemed to make a PET occurs when he pays or applies money or money's worth in or towards satisfying or reducing a debt which he has incurred or an encumbrance which he has created and which s.103 of the

---

[44] IHTA 1984 s.3(2).
[45] HMRC Inheritance Tax Manual para.14396.

Finance Act 1986[46] would prevent from being deductible from his estate immediately before he died. Section 103(5) provides that in such a case the individual is to be treated as having at that time made a PET equal in value to the money or money's worth so paid or applied. The purpose and effect of this provision is best shown by an example.

Assume X gives £10,000 to Y and Y lends £5,000 of this back to X. Two years later X repays Y. Section 103(2) prevents the £5,000 debt X owes to Y from being taken into account in valuing X's estate immediately before he dies, but this does not prevent it from being taken into account in valuing his estate immediately before he repays Y. That being the case, the repayment by X does not diminish the value of his estate and, in the absence of provision to the contrary, no charge to tax would arise. Section 103(5), in order to protect the charge that would arise on X's death if the liability were still outstanding at that time, accordingly provides that the repayment constitutes a PET by him. It may, of course, still be to X's advantage to discharge his indebtedness because, if he survives the repayment by seven years, he will have avoided the effects of s.103 altogether. Even if he does not do so, his position may be improved if he survives the repayment by more than three years.   **5–43**

Pre-March 22, 2006 contracts of life insurance

Section 46A (added by Finance Act 2006) provides that the payment of premiums in respect of life assurance policies taken out before March 22, 2006, and held in a life interest settlement created before that day, will be treated as potentially exempt transfers (if they would otherwise be transfers of value made by an individual). The policy must have been held in the settlement since March 22, 2006, on life interest trusts qualifying for protection as a pre-March 22, 2006 interest in possession, or as a transitional serial interest, or both; and no amendment to the policy which increases the benefits payable or extends the term is allowed, unless it is made by an exercise of rights applying under the policy terms in force immediately before March 22, 2006.   **5–44**

Similarly, s.46B treats the payment of premiums held in former accumulation and maintenance trusts, that on or after March 22, 2006 qualify as an 18–25 trust, an outright at 18 trust, or a bereaved minor's trust, as a PET if the payment would otherwise be a transfer of value made by an individual. The settlement must have been in existence on March 22, 2006 and the policy taken out before then; throughout the period since then the policy must have been held in the settlement and either s.71 or s.71A or s.71D applies, and there has been no variation to the policy terms except as set out in para.5–44 above.   **5–45**

It is worth noting that the terms of these two sections appear to override the concerns about indirect gifts noted at paras 5–23–5–26 above. If the settlor of a pre-March 22, 2006 accumulation and maintenance trust holding a life policy were now to pay the premiums direct to the insurance company, s.46B(5) states that it will be a PET, if it is not exempt as normal expenditure, since the estate of the donor is diminished and therefore it must be a transfer of value. This is in contrast to the position prior to the   **5–46**

---

[46] See paras 25–92 and following.

changes made in 2006, when such a payment direct to the insurance company would not qualify as a PET due to the restrictions on indirect gifts (see para.5–26 above).

V. REPORTING

5–47   There is no duty to report the making of a PET: a duty to report will arise only if the transferor dies within the following seven years so that the transfer becomes chargeable.[47] No machinery therefore exists for agreeing the value transferred by a PET and, giving that it is this "frozen" value which will usually be taxed in the event of the transferor dying within seven years,[48] this may give rise to practical problems. It is accordingly desirable that a PET should be fully documented when made and, in appropriate cases, a professional valuation obtained, although this valuation may eventually be disputed by HMRC. In cases where the PET is also a chargeable disposal for CGT purposes, and the gain that would otherwise be subject to charge is held over as a result of an election under TCGA 1992 s.165, valuations will have to be agreed with HMRC but this may not help in computing any subsequent IHT charge since CGT is not charged on the basis of the loss suffered by the disponor.

VI. FAILED PETs

5–48   The IHT consequences when the transferor dies within seven years after making a PET—so that the PET "fails"—are considered in the next chapter. The advantages of insuring against this eventuality are also discussed.

[47] See para.29–07.
[48] See para.5–02.

CHAPTER 6

CHARGEABLE LIFETIME TRANSFERS

I. INTRODUCTION

This chapter is concerned with the computation of IHT on chargeable lifetime **6–01** transfers and, as such, is divided into four sections. The first section (Pts III–V) explains the rules for determining the amount on which tax is chargeable, i.e. on the *value transferred* by a chargeable transfer.[1] Consideration is given to the distinction between the value transferred by a transfer of value and the value transferred by a chargeable transfer, the reliefs given to the value transferred by a transfer of value, the place of exemptions in determining the amount on which tax is charged and the

---

[1] IHTA 1984 s.1.

181

requirement, in certain circumstances, to "gross up" in order to arrive at the relevant value transferred. The second section (Pts VI and VII) is concerned with the calculation of the tax. The section begins by explaining the cumulation principle, and then considers how the rate structure operates in relation to lifetime transfers which attract an immediate charge, lifetime transfers which attract a supplementary charge and, finally, failed PETs. The third section (Pts VIII and IX) deals with various miscellaneous matters and the fourth (Pts X–XVI) with planning.

6–02   The Finance Act 2006 contained a number of significant changes to the IHT treatment of trusts. These changes, which are covered in detail in Chapters 10–24, have a considerable impact on trusts created both before and after 2006, whether created during the settlor's lifetime or arising on death. In the context of chargeable lifetime transfers, it is important to be aware of the impact of the changes in determining which lifetime transfers to trusts are chargeable. In essence, the ability to make PETs to most types of trusts has been lost, except in a small number of very specific scenarios.

It is also important to emphasise that, while the Finance Act 2006 affects which lifetime transfers to a trust are chargeable to IHT, it does not change the way in which tax is charged on a chargeable transfer. It also does not affect the IHT treatment of outright gifts as opposed to gifts to a trust.

II. OVERVIEW

6–03   It will be helpful, before considering the detailed provisions, for readers to have a general overview of how tax is charged on lifetime transfers. As is mentioned, there are two main considerations—the amount on which tax is charged and the rate at which it is charged. As will be seen below, there are, strictly speaking, only two rates of tax, i.e. the nil rate and the 40 per cent rate. The legislation does provide, however, that, in relation to lifetime transfers, only half the 40 per cent rate is applicable, and accordingly, in this book, a distinction is made between the "death rates", i.e. the nil rate and the 40 per cent rate, and the "lifetime rates", i.e. the nil rate and the 20 per cent rate.

The basic rules

6–04   The legislation effectively establishes three kinds of chargeable lifetime transfers —invulnerable lifetime transfers, vulnerable lifetime transfers and failed PETs.

Invulnerable lifetime transfers

6–05   The first kind of chargeable lifetime transfer is a transfer of value which is chargeable when it is made and which the transferor survives by at least seven years. Such a transfer is chargeable only at the time when it is made, only at the lifetime rates then in force and only on the value then transferred. There is no question of any further tax being chargeable or of the transferor's cumulative total being retrospectively affected. Such a transfer is referred to by the authors as an "invulnerable lifetime transfer".

Vulnerable lifetime transfers

6–06 The second kind of chargeable lifetime transfer is a transfer of value which is chargeable when it is made but which the transferor does not survive by at least seven years—referred to by the authors as a "vulnerable lifetime transfer". Here the treatment is more complicated:

(1) *Initial charge*: such a transfer is initially charged at the lifetime rates then in force on the value then transferred.
(2) *Supplementary charge*: on the transferor's death, tax is recharged at the full death rates then in force or, if the transferor has survived the transfer by more than three years, at a percentage thereof (see taper relief, discussed at para. 6–09), on the value transferred at the time of the transfer, but subject to any clawback of agricultural relief or business relief,[2] credit being given for any tax previously paid.[3] Revaluation relief[4] is given in the usual way in calculating the tax due. This second charge is referred to in this chapter as "the supplementary charge".
(3) *Cancellation of charge*: it may be that the tax previously paid exceeds the supplementary charge, e.g. because substantial taper relief is available. In that case no supplementary charge is imposed, but there is no refund of the tax previously paid.
(4) *Cumulative total*: the transferor's cumulative total is unaffected by any clawback of agricultural relief or business relief (see para.6–21 below).

Failed PETs

6–07 The third kind of chargeable lifetime transfer is a transfer of value which is a PET when it is made but which the transferor fails to survive by at least seven years—referred to by the authors as a "failed PET":

(1) *No initial charge*: no tax is charged when such a transfer is made.
(2) *Death charge*: tax is charged on the death of the transferor at the full death rates then in force[5] or, if the transferor has survived the transfer by more than three years, at a percentage thereof (see taper relief, discussed at para.6–09), on the value transferred at the time of the transfer, but subject to any clawback of agricultural relief or business relief.[6] Revaluation relief[7] is given in the usual way in calculating the tax due.
(3) *Cumulative total*: in contrast to the position where the transfer is a vulnerable lifetime transfer, the transferor's cumulative total is adjusted to take account of

[2] See paras 6–21 and 26–101 and following and paras 26–157 and following.
[3] IHTA 1984 s.7(2), (4) and (5). The credit arises because s.7(4) cancels out the earlier charge imposed by s.7(2) if the s.7(4) charge exceeds the earlier charge.
[4] See paras 6–38 and 25–109 and following.
[5] Unless the death rates when the transfer was made were lower; see para.6–45.
[6] See paras 6–21, 26–101 and following and paras 26–151 and following.
[7] See paras 6–38 and 25–109 and following.

any clawback of agricultural relief or business relief (see para.6–21 below). This will at the very least affect the transferor's cumulative total on his death and may also have a knock-on effect on lifetime transfers which he made after making the PET, possibly causing a recalculation of IHT due in respect of past events.[8] In this respect the failure of a transferor to survive a PET by at least seven years can have much more serious implications than failure to survive a vulnerable lifetime transfer by that period.

Relevant value transferred

6–08   As was just noted, where a supplementary charge is imposed on a vulnerable lifetime transfer or tax is charged on a failed PET, the charge is imposed on the value originally transferred by the transfer in question, but subject to any clawback of agricultural and/ or business relief and to any claim to revaluation relief. For convenience, the value transferred on which the supplementary charge is imposed or by reference to which the tax on a failed PET is charged will, in this chapter, be called the "relevant value transferred", which term means the original value transferred as affected by any such clawback or claim. So far as a claim for revaluation relief is concerned, note that although the tax charge is computed on the reduced value transferred, it is the original value transferred which remains in the cumulative total of the transferor.

Taper relief on rates

6–09   As was mentioned above, the legislation provides, in relation to the supplementary charge on vulnerable lifetime transfers and the charge if a PET fails, that tax is charged at the full death rates only if the transferor fails to survive the transfer by more than three years. If he survives it by more than three but less than seven years, the tax is charged at a tapering percentage of the death rates. The position[9] is as follows:

Years between transfer and death	Appropriate percentage
3 or less than 3	100
more than 3, up to 4	80
more than 4, up to 5	60
more than 5, up to 6	40
more than 6, up to 7	20

No taper relief on cumulation

6–10   Note that taper relief is given only in respect of the rate at which tax is charged. The seven-year cumulation rule is not subject to any taper relief. The value transferred by a transfer either cumulates or does not cumulate, and a transferor who dies just one day before the time when he would have survived a transfer by seven years cannot contend

---

[8] See paras 6–64 and following.
[9] IHTA 1984 s.7(4). The further charge is imposed in respect of a vulnerable lifetime transfer only if it produces a higher charge to tax than that imposed when the transfer was made: s.7(5).

that only a portion of the value transferred by that transfer should form part of his cumulative total.

THE VALUE TRANSFERRED

III. THE BASIC DISTINCTION

As we have seen, s.1 provides that where there is a chargeable transfer the value **6–11** transferred by that transfer is the amount on which tax is charged. The legislation does not in terms specify how this amount is to be computed. Rather, it specifies (in s.3(1)) how the value transferred by a *transfer of value* is to be computed. The fact that s.2(1) provides that a chargeable transfer is any transfer of value made by an individual that is not an exempt transfer means that, since no tax is charged on the exempt portion of a transfer of value, the value transferred by a transfer of value may be more than the value transferred by a chargeable transfer.

To make matters more complicated, the effect of certain provisions in s.5 is that, in computing the value transferred by a chargeable transfer, account may have to be taken of the fact that the transferor bears the tax on the transfer. The result is that a distinction must be drawn between the value transferred by a transfer of value and the value transferred by a chargeable transfer. This distinction is considered in more detail in the following discussion, which begins by examining the rules which govern the computation of the value transferred by a transfer of value.

IV. THE VALUE TRANSFERRED BY A TRANSFER OF VALUE

The rules for computing the value transferred by a transfer of value differ according **6–12** to whether the transfer is an actual or a notional one. In the case of an actual transfer, regard is had to the reduction that the transfer occasions in the value of the transferor's estate before taking into account any exemptions and before any grossing-up. Where the transfer is a notional one, regard is had (again, before taking account of any exemptions) to the specific value mentioned in the legislation, except where the transfer is made under s.94(1), in which case regard is had to the reduction in the value of the company's estate.

There is never any requirement to "gross up" a transfer of value. This follows from the fact that the requirement to gross up in the case of an actual transfer derives from the transferor bearing the IHT on the transfer, and IHT is charged on chargeable transfers, not on transfers of value. That being the case, no requirement to gross up can arise in respect of an actual transfer of value. So far as transfers of value treated as having been made under s.94(1) are concerned, the value transferred by such transfers is grossed up only for purposes of determining the value transferred by the chargeable transfer (if any) in question. This is discussed at para.2–87.

Once the value transferred by an actual or a notional transfer has been computed, it may be reduced by certain reliefs available to transfers of value generally; this is considered below.

Actual transfers

Where the transfer is an actual transfer of value, i.e. one made by a disposition, s.3(1) **6–13** provides that the value transferred is the amount by which the value of the transferor's

185

estate immediately after the disposition is less than it would be "but for" the disposition. Strictly, therefore, it is not the property actually transferred which forms the value transferred. Instead, the proper procedure is to compare the value of the transferor's estate before the transfer with the value of his estate thereafter: the difference is normally the value transferred by the transfer in question. This is subject to two qualifications. First, by s.5(4), the fact that, as a result of the transfer, the transferor has become liable for CGT, income tax or any other tax or duty is left out of account. Thus, if X gives Y a diamond ring with the result that X's estate is worth £40,000 less and X pays CGT of £10,000 on the gift, he makes a transfer of value of £40,000, not £50,000. Secondly, the use of the words "but for" in s.3(1) implies that only changes in value which are caused by the disposition fall to be brought into account. Accordingly, if part of the diminution is purely coincidental, that part will be left out of account. Conversely, any coincidental increases in the value of the transferor's estate will also be left out of account.

It may be that the diminution in the value of the estate exceeds—perhaps substantially—the value of the property disposed of. For example, if X owns 51 of the 100 shares in a company and gives away two of them his remaining 49 shares will be valued on a minority basis, with the result that the diminution in the value of his estate will exceed the value of the two shares he gave away. This is known as "the consequential loss rule": for a fuller discussion, see para.2–33.

Notional transfers

6–14   Notional transfers are made on the happening of three events, i.e.:

(1) on the termination (in certain circumstances) during a person's life of an interest in possession to which he was beneficially entitled;
(2) on a close company making a transfer of value, in which case the value transferred is apportioned to the participators in the company; and
(3) on a person's death.

Special rules govern the computation of the value transferred by each of these kinds of notional transfer.

Termination of an interest in possession

6–15   Section 52 provides that in certain circumstances a person is treated as making a transfer of value on the termination of all or part of an interest in possession, in which case the value transferred by that transfer is equal to the value of the property in which his interest subsisted. Regard is thus had to the value of the underlying assets, not to the value of the person's interest in possession. This means that if X is entitled to an interest in possession in £100,000 until he marries, on marrying X will make a transfer of value of £100,000, i.e. regard is had to the value of the underlying property, not to the value of X's interest per se and that value is computed without reference to assets which X owns absolutely.[10] As will be seen below, this can in certain circumstances create opportunities for tax planning.

[10] See para.6–18.

Until March 22, 2006, s.52(1) applied to any lifetime termination of an interest in possession. It should be noted, however, that with effect from March 22, 2006 s.52(1) only applies where either:

(a) X became beneficially entitled to his interest in possession before March 22, 2006; or

(b) (if he became entitled to it on or after that date) his interest is an immediate post-death interest, a disabled person's interest or a transitional serial interest.[11]

The termination of X's interest in possession will therefore *not* give rise to a deemed transfer under s.52(1) in other circumstances, i.e. where X became beneficially entitled to his interest in possession on or after March 22, 2006 and his interest is not an immediate post-death interest, a disabled person's interest or a transitional serial interest.[12] The reason for this is that in those circumstances the relevant property regime will apply and X will not be treated for IHT purposes as beneficially entitled to the property in which his interest subsists.

Close company transfers

Under s.94(1) the value transferred when a transfer of value is made by a close company is apportioned to the participators in the company. In computing the value transferred, regard is had to the diminution the transfer occasioned in the value of the company's estate. Against this amount is set off any increase in the value of the estate of the participator in question.[13] **6–16**

Death

Where a person is treated under s.4(1) as having made a transfer of value immediately before he died, the value transferred by that transfer is specified by s.4(1) to be equal to the value of his estate at that time. Regard is thus had to the value of a deceased person's estate immediately before he died, not to its value on or after his death. What property is comprised in a person's estate immediately before he dies, how that property is valued and the computation of tax on death is discussed in Chapter 8. **6–17**

Planning

The fact that the legislation provides different rules for determining the value transferred for different kinds of transfers of value may open up planning possibilities in certain circumstances. Assume, e.g. a company in which there are 300 issued shares. A owns 100 shares outright and has a pre-March 22, 2006 interest in possession in the remaining 200 shares.[14] Clearly, on his death he will be treated as though he owned all **6–18**

[11] See s.52(2A).
[12] However, it may trigger an exit charge under s.65 if the property in which his interest subsisted ceases to be relevant property as a result of the termination: see Ch.15.
[13] See paras 2–93 and following.
[14] As noted above, this type of planning will generally not be available if A became entitled to his interest in possession on or after March 22, 2006.

300 shares. Equally clearly, if during his life he makes a transfer of any of the 100 shares comprised in his free estate, the diminution in his estate will be calculated on the basis that the shares transferred formed part of a holding comprised of 300 shares. But what is the position if A disposes of his interest in, e.g. 50 of the shares held on trust? Any argument that there has been a transfer of value equal in amount to the difference between 300 and 250 shares is plainly wrong, because the value transferred under s.52 is the value of the property in which the assigned interest subsisted.

HMRC originally argued that, in valuing the 50 shares, account should be taken of the 100 shares in A's free estate, so that the 50 shares fell to be valued as part of a holding of 300 shares. However, since April 1990 HMRC have accepted that this is wrong and that the 50 shares fall to be valued in isolation from the 100 shares in A's free estate.[15] Having said that, note that although the shares in which A's interest in possession subsist are valued in isolation from the shares in his free estate:

(a) in determining the value of the shares in A's free estate, regard will be had to the shares in which he has an interest in possession; and
(b) in determining whether agricultural relief or business relief is available on the trust shares, regard will be had to the shares in A's free estate.

One further consideration remains, namely do the 50 shares in which A's interest in possession subsisted prior to the assignment fall to be valued in isolation from the other 150 shares in which his interest subsisted, or as part of a holding of 200 shares? The authors' view is that the shares fall to be valued as part of the holding of 200 shares, under s.52(4)(a).

The following additional points should be noted in relation to the termination of an interest in possession on or after March 22, 2006:

(1) The IHT consequences of the termination of A's interest in possession will depend on whether or not the trust itself then terminates. If it does, the transfer may be a PET by A. However, if the trust continues, A will in principle be treated as making a chargeable transfer to a relevant property trust.
(2) The reservation of benefit rules (see Chapter 7) were amended by the Finance Act 2006 so that they now apply to a lifetime termination of an interest in possession even if the person entitled to the interest in possession (in this case A) does not put the termination into effect or consent to it.

It should also be noted that the *appointment* of an interest in possession out of a discretionary trust on or after March 22, 2006 no longer has any IHT consequences unless the interest falls within s.59 as a "qualifying interest in possession" (see Chapter 12).

Reliefs

6–19   In two cases, the legislation makes provision to reduce the value transferred by a transfer of value, whether it is actual or notional. First, the value transferred may be

---

[15] See HMRC Manuals IHTM4093. HMRC have reserved their position where the Ramsay principle or the associated operations provisions are relevant.

reduced by agricultural or business relief. Secondly, the value transferred may be reduced by certain incidental expenses incurred by the transferee.

Agricultural relief and business relief

Sections 115–124C afford relief to the extent that the value transferred by a transfer **6–20** of value is attributable to the "agricultural value" of "agricultural property". The relief takes the form of a 50 per cent or a 100 per cent reduction of so much of the value transferred as qualifies for relief. Sections 103–114 afford relief in certain circumstances to the value transferred by a transfer of value to the extent that that value is attributable to the value of any "relevant business property". It may be that the same transfer qualifies for both agricultural relief and business relief. In that case, agricultural relief is given in priority to business relief. Both reliefs are discussed in detail in Chapter 26. Note that the reliefs do not reduce the value of the property concerned. This may be important for CGT, as well as IHT purposes; see para.25–34.

Clawback of reliefs

The Finance Act 1986 introduced provisions affecting the position where a trans- **6–21** feror dies within seven years of making a transfer in respect of which agricultural or business relief is available and on which, by reason of his death, tax is due, either in the form of the supplementary charge or because the transfer was a PET which has failed. In determining how much tax is payable in such a case the value transferred by the transfer of value in question is treated as not having been reduced by the relevant relief unless various conditions are satisfied. These conditions are discussed in detail at paras 26–101 and following and paras 26–157 and following. One of the main conditions is that the donee must have owned the gifted property[16] throughout the period beginning with the gift and ending with the earlier of the death of the transferor and the transferee. Assume, e.g., that X makes a PET to Y of shares qualifying for agricultural relief. Two years later Y sells the shares. Eighteen months after the sale X dies. The transfer to Y will thus have become chargeable. Although agricultural relief will initially have been available to the transferor, that relief will be clawed back because Y did not own the shares throughout the period beginning with the gift and ending with X's death. Or assume that A settles on discretionary trusts shares qualifying for business relief. Five years later A dies. At the time of his death the trustees still own the shares, but they have ceased to be relevant business property in their hands, e.g. because the company has become listed on the Stock Exchange. There is no need to reopen the calculations on which the original charge was based, but in determining how much additional tax is payable under the supplementary charge the value transferred by the transfer of value is treated as not being reduced by business relief.

It is important to note that the clawback operates in relation to transfers of value which are chargeable transfers ab initio for the purpose only of determining how much additional tax is payable under the supplementary charge. Thus, the amount that goes into the transferor's cumulative total will be the value transferred reduced by the business and/or the agricultural relief available at the time of the transfer, *not* the value

---

[16] The ability to pay by instalments tax due by reason of a transferor's dying within seven years of making a transfer may also be lost; see paras 29–100 and following.

transferred after the clawback of any relief, with the result that there is a kind of "double standard".[17]

Incidental expenses

6–22   By s.164, any expenses, e.g. legal fees, which are borne by the transferor in connection with a transfer of value (except his liability to IHT) are left out of account in determining the value transferred by the transfer in question. Where such incidental expenses are borne by the transferee (which would include the trustees of a settlement to which property is being transferred), they are taken as reducing the value transferred by the transfer. Relief for CGT borne by the transferee may be available under s.165 against the value transferred by the chargeable transfer which the transfer of value in question comprises; this is discussed below.

Interaction of reliefs

6–23   It is not clear from the legislation whether agricultural relief and business relief are to be given before the deduction of incidental expenses or vice versa. It is to the taxpayer's advantage if agricultural and/or business relief is given first, since if that is the case, the amount which qualifies for the percentage reduction is greater. HMRC accept that incidental expenses may be brought into account last: see IHTM24001 and IHTM25131.

V. THE VALUE TRANSFERRED BY A CHARGEABLE TRANSFER

6–24   As was noted above, the value transferred by a chargeable transfer may differ in two respects from the value transferred by a transfer of value, i.e. the value transferred by a transfer of value is the value transferred by the transfer in question:

(1) before taking any exemptions into account; and
(2) before any grossing-up that may be necessary.

Thus, the first step in computing how much of the value transferred by a transfer of value is transferred by the chargeable transfer which it comprises, is to reduce the value transferred by that transfer of value by any available exemptions. This follows from the fact that, by s.2(1), an exempt transfer is not a chargeable transfer. Accordingly, if X makes an actual transfer of value of £100,000 to trustees of a discretionary trust, he may be entitled to reduce the value transferred by his annual exemption. If the transfer is an actual one and X bears the tax, or if the transfer is one made by virtue of s.94(1), it will then be necessary to gross up the value transferred. As a last step, certain reliefs given against the value transferred by a chargeable transfer may fall to be taken into

---

[17] See HMRC Manuals IHTM14579.

account; if they do, the value transferred by the chargeable transfer in question will be reduced accordingly.

Exemptions

The exemptions available to actual and notional transfers are discussed in Chapter 3 **6–25** and their availability to transfers of value capable of being PETs is discussed at paras 5–05 and following. It will be recalled that the basic rule is that exemptions are applied first, and only so much of the value transferred as is not covered by an exemption is a PET.

Grossing-up: actual transfers

Perhaps the most controversial aspect of CTT when it first appeared on the scene was **6–26** the requirement that in certain circumstances tax had to be charged on tax. The satisfaction of this requirement involved a procedure known as "grossing-up". The general reaction to this requirement was that it was unfair, and to the procedure that it was bewildering, involved higher mathematics and would send us all to an early grave. In fact, this reaction, though understandable, was misfounded: the requirement is fair, and the procedure, once grasped, is fairly straightforward.

The requirement

The grossing-up requirement derives from the interaction of three provisions. The **6–27** first, s.3(1), was discussed above: it provides that the value transferred by an actual transfer of value is the amount by which the transfer diminishes the value of the transferor's estate. This diminution is arrived at by comparing the value of his estate before the transfer with the value of his estate after the transfer. The other two provisions are found in s.5 and are concerned with the valuation of a person's estate. By s.5(3), in determining the value of a transferor's estate at any time his liabilities at that time must be taken into account; and, by s.5(4):

> "The liabilities to be taken into account in determining the value of a transferor's estate immediately after a transfer of value include his liability for tax on the value transferred but not his liability (if any) for any other tax or duty resulting from the transfer . . . ".

The result of these three provisions is that when a person makes an actual chargeable transfer[18] on which he bears the IHT his estate is reduced by two distinct amounts. First, it is reduced by the amount of the chargeable transfer before any grossing-up; for case of reference, this amount will be referred to as the "gift". Secondly, it is reduced by the tax on the gift. This means that the transferor must pay tax on two amounts; first, he must pay tax on the gift and then, since his estate has also been diminished by that tax, he must also pay tax on that tax. This, alas, is not the end. Since the transferor's estate has also been diminished by that tax, i.e. by the tax on the tax, he must also pay tax on that tax, and so on. This process is not never-ending, however, since, as a

---

[18] Since he will not make a chargeable transfer at the time he makes a PET, no grossing-up is required; see para.6–35.

moment's reflection shows, each subsequent portion of tax is but a fraction of the one that preceded it. The amount of tax on which tax is due thus grows steadily smaller until a figure is reached on which it is pointless to charge tax.

6–28   Given that the payment of IHT on a chargeable transfer by the transferor will reduce his estate, the question arises whether grossing-up will invariably be required in these circumstances. However, IHTM14541–14542 suggests that grossing-up will be required in the following circumstances:

"— the account or correspondence states that the transferor is to bear the tax
— at the time of the transfer the transferor enters into a binding agreement to pay the tax
— after the transfer, the transferor pays the tax (even an instalment) direct to HMRC, or
— the tax is paid from the transferor's death estate"

but that in other situations the transferor's payment of IHT can, in principle, be treated as either a PET or a separate chargeable transfer.

Fairness

6–29   The charging of tax on tax is, in fact, perfectly fair, and is done only to preserve HMRC's position, not to improve it. This is shown by the following example, which assumes for simplicity's sake that tax is charged at a constant rate of 10 per cent on all gifts. Assume that on January 1, 2008, X had an estate worth £1,000,000, and that he died on January 5. On his death, tax would have been charged as follows:

$$10\% \times £1,000,000 = £100,000$$

If, on the other hand, X had made a gift on January 2, of, say, £200,000, then, in the absence of grossing-up, tax would have been charged at 10 per cent on the £200,000, with the result that £20,000 would have been paid to HMRC, and X's estate would have been worth:

		£
		1,000,000
Less gift		200,000
		800,000
Less tax		20,000
		780,000

On X's death on January 5, tax would have been charged as follows:

$$10\% \times £780,000 = £78,000$$

The result would thus have been that, as a result of X's lifetime gift, HMRC would have collected from X a total of £98,000 (£20,000 plus £78,000), i.e. £2,000 less tax than if X had died without having made the gift. Grossing-up prevents this, since it means that on his lifetime gift X pays tax as follows:

£			£	
200,000.00	@ 10% =		20,000.00	Tax on gift
20,000.00	@ 10% =		2,000.00 }	
2,000.00	@ 10% =		200.00 }	
200.00	@ 10% =		20.00 }	tax on gift
20.00	@ 10% =		2.00 }	
2.00	@ 10% =		0.20 }	
.20	@ 10% =		0.02	
			22,222.22	total tax

The value of X's estate after the gift is thus £777,777.78, with the result that if he died without making further gifts, tax would be charged as follows:

$$£777,777.78 @ 10\% = £77,777.78$$

When this is added to the tax previously collected, it is seen that the effect of grossing-up is that HMRC collect the same amount of tax that they would have collected had X not made the lifetime gift:

£22,222.22 tax during lifetime
£77,777.78 tax on death

£100,000.00 total tax

Procedure

Prior to the changes made by the Finance Act 1988, applicable to chargeable **6–30** transfers made on or after March 15, 1988, IHT was charged at progressive rates. The grossing-up procedure was therefore somewhat complex and in practice recourse was had to special grossing-up tables. This procedure is fully analysed in the second edition of this book at paras 5–17 and following. With the reduction in the IHT rates to two—a nil rate band on chargeable transfers up to, currently, £325,000[19] and (for lifetime transfers) a 20 per cent rate thereafter—grossing-up is now straightforward, as the following examples show. In these cases so much of the value transferred as is chargeable to tax at 20 per cent is multiplied by

$$\frac{100}{100 - 20} = \frac{100}{80} = \frac{5}{4}$$

EXAMPLE 1

A, who has exhausted his nil rate band, makes a chargeable lifetime transfer of £40,000, on which he bears the IHT. As the rate of tax applicable is 20 per cent, £40,000 is grossed up to £50,000 (£40,000 × 100/80). Accordingly, the tax payable is

---

[19] The nil rate band was increased to £312,000 with effect from April 6, 2008 and applies for the 2008–2009 tax year. The nil rate band is currently £325,000 and will remain at this level for transfers from April 6, 2009–April 5, 2015.

£10,000. Alternatively, the computation could simply gross up the tax payable as follows:

$$\text{tax on £40,000 at 20 per cent} = £8,000$$

$$\text{£8,000 grossed up at } \frac{5}{4} = £10,000$$

EXAMPLE 2

Assume that A makes a chargeable transfer of £100,000 at a time when £60,000 of his nil rate band is unused. The first £60,000 is thus taxed at the nil rate, while the remaining £40,000 of the chargeable transfer is grossed up at the 20 per cent rate as above to £50,000, with the result that the grossed up chargeable transfer made by A becomes £110,000 (£60,000 + £50,000).

EXAMPLE 3

A makes a chargeable transfer within his unused nil rate band. Since the transfer is subject to tax at the nil rate, no tax is due and there is no question of grossing-up.

6–31   Where grossing-up applies, the instalment option under s.227 will not be available (see s.227(1)(b) and IHTM14542).

Tax borne by transferee

6–32   It should be obvious from the foregoing that where the transferee of an actual transfer of value bears the tax, there is no question of grossing-up, since in that case the value of the transferor's estate is not reduced by any liability to pay tax.

Grossing-up: notional transfers

6–33   Strictly speaking, only one kind of notional transfer, that made under s.94(1) in consequence of an actual transfer of value by a close company, needs to be grossed up.[20] The fact that no grossing-up is required where the notional transfer is made under s.52(1) on the termination of an interest or under s.4(1) on a person's death follows from the fact that, as we have seen, both those provisions specify the value transferred by the transfer of value in question, with the result that the consequential loss rule in s.3(1) is overridden. This, of course, is what one would expect; otherwise, on death one could have been liable (when the rates exceeded 50 per cent) for an amount greater than

[20] See para.2–87.

the value of one's estate, while on the termination of an interest in possession, the tax could exceed the value of the property in which the interest subsisted.

De facto grossing-up

The legislation specifies the value transferred by a transfer made under s.52(1) as being equal to the value of the property in which the transferor's interest in possession subsisted. At first glance, this suggests that where a person makes such a transfer he should bear the tax on that transfer, since he would appear to be able to do so without having to suffer any grossing-up: the tax he paid would thus constitute a tax-free gift to the beneficiary, who would be spared having to pay any tax.[21] This is true up to a point, but other provisions preclude any real tax saving.

To begin with, s.201(1)(b) provides that where such a transfer is made, one of the persons liable for the tax is:

> "any person entitled (whether beneficially or not) to an interest in possession in the settled property . . . "

It is not entirely clear whether this means any person with an interest in the property before the transfer, or any person interested in the property after the transfer. If, as is thought to be the case,[22] it means the person entitled to the interest after the transfer, the transferor is not liable to pay the tax; therefore if he pays the tax he will, in effect, make a gift of the tax to the transferee, whose liability for the tax he will have discharged. In so far as this gift is not covered by any exemptions that may be available to the transferor such as the annual exemption, it will constitute a transfer by him.[23] If, as would presumably be the case, the transferor also bears the tax on this transfer, this transfer will have to be grossed up, with the result that there is de facto grossing-up. Alternatively, if the person entitled in s.201(1)(b) means any person entitled to an interest in the property before the transfer, the transferor is liable for tax, with the result that his payment of the tax does not of itself constitute a chargeable transfer. But, under s.212(2), he is entitled to a charge over the settled property in respect of which he paid the tax, and if he does not exercise his right to this charge, he will make a notional disposition under s.3(3) at the latest time he could have done so, with the result that, again, there may be de facto grossing-up. The one advantage if this is the case is that it would be possible for the transferor each year to release such a portion of the debt owed to him as was covered by his annual exemptions, with the result that he never makes a chargeable transfer. In appropriate cases, the normal expenditure out of income exemption might also be available, and the associated operations provisions should not affect this.[24]

PETs not grossed up

When an individual makes a PET no tax is chargeable at that time, and consequently there is no question of grossing up the value transferred at that stage. In the authors'

6–34

6–35

---

[21] HMRC's view, according to HMRC Manuals IHTM14546, is that no grossing-up is required for a s.52(1) transfer unless the s.52(1) charge is the result of a partition of the settled fund, in which case "if it is a term of the partition agreement that the tax shall be paid out of the property remaining in settlement, the claim extends to the property required to meet the tax".

[22] See para.29–59.

[23] It will, in appropriate circumstances, be a PET.

[24] See para.9–27.

view, there is also no question of grossing up the value transferred if that transfer subsequently proves to be a chargeable transfer and this is so even though the transferor has directed, or indeed bound, his personal representatives to pay such tax as subsequently may prove chargeable.[25] The transferor is not among the persons liable for the extra tax, and there is thus no possibility of taking into account any liability for IHT in computing the amount by which the transferor diminished the value of his estate.[26]

Reliefs

6–36   In two cases, the legislation makes provision to reduce the value transferred by a chargeable transfer after grossing-up, whether the transfer is an actual or a notional one. First, the value transferred may be reduced by the amount of certain taxes borne by the transferee. Secondly, where the transferor makes a lifetime gift and dies within seven years of making the transfer, the value transferred will be reduced in certain circumstances if the value of the property previously transferred has fallen in value since the making of the lifetime gift.

Taxes borne by the donee

6–37   By s.165(1), where a chargeable transfer involves the disposal of an asset in respect of which a chargeable gain accrues to the transferor (or, in the case of a transfer made under s.52(1), the trustees),[27] the value transferred by that transfer is reduced by so much of the CGT due on the gain as is borne by the donee.[28] Where CGT holdover relief is available, it is important to compare the results of relying on s.165 as against electing for that relief in cases where an onward sale is anticipated and where the effective rate of CGT exceeds the effective rate of IHT.

Revaluation relief

6–38   Section 131 takes account of the fact that the value of property, in respect of which a charge is levied by reason of the transferor dying within seven years of making a transfer, may have fallen in the period between the transfer and the death, and provides that in certain circumstances tax is to be calculated as if the value transferred by the transfer in question was reduced to take account of this fall in value. Provided certain conditions are satisfied, s.131(2) provides that the value transferred is reduced by the fall in market value of the property. The effect of this is that there is a reduction in the

---

[25] Note, however, that the payment of the tax will constitute the payment of a specific free of tax gift, and that gift may have to be grossed up; see para.8–51. In HMRC's view the whole of the lifetime gift should be grossed up in these circumstances.

[26] It is true that s.204(7), by overriding the qualification in s.204(6) concerning the absence of liability for tax attributable to grossing-up, might be taken as suggesting otherwise, but it must be borne in mind that s.204(7) can be relevant only if the transfer was grossed up to begin with. It thus appears relevant only where a person makes a transfer of value which is a chargeable transfer when it is made.

[27] IHTA 1984 s.165(2).

[28] Within the meaning of TCGA 1992 s.282. This reference suggests that s.165 operates only where the donor has failed to pay the CGT within 12 months from the date when the tax becomes payable and the donee has been assessed instead on a grossed-up sum. It is understood that in practice HMRC accept that any arrangement for the donee to pay which is complied with suffices, presumably on the footing that the words "within the meaning of s.282" modify only the word "donee" and not the words "borne by the donee".

supplementary charge payable on death in respect of the chargeable transfer, but note that it does not affect the transferor's cumulative total, nor does it affect the tax originally charged at lifetime rates.[29] If s.131 applies to a failed PET where the asset has reduced in value, the effect of the relief is to reduce the tax payable on the PET but, again, the cumulative total is unaffected and is based on the unrelieved value transferred at the date of transfer.[30]

It may be that the value transferred qualifies for agricultural or business relief (see Chapter 26). In that case, the fall in the market value is reduced by the percentage by which the agricultural or business relief was given.[31] The relief must be claimed by a person liable to pay the tax. No relief is available if the transferred property is tangible moveable property that is a wasting asset. For this purpose, property is a wasting asset if immediately before the transfer it had a predictable useful life, having regard to the purpose of which it is held by the transferor, of not more than 50 years. Plant and machinery are regarded as always coming within this category.[32] Although the relief operates to reduce the value transferred by the transfer in question, it will be convenient to discuss it in detail at the same time as the revaluation reliefs are considered, and the reader is accordingly referred to paras 25–110 and following.

No tapering

As was noted above, and as will be explained more fully below, tapering provisions apply in determining how much tax is payable in respect of a lifetime chargeable transfer. If, for example, X settles property on discretionary trusts and survives the transfer by, say, five years, he will pay less tax[33] than if he had survived it by more than four but less than five years, because, under the tapering provisions, tax will be charged at a smaller percentage than it would have otherwise been charged. No such tapering provisions apply, however, in computing the value transferred by a chargeable transfer.[34]   **6–39**

CALCULATING THE TAX

VI. THE CUMULATION PRINCIPLE

Inheritance tax is a cumulative tax: in order to ascertain the rate or rates that apply to a given transfer, it is necessary to take into account the total of the values transferred by earlier chargeable transfers made by the transferor in the seven-year period ending with the date of the last transfer.[35] Originally all transfers made by the transferor in his lifetime were taken into account without time limit and then between 1981 and 1986 a 10-year cumulation period operated. For all transfers since March 18, 1986, there has been a seven-year cumulation period.   **6–40**

The way the seven-year cumulation rule works is illustrated by the following example. Assume that X makes chargeable transfers of value of £100,000, £200,000,   **6–41**

[29] See HMRC Manuals IHTM14622.
[30] HMRC Manuals IHTM14622.
[31] IHTA 1984 s.131(2A).
[32] IHTA 1984 s.132.
[33] This is subject to any change in the rates of tax.
[34] This contrasts with the position under estate duty, where tapering relief was available in respect of the amount on which tax was charged.
[35] IHTA 1984 s.7(1)(b).

and £300,000 on January 1, 1997, January 1, 1998, and January 3, 2004. In computing the IHT to be charged on the 1998 transfer, A's cumulative total will include the £100,000 transfer made 12 months before. In computing tax on the 2004 transfer it will be necessary to look back over the previous seven years so that A's cumulative total will stand at £200,000, the 1997 transfer of £100,000 having dropped out of his total by that date (i.e. on the seventh anniversary from the date when it was made).

VII. THE RATES OF TAX

6–42 The rates of tax are set out in Sch.1 to the Act. For transfers made between April 6, 2008 and April 5, 2009, the rates are as follows:

Table of Rates of Tax

Portion of value		Rates of tax
Lower limit	Upper limit	Per cent
£	£	
0	312,000	Nil
312,000	–	40

The rates of IHT for transfers made in the 2009–2010 and 2010–2011 tax years will be as follows[36]:

Transfers between April 6, 2009 and April 5, 2010

Portion of value		Rates of tax
Lower limit	Upper limit	Per cent
£	£	
0	325,000	Nil
325,000	–	40

Transfers between April 6, 2010 and April 5, 2011

Portion of value		Rates of tax
Lower limit	Upper limit	Per cent
£	£	
0	350,000	Nil
350,000	–	40

[36] Announced by FA 2006 s.155(1)–(4) and FA 2007 s.4(1) respectively.

It should be noted that ss.8A–8C, introduced by the Finance Act 2008, contain provisions allowing unused nil rate band to be transferred between spouses or civil partners in cases where the second death occurs on or after October 9, 2007. These provisions are described in Chapter 4.

Since 1982 the rates of tax have been linked by what is now s.8 to the Retail Prices **6–43** Index: see para.4–02.

"Death rates" and "lifetime rates"

As was mentioned, the 40 per cent rate applies only to transfers made on death. **6–44** Where lifetime transfers are concerned, only half the 40 per cent rate is applicable, a distinction being made between the "death rates", i.e. the nil rate and the 40 per cent rate, and the "lifetime rates", i.e. the nil rate and the 20 per cent rate.[37] How the rates apply varies according to whether the transfer is an invulnerable lifetime transfer, a vulnerable lifetime transfer or a failed PET.

Change in rates regime

It may be, following a vulnerable lifetime transfer or a PET, that there is a reduction **6–45** in the tax rates. If the transferor dies within seven years of his transfer and after that there is a reduction in rates, tax is charged as if the reduced rates had applied to the transfer.[38] Accordingly, the taxpayer benefits from any reduction in the rates, but does not suffer an increased charge if the rates go up after the relevant transfer. In that event, tax will be charged at the rates in force at the date of the transfer.

Invulnerable lifetime transfers

The position where an invulnerable lifetime transfer is concerned is straightforward. **6–46** Assume, for example, that X, who died in 2008, had, on Christmas Day 1997, settled £228,000 on discretionary trusts, having made no previous chargeable transfers. The first £3,000 of this would have been exempt, with the result that, assuming the trustees bore the IHT on the gift, X would have made a chargeable transfer of £225,000. The tax on this would have been £2,000. (The first £215,000 of the transfer exhausts X's nil rate band at 1997/1998 rates and the remaining £10,000 is subject to tax at a 20 per cent rate.) Assume further that on New Year's Day 1998 X made a gift of £5,000 to a discretionary trust. If it is assumed that the trust bears the tax, X has made a chargeable transfer of £5,000. Having regard to the £225,000 previously transferred by X, the

---

[37] IHTA 1984 s.7(2); see para.6–03.
[38] IHTA 1984 Sch.2 paras 1A and 2.

£5,000 falls within the 20 per cent rate band with the result that £1,000 would be payable in tax.[39]

Vulnerable lifetime transfers

6–47   As was explained at para.6–06, where a vulnerable lifetime transfer is made IHT will be charged at the lifetime rates in force at the time when the transfer was made on the value then transferred. In computing that tax, transfers in the seven preceding years will have been included in the transferor's cumulative total. On his death, tax is charged on the relevant value transferred[40] normally at the full rate of IHT then in force,[41] subject to taper relief, but only if the tax chargeable exceeds that charged when the transfer was originally made. No tax refund is available if the tax charged when the transfer was originally made exceeds that due at the death rates.[42] This means that in most cases the taper ceases to be of value once the transferor has survived the transfer by five years.[43]

EXAMPLE

6–48   The basic calculation and operation of taper relief is illustrated by the following example:

Assume that A settles £400,000 on discretionary trusts in December 2000 (IHT being paid by the trustees). Consider the position if he dies on:

   (i) January 1, 2002;
   (ii) January 1, 2006;
   (iii) January 1, 2008.

The original transfer in 2000 was subject to IHT at half the rates in force during the year 2000–01.

In (i) he dies within three years of that transfer and accordingly a charge at the full tax rates for 2001–02 must be calculated and compared with the tax paid in 2000.

---

[39] In the above example the transfer of £225,000 will have dropped out of X's cumulative total on Christmas Day 2004. X can, of course, give away his nil rate band every seven years. If in the above example X had borne the IHT in the case of the settled gift on Christmas Day, grossing-up would have been necessary so the tax would have become £2,500 and X's chargeable transfer £227,500. In the case of the New Year's Day gift, the tax would be £1,250, X's chargeable transfer £6,250 and his cumulative total at that date £233,750. Note that the £5,000 transfer dropped out of X's cumulative total on New Year's Day 2005. Neither lifetime gift is subject to a further tax charge on X's subsequent death in 2008.

[40] See para.6–08.

[41] See IHTA 1984 Sch.2 paras 1A and 2 in which it is made clear that tax on a failed PET and extra tax on a chargeable lifetime transfer is computed on the rates of tax at the date of death when those rates are less than the rates current at the time when the chargeable transfers were made. In the event of a later increase in rates both transfers would be subject to charge at the rates of tax current when they were made; see para.6–45.

[42] IHTA s.7(5); see para.6–06.

[43] If agricultural and/or business relief is clawed back the taper may be valuable if the transferor survives the transfer by six years.

In (ii) he dies more than five but less than six years after the gift: therefore only 40 per cent of the full amount of tax chargeable at the date of death is to be calculated and compared with the tax paid in 2000.[44]

In (iii) he dies more than seven years after the transfer: therefore no supplementary charge is imposed.

Assuming for simplicity that the current rates of IHT apply throughout this period, the actual tax computations are as follows (assuming that the 2000 transfer was the first chargeable transfer made by A):

(1) IHT on the 2000 chargeable transfer is as follows:
  First £234,000—Nil;
  Remaining £166,000 at 20 per cent = £33,200;
  Total IHT paid by the trustees in 2000–01 is therefore £33,200.
(2) If death occurs within three years on January 1, 2002: tax on a transfer of £400,000 at the then death rates is:
  First £242,000—nil;
  Remaining £158,000 at 40 per cent = £63,200;
  Total IHT on the transfer is therefore £63,200 which, after giving credit for the £33,200 paid in 2000, leaves a further £30,000 to be paid.
(3) If death occurs on January 1, 2006, the calculation is as follows:
  (a) First £275,000 = nil;
  (b) Full IHT at death rates on remaining £125,000 = £50,000 (as above);
  (c) Take 40 per cent (taper relief) of that tax: £50,000 × 40 per cent = £20,000;
  (d) As that sum is less than the £33,200 actually paid in 2000, there is no extra tax to pay (and none of the £33,200 is refunded).

Failed PETs

Where a PET fails, tax is charged on the relevant value transferred,[45] normally by **6–49** reference to the rates in force at the date of the death,[46] having regard to the transferor's

---

[44] Under s.7(2) inter vivos chargeable transfers are taxed at half the table rates except when s.7(4) is applicable. Under s.7(4), transfers made within three years of death are subject to charge at full rates under s.7(1) and transfers made more than three but less than seven years before death at the taper rates (80%; 60%; 40%; 20%). However, s.7(4) will not apply if the tax chargeable under that subsection is less than the tax which would have been chargeable in accordance with s.7(2) if the transferor had not died within seven years of the transfer (this is provided for in s.7(5), to which s.7(4) is expressly made subject). As a result, when taper relief causes the rate of tax on death to fall below the 20% charge imposed at the time when the transfer was originally made, s.7(4) will not normally apply. Note, however, that tax on a failed PET will always fall to be assessed under s.7(4) and s.7(5) will not apply. Further, should tax on a chargeable transfer need to be recomputed because of a prior failed PET (see paras 6–66 and 6–67) then s.7(4) may apply since even allowing for the higher rates of taper relief the resulting tax charge may still be greater than the sum originally paid.

[45] See para.6–08.

[46] See IHTA 1984 Sch.2 paras 1A and 2, in which it is made clear that tax on a failed PET and extra tax on a chargeable lifetime transfer is computed on the rates of tax at the date of death when those rates are less than the rates current at the time when the chargeable transfers were made. In the event of a later increase in rates both transfers would be subject to charge at the rates of tax current when they were made; see para.6–45.

cumulative total at the date when the PET was made (i.e. taking into account the chargeable transfers made by him in the seven years immediately preceding the making of the PET), subject to taper relief.[47]

EXAMPLE

6–50   The following example illustrates the operation of these rules. Assume that in October 2003 Q gave a valuable Ming vase then worth £400,000 to her granddaughter R, thereby making a PET. Q dies in July 2007; R still owns the vase, which by Q's death has fallen in value to £350,000. Assuming that Q has made no other chargeable transfers during her life; ignoring exemptions and reliefs; and assuming that 2003–2004 rates apply throughout, the tax consequences are:

(1) The 2003 transfer was potentially exempt when made. As Q dies within seven years, it becomes a chargeable transfer.
(2) As on Q's death the vase is worth only £350,000, revaluation relief[48] is available and IHT is charged on £350,000.
(3) Tax at the rates current when Q died is:
    First £300,000 = nil
    Remaining £50,000 at 40 per cent = £20,000
    Total IHT = £20,000
(4) Taper relief is available since Q died more than three years after the gift therefore:
$$£20,000 \times 80 \text{ per cent} = £16,000$$

Note that although tax is calculated by reference to the reduced value of the vase, for cumulation purposes the original value transferred (£400,000) is retained.

Planning: beware of premature PETs

6–51   When a PET is made after an earlier chargeable transfer and the transferor dies in the following seven years, tax on that PET will be calculated by including that earlier transfer, if it was made within seven years before the PET, in the transferor's cumulative total. This means that the eventual IHT bill could turn out to be higher than if the PET had never been made.

Assume, e.g. that Y made a chargeable transfer of £275,000 on May 1, 2000, and on May 1, 2005, made a PET of £350,000. He dies after May 1, 2007 (when the 2000 transfer drops out of cumulation) but before May 1, 2008 (when taper relief begins to operate on the PET). Accordingly, IHT on the failed PET (at 2007–08 rates) is £130,000 ((£350,000 − £25,000) × 40%), because the 2000 transfer forms part of Y's cumulative total in 2005 so only £25,000 nil rate band was available. Tax on Y's death

---

[47] See para.6–09.
[48] See paras 25–110 and following.

estate will be calculated by including the 2005 transfer (the failed PET) in Y's cumulative total.

By contrast, had Y not made the PET, so that an additional £350,000 formed part of his death estate, tax thereon (ignoring the 2000 transfer which dropped out of cumulation by the date of death) would have been £20,000 ((£350,000 − £300,000 nil rate band) × 40%). On these facts, therefore, extra tax results from the making of the PET of £120,000 (£140,000 − £20,000). It follows that great care should be taken to ensure that sufficient time is left to allow previous transfers to fall out of cumulation before making a PET.

The consequences of a failed PET may be particularly adverse in circumstances **6–52** where the death estate is not chargeable to IHT at all, e.g. because the spouse exemption applies. This situation was illustrated in the case of *Jonathan Mayson Ogden (2) Brian Hutchinson (Executors of the Estate of Ronald Henry Samuel Griffiths) v Trustees of the RHS Griffiths 2003 Settlement.*[49] The deceased (G) made PETs to trusts in April 2003 and February 2004. However, G was diagnosed with lung cancer in autumn 2004 and died in April 2005, with the result that the PETs failed, triggering an IHT liability in excess of £1 million. Under G's will, he left a life interest in his residuary estate to his widow. Had the PETs not been made, therefore, there would have been no immediate liability to IHT on his death because the residuary estate qualified for spouse exemption.

This case is interesting because it involved an application by G's executors to set aside the transfers on the basis that they were made under a mistake of fact, i.e. that G mistakenly believed, at the time of the transfers, that there was a real chance that he would survive for seven years and would not have made the transfers had he known that his life expectancy was so short. Neither HMRC nor any of the other parties opposed the relief sought.

On the basis of medical evidence, the court found that G did not suffer from lung cancer in April 2003, but that he was suffering from lung cancer in February 2004 and his life expectancy at that time did not exceed three years.[50] Lewison J. was satisfied that in those circumstances G would not have made the February 2004 transfer and that this mistake of fact was sufficiently serious to bring into play the court's equitable jurisdiction to relieve the consequences of a mistake. He therefore found that the February 2004 transfer (but not the earlier transfer in April 2003) was voidable and exercised his discretion to set it aside.

MISCELLANEOUS

VIII. TRANSFERS MADE ON THE SAME DAY

Because of cumulation, the order in which chargeable transfers are made will be **6–53** important when the total of those transfers falls in part within the nil rate band and in

---

[49] *Jonathan Mayson Ogden (2) Brian Hutchinson (Executors of the Estate of Ronald Henry Samuel Griffiths) v Trustees of the RHS Griffiths 2003 Settlement* [2008] S.T.C. 776.

[50] The judge had some hesitation in making this finding based on the fairly limited medical evidence submitted and said that he might not have felt able to do so had the facts been contested.

part within the 20 per cent band.[51] When more than one transfer is made on the same day s.266 introduces two special rules.

The order of transfers

6–54   Section 266(1) regulates the position where a person makes two or more transfers by providing:

> "Where the value transferred by more than one chargeable transfer made by the same person on the same day depends on the order in which the transfers are made, they shall be treated as made in the order which results in the lowest value chargeable".

Accordingly, where a person makes more than one chargeable transfer on the same day, they must be so arranged that the lowest amount of tax is payable thereon. This provision will be important only if the aggregate value transferred by the transfers is taxable at more than one of the applicable lifetime rates (currently the nil rate and the 20 per cent rate) and the transferor bears the tax on some, but not all, of the transfers.[52] In such circumstances the section ensures that transfers which must be grossed up are treated as having been made before transfers which need not be grossed up, so that the grossing-up is carried out at the lowest possible rate.

Assume, for instance, that on June 1, 2007, A, who had a cumulative total of £287,000, and had exhausted his annual exemption, made two chargeable transfers. The first, made in the morning, was of £20,000 to the trustees of the A discretionary trust and the second, made after lunch, was of a further £20,000 to the trustees of the B discretionary trust. A is to pay any IHT due on the transfer to the B trustees but not on the transfer to the A trustees. In the absence of s.266(1), the transfers would have been taxed in the order in which they were made, as follows:

(1) *Transfer to the A trustees*
     First £13,000 taxed at 0 per cent = nil
     Remaining £7,000 taxed at 20 per cent = £1,400.
(2) *Transfer to the B trustees*
     £20,000 taxed at 20 per cent = £4,000
     £4,000 grossed up = £5,000
     Accordingly, total tax payable is £6,400 (£1,400 + £5,000).

On the other hand, by the operation of s.266(1), if the transfer to the B trustees were treated as being made first, the tax payable would be reduced as follows:

(1) *Transfer to the B trustees*
     First £13,000 taxed at 0 per cent = nil
     Next £7,000 taxed at 20 per cent = £1,400
     £1,400 grossed up = £1,750.
(2) *Transfer to the A trustees*

[51] When the taxpayer intends to make a number of transfers some of which will be subject to an immediate charge and some of which will be PETs, the order of such transfers is a matter needing careful consideration; see para.6–71.

[52] The order of transfers will be important when a PET and chargeable transfer are made on the same day and the transferor dies within seven years, since there is no question of grossing-up applying to tax charged on the PET whereas the other transfer may have been grossed up when made: see paras 6–26 and following.

£20,000 taxed at 20 per cent = £4,000
Total tax payable = £5,750 (£1,750 + £4,000).

Obviously less IHT will be payable in such cases if transfers which must be grossed up are actually made before transfers which are not in which case there will be no need to make the above comparison. Where there are more than two transfers, the order inter se of transfers which must be grossed up and transfers which need not be grossed up is unimportant.

Effective rate

Section 266(2) then completes the treatment of multiple transfers made on the same   **6–55**
day by providing, in relation to the rate of tax that is to be charged on such transfers, that:

> "Subject to subsection (1) above, the rate at which tax is charged on the values transferred by two or more chargeable transfers made by the same person on the same day shall be the effective rate at which tax would have been charged if those transfers had been a single chargeable transfer of the same total value."

The effect of this provision is to make chargeable transfers made on the same day bear rateably IHT due in respect of those transfers, assuming that s.266(1) has not already deemed one to have taken place before the other. Although not defined, the term "effective rate" presumably means the rate found by expressing the tax chargeable as a percentage of the amount on which it is charged. If we continue with the facts in the example given in the previous paragraph but assume that in both cases the trustees of the settlement bear the IHT, then it becomes immaterial whether one gift was completed earlier in the day than the other since the total tax payable is the same (and s.266(1) does not apply).[53] They will be treated as a single gift of £40,000 and the calculation of tax is:

First £13,000 at 0 per cent = nil
Remaining £27,000 at 20 per cent = £5,400

The effective rate of tax is therefore £5,400/£40,000 = 13.5 per cent. Accordingly, the tax chargeable on each transfer of £20,000 is:

£20,000 × 13.5 per cent = £2,700

IX. TRANSFERS REPORTED LATE

Section 264 deals with certain transfers of value that are reported late. By s.264(1),   **6–56**
the section applies where:

(1) HMRC are not notified of a transfer of value in an account or by information before the expiry of the period specified in s.216, for the delivery of accounts[54]; and

(2) this transfer is not discovered until after HMRC have accepted payment in full satisfaction of the tax due on the value transferred by another transfer of value

---

[53] The same result would follow if both gifts had been grossed up.
[54] See para.29–06.

subsequently made by the same person. If no tax is chargeable because the nil rate applies, payment is treated under s.264(8) as having been accepted by HMRC when the nil-rate transfer is notified in an account to HMRC.

Under s.256(1), HMRC may make regulations modifying s.264(8) in cases where the delivery of an account has been dispensed with under the relevant regulations.[55] Under these regulations, no account is required of an "excepted transfer" or an "excepted estate". It may be that where the regulations have dispensed with the need to submit an account an earlier transfer is discovered. The regulations provide that in such circumstances:

(1) an account of the excepted transfer will be treated as having been delivered on the last day on which it would otherwise have been due, i.e. normally 12 months after the end of the month in which it was made; and

(2) an account of the excepted estate shall be treated as having been delivered 35 days after issue of the grant of probate (in Scotland, 60 days after the date on which confirmation to the estate was first issued).

Prior to the Finance Act 1981, the legislation provided that where the above conditions were fulfilled, the earlier transfer was treated for the purposes of determining the rate of tax as if it had been made on the date on which it was discovered, unless the later transfer was made on death, in which case the earlier transfer was treated as having been made immediately before the later transfer. This was subject to the qualification that the section did not apply for the purpose of deciding whether the earlier transfer was made within three years of death.

6-57 With the introduction by the Finance Act 1981 of a 10-year cumulation period, a new procedure was needed, and this procedure should have been updated to take account of the seven-year cumulation period brought in by the Finance Act 1986. No such updating took place, however, and so the procedure introduced by the Finance Act 1981 as from July 27, 1981 continues to operate.

To begin with, no provision is made to treat the earlier transfer as having been made on the date on which it is discovered. Accordingly, the date on which it was in fact made is the relevant date. If this was more than 10 years before the later transfer, the earlier transfer will have ceased to cumulate, and no adjustments will be needed as regards the later transfer. Tax, together with, perhaps, substantial interest, will, of course, be due on the earlier transfer.

Where the earlier transfer was made within 10 years of the later transfer, tax is due on the earlier transfer in the usual way, i.e. by reference to the rates, exemptions, etc. in force at that date. In addition, by s.264(2), an extra amount of tax may be due on the earlier transfer, depending on whether more than seven years have elapsed. Any amount due is equal to the difference between the IHT properly chargeable, in the light of the earlier transfer, on the later transfer and the payment previously accepted by HMRC in full satisfaction of the tax due on the later transfer.[56]

6-58 It may be that within the 10-year period ending with the date of the later transfer there have been two (or more) earlier transfers. In that case, the tax due on each of the

---

[55] See paras 29–09 and following.

[56] This "extra" tax is not chargeable on the later transfer. Where the later transfer was a nil rate transfer the payment is treated as being nil: see s.264(8). Where no account of an excepted estate (see paras 29–10 and following) has been delivered and an earlier unreported lifetime transfer is discovered, an account of the estate will be treated as having been delivered on the last day of the prescribed period in relation to the estate. The fact that the transfer took place within ten years of a later transfer no longer automatically results in an extra tax charge: this follows from the reduction in the cumulation period to seven years.

earlier transfers is calculated and then all the extra tax on the later transfer as a result of the discoveries of the earlier transfers is aggregated and apportioned among the earlier transfers in proportion to the values transferred by them.[57] A further complication can arise where there are two or more such earlier transfers and HMRC have accepted an amount in full satisfaction of the tax due on one of these earlier transfers before the discovery of any of the other earlier transfers. In such circumstances, the earlier transfer in respect of which tax has been accepted is brought into account only for the purpose of determining what tax is properly chargeable on the later transfer and any other earlier transfers. This follows from s.264(5) which provides that:

(1) no further extra tax is charged under s.264(2) in respect of this transfer in consequence of regard being had to the effect of the other earlier transfers on the tax due on the later transfers;

(2) the amount of extra tax paid on this transfer reduces the amount of extra tax due on the other earlier transfers in respect of the later transfers; and

(3) this transfer is left out of account in apportioning among the other earlier transfers the extra tax due.

Where there are two or more earlier transfers in relation to a later transfer, one of those earlier transfers will be a later transfer in relation to the other earlier transfer. If the earliest transfer is discovered last, the additional tax due on it will include the tax due on both of the later transfers.

The intention behind the legislation appears to be to ensure that the correct figure is **6–59** brought into account for each transfer for the purpose of the 10-year cumulation period, regardless of the order in which the transfers are made. There is some doubt, however, as to whether the legislation achieves this. Where a later transfer involved grossing-up, the discovery of an earlier transfer may affect the rate at which the grossing-up was effected, so that the value transferred by that later transfer should also be altered. There is no express provision to ensure that this is done, and it does not follow that it must be done by necessary implication. Finally, the legislation does not make it clear who is responsible for the extra tax due when an earlier transfer is discovered. This could cause particular problems where a transferee had originally undertaken to pay the tax and the transferor failed to account for the transfer.

Interest

Under the original s.264, the fact that the earlier transfer was taxed at the rates that **6–60** would have been due had it been made on the date on which it was discovered could mean, given the cumulative nature of CTT, that more tax was payable in respect of the value transferred by that transfer than would have been the case if the tax had been chargeable by reference to the date on which the transfer was in fact made. In this connection, s.264(6) provides that for six months after the discovery of the transfer interest is calculated by reference to the tax that would have been charged if the transfer had not been reported late. After the expiry of the six-month "grace period" interest is charged by reference to the amount of tax actually charged. The six-month grace period is now necessary in order to ensure that extra tax charged on the later transfers (and

---

[57] IHTA 1984 s.264(3).

which is collected from the transfer reported late) does not attract interest for six months.

Exemptions

6–61   It may be that the earlier transfer would have been wholly or partly exempt because all or some of the value transferred by it fell within a limit, e.g. within the annual exemption. In that case, s.264(7) provides that if payment has been accepted by HMRC in full satisfaction of the tax due on the later transfer on the basis that the later transfer was *partly* exempt because part of the value transferred by that transfer fell within the limit in question:

> (1) tax is not chargeable on the part of the value transferred by the later transfer; and
> (2) a corresponding part of the earlier transfer is treated as falling outside the limit of the exemption in question.

Assume that the only exemption available to X is his annual exemption, and that he made two transfers. On Christmas Day 2007, he made a transfer of value to Y of £11,000, for which he failed to account; on February 1, 2008, he made a further transfer of value to Z of £4,000, for which X's annual exemption was given. On April 1, 2008, the earlier transfer of £11,000 is discovered. Applying s.264(7), the transfer to Y would be regarded as having taken place before that to Z, but under s.264(7) none of the transfer to Y would have been exempt, while £3,000 of the transfer to Z (for which exemption had previously been given) would not be regarded as chargeable to IHT. Had the transfer to Z been of only £2,000, then, since that transfer was wholly exempt, s.264(7) would not have applied, with the result that (i) the £3,000 exemption would have been available to the transfer to Y, and (ii) the transfer to Z would have been wholly chargeable.

PLANNING

6–62   The introduction by the Finance Act 1986 of the seven-year regime opened up a large number of planning possibilities. It is important to get these possibilities into perspective, and to realise that the position is not as straightforward as it might at first glance seem. The purpose of the following discussion is to bring out a number of the key points.

X. ESTATE FREEZING

6–63   It will be immediately apparent that lifetime transfers, even if made within three years of a transferor's death, have an inherent estate-freezing aspect. This follows from the fact that, even if tax is charged on the transferor's death, be it in the form of a supplementary charge or because a PET has failed, the charge is imposed on the value transferred by the transfer at the time it was made, not by reference to the value of the gifted property at the time of the transferor's death. Thus, subsequent appreciations in the value of gifted property escape IHT altogether.

XI. THE KNOCK-ON EFFECT OF A PET

There is a problem, not always fully appreciated, that afflicts failed PETs but not **6–64** vulnerable lifetime transfers. It is that the failure of a PET produces two results. The first affects the PET itself: it is that the failure of the PET may produce an immediate tax charge in respect of the PET itself. The second effect relates to other transfers made by the transferor: it is that the value transferred by the PET will retrospectively enter the transferor's cumulative total. Except where fairly small values are concerned this will, in the vast majority of cases, have at least one, and possibly two adverse effects.

Boosted death charge

The first adverse effect will be that on the transferor's death tax may be charged at **6–65** a higher rate than it would have been charged had the PET not failed. If, for example, the failed PET exhausted the transferor's nil rate band, the donee of the PET will not himself suffer any charge to tax by reason of the failure of the PET, but the nil rate band will be unavailable to shelter any of the value transferred on death, with the result that the donee of the PET will have benefited more, per pound of gift, than the deceased's heirs.[58] This is easily overlooked in practice. It may be possible to take out term assurance to ameliorate this result: see paras 6–82 and following.

Boosted lifetime charges

The second adverse effect is that lifetime transfers made subsequent to the failed **6–66** PET may, by reason of the transferor's nil rate band being wholly or partly absorbed by the failed PET, suffer tax at a greater effective rate than they would have done had the PET not failed. There may also be a knock-on effect where such a subsequent transfer has been made to a discretionary trust, as the following example shows.

Example

Assume that on August 1, 2004 S gave shares then worth £300,000 to his son and **6–67** that on March 1, 2005 he settled land worth £273,000 on discretionary trusts, paying the IHT himself so that grossing-up applies. Exactly 12 months later, on March 1, 2006, the trustees appointed one-quarter of the fund (then valued at £120,000) on interest in possession trusts, which under the rules applicable prior to March 22, 2006 resulted in an exit charge.[59] S himself dies in February 2008.

---

[58] No problem arises if the donee is himself the only heir, and the problem is less severe if he is included among the heirs.

[59] An appointment out of a discretionary trust on interest in possession trusts on or after March 22, 2006 would generally not result in an exit charge, as the property would (subject to certain limited exceptions) not cease to be relevant property following the appointment. See Ch.14.

Assuming that no other chargeable transfers were made by S, that there were no available exemptions and reliefs and that the rates of tax current in 2004–05 apply throughout, the consequences are as follows:

(1) The original gift of shares in 2004 to S's son was a PET and was therefore ignored when computing the tax charge on the creation of the discretionary settlement in March 2005. Accordingly, tax then payable by S was £2,500 (the first £263,000 falling within S's nil rate band and the remaining £10,000 being grossed-up at the 20 per cent rate). Accordingly, the chargeable transfer at that time was £275,500.

(2) The exit charge levied on the trustees at the time when the interest in possession was appointed in a part of the fund will be calculated on the basis of a settlement rate of 0.27 per cent (2,500 ÷ 275,500 × 30%) which will be further reduced on the basis that property has only been in the settlement for four quarters (this procedure is fully explained at paras 16–15 and following). Assuming that the tax is paid out of the appointed portion of the fund, the IHT charged on the appointment of £120,000 at that stage is therefore £32.40 (£120,000 × 0.27% × 4/40).

(3) As the result of S's death within seven years of the making of the PET, tax is levied as follows:

(a) On the failed PET tax is charged as follows:
On the first £263,000 = nil
On the remaining £37,000 at 40 per cent = £14,800

(b) The tax on the creation of the discretionary trust needs to be recomputed on the basis that at that time S had already made chargeable transfers equal to £300,000. Accordingly, the sum settled (£273,000) will, as a result of his death, be liable to charge at 40 per cent (tax of £109,200). After deducting tax paid in 2005, extra tax owing is £106,700.

(c) The tax paid by the trustees must also be recomputed on the basis that the settlement was created by a settlor who had already made chargeable transfers equal to £300,000. The settlement rate accordingly becomes six per cent and the effective rate charged 0.6 per cent. Accordingly, the tax charge is £720. After deducting the tax already paid of £32.40, the additional tax due is £687.60.

In this example, the total additional IHT due as a result of the failure of the PET is therefore £122,187.60 (£14,800 + £106,700 + £687.60).

XII. CLAWBACK OF RELIEFS

6–68 Account also has to be taken of the fact that agricultural and/or business relief on lifetime gifts made within seven years of a transferor's death may be clawed back. The person making a transfer which is chargeable when it is made has no better idea of whether or not it will prove to be an invulnerable lifetime transfer than a person making a PET has of whether that PET will succeed or fail. Accordingly, a person considering making a lifetime gift of property which qualifies for agricultural or business relief needs to consider very carefully whether or not such relief is likely to be clawed back. If it is, then further consideration will have to be given to whether:

(1) given the fact that no such clawback operates on death,[60] he should wait until then to make the gift; and

[60] See paras 26–101 and 26–157.

210

(2) the transfer should be by way of a PET or a transfer which is chargeable when it is made.

PET or chargeable transfer?

If the value transferred, with agricultural or business relief, will result in either: **6–69**

(1) no tax being charged (because the value transferred, with relief, falls within the transferor's unused nil rate band); or
(2) only a manageable amount of tax being due (as interest-free instalment relief may be available),[61]

it may be better for the transfer to be an immediately chargeable one, because even if a supplementary charge is imposed and relief clawed back, the transferor's cumulative total will be unaffected. This may be especially important with regard to the knock-on effect of a failed PET, discussed above.

XIII. NIL RATE BAND TRANSFERS

Where a transfer falls within a transferor's nil rate band the effect, subject to one **6–70** qualification, is the same whether the transfer is by way of a vulnerable lifetime transfer or a failed PET. This follows from the fact that in both cases the transferor's death within seven years of the transfer will affect only his cumulative total: no tax will actually be charged on the transfer per se. The qualification to this rule occurs where agricultural and/or business relief is available on a transfer. In that case the clawback of relief, besides meaning in both cases that tax may be chargeable on the transfer, will mean in the case of a failed PET, but not in the case of a vulnerable lifetime transfer, that the transferor's cumulative total is retrospectively increased, and this may affect the rate at which tax is charged on transfers made subsequent to the failed PET.

XIV. ORDER OF TRANSFERS

Where a transferor contemplates making two gifts,[62] one of which is to be a PET and **6–71** one of which is to be chargeable when made, the question arises which gift he should make first. There is no simple answer to this; the only safe course is to work through the permutations in each case. There are, however, a number of guidelines. First, if the gifts are to be separated by more than two years, it would generally be better to make the PET first, since under taper relief there is a full run-off for PETs while the run-off for vulnerable lifetime transfers, at least as the rates and taper provisions stand at present, generally[63] ceases after five years. Secondly, if one of the gifts will cause a disproportionate diminution in the value of the transferor's estate, e.g. where he owns 52 per cent of the shares in an investment company and proposes to give half the shares

---

[61] This, of course, may also be lost retrospectively as the result of a clawback: see paras 29–100 and following.
[62] See paras 6–53 and following where the gifts are made on the same day.
[63] If agricultural and/or business relief is clawed back, the run-off may continue for six years.

to his son and to settle the other half on discretionary trusts, it will generally be better for the first transfer to be a PET, so that a greater proportion of the aggregate value transferred by the gifts shelters under the PET regime.[64] Much will depend, obviously, on the values in question. Finally, the failure of the PET may have knock-on effects, as was discussed above.[65]

The failure of a transferor to survive a lifetime transfer by seven years can result in tax, or extra tax, being charged on that transfer and, because the transfer is then included in the cumulative total of the transferor, in an increased tax bill on his death estate. Taking out suitable insurance cover should be considered as a way of alleviating these problems, often at a relatively small cost.

XV. CAPITAL GAINS TAX

6–72 The interface of IHT and CGT in any case needs careful consideration. While the position can be straightforward or extremely complex, a few basic considerations are normally present.

Loss of CGT-free uplift on death

6–73 The first consideration is that, if the transferor is unlikely to survive the transfer by seven years, consideration will have to be given to the CGT effects of his failing to do so, i.e. such CGT-free uplift as would otherwise have been available on his death[66] will have been lost as the result of his having given the property away during his lifetime. This may not matter if, for example, the asset is showing little or no gain, a CGT exemption is available to him, or any gain can be sheltered by losses without any ill effects (he might be better off deploying them against other, e.g. commercial gains). But if no such amelioration is available, there may be a good case for doing nothing, especially if 100 per cent business relief or agricultural relief should be available on his death.

Upfront charge to CGT

6–74 Even if the loss of an uplift on death is not a concern, taxpayers are generally unwilling to attempt to achieve IHT savings if doing so involves an upfront charge to CGT. Having said that, the fact that the disposal of an asset will generate a gain may

---

[64] See also para.6–68. Note however the possibility HMRC might regard part of the first transfer as immediately chargeable anyway, see para.5–22.

[65] If the chargeable transfer is the creation of a trust, then it may be advantageous to make that transfer before any PET, since in the event of the PET failing not only will tax on the subsequent creation of a trust need to be recalculated but so too will any exit charges which may have been incurred by the trustees.

[66] See TCGA 1992 ss.62(1), 72(1)(b), 72(1A), 73(1)(a) and 73(2A). Note the loss of uplift in respect of post March 22, 2006 interest in possession (see para.10–03).

not preclude IHT planning if a CGT relief is available. The reliefs most likely to be relevant are considered below.

Reliefs for business assets

Taper relief (before April 6, 2008)

Prior to April 6, 2008, the availability of CGT taper relief for business assets meant that it was possible to reduce the effective CGT rate on gains on business assets to only 10 per cent, whilst IHT business relief would be likely to reduce the IHT cost to nil. Although this might mean that there was little incentive to give, cases could arise where there was concern about future loss of IHT business relief, in which case a donor might wish to take advantage of such IHT business relief as was available to him for the time being. **6–75**

Entrepreneurs' relief (from April 6, 2008)

The Finance Act 2008 introduced a number of changes to the way in which CGT is charged with effect from April 6, 2008. In particular, the rate of CGT was reduced to a single rate of 18 per cent and taper relief was withdrawn for disposals and held-over gains coming into charge on or after April 6, 2008—effectively increasing the CGT rate applicable to gains on business assets from 10 per cent to 18 per cent. Following extensive lobbying by businesses after the changes were announced in the Pre-Budget Report 2007, the government announced a partial concession in the form of a new entrepreneurs' relief with effect from April 6, 2008. **6–76**

It should be noted that entrepreneurs' relief is likely to prove considerably less generous than business asset taper relief. Where entrepreneurs' relief applies, the chargeable gain is reduced by four-ninths, which—like business asset taper relief —produces an effective CGT rate of 10 per cent. Unlike taper relief, however, entrepreneurs' relief is subject to a lifetime limit of £1 million of gains (i.e. a maximum benefit of £80,000 per taxpayer) and has considerably more restrictive qualification criteria. This means that some taxpayers who would have qualified for business asset taper relief will not qualify for entrepreneurs' relief, and even where the relief is available the taxpayer may be worse off.

It remains to be seen what impact the introduction of entrepreneurs' relief in place of taper relief will have on IHT planning, but it seems likely that it will militate against lifetime gifts of business assets, particularly in cases where IHT business relief is available at 100 per cent (see Chapter 26).

Holdover relief

The next consideration is the possibility of claiming one of the two types of holdover relief provided for by s.165 and s.260 of the Taxation of Chargeable Gains Act 1992 respectively.[67] **6–77**

---

[67] Bear in mind that where holdover relief is claimed on a gift into settlement, the held-over gain will not benefit from the CGT-free uplift conferred by ss.72(1)(b) and 73(1)(a); T.C.G.A. 1992 s.74. A further claim for s.165 or s.260 holdover relief may be available on the occasion of a s.71(1) or s.72(1)(a) deemed disposal.

Section 165 holdover relief basically operates in respect of gains arising on disposals of business assets, and is subject to certain restrictions where the disposal is of, e.g., shares in a trading company which owns investments.[68] Section 260 holdover relief basically operates in respect of gains arising on disposals which rank as immediate chargeable transfers for IHT purposes; a PET therefore cannot qualify for s.260 holdover (even if the PET fails because the transferor dies within seven years). Unlike s.165 holdover, s.260 holdover does not depend on the nature of the asset transferred. Where both reliefs are available, s.260 takes precedence[69] and, as will be seen below, this can be important.

6–78　　The availability of holdover relief has been affected by various legislative changes in recent years. In particular, as indicated in the previous edition of this book, the Finance Act 2004 introduced anti-avoidance provisions denying both ss.165 and 260 holdover relief for transfers to settlor-interested trusts after December 9, 2003.[70] Those provisions were mainly aimed at so-called "*Melville* schemes",[71] since aside from such schemes settlor-interested settlements were (given the effects of s.49(1) and the reservation of benefit rules) generally not attractive as tax planning vehicles to most taxpayers.

While holdover relief continues to be available for gifts to non-settlor interested settlements, it should be noted that with effect from April 6, 2006 the CGT definition of "settlor-interested" was extended to include trusts under which a dependent child[72] of the settlor can benefit.[73]

In addition to the CGT changes, the IHT implications of creating a trust have been radically affected by the Finance Act 2006 changes described in Chapter 10, as most gifts to a settlement (settlor-interested or otherwise) are now chargeable transfers for IHT purposes.

Section 165 holdover

6–79　　Where s.165 business assets holdover is available there is less of a pure tax incentive to make gifts because, as discussed, in such cases the assets in question will normally also qualify for IHT business relief. Where a gift is nevertheless to be made, the donor has the choice of either: (a) crystallising such entrepreneurs' relief as may be available to him so that, in an optimum situation, the gain is reduced and he pays CGT at only 10 per cent; or (b) claiming holdover relief in which case no CGT is payable at all on the occasion of the transfer, but such entrepreneurs' relief as has accrued in respect of the gifted asset is lost, the donee taking over the donor's historical base cost with the result that the held-over gain may be brought into charge in future, any entrepreneurs' relief then available being based on the donee's period of ownership.

It should be noted that s.165 holdover relief is not available where the transferee is neither resident nor ordinarily resident in the UK, or is resident or ordinarily resident but is regarded as resident in another country for the purposes of a double taxation agreement and would consequently not be liable to CGT on a subsequent disposal of

---

[68] TCGA 1992 Sch.7.

[69] TCGA 1992 s.165(3)(d).

[70] See TCGA 1992 ss.169B–169G.

[71] See para.25–14.

[72] For this purpose a "dependent child" means a child/stepchild under the age of 18 years who is unmarried and does not have a civil partner (TCGA 1992 s.169F).

[73] These changes do not affect outright gifts to a dependent child. Such gifts will generally be PETs and will therefore fall outside s.260, although they may qualify for s.165 holdover.

the asset (Taxation of Chargeable Gains Act 1992 s.166). The relief is also clawed back if the transferee ceases to be UK resident within six years of the transfer.

Section 260 holdover

A chargeable transfer which falls wholly within the transferor's unused IHT nil band **6–80** will qualify for s.260 holdover relief, so in appropriate cases a transfer to a non settlor-interested trust of an amount within the transferor's unused IHT nil band may be attractive. Section 260 holdover relief will generally also be available on a transfer of property out of the trust (unless, exceptionally, the transfer is not a chargeable event for IHT purposes, e.g. because it is made within three months after the creation of the trust or a ten-year anniversary).

Like s.165 holdover relief, s.260 holdover relief is not available where the transferee is neither resident nor ordinarily resident in the United Kingdom, or is resident or ordinarily resident but is regarded as resident in another country for the purposes of a double taxation agreement and would consequently not be liable to CGT on a subsequent disposal of the asset (Taxation of Chargeable Gains Act 1992 s.261). The relief is also clawed back if the transferee ceases to be UK resident within six years of the transfer.

Using section 260 instead of section 165

Curiously, in some cases it will be beneficial to structure matters so that holdover **6–81** relief under s.260 is available in respect of a transfer of shares in a company which qualify as business assets within s.165 and which qualify for IHT business relief. This is because, although s.165 limits the amount of the gain which can qualify on a disposal of shares in certain cases where the company in question, or any of its subsidiaries,[74] owns investments, s.260 imposes no such limitations. It follows that in such a case it would be useful from a CGT standpoint for a donor wishing to make a gift of shares to do so to a non settlor-interested trust so that s.260 holdover, which takes priority over s.165 holdover, would be available.

It might be thought that this would be problematic for IHT purposes on the basis that a similar restriction must operate for business relief purposes so that the transfer would not qualify entirely for IHT business relief, with the result that the value transferred might exceed the transferor's unused nil rate band, but this will not automatically follow, because the presence of investments in a company will not necessarily result in a loss of business relief.[75] It follows that where the circumstances are such that s.165 holdover relief will not extend to the whole of the gain to be realised, the intending donor should consider making a gift to a non settlor-interested trust so that s.260 holdover, which as noted above takes priority over s.165 holdover, will be available to shelter the whole of the gain.[76]

XVI. INSURANCE

Insurance can be used in a number of ways for UK tax planning. From an IHT **6–82** perspective, insurance-based planning will generally involve taking out a policy to fund

[74] TCGA 1992 Sch.7 Pt II.
[75] See paras 26–33 and following.
[76] See para.26–109 and *Private Client Business* (London: Sweet & Maxwell, 1993), pp.138–143.

an anticipated IHT liability while ensuring that the policy is held outside the taxpayer's estate.

Term assurance

6–83   Simple term assurance results in a specified sum being paid in the event of the death of the life assured before a specified date. A seven-year policy can therefore be taken out to deal with the IHT problems considered above in relation to a specific potential IHT liability. The same policy may cover both the risk of tax or extra tax on a lifetime gift and the charge on the death estate or, alternatively, separate policies may be taken out.

Whole life cover

6–84   Whole life cover involves the regular payment of premiums and gives insurance cover throughout the life of the assured. On death there will be an eventual payment of a fixed sum, a fixed sum with profits, or an index-linked sum. Often the prospective IHT bill is insured against by a combination of term and whole life insurance.

Holding the policy

6–85   Whichever policy or policies are decided upon, it is essential from an IHT per-spective that they are not held as part of the donor's estate: otherwise the proceeds will be subject to tax on his death,[77] thereby, in part, defeating the object of the exercise. In those cases where a donee takes out such a policy, he will obviously retain the benefit in his own name so that the problems discussed above will not arise. When, however, it is the donor who wishes to effect the policy (e.g. to ensure that his personal representatives are not made to pay tax on lifetime gifts out of his death estate or to cover the tax charge on that estate on death) it will usually be necessary to write the policy in trust for the relevant beneficiaries. Given that the donor's intention is to cover the potential tax liabilities both on the lifetime gifts and on the death estate, the most suitable vehicle to hold this policy will usually be a discretionary trust. The trustees should be given power to appoint capital and income amongst a wide beneficial class together with a power to add to that class. Ideally the trust should be created at a time when the settlor has made no other chargeable transfers: in this case it may be anticipated that no anniversary charge will ever arise and that payments out will suffer little or no tax. Obviously if the sums involved are substantial it may be more satisfactory to make separate arrangements for the donees' and the donor's estate: e.g. for the donor take out individual policies for each donee whilst setting up a discre-tionary trust for the benefit of those who will take his property on death.

Paying the premiums

6–86   Care must be exercised if premiums payable under the insurance policy are to continue to be discharged by the donor. Such premiums, unless they are within the

[77] See para.8–17.

normal expenditure out of income exemption, will themselves be PETs if the benefit of the policy has been assigned to the donee outright. However, if the benefit is assigned to a trust, the payments will (other than in very limited circumstances) fall outside the definition of a PET,[78] and therefore, unless they are exempted as normal expenditure out of income or fall within the settlor's annual exemption, will constitute chargeable transfers. See further paras 5–26 and 5–44–5–46.

---

[78] See para.5–26.

CHAPTER 7

RESERVATION OF BENEFIT

I. INTRODUCTION

The reservation of benefit provisions, like the PET regime, were introduced by the Finance Act 1986 and the statutory references in this chapter are to that Act unless otherwise indicated. It is fair to say that the reservation of benefit provisions are among the most difficult in the IHT legislation, and many issues remain to be resolved. They derive from the fundamental problem that they were lifted from the estate duty legislation and engrafted onto the capital transfer tax legislation (which was converted by the Finance Act 1986 to the IHT legislation) without, apparently, too much attempt genuinely to integrate them fully into the existing legislation. In particular, they do not link with the basic IHT concept of transfer of value and fail to take account of the rule under IHTA 1984 s.49(1) that a person entitled to an interest in possession in settled property is, in certain circumstances, treated as beneficially entitled to that property. **7–01**

The relevant provisions in the 1986 Act were originally found in s.102 and Sch.20; the Finance Act 1999 added ss.102A–102C, the Finance Act 2003 amended s.102(5) and added s.102(5A)–(5C) and the Finance Act 2006 added s.102ZA. The effect of these provisions is to make it difficult in many cases for a taxpayer to make a tax-efficient gift if the circumstances and/or terms of that gift are such that he may still derive some benefit from the subject-matter of the gift. This kind of gift is, of course, just the sort that many taxpayers wish to make. The reservation of benefit rules thus act as a disincentive to giving which to some extent balance out the incentives to giving introduced by the PET regime. Taxpayers contemplating gifts can thus be forgiven if they feel they are confronted with a schizophrenic tax code which appears on the one hand to be encouraging them to make gifts and on the other to be discouraging them from doing so. In fact, this is not quite accurate. What the reservation of benefit provisions do is not so much to discourage giving generally, but rather to discourage individuals from making the kind of gifts from which they may benefit in the future, e.g. if they fall on hard times.

The approach adopted in the 1986 Act aims to revive the concept of the reservation by a donor of a benefit from a gift made by him which was vital for estate duty. This concept was, unfortunately, pregnant with uncertainty under estate duty, and as such it provides a great deal of food for thought and not a little trouble for estate planners under IHT.

The scheme of this chapter in relation to the reservation of benefit provisions is to consider firstly, when the provisions apply generally and the effect of the provisions applying (Pt I); secondly, the relevant estate duty and IHT case law (Pts II and III); thirdly, the detailed conditions that must be obtained for the provisions to apply (Pts IV–VII); fourthly, certain ameliorating factors[1] that may oust the application of the provisions (Pt VIII); fifthly, certain anti-avoidance rules (Pts IX and X); sixthly, how

---

[1] Note also that the terms of a double tax treaty may prevent the reservation of benefit provisions from imposing a charge to IHT.

account is taken of agricultural and business relief (Pt XI); and finally, some aspects of reservation of benefit in practice (Pt XII).

The introduction by the Finance Act 2004 of the income tax preowned assets regime ("the Regime"), which took effect as from April 6, 2005,[2] has greatly complicated matters, both in respect of future tax planning and in respect of pre-existing arrangements. Although the Regime imposes a charge to income tax and is thus strictly outside the scope of this book it would be inappropriate not to comment on it, not least because under the Regime it is possible to elect for the reservation of benefit provisions to apply in respect of property instead of the Regime. The Regime is accordingly discussed briefly in the last part of this chapter.

When the provisions apply

7–02   The central provision in the reservation of benefit minicode for determining whether an individual has reserved a benefit is s.102(1), the essential part of which provides as follows:

> " . . . this section applies where, on or after 18th March 1986, an individual disposes of any property by way of gift and either—
>   *(a)* possession and enjoyment of the property is not bona fide assumed by the donee at or before the beginning of the relevant period; or
>   *(b)* at any time in the relevant period the property is not enjoyed to the entire exclusion, or virtually to the entire exclusion, of the donor and of any benefit to him by contract or otherwise;
> and in this section 'the relevant period' means a period ending on the date of the donor's death and beginning seven years before that date, or, if it is later, on the date of the gift."

7–03   Where these requirements are satisfied, the property in question is prima facie "property subject to a reservation"[3] and so caught by the reservation of benefit provisions. In certain cases, anti-avoidance provisions have the effect that property may be caught, even though these requirements are not satisfied.[4] Conversely, there are various ameliorating considerations that mean that notwithstanding that these requirements are satisfied or the anti-avoidance provisions prima facie infringed, the provisions will still not apply.[5]

7–04   The words and punctuation of s.102(1), which are essentially[6] identical to the relevant estate duty wording, do not make easy reading. The equivalent estate duty legislation effectively established three hurdles for a taxpayer to clear, and the following discussion proceeds on the basis that s.102(1) does as well.

The three hurdles

7–05   On this basis, s.102(1) establishes three hurdles which must be cleared to avoid the application of the provisions where there is a disposal of property by way of gift by an individual:

---

[2] FA 2004 s.84 and Sch.15.
[3] FA 1986 s.102(2).
[4] See paras 7–98–7–109.
[5] See paras 7–106 and 7–107.
[6] The estate duty legislation referred to "possession and enjoyment" but this is not thought to make much difference.

(1) *the first hurdle*: possession and enjoyment of the property must be bona fide assumed by the donee at or before the beginning of the relevant period;
(2) *the second hurdle*: at all times in the relevant period the property must be enjoyed to the entire exclusion, or virtually to the entire exclusion, of the donor; and
(3) *the third hurdle*: at all times in the relevant period the property must be enjoyed to the entire exclusion, or virtually to the entire exclusion, of any benefit to the donor by contract or otherwise.

These are examined in detail in Pts V, VI and VII of this chapter.

Relevant period

The definition of "relevant period" operates as follows. Assume that on March 30, **7–06** 1999, X made a gift, that he made a further gift on April 1, 2002, and that he died on December 15, 2007. The relevant period in relation to the first gift is December 15, 2000–December 15, 2007, i.e. the seven years preceding the death, while the relevant period in relation to the second gift is April 1, 2002–December 15, 2007, i.e. the period between the second gift and the death.

Reservations for spouses or civil partners

It will be noted that there is nothing in s.102(1) which makes property which the **7–07** donor's spouse or civil partner is capable of enjoying or from which he/she benefits "property subject to a reservation".[7] On the contrary, the legislation confers favourable treatment on some gifts to spouses or civil partners.[8] Difficulties may arise, of course, where a donee spouse/civil partner passes a benefit to the donor spouse/civil partner. To avoid uncertainty, there should be clear evidence that the donee spouse/civil partner has not used his/her benefits directly or indirectly to benefit the donor spouse/civil partner. Problems may also arise where the nature of the donee's spouse's/civil partner's enjoyment or benefit is such that the donor spouse/civil partner also partakes of it, but HMRC are likely to take a common sense view in such cases.

Effect of provisions applying

There are two dangers where property is subject to a reservation. First, if such **7–08** property exists in relation to a donor immediately before he dies, the property in question will be treated as property to which he was beneficially entitled immediately before his death, with the result that its value may be brought into charge on his death, in which case the death rates will, by definition, apply. The strings attached to the gift

---

[7] A benefit to the donor's spouse or civil partner is relevant under FA 1986 Sch.20 para.7; see para.7–109. Also, the fact that the donor's spouse or civil partner has a right may have adverse implications for the donor under s.102A; see para.7–102.

[8] See paras 7–90–7–94. The inclusion of a spouse as a beneficiary under a settlement may, of course, have adverse income tax or CGT consequences.

may thus—adjusting the metaphor—turn into a noose. The possibility of this happening is especially worrying since the position may not be known until the donor's death, by which time it will not be possible to take any corrective action.[9]

Secondly, it may be that property which is subject to a reservation ceases to be such property, because the strings attaching to it are severed. In such a case, the donor is treated as having at that time made a PET, which he will need to survive by seven years if he is to avoid a clawback charge.

Clawback on death: s.102(3)

7–09   Section 102(3) provides that if, immediately before the death of the donor, there is any property which in relation to him is property subject to a reservation then, to the extent that the property would not otherwise form part of the donor's estate[10] at that time, that property shall be treated as property to which he is beneficially entitled. In this context it is important to understand the interaction of the excluded property rules and the reservation of benefit rules, both in relation to a person's free estate and in relation to settled property.

Excluded property: free estate

7–10   The position is best explained by an example. Assume that X, who is domiciled abroad, gives property situated outside the United Kingdom to Y in circumstances such that the property given is property subject to a reservation. Two years later X dies, and under s.102(3) he is treated as being beneficially entitled to the property given, which, immediately before he died, was situated outside the United Kingdom. Under IHTA 1984 s.4(1) he is treated as having made a transfer of value on his death equal in amount to the value of his estate. IHTA 1984 s.5(1) defines his estate as being all of the property to which he was beneficially entitled immediately before his death, but goes on to provide that his estate does not include excluded property. Accordingly, if X was still domiciled outside the United Kingdom when he died, the property clawed back into his estate will not be brought into charge, because had he actually been beneficially entitled to it, it would have been excluded property. Conversely, if immediately before his death he was domiciled in the United Kingdom, the property would not have been excluded property, and so it would have been brought into charge.

Excluded property: settled property

7–11   The position with regard to settled property is more complex.

Assume that in the above example X had settled the property on discretionary trusts in circumstances, again, where he reserved a benefit. If, when he died, he was domiciled outside the United Kingdom, the position would have been as above on either of two analyses. First, if the effect of s.102(3) is, as at first reading it clearly appears to be, to treat X as beneficially entitled to the property, so that it ceases to be

---

[9] See e.g. *Daniels v Thompson* [2004] EWCA Civ 307, described in para.7–152.
[10] See para.25–02 for the meaning of "estate".

settled property, the analysis is as above, i.e. it would have been excluded property in his hands, and so does not form part of his estate.[11] If, on the other hand, the correct analysis is that, notwithstanding the fact that s.102(3) treats him as beneficially entitled to the property, it is still to be regarded as settled property, it remains excluded property because it is situated abroad and comprised in a settlement made by a person who was domiciled abroad when he made the settlement.[12]

Consider the position, however, if, immediately before his death, X was domiciled in the United Kingdom. In that case, the first analysis would be of no help to him because given his United Kingdom domicile, the property treated as belonging to him would not be excluded property in his hands. The position under the second analysis, on the other hand, would leave room for argument. On the one hand it could be said that the fact that the property is settled makes no difference—the legislation says he is treated as owning it. That being the case, it cannot, given his United Kingdom domicile, be excluded property in his hands.

Against this, it could be said that once property is comprised in a settlement the relevant rule for determining whether or not it is excluded property is found in IHTA 1984 s.48(3), which provides that property comprised in a settlement made by a person who was domiciled abroad when he made the settlement is excluded property if it is situated abroad, and this is unaffected by the fact that a person with an interest in possession in that property, and who is in certain circumstances therefore treated as beneficially entitled to that property under IHTA 1984 s.49(1), is domiciled in the United Kingdom.[13] That being the case, the fact that X was domiciled in the United Kingdom when s.102(3) of the Finance Act 1986 treated him as beneficially entitled to the property would not mean that the property ceased to be excluded property.

In correspondence following the introduction of the reservation of benefit rules HMRC made it clear that in their view the settled property rules took precedence so that in the above example the settled excluded property clawed back into X's estate retained its character as excluded property.[14] However, in late 2001 HMRC amended what was then para.D8 of the *CTO Advanced Instruction Manual* in a way that showed they were reviewing the position and the relevant part of IHTM (which replaced the *CTO Advanced Instruction Manual*) was rewritten as from October 2007. The new section contradicted itself but indicated that HMRC thought that the GROB rules could take precedence over the excluded property rules both in respect of a donor who died not having released the reservation and in respect of a donor who released the reservation and died within seven years.

However in January 2011 the Manual was again amended and now makes clear that HMRC accept that the excluded property rules take precedence over the gift with reservation rules.[15] Whether the reservation remains in place at the death of the settlor or is released during his lifetime, there will be no IHT charge or potential charge even though the settlor has acquired a UK domicile or is deemed domiciled. The Manual does however make the point that excluded property treatment will not of course be available in respect of any UK situs assets in the settlement at death/release of the reservation; and any asset added to the settlement when the settlor has become UK domiciled will not be excluded property. HMRC treat such assets as held in a separate settlement made by a UK domiciled settlor.

[11] IHTA 1984 ss.5(1) and following.
[12] See para.32–48.
[13] See paras 32–49–30–56.
[14] See *The Law Society Gazette*, December 10, 1986.
[15] HMRC Inheritance Tax Manual 14396.

It should be noted that s.102(3) does not apply in relation to property which is subject to an interest in possession to which IHTA 1984 s.49(1) applies (subject to s.102ZA): see para.7–13.

Impact on valuation

7–12   The operation of s.102(3) may have the effect of adversely affecting the value of other property already comprised in the deceased's estate. Assume that X owns two adjoining plots of land, the value of which, taken together, exceeds the value of the plots taken separately. He gives one plot to his son, but continues to enjoy the land in circumstances such that that plot is property subject to a reservation when he dies. The s.102(3) clawback of that land on his death will mean that both plots will be valued on the basis that they would be sold together[16] with the result that the value of the plot actually retained by X is regarded as being higher than it would be had the clawback not operated.

Property already comprised in estate

7–13   The legislation recognises that there is no point clawing back into a person's estate property which is already comprised in it for IHT purposes, and s.102(3) therefore expressly provides that it does not apply to such property. The fact that s.102(3) does not operate with respect to property which already forms part of the deceased's estate immediately before he dies means that s.102(3) will in certain circumstances not operate with respect to settled property in which the deceased had an interest in possession immediately before he died: since here he is treated by s.49(1) of the 1984 Act as being beneficially entitled to that property, it will accordingly be comprised in his estate.[17] This will not be the case, however, if the property in which his interest subsists is excluded property because in that case, although he will still be treated by s.49(1) of the 1984 Act as owning the property, the property will not be included in his estate.[18] This will be the case even if he has become domiciled in the United Kingdom since the creation of the settlement (see para.7–11).

Exemptions

7–14   The fact that s.102(3) operates to claw back property into the deceased's estate does not necessarily mean that that property will form part of any chargeable transfer made on the deceased's death. Such a result will be avoided if the property devolves on the deceased's death in such a way that it is comprised in an exempt transfer. If, for example, property subject to a reservation became comprised in the estate of the

---

[16] See para.25–27.
[17] The circumstances in which a person entitled to an interest in possession in property will be treated by s.49(1) of the 1984 Act as being beneficially entitled to that property are described in Ch.11.
[18] IHTA 1984 s.5(1)(b).

deceased's spouse or civil partner, there would appear to be no reason why the s.18 exemption[19] should not be available.

Misconception as to effect of s.102(3)

It will be noted that under s.102(3) the property caught by the reservation of benefit **7–15** rules is treated as forming part of the donor's estate only immediately before his death, i.e. s.102(3) does not provide that the property never leaves his estate. There are thus no grounds for contending that where a person makes a gift of property which is "property subject to a reservation" at the time of the gift, that gift is incapable of being a transfer of value on the footing that, since the property never leaves the person's estate, the gift cannot have diminished his estate.[20]

Liability for IHT

Where a person dies and property subject to a reservation is treated as being **7–16** comprised in his estate, his personal representatives will be among the persons liable for the tax, but they will be so liable only if the tax due remains unpaid 12 months after the end of the month in which the person in question died and to the extent only of the assets mentioned in s.204(1) of the 1984 Act.[21]

Capital gains tax implications

It might be thought, on the basis of the adage "nothing ventured, nothing gained", **7–17** that the application of the reservation of benefit provisions on death is not a sufficient disincentive to prevent individuals from making gifts which attempt to outflank the provisions, on the basis that even if the property is clawed back into their estates on their death they will be no worse off than if they had retained the property. Such an approach would overlook the CGT implications of such attempts. Where an individual dies owning property his personal representatives are treated on his death as if they had acquired that property at its then market value, but without there being any disposal by the deceased. The result is a CGT-free uplift in the deceased's base cost.[22] This uplift will not be available, however, in respect of property which is clawed back into the deceased's estate for IHT purposes under the reservation of benefit provisions. In such a case the deceased may thus have the worst of both worlds—a charge to IHT[23] without any compensating CGT-free uplift.

Cessation of reservation: s.102(4)

In the absence of provision to the contrary, there would be nothing to prevent a donor **7–18** from outflanking s.102(3) by making a disposal of property in circumstances such that

[19] See paras 3–29 and following.

[20] The double tax regulations may be relevant on the donor's death; see paras 8–36 and following.

[21] See para.29–74. The personal representatives will have a right of reimbursement under s.211(3) against the donee of the property in question.

[22] TCGA 1992 s.62(1). Note that this uplift erases losses as well as gains.

[23] Exceptionally this charge may be avoided if an exemption is available; see para.7–14.

225

the property was property subject to a reservation and then arranging matters so that before his death the property ceased to be property subject to a reservation, because the s.102(3) clawback would then have nothing on which to fasten. Section 102(4) accordingly provides that if, at any time before the end of the "relevant period" any property ceases to be property subject to a reservation, the donor is treated as having at that time made a disposition of the property by a disposition which is a PET. This provision is discussed at paras 5–38 and following.

II. BACKGROUND: THE ESTATE DUTY CASES

7–19   The IHT reservation of benefit provisions are modelled on the estate duty legislation, which contained similar provisions; see the Customs and Inland Revenue Act 1881 s.38(2)(a), the Customs and Inland Revenue Act 1889 s.11(1), the Finance Act 1894 s.2(1)(c) and the Finance (1909–10) Act s.59(3). The key provision was s.11(1) of the Customs and Inland Revenue Act 1889 which referred to:

> "property taken under any gift . . . of which property bona fide possession and enjoyment shall not have been assumed by the donee immediately upon the gift and thenceforward retained, to the entire exclusion of the donor, or of any benefit to him by contract or otherwise."[24]

Over the years, the Privy Council heard a number of cases on appeal from the High Court of Australia concerning the effect of s.102(2) of the Stamp Duties Act, 1920–1940, as amended, of New South Wales. At the material times, this provision charged duty on:

> " . . . any property comprised in any gift made by the deceased at any time . . . of which bona fide possession and enjoyment has not been assumed by the donee immediately upon the gift and thenceforth retained to the entire exclusion of the deceased or of any benefit to him of whatsoever kind or in any way whether enforceable at law or in equity or not and whenever the deceased died."

The concluding part of this provision is thus wider than the equivalent estate duty and IHT provisions, but it is thought that nothing in the decided cases turns on this. They have been accepted as authorities on the relevant UK legislation,[25] and they are treated as such in the following discussion.

Since the introduction of the IHT reservation of benefit provisions there have been two decided cases—*Ingram v IRC*[26] and *Eversden v IRC*,[27] decided respectively by the House of Lords and the Court of Appeal—which have made it clear that, while the court will be informed by the estate duty cases, the position in any case will have to be determined by reference to the IHT legislation. The estate duty cases, while not decisive, thus remain relevant. In particular, the estate duty cases drew a distinction, sometimes subtle, between a gift "with strings attached" and a gift of property out of which the donor had carved an interest, the principle being that one did not reserve a

---

[24] FA 1986 s.102(1), unlike s.11(1), makes no reference to enjoyment and possession of the property being retained by the donee, but, as will be seen, this is not material to the cases concerned with s.11(1) (or with its Australian equivalent).

[25] *Oakes v Commissioner of Stamp Duties of New South Wales* [1954] A.C. 57 at 71–72.

[26] *Ingram v IRC* [1999] S.T.C. 37; see paras 7–33 and following.

[27] *Eversden v IRC* [2003] S.T.C. 822; see paras 7–35 and following.

benefit out of that which one kept back. It will be helpful to consider those cases at this juncture, partly because they are important in their own right, and partly because they provide a useful introduction to the kind of issues that can arise in relation to IHT.

The *Munro* case—the classic "carve-out"

A useful starting point is the New South Wales case of *Munro v Stamp Duties* **7–20** *Commissioner (New South Wales)*.[28] The taxpayer carried on the business of a grazier on three pastoral holdings. He had four sons and two daughters. Shortly after the eldest son attained his majority the taxpayer entered into a verbal agreement with his children to carry on the business with them in partnership. The taxpayer was to contribute the whole of the capital and to take a quarter of the profits. The business was to be carried on on the existing land, and the taxpayer was to be the sales manager with the final say on all matters. About four years later the taxpayer transferred some of the land outright to his four sons; most of the rest he settled on his daughters. He continued the business, and on his death the New South Wales Revenue invoked their reservation of benefit provisions. The Privy Council held that what was comprised in the gift was the land shorn of the right which belonged to the partnership, so that the donee in each case assumed bona fide possession and enjoyment of the gift to the exclusion of the donor. As to an argument that under Australian land law, the transfers of the land, in the absence of any registration of the partnership's right, gave the donees a title which overrode the partnership right, Lord Tomlin, delivering the judgment of the court, said[29]:

> "In their Lordships' opinion it is the substance of the transactions which must be ascertained and if when so ascertained the substance does not fall within the words of the statute it cannot be brought within them merely because the forms employed did not give true effect to the substance. It is not always sufficiently appreciated that it is for the taxing authority to bring each case within the taxing Act, and that the subject ought not to be taxed upon refinements or otherwise than by clear words."

The limits of *Munro*

Munro is one of the leading authorities on what have become known as "carve-" **7–21** outs," i.e. the retention by a donor of one or more rights over property which he gives away. The case has its limits, however. In particular, it is to be noted that, in coming to their decision, the Privy Council did not determine the precise nature of the right of the partnership at the time of the transfers. The decision proceeded on the basis that the right was either a tenancy during the term of the partnership or a licence coupled with an interest.[30] It would thus be dangerous to seek to rely on the decision in *Munro* where the donor has merely licensed the occupancy by the partnership. Furthermore, the

---

[28] *Munro v Stamp Duties Commissioner (New South Wales)* [1934] A.C. 61.
[29] *Munro v Stamp Duties Commissioner (New South Wales)* [1934] A.C. 61 at 68.
[30] See also the discussion at para.7–31.

possibility of the children having conferred a benefit on the donor by not dissolving the partnership also appears not to have been considered.

The *Perpetual Trustee* case and gifts into trust

7–22   A second Australian case, *Commissioner of Stamp Duties of New South Wales v Perpetual Trustee Co Ltd*[31] is particularly useful, because there is to be found in the judgment of the Privy Council, as given by Lord Russell, a particularly clear exposition of the issues involved. A taxpayer transferred certain shares to trustees to hold the same on trust for his son should the latter attain 21, the trustees in the meantime having power to apply the income and capital of the fund for the maintenance, etc. of the son as they saw fit. Accumulated income was to go to the son on his attaining 21. The settlor was one of the trustees. The Australian Revenue attacked on three grounds. First, it was said that the settlor, as one of the trustees, was in possession of the property. Secondly, his remaining in possession meant he had a benefit. Thirdly, there was a resulting trust for him, so that he also had a benefit on that ground. Lord Russell gave the judgment. He said:

> "The questions to be determined are, (1) what was the property comprised in the gift, was it the shares themselves or only a particular type of interest in the shares? (2) Had bona fide possession and enjoyment been assumed by the donee immediately upon the gift? (3) Had bona fide possession and enjoyment been thenceforth retained by the donee to the entire exclusion of the settlor, and to the entire exclusion of any benefit to him of whatsoever kind or in any way whatsoever?"[32]

The answers to these questions were as follows:

> " . . . the property comprised in the gift was the equitable interest in the eight hundred and fifty shares, which was given by the settlor to his son. The disposition of that interest was effected by the creation of a trust, *i.e.*, by transferring the legal ownership of the shares to trustees, and declaring such trusts in favour of the son as were co-extensive with the gift which the settlor desired to give. The donee was the recipient of the gift; whether the son alone was the donee (as their Lordships think) or whether the son and the body of trustees together constituted the donee, seems immaterial. The trustees alone were not the donee. They were in no sense the object of the settlor's bounty. Did the donee assume bona fide possession and enjoyment immediately upon the gift? The linking of possession with enjoyment as a composite object which has to be assumed by the donee indicates that the possession and enjoyment contemplated is beneficial possession and enjoyment by the object of the donor's bounty. This question therefore must be answered in the affirmative, because the son was (through the medium of the trustees) immediately put in such bona fide beneficial possession and enjoyment of the property comprised in the gift as the nature of the gift and the circumstances permitted. Did he assume it, and thenceforth retain it to the entire exclusion of the donor? The answer, their Lordships think, must be in the affirmative and for two reasons: namely, (1) the settlor had no enjoyment and possession such as is contemplated by the section; and (2) such possession and enjoyment as he had from the fact that the legal ownership of the shares vested in him and his co-trustees as joint tenants, was had by him solely on behalf of the donee. In his capacity as donor he was entirely excluded from possession and enjoyment of what he had given to his son. Did the donee retain possession and enjoyment to the entire exclusion of any benefit to the settlor of whatsoever kind or in any way whatsoever? Clearly, yes. In the interval between the gift and his death,

---

[31] *Commissioner of Stamp Duties of New South Wales v Perpetual Trustee Co Ltd* [1943] A.C. 425.
[32] *Commissioner of Stamp Duties of New South Wales v Perpetual Trustee Co Ltd* [1943] A.C. 425 at 436.

the settlor received no benefit of any kind or in any way from the shares, nor did he receive any benefit whatsoever which was in any way attributable to the gift."[33]

Cochrane and *Earl Grey*

Attention was given by the court in the *Perpetual Trustee* case to two other, earlier cases. In the first, *Re Cochrane*[34] the taxpayer settled £15,000 on trust to pay each year out of the income a specified amount to his daughter for life, and to pay the surplus income to himself during her life. There was a resulting trust of the entire trust fund for the settlor if certain trusts in favour of the daughter's issue failed. HMRC contended that the subject-matter of the gift was the entire equitable interest in the sum settled. Lord Russell agreed with Palles C.B. that:

7–23

> "Gift in the context meant beneficial gift. A person who declares trusts of property only gives the beneficial interests covered by the trusts. Everything else he retains and does not give; and there is an entire exclusion of the donor from the property taken under the disposition of the gift. Sir Henry Cochrane obtained no benefit either by way of reservation out of the gift, or collaterally in reference to the gift. He held, therefore, that estate duty was not payable in respect of the £15,000."[35]

Lord Russell concluded that *Cochrane* had been correctly decided.

The next step was to reconcile that decision with the earlier case of *Grey (Earl) v Att Gen*.[36] In that case the taxpayer conveyed his real and personal estate to the donee to hold the same in fee simple, subject to certain annuities and mortgages, so that the taxpayer should during his life receive an annual rentcharge charged on the realty and have the right to occupy the mansion house. The deed of conveyance also contained certain covenants by the donee, inter alia, to pay the rentcharge and the donor's funeral and testamentary expenses. The House of Lords held that the donor had reserved a benefit. For HMRC in the *Perpetual Trustee* case, it was argued that *Cochrane* was inconsistent with this decision in that in *Cochrane* it was held that no benefit was reserved while in *Earl Grey* it was held that the rentcharge was reserved out of the property given. In the view of Lord Russell, there was nothing inconsistent in the decisions. The whole transaction in the *Earl Grey* case "reeked of benefits to the donor".[37] There was nothing in the *Cochrane* case that:

7–24

> "conflicts with the view that the entire exclusion of the donor from possession and enjoyment which is contemplated by s.11, sub-s.1, of the Act of 1889 is entire exclusion from possession and enjoyment of the beneficial interest in property which has been given by the gift, and that possession and enjoyment by the donor of some beneficial interest therein which he has not included in the gift is not inconsistent with the entire exclusion from possession and enjoyment which the subsection requires. With the suggestion that *In re Cochrane* is inconsistent with the decision in *Attorney-General v Worrall* their Lordships cannot agree. That was simply a case in which the Court of Appeal held on the facts and documents there disclosed that the donor had obtained a collateral benefit in reference to the

---

[33] *Commissioner of Stamp Duties of New South Wales v Perpetual Trustee Co Ltd* [1943] A.C. 425 at 439–440.

[34] *Re Cochrane* [1906] Ir.R. 200.

[35] *Commissioner of Stamp Duties of New South Wales v Perpetual Trustee Co Ltd* [1943] A.C. 425 at 441–442.

[36] *Grey (Earl) v Att Gen* [1900] A.C. 124.

[37] *Commissioner of Stamp Duties of New South Wales v Perpetual Trustee Co Ltd* [1943] A.C. 425 at 445.

gift which he had made. Possession and enjoyment of the property taken under the gift had not been assumed and retained to the exclusion of any benefit to the donor by contract or otherwise . . . "[38]

The *St Aubyn* case—a contemporaneous carve-out

7–25   The need for precision in analysis was stressed by the House of Lords in *St Aubyn v Att Gen*,[39] the facts of which the authors have simplified slightly for ease of explanation. The taxpayer's uncle, Lord St. Levan, was tenant for life under a strict settlement.[40] Lord St. Levan and one of the trustees sold the trust assets to a company for cash, some of which was payable by instalments over 40 years. The trustees used all the cash paid at the time of the sale, except for £100,000, to subscribe for ordinary shares in the company. Lord St. Levan and the trustee then appointed the £100,000 and the sums to be paid by instalments to be held on trust for Lord St. Levan absolutely. He used the £100,000 to subscribe for preference shares in the company. Lord St. Levan's life interest in the ordinary shares was then extinguished and he was excluded from all benefit from them and from all income from them. The transactions were effected in just over one week. On Lord St. Levan's death HMRC claimed duty on the ordinary shares.

The relevant provision was s.43 of the Finance Act 1940, which provided that duty was exigible unless Lord St. Levan had been entirely excluded from the shares and of any benefit to him by contract or otherwise.

The House of Lords found unanimously for the taxpayer. Of the judgments, Lord Radcliffe's is perhaps the most illuminating. He said that HMRC's case was that since, as part of the whole scheme, Lord St. Levan enjoyed a contractual benefit in the form of the right to receive the instalments, it could not be said that he was excluded from benefiting from the ordinary shares, even though they had been appointed away from him absolutely. This Lord Radcliffe was unable to accept. *Worrall's* case[41] was, it was true, authority for the proposition that the contractual benefit did not have to be reserved out of the subject-matter of the gift, but:

> " . . . I think it a very mistaken form of reasoning to deduce from a decision that a benefit, to be within the mischief of the section, need not necessarily be by way of reservation out of the subject-matter of a gift the general proposition that all benefits are within the mischief of the section, whether they are by way of reservation out of the subject-matter of the gift or not. To deny the validity of one general proposition is not to assert the general validity of its opposite. I suggest, therefore that your Lordships can safely put aside the case of *Attorney General v Worrall* as having no further bearing on this appeal than that of showing that the benefit of the instalment payments which Lord St. Levan retained was not without the mischief of the section merely because the company's contract to pay them was neither a charge upon nor a reservation out of the property which consisted of the ordinary shares."[42]

[38] *Commissioner of Stamp Duties of New South Wales v Perpetual Trustee Co Ltd* [1943] A.C. 425 at 446.

[39] *St Aubyn v Att Gen* [1952] A.C. 15.

[40] For those unfamiliar with them, a strict settlement was one created under the Settled Land Act 1925, which gave the tenant for life much wider powers than settlements made under the Law of Property Act 1925. If a settlement did not qualify as a 'trust for sale' under the Law of Property Act, it was a strict settlement by default. The Trusts of Land and Appointment of Trustees Act 1996 abolished strict settlements for the future but pre-existing ones may continue as such.

[41] See para.7–24.

[42] *Att Gen v Worrall* [1952] A.C. 45 at 48.

What Lord St. Levan had disposed of was the ordinary shares subject to his right to the instalments:

" . . . the possession and enjoyment of the rights which constituted the ordinary shares were only affected by the existence of the instalment debt in the sense that the half-yearly payment of the instalments reduced the resources which, had there been no debt, would have been available for the benefit of the shareholders of the company. But I think that there is formidable authority against the view that in such a situation the possession and enjoyment of the relevant property is not exclusive of a benefit to the donor or releasor of such property. A man may have an arrangement which gives him contractual benefits that affect an estate and may subsequently make a gift of his interest in that estate; if he does the donee has possession and enjoyment of what is given, to the entire exclusion of the donor or of any benefit to him. That is the *Munro* case. Shares may be made the subject of a trust for another person, the maker of the trust having the right under it to be one of the trustees, to retain in his control the voting-power in respect of the shares and to take an ultimate resulting interest; yet that benefit does not bring the property within the mischief of a similar provision. That is *Commissioner of Stamp Duties for New South Wales v Perpetual Trustee Co Ltd.* No more is possession and enjoyment of a gift compromised if a man vests property in trustees upon trust to provide out of it certain limited benefits for a donee, but subject thereto upon trust for himself. That is *Re Cochrane.* All these decisions proceed upon a common principle, namely, that it is the possession and enjoyment of the actual property given that has to be taken account of, and that if that property is, as it may be, a limited equitable interest or an equitable interest distinct from another such interest which is not given or an interest in property subject to an interest that is retained, it is of no consequence for this purpose that the retained interest remains in the beneficial enjoyment of the person who provides the gift.

My Lords, I think that the application of that principle is sufficient to destroy the Crown's claim under s.43. In substance the position of Lord St. Levan was the position of a man who creates a rentcharge in his own favour upon property which is in his absolute disposition and then makes a gift of that property subject to that charge. Nothing is then given except the interest charged."[43]

The *Oakes* case—a worrying development

An important Privy Council case, which further illustrates the subtlety of analysis **7–26** needed in this area, and the particular difficulties that may arise where an individual settles property on trustees of whom he is one, is *Oakes v Commissioner of Stamp Duties of New South Wales,*[44] decided two years after the *St Aubyn* case. The taxpayer, who owned grazing property, executed a deed under which he declared that he held the property on trust for himself and his four children as tenants in common in equal shares. Under the deed he had wide powers of management, and was entitled to remuneration for any work he did in managing the trust property. On his death, the New South Wales Revenue tried to charge tax on the value of the whole of the trust property because, inter alia, the reasonable remuneration which he took for managing the trust property constituted a benefit to him. Dealing with this point, Lord Reid, delivering the judgment, said first that the receipt by the taxpayer of reasonable remuneration for acting as a manager was "clearly" an advantage or benefit to him. But did this give the result contended for by HMRC?

"If a donor reserves to himself a beneficial interest in property and only gives to the donees such beneficial interests as remain after his own reserved interest has been satisfied, it is

---

[43] *Att Gen v Worrall* [1952] A.C. 45 at 49–50.
[44] *Oakes v Commissioner of Stamp Duties of New South Wales* [1954] A.C. 57.

now well established that such reservation of a beneficial interest does not involve any benefit to the donor within the meaning of the section . . . It follows that if the right to take remuneration could be regarded as a beneficial interest in the property reserved by the deceased when making the deed of trust, then his remuneration would not be a benefit within the scope of the section. But their Lordships cannot regard a right to take remuneration for managing property as a beneficial interest in the property. A trustee is not permitted to take remuneration for services performed by him unless he is authorized to do so: in this case the trustee was authorized to do so because the deceased provided in the deed of trust that he as trustee or the trustee for the time being should be entitled to remuneration as if he were not a trustee. If the deceased had resigned office and another trustee had taken his place it could hardly have been contended that this provision gave to the new trustee a beneficial interest in the trust property, and in their Lordships' judgment the deceased did not reserve to himself a beneficial interest in the property by inserting this provision in the deed of trust. Indeed, the terms of the deed of trust make it clear that the whole beneficial interest in the property passed to the deceased and his children in equal shares, so that the subject-matter of the gift to each child was one-fifth of the whole beneficial interest in the property . . . It is true that the deceased did not exact from his children his power to take benefits and that the benefits which he took were benefits which they neither permitted him to derive nor had any power to deny him. But in their Lordships' judgment the question is not whether the donees permitted the donor to take benefits. It is whether the donor took benefit out of that which was given. If a benefit arises by way of reservation out of interests which were given then no doubt the donees' interests are inherently insusceptible of being so possessed and enjoyed as to preclude the donor from taking that benefit, but the section applies because there is not entire exclusion of the donor or of benefit to him from the interests comprised in the gift. The contrast is between reserving a beneficial interest and only giving such interests as remain on the one hand, and on the other hand reserving power to take benefit out of, or at the expense of, interests which are given, and for the reasons already stated their Lordships are of opinion that the present case is within the latter class."[45]

The position on trustees' remuneration

7–27   HMRC do not apply the *Oakes* case under IHT where a settlor (or a settlor's spouse or civil partner) is entitled under a trust deed to remuneration for acting as a trustee, provided the remuneration is not excessive.[46] Although this helpful attitude is obviously to be welcomed, it is difficult to see how it can be justified, and in the authors' view the prudent course must be for a settlor who is a trustee of his own settlement not to be remunerated for so acting.

The *Way* case and transactions with trusts

7–28   It may be helpful to refer to a third Privy Council case concerning the position of a settlor who retains a link with a settlement made by him. In *Commissioner of Stamp Duties of New South Wales v Way*[47] the settlor had power during his lifetime to require the trustees to purchase from him any property, provided that the sale price to be paid to the settlor was no more than 95 per cent of the market value of the property, i.e. the settlor could not make a profit out of the trust fund by means of such a sale. The Privy Council held that this did not amount to a reservation to the settlor of a benefit in the

---

[45] *Oakes v Commissioner of Stamp Duties of New South Wales* [1954] A.C. 57 at 76–79.
[46] HMRC Manuals IHTM14394; see also para.7–135, IHTA 1984 s.90 is not relevant.
[47] *Commissioner of Stamp Duties of New South Wales v Way* [1952] A.C. 95.

settled property. In the context, the settlor's power was a fiduciary one. His power was to decide:

> "how the trustees should apply their trust funds, and in the absence of express provision to the contrary the presumption would be that his decision was to be given for the benefit of the settlement, not of himself . . . "[48]

The *Nichols* case and prior independent transactions

In *Nichols v IRC*[49] the Court of Appeal had to consider the effect of a gift of property   **7–29**
by a father to his son and a contemporaneous leaseback, made under a binding equitable obligation, of the property by the son to the father. The lease contained a full repairing covenant by the son. It subsequently proved necessary to adjust the lease somewhat in favour of the father. HMRC contended that the subject-matter of the gift was the unencumbered property, not the property subject to the lease. The Court of Appeal, following the *Earl Grey* case,[50] held that the existence of the covenant was sufficient to support HMRC's claim for duty. Goff J. giving the judgment of the court said:

> "The right to have the mansion house and outbuildings repaired under that covenant did not exist before, and therefore could not be something simply not given. Moreover, it was reserved out of that which was given, since it was a covenant immediately operative and running with the land. In any event, however, being a covenant for the benefit of the donor, at the expense of the donee, and one which he was as a condition of the gift obliged to enter into and for the protection and better enjoyment of the property by the donor, it must in our judgment be a benefit to the donor by contract or otherwise referable to the gift and so within the section. It appears to us to be just as much a benefit taken by the donor out of that which was given as the power to charge remuneration in the *Oakes* case."[51]

Effect of the leaseback

That was sufficient to deal with the case, and the court accordingly did not come to   **7–30**
a "final conclusion" concerning the effect of the gift and leaseback, although they were clearly of the view that the subject-matter of the gift was the entire property, not just the property shorn of the lease:

> "Having thus reviewed the authorities, we return to the question what was given, and we think that a grant of the fee simple, subject to and with the benefit of a lease back, where such grant is made by a person who owns the whole freehold free from any lease, is a grant of the whole fee simple with something reserved out of it, and not a gift of a partial interest leaving something in the hands of the grantor which he has not given. It is not like a reversion or remainder expectant on a prior interest. It gives an immediate right to the rent, together with a right to distrain for it, and, if there be a proviso for re-entry, a right to forfeit the lease. Of course, where, as in the *Munro* case, the lease, or, as it then may have been, a licence coupled with an interest, arises under a prior independent transaction, no question can arise because the donor then gives all that he has, but where it is a condition of the gift

---

[48] *Commissioner of Stamp Duties of New South Wales v Way* [1952] A.C. 95 at 107.
[49] *Nichols v IRC* [1975] S.T.C. 278.
[50] See para.7–24.
[51] *Nichols v IRC* [1975] S.T.C. 278 at 285c–e.

that a lease back shall be created, we think that must, on a true analysis, be a reservation of a benefit out of the gift and not something not given at all."[52]

The court also rejected an argument to the effect that the alteration of the lease in favour of the father constituted a new, more limited gift by the father. The improvement of the father's lease could not be regarded as something left with the father which he had not given. It was a cutting-down of the original gift, and it therefore could not be said that the son had retained possession of the property to the entire exclusion of the father or of any benefit to him.

Counsel for the taxpayer did not attempt to argue that reservation by the father of the lease was for full consideration in money or money's worth within the meaning of the estate duty equivalent of para.6(1)(a) of Sch.20 to the 1986 Act.[53]

The need for a prior independent transaction

7–31   It will be noted that in the *Munro*[54] case the donor's rights existed over the property before he gave it away, while in the *Nichols* case they arose contemporaneously with the gift.

In the quotation cited above at para.7–29 Goff J., while recognising the authority of *Munro*, referred to the need for the existence of what he called a "prior independent transaction", stating that only rights reserved by such a transaction could be enjoyed by a donor without infringing the estate duty reservation of benefit provisions. Prior to the House of Lords' decision in *Ingram* (described in para.7–33) HMRC placed considerable store by Goff J.'s statement. *Ingram* made it clear that there is no such requirement.

III. THE INHERITANCE TAX CASES

7–32   There have been two major IHT cases—*Ingram* and *Eversden*—on the reservation of benefit provisions. These have made it clear that although the estate duty cases provide guidance, they are by no means determinative. They have also made it clear that a number of issues still remain to be resolved.

The *Ingram* case

7–33   Lady Ingram owned property which she wished to give to her children and grand-children but subject to the right to occupy the property during her life. To achieve this, she transferred the property to her nominee. The next day, acting on her directions, the nominee granted her a 20-year rent-free lease and on the following day transferred the property, encumbered by the lease, to trustees who immediately executed declarations of trust whereby the property became held for the benefit of her children and grand-children, to the exclusion of Lady Ingram. Following her death HMRC issued a determination that, under the reservation of benefit rules, the property was deemed to

---

[52] *Nichols v IRC* [1975] S.T.C. 278 at 284h–285b; compare Walton J. [1973] S.T.C. 497 at 502e–f.
[53] [1973] S.T.C. 499 at 505a; and see paras 7–84 and following.
[54] See para.7–20.

be comprised in her estate immediately before she died. Her executors appealed directly to the High Court under IHTA 1984 s.222(3).[55]

HMRC argued that, on the basis of *Kildrummy (Jersey) Ltd v IRC*,[56] the lease was a nullity and that although the trustees and the beneficiaries were subject to an equitable obligation to give effect to the purported lease, the gift was of the property unencumbered by the lease because conceptually no obligation to give effect to the lease arose until the unencumbered freehold had been transferred. Therefore there had been a point in time when Lady Ingram had parted with the whole of the property. Furthermore, even if the lease was effective, it fell to be ignored under the *Ramsay* principle.

Ferris J.[57] agreed that the lease was a nullity but held that in substance there had never been a point in time at which the subject-matter of the gift had been the unencumbered freehold, for two reasons. First, Lady Ingram had never intended to give the property free from the lease. Secondly, the creation and existence of the lease did not depend upon the concurrence of the trustees and beneficiaries, still less on their performing some positive act.

A majority of the Court of Appeal[58] (Nourse and Evans L.JJ.) allowed HMRC's appeal on the basis that the lease was a nullity and the property given was therefore the freehold with the trustees' obligation to allow Lady Ingram possession of the property arising only after the gift. It was conceptually impossible for a lease to come into existence until the lessor had acquired the freehold interest. Millett L.J., dissenting, held that the lease was valid so that there was an effective carve-out; but even if the lease was a nullity, the subject-matter of the gift was what remained after the trustees had fulfilled their equitable obligation to grant the lease to Lady Ingram.

The House of Lords

The House of Lords[59] found unanimously for Lady Ingram's executors. The lease **7–34** was valid, but even if it was not, the gift was of the encumbered reversion. The *Ramsay* principle therefore did not apply.

In his leading speech, Lord Hoffmann said:

> "It is a curious feature of this case that both sides claim that their views reflect the reality and not the mere form of this transaction. But the Revenue's version of reality seems entirely dependent upon the scintilla temporis which must elapse between the conveyance of the freehold to the donee and the creation of the leasehold interest in favour of the donor. For my part, I do not think a theory based upon the notion of a scintilla temporis can have a very powerful grasp on reality . . . It is true that as a matter of conveyancing, no lease can come into existence until the freehold has been vested in the intended lessor. But s.102 is concerned not with conveyancing but with beneficial interests. It uses words like 'enjoyment' and 'benefit'. In *A-G v Worrall* [1895] 1 QB 99 at 104, a case on a predecessor of s.102 Lord Esher MR began his judgment with the words:
>
>> 'It has been held that in cases of this kind the Court has to determine what the real nature of the transaction was, apart from legal phraseology and the forms of conveyancing.'
>
> If one looks at the real nature of the transaction, there seems to be no doubt that Ferris J was right in saying . . . that the trustees and beneficiaries never at any time acquired the land free of Lady Ingram's leasehold interest. The need for a conveyance to be followed by a lease

---

[55] See para.29–153.
[56] *Kildrummy (Jersey) Ltd v IRC* [1990] S.T.C. 657.
[57] *Ingram v IRC* [1995] S.T.C. 564.
[58] *Ingram v IRC* [1997] S.T.C. 1234.
[59] *Ingram v IRC* [1999] S.T.C. 1234.

back is a mere matter of conveyancing form. As I have said, she could have reserved a life interest by a unilateral disposition. Why should it make a difference that the reservation of a term of years happens to require the participation of another party if the substance of the matter is that the property will pass only subject to the lease? . . . if, in addition to the leasehold estate which she reserved, Lady Ingram had obtained by covenant any additional benefits, as in *Nichols v I.R.C.* [1975] S.T.C. 278 . . . , they would have been benefits reserved. But in a case such as this, when she in fact received no such benefits, the contractual nature of the lease seems to be a matter of conveyancing theory rather than substance."[60]

Lord Hoffmann then went on to make some important general observations concerning s.102:

"Before parting with this aspect of the case, I should say something about the more general considerations involved in the application of s.102. Its policy has puzzled people for a long time. For one thing, it is in one sense a penal section. Not only may you not have your cake and eat it, but if you eat more than a few de minimis crumbs of what was given you are deemed for tax purposes to have eaten the lot. Secondly, a superficial reading of phrases like 'beneficial enjoyment of the property' and enjoyment of property 'to the entire exclusion . . . of the donor' has led to numerous occasions in the past century in which the Revenue has put forward the proposition that, as a matter of practical common sense, it simply must be contrary to the policy of the statute for a donor to be able to give away property such as a house and go on enjoying the benefit of the property by continuing to live there. This is the premise on which the Revenue claim the high ground of substance and reality . . . But this approach ignores the fact that 'property' in s.102 is not something which has physical existence like a house but a specific interest in that property, a legal construct, which can co-exist with other interests in the same physical object. Section 102 does not therefore prevent people from deriving benefit from the object in which they have given away an interest. It applies only when they derive the benefit from that interest.

If Lady *Ingram* has been dealing with a fund of investments instead of a house, she would have had no difficulty in achieving the same result, in economic terms, as the transaction in this case. She could have used part of the fund to purchase an annuity which would have guaranteed her exactly the same income as she had been receiving from the fund and given away the rest . . . Why should it make a difference that her asset happened to consist of land? The gift was a real gift of the capital value in the land after deduction of her leasehold interest in the same way as a gift of the capital of a fund after deduction of an annuity.

What, then, is the policy of s.102? It requires people to define precisely the interests which they are giving away and the interests, if any, which they are retaining. Once they have given away an interest they may not receive back any benefits from that interest. In *Lang v Webb* (1912) 13 CLR 503 at 513 Isaacs J suggested that the policy was to avoid the 'delay, expense and uncertainty' of requiring HMRC to investigate whether a gift was genuine or pretended. It laid down a rule that if the donor continued to derive any benefit from the property in which an interest had been given, it would be treated as a pretended gift unless the benefit could be shown to be referable to a specific proprietary interest which he had retained. This is probably the most plausible explanation and accepting this as the policy, I think there can be no doubt that the interest retained by Lady *Ingram* was a proprietary interest defined with the necessary precision."[61]

Lord Hutton adopted the reasoning of Ferris J. The correct approach in this context was to have regard to the substance of the transaction and that was that Lady Ingram had made a gift of the freehold shorn of the leasehold interest. Not long after the House

---

[60] *Ingram v IRC* [1999] S.T.C. 1234 at 43–44.
[61] *Ingram v IRC* [1999] S.T.C. 1234 at 44–45.

of Lords' decision, anti-avoidance legislation was introduced to counter such arrangements; see paras 7–101 and following.

The *Eversden* case

In 1988 a wife settled the family home, which she owned, upon trust to hold the same as to herself as to 5 per cent absolutely and as to 95 per cent upon the trusts of a settlement under which her husband was the life tenant. After his death the trust fund was to be held upon discretionary trusts for a class of beneficiaries which included the wife.

During their joint lives the spouses occupied the family home—Mr S under the terms of the settlement, and the wife by virtue of her retained interest as a tenant in common. After the husband's death in 1992 the wife continued to occupy the family home. In 1993 the trustees sold the family home and, out of the proceeds, including the wife's 5 per cent share, acquired a replacement property and an investment bond. Thereafter she had a 5 per cent interest in the replacement property and the bond. She died in 1998 having, in the interim, been in sole occupation of the replacement property, but having received no benefit from the bond.

HMRC argued that the entirety of the replacement property (and the bond) should, under the reservation of benefit provisions, be included in her estate immediately before she died by reason of her enjoyment of it.

7–35

The Special Commissioner's decision

A number of interesting points were made before the Special Commissioner.[62] First, the taxpayer (the wife's executors) contended that applying the reservation of benefit provisions would result in the property being charged to IHT twice—once on the husband's death by virtue of his interest in possession, and once on the wife's death, under the reservation of benefit provisions. HMRC countered that since the reservation of benefit provisions were penal the fact of double taxation was not determinative. The case is in this respect a salutary reminder of just how penal the provisions can be when they do apply.

7–36

The Special Commissioner held that, subject to the application of s.102(5), the wife had reserved a benefit. She did not do so, however, by reason of her actual occupation of the property, because that occupation was a right enjoyed by her as a co-owner of property. Therefore the "carve-out" principle applied. But she did reserve a benefit because, since as a discretionary beneficiary she had the right to be considered as a potential recipient of benefit, the trust property was not enjoyed to her sufficient exclusion.

The case therefore turned on whether the taxpayer could rely on s.102(5), which provided that s.102 did not apply if the disposal by way of gift was, inter alia, covered by the s.18 exemption. The taxpayer's argument was that on making the settlement the wife had, applying IHTA 1984 s.49(1), made a transfer of value to her husband of the whole of the property which had become comprised in the settlement; therefore the s.18 exemption was available to the whole of that transfer. That being the case, s.102(5) applied to prevent the reservation of benefit provisions from applying. HMRC sought to restrict the size of gift to which the s.18 exemption applied by contending that when

---

[62] [2001] S.T.C. (S.C.D.) 39.

the wife created the settlement she made a series of gifts consisting of the equitable interests given to the various beneficiaries under the settlement and that only the gift to the husband qualified for the s.18 exemption. HMRC relied upon the House of Lords' decision in *Ingram v IRC*,[63] but the Special Commissioner held that *Ingram* was concerned with the nature of what the settlor had retained, and noted the importance of s.49(1) of the 1984 Act to the scheme of the legislation. HMRC also cited the *Oakes*[64] case, but the Special Commissioner distinguished it on the ground inter alia that it had not involved successive interests and concluded that there had been a single gift to the husband. In doing so, the Special Commissioner noted that the wording of the Finance Act 1986 Sch.20 para.5(1) was consistent with the view that there was only one gift.

As a last resort, HMRC argued that the relevant date for determining whether s.102(5) applied was the date of the wife's death, not the date when she made the gift to her husband. This argument was rejected by the Special Commissioner.

The judgment of Lightman J.

7–37   Lightman J. at first instance[65] reached five conclusions on the basis of the arguments presented to him. First, the trust fund was clearly not enjoyed to the entire exclusion, or virtually to the entire exclusion, of the wife and of any benefit to her by contract or otherwise for purposes of s.102 because, per the Special Commissioner, the right to be considered as a potential recipient meant that she was not sufficiently excluded from enjoying the trust property. There was for this purpose no distinction between the nature of the right or interest of a person as an object of a discretionary trust and as an object of a power of appointment. Any argument that this right or interest fell within the carve-out principle was "hopeless". The wife therefore prima facie fell foul of the reservation of benefit provisions, but certain defences were available to her.

Lightman J. appears to have taken the view that her occupation of the *original* property did not infringe the reservation of benefit provisions because it was by reason of her beneficial interest as a tenant in common and this was so even after her husband's death:

> "She was not entitled to sole or exclusive possession, but for all practical purposes her occupation would be and was sole and exclusive unless the Trustees made a decision and took action to dilute or (through the medium of the Court) extinguish her right of occupation."[66]

The gist of his conclusion appears to be that the so-called "carve-out principle" prevented the wife from having reserved a benefit in respect of her occupation of the original property. The conditions of s.12 of the Trusts of Land and Appointment of Trustees Act 1996,[67] which came into force on January 1, 1997, were satisfied and the wife accordingly continued to be entitled to occupy the replacement property after January 1, 1997. It should be noted that had the settlement been made after March 8, 1999, s.102A of the Finance Act 1986[68] would have prevented this defence from being available.

---

[63] *Ingram v IRC* [1999] S.T.C. 1234; see paras 7–33 and following.
[64] See para.7–26.
[65] *IRC v Eversden* [2002] S.T.C. 1109.
[66] *IRC v Eversden* [2002] S.T.C. 1109 at 1127, para.21.
[67] See para.12–34, *IRC v Eversden* [2002] S.T.C. 1109 at 1130, para.34.
[68] See para.7–102.

The carve-out principle did not assist the wife, however, in relation to her occupation of the replacement property because Lightman J. *presumed* that the trustees and the settlor "agreed" that:

(a) the proceeds from the sale of the original property should be invested in the purchase of the replacement property and the bond; and

(b) the wife should become entitled to occupy the replacement property on the same footing as she had occupied the original property.

This meant that the wife did not occupy the replacement property under the carve-out principle but rather by reason of an agreement entered into between the trustees and her to benefit her. She therefore, at this stage in the analysis, reserved a benefit in respect of the replacement property and the bond.

Last, and most importantly, notwithstanding that the wife enjoyed benefits unprotected by the carve-out principle, she was prevented by s.102(5) from having reserved a benefit. Per Lightman J.:

> "The . . . question is accordingly whether the relevant disposal of property by way of gift (in this case the Settlement) was an exempt transfer between spouses. The language of Section 102(5) looks at this disposal at the date on which it is made and its character (as a transfer between spouses) must . . . be determined at that date. If the gift answers that character at that date, the provisions of Section 102 relating to property subject to a reservation have no application. For the purposes of Section 18 . . . the duration of the proprietary interest gifted to the spouse is irrelevant even as it is irrelevant how long the spouse retains the proprietary interest and whether the spouse gifts the proprietary interest on to someone else e.g., the children of the donor and donee. Likewise the duration of the proprietary interest is irrelevant for the purposes of Section 102(5)."[69]

HMRC again attempted unsuccessfully to contend that the relevant date for determining the application of s.102(5) was the date of the settlor's death, not the date of the settlement.

The judgment of the Court of Appeal

The Court of Appeal[70] unanimously rejected HMRC's appeal. The case was argued **7–38** entirely on the application of s.102(5). HMRC again sought to restrict the size of gift to which the s.18 exemption applied by arguing there was a mismatch in the legislation between "gift" and "transfer of value": although when the wife created the settlement she might for IHT purposes generally have made a transfer of value to her husband of her 95 per cent interest, for the purpose of the reservation of benefit provisions she made a series of gifts consisting of the equitable interests given to the various beneficiaries under the settlement and the let-out conferred by s.102(5) was confined to the gift she made to her husband.

Carnwarth L.J., with whom Brooke L.J. and Nelson J. agreed, rejected HMRC's argument. *Ingram* was concerned solely with the nature of the interest retained by the donor and was decided in a different context. The same applied to the *Perpetual Trustee* case. Neither was concerned with and neither addressed the position of successive interests forming part of a gift under a settlement. Carnwarth L.J. held that

---

[69] *IRC v Eversden* [2002] S.T.C. 1109.
[70] *IRC v Eversden* [2003] S.T.C. 822.

it was not possible to introduce such conceptual subtleties into s.102(5) without distorting the language:

> "Rightly or wrongly (from the purist's point of view), the draftsman clearly did find it possible to equate a disposal by way of gift with a transfer of value."[71]

Support for this view was to be found in the wording of s.3A, which also used the word "gift" and married it with the concept of "transfer of value". Given s.49(1) of the 1984 Act, the wife had clearly made a transfer of value of the whole of the settled property to her husband and to him alone. Section 102(5) applied to that transfer, and the wife did not reserve a benefit. There was nothing in s.102 to modify the effect of s.49(1). If this caused problems they were for Parliament to correct.

While it was fine for the Court of Appeal (and the Special Commissioner) to take the line that *Ingram* and *Eversden* were concerned with different issues, it does leave a nagging question—is one test being applied per *Ingram* to determine what the donor retained and another per *Eversden* to determine what he gave away? This would not seem to make much sense. Before addressing this question directly, it may be helpful to consider just what *Eversden* decided.

The ratio of *Eversden*

7–39   The ratio of *Eversden* appears to be that where property is settled upon trusts under which an individual has an interest in possession the subject-matter of the gift is the settled property and the sole donee of the gift is the individual who has that interest.

Implications of *Eversden*

7–40   So much for the strict ratio. What are the implications of *Eversden* for the operation of the reservation of benefit provisions generally? In the authors' view, there are three.

1. The subject-matter of the gift: settled property generally

7–41   The fact that under *Eversden* where an individual settled property upon trusts with an initial interest in possession the subject-matter of the gift was (as the law stood at that time) the settled property and not the interests arising under the settlement might be thought to be the inevitable effect of s.49(1) of the 1984 Act and so limited to trusts with an initial interest in possession falling within s.49(1). In the authors' view, however, there is a strong argument that the same approach should apply in relation to all settled property on the basis that it is the only approach consistent with para.5 of Sch.20 to the Finance Act 1986 (a point argued before the Special Commissioner[72]). Paragraph 5 is important because it is the only provision dealing expressly with how s.102 is to apply to settled property. Note that para.5 is concerned with property comprised in a gift which becomes settled property, not with interests in settled

[71] *IRC v Eversden* [2003] S.T.C. 822 at 830, para.22.
[72] See para.7–36.

property. If HMRC's arguments had prevailed, para.5 would have had no application to the settled property in *Eversden* because the subject-matter of the gift would have been the interests in the settled property (which interests were not themselves settled property), not to the settled property per se. *Eversden* avoids such an extraordinary result and it is clear that in *Eversden*, para.5 operated in the manner which in the authors' view was unmistakably intended by the draftsman.

Although it might be said that this approach is confined to settlements in which there is a pre March 22, 2006 initial interest in possession, in the authors' view it is likely to apply to all settled property. Assume X settles property upon initial discretionary trusts following which, e.g. A takes a life interest with remainder to B. The subject-matter of the gift should be the property settled by X, not the interests given to the discretionary class, A and B.

2. The subject-matter of the gift: the scope of the "carve-out" principle

The fact that the subject-matter of the gift where there is a pre-March 22, 2006 initial **7–42** interest in possession—and possibly regardless of the terms and/or date of the settlement—is the settled property arguably has important implications concerning the scope of the "carve-out" principle. Before *Ingram* the estate duty carve-out cases tended to be seen as concerned with identifying the subject-matter of the gift. *Ingram* was taken as continuing this approach; Lady Ingram never gave away the lease and therefore did not reserve a benefit by reason of her continued occupation of the property under the lease. On that basis, HMRC argued in *Eversden* that *Ingram* and the estate duty cases mentioned above meant that when a donor settled property upon trust the subject-matter of the gift was not the settled property but the interests of the beneficiaries under the trust. This appears to have assumed that *Ingram* and the estate duty cases were authority for the proposition that a settlor who enjoys settled property pursuant to a retained interest in it prima facie reserves a benefit in respect of it and that this result is to be avoided by regarding him as having made a series of gifts of the unretained equitable interests under the settlement rather than of the settled property per se.

The Court of Appeal, echoing the Special Commissioner, by implication rejected this line of argument—in their view *Ingram* (and the *Perpetual Trustee* case) was concerned solely with the nature of the interest retained by the donor in circumstances which were not concerned with the position of successive interests under a settlement.

But where does that leave us: is one test being applied per *Ingram* to determine what the donor retained and another per *Eversden* to determine what he gave away? The authors suggest otherwise and invite the view that *Eversden* is authority for the proposition that the retention by a donor of an equitable interest in settled property which he has disposed of by way of gift is not relevant in determining the subject-matter of the property given but is relevant in determining whether his enjoyment of the property given infringes the reservation of benefit provisions. In other words, HMRC's argument in *Eversden* unduly limited the carve-out principle. *Eversden* has, in this respect, reminded us of the full scope of the principle.

It must be said at once that this is not part of the ratio of *Eversden*. But it must also be said that such a view is arguably not inconsistent with *Ingram*; indeed, Lord Hoffmann's statement in *Ingram*, cited above,[73] that the policy behind s.102 was, per Isaacs J. in *Lang v Webb*,[74] that:

[73] See para.7–34.
[74] *Lang v Webb* (1912) 13 C.L.R. 503.

"It laid down a rule that if the donor continued to derive any benefit from the property in which an interest had been given, it would be treated as a pretended gift *unless the benefit could be shown* to be referable to a *specific proprietary interest which he had retained* [authors' italics] . . . "

is capable of embracing this view.

The approach is now arguably a two-tier one. First, one identifies the subject-matter of the property given. If, as in *Ingram*, the donor derives no benefit from the property given, he clearly does not reserve a benefit in respect of it. But even if the donor enjoys the subject-matter of the gift, the reservation of benefit provisions will not apply if his enjoyment derives from a proprietary interest which he retained over (but the retention of which did not affect the subject-matter of) the property given. Strictly, the latter point did not arise in *Ingram*, because in that case Lady Ingram enjoyed property which she retained. However, in the authors' view the ratio in *Ingram* is arguably an application of the wider principle alluded to by Lord Hoffmann, namely that whether or not a donor reserves a benefit depends not just on the subject-matter of the gift per se, but rather on the nature of the interests, if any, which the donor has retained in respect of the property given. Identifying the subject-matter of the gift is only the first step in a two-step process for determining whether or not a gift is caught by the provisions. Adopting this approach allows *Eversden* to sit comfortably with the carve-out principle, at least in relation to settled property involving successive interests. Having said that, there seems to be no reason why it should be limited to applying to such property.

3. Gifts and section 49(1)

7–43   *Eversden* suggested that where an individual settled property upon trusts under which he retained an interest in possession, he did not at that stage (under the law as it then stood) make a disposal of property by way of gift within the meaning of s.102(1). This follows from the decision in *Eversden* that the effect of IHTA 1984 s.49(1) was that where property was settled upon trusts under which an individual took an interest in possession the relevant gift was a gift of the whole of the settled property to that individual. Where that individual was the settlor for IHT purposes he was treated by s.49(1) of the 1984 Act as having continued to be the beneficial owner of the property. Consequently he did not make a transfer of value and the settled property was still generally treated as comprised in his estate. Why, then, should he be regarded as having made a disposal of property by way of gift for purposes of the reservation of benefit provisions?

Although s.49(1) of the 1984 Act will generally not apply to trusts created on or after March 22, 2006, it is still relevant in relation to interest in possession trusts created before that date. In that situation, if it is the settlor who has an interest in possession, the question has arisen how the reservation of benefit provisions will operate when his interest comes to an end, assuming that the transfer to the settlement was not a disposal by way of gift. Where the interest terminates on the settlor's death, the point is not important, because the property will normally already be treated by s.49(1) of the 1984 Act as forming part of his estate and therefore s.102(3) will not apply in any event. However, until 2006 the position was less clear where the settlor's interest terminated during his lifetime (e.g. because the trustees exercised a power of appointment to terminate his interest or his interest terminated after a specified period under the terms of the settlement) and the trust fund then became held on discretionary trusts. In such a case, there would arguably at that stage be no disposal by way of gift by the settlor (since neither case would involve the settlor acting or omitting to act in relation to the termination of his interest) and therefore, if there was no disposal of property by way of gift by him when he created the settlement, the reservation of benefit provisions would not apply in precisely the kind of circumstances in which they should do. In relation to lifetime terminations on or after March 22, 2006 of an interest in possession to which s.49(1) of the 1984 Act applies, the above issue has been resolved by s.102ZA, which explicitly provides that such a termination *will* be regarded as a disposal by way of gift for the purposes of the reservation of benefit provisions.[75]

IV. PRELIMINARY ISSUES

Before considering the three hurdles which a donor must clear in relation to a gift in order to avoid being caught by the reservation of benefit provisions, it will be helpful to consider some preliminary issues.

7–44

The reservation of benefit provisions can apply only if there has been a disposal of property on or after March 18, 1986 and that disposal has been both made, or deemed to be made, by an individual and by way of gift. Careful consideration needs to be given to each of these requirements.

7–45

Disposal of property on or after March 18, 1986

It is vital to note that s.102(1) applies where an individual "disposes of" property. This links with the use throughout s.102 and Sch.20 of "disposal", not "disposition". "Disposal" is also used in ss.102A and 102B.[76] The draftsman's use of "disposes of" and "disposal" in this way suggests that he intended a distinction to be drawn between "disposal" and "disposition". Such a distinction is important because although the legislation provides that a disposition can be effected by associated operations,[77] there is no provision extending the term "disposal" beyond its normal meaning. There are, however, indications that HMRC do not share this view and that they consider that a disposal of property by way of gift can be made by associated operations.[78]

7–46

Section 102 applies to disposals made on or after March 18, 1986, i.e. gifts made before that date cannot be the subject of a reservation of benefit claim. One consequence of this is that a settlement made before March 18, 1986 will not be caught by the reservation of benefit provisions unless further gifts into the settlement are made after that date. The provisions will then apply to the property settled by the further gifts only.[79]

Disposal by an individual

In principle, the fact that trustees require the consent of a beneficiary before exercising a power over his interest would not change the analysis, because of the

7–47

---

[75] See paras 7–99 and following.
[76] See paras 7–101 and following.
[77] IHTA 1984 s.272.
[78] HMRC Manuals IHTM14372.
[79] See HMRC Manuals IHTM14311.

requirement that the disposal of the property in question must have been made by an individual. In the authors' view there is a difference between making a disposal and consenting to a disposal, and this is the case even though the disposal cannot be made without the requisite consent. Where, e.g. trustees revoke a beneficiary's life interest, with the result that the interest of a remainderman is accelerated, under general principles no disposal is made by the life tenant of his life interest, because he is not effecting the termination himself.

In the past, the consequence of this was that if the trustees had power to revoke the remainderman's interest and appoint the fund back to the former life tenant, this generally did not mean that the former life tenant would have reserved a benefit. However, terminations of an interest in possession on or after March 22, 2006 are governed by the statutory rule in s.102ZA, described in paras 7–99 and following.

HMRC agree that a gift made by a close company will not be a disposal by an individual participator,[80] and this is so even though the gift is a transfer of value apportioned to its participators by s.94 of the 1984 Act.

It is clear, on the other hand, that the disposal need not to be made to an individual—it can be made, e.g. to a company.

Variations and disclaimers

7–48   Where a person validly enters into a deed of variation or a disclaimer that comes within s.142 of the 1984 Act, the reservation of benefit rules cannot apply to any gift made by him under that variation or disclaimer, even though the effect of the variation or disclaimer is that he is not precluded from enjoying the property which is the subject-matter of the variation or disclaimer. This follows from the fact that s.142 provides that in such a case the variation is to be treated (for IHT purposes) as having been effected by the deceased or, in the case of a disclaimer, as if the disclaimed benefit had never been conferred. Assume, for example, that X dies leaving his house to Y, and that Y enters into a deed of variation under which the house is rerouted to Z, who allows Y to continue living there. Under s.142(1) the variation is treated as having been effected by X, with the result that it cannot be said that Y has made any gift. This is understood to be the view taken by HMRC.[81]

Disposal by way of gift

7–49   The disposal of property must be made "by way of gift". The estate duty legislation referred to "property taken under any gift". Under estate duty, it was originally thought that "gift" meant simply "disposition", but the correct view was that to rank as a gift a disposition had to contain some element of bounty.[82] This is thought also to be the position for IHT purposes. The exercise by trustees of a power of appointment to defeat a beneficiary's interest by, e.g. advancing capital to another beneficiary will not constitute a disposal by the first beneficiary, and it is thought that this is the case even if the advance can be made only with the consent of the beneficiary whose interest is defeated.

[80] See HMRC Manuals IHTM14312.
[81] HMRC Manuals IHTM14312 and 35151.
[82] *A.G.(I) v Smith* (1905) 2 Ir.R. 533; *HM Adv v Heywood-Lonsdale's Trustees* (1906) 43 S.L.R. 529; *Re Fitzwilliam's (Earl) Agreement* [1950] Ch. 448; *Re D'Avigdor-Goldsmid* [1953] A.C. 347. See also *Berry v Warnett* [1982] 1 W.L.R. 698.

The requirement that there must be a gift of property before the reservation rules apply does not fit happily alongside the general requirement that for IHT to be charged there must be a transfer of value. Although in the majority of cases any gift will constitute a transfer of value, there are cases where a gift will not amount to a transfer of value and vice versa. Consider the situation where Adam owns a pair of Constable watercolours and sells one to his daughter Jennifer. He retains possession of the other picture. Each picture is worth £10,000: as a pair they are worth £35,000. Jennifer pays Adam £10,000 for the picture. On these facts, there is a transfer of value of £15,000 (the fall in value of Adam's estate) which will be a PET,[83] but since there is no gift of the property the reservation of benefit rules cannot apply.[84]

Since the draftsman based the rules on a gift of property, reference must be made to the estate duty cases on the meaning of "gift". A court might be persuaded that any disposition which diminishes the value of an individual's estate ranks as a gift for IHT purposes, but in the authors' view the (apparently) conscious choice by the draftsman of the words "gift" and "donor" in s.102(1) and elsewhere in the reservation of benefits minicode make this unlikely.

In *IRC v Eversden* Carnwath L.J. took the view that "the draftsman clearly did find it possible to equate a disposal by way of gift with a transfer of value".[85] Although in many cases a gift will be a transfer of value, to suggest that the terms are coterminous does not do justice to the complexity of the IHT legislation. A gift of excluded property, for example, would not normally be a transfer of value.[86] The assignment by a beneficiary of an interest in possession will be prevented by s.51(1)(a) of the 1984 Act from being an actual transfer of value but will be treated by s.51(1)(b) as the termination of his interest with the result that he will be treated by s.3(4) has having made a transfer of value. It is a nice question whether such a notional transfer of value would be regarded by Carnwarth L.J. as constituting a gift.[87]

Following *Eversden*, it was also arguable (prior to March 22, 2006) that where an individual settled property upon trusts under which he retained an interest in possession, he did not at that stage make a disposal of property by way of gift.[88]

The termination of an interest in possession, if brought about by the exercise by trustees of a power of appointment or advancement, though a notional transfer of value, would in principle not normally constitute a gift by the beneficiary whose interest was terminated. However, with effect from March 22, 2006 the termination of an interest in possession will in certain circumstances be deemed to be a disposal by way of gift under s.102ZA: see para.7–99.

Gifts to companies

Assume X owns all the shares in a company and that he gives property to that company. He has clearly disposed of the property but has he done so by way of gift? The question is not a simple one, but there is some judicial support for the view that he has not. The question becomes more difficult if X has an interest in possession in the shares.

7–50

---

[83] See para.5–22.
[84] See also the example given in HMRC Manuals IHTM14315. Note that in this example HMRC's starting assumption would be that there *was* a gift (and therefore the reservation of benefit provisions would potentially apply).
[85] *IRC v Eversden* [2003] S.T.C. 822 at 831, para.22.
[86] See para.2–36.
[87] See *IRC v Levy* [1982] S.T.C. 442.
[88] See para.7–43.

Where X owns all the shares, gives property to the company, and then settles the shares on discretionary trusts under which he can benefit he will clearly reserve a benefit in respect of the shares given. If he also reserves a benefit in respect of the property he gave to the company he will apparently have effectively doubled the value of his estate for IHT purposes.

Other subjective considerations

7–51   Note that motive is irrelevant, as is the existence of a moral obligation.[89] What matters is whether or not there is an element of bounty, not why it exists. If an individual enters into a deed of covenant and subsequently makes payments thereunder, those payments are gifts notwithstanding that they are made under an enforceable contract.[90]

Interest-free loans

7–52   In the authors' view a loan at less than a commercial rate of interest does not of itself constitute a gift with reservation. It is true that when a person lends money or other property otherwise than on commercial terms he thereby makes a gift, but only of the interest foregone. No benefit is retained by the donor in that foregone interest. There is no gift of the capital lent, and therefore s.102 (which requires a disposal by way of gift to have been made) cannot bite on it. HMRC appear to agree with this analysis.[91]

Sales at an undervalue

7–53   The definition of "gift" as a disposition containing an element of bounty means that a sale at an intentional undervalue will constitute a gift for these purposes.[92] The fact that a transaction contains an element of bargain does not prevent it from being a gift. In *Att Gen v Worrall*[93] a father gave to his son a sum secured on mortgage. The son, who had bought in the equity of redemption for a small sum, thereby became the owner of the property. In return, he covenanted to pay the father an annuity during the father's life. The effect was that the father continued to receive the income from the property. The Court of Appeal held that the transfer by the father was a gift.[94]

---

[89] *Att Gen v Chamberlain* (1904) 48 S.J. 332.

[90] *Att Gen Cobham* (1904) 98 S.J. 398; *HM Adv v Heywood-Lonsdale's Trustees* (1906) 43 S.L.R. 529.

[91] HMRC's analysis is that the foregone interest is property, but that the grant of such a loan is not, in itself, a gift with reservation: HMRC Manuals IHTM14317. However, loans to a settlement (interest-free or not) may be caught: see IHTM14401 and para.7–125.

[92] *Att Gen v Kitchin* [1941] 2 All E.R. 735; *Letts v IRC* [1957] 1 W.L.R. 201; (reported on this point at 1 W.L.R. 201 only). See also *Berry v Warnett* [1982] S.T.C. 396, per Lord Wilberforce at 399h, with whom Lords Scarman and Bridge agreed. The dissenting speech of Lord Roskill (with whom Lord Fraser agreed) adopts the reasoning of Buckley L.J. in the Court of Appeal, and the latter's judgment is based on the CGT context In which the term "gift in settlement" appeared: [1980] S.T.C. 645g–646g. Lord Wilberforce, on the other hand, gave the word its natural meaning.

[93] *Att Gen v Worrall* [1895] 1 Q.B. 99.

[94] The capitalised value of the annuity was less than the value of the equity of redemption together with the payment of the small sum, so there was an element of undervalue, though this did not figure in the judgments given in the Court of Appeal.

HMRC have expressed the view that a sale of property in consideration of an annuity may be a gift with reservation (rather than merely a sale for inadequate consideration) if the value of the annuity is less than the value of the property, e.g. if the annuity is equal to the income generated by the value of the property given.[95]

Where there is a sale at an intentional undervalue the question arises as to whether the vendor has reserved a benefit in the whole of the property sold. Assume A, knowing his house to be worth £500,000, sells it to his son for £400,000, thereby prima facie making a gift of £100,000. The son allows A to continue living in the house. A later ceases living in the house. Does he make a further PET of £500,000 under s.102(4)? In the authors' view, the court would strain against such a result. Perhaps more importantly, it is understood that HMRC's practice in these circumstances is to regard only the undervalue as the gift and in practice they will apply the reservation of benefit rules only to that portion of the value at the material date that reflects the gift element at the time of the disposal. Continuing with the example, suppose that, when the house is worth £600,000 the father dies while still living in the house. Under HMRC's practice the reservation of benefit rules would operate with respect to 100,000/500,000 × £600,000 = £120,000.[96]

Where, on the other hand, the purchase price is itself funded out of income arising from the property, the provisions may well apply. Difficulties may also arise where the purchase price is payable by instalments or is left entirely outstanding, especially if no interest or interest at less than a commercial rate is charged.

Note that a gift of mortgaged property on terms that the donee takes over the mortgage ranks as a sale at an undervalue. Thus, if a father wishes to give his farm to his son subject to the son taking over the mortgage concern might be felt that the discharge by the son of the mortgage over a period of time might infringe the reservation of benefit provisions. However, it appears from the pamphlet "PETs and Reservation of Benefit" published by the Country Landowners Association in June 1987 that HMRC may not seek to invoke the provisions in such a case (though note the SDLT implications of such a transfer).[97] An alternative approach would be for the son to borrow an amount equal to the outstanding mortgage on the security of the land and to use that sum to purchase the land from his father, in which case the transaction would be less likely to infringe the reservation of benefit provisions.

The property disposed of

It is essential to identify the property disposed of by the donor. This may raise difficult legal issues; see the discussion at paras 7–41 and following.   **7–54**

Gifts of more than one item of property

It may be that a settlor gives away on the same occasion more than one item of property and subsequently enjoys one of the items given. Does this mean that all the items are property subject to a reservation? HMRC were given the following example: **7–55**

---

[95] See HMRC Manuals IHTM14316.

[96] Which the double taxation regulations (see paras 8–36 and following) would not prevent from arising.

[97] HMRC have since indicated that in such cases they would regard there being an outright gift of the mortgaged property; see pp.34–35 of the Ninth Cumulative Supplement to the third edition of this book. See also HMRC Manuals IHTM14314.

assume Cedric gives away his 300 acre farm, including the buildings thereon, to his son. The total value of the property given is £500,000 and several years later, when its value has doubled, Cedric is allowed to occupy one of the cottages, worth £40,000, on the estate. HMRC replied that the de minimis let-out would not apply but that generally where a gift comprises several items of property and the benefit is reserved out of only one they would expect that only that item would be property subject to a reservation. On that basis, they expected that only the cottage occupied by Cedric would be property subject to a reservation.[98]

V. THE FIRST HURDLE: DONEE'S POSSESSION AND ENJOYMENT

7–56 The first hurdle is found in s.102(1)(a). It is that possession and enjoyment of the property given must be bona fide assumed by the donee at or before the beginning of the relevant period.[99] In the absence of his doing so, the property given is prima facie property subject to a reservation.[100]

Actual possession and enjoyment

7–57 The requirement is one of *actual* possession and enjoyment, and it is actual possession and enjoyment of the whole of the property, i.e. there is no de minimis let-out as is found in the second and third hurdles. It is insufficient that the donee has the *right* to possession and enjoyment.

In *HM Adv v McTaggart Stewart*[101] income was to be accumulated under the terms of a trust during the life of the taxpayer. Such accumulation became invalid in 1888. The income, by mistake, continued to be accumulated until her death. She was entitled to half of the unlawful accumulations. In 1894 she executed a deed of gift of the whole of her personal estate. She died in 1902, at which time her share of the unlawful accumulations was paid over to the donee. It was held that the accumulations were dutiable because the donee had not assumed possession and enjoyment of them immediately upon the gift by the taxpayer.

In determining whether the donee assumed the requisite possession and enjoyment one must have regard to the nature of the property given. If, e.g. the gift is of a freehold encumbered by a lease, the donee's actual possession and enjoyment would not extend to the occupation of the property. An example given by HMRC[102] is that of a farmer who takes his son into partnership and makes a gift to him of a share of all the partnership assets including the land, after which they share profits and losses in the same proportion as they own the partnership assets at commencement. HMRC accept that in these circumstances the son has taken possession and enjoyment of the partnership share given to him in the form of his share of profits. The father's share of profits is referable to his own partnership share, not the share given.[103]

---

[98] See pp.32–33 of the Ninth Cumulative Supplement to the third edition of this book.
[99] See para.7–06 for the meaning of "relevant period".
[100] FA 1986 s.102(2)(a).
[101] *HM Adv v McTaggart Stewart* (1906) 13 S.L.T. 945.
[102] HMRC Manuals IHTM14332.
[103] On the other hand, they point out that the reservation of benefit rules *would* apply to a gift of a share of land farmed by a partnership (but owned by one of the partners), where the donee is not a partner and the partnership remains in rent-free occupation of the land. Here the donee has not assumed possession and enjoyment of the land.

In *Sillars and Deeprose v IRC*[104] as part of a tax planning exercise, a mother had made gifts of £10,000 to each of her two daughters. A few days later, she transferred a bank account holding £43,701 into joint names with the daughters, again intending to make an immediate gift. Initially withdrawals were made only by the mother to cover her own expenses or gifts by her to other members of the family. In later years, withdrawals were made by the daughters on behalf of the mother. Payments into the account were only ever made by the mother. For income tax purposes, the interest on the account was returned by the mother and the two daughters equally and at all times the daughters regarded themselves as each owning one third of the balance in the account.

The mother was able to dispose of the balance if she chose, the withdrawals were made for her benefit and no-one paid attention to whether she withdrew more than her one-third share. In short, the mother had a power to deal with the account as she saw fit, and it was not to be regarded as inconsistent that while the daughters saw themselves as owning a third of the balance from time to time, it was also understood that the mother was free to withdraw funds from the account for her own benefit.

One of the arguments put forward by HMRC and which was accepted by the Special Commissioner was that the mother had reserved a benefit on the basis that the gift was of a chose in action consisting of the whole account and that possession and enjoyment of the chose had not been assumed by the daughters.

Property held on trust

Under estate duty, where the property was held on trust, the trustees' possession was **7–58** the beneficiaries' possession for this purpose. It did not matter that the donor was the sole trustee (the *Oakes*[105] case) or one of the trustees (the *Perpetual Trustee*[106] case). This approach was based on the view that a gift into settlement consisted of a gift of the interests under the settlement.

It is thought that the basic position will be the same for IHT purposes. HMRC's published view[107] is that where a gift is made to a trust, the donee is the beneficiary, not the trustees, and the reservation of benefit rules should be applied to the equitable interest created in persons other than the donor (and any equitable interest retained by the donor is not included in the gift). However, the *Eversden*[108] case raised questions about whether or not this is a result of the estate duty view of the nature of a gift into settlement. In *Eversden*, HMRC argued unsuccessfully that the gift to the trust should be analysed as a transfer of a number of distinct interests in the settled property, of which only the husband's life interest was outside the scope of s.102 by virtue of the s.18 exemption. The Court of Appeal rejected this argument as involving "an unwarranted extension of the reasoning of the House of Lords in *Ingram*[109] and an unwarranted extension of the statutory language" and held that there was nothing in s.102 to displace IHTA 1984 s.49, under which the acquisition of an interest in possession was (at that time) treated as the equivalent of the acquisition of the underlying property.

However, s.49 of the 1984 Act no longer applies to most gifts to an interest in possession settlement on or after March 22, 2006 and does not apply to gifts to non-interest in possession settlements whenever made. Where property is settled otherwise

---

[104] *Sillars and Deeprose v IRC* [2004] S.T.C. (S.C.D.) 900; see also para.25–08.
[105] See para.7–26.
[106] See para.7–22.
[107] HMRC Manuals IHTM14392.
[108] See paras 7–35 and following.
[109] *Ingram v IRC* [2000] 1 A.C. 293.

than on interest in possession trusts within s.49 of the 1984 Act, e.g. where trustees are to accumulate income for the beneficiaries, the authors' view is that the gift is a class gift, with the result that the fact that no individual beneficiary can be said to have possession or enjoyment should not prevent the hurdle from being cleared.

The position where trustees have a discretion over income and capital is more difficult. If the correct view is that a gift on such trusts is also a class gift, the same position should obtain. In principle, the inclusion of the donor among the class of beneficiaries would mean that the donor failed at the second hurdle, but it should not prevent the first hurdle from being cleared. However, in the 2007 case of *Personal Representatives of Lyon v Revenue and Customs Commissioners*,[110] the Special Commissioner held that not only did the inclusion of the settlor as a potential beneficiary of a discretionary trust constitute a reservation of benefit under the second hurdle (i.e. because it meant that the property given to the trust was not enjoyed to the entire exclusion or virtually to the entire exclusion of the settlor), but the first hurdle had also not been cleared as possession and enjoyment of the property given had not been assumed by the trustees. It is questionable whether the latter conclusion (which appears to have been based on the terms of the trust deed and the way in which the trust was actually operated during the donor's lifetime) is correct.

The fact that the donee's legal title is perfected after he has become beneficially entitled to the property given, the donor in the interim holding the property and its income on trust for the donee, does not infringe the condition, and this is so even though no income accrued in the interim.[111]

Premiums paid direct to Life Office

7–59   HMRC do not seek to invoke the reservation of benefit provisions, on the basis that s.102(1)(a) has been infringed, where an individual who has settled a policy of insurance on trustees subsequently makes payments direct to the Life Office concerned, notwithstanding the fact that on the face of it it would appear that the donee of those premiums (the trustees) does not satisfy the test of immediate possession and enjoyment.[112] The position is presumably the same where an individual is the donee.

Delay in taking possession and enjoyment

7–60   Note that in order to clear the immediate possession and enjoyment hurdle possession and enjoyment must be assumed by the donee no later than at the beginning of the relevant period. Failure to comply with this requirement can arguably be remedied only by subsequent action and effluxion of time.

Assume, e.g. that X gives property to Y but that Y does not take possession and enjoyment at the time of the gift. Three months later Y takes possession and enjoyment. X dies seven years and two months after making the gift. HMRC accept that X will be

---

[110] SpC 616, June 26, 2007. See also para.7–76.
[111] *Re Rose* [1952] Ch. 499.
[112] HMRC Manuals IHTM14453.

regarded as having made a PET under s.102(4) when Y takes possession and enjoyment.[113]

VI. THE SECOND HURDLE: DONOR'S ENJOYMENT OF PROPERTY GIVEN

The second hurdle is found in the first limb of s.102(1)(b). It is that during the **7–61** relevant period[114] the property must be enjoyed to the entire exclusion, or virtually to the entire exclusion, of the donor. In the absence of such an exclusion, the gifted property is prima facie property subject to a reservation.[115]

Position under estate duty

Under estate duty the test was a rigorous one. Per Viscount Simonds: **7–62**

> "Where the question is whether the donor has been entirely excluded from the subject matter of the gift, that is the single fact to be determined. If he has not been so excluded, the eye can look no further to see whether his non-exclusion has been advantageous or otherwise to the donee".[116]

Thus, it did not matter that the donor gave full consideration; what mattered was that he was excluded from the subject-matter of the gift. The position is well illustrated by two cases.

The *Chick* case

In *Chick v Commissioners of Stamp Duties*[117] the taxpayer gave his son land   **7–63** outright. Seventeen months later the father became a member of a partnership with the donee and another of his sons. Each of the partners owned property and each partner brought into the partnership livestock and land. The three properties were subsequently used by the partnership for the depasturing of partnership stock. The father was manager of the partnership business with power to make final and conclusive decisions on all matters relating to it. The arrangement continued until he died. Among the arguments put forward by the taxpayer to rebut a claim that the land given was subject to the reservation of benefit rules was that the partnership agreement was an independent commercial transaction for full consideration. As to this, Viscount Simonds said:

> " . . . the subsection says nothing about independent transactions. The sole question is one of fact—was the donor excluded? If he was not excluded, it is not relevant to ask why he was not excluded. Equally with regard to the transaction being 'commercial' and 'for full consideration.' Their Lordships see no reason why a gloss should be put upon the plain words of the subsection by excluding from its operation such transactions."[118]

[113] See *Capital Taxes and Estate Planning Quarterly* (1988), pp.12–13.
[114] See para.7–06 for the meaning of "relevant period".
[115] FA 1986 s.102(2)(b).
[116] *Chick v Commissioner of Stamp Duties* [1958] A.C. 435 at 449.
[117] *Chick v Commissioner of Stamp Duties* [1958] A.C. 435.
[118] *Chick v Commissioner of Stamp Duties* [1958] A.C. 435 at 446–447.

If X gives Y land and on the same day takes a lease of the land the condition is infringed,[119] and it makes no difference that Y can make no better use of the property given to him than by leasing it back to X:

"... the possession and enjoyment by the donee of the property given to him in the manner most advantageous to himself are by no means incompatible with the donor not being excluded from it ..."[120]

The *Permanent Trustee* case

7–64   In *Commissioner of Stamp Duties of New South Wales v Permanent Trustee Co, New South Wales*,[121] the taxpayer in 1924 transferred to the respondent trustee company certain property to apply the whole or such part of the income thereof, as that company should see fit, for the maintenance, education and general support of his daughter until she should attain 30 or marry. On attaining the age of 30 she became entitled to the balance of the trust fund and all accumulations. The daughter married in 1940. Shortly after her marriage, acting on her father's instructions, she gave him full authority over her bank account into which she instructed the trustee to pay the trust income. The father subsequently drew out practically all the money paid into the account and used most of it for his own purposes. These withdrawals were treated as interest-free loans to the father by the daughter. The High Court of Australia held that withdrawals by the father from the bank account did not constitute the use by him of trust income but rather involved his borrowing from his daughter money which had lost its identity as trust income. The daughter chose, the court held, to lend the money to him: she might equally have lent it to a stranger. The decision would have been different, on the other hand, if the father had taken the moneys free from any obligation of repayment. This view was rejected by the Privy Council, who held that the father was the master of the income and was not therefore entirely excluded from benefiting from the property given. Viscount Simonds said:

"The transaction must be viewed as a whole and, since an integral part of it was that the testator before the account was opened was authorised to draw on it for his own purposes, it is irrelevant whether, when he did draw on it, he was or was not under any obligation to repay. Gift or loan, he for his own advantage used her money paying no interest for it and by so much reduced her enjoyment of what was her trust income, nothing else. The obligation to repay it affected the quantum of the benefit obtained by him: it did no more."[122]

Occupation under estate duty

7–65   The condition was not infringed for estate duty where X gave Y a house and Y allowed X to remain in residence, as his guest. This, in any event, is what was held in *Att Gen v Seccombe*[123] by Hamilton J., although his decision appears to proceed on the

---

[119] *Lang v Webb* (1912) 13 C.L.R. 503, approved in *Chick* at 447.
[120] *Chick v Commissioner of Stamp Duties* [1958] A.C. 435 at 448.
[121] *Commissioner of Stamp Duties of New South Wales v Permanent Trustee Co, New South Wales* [1956] A.C. 512.
[122] *Commissioner of Stamp Duties of New South Wales v Permanent Trustee Co, New South Wales* [1956] A.C. 512 at 526.
[123] *Att Gen v Seccombe* [1911] 2 K.B. 688.

fact that the guest lacked any enforceable right of occupation, and, as is discussed below, that would appear to be relevant (if at all) only to the third hurdle. The *Seccombe* case is difficult to reconcile with the later decision in *Chick*, but HMRC accepted it in practice for estate duty. The same practice is thought not to apply, however, for IHT. Certainly the ameliorating provisions[124] in Sch.20 para.6(1) of the 1986 Act imply that retention or assumption of actual occupation of land does infringe the condition unless it satisfies the requirements laid down in that paragraph.

Position under IHT

The basic position—ignoring the *Seccombe* case—is likely to be the same under the IHT legislation. Note, however, that the IHT legislation differs from the estate duty legislation in two respects. First, it contains a de minimis let-out. Secondly, it provides that the donor's enjoyment of property shall be disregarded in certain circumstances. Since each of these let-outs apply to both limbs of s.102(1)(b), they are considered below under Statutory (And Other) Ameliorations; see paras 7–81 and following. **7–66**

VII. THE THIRD HURDLE: BENEFIT TO THE DONOR

The third hurdle is found in the second limb of s.102(1)(b). It is that during the relevant period[125] the property must be enjoyed to the entire exclusion or virtually to the entire exclusion, of any benefit to the donor by contract or otherwise. In the absence of such an exclusion, the property given is prima facie property subject to a reservation.[126] **7–67**

The same test applied for estate duty purposes. Although the subject of a considerable degree of judicial comment, its precise ambit was never finally decided. Over the years there were various decisions which had the effect of limiting the scope of the statutory prohibition in various ways. The best approach will be to note these limitations and then to consider the effect of the *Chick* case on them. Against that background, the position under IHT will then be discussed. **7–68**

The position under estate duty

Under estate duty, it was not enough that the donor had retained some links with the property given away. The correct approach was to analyse each and every benefit with a view to seeing if it came within the statutory prohibition. In the *Oakes* case, Lord Reid said: **7–69**

> "In their Lordships' judgment it is now clear that it is not sufficient to bring a case within the scope of these sections to take the situation as a whole and find that the settlor has continued to enjoy substantial advantages which have some relation to the settled property; it is necessary to consider the nature and source of each of these advantages and determine

[124] See paras 7–84 and following.
[125] See para.7–06 for the meaning of "relevant period".
[126] FA 1986 s.102(2)(b).

whether or not it is a benefit of such a kind as to come within the scope of the section ..."[127]

Ejusdem generis rule

7–70   The first limitation placed by the court on the statutory prohibition was that the words "by contract or otherwise" had to be construed in accordance with the ejusdem generis rule. This view was first propounded by Hamilton J. in *Att Gen v Seccombe*.[128]

The case concerned a taxpayer who had given, inter alia, his house to his great-nephew, who, as master of the house and without any prior understanding, allowed the taxpayer to continue to live there, as his guest. Hamilton J. said:

> "I think that the words 'by contract or otherwise' were merely intended to be an improvement in drafting upon the earlier and more diffuse expression. There is no reason why the rule of ejusdem generis construction would not apply to these words. The enactment might have stopped at the words 'or of any benefit to him,' or it might have said 'of any benefit to him of whatsoever kind.' It has not done so. The words 'by contract or otherwise' indicate a genus of which contract is one species, and all other species are intended to be swept in. I do not see the difficulty of saying that there is a genus of which contract is a species. There are two points to notice about the word 'contract' as used in this connection. In the first place it points to a legal obligation; and in the next place it points to a contract between the same persons as were parties to the gift. Hence I think that the words 'by contract or otherwise' are aimed at any contract between the parties to the deed of gift or any contract with third parties having the effect of conferring a benefit on the donor, and to any transaction enforceable at law or in equity which, though not in the form of a contract, may confer a benefit, such as a lien. It is therefore not necessary to give any unusual or exceptional construction to the words."[129]

Hamilton J.'s view was referred to without dissent by the Court of Appeal in *Att Gen v Hon Lionel Michael St Aubyn (No.2)*.[130] See para.7–73 below in relation to IHT.

Detriment to donee

7–71   Under estate duty there appears to have been a fundamental difference between the second and third hurdles, in that under the second hurdle it was irrelevant whether or not the donor's non-exclusion was disadvantageous to the donee. In the *Oakes* case,[131] the Privy Council held that that factor was relevant to the third hurdle, something being a reserved benefit only if it detracted from or impaired the donee's enjoyment of the gift.

The facts relevant to this point in *Oakes* were that the taxpayer settled property on himself and his four children. He was a trustee with wide powers of management who was given reasonable remuneration for his work. He lived on the property and applied his children's share of the income from the property during their respective minorities for their maintenance, etc. As was noted above,[132] HMRC argued, inter alia, that the

---

[127] *Oakes v Commissioner of Stamp Duties of New South Wales* [1954] A.C. 57 at 72.
[128] *Att Gen v Seccombe* [1911] 2 K.B. 688.
[129] *Att Gen v Seccombe* [1911] 2 K.B. 688 at 703.
[130] *Att Gen v Hon Lionel Michael St Aubyn (No.2)* [1950] 2 K.B. 429 at 449.
[131] See para.7–26.
[132] See para.7–26.

remuneration constituted a benefit to the taxpayer. The Privy Council rejected the taxpayer's contention that he had, in effect, carved his entitlement out of the subject-matter of the gift, and held that the remuneration was "clearly" a benefit to him, notwithstanding the fact that it was reasonable. HMRC also contended that the taxpayer enjoyed benefits in the form of the following:

(1) residing on the property;
(2) not having to spend his own money in maintaining his children during their minorities; and
(3) the linking together of his one-fifth interest as tenant in common with the interests of the other tenants in common.

With regard to the residence, it was held that it might well have been that the property needed a manager living there and that there was nothing to show that residing there was to the taxpayer's advantage. Nor was it clear that such residence went beyond the taxpayer's right as a tenant in common of the property.

Residing there was accordingly not regarded as a benefit. Turning to the other outstanding matters, Lord Reid said:

" . . . it was said that even if the income which accrued to the children was properly spent for their maintenance and they are to be held to have had full benefit and enjoyment of it, yet there was also a benefit to the deceased because if it had not been available he would have had to spend more of his own money. The findings in the case are not very specific, but their Lordships will assume that there was some advantage to the deceased; but that advantage was not at the expense of the children and did not impair or diminish the value of the gift to them or their enjoyment of it. It is possible for a donee in the full and unrestrained enjoyment of his gift to use or spend it in a way that happens to produce some advantage to the donor without there being any loss or disadvantage to the donee. But in their Lordships' judgment, any such advantage is not a benefit within the meaning of the section.

For similar reasons their Lordships are not able to accept the ground of judgment of the Supreme Court of New South Wales to the effect that the linking together of the one-fifth beneficial interests of the donor and the donees resulted in a benefit or disadvantage to each share, and that this advantage to the donor brought the case within the section. Even if this linkage was of advantage to the deceased (of which there is no evidence) that advantage did not in any way impair the enjoyment of the gift by the donees or trench upon their rights . . . "[133]

The *Oakes* case thus appeared to impose a very helpful limitation on the meaning of the word "benefit", but in the *Chick* case, heard by the Privy Council four years later, doubt was cast on the validity of this distinction. Viscount Simonds distinguished the *Oakes* case from *Chick* case on the basis that in *Oakes*:

"the Board appears to be dealing with the second limb of the subsection, the question being whether the donor was entirely excluded from any benefit to him of whatsoever kind or in any way whatsoever. It is possible that in the consideration of this very difficult part of the subsection it may be pertinent in some cases to enquire whether the benefit derived by the donor is one that impairs or detracts from the donee's enjoyment of the gift. Their Lordships, with great respect, think that this is a matter which may require further examination, but, as they have already said, they are clearly of the opinion that it is not a relevant consideration where the question arises under the first limb of the subsection . . . "[134]

---

[133] *Oakes v Commissioner of Stamp Duties of New South Wales* [1954] A.C. 57 at 73–75.
[134] *Chick v Commissioner of Stamp Duties of New South Wales* [1958] A.C. 435 at 450.

Thus, there was some doubt as to whether the "detriment" limitation really existed for estate duty.

Referability under estate duty

7–72   Under estate duty, the benefit did not have to be reserved out of the gift, but it was sometimes said that it did have to be "referable" or "related" to the gift by the donor.[135]

Position under IHT

7–73   In the authors' view, there must be serious doubt as to whether the limitations imposed by the Court in the *Seccombe* and *Oakes* cases can be relied on under IHT. As regards the ejusdem generis rule, see *R v Special Commissioners of Income Tax, Ex p Shaftesbury Homes and Arethusa Training Ship*[136] and *Re Stratton's Disclaimer*.[137] Even if the rule still exists, it may be irrelevant if the benefit is obtained by virtue of associated operations.[138] As regards the "detriment" limitation, the cloud cast by Viscount Simonds's comments in the *Chick* case can hardly be ignored. Furthermore, given the ameliorating provisions where full consideration is provided by the donor,[139] it is thought that no such limitation exists for IHT: if it did, there would be no need for those provisions to apply to both limbs of s.102(1)(b).

A further limitation referred to in the *Seccombe* case was that benefits were regarded as being within the scope of the reservation of benefit rules only if they were enforceable.[140] Under IHT, however, this practice does not appear to have been followed and HMRC now take the view that unenforceable benefits are also within the scope of the reservation of benefit rules.[141]

Referability under IHT

7–74   HMRC accept that a limitation geared to referability does exist under IHT. IHTM14333–14334, provides (inter alia) that: "The benefit must be referable to the gift, although it need not issue from the gifted property itself ", and gives the following example:

"A husband and wife each own 50% of the issued capital of a limited company. The company owns the freehold property in which they live. The spouses transfer their shares into an Accumulation and Maintenance Settlement. They continue to live in the house rent-free until the husband's death.

[135] See the Court of Appeal's judgment in *Att Gen v St Aubyn* [1950] 2 K.B. 429 at 450; cf. Lord Radcliffe's view in the House of Lords [1952] A.C. 15 at 47.
[136] *R v Special Commissioners of Income Tax, Ex p Shaftesbury Homes and Arethusa Training Ship* [1923] 1 K.B. 393.
[137] *Re Stratton's Disclaimer* [1957] 1 Ch. 32.
[138] See para.7–75.
[139] See paras 7–84 and following.
[140] See the reference to "legal obligation" at para.7–70.
[141] See HMRC Manuals IHTM14333.

This is not a GWR. The continued occupation of the property is not referable to the gift."

The limitation as to referability, however, has in practice been weakened by the associated operations provisions, which will be considered below.

Statutory extension—associated operations

Sch.20, para.6(1)(c) provides that: 7–75

"a benefit which the donor obtained by virtue of any associated operations . . . of which the disposal by way of gift is one shall be treated as a benefit to him by contract or otherwise."

The estate duty legislation contained a similar provision.[142] Although the inclusion of para.6(1)(c) militates against any argument to the effect that a benefit needs to be referable or related to the gift in question, the words "by virtue of" may leave room for argument[143] and, as indicated in the previous paragraph, HMRC accept that such a limitation exists. The inclusion of para.6(1)(c) also eliminates the ejusdem generis limitation (if that limitation still exists), but leaves unaffected the "detriment" limitation (to the extent that that limitation still exists). One question that remains is what is the effect, if any, of para.6(1)(c) in circumstances where a donor begins by carving out a right from property which he proposes to give away, following which he gives away the property, subject to that right? The carving out of the right will presumably be an operation associated with the later gift, but can it be said that the right is a "benefit" to the donor? The authors find it difficult to see how a person can confer a benefit on himself.[144]

In HMRC's view,[145] a gift of property to a person, subject to a reservation to the donor's spouse or civil partner, will not in itself be a gift with reservation, but if the donor shares the spouse's/civil partner's enjoyment or benefit in the property, it may be said that the donor has not been entirely excluded.

Potential benefit

Under estate duty there was a suggestion that it sufficed that the donor was excluded   7–76
from actual benefit. Under IHT, on the other hand, it seems, at least where the second hurdle is concerned, that the donor will in principle fail to clear the second hurdle unless he is also excluded from potential benefit.

The point arose in the *Eversden* case (see para.7–35) with reference to the position of a donor who was a discretionary beneficiary of a settlement of which she was the settlor. The Special Commissioner held that the settlor's entitlement to be considered as a potential recipient of benefit by the trustees precluded a finding that the trust fund was enjoyed to the entire or virtually to the entire exclusion of benefit to her under the settlement. It is not entirely clear whether the Special Commissioner came to this

---

[142] FA 1960 s.35(3).

[143] See the discussion in paras 9–13 and following of the judicial limits imposed on the application of the associated operations provisions.

[144] HMRC accept that a retention of rights will not, of itself, be treated as giving rise to a reservation: see HMRC Manuals IHTM14334, Example 9.

[145] See HMRC Manuals IHTM14338.

conclusion on the basis that the settlor's right to be considered was itself sufficient benefit to trigger the provisions or whether the fact that she might benefit was the relevant consideration.

Lightman J. endorsed the Special Commissioner's conclusion and made it clear that he was doing so on the basis of the latter reasoning:

> "I entirely agree. The insertion of the provision enabling benefit to be conferred on her creates the potential for the conferment of substantial benefit on her and the consequent diversion of benefit from others. The provision in her favour is not consistent with her entire exclusion or virtual entire exclusion. It cannot be discounted or virtually entirely discounted by evaluation of the probabilities or otherwise that occasion will arise for conferring benefits on her".[146]

The same point was again considered in the *Lyon* case.[147] The donor in this case made a gift of £2.7 million to a discretionary trust of which he was the settlor and a potential beneficiary: he also had power to revoke the trust and to regulate investment management. During the settlor's lifetime the trustees made distributions of £15,695 to him.[148] The appellants (the settlor's personal representatives) unsuccessfully submitted that HMRC's interpretation of Lightman J.'s ruling in *Eversden* was too restrictive and that whether a settlor's beneficial interest under a discretionary trust constituted a reservation of benefit depended on the facts of the individual case. They stated that *Eversden* was decided principally on the fact that the settlor in that case had enjoyed substantial benefits from the trust fund, whereas in *Lyon* the level of the benefits received by the settlor was insignificant and took the arrangements outside the scope of the reservation of benefit rules.

The Special Commissioner, however, held that the finding of a reservation of benefit in *Eversden* was clearly based not only on the actual benefit received by the settlor (in the form of rent-free occupation) but also on the fact that she was a beneficiary of the trust.

> "The fact that the *Eversden* settlor received a substantial benefit in her own lifetime was not relevant to the second ground, which undermined the Appellants' reliance upon the differences in *Eversden*. The reality was that this Appeal shared the identical factual basis with *Eversden* in respect of the second ground, namely, both settlors were potential beneficiaries under the trusts created by them."

He went on to reject the appellants' argument that the benefits received by the settlor were minimal (and therefore the reservation of benefit rules did not apply) as a misinterpretation of Revenue's *Tax Bulletin 9*,[149] which considered a range of situations in which a gift initially made without a reservation could be compromised by subsequent actions of the donor. In *Lyon*, the issue was not primarily about the donor's actions after the gift, but about whether a gift without reservation was made in the first place. The appellants' reasoning was flawed, because they had worked backwards from the final distribution of funds to justify their position, whereas they should have started with the initial gift to the trust and asked themselves the question whether it was a true gift or a "pretend gift". In this case, a proper analysis of the trust deed would have revealed that not only did the settlor stand to benefit from the whole trust fund as a

---

[146] *IRC v Eversden* [2002] S.T.C. 1109 at 1126, para.17.

[147] SpC 616, June 26, 2007: see also para.7–58 and the *Buzzoni* case referred to in para.7–83.

[148] A further £10,000 was distributed to a third party: it was assumed that these payments were made at the settlor's direction, as the third party was not a beneficiary and the appellants were unable to identify or locate her.

[149] Issued in November 1993.

potential beneficiary, but he also retained significant control by giving himself powers to revoke the trust and regulate investment management.[150]

A reservation of benefit potentially also arises where a settlor is not included as a **7–77** beneficiary at the outset, but the settlement includes a power for the trustees to add him to the class of beneficiaries at some future date. In these circumstances HMRC have indicated[151] that they will determine whether or not a reservation arises on the basis of the particular facts.

In *Eversden*, Lightman J. was concerned with the possibility of a donor benefiting **7–78** under a settlement of which he was the settlor. It is clear that the mere possibility of such a donor benefiting under the settlement meant the donor did not clear the third hurdle. What is less clear is whether a similar result would obtain in a case where Sch.20 para.6(1)(c) was relevant. That provision refers to "a benefit which the donor obtained by virtue of any associated operations" and the use of "obtained" arguably suggests that para.6(1)(c) is relevant only in relation to an actual and not merely a potential benefit.

Settlement powers

Assume X creates a settlement which he has power to revoke but from which he is **7–79** otherwise excluded from benefit. His power to revoke the settlement will be a "settlement power" within s.47A and so excluded by the definition of "property" in IHTA 1984 s.272 (in conjunction with s.5) from being comprised in his estate.[152] Does this mean that his power is to be ignored in deciding whether or not the third hurdle is cleared? The authors take the view that it is not, because the relevant question is whether the property comprised in the settlement is enjoyed to the entire exclusion of any benefit to X and, applying the "potential benefit" test he is not, as matter of fact, excluded from such benefit.[153]

Reversionary interests

The question arises whether the retention by a donor of a reversionary interest under **7–80** a trust could be regarded as a "benefit to the donor" within s.102(1)(b). HMRC appear to take the view that this will in principle not constitute a reservation of benefit. A letter of May 18, 1987 from HMRC contains the following statement:

> "In the case where a gift is made into trust, the retention by the settlor (donor) of a reversionary interest under the trust is not considered to constitute a reservation, whether the retained interest arises under the express terms of the trust or arises by operation of general law e g a resulting trust."

[150] Although (as in *IRC v Eversden* [2002] S.T.C. 1109) the mere fact that he was one of the beneficiaries was sufficient to find that the gifted property was not enjoyed to his entire exclusion or virtually to his entire exclusion. In view of this, the authors query whether the control aspects are really relevant: in the absence of a beneficial interest, the retention of a degree of control should not amount to a reservation of benefit.

[151] See HMRC Manuals IHTM14393.

[152] See para.25–07.

[153] The settlor's power of revocation was a factor (although not the sole deciding factor) in the finding of a reservation of benefit in the *Lyon* case described in para.7–76.

This statement provides some comfort in circumstances where, for example, life tenant A's interest in possession under a trust is terminated[154] and A is also a default beneficiary. However, the scope of the term "reversionary interest" in the statement is not entirely clear and on a cautious view it would therefore be advisable to ensure either that A could not derive any further benefit from the trust at all following the termination of his interest in possession, or that he could only do so after several contingencies fell in.

VIII. STATUTORY (AND OTHER) AMELIORATIONS

7–81   There are a number of cases in which the reservation of benefit provisions will be prevented from applying.

Lowering of second and third hurdles

7–82   The initial ameliorations operate by effectively lowering the second and third hurdles. The first hurdle, however, remains unaffected.

De minimis let-out

7–83   The second and third hurdles are subject to a de minimis let-out in that it suffices that the donor is virtually entirely excluded from enjoyment or benefit. Revenue Interpretation RI 55[155] states:

> "The word 'virtually' in the de minimis rule in s.102(1)*(b)* is not defined and the statute does not give any express guidance about its meaning. However, the shorter OED defines it as, amongst other things, 'to all intents' and 'as good as'. Our interpretation of 'virtually to the entire exclusion' is that it covers cases in which the benefit to the donor is insignificant in relation to the gifted property.
>
> It is not possible to reduce this test to a single crisp proposition. Each case turns on its own unique circumstances and the questions are likely to be ones of fact and degree. We do not operate s.102(1)(b) in such a way that donors are unreasonably prevented from having limited access to property they have given away and a measure of flexibility is adopted in applying the test.
>
> Some examples of situations in which we consider that s.102(1)(b) permits limited benefit to the donor without bringing the GWR provisions into play are given below to illustrate how we apply the de minimis test:
> - a house which becomes the donee's residence but where the donor subsequently
> - stays, in the absence of the donee, for not more than 2 weeks each year, or
> - stays with the donee for less than one month each year;
> - social visits, excluding overnight stays made by a donor as a guest of the donee, to a house which he had given away. The extent of the social visits should be no greater than the visits which the donor might be expected to make to the donee's house in the absence of any gift by the donor;

[154] With effect from March 22, 2006, s.102ZA provides that the lifetime termination of an interest in possession to which s.49(1) of the 1984 Act applies is deemed to be a disposal by way of gift (and therefore within the scope of the reservation of benefit rules) even if this would not otherwise be the case: see para.7–99.

[155] Reproduced in HMRC Manuals IHTM14333.

- a temporary stay for some short term purpose in a house the donor had previously given away, for example:
  - while the donor convalesces after medical treatment,
  - while the donor looks after a donee convalescing after medical treatment,
  - while the donor's own home is being redecorated;
- visits to a house for domestic reasons, for example baby-sitting by the donor for the donee's children;
- a house together with a library of books which the donor visits less than 5 times in any year to consult or borrow a book;
- a motor car which the donee uses to give occasional (i.e. less than 3 times a month) lifts to the donor;
- land which the donor uses to walk his dogs or for horse riding provided this does not restrict the donee's use of the land.

It follows, of course, that if the benefit to the donor is, or becomes, more significant, the GWR provisions are likely to apply. Examples of this include gifts of[156]:
- a house in which the donor then stays most weekends, or for a month or more each year;
- a second home or holiday home which the donor and the donee both then use on an occasional basis;
- a house with a library in which the donor continues to keep his own books, or which the donor uses on a regular basis, for example because it is necessary for his work;
- a motor car which the donee uses every day to take the donor to work."

A recent case in which the meaning of "virtually excluded" was considered was *Buzzoni* (though the case is to be appealed).[157] The taxpayer (prior to the enactment of the anti-*Ingram* provisions in 1999) granted an underlease commencing 10 years after the grant, under which the underlessee covenanted inter alia to pay the service charges due under the taxpayer's headlease. Other covenants included a covenant to repair and decorate. It was held that the service charges (of £9,000 p.a.) and other covenants were too substantial for the taxpayer to be considered virtually excluded from benefit, and the point was made that even if the covenants were not enforced there was a reservation, since it is the possibility of benefit not any actual benefit that was relevant.

Full consideration let-out

Following the decision in the *Chick* case, the position where a donor who retained   **7–84** or assumed actual enjoyment of land, an incorporeal right over the land or actual possession of chattels was eased, such occupation or possession being disregarded if the donor provided full consideration in money or money's worth.[158] Not surprisingly, the Finance Act 1986 contains a virtually identical provision in the form of Sch.6, para.(1)(a), which provides, in relation to s.102(1)(b), that in the case of property which is an interest in land or a chattel,[159] retention or assumption by the donor of actual occupation of the land or actual enjoyment of an incorporeal right over the land, or actual possession of the chattel is disregarded if it is for full consideration in money or money's worth. Note that the relief afforded by para.6(1)(a) is available only if the consideration is full, i.e. if the consideration is partial no relief is available at all. Assume that X owns a rundown cottage in the country which he gives to his son. Every August X lives in the cottage rent-free on terms that he will carry out agreed repairs,

---

[156] *Buzzoni v Revenue and Customs Commissioners* [2011] UKFTT 267 (TC).

[157] *Buzzoni v Revenue and Customs Commissioners* [2011] UKFTT 267 (TC).

[158] FA 1959 s.35(1) and (2).

[159] The rules apply in Scotland as if references to a chattel were references to a corporeal moveable; FA 1986 Sch.20 para.6(3).

the value of which is not less than the rent which the son could obtain if he let the cottage commercially. The making of the repairs will constitute full consideration in money's worth, and X's enjoyment of the cottage will be disregarded. If the repairs were worth less than the rent, para.6(1)(a) relief would not be available at all.

Revenue Interpretation RI 55 states that while HMRC take the view that full consideration is required throughout the relevant period—so that rent paid should be reviewed at appropriate intervals to reflect market changes—they do recognise that there is no single value at which consideration can be fixed as "full". Rather, they accept that what constitutes full consideration in any case lies within a range of values reflecting normal valuation tolerances, and that any amount within that range can be accepted as satisfying the statutory test. In practice, HMRC take the view that:

> "it is unlikely that any such arrangement could be overturned if the taxpayer can demonstrate that it resulted from
> - a bargain negotiated at arm's length
> - by parties who were independently advised and
> - which followed the normal commercial criteria in force at the time it was negotiated".[160]

This let-out is rarely used in relation to a gift of land, because it is normally too costly. It may, however, in appropriate cases, be useful in relation to a gift of chattels (see para.7–88).

7–85   It should be emphasised that the full consideration let-out does not apply in relation to assets other than land and chattels. HMRC give the following example[161]:

> "A, who is a partner, withdraws capital from his partnership capital account and gives it to B. B then lends the partnership an equivalent cash sum.
>   This is a reservation. Though A may pay B a commercial rate of interest for the loan, this payment will not prevent the loan being a reservation."

Ministerial statement

7–86   On June 10,1986, Mr. Peter Brooke, the then Minister of State, Treasury, said:

> " . . . it may be that my Hon. Friend's intention concerns the common case where someone gives away an individual share in land, typically a house, which is then occupied by all the joint owners including the donor. For example, elderly parents may make unconditional gifts of undivided shares in their house to their children and the parents and their children occupy the property as their family home, each owner bearing his or her share of the running costs. In those circumstances, the parents' occupation or enjoyment of the part of the house that they have given away is in return for similar enjoyment of the children of the other part of the property. Thus the donors' occupation is for a full consideration.
>   Accordingly, I assure my Hon. Friend that the gift with reservation rules will not be applied to an unconditional gift of an undivided share in land merely because the property is occupied by all the joint owners or tenants in common, including the donor."[162]

The thinking behind this statement is not entirely clear. One would have thought that the parents' occupation in the example was by virtue of their being tenants in common with the children, i.e. there is no question of the children "allowing" them to live

---

[160] See HMRC Manuals IHTM14341.
[161] HMRC Manuals IHTM14336.
[162] *Hansard*, Standing Committee G, June 10, 1986, Col.425.

there.[163] The views expressed in the statement appear to proceed upon the premise that the house is divided into "parts" so that the parents use of the children's' "part" is in return for letting the children use their "part". In reality, of course, the interest of a tenant in common is in the whole property: he is the owner of an undivided share. Accordingly, the parents' right to occupy the entire property is derived from the interest retained and does not amount to a reservation in the share given. In the authors' view, the benefit conferred by the children is arguably that of the children not enforcing the trust for sale,[164] because the result of a forced sale would be that the parents were no longer entitled to occupy the house. The parents provide consideration for this in that they do not force a sale, either. Brian Houghton, Inland Revenue Under Secretary for Capital Taxes and Rating, elaborating on this statement, subsequently indicated in correspondence with The Law Society that so long as all the joint owners remained in occupation the donor's occupation would not be treated as a reservation provided that the gift was unconditional and there was no collateral benefit to the donor. Moreover, an arrangement would not necessarily be jeopardised merely because it involved a gift of an unequal share in a house.[165]

The statement has since been overtaken by s.102B in relation to disposals after March 8, 1999; see paras 7–105 and following.

HMRC's practice

A key question is, what constitutes "full consideration in money or money's worth" **7–87** for purposes of para.6(1)(a)? A similar requirement appears in s.16 of the 1984 Act, which relieves the grant of a tenancy of agricultural property from being a transfer of value if, inter alia, the grant is for full consideration in money or money's worth.[166] HMRC's practice in applying s.16 appears to be to have regard to the entirety of the arrangement, not just to the rent initially chargeable. The authors agree with this approach. On this basis, it will clearly be necessary to include rent review clauses where a lease is granted. One point which is not absolutely clear is whether it suffices that the consideration is full at the time of the gift or whether it is necessary for the consideration to be full throughout the relevant period. In the authors' view, it is only prudent to proceed on the basis that full consideration is necessary throughout the relevant period and that therefore a donee must, e.g. exercise his right to increase rent under a rent review clause.[167]

HMRC appear, commendably, perhaps on the basis of one or more of:

(1) the ministerial statement;
(2) the estate duty case of *Att Gen v Boden*[168]; and/or
(3) common sense,

to be giving the words "for full consideration in money or money's worth" a wide reading.

---

[163] See *Oakes v Commissioner of Stamp Duties of New South Wales* [1954] A.C. 57, discussed at para.7–26.

[164] Much would depend on the actual terms of the trust for sale in question.

[165] See *Tolley's Yellow Tax Handbook Part 3, IHT Press Releases*, letter of May 18, 1987.

[166] See para.2–54. See also *IRC v Macpherson* [1988] S.T.C. 362, discussed at para.15–15 and *Att Gen v Boden* [1912] 1 K.B. 539 and *Att Gen v Ralli* [1936] 15 A.T.C. 523, both discussed at para.28–17.

[167] See HMRC Manuals IHTM14335. A reservation of benefit may arise at a later date even if the gift is made for full consideration at the outset.

[168] *Att Gen v Boden* [1912] 1 K.B. 539, discussed at para.28–17.

In the same correspondence with the Law Society, Mr Houghton, considering the case where a father who owns land which he farms in partnership with his son gives part of the land to his son, said that the "full consideration let-out" may be available to prevent the father's gift being caught by the reservation of benefit provisions, and that in considering the availability of the let-out:

> "... we shall take account of all the circumstances surrounding the arrangement including the sharing of profits and losses, the donor's and the donee's interests in the land, and their respective commitment and expertise."[169]

The message appears to be that HMRC will not seek to apply the reservation of benefit provisions in such a way as would frustrate normal planning within a commercial context. In particular, HMRC will probably not challenge arm's length, commercial arrangements entered into by independently advised parties, e.g. returning to the above example of father and son, if the father and son, having taken separate advice, revised the partnership sharing ratio to reflect their altered circumstances.[170]

Chattels leases

7–88   The "full consideration" requirement is potentially problematic in relation to assets such as country house chattels or valuable works of art for which there may be no meaningful rental market. In practice the convention has arisen that a rental fee of 1 per cent of capital value is regarded as an accepted norm for the purposes of meeting the full consideration requirement for chattels leases. The basis of the 1 per cent figure is not entirely clear, but it has regularly been applied in practice by valuers and accepted by HMRC.

Following the introduction of the pre-owned assets income tax charge in 2004, HMRC appeared to be signalling a change in their previous approach when they challenged the adequacy of the 1 per cent norm in a number of cases. The attack was heavily based on the decision, in a different context, in the Canadian case of *Lloyd Youngman v The Queen*,[171] in which the Federal Court of Appeal held that the appropriate basis for calculating the income tax benefit of occupation provided by a company of which the taxpayers were shareholders was the rate of return to the company, rather than the free-market rental rate. In the event HMRC accepted that the accepted norm of 1 per cent of capital value did constitute full consideration provided that the accepted procedures relating to the negotiation of the rent had been followed, and they subsequently abandoned such challenges.[172]

It should be noted that the 1 per cent figure is no more than a norm: each case will need to be considered on its own merits and it is important to take into account HMRC's guidance referred to above. In particular, the taxpayer will need to be able to demonstrate that the rental rate resulted from (1) a bargain negotiated at arm's length (2) by parties who were independently advised, and (3) which followed the normal commercial criteria in force at the time it was negotiated.[173] In practice this will

---

[169] See *Capital Taxes—A Quarterly Commentary* (1987) pp.49–51.
[170] For further discussion, see paras 7–145 and following.
[171] *Lloyd Youngman v The Queen* [1990] 90 D.T.C. 6322.
[172] HMRC's pre-owned assets guidance states that a chattels lease carve-out will not be subject to a reservation of benefit (and therefore *will* be within the scope of the pre-owned asset tax).
[173] See HMRC Manuals IHTM14341.

normally involve instructing independent valuers for each side to negotiate the "rent" and other terms of the lease.

The Chattels Valuation Fiscal Forum convened by HMRC on November 22, 2006 included a discussion of various matters relating to chattels leases. One of these was the question whether the figure of 1 per cent included certain costs (if paid by the lessee) such as insurance and security, as had commonly been assumed. However, HMRC indicated during the forum that in their view the 1 per cent figure did not include such costs. Another point raised was whether purely nominal rental rates are appropriate in respect of particularly important chattels, on the basis that in the real world a rate as high as 1 per cent could not be obtained for a chattel worth many millions of pounds. HMRC rejected this argument and made it clear that taxpayers who apply purely nominal rental rates can expect them to be vigorously challenged. The forum convened subsequently on December 7, 2009 and December 1, 2010 and confirmed on both occasions that the 2006 advice still stood.[174]

Some donors of chattels enter into leaseback arrangements under which the rent is capitalised. This arrangement avoids an income tax charge in the hands of the donee and will, assuming that the premium paid constitutes full consideration, still be effective for IHT purposes.

Disadvantaged donor let-out

The legislation also makes special provision to ease the position where a donor **7–89** makes a gift to a relative who subsequently looks after the donor in the donor's hour of need. Schedule 20 para.6(1)(b) provides that in the case of property which is an interest in land, but only in such a case, occupation by the donor of all or part of the land shall be disregarded in determining whether the conditions in s.102(1)(b) are infringed if the donee is a relative of the donor or the donor's spouse or civil partner and the occupation satisfies three further conditions, i.e. it:

(1) results from a change in the circumstances of the donor since the time of the gift, being a change which was unforeseen at that time and was not brought about by the donor in order to receive the benefit of para.6(1)(b);
(2) occurs at a time when the donor has become unable to maintain himself through old age, infirmity or otherwise; and
(3) represents a reasonable provision by the donee for the care and maintenance of the donor.

HMRC give the following example:

> "A perfectly healthy donor gives his house to his son, but five years later is struck down by motor neurone disease, as a result of which he has to move back to his former house to be cared for by his son. His occupation has resulted from an unforeseen change in his circumstances, and that occupation represents reasonable provision for his care and maintenance."[175]

[174] http://www.iemployee.co.uk/consultations/cuf.html [Accessed November 12, 2012].
[175] HMRC Manuals IHTM14342.

In the authors' view it is likely that inability to maintain oneself in this context relates to physical rather than financial maintenance, but the point is not entirely clear.

Exempt transfers blanket let-out

7–90   Section 102(5) provides that the reservation of benefit rules do not apply if, or to the extent that, the property is disposed of by way of a gift which is an exempt transfer under any of the following exemptions:

- section 18 exemption;
- small gifts exemption;
- marriage gifts exemption;
- charities exemption;
- political parties exemption;
- housing associations exemption;
- national purposes exemption;
- maintenance funds for historic buildings exemption; and
- employee trusts exemption.

The annual exemption and the normal expenditure out of income exemption are conspicuous by their absence from this list. A PET will also not come within it, even if made seven years or more before the death of the donor.[176]

Although the small gifts exemption is strictly only available in relation to outright gifts, HMRC accept that the mere fact that a donor has reserved a benefit in the property given should not, in itself, prevent the gift from being regarded as an outright one.[177]

Section 18 exemption anti-avoidance

7–91   The Finance Act 2003, s.185 introduced ss.102(5A)–(5C) in order to remove any doubt as to the application of s.102(5) in certain circumstances. The issue in doubt was the effect of s.102(5) where an individual settled property on terms under which his spouse[178] took an interest in possession which interest subsequently terminated leaving the property held upon discretionary trusts under which the settlor was capable of benefiting. Did s.102(5) mean that the reservation of benefit rules were incapable of applying on the basis that the initial disposal qualified for the s.18 exemption, or were the provisions capable of applying on the basis that the settlor had made two gifts—one to his spouse of the interest which he had given her and another of the reversionary interest to the discretionary class?

The issue arose in *Eversden v IRC*[179] which was decided in the taxpayer's favour before a Special Commissioner, Lightman J. and a unanimous Court of Appeal. The

---

[176] Although HMRC Manuals IHTM14319 refers only to PETs made seven years or more before the death of the transferor.

[177] See HMRC Manuals IHTM14319.

[178] In 2003 the s.18 exemption applied only to spouses: it was subsequently extended to civil partners with effect from December 5, 2005.

[179] *Eversden v IRC* [2003] S.T.C. 822; see paras 7–35 and following.

Special Commissioner's decision in late 2001 led to an increasingly feverish popularisation of so-called "*Eversden* schemes" which were finally reined in by the introduction of anti-avoidance legislation in late June 2003. These schemes basically involved a donor settling property on terms such that he retained an interest in possession in a small proportion of the property, his spouse taking an interest in possession in the remainder. Most of the donee spouse's interest was then terminated so that the property in which the spouse's interest previously subsisted became held upon discretionary trusts under which both spouses could benefit. The basic argument was that *Eversden* meant that the reservation of benefit provisions were prevented from applying to the property held upon discretionary trusts.

Section 102(5A)–(5C) have effect in relation to disposals made on or after June 20, 2003. Section 102(5A) provides that s.102(5)(a) does not apply if or, as the case may be, to the extent that the four conditions are satisfied:

(1) the property becomes settled by virtue of the gift;
(2) by reason of the donor's spouse or[180] civil partner (who is referred to as "the relevant beneficiary") becoming beneficially entitled to an interest in possession in the settled property, the disposal is or, as the case may be, is to any extent within the s.18 exemption because of s.49(1) of the 1984 Act;
(3) at some time after the disposal during the donor's lifetime the relevant beneficiary's interest in possession comes to an end; and
(4) on the occasion when the interest in possession comes to an end, the relevant beneficiary does not become entitled to the settled property or to another interest in possession in the settled property.

For this purpose (i) the disposal of an interest is treated as the termination of that interest, and (ii) references to any property or to an interest in any property include references to part of any property or interest.[181]

Section 102(5B) then provides that to the extent that s.102 applies by virtue of s.102(5A), s.102 has effect as if the disposal by way of gift had been made immediately after the beneficiary's interest in possession came to an end.

It should be noted that s.102(5A–5C) will rarely apply in relation to disposals made on or after March 22, 2006, because in most cases a gift to an interest in possession settlement will be a chargeable transfer and s.49(1) will not apply, i.e. a beneficiary who becomes entitled to an interest in possession on or after that date will generally not be treated as beneficially entitled to the property in which his interest subsists. This includes cases where the beneficiary is the spouse or civil partner of the donor.

The anti-avoidance provisions are targeted directly at *Eversden* schemes. The wording of condition (4) appears to be modelled on that in s.53(2) of the 1984 Act. The legislation appears to assume that the interest in possession in settled property of a beneficiary can terminate in circumstances where on that same occasion he acquires another interest in the same settled property. Perhaps the draftsman assumed that this occurred where, e.g., an individual with an interest for a term of years acquired a life interest expectant on that prior interest.

7–92

In view of this point, the question was raised in the fourth edition of this book (at para.6–87) whether it was possible to resuscitate *Eversden* by arranging matters so that a spouse was given an interest in possession which terminated in circumstances such that that spouse acquired another interest in possession, so that condition (4) remained unsatisfied and on the termination of the subsequent interest in possession the property

---

[180] With effect from December 5, 2005.
[181] FA 1986 s.102(5C).

267

could be held upon trusts under which the donor could benefit without infringing the reservation of benefit provisions. Although arrangements were apparently devised to achieve this effect, the authors concluded that this approach was unlikely to succeed. In any event, as indicated above, the creation of an interest in possession on or after March 22, 2006 (even if the settlement was established before that date) will generally be outside the scope of s.49(1) of the 1984 Act.

Charity exemption

7-93   Special care needs to be taken where, e.g., the charity exemption is relied on. One of the approaches to planning where the reservation of benefit provisions are concerned is for an intending donor, prior to making a gift, to "carve out" of property which he intends to give away such rights as he wishes to retain. Where, however, the gift is to a charity, such a "carve-out" may prevent the charity exemption from being available.[182]

Small gifts exemption

7-94   It may be possible, where 100 per cent business relief is available, to arrange matters so that the transferor, in addition to transferring the property qualifying for business relief, also transfers other property not qualifying for the relief but which nevertheless comes within the small gifts exemption.[183]

Premiums on pre-March 18, 1986 policies

7-95   Section 102(6) provides that s.102 does not apply if the disposal of property by way of gift is made under the terms of an insurance policy made before March 18, 1986, unless the policy is varied on or after that date so as to increase the benefit secured or to extend the term of this insurance.[184] For this purpose, any change in the terms of the policy which is made in pursuance of an option or other power conferred by the policy is deemed to be a variation of the policy.[185]

It may be that a pre-March 18, 1986, policy confers an option or other power under which benefits (and premiums) may be increased to take account of increases in the retail prices index (or any similar index specified in the policy). In such a case, the exercise of the option or power, before August 1, 1986, is disregarded for these

---

[182] See paras 3–38 and following.

[183] See *Private Client Business* (1993), p.7 and HMRC Manuals IHTM14319.

[184] HMRC take the view that if a pre-March 18, 1986 policy is varied on or after that date, the reservation of benefit rules apply in relation to all premiums paid after March 17, 1986 (i.e. not just those paid after the variation): HMRC Manuals IHTM14433.

[185] FA 1986 s.102(6).

purposes to the extent that the right to exercise the option or power would be lost if it had not been exercised on or before that date.[186]

Superannuation arrangements

HMRC's Statement of Practice SP10/86 provides as follows with regard to death benefits under superannuation arrangements[187]: **7–96**

> "The Board confirm that their existing practice (see SP E3) of not charging capital transfer tax on death benefits that are payable from tax-approved occupational pension and retirement annuity schemes under discretionary trusts also applies to inheritance tax.
> The practice extends to tax under the "gifts with reservation" rules as well as to tax under the ordinary inheritance tax rules."

The effect of this practice is that the reservation of benefit rules do not apply where death benefits payable under an approved scheme are held on discretionary trusts and the deceased member or his estate or personal representatives are potential beneficiaries. However, if the scheme is unapproved the reservation of benefit provisions do apply in this scenario and the death benefits will be chargeable to IHT on the member's death.[188]

Statutory right to reimbursement

A settlor who has paid CGT on gains attributed to him by s.86 of the Taxation of Chargeable Gains Act 1992 has the statutory right under para.6 of Sch.5 to that Act to recover that tax from the trustees of the settlement to whom the gains arose. Paragraph 9 of Statement of Practice SP5/92[189] provides that neither this right nor any provision in the trust deed either requiring the trustees to recognise the settlor's para.6 right or to reimburse the settlor is regarded as a reservation of benefit.[190] **7–97**

IX. DEEMED RESERVATION OF BENEFIT

The legislation contains anti-avoidance provisions targeted at particular instances where the basic provisions would not apply. Where these provisions operate, the property in question is treated in such a way that the clawback provisions in s.102(3) and (4) are not prevented from operating. It is perhaps worth noting that a similar situation obtains where an election is made under the preowned assets regime in the Finance Act 2004 (discussed at the end of this chapter) that the reservation of benefit **7–98**

---

[186] FA 1986 s.102(7).

[187] SP 10/86 (reproduced at HMRC Manuals IHTM17073); see also para.23–13.

[188] See HMRC Manuals IHTM17073.

[189] Reproduced in *Tolley's Yellow Tax Handbook*, Pt 2.

[190] A failure by the settlor to exercise his para.6 right may give rise to a deemed disposition under IHTA 1984 s.3(3); see para.2–21. In an ICAEW Guidance Note on December 14, 1992 (see *Tolley's Yellow Tax Handbook*, Pt 2), HMRC commented that the duration of the right is governed by the normal six-year limitation period. The question of when the settlor has done everything in his power to enforce payment was considered in correspondence reported in *Taxation Practitioner* of July 1998. If it can be shown that he has taken all reasonable steps to enforce his right, it cannot be said that his omission was deliberate.

provisions shall apply in respect of specified property, i.e. in that case the provisions apply when they would not otherwise do so, and the statutory ameliorations will not prevent the clawback provisions from operating (though they may be taken into account in determining whether the Regime applies in the first place; see paras 7–176 and following).

Termination of interests in possession: section 102ZA

7–99   Until s.102ZA was inserted into the Finance Act 1986 in 2006, the IHT legislation did not contain any specific provision governing the application of the reservation of benefit rules to the termination of an interest in possession. Consequently, if a beneficiary's interest in possession was terminated by the exercise of a power vested in the trustees, the termination did not constitute a "disposal by way of gift" by the beneficiary[191] and was therefore outside the scope of the reservation of benefit rules. On the other hand, if the beneficiary assigned or released his interest, this did constitute a gift and the reservation of benefit rules were capable of applying.

This lacuna was closed by the insertion of s.102ZA, which provides that in certain circumstances the reservation of benefit rules now apply to the lifetime termination of an interest in possession to which s.49(1) of the 1984 Act applies, even if this would not otherwise be the case (i.e. if the beneficiary takes no part in the termination of his interest). As indicated above, a termination in these circumstances would in principle not amount to a disposal by an individual and would therefore (in the absence of s.102ZA) be outside the scope of the reservation of benefit rules.

Section 102ZA provides that the termination of an interest in possession will be regarded, for the purposes of s.102 and Sch.20, as a disposal by way of gift by the beneficiary entitled to the interest if the following conditions are met:

(1) the beneficiary is an individual beneficially entitled to an interest in possession in settled property;
(2) that interest in possession is treated as part of his estate for IHT purposes, i.e.:
    (a) he became entitled to the interest before March 22, 2006; or
    (b) he became entitled to the interest on or after March 22, 2006 and the interest is an immediate post-death interest, a disabled person's interest or a transitional serial interest;
(3) the termination occurs on or after March 22, 2006; and
(4) the interest in possession comes to an end during the beneficiary's life.

Where the above conditions are met, the beneficiary will be deemed to make a gift of what the legislation elegantly calls "the no-longer possessed property" (i.e. the property in which his interest in possession subsisted immediately before it came to an end, other than any of it to which the beneficiary himself becomes absolutely and beneficially entitled in possession on the termination of his interest in possession). If the beneficiary benefits, or may be able to benefit, from the property following the termination, the reservation of benefit rules will therefore apply.

7–100   The following points should be noted in relation to s.102ZA:

---

[191] Even if the beneficiary's consent was required to the exercise of the trustees' power.

(1) Where s.102ZA applies, the object of the deemed gift by the beneficiary is the property in which his interest in possession subsisted, rather than the interest in possession.

(2) If the property remains settled following the termination of the interest in possession, the settled property tracing provisions in Sch.20 para.5 (described in para.7–122) will apply. These provisions are expressed to apply to disposals by way of gift where the property comprised in the gift becomes settled property by virtue of the gift. However, Sch.20 para.4A provides that these provisions (rather than the separate tracing provisions contained in Sch.20 paras 2–4) also apply to a termination of an interest in possession within s.102ZA as if the beneficiary had made a gift of the settled property in which his interest subsisted.

(3) Section 102ZA is expressed to apply for the purposes of s.102 and Sch.20. It therefore does not apply to sections 102A–102C.

(4) If the reservation of benefit ceases during the beneficiary's lifetime, this will be a PET in the usual way (s.102(4)).

(5) Section 102ZA does not apply to the termination of an interest in possession before March 22, 2006, which is governed by general principles. As indicated above, such a termination was regarded as being outside the scope of the reservation of benefit rules unless the life tenant himself terminated his interest by assigning or surrendering it.

"Anti-*Ingram* provisions": sections 102A and 102B

Not long after the House of Lords' decision in the *Ingram* case[192] anti-avoidance legislation intended to nullify the effect of *Ingram* in relation to land was introduced in the form of s.102A. The Paymaster General said the legislation would "restore the tax position as it was understood to be prior to the House of Lords' ruling in *Ingram*."[193] This, of course, was a bit rich, as the prevailing body of professional opinion was, to the authors' knowledge, that *Ingram* simply confirmed the existing law.

7–101

At the same time, legislation dealing with undivided interests in land and which took account of the Ministerial statement concerning shared occupation[194] was introduced in the form of s.102B. Note that:

(a) s.102A does not operate if s.102 already does so[195]; and

(b) neither s.102 nor s.102A applies if s.102B does so.[196]

Under both s.102A and s.102B the relevant disposal must be "by way of gift"; the same expression is used in s.102(1), and the same considerations apply.[197]

Both ss.102A and 102B operate by deeming subss.102(3) and 102(4) to apply. Since the statutory ameliorations are geared to the circumstances set out in s.102(1) and not to the consequence provisions in s.102(3) and (4), a third section—s.102C—ensures that certain statutory ameliorations are effectively available to prevent ss.102A and 102B from operating. Section 102C is also concerned with bringing ss.102A and 102B

[192] *Ingram v IRC* [1999] S.T.C. 1234; see paras 7–33 and following.
[193] *Hansard*, June 15, 1999.
[194] See para.7–86.
[195] FA 1986 s.102C(7).
[196] FA 1986 s.102C(6).
[197] See paras 7–49 and following.

into line with the reservation of benefit tracing provisions. Section 102C also provides that "relevant period" has the same meaning as in s.102[198] and governs the interaction of ss.102, 102A and 102B.

Interest in land: section 102A

7–102   Section 102A applies where an individual disposes, after March 8, 1999, of an interest in land by way of gift.[199] Where he disposes of more than one interest in land by way of gift, whether or not at the same time or to the same donee, s.102A applies separately in relation to each disposal.[200] The interest disposed of is referred to as property subject to a reservation and s.102(3) and (4) apply if at any time in the relevant period the donor, or his spouse or civil partner, enjoys a "significant right or interest", or is party to a "significant arrangement, in relation to the land".[201]

The scene is thus set for some tortuous definitions. The general rule is that a right, interest or arrangement in relation to land is significant only if it entitles or enables the donor either:

(a) to occupy all or part of the land; or
(b) to enjoy some right in relation to all or part of the land

otherwise than for full consideration in money or money's worth (e.g. under a lease at a full rent).[202] The focus is thus on the donor's occupation or enjoyment of the land, rather than on whether the donor has reserved an interest or benefit in the property given.[203] The fact that the donor's spouse or civil partner enjoys the right is problematic only if the spouse's/civil partner's enjoyment entitles or enables the donor to occupy the land or to enjoy some right in relation to it. The fact that the donor's spouse/civil partner enjoys the land is irrelevant. This is, of course, consistent with the general posture of the reservation of benefit provisions.[204]

Section 102A would clearly catch an *Ingram* arrangement[205] because the donor would enjoy a significant right in relation to the land given, namely the entitlement to occupy it. The distinction between being entitled and being enabled appears to contemplate cases where a donor is not in occupation but is entitled to occupy as opposed to cases where he is actually in occupation pursuant to a right enjoyed by his spouse/civil partner or an informal arrangement. The reference to "some right" is wide enough to catch, e.g. retained easements, sporting rights and mesne tenancies.

A right or interest (although not an arrangement) is not significant if it was granted or acquired before the period of seven years ending with the date of the gift.[206] Section 102A thus effectively countenances 14-year planning, i.e. on day one the donor carves out an interest for herself and seven years later she makes a PET of the encumbered freehold reversion and this is so even if she effected the carve-out with a view to making the PET. Most taxpayers, of course, prefer more truncated timeframes for achieving tax savings.

---

[198] See para.7–06.
[199] FA 1986 s.102A(1).
[200] FA 1986 s.102A(6).
[201] FA 1986 s.102A(6).
[202] FA 1986 s.102A(3).
[203] See HMRC Manuals IHTM14360.
[204] See para.7–07.
[205] As indicated in HMRC Manuals IHTM14360 and pre-owned asset guidance.
[206] FA 1986 s.102A(5).

A right, interest or arrangement is not significant in two cases. First, if it does not and cannot prevent the enjoyment of the land to the entire exclusion, or virtually to the entire exclusion, of the donor.[207] This simply aligns s.102A with s.102(1). Secondly, if it does not entitle or enable the donor to occupy all or part of the land immediately after the disposal, but would do so were it not for the interest disposed of.[208] This simply prevents s.102A from applying if X grants a lease to Y and retains a reversionary interest expectant on the expiry of the lease.

As indicated above, where a donor disposes of more than one interest in land by way of gift, s.102A applies separately in relation to each disposal. If the donor wishes to retain rights over only part of the land to be disposed of, it may therefore be advantageous to dispose of this part of the land separately from the rest.

Reversionary lease schemes

The area of greatest controversy in relation to s.102A, at least initially, was its impact **7–103** on reversionary lease schemes.[209] Typically, these schemes involve a donor giving away a long lease, at a low or nominal rent, which is to commence only after a specified period of years during which the donor wishes to remain in occupation of the property.

HMRC accepted that such arrangements effected before March 9, 1999, did not infringe the reservation of benefit rules. So far as post-March 8, 1999 arrangements are concerned, however, the question arose whether these schemes were caught by s.102A. Many practitioners believed that the "seven-year let out" in s.102A(5) prevented the encumbered freehold from being a "significant right or interest" in land so long as the donor had owned the unencumbered freehold for more than seven years before granting the deferred lease. However, HMRC initially took the view that s.102A did apply to reversionary leases. IHTM14360 states that

> "the donor's occupation, although acquired more than seven years before the creation of the lease, is nevertheless considered to be a 'significant right in relation to the land' within the meaning of s.102(A)3 and thus within the revised rules",

but on that basis it is unclear why the seven-year let-out would not apply.[210]

It appears, however, that HMRC have conceded that their initial view was incorrect. Although IHTM14360 has not yet been amended, Section 5 of HMRC's pre-owned asset guidance states as follows:

> "For reversionary lease schemes entered into on or after 9 March 1999, HMRC had previously held the view that section 102A Finance Act 1986 would apply to them because the donor's occupation would be a 'significant right in relation to the land'. If that analysis were correct, the reservation of benefit rules would apply and there would be no income tax charge. However, HMRC now consider that where the freehold interest was acquired more than seven years before the gift, the continued occupation by the donor would not be a significant right, and therefore, contrary to its previously held view, section 102A cannot apply to the gift because of section 102A(5). If the donor grants a reversionary lease within

---

[207] FA 1986 s.102A(4)(a).
[208] FA 1986 s.102A(4)(b).
[209] For a discussion, see *Private Client Business* (2000), pp.331–338.
[210] An alternative argument might have been that the encumbered freehold would be a significant interest in land because the donor's continuing occupation of it amounted to an arrangement (and was therefore not protected by the seven-year let-out). Again, this argument seemed unconvincing, as in the authors' view an "arrangement" must involve something more than the continuing enjoyment of an existing right.

7 years of acquiring the freehold interest, section 102A may apply to the gift depending on how the remaining provisions of that section apply in relation to the circumstances of the case.

> Bear in mind, however, that, whenever the freehold interest was acquired, a gift may be a gift with reservation of benefit under section 102 Finance Act 1986 if the lease contains terms beneficial to the donor. An example of this may be where the lessee covenants to pay the costs of maintaining the property."

The result of this, of course, is that the pre-owned assets tax may apply to reversionary leases made on or after March 9, 1999: see para.7–165.

Reversionary lease arrangements did, and continue to, involve CGT issues if the reversioner disposed of the property because the CGT principal private residence exemption was not available to him in respect of his period of non-occupation. It had been suggested prior to March 22, 2006 that this problem could be solved if X first created a trust with two funds, one in which he retained a life interest in possession and the other of which was held on interest in possession or accumulation and maintenance trusts for, e.g. his children and/or grandchildren, which trusts were expectant on his life interest. X then granted a reversionary lease to the trustees to hold on the life interest trusts, at the same time transferring the encumbered freehold reversion to the life interest fund. This arrangement addressed the CGT problem because the conditions in s.225 of the Taxation of Chargeable Gains Act 1992 for principal private residence relief should be satisfied when the trustees sold the property. However, it will no longer be effective for IHT purposes if effected on or after March 22, 2006, as the transfer to the trust will be a chargeable transfer.

An "internal" Ingram *arrangement*

7–104   Where land was already held on interest in possession trusts, it used to be suggested that the reservation of benefit rules could be circumvented if the land was appointed to a separate interest in possession fund (with separate trustees) for, say, the life tenant's son, after which the trustees of the separate fund could grant a lease at a low or nominal rent to the trustees of the main fund to hold on the existing interest in possession trusts. Although this effectively replicated the *Ingram* transactions, it was assumed that the reservation of benefit provisions should not apply because (assuming his consent to any of the transactions was not required and that he was not one of the trustees) the life tenant would not have made a disposal by way of gift. However, this arrangement is no longer effective following the introduction of s.102ZA with effect from March 22, 2006 (see para.7–99).

Undivided share of interest in land: section 102B

7–105   Section 102B applies where an individual disposes, by way of gift after March 8, 1999, of an undivided share of an interest in land. Remember that where this condition is fulfilled neither s.102 nor s.102A apply.[211] Where s.102B applies, unless the let-outs

---

[211] FA 1986 s.102C(6).

274

below apply, the share disposed of is treated at any time during the relevant period[212] as property subject to a reservation and s.102(3) and (4) apply.

Let-outs from section 102B

The share disposed of is not treated at any time during the relevant period as property subject to a reservation and s.102(3) and (4) do not apply in three cases. First, when the donor does not occupy the land.[213] It thus appears open to a non-occupying donor to receive benefits not relating to occupation, e.g. a share of the rents from the property. Secondly, where the donor occupies the land to the exclusion of the donee for full consideration in money or money's worth.[214] The relief for full consideration is similar to the statutory amelioration along those lines.[215] Thirdly, if the donor and the donee both occupy the land and the donor does not receive any benefit, other than a negligible one, which is provided by or at the expense of the donee for some reason connected with the gift.[216] This effectively rationalises the Ministerial statement that previously governed shared occupation[217] but note that the "no linked benefit" requirement does not require any proportionate sharing of expenses. It is perfectly acceptable for the donor to bear all the expenses; the problem arises in determining how much the donee can pay without benefiting the donor. HMRC are understood to have regarded the Ministerial statement as applying only in cases where the donor did not give away more than a 50 per cent interest in the property. Clearly, there is no such limit under s.102B, although if the donor retains only a small percentage the arrangements may be subject to closer scrutiny from HMRC. A major difficulty in relying on the third let-out is that it applies only so long as the donee occupies the land with the donor. This is likely to cause problems where, e.g. a parent occupies with a child who subsequently wishes to opt to live in separate accommodation.

7–106

Adapted statutory ameliorations: section 102C

Section 102C brings ss.102A and 102B into line with two general statutory ameliorations. First, an interest or share disposed of is not property subject to a reservation under s.102A(2) or s.102B(2) if or to the extent that the disposal is an exempt transfer by virtue of any of the provisions listed in s.102(5).[218] So, if the disposal in question is wholly exempt under the s.18 exemption neither s.102A nor s.102B will operate. Secondly, in applying ss.102A and 102B no account is taken of (a) occupation of land by a donor, or (b) an arrangement which enables land to be occupied by a donor, in circumstances where the occupation or the occupation pursuant to the arrangement would be disregarded under the statutory amelioration in the Finance Act 1986 Sch.20 para.6(1)(b) for disadvantaged donors.[219] That amelioration applies only in respect of

7–107

---

[212] "Relevant period" has the same meaning as in s.102 (s.102C(1)).
[213] FA 1986 s.102B(3)(a).
[214] FA 1986 s.102B(3)(b).
[215] See para.7–84.
[216] FA 1986 s.102B(4).
[217] See para.7–86.
[218] FA 1986 s.102C(2); see para.7–90.
[219] FA 1986 s.102C(3); see para.7–89.

a donor's occupation of land and will therefore not prevent s.102B from applying if the donor is paying less than his fair share of outgoings.

Tracing alignments

7–108   Section 102C(4) provides that the provisions of Sch.20 to the Finance Act 1986, apart from para.6, have effect for purposes of ss.102A and 102B as they have effect for the purposes of s.102, and that any question which falls to be answered under s.102A or s.102B in relation to an interest in land shall be determined by reference to the interest which is at that time treated as property comprised in the gift. It follows that the provisions concerning the availability of business relief and agricultural relief[220] will apply. Where property other than an interest in land is treated by virtue of para.2 of Sch.20 as property comprised in a gift, the provisions of s.102 apply to determine whether or not that property is subject to a reservation.[221] It follows that s.102B would cease to apply if the donee of a post-March 8, 1999 gift of an undivided share of an interest in land occupied by the donor exchanged on commercial terms his share for an interest in land which was not an undivided share.

Life insurance policies

7–109   As a general rule, gifts relating to insurance policies (e.g. the payment of premiums to a life or term insurance policy) are within the scope of the reservation of benefit rules.[222] The introduction of the reservation of benefit provisions in 1986 was aimed partly at certain types of insurance products then in circulation, such as PETA (Pure Endowment and Term Assurance) plans. However, there was some doubt as to whether the provisions were in fact equal to the task. In order to put matters beyond doubt, the general reservation of benefit rules were supplemented by a special provision aimed at avoidance involving the use of linked endowment and term assurance arrangements. Paragraph 7 of Sch.20 provides that certain gifts relating to insurance policies are deemed not to be enjoyed to the entire exclusion, or virtually to the entire exclusion, of the donor in circumstances where benefits accruing to the donee and the donor or[223] the donor's spouse or civil partner are linked under the terms of the insurance contracts.

The conditions for the application of para.7 of Sch.20 are as follows.

(1) There must have been a disposal by way of gift made on or after March 18, 1986, which consists of or includes, or is made in connection with, a policy of insurance on the life of the donor or his spouse or[224] civil partner or on their

[220] See para.7–129.

[221] FA 1986 s.102C(5). The tracing rules in FA 1986 Sch.20 para.5, on the other hand, apparently will not apply. Why this should be so is not clear.

[222] This is the case even if the gifts are regular premiums which are covered by the normal expenditure out of income exemption. As indicated in para.7–90, this exemption is outside the blanket let-out for exempt transfers under s.102(5). However, s.102(6) contains a transitional rule applicable to policies effected before March 18, 1986: see para.7–95.

[223] Contrary to the general rule referred to in para.7–07.

[224] With effect from December 5, 2005.

joint lives. This extends to a policy on their joint lives and on the life of the survivor.

(2) The benefits which will or may accrue to the donee as a result of the gift vary by reference to benefits accruing to the donor or his spouse/civil partner (or both of them) under that policy or under another policy (whether issued before, at the same time as, or after that referred to in the first condition).

Paragraph 7(2)(b) provides that, for the purposes of condition (2) above, benefits accruing to the donor or his spouse/civil partner include benefits which accrue by virtue of the exercise of rights conferred on either or both of them. It should be noted that the rights referred to in para.7(2)(b) need not be conferred by the policy. Having said that, HMRC accept that para.7(2)(b) does not displace the need for the accruer of benefits to the donor to be under the policy and not under the terms of trusts upon which the policy is held. Their IHTM14453, contains the following example:

> "On 1 April 1998 the donor effects a whole life policy on his own life in trust. The trustees have a power of appointment over the trust fund which can be exercised in favour of the donor's wife but not the donor.
>
> Paragraph 7 Schedule 20 FA 1986 does not apply. The provision is only relevant if benefits can accrue to the donor or his spouse or civil partner (IHTM11032) under the policy itself. It does not apply in a situation such as this where the spouse or civil partner can only benefit under the trust even though the assets of the trust include a policy of insurance."

X. IDENTIFICATION OF PROPERTY

In the absence of provision to the contrary, it would not be difficult to avoid the **7–110** harsher effects of the provisions concerning the reservation of benefit. Assume, for example, that X gives Y a new Rolls-Royce on condition that Y allows X to use it when Y goes on holiday for two months in the summer. Y, however, favours Ferraris, and exchanges the Rolls-Royce for a vintage Ferrari, which he allows X to use according to their agreement. In the absence of provision to the contrary the exchange would have resulted in the property given to Y ceasing to be subject to a reservation, because the Rolls-Royce was the property given by X to Y, and on its passing into the hands of the former Ferrari owner X would no longer have been able to use it. A somewhat similar result originally obtained under estate duty[225] but the Finance Act 1957 s.38 introduced provisions allowing property to be traced, and provisions similar but not identical to the relevant portions of the estate duty provisions are to be found in Sch.20 paras 2–6. The key provision is para.6(2), which provides that:

> "Any question whether any property comprised in a gift was at any time enjoyed to the entire exclusion of the donor and of any benefit to him shall (so far as that question depends upon the identity of the property) be determined by reference to the property which is at that time treated as property comprised in the gift."

Other provisions in Sch.20 specify which property is to be treated under the principal section, i.e. s.102, as comprised in the gift.

---

[225] *Sneddon v Lord Advocate* [1954] A.C. 257.

It may be helpful at this stage to note that the provisions are by no means of universal application; this is discussed at paras 7–115 and following, and 7–122 and following.

Substitutions

7–111   Paragraph 2 of Sch.20 lays down the important rule that where a donor makes a gift which is not a sum of money in sterling or any other currency and which does not become settled property by virtue of the gift, then if the donee ceases to have the possession and enjoyment of any of the property comprised in the gift, the property, if any, received by the donee in substitution for the property is treated as if it (in addition to any other property comprised in the original gift) had been comprised in that gift instead of the property which the donee has ceased to possess and enjoy. If the substituted property is itself then replaced by other property HMRC's view is that para.2(1) continues to operate.[226] Returning to the original example at para.7–110 of X who gave Y a Rolls-Royce which Y exchanged for a Ferrari, para.2(1) would operate to treat the Ferrari as the subject-matter of the original gift. If Y, tired of the Ferrari, exchanged it for an Aston Martin, para.2(1) would then, in HMRC's view, apply to the Aston Martin as though it had been the subject-matter of the original gift replacing, as it does, the Ferrari, which para.2(1) treated as the original gift. The authors take the view that this is also the way that the court would be likely to apply para.2(1).

7–112   Paragraph 2(3) of Sch.20 gives the following examples of the kind of substitutions caught:

(a) in relation to property sold, exchanged or otherwise disposed of by the donee, any benefit received by the donee by way of consideration for the sale, exchange or other disposition; and

(b) in relation to a debt or security, any benefit received by the donee in or towards the satisfaction or redemption thereof; and

(c) in relation to any right to acquire property, any property acquired by the donee in pursuance of that right.

Where the substituted property is property acquired in pursuance of a right falling within para.2(3)(c) above, the value of any consideration in money or money's worth given by the donee for the acquisition is allowed as a deduction in valuing the property comprised in the gift at any time after the consideration is given.[227] This is subject to the qualification that if any part of that consideration which is not a sum of money consists of property comprised in the same or another gift from the donor and is subject to a s.102(3) clawback or is attributable to a PET made by him under s.102(4), then no deduction can be made in respect of it.[228] Assume X gives Y a valuable option to acquire shares worth £30,000, for £10,000. Y exercises the option. The relevant property is first the option, but, on Y's exercising the option, then becomes the shares. The value of the shares for the purpose of these rules is reduced to £20,000, i.e. their value less the consideration given for them. If, in addition to the option, X has given Y a painting worth £10,000, which Y gives as consideration for acquiring the shares

---

[226] See HMRC Manuals IHTM14373.
[227] FA 1986 Sch.20 para.3(1)(a).
[228] FA 1986 Sch.20 para.3(1)(b); and see para.3(2) and (3).

under the option, the relevant property is first the option and the painting, but, on Y's exercising the option, then becomes the shares, the value of which is £30,000.

HMRC take the view that a gift of land which the donee subsequently builds on, or a gift of a house subsequently improved at the donee's expense, will only be a gift with reservation to the extent of the property originally given.[229]

Gift by donee

Paragraph 2(4) of Sch.20 qualifies the general rule in para.2(1) by providing for special treatment where the donee makes a gift of property comprised in the gift to him, or otherwise voluntarily divests himself of any such property. In such a case he is treated as continuing to have possession and enjoyment of that property, unless he gives the property to the original donor. This provision does not apply if the property is transferred for a consideration in money or money's worth that is not less than the value of the property at that time. Thus, if the sale is for full consideration, para.2(1) applies; otherwise para.2(4) is the relevant provision. Assume X gives Y property, half of which Y subsequently gives to Z and half of which Y subsequently returns to X. Y will be treated as still owning the property given to Z, so that if Z allows X to use it, it will be property subject to a reservation in relation to X.

7–113

A donee is treated as divesting himself, voluntarily and without consideration, of any interest in property which merges or is extinguished in another interest held or acquired by him in the same property.[230] A disposition made by the donee by agreement is not deemed to be made voluntarily if it is made to any authority who, when the agreement is made, is authorised by, or is or can be authorised under any enactment to acquire the property compulsorily.[231]

While the rule in para.2(4) is relatively easy to state, applying it may be difficult in practice, because in the real world the donee will not retain the asset given, and the effect of para.2(4) is that it is by reference to that asset that any charge will be imposed. It will presumably be necessary in appropriate cases to attempt to follow that asset in order to determine its value on any chargeable occasion, but depending on the nature of the asset, this may be hard to do.

The Battle case

Paragraph 2(4) can give rise to some subtle points. In the estate duty case *Battle v IRC*[232] two donees were given shares worth £98,000 which they exchanged for an issue of two 49 per cent shareholdings in a private company in which they already owned the remaining 2 per cent of the shares. Subsequently these two 49 per cent shareholdings were converted from ordinary shares into 10 per cent preference shares with a consequent diminution in the value of the shares so that each holding was worth only £49 each. On the death of the original donor it was argued for estate duty purposes that under what is now para.2(1) the 49 per cent holding represented the original shares given so that the value of that gift had been reduced to £49 in each case. However,

7–114

---

[229] See HMRC Manuals IHTM14373.
[230] FA 1986 Sch.20 para.2(5)(b).
[231] FA 1986 Sch.20 para.2(5)(a).
[232] *Battle v IRC* [1980] S.T.C. 86.

HMRC succeeded in arguing that the original share exchange was not for full consideration since a 49 per cent holding must always be discounted (i.e. it is never worth 49 per cent of the corporate assets) and therefore an element of gift was present in that exchange, which meant that under what is now para.2(4) the original property given must be treated as still being retained by the two donees. It has been suggested that the arrangement would have worked had each donee transferred his shareholding to a separate private company, thereby obtaining for that shareholding a majority of shares in the company. It is worth noting, however, that Balcombe J. in the *Battle* case felt that even an allotment of a 98 per cent holding in a private company would still result in a diminution in the value of the assets, since a prospective purchaser would prefer to hold the original shares outright rather than be faced with a shareholding in a private company.

Cash gifts

7–115   Paragraph 2(1) does not apply to outright gifts of "a sum of money in sterling or other currency".[233] The reason for this is a practical one, namely that each and every unit of currency is a separate item of property, and it would in practice be impossible to trace through them. Where, for example, a person is given 50 £5 notes, each of those notes is a separate item of property. If he buys a newspaper and is given change, the £5 note he uses to buy the newspaper becomes the property of the newsagent, while the coins given in change become the property of the person buying the newspapers.

Where the original gift is of money and the money is subsequently used to purchase property, the property which was the subject of the original gift will, in principle, cease to be subject to a reservation. Under estate duty it appears that this was the case even though the gift of money was made with instructions to buy the property in question.[234] Under IHT, however, it is possible that in such circumstances this would be regarded as a gift of the property by associated operations. HMRC have stated that, although they will not normally raise any enquiries to see if a gift which appears to be of cash may in fact be a gift, by associated operation, of other property, they *will* ask questions if the gift is of an odd amount, which suggests that it may be related to a purchase by the donee, or if there is specific information that the gift was related to the acquisition of property by the donee, especially if the acquisition is from the donor.[235]

If a cash gift with reservation is made direct to a settlement, or if the original gift is an outright gift but the donee subsequently settles it, the tracing provisions in para.5 of Sch.20 will apply (see para.7–122).[236]

Use of cash gifts in planning

7–116   The fact that the tracing provisions do not apply to outright gifts of cash means that, in principle, the reservation of benefit rules will cease to apply if the donee spends the cash. Where X gives Y cash and Y uses the cash to purchase an asset from which X

[233] *Gresham Life Assurance Society Ltd v Bishop* [1902] A.C. 287; and see the discussion by the Court of Appeal in *Thomson v Moyse* [1960] 39 TC 291; *Central Electricity Board v Halifax Corp* [1963] A.C. 785.

[234] *Potter v IRC* [1958] S.C. 213; *Sneddon v Lord Advocate* [1954] A.C. 257 at 280.

[235] See HMRC Manuals IHTM14372.

[236] For this purpose para.5(3) of Sch.20 provides that property which becomes settled property under any testamentary disposition of the donee or on his intestacy (or partial intestacy) is treated as settled by him.

subsequently benefits it is not in theory possible to identify the asset with the cash. As indicated in the previous paragraph, however, HMRC will consider the terms of the gift closely and will be alert to any indications that an apparent cash gift may in fact be a gift of other property by associated operations, although they will not normally raise any enquiries unless there is a positive indication for doing so.

A common planning technique under estate duty was for the donee to use the cash given to purchase an asset from the donor. Under IHT, HMRC would be likely to regard such an arrangement as a gift of the asset by associated operations.

The converse situation also needs considering. Assume a donor gives property to a donee who sells the property for cash. The original property will be within para.2(1), the effect of which will be to substitute the cash for that property. But if the donee then uses the cash to buy further property, para.2(1) will not apply, and the effect of the transactions will apparently be that the property ceased to be subject to a reservation when the proceeds of sale were used to acquire the second property. If this is so, then presumably it will mean that the donor has made a deemed PET under s.102(4).[237]

Nature of property given

The fact that the property given is of a wasting nature, e.g. where a lease or annuity   **7–117** is concerned, does not matter. The fact that income accrues in respect of the property is also irrelevant, i.e. there is no question of any clawback being imposed on that income.[238] The position where property is lost or destroyed is not entirely clear. If insurance money is received, presumably para.2(1) applies. If no such money is received and nothing else is received by the donee, it is arguable that no PET is treated as made under s.102(4), on the basis that that provision operates only where property in existence ceases to be subject to a reservation, not where property ceases to exist altogether.

Shares and debentures

It may be that shares or debentures are given to someone and that, as the holder   **7–118** thereof, he is issued with shares in or debentures of the same or another company, or granted a right to acquire such shares or debentures. Paragraph 2(6) provides that in such a case the shares, debentures or the right, as the case may be, are treated as having been comprised in the gift in addition to any other property so comprised. The rule does not apply, understandably, if the issue or grant is made by way of exchange for the shares or debentures originally given by the donor, because in that case the basic "exchange" rule in para.2(1) will apply.[239] Assume X gives Y shares in Z Ltd. Z Ltd then makes a bonus issue. The bonus shares will be treated as having been comprised in the gift of the original shares to Y. Now assume that A gives B shares in C Ltd. and that B exchanges these shares with D for shares in ICI Plc. The basic rule in para.2(1)

---

[237] In which case the double tax regulations may be relevant; see paras 8–48 and following.
[238] Compare the rules for settled property; see para.7–122.
[239] See FA 1986 Sch.20 para.2(3)(a).

will apply, and the ICI shares will be treated as the property comprised in the gift by A.

No double counting against taxpayer

7–119   The value of any consideration in money or money's worth given by the donee for the above-mentioned issue of the shares or debentures or the grant of the right is allowed as a deduction in valuing the property comprised in the gift at any time after the consideration is given.[240] This is subject to the qualification that if any part of the consideration, other than a sum of money, consists of property comprised in the same or another gift from the donor and is within s.102(3) or (4), no deduction is made in respect of it.[241] There is left out of account so much, if any, of the consideration for any shares or debentures, or for the grant of any right to be issued with such shares or debentures, as consists in the capitalisation of reserves of the company in question, or in the retention by that company, by way of set-off or otherwise, of any property distributable by it, or is otherwise provided directly or indirectly out of the assets or at the expense of that or any associated company.[242] For this purpose, two companies are associated if one has control of the other or if another person controls both of them.[243]

Former shareholders

7–120   Paragraph 2(7) extends para.2(6) to cover the case where an issue or grant is made to the donee as having been the holder of the shares or debentures, or is made to him in pursuance of an offer or invitation made to him as being or having been the holder of those shares or debentures, or an offer or invitation in connection with which any preference is given to him as having been the holder thereof.

Early death of donee

7–121   It may be that the donee dies before a clawback charge is imposed. Paragraph 4 provides that in such a case the provisions considered above apply as if:

(1) the donee had not died and his personal representatives' acts were his acts; and
(2) property taken by any person under the donee's testamentary dispositions or total or partial intestacy were taken under a gift made by him at his death.

Thus, if the personal representatives sell any property, para.2(1) will apply to the proceeds of sale, and para.2(4) will apply to any property passing under the deceased's will or intestacy.

---

[240] FA 1986 Sch.20 para.3(1)(a).
[241] FA 1986 Sch.20 para.3(1)(b).
[242] FA 1986 Sch.20 para.3(2).
[243] FA 1986 Sch.20 para.3(3).

It should be noted that if the property is settled by the donee's will or intestacy, the tracing rules applicable to settled property described in the following paragraphs will apply.[244]

Settled property

Paragraph 5 of Sch.20 establishes special rules where property (whether money or **7–122** not) comprised in a gift becomes settled property by virtue of the gift. In such a case, the property comprised in the settlement when the clawback provisions are activated is treated as the property comprised in the gift, except in so far as that property neither is, nor represents, nor is derived from, property originally comprised in the gift.[245] This is subject to the qualification that where income arising from the property after the date on which either of the clawback provisions is activated is accumulated the accumulations are not treated as having been derived from the property.[246]

Assume X settles £300,000 on trust for his children. The trustees invest in quoted securities, and accumulate the income therefrom. Both the securities and the accumulated income will be taken into account in respect of any clawbacks, but income arising to the trust after the clawback is imposed will not be taken into account. Given that the reservation of benefit ceases on the clawback, this provision appears to be superfluous.

It should be noted that a settlement made before March 18, 1986 will not be caught **7–123** by the reservation of benefit provisions unless further gifts are made to the settlement after that date, in which case the provisions only apply to the property settled by the further gifts.[247]

Theoretical difficulties

Although it is generally assumed that para.5 is the relevant provision for identifying **7–124** what property is subject to a reservation where property has become comprised in a settlement as a result of a gift, the point is not free of doubt. Its practical importance has been substantially reduced by the changes introduced by the Finance Act 2006. However, until March 22, 2006 it was somewhat unclear whether the subject-matter of a gift to an interest in possession trust was the reversionary interest or the property settled.[248] If the subject-matter of the gift was the reversionary interest, then the relevant paragraph of Sch.20 would presumably be para.2, not para.5, and the only time para.5 would have applied would be where property was settled on discretionary trusts with no qualifying interest in possession. As discussed further at para.6–116 of the previous edition of this book, it seems clear that this is not the result that the draftsman

---

[244] See FA 1986 Sch.20 para.5 and para.7–128 below.
[245] FA 1986 Sch.20 para.5(1).
[246] FA 1986 Sch.20 para.5(5); and see para.14–04.
[247] See HMRC Manuals IHTM14311.
[248] See paras 7–41 and following.

intended and that the approach he presumably did envisage achieved the desired result.

Loans to trustees

7–125   The legislation makes special provision in para.5(4) to deal with the case where the property comprised in a settlement on the date when either of the clawbacks operates derives (whether directly or indirectly) from a loan made by the settlor to the trustees of the settlement. In such a case, the property deriving from the loan is treated as derived from the property which was originally comprised in the gift.

Paragraph 5(4) was introduced to nullify the effectiveness of an arrangement known as a "loan-based inheritance trust". Under this arrangement a donor settled a small sum on trustees and then lent them a larger sum. The trustees then used the sums to purchase a single premium bond, part of which they encashed each year. They then used the proceeds of the encashment to discharge part of their indebtedness to the settlor. The arrangement was seen as objectionable by HMRC, presumably because it involved the settlor effectively retaining access to the trust income while alienating the growth in the trust fund. Paragraph 5(4) renders this approach ineffective in relation to structures brought into being on or after March 18, 1986 which do not differ in any way from the traditional arrangement.

Paragraph 5(4) can operate only if the person who makes the loan is also a donor in relation to a gift made to the trustees, i.e. it does not apply to a loan by someone other than the donor, such as the donor's spouse or civil partner. HMRC accept this.[249] Note that para.5(4) applies to any loan, not just to one that is interest-free.

Paragraph 5(4) seems to involve an element of overkill. This follows from the fact that it appears that although para.5(4) was intended only to prevent the lender from alienating the growth in value in the property in which the trustees invested the sum lent to them, the effect of para.5(4) is to bring into charge the whole of the value of that property without any compensating adjustment for the fact that the value of the right to be repaid the sum lent will also be included in the donor/lender's estate. There will thus be an element of double taxation which will not be relieved by the double taxation regulations.[250]

Termination of settlement

7–126   It may be that property is settled by a gift and that the settlement comes to an end (wholly or partly) before either of the clawback provisions is activated, i.e. while the reservation of benefit still exists. In that case, the property leaving the settlement is treated as comprised in the gift, in addition to any other property so comprised. If, on the termination of the settlement, the donor becomes absolutely and beneficially entitled in possession to any of the property, that property is not treated as comprised in the gift. However, any consideration given by him for any of the property to which

---

[249] See HMRC Manuals IHTM14401.
[250] See para.8–57.

284

he so becomes entitled, save such consideration as consists of rights under the settlement, *is* also treated as comprised in the gift.[251]

Termination of interests in possession

The settled property tracing rules in para.5 of Sch.20 can also apply to the termina- **7–127** tion on or after March 22, 2006 of an interest in possession during the lifetime of the beneficiary. Paragraph 4A of Sch.20 provides that where such a termination is treated as a deemed disposal by way of gift under s.102ZA (see para.7–99), and the property continues to be settled property immediately after the disposal, the provisions of s.102 and para.5 apply as if the property comprised in the gift consisted of the property comprised in the settlement on the material date.[252]

Settlement by donee

Circumstances may arise where the gift by the donor is not a gift in settlement, but **7–128** before either of the clawback provisions is activated the donee settles the property. In such a case, the settlement made by the donee is treated as having been made by the donor's gift. For this purpose, property which becomes settled property under the donee's testamentary dispositions or on his total or partial intestacy is treated as having been settled by him.[253]

For the period between the original gift and the settlement by the donee, the normal tracing rules apply as described above.[254]

XI. AGRICULTURAL RELIEF AND BUSINESS RELIEF

Paragraph 8 of Sch.20 deals with a donor who has given away property in respect of **7–129** which agricultural and/or business relief is relevant. Assume that X gives to Y property which in X's hands qualified for agricultural or business relief, and that, e.g., X retains a benefit in respect of the property so that, in relation to him, it is "property subject to a reservation." Sometime later the property ceases to be subject to a reservation, so that X then makes a notional PET of the property or, failing that, X dies, with the result that the property is at that stage clawed back into his estate. In such a case, in the absence of provision to the contrary, agricultural and business relief might well not have been available in respect of the property brought into charge by virtue of s.102(3) or (4), and this would have been unfair given the fact that if X had retained the property relief

---

[251] FA 1986 Sch.20 para.5(2).
[252] Including any property in the settlement which is directly or indirectly derived from a loan by the beneficiary to the trustees, but excluding property which neither is, nor represents, nor is derived from, property originally comprised in the gift (para.5(2) & (3)).
[253] FA 1986 Sch.20 para.5(3).
[254] See HMRC Manuals IHTM14403.

would have been available in respect of it. Paragraph 8 deals with this problem in a special way which is discussed in detail at paras 26–189 and following.

XII. ASPECTS OF RESERVATION OF BENEFIT IN PRACTICE

7–130   This part of this chapter comments on various aspects of the reservation of benefit rules in practice.

HMRC's attitude generally

7–131   HMRC have traditionally taken a reasonable approach to the reservation of benefit provisions. Rather than operating the provisions as a kind of anti-avoidance microscope under which all transactions fall to be painstakingly scrutinised, they have tended to hold the provisions in reserve as a threat to be deployed against arrangements HMRC find objectionable.

In recent years, however, the tax climate has been changing as HMRC and the Government have become less tolerant of tax planning arrangements which would in the past have been regarded as normal estate planning. The development of IHT saving schemes intended to circumvent the reservation of benefit rules resulted in amendments to the rules to reverse the decisions in the *Ingram* and *Eversden* cases in 1999 and 2003 respectively. However, the amendments failed to stifle attempts by donors to "have their cake and eat it" and the Government eventually lost patience. In 2004 it introduced a further deterrent to such attempts, not by tightening the reservation of benefit rules again, but in the form of an income tax charge, the preowned assets regime (discussed at paras 7–155 and following), which is designed to apply only when the reservation of benefit provisions do not apply for whatever reason. So far the preowned assets regime does not appear to have signalled the death of IHT planning, but it does present a significant potential disincentive. Also, under self-assessment taxpayers must take a view as to whether or not the preowned assets regime applies in respect of arrangements they have entered into—often many years ago—and this may require them to take a view on the reservation of benefit provisions. In this respect they may need to seek confirmation from HMRC, thereby causing HMRC to consider various arrangements not previously scrutinised or to reconsider arrangements where their previously held views call for fresh examination.

HMRC's current published guidance in relation to reservation of benefit indicates that, while they will adopt an "investigative approach", they will not invoke the provisions "unless and until all relevant facts have been fully established and clearly point to there being such a claim."[255]

Giving shares while keeping salary, pension and control

7–132   Under the PET regime many individuals owning shares in family companies wish to give away some or all of their shares. In many cases, they also wish to continue working for the company, drawing directors' fees, participating in the company pension scheme and, sometimes, keeping control of the company. The question arises

[255] See HMRC Manuals IHTM14302.

as to whether the receipt of such fees and such continuing participation in the pension scheme will infringe the reservation of benefit rules.

Directors' remuneration

As was discussed above, in *Oakes v Commissioner of Stamp Duties of New South Wales*[256] the Privy Council held that an individual who settled property on trusts of which he was one of the trustees reserved a benefit in respect of the whole of the property comprised in the trust fund by reason of the fact that he was entitled to be reasonably remunerated as a trustee. The basis of the decision was that his right to be remunerated did not constitute a beneficial interest in the trust fund.

7–133

In the previous edition of this book the question was raised whether the *Oakes* case had any implications in circumstances where an individual gives away shares in a company and continues to be a reasonably remunerated director of that company. In practice this point has not been taken and HMRC do not regard the reservation of benefit rules as applying where a donor of shares continues to receive remuneration or other benefits for his services as a director, provided that this is a continuation of existing reasonable commercial arrangements and the benefits are in no way linked to or affected by the gift.[257] However, in other circumstances (e.g. if the remuneration package is altered as part of the overall arrangements), HMRC may scrutinise the arrangements and it is possible that the donor may be treated as reserving a benefit. HMRC give the following example:

> "A makes a gift of shares to B, it being part of the package that B would appoint A to the Board of Directors, a salaried position entitling him to a company car and other fringe benefits.
>   This would be regarded as the reservation of a benefit to the donor 'by contract or otherwise'."[258]

Reservation of benefit may be a concern where, as is often the case, under the existing arrangements the intending donor is underpaid and/or has made inadequate pension provision. It has been suggested that the solution lies in the donor taking out a generous remuneration package before the gift but, given the associated operations provisions, the authors doubt the efficacy of such an approach.

Settling shares—donor as trustee and fiduciary accountability

It is a fundamental principle of trust law that, unless he is expressly authorised to do so, a trustee cannot profit from his position. This means that, in the absence of provision to the contrary in the trust deed, a trustee who is a director of a company must prima facie account to the trust for any director's fees he receives which accrue to him by reason of his trusteeship. It is thus standard practice for a trust deed to provide that a trustee in such a position need not account to the trust in respect of any director's fees he receives as a director notwithstanding, e.g. "that his position as a director may have been obtained or may be held or retained in right or by means or by reason of his

7–134

---

[256] *Oakes v Commissioner of Stamp Duties of New South Wales* [1954] A.C. 57; see para.7–26.
[257] *Capital Taxes—A Quarterly Commentary* (1987), pp.1 and 50; HMRC Manuals IHTM14337 and IHTM14395.
[258] HMRC Manuals IHTM14334.

position as one of the trustees or of any shares stock property rights or powers comprised in or connected with the trust fund." Does the inclusion of such a clause activate the reservation of benefit rules?

7–135   HMRC have indicated that they generally do not propose to take this point so long as the director's remuneration package is on a reasonable commercial basis, and that they will disregard any rights over the property given which the donor retains but which can be exercised solely in a fiduciary capacity for the benefit of the donees/settlement.[259]

For the position where a settlor is entitled to remuneration for acting as a trustee, see para.7–27.

Voting arrangements

7–136   Individuals minded to give away shares are often unwilling to do so if they will thereby lose control of the company, because they will no longer be able to control how the votes attaching to the shares given are exercised. One solution to this problem is for the shares to be given into trust and for the settlor to be one of the trustees, as he will then be in a position to influence how the trust shares are voted. This course of action may, of course, expose the settlor/trustee to a conflict of interest. HMRC do not invoke the reservation of benefit provisions so long as the settlor/trustee exercises his votes in the interests of the beneficiaries.[260]

Voting carve-outs

7–137   A prospective settlor of family company shares wishing to keep control of the company may, instead of settling them and being a trustee, wish to consider the possibility of reorganising the company share capital into voting shares and non-voting equity shares, following which he would give away or settle the non-voting equity shares.

It seems clear that such an arrangement would not, of itself, infringe the reservation of benefit rules. There would be a partial gift, not a gift with a reservation.

Is there a PET?

7–138   In the overwhelming majority of cases, the donor will wish to make a PET when he gives away the non-voting equity shares. In this connection it is relevant to remember that s.98(3) of the 1984 Act provides that a notional disposition made under s.98(1) by virtue of a company reorganisation is incapable of qualifying as a PET.[261] Here the reorganisation itself does not constitute a transfer of value, but there may be a danger that HMRC will contend that the reorganisation and the gift of the non-voting equity shares, which are clearly associated operations, fall within s.98(3) as, in effect, an

---

[259] *Capital Taxes—A Quarterly Commentary* (1987), p.51; HMRC Manuals IHTM14337 and IHTM14395.
[260] HMRC Manuals IHTM14394.
[261] See para.5–13.

extended reorganisation, with the result that the gift of the non-voting equity shares is barred from being a PET.

Home loan schemes

Various arrangements have been promulgated over the years for sheltering the family home from IHT. One such arrangement was the so-called "home loan scheme" (also referred to as the double trust scheme), which was widely employed prior to the introduction of the preowned asset tax described later in this chapter. There were various permutations of the scheme, typically including the following steps:

7–139

(1) Assume X owned a valuable house, Purple Acre. X established a UK resident trust ("the House Trust") under which X was entitled both to the trust income for his life and to occupy any dwelling-house owned by the House Trust;

(2) X sold Purple Acre to the House Trust for a purchase price left outstanding ("the Debt"[262]). X continued to live in Purple Acre;

(3) X settled the Debt on the trustees of an existing or a new accumulation and maintenance trust or interest in possession trust ("the Debt Trust") under which he was excluded from benefit.

The thinking was that if X survived settling the Debt by seven years there would be a charge to IHT on X's death on Purple Acre, but to the extent only that its then value exceeded the amount of the Debt.[263]

Although X would be regarded as having reserved a benefit[264] in Purple Acre under s.102A, this did not matter, because he would already be treated as owning Purple Acre because of his interest in possession, by virtue of s.49(1) of the 1984 Act (as it applied prior to March 22, 2006: see Chapter 12).[265] The more important question was whether X had reserved a benefit in relation to the Debt, as the consequence of doing this would be that both the Debt and the value of Purple Acre in excess of the amount of the Debt (i.e. the full value of Purple Acre) would be subject to IHT on X's death. In HMRC's view X *would* be treated as having reserved a benefit if the Debt was repayable on demand, until such time as the trustees of the Debt Trust called in the Debt. The basis for this conclusion is that failure to call in the Debt constituted a reservation of benefit in it by associated operations, since if the Debt were to be called in, the trustees of the House Trust would either have to sell Purple Acre (in which case X would be unable

---

[262] The terms of the Debt varied, e.g. it might be repayable on demand or repayable after the death of X, interest-free or interest-bearing with interest rolled up and added to principal.

[263] So far as CGT was concerned, provided the land associated with Purple Acre was required for the reasonable enjoyment of Purple Acre and there had been no exclusive business user any gain realised by X on the sale of Purple Acre to the House Trust would be eligible for the principal private residence exemption. In addition, any gain realised on a sale by the trustees during X's life (so long as at all relevant times X had been entitled under the terms of the Settlement to occupy Purple Acre) would have been within the principal private residence exemption. On X's death there would be a CGT free uplift in respect of assets then comprised in the House Trust. Any gain realised by the trustees of the House Trust on the sale within 36 months of X's death after the sale of Purple Acre would be within the CGT principal private residence exemption so long as at all relevant times X was entitled under the terms of the settlement to occupy Purple Acre; see Taxation of Chargeable Gains Act 1992 s.225.

[264] If the initial disposal was a disposal by way of gift; see para.7–49.

[265] Even if X's s.49(1) deemed ownership of the House pre-empted the operation of the reservation of benefit clawback rule on his death, the reservation of benefit rules would not be wholly irrelevant. If X ceased to be interested in the House Trust during his lifetime he would then prima facie make a notional PET under FA 1986 s.102(4). This, however, was not envisaged.

to occupy it) or obtain third party financing (which might not be possible and in any event could only be justified if the trustees were financed by X).[266]

HMRC now take the view that that X would also be treated as having reserved a benefit in the debt if it was only repayable after death, because X has thus ensured that his occupation of the house cannot be disturbed during his lifetime. This benefit in HMRC's view arises directly from the terms of the loan given away.[267] HMRC have also put forward two further arguments in this respect.[268] The first is that the debt is caught by s.103 of the Finance Act 1986 (disallowing the deduction of a debt against the estate) because the debt is, as result of the trustees' lien on the house, an incumbrance on the property, and the consideration for the debt was derived from the deceased. Second, HMRC consider that the scheme can be regarded as a pre-ordained series of transactions which taken together deem the vendor to have made a gift of the property which he continues to occupy.

7–140   Home loan schemes are no longer in use and many existing such schemes have now been wound up. The main reason for this is the introduction of the preowned assets regime with effect from April 6, 2005.[269] The regime was intended as a deterrent to the use of what were seen as aggressive IHT planning schemes (although as described later in this chapter it is wide enough to catch arrangements which do not involve any IHT avoidance) and the home loan scheme was one of its main targets. Ironically, there was a good deal of debate as to whether the scheme was in fact caught by the new regime, but the general conclusion was that the regime did apply.[270]

It is now known that HMRC are claiming that the reservation of benefit provisions apply to almost all home loan schemes and the matter is being litigated.[271]

Partnership arrangements

7–141   Partnerships give rise to many problems under the reservation of benefit provisions. The simplest situation one encounters is that of a partner who wishes to give away part of his partnership share. The question often arises as to whether his continuing occupation of partnership property will infringe the reservation of benefit provisions. In the authors' view it should not, because he will continue to be entitled to occupy that property by virtue of his ongoing participation as a partner, not by virtue of any act or omission of the donee.

Gift of land owned by partner and used by partnership

7–142   Another situation which is often met in practice is that of a partner who owns land which he farms in partnership with his wife and child and who wishes to give part of the land to the child, following which the partners will continue to farm it as they have

---

[266] See HMRC's *Pre-owned assets guidance*, s.5.

[267] HMRC Manuals IHTM 44105.

[268] HMRC Manuals IHTM44106. For a refutation of these arguments, see C. Whitehouse & E. Chamberlain, "HMRC's attack on home loan schemes", *Taxation* (2011), Vol.167, Issue 4290.

[269] Although home loan schemes have also been adversely affected by the introduction of stamp duty land tax and the FA 2006 changes imposing an IHT charge on gifts to an interest in possession or accumulation and maintenance trust.

[270] On the basis that the Debt was an "excluded liability" for the purposes of para.11(7) of Sch.15 to the FA 2004.

[271] HMRC Manuals IHTM 44103.

done previously. In such a case it is clear that the subject matter of the gift is the land and that the prohibition against the donor's continuing enjoyment of the subject matter will prima facie be infringed. What can be done in such a situation?

The most obvious and straightforward means of staying out of the reservation of benefit provisions would be for the partnership to pay the child a market rent, in which case the full consideration let-out would apply.[272] Unfortunately, this is not an approach which will normally recommend itself.[273]

It should be possible in most cases to arrange matters, by adjusting the entitlements under the partnership agreement of the partners concerned, so that reliance can be placed on the full consideration let-out on the basis that, by taking a smaller share of the profits, the donor provides full consideration for his continuing occupation of the land.[274]   **7–143**

It is important to emphasise that, as indicated earlier in this chapter, the full consideration let-out does not apply in relation to assets other than land or chattels. In the context of partnerships, HMRC give the following example[275]:   **7–144**

> "A, who is a partner, withdraws capital from his partnership capital account and gives it to B. B then lends the partnership an equivalent cash sum.
> This is a reservation. Though A may pay B a commercial rate of interest for the loan, this payment will not prevent the loan being a reservation."

Lopsided arrangements

More adventurous arrangements may attract a challenge from HMRC. Assume that Adam farms Blackacre in partnership with his daughter Berta. Assume that there is a 20 year partnership agreement under which Adam is entitled to 80 per cent of the profits and surplus assets. Adam assigns to Berta a fraction of his share in surplus assets so that they are now held equally. He retains, however, his 80 per cent share of the profits.   **7–145**

There are two views on what IHT consequences flow from the rearrangement carried out by Adam and Berta. First, there is the simple view that Adam has given away a share in the underlying assets of the firm so that by continuing to receive 80 per cent of the profits he has continued to derive a benefit from the share given. This view assumes that profits follow assets and, if correct, will mean that the property given away by Adam is caught by the reservation of benefit rules and will form part of his death estate.

A second view of the foregoing involves analysing what is included in the phrase "a share of a partnership". Typically this will include a share in profits, the right to a return of capital on dissolution and a share in surplus assets. On this analysis the partnership share does not therefore include a direct interest in the partnership property itself and is merely a chose in action (akin to a share in a company). Hence, the gift by Adam represents a transfer of a part of his chose in action and there would appear to be no reason why Adam cannot give away part of his interest in surplus assets whilst retaining in full his share of the profits. On this analysis, Adam never gave away any

[272] See para.7–84.
[273] Aside from the obvious commercial implications, it will, by reducing the partnership's profits, affect the ability of the partners to get income tax relief on their pension contributions.
[274] See para.28–17 and HMRC Manuals IHTM14341.
[275] See HMRC Manuals IHTM14336.

interest in the profits, but merely gave away a quite separate interest in surplus assets.[276]

7–146   Assume now that a husband and wife, A and B, are in partnership with their son C. A and B feel that C is working the hardest and making a substantial contribution to profits so they transfer a sum from their capital accounts to him to recompense him for his additional efforts. In these circumstances HMRC accept that, if the transfer was commensurate with the additional contribution C was expected to make, the transfer will not be a gift and there will therefore be no question of a reservation of benefit. However, in practice they will not assume that this is the case and will initially proceed on the basis that the transfer was a gift.[277]

Retirement annuities

7–147   If a retiring partner's share is unfettered by accruer or option arrangements and he voluntarily transfers his capital account to the continuing partners in exchange for an annuity which proves to be worth less than the value of his capital account, HMRC's view is that the reservation of benefit provisions can apply on the basis that the sale of the retiring partner's share will have been for less than full consideration.[278] The position would probably turn on whether the retiring partner was aware that he was transferring his capital account for less than it was worth, since a sale at an intentional undervalue would be within the scope of the reservation of benefit rules.[279]

Partnerships as trust substitutes

7–148   The amended IHT regime for trusts which was introduced by the Finance Act 2006 has significantly restricted the scope for tax and succession planning for UK domiciled individuals using trusts. Subject to certain very limited exceptions, lifetime transfers to trusts of any kind in excess of the nil rate band will trigger an immediate IHT charge at 20 per cent and 10-yearly and exit charges will subsequently be due under the relevant property regime. In addition, with effect from April 6, 2006 capital gains tax holdover relief is excluded for trusts from which the settlor, his spouse/civil partner or his minor children can benefit.[280] Consequently a transfer to such a trust will frequently trigger an immediate charge to CGT in addition to any IHT due.

In view of these changes, there has been increasing interest in the use of alternative structures for holding assets and transferring them from one generation to the next. In certain cases a partnership may be worth considering in this context. Although a partnership will not always be a suitable alternative to a trust, in appropriate circumstances it can provide a tax-efficient and comparatively flexible means of facilitating transfers of assets to younger generations.

From a tax perspective, one of the main potential attractions of a partnership is that it will in principle not be regarded as a settlement for IHT purposes. The structure can therefore be funded without an immediate IHT charge and a subsequent gift of a partnership interest will qualify as a PET for IHT purposes. On the other hand, there

[276] See para.28–03.
[277] See HMRC Manuals IHTM14315.
[278] HMRC Manuals IHTM14316.
[279] See paras 7–49 and following.
[280] See TCGA 1992 s.260(1) in conjunction with s.169B.

will be a potential reservation of benefit if a donor has any ability to claw back or benefit from the interests given away. This means that it is unlikely to be possible to maintain the same level of flexibility as a trust, since if the partnership structure is to be effective, it will be necessary to ensure not only that the donor cannot reduce or take away an interest following the gift, but also that any distributions to partners must be made pro rata to their capital entitlement.

It has also been suggested that a reservation of benefit will arise if the donor is a partner. However, in the authors' view this will not be an issue provided that the donor's entitlement under the partnership is referable to his own partnership share rather than the share he has given away.[281]

Insurance arrangements

The Finance Act 2006 changes have also generated increasing interest in insurance-based IHT planning. There are various products in the market, the commonest of which include discounted gift schemes and gift and loan trusts. **7–149**

Discounted gift schemes

Discounted gift schemes (also known as estate planning bonds) are intended to enable donors to reduce their capital while retaining an income stream, without a reservation of benefit. Various different schemes exist, but broadly they involve a gift of a bond issued by a life insurance company and held on trust for the intended beneficiaries, with certain rights retained for the donor to provide him with regular payments during his life. The transfer to the trust will be either a PET (if a bare trust is used) or a chargeable transfer. In either case, the donor's retained rights normally enable the value of the gift to be discounted: the level of discount will vary according to the level of income and the donor's age, sex and state of health. **7–150**

HMRC appear to regard discounted gift schemes as being acceptable in principle and have confirmed that the retained rights are sufficiently well defined to preclude a reservation of benefit.[282] However, in certain cases they may seek to challenge the insurance company's valuation of the retained rights as at the date of the gift. Where the donor is older than 90 on their next birthday (actual age or deemed age following underwriting) or is considered to be uninsurable per se as at the transfer date, HMRC take the view that only a nominal value can be attributed to the retained rights and the value transferred to the gift will extend to a sum adjacent to the whole amount invested in the scheme (i.e. the value of the gift cannot be significantly discounted).[283]

Gift and loan trusts

Gift and loan trusts are intended for use by donors who still require access to capital during their lifetime but want to take future growth outside their estates. They involve **7–151**

---

[281] See para.7–57 above and HMRC Manuals IHTM14332, example 4.

[282] See HMRC's technical note issued on May 17, 2007 (available at *http://www.hmrc.gov.uk/cto/dgs-tech-note.pdf* [Accessed October 2, 2012]) and *Preowned assets Technical Guidance,* Appendix 1.

[283] See HMRC Brief 21/2009 issued following the High Court's decision in the case of *Revenue and Customs Commissioners v Bowers (executors of Bower (Deceased))* [2009] S.T.C. 510.

the creation of a trust for the intended beneficiaries followed by an interest-free loan by the donor to the trustees. The loan is invested in an insurance bond and can be partly encashed as and when the donor requires a repayment. These trusts do not produce an immediate IHT saving as the benefit of the loan (although not any future growth in the value of the bond) remains within the settlor's estate. Any subsequent loan repayments which are used by the donor to fund living expenses, etc. will reduce his estate.

HMRC have confirmed that this arrangement is not a gift with reservation, as the donor is not a beneficiary of the trust itself and the making of the loan does not constitute a settlement for IHT purposes.[284]

Negligence and reservation of benefit

7–152   The solicitor's duty of care in relation to reservation of benefit was considered in the 2004 Court of Appeal case of *Daniels v Thompson*.[285] The claimant was the son of the late Mrs Daniels and the defendant was a solicitor whom she had consulted for advice on IHT mitigation in 1989, at the age of 85. On the defendant's advice, she transferred her house to the claimant and took out insurance to protect her estate against the risk of an IHT charge in the event of her death within seven years of the transfer. However, the defendant did not advise her about the possible application of the reservation of benefit rules and she continued to live in the house rent-free until her death in 1998, when the house was charged to IHT in her estate. The claimant, who was both her executor and a beneficiary, brought a claim (in his capacity as personal representative) against the defendant for breach of his duty of care towards Mrs Daniels.

The judge at first instance dismissed the claim on the basis that the cause of action arose on the execution of the deed of gift in 1989 (rather than on Mrs Daniels' death as the claimant contended) and was therefore statute barred under the Limitation Act 1980. The Court of Appeal agreed that the relevant date for limitation purposes was the date of the deed of gift rather than the date of death, but also took the view that Mrs Daniels had not suffered any loss. The only loss pleaded was the liability to pay IHT on the value of her house. However, because this liability arose only on Mrs Daniels' death, it could only be a liability of the estate and she herself was never at risk of having to pay it. Although she had suffered the detriment that the defendant's negligence frustrated her wish to confer a benefit on her son (in the form of a reduction of the IHT liability of her estate), this was not a detriment which was recognised by law as being capable of assessment in money terms. Effectively the claimant was faced with a fundamental dilemma, in that his argument on the limitation issue, i.e. that the loss was not suffered until Mrs Daniels died, meant that she could not have suffered any loss. Alternatively, if she did suffer any loss, it must have occurred more than six years before the proceedings were issued and was therefore statute barred.

During the course of argument, the claimant applied for permission to plead an alternative case on the basis that the defendant owed a duty of care in tort to the claimant as Mrs Daniels' personal representative. The Court of Appeal refused permission on the ground that the application had been made too late, and also expressed the view that the amended claim had no real prospects of success, as the claimant had suffered no loss in his capacity as personal representative.

Although this case appears to limit the potential for negligence claims in relation to reservation of benefit, there are two points which should be noted. The first is that the Court of Appeal emphasised that the claimant had not attempted to argue that the

[284] See HMRC Manuals IHTM44113.
[285] *Daniels v Thompson* [2004] EWCA 307.

defendant owed him a duty of care in his capacity as a potential beneficiary (under the principles in *White v Jones*[286]) and this issue was therefore not considered. The second point is that *Daniels v Thompson* does not mean that a transferor can never bring a negligence claim in relation to a gift with reservation. Although Mrs Daniels could never have been liable to pay IHT on the gift of her house, the Court of Appeal pointed out that if she had become aware of the negligent advice during her lifetime and obtained legal advice from another solicitor to remedy the position, she would then have been able to recover the cost of obtaining the legal advice and any reasonable remedial steps to make good the original deficiency.

Agreements to bear tax

Where a transferor dies within seven years of making a PET the primary liability for **7–153** the tax due is that of the transferee, but the tax is also a liability of the transferor's personal representatives if it remains unpaid for more than 12 months after the death.[287] It may therefore be desirable for the parties to agree that any tax which should prove to be payable will be borne by the transferee. HMRC have confirmed that such an agreement will not activate the reservation of benefit provisions.[288]

Agricultural relief and the counterproductive carve-out

A taxpayer who lives in a farmhouse on a farm which he owns may want to give the **7–154** farm to, e.g., his son, but to continue living in the farmhouse. This prima facie causes problems under the reservation of benefit provisions. It might occur to the would-be donor, geography permitting, that he simply gives away the farm, but retains the land on which the farmhouse is built. This will clearly solve his reservation of benefit problems, but it will result in his losing agricultural relief on the farm, because the relief is given by reference to "agricultural property" and a farmhouse is such property to extent only that it is "of a character appropriate to" agricultural land or pasture.[289] If the taxpayer gives away most of the his land and pasture, it will be difficult to satisfy this test.

THE PREOWNED ASSETS REGIME

I. INTRODUCTION

The Finance Act 2004 Sch.15 introduced an entirely new charging regime ("the **7–155** Regime") under which an individual resident[290] in the United Kingdom is, from April 6, 2005,[291] charged to income tax on an annual basis in respect of benefits they enjoy—or, in some cases, are capable of enjoying—from certain kinds of property

---

[286] *White v Jones* [1995] 2 A.C. 207.
[287] See para.29–69.
[288] *The Law Society Gazette* (April 8, 1987), p.1041.
[289] IHTA 1984 s.115(2).
[290] FA 2004 Sch.15 para.12(1).
[291] FA 2004 s.84(2).

owned by others which, broadly speaking, that individual previously owned or the acquisition of which they financed. The charge is intended to perform two functions: first, to operate as a kind of fine on individuals who have escaped the clutches of the IHT reservation of benefit provisions by what HMRC regard as unacceptable means; secondly, as a disincentive to further attempts at IHT avoidance. As the Regime imposes a charge to income tax it is outside the scope of this book, but it is so closely linked to IHT generally and the reservation of benefit provisions in particular that the authors thought they should summarise the principal issues.[292]

7–156   One might have thought that the natural response to the avoidance of IHT would have been the introduction of IHT anti-avoidance provisions, but HMRC were apparently concerned both by the perceived scale of the avoidance and by the risk that tax advisers would find ways around any additional IHT anti-avoidance legislation. A new approach was therefore thought to be needed.[293]

Retroactive, not retrospective

7–157   A particularly noteworthy feature of the Regime is that the only time limit as to its application is that the Regime does not operate with respect to arrangements put into effect before March 18, 1986 (which is also the starting date for the application of the reservation of benefit provisions),[294] except in certain cases where a gift of cash falls out of account after seven years (see para.7–188 below). Representations were made that the Regime was retrospective and should apply only to arrangements put into effect after, e.g., December 9, 2003, the date on which it was announced that the Regime was to be introduced. The government resisted this view: although the Regime affected structures put into place before the introduction of the Regime, it imposed a charge only on benefits enjoyed after the introduction of the Regime. The Regime was therefore retroactive, but not retrospective.

Impact on existing arrangements

7–158   The Regime applies to a wide range of arrangements implemented since March 18, 1986 which have successfully avoided IHT, notably successful *Ingram*-based schemes[295] and *Eversden*-based schemes,[296] and to home loan schemes.[297] Many other arrangements, some "innocent", may also be caught, including policies taken out in connection with cross option arrangements, despite their commercial nature. HMRC have provided guidance ("the Guidance") on a number of types of arrangements, which can be found on their website. The Guidance has recently been re-written and has been moved to the IHT Manual, paras 44000 to 44116 and it can also be found in Part 2 of Tolley's *Yellow Tax Handbook*. Reference should also be made to the Code

---

[292] Detailed commentary can be found in E. Chamberlain & C. Whitehouse, *Preowned Assets and Tax Planning Strategies*, 2nd edn (London: Sweet & Maxwell, 2005).

[293] *Hansard*, Standing Committee Debates, col.238 (May 28, 2004).

[294] FA 1986 s.102(1).

[295] See paras 7–33 and following.

[296] See paras 7–35 and following.

[297] See para.7–172.

of Practice Letter submitted by STEP, CIOT and the Low Income Tax Reform Group on July 14, 2005 ("POAT COP 10 Letter").[298]

The re-written Guidance does not in most cases differ substantively from the earlier version, but there are some changes that may be significant and these have been highlighted below. It includes many more examples of how HMRC consider the charge operates in practice and also explains the current HMRC approach to home loan schemes: see further below.

Guiding principles

The Regime appears to be based on the following guiding principles:　　　　　**7–159**

- value which is subject to IHT should not be subject to the Regime;
- property and transactions which resulted in IHT not being payable either by reason of qualifying for favoured IHT treatment or by reason of what HMRC regarded as "acceptable" IHT planning should not be caught by the Regime; and
- land, chattels and settled "intangible" property not subject to IHT and to which no favoured treatment is expressly given by the Regime are within the scope of the Regime.

Unfortunately, the actual provisions do not always give effect to these principles. In particular, it should be noted that the tax does not apply only where there has been a gift, but potentially in the case of any kind of disposal even at full value (where one would expect therefore there would be no IHT planning motive or advantage). There are major exceptions, but this rule can cause many problems especially in the case of disposals of part of an interest in property.

Statutory links with IHT

Although the Regime is a freestanding regime, it is intimately linked with IHT in a　　**7–160**
number of ways:

(a) not only is property comprised in an individual's estate for IHT purposes outside the scope of the Regime, but so is other property not comprised in the individual's estate but from which property which is comprised in his estate derives its value. This is intended to prevent the same value being subject both to IHT and to the Regime;

(b) subject to certain qualifications, property which would fall to be treated as property subject to a reservation in relation to the person chargeable under the Regime is outside the scope of that Regime so that the same property is not subject to both IHT and to the Regime. Furthermore, it is open to a person to opt out of the Regime in relation to property by electing to subject himself to the reservation of benefit rules in relation to that property;

(c) the territorial scope of the Regime is framed by reference to the territorial scope of IHT in some respects—there are notable mismatches—and the IHT deemed domicile provisions apply;

---

[298] See *http://www.step.org/policy_and_technical/uk_policy/2006/pre-owned_assets_-_responses.aspx ?link=contentMiddle* [Accessed November 15, 2012].

(d) favoured treatment given to posthumous transactions is linked to the IHT favoured treatment given to such transactions so this remains a fruitful area for planning;

(e) certain reliefs and exemptions are framed by reference to IHT reliefs and exemptions; and

(f) various IHT definitions apply for the purpose of the Regime.

Basic structure

7–161   The broad structure of the Regime is to establish a separate charging system for each of three different kinds of property:

- land;
- chattels; and
- "intangible" property comprised in a settlor-interested settlement.[299] Note that the use of the word "intangible" is remarkably misleading—it includes cash and any other asset which is not land or chattels.

Parallel charging codes

7–162   More than one of the charging codes can apply to an arrangement. Assume that X lives in a house owned by a company all the shares in which are owned by a discretionary trust of which he is the settlor and under which he can benefit. The Regime is capable of applying to two assets: first, the house in which X lives under the charge on land; secondly, the shares in the company, under the charge on settled intangible property.[300]

Reliefs and exemptions

7–163   Certain conditions, which vary according to the type of property concerned, must be satisfied before the Regime can apply to that kind of property. Where land and chattels are concerned these conditions must be satisfied otherwise than by certain transactions called "excluded transactions". Even if the conditions are satisfied, certain exemptions may prevent the Regime from applying.

Associated operations

7–164   It is worth mentioning that the IHT associated operations provisions are of limited relevance under the Regime. They generally[301] do not apply for purposes of the Regime

---

[299] "Chattel" and "intangible property" are defined as follows: (a) "chattels" means any tangible moveable property (or, in Scotland, corporeal moveable property); "intangible property" means any property other than chattels or interests in land. "Intangible property" is thus a default term in that it applies to all property other than chattels and interests in land: FA 2004 Sch.15 para.1.

[300] There are provisions in Sch.15 para.18 to prevent double taxation arising in such a case, but the point to bear in mind is that each situation must be carefully analysed for its consequences under the Regime.

[301] They are relevant for determining what is an "excluded liability": see para.7–172.

(though they can be indirectly relevant in that they may apply for the purpose of determining whether or not property is subject to a reservation). In particular, although the Regime uses the term "disposition" it does not adopt the extended IHT definition of that term whereby a disposition includes a disposition effected by associated operations.[302] Indeed, as a general rule the legislation uses the term "disposal" rather than "disposition".

II. THE CHARGING CODES

The paragraph 3 charge on land

The charge on land, under para.3, operates where in any year of assessment an individual occupies any land, whether alone or together with other persons and either of two conditions are met. The first condition—"the disposal condition"—is broadly that the land was previously owned by the individual or represents property which he previously owned. The second condition—"the contribution condition"—is broadly that he provided the money with which the land was acquired.[303] Where para.3 applies an amount equal to "the chargeable amount" is treated as the income of the individual chargeable to income tax.[304] The "chargeable amount" is, very broadly speaking, the rent which, applying various rules based on the rental value of the property, is regarded as appropriate in the circumstances.[305]

7–165

Property does not need to be valued for these purposes more than once every five years,[306] unless it is sold and a new property purchased. The charge applies only to the "relevant land" actually occupied, so if the house is sold and a smaller one purchased, the rental value of the smaller property becomes the relevant figure. It may be that the individual is already paying a commercial rent. The rules regulating the computation of the notional rent are such that the notional rent may exceed the commercial rent actually being paid, in which case the Regime applies to the excess of the notional rent over the actual rent. In practice this is unlikely to be a concern because where a full commercial rent is chargeable the full consideration let-out in the Finance Act 1986 Sch.20 para.6(1)(a) will normally apply: see para.7–84.

"Occupation" will be widely construed for the purposes of the Regime by HMRC, in line with their view on the meaning of "occupation" for the reservation of benefit rules, e.g. visits of more than two weeks a year to a house formerly owned if the new owner is absent, will be regarded as occupation.[307] The new guidance states that occupation requires an element of control, and states that a visitor may therefore not be in "occupation" even if staying for an extended period. This does not seem consistent with the reference to the GROB guidance on occupation, which implies that visits to one's former home, now occupied by the donee, of more than one month a year are likely to be regarded as being occupation. However, the Manual now also states that merely storing possessions in a property will be insufficient for occupation and that a right of access (evidenced by having the key) will be needed for occupation to arise. There is also now a reference to persons occupying a part of a property given away but

---

[302] IHTA 1984 s.272.
[303] FA 2004 Sch.15 para.3(1)–(3).
[304] FA 2004 Sch.15 para.3(5).
[305] FA 2004 Sch.15 para.4.
[306] SI 2005/724 para.4.
[307] HMRC Manuals IHTM44003.

using the rest, where HMRC will regard them as remaining in occupation of the whole.

A sale of the whole property at an undervalue is referred to as a "non-exempt sale" and a formula is applied to calculate the tax only on the part given, not sold. However, since the taxpayer will be subject to the charge only if he is in occupation of the land, HMRC take the view that in such a case the gift element is subject to a reservation and therefore exempt from the charge anyway.

A sale of part of the property at an undervalue is however not a "non-exempt sale". As a result, although the gift element is still a GROB (assuming the vendor is in occupation) the sale element is subject to the Regime—since neither the excluded transaction rules, nor the sale of part rules, nor the non-exempt sale provisions, apply. This is one of the better illustrations of the sometimes unfathomably bizarre operation of the tax.

The Manual deals with certain specific arrangements affected. Pre-June 20, 2003 *Eversden* schemes will not be caught by the gift with reservation legislation, and will not be caught by the Regime either unless or until the life interest of the second spouse/civil partner ends during his lifetime—until then para.10(1)(c) will exempt it.[308]

Pre-March 10, 1999 reversionary leases are caught by the tax since they are not usually regarded as gifts with reservation, provided there are no terms of the lease which benefit the donor. HMRC now accept that post-March 9, 1999 reversionary leases, provided that the freehold was acquired over seven years before the gift, are not GROBs either so the Regime will also apply.[309]

The Guidance states that pre-March 10, 1999 lease carve out (or *Ingram*) schemes will be affected by the Regime charge, since they cannot be regarded as GROBs. However such a scheme made after that date will be caught by the amended GROB rules and therefore no charge will arise.[310]

A sale of the whole interest in a property at full market value followed by rent free occupation will not, in HMRC's view, be caught by the charge as it will be regarded as an excluded transaction, provided there has not been a gift of money from the donor to the donee in the past.[311]

However, a sale of part only at full market value is not an excluded transaction, and therefore rent-free occupation by the donor of the part given will be subject to the charge, unless the sale was to an unconnected party at arm's length (as above); or the arrangement otherwise comes within the limited exemption for disposals of part (see para.7–189).[312] In view of the limits on the exemption a sale of part to a connected person should be avoided as it is likely to be caught by the tax.

Equity release schemes were potentially caught by the charge since excluded transactions did not include sales of part. However the regulations referred to above should ensure that provided the transaction is at arm's length to an unconnected party, such schemes will be exempted (see para.7–189).[313]

The paragraph 6 charge on chattels

7–166   The charge on chattels, under para.6, applies where an individual is in possession of, or has the use of, a chattel, whether alone or together with other persons, and either of

[308] HMRC Manuals IHTM44101.
[309] HMRC Manuals IHTM44102.
[310] HMRC Manuals IHTM44100.
[311] HMRC Manuals IHTM44031.
[312] SI 2005/724 para.5 and HMRC Manuals IHTM44059.
[313] SI 2005/724 para.5.

two conditions are met. The first condition—"the disposal condition"—is broadly that the chattel was previously owned by the individual or represents property which he previously owned. The second condition—"the contribution condition"—is broadly that he provided the money with which the chattel was acquired.[314] Where para.6 applies an amount equal to "the chargeable amount" is treated as the income of the individual chargeable to income tax.[315] The "chargeable amount", although couched in terms of "notional interest", is essentially what the legislation regards, applying the official rate of interest as at the valuation date, as the price which would be paid to use or possess the chattel in the circumstances.[316] Assuming at current rates a notional 4 per cent return, the chargeable amount in respect of a chattel worth £500,000 would be £20,000.

On the basis of the foregoing, concern might be felt that problems would arise under the Regime in respect of various arrangements entered into under which individuals have sought to avoid the reservation of benefit provisions by sheltering under the full consideration let-out in para.6(1)(a) of Sch.20 to the Finance Act 1986 by paying a "full rent" for the use of chattels which they had given away but which they still enjoyed or had the use of—typically, works of art. The payment of full consideration was generally not onerous because normally independent experts engaged by the parties advised that only a relatively small rent was appropriate, taking into account the costs of insurance and security.

In the absence of provision to the contrary, individuals would now have to pay the annual para.8 charge on the notional interest calculated by reference to the value of the chattels. However, as is explained below, there is a blanket exemption for property which is subject to a reservation or which would be subject to a reservation but for, inter alia, para.6 of Sch.20 to the Finance Act 1986, which contains the full consideration let-out in para.6(1)(a). Accordingly, the Regime will not apply in cases where existing IHT arrangements are within para.6(1)(a). Although HMRC have argued that there is no market for rented chattels and that, in the absence of any such market, it is impossible to determine what constitutes "full consideration", the most recent position (set out by HMRC at the annual Chattels Valuation Fiscal Forum, of November 2006) is that HMRC state they will be unlikely to challenge the rental rate provided that the parties can show that there has been a proper process of negotiation, with independent advice on both sides, following normal commercial criteria. On that basis, they accept that a norm of 1 per cent of capital value has arisen. HMRC consider however that the costs of insurance and security should not be deducted from this amount. If that is not the case then the reservation of benefit provisions will apply, in which case the Regime will not: see para.7–177.

The current Manual is misleading on this issue (as the Guidance was); IHT Manual para.44018 refers to rent being paid for the use of chattels, and that this will reduce the chattels charge, but does not cross-refer to para.44048 which discusses the full consideration let out. Provided the conditions are all met, it is likely that payment of rent will take the use of the chattels out of charge altogether.

It is understood that HMRC accept that an arrangement such as a chattels lease made within a trust, where there is no actual disposal by an individual, falls outside the charge. If trustees own chattels on pre-2006 life interest trusts, and the life interest is revoked and a lease granted to the life tenant, the life tenant has not disposed of anything and so is not within para.6 albeit that the life tenant is treated as having made

---

[314] FA 2004 Sch.15 para.6(1)–(3).
[315] FA 2004 Sch.15 para.6(5).
[316] FA 2004 Sch.15 para.7.

a PET or chargeable transfer (depending on the nature of the trusts arising after the revocation).

The paragraph 8 charge on intangible property comprised in a settlor-interested settlement

7–167   The charge under para.8 applies where the terms of a settlement, as they affect any intangible property comprised in the settlement which is or represents property which the individual contributed to the settlement, are such that any income arising from that property would be treated as the income of the settlor by ITTOIA 2005 s.624.[317] Section 624 is applied ignoring any benefit or possible benefit to the settlor's spouse or civil partner from the settlement.[318] The fact that no actual income arises is irrelevant.

Paragraph 8 is framed by reference to ITTOIA s.624. This raises the question of whether the term "settlement" in the context of para.8 should be given the meaning it has for IHT purposes, in accordance with the definition given in para.1 of the Schedule, or whether for para.8 it should be a hybrid definition, requiring both the IHT definition and the income tax definition to be fulfilled. Thus, an element of bounty would be required, in accordance with ITTOIA s.620(1) which applies for the purposes of s.624. Further, the extension of the meaning of "settlement" to include "any disposition, trust, covenant, agreement, arrangement or transfer of assets" under ITTOIA s.620 would not, it may be argued, apply since it would appear that the opening words of para. 8(1)(a) of Sch.15 refer to the IHT definition, given that the reference to "the terms of the settlement" could not easily be applied to a disposition, etc.

HMRC make clear in the Guidance that they consider the IHT meaning applies, where no element of bounty is required,[319] but the Manual now also states that the POAT legislation requires the taxpayer to have "settled" property on the settlement. HMRC state therefore that a sale at full market value to the settlement would not be a settlement or addition by the taxpayer. However, the Manual seems to contradict itself, since the section dealing with life assurance policies held in trust for business purposes continues to state that such arrangements may be caught by POAT because although "there is no gift for inheritance tax [of the policy into trust for the other partners] . . . the trust remains a settlement".[320]

The contrary interpretation of the meaning of settlement for these purposes is, at least, arguable. It is unclear why the reference to ITTOIA should have been brought in unless the definition of settlement it contains was intended to be used for this paragraph. Paragraph 8(1)(a) refers to "income of a person . . . who is *for the purposes of [ITTOIA]* the settlor . . . " (emphasis added). An arrangement which was not for ITTOIA purposes a settlement, as there was no element of bounty, would have no settlor. Further, taking a purposive approach to the matter, the Regime was intended to discourage arrangements involving "unacceptable" IHT planning; commercial arrangements generally do not do so. Whilst the meaning of the paragraph is far from clear, therefore, this interpretation has, in the authors' view, much to recommend it.

Any planning taken on this basis would of course have to take into account HMRC's clearly expressed view to the contrary; and also should bear in mind the possibility of

---

[317] FA 2004 Sch.15 para.8(1)(a) and (c) and (2).
[318] FA 2004 Sch.15 para.8(1)(b).
[319] HMRC Manuals IHTM44009.
[320] HMRC Manuals IHTM44115.

HMRC arguing that, if the income tax definition is relevant, the wider meaning of settlement, including a disposition, etc., is imported.

As indicated above, "intangible property" for this purpose means any property other than chattels or interests in land.[321] The most common kinds of property that it will catch are shares, securities, insurance policies and bank accounts. Land or chattels comprised in a settlement would not be within para.8. Nor, if the settlor did not occupy the land or use or enjoy the chattels, would the land be within para.3 or the chattels within para.6.

The Manual sets out HMRC's view of the application of the charge to a number of situations.[322] It does not apply to discounted gift schemes since HMRC take the view that the settlor's retained right to "income" is held on a bare trust and this is separate from the trusts of the part given away (even though, in fact, these two parts are usually not separate). Nor will registered pension policies come within the charge. Arrangements such as cross options backed by term assurance, despite their commercial nature, can however be caught, in HMRC's view (as discussed above), if the donor of the life policy has retained a benefit in it, e.g. the ability to cash in the policy on leaving the partnership. Whilst the value chargeable may be within the de minimis limit, if the donor is in good health, the charge could well arise if he is not. Thus the donor could find he is unexpectedly liable to an additional tax charge, as a result of critical illness, in respect of what is normally a fully commercial arrangement not entered into for IHT reasons. The problem would not arise if the argument above, that "settlement" in this context does require an element of bounty, is correct, despite HMRC's view.

Where para.8 applies an amount equal to "the chargeable amount" is treated as the individual's income chargeable to income tax.[323] The "chargeable amount" is the notional interest return on the property found by applying the official rate of interest.[324] Assuming a 4 per cent rate of interest (current as at July 2012), the chargeable amount in respect of an insurance policy worth £250,000 would be £10,000. There is deducted from this amount certain other taxes payable in respect of the property, e.g. under s.624 itself or where the individual is assessed to CGT on chargeable gains attributed to him by s.86 of the Taxation of Chargeable Gains Act 1992.[325]

A radically different approach

It is essential to understand that para.8 adopts an entirely different approach to that **7–168** adopted under the para.3 land provisions and the para.6 chattels provisions, in several ways. First, under the para.3 and para.6 provisions the taxpayer must have actually benefited. Under para.8, on the other hand, what matters is the mere possibility of benefiting. Secondly, none of the "excluded transactions" let-outs (i.e. broadly transactions at arms' length and between spouses/civil partners) apply to prevent para.8 from operating.

However the exemptions from charge set out in para.11 do apply, so for para.8 to be in issue there must for example be no life interest retained by the settlor, or gift with reservation, which will take many cases out of the charge. It is for this reason that the paragraph may disproportionately affect commercial arrangements (again assuming no

---

[321] FA 2004 Sch.15 para 1.
[322] HMRC Manuals IHTM44111 ff.
[323] FA 2004 Sch.15 para.8(1) and (3).
[324] FA 2004 Sch.15 para.9(1).
[325] FA 2004 Sch.15 para.9(1).

element of bounty is needed) which do not involve gifts and so the GROB provisions cannot apply.

III. EXEMPTIONS AND RELIEFS

7–169   The legislation provides certain exemptions and reliefs. It is important to understand their scope. The "blanket exemptions" discussed below apply to all three charging codes. The relief given to "excluded transactions", on the other hand, applies only in respect of the codes dealing with land and chattels. A further exemption was added by Regulations made in 2005, for disposals of part at arm's length, which also applies only to the land and chattels charges. Last, the £5,000 annual exemption operates very differently from the IHT £3,000 annual exemption, as is explained below.

Blanket exemptions

7–170   Five blanket exemptions operate to prevent any of the three charging codes from operating.

1. Ownership exemption

7–171   Subject to two qualifications, none of the three charging codes applies to an individual at a time when for IHT purposes his estate includes the Regime property.[326] The purpose of this rule is straightforward enough—property already within a person's estate is already prima facie within the scope of IHT. Were the Regime also to apply to it there would be an element of double taxation.

Qualification one: excluded liabilities

7–172   Where at any time the value of a person's estate for IHT purposes is reduced by an excluded liability affecting any property, that property is not treated as comprised in his estate except to the extent that the value of the property exceeds the amount of the excluded liability.[327] A liability is an "excluded liability" if (a) the creation of the liability and (b) any transaction by virtue of which the person's estate came to include the Regime property or property derived directly or indirectly therefrom, were associated operations.[328]

The purpose of this provision is thought to be to nullify the effectiveness of certain IHT arrangements known as "home loan" schemes, discussed at para.25–97. In essence, these operated as follows. Assume X's family home was worth £500,000. He created a trust under which he had an interest in possession and sold his home to the trust for a purchase price left outstanding interest-free. He then settled the debt owed to him on interest in possession trusts for his children, or trusts that were at the time

[326] FA 2004 Sch.15 para.11(1)(a).
[327] FA 2004 Sch.15 para.11(6).
[328] FA 2004 Sch.15 para.11(7).

accumulation and maintenance trusts, thereby making what was at the time a PET. On his death the value of the home was reduced by the amount of the debt. So, if on his death the home was worth £700,000 and the debt was for £500,000, the value of the home for IHT purposes was £200,000. If X survived the PET by seven years he had therefore reduced the amount on which IHT was due on the home from £700,000 to £200,000.

If under the Regime the debt is an excluded liability the result will be that (a) the ownership exemption is not available in respect of the home save as to £200,000, which sum will, of course, be within the scope of IHT, and (b) the remaining £500,000 will be within the scope of the Regime.

As a result of the introduction of the Regime, most home loan schemes have now been dismantled or elections made to disapply the tax, in return for accepting that the property is treated as back in the donor's estate (see section V below), except in cases where the taxpayer decides he will accept the income tax cost as the price of retaining the IHT advantage. In considering how to deal with any schemes which have not yet been unwound the following points should be noted:

(a) unwinding the scheme is likely to be a better option than electing for several reasons, including the possible income tax implications. Where as is often the case the debt is a deeply discounted security the eventual income tax charge on repayment of the loan could well equal or outweigh the IHT saving. Further, if a married couple entered into the scheme, both elect and then one dies, HMRC consider that the spouse exemption is only available to the extent that the value of the house exceeds the debt[329];

(b) whilst post-March 22, 2006 a waiver of the debt might be thought to have IHT implications, as it could be seen as, in effect, adding property to the trust holding the house (by reducing the loan owed by the trustees to nil) HMRC have confirmed in writing, in several individual cases in the writers' experience, that they consider that a waiver is a PET by the life tenant of the trust holding the debt. It thus appears still to be possible to terminate the scheme in this way without giving rise to an immediate IHT charge;

(c) unwinding does however give rise to possible double charges to IHT, if the original donor and the person who waives the benefit of the loan note die within seven years of the relevant dates. The double charges regulations do not give relief in that situation, only on the double charge on the donor's death because he has made a PET which has become chargeable, but (because of the waiver) the value of the house is back in his estate; and

(d) HMRC are challenging the validity of some widely marketed schemes, where the donor has died, on the grounds that the scheme gives rise to a reservation of benefit. The amended Guidance, now the Manual, first published in October 2010 indicated that HMRC had changed their former view (published in the original POAT Guidance) to the effect that schemes where the loan was not repayable until after the donor's death would now be regarded as caught by the gift with reservation rules as the donor will be regarded as having reserved a benefit in the debt. The earlier version of the Guidance stated that the donor will be regarded as having reserved a benefit in the debt only where the debt was repayable on demand, and that it was "generally thought" that there would be no reservation if the loan was not repayable in the donor's lifetime. The matter is now being litigated. In either case, however, HMRC consider that POAT will still apply, as in each case—on HMRC's analysis—it is the loan in which the benefit is reserved, not the house, and POAT is therefore payable in respect of

[329] Regime COP10 letter, question 18.

305

the occupation of the house.[330] In these cases it is therefore possible for both POAT and an IHT charge to arise. Retention of the scheme and payment of tax under the Regime may not therefore succeed in achieving any IHT saving.

Qualification two: Interests in possession

7–173   It was widely noted after the Regime was introduced that the reverter to settlor exemption could be used in order to avoid the impact of the charge on existing schemes by (say) a donee under a lease carve out scheme settling the freehold of the property on life interest trusts for the donor, with reverter back to the donee on the donor's death. This meant that provided the original donor died first there was no IHT on the value of the freehold passing back to the original donee, and the Regime was avoided as both freehold and lease would be in the orginal donor's estate.

Therefore para.11(11) was added to Sch.15 with effect from December 5, 2005 to counter this. A person's interest in possession in relevant property (whether created before or after December 5, 2005) will not cause that property to fall outside the Regime charge if at an earlier time the person had provided consideration for the acquisition of the property; or previously the property had ceased to be comprised in the person's estate (before coming back into the estate, as under the example given above). HMRC have confirmed in correspondence that, for para.11(11) to apply, the consideration or property must leave the donor's estate, causing a reduction in value for IHT purposes, so the paragraph will not bite if the donor has had an interest in possession in the property concerned throughout.

Nonetheless, as noted in the correspondence between STEP and HMRC[331] on the matter, the exception is clearly wide enough to catch many arrangements which do not involve a reverter to settlor trust. The example is given of a trust holding UK property funded by a resident non-domiciliary which is converted into an interest in possession trust before March 22, 2006. After conversion the settlor would be chargeable under the Regime. The Manual confirms that arrangements other than reverter to settlor trusts can be caught and gives examples, one involving a gift from son to mother to enable her to buy her house.[332] If the mother leaves the house to the son in her will on a life interest trust, the son will be caught by the charge despite the fact that the house is in his estate and it will be charged on his death. In such a case the son should elect—provided he is properly advised and so able to do so within the necessary time period. The Manual also gives an example involving a settlement between spouses (not caught at the outset because of the exemption for gifts between spouses) which is later caught where, following divorce, the spouse who made the settlement acquires an interest in possession where he did not have one before.

2. Derivative ownership exemption

7–174   The second exemption is that, subject to two qualifications, none of the three charging codes applies to an individual in respect of Regime property if that individual's estate includes property which derives its value from that Regime property.[333]

---

[330] HMRC Manuals IHTM44103–44106.
[331] STEP correspondence Sept/Dec 2006: see STEP website.
[332] HMRC Manuals IHTM44050.
[333] FA 2004 Sch.15 para.11(1)(b)(i).

This rule is more subtle than the first rule. It means that although an individual does not own property or have an interest in possession in property, the exemption will apply if other property to which he is beneficially entitled derives its value from that property. Assume X occupies land owned by a company of which he is the sole shareholder. The land is not in his estate and so is not covered by the ownership exemption; but the shares derive their value from the land and so are covered by the basic derived value exemption.

Qualification one: the "substantially less" rule

It may be that the value of the derivative property—in the example just given, the **7–175** shares—is less than the value of the property from which it derives its value, i.e. the land. In that case if the value of the derivative property is "substantially less", then the amount on which tax is charged under the Regime[334] is reduced by such proportion as is reasonable to take account of the inclusion of the derivative property in his estate.[335]

HMRC regard "substantially less" as meaning a reduction in value of 20 per cent or more.[336]

HMRC may consider that the "substantially less" rule may apply where a company holding property is funded by a loan. The COP10 letter stated that HMRC considered that the loan did not derive its value from the house[337] and the charge may therefore apply to a rental applied to the value of the property without deducting the loan. However, the example in the Manual dealing with a transfer of a house to a company has been altered. The former Guidance stated that if the donor had lent money to the company "we take the view that the company's value is less than the house unless (possibly) the loan is charged on the house"; this has been deleted from paragraph IHTM 44043. This may suggest a change of view on the part of HMRC.

Qualification two: excluded liabilities

The excluded liabilities restriction that operates in respect of the ownership exemp- **7–176** tion also operates in respect of the derived value exemption, regardless of whether or not the "substantially less" rule applies.[338] In applying the "substantially less" rule the procedure is thus first to apply the excluded liabilities rule and then to apply the substantially less rule.

3. Reserved benefit exemption

None of the three charging codes applies to a person by reference to any Regime **7–177** property at a time when that property satisfies any one of four conditions framed by

---

[334] Strictly, the appropriate rental value in para.4, the appropriate amount in para.7 and the chargeable amount in para.9 (as the case may be); FA 2004 Sch.15 para.11(2).
[335] FA 2004 Sch.15 para.11(1)(b)(ii) and (2).
[336] HMRC Manuals IHTM44043.
[337] Regime COP10 Letter, question 33.
[338] FA 2004 Sch.15 para.11(6).

reference to the IHT reservation of benefit provisions.[339] The purpose of this exemption is to take out of the Regime property which is already caught by the IHT reservation of benefit provisions or which is excused from the operation of those provisions by certain let-outs in the reservation of benefit rules, including that in the Finance Act 1986 s.102B for sharing arrangements and that in para.6(1)(a) of Sch.20 to that Act where full consideration is provided.[340] We will for convenience refer to such property as "reserved benefit property".

4. Derivative reserved benefit exemption

7–178   Subject to the "substantially less" rule discussed at para.7–175,[341] none of the three charging codes applies to Regime property from which reserved benefit property derives its value.[342] The purpose of this exemption is subtler than the reserved benefit exemption. Assume X owns shares in a company which owns a house in which X lives. If X gives the shares to his son and lives in the house free of charge X will reserve a benefit in respect of the shares but not the house. Therefore the reserved benefit exemption will not apply. But the shares will derive their value from the house, and so the house will be exempt under the fourth exemption. But note the problem arising if the purchase of the house had been funded by a loan: see para.7–196 below.

5. Posthumous arrangements

7–179   Under the fifth blanket exemption, any disposition made by a person in relation to an interest in the estate of a deceased person is disregarded for Regime purposes if, under para.16, that disposition is not treated as a transfer of value for IHT purposes "by virtue of" IHTA 1984 s.17. Section 17 provides that none of the following is a transfer of value: under s.17 of the 1984 Act that disposition is not treated as a transfer of value for IHT purposes.[343] This covers:

(a) variations coming within s.142[344];
(b) dispositions made pursuant to precatory trusts within s.143[345];
(c) an election by a surviving spouse/civil partner under s.47A of the Administration of Estates Act 1925[346]; and
(d) the renunciation of a claim to legitim within the period mentioned in s.147(6).[347]

HMRC have confirmed that, in cases where a variation does not in fact give rise to a transfer of value (such as the creation by variation of an IPDI for the spouse/civil

---

[339] FA 2004 Sch.15 para.11(3) and (5). See para.11(8) for the position in relation to cash gifts.
[340] See paras 7–105 and 7–84 and following respectively.
[341] Where the rule applies the relevant amounts above fall to be reduced by such proportion as is reasonable to take account of that fact: FA 2004 Sch.15 para.11(4).
[342] FA 2004 Sch.15 para.11(3)(b) and (5).
[343] FA 2004 Sch.15 para.16.
[344] See paras 8–114 and following.
[345] See paras 8–205 and following.
[346] See para.2–110.
[347] See paras 8–215 and following.

partner), the Regime does not apply even though it is arguable that s.17 is not in point.[348]

Excluded transactions

Certain transactions, called "excluded transactions" are given favoured treatment in that they are ignored in determining whether the disposal condition or the contribution condition in relation to the occupation of land and the use of chattels are satisfied, thus potentially taking the arrangement concerned out of the Regime. It is vital to note that excluded transactions are relevant only to chattels and land; they have no bearing on the treatment of intangible property comprised in a settlor-interested settlement.[349]   **7–180**

"Excluded transactions" fall into two categories. One category is framed in general terms—"the general excluded transactions"—while the other—"the special excluded transactions"—is framed by reference to the provisions identifying the particular circumstances which cause land or chattels to be within the Regime.

General excluded transactions

The disposal of any property, or the provision of consideration for another's acquisition of it, is an excluded transaction in relation to the individual who made the disposal or provided the consideration in four cases.   **7–181**

1. Transfer to or acquisition by spouse/civil partner

A transfer of property is an excluded transaction if the property was transferred to his spouse (or where the transfer has been ordered by a court, to his former spouse). The provision of consideration by a spouse for the acquisition of property by the other spouse is an excluded transaction (or where the transfer has been ordered by a court, by his former spouse).[350]   **7–182**

2. Spouse/civil partner entitled to interest in possession

A disposal is an excluded transaction if it was a disposal by way of gift[351] (or, where the transfer is for the benefit of his former spouse or former civil partner, in accordance with a court order) by virtue of which the property became settled property in which the individual's spouse, civil partner, former spouse or former civil partner is beneficially entitled to an interest in possession, but this condition ceases to be satisfied if the spouse/ civil partner or former spouse/former civil partner's interest comes to an end during his/her lifetime.[352] This provision applies to both pre and post-March 22, 2006 life interests.   **7–183**

---

[348] Regime COP10 letter, question 1.
[349] FA 2004 Sch.15 para.10(1).
[350] FA 2004 Sch.15 para.10(b) and 10(2)(a).
[351] See paras 7–49 and following.
[352] FA 2004 Sch.15 para.10(1)(c) and (3).

Similarly, the provision of consideration by a spouse for the acquisition of property by a settlement in which the other spouse is beneficially entitled to an interest in possession, is an excluded transaction, but this condition ceases to be satisfied if the spouse/civil partner or former spouse/former civil partner's interest comes to an end during his/her lifetime.[353]

3. Family maintenance dispositions

7–184   A disposal is an excluded transaction if the disposal was a disposition within the relief afforded to family maintenance dispositions by s.11 of the 1984 Act. If the provision of consideration for the acquisition of property is within the family maintenance relief, it will be an excluded transaction.[354]

4. Annual and small gifts exemptions

7–185   A disposal or the provision of consideration is an excluded transaction if the disposal/provision of consideration is an outright gift to an individual and is for IHT purposes a transfer of value that is wholly exempt by virtue of the annual exemption or the small gifts exemption.[355]

Special excluded transactions

7–186   The para.3 charge on land and the para.6 charge on chattels both operate only if either a "disposal condition" or a "contribution condition" is satisfied. The legislation provides for two excluded transactions that are framed by reference to these conditions:

(a) a transaction at arm's length of the whole property is an excluded transaction in relation to the disposal condition that exists in relation to land and chattels respectively; and

(b) an outright gift of money seven or more years earlier than the occupation/enjoyment arises is an excluded transaction in relation to the contribution condition that exists in relation to land and chattels respectively.

1. Arm's length transaction or its equivalent

7–187   For purposes of the disposal condition in the land code and the chattels code a disposal is an excluded transaction if it was of the individual's *whole* interest in the property, except for any right expressly reserved by him over the property, either:

(a) by a transaction made at arm's length with a person not connected with him; or

---

[353] FA 2004 Sch.15 para.10(2)(b) and (3).
[354] FA 2004 Sch.15 para.10(1)(d) and (2)(d); see paras 2–54 and following.
[355] FA 2004 Sch.15 para.10(1)(e) and (2)(e); see paras 3–04 and following.

(b) by a transaction such as might be expected to be made at arm's length between persons not connected with each other.[356]

With one exception, the arm's length or equivalent transaction test is the same as that in s.10(1)(a) and (b) of the IHTA 1984.[357] The qualification is that the definition of connected persons is modified so that:

(a) "relative" includes uncle, aunt, nephew and niece; and
(b) "settlement" "settlor" and "trustee" have the same meanings as in IHTA 1984.

For disposals of part, see below at para.7–189.

2. Potentially exempt currency contribution

For the purposes of the contribution condition in the land code and the chattels code **7–188** the provision by a person of consideration for another's acquisition of any property is an excluded transaction if it constitutes an outright gift of money in any currency by the individual to the other person and was made at least seven years before the earliest date on which:

(a) in the case of land, the individual occupies the land, whether alone or together with any persons[358]; or
(b) in the case of a chattel, the individual is in possession of, or has the use of, the chattel, whether alone or together with other persons.[359]

This means that if X gives Y £100,000 which Y uses to purchase a house, and X occupies the house, but does not start to do so until seven years or more after the cash gift, the contribution condition will not be satisfied.

HMRC accept that any cash gift made prior to April 6, 1998 will be excluded from the Regime by this provision (even if the occupation/possession commenced before then).

Disposals of part

In the Standing Committee debates and at Report Stage the point was taken that the **7–189** requirement for the excluded transaction exemption to apply, that the disposal had to be of the vendor's whole interest in the property, was unfair. It would not, e.g. cover a sale of a half share in a property. A new exemption was given by Regulation 2005/724 in respect of sales of part (see also the final two paragraphs of para.7–165 above). However the exemption is limited to circumstances where there is a disposal of part and:

---

[356] FA 2004 Sch.15 para.10(1)(a).
[357] For the definition of connected persons, see ITA 2007 s.993; FA 2004 Sch.15 para.2.
[358] FA 2004 Sch.15 para.10(2)(c) and para.3(1)(a).
[359] FA 2004 Sch.15 para.10(2)(c) and para.6(1)(a).

(a) the disposal was a transaction at arm's length with a person not connected with the taxpayer; or

(b) the disposal was such as might be expected to be made at arm's length *and* either (i) the consideration was not in money or money's worth; or (ii) it was made before March 7, 2005.[360]

Thus, for example, a sale of a share in one's house to a child for full market value in cash followed by continued occupation by the donor would not be covered, with the result that the donor would be liable for tax under the Regime in respect of the sold part. Shared occupation with the child would appear to make no difference to the position. It may be better for the part share to be given, not sold, to the child as in that case, provided the child and donor share occupation of the property and share the expenses, the exemption from the IHT GROB rules in Finance Act 1986 s.102B should apply and consequently there would be no charge under the Regime either.

The exemption for cases where the consideration is not in money or money's worth is apparently intended to allow a parent, for example, to give a share of the family home to a child who gives up work to care for him, provided that the acquirer can show that he has suffered detriment. In the Manual, HMRC state that such detriment could fulfil the requirement in the Regulation for consideration. However, it should be noted that the further commentary which was in the Guidance has now been removed. This referred to the case law on persons acquiring an interest in property by acting in reliance on promises, to their detriment, and stated HMRC would not expect the parties to have obtained separate advice or a court order. The former Guidance and the COP10 Letter appeared to be at odds on this point, with the Letter stating that HMRC would want to see evidence of such advice being taken.[361] The implication would seem to be that HMRC will now expect advice to be taken and possibly other steps suggestive of an arm's length arrangement.

The common situation where father and son farm father's land and the father gives the son half the land in consideration of the son's efforts in the partnership might be covered by the new exemption, if the transaction could be shown to be at arm's length. Alternatively, in such cases HMRC practice is normally to regard the full consideration let-out in the Finance Act 1986 Sch.20 para.6(1)(a) as preventing the father from having reserved a benefit on the basis of *Att Gen v Boden*,[362] and in that case the fact that para.6(1)(a) applies would also prevent the Regime from applying (see para.7–177 above).

£5,000 annual exemption

7–190   An individual is not chargeable in a year of assessment if the aggregate of:

(a) the appropriate rental value for the land charge

(b) the appropriate amount for the chattels charge; and

(c) the chargeable amount for the settled intangible property charge

---

[360] SI 2005/724 para.5(1).
[361] HMRC Manuals IHTM44059; Regime COP10 letter, question 25.
[362] *Att Gen v Boden* [1912] 1 K.B. 539; see para.28–17.

does not exceed £5,000.[363] Taking the official rate in August 2008 of 6.25 per cent, the broad effect of this exemption is to take out of the charge at these rates of return chattels or intangible property worth up to £80,000. This figure does not, however, constitute an equivalent to the IHT nil rate band because once the £5,000 exemption is exceeded the exemption is lost altogether.

Tax trap: the ungenerous exemption

The exemption is perhaps less generous than it looks. Assume A gives B land worth £150,000 and occupies it, that the appropriate rental value is £7,500 and that A pays B £5,000 per year in rent. The amount on which A is actually chargeable is only £2,500 (£7,500 less £5,000) but the exemption operates by reference not to that amount but by reference to the appropriate rental value, i.e. £7,500.[364] The exemption therefore does not apply. The exemption also operates in this way in relation to chattels.[365]

7–191

IV. FOREIGN RESIDENTS AND DOMICILIARIES

Foreign residents or domiciliaries (the IHT deemed domicile rules apply)[366] generally have little to fear under the Regime, though in some cases they may be troubled by the "excluded liability" rules or by the problems caused by HMRC's interpretation of the "derived property" rules. Before considering the application of the Regime in practice, it will be helpful first to consider two reliefs provided by the Regime for foreign residents or domiciliaries—a basic relief and a settled property relief—and then, against that background, to discuss how the blanket exemptions assist foreign domiciliaries in situations where the reliefs do not do so.

7–192

The basic relief

The basic relief is firstly that the Regime does not apply at all in relation to a person who is not resident in the UK; and secondly that where an individual is not domiciled in the United Kingdom for IHT purposes, the Regime does not apply to him unless the property by reference to which the Regime operates is situated in the United Kingdom.[367] Note that one simply focuses on the Regime property; it is irrelevant whether it is held by an individual, a company or a trust. Assume Boris, a foreign domiciliary, occupies a Spanish villa owned by a UK company the shares in which are owned by a trust of which he is the settlor. Both the shares and the villa are prima facie within the Regime (under paras 8 and 3, respectively). The relief applies in relation to the

7–193

---

[363] FA 2004 Sch.15 para.13.
[364] FA 2004 Sch.15 para.13(1)–(3).
[365] The payment of consideration is irrelevant under para.8.
[366] FA 2004 Sch.15 para.12(4); see paras 30–14 and following.
[367] FA 2004 Sch.15 para.12(2).

villa, which is situated abroad, but not to the shares,[368] which are situated in the United Kingdom. If Boris becomes domiciled in the United Kingdom the relief for the villa will no longer be available.

The settled property relief

7–194   Under the settled property relief, in determining the application of the Regime to a person who was at any time[369] domiciled outside the United Kingdom no regard is had to settled foreign situs property which is excluded property for IHT purposes by reason of being comprised in a settlement made by an individual who was not domiciled in the United Kingdom when he made the settlement.[370] Assume Svetlana, a foreign domiciliary, occupies a Spanish villa owned by an offshore company the shares in which are owned by a trust of which she is the settlor. Both the shares and the villa are prima facie within the Regime (under paras 8 and 3, respectively). Since both the shares and the villa are situated abroad, the basic relief applies in relation to both of them. If Svetlana becomes domiciled in the United Kingdom, the basic relief will cease to be available, but the settled property relief will be available in respect of the shares but not the villa (which is not settled property and therefore not excluded property).

Relevance of blanket exemptions

7–195   It might be thought that the example in the previous paragraph concerning Svetlana departs from the basic principle that individuals who have arranged their affairs in "an acceptable manner" to take advantage of IHT favoured treatment, e.g. that accorded to foreign domiciliaries, should not be caught by the Regime. This follows from the fact that for IHT purposes the only relevant asset would have been the shares, which would have been excluded property and so outside the scope of IHT. In fact, that is unlikely to be the case, because in the vast majority of cases the blanket exemptions will apply so as to make up for any apparent deficiencies in the reliefs for foreign domiciliaries.

In the above example of Svetlana, although neither the basic relief nor the settled property relief will be available:

(a) if the settlement is one in which she has an interest in possession, the second blanket exemption will apply in respect of the villa on the basis that property—the shares—which she is treated as owning by virtue of her interest in possession derives its value from the villa[371]; and

(b) if the settlement is discretionary and therefore, as is likely to be the case, one in respect of which she has reserved a benefit, the fourth blanket exemption will

---

[368] Depending on the terms of the trust, the shares should be taken out of the Regime under either the second blanket exemption in FA 2004 Sch.15 para.11(1)(b) or the fourth exemption in para.11(3)(b) and (5)(a).

[369] It is not clear whether "at any time" means that the individual must have become a UK domiciliary, but nothing appears to turn on the point.

[370] FA 2004 Sch.15 para.12(3). Since the relief is framed by reference to IHTA 1984 s.48(3)(a), ss.80–82 will not be relevant.

[371] FA 2004 Sch.15 para.11(1)(b). See para.25–06.

apply on the basis that property—the shares—in respect of which she has reserved a benefit derive their value from the villa.[372]

Companies funded by loans

In either case however a problem may arise if there is a loan outstanding from the company, due to the trustees (usually made to enable the property to be purchased). HMRC have stated that they do not consider that such a loan should be regarded as derived property, with the result that the value of the underlying property will exceed the value of the shares so that the exemption is limited in effect.[373] Most commentators think that HMRC are wrong[374] and changes to the Manual from the Guidance may suggest that they no longer intend to pursue this point (see para.7–175 above). HMRC have stated that, in the case of *commercial* borrowing, the relevant property for the purposes of the charge would be the house net of such borrowing, thus reducing its value to the value of the shares and allowing the full exemption to apply.[375] HMRC also accept that a loan, as opposed to a gift, does not fall within the contribution condition for land or chattels.[376] If therefore the house is owned by a company owned directly by the occupier of the house, and the occupier has loaned the funds to the company, the contribution condition is not satisfied by the occupier and the Regime will not apply. **7–196**

One other case is worth mentioning, i.e. that where the Regime property is held by a company the shares in which are not settled. Consider the following examples: **7–197**

(a) Catherine owns a company which owns a chattel which she uses. If she is domiciled abroad and the chattel is situated abroad the basic relief will apply. If she becomes domiciled in the United Kingdom the second blanket exemption will apply.[377]

(b) Peter occupies a villa owned by a company the shares in which he has given to his son. If he is domiciled abroad and the villa is situated abroad the basic relief will apply. If he becomes domiciled in the United Kingdom and, as is likely to be the case, he has reserved a benefit in respect of the shares, the fourth blanket exemption will apply.[378] If Peter has lent the funds to the company to buy the villa, the contribution condition will not apply anyway—see above.

Accommodation arrangements

For many years a foreign domiciliary who wished to own, e.g. a house in London, was advised to establish a trust which owned all the shares in an offshore company which in turn owned the house. The thinking was that the relevant asset for IHT purposes would be the shares in the company which would be excluded property for **7–198**

---

[372] FA 2004 Sch.15 para.11(3)(b) and (5)(a).
[373] Regime COP10 Letter, question 33.
[374] e.g., see E. Chamberlain & C. Whitehouse, *Preowned Assets and Tax Planning Strategies*, 2nd edn (London: Sweet & Maxwell, 2005), para.20–31.
[375] Regime COP10 Letter, question 13.
[376] HMRC Manuals IHTM44005 and 44009.
[377] FA 2004 Sch.15 para.11(1)(b).
[378] FA 2004 Sch.15 para.11(3)(b) and (5).

IHT purposes. Following the *Dimsey*[379] and *Allen*[380] cases, however, the risk of a "shadow director" charge under ITEPA 2003 Ch.5 became much greater and new approaches were developed which did not involve a company owning the house.

Offshore "home loan" arrangements

7–199   Often a two trust solution was used which was a variant of the home loan schemes mentioned at para.7–172. The essence of the arrangement was that the foreign domiciliary created two trusts. He funded the first trust, which could be discretionary, which in turn funded a company wholly-owned by that trust. The company lent the funds to the second trust, which would normally be an interest in possession trust, which used the funds to purchase the house. The loan, which was secured on the house, was left outstanding interest-free and repayable on demand.

Assume the company lent the trust £1,500,000 which the trust used to purchase the house and that 10 years later, when the foreign domiciliary died, the house was worth £2,000,000. For IHT purposes the value of the house would have been reduced by the debt owed to the company and so worth £500,000. Even if the debt was a United Kingdom situs asset, the relevant asset for IHT purposes was the shares in the company, which were excluded property. The net result was to take the amount of the debt outside the scope of IHT. In many cases the foreign domiciliary and his spouse had successive life interests in the house, so that if the foreign domiciliary's spouse survived him any charge on his death was deferred until the death of his spouse.

7–200   Under the Regime both the basic relief and the settled property relief will operate in respect of the shares in the company. Neither of the reliefs will be available in respect of the house, because it is UK situs property. If, as is usually the case, the trust which owns the house is an interest in possession trust, the ownership exemption will be available in respect of it, but if the "excluded liability" rules apply, the value of the debt will be within the Regime. This will depend on whether the trust holding the shares in the company is a relevant property trust or one under which the settlor has a pre-March 22, 2006 interest in possession. If the latter, the debt will *not* be an excluded liability because, since the settlor is treated as owning the shares, the value of which are the same as the debt, the debt will not reduce the value of his estate. The fact that the shares in the company are excluded property does not affect this analysis because where a person owns excluded property that property is included in his estate for IHT purposes except immediately before he dies (see para.25–18). If, on the other hand, the trust is discretionary, or the occupier has a post-March 22, 2006 interest in possession, the debt will reduce the value of the settlor's estate and therefore be an excluded liability.

7–201   Finally, to put matters in perspective, consider the position under the Regime of a traditional property owning structure of the kind mentioned above, i.e. the UK property is owned by an offshore company all the shares in which are owned by a settlement made by a foreign domiciliary. The shares in the company will be prevented by both the basic relief and the settled property relief from being within the Regime, but what about the UK property? If the foreign domiciliary has a pre-March 22, 2006 interest in possession in the trust he will be treated as owning the shares in the company, which derive their value from the house with the result that the house will be within the

---

[379] *R. v Dimsey* [2001] S.T.C. 1520.
[380] *R. v Allen* [2001] S.T.C. 1537.

derivative ownership exemption. If he does not then, assuming he has reserved a benefit under the trust, the derivative reserved benefit exemption will operate in respect of the house, with the same result (but the position is uncertain where there the trust was funded by a loan, see para.7–196 above).

Interaction of reliefs and exemptions

The legislation does not establish any hierarchy between the reliefs and the blanket **7–202** exemptions. In practice it is simpler to apply the reliefs first because they are easier to apply conceptually than the exemptions and unlike the exemptions, are not subject to any qualifications.

V. OPT OUT ELECTIONS

Taxpayers can, by an election made on or before January 31 in the year of **7–203** assessment that immediately follows the first year of assessment in which the Regime applies to the property in question, opt out of the Regime and into the reservation of benefit provisions with respect to that Regime property[381] on a once and for all basis. Where land or a chattel is concerned only the "chargeable proportion", i.e. broadly speaking, the value of the property not subject to IHT in the year of assessment in question, is treated for IHT purposes as property subject to a reservation.[382] HMRC have confirmed that the election will have effect only to the extent that the property concerned is not in the taxpayer's estate in any event, e.g. in the case of a home loan scheme where the election is made and the scheme is subsequently unravelled.

To opt or not to opt

Whether or not it makes sense to opt into reservation of benefit will need careful **7–204** consideration in each case. The election cannot be revoked after the relevant filing date has passed. Therefore, the opportunity has gone for those taxpayers whose arrangements were already within the Regime on April 6, 2005. Note also the potential loss of spouse exemption in respect of an election in the context of a home loan scheme, see para.7–172 above.

It may be that opting into reservation of benefit has no adverse IHT implications for one or more of the following reasons:

(1) *Business/agricultural relief*: the property in question may qualify for 100 per cent business relief or agricultural relief by virtue of para.8 of Sch.20 to the 1986 Act.

(2) *IHT exemption*: exceptionally the property in question may qualify for an IHT exemption on the taxpayer's death.[383]

---

[381] Or in the case of para.3 or para.6 property which has been substituted for the Regime property and in the case of para.8 property which represents or is derived from the Regime property: FA 2004 Sch.15 paras 21(2) and 22(2).

[382] FA 2004 Sch.15 paras 21 and 22.

[383] See para.7–14.

(3) *Nil rate band*: the property may fall within the taxpayer's unused IHT nil rate band.

(4) *Double tax treaty*: in exceptional cases, a double tax treaty may prevent any charge to IHT from arising.

On the other hand, the taxpayer may prefer to be taxed under the Regime because, e.g. the taxpayer's life expectancy is such that it is less expensive to pay the annual charge under the Regime than it is to bear IHT on the property. In some cases the taxpayer may wish not to burden the donee with the IHT on the property.

7–205   The fact that a taxpayer has opted to pay charges under the Regime during his life does not of itself preclude HMRC from invoking the reservation of benefit provisions on his death or, for that matter, during his lifetime should he cease while still alive to reserve a benefit in respect of property. Should HMRC adopt such a course of action they would have to refund the Regime charges for up to six years but, depending on the sums, they might conclude it was in their interest to claim IHT on the basis of the reservation of benefit provisions. Taxpayers who opt to pay under the Regime should therefore be confident that they are not subject to the reservation of benefit provisions.

VI. MISCELLANEOUS

Avoidance of double taxation

7–206   The legislation makes provision in two ways to prevent the imposition of certain double charges to income tax.

Employment benefits charge

7–207   It may be that in a year of assessment a person is chargeable to income tax in respect of his occupation of any land or his possession or use of any chattel under both the benefits code in Pt 3 of the ITEPA 2003 and the Regime. In that case the Pt 3 charge takes priority and displaces the Regime, except to the extent that the amount chargeable under the Regime exceeds the amount treated as earnings under Pt 3.[384]

Double charges under the regime

7–208   It may be that a person is chargeable under para.3 or para.6 by reason of his occupation of land or his possession or use of a chattel and under para.8 by reference to intangible property which derives its value, whether in whole or in part, from that land or chattel. In that case he will be charged only under the paragraph that produces the higher amount.[385]

---

[384] FA 2004 Sch.15 para.19.
[385] FA 2004 para.18(1) and (2).

In addition regulations were passed (2005/724 and 2005/3441) to avoid double charges where:

(1) the taxpayer has elected into the GROB regime and dies within seven years of the original gift into a settlement; or
(2) a debt scheme was entered into and the benefit of the debt was waived, and the taxpayer dies within seven years of the original gift of the debt.

In each case the tax is calculated as the greater of the tax on the gift and on the death, and the other occasion of charge is ignored.

Both sets of Regulations were aimed at giving relief in specific cases, in the first case only in respect of gifts into settlement where there was an election, and in the second case to allow home loan schemes to be dismantled without electing. They are not wide enough necessarily to cover many other situations, e.g. not involving a settlement in the first case or not involving a debt in the second.

CHAPTER 8

THE CHARGE ON DEATH, PARTLY EXEMPT TRANSFERS AND POSTHUMOUS ARRANGEMENTS

I. INTRODUCTION

This chapter is concerned with a number of related topics. It begins by considering **8–01** how a charge to IHT is imposed when a person dies. Of particular interest in this connection is how tax is charged when there is what is known as a "partly exempt transfer". There are special, complicated, rules governing the treatment of such transfers. These rules are, unfortunately, both difficult to understand and frequently relevant: whenever an individual leaves part of his estate to his surviving spouse or civil partner and part to his children the rules may apply, as well as in the common case where there is no surviving spouse or civil partner and part of the estate is left to charity and part is left to various relations. Given the fact that they have a significant impact on precisely how much a beneficiary under a will or intestacy receives, the authors think it right to stress their importance by including them as an integral part of the discussion of the charge on death. Finally, regard is had to the various provisions that, remarkably, allow taxpayers to reduce, after a person has died, the tax that was chargeable on his death. The importance of these provisions in practice can hardly be overstressed; indeed, they have taken on increased significance with the introduction by the Finance Act 2004 of the pre-owned assets regime.

THE CHARGE ON DEATH

II. INTRODUCTION

When a person dies he is treated by s.4(1) as if he had made a transfer of value **8–02** immediately before he died and as if the value transferred by that transfer had been equal to the value of his estate at that time. This is, of course, the last transfer he ever makes. Given the nature of the occasion of the transfer, what will be in issue is the amount to be brought into charge and the extent, if any, that the prima facie charge will not apply as the result of any reliefs or exemptions. No grossing-up is required, because s.4(1) specifies the value transferred.

Active service deaths

Section 4 does not apply to a death which occurred while the deceased was on active **8–03** duty (or which was caused by a wound sustained or disease contracted by him while he was on such duty), provided the Defence Council or the Secretary of State certifies that certain conditions are satisfied. These conditions are discussed at para.8–29.

III. THE OCCASION AND TIME OF THE TRANSFER

8–04   Two preliminary points concerning the occasion and time of the transfer should be noted. First, the occasion of the transfer is the deceased's death, not the devolution under his will or intestacy of the property comprised in his estate. This means that the reliefs available only to actual transfers of value will never apply: in particular, the relief for family maintenance dispositions will not be available. This follows from the fact that those reliefs apply only to transfers made by dispositions, and here the occasion of the transfer is a natural event, the deceased's death, not a disposition.[1] In much the same way, since the transfer is a notional one, only those exemptions available to actual and notional transfers alike will be relevant.[2]

Although the occasion of the transfer is the deceased's death, the transfer is treated as having been made immediately before that death. This means that the value of certain property will be brought into account even though that property does not form part of the deceased's estate after his death. In particular, it means that the value of any property in which the deceased had a life interest or a joint interest will be brought into account even though the former interest ceased on his death and the latter interest evaporated from his estate on his death under the operation of the right of survivorship.

Donatio mortis causa

8–05   A *donatio mortis causa*, i.e. a gift made before death in anticipation of that death and conditional upon it happening,[3] remains part of the donor's estate under s.5(2) and is taxable under s.4(1) in the same way as other revocable gifts. The gift is not a transfer of value when made and if the donor dies shortly after making it there are subtle differences between a *donatio mortis causa* and a failed PET; the former does not qualify for lifetime exemptions but may qualify for reliefs available on death, e.g. quick succession relief,[4] a *donatio mortis causa* is valued at the date of death not at the date of the gift, and the donor's personal representatives and donee are concurrently liable for the IHT.[5]

Commorientes

8–06   In the absence of special provision the fact that the transfer is made immediately before the deceased's death could yield harsh results in the case of commorientes. This is because normally when persons die in circumstances in which it is not possible to

---

[1] See para.2–39.
[2] See paras 3–01 and following.
[3] *Tate v Hilbert* (1793) 2 Ves. 111, 119; and *Sen v Headley* [1991] 2 W.L.R. 1308.
[4] See paras 8–32 and following.
[5] IHTA 1984 s.200(1)(a) and (c), although their liability is limited by s.204(1) and (3); cf. the donee being primarily responsible for the IHT on a failed PET under ss.199(1)(b) and 204(7) with the personal representatives being secondarily liable under ss.199(2) and 204(8).

determine who was the last to expire the youngest is presumed to have died last,[6] with the result that there could be a double charge on the same property in circumstances where only one charge was justified.

Assume a father leaves his estate to his son and both are killed simultaneously. The father would be presumed to have predeceased his son, and tax would be charged on his estate accordingly. The property would then be seen as having passed to the son, on whose estate—now increased by the property his father left him—tax would also be charged. Section 4(2) remedies this by providing that, for these purposes, when it cannot be known which of two or more persons who have died survived the other or others they shall be assumed to have died at the same instant. The result is that the son in the above example is treated as having made his notional transfer before his estate was swollen by his father's death. Thus a double charge on the same property is avoided.[7] Compare this to the position where the son survives the father by one week or where it is known who died first; here s.4(2) would not apply and therefore a double tax charge would arise. This would be alleviated to a certain extent by quick succession relief.[8]

An interesting interaction

In the case of a husband and wife or civil partners dying together, in circumstances **8–07** where it is unclear who died first, the interaction of ss.4 and 18 and 184 of the Law of Property Act 1925 can produce unexpected results. Assume that the husband and wife or civil partners each have an estate of £400,000 in their own names and have in place wills in which they leave the entirety of their respective estates (with no survivorship requirement) to each other, with gifts over to their children. Under s.184 the elder spouse or civil partner, will be deemed to have died first and for succession purposes his estate of £400,000 will pass to the younger spouse or civil partner. By s.18, this will be exempt from IHT (on the assumption that the couple were both domiciled in England and Wales). As a result of s.4(2), however (which only applies to s.4), for IHT purposes the husband and the wife or civil partners will be deemed to have died at the same time and, consequently, the younger spouse or civil partner will not be treated as having inherited the elder one's estate. Only the younger spouse or civil partner's own assets of £400,000 (less the nil rate band) will be taxable in their estate and the elder spouse or civil partner's estate will pass to the children under the younger spouse or civil partner's will free of tax.[9] This is one instance where it would be detrimental to have a survivorship clause in the older spouse or civil partner's will; although it seems it would still be possible to enter an instrument of variation posthumously to amend the will.[10] The introduction of the transferable nil rate band[11] means that the estate of the younger spouse or civil partner will be able to utilise any unused portion of older spouse's nil rate band thus reducing the amount of IHT payable by the younger spouse's estate.

The above anomaly would not apply in respect of the death of husband and wife or civil partners where the older spouse or civil partner died intestate; s.1(4) of the

[6] Law of Property Act 1925 s.184.

[7] It is possible to effectively override s.4(2) by including a survivorship clause in the will; see para.12–45.

[8] See paras 8–32 and following.

[9] HMRC appear to accept this interpretation; see *Trusts and Estates Tax Journal*, July/August 2000, p.4, for a full discussion.

[10] See paras 8–115 and following.

[11] See paras 4–14 and following.

Intestate's Estates Act 1952 provides that no benefit under the intestacy accrues to the younger spouse or civil partner's estate. Further, s.1(1) of the Law Reform (Succession) Act 1995 provides that for deaths on or after January 1, 1996, a survivorship period of 28 days is imposed.

IV. THE VALUE TRANSFERRED

8–08   Section 4(1) provides that the value transferred is equal to the value of the deceased's estate immediately before he died. Two questions thus arise:

(1) Identifying property: what property is for IHT purposes comprised in the deceased's estate immediately before he died?
(2) Valuing property: how is that property valued?

Identifying the property comprised in a person's estate immediately before he dies

8–09   Section 5(1) provides that a person's estate is the aggregate of all the property to which he was beneficially entitled, except that the estate of a person immediately before his death does not include excluded property. This leads on to four considerations.

Free estate

8–10   The starting point is the property comprised for IHT purposes in an individual's free estate. For this purpose the general legal rules apply, subject to certain modifications under the IHT rules. The position is considered in detail in Chapter 25.

Interests in possession

8–11   Although as a matter of general law settled property in which an individual has an interest in possession (or is deemed for IHT purposes to have such an interest) is not comprised in his estate, such an individual is treated by s.49(1) as beneficially entitled to such property. The result is that the settled property, and not just his interest in it, is comprised in his estate for IHT purposes. Since the transfer of value occurs immediately before the individual died, the fact that his interest in possession terminated on his death is irrelevant. The circumstances in which an individual has an interest in possession, or is deemed to have such an interest, are discussed in Chapter 12. The Finance Act 1986 amended s.49 significantly in respect of post-March 22, 2006 interest in possession trusts; these will only be subject to s.49(1) if they are either an immediate post-death interest trust, or a disabled person's interest trust, or a transitional serial interest trust. The position in respect of these trusts is considered in detail in Chapter 12.

Excluded property

Although excluded property is generally included in a person's estate, by s.5(1) it is **8–12** not included in his estate immediately before he dies. Such property is therefore outside the charge on death and the value of such property is disregarded in valuing other property comprised in the individual's estate immediately before he died. Where settled property in which the deceased had an interest in possession is concerned, the relevant consideration is whether the settled property was excluded property, i.e. the fact that the individual is treated as beneficially entitled to the property does not deprive the property of its character as settled property. The circumstances in which property and settled property are excluded property are discussed in Chapter 32. The 2011 and 2012 budgets have seen the introduction of anti-avoidance measures to prevent the use of excluded property as a means of reducing IHT liabilities; this is discussed further in Chapter 32.

Reservation of benefit

By s.102(3) of the Finance Act 1986, property in respect of which an individual has **8–13** reserved a benefit is treated as property to which he was beneficially entitled immediately before his death. The position so far as excluded property is concerned in relation to such property is discussed in detail at paras 7–10 and following. The basic position is as follows:

Free estate

Where the property subject to a reservation is not settled property the position **8–14** depends on the deceased's domicile immediately before he died and the nature of the property concerned. So if, e.g. he reserved a benefit in respect of foreign situs property and immediately before his death he was not domiciled in the United Kingdom the property will be excluded property and therefore, although he is treated as beneficially entitled to it by s.102(3), s.5(1) prevents it from forming part of his estate.

Settled property

Where the property subject to a reservation is settled property which is excluded **8–15** property, e.g. because it is foreign situs property comprised in a settlement the settlor of which was domiciled outside the United Kingdom when he made the settlement, HMRC practice has traditionally been to regard the property as retaining its status as excluded property notwithstanding the fact that under s.102(3) the deceased is treated as having been beneficially entitled to the property immediately before he died.

Although HMRC are reviewing this practice, the authors understand that it continues to apply. For a full discussion, see para.7–11.

Valuation of deceased's estate: special rules

8–16   The various IHT general rules for valuing property are discussed in Chapter 25. In addition to these rules, the basic rule that regard is to be had to the value of the deceased's estate immediately before he died is subject to two qualifications, namely that:

(1) Certain changes which occur in the value of a person's estate after his death must be brought into account.
(2) The value of certain property comprised in the deceased's estate immediately before he died must be left out of account.

Changes in value after death[12]

8–17   In the absence of provision to the contrary, the fact that the transfer is treated as having been made immediately before the deceased's death would mean that changes in the value of his estate that occurred after his death, e.g. where money was paid to his personal representatives under an insurance policy, would not be brought into account. Sections 171(1) and (2) accordingly provide that a change in the value of a person's estate which occurs on or after his death is to be taken into account as if it had occurred before his death if:

(1) the change occurred by reason of his death; and
(2) the change constitutes:
  (a) an addition to the property comprised in his estate immediately before his death, or
  (b) an increase in the value of property comprised in his estate immediately before his death, or
  (c) a decrease in the value of the property comprised in his estate immediately before his death, other than a decrease resulting from an alteration in a close company's share or loan capital under s.98(1) which is not taken into account. This qualification is intended to prevent an individual avoiding tax by holding shares in a close company whose articles of association provide that on his death his shares lose the rights which had previously attached to them.

Sums paid to the deceased's estate under, e.g., an insurance policy, are thus brought into charge (rather than the surrender value of the policy immediately before the death).

---

[12] For the implications of s.171 on valuing property on death generally, see para.25–50.

A termination on the deceased's death of any interest, or the passing of any interest by survivorship are left out of account, i.e. the position regarding life interests and joint interests is unaffected.

Value left out of account

The legislation provides that the value of certain property comprised in a person's estate is to be left out of account in determining the value of his estate immediately before he dies. Please note that the following references to interest in possession trusts refer to pre-March 22, 2006 trusts, immediate post-death interest trusts, disabled person's interest trusts, and transitional serial interest trusts. This happens in seven cases. **8–18**

1. Acquisition of the property or another interest in possession

By s.54(1), where a person is entitled to an interest in possession in settled property and on his death, but during the settlor's life, that property reverts to the settlor, the value of the property in which the deceased's interest subsisted is left out of account in determining the value of his estate immediately before his death. Thus, if A settles Blackacre on B for life, remainder to A, on B's death the value of Blackacre will be left out of account in determining the value of B's estate. **8–19**

This relief is analogous to that given under s.53(3).[13] Like that relief, it is given to preclude a double charge in respect of the same property—once on the creation of the settlement, and again on the reversion to the settlor—and it is subject to the same qualifications, namely that it does not apply if (a) the settlor or his spouse or civil partner acquired a reversionary interest[14] in the property for a consideration in money or money's worth, or (b) the relief depends upon a reversionary interest having been transferred into a settlement on or after March 10, 1981.[15] The relief applies only if the property reverts to the settlor, but this does not mean that the settlor must become absolutely entitled to the property. It suffices that he acquires an interest in possession since he will then be treated by s.49(1) as being beneficially entitled to the property in which his interest subsists with the result that the property will be treated as having reverted to him even though he is not as a matter of general law absolutely entitled to it. In determining the availability of this relief the identity of the settlor is crucial and has been the subject of complicated judicial analysis. Particular problems may arise where there is more than one settlor of a settlement.[16]

2. Settlor's spouse or civil partner becomes beneficially entitled

By s.54(2), where a person is entitled to an interest in possession in settled property and on his death the settlor's spouse or civil partner becomes beneficially entitled to that property the value of the property in which the deceased's interest subsisted is left **8–20**

---

[13] See para.2–116.

[14] The fact that the reversionary interest acquired is not the interest as a result of which the property reverts to the settlor but comes into effect only subsequently is, on a strict reading of the statute, irrelevant.

[15] See para.2–117 for an explanation of these qualifications.

[16] See paras 11–43 and following.

out of account in determining the value of his estate immediately before his death, provided that at the time of the death the spouse or civil partner was a UK domiciliary (the deemed domicile rules apply).[17] The availability of the relief is subject to the same qualifications that apply to s.54(1). As above, the spouse or civil partner need not take absolutely, it suffices that an interest in possession is acquired. Again, difficulties may arise if there is more than one settlor.[18]

3. Settlor's widow/widower or surviving civil partner becomes beneficially entitled

8–21 By s.54(2), where a person is entitled to an interest in possession in settled property and on his death the settlor's widow/widower or surviving civil partner becomes beneficially entitled to the property the value of the property in which the deceased's interest subsisted is left out of account in determining the value of the estate immediately before he died if:

(1) at the time of his death the widow/widower or surviving civil partner was a UK domiciliary (the deemed domicile rules apply)[19]; and
(2) the settlor died less than two years before the deceased.

The relief is not available if either the settlor or the widow/widower or surviving civil partner acquired[20] a reversionary interest in the property for a consideration in money or money's worth. As above, the widow/widower or surviving civil partner need not take absolutely, it suffices that he or she acquires an interest in possession. HMRC's view is that a widow/widower or surviving civil partner does not lose that status if they remarry. Again, difficulties may arise if there is more than one settlor.[21]

4. Section 18 exemption

8–22 Under estate duty, property in which the surviving spouse or civil partner was left a life interest was exempt from duty on his or her death. The legislation honours this exemption in relation to the charge arising under s.4(1) on death by providing in para.2 of Sch.6 that where one party to a marriage dies before November 13, 1974, and the other party dies after March 12, 1975, then, in determining the value of the survivor's estate immediately before he or she died there is left out of account the value of any property which, if estate duty were chargeable in respect of the survivor's death, would have qualified for the s.18 exemption under s.5(2) of the Finance Act 1894. Similar relief, as was seen previously, is available under para.2 of Sch.6 where the survivor's interest comes to an end during his lifetime.[22]

It is to be noted that para.2 applies only where the first spouse died before November 13, 1974. If the first spouse (or civil partner in these circumstances) died on or after that date then para.2 does not apply and tax is charged in the usual way. This is because after November 12, 1974, the estate duty "surviving spouse exemption" was abolished, exemption from estate duty in respect of deaths between November 13, 1974, and

---

[17] IHTA 1984 s.267.
[18] See paras 11–43 and following.
[19] IHTA 1984 s.267.
[20] See para.8–19.
[21] See paras 11–43 and following.
[22] See para.2–115.

March 12, 1975, instead being given on the death of the first spouse rather than on the death of the surviving spouse.[23]

For a deceased domiciled spouse giving to a non-domiciled spouse, the position is less attractive than for domiciled couples (who can take advantage of an unlimited spouse exemption on the first death). For a lifetime gift, or a gift on death, from a domiciled spouse to a non-domiciled spouse, the inheritance tax exemption is capped at £55,000. This limit is, however, set for review and the government will publish a consultation document in summer 2012 to prepare for a change to the current legislation in the Finance Bill 2013.[24]

Tax trap

It must be borne in mind that what is left out of account in each of the above four cases is the value of the property in which the deceased's interest subsisted, not the property itself, which remains part of the deceased's estate. Normally, leaving the value of the property in question out of account will have the same result as treating that property as not being comprised in his estate. Exceptionally, however, the fact that the property remains part of the deceased's estate may be important.   **8–23**

Assume A, a widow, owns 45 shares in B Ltd, an investment company with 100 issued ordinary shares, and also has an interest in possession in 10 shares in B Ltd in circumstances such that the estate duty surviving spouse exemption is available. If immediately before A's death she still has an interest in possession in the 10 shares no charge will arise in respect of those shares, but they will be taken into account in valuing the 45 shares, which will accordingly be valued on a majority rather than a minority basis. If, on the other hand, A's interest in possession is terminated during her lifetime, there will still be no charge on the 10 shares, but on her death the 45 shares will be valued on a minority basis.[25]

In the example just given no business relief is available because B Ltd is an investment company. Circumstances may arise where the aggregation of the shares in A's free estate and those in which she has an interest in possession mean that the impact of the property held in trust on the valuation of property held in the deceased's free estate is unimportant.

5. Overseas pensions

In determining the value of a person's estate immediately before his death there is left out of account under s.153(1) any pension payable under either: **8–24**

(1) s.273 of the Government of India Act 1935; or
(2) s.2 of the Overseas Pensions Act 1973.

In addition, certain pensions paid in the United Kingdom are treated by s.153 as paid abroad. This is important since it means that if the holder of the pension is a foreign

---

[23] FA 1975 s.49(1) and Sch.11 Pt 1 para.2 and Pt II para.4. If the deceased was domiciled in the UK but his spouse was not, the exemption was limited to the first £15,000: see paras 2(4) and 4(4).
[24] For practical examples of the non-domiciliary spouse exemption see IHTM111033.
[25] See also para.2–115.

domiciliary the pension will be excluded property.[26] The following pensions are to be treated as paid abroad:

(1) a pension paid under a scheme made under s.2 of the Overseas Pensions Act 1973 which is constituted by the Pensions (India, Pakistan and Burma) Act 1955 or is certified by the Secretary of State for the purposes of s.153 to correspond to the 1955 Act;

(2) a pension paid out of any fund established in the United Kingdom by the government of any country which, at the time when the fund was established, was, or formed part of, a colony, protectorate, protected state or UK trust territory if the fund was established for the sole purpose of providing pensions payable in respect of service under that government;

(3) a pension paid out of the Central African Pension Fund established by s.24 of the Federation of Rhodesia and Nyasaland (Dissolution) Order in Council 1963[27]; and

(4) so much of the pension paid in the United Kingdom under s.1 of the Overseas Pensions Act 1973 as is not paid by virtue of the Pensions (Increase) Act 1971 or any other enactment repealed by the 1971 Act.[28]

6. Woodlands

8–25   The legislation recognises that it would be unfair to tax growing trees which might take several generations to mature. In addition, such taxation could easily discourage afforestation. The legislation accordingly provides a special deferral relief where the value of a person's estate immediately before he dies is attributable partly to the value of land in the United Kingdom on which trees or underwood are growing. In such a case it may be possible for the deceased's personal representatives or any other person liable for the whole or part of the tax to elect to leave the value of the growing timber (but not the land itself) out of account in determining the value transferred on the deceased's death, and instead to pay tax when the trees are actually disposed of. If there is no disposal, tax is charged on the next death in the usual way, unless, of course, another election is made to defer tax. Any election to defer tax must be made in writing to the Board within two years of the death or such longer time as the Board may allow. The details of the relief are set out at paras 26–194 and following.

7. Sales and mortgages of reversionary interests before March 27, 1974

8–26   Where a reversionary interest has been sold or mortgaged for full consideration in money or money's worth before March 27, 1974, a restriction is placed on the amount of IHT payable by the purchaser or mortgagee; when the interest falls into possession the IHT payable will be capped at the amount of estate duty which would have been payable, in order to prevent the purchaser or mortgagee from being unduly prejudiced. In addition, any IHT which is payable by the mortgagor will rank as a charge

---

[26] IHTA 1984 s.6(1).
[27] IHTA 1984 s.153(2)(c).
[28] IHTA 1984 s.153(2)(d).

subsequent to that of the mortgagee.[29] In practice, as IHT is charged at a flat rate of 40 per cent rather than ascending bands under the estate duty legislation, it will often be the case that the IHT will be less than the estate duty which would have been payable.

Where the reversionary interest was sold or mortgaged to a close company in which the person entitled to the interest was a participator the relief is limited to the extent that other persons had rights and interests in the company.[30] The reason for this restriction is to avoid, e.g. the case where a reversioner sells his reversion to a close company in which he is a shareholder, i.e. in effect selling to himself.

Reliefs

Business relief and/or agricultural relief may be available; this is discussed in Chapter 26. **8–27**

Allowances for expenses

The legislation is framed so that expenses incurred after a death which are paid out **8–28** of the deceased's estate, the expense of obtaining probate, are not normally deducted in determining the value of his estate. This follows from the fact that such expenses are incurred after his death, and therefore can be brought into account only if they come within s.171. But to come within s.171, the expense must decrease the value of property comprised in the deceased's estate, and this requirement will not be satisfied since the value of the property comprised in the deceased's estate will remain unchanged.

In two cases, an allowance is made for expenses. First, by s.172 allowance is made for reasonable funeral expenses. HMRC published, on July 15, 1987, a Statement of Practice (SP 7/87) to the effect that they take the view that the term "funeral expenses" allows a deduction from the value of the deceased's estate for the cost of a tombstone or a gravestone. In addition, extra-statutory concession F1 allows a reasonable amount for mourning for family and "servants". Each case will be looked at on its own facts, but generally the larger the estate and the more well known the deceased the more likely it is that HMRC will allow additional expenses such as the cost of airfares to travel to the funeral.

Secondly, by s.173 there is an allowance against the value of property situated outside the United Kingdom for any expense shown to be attributable to the situation of the property which is incurred in administering or realising the property. This is subject to the qualification that the allowance cannot exceed 5 per cent of the value of the property. In practice HMRC only allow a deduction for foreign expenses over and above what would have been paid if the property were situated in the United Kingdom so claiming a blanket reduction will not succeed. HMRC interpret s.173 as if the words

---

[29] IHTA 1984 Sch.6 para.3(1).
[30] IHTA 1984 Sch.6 para.3(2).

"additional expenses" had been inserted. The authors' view is that this is inconsistent with the actual wording of the section which states "any expense incurred".

Active service deaths

8–29   By s.154(1), s.4 does not apply to a death[31] if the Defence Council or the Secretary of State certifies that the following conditions are satisfied:

(1) the deceased was:
   (a) a member of any of the armed forces of the Crown[32]; or
   (b) was subject to the law governing any of those forces by reason of association with or accompanying any body of those forces; and

(2) the deceased was or had been:
   (a) on active service against an enemy; or
   (b) on other service of a warlike nature; or
   (c) on other service which in the Treasury's opinion involved the same risks as service of a warlike nature; and

(3) the deceased died:
   (a) from a wound inflicted, or an accident which occurred or a disease contracted at the time while on the above-mentioned service[33]; or
   (b) from a disease contracted prior to such service provided the death was due to or hastened by the aggravation of the disease during that service.

It is thought that "active service" in wartime means being under a military, naval, or air force discipline, and that it does not matter whether the cause of death occurred when the deceased was on duty, off duty or absent on leave. The "armed forces of the Crown" are understood to include Dominion and Colonial forces, but not forces of the Republics associated with the Commonwealth, e.g. India. A strictly limited category of non-members of the forces, such as war correspondents, are included in para.1(b).

Individuals wounded in active service in the Falkland Islands conflict will be included: Revenue Press Release, June 23, 1982. There does not appear to have been any similar press release relating to the Gulf wars and the war in Afghanistan. It is assumed that those killed in such conflicts will also qualify for the exemption provided the above conditions are satisfied and the Defence Council or Secretary of State issue the required certificate. A more tenuous position is where a civilian dies very many years after leaving active service as the causal link will be much more difficult to prove.

By extra-statutory concession F5 the above conditions are taken to be satisfied in the case of a death of a member of the Police Service of Northern Ireland (or the previous police authority, the Royal Ulster Constabulary) where the death is from injuries caused in Northern Ireland by terrorist activity.

The procedure is to apply to the appropriate issuing department for a certificate. That department will then send the certificate to HMRC, who have no discretion in this area:

---

[31] But only in relation to tax which would otherwise be chargeable under s.4. Therefore the exemption would not extend to any lifetime transfer on which tax (or more tax) is due because of a death. See further IHTM11282 and IHTM11321.

[32] See IHTM11312 for details of who was considered to be a member of the armed forces prior to the Armed Forces Act 1981.

[33] It suffices that the wound was one of the causes of the death: see *Barty-King v Ministry of Defence* [1979] 2 All E.R. 80; [1979] S.T.C. 218.

they can grant relief only if they have received the necessary certificate. The certifying departments are as follows:

>Service Personnel and Veterans Agency
>Joint Casualty and Compassionate Centre (Attn SO3 Deceased Estates)
>Imjin Barracks
>Innsworth
>Gloucester
>GL3 1HW
>(Tel 01452 712 612 Extension 5680/8174)

By extra statutory concession F13, where a person died before March 12, 1952 and his estate was wholly exempted from estate duty as the property of a common seaman, marine or soldier who died in the service of the Crown, and under his will he left a limited interest to someone who dies on or after March 13, 1975, tax is not charged on any property exempted on the original death which passes under the terms of the will on the termination of the limited interest.

World War II compensation payments

8–30 By extra-statutory concession F20 (effective from February 1, 2001) the £10,000 ex gratia payments to surviving prisoners of war (or their spouses) of the Japanese will be left out of account when determining the chargeable value of the deceased's estate. It does not matter whether the payment was made during their life or to their personal representatives after their death.

ESC F20 was extended in October 2001 and March 2002 to include compensation payments made by:

(1) German Foundation "Remembrance, Responsibility and Future";
(2) Austrian Reconciliation Fund;
(3) Holocaust Victim Assets Litigation (Swiss Bank Settlement);
(4) Swiss Refugee Programme;
(5) Stichting Maror-Gelden Overheid (Dutch Maror);
(6) Federal German Government (the Hardship Fund);
(7) Austrian National Fund for Victims of Nazi Persecution; or
(8) French Orphan Scheme.

By ESC A100, all compensation payments paid by the "Restore UK" initiative to holocaust victims (or their beneficiaries) will be exempt from IHT (and all other taxes).

V. THE RATE OF TAX

8–31 Once the chargeable value transferred has been ascertained, the next step is to apply the appropriate rates of tax to it. As was explained earlier,[34] there are now only two

---

[34] See para.6–03.

rates. First, tax is charged at a nil rate on the first £325,000[35] of chargeable value transferred. Thereafter tax is charged at 40 per cent. In determining how much, if any, of the deceased's nil rate band is available, regard will be had to the value transferred by any chargeable transfers made by him in the seven years immediately preceding his death.[36] In taking account of such chargeable transfers, regard will have to be had to any PETs which he made within those seven years and which have become chargeable as a result of his dying within seven years of making them. For example, if on his death on May 1, 2008, X made a chargeable transfer of £300,000 and during the preceding seven years he had made chargeable transfers totalling £100,000 plus a failed PET of £80,000, £145,000 of the transfer made on death would fall within his nil rate band and the remaining £155,000 would be charged at 40 per cent with the result that £62,000 in tax was due.[37] Lifetime gifts will use up the nil rate band first, any balance then being applied to the chargeable transfer on death.

When calculating the tax that falls due, any unused part of the deceased spouses or civil partners nil rate band should be taken into account.[38]

Reduction in tax: quick succession relief

8–32   Under s.141 relief is available, generally speaking, where a person's estate has been increased in value by a chargeable transfer made to him and within five years he himself makes a chargeable transfer either on his death or under s.52(1), i.e. as a result of the termination during his lifetime of an interest in possession. The relief is thus not available to actual transfers. This, of course, is to be expected, since the relief is intended to prevent tax being charged twice in quick succession in circumstances which are beyond a person's control; if a person chooses to incur a charge, he has no cause to complain. The relief takes the form of a reduction in tax and is calculated on a sliding scale: the greater the interval between the transfers, the smaller the reduction. The relief is available in two cases, as follows.

Transfers on death

8–33   The relief is available where the value of a person's estate was increased by a chargeable transfer (whether made to him or not)[39] and within five years that person makes a chargeable transfer on his death. It is important to note that in such a case it does not matter that the property which was given to him, if that is how the value of his estate was increased, remains comprised in his estate at the time of his death: all that matters is that the value of his estate was increased by a chargeable transfer made within five years of his death.

By s.141(6), in determining whether or to what extent a person's estate was increased by a chargeable transfer the value of a reversionary interest which is excluded property is disregarded if he became entitled to it on the occasion of or before the chargeable transfer. This is intended to prevent certain anomalies from arising. Assume, for example, that by a chargeable transfer A settles property worth, say,

---

[35] From April 6, 2010.

[36] See paras 6–40 and following.

[37] For the position where transfers are reported late, see paras 6–56 and following.

[38] See paras 4–06 and following.

[39] A transfer to his spouse or civil partner could increase the value of his estate under the related property rules.

£100,000 on B for life (and s.49(1) applies), remainder to C, thereby increasing the value of B's estate by £100,000 and the value of C's estate by, say, £45,000. If C dies within five years while B is still alive, quick succession relief will be available in respect of £45,000 on the transfer made on his death notwithstanding the fact that his reversion does not at that stage form part of his estate. This would, in the absence of s.141(6), prejudice HMRC. If, on the other hand, B dies, so that C becomes absolutely entitled to the trust property, and then within five years C also dies, C would be unfairly disadvantaged. This follows from the fact that the effect of B's death would be to increase the chargeable portion of C's estate by more than the amount by which it was in fact increased. Before B's death, C owned excluded property worth £45,000, while after the death he owned property worth £100,000 which was not excluded property. On his death, in the absence of s.141(6), relief would be available in respect of only the £55,000 by which B's transfer increased the value of C's interest; this would be plainly unfair, and is prevented from happening by s.141(6).

Lifetime termination of an interest in possession created before March 22, 2006 or under an immediate post-death interest, a disabled person's interest or a transitional serial interest

The relief is also available where a person's estate is increased by a chargeable **8–34** transfer, and within five years he makes a notional transfer under s.52(1) in respect of which the following conditions are satisfied:

(1) the first transfer must either have been or have included the making of the settlement in question or must have been made after the making of that settlement; and
(2) the value transferred by both transfers, unlike the relief given on death, must fall to be determined by reference to the same property.

Section 141 thus contemplates three possibilities under this head, namely the coming to an end of an interest in possession within five years of:

(a) the creation, by a chargeable transfer, of the settlement in which that interest subsisted;
(b) the settlor adding property, by a chargeable transfer, to the settlement[40]; and
(c) a chargeable transfer made on the coming to an end of a prior interest in the settled property in question.

As was mentioned above, the relief is not available to actual transfers. At first glance, it might seem possible to outflank this restriction. Assume that A has been given property which one year later he wishes to transfer to B. If he gives the property to B as an outright gift, no quick succession relief will be available. If, on the other hand, he settles the property on himself for a short period, remainder to B, the property will pass to B on the termination of A's interest in possession, so that the relief appears to be available. This, however, overlooks the first of the two conditions mentioned above which must be satisfied for the relief to be available on the termination of an interest in possession, i.e. that the first transfer must have been or included the making of the settlement in question or must have been made after the making of that settlement.

---

[40] If the property is added by someone other than the settlor the addition will therefore normally constitute the making of a separate settlement: IHTA 1984 s.44(2); see para.11–20.

Since A will not have made a chargeable transfer when he created the settlement this condition will not have been satisfied.

How the relief is given

8–35   The relief is given by reducing by a specified amount the tax that would otherwise be chargeable on the later transfer. The specified amount is expressed by s.141(3) to be a percentage of the tax charged on so much of the value transferred by the earlier transfer as is "attributable to" the increase occasioned by that transfer in the value of the transferor's estate. The percentage is geared to the period between the two transfers, as follows:

Period between transfers	*Per cent of tax available as credit*
1 year or less	100
Between 1 and 2 years	80
Between 2 and 3 years	60
Between 3 and 4 years	40
Between 4 and 5 years	20

Although the relief seems straightforward, certain complications can arise from the words "attributable to" in s.141(3). To begin with, the value transferred by the transfer which increases the value of the deceased's estate will normally exceed the amount by which his estate was increased in value by that transfer. This is because he receives the gift net of tax. Assume A, who had made previous transfers totalling £325,000, on June 1, 2006 made a chargeable transfer of £10,000 to B and died within three years. The IHT on the transfer would have been £4,000, with the result that although the value transferred by the transfer was £10,000, the amount by which B's estate increased was only £6,000. Therefore the tax attributable to the increase in B's estate is £6,000/£10,000 × £4,000 = £2,400 not £4,000. The remainder is attributable solely to the decrease of value in A's estate.

The position where one chargeable transfer increases the estates of two or more persons in different proportions is particularly tricky. This will normally occur where a person gives shares in equal proportions to different persons one or more of whom already own shares in the company. Assume, for example, that A Ltd. has a share capital of 25,000 £1 shares; A owns 15,000 shares worth, say, £2 each, while B and C respectively own 7,500 shares and 2,500 shares valued at, say, £1 each. A gives 7,500 shares to B and C respectively, with the result that B's holding becomes a majority holding, while C's holding remains a minority one. Before the transfer B's shares were worth £7,500, while after it they are worth £30,000. C's shares, on the other hand, have increased in value from £2,500 to only £10,000, with the result that three times as much of the value transferred by A's transfer is attributable to the increase in the value of B's estate as is attributable to the increase in value of C's estate. That being the case, three times as much of the tax charged on the transfer should be apportioned to B as to C. Thus, if the effective rate of tax on A's transfer was 40 per cent, tax of £12,000 (£30,000 × 40 per cent) would have been charged, and of that amount £9,000 would have been apportioned to B and £3,000 to C (subject, of course, to a reduction according to the period that had elapsed between A's transfer and the death of B and/or C, as the case might be).

Notwithstanding the above, it is understood that the official practice in such cases is to apportion the tax equally, so that in the above example £6,000 would have been apportioned to both B and C. This appears to be inconsistent with the wording of s.141(3).

It may be that within five years of a chargeable transfer being made to a person he makes more than one transfer which qualifies for quick succession relief. In that case, the relief is given to the transfers in chronological order until the "tax credit" is exhausted.[41]

VI. DOUBLE CHARGES RELIEF

8–36 The framers of the Finance Act 1986 foresaw that the changes they were introducing might result in a taxpayer being charged more than once on the same property. They also appreciated that any provisions aimed at eliminating such double charges would be complex and so s.104 of that Act empowered HMRC to make regulations, exercisable by statutory instrument subject to annulment in pursuance of a resolution of the House of Commons, to eliminate certain kinds of double charges. These are listed in s.104(1) of the Finance Act 1986 as arising where:

(1) a PET proves to be a chargeable transfer and, immediately before the transferor's death, his estate includes property acquired by him from the transferee otherwise than for full consideration in money or money's worth;

(2) an individual disposes of property by way of a transfer of value which is or proves to be chargeable and the property is caught by the reservation of benefit provisions;

(3) in determining the value of a person's estate immediately before his death a liability of his to any person is abated under s.103 and before his death he made a transfer of value increasing that other person's estate or by virtue of which property became comprised in a settlement of which that person is a trustee; and

(4) the circumstances are such as may be specified in the regulations as similar to those mentioned above.

To solve the problems envisaged, s.104(2) provided that the regulations could:

(1) treat the value transferred by a transfer of value as reduced by reference to the value transferred by another transfer of value; and/or

(2) treat the whole or any part of the tax paid or payable on the value transferred by a transfer of value as a credit against the tax payable on the value transferred by another transfer of value.[42]

The Regulations

8–37 Regulations came into force on July 22, 1987, and apply to transfers of value made after March 17, 1986. Accompanying the Regulations was a schedule of examples. These are, however, non-binding; para.9 of the Regulations expressly provides that the

---

[41] IHTA 1984 s.141(4) and (5).
[42] See paras 25–92 and following.

Regulations shall prevail in the event of any conflict between them and the Schedule.

Extent of the Regulations

8–38   The Regulations deal with the first three circumstances laid down in s.104(1)(a)–(c). They also deal with a fourth circumstance, as being similar to the circumstances mentioned in the first three circumstances. The best approach will be to take the regulations and the relevant examples in a slightly different order from that in which they appear, for reasons which will appear below. The examples in the Regulations are based on rates and bands in force as at March 18, 1987. These have been updated in the text below to more relevant dates and rates and the nil rate band in force as at April 6, 2012. As there are no longer different bands at different rates the examples are therefore slightly simpler than those given in the Regulations, transfers on death being taxed at a flat rate of 40 per cent and lifetime chargeable transfers taxed at a flat rate of 20 per cent.

Terminology and assumptions in the examples

8–39   Note the following with regard to the examples. First, terminologically:

"cumulation" means the inclusion of the total chargeable transfers made by the transferor in the seven years preceding the current transfer;
"GWR" means gift with reservation; and
"taper relief" means the reduction in tax provided under s.7(4) of the 1984 Act, inserted by para.2(4) of Sch.19 to the 1986 Act.

Secondly, except where otherwise stated, the examples assume that:

(1) tax rates and bands remain as at April 5, 2009;
(2) the transferor has made no transfers other than those shown in the examples;
(3) no exemptions (including annual exemptions) or reliefs apply to the value transferred by the relevant transfer;
(4) "grossing up" does not apply in determining any lifetime tax (the tax is not borne by the transferor); and
(5) any references to interest in possession trusts refer to pre March 22, 2006 trusts, an immediate post-death interest trust, a disabled person's interest trust or a transitional serial interest trust.

Against this background, let us now consider the detailed provisions in the Regulations.

Gifts back: paragraphs 4 and 7

8–40   As was seen above, s.104(1)(a) contemplates a double charge arising by virtue of a person having made a failed PET of property which he owned on his death, having re-acquired it from the transferee otherwise than for full consideration. No reference, however, was made anywhere in s.104(1) to a very similar situation, namely where a person made a transfer which was chargeable when it was made of property which the transferor owned on his death, having acquired it from the transferee otherwise than for full consideration. It was subsequently realised that this was the kind of "similar circumstance" envisaged by s.104(1)(d), and the Regulations accordingly make provision to deal with it. Since the two circumstances mentioned above are so alike, it will be convenient to consider them together even though the Regulations deal with them separately (in paras 4 and 7 respectively).

Tax planning

It may be that reg.4 is capable of being exploited to the benefit of the taxpayer and **8–41** could be a useful tool for deathbed planning, as illustrated in the following example. Assume that Adam gives property worth £100,000 to his daughter Berta in 2006 and then buys the property back for £75,000 (which represents less than full consideration) in 2008. He then dies. Under reg.4 the value of the property (£100,000) will remain subject to IHT but Adam's estate has been reduced by the £75,000 paid for the property (see especially reg.4(3)(a)).[43] Care must be taken to ensure that the original gift and the buy-back are unconnected.

Relevant conditions

The conditions that must be satisfied for paras 4 or 7 to apply are as follows: **8–42**

(1) the deceased must have made a transfer of value on or after March 18, 1986, which is a failed PET (reg.4) or which was chargeable when it was made and he has died within seven years (reg.7); and
(2) immediately before his death the deceased must have been beneficially entitled to property:
  (a) which the deceased, after making the aforesaid transfer, acquired from the transferee otherwise than for full consideration in money or money's worth, and
  (b) which is property which was transferred to the transferee by the aforesaid transfer or which is property directly or indirectly representing that property, and
  (c) which is property comprised in the estate of the deceased immediately before his death (within the meaning of s.5(1)), the value attributable to which is transferred by a chargeable transfer (under s.4).

How relief is given

The rules for giving relief vary according to whether the original transfer was a **8–43** failed PET or chargeable when made.

Original transfer a failed PET

The rules, as stated in para.4(4) and (5), may be summarised as follows: **8–44**

[43] For criticism of this interpretation, see *Personal Tax Planning Review*, Vol.2, Issue 3, p.221.

(1) *Disregard the failed PET*: calculate the total tax chargeable as a consequence of the death, disregarding so much of the value transferred by the failed PET as is attributable to the property the value of which is transferred by the chargeable transfer made on death.

(2) *Disregard the death transfer*: calculate the total tax chargeable as a consequence of the death, disregarding so much of the value transferred by the chargeable transfer made on death as is attributable to the property, the value of which was transferred by the failed PET.

(3) *Compare the amounts of tax payable*: the lower of the two amounts just calculated is reduced to nil. If the calculation means that the failed PET falls to be disregarded, so much of the value transferred by it as is attributable to the property in question is disregarded for all lHT purposes. Thus, if after the PET the transferor made, e.g., a transfer to a discretionary trust in respect of which exit charges were subsequently imposed, those charges will be unaffected by the failure of the disregarded PET.[44]

8–45   The following example is given in the Schedule (although updated to use rates as at April 6, 2012).

Example

July 2011	A makes PET of £330,000 to B.
July 2012	A makes gift into discretionary trust of £350,000; tax paid £5,000.
January 2013	A makes further gift into same trust of £50,000; tax paid £10,000.
January 2014	B dies and the 2011 PET returns to A.
April 2015	A dies. His death estate of £700,000 includes the 2011 PET returned to him in 2014, which is still worth £330,000.

First calculation under reg.4(4)(a)

Charge the returned PET in A's death estate and ignore the PET made in 2011.

		Tax
July 2011	PET £330,000 ignored	NIL
July 2012	Gift £350,000	
	Tax £10,000 less £5,000 already paid	£ 5,000
January 2013	Gift £50,000 as top slice of £400,000	
	Tax £20,000 less £10,000 already paid	£ 10,000
April 2015	Death estate £700,000 as top slice of £1,100,000	£280,000
	Total tax due as result of A's death	£295,000

In the first calculation the tax of £295,000 on the death estate does not allow for any successive charges relief (under s.141) that might be due in respect of the returned PET by reference to any tax charged on that PET in connection with B's death.

Second calculation under reg.4(40)(b)

Charge the 2011 PET and ignore the value of the returned PET in A's death estate.

[44] See paras 6–64 and following.

340

		Tax
July 2111	PET £330,000; tax with taper relief	£ 1,600
July 2012	Gift £350,000 as top slice of £680,000; tax £140,000	
	less £5,000 already paid	£135,000
January 2013	Gift £50,000 as top slice of £730,000; tax £20,000	
	less £10,000 already paid	£ 10,000
April 2015	Death estate £370,000 as top slice of £1,100,000	£148,000
	Total tax due as result of A's death	£294,600

Result*

First calculation gives higher amount of tax. So PET reduced to nil and tax on other transfers is as in first calculation.

* If after allowing any successive charges relief, the second calculation gives higher amount of tax, the 2008 PET will be charged and tax on other transfers will be as in second calculation.

Original transfer chargeable when made

The rules as stated in para.7(4) and (5), may be summarised as follows:

8–46

(1) *Disregard the lifetime transfer*: calculate the total tax chargeable as a consequence of the death, disregarding so much of the value transferred by the lifetime transfer as is attributable to the property, the value of which is transferred by the chargeable transfer made on death.

(2) *Disregard the death transfer*: calculate the total tax chargeable as a consequence of the death, disregarding so much of the value transferred by the chargeable transfer made on death as is attributable to the property, the value of which was transferred by the lifetime transfer.

(3) *Compare the amounts of tax payable*: if disregarding the death transfer gives a higher amount, the amount of tax chargeable on death that is attributable to the property in question is reduced to nil. If, on the other hand, disregarding the lifetime transfer gives a higher amount, the position is slightly more complicated. In that case, the amount of tax chargeable on the lifetime transfer is reduced to nil, and credit is given against the tax due on death for any tax payable in respect of the lifetime transfer. Furthermore, so much of the value transferred by the lifetime transfer as is attributable to the property in question is reduced to nil for all IHT purposes, subject to one qualification, namely that it is not so reduced in respect of any exit charges that arose prior to the death. So if, e.g., the lifetime transfer was into a discretionary trust, any exit charges are unaffected by the regulations.[45]

---

[45] See paras 6–66 and following.

8–47   The following example is given in the Schedule (although updated to use rates as at April 6, 2012):

May 2007	S transfers into discretionary trust property worth £330,000. Immediate charge at the rates then in force.	Tax paid £6,600
October 2007	S gives T a life interest in shares worth £120,000. PET (in example in Regulations this was a gift in October 1996 and therefore chargeable immediately at the rates then in force).	Tax paid Nil
January 2012	S makes a PET to R of £40,000.	
December 2013	T dies, and the settled shares return to S who is the settlor and therefore no tax charge on the shares on T's death.	
August 2014	S dies. His death estate includes the shares returned from T which are currently worth £100,000 and other assets worth £400,000.	

First calculation under reg.7(4)(a)

Charge the returned shares in the death estate and ignore the October 2007 gift. Tax rates and bands are those in force at the date of S's death.

		Tax
May 2007	Gift into trust made more than 7 years before death—so no adjustment to tax already paid but the gift cumulates in calculating tax on other gifts	NIL
October 2007	Gift ignored	NIL
January 2012	PET of £40,000 as top slice of (£333,000 + £40,000) £373,000	£ 16,000
August 2014	Death estate £500,000 as top slice of £540,000	£ 86,000
	Total tax due as result of S's death	£102,000

Second calculation under reg.7(4)(b)

Charge the October 2007 gift and ignore the returned shares in the death estate. Tax rates and bands are those in force at the date of S's death.

		Tax
May 2007	Gift into trust made more than 7 years before death—so no adjustment to tax already paid but the gift is taken into account calculating the tax on the other gifts	NIL
October 2007	Gifts of £120,000 as top slice of £453,000; tax with taper relief	£ 9,600
January 2012	PET of £40,000 as top slice of £493,000	£ 16,000
August 2014	Death estate (excluding the returned shares) £400,000 as top slice of £560,000 (£120,000 + £40,000 + £400,000)	£ 94,000
	Total tax due as result of S's death	£119,600

Result

Second calculation gives higher amount of tax. So tax is charged as in second calculation by excluding the shares from the death estate.

Reservation of benefit: para.5

Section 104(1)(b) contemplates a double charge arising by virtue of a person having **8-48** gifted property by a failed PET or a transfer which is chargeable when it is made, the property subsequently being caught by the reservation of benefit rules. Paragraph 5 of the Regulations deals with this.

Relevant conditions

The relevant conditions that must be satisfied for para.5 to apply are as follows: **8-49**

(1) the deceased must have made a lifetime chargeable transfer or a failed PET on or after March 18, 1986; and
(2) the property given by the chargeable transfer or the failed PET either:
   (a) ceases to be subject to a reservation so that the deceased makes a failed PET of value attributable to the gifted property,[46] or
   (b) is treated as property to which he was beneficially entitled immediately before his death.[47]

How relief is given

The rules, as stated in para.5(3)–(5), may be summarised as follows: **8-50**

(1) *Disregard the original transfer*: calculate the total tax chargeable as a consequence of the death disregarding so much of the value transferred as is attributable to the original gift.

---

[46] See para.5–38.
[47] See para.8–09.

(2) *Disregard the clawback*: calculate the total tax chargeable as a consequence of the death, disregarding so much of the value of the gifted property as is brought into charge under the reservation of benefit rules.

(3) *Compare the amounts of tax payable:* if disregarding the original transfer gives a lower amount, the value of the property caught by the reservation of benefit rules is reduced to nil. If disregarding the amount brought into charge under the reservation of benefit rules gives a lower amount, the position is the same as under reg.7, i.e. the amount of tax chargeable on the lifetime transfer is reduced to nil, and credit is given against the tax due under the reservation of benefit rules for any tax payable in respect of the original transfer. Furthermore so much of the value transferred by the original transfer as is attributable to the property in question is reduced to nil for all IHT purposes, subject to one qualification, namely that if the original transfer was chargeable when it was made the value transferred by it is not reduced in respect of any exit or periodic charges that arose prior to the death.[48] Any exit or periodic charges will thus stand. This follows from the fact that if the original transfer was chargeable when made the regulations expressly provide that those charges are to be unaffected, while if the original transfer was a PET which now falls to be disregarded the fact that the PET has failed will not involve reopening the calculations.

EXAMPLES

8–51   The following examples are given in the Schedule (although, again, updated to use rates as at April 5, 2012).

EXAMPLE 1

June 2008	A makes PET of £350,000 to B	
August 2012	A makes gift of land worth £350,000 into a discretionary trust of which he is a potential beneficiary. The gift is a "GWR".	Tax paid £5,000
July 2015	A dies without having released his interest in the trust. His death estate valued at £900,000 includes the GWR land currently worth £400,000.	

First calculation under reg.5(3)(a)

Charge the GWR land in A's estate and ignore the GWR

		Tax
June 2008	PET (now exempt)	NIL
August 2012	GWR ignored	NIL

---

[48] See paras 6–66 and following.

		Tax
July 2015	Death estate £900,000	
	Tax £230,000 less £5,000 already paid on GWR*	£225,000
	Total tax due as result of A's death	£225,000

* Credit for the tax already paid cannot exceed the amount of the death tax attributable to the value of the GWR property. In this example the tax so attributable is £102,222:

$$\frac{230,000}{900,000} \times 400,000$$

So credit is given for the full amount of £5,000.

Second calculation under reg.5(3)(b)

Charge the GWR and ignore the GWR land in the death estate.

		Tax
June 2008	PET (now exempt)	NIL
August 2012	GWR £350,000	
	Tax £10,000 less £5,000 already paid	£5,000
July 2015	Death estate £500,000 (ignoring GWR property)	
	as top slice of £850,000	£200,000
	Total tax due as result of A's death	£205,000

Result

First calculation yields higher amount of tax. So the value of the GWR transfer is reduced to nil and tax on death is charged as in first calculation with credit for the tax already paid.[49]

EXAMPLE 2

April 2008	A makes gift into discretionary trust of £340,000	Tax paid £3,000
January 2009	A makes further gift into same trust of £80,000	Tax paid £16,000

---

[49] It is interesting to note that whilst HMRC have no choice but to opt for the result producing the higher IHT liability this can make a considerable difference as to who is liable for the tax, i.e. the personal representatives would not be liable for the IHT due under the reservation of benefit provisions and HMRC would have to seek payment from the beneficiary of the GWR (in this example the trustees of the trust) or against anyone who had received benefits from the trust. If the personal representatives pay this tax without the authority of the trustees they would potentially commit a devastavit.

| March 2014 | A makes PET of shares valued at £150,000 to B |
| February 2017 | A dies. He has continued to enjoy the income of the shares he had given to B (the 2014 PET is a GWR). His death estate, valued at £600,000 includes those shares currently worth £200,000 |

First calculation under reg.5(3)(a)

Charge the GWR shares in the death estate and ignore the PET.

		Tax
April 2008	Gift £340,000. No adjustment to tax as gift made more than 7 years before death	NIL
January 2009	Gift £80,000. No adjustment to tax as gift made more than 7 years before death	NIL
March 2014	PET £150,000 reduced to NIL	NIL
February 2017	Death estate including GWR shares £600,000 No previous cumulation	£110,000
	Total tax due as result of A's death	£110,000

Second calculation under reg.5(3)(b)

Charge the PET and ignore the value of the GWR shares in the death estate.

		Tax
April 2008	Gift £340,000—no adjustment to tax as gift made more than 7 years before death	NIL
January 2009	Gift £80,000—no adjustment to tax as gift made more than 7 years before death	NIL
March 2014	GWR £150,000 as top slice of £570,000 (i.e. previous gifts totalling £420,000 + £150,000)	£60,000
February 2017	Death estate (excluding GWR shares) £400,000 as top slice of £550,000 (the 2008 and 2009 gifts drop out of cumulation)	£ 90,000
	Total tax due as result of A's death	£150,000

Result

Second Calculation yields higher amount of tax. So, tax is charged by reference to the PET and the value of the GWR in the death estate is reduced to nil.

Loanbacks: paragraph 6

8–52   Section 104(1)(c) envisages a double charge arising by virtue of a person having made a failed PET or a transfer which is chargeable when it is made and on his death being indebted to the transferee in circumstances such that the indebtedness falls to be abated under s.103 of the 1986 Act,[50] e.g. because the debt arises by reason of the transferor having borrowed back from the transferee the subject matter of the original gift. This is dealt with in para.6 of the Regulations.

Relevant conditions

The conditions that must be satisfied for para.6 to apply are as follows: **8–53**

(1) the deceased must have made a failed PET or a transfer which was chargeable when it was made on or after March 18, 1986;
(2) that transfer must have increased the value of the transferee's estate or resulted in property becoming comprised in a settlement of which the transferee was a trustee when the transfer was made; and
(3) the deceased must before his death have incurred a liability to the transferee which was subject to abatement under s.103 on his death.

How relief is given

The rules, as are stated in para.6(3)–(5), may be summarised as follows: **8–54**

(1) *Disregard the transfer*: calculate the total tax chargeable as a consequence of the death of the deceased, disregarding so much of the value transferred by the original transfer as is:
  (a) attributable to the property by reference to which the liability falls to be abated, and
  (b) equal to the amount of the abatement of the liability.
(2) *Take account of the transfer and the liability*: calculate the total tax chargeable as a consequence of the death of the deceased, taking account of the value transferred and the liability.
(3) *Compare the amounts of tax payable*: where taking account of the value transferred and the liability produces a higher amount, that amount is payable. Where disregarding the original transfer gives a higher amount, the amount is reduced, as a credit, by a sum equal to so much of the tax as became payable before the death as was attributable to the property by reference to which the liability falls to be abated. This credit cannot exceed the difference between the amount of tax arrived at under the first calculation mentioned above and the amount of tax that would have fallen to be calculated under the second calculation mentioned above if the liability had been taken into account. Furthermore, so much of the value transferred by the original transfer as is:
  (a) attributable to the property by reference to which the liability is abated, and
  (b) equal to the amount of the abatement,
  is treated as reduced to nil for all IHT purposes, except for the purpose of exit charges on discretionary trusts.
(4) *More than one transfer:* it may be that there have been a number of transfers relevant to an abated liability. In that case, the regulations apply to the transfers in reverse order of their making, i.e. as taking the last first and the first last, but

[50] See paras 25–92 and following.

347

to the extent only that in aggregate the value of the transfers does not exceed the amount of the abatement in question.

8–55 The following examples are given in the Schedule (although, again, updated to use rates as at April 5, 2012):

EXAMPLE 1

November 2008	X makes a PET of cash of £330,000 to Y
December 2008	Y makes a loan to X of £330,000
May 2009	X makes a gift into a discretionary trust of £100,000
April 2014	X dies. His death estate is worth £350,000. A deduction of £330,000 is claimed for the loan from Y

First calculation under reg.6(3)(a)

No charge on November 2008 gift, and no deduction against death estate.

		Tax
November 2008	PET ignored	NIL
May 2009	Gifts £100,000	NIL
April 2014	Death estate £350,000 as top slice of £450,000	£50,000
	Total due as result of X's death	£50,000

Second calculation under reg.6(3)(b)

Charge the November 2008 PET, and allow the deduction against death estate.

		Tax
November 2008	PET £330,000. Tax with taper relief	£800
May 2009	Gift £100,000 as top slice of £430,000. Tax with taper relief	£24,000
April 2014	Death estate (£350,000 – loan £330,000) £20,000 as top slice of £450,000	£8,000
	Tax due as a result of X's death	£32,800

Result

First calculation gives higher amount of tax. So debt is disallowed against death estate, but PET of £330,000 is not charged.

EXAMPLE 2

August 2009	P makes a PET of cash of £340,000 to Q

September 2009	Q makes a loan to P of £340,000	
October 2010	P makes a gift into a discretionary trust of £350,000	Tax paid £5,000
November 2013	P dies—death estate of £350,000 less allowable liabilities of £250,000 (which do not include the debt of £320,000 owed to Q)	

First calculation under reg.6(3)(a)

No charge on August 2009 PET, and no deduction against death estate for the £320,000 owed to Q.

		Tax
August 2009	PET ignored	NIL
October 2010	Gift £350,000	
	Tax (with taper relief) £8,000 less £5,000 already paid	£3,000
November 2013	Death estate £100,000 as top slice of £420,000	£40,000
	Total tax as result of P's death	£43,000

Second calculation under reg.6(3)(b)

Charge the August 2009 PET, and allow deduction against death estate for the £340,000 owed to Q.

		Tax
August 2009	PET £340,000. Tax with taper relief	£3,600
October 2010	Gift £350,000 as top slice of £690,000. Tax (with taper relief) £112,000 less £5,000 already paid	£107,000
November 2013	Death estate £100,000 − £340,000 (owed to Q)	NIL
	Total tax due as result of P's death	£110,600

Result

Second calculation gives higher amount of tax. So the PET to Q is charged, and deduction is allowed against death estate for the debt to Q.

EXAMPLE 3

May 2008	A makes PET to B of £335,000	
January 2009	A makes PET to B of £40,000	
July 2009	A makes gift into discretionary trust of £340,000	Tax paid £3,000
January 2010	A makes PET to B of £30,000	
July 2010	B makes a loan to A of £100,000	
December 2011	A dies. Death estate £200,000 against which deduction is claimed for debt of £100,000 due to B	

First calculation under reg.6(3)(a)

Disallow the debt and ignore corresponding amounts (£100,000) of PETs from A to B starting with the latest gift.

		Tax
May 2008	PET now reduced to £305,000	NIL
January 2009	PET now reduced to NIL	NIL
July 2009	Gift into trust £340,000 as top slice of £645,000	
	Tax £128,000 less £3,000 already paid	£125,000
January 2010	PET now reduced to NIL	NIL
December 2011	Death estate £200,000 as top slice of £845,000	£80,000
	Total tax due as result of A's death	£205,000

Second calculation under reg.6(3)(b)

Allow the debt and charge PETs to B in full.

		Tax
May 2008	PET £335,000. Tax with taper relief	£3,200
January 2009	PET £40,000 as top slice of £375,000	£16,000
July 2009	Gift into trust £340,000 as top slice of £715,000	
	Tax £136,000 less £3,000 already paid	£133,000
January 2010	PET £30,000 as top slice of £745,000	£12,000
December 2011	Death estate £100,000 as top slice of £845,000	£40,000
	Total tax due as result of A's death	£204,200

Result

First calculation yields higher amount of tax. So the debt is disallowed and corresponding amounts of PETs to B are ignored in determining the tax due as a result of the death.

EXAMPLE 4

April 2008	A makes a gift into discretionary trust of £350,000	Tax paid £5,000
January 2011	A makes PET to B of £200,000	
January 2012	A makes a further gift into same trust of £70,000	Tax paid £14,000
January 2013	Same trust makes a loan to A of £310,000	
June 2015	A dies—death estate is £320,000 against which deduction is claimed for debt of £310,000 due to the trust	

First calculation under reg.6(3)(a)

Disallow the debt and ignore corresponding amounts (£310,000) of gifts from A to trust, starting with the latest gift.

		Tax
April 2008	Gift now reduced to £110,000. No adjustment to tax already paid as gift made more than 7 years before death	NIL
January 2011	PET £200,000 as top slice of £310,000 Gift now reduced to NIL	NIL
January 2012	No adjustment to tax already paid	NIL
June 2015	Death estate £320,000 as top slice of £520,000 (the 2008 gift of £110,000 drops out of cumulation)	£78,000
	Less credit for tax already paid £5,000 + £14,000	£(19,000)
	Total tax due as result of A's death	£59,000

Second calculation due under reg.6(3)(b)

Allow the debt and no adjustment to gifts into the trust.

		Tax
April 2008	Gift £350,000. No adjustment to tax already paid as gift made more than 7 years before death	NIL
January 2011	PET £200,000 as top slice of £550,000. Tax with taper relief	£48,000
January 2012	Gift £70,000 as top slice of £620,000 Tax (with taper relief) £22,400 less £14,000 already paid	£8,400
June 2015	Death estate £10,000 as top slice of £280,000. (The 2008 gift drops out of cumulation. No credit for tax paid on that gift.)	NIL
	Total tax due as result of A's death	£56,400

Result

First calculation yields higher amount of tax. So the debt is disallowed and corresponding amounts of gifts into trust are ignored in determining the tax due as a result of the death.

Equal calculations

It may be that the total tax chargeable as a consequence of death under the two **8–56** separate calculations provided by paras 4(4), 5(3), 6(3) or 7(4) is equal in amount.

Paragraph 8 provides that in such a case the first calculation is treated as producing a higher amount for the purposes of the regulation concerned.

Commentary

8–57   The Regulations do not cover all the circumstances in which the same property may be charged more than once. Consider the case where, e.g. X settles £100,000 on discretionary trusts under which he is a beneficiary and the trustees subsequently lend the money back to him. On his death X will be treated under the reservation of benefit rules as beneficially entitled to the trustees' right to be repaid the £100,000 and s.103 will prevent his indebtedness to the trustees from being taken into account in valuing his estate. So, if he still has the £100,000, or property representing it, he will be taxed twice on, in effect, the same property. Neither para.5 nor para.6 will prevent this. Consider also the case of a person who makes a gift, borrows from the donee and then discharges his indebtedness. If the original transfer is or proves to be a chargeable transfer and the PET which the transferor makes under s.103(6) when he discharges his indebtedness fails he will be charged twice and nothing in para.6 will prevent this. Had, on the other hand, the transferor not discharged his indebtedness but instead died with his liability abated under s.103, para.6 will prevent a double charge.

PARTLY EXEMPT TRANSFERS

VII. INTRODUCTION

8–58   The provisions governing the treatment of partly exempt transfers are found in Ch.III of Pt II of the Act. Although Ch.III is concerned with determining what portion of the value transferred by a partly exempt transfer is attributable to the exempt part of the transfer, and not with the value transferred by a transfer as such, it was thought best to defer discussion of Ch.III until now. This is because the provisions are most likely to be relevant to a transfer made on death.

The provisions contained in Ch.III, which are often overlooked, can be vitally important, especially in relation to the drafting of wills. Their application at one stage caused consternation in the IHT planning community[51] and they still offer planning opportunities. They therefore deserve careful study. Although Ch.III is generally regarded as containing provisions which are among the most bewildering to be found in the legislation, the difficulties encountered derive primarily from the somewhat elliptical language of Ch.III, not from the conceptual problem with which Ch.III is designed to deal. It will therefore be helpful to consider the legislation in general terms first, identifying the basic problem which a partly exempt transfer may cause and indicating how the legislation deals with that problem, and then, against that background, to consider in detail the statutory provisions contained in Ch.III.

8–59   For the sake of convenience, all transfers given in the examples below are assumed to have occurred on October 1, 2008, so that the rates of tax relevant to the examples are those that were then in force. Grossing-up at 40 per cent is simple—all that is necessary is to multiply the sum that is to be grossed-up by four-sixths (or two-thirds)

---

[51] See paras 8–110 and following.

and to add the resulting sum to the sum to be grossed-up. Thus, if one wishes to gross-up £60,000, one simply multiplies it by two-thirds = £40,000 and then adds the £40,000 to the original £60,000 = £100,000, which represents £60,000 grossed-up at 40 per cent. Alternatively, one can simply multiply the sum to be grossed-up at ten-sixths (or five-thirds). It may be, of course, that not all of the sum falls to be grossed-up. This would occur where part of the sum falls within the nil band. Assume, for example, that on his death X makes a chargeable transfer of £140,000, £20,000 of which falls within his nil rate band. In that case, only £120,000 would be grossed-up. The grossed-up amount would be £120,000 × five-thirds = £200,000.

Since the introduction of the reduced charitable rate of 36 per cent (see para.3–43), the "simple" grossing-up fraction would be 100/64 in estates where the reduced charitable rate is applicable. Please note that all the following examples are based on a tax rate of 40 per cent, although some may qualify for the new rate of 36 per cent. An example of the reduced charitable rate (for the general component) and grossing-up (in relation to other components not reduced) can be found in the IHT Manual.[52]

The problem

A partly exempt transfer may give rise to two basic problems, which, for the sake of convenience, will be referred to as the problems of quantum and of competition. The nature of these problems is best shown by an example. Assume that Atlas died on June 1, 2008, possessed of a net estate worth £800,000 and that by his will he left £517,000 free of tax to his son and the residue to his widow. In such a case, the problems of quantum and competition would have arisen in the following way.

8–60

First, from HMRC's standpoint, there might have been a shortfall of tax. Normally (assuming that the full nil rate band was available) it would take a chargeable estate of £645,000 to produce a net chargeable gift of £517,000, i.e. a chargeable gift of £517,000 would normally give rise to a charge of £128,000. If tax is charged on only the free of tax gift to Atlas's son, i.e. on only £517,000, and not on £645,000, HMRC will be entitled to recover only £76,800, a shortfall of £51,200. This is the problem of quantum.

Secondly, it would not be easy to decide whether to make the chargeable part of the transfer, the gift to the son, bear the tax due, or to make the exempt part of the transfer, the gift to the widow, do so. To make the chargeable part bear the tax would have been to disregard the transferor's wishes; to make the exempt part bear the tax would have been to force that part to bear tax which was not attributable to it. This is the problem of competition.

The solution

The legislation solves each problem by a separate process. The first process, which is designed to solve the problem of quantum, is known as the attribution of the value transferred. The second process, which is designed to solve the problem of competition, is known as the allocation of the burden of tax.

8–61

The first process involves attributing to the chargeable gifts a portion of the value transferred by the transfer of value in question. This is done in such a way as to ensure

---

[52] *http://www.hmrc.gov.uk/manuals/ihtmanual/IHTM45030.htm* [Accessed November 19, 2012].

that enough of the value transferred is brought into charge to secure HMRC's position.[53] This affects the position between HMRC and the taxpayers only; it does not affect the position of the transferees among themselves. The process of attributing the value transferred thus solves the problem of quantum but leaves the problem of competition. The second process, the allocation of burden, comes into play at this stage, i.e. once the amount of tax due has been ascertained. It determines how much, if anything, each transferee will receive out of the transfer after tax. An example will help to show how these processes work.

Assume the same facts, a net estate of £800,000, a free of tax gift of £517,000 to the testator's son, residue to his widow. The legislation provides that in such a case the part of the value transferred that is attributable to the chargeable part of the transfer (i.e. the gift to the son) is the amount of the value transferred that corresponds to the grossed-up value of the gift. The grossed-up amount of the gift of £517,000 to the son is £645,000 (i.e. the nil rate band of £325,000 plus five-thirds of the amount by which the gift exceeds the nil rate band—see table below) with the result that the amount of value transferred attributable to that gift is £645,000, not just £517,000. This is the process of attributing the value transferred.

Value of estate	£800,000
Gift free of tax	£517,000
Threshold at death	£325,000
Gift less threshold at death (£517,000 − £325,000)	£192,000
5/3 of the above balance (£192,000 × 5/3)	£320,000
Plus threshold at death (£320,000 + £325,000)	£645,000
Residue (£800,000 − £645,000)	£155,000

The fact that £645,000 of the £800,000 transferred is regarded as being attributable to the chargeable part of the transfer means that £128,000 of tax is due. At this stage it thus becomes necessary to determine how this tax is to be borne, i.e. to allocate the burden of tax. In these circumstances, the £128,000 due in respect of the gift to the son is borne by the residuary gift to the widow, so that, after payment of this tax, £517,000 would have passed to the son in accordance with the terms of the will, and £155,000 would have been left for the widow. The net result would thus have been that the tax on the chargeable gift to the son was preserved at the expense of the exempt residuary gift to the widow.[54]

Anomalies

8–62   It is important to note that the rules governing the attribution of the value transferred by a transfer of value to chargeable gifts may yield some interesting results. In some cases, they may render wholly chargeable what appears to be a partly exempt transfer; in other cases, they may result in what appears to be a partly exempt transfer becoming wholly exempt. Given the fact that it is possible, in effect, to rewrite a will by entering into a deed of variation, a taxpayer may be in a position to manipulate the rules

---

[53] As will be seen below, this is done with a vengeance sufficient sometimes to render wholly chargeable what appears to be a partly exempt transfer: see para.8–81.

[54] The legislation also makes provision to deal with specific subject to tax gifts, specific exempt gifts and chargeable residue; this is discussed below.

governing the attribution of the value transferred to his own advantage: see para.8–121.

When Chapter III applies

By s.36, Ch.III applies when a transfer of value is partly exempt because it is covered **8–63** only partially by one or more of:

(1) the exemptions that apply under ss.18 and 23–26 to actual and notional transfers alike[55]; or
(2) the exemption that applies under s.30 to transfers of national heritage property[56]; or
(3) the exemption that applies under s.27 to transfers to maintenance funds.[57]

A transfer of value may be covered only partially by one of the above-mentioned exemptions for one of two reasons, i.e. because it includes:

(1) a gift to a non-exempt person, e.g. where a deceased person leaves part of his estate to his son and the remainder to his widow; or
(2) a gift which falls within s.18(3) and other parallel provisions, e.g. where a deceased makes a gift which does not carry the intermediate income to his widow and part of the gift is conditional on the widow's surviving for more than 12 months.[58]

Since s.36 provides that Ch.III applies where a transfer of value is covered only partly by one of the Ch.I exemptions, on a strict reading Ch.III therefore applies where a transfer to a *single* transferee exceeds an exemption limit, e.g. where a UK domiciled husband or civil partner makes a transfer to his foreign domiciled wife or civil partner in excess of the exemption limit that applies to such transfers (see para.3–35). In the authors' view, however, it seems unlikely that Ch.III will be construed as applying to such transfers.

If it is correct that Ch.III applies only when there is more than one transferee, most partly exempt transfers will be made on death. This follows from the fact that if a transferor makes an inter vivos gift to two or more transferees, he will usually be regarded as having made a separate transfer to each of them, so that each transfer is either wholly chargeable or wholly exempt. Exceptionally, an inter vivos transfer to two or more transferees may be regarded as a single transfer. This would be the case, it is thought, where a transferor makes an actual transfer of value under s.3(1) by transferring property to trustees on terms, e.g. that they hold the income from the property in equal shares for A (a chargeable person) and B (an exempt person) for a specified period, remainder to C, or where a transferor transfers property to two or more persons jointly, one of whom is exempt. In a similar fashion, a single inter vivos

[55] See paras 3–04 and following.
[56] See paras 27–04 and following.
[57] See paras 27–71 and following.
[58] See paras 3–50 and following. At one time there was a third reason why a transfer of value might be covered only partially by an exemption. This was because under the exemptions given to gifts to charities and political parties there used to be a £100,000 limitation on gifts made within a year of death. Certain exemptions are, of course, still limited—see the annual, small gifts, marriage and normal expenditure out of income exemptions—but in the authors' view it is most unlikely that those exemptions will be relevant in Ch.III computations.

notional transfer might be made under s.52(1) to more than one person where on the termination during a person's lifetime of his interest in possession in settled property that property fell to be held on trust for two or more persons, one of whom was exempt. Where such circumstances arise the procedure set out below for dealing with transfers made on death should be followed but using the lifetime rate of tax.

Deemed operation

8–64   In one case, Ch.III is effectively deemed to operate. This occurs in certain cases where the transferee of an exempt transfer made on death makes a disposition of property which was the subject matter of that transfer.[59]

Rules governing attribution of value transferred

8–65   In the example given earlier, the chargeable part of the transfer consisted solely of a specific gift expressed to be made free of tax. Partly exempt transfers may involve other kinds of gifts, and it will be helpful at this point to outline how the slightly complicated rules governing the attribution of the value transferred operate in respect of gifts generally. It should be borne in mind that the purpose of applying these rules is to find what part of the value transferred is chargeable, so that the tax due in respect of the transfer may be calculated.

8–66   First, by s.39, the value transferred by a partly exempt transfer is always attributed to specific gifts[60] first. So much of the value transferred, if any, that is not attributed to specific gifts is then attributed to residue.

8–67   Secondly, the amount of value transferred that is attributable to a specific gift is taken to be "such part of the value transferred . . . as corresponds" to the value of that gift.[61] The procedure for determining how much of the value transferred is regarded for the purposes of Ch.III as corresponding to the value of a gift is thus crucial. This procedure varies according to whether the gifts are:

     (1) subject to tax;
     (2) exempt; or
     (3) free of tax.

Where specific gifts are *subject to tax or exempt* there are no special rules for determining how much of the value transferred corresponds to the value of the gifts. The part of the value transferred which is taken to be attributable to the specific gifts is thus simply that part of the value transferred that in fact corresponds to the value of those gifts. Assume for example, that Caesar, who has a nil cumulative total and whose net estate is worth £1,000,000, dies, leaving £150,000 to his son subject to tax, £330,000 to his daughter subject to tax, £100,000 to charity, the residue to his widow. The value transferred would be attributed as follows:

---

[59] See paras 8–83 and following.
[60] See paras 8–74 and 8–91.
[61] IHTA 1984 s.38(1).

	Value of gift	Amount of value transferred corresponding to value of gift
To son	£150,000	$\dfrac{150,000}{1,000,000} \times £1,000,000 = £150,000$
To daughter	£330,000	$\dfrac{330,000}{1,000,000} \times £1,000,000 = £330,000$
To charity	£100,000	$\dfrac{100,000}{1,000,000} \times £1,000,000 = £100,000$
To widow	£420,000	$\dfrac{420,000}{1,000,000} \times £1,000,000 = £420,000$

Where, on the other hand, free of tax gifts are concerned, there are special rules for determining how much of the value transferred corresponds to the value of the gifts. The position varies according to whether all the chargeable gifts are free of tax, or there is a mix of chargeable subject to tax and free of tax gifts. If all the chargeable gifts are free of tax, the gifts are added together and the total is grossed-up at the appropriate rate or rates of tax.[62] The value transferred that is attributable to the chargeable part of the transfer is then taken to be so much of the value transferred as corresponds to this grossed-up value. Returning to the previous example, assume that the gifts of £150,000 and £330,000 to Caesar's children were both free of tax gifts. The procedure would then have been to add those gifts together so as to find the total of the chargeable free of tax specific gifts, in this case £480,000. This figure would then have been grossed-up to £583,334 which would have been the amount of the value transferred that corresponded to the value of the specific chargeable gifts and that was therefore attributable to them. The amount of value transferred corresponding to the value of (and therefore attributable to) all the specific gifts (both chargeable and exempt) would have been £683,334 (£583,334 + £100,000); the remainder of the value transferred—£316,666 —would have been attributable to the residual gift to the widow. **8–68**

If there is a mix of chargeable subject to tax and free of tax gifts, the position is more complicated and two rounds of grossing-up are in theory necessary.[63] Assume the facts are as above, except that the £150,000 gift to the son is subject to tax, while the £330,000 gift to the daughter is free of tax. It seems obvious that the amount by which the gift to the daughter is grossed-up should take account of the fact that the subject to tax gift to the son (which is also chargeable) forms part of the same transfer; otherwise the charge to tax would be artificially low. But it is not at all obvious how this should be done. The statutory solution is to provide that the amount of value transferred attributable to the free of tax gifts is determined by grossing-up those gifts at an average rate, known as the "assumed rate". The method used for finding this assumed rate looks rather tricky, but is in fact basically quite simple[64]: **8–69**

---

[62] IHTA 1984 s.38(1) and (3).

[63] IHTA 1984 s.38(1), (4) and (5).

[64] It is no longer necessary to find the assumed rate if the Grossing-Up Calculator at *http://www.hmrc. gov.uk/cto/g_up.pdf* [Accessed October 3, 2012] is used.

(1) The free of tax gift is grossed-up in the usual way, i.e. by the amount of tax which would be correct if there were no subject to tax gifts. This yields the amount of value transferred provisionally attributable to the free of tax gift.

(2) The remainder of the value transferred is provisionally attributed to the rest of the gifts, and then to residue.

(3) Tax is calculated in the ordinary way on the amount of value transferred provisionally attributed to the chargeable part of the transfer.

(4) The tax on this amount is then divided by this amount. This is the assumed rate and is conveniently expressed as a percentage.

(5) The free of tax gifts are now grossed-up at the assumed rate. This yields how much of the value transferred is attributable to the free of tax gifts.

To reach the solution, then, one has first to make all the calculations on a provisional basis in order to find the assumed rate; and then, to repeat the calculations using the assumed rate itself. Returning to the above example, the following procedure would be used:

(1) Provisionally gross-up the tax-free gift to the daughter to £333,334.

(2) Add to the grossed-up gift the subject to tax gift to the son of £150,000 to give a provisional value of £483,334.

(3) Tax this figure in the usual way; the result is that £63,334 in tax would be due.

(4) Find the assumed rate $\dfrac{63,334}{483,334} = 13.104\%$

(5) Gross-up[65] the free of tax gift of £330,000 at the assumed rate:

$$£330,000 \times \frac{14.104}{86.896} = £49,764$$

The result is that £379,764 of the value transferred is attributable to the £330,000 gift to the daughter (i.e. £330,000 + £49,764), so that the chargeable portion of the value transferred is £529,764 (£379,764 + £150,000).

Although two rounds of grossing-up are necessary in theory and were necessary in fact in the example just given, it will be appreciated that if the only rate of tax that applies to the estate is 40 per cent (e.g. if there is no available nil rate band) that will necessarily be the assumed rate, and thus in practice only one round of grossing-up will be necessary.

The above indicates the general shape of the rules governing the attribution of the value transferred. The detailed rules are considered below, but before turning to them it may be helpful to outline briefly the various considerations that may have to be taken into account in a Ch.III calculation.

VIII. OVERVIEW

8–70   Normally the first task is to attribute the value transferred by the partly exempt transfer in question to the various gifts comprised in that transfer. This will disclose

---

[65] For an explanation of this formula, see para.6–30.

how much of the value transferred is attributable to the chargeable portion of the transfer, with the result that the amount of tax payable in respect of the transfer can be found. This tax is then deducted from the total estate,[66] leaving the amount to be distributed to the various transferees. The last step is to allocate this net amount among the transferees.

Exceptionally, before attributing any of the value transferred it may be necessary as a matter of general law to abate the gifts made by the transferor. This would be the case where, for example, even before tax a testator's estate was insufficient to fund the various gifts he made in his will. In such a case, the gifts are abated in the order prescribed by the general law, and then the value transferred is attributed to the abated gifts in the usual way.[67]

Occasionally, the process of attributing value to specific gifts will result in the value transferred attributable to those gifts exceeding the value transferred by the partly exempt transfer in question. This would come about when a free of tax gift is grossed-up to such an extent that the residue, if any, is exhausted. Assume, for example, that Euripides, whose nil rate band was exhausted, died with a net estate of £190,000 and that he left £120,000 free of tax to his son, residue to charity. The free of tax gift would have been grossed-up to £200,000, with the result that the value attributable to the specific gift exceeded the value transferred by the transfer Euripides made on his death. In such a case it will be necessary to reduce the value of the specific gifts to an aggregate amount equal to the value transferred by the partly exempt transfer in question, and to adjust the amounts of value transferred attributable to the various gifts accordingly.[68]

IX. CHAPTER III IN DETAIL

It is now time to consider the provisions of Ch.III in detail. In all, Ch.III contains only eight sections, but as was mentioned above, they are rather daunting, even to the experienced reader of complicated fiscal legislation: a person whose first exposure to IHT involved confronting a partly exempt transfer would certainly be entitled to sympathy. Against the background of the preceding discussion, however, the Ch.III provisions should be less impenetrable. It will he helpful to begin by considering the definitions that apply for purposes of Ch.III.   **8–71**

Definitions

The definitions in Ch.III are contained in s.42, which defines "gift" and "specific gift", and which also indicates when a gift is to be regarded as bearing its own tax, i.e. is a subject to tax gift. The provisions are as follows.   **8–72**

Gift

Section 42(1) provides that in relation to any transfer of value "gift":   **8–73**

---

[66] Or gift, as the case may be.
[67] See para.8–77.
[68] See paras 8–08 and following.

"... means the benefit of any disposition or rule of law by which, on the making of the transfer, any property becomes (or would but for any abatement become) the property of any person or applicable for any purpose; 'given' shall be construed accordingly ... "

"Gift" is thus widely defined and will include the benefit of any disposition, whether it is made inter vivos, by will, or on an intestacy. There must be some doubt as to whether a "gift" is made where a benefit accrues to a surviving joint tenant by virtue of his right of survivorship, since in such a case the interest of the deceased joint tenant is extinguished and therefore cannot be said to "become" the property of the survivor. It is to be noted that "gift" is defined to mean a benefit; this seems to imply that where a gift is made subject to a condition precedent that condition will have to be taken into account in measuring the benefit conferred by the gift.

Specific gift

8–74   Section 42(1) defines a "specific gift" as any gift other than a gift of residue or of a share in residue.[69] Here four points should be noted. First, by s.38(6), for the purposes of s.38 (i.e. for the purposes of attributing the value transferred) any liability of the transferor which does not fall to be brought into account under s.5(5) is treated as a specific gift. Under s.5(5), a liability falls to be taken into account to the extent only that it was imposed by law or incurred for a consideration in money or money's worth.[70] Thus, a person who had during his life entered into a covenant which remained in force after his death would on his death be regarded as having made a specific gift of an amount equal to the capitalised value at that time of his liability under the covenant.

Secondly, it may be that on making a lifetime transfer a person undertakes to bear any tax that may become chargeable by reason of his dying within seven years of making that transfer and binds his personal representatives to do likewise. The liability he undertakes, having been assumed voluntarily, will not be taken into account in valuing his estate for IHT purposes. Difficulties may arise, however, when the personal representatives honour the undertaking, because the payment of the tax will constitute the making of a specific free of tax gift, and that gift may have to be grossed-up.

Thirdly, in relation to Scotland, s.42(4) provides that where on a death legal rights are claimed by a person entitled to claim such rights, those rights should be treated as a specific gift which bears its own tax. The position with regard to legal rights in Scotland is discussed below.[71]

Finally, in certain cases where the transferee of an exempt transfer made to him on death makes a disposition of property which was the subject matter of that transfer that disposition is treated as a specific gift made by the deceased individual who made the exempt transfer.[72]

Subject to tax gifts

8–75   As was noted above, the question of whether a gift bears its own tax or is free of tax is important in two ways in the context of attributing the value transferred. First, if a

---

[69] For the constructional difficulties this can cause, see *British Tax Review* (1986), pp.27–29.
[70] Subject to FA 1986 s.103; see paras 25–79 and following.
[71] See para.8–76.
[72] See para.8–83.

chargeable gift is free of tax, it will have to be grossed-up. Secondly, if the chargeable part of a transfer includes both free of tax and subject to tax gifts, the grossing-up will have to be done in the special way, using the "assumed rate", outlined above.[73]

It is thus vital to know whether or not a chargeable specific gift bears its own tax or not. For this purpose, s.42(2) provides that a gift bears its own tax if the tax attributable to it:

(1) falls on the person who becomes entitled to the property given; or
(2) as the case may be, is payable out of property applicable for the purposes for which the property given becomes applicable.

In deciding whether a gift bears its own tax within the meaning of s.42(2), regard will have to be had first of all to the terms of the gift, and then to the general law and the specific provisions in s.41.[74] Normally no problems will arise in respect of a transfer inter vivos, since the terms of such a transfer will usually be clear. The position on death is that, subject to contrary provision in the will, specific gifts are generally free of tax.

Legal rights in Scotland

Section 42(4) makes special provision to deal with claims of legal rights in Scotland.[75] Where such rights are claimed by a person entitled to claim them the rights are treated as a specific subject to tax gift. In determining the value of such rights any IHT payable on the estate is ignored. The rights are legitim[76] and the right of a surviving spouse or civil partner to one-third (one-half if there are no surviving descendants) of the "net movable estate", i.e. the chargeable estate after the deduction of debts, funeral expenses and costs of administration (but not legacies).

8–76

Abatement: section 37(1)

Abatement is the rule of general law under which if a deceased person's estate is insufficient to satisfy the gifts made by him those gifts must be reduced to the point where the estate becomes sufficient.

8–77

---

[73] Please note that, with the provision by HMRC of the Grossing-Up Calculator on their website, it is no longer necessary to find the assumed rate as the Calculator completes all the calculations once the basic information has been given: *http://www.hmrc.gov.uk/cto/g_up.pdf* [Accessed October 3, 2012].

[74] See paras 29–84 and following.

[75] For the special planning opportunities afforded by the Scottish forced inheritance rules, see *Private Client Business* (1992), p.57. Section 42(4) only refers to legal rights in Scotland. The position in relation to other forced heirship regimes (see paras 34–14 and following) is not covered by s.42(4); the existence of s.42(4) might imply that other similar situations will be treated in the same way or it might imply the opposite, i.e. as specific provision has been made only in relation to legal rights in Scotland the assumption must be that it is the only exception to the general rule. The authors would favour the first approach on the basis that the draftsman was concerned only with the position in the United Kingdom and that one would not expect to find foreign forced heirship regimes addressed in the same way as, e.g., "settlement equivalents" are addressed in the closing portion of s.43(2) (see paras 34–48 and following). The position will probably depend on the precise nature of the forced heirship regime in question.

[76] See paras 8–216 and following.

In any case where it is necessary to abate a gift under the general law before taking into account any tax that may be payable, that abatement is to be effected *before* applying any of the special rules found in Ch.III. This follows from s.37(1), which provides that:

"Where a gift would be abated owing to an insufficiency of assets and without regard to any tax chargeable, the gift shall be treated for the purposes of the following provisions of this Chapter as so abated."

The manner in which pecuniary legacies are abated is quite straightforward. Assume, for example, that Achilles died owning an estate which after liabilities other than tax was worth £240,000, and that by his will he left £50,000 to his son, £100,000 to his daughter and £150,000 to his widow. Since the aggregate of the pecuniary legacies exceeds the net estate the legacies must be abated rateably, i.e. so that they share in the actual estate in the proportions:

son	daughter	widow
$\dfrac{50,000}{300,000}$	$\dfrac{100,000}{300,000}$	$\dfrac{150,000}{300,000}$

Thus,

son's gift is abated to $5/30 \times £240,000$	=	£40,000
daughter's gift is abated to $10/30 \times £240,000$	=	£80,000
widow's gift is abated to $15/30 \times £240,000$	=	£120,000
		£240,000

Attribution of value transferred: sections 38 and 39

8–78   The main process that comes into play in dealing with a partly exempt transfer involves attributing the value transferred by the transfer to the specific gifts and to residue, if any, so as to find what part of the value transferred is chargeable. Under the rules laid down in ss.38–40, the value is attributed to specific gifts first, and then to such residue as there may be.[77]

The general rule: section 38(1)

8–79   Section 38(1) provides that:

"Such part of the value transferred shall be attributable to specific gifts as corresponds to the value of the gifts: but if or to the extent that the gifts—

---

[77] IHTA 1984 s.39.

(a) are not gifts with respect to which the transfer is exempt or are outside the limit up to which the transfer is exempt, and

(b) do not bear their own tax,

the amount corresponding to the value of the gifts shall be taken to be the amount arrived at in accordance with subsections (3) to (5) below."

Section 38(1) thus lays down the general rule that the amount of value transferred by a transfer of value attributable to a specific gift is the amount that corresponds to the value of that gift. A distinction is then drawn between:

(1) chargeable subject to tax specific gifts and exempt specific gifts; and

(2) chargeable free of tax specific gifts.

Where subject to tax and exempt gifts are concerned the amount of the value transferred attributable to the gift in question is the part of the value transferred that corresponds to the value of the gift. Where free of tax gifts are concerned, the amount of the value transferred attributable to the gift in question is taken to be an amount which is arrived at by grossing-up the value of the gifts in accordance with the special rules laid down by subs.(3)–(5). It is thus important in all cases to know the value of the gifts in question. Normally the value of a gift will be the market value of the gift at the time the transfer was made. This is subject to two qualifications. First, if one of the revaluation reliefs discussed at paras 25–123–25–130 applies in relation to a transfer made on death[78] a different value will be substituted. Secondly, s.42(3) makes provision to deal with the case where the value transferred by a partly exempt transfer exceeds the aggregate value of the property which is the subject matter of the gifts involved. This covers the case where, for example, an individual who owns, say, 75 of the 100 ordinary shares in an investment company dies leaving, say, 24 of the shares to his son and 51 of the shares to his widow. In the absence of special provision, there might have been some doubt as to whether or not the shares given to the son were to be valued as a minority holding. Section 42(3) accordingly provides that in such a case the value of each of the gifts is taken to be the "relevant proportion of the value transferred", i.e. the proportion which the value of each gift bears to the aggregate of the values of the gifts in question. The result is that the gift to the son will be valued as part of a 75 per cent holding.

As was mentioned above, the position is straightforward when the only specific gifts involved are subject to tax gifts and/or exempt gifts, since in that case the amount of value transferred attributable to the gift is the amount of the value transferred which corresponds to the value of the gift without any grossing-up.

Consider the following examples.

8–80

EXAMPLE 1

Subject to tax specific gift, exempt residue.
Assume that Darius, whose net estate is £400,000 dies leaving £100,000 subject to tax to his son, residue to his widow. £100,000 of the value transferred is attributable to the gift to the son, £300,000 to the residuary gift to the widow.

---

[78] If the revaluation relief available under IHTA 1984 s.131 (see paras 25–109 and following) applies in relation to a transfer of value made within seven years before the death the value transferred by that transfer is reduced, not the value of the property which was the subject matter of the transfer.

EXAMPLE 2

Exempt specific gift, chargeable residue.

The facts are as above, except that £100,000 is left to the widow, and the residue to the son. £100,000 of the value transferred would be attributable to the gift to the widow, £300,000 to the residuary gift to the son.

EXAMPLE 3

Subject to tax specific gift, exempt specific gift, chargeable residue.

Assume that Darius left £80,000 to his son subject to tax, £120,000 to the Labour Party, residue to his brother. The value attributable to the specific gifts would be £80,000 and £120,000 respectively, and the value attributable to the residue would be £200,000.

All chargeable gifts free of tax specific gifts: section 38(3)

8–81 Section 38(3) governs the position where the only gifts with respect to which a transfer is or might be chargeable are free of tax specific gifts. It thus applies where any other gifts (whether specific or of residue) are exempt. In such a case s.38(3) provides that the amount of the value transferred which is taken to correspond to the value of the specific free of tax gift is:

> "the aggregate of—
>   (a) the sum of the value of those gifts, and
>   (b) the amount of tax which would be chargeable if the value transferred equalled that aggregate."

This means that where s.38(3) applies it is necessary to gross-up the aggregate value of any specific free of tax gifts at the rate (given the transferor's cumulative total) that would apply if the value transferred by the transfer in question were equal to that aggregate. As will be seen below, this may give the strange result that what at first appears to be a partly exempt transfer turns out to be a wholly chargeable one.

EXAMPLE 4

Free of tax specific gifts, exempt residue.

Assume that Ulysses, who died with a net estate of £800,000, left £360,000 free of tax to his son, residue to his widow. If Ulysses' nil rate band was exhausted, the gift of £360,000 would be grossed-up to £600,000, and the £600,000 of the value transferred would be attributable to the gift to the son. The remainder, £200,000, would be attributable to the exempt residue. Had Ulysses left £480,000 to his son, the entire value transferred of £800,000 would be attributable to the gift to the son, with the result that the transfer, although ostensibly partly exempt, was wholly chargeable.[79]

EXAMPLE 5

Free of tax specific gift, exempt specific gift, exempt residue.

Assume the above facts, but that Ulysses also left £100,000 to charity. In that case £600,000 would have been attributable to the gift to the son, £100,000 to the gift to charity, and the remainder, £100,000, to the exempt residue. Had the gift to charity been £200,000, the residue would have been wiped out.[80] (Had Ulysses' net estate been less than £800,000 the residue would have been wiped out and it would also have been necessary to reduce the grossed-up gift to the son and the gift to charity; see para.8–98.)

Not all chargeable gifts free of tax specific gifts: section 38(4) and (5)

Section 38(4) and (5) govern the position where specific free of tax chargeable gifts are not the only gifts with respect to which the transfer of value in question is or might be chargeable. Section 38(4) and (5) thus apply where there is at least (a) one free of tax chargeable specific gift, and (b) one subject to tax specific gift and/or chargeable residue. Section 38(4) provides that in such circumstances the amount of the value transferred which is to be taken as attributable to each free of tax specific gift is equal to the value of that gift grossed-up at the "assumed rate". Section 38(5) provides in turn that: **8–82**

"For the purposes of subsection (4) above—
(a) the assumed rate is the rate found by dividing the assumed amount of tax by that part of the value transferred with respect to which the transfer would be chargeable on the hypothesis that—
  (i) the amount corresponding to the value of specific gifts not bearing their own tax is equal to the aggregate referred to in subsection (3) above, and
  (ii) the parts of the value transferred attributable to specific gifts and to gifts of residue or shares in residue are determined accordingly; and
(b) the assumed amount of tax is the amount that would be charged on the value transferred on the hypothesis mentioned in para.(a) above."

As was discussed above at para.8–69, this puzzling formulation means that two rounds of grossing-up are necessary, as follows:

(1) the aggregate of the free of tax gifts are grossed-up at the rate appropriate to them, so as to determine how much of the value transferred is to be provisionally attributable to the free of tax gifts;
(2) the remainder of the value transferred is provisionally attributed to the rest of the gifts and then to residue;

---

[79] It is worth noting that this result is not at odds with the wording of s.36, which by providing that Ch.III applies where a transfer is not "wholly exempt" leaves open the possibility of Ch.III applying to wholly chargeable as well as to partly exempt transfers. Where residue is depleted or substantially reduced an application under the Inheritance (Provision for Family and Dependants) Act 1975 may be in order.
[80] IHTA 1984 s.39.

(3) tax is charged in the ordinary way on the value transferred provisionally attributed to the chargeable part of the transfer;

(4) the average rate of tax on the value transferred provisionally attributed to the chargeable part of the transfer is found; this is the "assumed rate"; and

(5) the free of tax gifts are grossed-up at the assumed rate. This yields the amount of the value transferred attributable to the free of tax gifts.

EXAMPLE 6

Free of tax specific gift, subject to tax specific gift, exempt residue.

Assume that Socrates dies with a net estate of £1,000,000, a cumulative total of £252,000, and that he leaves £150,000 free of tax to his son, £210,000 subject to tax to his daughter, residue to his widow. The £150,000 gift to the son would be grossed-up to £201,333, and this figure would be added to the £210,000 gift to the daughter so that £411,333 was provisionally attributable to the chargeable gifts. Given a cumulative total of £252,000, tax on £411,333 would be:

$$
\begin{array}{rr}
 & \text{£} \\
252{,}000 - 325{,}000 \text{ @ } 0\% = & 0 \\
325{,}000 - 663{,}333 \text{ @ } 40\% = & \underline{135{,}333} \\
 & \overline{135{,}333}
\end{array}
$$

The assumed rate would thus be:

$$
\frac{135{,}333}{411{,}333} = 32.901\%
$$

The free of tax gift would then be grossed-up at the assumed rate[81]:

$$
150{,}000 \times \frac{32.901}{67.099} = 73{,}551 + 150{,}000 = £223{,}551
$$

The value transferred by Socrates' transfer would thus be attributed as follows:

gift to son	£223,551
gift to daughter	£210,000
residue to widow	£556,449
	£1,000,000

EXAMPLE 7

Specific free of tax gift, specific subject to tax gift, chargeable residue and exempt residue.

Assume the facts are as above, but that the residue passed in equal shares to Socrates' widow and brother. Again, the £150,000 free of tax gift to the son would be grossed-up to £201,333. The value transferred attributable to the specific gifts would thus be £411,333 and the value transferred attributable to residue £588,667. Half of this

[81] See para.6–30 for an explanation of this formula.

£588,667, i.e. £294,334, would be chargeable (the brother's share), so that the value transferred provisionally attributable to the chargeable part of the transfer was £705,667 (£411,333 + 294,334).

Given a cumulative total of £252,000, tax on £710,000 would be:

$$\begin{array}{lr}
 & \text{£} \\
252,000 - 325,000 \ @ \ 0\% = & 0 \\
325,000 - 957,667 \ @ \ 40\% = & \underline{253,066} \\
 & \underline{£253,066}
\end{array}$$

The assumed rate would thus be:

$$\frac{253,066}{705,667} = 35.86\%$$

The free of tax gift would then be grossed-up at the assumed rate:

$$150,000 \times \frac{35.86}{64.14} = 83,863 + 150,000 = £233,863$$

The value transferred by Socrates' transfer would thus have been attributed as follows:

gift to son	£233,863
gift to daughter	£210,000
exempt residue	£278,069
chargeable residue	£278,068
	£1,000,000

EXAMPLE 8

Two specific free of tax gifts, two specific subject to tax gifts, one specific exempt gift, exempt residue, chargeable residue.

Assume the facts are as above, but that the gifts made by Socrates were as follows: £100,000 free of tax to his son, £50,000 free of tax to his stepson, £150,000 subject to tax to his daughter, £50,000 subject to tax to his stepdaughter, £100,000 to charity, residue in equal shares to his brother and his widow. The gifts to the boys would be aggregated and the resulting £150,000 grossed-up to £201,333 as in the above example; £201,333 of the value transferred would thus be provisionally attributable to the specific chargeable free of tax gifts. The value transferred would thus have been provisionally attributed as follows:

	Chargeable	Exempt	Total
Specific free of tax gifts	£201,333		
Specific subject to tax gifts	£200,000		
Specific exempt gift		£100,000	
Chargeable residue	£249,334		
Exempt residue		£249,333	
	£650,667 +	£349,333 =	£1,000,000

367

The assumed tax would be:

$$
\begin{array}{lr}
 & £ \\
252{,}000 - 325{,}000 \ @ \ 0\% = & 0 \\
325{,}000 - 902{,}667 \ @ \ 40\% = & \underline{231{,}066} \\
 & £231{,}066
\end{array}
$$

The assumed rate would thus be:

$$\frac{231{,}066}{650{,}667} = 35.512\%$$

The free of tax gifts would be grossed-up at the assumed rate:

$$150{,}000 \times \frac{35.512}{64.488} = 82{,}601 + 150{,}000 = £232{,}601$$

The value transferred would thus have been attributed as follows:

Gifts	Chargeable	Exempt	Total
To boys	232,601		
To girls	200,000		
To charity		100,000	
To widow		233,699	
To brother	233,700		
	666,301 +	333,699	= £1,000,000

Rerouted exempt transfers: section 29A

8–83 Section 29A[82] was introduced as an anti-avoidance measure and has a similar effect to s.142(3).[83] The section applies where:

> "(a) apart from this section the transfer of value made on the death of any person is an exempt transfer to the extent that the value transferred by it is attributable to an exempt gift, and
>
> (b) the exempt beneficiary, in settlement of the whole or part of any claim against the deceased's estate, effects a disposition of property not derived from the transfer."

The application of s.29A is best shown by an example. Assume X by his will leaves his estate to his widow. His mistress makes a claim which the widow satisfies by paying the mistress £100,000 out of her own resources (i.e. not out of the property inherited from X) in circumstances where s.146[84] did not apply. Section 29A will apply. Note

[82] By FA 1989 s.172 re deaths occurring after July 26, 1989.
[83] See para.8–141 below.
[84] See para.8–210 below.

368

that s.29A affects not only spouses or civil partners, but also charities and all exempt beneficiaries contained in ss.24–28.[85]

How section 29A works

If the above conditions in s.29A(1) are satisfied the transactions entered into by the parties are rewritten in a most unusual way. First, returning to the example, although the widow paid the mistress, under s.29A the deceased (not the widow) is treated as having made a chargeable free of tax specific gift to (somewhat bewilderingly) the exempt beneficiary, i.e. the widow.[86] Since the deemed chargeable specific gift is deemed to be free of tax, it must be grossed-up. **8–84**

The amount of deemed gift

The amount of the deemed gift is equal to the amount by which the disposition made by the widow to the mistress diminished the value of her estate.[87] In determining the value of the widow's estate for this purpose no deduction is made in respect of the mistress's claim and where the disposition made by the widow is a transfer of value no account is taken of any liability of the widow for any tax on the value transferred. Section 29A(4)(ii) also provides that business relief and agricultural relief are disregarded,[88] but this indicates a misunderstanding of the nature of those reliefs because, since those reliefs operate by reducing the value transferred by a transfer of value, not by reducing the value of any property, those reliefs would in any event fall to be disregarded. **8–85**

The mischief

The purpose of s.29A is to prevent certain dispositions having the benefit of exemptions when they should not. Returning to the above example, in the absence of s.29A £100,000 would have passed free of tax to the mistress. On X's death the £100,000 would have had the benefit of the s.18 exemption and when the widow paid the mistress she could have contended, e.g., that s.10 prevented her from making a transfer of value.[89] **8–86**

The curious cure

It is worth stressing how s.29A operates: it is by retrospectively withdrawing the s.18 exemption from the £100,000 but not, as might be expected, on the basis that X had made a gift of £100,000 free of tax to the mistress. Rather, it—curiously—converts the **8–87**

---

[85] IHTA 1984 s.29A(6).
[86] IHTA 1984 ss.29A(3) and 38(1).
[87] But not exceeding so much of the value transferred on the deceased's death as is attributable to the exempt gift in question: IHTA 1984 s.29A(2)(b) and (6).
[88] IHTA 1984 s.29A(4).
[89] See para.2–41.

£100,000 into a chargeable free of tax specific gift to the widow (notwithstanding that she is an exempt beneficiary). The operation of s.29A is to be contrasted with that of s.146 which operates by simply treating the gift made to the mistress as having been made by the deceased.[90]

Anomalies

8–88 Section 29A can produce some seriously unfair results. Assume Y leaves his entire estate to charity and that his widow makes a £50,000 claim which the charity satisfies otherwise than out of the residuary estate in circumstances such that s.146 does not apply. In that case s.29A will apply and the charity will be treated as having received a chargeable free of tax specific gift of £50,000, and this is so even though the £50,000 moves from one exempt beneficiary to another. If, on the other hand, s.146 applied, Y would be treated as having left the £50,000 to his widow and the s.18 exemption would have been available.

A side exit

8–89 Although s.29A is rather terrifying, it is thought that it is easily sidestepped by the simple expedient of the exempt beneficiary satisfying the claim out of property derived from the deceased's estate.[91] The explanation for the effectiveness of this approach is historical.

As part of a proposed reform of the IHT treatment of posthumous transactions the Finance Bill 1989 contained new, related proposals, only some of which were eventually enacted. First, it was proposed to replace the existing, relatively wide s.142 relief for instruments of variation with a new, much narrower s.142 under which the rerouting of benefits was no longer possible, the relief being restricted to disclaimed benefits. Secondly, it was proposed to introduce a new s.146A which would apply where benefits conferred by a deceased were varied, but only if the variation was effected in bona fide settlement of a claim. Where these conditions were satisfied then, if the terms of the variation could have been included under an order under the Inheritance (Provision for Family and Dependants) Act 1975 the variation was for IHT purposes to be treated as if it had been effected by the deceased. This section thus had the basic effect of capturing variations of property which had devolved from the deceased which were not within s.146 if, having satisfied the aforesaid conditions, they could have been included in an order under the 1975 Act. Thirdly, it was proposed to introduce what is now s.29A.

The result of these proposals being implemented would have been that s.146 and proposed s.146A would have dealt with the satisfaction of claims out of assets which devolved from the deceased's estate, while s.29A would have dealt with the satisfaction of claims out of assets which did not so devolve.

In the event, it was decided to retain s.142. It appears to have been assumed that s.146A was therefore inappropriate and accordingly only s.29A was enacted. The result

---

[90] See para.8–210.

[91] Where the exempt beneficiary is a charity regard will have to be had to IHTA 1984 s.23(5) and (6). The authors incline to the view that, depending on the facts, the satisfaction of the claim could be an application for charitable purposes.

is that the satisfaction of a claim with assets which devolved from the deceased is outside s.29A and in the authors' view will not be within s.146.[92]

Other limitations

In two cases, the value of the deemed gift should be nil. First, if someone without **8–90** an estate, e.g. trustees of a charitable trust,[93] satisfies a claim, s.29A should be harmless because the value of that person's estate will not have been diminished by the satisfaction of the claim; accordingly, the amount of the deemed chargeable free of tax specific gift will be nil.[94] Secondly, if the person satisfying the claim does so out of excluded property, s.3(2) will prevent the value of the excluded property being taken into account in determining the value of their estate after the satisfaction of the claim.

Residue: section 39

As was mentioned at para.8–66 and illustrated above, the value transferred by a **8–91** partly exempt transfer is always attributed to specific gifts first, and then to residue. This follows from s.39, which provides:

> "Such part only of the value transferred shall be attributed to gifts of residue or shares in residue as is not attributed under s.38 above to specific gifts."

Specific gifts made separately out of different funds: section 40

It may be that a person makes what might be called a "compound" transfer of value, **8–92** i.e. a transfer such that gifts are made out of different funds. This would be most likely to happen where immediately before he died a person was beneficially entitled to an interest in possession in one or more settlements, so that on his death he was regarded as making gifts out of both his free estate and the settlement(s). Section 40 takes account of this disconcerting possibility by prescribing that:

> "Where gifts taking effect on a transfer of value take effect separately out of different funds the preceding provisions of this Chapter shall be applied separately to the gifts taking effect out of each of those funds, with the necessary adjustments of the values and amounts referred to in those provisions."

Although s.40 gives rise to a number of questions to which there are no clear **8–93** answers, its basic purpose in providing that ss.36–39 are to be applied to each fund separately seems to be to prevent the rate at which free of tax gifts in a fund are

---

[92] It is perhaps worth noting that CTO Advanced Instruction Manual M.246, after commenting on how s.29A operates, stated: "The text at this point has been withheld under the Code of Practice on Access to Government Information", and adds: "Refer any general enquiry on the operation of I.H.T.A. 1984 s.29A to Controller's Division/your Group Leader (Sco)". There now appears to be no reference at all in the IHTM.

[93] IHTA 1984 s.3(3) recognises that trustees of a discretionary trust do not have an estate. See also para.25–90.

[94] See para.8–84 above.

grossed-up from being affected by the size and nature of gifts made out of one or more other funds to which that fund bears no relation as a matter of general law. Assume, for example, that on July 1, 2008, Adam, who had a nil cumulative total, died, leaving a free estate of, say, £750,000, out of which he left £350,000 free of tax to his son, residue to his widow, Eve, and that immediately before he died he had an interest in possession in a trust fund worth, say, £1,000,000, some of which passed to his children. The entitlements under the trust fund would, it is thought, have amounted to specific gifts subject to tax, with the result that two rounds of grossing-up would, in the absence of s.40, have been necessary. The tax due in respect of the £350,000 gift would thus have been increased and the residue passing to Eve reduced accordingly. The parliamentary draftsman, notwithstanding his previous efforts to safeguard HMRC's position, apparently felt that such "guilt by accidental association" should be prevented, probably so as to prevent a fund from not bearing tax properly attributable to it, and thus s.40 provides that ss.36–39 are to be applied to different funds separately. The extent to which this separate treatment is affected by "necessary adjustments", an exquisitely enigmatic qualification,[95] is, as will be seen below, unclear.[96]

8–94   As was mentioned above, s.40 raises a number of difficult questions. To begin with, there is some doubt as to when s.40 applies. Although the heading reads "Gifts made separately out of different funds", s.40 is in terms expressed to apply only where gifts (a) are made out of different funds, and (b) "take effect separately". Section 40 thus appears to assume that gifts made out of different funds may take effect other than "separately"; otherwise that word is otiose.[97] What the words "take effect separately" mean is uncertain (it is unfortunate that the legislation does not simply say "are made"). Presumably they refer to the manner in which the gifts take effect, and not the time at which they do so. Even then, it is not clear what test is to be applied. The test does *not* appear to be whether the gifts take effect under different instruments—otherwise a gift made under a testator's will out of his free estate and a gift made under a trust as a result of the exercise by him in his will of a testamentary power of appointment might not be regarded as taking effect separately. These, however, are just the kind of circumstances in which it is thought that s.40 is intended to operate. In the end, the only definite thing that can be said about the words, "take effect separately" in the first line of s.40 is that s.40 would read far more clearly without them.

8–95   The next question that arises in connection with s.40 concerns its operation. Section 40 first states quite categorically that where gifts take effect separately out of different funds, ss.36–39 are to be applied separately to those gifts and then adds that this application is to include the "necessary adjustments" of the values and the amounts referred to in those paragraphs. In analysing these two directions it seems clear that s.40 must be intended to yield a result other than that which would obtain if ss.36–39 were applied to the various gifts in question as though they had all been made out of one fund; otherwise s.40 is pointless. This, in turn, gives rise to two possibilities. The first is that the correct procedure is to apply ss.36–39 to the funds separately, making certain minor adjustments (see below), but doing no more. In most cases, given the fact that (a) IHT is charged at progressive rates, and (b) Ch.III will often involve grossing-up, this approach may be to the taxpayer's advantage, since it means that the value transferred attributable to the chargeable part of the transfer may be smaller than if

---

[95] This is the sort of formation to which one suspects the draftsman has recourse in such difficult circumstances: see "Legislative technique", *New Law Journal* (1980), p.293.

[96] For another view on these difficult provisions, see *British Tax Review* (1986), pp.29–33.

[97] Precisely what constitutes a "fund" for those purposes is also not free from doubt. If, for example, a settlement is divided into different funds, is each of those funds an IHTA 1984 s.40 fund or is the settlement just one big IHTA 1984 s.40 fund?

ss.36–39 were applied to the aggregate of the funds. To take an extreme example, assume that Nero has £1,200,000, a nil cumulative total, and that he wishes to leave £500,000 to his son after tax and the rest to his widow. Aside from s.40, there appears to be only one course of action open to Nero: he must leave £500,000 free of tax to his son. In the circumstances, this would gross-up to £616,666, so that the son would receive £500,000, HMRC £116,666, and the widow £583,334.

The position might be quite different, however, if Nero had, before March 22, 2006, created five settlements of £240,000 each under which he retained life interests. The terms of each settlement would be that on his death £100,000 of each settlement passed to his son free of tax, residue to his widow. The position is now changed for self settled settlements on interest in possession terms made post-March 22, 2006. On Nero's death under the old regime he would make a partly exempt transfer of value of £500,000, but, applying ss.36–39 to each settlement separately, each of the £100,000 gifts to the son would be grossed-up under s.38(3) at a nil rate (using the rates in effect on April 6, 2012), with the result that the total value transferred attributable to the aggregate gift of £500,000 to the son was only £500,000, not £616,666. The IHT due on this £500,000 would be £70,000, leaving £500,000 for the son and £630,000 for the widow, i.e. a saving of £46,666. It follows from the above example that the advantage gained will depend on how much of a taxpayer's nil rate band is unused. The best result will be if the entire nil rate band is unused. If, on the other hand, the nil rate band is completely exhausted, no advantage at all will be gained: in the above example, each of the five funds would be grossed up at 40 per cent.

This brings us to the second possibility, namely that in order to prevent such a result, in applying s.40 it is necessary to undertake three different sets of calculations. The first set of calculations is the set just undertaken; but now its purpose is not to find the amount of value transferred attributable to the chargeable part of the transfer, but to find out how that amount, once found, is to be apportioned among the chargeable gifts.

The second and third calculations are undertaken by way of "necessary adjustment" to the first set, which would otherwise yield the tax savings seen above. The second set of calculations involves determining how much of the value transferred would have been attributable to the chargeable part of the transfer, if s.40 had been ignored altogether. The purpose of this set of calculations is to safeguard HMRC's position. In the above example it would mean aggregating the five £100,000 free of tax gifts and grossing them up to £616,666, so that £616,666, not just £500,000, was attributable to the chargeable part of the transfer.

The third set of calculations involves apportioning the value transferred attributable to the chargeable part of the transfer among the various chargeable gifts on the basis of the amounts of value transferred attributed to those gifts under the first set of calculations. This would introduce an element of equity among taxpayers concerned.

In the authors' view it is unlikely that the direction in s.40 concerning "necessary adjustments" will be regarded as authorising all these sets of calculations, both because they seem to be unduly complicated and because they can hardly be regarded as mere "adjustments". Indeed, under this system the initial calculations undertaken on the footing that the funds fell to be treated separately would more properly be regarded as the adjustment. It seems, therefore, that the proper approach is the first, simpler one, even though it may result in certain tax savings. This does not deprive the direction to make necessary adjustments of all meaning, since adjustments may have been made where, for example, the aggregate of gifts made out of different funds exceeds an exemption limit even though the aggregate of the gifts made out of a particular fund does not do so.

8–96 HMRC now accept the first interpretation of s.40, i.e. that the grossing-up computation should proceed on the basis of looking at each fund separately and in isolation. In the IHTM this view was unequivocally stated[98]: the effect of s.40 is that ss.36–39A apply to different funds individually and the calculations required by those sections should therefore be made separately for each fund. The IHTM[99] set out a useful summary of what HMRC would consider to be "different funds" for the purposes of s.40:

- each will trust or settlement under which the deceased had an interest in possession;
- property passing by survivorship in joint tenancy or under a survivorship destination in the title to property;
- nominated property;
- where the free estate is expressly divided into different funds, e.g. a Spanish villa devolving under the lex situs or under a Spanish will, with the remainder of the assets being disposed of under an English will;
- occasionally where the estate includes an interest in a partnership (e.g. if the surviving partners take over the deceased's share by paying a sum to the personal representatives which is based on criteria which are lower than the value of the interest for IHT purposes, then the taxable difference accrues to the surviving partners under the terms of their partnership agreement and is thus a different fund, separate from the deceased's free estate); and
- each gift with reservation which is charged as part of the death estate must be treated as a different fund from the deceased's free estate.[100]

HMRC emphasises that the deceased's previous lifetime cumulative total, which is not a gift that takes effect as part of the transfer on death, is *not* a different fund.

8–97   One final point concerns the position where it is necessary under s.38(4) to gross-up at an assumed rate. Section 38(5) defines the "assumed rate" in terms of the value transferred "with respect to the transfer" in question. This gives some ground for saying that if it is necessary to gross-up at an "assumed rate" a single assumed rate is to be applied to all free of tax gifts out of all the funds involved. This approach, however, conflicts with the express direction in s.40 that ss.36–39 are to be applied to each fund separately, and is, in the authors' view, incorrect. Indeed, if it is correct, free of tax gifts which fell to be grossed-up under s.38(3) would also have to be grossed-up in aggregate, ignoring s.40, since s.38(3) also refers to "the transfer."

Reduction for tax

8–98   It may also become necessary to "abate", more properly, to reduce, gifts *as a result of* applying the Ch.III rules governing attribution of value.[101] This will be the case where after grossing-up one or more free of tax gifts the value transferred attributable

---

[98] HMRC Manuals IHTM26211.
[99] HMRC Manuals IHTM26212.
[100] A gift with reservation which is subsequently charged as part of a deceased's free estate is nevertheless treated as a different fund from the free estate for the purposes of s.40. However, where a gift with reservation was made within the cumulative period, it may instead be charged as a PET under the Double Charges Regulations (see paras 8–36 and following). Calculations under the Double Charges Regulations must reflect the fact that the charging of such a gift as PET could have an impact on the grossing up calculations which it would not have if it were to be treated as a gift with reservation.
[101] For the rule governing abatement, see para.8–77.

to specific gifts exceeds the value actually transferred by the transfer in question. Section 37(2) takes account of this possibility by providing that:

> "Where the value attributable in accordance with section 38 below, to specific gifts exceeds the value transferred the gifts shall be treated as reduced to the extent necessary to reduce their value to that of the value transferred."

It is to be noted that although s.37 is entitled "Abatement of gifts", s.37(2) does not itself make any reference to the term "abatement" as such, and it is clear there is nothing in the wording of s.37(2) to suggest that s.37(2) does not apply to inter vivos gifts. Accordingly the process prescribed under s.37(2) will be referred to as "reduction" rather than as "abatement", so that this point may be borne in mind. Where a reduction falls to be made under s.37(2), it is provided that this reduction should be made:

> " . . . in the order in which, under the terms of the relevant disposition or any rule of law, it would fall to be made on a distribution of assets."

Where the disposition is made by will, the reduction will thus be made (subject to any provision to the contrary in the will) out of property in the order prescribed by s.34(3) of the Administration of Estates Act 1925 Pt II of Sch.1, i.e. out of:

> "1. Property of the deceased undisposed of by will, subject to the retention thereout of a fund sufficient to meet any pecuniary legacies.
> 2. Property of the deceased not specifically devised or bequeathed but included (either by a specific or general description) in a residuary gift, subject to the retention out of such property of a fund sufficient to meet any pecuniary legacies, so far as not provided for as aforesaid.
> 3. Property of the deceased specifically appropriated or devised or bequeathed (either by a specific or general description) for the payment of debts.
> 4. Property of the deceased charged with, or devised or bequeathed (either by a specific or general description) subject to a charge for the payment of debts.
> 5. The fund, if any retained to meet pecuniary legacies.
> 6. Property specifically devised or bequeathed, rateably according to value.
> 7. Property appointed by will under a general power, including the statutory power to dispose of entailed interests, rateably according to value.
> 8. The following provisions shall also apply—
> (a) The order of application may be varied by the will of the deceased.
> (b) . . . "[102]

Assume that Plato's net estate at the time of his death was £400,000, that he gave £80,000 and £100,000 in pecuniary legacies to his son and daughter respectively and £150,000 to his widow (so that no abatement was necessary as a matter of general law), and that his IHT cumulative total was £325,000. In that case the £180,000 given to the children would be grossed-up at 40 per cent to £300,000, with the result that the value attributable to all the specific gifts totals:

$$\begin{array}{r} £300,000 \\ \underline{£150,000} \\ £450,000 \end{array}$$

Since this figure exceeds the value transferred, it would be necessary under s.37(2) to reduce the aggregate value of the gifts to £400,000. This would be done in two stages as follows:

---

[102] Words omitted repealed by the F(No.2)A 1983 s.16(4) Sch.2 Pt II in relation to deaths on or after July 26, 1983.

(1) Apportion £300,000 between son and daughter:

Son $\dfrac{4}{9} \times £300,000 = £133,333.33$

Daughter $\dfrac{5}{9} \times £300,000 = £166,666.67$

(2) Apportion £400,000 among son, daughter and widow:

Son $\dfrac{133,333}{450,000} \times £400,000 = £118,518$

Daughter $\dfrac{166,667}{450,000} \times £400,000 = £148,148$

Widow $\dfrac{150,000}{450,000} \times £400,000 = \dfrac{£133,334}{£400,000}$

The amount of the value transferred attributable to the chargeable portion of the transfer would thus have been £266,666 (£118,518 + £148,148) and the amount attributable to the exempt portion would have been £133,334, making the required total £400,000.

Had the gift to the widow been of residue, there would have been no reduction in tax. This follows from the fact that the £300,000 attributable to the specific gifts would not have exceeded the £400,000 value, transferred on Plato's death; therefore s.37(2) would not have come into operation. The value transferred would have been attributed first to specific gifts and then to residue.[103] In the circumstances, this would have meant that only £100,000 of the value transferred was attributable to the gift to the widow.

Abatement and reduction

8–99 It may be that gifts must be both abated and reduced. Assume that Aristotle died with a net estate of £240,000, and that he left £50,000 to his son free of tax and £250,000 to his widow. Plainly, the gift to the son and widow would have to be abated, as follows:

gift to son $\dfrac{50,000}{300,000} \times £240,000 = £40,000$

gift to widow $\dfrac{250,000}{300,000} \times £240,000 = £200,000$

Aristotle, a generous man, had a cumulative total of £350,000. The abated gift of £40,000 to the son must therefore be grossed-up to £66,667, and then the gifts to the son and widow will need to be reduced as follows:

103 IHTA 1984 s.39.

376

$$\text{gift to son} \qquad \frac{66,667}{266,667} \times £240,000 = £60,000$$

$$\text{gift to widow} \qquad \frac{200,000}{266,667} \times £240,000 = £180,000$$

$$£240,000$$

Business and agricultural relief: section 39A

It was thought that there was an anomaly in the existing legislation where an individual made a partly exempt transfer and all or some of the value transferred by that transfer was attributable to the value of property which qualified for agricultural or business relief. The Finance Act 1986 appeared to confirm that this was the case by adding to the relevant provisions a new section designed to make the position what, in fairness both to taxpayers and HMRC, it should have been all along. **8–100**

The apparent anomaly is best shown by an example.[104] Assume that Frank, who has made no previous chargeable transfers, dies owning property worth £1,200,000, £750,000 of which is attributable to business property which qualifies for 50 per cent business relief. In his will he makes a specific gift of the non-business property and one third of the business property to his widow and leaves the residue of his estate to his children. The transfer would, under the old rules, appear to have been entirely exempt. The reasoning was as follows. The transfer was a partly exempt one, because some of the property passed to an exempt person (the widow) while the rest of the property passed to chargeable persons (the children). That being the case the special provisions in Ch.III would have applied. Although the effect of agricultural relief and business relief was to reduce the value transferred by the transfer of value in question, there was nothing in the legislation to the effect that where a specific gift was made out of property qualifying for agricultural or business relief that relief was to be taken into account in determining the value of that gift. There thus appeared to be a double standard which could work for or against the taxpayer.

Returning to the above example, the value transferred by Frank, after business relief, was £825,000. The value of the specific gifts made by him, it was argued, was £700,000, i.e. £450,000 in non-business property and one-third of his business property of £250,000. That being the case, it was argued, all of the value transferred fell to be attributed to the transfer to his widow. That transfer was, of course, exempt, with the result that property worth £500,000 passed free of IHT to the children, i.e. with a full reduction of 50 per cent business relief bringing the value within the nil rate band. If, on the other hand, Frank had adopted a different course and made a specific gift of his non-business assets to his children, leaving the residue of his estate to his widow, the rules would have worked against the family, because £450,000 of the value transferred would have been attributed to the gift to the children, so that business relief was wasted.

The Finance Act 1986 remedied this unhealthy situation by inserting a new section, s.39A, the effect of which is as follows. First, s.39A(2) provides a new rule for determining the value of specific gifts and gifts of residue or shares of residue where

[104] See also *IRC v Russell* [1988] S.T.C. 195, discussed at para.8–147.

any part of the value transferred by a partly exempt transfer qualifies for agricultural or business relief. In such a case the value of specific gifts of relevant business property or agricultural property is "to be their value as reduced" by the relief in question. The drafting thus leaves something to be desired, because both the reliefs in question operate only to reduce the value transferred by a transfer, i.e. they do not reduce the value of the property which is the subject-matter of the transfer in question.

It may be, of course, that other specific gifts are involved, i.e. gifts not qualifying for relief. In such a case, s.39A(3) provides that their value is taken to be the "appropriate fraction" of their face value. The numerator of this fraction is the value transferred by the transfer (as reduced by agricultural or business relief), less the value of the specified gifts of relievable property also as reduced by agricultural or business relief. The denominator is the value transferred by the transfer (before any reduction for agricultural or business relief), less the value of any specific gift of relievable property at its value before reduction.[105] It should be noted that, where there are gifts out of different funds, s.39A has to be applied separately to each fund.

If grossing-up is necessary, the gift is grossed up at its reduced value.

HMRC's approach

8–101   HMRC recommends that the following six steps are followed to arrive at the value of the estate where s.39A applies[106]:

(1) allow business and agricultural relief as normal to establish the value transferred by the transfer of value, excluding any property devolving from a different fund;

(2) identify any specific gift of relievable property and use its value after relief;

(3) if there is any other relievable property in the free estate, reduce all other specific gifts by the fraction set out in s.39A(4) and use their reduced values;

(4) if grossing-up is necessary, gross-up the reduced value;

(5) calculate the residue using the reduced values; and

(6) calculate the extent to which the free estate is chargeable by deducting the total of the reduced values of the exempt specific and residuary gifts from the value transferred ascertained in (1) above.

EXAMPLE

8–102   The following example (based on an example given in the Inheritance Tax Manual)[107] shows how this works:

Henry dies in January 2012 with a free estate worth £1,800,000 and a lifetime cumulative total of £200,000. Henry also had an interest in possession in his father's will trust comprising quoted securities worth £500,000 on Henry's death. Henry's free estate comprised shares in his own company worth £600,000 and qualifying for 100 per

---

[105] If all the relievable property is specifically given and therefore gets full relief under s.39A(2), the numerator and denominator of the fraction are the same so there will be no reduction of the value of any other gifts.

[106] HMRC Manuals IHTM26104.

[107] HMRC Manuals IHTM26158.

cent business relief, land which he let to his company worth £400,000 and qualifying for 50 per cent business relief, a house and chattels worth £200,000 and other property worth £600,000. In his will Henry gave the land let to the company to his son subject to tax, the house and chattels to his widow, pecuniary legacies free of tax of £300,000 to each of his widow and his daughter, with the residue to be divided as to half to his widow and as to the other half equally to his son and daughter.

Step 1—allow business and agricultural relief as normal

Value of the estate		£1,800,000
Less business relief		
On unquoted shares at 100%	(£600,000)	
On land at 50%	(£200,000)	
		(£800,000)
Value transferred		£1,000,000

Step 2—identify any specific gift of relievable property:

Gift of land to the son—value after relief   £200,000

Step 3—if there is any other relievable property in the free estate, reduce all other specific gifts by the s.39A(4) fraction. As there is other relievable property in this example, the specific gifts to the widow and the daughter have to be reduced. The fraction is based solely on the property comprised in the free estate (excluding the settled property) and ignoring the lifetime cumulative total:

$$\frac{850,000 \quad \text{(i)}}{1,400,000 \quad \text{(ii)}}$$

(i) = Reduced value of the free estate (£1,000,000) less the reduced value of the specific gift (£200,000)

(ii) = Unreduced value of the free estate (£1,800,000) less the unreduced value of the specific gift (£400,000)

Accordingly, the reduced values are:

Gifts to the widow (house, chattels, legacy)

$$£500,000 \quad \times \quad \frac{800,000}{1,400,000} \quad = \quad £285,714$$

Legacy to the daughter

$$£300,000 \quad \times \quad \frac{800,000}{1,400,000} \quad = \quad £171,429$$

Step 4—gross-up the reduced value

(a)   gross-up the free of tax gift to the daughter:

Value of gift (as reduced)	£171,429
Add cumulation	£200,000
Balance	£371,429
5/3 of above balance	£77,381
Plus threshold	£325,000
Grossed up value of legacy	£202,381

(b)   make an initial determination of the chargeable estate:

Grossed up gift to daughter	£202,381
Gift to son subject to tax	£200,000
Exempt specific gifts	£285,714
Total specific gifts	£688,095
Total free estate	£1,000,000
Less total specific gifts	(£688,095)
Residue	£311,905
half exempt	£155,953
half chargeable	£155,952

The chargeable free estate is:

£202,381 + £200,000 + £155,952	=	£558,333

(c)   re-gross the chargeable free of tax specific gifts:

Lifetime cumulation	£200,000
Chargeable free estate	£558,333
Balance	£758,333
Tax on that value	£173,333
Less tax on lifetime transfer death rates	Nil
Tax on death estate	£173,333
Chargeable free estate net of tax	£385,000

The gross equivalent of the specific gift of £171,429 is:

$$£171,429 \times \frac{558,333}{385,000} \quad = \quad £248,609$$

Step 5—calculate the residue using the reduced values:

Value of the estate	£1,000,000
Less grossed up value of all chargeable specific gifts	(£248,609)
Less specific gift to son	(£200,000)
Less exempt gifts	(£285,714)
Residue	£265,677
half exempt	£132,839
half chargeable	£132,838

Step 6—calculate the extent to which the free estate is chargeable:

Value of the estate	£1,000,000
Less exempt specific gift to widow	(£285,714)
Less exempt residuary gift to widow	(£132,839)
Chargeable estate	£581,447
Total chargeable estate with lifetime cumulative total of £200,000 to be taken into account:	
Free estate	£581,447
Settled property	£500,000
Total	£1,081,447
Plus lifetime cumulative total	200,000
Total subject to IHT	£1,281,447

Where there are chargeable gifts which exceed the threshold and the residue is wholly exempt, it will be necessary to consider the nature and value of the whole estate simply to establish the s.39A(4) fraction.

HMRC had previously stated at page M26105 of the Inheritance Tax Manual that "sensible discretion" should be exercised when examining such cases, particularly in smaller estates or in cases where the amount chargeable or the property qualifying for relief is small in relation to the size of the estate. This text has since been removed from the manual, which states instead "This text has been withheld because of exemptions in the Freedom of Information Act 2000". It is unclear whether the view HMRC previously stated, that it would exercise sensible discretion in these cases and not examine them in unnecessary detail, still applies.

Quick succession relief

8–103 Under this relief the tax chargeable is reduced by a specified percentage.[108] This relief therefore falls to be taken into account after applying the Ch.III provisions and after calculating any tax due. Strictly speaking, it would therefore be more logical to consider it after discussing how tax on a partly exempt transfer is calculated (the next subject for discussion) but it is convenient to deal with it here with the other reliefs. It is thought that once the part of the value transferred attributable to the chargeable portion of the transfer has been found under Ch.III and the amount of tax chargeable has been ascertained, effect is given to this relief by reducing by the appropriate percentage so much of the tax as may be attributable to the value of property qualifying for this relief.[109]

Calculation of tax

8–104 Once the portion of the value transferred which is attributable to the chargeable part of the transfer has been found the next step is to calculate the IHT due on that portion.

---

[108] See paras 8–32 and following.

[109] The alternative view is that the relief is taken into account in determining the rate at which free of tax gifts are grossed-up.

Here, subject to one (and possibly a second) qualification, the position is straightforward,[110] tax being charged at the relevant lifetime or death rates on the value transferred attributable to the chargeable part of the transfer. In particular, it is to be noted that there is no question of tax being charged at the assumed rate. The qualifications arise in the unusual case where the transfer is an actual one.[111] In such cases it is important to keep in mind that the effect of applying Ch.III is only to find how much of the value transferred is attributable to the chargeable part of the transfer and how much of the value transferred is attributable to the part exempted under the exemptions taken into account under Ch.III. It follows from this that once the value transferred attributable under Ch.III to the chargeable part of the transfer has been found at least one, and perhaps two, further steps may be necessary before it is possible to calculate the tax due.

Exemptions outside Chapter III

8–105   The first additional step that may be necessary is to reduce the value transferred attributable under Ch.III to the chargeable part of the transfer by any exemptions (e.g. the annual exemption) not taken into account under Ch.III that may be available to the transferor.[112] This follows from the fact that IHT is charged on the value transferred by a chargeable transfer, and that value transferred is arrived at only after applying *all* available exemptions.[113]

8–106   The second step that might be thought to be necessary before tax can be calculated involves the grossing-up of so much of the value transferred of the transfer in question as remains after the application of all available exemptions.[114] At first glance it appears strange that any further grossing-up should be necessary, but regard must be had to the fact that any grossing-up effected under the provisions of Ch.III is effected because of those provisions, which operate quite independently of the provisions requiring grossing-up generally when the transferor bears the tax. Chapter III, the argument would run, operates only to determine how much of the value transferred by a partly exempt transfer is exempt after the application of certain exemptions; it therefore might be necessary where the transferor is to bear the IHT to take further steps to determine the value transferred by the chargeable transfer comprised by that partly exempt transfer.

In the authors' view this argument is misconceived and no further grossing-up should be necessary. The requirement to gross-up where a transferor bears the IHT on an actual transfer of value derives from the interaction of two provisions—s.3(1) and s.5(4). The effect of the interaction of these two provisions is to bring into account in

---

[110] If the transfer is a notional one made under a s.52(1) de facto grossing up may be necessary; see para.6–34.

[111] Or a notional one made under IHTA 1984 s.94(1); this would be extremely rare.

[112] It is thought that these exemptions are brought in at this stage and not before applying Ch.III since the purpose of applying Ch.III is to find what part of the value transferred is not attributable to the Ch.III exemptions. The part of the value transferred not so attributable falls to be reduced by any other available exemptions.

[113] See para.6–25.

[114] If the transfer is made under IHTA 1984 s.52(1), grossing up will be mandatory. If the transfer is made under IHTA 1984 s.94(1) there will be de facto grossing up; see para.6–34.

determining the value transferred by a chargeable transfer any diminution occasioned in the value of the transferor's estate by his undertaking to bear all or some of the IHT on that transfer. This is done by grossing-up the transfer. Where the provisions of Ch.III apply to an actual transfer, precisely the same result obtains, and for precisely the same reason: because the transferor bears the tax on a gift, that gift is grossed-up. That being the case, the lHT borne by the transferor is taken into account in computing the value transferred by the transfer in question, and therefore there should be no question of any further grossing-up under s.3(1); such further grossing-up would involve taking into account twice the lHT to be borne by the transferor, and that cannot have been intended.

With regard to specific free of tax gifts allowance is made for the relief by reducing the value of those gifts by the amount required to produce quick succession relief before grossing up. To provide an example of this, suppose that Jane dies having used up her nil rate band but leaves in her will specific free of tax legacies of £200,000 to chargeable beneficiaries and her residue wholly to charity. There is quick succession relief of £20,000 which is the equivalent to the tax at 40 per cent on £50,000:

Legacies	£200,000
Less "gross" sum of quick succession relief	(£50,000)
Balance	£150,000
Grossed-up balance (i.e. × 5/3)	£250,000
Plus "gross" sum of quick succession relief	£50,000
Grossed up legacies	£300,000

Allocation of burden of tax[115]

8–107   Once the IHT due in respect of a partly exempt transfer has been calculated the next, and last, step is to determine how that tax is to be borne. The rules relating to burden of tax generally are discussed at paras 29–84 and following. These general rules are subject to two qualifications laid down by s.41 which provides that:

> "Notwithstanding the terms of any disposition—
> (a) none of the tax on the value transferred shall fall on any specific gift if or to the extent that the transfer is exempt with respect to the gift; and
> (b) none of the tax attributable to the value of property comprised in residue shall fall on any gift of a share of residue if or to the extent that the transfer is exempt with respect to the gift."

Before considering the effect of these rules, it is important to bear in mind that the preceding process of attributing the value transferred was concerned solely with determining what part of the value transferred was attributable to the chargeable gifts comprised in the transfer: in particular, the process of attributing value did not in itself in any way affect the actual size of any gift in the hands of the donees. What will affect the size of the gifts in their hands is how the tax on the respective gifts is borne. The

---

[115] See also *British Tax Review* (1986), pp.24–35.

rules governing the allocation of the burden of the tax set out in s.41 expressly override the terms of the deceased's will or other relevant disposition.

The effect of s.41 is that the tax will be borne as follows:

(1) The tax on any subject to tax specific gifts is deducted from these gifts; this follows from the terms of the disposition in question, under which these gifts are directed either expressly or impliedly to bear their own tax.

(2) Any exempt specific gift is paid gross, i.e. without deduction of tax.

(3) Any specific chargeable free of tax gift is also paid gross, without deduction of tax. The tax on such gifts is paid out of residue, so that such gifts do not bear their own tax. As will be seen below, it is important, to bear this in mind from a planning standpoint, since it means that residue may be severely reduced or even eliminated altogether, even where the residue is exempt (in whole or in part).

(4) At this point, all that remains is the residue. The tax due in respect of the free of tax specific gifts is deducted, and the residue divided according to the terms of the disposition. The tax due in respect of the chargeable part of the residue is then borne by that part, and this is so despite any provisions to the contrary in the will.

EXAMPLE 9

Assume that Socrates has made the following gifts[116] (with a cumulative total of £252,000), to which the following amounts of the value transferred are attributable:

Gift	Amount of value transferred attributable		
	Chargeable	Exempt	Total
	£	£	£
£150,000 free of tax to boys	232,601		
£150,000 subject to tax to daughter	150,000		
£50,000 subject to tax to stepdaughter	50,000		
£100,000 to charity		100,000	
Half residue to brother	233,700		
Half residue to wife		233,699	
	667,805 +	332,195 =	1,000,000

The tax on £666,301 would have been:

	£
252,000 – 325,000 @ 0% =	0
325,000 – 918,301 @ 40% =	237,320
	237,320

The tax would have been apportioned among the gifts as follows:

[116] See Example 8 above at para.8–82.

384

Gift	Value attributable to gift	Tax
£150,000 free of tax to boys	$\dfrac{232,601}{666,301} \times 237,320$	= £82,847
£150,000 subject to tax to daughter	$\dfrac{150,000}{666,301} \times 237,320$	= £53,426
£50,000 subject to tax to stepdaughter	$\dfrac{50,000}{666,301} \times 237,320$	= £17,809
£233,700 residue to brother	$\dfrac{233,700}{666,301} \times 237,320$	= £83,238

Total Tax £237,320

The tax would have been borne as follows:

1. The tax on the subject to tax gifts to the girls would have been borne by those gifts, so that, after tax, the girls would have been entitled to:

    daughter
    £150,000
    − 53,426
    £96,574

    stepdaughter
    £50,000
    − 17,809
    £32,191

2. The gift to charity was exempt, so the charity would have received £100,000.
3. The gifts to the boys were free of tax, so they would have been entitled to £150,000. At this point £550,000 would have remained in the estate. The tax on the free of tax gift would have been borne by this, leaving:

    £550,000
    − 82,847
    £467,153

4. This remaining residue of £467,153 would have been divided equally, £233,576 each, between the brother and widow. The £83,238 in tax due in respect of the brother's share would have been borne by his share, leaving him:

    £233,576
    − 83,238
    £150,338

Planning

Probably the most obvious point that occurs to any adviser when considering the **8–108** provisions affecting partly exempt transfers is that it is in the best interests of his own sanity to advise his clients not to make any such partly exempt transfers. In practice, however, partly exempt transfers will be common, and the best way to avoid problems will be to make sure that all gifts bear their own tax. As was seen above, the tax charged on free of tax gifts must be borne by residue, and this may result in residue being depleted or even exhausted. Assume, for example, that Hercules died leaving an estate of £100,000, £60,000 of which was to pass free of tax to his son, residue to his widow. If Hercules' nil rate band was exhausted, the gift to the son would be grossed-up to £100,000 with the result that the entire value transferred would be attributable to the chargeable gift to the son. The £40,000 due on this would be found out of residue, with the result that (a) nothing would be left for the widow, and (b) a transfer which appeared to be partly exempt turns out to be wholly chargeable.[117] Unfortunately, testators are often reluctant to make subject to tax gifts because there is an element of uncertainty about how much the donee will actually receive from such a gift (the tax rates may change, among other things). Where a testator wishes to make one or more free of tax gifts and to leave residue to his widow it will thus normally be wise to ensure that a specific free of tax gift of an appropriate amount is also made to the widow in addition to residue.

It may be that a testator wishes to divide his residue after payment of tax equally (or in some other fixed proportions) between chargeable and exempt persons. Given the Ch.III rules, it is hard to see how this can be done otherwise than by defining the shares in terms of such amount as after payment of tax would leave shares of equal value. This should yield the desired result, and, so long as the whole of the value transferred by the deceased on his death fell within one IHT band, so that a single rate applies, the arithmetic is not too daunting. Assume, for example, that the deceased's nil rate band is exhausted, and that under his will what remained of residue after payment of tax was to pass to his widow and son in equal shares. In such a case, the sums would be worked out by determining the proportions in which the residue was to be divided among HMRC, the son and the widow.

To begin with, it is clear that the *chargeable* residue will be divided between HMRC and the son in the ratio of 40 to 60. Secondly, it is equally clear that, whatever the amount of chargeable residue to which the son may be entitled, the widow will be entitled to an equal amount out of exempt residue; indeed, that amount will be the exempt part of the residue. Thus, HMRC, the son and the widow will be entitled to share the residue in the ratio 40:60:60.

If, for example, the residue was £280,000, the respective entitlements would be:

$$\text{Revenue} \quad \frac{40}{160} \times £280,000 = £70,000$$

$$\text{Son} \quad \frac{60}{160} \times £280,000 = £105,000$$

$$\text{Widow} \quad \frac{60}{160} \times £280,000 = £105,000$$

The chargeable residue would thus have been £175,000, of which 40 per cent, £70,000, would have gone to HMRC. The remaining £210,000 would have been divided equally, £105,000 each, between the son and the widow.[118]

[117] In such a case an application under the Inheritance (Provision for Family and Dependants) Act 1975 may be in order.

[118] This very neat solution was provided by Patrick Eyre, Barrister.

If the transferor's cumulative total is such that tax is charged at more than one rate, computational difficulties may arise. That being the case, proportional gifts after payment of tax, intentionally or inadvertently (see below), should be assiduously avoided.

Drafting

When drafting wills, it is important to make sure that the burden of tax falls in the **8–109** intended way. Section 41 precludes the burden of tax falling on exempt specific gifts at all, and also precludes tax attributable to a chargeable share of residue falling on any exempt share of residue. It does not preclude tax attributable to chargeable specific gifts falling on exempt shares of residue.[119] A will should therefore be drafted in such a way as (a) makes clear exactly how tax is to be borne, and (b) is not rendered ineffective for that purpose by s.41.

Regard should also be had to the burden of tax when drafting instruments of variation: see for instance *Lake v Lake*.[120] If the instrument makes no provision for the tax liability the general rules will apply. For instance, if the instrument carves a specific legacy out of residue, tax on that legacy will (in the absence of any provision to the contrary) fall on the remaining residue.

The *Benham* saga

In the common case where, say, residue has been left partly to charity and partly to **8–110** non exempt beneficiaries, the perceived correct procedure before the decision in *Re Benham's Will Trusts; Lockhart v Harker, Read and the Royal National Lifeboat Institution*[121] was to divide the "gross" residue between the residuary beneficiaries and then to deduct the full amount of IHT payable in respect of the non exempt residue from the non exempt beneficiaries' share. The result would be that the charity (or other exempt beneficiary) would receive their share of residue without any deduction of IHT payable in respect of the non-exempt share of residue. In effect, therefore, the charity (or exempt beneficiary) would often receive a quite significantly larger distribution than the non exempt beneficiary, even though on the face of the will the residue was shared equally between them. This common practice was seemingly reversed by the decision in *Re Benham* which caused enormous consternation at the time.

The *Benham* case

The facts in *Re Benham* were that the testator left his residuary estate on the **8–111** following terms:

(a) upon trust to pay debts, funeral and testamentary expenses; and

[119] Because of the provisions of Ch.III this will not prejudice HMRC.
[120] *Lake v Lake* [1989] S.T.C. 865 (discussed at para.8–173 below).
[121] *Re Benham's Will Trusts; Lockhart v Harker, Read and the Royal National Lifeboat Institution* [1995] S.T.C. 210.

(b) after such payment "to pay the same to those beneficiaries as are living at my death and who are listed in List A and List B hereunder written in such proportions as will bring about the result that the aforesaid beneficiaries named in List A shall receive 3.2 times as much as the aforesaid beneficiaries named in List B and in each case for their own absolute and beneficial use and disposal".

List A contained one charity and a number of non-charitable beneficiaries; and List B contained a number of charities and non-charitable beneficiaries.

By an originating summons, the executor sought, inter alia, the opinion of the court on the following issues:

(1) whether the non-charitable beneficiaries received their respective shares subject to IHT, which would mean that they would receive less than the charities;

(2) whether the non-charitable beneficiaries should have their respective shares grossed up, so that they received the same net sum as the charities; or

(3) whether the IHT was paid as part of the testamentary expenses under cl.3(A), and the balance was distributed equally between the non-charitable beneficiaries and the charities.

The deputy judge agreed that the third possibility was precluded by s.41. However, he did not agree that the charities should receive more than the non-charitable beneficiaries. The "plain intention of the testatrix" was that each beneficiary, whether charitable or non-charitable, should receive the same as the other beneficiaries on the relevant list. That result, he concluded, was consistent with the express terms of the will and s.41. Thus, he considered that the non-charitable beneficiaries' shares should be grossed up.[122] The decision was not appealed.

Following this decision, advisers were in an unenviable position; if they ignored the decision in *Re Benham* (on the grounds that the facts could be distinguished) the exempt beneficiary would benefit from the "gross" distribution to them before deduction of IHT, but they were in danger of the non-exempt beneficiary claiming that the estate had not been distributed correctly and that they were owed more, i.e. that they should benefit from the *Re Benham* "net" distribution. Without agreement between all the residuary beneficiaries the executors and their advisers would be at risk whichever way they chose to distribute the estate unless they first obtained the court's approval. Interestingly, HMRC's approach was generally to follow the pre *Benham* approach even though this resulted in less tax being payable.

The effect of the approach adopted in *Re Benham* is best shown by an example (and see para.8–108 above). Assume a testator, with no available nil rate band, leaves an estate worth £1,000,000. Under his will the residue, after payment of funeral and testamentary expenses and any debts, is left equally between his sister and a charity. The sister's half of the residue is subject to IHT at 40 per cent and needs to be grossed up. The following formula may be applied:

---

[122] The deputy judge referred approvingly to the analysis in the third edition of this book.

	£
Total residuary estate	1,000,000

If A is the gross non-exempt residue:

A × 0.4 = shares taken in tax
A × 0.6 = sister's share after tax
A × 0.6 = charity's share
1.6A = 1,000,000

$$A = \frac{1,000,000}{1.6} = \quad 625,000$$

Therefore:

IHT = £625,000 × 40 per cent =	250,000
Net residue for distribution =	
£1,000,000 − £250,000 =	750,000
To be divided:	
One-half to charity	375,000
One-half to sister	375,000

The *Ratcliffe* case

Thankfully, the chaos caused by *Re Benham* was for the most part remedied by **8–112** Blackburne J. in *Re Ratcliffe (Deceased) Holmes v John McMullan*.[123] The facts in *Re Ratcliffe* were that the testator left his residuary estate on the usual trusts for sale, conversion and payment of debts and expenses and subject thereto to be divided as to one-half between the first and second defendants (who were the deceased's cousins) and as to the other half in trust for the third, fourth, fifth and sixth defendants (all charities). The case was an application for a declaration as to the true construction of the deceased's will. The question arising for decision was whether or not the tax should be paid out of residue as a testamentary expense, and the balance then distributed in equal net shares between the cousins and the charities; or whether the charge to tax fell wholly on the cousins' shares and the charities received their shares gross.

Blackburne J. held that, on the true construction of the will, it was the testatrix's intention that the cousins' shares should bear the tax and the charities' shares should be received gross without any deduction of tax. The IHT attributable to the cousins' shares was part of the deceased's gift to them and as such was part of her disposable residue. He declined to follow *Re Benham* stating that:

> "If I had thought that *Re Benham's Will Trusts* laid down some principle, then, unless convinced that it was wrong, I would have felt that I should follow it. I am not able to find that it does and, accordingly, I do not feel bound to follow it."

Blackburne J. stated that if a testator wished to achieve a *Re Benham* distribution this could still be achieved but much clearer wording than the "common form wording" would have to be included in the will.

Where there are conflicting first instance judgements the leading authority on the proper approach is provided by Denning J. in *Minister of Pensions v Higham*[124]:

> "Where there are two conflicting decisions . . . the later decision is to be preferred, if it is reached after full consideration of the earlier decision."

[123] *Re Ratcliffe (Deceased) Holmes v John McMullan* [1999] S.T.C. 262.
[124] *Minister of Pensions v Higham* (1948) 2 K.B. 153.

That ruling was subsequently applied by Nourse J. in *Colchester Estates (Cardiff) v Carlton Industries Plc.*[125] Blackburne J. having given full consideration to *Re Benham, Re Ratcliffe* is to be preferred.

The effect of the approach adopted in *Re Ratcliffe* is best shown by an example. Assuming the same facts as at para.8–111 above:

	£
Total residuary estate	1,000,000
Less exempt half to pass to charity free of tax	(500,000)
Balance	500,000
Sister's half of residue, subject to tax	500,000
Less IHT on £500,000.00 @ 40 per cent	(200,000)
Sister's net share of residue	300,000

Although the net shares are unequal, £50,000 less IHT is payable than if the *Re Benham* calculation is used to give the sister and the charity equal net shares.

Conclusion

8–113   It is generally accepted that *Re Ratcliffe* was correctly decided. HMRC has confirmed that it will use the *Ratcliffe* style calculation in all cases unless specific wording appears in the will to rebut that approach.

Some testators, however, may still wish their residuary estate to be distributed so that the exempt and the non-exempt beneficiaries receive equal net shares. Blackburne J. agreed that this could be achieved but much clearer wording than the "common form wording" would have to be included in the will. An example of the sort of clause which would achieve a *Benham* type division but still fulfil the conditions of s.41 would be along the lines of the following:

> " . . . shall divide my estate into x shares such that each share which bears inheritance tax shall be equal in size after payment of inheritance tax to any share which is free of inheritance tax . . . "

In all estates where a common form of wording is adopted in the will for a proportionate division of the residue, the principle laid down in *Re Ratcliffe* is that the exempt beneficiaries should receive their share gross without any deduction of tax. If executors calculate the division of residue incorrectly (e.g. on a *Benham* type of net division) and fail to distribute the residuary estate in the proper proportions, they will be personally liable to the exempt beneficiaries for any overpayment of IHT that they cannot recover from HMRC, or any overpayment of residue that they cannot recover from a non-exempt beneficiary.

If there is any doubt as to whether the *Benham* or the *Ratcliffe* method of division applies, executors would be well advised to reserve sufficient funds from the residue

---

[125] *Colchester Estates (Cardiff) v Carlton Industries Plc* (1986) 1 Ch. 80.

until the position is resolved (e.g. through consent of all the adult beneficiaries or by application to the court) and to obtain indemnities from all the adult beneficiaries.

POSTHUMOUS ARRANGEMENTS

X. INTRODUCTION

The legislation contains a number of provisions under which transactions carried out **8–114** after a person's death can affect the tax that would otherwise have been payable on his death. The provisions, which confer on taxpayers unusual planning opportunities, are concerned with the following:

- variations;
- disclaimers;
- two year discretionary will trusts;
- precatory trusts;
- orders under the Inheritance (Provision for Family and Dependants) Act 1975; and
- legitim.

Each of these will be considered in turn below. Note also that certain posthumous elections concerning the value which is to be attributed to property comprised in a person's estate immediately before he died may affect the amount of tax due on his death; see paras 25–109 and following.[126] Note also that posthumous arrangements involving the transferable nil rate band are also possible and are discussed at paras 4–28 and following.

XI. VARIATIONS

Section 142(1) provides relief to certain variations of dispositions of property made **8–115** by a person on his death:

"(1) Where within the period of two years after a person's death—
(a) any of the dispositions (whether effected by will, under the law relating to intestacy or otherwise) of the property comprised in his estate immediately before his death are varied, or
(b) the benefit conferred by any of those dispositions is disclaimed,
by an instrument in writing made by the persons or any of the persons who benefit or would benefit under the dispositions, this Act shall apply as if the variation had been effected by the deceased or, as the case may be, the disclaimed benefit had never been conferred."

It will be helpful to begin by considering the circumstances in which this relief is intended to operate. When a person dies, his estate may pass under his will or intestacy in a way that is not in the best interests of those concerned, and they may therefore wish to rearrange matters. They could easily do this, of course, by making appropriate

---

[126] See also the election which a surviving spouse or civil partner can make under an intestacy, discussed at para.2–112, and the possibility of retrospective exemption on heritage property, discussed at para.27–24.

dispositions. But, in the absence of provision to the contrary, such dispositions might give rise to an IHT charge. The result would be that there would be two charges: one on the deceased's death, and one on the making of the subsequent "corrective" disposition. Had, on the other hand, the property passed on the deceased's death directly to the person to whom it passes as a result of the disposition, there would have been but one charge. The Finance Act 1975 made provision to relieve such dispositions from this possible double charge by giving relief to "deeds of family arrangement and other similar instruments". Section 68(1) of the Finance Act 1978 (now s.142) broadened and simplified the relief, and eliminated many of the problems of interpretation, including precisely what constituted a "deed of family arrangement or other similar instrument".

Favoured treatment and planning

8–116   A variation coming within s.142(1) qualifies for two kinds of special statutory treatment. First, by s.17(a), a s.142 variation is relieved from being a transfer of value. Thus, a s.142 variation will not itself result in the person or persons effecting it sustaining a charge to IHT in respect of the disposition made by the variation. This is obviously important, because it removes any threshold IHT disincentive to making a variation. Secondly, s.142(1) provides that the one or more dispositions effected by a s.142 variation are to be treated as having been effected by the deceased. This is enormously important, because it opens up a wide number of tax planning possibilities which the authors think it will be helpful to mention at the outset so that the reader will have them in mind when considering the detailed rules governing variations.

Availability of exemptions

8–117   Assume that X dies leaving all his property to his adult children. They decide that the property would have been better left to their mother and enter into a variation providing that the property passing under their father's will should devolve as though it had been left to their mother. This will be relieved by s.17(a) from being a transfer of value by the children, but s.17(a) will not displace the charge which arose on the father's death by reason of his testamentary gift to the children. That is why the provision in s.142 that the disposition effected by the children's variation shall be treated as having been effected by the father is important: it means that the father will be treated as having made the gift to the mother, with the result that the s.18 exemption becomes available to displace the charge that would otherwise have arisen on his death.

Availability of reliefs

8–118   A deceased person may have owned property qualifying for agricultural, business or interest free instalment relief which was effectively wasted, e.g. a husband might have left his business interests to his widow. If she enters into a variation rerouting these interests to her children they may enjoy the benefit of business and interest-free instalment relief; see e.g. the *Russell* case, discussed below at para.8–147.[127] Care

---

[127] See also the partly exempt transfer rules at paras 8–58 and following.

needs to be taken though to ensure that any such re-arrangement does not fall within the provisions of s.39A, discussed at paras 8–100 and following.

Changes in rates

Whilst there remains in force a flat rate of 40 per cent IHT there will no advantage in effecting a variation to gain a benefit in changes in rates.[128]   **8–119**

Planning: deemed settlors

The fact that the deceased is treated as having made the dispositions effected by the variation can also be important where the deceased died domiciled abroad. Assume that X dies domiciled abroad, owning property situated outside the United Kingdom. The property was thus excluded property when he died.[129] Under X's will the property passes to Y, his son, who is domiciled in the United Kingdom. Thus, as matters stand, no charge arose on X's death in respect of the property,[130] but, as property comprised in Y's estate, it is now within the scope of IHT. Had X settled the property, on the other hand, it might have remained outside the scope of IHT.[131] Accordingly, Y should consider entering into a variation under which he directs that the property should be held on trusts for, e.g., Y and his family. For IHT purposes,[132] X, not Y, will be the settlor, with the result that so long as the property comprised in the settlement is situated abroad, the property may be excluded property and so immune from any charges to IHT.[133]   **8–120**

Planning: freezer legacies

The fact that the deceased is treated as having made the dispositions means that the variation is treated for IHT purposes as taking effect from his death. This has the result that a variation may be employed to redirect a posthumous increase in value of an estate without any IHT charge. Assume, for instance, that a death estate of £400,000 was left to the testator's wife and that, within the two year period, it had increased in value to £650,000. The wife could vary the will to provide for a specific legacy of £400,000 to herself with the residue passing to her daughter. Under ss.36–42, the value   **8–121**

---

[128] As compared to earlier years when IHT was charged at different bands and therefore a variation could have the effect of indirectly changing the rate at which property was taxed where the rates of tax changed since the death, for example, X died in 1987 in circumstances where the effective rate of tax on his estate was 60 per cent. If he died leaving a widow, but left all or some of his property to his children, the children could enter into a variation under which the property in question was rerouted to the widow. If she died while the rates at present in force applied, the property would bear tax at a maximum rate of 40 per cent.

[129] IHTA 1984 s.6(1).

[130] IHTA 1984 s.4(1) and 5(1).

[131] See paras 32–49 and 10–23 and following.

[132] But not for CGT or income tax purposes; see paras 8–151 and 8–154.

[133] See paras 32–49 and 10–23 and following. Section 142(1) uses the word "effected", while s.48(3)(a) uses the word "made", but nothing appears to turn on this. The interaction of s.142(1) and s.44(1) (associated operations) is far from clear. In practice, HMRC accept the view stated in the text. In an extreme case, however, there is a danger that they would invoke s.144(1) to argue that the son was the settlor on the footing that he had provided funds indirectly.

of the deceased's estate (£400,000) would be attributed to the exempt legacy to the wife, with the result that the remaining £250,000 passed free of IHT to the daughter.[134]

Planning: outflanking reservation of benefit

8–122   A variation may be used to outflank the reservation of benefit rules, e.g. a beneficiary can set up a discretionary trust by an instrument of variation with himself as one of the objects without the reservation of benefit rules coming into play, because under s.142(1) the beneficiary is not the settlor for IHT purposes.[135]

Possible withdrawal of favoured treatment

8–123   Proposals to repeal the IHT benefits enjoyed by instruments of variation entered into within two years of a testator's death (save only for compromise arrangements falling within the general guidelines laid down in the Inheritance (Provision for Family and Dependants) Act 1975) have been muted since the 1989 Budget. It was then, and has since, been argued that 'rearrangements are being increasingly exploited to avoid IHT.

Although nothing has happened to date, given this threat of future legislation the use of instruments of variation has come under close scrutiny. In the authors' view the various changes of government since 1989 have not lessened the potential future threat. Notwithstanding the above view, the present law is that a wide variety of posthumous arrangements is possible for tax planning purposes.

Positive conditions that must be satisfied

8–124   The legislation establishes both positive and negative conditions that need to be satisfied if a variation is to come within s.142. Each kind of condition will be considered in turn, starting with the five positive conditions, which are as follows:

(1) the variation must be made within two years of the death of the deceased person in question;

(2) the variation must be effected by a written instrument;

(3) the variation must be of a disposition, whether effected by will, under the law relating to intestacy, or otherwise of property which was comprised in the estate of a deceased person immediately before he died;

(4) the instrument of variation must contain a statement made by all the relevant persons to the effect that they intend the subsection to apply to the variation; and

[134] See paras 8–58 and following.
[135] HMRC Manuals IHTM35151.

394

(5) the variation must be a "real" variation.

Each of these will be considered in turn.

1. Two-year time period

The variation must be effected within two years of the deceased's death. This is an ironclad rule, i.e. HMRC have no authority to extend the two-year period.[136] Occasionally it will not be clear precisely when a person died. In such a case his advisers should establish the earliest possible date on which he died and base the two-year period on that date. **8–125**

2. Written instrument

It suffices that the variation is by a "written instrument". Normally, a deed will be necessary, for a number of reasons. First, it will mean that the parties are legally bound.[137] Secondly, certain forms of property can be transferred only by deed. Finally, it is essential that the variation is effected *by* the written instrument.[138] It may be that title to the property in question passes by delivery where a chattel is concerned. In such cases, relief may only be available if ownership is transferred by a deed before delivery takes place. **8–126**

3. Property comprised in the deceased's estate

The variation must be of a disposition of property which was comprised in the deceased's estate immediately before he died. The rule has a number of ramifications. **8–127**

Included excluded property

Section 142(5) expressly provides that a person's estate immediately before he dies includes excluded property. In the absence of this provision the kind of variation envisaged at para.8–120 would be impossible, because the normal rule is that immediately before a person dies his estate does not include excluded property.[139] **8–128**

Deed of variation cannot exclude assets from being comprised in the Deceased's Estate

It is not possible to utilise a deed of variation to remove assets from the deceased's estate for IHT purposes so that the assets are no longer part of the estate and subject **8–129**

---

[136] cf. the position on elections pre August 1, 2002; see para.8–136.

[137] The alternative is for the parties to provide consideration, but this may lead to problems; see paras 8–141 and following.

[138] See *The Law Society Gazette* (1985), p.1454.

[139] IHTA 1984 s.5(1).

to the deemed transfer of value on death under s.4. In *Wells (Personal Representatives of Glowacki, Deceased) v Revenue & Customs Commissioners*[140] the Special Commissioner held that a deed of variation which had purported to treat the deceased's house as having been given away as a lifetime gift immediately before the deceased died, thereby removing the house from the estate for IHT purposes, was not capable of taking effect under s.142. It was the disposition that has to be varied and this does not include substituting a disposition that purportedly takes effect otherwise than on death.

Existing settled property

8–130   In the absence of provision to the contrary, where an individual with an interest in possession in settled property exercises a testamentary power of appointment over that property it might have been possible for the beneficiaries who benefitted from that exercise to vary the appointment because the property would by virtue of s.49(1) have been comprised in his estate for IHT purposes on the basis that they would have been varying a testamentary disposition of that property made by that individual. Section 142(5) prevents such a variation from falling within s.142(1) by providing that settled property to which a person is treated by s.49(1) as being beneficially entitled because he has an interest in possession does not for these purposes form part of his estate.

Newly settled property: variations by beneficiaries

8–131   It is possible for beneficiaries to vary their interests under a trust *created* by the deceased. Assume, for instance, that on A's death property is settled on B for life with remainder to C. B and C could effect a variation whereby the property is to pass on A's death to D absolutely or, alternatively, B could assign his life interest to D and read that assignment back into A's will with the result that D's interest *pur autre vie* would be treated as arising under that will.

Newly settled property: variations by personal representatives

8–132   More difficult is the position when the relevant life interest under a settlement created by the deceased has terminated at the time when a variation is to be carried out. In this situation it is obviously the remainderman who will desire the variation. A typical case would occur where A left property to his widow for life with remainder to his two daughters B and C. The widow dies within a short time of A and it transpires that it will be advantageous for the daughters to take their property, not on the death of their mother, but on the death of A. HMRC have now adopted a far harder line in relation to variations of such interests and no longer accept that such variations can be effective under s.142.[141] HMRC argue that:

> "It is a pre-requisite if the provisions are to have any impact that a real life disposition or transfer took place so that the transferor can decide whether or not to make an election in order to trigger the deeming provisions."

---

[140] *Wells (Personal Representatives of Glowacki, Deceased) v Revenue & Customs Commissioners* 2007 SpC. 631.
[141] The Inland Revenue Capital Taxes December 2001 newsletter.

The basis of HMRC's argument was that it is a requirement for a valid instrument of variation that there is an actual asset for it to vary and, as the interest of the widow in the above example no longer exists as at the date of the deed, B and C cannot now execute a variation over it. This view was supported by the Special Commissioner's decision in *Soutter's Executry v IRC*.[142] The deceased, S, died in November 1999 leaving a liferent in her house to G. The estate was within the IHT nil rate band. G lived in the house until she became ill and then died in November 2000, with an estate substantially over the nil rate band. The Executors and beneficiaries of both estates executed an instrument of variation removing G's liferent. The Special Commissioner found in favour of HMRC stating that there can be no assignment of something that does not exist. He further held that whilst a deed of variation will be deemed to be made by the deceased it is only so deemed for tax purposes and therefore cannot affect the law of property or the question of whether those making the variation had any right to do so.

The alternative argument is that the whole sense of s.142 is to deem the variation to take effect at S's death and therefore the fact that the liferent did not exist at G's death is irrelevant; it did exist at S's death and accordingly G's executors could vary it. The executors further argued that the position here was no different than if a beneficiary had already spent all the cash legacy left to him by will and then varied the gift. In the authors' view, however, such a variation would be unlikely to be effective; see para. 8–135.

It should be noted that, in *Soutter*, G's interest had solely been in a property. Had there been actual income arising, represented by cash or assets in a form that the executors could have transferred after his death, the outcome may have been different, particularly if the life interest had been in income producing property and income arising between the two deaths had to be apportioned. Interestingly, HMRC did accept that the executors could have disclaimed the liferent if it had not been accepted by G and where it is possible as a matter of general law.[143]

Reservation of benefit

Section 142(5) also provides that property to which a person is treated as being **8–133** beneficially entitled under the reservation of benefit rules by virtue of s.102 of the Finance Act 1986 does not form part of his estate, though why this was thought necessary is not clear since such property will not be comprised in his estate as a matter of general law and so could not be disposed of by him.

Property passing by survivorship

Property passing by survivorship raises special problems under s.142. Where a **8–134** person has a joint interest in property, e.g. where a husband and wife or civil partners own the matrimonial home as beneficial joint tenants, each of their respective joint interests will be comprised in their respective estates immediately before they die, and this is so notwithstanding the fact that the property will pass by way of survivorship and not under their wills or intestacies. This gives rise to the question of whether a joint interest is within s.142 at all. The answer is "yes" because it was comprised in the

[142] *Soutter's Executry v IRC* [2002] S.T.C. (S.C.D.) 385.
[143] Also see HMRC Manuals IHTM35042 and IHTM35164.

deceased's estate immediately before he died. Can it be said, however, that he disposed of it? Section 142(1)(a) refers to dispositions "whether effected by will under the law relating to intestacy *or otherwise*". The prevailing view is that the words "or otherwise" extend to property passing by survivorship. This is certainly the practice of HMRC[144]:

> "Beneficiaries of the estate of a deceased person—whether under the will, rules relating to intestacy or otherwise—may wish to change their inheritances. There are special IHT rules for changes or variations made within 2 years after the deceased's death.
>
> If a variation made within the 2-year period satisfies certain other conditions, IHT is charged on the death as though the deceased person had made the variation and the beneficiaries do not have to pay tax on any gift of their inheritance. The main conditions are that the variation is made in writing and that, within 6 months after the variation, the persons making the variation give written notice to HMRC electing for the IHT rules to apply.
>
> Similar rules apply for certain purposes of capital gains tax (CGT).
>
> Recently, we have seen suggestions that these rules do not apply to a variation of the deceased's interest in jointly held assets, which passed on the death to the surviving joint owner(s).
>
> For example, the family home was owned by a mother and her son as beneficial joint tenants and on the mother's death, her interest passed by survivorship to the son who then became the sole owner of the property. It has been suggested that, in this example, the son cannot, for IHT/CGT purposes, vary his inheritance of his mother's interest by redirecting it to his children.
>
> We do not share this view.
>
> Both IHT and CGT rules apply not only to dispositions/inheritances arising under will or the law of intestacy but also to those effected 'otherwise'. In our view, the words 'or otherwise' bring within the rules the automatic inheritance of a deceased owner's interest in jointly held assets by the surviving joint owner(s)."[145]

Posthumous changes in property

8–135   Cases sometimes arise where, following a person's death, the property comprised in his estate immediately before he died is sold, with the result that when it comes time to enter into a variation the property comprised in the deceased's estate immediately before he died is no longer comprised in his estate. This is a difficult area where there are no general rules. HMRC have indicated that each case falls to be considered individually but appear to accept that the variation succeeds so long as the property in existence at the time of the deed represents and can be traced back to the original property that is the subject of the variation. It is thought that if under a variation an individual is given a cash sum HMRC will accept that the deed is valid notwithstanding the fact that at death there were insufficient liquid assets to satisfy that gift.[146]

---

[144] A joint tenant can dispose of his interest in the land: he has the full power of alienation inter vivos but any such conveyance will destroy the joint tenancy by severance and turn the interest into a tenancy in common. However, a joint tenant cannot sever and transfer his interest by will or under intestacy. Accordingly, the question arises whether the variation of a joint tenancy must contain words of severance. It is thought that this is unnecessary since although s.142(1) provides that the variation is deemed to have been made by the deceased, the section does not say that it is deemed to have been made by will or intestacy. Hence, the rule that a joint tenancy cannot be severed by will or on intestacy is irrelevant. Under the CGT legislation (see TCGA 1992 s.62(6)) the wording is similar to s.142 in that it includes dispositions by will or intestacy or otherwise. However, it also requires the deceased to have been competent to dispose of the property in question, but these additional words do not prevent a CGT variation of a joint tenancy: see s.62(10).

[145] *Inland Revenue Tax Bulletin* (October 1995), p.254.

[146] See *Russell v IRC* discussed at para.8–147.

Care should be taken when drafting the deed of variation to ensure that any changes in the identification of the property are clearly traced back to the date of death, for example, where company shares held at the date of death have changed by way of capital reorganisation and are represented by different shares as at the date of the deed of variation.[147]

4. Requisite statement

As was noted above, no relief is available unless the instrument of variation contains a statement, made by all the "relevant persons", to the effect that they intend s.142(1) to apply to the variation.[148] This simplified procedure applies in respect of all variations executed on or after August 1, 2002. Instruments executed before that date had to have an election in writing to HMRC within six months (or such longer time as HMRC might allow) after the date of the variation. Another important change introduced by the Finance Act 2002 is that it is no longer possible to make the statements outside the instrument of variation as the statements must be contained in the instrument itself.[149]

8–136

The "relevant persons" are defined as the person or persons making the instrument and, if the variation results in extra tax being payable—e.g. where a spouse or civil partner effects a variation with the result that less of the transfer made by the deceased is exempt—the deceased's personal representatives. For this purpose, personal representatives may decline to make such a statement only if they hold insufficient assets in their capacity as personal representatives to discharge the additional tax.[150] This might occur where, e.g., the administration of an estate had been completed and it was proposed to enter into a variation which would increase the tax due from the estate.

Although there will not be many occasions when a variation results in additional tax being payable, it is interesting to note that if it does, s.218A still obliges the relevant persons to deliver a copy of that instrument to HMRC within six months after the date of execution of the variation.

Tax trap for trustees

Trustees, whose liability may be increased as the result of a deed of variation, are in a vulnerable position. Assume, for instance, that when X dies he was entitled to an interest in possession in settled property and that a deed of variation is subsequently entered into which increases the tax chargeable in respect of his free estate. If the settled property is also chargeable, this may have the effect of increasing the effective rate of tax on that property and there is nothing that the trustees can do about this. They will not be parties to the variation and there is no provision allowing them to recover from the beneficiaries who made that variation such additional tax as may become payable in respect of the settled property.[151] Cautious trustees may therefore wish to

8–137

---

[147] HMRC Manuals IHTM35026.
[148] IHTA 1984 s.142(2) substituted by FA 2002 s.120(1).
[149] cf. elections pre-August 2002 where the election did not need to be part of the instrument itself.
[150] IHTA 1984 s.142(2A).
[151] HMRC Manuals IHTM35153.

retain assets until two years after a death if they believe that there is any danger that they may have to pay additional tax as the result of a variation.

Infants and unborn beneficiaries

8–138   A variation will not be effective unless it has been effected by everyone who might have benefited from the disposition that is being varied. Where the variation could adversely affect the interests of any minor or unborn beneficiaries[152] it will be necessary for the court to approve the variation on their behalf.[153]

5. The variation must be a "real" variation

8–139   This condition is not expressly established by s.142. Rather, it is the authors' way of drawing attention to certain considerations which can easily be overlooked. The first and most important is that the variation must genuinely vary the dispositions effected by the deceased. Assume that X dies leaving his entire estate to his children. It occurs to their advisers that the charge to IHT that arose on the father's death could be avoided if the children entered into a variation under which the children reroute their late father's estate to their mother. The advisers (or the children, as the case may be) may, however, not be content to leave matters there. The temptation will exist to arrange for the mother to make a PET of the property back to the children. If this is done, the problem is that it may be difficult to contend that the variation genuinely varied the dispositions effected by the deceased; after all, the children end up with all the property. This is a point which HMRC are known to take. Indeed, it now appears to be standard practice on their part to inquire, at the time the variation is submitted to them, as to the intentions of the parties to the variation at the time they effected it. There could, of course, also be an attack under the *Ramsay* principle and/or under the "extraneous consideration" rule.[154]

In an appropriate case it may be possible to adopt a subtler approach. Assume the facts are the same as those just mentioned but, instead of passing back to the children the property which they originally took under the will, the widow gave to the children property which she originally took under the will or which was comprised in her free estate at the time of the death. In that case there would be a "real variation" and it might be difficult to apply the *Ramsay* principle; the "extraneous consideration" rule would need watching though.

Another possibility would be for the children's deed to settle the property on trust for the widow for life, with appropriate remainders over, with the trustees having power to revoke all or (preferably) part of the widow's interest. After an appropriate period[155] the trustees could revoke all or part of the widow's interest. So long as the trustees acted independently and, in particular, were unaware of any understanding that may have existed between the widow and the children, HMRC might find it very difficult

---

[152] Or others incapable of consenting.

[153] It has been suggested that an order of the court might be required regardless of how the interest of the person unable to consent is being varied, i.e. even if he benefits from the variation. HMRC Manuals IHTM reflected the authors' view that only those variations which adversely affect the interest of the person unable to consent require the approval of the court.

[154] See paras 8–141 and following.

[155] See paras 8–161 and following as to the "short term interest" trap.

to establish the requisite degree of preordination.[156] However, in real life, such a lack of awareness might, perhaps with justification, be viewed with suspicion by HMRC.

Negative conditions that must be satisfied

There are two negative requirements, one concerning consideration, the other concerning the effects of previous variations. **8–140**

1. Extraneous consideration

By s.142(3), a variation does not qualify for relief under s.142(1) if it is made for any consideration in money or money's worth, other than consideration consisting of the making, in respect of another of the dispositions of the deceased, of a variation or disclaimer which qualifies for relief under s.142(1). **8–141**

The purpose of this provision is primarily to prevent advantage being taken of the spouse or civil partner or charitable exemption in order to pass property on to non-exempt beneficiaries. Assume, e.g. that X dies, leaving £200,000 to his widow and £350,000 to his son. The transfer to his spouse is an exempt transfer. Accordingly, but for s.142(3), the widow and son could effect variations under which the son agreed to redirect his £350,000 to his mother in return for her:

(1) redirecting the £200,000 to him; and
(2) paying him £150,000 equality money.

The result would be that the son still received £350,000 and the mother £200,000 but the exempt part of the transfer on X's death was increased from £200,000 to £350,000. This follows from the fact that after the variation £350,000 would have been treated as going to the widow under the deceased's will. The transfer of the £150,000 from the widow would have had no adverse IHT consequences since it would not have diminished the value of her estate. To prevent this result, under s.142(3) only £200,000 of the £350,000 passing from the son will qualify for relief under s.142(1). No IHT charge will arise because neither the widow's nor the son's estate is diminished in value; but the widow will be regarded as having received under her deceased husband's will only £200,000 of the £350,000 redirected to her by her son so that the exempt portion of the deceased's estate remains £200,000.

Legal costs

HMRC consider that if the beneficiary under an instrument of variation agrees to pay the legal costs of the other party, this will amount to consideration within s.142(3). **8–142**

Obligation to discharge indebtedness

Circumstances may arise where a variation is made of property on the basis that the recipient of the property will be responsible for discharging some form of indebtedness. **8–143**

---

[156] See *Schneider v Mills* [1993] S.T.C. 430.

In such a case the question arises as to whether the recipient, by assuming responsibility for the debt, provides "consideration" for the purposes of s.142(3). This would clearly be the case if the property was not charged with the debt, but where the property is charged s.142(3) is arguably not infringed.

Compromise of a claim

8–144   At first sight, the compromise of a claim against the deceased's estate under the Inheritance (Provisions for Family & Dependants) Act 1975, even if made within two years of the death, would seem incapable of amounting to a variation within s.142 because of consideration furnished by the recipient in giving up his claim against the estate. In practice, it is believed that HMRC do not take this point.[157] If agreement is reached in such cases more than two years after the death and "reading back" is desired it will be necessary to obtain a court order approving the compromise so that s.146 will then apply (see paras 8–208 and following).

Understandings

8–145   Often a variation will be made on the "understanding" that the appropriate beneficiary will then deal with the assets in a particular way, e.g. a child of the deceased may agree to re-route property to his widowed mother on the understanding that in due course she will make a PET to him or to his children. Apart from the artificiality of this arrangement, the understanding with his mother may amount to consideration within the meaning of s.142(3). Should this be the case, it will presumably follow that the variation will be ineffective for the purposes of s.142; the transfer by the mother will not be a transfer of value since she will have given effect to an obligation which she was under; and whether or not the transfer by the son will constitute a transfer of value must depend upon the ultimate destination of the property. If it is to come back to him there will be no such transfer; if, on the other hand, it is to pass, e.g. to his children, then he will presumably have made a PET.

2. No previous variation of the deceased's disposition

8–146   The property the disposition of which is sought to be varied must not itself have been the subject of a previous variation coming within s.142. Thus, if X dies leaving property to his children and they enter into a s.142 variation with respect to some[158] of it, it is not open to the persons taking under that variation to argue that they themselves can enter into a s.142 variation with respect to that property on the basis that s.142 treats them as having taken under X's will. This was a matter of controversy for some time. HMRC's view was stated as follows in *The Law Society Gazette* of May 22, 1985, p.1454:

> "There have been some cases in which a number of instruments of variation have been executed in relation to the same will or intestacy. The Revenue emphasise that these cases must be considered on their precise facts, but in broad terms their views will be as follows:

---

[157] HMRC Manuals IHTM35100.

[158] There is nothing to prevent the children from subsequently entering into a variation of the property unaffected by the first variation.

(i) an election which is validly made is irrevocable;

(ii) an instrument will not fall within s.142 it if *further* redirects any item or any part of an item that has *already* been redirected under an earlier instrument; and

(iii) to avoid any uncertainty, variations covering a number of items should ideally be made in one instrument.

Whilst multiple variations should therefore be avoided when not essential, the Revenue recognise that they are not as such prohibited by s.142. For example, a widow left all her husband's estate and who makes a small gift to her children soon after the death is not thereby precluded from making considered provision for those children out of the remainder by a further variation involving the relocation of different property towards the end of the two year period."

Many advisers were of the view that multiple variations of the same property were possible, but Knox J. held to the contrary in *Russell v IRC*.[159]

The facts in *Russell v IRC* were that the deceased died in 1983 survived by his wife **8–147** and four daughters. His estate included his interest as a Lloyds Underwriter, which qualified for business relief. Under his will most of his estate passed to his widow and was not, therefore, subject to an IHT charge. Accordingly, the business relief was wasted, as was the nil rate band. The family decided to vary the dispositions of the will by providing that each daughter should receive a pecuniary legacy of £25,000 to be raised out of the business property. By giving away business property worth in total £100,000 (4 × £25,000) which would qualify for business relief at 50 per cent, it was intended that some £50,000 of the testator's nil rate band would then be utilised. HMRC, however, took the view that the legacies as drafted were gifts of cash and not of qualifying business assets, so that the 50 per cent relief was unavailable and a tax charge arose since part of each legacy fell outside the nil rate band. Although the family did not accept this interpretation, in 1985 they executed a fresh deed of variation whereby each daughter was to receive instead of the cash legacy a proportionate share of business assets worth £25,000 each.

Knox J. had to decide whether this second deed was effective in carrying out the family's intentions. He held that under s.142 a benefit which had already been redirected once could not be further redirected and read back into the testator's will. Accordingly, as there had already been a valid variation in favour of the daughters in 1983, those beneficiaries could not further amend what they had already done:

"My principal reason for accepting the Crown's submission that the hypothesis contained in s.68(1) of the Finance Act 1976[160] should not be applied to that subsection itself is that this involves taking the hypothesis further than is necessary. No authority was cited to me of a statutory hypothesis being applied to the very provision which enacts the hypothesis. Such a tortuous process would merit a specific reference in the enactment to itself . . ."[161]

It should be noted that there is a difference between multiple variations of different property within an estate, which are normally acceptable and multiple variations of the same property.[162]

Disclaimers

It is the author's opinion that it should be possible to have a disclaimer within s.142 **8–148** followed by a deed of variation of the same property, on the basis that it would be a

[159] *Russell v IRC* [1998] S.T.C. 195.
[160] Now IHTA 1984 s.142.
[161] *Russell v IRC* [1988] S.T.C. 195 at 204.
[162] HMRC Manuals IHTM35083.

variation of dispositions of property actually arising on the deceased's death if the disclaimed gift does not take effect. to the reverse, where a deed of variation is followed by a disclaimer of the same property, would not be accepted under *Russell v IRC*. The Revenue are, however, ambiguous in their guidance, stating that all cases involving a disclaimer and deed of variation (in whatever order) should be referred for consideration.[163]

Non-requirements

8–149   It may be helpful to note at this stage the following "non-requirements", i.e. conditions which are occasionally thought to exist but which in fact do not:

(1) there is no requirement that the person entering into the deed can only do what the deceased himself could have done. For example, the persons effecting the deed can, it seems, settle the property on trustees of a trust which was not in existence when the deceased died, e.g. which is set up by, or contemporaneously with, the variation. In the same way, the fact that the deceased was a beneficial joint tenant of property does not preclude a variation being entered into in respect of that property;

(2) there is no requirement that the property must go to someone else who benefited under the deceased's will or intestacy. It can go to whoever the person entering into the variation wishes it to go to. It could go to someone, for example, who the deceased expressly excluded from benefiting under his will for reasons stated or unstated;

(3) there is no requirement that the estate must still be in the course of administration. On the contrary, s.142(6) expressly provides that a deed can be entered into "whether or not the administration of the estate is complete or the property concerned has been distributed in accordance with the original dispositions." Thus, there is no requirement that the property must still be in the hands of the personal representatives, still less that it somehow must pass through their hands on its way from the person entering into the deed to the person intended to benefit under the deed; and

(4) there is no requirement that the person redirecting the property must not have benefited from it, e.g. by receiving dividends; cf. disclaimers below.

Capital gains tax

8–150   The CGT legislation also confers favourable treatment on qualifying deeds of variation. The following points should be borne in mind.

Treatment generally

8–151   Similar relief from CGT for variations and disclaimers is available under the Taxation of Chargeable Gains Act 1992 s.62(6)–(10), but with the important difference that the variation is not read back for purposes of determining the donor. In *Marshall*

[163] HMRC Manuals IHTM35082.

v Kerr[164] the House of Lords held that the CGT settlor of a settlement made by a deed of variation was the original beneficiary who entered into the deed, not the testator, on the basis that s.62(6)(b) states that "this section" shall apply as if the variation had been effected by the deceased. Section 142, on the other hand, provides that "this Act" shall apply as if the variation had been effected by the deceased or the disclaimed interest had never been conferred. This point can be important when it is intended to take advantage of the deemed settlor provisions discussed at para.8–120.[165]

Extraneous consideration

The CGT legislation contains[166] a restriction similar, but not identical to, the IHT   **8–152** restriction that prohibits the giving of any consideration in money or money's worth other than consideration consisting of the making of a variation in respect of another of the dispositions. Both ss.142(3) and 62(8) are concerned with "extraneous consideration", i.e. there is no objection to, e.g., beneficiaries under a will each entering into a variation in consideration of the other doing so.

Election

The requisite CGT statement is independent of the IHT statement (see para.8–136   **8–153** for the IHT statement) so that although it is likely that a statement electing both sections to apply will normally be made, there may be circumstances where one but not the other is desirable.

Income tax

No income tax favoured treatment is conferred on variations, but there are the   **8–154** following income tax considerations.

Although variations are read back for all IHT purposes and some CGT purposes, they are not read back for any income tax purposes. This has two main consequences in practice. First, a person who effects a variation will remain assessable to income tax up to the date of the instrument of variation. Secondly, if a person effects a variation creating a settlement, he will be the settlor of that settlement.

Whilst it remains the case that instruments of variation will not be read back for income tax purposes, the rules governing the taxation of estate income may in fact achieve something of the same result. The effect of s.698(1A), (1B) and (2) of the Taxes Act 1988 is that so long as no payments are made to the original beneficiary all income from the estate will be assessed on the beneficiary under the variation as and when payments are made to him. (This assumes that the variation makes it clear that

---

[164] *Marshall v Kerr* [1994] 2 All E.R. 106; [1994] S.T.C. 638.
[165] See *Inland Revenue Tax Bulletin* (February 1995), p.194.
[166] TCGA 1992 s.62(8).

the original beneficiary is giving up any right that he may have to income accrued up to the date of the variation.)[167]

Gift Aid double dip

8-155   Under the Gift Aid rules in the Income Tax Act 2007 s.414(2)(b) a higher rate taxpayer who makes a cash gift qualifying for relief under s.25 is deemed to have deducted income tax at the basic rate from a larger gross sum: the charity can reclaim that tax while the taxpayer, if a higher rate taxpayer, can reclaim tax at the difference between the higher rate and the basic rate. This in itself was attractive but the question arose as to whether the asymmetry between the IHT and income tax treatment of variations meant the position could be made even more attractive.

Assume that in his will X leaves £75,000 to Y, who decides to pass the £75,000 on to charity. If Y simply gives the £75,000 to charity he will qualify for Gift Aid relief, but that is all. But what is the position if he uses a deed of variation to pass the £75,000 to charity? It is clear that X will be treated for IHT purposes as the donor, so that the IHT charity exemption prevents any IHT being chargeable on X's gift of the £75,000 to Y (which ends up with the charity). It is also clear that Y, not X, is the donor for purposes of Gift Aid. Does this mean that Gift Aid relief, as well as the IHT charity exemption, is available in respect of the £75,000 rerouted to the charity via the deed of variation?

This was the question that arose in *St Dunstan's v Major*.[168] The facts were that P was the sole executor and beneficiary of his mother's estate. Prior to the completion of administration he varied his mother's will to provide for the payment of a legacy of £20,000 to St Dunstan's (a charity). That sum was duly paid some months later at the conclusion of the administration. It was accepted that the variation was effective for IHT purposes and so took effect as if the deceased had made an exempt charitable gift, so that an IHT saving of some £8,000 was achieved, which benefited P as the sole beneficiary. The case was concerned with whether the gift made by the instrument of variation attracted Gift Aid relief from income tax under the provisions of the Finance Act 1990 s.25. This was denied by HMRC for two reasons.

First, because the gift did not take the form of "a payment of a sum of money" as required by the Finance Act 1990 s.25(2)(a) since it was made at a time when the estate was unadministered with the result that P had no right to be paid £20,000 but merely enjoyed a chose in action. This argument was shortly rejected by the Special Commissioner and it is considered that it had no merit for the following reasons:

(a) a payment to charity in the form of a cheque is not the payment of a cash sum because the payee, until such time as the cheque is duly cashed, owns a chose in action;

(b) similarly, a deed of gift of a sum of money to charity entitles the charity to sue on that deed (i.e. a chose in action) and this right is subsequently extinguished by the receipt of the promised cash;

---

[167] Previously the original beneficiary was chargeable on income arising prior to the variation even if it was never received by him. This change has occurred as an incidental effect of the new rules for taxing estate income resulting from the introduction of self assessment.

[168] *St Dunstan's v Major* [1997] S.T.C. (S.C.D.) 212.

(It is understood that HMRC accept that in both these situations Gift Aid remains available and it is difficult sensibly to distinguish them from the argument taken in the *St Dunstan's* case);

(c) the wording of the deed of variation indicates that the obligation to pay only arose when the taxpayer became entitled to the residue. Further the claim to Gift Aid was only made after the cash payment had been made. It is hard to see on these facts that the taxpayer assigned any part of his interest as residuary beneficiary to the charity: rather the payment was charged on and payable out of the residuary estate as and when the taxpayer received (or was entitled to receive) that estate; and

(d) it was suggested by HMRC that the cash payment was made by the personal representative rather than by the taxpayer (obviously this argument was obscured by the fact that the taxpayer was the sole personal representative). However, any payment could only be made by the personal representative at the direction of the beneficiary (the taxpayer) and, in effect, as his agent. Further, if the payment had been made before the completion of the administration it would represent an assent by the personal representative of the relevant cash sum in favour of the beneficiary (in this case although the facts are not entirely clear it would seem that payment was only made when the administration of the estate had been concluded).

HMRC's second—and winning—argument was that under s.25(2)(e) of the Finance Act 1990, Gift Aid is not available if the donor receives a benefit in excess of a de minimis limit of 2.5 per cent of the value of the gift in consequence of making the gift and P, as the sole beneficiary under his mother's estate, had infringed this by receiving a benefit in the form of the IHT savings of some £8,000.

In the authors' view this decision is not convincing. The main fiscal consequence of **8–156** a Gift Aid claim is income tax relief for the donor. The sum paid to the charity reduces his total income and accordingly, in the case of a higher rate taxpayer, such as P in this case, results in a saving of income tax at the higher rate. In this sense a higher rate donor will always receive a fiscal benefit consequent upon the Gift Aid payment but this result is inherent in the legislation and it would make a mockery of the whole intent behind that legislation if it were to invalidate any claim for Gift Aid. It has therefore to be accepted that income tax benefits are not within the "benefit" envisaged by the legislation. Why, therefore, should benefits in the form of an IHT adjustment be treated any differently?

Looking at the Parliamentary Debates at the time of the introduction of the Gift Aid legislation, it would appear that the purpose of the restriction was to deal with gifts or benefits received from the charity as consideration for the making of the payment. The first Gift Aid leaflets produced by HMRC supported this view.[169]

The case effectively destroys what had been known as the "double-dip" arrangement.[170] It will be appreciated that Gift Aid arrangements effected under a precatory trust are similarly affected by this decision (for precatory trusts see paras 8–206 and following.

The issue was raised again in *Harris v Revenue and Customs Commissioners*[171] under a similar fact pattern. The tribunal regrettably reached the same decision as *St*

---

[169] It should, of course, be remembered that recourse to Hansard debates as an aid to statutory construction is only permitted in the courts in the limited circumstances set out in *Pepper (Inspector of Taxes) v Hart* [1993] A.C. 593 and subsequent cases, and specifically when the relevant legislation is ambiguous.

[170] See *Private Client Business* (1994), pp.48, 183 and 264.

[171] *Harris v Revenue and Customs Commissioners* [2010] UKFTT 385 (TC).

Dunstan's, finding that the two residuary legatees to a will, having diverted a portion of their legacies to a charity by a deed of variation thereby benefitting from a reduction in IHT liability, had received a benefit in consequence of making the gift of sufficient value to fall foul of s.25(2).

However, if the income tax savings and IHT savings are achieved by different people the "double-dip" arrangement may still be possible, i.e. where a variation is made by a legatee then he may benefit from the higher rate income tax saving but it is the residuary estate (not the legatee) that benefits from the IHT saving.

It has also been argued that the arrangement will still be effective in the context of a discretionary trust of residue where there is an appointment out of the trust to a family member under s.144 and then he gives the assets to a charity by an instrument of variation under s.142[172] and claims higher rate tax relief. The discretionary trust residue will still get the benefit of the IHT saving.

Share Aid—a subtle sharing

8–157   The Finance Act 2002, by inserting s.587B into the Taxes Act 1988, introduced "Share Aid" rules similar but not identical to the Gift Aid rules. A key difference is that s.587B modifies the rule disallowing relief where a benefit had been received.

Under s.578B(5), where a donor received a benefit the relief is not completely disallowed; rather, the amount of the gift on which tax relief can be claimed is reduced by the value of the benefit reduced by the donor.

It should, therefore, be possible for a beneficiary who pays IHT and income tax at 40 per cent to redirect his entitlement to shares to a charity, claim 40 per cent IHT relief on the whole of the gift and 40 per cent income tax relief on the net 60 per cent of the gift. It is also worth noting that the income tax relief would inure entirely to the benefit of the donor rather than being split between the charity (as to basic rate income tax) and the donor (as to higher rate income tax).

If a deed of variation of this sort is envisaged, it would be prudent for the executors to transfer the shares to the beneficiary in advance of the deed so as to preclude any argument that when he entered into the deed the donor did not have any proprietary rights over the shares themselves (as opposed to a chose in action in respect of the administered estate).

Where shares have increased in value between the date of the death and the date of the deed the potential benefit is even greater, because the income tax relief should be on the current value of the shares while the IHT savings will be calculated by reference to their lower probate value.

Reduced charitable rate

8–158   The new provisions, as outlined at para.3–43, will also apply to charitable legacies made by a Deed of Variation. The reduced rate will only apply if it is shown that the

---

[172] See para.8–203 below for the interaction of ss.142 and 144.

charity has been notified that the devolution of the estate has been varied in its favour.[173]

I Grossing-Up Calculator

HMRC have produced an additional grossing-up calendar at the reduced 36 per cent rate.[174]

II Example

Jess has gross free estate of £500,000 and no qualifying interest in possession or jointly held property. She had made no gifts with a reservation of benefit. Under her original will, Jess was to leave £15,000 to charity and the residue of her estate to her brother.

Gross value of estate	£500,000
Gift to charity	£10,000
Value of free estate minus gift to charity	£490,000
Inheritance tax nil rate band applied	£325,000
Value of free estate minus nil rate band	£175,000
Minimum charitable gift to meet the ten per cent test	£17,500

Jess's charitable gift is not sufficient to reduce the rate at which she pays IHT to 36 per cent and the IHT liability on her estate is as follows:

Gross value of estate	£500,000
Less exempt gift to charity	(£15,000)
Net estate	£485,000
Less nil rate band	(£325,000)
IHT payable at 40%	£160,000 @ 40% = £64,000
Gift to brother	£421,000

In this scenario, Jess is gifting £17,5000 to charity under her will; here her estate would qualify for the reduced nil rate band and her liability would be as follows:

Gross value of estate	£500,000
Less exempt gift to charity	(£17,500)
Net estate	£482,500
Less nil rate band	(£325,000)
IHT payable at 40%	£157,500 @ 36% = £56,700
Gift to brother	£425,800

---

[173] See HMRC Manuals IHTM45039.
[174] *http://www.hmrc.gov.uk/cto/g_up36.pdf* [Accessed November 20, 2012].

This simple example is used, therefore, to describe a situation in which increasing a charitable gift under a will can reduce the IHT liability and increase the residuary gift over.

Pre-owned assets

8–159   Deeds of variation are expressly excluded from the scope of the pre-owned asset tax in the Finance Act 2004 Sch.15. This is discussed at paras 7–179 and following.

Stamp duty and stamp duty land tax

8–160   HMRC have confirmed that the only occasion when an instrument of variation will require a stamp duty exemption certificate pursuant to the Stamp Duty (Exempt Instruments) Regulations 1987[175] is where the instrument effects a variation in the destination of stocks and shares or marketable securities and where (unusually) the instrument itself acts as a transfer form for the shares.[176] Stamp duty land tax is not payable on instruments of variation[177] and there is no need to include a certificate on the variation itself.[178]

Some practical points for variations

8–161   The following practical points should be borne in mind.

The short-term interest trap

8–162   Difficulties can arise if by a variation falling within s.142(1) property is held in trust for a person for a period which ends within two years of the relevant death. This matter is dealt with in the unhappily worded s.142(4) which provides that:

> "Where a variation to which subsection (1) above applies results in property being held in trust for a person for a period which ends not more than two years after the death, this Act shall apply as if the disposition of the property that takes effect at the end of the period had had effect from the beginning of the period; but this subsection shall not affect the application of this Act in relation to any distribution or application of property occurring before that disposition takes effect."[179]

The subsection may be relevant if a variation falling within s.142(1) establishes a trust in favour of a person and that trust then comes to an end within two years of the death. Usually the relevant trust will create an interest in possession which terminates but the section is not so limited. A typical example falling within the words of s.142(4) would

---

[175] IHT Newsletter of April 2004.
[176] The stock transfer form itself would otherwise normally require the relevant stamp duty certificate.
[177] FA 2003 Sch.3.
[178] HMRC Manuals IHTM35060.
[179] Note that s.142(4) does not apply to disclaimers, nor to appointments under s.144.

be where the deceased had left his entire estate to his two sons and they had entered into a variation whereby each took a pecuniary legacy thereby exhausting the deceased's nil rate band and then settled the remainder of his estate on life interest trusts for their mother, the deceased's surviving spouse. That variation, to the extent that it creates settled property, would fall within the subsection.

The subsection provides that if the trust so created ends within two years of the death **8–163** the interest of the beneficiary under that trust is effectively ignored in determining the IHT consequences of the variation: thus the disposition of the property that takes effect from the ending of the trust interest is read back to the beginning of "the period". The effect of this appears to be that the variation is treated as having been effected by the deceased although the position is less clear than under s.142(1) where it is expressly provided that the variation is not a transfer of value but is instead regarded as having been effected by the deceased. It is also worth noting here that HMRC will scrutinise variations where the life interest is for a period "slightly" longer than the two years covered by subs.(4).[180]

The effect of subs.142(4) can be catastrophic. In the example considered at **8–164** para.8–162, for instance, if the widow's interest in possession came to an end within two years of her late husband's death the s.18 exemption which had been available as a result of the original instrument of variation would retrospectively be revoked so that the charge on the husband's death would be reinstated. As a corollary the termination of the life interest would not be a PET by the widow.

Section 142(4) is not worded very happily. It provides that where a *variation* within **8–165** subs.(1) *results* in property being held in trust for a person for a period ending within two years of the death, the short-term interest is in effect to be disregarded. HMRC's view is that it follows from the words *"where a variation . . . results"* that s.142(4) does not apply where a variation creates an interest which is not limited to cease with the s.142(4) period but which does cease within that period because of some other event, e.g. the death of the person entitled to the interest.[181]

The view has been expressed that s.142(4) is not infringed where an interest in possession is brought to an end within the two year time limit by an act of the trustees, by their exercising an overriding power of appointment, but the authors' view is that this is optimistic because the trusts created by a power of appointment are to be read back into the original settlement.

A silver lining

Exceptionally, it may be possible to use s.142(4) to the taxpayer's advantage. **8–166** Assume a testator died owning a valuable freehold property. Under his will he left the property to charity subject to licence allowing his long time companion the right to live in the property rent free for, say, 18 months. The existence of this licence meant that there was a very serious risk that s.23(2)(a)[182] would operate to prevent the charitable exemption from being available. The companion was unwilling to give up her licence so as to accelerate the charity's entitlement. The solution acceptable to all parties was for a deed of variation under which the companion was given an interest in possession

---

[180] HMRC Manuals IHTM35095, p.65.
[181] HMRC Manuals IHTM35133, p.56.
[182] See paras 3–49 and following.

for 18 months. This provided the companion with security of tenure while at the same time ensuring that the charitable exemption would be available on the death of the testator on the basis that the short term interest in possession was ignored, the gift to charity being treated by s.142(4) as having taken place on the death of the testator.

Variations by personal representatives[183]

8–167   There is nothing to prevent personal representatives of a dead beneficiary from themselves making a variation which reduces the value of the estate of the deceased person they represent. Before the introduction of the transferable nil rate band by the Finance Act 2008, this could result in a very useful means of not 'wasting' each spouse/ civil partner's nil rate bands, as illustrated in the following example. If A dies leaving property to B, and B dies within two years of A's death, B's personal representatives can make a variation under which they redirect the property that would otherwise have accrued to B's estate under A's will.[184] Assume that H dies with a nil cumulative total leaving his £325,000 estate to his widow. One year later the widow dies with a nil cumulative total and an estate worth (disregarding the £325,000 inherited from her husband) £325,000. Under her will her entire estate passed to her adult children. The obvious way forward is for the widow's executors (having obtained the consent of the beneficiaries) to enter into a deed of variation rerouting the husband's estate so that it passes direct to the children rather than through the widow's estate. HMRC accept that the executors of the deceased person can enter into such a deed but it will in any event be prudent to join the beneficiaries as parties to the deed. Where B has been left a life interest in A's estate care needs to be taken to avoid the *Re Soutter's* trap discussed at para.8–132.

For deaths of the surviving spouse or civil partner on or after October 9, 2007, it is now possible to claim the unused portion of the nil rate band which was not utilised on the death of the first spouse or civil partner (at the prevailing rates on the death of the second to die).[185] Therefore there would not be the need to vary the estate of the first to die as shown in the above example in order to benefit from both nil rate bands.

8–168   It is equally possible for the estate of a deceased person to be increased in value by a variation so long as that person was alive at the testator's death. Assume that H dies leaving his estate worth £500,000 to his adult children. Shortly thereafter H's widow dies, leaving her estate of £150,000 to her adult children. It appears that it will be open to the children, as beneficiaries under their father's will, to execute a deed of variation under which £175,000 passes to their mother's estate and to elect to read that variation back into their father's estate. This would utilise their mother's IHT nil rate band. It is not possible, however, to increase the estate of a person who predeceased the testator.[186]

Legacies

8–169   If a variation provides for notional legacies then it is desirable to provide expressly that those legacies, whenever paid, are not to carry interest. In practice it is commonly

---

[183] See also para.8–132.

[184] In such cases personal representatives should only act if so instructed by those persons who would otherwise receive A's property on B's death.

[185] IHTA 1984 ss.8A–8C inserted by FA 2008 s.10 Sch.4.

[186] See *Re Corbishley's Trusts* (1880) 14 Ch. D. 846; and *Re Tilt, Lampet and Kennedy* (1896) 74 L.T. 163.

the case that by the time a variation is prepared the executor's year will have passed. Given that recipients of these notional legacies are, in reality, receiving a gift rather than a legacy it is arguable that no interest would be payable; however, to put the matter beyond doubt it is advisable for the variation to provide so expressly.

Variations in favour of a surviving spouse or civil partner: accrued income

There may be a hidden danger if the object of the variation is to increase that part **8–170** of the estate to which the IHT s.18 exemption applies. In the past HMRC are understood to have taken the view that if such a variation included a provision whereby the recipient spouse or civil partner was not entitled to income accrued between the date of death and the date of the variation, then the s.18 exemption did not apply. In any event it will be desirable in such cases to provide that the recipient spouse or civil partner is to be entitled to all income accruing between the date of death and the date when the interest was redirected or to give the spouse or civil partner a short term interest in possession as discussed at paras 8–161 and following.

Variations and two-year discretionary will trusts

Circumstances may arise in which trustees of a two-year testamentary trust, e.g. **8–171** appoint property to a beneficiary who then wishes to enter into a deed of variation in respect of that property. Such a variation is possible.[187]

Drafting

HMRC at one stage argued that for a variation to fall within s.142, the operative **8–172** clause in the instrument of variation had to state that the transfer of property was taking effect as a variation of the provisions of a will or intestacy to avoid it being construed as a lifetime gift. Accordingly, it was suggested that any variation should follow the wording of that section and provide as follows:

> "The dispositions of property comprised in the estate of the testator (intestate) immediately before his death, shall be varied as follows . . . "

This view was thought by many advisers to be misconceived, and after taking advice, HMRC abandoned it setting out their understanding of the requirements an instrument must satisfy to be valid under s.142[188] stating, inter alia, that

> "the instrument must clearly indicate the dispositions that are the subject of it, and vary their destination as laid down by the deceased's will, or under the law relating to intestates' estates, or otherwise; . . . It will not be contended that the instrument of variation, to be eligible, has in terms to purport to vary the will or intestacy provisions themselves: it is

---

[187] See para.8–203.
[188] *The Law Society Gazette* (May 22, 1985), p.1454.

sufficient if the instrument of variation identifies the disposition to be varied and varies its destination."

Rectification

8–173   Where there is a valid variation, even if it does not achieve the required result, either due to a mistake or otherwise, the variation will still be binding unless the instrument can be rectified.[189] In *Lake v Lake*,[190] Mervyn Davies J. held that a deed of variation can be rectified by the court if words mistakenly used mean that it does not give effect to the parties' joint intention. It does not matter that the rectification achieves a tax advantage nor that it is made more than two years after the death. The court must, however, be satisfied that the deed as executed contains errors: in *Lake* the variation was designed to give legacies to children of the deceased but as a result of a clerical error such gifts were expressed to be "free of tax". As residue passed to an exempt beneficiary (the surviving spouse) grossing up was necessary (see para.8–63, above). The order for rectification substituted "such gifts to bear their own tax" for "free of tax".[191]

In *Wills v Gibbs*[192] the claimant (R), being the testator's cousin's son, claimed for the rectification of a deed of variation, which varied the dispositions taking effect under the last will and codicil of a testator who died in 2005. The application was not opposed by the defendants. (P), the third defendant (the testator's cousin and R's father) was given gifts of land and a farming business under the testator's will, all expressed free of inheritance tax. P wished to vary the gifts in R's favour by deed of variation. The deed of variation would divert the gifts as if they had taken effect under the testator's will, to avoid the disposition being a lifetime gift from P to R which would have created an inheritance tax liability had P not survived the gift by seven years.

P engaged a solicitor, M, who was also the testator's executor, to prepare the deed. However, the deed did not include the statements prescribed by s.142(2) of the Inheritance Tax Act 1984 or the Taxation of Chargeable Gains Act 1992 s.62(7). As a result, the deed would take effect as a lifetime disposition by P and not as a variation of the testator's disposition, with the inevitable tax consequences.

R argued that only if the deed were rectified so as to include the prescribed statements would it achieve the legal effect intended by P and submitted that the failure of the deed to achieve its intended result was attributable to an unintended mistake by M.

Rimer J. accepted that there was an issue capable of being contested between the parties, *Racal Group Services Ltd v Ashmore* [1995] S.T.C. 1151 applied. Although the purpose of the claim was to achieve a tax advantage, this was not a bar in itself to rectification as it was not the only effect of rectification; the parties' rights would also be affected by the rectification. P had intended that the deed should comply with the relevant formalities and its omission was an unintended mistake on M's part. Rimer J. ordered that the deed of variation be rectified to include the relevant formalities.

Rectification of the will was ordered on the basis that, although a tax advantage was the result of rectification, it was not the only result. The parties' rights were also to be

---

[189] See *Russell v IRC* [1988] S.T.C. 195 discussed at para.8–147.

[190] *Lake v Lake* [1989] S.T.C. 865.

[191] See also *Matthews v Martin* [1991] S.T.I. 481 and *Schneider v Mills* [1993] S.T.C. 430. Whilst HMRC would insist on rectification of an instrument of variation, even in cases where it is clear that the variation does not give effect to the parties' intentions, it is arguable that if HMRC are not joined as a party to the rectification proceedings they may not be bound by the court's decision.

[192] *Wills v Gibbs* [2007] EWHC 3361 (Ch).

effected; had rectification not been allowed the testator's executors would have had to hold onto the gifts as security against any potential inheritance tax liability. However, with the rectification, the gifts could pass freely to R; this was sufficient to satisfy Rimer J. that there was more than a fiscal benefit to the rectification of the deed.

Foreign element

Foreign tax systems generally do not contain equivalents to IHT deeds of variation **8–174** and confusion sometimes arises as to the effect of such a deed under foreign law and foreign tax; this is discussed at para.34–103.

XII. DISCLAIMERS

There are two distinct provisions regulating the IHT treatment of disclaimers. **8–175** Section 142(1) deals with disclaimers generally and establishes certain requirements in relation to them. Section 93, on the other hand, deals exclusively with the disclaimer of an interest in settled property. It lays down requirements that are simpler than those established by s.142.

Spouses can use disclaimers to preserve the nil rate band for the death of the second spouse. For further discussion of this see paras 4–29 and following.

Section 142 disclaimers

A disclaimer will come within s.142 only if it involves the disclaiming of a benefit **8–176** conferred by any of the dispositions of the property comprised in a deceased person's estate immediately before he died.

Favoured treatment

A disclaimer coming with s.142 qualifies for two kinds of special statutory treat- **8–177** ment.[193] The relevant statutory provisions are s.17(a) and s.142(1). Section 17(a) provides that a disclaimer coming within s.142 is relieved from being a transfer of value. Thus, a s.142 disclaimer will not itself give rise to a charge to tax. Section 142(1) provides that the disclaimed benefit is to be treated as never having been conferred.

Positive conditions that must be satisfied

Four positive conditions must be satisfied if a disclaimer is to come within s.142(1), **8–178** as follows:

---

[193] Exceptionally, a benefit which a person has disclaimed may nevertheless devolve on him, e.g. where a person who is a residuary legatee disclaims a pecuniary legacy which then falls into residue and to which he is then entitled in part. Since the gift of residue will be regarded as having been made by the deceased testator, there will be no question of the reservation of benefit rules applying in respect of that part of the pecuniary legacy passing to the other residuary legatees.

(1) the disclaimer must be made within two years of the death of the deceased person in question;

(2) the disclaimer must be effected by a written instrument;

(3) the disclaimer must be of a disposition, whether effected by will, under the law relating to intestacy, or otherwise, of property which was comprised in the estate of a deceased person immediately before he died; and

(4) the disclaimer must be a "real" disclaimer.

Commentary generally

8–179   The comments in relation to variations concerning the two year time period; the existence of a written instrument and the desirability, in most cases, of using a deed; precisely what property is treated for these purposes as having been comprised in a person's estate immediately before he died, and the need for the disclaimer to have been a genuine one (HMRC can be expected to challenge disclaimed benefits which, soon after the disclaimer, find their way back into the estate of the person who disclaimed them) all apply equally here.

No section 142(2) statement of intention needed

8–180   In contrast to the position where a variation is effected, no s.142(2) statement need be made in respect of a disclaimer.

Negative conditions that must be satisfied

8–181   There are two negative conditions that must be satisfied. The first is statutory, the second a requirement of general law. The statutory condition is that the disclaimer must not be made for any consideration in money or money's worth other than consideration consisting of the making of a s.142 disclaimer in respect of another of the dispositions effected by the deceased on his death. The comments made at paras 8–141 and following with regard to this "extraneous consideration" condition in relation to variations apply equally here. The requirement of general law is, simply, that the purported disclaimer must be one that the person in question is capable of making as a matter of general law. Here there are two points.

Previous benefits

8–182   As a matter of general law a person cannot disclaim a benefit which he has enjoyed in any way[194]; it is thus impossible to disclaim an interest in possession once the beneficiary has accepted that interest, e.g. by receiving income from the trust. Nor can a person disclaim part[195] only of a benefit although if, for instance, a specific legacy

---

[194] See also HMRC Manuals IHTM35161.

[195] This is clearly HMRC's view but two Ontario cases (*Re Coulson* (1977) 78 D.L.R. (3d) 435 and *Re Graydon* (1942) 2 D.L.R. 306) afford support for the proposition.

and a share of residue are left to the same person, the benefit of one can be accepted and the other disclaimed.[196] It appears possible to disclaim entitlement on an intestacy. In such a case it is thought that the disclaimed property does not pass to the Crown as bona vacantia.[197] Prior to the Finance Act 2002, HMRC had been known to treat ineffective disclaimers as effective variations,[198] but since a variation must now contain a statement (see para.8–136) to the effect that it is intended that s.142(1) is to apply to the variation, it will not be possible for a disclaimer to qualify as a variation because it will not contain such a statement.

Joint tenancies

So far as joint tenancies are concerned, it is thought that a single joint tenant cannot disclaim property: he can only release it in favour of the other joint tenants. On the other hand, all joint tenants can together disclaim a gift. In *Re Schar*, Vaisey J., said: **8–183**

> "I do not believe that a disclaimer can be made by one of several joint tenants, for I think that the unity of the estate and of the interest in it enures for the benefit of each and all; and each and all have one undivided and indivisible property in the subject matter of the gift . . . I think that the only disclaimer which can be made by joint tenants is a disclaimer which is made by them all."[199]

Accordingly, if there were only two joint tenants and one of them dies, it does not seem possible that a disclaimer executed by the survivor can be effective because there is no-one in whose favour it can operate.

Effect of a disclaimer

A disclaimer is a refusal to accept property[200] and it is therefore important to realise that it is not possible to disclaim *in favour* of a particular person. Instead entitlement to property disclaimed passes according to operation of law. Thus, a disclaimed specific gift or pecuniary legacy will form part of the residue, whereas, pre-February 1, 2012, a disclaimed gift of residue or of a share therein will pass on intestacy. The Estates of Deceased Persons (Forfeiture Rule and Law of Succession) Act 2011, which came into effect on February 1, 2012, provides that a will is to be interpreted as if the person disclaiming had died immediately before the testator. The effect of this being that the person next entitled to the property will be able to inherit, rather than, e.g. in the case of a disclaimer of residue, the disclaimed property passing on intestacy. This equally applies on an intestacy. Further, a disclaimer of a residuary gift does not constitute a disclaimer of entitlement on intestacy: a person can disclaim under the will but take the property under the intestacy. If a life interest in property is disclaimed the fund will be held for the remainderman (unless, of course, there is a subsequent life interest). The   **8–184**

---

[196] *Re Joel; Rogerson v Joel* [1943] Ch. 311; and see Fray L.J. in *Guthrie v Walrond* (1883) 22 Ch. D.573: "It appears to me plain that when two distinct legacies or gifts are made by will to one person, he is, as a general rule, entitled to take one and disclaim the other, but that his right to do so may be rebutted if there is anything in the will to show that it was the testator's intention that the option should not exist".

[197] *Re Scott; Widdows v Friends of Clergy Corp* [1975] 2 All E.R. 1066.

[198] Provided a timely election had been made.

[199] *Re Schar* [1951] Ch. 280 at 285.

[200] *Re Stratton's Disclaimer* [1958] Ch. 42.

disclaimer of a remainder interest under a settlement has the effect that on the termination of prior interests (e.g. on the death of life tenants) the settled property will revert to the settlor.

There is nothing to stop a will being drafted so as to set out who will obtain property in the event of its disclaimer.[201] Assume, for instance, that property is to be left by a will to a surviving spouse or civil partner but the testator is aware that when the time comes it may be desirable for that spouse or civil partner to disclaim it. The will could be drafted to provide that in the event of such a disclaimer the property should pass to the grandchildren of the testator on trust. In this way the vagaries of the general law in this area can be avoided. Further, a provision enabling the relevant beneficiary to disclaim all "or any part" of the property in favour of the grandchildren would be equally effective and thereby circumvent the limitation noted in para.8–181.

Intestacies

8–185   Special care needs to be taken where a disclaimer is entered into with respect to property passing on the deceased's intestacy. The problem is that the intestacy rules will continue to operate. Thus, if someone taking under the intestacy disclaims his entitlement, that entitlement will pass under the rules of intestacy which may not yield the desired result. Assume that X died intestate survived by his widow but that he was childless. He was also survived by his father and two brothers. Under the current intestacy rules the widow became entitled to the deceased's personal chattels, £450,000 and one half of the net residuary estate. The father became entitled to the other half of the net residuary estate. On these facts, if the father decided that he did not want half of the residuary estate but that it should pass to the widow and if he therefore disclaimed his interest under the intestacy rules, the two brothers and not the widow would become entitled to that half share of residue. In the case of an intestacy, therefore, it is often more satisfactory for a variation to be effected whereby the relevant property is directed to the intended beneficiary. As an alternative it is always possible to provide that the intestacy rules shall apply as if certain individuals had predeceased the deceased. This is now the general law in any event under the Estates of Deceased Persons (Forfeiture Rule and Law of Succession) Act 2011.

Section 93 disclaimers

8–186   Section 93 provides that where a person becomes entitled to an interest in settled property but disclaims that interest, he is to be treated as never having become entitled to the interest, provided that he did not make the disclaimer for a consideration in money or money's worth. The interest need not have arisen in any particular way, no election need be made, and there is no time limit, but it must be borne in mind that the disclaimer will be effective for s.93 purposes only if it is effective as a matter of general law. This means that, if the interest is an interest in possession, the person entitled to it will normally need to disclaim it fairly soon after becoming entitled to it, so that he conforms to the general requirement that he must not have benefited from the interest that he is disclaiming.

8–187   The relief afforded by s.93 may be particularly useful where an individual with an interest in possession dies. Assume, for example, that the terms of a trust are A for life,

---

[201] See *Guthrie v Walrond* [1883] 22 Ch. 573.

B for life, remainder to C. A dies, and B wishes the trust fund to vest absolutely in C. B cannot achieve this result by entering into a variation or disclaimer under s.142, because the trust fund was not comprised in A's estate for purposes of that section.[202] But he can disclaim his interest under s.93.

The s.93 relief is not confined to an interest in possession. It extends also to reversionary interests and intermediate interests.[203]

Other tax regimes

Under s.62(6)(a) of the Taxation of Chargeable Gains Act 1992 the disclaimer is **8–188** prevented from being a disposal and then s.62 applies as if the disclaimed benefit had never been conferred.[204] Since a disclaimer operates as a refusal to accept property and not as a redirection of property, a person who disclaims property in circumstances such that the property becomes comprised in a settlement for CGT or income tax purposes. There thus may be a significant advantage in using (circumstances permitting) a disclaimer rather than a variation. The pre-owned assets regime introduced by the Finance Act 2004 Sch.15 generally affords favoured treatment to disclaimers; see paras 7–155 and following. There is no general income tax favoured treatment. There is no stamp duty land tax payable on disclaimers.[205]

XIII. TWO-YEAR DISCRETIONARY WILL TRUSTS

Section 144 confers favoured treatment where property comprised in a person's **8–189** estate immediately before his death is settled by his will and, within the period of two years after his death and before any interest in possession has subsisted in the property, there occurs either:

(1) an event on which an exit charge would be imposed; or
(2) an event which would have resulted in such a charge were it not prevented from being imposed by:
   (a) the relief given by s.75 to property becoming subject to employee trusts,
   (b) the relief given to property by s.76 to property becoming held on charitable trusts only without limit of time; property of a qualifying political party; property becoming held for national purposes or property of a body not established or conducted for profit, or
   (c) the relief given by s.144 itself.[206]

In such a case, s.144(2) provides two kinds of relief.

Reliefs

The first kind of relief is that no tax is charged on the event in question. The second **8–190** relief is that the IHT legislation is treated as having effect as if the will had provided

[202] See para.8–130.
[203] See para.11–65.
[204] TCGA 1992 s.62(6)(b).
[205] FA 2003 Sch.3.
[206] IHTA 1984 s.144(1), (3)(c) and (5)(c) inserted by FA 2006 s.156 Sch.20 paras 7, 27 with effect from March 22, 2006.

that on the testator's death the property should be held as it is held after the event in question. The reliefs are thus similar to those provided under s.142, and many of the comments made at paras 8–116 and following with regard to the two statutory reliefs provided by s.142(1) will be relevant here.

Property comprised in the deceased's estate[207]

8–191   Unlike s.142(5), s.144 contains no special rules for determining what property was comprised in a deceased person's estate immediately before he died. Thus, if he settled excluded property by his will, s.144 will not apply. Settled property in which a person had an interest in possession and over which he had a general power of appointment which he exercised by his will to settle the property on discretionary trusts will be within s.144, unless the property was excluded property.

Precipitate appointments

8–192   It is vital to note that s.144 will apply only in circumstances where, in its absence, an exit charge would arise or would have arisen but for the aforementioned reliefs under ss.75 and 76. It follows that no relief will be available if an appointment is made within three months of the testator's death, because in such a case the exit charge that would otherwise have arisen will not apply because of s.65(4). This will have no ill effects as far as the exit charge itself is concerned, but it could have disastrous effects if the appointment is made in favour of the testator's surviving spouse or civil partner with a view to securing the s.18 exemption retrospectively, because this will not be achieved.

8–193   In *Frankland v IRC*[208] the testatrix died on September 26, 1987, leaving property on discretionary trusts for her spouse and issue. On December 22, 1987, the property was transferred to a trust in which the testatrix's surviving spouse was the life tenant. The will trustees claimed that as a result of s.144(2) the interest of the spouse was deemed to arise under the testatrix's will, the spouse exemption was applicable and no IHT was payable on the testatrix's death. However, the settlement made by the testatrix commenced on her death when the trust was completely constituted by the vesting in the trustees of a chose in action. Accordingly, the relevant event, the December appointment, occurred within the first quarter and so the conditions for the operation of s.144(2) were not satisfied. IHT was therefore charged in full on the death of the testatrix and the appointment in favour of the spouse was, as a consequence of s.65(4), not subject to charge. The result was disastrous since some £2 million of tax was in issue.

Counsel for the surviving trustee bravely argued that words should be implied into s.144(2) whereby the actual time when the appointment occurred, provided that it was within two years of death, should be disregarded. It is not surprising, given that the

---

[207] See paras 8–09 and following.
[208] *Frankland v IRC* [1996] S.T.C. 735.

wording of the section is crystal clear and lacks any ambiguity, that this argument was unsuccessful.

In *Harding (Exec. of Loveday Deceased) v IRC*[209] the Special Commissioner decided **8–194** that the *Frankland* decision could not be sidestepped by relying on the provisions of s.143 ("precatory trusts"—see para.8–206). On the relationship between s.143 and s.144 he commented:

> "Reading s.143 as a whole seems to convey a legacy to a person beneficially entitled who carries out the testator's wishes in transferring the asset to another person, rather than trustees exercising fiduciary powers. In 1976 in the absence of this provision the legatee would be making a gift which would have been immediately taxed. Since he was carrying out the deceased's wishes it was natural that he should be exempted from being taxed as having made a gift. The same argument does not apply to trustees who are exercising a power given to them by the testator. Why should trustees in another case, otherwise identical to this one, be taxed differently when they made an identical appointment in the exercise of their own discretion but not carrying out the deceased's wishes? I accept that in some contexts a legatee may include a trustee but this does not seem to me to be such a context. The fact that a transfer under s.143 is not a transfer of value, while not conclusive in saying that it must have been one apart from the section, does indicate that the normal ambit of the section is limited to cases where there would be a transfer of value. Trustees making an appointment like the one in this case were protected by s.144 which was originally s.47(1A) of the Finance Act 1975, immediately preceding s.47(1B) which became s.143. The *Frankland* trap did not exist under the original legislation and so there was no need for s.143 to operate in this area. I appreciate the existence of the overlap between ss.142 and 143 but s.142 was a later addition [see s.68(1) of the Finance Act 1978] while ss.143 and 144 were both introduced at the same time [see s.121 of the Finance Act 1976] and one would not expect them to overlap."

Practical problems with two-year trusts

A major difficulty with these flexible trusts is to determine the moment when the **8–195** trust is constituted so that the trustees' discretionary powers become exercisable. Assume, for instance, that on the death of the testator it is obvious that all the property comprised in the trust should be appointed in favour of his surviving spouse or civil partner. Can the trustees, before the commencement of administration (even before the grant of probate) appoint to her the fund? HMRC's original view seemed to be that appointments are not possible until the completion of administration—a view which would imply that until that time nothing is owned by the trustees so that the trust is incompletely constituted.

The correctness of this view is open to some doubt since, although on death legal and **8–196** equitable title to assets forming the residue of the estate vests in the personal representatives *(Commissioner of Stamp Duties (Queensland) v Livingston)*[210] the beneficiaries under the will have the right, inter alia, to compel due administration of the estate and this right is a transmissible chose in action *(Re Leigh)*.[211] It follows that trustees appointed under the will must likewise possess this chose in action and they should, of course, be vigilant to ensure that the estate is duly administered. Further, it may therefore be argued that the chose constitutes the trust from the moment of death

---

[209] *Harding (Exec. of Loveday Deceased) v IRC* [1997] S.T.C. (S.C.D.) 321.
[210] *Commissioner of Stamp Duties (Queensland) v Livingston* [1965] A.C. 694.
[211] *Re Leigh* [1970] Ch. 277.

with the result that the trustees dispositive powers may be exercised immediately and beneficiaries appointed to all or a portion of the trust fund.[212]

8–197 It has also been suggested that this view of HMRC could be challenged under s.91 which provides as follows:

> "(1) Where a person would have been entitled to an interest in possession in the whole or part of the residue of the estate of a deceased person had the administration of that estate been completed, the same consequences shall follow under this Act as if he had become entitled to an interest in possession in the unadministered estate and in the property (if any) representing ascertained residue, or in a corresponding part of it, on the date as from which the whole or part of the income of the residue would have been attributable to his interest had the residue been ascertained immediately after the death of the deceased person."

This section is designed to ensure that the normal IHT principles apply to residuary beneficiaries under a will from the moment of death. When the residue is settled, for instance, and the life tenant dies before completion of administration, IHT is charged not on the value of his interest, but on the assets in which his interest subsists. Although intended for this particular purpose the section may also be relevant to an appointment out of a two year discretionary will trust: assume, for instance, that the trustees determine, despite the fact that the estate is still unadministered, to appoint all the property to the testator's daughter. Under s.91 she is now treated as owning all the assets in that residuary estate.

8–198 Although this argument may appear convincing at first sight, it does assume the very point in issue, i.e. that trustees can make a valid appointment of property before administration of the estate has been completed. Therefore, to counter HMRC 's view, it must be necessary to rely on the argument deployed earlier that the trust is constituted at death by the vesting of the chose in action.

8–199 It has been suggested that careful drafting of the will can overcome HMRC's objections and ensure that property can be appointed before the completion of administration of the estate. One suggestion, to confer upon the *trustees* an express power to appoint property before the completion of the administration of the estate, appears doomed to fail since ex hypothesi if nothing is owned at that stage nothing can be appointed. Alternatively, however, and more satisfactorily, the executors of the will should be given the power to exercise, during the administration period, those discretions which the trustees could undoubtedly exercise after administration. Even if wills are not so drafted it will commonly be the case that the executors and trustees are the same persons and difficulties may be overcome if before any such appointment the property is assented from the executors to themselves qua trustees.[213] Care should, however, be taken over the CGT implications of so doing. If the executors as trustees appoint an asset to a beneficiary absolutely there will be a disposal chargeable to CGT under s.71 of the Taxation of Chargeable Gains Tax Act 1992. HMRC's view is that no such charge arises where the appointment is made by the executors during the administration of the estate (where executors can validly make such an appointment); see further the discussion at para.8–205.

---

[212] Assuming that the trustees can make such appointments considerable care will be needed to appoint part only of the trust fund to a particular beneficiary. No difficulties arise if the trustees determine that all of the estate shall be appointed but what if (say) only one quarter is to be appointed to the surviving spouse or civil partner. It is thought that the trustees should recite that they appoint an undivided share of the appropriate size in favour of that beneficiary. The *chose* that is owned by the trustees is thought to be capable of fragmentation in this fashion (see *Williams v CIR* (1965) N.Z.L.R. 395; *Shepherd v Taxation Commr* (1965) 133 C.L.R. 385).

[213] In the case of land this must be done in writing: see *Re King's Will Trust* [1964] Ch. 542.

It is worth noting, in this context, what happened in *Fitzwilliam v IRC*.[214] The testator's residuary estate was settled on trusts which gave the trustees power in the 23 months following the death to appoint amongst a discretionary class of beneficiaries. After the expiration of that period the trustees were to pay the income to the testator's widow for the remainder of her life. The executors indicated that they intended to appoint the property to the surviving spouse and the Winchester District Probate Registry therefore accepted that the estate was spouse exempt. This conduct was criticised by HMRC but Vinelott J. did not join in that criticism and pointed out that because the estate was largely composed of agricultural land and chattels it would have been very difficult for the executors to have paid such a bill. This matter was not raised in subsequent appeals to the higher courts.

However, HMRC now accept that a power of appointment under a will is vested in **8–200** the executors/trustees as from the death and is exercisable over all residue whether or not residue has been ascertained, unless there is a clear contrary intention under the will.[215] It is therefore advisable to confer express power under the will for the executors in that capacity to be able to exercise the power of appointment during the administration, even before obtaining the grant of probate, thereby being able to claim, e.g., spouse/civil partner relief, and to avoid paying IHT up front on the application for the grant—care always being taken not to exercise the power within three months of the date of death.

Advantages of two-year discretionary trusts

It will often be preferable to use a two year discretionary will trust rather than rely **8–201** on a deed of variation, for five reasons:

(1) *No consents:* an appointment under such a trust will not need the consent of the beneficiaries. Thus, problems that would otherwise arise where there are infant beneficiaries and/or uncooperative beneficiaries can be avoided.
(2) *No new settlors:* none of the beneficiaries adversely affected by an appointment will be treated as settlors for the purposes of CGT or income tax.
(3) *Changes in assets:* the fact that the assets comprised in the estate have changed since the death does not matter.
(4) *Short term interests/extraneous consideration:* there is no short term interest or extraneous consideration trap.
(5) *No "election":* there is no need to "elect" that s.144 should apply.

Note also that two year discretionary will trusts can, in effect, give a two year survivorship period. Section 144 applies to the extent that a trust satisfying the above requirements is ended (in whole or in part) within two years of the testator's death and it is not necessary (although it is often done as a matter of practice) to limit the trust to two years.

Disadvantages of two-year discretionary trusts

The two year discretionary trust does, however, have a number of disadvantages. **8–202** First, when created IHT will be charged on the property comprised in the trust.

[214] *Fitzwilliam v IRC* [1993] S.T.C. 65.
[215] HMRC Manuals IHTM35181.

Accordingly, there will be a cash flow disadvantage although if any portion of the trust fund is appointed within the appropriate two year period to the testator's surviving spouse or civil partner, a repayment of IHT will result and interest on over-paid tax may be payable under s.235—although see para.8–199 above. Secondly, difficulties may arise in the case of wills establishing such discretionary trusts which include, as part of the trust property, chattels. Commonly in such cases the beneficiaries will continue to enjoy the use of the chattels as they had done during the testator's life. It is arguable that by so doing the beneficiaries will have an interest in possession in the relevant property with the result that the relevant property regime may come to an end at that point.[216] Finally, it is important to realise that while s.144 confers relief from IHT there is no equivalent provision affording relief from CGT (contrast the position with variation and disclaimers).

Interaction of sections 142 and 144

8–203   Two questions arise as to the interaction of ss.142 and 144. First, can s.144 apply where the discretionary trusts arise under a variation to which s.142 applies? It is thought that s.144 relief should not be available because s.144(1) requires the property to be settled by the deceased's will. However, HMRC have accepted that there can be a s.144 appointment after a variation within s.142 and have cited the example of a variation under s.142(1) creating a discretionary trust and then there being an appointment out of that trust within two years of the testator's death.[217]

Secondly, can s.142 apply in relation to property in respect of which s.144 has applied, e.g. X leaves property on discretionary trusts, the trustees more than three months[218] after but within two years of X's death appoint the property to Y who then, also within two years of X's death, effects a variation giving the property to Z? In the authors' view s.142 can apply in such a case and this is understood also to be HMRC's view.[219]

Possible withdrawal of favoured treatment

8–204   The 1989 Budget proposals noted in para.8–89 above would have removed the favoured treatment of these settlements.

Capital gains tax and income tax

8–205   Neither the CGT legislation nor the income tax legislation contains the equivalent to s.144. Where an appointment is made by the trustees after the assets of the estate have vested in the trustees, i.e. after the assets have passed out of the estate into the hands of the trustees the CGT position will be as follows. If the occasion on which s.144 prevents an IHT exit charge from being incurred is also the occasion of a deemed market value disposal under s.71(1) of the Taxation of Chargeable Gains Act 1992, e.g.

---

[216] *Sansom v Peay* [1976] 3 All E.R. 375 and see para.12–45.
[217] HMRC Manuals IHTM35085.
[218] See *Frankland v IRC* [1996] S.T.C. 735, discussed at para.8–192.
[219] HMRC Manuals IHTM35085.

because a beneficiary becomes absolutely entitled to trust property, the trustees will realise a chargeable gain if the trust assets have appreciated in value since the testator's death.[220] The question may then arise as to whether the condition for CGT holdover relief under s.260(2)(a) of the 1992 Act is satisfied. That section refers to the need for a chargeable transfer, and as is discussed at para.8–33 an exit charge for this purpose ranks as a chargeable transfer. Nevertheless, in the view of both the authors and HMRC the s.260(2)(a) condition will not be satisfied, because the effect of s.144 applying will be to prevent any exit charge from arising.

The position for CGT is different if the trustees make an appointment during the administration of the estate, i.e. before the assets have vested in them. Assets will normally vest on the ascertainment of residue[221] but when an appointment is made in advance of residue being ascertained in this case the appointment is not treated as a disposal for CGT purposes and the appointee will take the assets as legatee and therefore acquire them at their probate value[222]; see also the discussion at paras 8–198–8–199.

XIV. PRECATORY TRUSTS

It may be that a testator bequeaths property (e.g. his personal chattels) by his will to **8–206** a person expressing a wish that that person should transfer the property to someone else. The person to whom the property is bequeathed is regarded (somewhat mislead-ingly) as holding the property on "precatory trusts". In fact, he owns the property beneficially and is under no legal obligation to comply with the testator's wishes. Thus, if he were to comply with the testator's wishes he would, in the absence of provision to the contrary, make a transfer of value. The legislation accordingly provides that where such a person transfers any such property in accordance with a testator's wish within two years of the latter's death:

(1) the transfer is not a transfer of value[223]; and
(2) the property is treated as having been bequeathed by the testator's will to the transferee.[224]

Care should be taken where the testator leaves a letter of wishes. If a surviving spouse or civil partner distributes assets in accordance with the deceased's written wishes then those distributions will be retrospective and charged under s.143. If there is a letter of wishes that sets these out it is difficult for the surviving spouse or civil partner to argue that he is distributing them to those beneficiaries otherwise than in accordance with the deceased's expressed wishes. To avoid being caught by s.143 it would be preferable if the letter of wishes is phrased as expressing the testator's wishes as to what would happen to the assets on the death of the survivor. If, therefore, the surviving spouse or civil partner wanted to make these distributions during his own lifetime then he himself is making this choice and he is not transferring the property in accordance with the deceased's wishes.

---

[220] See TCGA 1992 s.62(1)(a) and (4).
[221] Capital Gains Manual CG31431; cf. the position if the trustees considered to be entitled to a chose in action.
[222] See TCGA 1992 s.62(4).
[223] IHTA 1984 s.17(b).
[224] IHTA 1984 s.143.

The 1989 Budget proposals noted in para.8–89 above would also have removed the favoured treatment of precatory trusts.

Other taxes

8–207 The pre-owned assets regime introduced by the Finance Act 2004 Sch.15 generally affords favoured treatment to dispositions made pursuant to precatory trusts under s.143: see para.7–179. No particular CGT or income tax treatment applies.

XV. ORDERS UNDER THE INHERITANCE (PROVISION FOR FAMILY AND DEPENDANTS) ACT 1975

8–208 Under the Inheritance (Provision for Family and Dependants) Act 1975, hereafter referred to as the "Inheritance Act", the court has power to order financial provision where the dispositions of the estate of a person who died domiciled in England and Wales do not make reasonable financial provision for his family and dependants. Under s.2 of the Act, the court may order payments to be made or property transferred out of the deceased's "net estate" in order to make up any insufficiency. The court may also order that the net estate is to be applied in acquiring property, and may vary any marriage settlement of the deceased.

8–209 Under s.8 of the Act, nominated property and *donationes mortis causa* are treated as part of the deceased's net estate to the extent of their value at death, after deducting any IHT payable in respect of them. This is subject to the qualification that the tax so deducted is limited to the amount of tax borne by the nominee or donee. Under s.9, so much of the value of any severable share of a joint tenancy as appears just (having regard, inter alia, to the tax payable in respect of it) to which the deceased was entitled may also be included in his estate. Where an order is made, s.19(1) of the Act provides that:

> " . . . for all purposes including the purposes of the enactments relating to capital transfer tax,[225] the will or the laws relating to intestacy, or both the will and the law relating to intestacy, as the case may be, shall have effect and be deemed to have had effect as from the deceased's death subject to the provisions of the order."

Orders under sections 2, 8 or 9

8–210 The IHT legislation takes account of the above provisions by providing in s.146(1) that, where an order[226] is made under s.2 of the Inheritance Act in relation to any property forming part of the net estate of a person who died after April 6, 1976, then, without prejudice to s.19(1), that property is treated as if on his death it had devolved subject to the provisions of the order. Section 146(1) thus echoes s.19(1); in addition, it also operates with respect to property dealt with under ss.8 or 9 of the Inheritance

---

[225] Now IHT: FA 1986 s.100(1)(b).
[226] Frequently no specific order is made under s.2. Instead proceedings under the Inheritance Act are stayed or dismissed by an order embodying such terms as might be included in an order under s.2. To avoid doubt such terms are treated for the purposes of s.146 as provisions of an order under s.2: see s.146(8).

Act. This is necessary, since as the destination of such property is not governed by a person's will or the law relating to intestacy, such property is not affected by s.19(1).

Section 10 dispositions

Section 10 of the Inheritance Act deals with dispositions made by the deceased **8–211** within six years of his death where the disposition was made for less than full consideration in money or money's worth, and with the intention of defeating an application for financial provision under the Act. In such a case, the court may make an order under which the person to whom the disposition was made must provide property or a sum of money not exceeding the value of the property transferred (less any IHT borne by that person on that transfer) to him by the deceased. The IHT legislation takes account of s.10 by providing in s.146(2) that where in relation to a death occurring after April 6, 1976, a person is required by an order made under s.10 to provide any money or property, the money or property is to be included in the deceased's estate for the purposes of the transfer of value made by him on his death.

In addition, if the earlier disposition made by the deceased was a chargeable transfer, and his personal representatives make a claim:

(1) any tax paid (plus the interest thereon) or payable on the value transferred by the chargeable transfer is repaid to the personal representatives (whether or not they paid it), or ceases to be payable, as the case may be; and

(2) the deceased's cumulative total is adjusted so as to exclude the value transferred by that chargeable transfer.

The claim should be made in writing, be signed by the personal representatives, and include a copy of the court order.[227]

Adjustments and tax repayments

The application of s.146 may have significant IHT implications: it could result in **8–212** extra tax being payable, e.g. where the effect of the order is that a smaller portion of the deceased's estate devolves on his surviving spouse or civil partner; conversely, it may result in less tax being paid, e.g. where the order results in a greater portion of the deceased's estate being transferred to his surviving spouse or civil partner. The legislation accordingly contains a number or rules to take account of the impact of an order.

On a preliminary matter, by s.146(4), any adjustment in consequence of the provisions of either s.146 or under s.19(1) of the Inheritance Act of the tax payable in respect of the transfer of value made by the deceased on his death does *not* affect either:

(a) the amount of any deduction to be made under s.8 of the Inheritance Act in respect of tax born by the person mentioned in s.8(3) of that Act; or

---

[227] In such cases the deceased's cumulative total of chargeable lifetime transfers in the previous seven years is reduced by the gift reclaimed for the estate. This, of itself, may affect the rate at which tax is charged on the deceased's estate on death. Also the value of the reclaimed property and any tax repaid on it falls into the estate at death thus necessitating a recalculation of IHT payable on death.

(b) the amount of tax to which regard is to be had under s.9(2) of that Act.

Where a person is ordered to make a payment or to transfer property by reason of holding property treated as part of the deceased's net estate under s.8 or s.9 of the Inheritance Act and tax borne by him is taken into account for the purpose of the order then, by s.146(4), any repayment of that tax shall be made not to that person but to the deceased's personal representatives.

In addition to the rule just noted concerning the destination of a repayment of IHT, there are two rules concerning the treatment of repayments of IHT (including, under s.146(7), any interest thereon):

(a) where IHT is repaid to a deceased's personal representatives pursuant to a claim made by them under s.146(2) in respect of a chargeable transfer made by the deceased during his lifetime that tax is included in his estate for purposes of the transfer of value made by him on his death; and

(b) where IHT is repaid as just stated or under s.146(4) that tax forms part of the deceased's net estate for purposes of the Inheritance Act.

Exemption from settled property charges

8–213   The legislation also takes account of the possible IHT impact on settled property of orders under the Inheritance Act. By s.146(6), anything which is done in compliance with an order under the Inheritance Act or which occurs on the coming into force of such an order, and which would constitute a chargeable occasion under the special charging provisions[228] is relieved from being a chargeable occasion. Where an order provides for property to be settled or for the variation of a settlement s.146(6) prevents any charge from arising under s.52(1).

Rerouted exempt transfers

8–214   It may be that a claim is settled in circumstances such that a beneficiary to whom an exempt transfer has been made effects a disposition of property not derived from that transfer in settlement of the whole or part of that claim. In that case regard needs to be had to s.29A, discussed at paras 8–83 and following.

Other taxes

8–215   The CGT and income tax legislation itself confers no special treatment in respect of Orders under the Act. However, s.19(1) of the Act gives limited provision which would seem to cover CGT and income tax. Where an order is made under s.2 of the Act it shall have effect "for all purposes" as from the date of the deceased's death subject to

---

[228] But not under IHTA 1984 s.79.

the provisions of the order. Therefore s.19(1) would not apply for example to an approved compromise agreement.

XVI. LEGITIM

Under Scots law, the infant children and certain remoter issue of a deceased person **8–216** have certain legal rights against one-third of the deceased's net moveable estate. These rights exist as an alternative to any testamentary provision which may exist in favour of the child in question; if the child claims his rights he forfeits any provision made in his favour. The rights must be satisfied unless the child renounces them, or elects to take under the will.

Before the Finance Act 1976, the existence of these rights gave rise to difficulties, because the final destination of the portion of the deceased's estate against which a child was entitled to claim legitim often remained undetermined for periods exceeding a year. In addition, the CTT effects of certain disclaimers of legitim were unclear. Section 147 has effectively resolved these problems. The section, which extends to Scotland only, has effect in relation to the estates of any testator who died after November 2, 1974. It provides two alternative courses of action where a testator dies leaving a surviving spouse or civil partner, one or more infants entitled to claim legitim, and a will (or other testamentary document) under which a disposition is made to the spouse or civil partner, the effect of which would be to leave insufficient property to satisfy the claims of the infant or infants in respect of legitim. The position where the insufficiency is caused by one or more dispositions to someone other than the surviving spouse or civil partner is not clear, but it is thought that HMRC are likely to apply the relief in a generous manner.

Claim is made

The first course of action is provided for in s.147(2), and assume, in effect, that the **8–217** person entitled to claim legitim has done so. Under this alternative, tax is charged as if the disposition to the surviving spouse or civil partner did not include any amount in respect of legitim, i.e. any claims are assumed to have been enforced. If any claims to legitim subsisting against the estate are in fact renounced within certain time limits (see below), tax is recalculated on the basis that the disposition to the spouse or civil partner included the amount renounced. Such a renunciation will normally increase the exempt portion of the testator's transfer, and s.147(2) provides that in such a case tax shall be repaid to the estate accordingly. The repaid tax carries interest from the date on which the tax was paid at the rate prescribed by s.233(1)(b). By s.147(8), the tax repayments need not be within the normal limits established by s.241 (discussed at para.29–161).

A person's renunciation will be within the above mentioned time limits only if he renounces his claim:

(1) before attaining the age of 18; or
(2) within two years of attaining the age of 18; or
(3) within such longer period as HMRC permit.[229]

---

[229] IHTA 1984 s.147(9).

429

A person is assumed to have claimed legitim unless he renounces his claim within these time limits.[230] If he in fact renounces his claim within these limits, the renunciation is not a transfer of value.[231]

Other taxes

8–218   The pre-owned assets regime introduced by the Finance Act 2004 Sch.15 generally affords favoured treatment where relief is available under s.147; see para.7–179. No particular CGT or income tax treatment applies.

Election

8–219   The alternative course of action is one which applies only if the testator's executors or judicial factor so elect. By s.123(5), any such election must be made in writing to the Board within two years from the date of the death or such longer period as the Board may allow. Under this alternative, any claims to legitim are initially ignored, and the tax is charged as if the disposition to the spouse or civil partner had taken effect. If the children do not renounce their claim to legitim within the above mentioned time limits,[232] tax is subsequently charged as if the legitim fund had not passed to the spouse or civil partner, but had in fact been paid out in full at the testator's death, any tax chargeable thereon being calculated as though the legitim fund had been paid out in full on the testator's death and the tax chargeable thereon had been apportioned rateably among the persons entitled to claim legitim. Amounts renounced are left out of account, and no apportionment is made to any child who has renounced his claim. The tax charged begins to carry interest at the above mentioned rates six months after the beginning of the month in which the deceased died. By s.209(2), the deceased's personal representatives are not liable for this tax. Instead, the persons to whom the tax is apportioned are liable and so far as the tax due is attributable to the value of any property, any person in whom that property is vested, whether beneficially or otherwise, at any time after the death or who at any such time is beneficially entitled to an interest in possession in that property is also liable for the tax so attributable. The liability of a person to whom tax is apportioned under s.147(4) is limited in the same way as the liability of a personal representative.[233] By s.147(9), a certificate of discharge may be given under s.239 in respect of the whole estate: this certificate does not preclude HMRC from claiming tax without any time limit.

Children

8–220   Finally by s.147(7), where a child dies under the age of 18, or before renouncing within the above-mentioned time limits his right to legitim, the provisions of s.147 apply to his executors or judicial factor as they would have applied to the child if he had attained 18; the date of the child's death is substituted for his 18th birthday for the

---

[230] IHTA 1984 s.147(6).
[231] IHTA 1984 s.17.
[232] IHTA 1984 s.147(6).
[233] See paras 29–62 and following.

purpose of determining the time limits. Where the executors or judicial factor of a deceased person renounce a claim to legitim, the amount renounced is not treated as forming part of that person's estate.

Long shelf life

Legal rights can subsist for up to 20 years after the death. On the ending of this long negative prescription there will then be a PET by the child in favour of his surviving parent flowing from the omission to exercise this right. If a parent dies within the 20 year period and has received (during that same period) property from his own pre-deceasing spouse or civil partner, the children could then have a valid claim against that estate which relates back to the legal rights which they enjoyed in the estate of the first parent to die. Such a claim would inevitably have to be satisfied out of the estate of the second parent to die but would have the effect of reducing his estate for IHT purposes.

8–221

PLANNING OVERVIEW

XVII. TESTAMENTARY AND POSTHUMOUS PLANNING GENERALLY

Strategic overview

Various specific planning points have been mentioned in the foregoing discussion. The purpose of the following discussion is to suggest some general approaches to testamentary and posthumous planning.

8–222

The advantages of testamentary trusts generally

There are a number of attractions, from both a general planning standpoint and so far as tax is concerned, to leaving property on trust. From a general planning standpoint, trusts offer flexibility and the opportunity for a testator to exercise some posthumous influence over the application of his property. This may be particularly attractive where, as is increasingly the case, the testator leaves a surviving spouse or civil partner and children from an earlier relationship.

8–223

So far as flexibility is concerned, the advantages of discretionary trusts are obvious, but the position is not so different where one or more beneficiaries are left interests in possession—typically a surviving spouse or civil partner is given a life interest—so long as the trustees are given wide overriding powers of appointment.

IHT

Before March 2006 the reservation of benefit provisions would not normally apply in relation to appointments made by the trustees. If X left property on trust for his

8–224

widow for life with remainder over to their children, conferring on the trustees a wide overriding power of appointment, the trustees could, e.g. exercise their power to terminate the widow's interest in a portion of the trust fund equal to her unused IHT nil rate band and appoint that that portion should be held on discretionary trusts under which the widow could benefit, if circumstances developed such that she needed financial help.[234] This did not result in the widow reserving a benefit and if she survived the appointment by seven years her IHT nil rate band will have been recycled with respect to the value of that portion. If, on the other hand, X had left his estate to his widow outright and she subsequently settled it on discretionary trusts under which she could benefit from the property, the latter would remain in her estate for IHT purposes.

However, as a result of the amendments to the gift with reservation of benefit rules in Finance Act 1986 s.102ZA, the life tenant will have to be excluded from any future benefit in the property so as not to be treated as having reserved any benefit (see paras 7–99 and following).

Capital gains tax

8–225   A trust is a taxable entity for CGT purposes. This has two major consequences:

(1) the fact that property comprised in a trust is appointed by trustees on new trusts, or becomes held on new trusts under the terms of a trust deed, is not the occasion of a disposal for CGT purposes.[235] Returning to the previous example, the appointment by the trustees will not be a chargeable occasion. If, on the other hand, the estate had been left to the widow, the transfer by her to the trustees would have involved a disposal by her (with a 20 per cent IHT charge going in) and any gain arising would have, prima facie, been subject to CGT; and

(2) the fact that property comprised in a trust is appointed by trustees on new trusts, or becomes held on new trusts under the terms of the trust deed, will leave the trust's taper relief unaffected.[236] Where, on the other hand, a person transfers property to a trust the transfer crystallises any available taper relief and the trust starts its own taper relief.

Discretionary trusts vs interest in possession trusts

8–226   Whether discretionary trusts or interest in possession trusts are appropriate will vary from case to case. In many cases, of course, both kinds of trust will be used in the same will, e.g. discretionary trusts to hold property equal in value to the testator's unused nil rate band, and interest in possession trusts for the remainder.

Using nil rate band discretionary trusts

8–227   In order to give the greatest flexibility under a will it is very common for there to be a nil rate band legacy, on discretionary trusts. Care needs to be taken in ascertaining the

[234] In the authors' view this was the case even if the trustees can exercise their power only with the widow or surviving civil partner's consent; see para.7–47.
[235] Unless a beneficiary becomes absolutely entitled to the trust fund: TCGA 1992 s.71(1).
[236] TCGA 1992 s.71(1).

testator's wishes as to exactly how much he intends to be included in this legacy. For example, if the discretionary legacy included all property attracting full 100 per cent business and agricultural relief plus the nil rate band of £325,000, the result might be that nothing is left to fall into residue. For discussion of how the transferable nil rate band can be used for tax planning purposes see paras 4–22 and following.

Such nil rate band discretionary trusts should specify a wide class of beneficiaries, including the surviving spouse or civil partner, so the greatest flexibility is attained: the nil rate band will not be known until the date of death and the needs of all the potential beneficiaries may be very different at the time of death as compared to when the will was made as may be the deceased's assets.[237] For problems which can arise in relation to nil rate band trusts where business relief or agricultural relief is available see paras 16–18 and following.

8–228 The most obvious way of taking advantage of the nil rate band and agricultural and business reliefs is to ensure that the maximum amount possible passes to non exempt beneficiaries, rather than "wasting" the exemptions when assets qualifying for such relief pass to exempt beneficiaries such as the surviving spouse or civil partner.

The will should give specific legacies of assets qualifying for agricultural and business relief to chargeable beneficiaries, because this will make full use of the availability of the reliefs. For the risks associated with such legacies and alternative strategies, see paras 26–177 and following.

It is not thought that an appropriation of assets to a particular beneficiary under an express power in the will nor under the Administration of Estates Act 1925 s.41 will suffice to ensure that full business relief is available, but a carefully worded appointment out of a discretionary trust within two years of the death may be treated as a specific gift.

Defeasible life interest trusts of residue

8–229 Where the testator is survived by a spouse or civil partner there may be an easy IHT saving opportunity. In simple terms the will is drafted so as to leave the surviving spouse or civil partner with a life interest (which would be an IPDI, therefore a qualifying interest in possession trust to which s.49 will apply) in the deceased's estate (after exhausting the deceased's nil rate band—see para.8–227). No IHT will be charged on death since the remaining property will fall under the s.18 exemption. Under the terms of that will trust it should be provided, first, that the trustees have power to advance capital to the surviving spouse or civil partner and, secondly, that they have the power to terminate the life interest in favour of an appropriate class of discretionary beneficiaries, including the surviving spouse or civil partner.[238] The end result is that (in much the same way as under full discretionary trusts) there is flexibility in the testator's will. Should the trustees decide that the spouse or civil partner's interest is to be terminated, in whole or in part, in favour of a particular beneficiary, then that termination will result in the surviving spouse or civil partner making a transfer of value, which if the property becomes held for one or more individuals absolutely, will be a PET. IHT will be avoided unless the spouse or civil partner dies within seven years.

There would be no objection to the trustees exercising their powers in this way soon after the testator's death. Care needs to be taken, though, to ensure that the spouse or

[237] For drafting options see *Practical Will Precedents* at F5 and following.
[238] For a precedent refer to *Practical Will Precedents*, B2.

civil partner has a "real" life interest to avoid any potential argument by HMRC that the life interest was a sham, and to avoid the associated operations rules applying (see para.9–06). It is believed that to date HMRC's practice has been not to query such arrangements but where the sums concerned are large it is possible that HMRC may scrutinise the appointment more closely. Obviously the longer the time span between the date of death and the date of the termination of the life interest the better. Equally, the executors and trustees should ensure that the decision to appoint is taken after a comprehensive review of the financial position, such a review as could not in practice have been carried out during the testator's lifetime, in order to avoid accusations that the appointment was in fact "preordained" by the deceased. Ideally, the life tenant should also have received some income from the assets before the life interest is terminated.

Drafting a flexible will along these lines has advantages over the use of discretionary trusts under s.144 (see para.8–188) as it avoids any tax charge on the death of the testator and further may avoid a tax charge on the termination of the interest in possession provided that the surviving spouse or civil partner lives for the requisite seven year period. There is also the additional advantage of great flexibility with such wills, including giving the testator a greater degree of influence over the ultimate destination of his estate, thus making this type of will particularly suitable where the testator leaves a surviving spouse or civil partner and children from an earlier relationship.

Prima facie, an appointment to an individual absolutely will crystallise a charge on any gains but, given the CGT free uplift on death, this will often not be a problem. Even if there were a substantial gain, CGT should be avoided on such an appointment provided the appointment has been made by the personal representatives from the unadministered estate.[239] The argument that no CGT is payable is based on s.62(4) of the TCGA 1992 which provides that "on a person acquiring any asset as legatee, no chargeable gain shall accrue to the personal representatives and the legatee shall be treated as if the personal representatives' acquisition of the asset had been his acquisition of it". "Legatee" is defined in s.64 as "including any person taking under a testamentary disposition . . . ". HMRC's published view[240] is that "the exercise of the power of appointment is, however, read back into the original will. The beneficiary therefore takes the asset as legatee under TCGA 1992 s.64(2) and TCGA 1992 s.64(4) applies".

One drawback to this approach is that it would always be open to the surviving spouse or civil partner to disclaim his or her interest which would defeat the tax benefit of using this type of will by making the residuary estate immediately chargeable. The threat of disclaiming could be used by the surviving spouse or civil partner as a negotiating tool in the ultimate division of the deceased's estate perhaps in relation to an Inheritance Act claim.

Where the will is not as IHT efficient as it could be

8–230   All is not lost in tax planning terms if the testator's will does not, as drawn, result in the most beneficial IHT result. As is discussed at paras 8–115 and following, it is possible to vary the terms of the deceased's will. Assume, e.g., that Jill dies owning an

---

[239] See paras 8–198 and following.
[240] In reply to a letter from the Chairman of the Accountancy Institute's Capital Taxes Sub-Committee in September 1995; see *Taxation Practitioner* (September 1995), p.23 and *Capital Gains Manual*, Ch.4, paras 31430–3 and 37910.

estate worth £1 million including, inter alia, property used in a business worth £600,000 which qualifies for 50 per cent relief and quoted shares worth £400,000 which do not qualify for any relief. Her £325,000 nil rate band is intact. Under her will the property used in the business passes to her husband[241] and the quoted shares pass to her son. Consideration should be given to her husband and son entering into a deed of variation under which the property used in the business and £25,000 of the quoted shares go to her son, residue to her husband. In this way, £325,000 of the value transferred would be attributable to the specific gift to the son, but all of that value transferred will be within the nil rate band. In both *Russell v IRC*[242] and *Lake v Lake*,[243] variations were entered into in order to achieve this kind of result.

Whether such an approach will in fact be desirable will depend on the circumstances of the case. An alternative approach would be for the son to take quoted shares worth only £325,000 and for the husband subsequently to make a PET to the son of the property used in the business. There would still be no charge on death and if the husband failed to survive the PET by seven years business relief would be available so long as the son still owned the property.[244] There could, of course, be no undertaking by the husband to make the gift. It is thought that the *Ramsay* principle will not apply.

A duty to advise

An interesting question is whether advisers have a duty of care to advise bene- **8–231** ficiaries of the tax planning opportunities afforded by instruments of variation.[245] In *Cancer Research Campaign v Ernest Brown & Co (a firm)*[246] the defendants were instructed to draw up a will and did not advise the testatrix on the tax advantages that would accrue if she varied the will of her recently deceased brother in favour of charity. In deciding that the defendants had not been negligent Harman J. commented:

> "It is clear from *White v Jones* [[1995] 2 A.C. 207] that, contrary to a good deal of classical legal thinking, there does arise a duty to take care to ensure that the intended beneficiary receives the benefit intended. The solicitor must draw the will with reasonable expedition so that the beneficiaries' expectations are not defeated by the testator dying in short order before the will is executed. That is *White v Jones* itself. The solicitor must advise the testator as to the proper execution of the will. In *Ross v Caunters (a firm)* [1980] Ch. 297 that was the vice which resulted in the will failing to take effect. I do not doubt the solicitor, in considering the will, must consider what inheritance tax complications that testator will cause by the bequests for which he is given instructions.
>
> But we refuse to hold, extending the duty to advise by, it was said, analogy, that there arises a duty to inform the intended testator, who has come in to instruct a solicitor about his or her will, about tax avoidance schemes in connection with some quite other estate. It is that departure which seems to us to make it impossible to imply any duty upon Ernest Brown & Co. during [the testatrix's] lifetime. It seems to us that the obligation to advise [the testatrix] as to her possible giving up of an interest under [her brother's] will (which is what would have to take place if a deed of variation were executed during her lifetime) raises so many difficulties that the court should approach it with extreme caution. If the duty to advise arises because the legal executive or solicitor taking instructions knows of some

[241] Note that a surviving spouse or civil partner will inherit his spouse or civil partner's ownership period for IHT purposes, see para.26–62.
[242] *Russell v IRC* [1988] S.T.C. 195 (discussed at para.8–147).
[243] *Lake v Lake* [1989] S.T.C. 865 (see para.8–173).
[244] See paras 26–101 and following.
[245] See *Capital Tax Planning* (May 1996), p.82.
[246] *Cancer Research Campaign v Ernest Brown & Co (a firm)* [1997] S.T.C. 1425.

other estate disposed of by a will which is within the permitted two-year period for variation by deed then I can foresee all sorts of claims that inheritance tax advantages were not obtained may be made. A family solicitor asked to draw a will for a member of that family would have to review all recent estates under which his immediate client did or could have been benefited. So wide and vague a duty is far from analogous to *White v Jones*."[247]

[247] *White v Jones* [1997] S.T.C. 1425 at 1433 and following.

CHAPTER 9

ASSOCIATED OPERATIONS

I. INTRODUCTION

The associated operations provisions have been the subject of concern since the **9–01** inception of the tax. Widely drawn, on a literal reading they appear to be capable of applying to a staggering range of transactions, in much the same way that, on one view, we are all related to each other if matters are traced back far enough. Fortunately, the courts have introduced a limit to the scope of the provisions[1]—though many operations may be associated with each other, regard is had only to those associated operations which are "relevant" within the statutory context in question; this is discussed in detail below.

II. THE IMPORTANCE OF OPERATIONS BEING ASSOCIATED

The fact that operations are associated is important both for IHT purposes generally **9–02** and in a number of specific contexts.

---

[1] See para.9–24 below.

Importance generally—definition of "disposition"

9–03   The reason why associated operations are important generally is that s.272 defines the crucial term "disposition" as including a disposition "effected by associated operations".

Relevance in specific statutory contexts

9–04   The specific statutory contexts in which associated operations may be important are summarised below. Each of these topics is discussed in more detail elsewhere in this book (readers should refer to the footnote references for details).

Relief for essentially commercial transactions. Under s.10(1), a disposition which diminishes the value of the estate of the person who made the disposition is not a transfer of value if it is shown, broadly speaking, that the disposition:

(1) was made in an arm's length transaction between persons not connected with each other (or in a transaction as might be expected to be made at arm's length between unconnected persons); and

(2) was not made in a transaction intended to benefit anyone gratuitously.

For these purposes "transaction" includes a series of transactions and any associated operations.[2]

Back-to-back policies. Under s.263, a person is treated as having made a disposition where, in effect, he has taken out back-to-back policies, unless he can show that the purchase of the annuity and the making of the insurance were not associated operations.[3]

Definition of "settlement". Under s.272, "disposition" includes a disposition effected by associated operations. The general effect of s.272 is discussed below. What is important to note at this stage is that it has the effect of widening the definition in s.43(2) of "settlement", and thus, indirectly, of related expressions such as "settlor" and "trustee".[4]

Secondary exit charge. Section 65(1)(b) provides that there is a secondary exit charge under the special charging provisions regulating the treatment of trusts within the relevant property regime where the trustees of a settlement make a disposition as a result of which the value of relevant property comprised in the settlement is less than it would be but for the disposition in circumstances where no primary exit charge is imposed.[5] The extended definition of "disposition" may thus also be relevant in this context.

Reservation of benefit. By the Finance Act 1986 Sch.20 para.6(1)(c), a benefit which a donor obtained by virtue of any associated operations of which a disposal made by him by way of gift is one is treated as falling within the second limb of the Finance Act 1986 s.102(1)(b).[6] HMRC have recently put forward arguments based on the associated operations provisions in challenging the effectiveness of "Home Loan" schemes.[7]

---

[2] Subsection 10(3). See paras 2–41 and following.
[3] See paras 2–25 and following.
[4] See paras 11–02, 11–08, 11–40 and following and 9–22.
[5] See para.15–08.
[6] See para.7–75.
[7] See IHTM44103–44105. As to Home Loan schemes generally, see para.25–97. For a summary of HMRC's arguments, including those based on associated operations, see C. Whitehouse, "HMRC's attack on home loan schemes", *Private Client Business* (2011), Vol.2, pp.72–76.

Abatement of liabilities. Under the Finance Act 1986 s.103, the extended definition of "disposition" may be relevant in determining whether a liability falls to be abated.[8]

III. DEFINITION OF "ASSOCIATED OPERATIONS"

The definition of "associated operations" is found in s.268(1), which provides that "associated operations" means "any two or more operations" of any kind, being: **9–05**

> "(a) operations which affect the same property, or one of which affects some property and the other or others of which affect property which represents, whether directly or indirectly, that property, or income arising from that property, or any property representing accumulations of any such income; or
> (b) any two operations of which one is effected with reference to the other, or with a view to enabling the other to be effected or facilitating its being effected, and any further operation having a like relation to any of those two, and so on,
> whether those operations are effected by the same person or different persons, and whether or not they are simultaneous; and 'operation' includes an omission."

It follows from this that two questions arise in deciding whether or not an act or omission is an associated operation. First, is the act or omission an "operation" within the meaning of s.268(1)? Secondly, if it is, does that operation stand in a relationship with another operation such that they are "associated" within the meaning of s.268(1)?

Meaning of "operation"

"Operation" is a word of wide meaning, and will include virtually any act done by any person: the opening words of s.268(1) refer to "operations of any kind". Normally an omission act does not constitute an operation,[9] but the closing words of s.268(1) make it clear that for these purposes an omission can constitute an operation.[10]   **9–06**

The term "operation" is, however, not of unlimited scope. In particular, an event, such as a person's birth or death, will not be an operation,[11] nor, generally speaking, should the vesting of an interest on the termination of another interest on the satisfaction of a contingency,[12] e.g. the attainment of a specified age. The position is less clear where the contingency is satisfied by some act of the beneficiary, e.g. where he marries, but it is thought that in such circumstances the position remains unchanged, i.e. that an event precipitated by an act is generally not itself an operation. The position where the precipitating factor has been "engineered" with a view to securing a tax advantage,

---

[8] See paras 25–94 and following.
[9] See *IRC v Nichols* [1975] 1 W.L.R. 534.
[10] The Inheritance Tax Manual (at IHTM14826) notes that the term "operation" "expressly includes an omission but is otherwise undefined"; also that that it "extend[s] to wider activities such as making of a will or the exercise of votes as a controlling shareholder at a company meeting."
[11] See *Bambridge v IRC* discussed at para.9–07. See also IHTM14826.
[12] Some support for this view is implicit in the approach adopted by HMRC in *Hatton v IRC* [1992] S.T.C. 140, discussed below at para.9–20.

e.g. where a short term interest is created under a settlement, may, obviously, be different.

"Associated operations"—other taxes: ITA section 721

9–07   The term "associated operations" also appears in the estate duty and income tax legislation, though it is mainly in respect of the latter, in connection with what is now s.721 of the Income Tax Act 2007, that there have been judicial pronouncements.[13] For the purposes of s.721, "associated operations" means:

> "in relation to a transfer of assets . . . an operation of any kind effected by any person in relation to
> (a) any of the assets transferred;
> (b) any assets directly or indirectly representing any of the assets transferred;
> (c) the income arising from any assets within paragraph (a) or (b); or
> (d) any assets directly or indirectly representing the accumulation of income arising from any assets within paragraph (a) or (b)."

Probably the most important income tax case for IHT purposes is *Bambridge v IRC*,[14] in which HMRC successfully raised assessments under what is now s.721 on the daughter of Rudyard Kipling. The facts of the case were that Mr and Mrs Kipling sold investments to a Canadian company in exchange for shares and debentures of that company. About a month later Mr Kipling settled his shares and debentures on himself for life, remainder to his wife for life, remainder to his daughter for life. About six years later Mrs Kipling made a will which did not expressly refer to her shares and debentures, but the effect of which was that following her death her shares and debentures were to be held for her daughter for life. After the deaths of her parents, the Revenue (as it then was) raised assessments on the daughter on the basis that by virtue or in consequence of the original transfers of the investments by her parents to the Canadian company and in conjunction with associated operations she had power to enjoy the income of the Canadian company. So far as the income relating to her father's securities was concerned, the associated operation was the making by him of the settlement; so far as the income relating to her mother's securities was concerned, the associated operation was the making by her mother of her will. The daughter contended that HMRC had to establish that her power to enjoy the income in question was wholly the result of the transfer, either alone or in conjunction with associated operations, and that, in the circumstances, this was not the case. So far as her father's securities were concerned, her power to enjoy the income of the Canadian company was attributable partly to her father's death, and death was not an associated operation. So far as her mother's securities were concerned, her power to enjoy the income of the Canadian company was attributable to her mother's will, and the making of that will was not an associated operation:

(1) because her power to enjoy the income depended on her mother dying in the daughter's lifetime without having revoked her will; and

(2) because the will contained no specific reference to her mother's holdings in the Canadian company,

---

[13] The term does not appear in the CGT or stamp duty legislation; the latter refers to a "series of transactions", a term which is discussed at para.2–44.

[14] *Bambridge v IRC* [1955] 1 W.L.R. 1329; [1955] T.R. 295.

so that the will could not be said to be, as was required by what is now s.719(1) "effected by any person in relation to any of the assets transferred". Even if this was correct, the daughter contended that her power to enjoy the income derived not only from the will but also from the probate thereof, and probate was not an associated operation.

The House of Lords found for HMRC. So far as the settlement was concerned, it was held that where an interest in remainder or a contingent interest was given by a settlement it was given by means of the settlement and not by means of the happening of the event which brought the interest into possession or, as the case may be, fulfilled the contingency. That being the case, the fact that death was not an associated operation, which the House of Lords accepted, was not in point, and the daughter's power to enjoy the income of the Canadian company derived wholly from the transfer of assets and the operation (the making of the settlement) associated therewith. Their Lordships also found against the daughter on her contentions concerning the will. First, it was not possible to accept the view that until a testator died his will was not an operation effected in relation to any of the assets to which it referred. This followed from the fact that no further action by a testator is required to make his will effective after his death in relation to assets comprised in his estate; it was immaterial that during his lifetime it was not possible to be sure what assets stood to be affected by the provisions of the will. Secondly, so far as the absence in the will of any specific reference to the mother's securities in the Canadian company was concerned, it simply was not reasonable to say that a will which disposed of property was not made in relation to the property of which it disposed; nor was there any justification for distinguishing between properties specifically disposed of and property comprised in a residuary gift and holding that the will relates to the former but not the latter. Finally, the fact that probate, not being effected by any one person, could not be an associated operation did not help the daughter since an executor derived his title and authority not from any grant of probate but from the testator's will. Thus, the daughter's power to enjoy the income depended on her mother's will, and not on the probate of that will. Probate, although necessary, was merely a question of evidence and not of title.

A second case under what is now s.721 which provides some guidance as to the meaning of "operation" is *IRC v Herdman*.[15] In this case, the taxpayer sold assets for £87,000 to a company in return for shares with a par value of £10,000; the remaining £77,000 was left as a debt owed to the taxpayer. The company subsequently paid no dividends, but did pay the taxpayer £15,000 in respect of the debt. The Court of Appeal held that the company's accumulation of profits and its management of the assets transferred by the taxpayer as a result of which funds were used to repay the taxpayer's loan were associated operations. Although the point was not argued in the House of Lords, the taxpayer having succeeded on another point, Lord Pearce said:

"The transfer of the taxpayer's assets to the company incorporated in the Irish Republic gave him rights as a shareholder in respect of its shares and a right to repayment of a capital sum which it owed him on the transfer . . . His 'rights' by virtue of which he (had) 'power to enjoy' the repayment of his debt were exactly the same whether the company distributed or accumulated parts of its income. The promptitude with which his rights were honoured might be affected thereby, but his right to repayment remained unaltered. A creditor's rights are not altered when a debtor saves or spends his income. There is therefore nothing in any associated operation of accumulating income by the company, if it can properly be called an associated operation at all, which contributed to any rights by virtue of which the taxpayer had power to enjoy."

---

[15] *IRC v Herdman* [1969] 1 W.L.R. 323; [1969] T.R. 1.

It might be, of course, that the failure by a company to pay dividends would constitute an associated operation for IHT purposes if such a failure could be said to be an "omission" within the meaning of s.268(1), which, as was noted above, defines "operation" to include an omission.

Finally, in *Congreve v IRC*[16] the House of Lords held that there is an operation when a person resident in the United Kingdom becomes resident outside the United Kingdom, or when a person domiciled in the United Kingdom becomes domiciled outside the United Kingdom. This, however, should not normally be significant for IHT purposes, since such changes will not diminish the value of a person's estate, and, as will be seen below, the effect of s.268(3) is that any disposition made after a person has become non-domiciled will be treated as made at the time of that final disposition, by which stage the property disposed of may have become excluded property.

Requisite association

9–08 Two operations will be associated only if they satisfy one of two tests. The first test, which is provided by s.268(1)(a), will be referred to as the "objective test", while the second, which is provided by s.268(1)(b), will be referred to as the "subjective test": the reasons for this will become apparent below. Each test will be considered in turn.

Objective test

9–09 Under s.268(1)(a), in order for operations to be associated, they must satisfy one of the following requirements:

(1) they must affect the same property; or
(2) one must affect some property and the other (or others) must affect property which directly or indirectly represents
    (a) the first property, or
    (b) income arising from the first property, or
    (c) property representing accumulations of income arising from the first property.

The operations need not be effected by the same person, nor need they be simultaneous.

This test is largely the same as that which applies for the purposes of s.721, and two cases under what is now s.721 illustrate the circumstances in which it will be satisfied:

In *Corbett's Executrices v IRC*[17] investments and sinking fund policies transferred to an English company in July 1933 were sold to a Canadian company in March 1935. The High Court upheld the Special Commissioners' finding that the 1935 sale was an operation associated with the 1933 transfer.

In *Beatty's Executors v IRC*[18] the taxpayer in 1933 transferred securities to a company in exchange for shares and debentures, which he subsequently settled on

[16] *Congreve v IRC* [1948] 1 All E.R. 948; 30 T.C. 168.
[17] *Corbett's Executrices v IRC* [1943] 2 All E.R. 218; 25 T.C. 305.
[18] *Beatty's Executors v IRC* [1940] 23 T.C. 574.

himself for life. His brother made a similar sale to a different company, and made a similar settlement. In 1937 each revoked his settlement, and, on the following day, transferred the shares and debentures (which each now owned absolutely) to the other. Lawrence J., held that the transfers in 1933 and the gifts in 1937 were associated operations.

One difference between the s.721 and the IHT definitions of associated operations is that the former refers to "an operation of any kind effected by any person *in relation to* . . . any of the assets . . ." while s.268(1) refers to operations which "affect" property. Section 268(1) would thus appear to posit a slightly narrower test. Property will presumably be affected only if there is a change in its legal or beneficial ownership, its situs, or in its physical or legal character; by way of contrast, an operation might be effected "in relation to" property notwithstanding the absence of any such change.

Subjective test

Under s.268(1)(b), in order for operations to be associated, they must satisfy one of **9–10** the following requirements:

(1) one must be effected with reference to the other; or
(2) one must be effected with a view to enabling the other to be effected; or
(3) one must be effected with a view to facilitating the other being effected.

In practice, HMRC will probably attempt to satisfy the above tests in either or both of two ways: first, by adducing evidence, such as correspondence; secondly, by contending that in the circumstances any reasonable man would conclude that operation A must have been effected with, e.g., a view to facilitating operation B being effected, thereby raising an inference which it falls to the taxpayer to rebut. It seems clear that the operations in question must have been effected by the person in question with the requisite intention, and that it is insufficient merely to establish that in the normal course of events operations of the kind referred to are usually effected with such an intention. It also seems beyond dispute that no reciprocal element is required, and that where operation A is effected, e.g. with reference to operation B, operation A is associated with operation B and operation B is associated with operation A regardless of whether operation B was effected by reference to or with a view to facilitating operation A being effected.

In *Rysaffe Trustee Co (CI) v IRC*,[19] discussed below, Park J. expressed the view that the mere fact that certain operations were all part of a single plan or scheme did not of itself necessarily mean that they had been "effected with reference to each other".

Different "operators", different times

Section 268 expressly provides that operations may be "associated" whether they **9–11** are effected by the same person or different persons, and whether or not the operations are simultaneous. Subject to the qualification in s.268(2), discussed below, time, at least in theory, has no bearing on whether operations are associated—although, having said

[19] *Rysaffe Trustee Co (CI) v IRC* [2002] S.T.C. 872.

that, as a general rule, operations not proximate in time are far less likely to fall within s.268.

Excepted operations

9–12   Section 268(2) specifically provides for two exceptions to the general rule, as follows.

Pre-March 27, 1974 operations. An operation effected on or after March 27, 1974, is not associated with any operation effected before that date, and this is so even if the earlier operation would have been an associated operation for purposes of estate duty.

Leases. The grant of a lease for full consideration in money or money's worth is not associated with any operation effected more than three years after the grant.

It is to be noted that while s.268(2) provides that the grant of a lease for full consideration in money or money's worth is not associated with any operation effected more than three years after that grant, it does not expressly provide that the later operation is not to be associated with that grant. It is nevertheless thought that it has this effect, and that there is no danger of the later operation being associated with the earlier grant. The fact that s.268(2) specifies a period of three years, a period which the draftsman of the legislation finds appropriate in a number of contexts, underlines the fact that, at least in theory, the passage of time does not prevent operations from being associated with each other.

Effect of operations being associated: section 268(3)

9–13   As was noted above, s.272 provides that "disposition" includes a disposition "effected by associated operations". If this means that if A gives property to B, and B gives the same property to C, A has therefore made a disposition to C of the property, a number of questions arise. When did A make the disposition to C? Did A also make a transfer to B? Did B make a transfer to C, or is his transfer subsumed in A's transfer to C? If B did make a transfer to C, does A get any credit for it?

The answers to some of these questions are to be found in s.268(3), which provides that:

> "Where a transfer of value is made by associated operations carried out at different times it shall be treated as made at the time of the last of them; but where any one or more of the earlier operations also constitute a transfer of value made by the same transferor, the value transferred by the earlier operations shall be treated as reducing the value transferred by all the operations taken together, except to the extent that the transfer constituted by the earlier operations but not that made by all the operations taken together is exempt under section 18 above."

Section 268(3) may thus be divided into three limbs. The first consists of the statement to the semicolon, and may be referred to as the "timing limb"; the second runs from the semicolon to the next natural break, i.e. to the word "together", and may be referred to as the "credit limb"; the last limb may be referred to as the "spouse/civil partner exemption limb". The function of each of these limbs is as follows.

The *timing limb* ("Where a transfer of value is made by associated operations carried out at different times it shall be treated as made at the time of the last of them") simply fixes the time at which the transfer is made. This ensures that the value transferred by all the operations is brought into account, and may affect the rate of tax chargeable in respect of a transfer, either because it means the transferor's cumulative total at the time of the transfer is higher than it might otherwise have been (where there have been intervening non-associated transfers), because it means the transfer was made within seven years of death, or because a new rate scale has been introduced. In addition, it may affect the availability of certain reliefs and exemptions, either because they are defined quantitatively or because there has been a change in the law. Finally, the timing limb may be important in fixing the date by reference to which any valuation is to be effected.

The *credit limb* ("but where any one or more of the earlier operations also constitute a transfer of value made by the same transferor, the value transferred by the earlier operations shall be treated as reducing the value transferred by all the operations taken together,") prevents the same person being charged twice in respect of the same value; it does not, however, prevent different persons being charged in respect of the same value.

The purpose of the spouse/civil partner exemption limb ("except to the extent that the transfer constituted by the earlier operations but not that made by all the operations taken together is exempt under section 18 above") appears to be to prevent "channelling operations", i.e. transfers by one spouse to another so as to enable the recipient spouse to take advantage of certain exemptions, such as the annual exemption, which are not available without limit to the spouse providing the funds. Two examples will help to illustrate how s.268(3) works.

Assume that X, who wishes to give his son £6,000, transfers £3,000 outright to his son, and £3,000 to his wife, on condition that she passes it on to the son, which she duly does. Both X and his wife subsequently die in circumstances such that the availability of the annual exemption to their gifts is relevant. In the absence of the associated operations provisions, all the transfers would be exempt: both gifts to the son would be covered by each parent's annual exemption, and the transfer of the £3,000 from husband to wife would be exempt under the spouse exemption. In the event, since the gift to the wife is conditional on her passing it on, her transfer to the son is an associated operation under s.268(1)(b). Therefore, under ss.272 and 268(3), the father is treated as prima facie having made a transfer of value of £6,000 to the son by associated operations. He would be given credit for the earlier transfer of £3,000 made to his son, but not for the transfer to his wife, with the result that he made three transfers—two to his son, the first of which was exempt, and one to his wife.[20]

Assume that the facts remain the same, except that the intermediary was someone other than the father's spouse, say, his brother. In that case, the father would have been regarded under the first limb of s.268(3) as prima facie making a transfer of value of £6,000 at the time of his brother's gift. But under the credit limb of s.268(3), the amount of the transfer would have been reduced to nil. This follows from the fact that credit would have been given for both of the earlier transfers made by the father. Where the wife was the intermediary, on the other hand, the spouse limb of s.268(3) prevented credit being given to the father in respect of the transfer he made to his wife.

By way of further example, assume that a father sells an asset for full market value **9–14** to his son (so that the sale does not reduce the value of the father's estate), the purchase price being left outstanding and subsequently released by instalments equal to the annual exemption. The sale, although a disposition, does not reduce the value of the father's estate, and so is not a transfer of value. Each of the annual releases is, of course, both a disposition and a transfer of value. The releases may well be "associated operations". HMRC have indicated that they will consider such cases in relation to

---

[20] It is thought that the wife would not be treated, for IHT purposes, as having made a gift to son.

their specific facts (see para.9–27 below) but it is arguable that they do not constitute a single transfer of value made by associated operations but rather a series of transfers of value. Alternatively, if there is only a single transfer of value, the subject matter of that transfer could be regarded as the debt rather than the original asset; if so, then the value of the transfer may effectively be frozen rather than reflecting any increase in value of the original asset.

IV. THE CASE LAW: AN EMERGING PRINCIPLE?

9–15   There have been a number of cases in which HMRC have invoked the associated operations provisions. Some of these cases involved HMRC contending that a disposition had been effected by associated operations, while others arose in some of the specific statutory contexts mentioned above.

What emerges from these cases is that HMRC entertained a generous view of the application of the provisions which they have generally been incapable of sustaining in litigation. We will begin by reviewing the decided cases and then suggest that a general principle has emerged from those cases which limits the application of the provisions.

The cases

9–16   The cases are considered in chronological order. Some of the cases have also given rise to other IHT issues, and are discussed in relation to those issues in the relevant sections of this book.

IRC v Brandenburg[21]

9–17   This case involved a taxpayer resisting before the Special Commissioners a Revenue attack on the basis of a disposition effected by associated operations. In the event, Warner J. found for HMRC on other grounds, and declined to comment on the applicability of the provisions. The case is nevertheless of considerable interest because the submissions made by the taxpayer's counsel, Robert Walker, now Lord Walker, as to the scope of the associated operations provisions, make fascinating reading, not least because they anticipate subsequent judicial findings in the *Rysaffe* case, discussed below,[22] as to the scope of the provisions.

The case involved an attempt to exploit a perceived asymmetry in the legislation. Mrs B, who was domiciled, resident and ordinarily resident in the United Kingdom, wished to make a gift free of CTT to her daughter, R, who was not so domiciled, resident or ordinarily resident. To this end Mrs B transferred £40,000 to be held on protective trusts during a "trust period" for Cockpit Investments Limited, a company incorporated (and therefore domiciled) and resident in Jersey and in which she held all the shares. The trustees had power to terminate the trust period. At the end of the trust period the trust fund passed to R. Since Mrs B owned all the shares in Cockpit, she was

---

[21] *IRC v Brandenburg* [1982] S.T.C. 555.
[22] *Rysaffe Trustee Co (CI) v IRC* [2003] S.T.C. 536; see para.9–22.

446

treated by a deeming section, now s.101, as owning Cockpit's protected interest, so that the initial transfer into settlement did not give rise to a charge to CTT.

Cockpit used the £40,000 to buy exempt gilts. Steps were then taken, including the termination by the trustees of the trust period, so that the trust fund vested in R. The taxpayer's argument was that since Cockpit was a person neither domiciled nor ordinarily resident in the United Kingdom, the gilts were excluded property under what is now s.48(4)(a) and although what is now s.101 applied for determining whether or not Mrs B was to be treated as owning Cockpit's protected interest for the purpose of determining whether there was a charge when she made the settlement, on a strict reading of the legislation s.101 did not apply (presumably because of defective drafting) in determining whether the gifts were excluded property when Cockpit's interest terminated. That being the case, no charge arose on that occasion.

HMRC invoked the associated operations provisions to contend that Mrs B had, by a disposition effected by associated operations, made a transfer of value of the gilts directly to R. Counsel for the taxpayer commenced his argument with the proposition that the associated operations provisions, if read literally, are impossibly wide and would lead to chaos which could be relieved only at HMRC's discretion, and that approach had been comprehensively rejected by the House of Lords in *Vestey v IRC*.[23] The way to avoid this was to limit the circumstances in which the extended definition of "disposition" was capable of applying, and this should be done by regarding the extended definition as inapplicable where dispositions existed in their own right. The essence of this argument was that a disposition *by* associated operations was not the same as two dispositions which happened to be associated operations. The extended definition could not be used to turn two transactions which were in themselves dispositions into a single composite disposition effected by associated operations.

The provisions applied where, e.g., a taxpayer guaranteed his son's borrowing, with a right of recourse against his son. This disposition did not in itself diminish the taxpayer's estate unless and until the son drew on the facility. Once he did, and the bank enforced their security against the taxpayer, the taxpayer suffered a diminution in the value of his estate, but at that stage made no disposition. But he did make a disposition by associated operations.

Counsel for the taxpayer also gave the following example by way of demonstrating the need to limit the ambit of the provisions. X, domiciled abroad, wants to help his son buy a house in the United Kingdom. He makes in Switzerland a cash gift to his son, who uses it to buy the house. The gift and the purchase are associated operations. Therefore, unless the ambit of the provisions is limited, X has made a gift of UK situs property—the house—and such a gift would be chargeable. The "credit limb" in s.268(3) would be of no assistance because since the first gift was of excluded property, it would not have constituted a transfer of value.

HMRC argued that what are now s.268(2) and (3) implied that it was possible to link two separate dispositions to form a composite disposition effected by associated operations; s.268(2) by referring to the grant of a lease and the gift of a reversion and s.268(3) by referring to two separate transfers of value, each of which would have necessarily involved a disposition. The taxpayer's rejoinder was twofold: first, that two separate dispositions could be relevant in determining if, e.g., what is now s.10 applied, but not in relation to the extended definition of "disposition"; secondly, so far as what is now s.263(3) was concerned, there could be an estate-diminishing disposition followed by a diminution caused by an omission.

It is interesting to note that HMRC did not seek to rely on the "objective limb" in what is now s.268(1), but argued that the "subjective limb" applied where, as in this case, there was a pre-planned course of action. So far as the example cited by the

[23] *Vestey v IRC* [1980] S.T.C. 10.

taxpayer concerning the funding of the house purchase was concerned, T would not have suffered a charge to tax because an operation which did not cause anything to leave his estate was not an associated operation; the only gift by T would therefore have been of the cash and would not have extended to the house purchased with the cash.

The Special Commissioners held that there had been an extended disposition by associated operations but that since it was made at the time of the last disposition, the relief given to exempt gilts was available. As was noted above, their decision was subsequently overturned by Warner J. on grounds which did not involve the application of the associated operations provisions. As will be seen below, echoes of the arguments put forward by Counsel for the taxpayers can be found in the *Rysaffe* case, discussed below.

Macpherson v IRC[24]

9–18   *Macpherson* involved an attempt by trustees of a discretionary trust to avoid the imposition of an exit charge on a depreciatory transaction under what is now s.65(1)(b). The trustees had on day one entered into a bona fide commercial transaction reducing the value of trust property and on day two appointed a protected life interest in the property. HMRC imposed an exit charge by reference to the depreciatory transaction. The trustees sought to rely on what is now s.65(6), which provides that no exit charge can be imposed if the disposition by which the depreciatory transaction was effected was such that, if the trustees were beneficially entitled to the settled property, what is now s.10[25] would prevent the disposition from being a transfer of value. HMRC contended that the s.10 relief was unavailable because the appointment of the interest was an operation associated with the depreciatory transaction and that operation conferred a gratuitous benefit.

It was common ground that the appointment of the interest was an associated operation. The House of Lords found for HMRC, but in doing so held that, had the events been reversed, so that the appointment of the interest in possession preceded the depreciatory transaction then, although the depreciatory transaction would have been an operation associated with the appointment, it would not have been a relevant associated operation because it would have contributed nothing to the gratuitous benefit that had already been conferred by the appointment. Lord Jauncey (with whom the other Law Lords agreed) identified the boundaries of the associated operations provisions as follows:

> "If an individual took steps which devalued his property on a Monday with a view to making a gift thereof on Tuesday, he would fail to satisfy the requirements of s.20(4) (now s.10(1)) because the act of devaluation and the gift would be considered together . . . The definition in s.44 (now s.268) is extremely wide and is capable of covering a multitude of events affecting the same property which might have little or no apparent connection between them. It might be tempting to assume that any event which fell within this wide definition should be taken into account in determining what constituted a transaction for the purposes of s.20(4). However, counsel for the Crown accepted, rightly in my view, that some limitation must be imposed. Counsel for the trustees informed your Lordships that there was no authority on the meaning of the words 'associated operations' in the context of capital transfer tax legislation but he referred to a decision of the Court of Appeal in

[24] *Macpherson v IRC* [1988] S.T.C. 362.
[25] See paras 2–41 and following.

Northern Ireland, *Herdman v I.R.C.* [1967] 45 TC 394 in which the tax avoidance provisions of ss.412 and 413 of the Income Tax Act 1952 had been considered. Read short, s.412(1) provided that a charge to income tax arose where the individual had by means of a transfer of assets either alone or in conjunction with associated operations acquired rights whereby he could enjoy a particular description of income. Lord MacDermott CJ (at 406) upheld a submission by the taxpayer that the only associated operations which were relevant to the subsection were those by means of which, in conjunction with the transfer, a taxpayer could enjoy the income and did not include associated operations taking place after the transfer had conferred upon the taxpayer the power to enjoy income. If the extended meaning of 'transaction' is read into the opening words of s.20(4) the wording becomes:

> 'A disposition is not a transfer of value if it is shown that it was not intended, and was not made in a transaction including a series of transactions and any associated operations intended, to confer any gratuitous benefit . . . '"

The case thus establishes that regard must be had only to associated operations which are relevant within the statutory context in question—in *Macpherson*, what is now s.10.

Countess Fitzwilliam v IRC[26]

In *Fitzwilliam* the associated operations provisions were not in issue but Vinelott J. remarked[27] that the provisions had very limited scope.   **9–19**

Hatton v IRC[28]

This case involved what was known at the time as "the reverter to settlor scheme".   **9–20**
The facts were that Mrs C ("the mother"), who was seriously ill, wished to pass property free of IHT to her daughter. Towards this end, two settlements were created within 24 hours. Under the first, made by the mother, the mother reserved an interest in possession for herself for just over 24 hours, with a reversionary interest to her daughter. In substance, she had thus made a very valuable gift, but her retained interest in possession meant that for IHT purposes she was still treated as owning the whole of the settled property. As a corollary of the mother's being treated as still owning the settled property, the daughter's reversionary interest was excluded property. On the following day, the daughter settled her reversionary interest on terms that her mother took an interest in possession in it for a 24-hour period following the termination of her mother's interest under the first settlement, with the property then becoming held absolutely for the daughter. The mother died shortly after the scheme had been effected.

The taxpayer's argument was that: (a) the original settlement by the mother was not a transfer of value because, since she retained an interest in possession in the property she settled, the value of her estate was undiminished; (b) the subsequent settlement by her daughter was not a chargeable event because the reversionary interest the daughter settled was excluded property and therefore the settlement did not for IHT purposes diminish the value of her estate; (c) when the mother's interest in possession in the first settlement terminated no charge to IHT arose because on that occasion she became

---

[26] *Countess Fitzwilliam v IRC* [1990] S.T.C. 65; discussed at para.8–199.
[27] *Countess Fitzwilliam v IRC* [1990] S.T.C. 65 at 99.
[28] *Hatton v IRC* [1992] S.T.C. 140.

interested in an interest in possession in the second settlement; and (d) when the mother's interest in possession in the second settlement terminated no charge to IHT arose because on that occasion her daughter became absolutely entitled to the property with the result that the reverter to settlor relief in what is now s.53(3) applied.

Not surprisingly—after all, if the taxpayer was right, there had been, by a naked tax avoidance scheme effected over a few days, a tax-free gift by the mother to her daughter of the property comprised in the trust fund—HMRC resisted this result. In the event, Chadwick J. decided against the taxpayers on two grounds. The first was that, under the *Ramsay* principle, the two settlements constituted a preordained series of transactions, the result of which was that the mother made a single composite transaction such that the reverter to settlor relief did not apply.

In case he was wrong on this, and the *Ramsay* principle did not apply to produce such a result, he also considered the Revenue's (as it then was) argument that for IHT purposes the mother was the settlor of the second settlement with the result that, again, but for a different reason, the reverter to settlor relief did not apply. He accepted HMRC's argument that the first settlement was made with a view to enabling or facilitating the making of the second settlement and that the two settlements were therefore associated operations. That being the case, they were to be regarded as having together effected a single disposition for purposes of the settled property regime, and that single disposition was a settlement for the purposes of what is now s.43(2).

This, in turn, gave rise to an intriguing question—who was the settlor of this composite settlement. Chadwick J. concluded that the correct analysis was that the mother and her daughter had each made the entirety of the settlement and that while the reverter to settlor relief applied to the settlement made by the mother, it did not do so in relation to the settlement made by her daughter.[29]

This intriguing conclusion should not be allowed to obscure the twofold importance of the *Hatton* case in the context of associated operations. First, it established that, depending on the facts, two settlements can be regarded as constituting a single settlement made by a disposition effected by associated operations. As will be seen below in connection with the *Rysaffe* case, HMRC may encounter serious difficulties in sustaining such a construction other than in extreme cases such as *Hatton*. Secondly, it is interesting to note that HMRC sought to defeat the *Hatton* scheme by denying the reverter to settlor relief, notwithstanding the intellectual difficulties this involved, rather than by simply contending that the mother had made an extended disposition by associated operations of the property to her daughter. As noted above, the legislation expressly provides that operations may be effected by different persons. It may be that HMRC were deterred from adopting this approach by the possibility that the termination of an interest under a settlement might not constitute an operation, and did not wish to have a finding to that effect on the record against them.

Reynaud v IRC[30]

9–21   In this case HMRC returned to the argument that a taxpayer had made a chargeable transfer by a disposition effected by associated operations. Four brothers each transferred shares qualifying for business relief into four separate discretionary settlements. On the following day the company in which the shares were held bought back from the trustees some of the shares; the trustees then sold the remaining shares to a third party purchaser. HMRC contended that the purchase by the company of the shares was an

---

[29] See para.11–13.
[30] *Reynaud v IRC* [1999] S.T.C. (S.C.D.) 185.

operation associated with the transfer of the shares into the settlements and that therefore there had been an extended disposition the effect of which was that the brothers had transferred cash to the trustees rather than the shares that had been purchased by the company from the trustees, with the result that no business relief was available.

The Special Commissioner agreed that the transfers into settlement and the purchases were associated operations. But in his view in the context of s.268(3) an operation was relevant

" . . . only if it is part of the scheme contributing to the reduction of the estate . . . Here the value of the estates of the brothers were diminished as a result of the gift into settlement alone. The purchase of own shares contributed nothing to the diminution which had already occurred and was not therefore a relevant associated operation."[31]

His authority for this view was Lord Jauncey's speech in *Macpherson*: an operation was a relevant operation in the context of determining whether or not there had been a transfer of value only if it contributed to a diminution in the value of the transferor's estate.

Rysaffe Trustee Co (CI) v IRC[32]

In *Rysaffe*, the last decided case on associated operations, a settlor sequentially made **9–22** five separate discretionary settlements of five parcels of 6,900 shares each. HMRC contended inter alia that the making of all the settlements were associated operations and that therefore the settlor had made one composite settlement by an extended disposition. The reason was that on that construction more IHT would be due than if each of the settlements was regarded as separate from the others.

The Special Commissioner found[33] for HMRC, but her decision was overturned[34] by Park J. on the fundamental ground that all of the property comprised within the five settlements was already within the 10-yearly charge because each settlement was created by a "disposition" in the ordinary sense. Therefore, in order to bring the property within charge, it was not necessary or appropriate to consider whether the five settlements were created by associated operations.

Park J. then went on to consider what the position would be if this fundamental point was incorrect. While accepting that the point was not clear cut, Park J. thought that, on balance, the making of the settlements were not associated operations because they had not been "effected with reference" to each other[35] even though they were all part of a single plan or scheme:

"Each transfer was effected in the knowledge that the other was being effected as well, but that does not seem to me to be the equivalent of saying that each transfer was effected 'with reference' to the other."[36]

---

[31] *Reynaud v IRC* [1999] S.T.C. (S.C.D.) 185 at 190g and 191e.
[32] *Rysaffe Trustee Co (CI) v IRC* [2003] S.T.C. 536.
[33] *Rysaffe Trustee Co (CI) v IRC* [2001] S.T.C. (S.C.D.) 225.
[34] *Rysaffe Trustee Co (CI) v IRC* [2002] S.T.C. 872.
[35] In *Smith v Revenue and Customs Commissioners*, discussed below at para.9–23, in referring to *Rysaffe*, the Special Commissioner noted that: "Park J stated in his judgement that the arguments were not 'clear cut' and, given the context, I consider that his remarks related to the particular circumstances before him, and that he was not proposing that in all cases and circumstances the relevant documents must make express reference to each other for the relevant operations to be effected 'with reference to' each other."
[36] *Rysaffe Trustee Co (CI) v IRC* [2002] S.T.C. 872, at 898h–j.

Park J. acknowledged the contrary argument, namely that:

"... if more operations than one are all part of an overall scheme, that is in itself enough to mean that each of them is effected with reference to the others."[37]

He then went on to express a "tentative view" as to whether the effect of the making of the settlements being associated operations was that there was a single settlement:

"That view is that the result would not follow. Each of the five parcels of 6,900 shares was held on discretionary trusts by virtue of a disposition. Suppose that, contrary to my opinion, each of the five dispositions was an operation associated with the other four. Why should it follow that all the five parcels of shares have to be regarded as held on the trusts of one settlement, not five? It seems to me that, if the five settlements were operations associated with each other, that may be of passing interest to specialists in this field, but it is irrelevant to the operation of the inheritance tax charge under s.64."[38]

The Court of Appeal adopted an even more robust approach. Mummery L.J., with whom Dyson and Schiemann L.JJ. concurred, held that the questions of (1) what is a settlement and (2) what property is comprised in a settlement,

"... can be determined without asking any additional questions, such as whether the dispositions were 'associated operations' ... The inclusion of the 'associated operations' in the statutory description of 'disposition' is not intended for cases, such as this, where there is no dispute that there was a 'disposition' of property falling within s.43(2). *They are intended for cases where there is a dispute as to whether there was a relevant 'disposition' at all. The CIR may be entitled to invoke the extended description to catch a case which would not be regarded as a 'disposition' of property in its ordinary and natural sense.*"[39]

This, of course, harks back to the arguments presented by the taxpayer in *Brandenburg* and suggests that the associated operations provisions may be of very limited application.

Smith v Revenue and Customs Commissioners[40]

9–23   In *Smith*, a husband and wife died within seven years of having taken out three annuities and three life assurance policies with the Equitable Life assurance Society as part of an investment plan. HMRC issued an assessment to IHT against the father's estate on the basis that the arrangements were associated operations and constituted a transfer of value by the husband to his three children. The children appealed. Before the Special Commissioner,[41] they put forward arguments that the purchase of the annuities and the life policies were not associated operations; the documentation for the annuities on the one hand and the policies on the other did not expressly refer to each other and therefore could not be regarded as having been purchased "with reference to each other" and the annuities were not purchased with a view to "enabling or facilitating"

---

[37] *Rysaffe Trustee Co (CI) v IRC* [2002] S.T.C. 872 at 899a.
[38] *Rysaffe Trustee Co (CI) v IRC* [2002] S.T.C. 872 at 899d–e.
[39] *Rysaffe Trustee Co (CI) v IRC* [2003] S.T.C. 536 at 541, para.23 (author's italics).
[40] *Smith v Revenue and Customs Commissioners* [2007] S.T.C. (S.C.D.) 506; [2008] S.T.C. 1649; the case is also discussed at para.2–29.
[41] Only the argument based on SP E4 was appealed to the High Court.

the effecting of the policies as there was nothing in the arrangements that required that the annuity payments be used to pay the premiums on the policies.

The Special Commissioner rejected these arguments. The purchase of each annuity and the making of each life assurance policy were more than "just mere elements in an overall scheme"; the application to the insurance company was, in each case, for an "Investment Plan" and that Plan was a combination of the annuity and the life assurance policy in each case. Although the annuity and the life assurance policy were evidenced by separate documents which did not refer to the other, there were references to both in the illustration included in the total package of documents, the proposal form referred to both and each pair formed part of a single contract with the company. The policy did not need expressly to mention the annuity (or vice versa) for the two to have been made with reference to each other, and even if some form of express statement was required, the references in either the Illustration or the proposal forms would have been sufficient.

With regard to the second argument, although the Special Commissioner agreed that the purchase of the annuities was not undertaken to enable the taking-out of the policies, he was not persuaded that the annuities did not facilitate the payment of the premiums on the life assurance policies. "Facilitation" did not require there to be a contractual link but only for something to make the other thing easy or easier; although there was nothing in the contractual terms of the annuity or the life assurance policy which required the annuity payments to be applied in paying the life assurance premiums, the illustration in the documentation stated that the income from the annuity "is designed to provide the remaining premiums for the endowment assurance policy . . . " and the Special Commissioner therefore found that receipts from the annuity made it easier for the premiums on the policy, in each case, to be paid.

The Special Commissioners also rejected a further argument, as did the High Court on appeal, that the arrangements fell within Statement of Practice E4 (which provides that life assurance policies and annuities are not to be treated as affected by the associated operations rules if the policy was issued on the basis of "full medical evidence" of the assured's health and would have been issued even without the purchase of the annuity) as the medical evidence provided in respect of the wife was held by both the Special Commissioners and the High Court not to meet the standard of "full medical evidence" required.

An emerging principle?

These cases show that the courts (and in the *Reynaud* case, the Special Commis- **9–24** sioners) have been generally reluctant (but not wholly unwilling) to import the associated operations provisions into the analysis of the IHT effects of a transaction. Besides what may be some judicial reluctance (see Park J. in *Rysaffe*) to conclude that operations are associated with each other, this reluctance has been manifested mainly in the approach that:

(1) associated operations must be relevant within the given statutory context; and
(2) in determining whether associated operations are relevant within a given statutory context the Court (and in the *Reynaud* case, the Special Commissioners) has regard to basic IHT consequences only and not to the possibility of an increased charge as a result of, e.g., disallowed business relief (*Reynaud*) or aggregated settlements (*Rysaffe*).

It is possible to see this reluctance as a principle which we will attempt to articulate. Before doing so, we think it may be helpful to identify HMRC's approach; this has been to identify all operations that are associated with each other within the statutory definition and then, if that extended disposition produces a higher charge to tax than would otherwise be the case, to contend that that is the relevant disposition for IHT purposes. This was expressly stated in *Brandenburg* to be their view as to the operation of the provisions and was the basis of their approach in *Reynaud* and *Rysaffe*. (It is also the approach adopted by the Special Commissioners in the *Brandenburg* and *Rysaffe* cases.)

The principle that appears to have emerged from the cases does not reflect this approach but instead looks to identify the substantial disposition and then to see whether or not associated operations contributed to it. If they did not, they were not relevant associated operations (*Reynaud* and *Rysaffe*); if they did, they were (*Hatton* and *Smith*). The fact that including associated operations within the extended disposition contended for by HMRC produced a greater charge to tax did not of itself alter the character of the substantial disposition and so render those operations relevant. The point is brought out neatly in Park J.'s judgment:

> "All the parcels of shares were property comprised in settlements for the purposes of s.64. The associated operations provisions had nothing to do with that analysis. There were ten-yearly charges on all of the parcels of shares. It is (I assume) true that in aggregate the five ten-yearly charges would be lower than the single charge which would have applied if there had been only one settlement. But that is not a valid reason for artificially importing the associated operations provisions into the exercise and using them to impose the false hypothesis that there was only one settlement when in fact and in law there were five."[42]

The Court of Appeal's decision in *Rysaffe* went rather further, indicating that an issue will arise as to whether or not there was a relevant disposition only in cases where, in the absence of the associated operations, there would be no disposition at all—in such a case the question will then be whether a disposition was made by associated operations, not whether operations can be associated with each other in such a way as to produce a charge where one would not otherwise exist or to increase an existing charge. This is, of course, the approach espoused before the Special Commissioners on behalf of the taxpayer in *Brandenburg*.

V. APPLICATION IN PRACTICE

9–25   It may be helpful to conclude this discussion by considering how the associated operations provisions may or may not apply in certain situations.

Channelling operations

9–26   As was mentioned above, the associated operations provisions are in part designed to prevent spouses/civil partners taking unfair advantage of the spouse/civil partner exemption. This, however, is subject to the recognition that it is unfair to penalise

---

[42] *Rysaffe Trustee Co (CI) v IRC* [2002] S.T.C. 872 at 897e–f.

straightforward transfers between spouses/civil partners. The Chief Secretary of the Treasury commented during the parliamentary debates on the Finance Act 1975[43]:

> "It is reasonable for a husband to share capital with his wife when she has no means of her own. If she chooses to make gifts out of the money she has received from her husband, there will be no question of using the associated operations provisions to treat them as gifts made by the husband and taxable as such."

HMRC accept this.[44] However, the Chief secretary went on to address more sophisticated transactions that might fall within the provisions:

> "In a blatant case, where a transfer by a husband to a wife was made on condition that the wife should at once use the money to make gifts to others, a charge on a gift by the husband might arise under the clause. The Hon. Gentleman fairly recognised that.
>
> I want to give an example of certain circumstances that could mean the clause having to be invoked. There are complex situations involving transactions between husband and wife and others where, for example, a controlling shareholder with a 60 per cent holding in a company wishes to transfer his holding to his son. If he gave half to his son, having first transferred half to his wife and later his wife transferred her half share to the son, the effect would be to pass a controlling shareholding from father to son. The Revenue would then use the associated operations provisions to ensure that the value of a controlling holding was taxed . . .
>
> Transfers between husband and wife will not be liable to tax except in certain circumstances of the kind that I have outlined."

By way of example of the mischief aimed at, assume that a husband holds 51 per cent of the shares of a company, and that he transfers 2 per cent to his wife, who, in turn, transfers the 2 per cent to their son, to whom the husband subsequently transfers his remaining 49 per cent holding. Given the related property provisions,[45] the transfer by the husband to the wife would diminish the value of the husband's estate by only the value of the two shares (valued on a majority basis). In the absence of the associated operations provisions, the value transferred by the wife's transfer would also be computed by reference to the value of the 2 per cent holding (again, valued on a majority basis under the related property rules), notwithstanding the fact that the effect of the two transfers would have been that the husband managed to divest himself of control without incurring a charge on the consequential fall in the value of his estate. The net effect of the two transfers by the husband and the transfer by the wife would thus have been that although the husband transferred a 51 per cent shareholding, only two fifty-firsts of that shareholding would have been taxed as part of a majority shareholding; the balance of the shares would, of course, be taxed on a minority basis on their being transferred to the son.

It is thought that s.268(3) on its own would not counteract this because it provides only that the aggregate transfer is to be treated as having been made at the time of the last of the associated operations; it seems to follow from this that under s.268(3) regard is had only to the wife's transfer of the 2 per cent holding. Under s.272, on the other hand, there would be a very real danger that the husband effected a disposition by associated operations, with the result that, at the time of the wife's transfer, he would be regarded as having transferred the two shares, so that, at that stage, tax would fall to be charged on the diminution in the value of his estate occasioned by the fall in the value of the spouses' aggregate shareholding. It is not clear whether the wife would

---

[43] *Hansard*, col.56 (March 10, 1975), p.897e–f.
[44] See also IHTM14833.
[45] See paras 25–65 and following.

also be regarded as having made a transfer of a 2 per cent holding, or whether her transfer is subsumed to his.

Purchase price left outstanding

9–27   One planning technique is for a taxpayer to take advantage of the various exemptions available to him (such as the annual exemption) to make gifts. Unfortunately, the financial position of many taxpayers is such that they are unable to do this by means of cash gifts or outright transfers of assets on a regular basis. One approach open to a taxpayer otherwise unable to take advantage of his exemptions is for him to sell the asset which he wished to transfer for a purchase price left outstanding, and then to release appropriate amounts of the debt at suitable intervals. The approach of HMRC means, however, that the value attributed to the asset for IHT purposes may well exceed the value of the debt.

Assume, for example, that X owns an asset which he wishes to transfer to his son. First, he sells for market value the asset to his son; this does not give rise to a transfer of value. The purchase price is left outstanding on demand, and each year X releases a portion of the debt equal to his annual exemption. The sale and each subsequent release of part of the amount due will be operations which are associated under s.268(1)(b), but this should have no adverse effects, since against the value transferred by the entire operation can be set under the credit limb of s.268(3) the aggregate of the value transferred by the transfers of value made by X by virtue of the annual releases.

However, if the assets appreciate in value, the value transferred by the entire operation, given the "timing limb" of s.268(3), will exceed the credit available to X. This point was the subject of correspondence published in the March 1, 1978 issue of *The Law Society Gazette* between the tax editor of that publication and the Revenue (as it then was). In his letter, the tax editor said:

> "I have received various queries regarding section 44 (associated operations) from readers of the Gazette, and I would be most grateful if you could give me the Revenue's view regarding the following two specific examples.
>
> The first concerns the sort of case where A sells to B for, say, £20,000 but the price is left outstanding on loan and is written off at the rate of £2,000 per annum making use of the £2,000 annual exemption of the vendor/donor. Would the Inland Revenue regard the annual writing off/releasing of £2,000 of the deferred purchase price as being associated with the transfer of the asset comprised in the original sale? If so, would the Inland Revenue consider that s.44(3) means that the asset comprised in the original sale is the subject matter of the transfer of value to which s.44 applies, with the result that one would have to look at the value of the asset at the date of the last payment and treat the excess over £20,000 as a transfer of value made by the vendor/donor at that date? Could you please also tell me whether the answers to the questions raised in the preceding paragraph depend at all upon whether interest is payable on the deferred purchase price?"

HMRC replied:

> "Your first example concerned the case where A sold an asset to B but left the price outstanding on loan, part of which was written-off each year. We will obviously need to consider any actual case of this kind in the light of the full facts, but on the facts as given in the example it seems clear that the sale of the asset and the writing-off of the loans are associated with each other as a single arrangement and, *prima facie*, we would consider section 44 relevant, whether or not interest was payable on the loan. If section 44 does apply

it may well follow that under section 44(3) we would have to look at the value of the asset at the date of the release of the last part of the debt."[46]

Funding of IHT

The second point dealt with in the abovementioned letter was the effect of a **9–28** transferor using his annual exemption to fund a transferor's liability to IHT. The point was covered by the tax editor as follows:

"The second example concerns a situation in which the controlling shareholder of a family company gives away all his shares to, say, his son on the basis that the son will pay the capital transfer tax by instalments. Let us assume for the purposes of the example that the donee/son finds himself having to pay £2,000 per annum capital transfer tax in respect of the shares which he has received and that the donor/father makes gifts of £2,000 per annum to enable him to do so which are covered by the basic annual exemption. Has the value of the original gift of shares been crystallised for capital transfer tax purposes when it was made, or does section 44(3) mean that it has to be reviewed at the time when the donor/father make the gift which is used to pay the final instalment of capital transfer tax?"

HMRC replied:

"Your second example involved a gift of shares on terms that the son would pay the capital transfer tax by instalments, the father subsequently making further gifts of cash to the son. In this case we agree that section 44 does not apply: the mere fact that the father made later gifts within the annual exemption to enable the son to pay the tax would not therefore require the value transferred by the original gift to be reviewed."

The introduction of the PET regime means, of course, that the above example is now outdated, but a like question would arise today if, instead of transferring the shares to his son, the father transferred the shares to the trustees of a trust within the relevant property regime.

Depreciatory transactions

What is the effect of ss.272 and 268(3) where there is a transfer of property the value **9–29** of which has been previously depreciated? By way of example, assume that in September 2008 X owns 51 of the 100 issued shares in X Ltd; the 51 shares are worth £51,000, but 49 shares would be worth only, say, £20,000. With a view to avoiding IHT, X after bona fide commercial negotiations sells his son two shares for, say, £300, their market value at that time. As the remaining shares are worth only £20,000, the sale depreciates the value of X's estate by £30,700; but, assuming relief under s.10(1) is available, X has not made a transfer of value. Three and a half years later, in 2012, he gives the remaining 49 shares, still worth £20,000, to his son. This gift would appear to have three effects. First, the relief granted under s.10(1) in respect of the earlier sale might be lost, in which case there would have been a transfer of value of £30,700 in 2008. Secondly, the gift of the 49 shares would itself constitute a transfer of value of £20,000. Thirdly, under the first limb of s.268(3), the two transfers would be aggregated and treated as having been made in 2012. The gift in 2012 would thus be regarded as being of 51 shares, so that the value transferred was prima facie £50,700

---

[46] See also IHTM14834.

(£51,000 less the £300 purchase price) but this would be reduced under the credit limb of s.268(3) to £20,000, credit being given in respect of the earlier transfer of £30,700.

If s.268(3) governs the time when the transactions are to be treated as having been made, it may be that the earlier sale is to be treated as having been made at the time of the later gift and this might result in the earlier transfer being made within seven years of death; it might also adversely affect the availability of certain exemptions. On the other hand, it could operate to the taxpayer's advantage if the value of the shares had fallen between the sale and the gift. Assume, for instance, that in the above example the value of the 51 shares at the time of the gift to the son was only £10,000. If the earlier transfer is ignored, the value transferred by the operations as a whole is £10,000. If, on the other hand, the earlier transfer is not subsumed into the later gift, the position is much less happy. In that case, there would have been two transfers—one of £30,700, and one of £10,000, against which the previous transfer of £30,700 could be set, with the result that the total amount to be brought into charge would have been £30,700. Given the credit limb of s.268(3), it is thought that s.268(3) does not have the effect of subsuming the two transfers; otherwise credit would never be given for the value transferred by earlier operations. That being the case, it appears that, at least as far as most depreciatory transactions are concerned, ss.272 and 268(3) are quite superfluous.

For the sake of completeness, it should be noted that the position would be no different in the above example if X had sold the 49 shares to Y, since in that case the s.10(1) relief would have been lost on the grounds that the transactions entered into by X were not, taken together as associated operations, arm's length or equivalent bargains entered into without any gratuitous intent.

VI. THE *RAMSAY* PRINCIPLE

9–30   It is to be noted that a taxpayer who escapes unscathed from an associated operations attack by HMRC may still have invoked against him the *Ramsay* principle[47] to frustrate measures taken to avoid tax which do not fall foul of the letter of the IHT code.[48]

It remains to be seen how successful such an attack will prove. In particular, neither the CGT legislation nor the income tax legislation contains any equivalent to the associated operations provisions. It is arguable that Parliament intended the IHT effects of transactions to be determined by reference only to the IHT legislation, which, unlike the CGT and income tax legislation, is specifically designed to deal with transactions containing a number of separate but related steps forming what is in effect a single composite transaction. In *Eilbeck v Rawling*[49] Lord Wilberforce said that

> "it would be quite wrong, and a faulty analysis, to segregate, from what was an integrated and inter-dependent series of transactions, in one step . . . and to attach fiscal consequences to that step regardless of the other steps or operations with which it was integrated",[50]

but given the fact that s.268(3) appears to require that in appropriate circumstances individual steps or operations must be segregated in order to determine whether one

---

[47] *WT Ramsay Ltd v IRC* [1981] UKHL 1.
[48] HMRC have put forward arguments based on both the associated operations provisions and *Ramsay* in seeking to challenge the effectiveness of "Home Loan" schemes. See IHTM44106 and fn.7 above.
[49] [1981] S.T.C. 174.
[50] [1981] S.T.C. 174 at 186e.

operation of a series of operations can be regarded as a transfer of value, there must be some question as to how far this statement applies to the IHT legislation.

Some judicial support for the view that the *Ramsay* principle does not apply for IHT purposes may be found in the judgments of Peter Gibson J. (at first instance) and Slade L.J. (in the Court of Appeal) in *Craven v White*,[51] a case involving avoidance of CGT. Peter Gibson J. said that:

> "It seems to me that what I am being invited to hold by the Crown would amount to judicial legislation. Parliament in other fiscal contexts, such as estate duty and capital transfer tax, has enacted provisions relating to associated operations so that a disposal by two or more such operations is made subject to tax. I am not prepared to do what Parliament has not thought fit to enact."[52]

Slade L.J., for his part, said that:

> "Various fiscal statutes expressly state that the term 'disposition' includes a 'disposition effected by associated operations'. Simply, for example (what is now s.272) (in the context of capital transfer tax) so provides; and (what is now s.268(1)) provides that associated operations means 'any two operations of which one is effected with reference to the other or with a view to enabling the other to be effected or facilitating its being effected'. If the capital gains tax legislation had included similar provisions the Crown's basic contention might have been easily sustainable. In my judgment, however, the gap cannot be filled by judicial legislation."[53]

In the House of Lords in *Fitzwilliam v IRC*[54] (see above) Lord Browne-Wilkinson cast doubt upon whether the *Ramsay* principle (as it was formulated) could apply to IHT (CTT),[55] given that the Act itself already included specific associated operations provisions:

> "Finally I must mention a point I wish to reserve. The Capital Transfer Tax legislation (considered in *Ramsay* and the other cases) contains provisions which render taxable dispositions effected by 'associated operations'. Associated operations are defined . . . to include:
>
> > 'Any two operations of which one is effected with reference to the other, or with a view to enabling the other to be effected or facilitating its being effected, and any further operation having a like relation to any of those two and so on.'
>
> This amounts to a statutory statement, in much wider terms, of the *Ramsay* principle which deals with transactions carried through by two or more operations which are interrelated. In the present case, the Revenue originally claimed tax in reliance on statutory associated operations provisions. The *Ramsay* principle is essentially based on the construction of statutory taxing provisions. It can therefore be argued that there is no room for the Court to adopt the *Ramsay* approach in construing an act which expressly provides for the circumstances and occasion on which transfers carried through by 'Associated Operations' are to be taxed. It is not necessary in the present case to express any concluded view on this subject."[56]

---

[51] [1987] S.T.C. 297.
[52] [1985] S.T.C. 531 AT 562f–g.
[53] [1987] S.T.C. 297 at 309j–310a.
[54] *Fitzwilliam v IRC* [1993] S.T.C. 502; see para.8–199.
[55] See also the judgments of Peter Gibson J. (at first instance) and Slade L.J. (in the Court of Appeal) in *Craven v White* [1985] S.T.C. 531 at 562f–g; [1987] S.T.C. 297 at 309j–10a.
[56] *Craven v White* [1985] S.T.C. 531 at 536.

Following a line of cases,[57] the *Ramsay* principle has evolved from the description given by Lord Browne-Wilkinson; no longer a specific doctrine targeted at tax avoidance schemes, it is now a more general principle of purposive construction to be applied to all legislation. A clear summary of the modern approach to the *Ramsay* principle is set out by Lewison J. in *Berry v Revenue and Customs Commissioners*.[58] However, Lord Browne-Wilkinson's view that, where a statute already provides for an anti-avoidance framework, there is no occasion for superimposing a further set of principles arguably retains its force.

HMRC have not been deterred from invoking the *Ramsay* principle in a number of IHT cases (see, e.g., the *Hatton* case,[59] discussed above). However, even where the court has implicitly accepted that the *Ramsay* principle may apply in principle to IHT, there has been little enthusiasm for applying it in practice (see, for example, the Court of Appeal[60] and the House of Lords[61] decisions in *Ingram v IRC*), possibly because the prescriptive code created by the IHT legislation makes purposive constructions difficult.

9–31   Other anti-avoidance provisions are considered in Chapter 30.

---

[57] See, inter alia, *Furniss (Inspector of Taxes) v Dawson* [1984] S.T.C. 153 (HL); *MacNiven (Inspector of Taxes) v Westmoreland Investments Ltd* [2001] S.T.C. 237; *Collector of Stamp Revenue v Arrowtown Assets Ltd* [2003] HKCFA 46; *Barclays Mercantile Finance Ltd v Mawson (Inspector of Taxes)* [2005] S.T.C. 1; *Tower MCashback LLP 1 v HMRC* [2011] UKSC 19. See also *HMRC v Mayes* [2011] EWCA Civ 407.

[58] [2011] UKUT 81 (TCC); [2011] S.T.C. 1057.

[59] See para.9–20.

[60] *Ingram v IRC* [1997] S.T.C. 1234; see paras 7–33 and following.

[61] *Ingram v IRC* [1999] S.T.C. 37.

PART TWO

THE SPECIAL CHARGING PROVISIONS

CHAPTER 10

OVERVIEW: CHARGING PROVISIONS APPLYING TO SETTLED PROPERTY AND OUTLINE OF THE SPECIAL CHARGING PROVISIONS

I. INTRODUCTION

Tax treatment of settled property: structure of the legislation

Settled property falls into two broad categories and is taxed accordingly, namely: **10–01**

(1) settled property in which there is a qualifying interest in possession;
(2) settled property in which there is no such interest.

Settled property in which there is a qualifying interest in possession is dealt with under the main charging provisions discussed in Pt I. Under those provisions, a charge can arise in one of two ways: first, under s.52(1), on the actual, notional or deemed termination during a person's life of a qualifying interest in possession to which he is entitled; secondly, under s.4(1), on the death of a person who was entitled to a qualifying interest in possession immediately before he died. The categories of interest

463

which fall to be treated as qualifying interests in possession are considered at paras 11–49 and following and an outline of the changes to the tax treatment of interest in possession settlements introduced by the Finance Act 2006 can be found at paras 12–02–12–19.

Settled property in which no qualifying interest in possession subsists is dealt with under the special charging provisions considered here in Pt II. If no qualifying interest in possession subsists in settled property[1] the tax treatment which will be applied depends upon whether the property falls to be taxed under the relevant property regime, or whether favoured treatment applies under the categories set out at para.10–08 below. Note, though, that favoured treatment is sometimes applied by treating settlements in which no interest in possession subsists as settlements with qualifying interests in possession.[2]

Historical background: special charging provisions applying to certain categories of settled property

Outline

10–02   Special charging provisions which applied to all discretionary trusts[3] were originally introduced by the Finance Act 1975. A new set of charging provisions applying to discretionary trusts was introduced in 1982 and are described at para.13–03. Until the enactment of the Finance Act 2006, the special charging provisions again applied only to discretionary trusts: favoured treatment being afforded only to certain categories of discretionary trust. While the rates of tax applicable under those special charging provisions were reduced in 1984 and 1988, the types of trusts to which the provisions applied remained largely unchanged until the enactment of the Finance Act 2006.

The Finance Act 2006 has extended the scope of the relevant property regime. It is still the case that all settled property falls to be taxed under that regime, unless a different treatment applies, either because a qualifying interest in possession subsists in it or because favoured treatment applies. However, since the Finance Act 2006, not all interests in possession are qualifying interests in possession. This means that a subsisting interest in possession is no longer the principal factor which defines the way that a settlement is to be treated for inheritance tax purposes: the relevant property regime has become the default regime that applies to all settled property, unless exemptions apply. Although the original structure of the legislation remains, the effect of the Finance Act 2006 has in essence been to convert the treatment of all qualifying interest in possession trusts into a form of favoured treatment applying only to limited categories of settled property.

From Budget Note 25 to the Finance Act 2006

10–03   The main changes brought about by the Finance Act 2006 were first announced on March 22, 2006 in Budget Note 25 ("BN 25") which was entitled "Aligning The Inheritance Tax Treatment for Trusts". BN 25 referred to the relevant property regime as the "mainstream IHT regime" within which interest in possession trusts and accumulation and maintenance trusts were going to be brought. BN 25 outlined the "special rules" for accumulation and maintenance trusts and interest in possession trusts—lifetime transfers into these trusts were exempt from charge if the settlor survived the transfer by seven years (see below) and that the trusts were not subject to periodic or exit charges. It announced that these "special rules" would henceforth be limited to the following: first, trusts created on death by a parent for a minor child who

---

[1] The term "qualifying interest in possession" is defined in IHTA s.59 and discussed at para.11–50.
[2] See paras 11–50 and following and Ch.17.
[3] This term is used here to describe all trusts in which no interest in possession subsisted.

will be absolutely entitled to the assets in the trusts by the age of 18 (i.e. announcing the introduction of bereaved minors' trusts); second, trusts created on death for the benefit of a single life tenant in order of time whose interest cannot be replaced (i.e. immediate post-death interests); and, third, trusts created either in the settlor's lifetime or on his death for a disabled person (i.e. this was an extension of the category of settlements that would qualify for favoured treatment under this head). BN 25 also announced that the favoured treatment for existing accumulation and maintenance trusts would continue only so long as the terms of the trust provided that the settled property would vest absolutely at the age of 18.[4] BN25 indicated that it would be possible for the terms of existing accumulation and maintenance trusts to be amended before April 6, 2008 to achieve absolute entitlement at 18.

Widespread protests followed this announcement, focusing in particular on the fact that, contrary to the principle originally accepted in relation to accumulation and maintenance settlements, i.e. that it was not desirable to vest income or assets in the hands of young beneficiaries, the new provisions encouraged absolute vesting at the age of 18. This led to a partial relaxation of the insistence on absolute entitlement at the age of 18 in the form of the introduction, by virtue of the Finance Act 2006, of a further new category of favoured property, namely the age 18-to-25 trust.[5]

A transitional period to April 5, 2008 (extended in the case of appointments of s.49C transitional serial interests[6] to October 5, 2008) was enacted, enabling some taxpayers to re-arrange their affairs so as to minimise the impact of the changes. The mechanism for transitional relief was to secure the pre-March 22, treatment in respect of certain categories of interests in possession.[7]

Consequential amendments were made to TCGA 1992. In particular, the application of the capital gains tax uplift on death under both ss.72 and 73 of the 1992 Act is now limited to terminations on death of general law interests in possession[8] which are also qualifying interests in possession for IHT purposes (i.e. the uplift does not apply where a qualifying interest in possession terminates on death but the settlement is, for example, a discretionary settlement under the general law). Consequential amendments were also made to the provisions affording holdover relief (see para.10–37).

Other changes introduced by the Finance Act 2006 included extending the application of the gifts with reservation of benefit provisions to terminations by trustees of qualifying interests in possession (see para.10–06 below).

Illustration of main changes introduced by Finance Act 2006 Sch.20

Lifetime transfers

Prior to the changes introduced by the Finance Act 2006, a gift into a settlement **10–04** could either be an immediately chargeable transfer (e.g. a gift into a discretionary trust) or a potentially exempt transfer (i.e. a gift into an accumulation and maintenance trust, or a gift into an interest in possession trust). If it was an immediately chargeable transfer, the entry charge on the gift of assets into such a settlement would be chargeable at half the lifetime rate, i.e. 20 per cent (or more if death followed within seven years).[9] If the gift was a potentially exempt transfer, there would be no immediate charge to inheritance tax and no charge in fact unless the settlor died within seven years of making the gift into the settlement.

---

[4] For an outline of the changes introduced to the tax treatment of accumulation and maintenance settlements, see para.18–33.

[5] See Ch.20.

[6] As to which see para.11–56.

[7] Extended correspondence between professional bodies and HMRC attempted to clarify the operation of the new provisions, and in particular the transitional regime. This can be accessed on STEP's website.

[8] For the general law meaning of interest in possession, see Ch.12.

[9] See paras 6–04 and 6–44.

The Finance Act 2006 changes have altered all this. The important point to note is that unless a settlement created after March 22, 2006 is one in which there is a "qualifying interest in possession" (as defined in s.59),[10] the lifetime transfer of assets into such a settlement will be an immediately chargeable transfer. Further, the assets within such a settlement will be subject to the relevant property regime. The one exception to the application of the relevant property regime to inter vivos settlements created after March 22, 2006 is a gift into a disabled person's trust, i.e. a trust in which a beneficiary has a "disabled person's interest" as defined in IHTA 1984 s.89B.[11]

Some key points to note in relation to the new regime:

(1) It is irrelevant that the settlor has an initial interest in possession in a post-March 22, 2006 new lifetime settlement. Such an interest in possession is not a "qualifying interest in possession". The property is, therefore, relevant property taxed under the relevant property regime (s.58). Consequently, even though the settlor has an interest in possession for the purposes of income tax and capital gains tax, his interest is, in effect, disregarded for the purposes of inheritance tax. There is therefore an immediate charge to inheritance tax on the value of the gift of assets into the settlement, to the extent that gift exceeds the settlor's unutilised nil rate band.

Given that the settlor's interest is not a "qualifying interest in possession", s.49(1) does not apply: in other words, the value of the underlying property in the settlement does not form part of the settlor's estate[12] (though, on death, this is subject to the possible application of the reservation of benefit provisions).[13] Once the assets become settled property, subject to falling within one of the favoured property regimes, the relevant property regime will apply: i.e. periodic and exit charges will apply (discussed in detail in Chs 14 and 15).

(2) The spouse exemption under s.18 is not available on the transfer of assets into a settlement in which the spouse has an interest in possession. This makes a post-March 22, 2006 settlement in favour of the settlor's spouse a less attractive option than an outright gift to the spouse, though there are two exceptions to this rule. First, there may not be an immediately chargeable transfer on the gift to a settlement in which the spouse has an initial interest in possession (whether or not the interest is a qualifying interest in possession) if the transfer of value is itself exempt, for example, by virtue of being a disposition for the maintenance of the family (s.11).[14] Second, the transfer will not be immediately chargeable if the interest of the spouse under the post-March 22, 2006 settlement is a disabled person's interest (see Ch.21).

Deathtime transfers

10–05   For settlements created on death after March 22, 2006, the charge under s.4[15] will arise unless the transfer into the settlement falls within certain exemptions, for example, the spouse exemption under s.18.[16] However, note that s.18(1) IHTA 1982 stipulates that the exemption applies only:

[10] See para.11–50.
[11] See Ch.21.
[12] See paras 10–14 and 12–02–12–04.
[13] See Ch.7.
[14] See also paras 2–55–2–57.
[15] See para.8–02.
[16] For other exemptions from charge, see paras 3–28–3–45.

" . . . to the extent that value transferred is attributable to property which becomes comprised in the estate of the transferor's spouse or civil partner or so far as the value transferred is not so attributable to the extent that that estate is increased."

Where the spouse's interest is not a "qualifying interest in possession" (because it is not an immediate post-death interest, a disabled person's interest or a transitional serial interest)[17] a charge under IHTA 1984 s.4 will arise. Generally, interest in possession settlements created on death will qualify as immediate post-death interests and therefore as "qualifying interests in possession". As such, there will be no charge under s.4 where property is transferred to an interest in possession settlement in favour of a spouse.[18]

The reservation of benefit provisions post-Finance Act 2006

Since the Finance Act 2006, situations in which the reservation of benefit provisions now apply include the following: **10–06**

(1) Where the settlor settles assets into the settlement and the trustees use that cash to purchase property in which the settlor then lives. Paragraph 5 of Sch.20 to Finance Act 1986 treats this as a reservation of benefit by the settlor in the property acquired using the gifted cash. Previously, this applied only to discretionary settlements where the settlor included himself within the class of discretionary beneficiaries of the settlement he created.

(2) Where the trustees of a qualifying interest in possession settlement terminate the beneficiary's interest in possession in property which the beneficiary continues to benefit in some way from the asset. Both pre- and post-Finance Act 2006, the termination of the interests is a transfer of value for the purposes of s.52. However, pre-March 22, 2006, it was not a "gift" for the purposes of the gifts with reservations provisions. New Finance Act 1986 s.102ZA now deems such terminations of qualifying interests in possession by trustees to be "gifts"—so that there is no longer any doubt that the reservation of benefit provisions apply.[19]

For a full discussion of situations where the gift of reservation of benefit provisions apply and of the extent to which it is possible to claim that the settlor has carved-out an interest before transferring property subject to that interest into the settlement, see Chapter 7 (gift with reservation of benefit provisions). The possible application of the pre-owned assets provisions should also be considered.[20]

Planning: access to holdover relief

Prior to the Finance Act 2006, from the CGT perspective, the transfer of property to a discretionary trust was more attractive than a transfer to an interest in possession settlement because where the conditions of the Taxation of Chargeable Gains Tax Act **10–07**

---

[17] For the definitions of these terms see Ch.11 at paras 11–50–11–63.
[18] HMRC considers that this will also apply where property is transferred to an existing interest in possession settlement in favour of a spouse.
[19] This is considered in detail at paras 7–99 and 7–100.
[20] See paras 7–155–7–204.

1992 s.260 were satisfied the settlor could elect to hold over the gain arising on the disposal: s.260 applies only where the disposal is a "chargeable transfer within the meaning of the Inheritance Tax Act 1984"[21] and is available even if no IHT is paid on the transfer because it is within the settlor's annual exempt amount, or his nil rate band or the property qualifies for 100 per cent agricultural relief or business relief.[22] The efficiency of this approach became somewhat circumscribed because, from December 10, 2004, holdover relief was no longer available in respect of transfers to "settlor interested" discretionary trusts[23] and from April 6, 2006, the meaning of "settlor interested" was extended. For these purposes a trust is "settlor interested" if someone who is a "settlor" in relation to the trust or his spouse has an interest in the settlement (or he or his spouse acquires an interest within six years of the date of the settlement). A "settlor" has an "interest in the settlement" if any property comprised in the settlement is payable to, or applicable for the benefit of the settlor or his spouse in any circumstances whatsoever, or is or will become so, or will or may become so payable to or applicable for the benefit of a dependent child of a settlor, i.e. a child of the settlor (including a stepchild) who is under the age of 18 and is unmarried.[24] A person is a "settlor" in relation to a trust if any of the settled property originates from him. As the definition of "settlor interested" is limited to the settlor and his spouse and dependent children, holdover relief is still available on a transfer of assets to a relevant property trust for the benefit of the settlor's adult children,[25] or grandchildren.

The changes introduced by the Finance Act 2006 mean that most inter vivos settlements, including most interest in possession settlements, will be relevant property trusts: transfers of property into such settlements will be immediately chargeable for IHT purposes and, subject to the other conditions for the availability of that relief being satisfied, s.260 holdover relief will apply.[26]

Section 260 holdover relief also applies to transfers out of settlements which are chargeable to IHT, and to certain transfers which are exempt, for example: transfers out of bereaved minors' trust where the bereaved minor becomes absolutely entitled to the trust property before the age of 18.[27]

II. BASIC STRUCTURE OF THE SPECIAL CHARGING PROVISIONS APPLYING TO SETTLED PROPERTY: I.E. THE PROVISIONS APPLYING TO SETTLED PROPERTY IN WHICH NO QUALIFYING INTEREST IN POSSESSION SUBSISTS

10–08   As seen in para.10–01 above, the legislation divides settled property in which no qualifying interest in possession subsists into two categories—"relevant property", and

[21] For the provision which treats an occasion of charge to inheritance tax as a chargeable transfer, see para.10–37.

[22] See paras 26–12–26–193.

[23] TCGA 1992 s.169B. Note that the limitation by reference to a settlor's interest does not apply in relation to a disabled person's trust: TCGA 1992 s.169D. Despite TCGA 1992 s.169D, holdover relief under s.260 will not be available for transfers into self-settlements which are disabled person's interests (as to which see Ch.21), as the transfer of property by a settlor into a self-settlement will not be chargeable for inheritance tax purposes.

[24] TCGA 1992 s.169F.

[25] But note the provisions for clawback of relief if a settlement becomes settlor-interest, for example because a dependent child becomes a beneficiary of the settlement within six years of a transfer of property to the settlement (TCGA s.169C).

[26] Section 260 holdover relief will potentially be available to all inter vivos transfers of property into settlements if HMRC's interpretation of the effect of post-March 22, 2006 additions to existing qualifying in possession settlements is correct (as to which see paras 11–19–11–20 and 12–17–12–19).

[27] See TCGA 1992 s.260(2)(b)–(f).

what for convenience will be called "favoured property". Post-Finance Act 2006, which introduced two new categories, the following categories of settled property qualify as "favoured property", i.e.:

(1) property held for a limited time for charitable purposes only;
(2) property held indefinitely for charitable purposes only;
(3) property held on accumulation and maintenance trusts;
(4) property held on bereaved minors' trusts;
(5) property held on age 18-to-25 trusts;
(6) property held by trustees of superannuation funds[28];
(7) property held on employee trusts;
(8) property held on protective trusts;
(9) property held on trusts for disabled persons;
(10) property comprised in a trade or professional compensation fund;
(11) property forming part of a premiums trust fund or ancillary trust fund of a corporate member of Lloyd's Underwriters;
(12) property held in a maintenance fund;
(13) excluded property.

In one sense, "relevant property" is a residual category: it is property held on trusts in which no-qualifying interests in possession subsist and which is not favoured property. In fact, that is how it is defined in the legislation (see s.58). However, as most inter vivos settlements created post-March 22, 2006 will not be settlements with qualifying interests in possession, this residual category of trusts is likely to be the one which is most frequently encountered.

The legislation establishes a single, separate code for dealing with relevant property and a series of mini-codes for dealing with each kind of favoured property. The code regulating the treatment of relevant property has a number of features in common with each of these mini-codes, which in turn share a number of common features. The position is thus that:

(a) some rules apply generally to settled property in which no qualifying interest in possession subsists (i.e. to both relevant property trusts and to favoured property trusts);
(b) some rules apply only to relevant property;
(c) some rules apply only to favoured property;
(d) some rules apply only to certain kinds of favoured property.

Main features of the special charging provisions as they apply to relevant property

These are outlined in Chapter 13. At the time of writing, a consultation is in progress **10–09** (the consultation document was published on July 13, 2012, the closing date for comments is October 5, 2012), with the aim of simplifying the regime of periodic and

---

[28] Exceptionally, such property may be relevant property; see para.23–05.

exit charges for relevant property trusts. Changes to the regime outlined in Chapter 13 are, therefore, probable.

Main features of the special charging provisions as they apply to favoured property

10–10 The special charging provisions have the following main features in relation to favoured property:

(1) *Exemption from periodic charge*: the periodic charge which is imposed on relevant property is not imposed on favoured property.

(2) *Exit charges*: the legislation divides favoured property into two categories —that on which an exit charge may be imposed, and that on which it may not.[29] The exit charges imposed on favoured property are largely identical to those imposed on relevant property. The terminology of "primary" and "secondary" exit charges or "special" exit charges is used in this book to distinguish between the different occasions which give rise to charges. The terminology adopted is explained at para.15–01 in relation to relevant property. Certain reliefs from exit charges available to relevant property are also available to favoured property.[30]

(3) *Rate of tax*: except in the case of the primary exit charge for age 18-to-25 trusts,[31] the rate at which an exit charge is imposed on favoured property is determined in a much simpler way than that prescribed where an exit charge is imposed on relevant property. The rate is found by multiplying one or more percentages, ranging from 0.25 per cent down to 0.05 per cent, by a specified number of quarters geared to take account, broadly speaking, of the period during which the property in question has been held on favoured property trusts.

III. PROVISIONS OF GENERAL APPLICATION

10–11 As was mentioned above, certain provisions apply to both relevant property and favoured property. The provisions can be vitally important, and it will be convenient to consider them now.

Commencement of a settlement

10–12 The legislation establishes a special rule for determining the time when a settlement is to be regarded as having commenced for purposes of the special charging provisions, i.e. the provisions that apply to relevant property and to favoured property. This rule, which can be of crucial importance, seems simple: by s.60, a settlement commences when property first becomes comprised in it. This, however, merely begs the question,

---

[29] See para.17–01.
[30] But see paras 10–23 and following below in relation to excluded property and favoured property trusts.
[31] See para.17–20.

when is property regarded as having become comprised in a settlement? There is no general provision fixing the time when property becomes comprised in a settlement. There are, however, three special rules. It is to be noted that these rules apply only for purposes of the special charging provisions and not, for example, for purposes of determining liability.

Death

By s.83, property which becomes comprised in a settlement in pursuance of a will **10–13** or intestacy is treated as having become comprised in that settlement on the death of the testator or intestate, whenever that death may have occurred. The period during which an estate is administered is thus ignored.

Initial interest of settlor, etc.

It may be that on or after March 26, 1974, property becomes comprised in a **10–14** settlement in circumstances such that the settlor, or his spouse or widow, is beneficially entitled to an interest in possession in that property immediately after it becomes so comprised. By s.80, a special rule applies if the property or any part of it subsequently becomes held on trusts such that none of those persons is beneficially entitled to an interest in possession. But note that where one of those persons becomes entitled to an interest in possession in a settlement post-March 22, 2006, this rule applies only if the interest of that person is a "postponing interest" as defined, i.e.: a disabled person's interest; or an immediate post-death interest.[32] In such a case, the property is treated for purposes of the special charging provisions, other than for the purposes of determining the dates of the 10-year anniversaries of the settlement, as not having become comprised in the settlement when it was made; instead, the property is treated as having become comprised in a separate settlement at the time when the last of the settlor, his spouse or widow ceased to be beneficially entitled pre-March 22, 2006, to an interest in possession in it and post-March 22, 2006, to a "postponing interest" in it. This is so regardless of the trusts on which it then becomes held. If the person with the pre-March 22, 2006 interest in possession or, as appropriate, the person with postponing interest ceases to have an interest in possession in only part of the property, then that part is regarded as having become comprised in a separate settlement on that occasion. The separate settlement is treated as having been made by the person the cessation of whose interest resulted in the property being regarded as having become comprised in the separate settlement. This rule was apparently introduced for the administrative convenience of HMRC. Given the availability of the spouse exemption pre-Finance Act 2006, there would be no chargeable transfer when the settlement was made, with the result that there would be no need to value the settled property at that time. On the occasion of subsequent charges under the special charging provisions it would thus be necessary to value the property in question retrospectively. Section 80 avoids this problem.

---

[32] IHTA 1984 s.80(4).

The following examples illustrate how s.80 operates:

(1) In 1967, A settled property on himself for life, remainder on discretionary trusts for his children. On January 1, 1988, he released his life interest, so that the property became held on discretionary trusts. Since A's interest vested before March 27, 1974, s.80 does not apply, and the property is regarded as having become comprised in the settlement in 1967.

(2) In 2000, B settled property on his wife for life, remainder to his children on discretionary trusts. On January 1, 2004 his wife released her interest, so that the property became held on discretionary trusts for the children. The property is regarded as having become comprised in the settlement on January 1, 2004, and B's wife, not B, is regarded as having made the settlement.

(3) In 2000, C settled property on himself for life, remainder to his sister for life, remainder on discretionary trusts for their children. On January 1, 2003, C died, and on February 1, 2004, his sister released her interest, so that the property became held on discretionary trusts. The property is regarded as having become comprised in the settlement on January 1, 2003, and C, not his sister, is regarded as having made the settlement.

(4) In 2000, D settled property on himself for life, remainder to his wife for life, remainder on discretionary trusts for their children. On January 10, 2004, D died. On February 29, 2012 D's wife died and the property became held on discretionary trusts. The property will be regarded as having become comprised in the settlement on February 29, 2012. D's wife will be regarded as having made the settlement.

(5) In 2002, E settled property for himself for life, remainder to his wife for life, remainder on discretionary trusts for his sister's children. E died on April 10, 2007. His wife died on November 17, 2018. The property is regarded as having become comprised in the settlement on April 10, 2007 and E will be regarded as having made the settlement. This is because E's wife's life interest is not a postponing interest: it is not an immediate post-death interest.[33] Although the wife's interest would be a transitional serial interest within s.49C[34] and therefore a qualifying interest in possession, that interest is not treated as a postponing interest for the purposes of s.80.[35]

(6) On December 10, 2008, F died. His will provided for the residue of his estate to be settled on a life interest trust for his wife, remainder on life-interest trusts for his children. F's wife died on June 16, 2020. The property will be regarded as having been comprised in the settlement on June 16, 2020. F's wife will be regarded as having made the settlement.

Ten-year anniversaries

10–15   As was mentioned above, s.80 applies for all but one of the purposes of the special charging provisions. The one purpose for which it does not apply is for determining the dates of the 10-year anniversaries of the settlement. Section 61(2) provides that for that

---

[33] For the definition of immediate post-death interest, see para.11–51.
[34] For the definition of transitional serial interest, see para.11–56.
[35] IHTA 1984 s.80(4).

purpose the relevant date is the date on which the settlement actually commenced, not the date on which is to be treated under s.80 as having commenced; see para.10–20.

Transfers between settlements

It may be that property ceases to be comprised in one settlement and becomes **10–16** comprised in another, e.g. where trustees advance assets to another trust. Section 81(1) provides that in such a case, subject to two qualifications, the property in question is to be treated for purposes only of the special charging provisions as having remained comprised in the first settlement. The purpose of s.81(1) appears to be to prevent the avoidance of tax by the slimming of trusts. Under the special charging provisions, the rate at which tax is charged depends on the history of the trust. If trustees advanced property to another settlement the rate of tax on the advanced property might be lower than it would have been if the advanced property had remained part of the original settlement—hence s.81(1). It is to be noted that in theory s.81 will apply to a sale between settlements even though such a sale does not result in any reduction in the rate at which tax would be charged on the vendor settlement. In practice HMRC may apply s.81 only to the extent that the value of the property comprised in the first settlement is diminished, e.g. where the sale is at an undervalue.

Qualifications

As was mentioned, s.81(1) is subject to two qualifications. First, it does not apply if **10–17** a person becomes beneficially entitled to the property in question (and not just to a qualifying interest in possession in it) before the property becomes comprised in the second settlement. Secondly, s.81(1) applies only to property which ceased to be comprised in the settlement on or after December 10, 1981. There is a special rule where property ceased to be comprised in the settlement before that date and after March 26, 1974. In such a case, s.81(2) provides that the property is to be regarded as having remained comprised in the first settlement only if it ceased to be comprised in that settlement and became comprised in the second settlement by the same disposition. Therefore, s.81(2) will not apply where:

(a) an individual with a reversionary interest under a settlement settled that interest on trustees of another settlement; and
(b) the interest which he settled subsequently vested in possession.

This follows from the fact that the property in question, i.e. the property in which the interest subsequently vested in possession, did not cease to be comprised in the first settlement and becomes comprised in the second settlement by the same disposition. It is understood that HMRC accept this. It is to be noted that s.81(2) applies only when both the settlement and the vesting of the interest occurred before December 10, 1981. It may be, of course, that the individual resettled his interest before December 10, 1981, and that that interest vested in possession on or after that date. In that case, s.81(2) will be of no assistance. Section 81(3) therefore provides that s.81(1) does not apply where a reversionary interest which vested on or after December 10, 1981, was settled before that date. Note that s.81(3) applies only where the interest which was settled was a reversionary interest expectant on the determination of a qualifying interest in possession. Thus, it will not apply where trustees of a discretionary trust appointed a

473

contingent interest to a beneficiary which he then resettled and which subsequently vested in possession. This will not normally be a cause for concern, since in such cases the contingency will normally have been satisfied shortly after the appointment, with the result that it will be exceptional for the two events to have straddled December 10, 1981.

EXAMPLE

10–18   The following example illustrates how s.81 operates. Assume that on March 1, 1986, a testator (T) dies leaving a will which settled his residuary estate on trust for his widow (Mrs T) for life with remainder to his son absolutely. Assume further that in November 2000 during Mrs T's life the son settled his remainder interest (along with other property) on discretionary trusts. Mrs T dies in January 2004 when the remainder interest fell into possession and it is now intended to break up the discretionary trust and distribute the property.

Section 81 is limited to property moving between settlements, i.e. settled assets must become comprised in a new settlement. The settlement by the son of his remainder interest in November 2000 does not fall within the provision since there is a distinction between his interest and the property subject to that interest which is comprised in the 1986 will trust. Accordingly, s.81 will be relevant only when the remainder interest falls into possession (i.e. in January 2004) since only then will assets cease to be comprised in one settlement (the 1986 will trust) and become comprised in a different settlement (the 2000 discretionary trust). When this occurs s.81 will then be relevant for the purposes of Ch.III of the 1984 Act. The effect of s.81 applying is that the property to which the trustees of the 2000 discretionary trust become entitled is treated as always having been comprised in the 1986 will trust. Accordingly, for the purpose of computing the IHT charge on such property, 10-year anniversary periods will start to run from March 1, 1986, and therefore the first anniversary occurred on March 1, 1996. Given that the 1986 will trust did not at that date contain any relevant property this is obviously irrelevant in the context of any tax charge. The next 10-year anniversary date will not be until March 2006. Curiously therefore the property comprised in the discretionary trust created in November 2000 must therefore be segregated: that deriving from the 1986 will trust is subject to future charges on the basis that it has remained comprised in the 1986 will trust, whereas the other property settled in 2000 will be taxed as being comprised in a separate discretionary trust with its own periodic charges, rates of tax, etc.

Problem area: pre-March 22, 2006 transfers from relevant property trusts to trust with qualifying interests in possession

10–19   It is to be noted that s.81(1) caused problems where there was a qualifying interest in possession subsisting in the settlement to which property was advanced prior to March 22, 2006. Assume, e.g. that an advancement was made on December 16, 2002 out of a discretionary trust into a trust in which there was a qualifying interest in possession. For the purposes of the special charging provisions the advanced property would, under s.81(1), have been treated as having remained comprised in the first settlement, with the result that, inter alia, it is subject to the periodic charge. For the purposes of the main charging provisions, on the other hand, the property is treated as being comprised in the second settlement with the result that it may be subject to a charge under those provisions as well.[36] It may be possible to interpret s.81 as meaning that although the property in question is treated as remaining comprised in the first settlement it is nevertheless subject to the trusts of the second settlement, i.e. the settlement in which it is in fact comprised, with the result that in the example just given the property would cease to be subject to the special charging provisions and would not affect the rate of tax charged on property which remained comprised in the first settlement as a matter of general law. Other interpretations are, however, possible.

Ten-year anniversary

A settlement's 10-year anniversary is defined as being the tenth anniversary of the **10–20** date on which the settlement commenced and subsequent anniversaries at 10-yearly intervals,[37] subject to three qualifications, as follows:

(1) No date falling before April 1, 1983, is a 10-year anniversary.[38] Thus, if a settlement commenced on June 26, 1962, its first 10-year anniversary would have been June 26, 1992.

(2) In exceptional circumstances, the first 10-year anniversary is taken to have been April 1, 1984. This will occur where the first 10-year anniversary would otherwise have fallen between April 1, 1983, and March 31, 1984, and during that period an event occurs in respect of the settlement on which tax is (or would in the absence of an election)[39] be chargeable under the special charging provisions if that event could not have occurred except as the result of some proceedings before a court. In such a case, the first 10-year anniversary is taken to have been April 1, 1984, but this does not affect the date of later 10-year anniversaries.[40] If, for example, trustees of a settlement which commenced on September 30, 1953, made a payment on July 1, 1984, which they could not have made except as a result of court proceedings, the settlement's first 10-year anniversary will have fallen on April 1, 1984, while its second 10-year anniversary will have fallen on September 30, 1993.

(3) It may be that under s.80 (previously s.120 of the Finance Act 1982) property is treated as not having become comprised in one settlement but instead as having become comprised in another, separate settlement.[41] In such a case, the 10-year anniversaries of the separate settlement are the same as those of the first settlement,[42] as the following exchange of letters between the Editor of *The Law Society Gazette* and HMRC[43] shows[44]:

---

[36] This problem is to be distinguished from the problem which can arise where trustees of one discretionary trust have an interest in possession in another discretionary trust; see paras 12–49, 12–50.

[37] IHTA 1984 s.61(1).

[38] IHTA 1984 s.61(3).

[39] As to which, see para.13–06.

[40] IHTA 1984 s.61(4).

[41] See para.10–14.

[42] IHTA 1984 s.61(2).

[43] *The Law Society Gazette* (2002), pp.12, 13.

[44] Note that references in the correspondence to "interests in possession" should, post-FA 2006 and for interests created post-March 22, 2006 be read as references to "postponing interests" (as to which see s.81(4) and para.10–14 above). References to "discretionary settlements" should be read as references to all settlements to which the special charging provisions apply.

"Dear Sir,

Section 120, Finance Act 1982

We have recently been called upon to advise on the provisions of s.120 of the Finance Act 1982.

The provisions of the said s.120 are expressed as being for the purposes of 'this Chapter.' The reference to 'this Chapter' is Chapter II of the Finance Act 1982 which sets out the provisions relating to settlements without interest *(sic)* in possession, *i.e.* discretionary settlements. Quite clearly therefore, these provisions exclude from the rules set out in s.109 of the Finance Act 1982 (now s.66 dealing with the rate of tax) any property comprised in a settlement that was, at the time the settlement was created and has since remained, outside of the discretionary settlement regime in which the settlor or his spouse, or the settlor's widow or widower, has an interest in possession in the settlement from the time of its inception.

However, what is not so clear is whether or not the provisions of s.120 of the Finance Act 1982 are intended to apply to those settlements in which the settlor or his spouse, or the settlor's widow or widower, has an interest in possession in the whole of the property of the settlement from its inception and which is followed on the termination of such an interest in possession by discretionary trusts. Our grounds for not being fully convinced that it is intended that the said provisions should apply in these circumstances is the inclusion of the word 'separate' in subs. (1) of the said section, as in our submission by the inclusion of the word 'separate' it could indicate that the provisions do not relate to a settlement in which there is an interest in possession in the whole of the property of the settlement and is followed on the termination of the interest in possession by discretionary trusts, as such a settlement would *ab initio* be a separate settlement.

We would also mention that note 21 of your Department's press release of 26 March 1982 dealing with the changes in the capital transfer tax legislation relating to discretionary trusts infers that the provisions of s.120 are limited to applying to the rules set out in s.109 of the Finance Act 1982.

We shall therefore be grateful if you could let us know if in your opinion the provisions of s.120 of the Finance Act 1982 are limited to applying to the rules set out in s.109 of the said Act, or whether these provisions are intended to apply to those settlements where there is an interest in possession in the whole of the property from the inception of the settlement and which is followed on the termination of such an interest by discretionary trusts.

Yours faithfully,

[Martyn Gowar]"

"Dear Sirs

Section 120, Finance Act 1982 6 October 1982

Thank you for your letter of 27 August.

You will appreciate that any question about the existence and/or extent of any liability to capital transfer tax in connection with a given event can only be determined in accordance with the facts as they are when the event occurs and on the basis of the law as it is then understood to be. My general remarks in this letter, therefore, are made simply with the object of being as helpful to you as possible, do not commit the Board of Inland Revenue in any way and will not preclude the Board from raising in connection with any event such claims for tax as may be justified by the circumstances.

On this understanding and on the basis of the law as it is at present understood to be, I can accept that s.120 has the broad effect set out in your second paragraph whilst the interest in possession of the settlor, his spouse or the settlor's widow or widower subsists. But the provisions of s.120 relate also to the situation referred to in the opening sentence of your third paragraph. The section entails an exception to the rule in s.105(1) which fixes the date of the ten-year anniversary. Section 105(2) makes special provision for a settlement which has entered the discretionary trust regime on or after the termination of an initial interest in possession held by the settlor or his spouse under a settlement which commenced after 26 March 1974. Where the settlor or his spouse is beneficially entitled to an interest in possession in property immediately after it becomes comprised in a settlement, s.120(1) disregards the actual commencement of the settlement. For the purposes of the discretionary trust code, when the settled property becomes held on trusts under which neither the settlor nor his spouse (including the widow or widower of the settlor) is beneficially entitled to an interest in possession, the property is treated as then becoming comprised in a separate settlement made by whichever of the settlor or his spouse was last beneficially entitled to an interest in possession in it. Notwithstanding that a new separate settlement is deemed to commence when the settlor's or his spouse's interest terminates, that new settlement is to have the same ten-year anniversary as the actual settlement which conferred on the settlor or spouse a beneficial interest in possession.

To illustrate the point, I think an example would be helpful. On 1 July 1977 A settled funds on himself for life, then to his wife for life, remainder on discretionary trust. A died on 9 May 1981; his wife dies on 4 April 1985. Under s.120(1) the property is treated as becoming comprised in a separate settlement made by the wife on 4 April 1985 but the ten-year anniversary dates of that settlement are fixed by reference to 1 July 1977, *e.g.* the first anniversary will be 1 July 1987. It is worth noting that the treatment of the wife as the settlor may be material for determining the tax payable on relevant property from time to time comprised in the settlement. In the example, the wife is to be treated as the settlor and it is her chargeable transfers in the ten-year period before 4 April 1985 which will be material. If she made a further settlement on 4 April 1985 that will be a related settlement unless it comes within s.106(2).

I trust the above is of some assistance to you.

Yours faithfully,

P.W. Legg"

Circumstances may arise in which the result of property being treated as having become comprised in a separate settlement is that the original settlement, given the fact that no property is comprised in it, has no 10-year anniversary. In that case, the 10-year anniversaries of the separate settlement are the same as those the first settlement would have had in the absence of s.80.

Settlor's additions

The special charging provisions now in force (unlike the original special charging provisions) make no provision for treating additions to a settlement by a settlor as being comprised in a separate settlement. Whether or not property added by a settlor to a settlement is comprised in that settlement is discussed at paras 11–19, 11–20 and 12–17–12–19. For the dangers of adding property to existing relevant property trust, see paras 16–27–16–29.

10–21

Quarters and payments

Section 63 defines a "quarter" as meaning a period of three months, and "payment" as including a transfer of assets other than money. Neither "transfer" nor "assets" is

10–22

defined, and there must be some question as to whether the creation of rights amounts to a transfer of assets for these purposes. The question may be important since if the creation of a right which diminishes the value of a trust fund does not constitute a payment it may be to the taxpayer's advantage, because a special relief may be available in such a case.[45]

IV. EXCLUDED PROPERTY

10–23   One kind of property which for a number of reasons deserves special attention is excluded property. Under the original special charging provisions:

(1) excluded property was not within the definition of settled property at all, with the result that it was altogether outside those provisions, from which it consequently enjoyed complete immunity; and

(2) no charge could be imposed when property held on discretionary trusts was converted into excluded property.

Neither of these rules remains in force under the current special charging provisions. Now, anomalously, given the favoured treatment intended to be given to excluded property, a charge may in certain circumstances be imposed when relevant property is converted into excluded property.[46] More surprisingly, and what is less likely to be appreciated, is that excluded property may itself be subject to an exit charge.

Tax trap

10–24   Assume that pre-March 22, 2006, X, a foreign domiciliary, wished to settle property situated outside the United Kingdom on trust for his children, and that he was advised to settle the property on accumulation and maintenance trusts. Given the settlor's domicile and the situs of the property, the property would be excluded property. If, as desired, the trusts qualified for favoured treatment by virtue of being held on favoured accumulation and maintenance trusts[47] and the trustees subsequently incur an exit charge, e.g. by entering into a depreciatory transaction, there appears to be nothing in the legislation to prevent this charge from being imposed notwithstanding the fact the trust property is actually excluded property. Problems could also arise if an exit charge was imposed because the property ceased, by effluxion of time, to be held on qualifying accumulation and maintenance trusts; see para.18–31. Post-Finance Act 2006, the same problem applies in a case where property is held on bereaved minors' trust or age 18-to-25 trusts. Because, usually, property will cease to receive favoured treatment on an occasion where the exit is exempt from charge, the possibility of such a charge being imposed is not likely often to arise in practice. Given the potential problems raised by the interaction of excluded property status and favoured property treatment, the counsel

[45] See para.15–15.
[46] See para.10–24.
[47] See para.18–33.

of perfection for foreign domiciliaries is to avoid settling property on favoured property trusts, and to rely exclusively on excluded property status.

Stricter definition of excluded property

A more fundamental point concerns the definition of excluded property, namely that s.82 provides that where s.80 or s.81 applies an extra requirement must be satisfied if property which would otherwise be excluded property is to be excluded property for the purposes of Ch.III of Pt III of the 1984 Act[48] (i.e. ss.58–85 regulating the treatment of settled property in which there is no qualifying interest in possession).

10–25

Scope of stricter definition

It is essential to understand that this stricter definition applies only for the purposes of Ch.III and not, e.g. for determining if settled property in which there is a qualifying interest in possession is excluded property or whether property held on relevant property trusts which is subject to the reservation of benefit provisions is excluded property.

10–26

The interaction of ss.80 and 82: double domicile test

It will be recalled[49] that under s.80 a special rule applies where (a) after March 26, 1974, property becomes comprised in a settlement in circumstances such that the settlor, or his spouse, widow or widower is beneficially entitled to an interest in possession in that property immediately after it becomes so comprised, and (b) that the property or any part of it subsequently becomes held on trusts under which none of those persons is beneficially entitled to a pre-March 22, interest in possession or a postponing interest (as defined). In such a case, the property in question is treated for purposes of the special charging provisions as not having become comprised in the settlement when it was made. Instead, the property is treated as having become comprised in a separate settlement at the time when the last of the persons just mentioned ceased to be beneficially entitled to a pre-March 22, 2006 interest in possession in it or to a postponing interest in it, and this is so regardless of the nature of the trusts on which the property becomes held. The last of the persons to be so entitled is treated as the settlor of a separate settlement.

In such a case, in determining whether the property will be excluded property by virtue of being foreign situs property comprised in a settlement made by a settlor when he was not domiciled in the United Kingdom, not only must the settlor of the new settlement, i.e. the last of the settlor, the settlor's spouse or widow or widower to have a pre-March 22, 2006 interest in possession or a postponing interest in the settlement, not have been domiciled in the United Kingdom but, by ss.81(1) and (3)(a), the settlor

10–27

---

[48] Except for the purposes of ss.78 and 70; IHTA 1984 s.82(1).
[49] See paras 10–12 and following.

of the original settlement must also not have been domiciled in the United Kingdom when he made the original settlement.

EXAMPLE: PRE-MARCH 22, 2006 SETTLEMENTS

10–28 Assume X settled property on trusts on December 1, 1990 under which he had a life interest, followed by a life interest for his wife, with the trust fund thereafter being held on discretionary trusts. At all relevant times all the property comprised in the settlement was situated outside the United Kingdom. X died on January 15, 1998, survived by his wife and children. On his death the property was not held on discretionary trusts and therefore Ch.III did not apply to it. Section 82 was therefore irrelevant. On his death, the only issue would have been where X was domiciled when he made the settlement. On the death of Mrs X on March 25, 2003, s.82 was also irrelevant in determining whether or not IHT was chargeable in respect of her death because immediately before her death she had a pre-March 22, 2006 interest in possession in the trust fund. Chapter III did not apply to the settlement at that stage: the only issue with regard to the excluded property status of the property in the trust fund was the domicile of X when he made the settlement. Immediately after Mrs X's death the property became held on discretionary trusts, and Ch.III did apply to it. Therefore s.82 was relevant in determining whether or not the property was excluded property in relation to exit and periodic charges. That being the case, regard had to be had both to the domicile of X when he made the settlement and the domicile of Mrs X when she died.

10–29 It follows from the foregoing that if the trusts had provided that, following the death of the survivor of X and Mrs X, the trust fund was to be held on interest in possession trusts for their children or failing that, if prior to the death of the said survivor the trustees appointed that the trust fund was to be held on interests in possession trusts for the children, and all of these events had happened prior to March 22, 2006, Ch.III would never have applied.

Planning pre-March 22, 2006

10–30 In some cases particularly where children were relatively young, or substantial sums were involved, or both, it was thought unattractive or inappropriate to give the children interests in possession. In such cases the settlement could have provided that following the death of X and Mrs X, the trust fund be held on accumulation and maintenance trusts for the children. In such a case Ch.III would have applied, but even if s.82 operated to disqualify the trust fund from being excluded property, favoured treatment would still have been available under s.71[50] so that the application of s.82 would not materially affect the position. The vesting of interests in possession in the children would have be prevented by that favoured treatment from being a chargeable occasion, and once a child had an interest in possession Ch.III would no longer have applied to the property in which his interest subsisted.

EXAMPLE: POST-MARCH 22, 2006 SETTLEMENTS

10–31 Assume that in his will X, who is non-UK domiciled and not deemed domiciled, settles property on trusts for his wife for life, remainder to his children for life. X dies

---

[50] See paras 18–02–18–32.

and is survived by his wife and children. On his death the property—at all relevant times situated outside the United Kingdom—will be held on trust for his wife for life. Her interest will be an immediate post-death interest, and therefore a postponing interest. Immediately after Mrs X's death the property will be held on relevant property trusts for her children and Ch.III will apply to it. Therefore s.82 will be relevant to determining whether or not the property held in trust for children is excluded property: regard will have to be had both to the domicile of X when he made the settlement (i.e. on his death) and to the domicile of Mrs X when she died.

The inter-action of ss.81 and 82: double domicile test

Under s.81 where property ceases to be comprised in one settlement and becomes **10–32** comprised in another it is treated for the purposes of the special charging provisions as remaining comprised in the first settlement unless before it becomes comprised in the second settlement a person becomes beneficially entitled to the property.[51] In the absence of provision to the contrary in determining whether the property will be excluded property by virtue of being foreign situs property comprised in a settlement made by a settlor who was not domiciled in the United Kingdom the only requirement would be, per s.48(3)(a), that the settlor of the original settlement was not domiciled in the United Kingdom when he made that settlement. However, under ss.82(1) and 3(b) there is a further requirement, namely that the settlor of the transferee settlement must also have not been domiciled in the United Kingdom when he made that settlement.

The interaction of ss.81 and 82 is in practice likely to be less worrying than the interaction of ss.80 and 82. This follows from the fact that s.81 is most likely to apply where trustees of a settlement advance property from that settlement into an ad hoc settlement, and in such circumstances the settlor of the original settlement will also be regarded as the settlor of the ad hoc settlement.[52] The position in such a case will thus be adversely affected by s.82 only if the settlor, having been domiciled abroad when he made the first settlement, has since become domiciled in the United Kingdom, whether under the law generally or as a result of the deemed domicile rules.

The interaction of ss.81 and 82 could also cause difficulty where a reversionary interest is settled on trustees. Assume, for example, that X, a UK domiciliary, settles property in his will on A for life, remainder to B, a foreign domiciliary, in circumstances such that B's reversionary interest is situated abroad. If B settles his reversion, the position when his reversion vests and the trustees of his settlement become entitled to the property comprised in the settlement made by X will vary according to the nature of the trusts on which it is settled. If B's settlement is a relevant property trust regard will have to be had to the domicile of X and B when they made their respective settlements. If, on the other hand, B's settlement is, say, a disabled person's interest Ch.III will not apply to it and regard will have to be had only to B's domicile.

Planning for ss.80–82 generally

Section 82 can be circumvented by ensuring that settled property is held on relevant **10–33** property trusts from the start. It used to be the case that frequent changes in interests in possession could be made without any adverse tax consequences: so long as a

---

[51] See para.10–16.
[52] See para.11–39.

qualifying interest in possession subsisted in the property the property continued to be excluded property. Post-Finance Act 2006, it is also true that frequent changes in interests in possession can be made without any adverse tax consequences: so long as no qualifying interest in possession subsists in the settled property at any time.

Double tax treaties

10–34   It is worth mentioning that in certain cases the terms of a double tax treaty can transform a settlement which is prevented by ss.80–82 from being an excluded property settlement into a settlement which effectively qualifies for the kind of treatment conferred on an excluded property settlement. For example, under art.11(2) of the United Kingdom-Netherlands Treaty the United Kingdom cannot impose tax on settled property if when the settlement was made the settlor was (a) domiciled in the Netherlands under the Treaty and (b) not a UK national who had been domiciled in the United Kingdom under the Treaty at any time within the immediately preceding ten years.[53] Article 11(2) could therefore mean that the fact that a settlor domiciled in the Netherlands for both Dutch and UK purposes when he made a settlement subsequently became domiciled in the United Kingdom for IHT purposes in circumstances such that ss.80–82 prevented the property comprised in the settlement from being excluded property would not matter, because art.11(2) would supply sufficient protection from charge.

Exit charges on conversion of relevant property into excluded property

10–35   In the absence of provision to the contrary, the conversion of relevant property into excluded property would result in an exit charge because the relevant property would have ceased to be relevant property. Special rules apply to prevent such a conversion from being chargeable. First, by s.65(7), no such charge arises where the property becomes excluded property by virtue of s.48(3)(a), i.e. because the settlor was not domiciled in the United Kingdom when he made the settlement; see paras 15–38 and 15–44. Secondly, by s.65(8), no such charge arises in respect of certain exempt gilts provided certain conditions are satisfied. For this purpose the special rules in ss.80–82 are relevant. Since these rules operate in relation to exempt gilts only for the limited purpose of s.65(8) they are considered at paras 15–39 and following in relation to exit charges.

V. SETTLED PROPERTY: RELATIONSHIP BETWEEN THE MAIN CHARGING PROVISIONS AND THE SPECIAL CHARGING PROVISIONS

10–36   The main charging provisions and the special charging provisions are best regarded as operating completely independently of each other notwithstanding the fact that they have a number of common features. In particular, subject to one or two qualifications, the reliefs and exemptions available under the main charging provisions do not apply to the special charging provisions.

One provision, s.2(3), deserves special mention. This provides that, inter alia,

---

[53] See para.33–85.

"except where the context otherwise requires, references in this Act to chargeable transfers or to the values transferred by them shall be construed as including references to occasions on which tax is chargeable under Chapter III of Part III of this Act (apart from s.79) or to the amounts on which tax is then chargeable."

Section 2(3) is essentially a tidying-up provision, the main effect of which is to ensure that various administrative provisions which in terms refer only to chargeable transfers apply also, where appropriate, to occasions on which tax is chargeable under the special charging provisions. A good example of the operation of s.2(3) is its effect on ss.199 and following. These sections establish who is liable to pay once a charge to tax has in fact arisen: no other sections perform this function. Yet they make no reference whatsoever to charges arising under the special charging provisions. Thus, in the absence of s.2(3), there would be no provision establishing who was liable to pay the tax due in respect of such a charge. Section 201(1) does apply where, inter alia, " . . . the chargeable transfer is made under Part III of this Act", with the result that the riddle is solved.

It is to be noted that s.2(3) has no effect other than so to extend various provisions relating to *chargeable transfers*. In particular, it does not operate to make the reliefs and exemptions available under the main charging provisions to *transfers of value* apply to the special charging provisions. To achieve that effect, an extra provision is required. Accordingly, e.g. to ensure that business relief is available to property chargeable under the special charging provisions, the legislation specifically provides in s.103(1) that for purposes of business relief references to a transfer of value include references to the occasion on which tax is charged under Ch.III, with references to the value transferred by a transfer of value including for this purpose references to an occasion on which tax is charged under Ch.III and references to the transferor including references to the trustees of the settlement concerned.

Capital gains tax holdover relief

Section 2(3) can also be important for CGT purposes. Provided certain other conditions are satisfied, holdover relief is available under s.260(2)(a) where a disposal is a chargeable transfer for IHT purposes.[54] Where, e.g. trustees of a relevant property trust appoint property to a beneficiary absolutely the appointment will give rise to a deemed market value disposal by the trustees under s.71(1) of the Taxation of Chargeable Gains Act 1992 and if a gain arises the trustees may well wish to hold it over. The disposal is not a chargeable transfer for IHT purposes, but it is an occasion on which tax is chargeable under Ch.III of Pt III of the 1984 Act and by virtue of s.2(3) is therefore treated as a chargeable transfer for the purposes of s.260(2)(a). **10–37**

---

[54] See para.10–07.

CHAPTER 11

SETTLED PROPERTY DEFINITIONS

I. INTRODUCTION

11–01   This chapter is concerned with the definition of certain terms that have been used in the main text in connection with settled property. The meaning of "interest in possession" is discussed in Chapter 12.

Considered in isolation, definitions tend to be uninteresting, so reference is also made to the importance of the terms in question.

II. SETTLEMENTS AND SETTLED PROPERTY

11–02   Under the legislation property is settled if it is comprised in a settlement.[1] A settlement, in turn, can be actual, or, in the case of certain leases, notional. By s.43(2), an actual settlement is defined as meaning:

"any disposition or dispositions of property, whether effected by instrument, by parole or by operation of law, or partly in one way and partly in another, whereby the property is for the time being
   (a) held in trust for persons in succession or for any person subject to a contingency; or

---

[1] IHTA 1984 s.43(1). By concession, certain partnership assurance schemes are regarded by the Revenue as not constituting settlements: see para.28–27.

484

(b) held by trustees on trust to accumulate the whole or part of any income of the property or with power to make payments out of that income at the discretion of the trustees or some other person, with or without power to accumulate surplus income; or

(c) charged or burdened (otherwise than for full consideration in money or money's worth paid for his own use or benefit to the person making the disposition), with the payment of any annuity or other periodical payment payable for a life or any other limited or terminable period;

or would be so held or charged or burdened if the disposition or dispositions were regulated by the law of any part of the United Kingdom; or whereby, under the law of any other country, the administration of the property is for the time being governed by provisions equivalent in effect to those which would apply if the property were so held, charged or burdened."

HMRC's August 2004 Consultation Document "Modernising the Tax System for Trusts" proposed using this definition as the basis for a common definition of "trust" for income tax and CGT purposes.[2] However, the proposal was not implemented.

11–03 This definition is extended to take account of the law of Northern Ireland and the law of Scotland. By s.43(5), for purposes of the law of Northern Ireland it has effect as if references to property held on trust for persons included references to property standing limited to persons. By s.43(4), in relation to Scotland "settlement" also includes:

(1) an entail;

(2) any deed by virtue of which an annuity is charged on, or on the rents of, any property (the property being treated as comprised in a settlement); and

(3) in relation to any transfer of value made after April 17, 1980, any deed creating or reserving a proper liferent of any property, whether it is heritable or moveable, the property that is from time to time subject to the proper liferent being treated as the property comprised in the settlement.

Section 43(4)(c) extends the definition of "settlement" in relation to Scotland to include any deed coming within (3), because the law of Scotland is such that in the absence of (3), liferented property held on "proper liferent" would not be a settlement. This is because such property is conveyed directly to the liferenter (or to a fiar, the grantor reserving the liferent). "Deed" for this purpose "includes any disposition, arrangement, contract, resolution, instrument or writing".[3]

11–04 The settlement definition in s.43(2) clearly contemplates the possibility that an entity governed by a foreign law may nevertheless constitute a "settlement" for inheritance tax purposes:

"or would be so held or charged or burdened if the disposition or dispositions were regulated by the law of any part of the United Kingdom; or whereby, under the law of any other country, the administration of the property is for the time being governed by provisions equivalent in effect to those which would apply if the property were so held, charged or burdened."

Practitioners are most likely to come across the question of whether a foreign entity is a "settlement" for inheritance tax purposes where the entity is either a "Foundation" or an "Establishment". If such an entity is a trust, UK situs assets held by it may not

---

[2] Whether the IHT or another definition of "settlement" applies in particular situations continues to be a live issue, see para.7–167.

[3] IHTA 1984 s.43(4).

be excluded property. However, if it is a company, the interest in it is likely to be excluded property even if it holds UK situs assets.

11–05   A "Foundation" has characteristics similar to a company as well as those of a trust. The characteristics of a Foundation which resemble a company are its separate legal personality and the fact that it owns its assets beneficially. However, a Foundation resembles a trust because it tends to have property held "for persons in succession" and/or may provide the Board (the governing body of the Foundation) with the discretion "to make payments out of [the Foundation's] income". It is necessary to look at the precise terms (by-laws) of the Foundation to see on which side of the company/ trust line it falls. Further, the Foundation may be "equivalent in effect" to a family settlement.[4] In fact, HMRC issued a helpful statement in the context of Tax Deduction Scheme for Interest (Mailshot 6, May 17, 2004), that a Liechtenstein Foundation (Stiftung) was a trust for UK tax purposes.[5] An "Establishment" also has separate legal personality and owns its assets beneficially. Although similar in several respects to Foundations, Establishments tend to be used as vehicles through which to conduct commercial activities. Much will depend on the terms of the Establishment when determining whether it is "equivalent in effect" to a settlement. Note, however, that HMRC regard a Liechtenstein Establishment (Anstalt) as if it were a company[6] and as opaque for income tax purposes.[7]

Actual settlements

11–06   It follows from s.43(2) that there is an actual settlement only if, as a result of a disposition,[8] property is held, charged, or burdened in one of the following ways:

    (1) the property must be held in trust for:
        (a) persons in succession; or
        (b) any person subject to a contingency; or
    (2) the property must be held by trustees on trust:
        (a) to accumulate the whole or part of any income of the property; or
        (b) with power to make payments out of that income at the discretion of the trustees or some other person, with or without power to accumulate surplus income; or
    (3) the property must be charged or burdened[9] with the payment of an annuity or other periodical payment payable for a life or any other limited or terminable period.

11–07   HMRC practice has been to treat separate funds established under a will or deed that are held on separate trusts as separate settlements. This is so regardless of the fact that the funds are administered by the same trustees. The existence of cross-accruers or the possibility that one settled fund may become added to another by partial intestacy are

---

[4] In fact, some commentators believe this to be the case: *Biedermann* [1993] P.C.B. 283. See also Lorenz, *Disputes involving Trusts*, edited by Ledim Vogt (1999), p.213.

[5] See *http://www.hmrc.gov.uk/tdsi/guidance-notes.pdf* [Accessed November 23, 2012].

[6] See TDSI Mailshot 6 (fn.6).

[7] See Tax Bulletin 83 superseded by INTM180030. For fuller discussion see paras 32–44 and following.

[8] By IHTA 1984 s.272, a disposition includes a disposition effected by associated operations.

[9] Otherwise than for full consideration in money or money's worth paid for his own use or benefit to the person making the disposition; IHTA 1984 s.43(2)(c).

not regarded as reasons for arguing that there is a single settlement. The fact that the funds later merge, e.g. as a result of the exercise of a power of appointment or the failure of trusts, will not prevent HMRC from continuing to regard them as separate settlements.[10]

It is far from clear that HMRC's view is correct. Many Chancery lawyers would take a different view. In the past, HMRC appeared to accept that theoretically the definition of "settlement" contemplated the possibility that several dispositions made in a single instrument could comprise a single settlement within s.43 even if each could have created a settlement on its own, but they used to advise their staff that such an argument should be used with "great discretion", bearing in mind the normal rule stated above.[11] The position now appears to be somewhat different: Budget Note 25, which preceded the FA 2006 changes, suggests that in HMRC's view each disposition of property represents a separate settlement.[12] However, practitioners consider that this view is also incorrect as a matter of trust law and, in the authors' view, also as a matter of tax law: in particular, s.43(2) envisages the creation of a single settlement by "dispositions".

Consequences of definitions

It follows from the above definitions that in practice virtually all real and personal property held on trust is settled property. To this general rule there are two exceptions. First, property held on trust for sale for persons with concurrent interests, e.g. where land is held on trust for sale for A and B jointly, is not settled property. Such property is not charged or burdened with any payment, nor is it held on any accumulation trusts. Although it is held in trust for persons, it is not held in trust for "persons in succession", or "for any persons subject to a contingency". This point, however, is not entirely free from doubt. It may be that s.5(2)[13] is directed to general powers over property which is not settled in any ordinary sense, though it is not easy to think of plausible examples. One possibility is a bank account in A's name with money provided by A but B having an unrestricted right to draw on the account for his own purposes. **11-08**

The second exception occurs where a person is absolutely entitled to property held on trust.[14] If, for example, A holds property on trust for B absolutely, the property is not held, charged or burdened in the manner required by s.43(2). Instead, B owns the property, and this is so even if B is an unmarried infant. The position where property is held on a bare trust for an infant beneficiary was not regarded as absolutely clear since, if during his minority where s.31 of the Trustee Act 1925 applies,[15] income will be accumulated, albeit that those accumulations belong to the infant's estate.[16] Following correspondence on this issue with STEP and the CIOT in the aftermath of the Finance Act 2006, HMRC now accept that a bare trust for a minor is not a settlement

---

[10] This practice was referred to in the CTO Advanced Instruction Manual, E.5, but appears not to be repeated in the HMRC Manuals IHTM.

[11] This was stated in the CTO Advanced Instruction Manual, E.4, but appears not to be repeated in the HMRC Manuals IHTM.

[12] See para.12–17.

[13] See para.25–07.

[14] HMRC accept that property held on bare trusts is not settled property: HMRC Manual IHTM16030.

[15] For example, the Trustee Act 1925 s.31 does not apply in Scotland. Legal capacity is acquired in Scotland at the age of 16.

[16] On this problem and precedent settlement, see *Capital Taxes—A Quarterly Commentary*, 1984, pp.66–71.

for these purposes.[17] If A holds property on trust for B and C absolutely in equal shares, then B and C are each normally[18] absolutely entitled to half the property. The consequence of a bare trust not falling within the definition of "settlement" for inheritance tax is that transfers to such trusts are, in effect, transfers to the individuals who are absolutely entitled to the property held on such bare trusts. Consequently, such transfers, now including such transfers to bare trusts for minor beneficiaries, will be PETs. The position is different when A holds property on trust for B, but B's interest is defeasible, e.g. on his marrying. In such a case the property will be settled property, either because it is held in trust "subject to a contingency", or because it is held in trust "for persons in succession", namely for B and for whoever takes the property on B's interest being defeated. It is thought that the fact that an absolute interest is defeasible by the exercise of a general power of appointment should not mean that property is settled property; support for this view is to be found in s.5(2), which clearly contemplates a person having a general power over property other than settled property.

Where, on the other hand, an absolute interest is defeasible by the exercise of a special power of appointment or property is revocably appointed out of a trust fund to a beneficiary the property will remain settled property.

The rule in *Saunders v Vautier*

11–09   The rule in *Saunders v Vautier*[19] is important in deciding whether or not property is settled property. Under this rule a beneficiary who:

(1) has an absolute, vested, indefeasible interest in property; and
(2) is of full age,

may at any time require the trustees to terminate any accumulation and to transfer to him the property and the accumulations therefrom. This means that if the terms of a trust are, e.g. "Accumulate the income for 21 years, then to A absolutely", the property will cease to be settled property on A attaining his majority at 18, since at that time, notwithstanding the direction to accumulate, A will under the rule in *Saunders v Vautier* become absolutely entitled to the property and to the accumulations therefrom. This will be the case even if A allows the income accruing to the trust to continue to be accumulated until he attains 21, since after he attains his majority it is accumulated because he allows it to be accumulated, not because it is held on accumulatory trusts. Once A attains 18 the property in such a trust ceases to be settled property.

11–10   Under another (and today probably more important) branch of the same rule, it is also possible for a number of adult beneficiaries to bring a trust to an end, provided that between them they are entitled to every vested or contingent interest in the property or are the only possible beneficiaries under a discretionary trust.[20] Their position, however, is to be distinguished from that of the person who, like A in the above example, can unilaterally bring the accumulation to an end. Under the rule in *Saunders v Vautier* he is absolutely entitled whether he acts or not. Where the action of more than one

---

[17] See Question 33 of questions put by STEP/CIOT to HMRC and answered on November 3, 2006. The document containing the questions and answers is available on the STEP website and was last updated on October 3, 2008.

[18] See *Stephenson v Barclays Bank Trust Co Ltd* [1975] S.T.C. 502 and *Crowe v Appleby* [1975] S.T.C. 555.

[19] *Saunders v Vautier* (1841) Cr. & Ph. 240.

[20] *Re Smith* [1928] Ch. 915.

person is required, on the other hand, there is no absolute entitlement until the rule is in fact invoked, or until the persons act to end the trust in some other way.[21]

Notional settlements

Certain leases of property are treated as settlements. By s.43(3), four kinds of lease **11–11** fall into this category:

(1) a lease for life or lives;
(2) a lease which is terminable on a death;
(3) a lease for a period ascertainable only by reference to a death;
(4) a lease which is terminable at a date ascertainable only by reference to a death.

The above is subject to the qualification that a lease granted for full consideration in money or money's worth is not treated as a settlement.[22]

HMRC have previously published guidance saying that they do not regard s.43(3) as applying where an occupying owner transfers the property to another person reserving a lease for life for himself, or where the transfer is made on condition that the transferee grants him such a lease at less than a rack rent.[23] It is to be noted that s.43(3) provides that where a lease not granted at a rack rent is at any time to become a lease at an increased rent it shall be treated as terminable at that time. Thus, if on the death of the lessee the rent could be increased, the lease will be treated as terminable on his death and thus fall within the second category above. In relation to Northern Ireland, a lease for these purposes does not include a lease in perpetuity within the meaning of s.1 of the Renewable Leasehold Conversion Act 1849, or a lease to which s.37 of that Act applies. It should also be noted that in England and Wales a lease for a life or lives or which is terminable on a death and which is granted at a premium is, by s.149 of the Law of Property Act 1925, converted into a lease held for 90 years determinable after the end of the life or lives, with the result that such a lease will come within the fourth category above. Under estate duty a statutory tenancy was not regarded as a lease for life; and HMRC accept that the position is the same for IHT.[24]

Composite settlements

Since "settlement" is defined as meaning any disposition of property whereby **11–12** property becomes held in certain stipulated ways and "disposition" is defined as including a disposition effected by associated operations, this opens up the possibility of two settlements made by associated operations constituting a single composite

---

[21] See *Re Davidson* (1879) 11 Ch. D. 341.
[22] For HMRC's interpretations of this requirement in other contexts, see paras 2–51 and 7–59.
[23] CTO Advanced Instruction Manual, E.15: this statement does not reappear in HMRC Manuals IHTM —it is not known whether HMRC have resiled from this view.
[24] See HMRC Manuals IHTM16191.

settlement made by a disposition effected by associated operations. This possibility has been considered in two cases.

Hatton v IRC

11–13   In *Hatton v IRC*[25] Chadwick J. held that where two settlements were made by reference to each other they constituted a single settlement made by a disposition effected by associated operations. The case involved what was known at the time as "the reverter to settlor scheme". The facts were that Mrs C ("the mother"), who was seriously ill, wished to pass property free of IHT to her daughter. Towards this end, two settlements were created within 24 hours. Under the first, made by the mother, the mother reserved an interest in possession for herself for just over 24 hours, with a reversionary interest to her daughter. In substance, she had thus made a very valuable gift to her daughter, but her retained interest in possession meant that for IHT purposes she was still treated as owning the whole of the settled property. As a corollary of the mother being treated as still owning the settled property, the daughter's reversionary interest was excluded property. On the following day, the daughter settled her reversionary interest on terms that her mother took an interest in possession in it for a 24-hour period following the termination of her mother's interest under the first settlement, with the property then becoming held absolutely for the daughter. The mother died shortly after the scheme had been effected.

The taxpayer's argument was that (a) the original settlement by the mother was not a transfer of value because, since she retained an interest in possession in the property she settled, the value of her estate was undiminished, (b) the subsequent settlement by her daughter was not a chargeable event because the reversionary interest the daughter settled was excluded property and therefore the settlement did not for IHT purposes diminish the value of her estate, (c) when the mother's interest in possession in the first settlement terminated no charge to IHT arose because on that occasion she became interested in an interest in possession in the second settlement, and (d) when the mother's interest in possession in the second settlement terminated no charge to IHT arose because on that occasion her daughter became absolutely entitled to the property with the result that the reverter to settlor relief in what is now s.53(3) applied.

Not surprisingly, HMRC resisted this result; after all, if the taxpayer was right, there had been, by a naked tax avoidance scheme effected over a few days, a tax-free gift by the mother to her daughter of the property comprised in the trust fund. Chadwick J. decided against the taxpayers on the grounds that, under the *Ramsay* principle, the creation of the two settlements constituted a preordained series of transactions, the result of which was that the mother made a single composite transaction such that the reverter to settlor relief did not apply.

In case he was wrong on this he also considered HMRC's argument that for IHT purposes the mother was the settlor of the second settlement with the result that, again, but for a different reason, the reverter to settlor relief did not apply. He accepted HMRC's argument that the first settlement was made with a view to enabling or facilitating the making of the second settlement and that the two settlements were therefore associated operations. That being the case, they were to be regarded as having together effected a single disposition for purposes of the settled property regime, and that single disposition was a settlement for the purposes of what is now s.43(2).

This, in turn, gave rise to an awkward question—who was the settlor of the composite settlement effected by this disposition? Chadwick J. concluded that the

[25] *Hatton v IRC* [1992] S.T.C. 140.

correct analysis was that the mother and her daughter had each made the entirety of the settlement and that while the reverter to settlor relief applied to the settlement made by the mother, it did not do so in relation to the settlement made by her daughter. For a full discussion, see paras 11–44 and following.

Rysaffe Trust Co (CI) v IRC

Hatton is to be contrasted with *Rysaffe Trustee Co (CI) v IRC*,[26] in which a settlor **11–14**
sequentially made five separate discretionary settlements of five parcels of 6,900 shares each with a view to reducing the rate of IHT that would apply to the property comprised in each of the settlements. HMRC contended inter alia that the making of all the settlements were associated operations and that therefore the settlor had made one composite settlement by a disposition effected by associated operations. The Special Commissioner, Park J. and a unanimous Court of Appeal all found that the settlor had not made such a disposition.

Following *Rysaffe*, which was a serious blow to HMRC aspirations as to the application of the associated operations provisions, HMRC may encounter serious difficulties in relying on s.272 to produce composite settlements otherwise than extreme cases such as *Hatton*—in this regard it is worth noting that *Hatton* was not referred to in *Rysaffe* which seems to suggest that *Hatton* may not be a case that is often applied by the courts. For a full discussion of the *Rysaffe* case, see para.9–22.

Excluded property

Excluded property is not prevented from being settled property, and for a full **11–15**
discussion see paras 32–49 and following. In certain exceptional cases excluded property may even be subject to the special charging provisions; see paras 10–23 and following.

Bona fide commercial dispositions

The fact that a disposition is bona fide commercial will not prevent it from being a **11–16**
settlement, except of course, where s.43(2)(c) is concerned. But commercial contexts sometimes throw up interesting issues concerning the meaning of "held in trust" as used in s.43(2)(a) and the meaning of "held by trustees on trust" as used in s.43(2)(b): is the fact of a contingency or power to accumulate in itself sufficient to render a contractual arrangement which gives rise to those features a "settlement" as defined? In the authors' view, there is a requirement that property be held "in trust" and accordingly, some bona fide commercial arrangements that do not create trusts are

---

[26] *Rysaffe Trustee Co (CI) v IRC* [2003] S.T.C. 536.

outside the scope of the definition of "settlement." The more difficult question is whether or not such arrangements do result in property being held "in trust".

III. WHICH SETTLEMENT?

11–17   Normally it will be clear whether or not property is settled property. What may be less clear is in which settlement property is comprised. Difficulties can arise in three contexts, i.e.:

    (1) where more than one person is a settlor;
    (2) where a settlor adds property to an existing settlement;
    (3) where property is resettled.

Multiple settlors

11–18   As a matter of general law, more than one person can be the settlor of the same settlement. This would normally be the case where more than one person creates a settlement, or where a person other than the original settlor adds property to an existing settlement. For IHT purposes, the existence of more than one settlor in relation to the same settlement could, in the absence of special provision, cause certain difficulties. To begin with, settled property may be excluded property if the settlor was domiciled abroad at the time he made the settlement. Where only one of two or more settlors was a foreign domiciliary when he made the settlement, problems could arise in determining which of the settled property was excluded property, and which was not. Secondly, the reverter to settlor exemption is available only in respect of reversions to the settlor, his spouse, or widow/widower; certain exemptions are also available in respect only of property to which such an individual becomes entitled. Next, rates of tax charged in respect of some discretionary trusts are based on the cumulative total of the settlor when he made the settlement (although this is subject to review, pending the outcome of the consultation referred to at para.10–09 above). Finally, the settlor of a settlement, the trustees of which are non-resident, may be liable for tax on any charge imposed in respect of the property comprised in that settlement.[27] The question of who is a settlor of a settlement is considered below at paras 11–40 and following.

Settlor's additions

11–19   Where a person adds property to an existing settlement of which he is the settlor, the property will prima facie be regarded as being comprised in the original settlement. This follows from the fact that the legislation makes no provision to deal with such an addition as a separate settlement. Problems may arise where the property comprised in the original settlement is excluded property and the added property is not, or vice versa. This could happen where the settlor's domicile had changed or where part of the property was situated abroad and part was not. HMRC's views (and the authors' doubts as to its correctness) are set out at paras 12–17–12–19, and 32–50–32–51, below.

---

[27] IHTA 1984 s.205(1)(d).

Settlors contemplating such additions should, other things being equal, put the additional property to a separate settlement, so as to avoid disputes as to which property is excluded property and which is not.

The issue of additions of property by the settlor to an existing settlement is of **11–20** increased importance in the context of the Finance Act 2006 changes. Assume that there is a pre-March 22, 2006 interest in possession settlement to which the settlor adds property post-March 22, 2006: is the addition regarded as adding property to a single pre-March 22, 2006 settlement or is the effect of adding the property that there are now two settlements—one that was a pre-March 22, 2006 settlement and another which is a post-March 22, 2006 settlement? If the post-March 22, 2006 settlement is not one in which there is a qualifying interest in possession, the property in the post-March 22, 2006 settlement will fall within the relevant property regime.[28] A similar problem arises in the context of additions to disabled person's trusts (discussed at para.21–21).

In the authors' view, the addition of value, rather than property, to an existing settlement does not create a new settlement. It is the authors' view that the addition of *property* is central to the creation of a settlement as defined in s.43. Further, although the addition of *value* to an existing settlement by a person other than the settlor may constitute an indirect addition of funds for the purpose of or in connection with a settlement (s.44), this is on the assumption that "funds" in this context means value rather than property. However, s.44 defines "settlor" in relation to a "settlement" and it is difficult to see how the person adding value has made any disposition of property as required by s.43.[29]

Resettlements

Trustees of a settlement may exercise one or more of their powers in such a way that **11–21** all or some of the property comprised in that settlement becomes held on such substantially different trusts that it is said to be "resettled". In such a case the question arises as to whether that property falls to be regarded as comprised in a new, separate settlement, different from that in which it was formerly held, or as still comprised in the original settlement. In some cases the same persons may be both the trustees of the original settlement and the trustees of the newly created settlement; there is no requirement that the property in question will be resettled only if the trustees of the new settlement differ from those of the existing settlement, though in practice separate trustees are often appointed.

Resettlements are normally effected in three[30] ways: by the trustees exercising a power of advancement; by the trustees exercising a special power of appointment; and under the Variation of Trusts Act 1958. Where trustees exercise a power they may create a new settlement into which they then decant property or they may simply

---

[28] See para.12–17.

[29] See further at paras 12–17–12–19 below.

[30] A fourth method of resettlement is by the beneficiaries themselves; historically this was the most common form of resettlement of all, under the classical disentail and resettlement by father and son, which is still not quite obsolete. The straightforward assignment by a beneficiary of his interest, be it an interest in possession or a reversionary interest, should not create a separate settlement as a matter of general law; see *Thomas v IRC* [1981] S.T.C. 382 discussed at para.22–04. If on the other hand, a beneficiary settles his interest on separate trustees on new trusts he may well create a separate settlement, but this should not of itself give rise to a deemed disposal under s.71 of the TCGA 1992, since the assignment will not affect the underlying trust assets.

appoint that property is to be held upon new trusts of the same settlement and subject to new powers and provisions.

Whether or not the exercise by trustees of their powers has the effect that property becomes comprised in a new settlement or remains comprised in an existing settlement has been considered in a series of CGT cases over the last 20 years or so and the principles that have emerged from those cases are relevant for IHT purposes. Before considering those cases, regard needs to be had to s.81(1).

Section 81(1)

11–22 At first glance, s.81(1)[31] appears to make the whole issue of resettlements academic, because it provides that:

> "Where property which ceases to be comprised in one settlement becomes comprised in another then, unless in the meantime any person becomes beneficially entitled to the property (and not merely to an interest in possession in the property), it shall for purposes of this Chapter be treated as remaining comprised in the first settlement."

This is subject to a qualification where property ceased to be comprised in one settlement and became comprised in another settlement after March 26, 1974, but before December 10, 1981. Section 81(2) provides that in such a case the property is to be treated as remaining comprised in the first settlement for purposes of the special charging provisions only if it ceased to be comprised in that settlement and became comprised in the second settlement by the same disposition. Assume, for example, the trustees appointed a reversionary interest to a beneficiary, that he assigned his interest to trustees of another settlement, and that that interest subsequently vested in possession. HMRC accepted that para.11(4) of Sch.5 to the Finance Act 1975, the relevant provision under the original special charging provisions, did not apply because the resettlement was not made by a single disposition,[32] and s.81(2), which is cast in terms similar to para.11(4), preserves this position in relation to events which transpired prior to the publication on December 10, 1981, of the proposed changes to the special charging provisions.

It may, of course, be that the individual resettled his interest before December 10, 1981, but that the interest vested in possession on or after that date. Section 81(3) accordingly provides that s.81(1) does not apply where a reversionary interest which vests on or after December 10, 1981, was settled before that date. Note that s.81(3) applies only where the interest which was settled was a reversionary interest expectant on the termination of a qualifying interest in possession. Thus, s.81(3) does not apply where trustees of a discretionary trust appointed a contingent interest to a beneficiary which he then resettled and which subsequently vested in possession. This will not normally be a cause for concern, since in such cases the contingency will normally have been satisfied shortly after the appointment with the result that it will be exceptional for the two events to have straddled December 10, 1981.

---

[31] For a full discussion of s.81, see paras 10–16 and following.

[32] The argument that the actions and events mentioned above constitute associated operations by means of which a single disposition effected under s.272 is apparently not taken, perhaps because the use of the words "by the same disposition" in s.81(2) implies that s.81(2) cannot apply where there is more than one actual disposition notwithstanding the fact that each of those dispositions is an associated operation capable or being amalgamated into one composite disposition by s.272.

Notwithstanding the terms of s.81(1), the question of whether or not property ceases to be comprised in one settlement and becomes comprised in another settlement can in certain circumstances be important in a number of ways, as follows.

Trusts with Qualifying Interests in Possession

To begin with, it is clear that s.81 applies only to resettlements of settled property in which there is no qualifying interest in possession. This follows from the fact that the section is expressed to apply for purposes of Ch.III of Pt III of the Act only, and that chapter has no application to settled property in which there is a qualifying interest in possession.

11–23

Settlor's liability

Secondly, s.81 does not apply in determining whether a settlor is liable under s.201(1)(d) for tax charged in respect of trust property. This, too, follows from the fact that s.81 applies for purposes of Ch.III only. The result is that a settlor's liability follows, as it were, the settled property in question. If the property is resettled from trustees resident in the United Kingdom to non-resident trustees, s.201(1)(d) comes into play; if on the other hand, the property is resettled from non-resident trustees to UK resident trustees, s.201(1)(d) ceases to apply.

11–24

Trustees' residence

Thirdly, in determining the residence of trustees, no regard is had to s.81, since that section applies for purposes of Ch.III only, and the residence of trustees is not relevant for purposes of that chapter. Thus, where property becomes resettled, regard is had to the residence of the trustees of the settlement to which the property was transferred, not to the residence of the trustees of the composite settlement comprised of the "old" and the "new" settlements.

11–25

Payment of IHT by instalments

Fourth, s.81 does not apply in determining whether property is comprised in a settlement for purposes of deciding whether tax may be paid by instalments.[33]

11–26

Court orders

The fifth case in which s.81 may not result in resettled property remaining comprised in the original settlement is where the resettlement is connected with the coming into force of an arrangement approved by the court under the Variation of Trusts Act 1958.

11–27

---

[33] See paras 29–110 and following.

495

Here two points fall to be considered. The first concerns the effect of a variation of trusts under the 1958 Act. In the leading case of *IRC v Holmden*[34] Lords Reid and Wilberforce took the view that before new trusts were substituted by a variation there was a point in time at which, as a result of the consent of the beneficiaries who were sui juris and of the court on behalf of the beneficiaries who were not, the old trusts were brought to an end. This meant that at that point the property ceased to be settled property, with the result that, in consequence of the variation, the property became comprised in a new and different settlement. This view had as its basis the rule in *Saunders v Vautier*, as applied in *Re Smith*[35] under which beneficiaries can together bring trusts to an end.[36] They cannot, however, vary trusts: trustees accept only the trusts imposed by the settlor, and beneficiaries cannot force different trusts on them against their will. But, under the rule in *Saunders v Vautier*, beneficiaries can declare new trusts, and trustees may acquiesce in those trusts. If they do so they become trustees of a new settlement, which differs from the old.

11–28   The majority of the House of Lords in *IRC v Holmden* took the view that, in the circumstances, it was not necessary to have regard to the conceptual hiatus between the cessation of the old trusts and the creation of the new, and that, on the facts of the case there was no new settlement. Lord Guest stated that in every case it was a question of construction whether the old trusts were revoked or merely varied. This clearly envisages circumstances in which a variation can result in the creation of a new set-tlement.[37]

Note that where such new trusts come into being post-March 22, 2006, they will fall within the relevant property regime unless they benefit from favoured treatment, for example, if they comprise qualifying interests in possession by virtue of being disabled person's interests.[38] And even if a variation does not result in a new settlement, the creation of a new interest in possession in the same settlement post-March 22, 2006 may result in the settled property falling within the relevant property regime. Accord-ingly, great care should be taken with variations of subsisting interest in possession settlements, where that interest is a qualifying interest in possession.

11–29   Coming back to *Holmden,* all their Lordships seemed to have agreed that a Variation of Trusts Act arrangement is not essentially different from an out-of-court family arrangement under the rule in *Saunders v Vautier* above; where they differed was in their views as to the effect of such an arrangement. Some said or implied that such an arrangement necessarily produced a new settlement; others said or implied that whether or not there was a new settlement depended on the particular circumstances in question. While it is true that trustees cannot be compelled to accept varied trusts against their will, it seems contrary to common sense (and is not supported by any authority) that this in itself should mean that an arrangement, which may only, e.g. confer a new investment power, necessarily produces a new settlement. The better view in the authors' opinion is, as Lord Guest said in *Holmden*, that in each case it should be a matter of construction, trustees perhaps being regarded as having acquiesced in the modified or varied trusts rather than having had those trusts imposed on them against

---

[34] *IRC v Holmden* [1968] A.C. 685. See also *Re Brockbank* [1948] Ch. 206; *Re T's Settlement Trusts* [1964] Ch. 158; *Re Ball* [1968] 1 W.L.R. 899; [1968] 2 All E.R. 438.

[35] *Re Smith* [1928] Ch. 915. See para.11–10.

[36] For a consideration of the operation of the Variation of Trusts Act 1958 see *Private Client Business* (1996), p.389 and of the Trusts (Scotland) Act 1961 see *Private Client Business* (1997), p.184.

[37] A variation of a trust under the 1958 Act, or in Scotland under the Trusts (Scotland) Act 1961, can create a new trust, at least for the purposes of the accumulation periods; see *Re Ball* [1968] 1 W.L.R. 899; [1968] 2 All E.R. 438 and *Re Aikman*, 1968 S.L.T. 137.

[38] As to which see paras 11–50 and 11–63.

their will. This approach appears to have been favoured by the courts in recent cases (in which the question of whether or not a new settlement has been created has been considered in a context different from that of the *Holmden* case).[39]

This brings us to the second point, namely, even if a variation results in a new **11–30** settlement, is such a resettlement a resettlement to which s.81 applies? It is clear that s.81 will apply if the variation occurs after December 9, 1981, but it may be argued that a variation effected before that date does not necessarily come within s.81(2). This follows from the fact that s.81(2) applies only where property ceases to be comprised in one settlement and by the *same disposition* becomes comprised in another settlement. "Disposition" is not defined, though, by s.272, it includes a disposition effected by associated operations. The meaning of disposition is a wide one,[40] as is the s.272 definition of "associated operations". If the view of Lords Reid and Wilberforce is correct, it is at least arguable that where, as the result of a variation, a new settlement comes into being, it does not do so by a disposition at all, but this will be cold comfort since in such a case there will be no new settlement. This is because in the absence of a disposition there can be no settlement at all. Exceptionally, it may be possible to contend that the property in question did not cease to be comprised in the old settlement and become comprised in the new settlement "by the same disposition", as is required if s.81(2) is to apply; in particular, the words "by the same disposition" should exclude a disposition effected by associated operations.[41]

Capital gains tax

It has been important to know in a number of CGT contexts whether or not a **11–31** settlement came to an end, and, as will be seen below, most of the cases in this area arose in these contexts. The introduction of holdover relief made the issue less pressing, where, by virtue of a resettlement, one set of trustees became absolutely entitled as against another set of trustees so that there was a deemed disposal under what is now s.71(1) of the TCGA 1992 and therefore the possibility of a charge to CGT, but the limitations on holdover relief introduced by the Finance Act 1989 and, to a lesser extent, the Finance Act 2004, mean that a CGT charge on the termination of a settlement is now commonplace, so that the issue has regained much of its importance.

The evolving approach

The cases about to be discussed demonstrate a significant evolution in the law in this **11–32** area. Prior to these cases a resettlement effected by the exercise of a power of advancement was regarded, at least by HMRC, as invariably creating a new settlement, while a settlement effected by the exercise of a special power of appointment was

---

[39] See para.11–33.
[40] See paras 2–05 and following.
[41] See fn.30 above and paras 11–12 and following.

regarded as never doing so. While this approach had some basis in law,[42] it was criticised by the authors in the third edition of this work as simplistic and was replaced by a less mechanical approach, as is shown by the following cases.

Roome v Edwards[43]

11–33   *Roome v Edwards* was concerned with the question of when a new settlement is created and with the effects of the creation of such a settlement. The facts of the case, greatly simplified, were that in 1944 a settlement (the "main fund") was made and that in 1955 certain investments (the "appointed fund") were appointed out of the main fund. The trusts under the 1955 appointment were not exhaustive; they were liable to fail at all material times, and in the event of failure, the trusts declared in the original 1944 settlement would have become relevant. In 1972 the trustees of the main fund were replaced by trustees resident in the Cayman Islands, and these non-resident trustees subsequently made large capital gains. HMRC contended that the 1955 appointment of the new trusts had not created a new settlement, and that therefore, the trustees resident in the United Kingdom and the non-resident trustees were to be regarded as a single body of trustees who were to be regarded as resident in the United Kingdom. That being the case, HMRC were authorised to assess the UK trustees to CGT in respect of the gains made by the non-resident trustees. The House of Lords unanimously held that:

(1) the 1955 appointment did not create a new settlement; and
(2) the UK trustees were liable in respect of the gain made by the foreign trustees.

Lord Roskill, the only judge to deal with the point, said obiter that if an appointment did create a new settlement then, that appointment would necessarily give rise to a deemed disposal under what is now s.71(1) of the TCGA 1992.

While the immediate outcome of the case was satisfactory, the decision gave little guidance on the subject of resettlements generally.[44] Such guidance as was to be had on the subject is to be found in Lord Wilberforce's speech in *Roome*, in which he expressed the following views:

> "There are a number of obvious indicia which may help to show whether a settlement, or a settlement separate from another settlement, exists. One might expect to find separate and defined property; separate trusts and separate trustees. One might also expect to find a separate disposition bringing the settlement into existence. These indicia may be helpful, but they are not decisive. For example, a single disposition, e.g., a will with a single set of trustees, may create what are clearly separate settlements, relating to different properties, in favour of different beneficiaries, and conversely separate trusts may arise in what is clearly a single settlement, e.g., when the settled property is divided into shares. There are so many

---

[42] Although the rule against perpetuities operates in the same way regardless of the nature of the power in question (*Pilkington v IRC* [1984] A.C. 612), powers of appointment are in some respects narrower than powers of advancement. Where a power of appointment is exercised in favour of a non-object, for example, the exercise is void for excessive execution; but the execution of a power of advancement so as to create trusts under which a non-object may take some (normally remote) benefit is valid so long as it benefits an object of the power. Also, while a power of appointment cannot be delegated unless delegation is authorised expressly or by necessary implication, the test of whether the delegation of a power of advancement is valid is more liberal.

[43] *Roome v Edwards* [1981] S.T.C. 96.

[44] This may not be entirely their Lordships' fault; it is understood that the subject was not dealt with in general terms by Counsel for either side.

possible combinations of fact that even where these indicia or some of them are present, the answer may be doubtful, and may depend on an appreciation of them as a whole.

Since 'settlement' and 'trusts' are legal terms, which are also used by business men or laymen in a business or practical sense, I think that the question whether a particular set of facts amounts to a settlement should be approached by asking what a person, with knowledge of the legal context of the word under established doctrine and applying this knowledge in a practical and common sense manner to the facts under examination, would conclude. To take two fairly typical cases. Many settlements contain powers to appoint a part or a proportion of the trust property to beneficiaries: some may also confer power to appoint separate trustees of the property so appointed, or such power may be conferred by law (Trustee Act 1925, s.37). It is established doctrine that the trusts declared by a document exercising a special power of appointment are to be read into the original settlement (*Muir v Muir* [1943] AC 468). If such a power is exercised, whether or not separate trustees are appointed, I do not think that it would be natural for such a person as I have presupposed to say that a separate settlement had been created: still less so if it were found that provisions of the original settlement continued to apply to the appointed fund, or that the appointed funds were liable, in certain events, to fall back into the rest of the settled property. On the other hand, there may be a power to appoint and appropriate a part or portion of the trust property to beneficiaries and to settle it for their benefit. If such a power is exercised, the natural conclusion might be that a separate settlement was created, all the more so if a completely new set of trusts were declared as to the appropriated property, and if it could be said that the trusts of the original settlement ceased to apply to it. There can be many variations on these cases each of which will have to be judged on its facts."

Initial Statement of Practice

On September 23, 1981, following the House of Lords' decision in *Roome v Edwards*, HMRC issued the following Statement of Practice: **11–34**

"Following discussions with the Law Society, the Board has decided that it might be helpful if it were to give some indication of how it proposes in practice to decide whether a new settlement has been created. In accordance with the judgment of Lord Wilberforce, this must be by applying established legal doctrine to the facts in a practical and common sense manner. On this basis, the Board considers it unlikely, for example, that a charge under s.54(1)[45] will arise in any of the following circumstances:
  (a) If the appointment is revocable.
  (b) If the trusts declared of the advanced or appointed funds are not exhaustive so that there exists a possibility at the time when the advancement or appointment is made that the funds covered by it will on the occasion of some event cease to be held upon such trusts and once again come to be held upon the original trusts of the settlement.
  (c) If reference has still to be made to the original settlement to ascertain the nature or extent of any of the trustees' dispositive powers of administration (whether or not the advancement or appointment document incorporates such a power by reference to the original settlement). While it is not possible to attempt a precise definition of all dispositive powers, dispositive powers clearly include powers of maintenance and advancement on the lines of s.31 and 32, Trustee Act 1925.
Furthermore, in deciding whether there is a new settlement, it seems irrelevant whether new trustees are appointed or the same trustees continue to be trustees of the advanced or appointed fund; or whether the mechanical powers of administration are to be found in the advancement or appointment document or in the original settlement (mechanical powers cannot be defined with precision but can be taken as common clauses in settlements such as powers of investment and professional charging clauses)."

[45] Now TCGA 1992 s.71.

Finally, the Board accept that a power of appointment can be exercised over only part of the settled property and that the above consequences would apply to that part."

Bond v Pickford

11–35   In *Bond v Pickford*,[46] HMRC contended that the exercise of two powers by trustees created separate settlements for CGT purposes. The appointments were made under cl.3(ii) of a settlement, which provided that:

> "... the Trustees may apply capital for the benefit of any one or more of the Beneficiaries ... by (a) allocating or appropriating to such Beneficiary such sum or sums out of or investments forming part of the capital of the Trust Fund as the Trustees shall think fit either absolutely or contingently ... and so that the provisions of s.31 of the Trustee Act 1925 under the powers of the Trustees to invest and vary investments shall apply to any moneys or investments so allocated or appropriated (b) settling the same on such trusts for the benefit of any such Beneficiary ... as the Trustees may think fit and so that any such settlement may confer on the Trustees thereof ... such powers of appointment and otherwise in relation to the fund thereby settled and the income thereof as the Trustees may determine."

Slade L.J. said that he felt:

> "... no doubt that as a matter of trust law trustees, who are given a discretionary power to direct which of the beneficiaries shall take the trust property and for what interests, do *not* have the power thereby to remove assets from the original settlement, by subjecting them to the trusts of a separate settlement, unless the instrument which gave them the power expressly or by necessary implication authorises them so to do. In the absence of such authority, any exercise of the power, other than one which renders persons beneficially absolutely entitled to the relevant assets, will leave those assets subject to the trusts of the original settlement, in accordance with the principles explained by Lord Romer in *Muir or Williams v Muir*; and the trustees of the original settlement will remain responsible for them accordingly, in that capacity.
>
> Thus, there is in my opinion a crucial distinction to be drawn between (a) powers to alter the presently operative trusts of a settlement which expressly or by necessary implication authorise the trustees to remove assets altogether from the original settlement (without rendering any person absolutely beneficially entitled to them); and (b) powers of this nature which do not confer on the trustees such authority.
>
> I will refer to these two different types of powers as 'powers in the wider form and powers in the narrower form'. The distinction between them is in my opinion of great importance and is reflected in the relevant decisions.
>
> Counsel for the Crown has submitted that for present purposes the effect of the exercise of the trustees' powers in 1972 is much more important than the terms of the powers that were exercised. I cannot agree. In my opinion, it is essential to examine the nature of the powers which the trustees were purporting to exercise, both in order to see whether they were acting intra vires and also to determine how they themselves viewed the matter; it seems clear from Lord Wilberforce's speech that the intention of the parties, viewed objectively, is a relevant consideration in this context: (see [1981] S.T.C. 96 at 101, [1982] AC 279 at 294–295)."

---

[46] *Bond v Pickford* [1983] S.T.C. 517.

He concluded that the power in cl.3(ii)(a) was indubitably a power in the narrower form. Oliver L.J., who agreed with Slade L.J., emphasised that the nature of the power in question was important (though not necessarily conclusive).

Revised Statement of Practice

On October 11, 1984, HMRC, following the Court of Appeal's judgment in *Bond v* **11–36** *Pickford*, revised their earlier Statement of Practice as follows:

"The Board's Statement of Practice SP9/1981, which was issued on 23 September 1981 following discussions with the Law Society, set out the Revenue's views on the CGT implications of the exercise of a Power of Appointment or Advancement when continuing trusts are declared, in the light of the decision of the House of Lords in *Roome & Denne v Edward*. Those views have been modified to some extent by the decision of the Court of Appeal in *Bond v Pickford*.

In *Roome & Denne v Edwards* the House of Lords held that where a separate settlement is created there is a deemed disposal of the relevant assets by the old trustees for the purposes of s.54(1), CGTA 1979 (formerly s.25(3), Finance Act 1965). But the judgments emphasised that, in deciding whether or not a new settlement has been created by the exercise of a Power of Appointment or Advancement, each case must be considered on its own facts, and by applying established legal doctrine to the facts in a practical and common sense manner. In *Bond v Pickford* the judgments in the Court of Appeal explained that the consideration of the facts must include examination of the powers which the trustees purported to exercise, and determination of the intention of the parties, viewed objectively.

It is now clear that a deemed disposal under CGTA 1979, s.54(1)[47] cannot arise unless the power exercised by the trustees, or the instrument conferring the power, expressly or by necessary implication, confers on the trustees authority to remove assets from the original settlement by subjecting them to the trusts of a different settlement. Such powers (which may be powers of advancement or appointment) are referred to by the Court of Appeal as 'powers in the wider form'. However, the Board considers that a deemed disposal will not arise when such a power is exercised and trusts are declared in circumstances such that:
(a) the appointment is revocable, or
(b) the trusts declared of the advanced or appointed funds are not exhaustive so that there exists a possibility at the time when the advancement or appointment is made that the funds covered by it will on the occasion of some event cease to be held upon such trusts and once again come to be held upon the original trusts of the settlement.
Further, when such a power is exercised the Board considers it unlikely that a deemed disposal will arise when trusts are declared if duties in regard to the appointed assets still fall to the trustees of the original settlement in their capacity as trustees of that settlement, bearing in mind the provision of CGTA 1979, s.52(1),[48] that the trustees of a settlement form a single and continuing body (distinct from the persons who may from time to time be the trustees).

Finally, the Board accept that a Power of Appointment or Advancement can be exercised over only part of the settled property and that the above consequences would apply to that part."

Swires v Renton

In *Swires v Renton*[49] Hoffmann J. stressed that the classic case involving a new **11–37** settlement occurred where particular assets were segregated, new trustees appointed,

[47] Now TCGA 1992 s.71(1).
[48] Now TCGA 1992 s.69(1).
[49] *Swires v Renton* [1991] S.T.C. 490.

and fresh trusts created exhausting the beneficial interest in the assets and providing full administrative powers so that further reference back to the original settlement became redundant. The absence of one or more of these features leaves open the question of whether a new settlement has been created, in which case the question would be determined on the basis of intention. In *Swires v Renton*, despite exhaustive beneficial trusts, the administrative powers of the original settlement were retained and the appointment made references to the original settlement, so indicating that a new settlement had not been created.

Summary

11–38   The CGT cases provide valuable guidance to the IHT effects of a resettlement. The basic authority is now *Bond v Pickford* and the HMRC Statement of Practice of October 11, 1984. Depending on the powers they possess, well-advised trustees should be able to resettle property or retain it within the existing settlement as they wish by choosing between "narrow" and "wide" powers and exercising those powers in a manner appropriate to achieve their goal.

Settlor of a resettlement

11–39   The last point to be noted is that a resettlement does not normally affect the identity of the settlor; it is clear from *Pilkington* that the settlor of the original settlement is also the settlor of the new settlement. This is subject to the qualification that if the views of Lords Reid and Wilberforce in the *Holmden* case are correct, it would appear that where the resettlement is made under the Variation of Trusts Act 1958, the settlor is the original settlor, plus all the beneficiaries who consented, either by themselves, or through the court, to the variation.[50] For capital gains tax purposes, the position has now been put beyond doubt by TCGA 1992 s.68B.[51] Under this provision, where there is a non-arm's length transfer of property from the transferor settlement to the transferee settlement, the settlor of the transferor settlement is treated as the settlor of the transferee settlement. Where there are numerous settlors of the property transferred by the transferor settlement, each of those settlors is treated as a settlor of a proportionate part of the property transferred to the transferee settlement.

IV. SETTLOR

11–40   The definition of "settlor" can be important for the purposes of determining:

    (1) in what settlement property is comprised;
    (2) whether the settled property is excluded property;
    (3) whether a charge to tax arises;
    (4) who is liable for tax; and

---

[50] These comments would not necessarily apply to an "old-fashioned" resettlement by life-tenant and reversioner; cf. the comments at paras 11–44 and following.
[51] Inserted by FA 2006 s.88 Sch.12 para.1(2), (4) with effect from April 6, 2006 in relation to settlements whenever they were created.

(5) in the case of a relevant property trust, what tax rates apply.

By s.44(1), the "settlor" of a settlement includes any person by whom the settlement was directly or indirectly made. In particular, it includes any person who has provided funds directly or indirectly for the purpose of or in connection with the settlement, or who has made with any other person a reciprocal arrangement with that other person to make the settlement. This definition is very similar to the income tax definitions of "settlor" in the income tax settlements provisions, ITTOIA ss.620 and following,[52] and cases such as *Mills v IRC*[53] will be relevant. It is to be noted, however, that for both IHT and income tax purposes "settlor" is defined by reference to the "settlement" in question. Thus, although the definitions of "settlor" are ostensibly the same, a person who is a settlor for income tax purposes may not be a settlor—given the way the income tax definition of "settlement" differs from the IHT definition of that term—for IHT purposes, and vice versa. However note the definition of settlement as used in para.8(1)(a) of Sch.15 to the Finance Act 2004 in the context of the pre-owned assets provisions. There the income tax definition of settlor is expressly incorporated into that provision which, in the authors' view, gives rise to a hybrid definition of settlement for those purposes.[54]

A settlor too far

The issue of the settlor's identity arose in *IRC v Fitzwilliam*,[55] a case in which taxpayers managed via a complex scheme to transfer £3.9 million free of CTT. The facts relevant to the issue were that the trustees of the late Earl Fitzwilliam's will had power to appoint the residuary estate among a class of beneficiaries. Between December 1979 and February 1980 the following five steps were taken:

(1) on December 20, 1979 the trustees appointed £4 million to the late Earl's widow;
(2) by cheque, post-dated to January 9, 1980, the widow gave £2 million to her daughter;
(3) on January 14, £3.8 million was appointed in trust as follows. The income was to be paid to the widow until the earlier of her death and February 15, 1980. At that stage half the £3.8 million was to pass to the daughter absolutely, and half to her daughter if she was living when the widow's interest in possession terminated. The daughter thus had an interest vested in interest in half the £3.8 million and a contingent interest in the other half of the £3.8 million;
(4) on January 31, in consideration of being paid £2 million by the daughter, the widow assigned to her daughter the widow's income interest in half of the fund to which the daughter was contingently entitled. This meant that the widow prima facie made a notional transfer of value of £1.9 million under what is now s.52(1). But by what is now s.52(2), an anti-avoidance provision, CTT was charged only on the excess of the value of the property in which that interest

---

[52] In relation to the historic provisions, ss.670 and 681(4) of the Taxes Act 1988, these definitions did not extend to a testator or intestate; see FA 1980 s.78(7) and *Hansard,* Standing Committee A, cols 759–760 (June 24, 1980); cf. FA 1981 s.80(7). See also FA 1988 Sch.10 para.6.
[53] *Mills v IRC* [1975] A.C. 38.
[54] See para.7–167.
[55] *IRC v Fitzwilliam* [1993] S.T.C. 502.

subsided over the consideration paid. Since the daughter had paid £2 million, no CTT was chargeable. Furthermore, the (since abolished) mutual transfer rules allowed a gift to be "nullified" if the value of the gifted property was returned to the donor. That, of course, is exactly what happened, with the result that the widow's original gift to the daughter was cancelled out and £1.9 million was transferred to the daughter free of CTT. This left the widow with £2 million, which she also wished to transfer free of CTT to her daughter;

(5) on February 5 the daughter settled a nominal sum upon trusts under which the widow was entitled to a life interest determinable on the earlier of her death and March 15, 1980, with remainder to the daughter. Two days later the daughter assigned her absolute remainder interest (created at step 3) to the trustees to the same trusts. This meant that the widow's interest did not determine on February 15, but continued for a further month. When it did determine the property in this settlement passed to the daughter. If the tax-payers' argument that the reverter to settlor relief in what is now s.53(2)[56] prevented the widow from making a notional transfer of value under s.52(1) was correct, a further £1.9 million passed free of CTT to the daughter.

HMRC's main line of attack against the arrangements was to invoke (unsuccessfully) the *Ramsay* principle. They also argued—rather desperately—in relation to the arrangement under step 5 that the real settlor of the daughter's absolute remainder interest was not the daughter but the deceased Earl on the basis that the appointment made by the trustees fell to be read back into his will under the principle of *Muir v Muir*[57] and *Pilkington v IRC*.[58] Although the House of Lords accepted that the Earl was the settlor for trust law purposes (such as the Scottish rule against successive liferents and the English rule against perpetuities) because for those purposes the exercise of a power of appointment must be written into the settlement creating the power, he could not reasonably be regarded as having provided property directly or indirectly for the purpose of or in connection with the settlement made by the daughter at step 5 because the words "for the purpose of or in accordance with" connote that there must be at least a conscious association of the provider of the funds with the settlement in question. It was not sufficient that the settled funds should historically have been derived from their provider.

Multiple settlors

11–43   There may be more than one settlor of a settlement. Section 44(2) provides in this connection that:

> "Where more than one person is a settlor in relation to a settlement and circumstances so require, this Part of this Act (except s.48(4) to (6)) shall have effect in relation to it as if the settled property were comprised in separate settlements."

---

[56] See para.2–114. Section 53(5)(b) has since robbed this approach of its effectiveness. For a case involving an unsuccessful reverter to settlor arrangement, see *Hatton v IRC* [1992] S.T.C. 140, discussed below at para.11–44.

[57] *Muir v Muir* [1943] A.C. 468.

[58] *Pilkington v IRC* [1964] A.C. 612.

The application of s.44(2) was carefully considered by Chadwick J. in *Hatton v IRC*.[59]

The *Hatton* case

This case was discussed at para.11–13. It will be recalled that a mother settled **11–44** property upon herself for a very short period, remainder to her daughter, and that her daughter then settled her reversion under her mother's settlement upon trust for her mother for a very short period, remainder to herself. The issue was whether the daughter was the settlor of the second settlement such that the reverter to settlor relief in what is now s.53(3) applied. Chadwick J. accepted HMRC's argument that the first settlement was made with a view to enabling or facilitating the making of the second settlement, that the two settlements were therefore associated operations, that they were to be regarded as having together effected a single disposition for purposes of the settled property regime, and that single disposition created a composite settlement for the purposes of what is now s.43(2).

This, in turn, gave rise to an awkward question—who was the settlor of this composite settlement? HMRC argued that the mother—as the "dominant settlor" —should be regarded as the only settlor. Chadwick J. concluded that the correct analysis was that the mother and her daughter had, given the wording of what is now s.44(1), each made the entirety of the composite settlement and that while the reverter to settlor relief applied to the settlement made by the mother, it did not do so in relation to the settlement made by her daughter.

Chadwick J. held that circumstances in which what is now s.44(2) is commonly found to apply include those where two or more persons have separately provided funds out of their own independent resources to be held upon the trusts of the same settlement, and that in such a case the effect of s.44(2) was likely to be that a proportion of the settled property was held in one settlement and one or more other proportions held in one or more other settlements, as the case might be, each settlement having its own notional settlor. But, he went on:

> " ... examination of (what is now s.44(1)) shows that there may well be more than one person who is a settlor in relation to a settlement in circumstances in which the settled property cannot sensibly be apportioned or partitioned amongst a series of notionally separate settlements. In such a case . . . (what is now s.44(1)) requires that (what are now the settled property rules and s.201(1)(d)) are to apply as if there were a number of separate settlements each with its own single settlor and each comprising the whole of the settled property."[60]

An example of this would occur where there were reciprocal settlements. Suppose A settled property on B's son X for a limited period, with remainder to himself, and B reciprocated, settling property on A's son Y for a limited period, e.g. as a way of paying the school fees of X and Y. In the circumstances, even if the dominant settlor test was applicable it was not satisfied, and it was not possible to avoid the conclusion that A was the settlor of both settlements and that B was also the settlor of both settlements.

After applying this approach, Chadwick J. decided that the mother and daughter had each made a single composite settlement consisting of the two settlements actually made, and although the reverter to settlor relief was available to the daughter in respect

[59] *Hatton v IRC* [1992] S.T.C. 140.
[60] *Hatton v IRC* [1992] S.T.C. 140 at 159.

of the settlement of which she was the settlor, it was not available in respect of the settlement of which her mother was the settlor.

11–45   Although the authors admire the ingenuity of Chadwick J.'s approach in defeating the naked tax avoidance arrangement in *Hatton*, they are concerned that it may, by effectively creating property for IHT purposes, cause as many problems as it solves. What would have happened in *Hatton* had both the settlements been discretionary? Would each of the settlors have been regarded as having made a chargeable transfer of the same property?

For HMRC's practice,[61] in light of Chadwick J.'s decision, in applying the excluded property rules to settlements to which more than one person has contributed, see para.32–51. Although that practice is expressed within the context of the excluded property rules, it would seem reasonable to assume that the practice is not confined to that context.[62]

A difficult case concerning multiple settlors may be that of a life-tenant and reversioner who join in a resettlement. For income tax purposes, the life-tenant would be treated as the settlor of any income arising during his lifetime. But can the same treatment possibly be applied in the case of a tax on capital? HMRC at times seem to suggest that in such cases some kind of actuarial apportionment should be made, but whether this is so is open to question.

V. TRUSTEES

11–46   Normally it will be clear who the trustees of a settlement are, and it is not surprising to find that the term is not defined except in default terms. By s.45, where there are no trustees, "trustee" means any person in whom the settled property or its management is for the time being vested. This provision appears to be relevant in two contexts. First, in the event of a notional settlement under s.43(3), there probably will be no trustee in the ordinary sense of the word; in that case, the lessor will be the trustee. Secondly, certain settlements governed by foreign law may not have trustees: in that case, the person in whom the settled property or its management is for the time being vested will be the trustee.

The operation of s.81 does not affect the question of who the trustees are.

Residence of trustees

11–47   The residence of trustees is important in four contexts. First, where the trustees of a settlement are non-resident, the balance of any foreign currency account in which a foreign domiciliary has an interest in possession may be left out of account in valuing his estate on his death.[63] Secondly, under s.201(1)(d), the settlor of a settlement which has non-resident trustees may be liable for any tax charged in respect of the trust property.[64] Thirdly, under s.218, in certain circumstances a person who has been concerned with the making of a settlement and who knows or has reason to believe that the trustees of the settlement are not or will not be resident in the United Kingdom may

[61] Revenue Interpretation RI 166.
[62] See HMRC Manuals IHTM42253.
[63] See para.32–43.
[64] See para.29–70.

be required to make a return to HMRC.[65] Finally, trustees of a maintenance fund for an historic building must be UK resident for a Treasury direction to be given.[66]

In the first three of the above-mentioned contexts trustees are assumed to be non-resident, unless both:

    (1) the general administration of the trust is ordinarily carried on in the United Kingdom; and

    (2) the trustees or a majority of them are for the time being resident in the United Kingdom; where there is more than one class of trustees, a majority of each class are resident in the United Kingdom.[67]

11–48

The position where maintenance funds are concerned is more subtle. Under para.2(2) of Sch.4, trustees are regarded as resident in the United Kingdom at a particular time if the general administration of the trust is ordinarily carried on in the United Kingdom and the trustees or a majority of them (and, where there is more than one class of trustees, a majority of each class) are resident in the United Kingdom, i.e. there is no presumption of non-residence unless certain conditions are satisfied, but the net result appears to be the same. Where the trustee is a trust corporation its residence is determined as for purposes of corporation tax, so that the trust corporation will be regarded as resident where its central management and control abides unless it is incorporated in the United Kingdom, in which case the special rules in the Finance Act 1988 s.66 will apply.

VI. INTERESTS IN SETTLED PROPERTY

Under the pre-Finance Act 2006 legislation, interests in settled property fell into three categories: interests in possession; reversionary interests; and intermediate interests (broadly, interests that fell between the first two kinds of interest). However, post-Finance Act 2006, the category of interests in possession afforded special treatment has been amended: special treatment that was afforded to all interest in possession is henceforth only afforded to "qualifying interests in possession". Even so, the meaning of the term "interest in possession" remains vitally important. There are a number of provisions in the legislation which bear on the meaning of the term, but these are of secondary importance to the meaning of the term as a matter of general law. Detailed consideration is given to the general law meaning of "interest in possession", and the effect of the statutory provisions that bear upon its meaning in Pts III and IV of Ch.12. The discussion here is limited to a description of the categories of interest in possession which are "qualifying interests in possession", and the conditions that need to be satisfied for such interests to fall within the relevant categories.

11–49

Qualifying interests in possession, reversionary interests and intermediate interests are each considered here in turn.

Qualifying interests in possession

The Finance Act 2006 Sch.20 para.20 amended the meaning of a "qualifying interest in possession" in s.59(1). Previously s.59(1) provided:

11–50

---

[65] See para.29–52.
[66] See para.27–82.
[67] See IHTA 1984 ss.201(5) and 218(3).

"In this Chapter 'qualifying interest in possession' means an interest in possession to which an individual, or where subsection (2) below applies a company, is beneficially entitled."

As a result of the Finance Act 2006 amendment, s.59(1) now provides:

"In this chapter 'qualifying interest in possession' means—
    (a) an interest in possession—
        (i) to which an individual is beneficially entitled, and
        (ii) which, if the individual became beneficially entitled to the interest in possession on or after March 22, 2006, is an immediate post death interest, a disabled person's interest or a transitional serial interest, or
    (b) an interest in possession to which, where subsection (2) below applies, a company is beneficially entitled."

As is apparent, the amended definition of 'qualifying interest in possession' introduces new terms (immediate post-death interest, disabled person's interest and transitional serial interest) for which further definitions are required. These definitions are found in ss.49A–E (immediate post-death interest and transitional serial interest) and s.89B (disabled person's interest). These definitions are discussed below.[68]

Immediate post-death interest

11–51   An "immediate post-death interest" is defined at s.49A[69] as follows:

"(1) Where a person ('L') is beneficially entitled to an interest in possession in settled property, for the purposes of this Chapter that interest is an 'immediate post death interest' only if the following conditions are satisfied.
(2) Condition 1 is that the settlement was effected by will or under the law relating to intestacy.
(3) Condition 2 is that L became beneficially entitled to the interest in possession on the death of the testator or intestate.
(4) Condition 3 is that—
    (a) section 71A below does not apply to the property in which the interest subsists, and
    (b) the interest is not a disabled person's interest.
(5) Condition 4 is that Condition 3 has been satisfied at all times since L became beneficially entitled to the interest in possession."

As is apparent from the name and from Conditions 1 and 2, an immediate post-death interest (referred to by practitioners as "IPDIs") can only be created on death: it is not possible to create an immediate post-death interest by a lifetime transfer.

Condition 1

11–52   An IPDI may be created by will or arise on intestacy. There are a few points to note. First, there is no restriction on who may be granted an immediate post-death interest. This gives great flexibility to a testator in choosing possible beneficiaries, including

---

[68] The consequences of this definition is considered in Ch.12—its application in relation to close companies is considered in para.12–43.
[69] Inserted by FA 2006 s.156 Sch.20 para.5.

minors. This freedom is clearly curtailed, however, in the case of intestacy because the intestacy rules themselves set out the identities of the beneficiaries.

Second, it appears possible to create an immediate post-death interest by a post-death variation falling within s.142(1),[70] since dispositions under such variations are deemed to have been effected by the deceased. One concern is whether, although deemed to be effected by the deceased, such a disposition is sufficient to satisfy condition 1. Condition 1 requires that the settlement is effected by will or by intestacy. It is the authors' view that condition 1 is satisfied by necessary implication: the deceased can conceivably only effect the dispositions by will (generally with the terms of the instrument standing in place of the terms of the original will or intestacy).

Third, despite the fact that Condition 1 itself states that "the settlement" is effected by will or on intestacy, it appears to be possible to create an immediate post-death interest by transferring settled property into an existing settlement. One argument for contending that Condition 1 is satisfied is that the property becomes settled by virtue of the will. However, arguably this does not itself seem to comply with the strict words of Condition 1 because "the settlement" is not created by the will. HMRC have confirmed that the interest in property added to an existing settlement will qualify as an immediate post-death interest.[71] The reason given is that "settlement" in the context of Condition 1 "relates to the contribution of property into the settlement rather than the document under which it will become held". An additional reason, although not one expressly stated by HMRC, could be that, according to the view generally held by HMRC, each addition of property to an existing settlement results in the added property forming a new settlement. Consistent with this view, it is arguable that the addition of property to an existing settlement satisfies the strict words of Condition 1.

Condition 2

The requirement is that L should become entitled to an interest in possession on the **11–53** death of the deceased. An interest in possession acquired at a later date in a settlement created by the will of the deceased will not, therefore, qualify as an immediate post-death interest. Where a post-death arrangement giving a beneficiary an interest in possession is entered into and falls within s.142 or s.144, that interest in possession is deemed to take effect on the death of the deceased and so will qualify as an immediate post-death interest.

Condition 3

The intention here is to ensure that the interest of the beneficiary is not a bereaved **11–54** minor's interest or a disabled person's interest. If it is either of those types of interest, it cannot be an immediate post-death interest.

Condition 4

In order to satisfy Condition 4, it is imperative that, at no time since the beneficiary **11–55** became entitled to an interest in possession, has that interest been a disabled person's

[70] See paras 8–115 and following.
[71] See Question 18 of questions put to HMRC BY STEP/CIOT and answered on November 3, 2006, last updated on October 3, 2008, available on the STEP website.

interest nor has the settlement been one to which the bereaved minors trust provisions apply. It is therefore possible for an interest in possession which has qualified as an immediate post-death interest to cease so to qualify as a result of a later event. For example, assume that a minor beneficiary was given an interest in possession in settled property under a disposition made by his mother's will but that at a later date the trustees exercised their power of appointment and appointed the capital to him absolutely at the age of 18 years. The interest would have been an immediate post-death interest until the appointment of capital to the beneficiary at the age of 18 years at which point the bereaved minors' trust provisions (s.71A) would have started to apply.

Transitional serial interests

11–56   An interest in possession is a transitional serial interest (referred to by practitioners as "TSIs") if it satisfies the requirements of ss.49C, 49D or 49E.[72]
Section 49C: interest to which a person becomes entitled during the period March 22, 2006 to October 5, 2008

11–57   Section 49C deals with the situation where a person ("B") becomes entitled, during the period from March 22, 2006 to October 5, 2008,[73] to an interest in the settled property. That interest ("the current interest") is a TSI if the following conditions are met.
Condition 1 is that the settlement commenced before March 22, 2006 and, immediately before that date, B or another person had an interest in possession in the property comprised in the settlement. This interest of B or another person is known as "the prior interest".
Condition 2 is that the prior interest came to an end at a time on or after March 22, 2006 but before October 6, 2008.
Condition 3 is that B became beneficially entitled to the current interest at that time.
Condition 4 is that the settled property is not subject to the bereaved minors' trust provisions nor is the interest a disabled person's interest.

11–58   It was only possible to have one change of interest in possession in the period from March 22, 2006 to October 5, 2008 in order to ensure that the interest acquired by beneficiary, B, qualified as a s.49C transitional serial interest. This follows from the combined effect of Conditions 1 to 3 inclusive. In effect, there must have been an interest in possession in the pre-March 22, 2006 settlement ("the prior interest") which came to an end during that period and on that occasion the beneficiary B became entitled to "the current interest".[74]

---

[72] Inserted by FA 2006 Sch.20 para.5.

[73] The date was originally April 5, 2008 but was extended to October 5, 2008 by FA 2008 s.141(1) with effect from April 6, 2008.

[74] There were concerns among practitioners about when s.49C transitional serial interests would arise, dealt with by STEP and CIOT in correspondence with HMRC. HMRC's responses, available on STEP's website, were not always consistent with the authors' views, but the guidance gives a helpful indication of HMRC's views.

Section 49D: interest to which a person becomes entitled on death of spouse on or after October 6, 2008

Section 49D deals with the situation where a person ("E") becomes entitled to an **11–59** interest in possession on the death of a spouse or civil partner on or after October 6, 2008[75] ("the successor interest") and provides that the successor interest will qualify as a transitional serial interest if Conditions 1–5 are met.

Condition 1 is that the settlement commenced before March 22, 2006 and immediately before that date a person other than E ("F") was beneficially entitled to an interest in possession in the settled property ("the previous interest").

Condition 2 is that the previous interest came to an end on or after October 6, 2008 on the occasion of the death of F.

Condition 3 is that, immediately before the death of F, F was E's spouse or civil partner.

Condition 4 is that E became beneficially entitled to the successor interest on the death of F.

Condition 5 is that the settlement is not a bereaved minors' trust and that the interest is not a disabled person's interest.

It is clear from the conditions that in order for a surviving spouse or civil partner's **11–60** interest in possession to qualify as a transitional serial interest under s.49D, it is necessary that the surviving spouse or civil partner should have acquired the successor interest on the death of the spouse or civil partner so that lifetime terminations of the spouse or civil partner's interest in possession in favour of the other spouse will not qualify as transitional serial interests.[76]

Further, it is to be noted that there appears to be no requirement that the successor interest has to be identical to the interest in possession to which the deceased spouse or civil partner was entitled, i.e. the previous interest: it is, therefore, possible for the successor interest to be in different property in the settlement and greater or lesser in scope than the previous interest.

It was possible until October 6, 2008 to terminate an existing interest in possession of a spouse or civil partner during that person's lifetime in favour of the other spouse or civil partner without triggering an immediate charge to inheritance tax. For example, if the Husband's pre-March 22, 2006 interest in possession was terminated during his lifetime but before October 5, 2008 in favour of his Wife, the Wife's interest will have satisfied the conditions of being a transitional serial interest under s.49C. The termination of the Husband's interest in possession would have been protected from charge by the s.18 spouse exemption. If, however, the termination occurs on or after October 6, 2008, and subject to favoured treatment applying, the termination will be the occasion on which property enters the relevant property regime: the Wife's interest is not a transitional serial interest under either s.49C or s.49D.

For further discussion of s.49D, see para.12–04.

Section 49E: contracts of life insurance

Section 49E deals with the situation where a person ("C") is beneficially entitled to **11–61** an interest in possession in settled property ("the present interest") and on C's

---

[75] The date was amended from "April" to "October" by the FA 2008 s.141(1) with effect from April 6, 2008.

[76] But see para.12–04.

becoming beneficially entitled to the present interest, the settled property consisted of or included rights under a life insurance contract entered into before March 22, 2006. The present interest is a transitional serial interest provided that Conditions 1–4 are satisfied. Note that only that part of the present interest that subsists in rights under the life insurance contract or in property comprised in the settlement that represents (whether directly or indirectly) rights under the life insurance contract can qualify as a transitional serial interest.

Condition 1 is that:

(a) the settlement containing the life insurance contract commenced before March 22, 2006; and
(b) that immediately before that date the following conditions were met, namely:
   (i) the property then comprised in the settlement consisted of or included rights under the contract; and
   (ii) those rights were property in which C, or some other person, was beneficially entitled to an interest in possession ("the earlier interest").

Condition 2 is that:

(a) (i) the earlier interest comes to an end on or after October 6, 2008 ("the earlier interest end time");
   (ii) on the death of the person beneficially entitled to it; and
   (iii) C became entitled to the present interest;
       1. at the earlier interest end time; or
       2. on the coming to an end, on the death of the person beneficially entitled to it, of an interest in possession to which that person became beneficially entitled on the earlier interest end time; or
       3. on the coming to an end of the latest in an unbroken line of two or more consecutive interests in possession to the first of which a person became beneficially entitled at the earlier interest end time and each of the consecutive interests in possession ended on the death of the person beneficially entitled to it; or
(b) C became beneficially entitled to the present interest—
   (i) on the coming to an end, on the death of a person entitled to it, of an interest in possession that is a transitional serial interest under s.49C (interest to which a person becomes entitled between March 22, 2006 and October 5, 2008), or
   (ii) on the coming to an end of the latest in an unbroken line of two or more consecutive interests in possession the first of which was a transitional serial interest under s.49C and each of the consecutive interests in possession ended on the death of the person beneficially entitled to it.

Condition 3 is that the rights under the life insurance contract were comprised in the settlement throughout the period beginning with March 22, 2006 and ending with the date on which C became entitled to the present interest.

Condition 4 is that the settlement is not a bereaved minors' trust and that the interest is not a disabled person's interest.

11–62 First, it is important to note that treatment as a transitional serial interest is only available for settlements that contained rights under life insurance contracts before March 22, 2006. The treatment in not, therefore, available in respect of rights that became comprised in a settlement after March 22, 2006 even where the settlement existed pre-March 22, 2006.

512

Second, there must, before March 22, 2006, have been an interest in possession in the rights under the life insurance contract: an interest under a discretionary settlement that held the rights under the contract of life insurance will not satisfy this requirement.

Third, it appears to be the case that only rights under life insurance contracts are covered by s.49E: the favourable treatment does not appear to apply to, for instance, settled capital redemption policies or pension policies (with provisions for pay-out on death).

Fourth, the present interest must arise on the death of the previous beneficially entitled person (or persons—where there is an unbroken line of successive interests in possession in the life insurance contract): lifetime terminations of prior interests in possession would disqualify the present interest from being a transitional serial interest under s.49E. There is, however, an exception to this requirement in relation to the first interest in possession to which s.49C applies: that interest in possession, it appears, may arise inter vivos or on death (see s.49E(3)(b)).

Fifth, Condition 3 is apparently satisfied only if the rights under the contract of life insurance are comprised in the settlement throughout the period stipulated in Condition 3. Consequently, if the settlement contained rights under a life insurance contract immediately before March 22, 2006, and these rights were replaced, at a time before C became entitled to the present interest, by other rights under life insurance contracts which directly or indirectly represent the prior rights, Condition 3 will not be satisfied. It does, however, seem possible for the present interest to qualify for transitional serial interest treatment where C becomes entitled to the present interest at a time before the rights under the contract of life insurance are replaced by rights representing them.

Sixth, while s.49E requires C to have an interest in possession, it does not appear to require that C's interest in possession must be essentially the same as the prior interest(s) in possession: trustees may therefore be able to alter the terms of the settlement without jeopardising s.49E treatment provided that before and after the alternation to the settlement terms, C retains an interest in possession.[77]

Disabled person's interest

Section 89B sets out the definition of "disabled person's interest". It provides: **11–63**

"(1) In this Act 'disabled person's interest' means—
    (a) an interest in possession to which a person is under s.89(2) above treated as beneficially entitled,
    (b) an interest in possession to which a person is under s.89A(4) above treated as beneficially entitled,
    (c) an interest in possession in settled property (other than an interest within paragraph (a) or (b) above) to which a disabled person becomes beneficially entitled on or after 22 March 2006, or
    (d) an interest in possession in settled property (other than an interest within paragraph (a) or (b) above) to which a person ("A") is beneficially entitled if—
      i A is the settlor,
      ii A was beneficially entitled to the property immediately before transferring it into the settlement,
      iii A satisfies [HMRC] as mentioned in s.89A(1)(b) above,

---

[77] Some commentators have highlighted anomalies in the interaction between s.49E transitional serial interests and disabled person's interests which are not discussed here.

iv The settled property was transferred into settlement on or after 22 March 2006, and

v The trusts on which the settled property is held secure that, if any of the settled property is applied during A's life for the benefit of a beneficiary, it is applied for the benefit of A.

(2) Subsections (4) to (6) of section 89 above (meaning of 'disabled person' in subsection (1) of that section) have effect for the purposes of (1)(c) above as they have effect for the purposes of subsection (1) of that section."

Four categories of interest, therefore, qualify as a "disabled person's interest", namely:

(1) a deemed interest in possession in a trust for a disabled person under s.89(2) IHTA 1984;

(2) a deemed interest in possession in a self-settlement created by a potentially disabled person under IHTA 1984 s.89A;

(3) an actual interest in possession in settled property (other than an interest within (1) and (2) above) to which a disabled person has become entitled on or after March 22, 2006; and

(4) an actual interest in possession in a self-settled trust (other than an interest within (1) and (2) above) into which settled property was transferred on or after March 22, 2006, which meets the requirements of potential disability set out in s.89A(1)(b), and which secures that if the capital is applied for any beneficiary's benefit it is applied only for the benefit of the settlor.

For a full discussion of the categories of interest that qualify as a disabled person's interest, see paras 21–11 and following.

Reversionary interests

11–64   Unlike the term "interest in possession", the term "reversionary interest" is statutorily defined by s.47. It means:

> "a future interest under a settlement, whether it is vested or contingent (including an interest expectant on the termination of an interest in possession which, by virtue of s.50 below, is treated as subsisting in part of any property) and in relation to Scotland includes an interest in the fee of property subject to a proper liferent."

Intermediate interests

11–65   A person can be entitled to an interest which falls somewhere between an interest in possession and a reversionary interest. Where, for example, as in the *Pearson* case, a person is entitled to the income from a trust fund unless the trustees accumulate that income, he does not have an interest in possession; equally, however, he cannot be regarded as having a reversionary interest. Such an interest might be called, for want of a better term, an "intermediate interest". The legislation makes no special provision for dealing with such interests; it therefore follows that they will be valued and brought into account in the usual way, so that, e.g. if a person disposes of such an interest or

514

dies owning such an interest tax will normally be charged on the market value of that interest. This should usually be negligible.[78]

Settlement powers

The Finance Act 2002 introduced a new term, "settlement power" into the IHT legislation by inserting into the legislation a new section, s.47A. For a discussion of this term, see paras 25–12 and following. **11–66**

---

[78] See para.25–49.

CHAPTER 12

INTERESTS IN POSSESSION

I. INTRODUCTION

12–01   Since the enactment of the Finance Act 2006, the tax treatment of settled property in which an interest in possession subsists is dependent upon whether the interest is a "qualifying interest in possession" within s.59. If the interest is not a "qualifying interest in possession", then, by virtue of s.58, the settled property will fall to be taxed under the special charging provisions: the relevant property regime will apply to the settled property, unless it falls within one of the categories of settled property which benefits from favoured treatment.

The categories of interests which post-March 22, 2006 fall to be treated as qualifying interests in possession are defined at para.11–50. The tax treatment of qualifying interests in possession has been considered in various places in this work. For ease of reference and to give an overall picture of how the changes brought about by the Finance Act 2006 affect the taxation of interest in possession settlements, the changes are described in outline in Pt II below.

In some cases, settled property is treated for IHT purposes as if a qualifying interest in possession subsists in it, even where no interest in possession subsists in it as a matter of the general law. This applies, for example, in relation to two categories of disabled person's interests,[1] and to pre-March 22, 2006 protective trusts where the life interest of the principal beneficiary has been forfeited and replaced by statutory discretionary trusts.[2] In all other cases, and in order to determine whether an interest in possession falls to be treated as a qualifying interest in possession, it is still vitally important to know whether an interest in possession subsists in settled property as a matter of the general law. Accordingly, the meaning of the term "interest in possession" in the general law is considered in Pt III of this chapter.

This is followed in Pt IV by consideration of the provisions in the legislation which bear on the meaning of "interest in possession".

II. TAX TREATMENT OF INTERESTS IN POSSESSION BEFORE AND AFTER MARCH 22, 2006

Tax treatment of interest in possession trusts before March 22, 2006

For settlements created[3] before March 22, 2006 in which any interest in possession subsisted, s.49 provided that:

12–02

> "(1) A person beneficially entitled to an interest in possession in settled property shall be treated for the purposes of this Act as beneficially entitled to the property in which the interest subsists."

The effects of the words of s.49(1) were as follows. First, because the estate of the interest in possession beneficiary included the settled property in which the interest in possession subsisted, on the death of the beneficiary with the interest in possession, the value of that settled property formed part of his estate, was deemed to be disposed of by him, and would generally (i.e. subject to the availability of any reliefs and/or any unused nil-rate band) give rise to an inheritance tax charge. Second, the disposal or termination of that interest in possession during the lifetime of the beneficiary with the interest in possession would trigger an inheritance tax charge under s.51 and s.52[4] except where the exemptions from charge under s.53 applied. Third, the lifetime termination of an interest in possession, whether by way of disposal or by way of a termination by the trustees of a settlement, could be the occasion of a potentially exempt transfer by the interest in possession beneficiary whose interest in possession terminated provided that another individual became entitled either to the property absolutely or to an interest in possession in such property. Fourth, if the person who became entitled to an interest in possession on the lifetime termination of an interest in possession in settled property was the spouse of the erstwhile interest in possession beneficiary, the spouse exemption under s.18 would apply: the estate of the spouse had

---

[1] Namely disabled person's interests within s.89B(a) and (b), i.e. where no interest in possession subsists in the settled property. See Ch.21.

[2] See Ch.22.

[3] The rules about when settlements are created are considered at paras 10–12–10–19.

[4] See paras 2–95–2–123.

517

been increased by virtue of the transfer of value deemed to have been made by the interest in possession beneficiary.

Post-March 22, 2006 tax treatment of interests in possession subsisting before March 22, 2006

12–03   Section 49 was amended by Finance Act 2006 Sch.20 para.4 with effect from March 22, 2006. Section 49 now contains two new provisions, subss.(1A) and (1B) which provide as follows:

> "(1A) Where the interest in possession mentioned in subsection (1) above is one to which the person becomes beneficially entitled on or after 22 March 2006, subsection (1) above applies in relation to that interest only if, and for so long as, it is—
> (a) an immediate post-death interest,
> (b) a disabled person's interest;
> (c) a transitional serial interest.
> (1B) Where the interest in possession mentioned in (1) above is one to which the person became beneficially entitled before March 22, 2006, subsection (1) above does not apply in relation to that interest at any time when s.71A below applies to the property in which the interest subsists."

The effect of s.49(1A) is to treat the settled property in which an interest in possession subsists as property to which the interest in possession beneficiary is beneficially entitled only where the interest which arises on or after March 22, 2006 is an immediate post-death interest, a disabled person's interest or a transitional serial interest.[5] Section 49(1A) does not alter the tax treatment of interests in possession that subsisted prior to March 22, 2006: interests in possession that subsisted before March 22, 2006 will continue to have s.49(1) treatment until such time as those interests are terminated.[6]

Post-Finance Act 2006 tax treatment of the termination of pre-March 22, 2006 interests in possession on the death of the interest in possession beneficiary

12–04   If a pre-March 22, 2006 interest in possession terminates on the death of the interest in possession beneficiary, then by virtue of s.49, the estate of the interest in possession beneficiary is deemed to include the settled property in which the interest in possession subsisted. A charge under s.4 will arise.[7] This is so unless, on the occasion of the interest in possession beneficiary's death the property passes to the spouse of the beneficiary absolutely, in which case s.18 (the spouse exemption) would apply. If, on the occasion of the interest in possession beneficiary's death, the spouse becomes entitled to an interest in possession in that property, s.49D provides that the spouse's interest will be a transitional serial interest, with the result that the spouse will be deemed to be beneficially entitled to the settled property in which this transitional serial interest subsists so that the spouse exemption can then apply.

Section 49D(1) provides:

---

[5] For the definitions of these terms see para.11–50.

[6] At which point the prior rules may continue to apply if the succeeding interest is one that attracts beneficial treatment, i.e. is a transitional serial interest, a disabled person's interest or an immediate post-death interest.

[7] See paras 8–02 and following.

"(1) Where a person ('E') is beneficially entitled to an interest in possession in settled property ('the successor interest'), that interest is a transitional serial interest for the purposes of this Chapter if the following conditions are met.

(2) Condition (1) is that—

(a) the settlement commenced before March 22, 2006, and

(b) immediately before March 22, 2006, the property then comprised in the settlement was property in which the person other than E was beneficially entitled to an interest in possession ('the previous interest').

(3) Condition (2) is that the previous interest came to an end on or after October 6, 2008 on the death of that other person ('F').

(4) Condition (3) is that, immediately before F died, F was the spouse or civil partner of E.

(5) Condition (4) is that E became beneficially entitled to the successor interest on F's death.

(6) Condition (5) is that—

(a) s.71A below does not apply to the property in which the successor interest subsists, and

(b) the successor interest is not a disabled person's interest."

There are a few points to note in relation to the conditions in s.49D in addition to the points made at paras 11–59–11–60. First, the interest in possession of the deceased beneficiary must have commenced and subsisted immediately before March 22, 2006. This is known as "the previous interest". It is an absolute requirement of condition 2 that "the previous interest" came to an end on the death of the beneficiary with the interest in possession on or after October 6, 2008. It is, therefore, not possible for an inter vivos termination of a beneficiary's interest in possession in favour of the spouse to qualify for s.49D "transitional serial interest" treatment. If the spouse inherits a right to income not limited by reference to the deceased's life, the inherited interest will not be a transitional serial interest, unless it could be said that the interest "came to an end" by virtue of s.51(1)(b) on the death of the spouse. Condition 3 raises the prospect of possible deathbed planning in that it is a requirement that immediately before the interest in possession beneficiary died, the spouse who acquires an interest in possession on the spouse's death, i.e. F, was the spouse or civil partner of E. It therefore makes it possible, subject of course to the usual anti-avoidance case law, for an individual interest in possession beneficiary to marry or acquire a civil partner as a deathbed planning scheme. Condition 4 imposes an additional limitation: it requires that E, (the spouse of the deceased beneficiary with the interest in possession) acquires the "successor interest" (i.e. the interest in possession to which E is beneficially entitled) only on the death of his or her spouse or civil partner. It is, therefore, not possible for s.49D "transitional serial interest" treatment to apply to a situation where E becomes entitled to the successor interest inter vivos. It also precludes qualification as a transitional serial interest where E does not become entitled immediately on F's death but on some later occasion, another interest having subsisted in the interim.

Pre-March 22, 2006 interest in possession beneficiary acquiring a successive interest in possession under the same trust post-March 22, 2006

A point sometimes overlooked is that the termination of an interest in possession **12–05** held by a beneficiary, B, in favour of another interest in possession in favour of B, even if it is in the same property and to the same extent triggers the termination of the prior interest in possession and the acquisition of the subsequent interest in possession. Before the Finance Act 2006 changes, a charge to inheritance tax would in any event have been protected by the fact that there was arguably no transfer of value provided that B's prior interest and B's subsequent interest did not represent any change in the value of his estate. The fact that the termination of B's prior interest could be the occasion of a charge under s.51 and s.52 is apparent because s.53(2) excludes a charge on that occasion s.53(2) contemplates that B's interest in property comes to an end and he becomes on the same occasion beneficially entitled to the property or to another interest in possession in it and exempts a charge in such circumstances (except in such circumstances that fall within s.52(4)(b)).[8]

12–06   Post the Finance Act 2006 changes, the date when the subsequent interest in possession arises is important. If the subsequent interest in possession arose within the transitional period (which ended on October 5, 2008), the subsequent interest will qualify as "a transitional serial interest", even if it is in favour of the same beneficiary (B). However, if the subsequent interest arises after the end of the transitional period (i.e. after October 5, 2008), the subsequent interest will not be a transitional serial interest even if it is in favour of the same beneficiary (B) and will, therefore, not be a "qualifying interest in possession" (unless it is a disabled person's interest).[9] As a result, the property in which the subsequent interest in possession subsists will fall within the relevant property regime.

It is to be noted that in certain circumstances, s.53(2) will have operated to prevent a charge arising on the occasion when the pre-March 22, 2006 interest in possession terminated: in other words, there would have been no charge to tax on the termination of the pre-March 22, 2006 interest in possession even if, say, on that occasion the property in which the terminated interest in possession subsisted entered the relevant property regime. But by virtue of s.53(2A), the exclusion from charge under s.53(2) does not apply to a termination of an interest in possession after March 12, 2008 in favour of another interest in possession unless the subsequent interest in possession is itself a disabled person's interest or a transitional serial interest. This treatment applies regardless of when the previous interest in possession, i.e. the one that comes to an end, was acquired, i.e. before, on or after March 22, 2006. In other words, where a beneficiary's interest in possession terminates on or after March 12, 2008 and on that occasion he does not become entitled beneficially to the underlying property or to a disabled person's interest or to a transitional serial interest, the termination of the previous interest will be the occasion of a charge under s.52: it will not be protected by s.53(2). Do note that s.53(2A), as now appears in the statute book, was introduced by the Finance Act 2008 and is treated as having come into force on March 22, 2006. Paragraph 14(3) of Sch.20 to the Finance Act 2006 which originally introduced a different s.53(2A) is treated as never having come into effect. The reason for this amendment was that, as originally enacted, s.53(2A) prevented a charge arising both on the occasion where a beneficiary with a qualifying interest in possession became entitled to the property or to another interest in possession in the property—whether or not that interest was a qualifying interest in possession. This gave rise to planning opportunities which were subsequently blocked.

EXAMPLE 1

12–07   A is a beneficiary with an interest in possession under a trust created on March 2, 2000. A's interest in possession terminates on March 10, 2008 and on that occasion he

---

[8] Broadly where the value of the property to which or to an interest in possession in which a person becomes beneficially entitled is less than the value on which tax would be chargeable apart from s.53(2).
[9] See Ch.21.

becomes entitled to another interest in possession in the property. The termination of the previous interest in possession and acquisition of a subsequent interest in possession is subject to the pre-Finance Act 2006 rules: although the termination of the previous interest in possession is the occasion of a coming to an end of the previous interest in possession so that s.52 applies, there will be no charge because of the exclusion from charge provided by s.53(2).

EXAMPLE 2

Assume the same facts as before except that A's previous interest in possession **12–08** terminates on April 1, 2008 on which occasion he acquires another interest in possession. The subsequent interest in possession will be a transitional serial interest.[10] As a result, the s.53(2) exclusion from a charge under s.52 will apply (s.53(2A)).

EXAMPLE 3

Assume the same facts as before except that A's previous interest in possession **12–09** terminates on October 12, 2008 on which occasion he becomes beneficially entitled to the settled property in which his previous interest in possession subsisted. The s.52 charge that would otherwise arise on the termination is excluded by s.53(2) itself because on the occasion of the termination of the previous interest in possession A becomes entitled to the underlying property.

EXAMPLE 4

Assume the same facts as before except that A's previous interest in possession in **12–10** the settled property terminates on October 12, 2008 and on that occasion he becomes entitled to another interest in possession in the settled property. The s.52 charge is not excluded by s.53(2) because on the termination of the previous interest in possession A does not become beneficially entitled to the property or to a disabled person's interest or to a transitional serial interest (s.53(2A)).

Finance Act 2006 changes and the reverter to settlor exemption

On the occasion where there is an inter vivos termination of an interest in possession, **12–11** and on that occasion the property in which the interest subsisted reverts to the settlor or to the settlor's spouse or civil partner, the s.52 charge that would arise on the termination of the settlor's interest in possession is excluded by s.53(3) and (4). However, the Finance Act 2006 changes have affected the manner in which the exclusion in s.53(3) and (4) apply.[11] Broadly, property "reverts" to the settlor if the settlor is beneficially entitled to it or if he has a qualifying interest in possession in it. This was true of all pre-March 22, 2006 interests in possession because an individual

[10] See definition in paras 11–56 and following.
[11] See also para.2–116.

521

with an interest in possession was deemed to be beneficially entitled to the property in which the interest in possession subsisted. However, post-March 22, 2006, the beneficiary with an interest in possession is only deemed to own the underlying property if the interest in possession is one that falls within s.49(1A), i.e. the subsequent interest in possession is an immediate post-death interest, a disabled person's interest or a transitional serial interest.[12]

EXAMPLE 1

12–12   A, the settlor, has an interest in possession that subsisted before March 22, 2006. His interest terminates on March 10, 2008 and on the occasion when A's interest in possession terminates A becomes beneficially entitled to the underlying property. This is an occasion on which the reverter to settlor exemption applies because A on the termination of his interest in possession becomes beneficially entitled to the underlying property. As such, s.53(3) should apply to exclude the s.52 charge.

EXAMPLE 2

12–13   A, the settlor's pre-March 22, 2006 interest in possession is terminated on March 10, 2008 and on that occasion A becomes beneficially entitled to an interest in possession in the settled property. The interest that A acquires on the termination of his previous interest in possession is a transitional serial interest because it is acquired before October 5, 2008. Consequently, the reverter to settlor exemption in s.53(3) will apply to preclude the s.52 charge.

EXAMPLE 3

12–14   A, the settlor's pre-March 22, 2006 interest in possession is terminated on January 1, 2009 and on that occasion A becomes entitled to another interest in possession in the settled property. A's subsequent interest in possession is not a transitional serial interest. As such, he is not treated as being beneficially entitled to the underlying property in which that interest in possession subsists. It can, therefore, not be said that on the occasion where A's interest in possession terminated, the property "reverts to the settlor".

EXAMPLE 4

12–15   A, the settlor's pre-March 22, 2006 interest in possession is terminated on April 7, 2008 and on that occasion A's spouse acquires an interest in possession in the settled property. The interest in possession acquired by the settlor's spouse is a transitional serial interest. Consequently, the spouse is regarded as beneficially entitled to the

---

[12] Alternatively if, on that occasion when the interest in possession terminates, the settlor with the interest in possession becomes beneficially entitled to the underlying property.

underlying property in which the interest in possession subsists (s.49(1A)). Accordingly, the s.52 charge is excluded by s.53(4).

EXAMPLE 5

A, the settlor's pre-March 22, 2006 interest in possession is terminated on October **12–16**
10, 2008 and on that occasion his spouse acquires an interest in possession in the settled
property. The spouse's interest will not be a transitional serial interest, being acquired
after the end of the transitional period (ending on October 5, 2008). Consequently, the
spouse will not be deemed to beneficially own the property in which the interest in
possession subsists. It cannot, therefore, be said for the purposes of s.53(4) that the
settled property "reverts to the settlor's spouse".

Property added to a settlement with a pre-March 22, 2006 interest in possession[13]

According to Budget Note BN25, an interesting situation is created where property **12–17**
is added to an interest in possession settlement that existed before March 22, 2006.
BN25 states that:

> "The new rules will apply . . . to new trusts, additions of new assets to existing trusts and
> to . . . other IHT-relevant events in relation to existing trusts."

The effect of this appears to be clear, as least as far as HMRC are concerned. Consistent
with their view on additions to excluded property settlements,[14] HMRC's view appears
to be that where property is added after March 22, 2006 to a settlement with a pre-
March 22, 2006 and therefore qualifying interest in possession, the added property
forms part of a new settlement. Given that this new settlement arises after March 22,
2006, the settlement will be within the relevant property regime and will not be subject
to the interest in possession regime that subsisted before March 22, 2006. It is highly
questionable whether HMRC are justified in taking the stance that all additions of
property to existing settlements create separate settlements. Certainly a trust lawyer
would object to such an analysis. HMRC's view appears to be based on their reading
of the words in s.43(2) (definition of "settlement"):

> "Any disposition or *dispositions* of property . . . "

However, s.43 equally (if not more forcibly, given the total context of inheritance tax
on trusts) supports the view that a single settlement may be created by several
dispositions. To state otherwise is arguably to fly in the face of the concept of creating
a pilot trust and then adding property to the trust. This has been established practice.
It would surprise most practitioners that each addition of property to such a settlement
would be regarded as a separate settlement. However, this appears to be HMRC's
position. Consequently, it would be prudent for practitioners to proceed on the basis
that additions of property post-March 22, 2006 to settlements that subsisted pre-March
22, 2006 create separate settlements. This is so unless and until the matter is actually
tested in, and settled by, the courts.

---

[13] See also paras 11–19–11–20 and the passages referred to therein.
[14] See para.32–50.

A corollary to the separate settlements point is that, in the authors' view, the relevant property regime only applies to that part of the settled property that is added post-March 22, 2006. In effect, the logical conclusion from the separate settlements analysis is that the settled property that formed part of the settlement prior to March 22, 2006 continues to be subject to the pre-March 22, 2006 rules. Consequently, interest in possession settlements that were created before March 22, 2006 should continue to have the interest in possession trust treatment that subsisted before the Finance Act 2006 changes. Additionally, it seems to follow from the separate settlements point that the commencement date for the added property settlement (that is subject to the relevant property regime) is the date that the property was added.[15]

12–18   A better argument for HMRC might be based on the words of s.49(1) itself. That provides that a person beneficially entitled to an interest in possession in settled property shall be treated as beneficially entitled to the property in which the interest subsists. Section 49(1A) extends this treatment to an interest in possession to which an individual becomes entitled on or after March 22, 2006 only if the interest is either an immediate post-death interest, a disabled person's interest or a transitional serial interest. It could be argued that the words of s.49(1) and (1A) only apply to settled property that formed part of the settlement before March 22, 2006. Consequently, it would logically follow that where property is added post-March 22, 2006 it is not possible to rely on s.49(1) or (1A).

12–19   Where *value* but not property is added to a settlement with a pre-March 22, 2006 interest in possession by an individual, this issue will not arise because there is no transfer of property: for example, if a person (whether or not it is the settlor) pays for improvements of a property which is the subject of a pre-March 22, 2006 interest in possession settlement, value but no property is added: no new settlement arises.

III. MEANING OF INTEREST IN POSSESSION IN THE GENERAL LAW

The general law: background

12–20   The meaning of "interest in possession" was considered by the House of Lords in *Pearson v IRC*.[16] Before examining *Pearson* it may be useful to consider what the position was thought to be before the case was decided. The leading case on the meaning of "interest in possession" for estate duty purposes was *Gartside v IRC*,[17] in which Lord Reid distinguished between an interest in possession and an interest which one merely possesses. He said that if the terms of the settlement are to A for life, remainder to B, B possesses an expectant interest, but that expectant interest is not an interest in possession:

> " . . . 'In possession' must mean that your interest enables you to claim now whatever may be the subject of the interest. For instance, if it is the current income from a certain fund

[15] Note that there has been an attempt to address some of the practical consequences of HMRC's view in published guidance, but no adequate guidance has yet been given by HMRC. They have indicated that they are reconsidering the guidance already given (see Q 37(1) and (2) of the questions put by STEP/CIOT to HMRC and answered on November 3, 2006, available on the STEP website) with a view to producing further guidance in due course.
[16] *Pearson v IRC* [1981] A.C. 753.
[17] *Gartside v IRC* [1968] A.C. 553.

your claim may yield nothing if there is no income, but your claim is a valid claim, and if there is any income you are entitled to get it; but a right to require Trustees to consider whether they will pay you something does not enable you to claim anything."

Thus, a reversioner does not have an interest in possession; nor does the object of a discretionary trust[18]; nor do the beneficiaries under an exhaustive discretionary trust collectively have an interest in possession.[19] Conversely, it follows from Lord Reid's above quoted statement that a person can have an interest in possession in property even though that property in fact produces no income. What matters is that if it did produce income the person in question would be entitled to that income. If the trustees have a discretion not to pay income to the beneficiary, but instead, e.g. to accumulate it, or to divert it to another class of beneficiaries, then the beneficiary in question was thought not, on the basis of the *Gartside* case, to have the necessary entitlement to give him an interest in possession.

On February 12, 1976, the Revenue issued a press release giving their view as to the meaning of "interest in possession" for both CTT and CGT purposes, as follows: **12–21**

" . . . The Board of Inland Revenue are aware that doubts have been expressed in the legal press and elsewhere concerning the precise scope of the term 'interest in possession' as used in F.A. 1975, Part III, and in particular about its application where an interest in settled property is subject to a discretion or power to accumulate the income of the property or to divert it elsewhere.

The Board therefore feel it appropriate, in view of the importance of the expression in F.A. 1975, Sch.5, to make known their understanding of the meaning of the expression. This is that an interest in possession in settled property exists where the person having the interest has the immediate entitlement (subject to any prior claim by the trustees for expenses or other outgoings properly payable out of income) to any income produced by that property as the income arises; but that a discretion or power, in whatever form, which can be exercised after income arises so as to withhold it from that person negatives the existence of an interest in possession. For this purpose a power to accumulate income is regarded as a power to withhold it, unless any accumulations must be held solely for the person having the interest or his personal representatives.

On the other hand the existence of a mere power of revocation or appointment, the exercise of which would determine the interest wholly or in part (but which, so long as it remains unexercised, does not affect the beneficiary's immediate entitlement to income) does not in the Board's view prevent the interest from being an interest in possession.

Capital Gains Tax

This understanding of the expression equally applies for the purposes of Finance Act 1965, s.25(4)."

HMRC's view was accepted by most practitioners, although some had reservations as to whether the existence of a power of accumulation necessarily precluded the existence of an interest in possession. This was the point at issue in the *Pearson* case, in which the House of Lords held by a bare majority (overruling the Court of Appeal and Fox J. at the first instance) that HMRC's view was correct.

The *Pearson* case

The relevant facts of the case were that under cll.2 and 3 of a 1964 settlement the trust fund was to be held on trust absolutely in equal shares for such of the settlor's   **12–22**

---

[18] Except, prior to April 6, 1981, for some CGT purposes; see *Leedale v Lewis* [1982] 1 W.L.R. 1319; [1982] S.T.C. 835.
[19] See *Sainsbury v IRC* [1970] Ch. 712.

children as attained the age of 21 years. This was subject to certain qualifications. First, the trustees had an overriding power of appointment as to both income and capital. Secondly, the trustees had power to accumulate income for a specified period. In addition, the trustees had two other powers. First, by cl.14, the trustees had in relation to the trust property "all the powers of management and exploitation of an absolute owner". Secondly, by cl.21, the trustees might

> "at any time or times apply any income of the Trust Fund in or towards the payment or discharge of any duties, taxes, costs, charges, fees or other outgoings, which but for the provisions of this clause would be payable out of or charged upon the capital of the Trust Fund or any part thereof".

By the end of February 1974, and thus before the introduction of CTT, the settlor's three children, Fiona, Serena and Julia, had all attained 21 years of age. Thus, subject to the exercise by the trustees of their powers of accumulation and appointment, and to the possibility of partial defeasance on the birth of further children to the settlor, Fiona was absolutely entitled to a one-third share of the income and capital. On March 20, 1976, the trustees, who had accumulated all the income which had arisen to them, by deed appointed £16,000 to be held on trust absolutely and irrevocably for Fiona.

It was common ground between HMRC and the taxpayer that:

(1) the trustees' overriding power of appointment did not preclude the existence of an interest in possession; and

(2) following the appointment Fiona had an interest in possession in the £16,000.[20]

Where they differed was on the consequences of the appointment. HMRC contended that Fiona acquired her interest in possession as a result of the appointment, with the result that tax was chargeable.[21] The trustees, on the other hand, contended that Fiona had acquired an interest in possession in one-third of the fund on attaining 21 years of age, and that consequently the 1976 appointment was not chargeable.[22] They sought a declaration that on attaining 21 Fiona had acquired an interest in possession in her share of the fund.

Decision at first instance

12–23 The case was first heard by Fox J., before whom the argument proceeded by agreement of both sides on the footing that the expression "interest in possession" had the same meaning for CTT purposes as it did for estate duty, and a great deal of both the argument before Fox J. and his subsequent judgment was concerned with the meaning of the term for estate duty purposes: as will be seen below, this approach was improper. Regard was also had to the meaning of "interest in possession" as a matter of general trust law. Fox J. noted the traditional distinction between an interest which

---

[20] It was agreed that:

(1) the possibility of Fiona's interest being partially defeated by the birth of a further beneficiary did not prevent her from having an interest in possession; and

(2) the fact that the trustees had accumulated all the income arising to them did not affect the issue in question.

[21] Under FA 1975 Sch.5 para.6(2).

[22] The £16,000 did not exceed the value of one-third of the fund.

is vested in possession (i.e. an interest which gives a present right of *present* enjoyment) and an interest which is vested in interest only (i.e. an interest which gives a present right of *future* enjoyment), and concluded:

> "For the purposes of that traditional distinction, it seems to me that the interest of a person who is entitled to the income of property subject only to a power in the trustees to accumulate is an interest in possession and not in reversion or remainder. The latter interests are future interests, which the former is not: it is a present interest, giving a present right to whatever income is not accumulated."

He went on to say that the terms of the settlement were in his view such that on attaining the age of 21

> " . . . the daughters would be entitled as of right to income of their shares in each of the following circumstances: (a) if the trustees decide not to accumulate that income: (b) if the trustees fail to agree as to whether they should accumulate or not: (c) if the trustees, having allowed a reasonable period to elapse after receipt of income, have reached no decision whether to accumulate or not. In each of those cases the daughter will be entitled to the income as of right. She will be entitled to it, not because the trustees have decided to give it to her . . . but because she is entitled to it in right of what is, beyond doubt, her interest in the trust fund . . . "

Moreover, the approach espoused by HMRC gave rise to a number of difficulties:

> " . . . First, it has been common form for many years now for settlements to confer upon trustees wide powers of applying income for all sorts of purposes; for example, in payment of the cost of improvements to land and in payment of capital taxes. Clause 21 of the present settlement contains such powers; it authorises payment out of income of any duties, taxes, charges, fees or other outgoings which but for the provisions of this clause would be payable out of capital. That is a convenient provision. But if the Revenue are correct, it seems to me that if a fund is held upon trust for A for life and the settlement includes, such a power, then the life interest is not in possession during periods when the practical situation is such that the power could be exercised to absorb the income (or would not be in possession as to the whole when the power could be exercised to absorb part). Such a power would plainly be exercisable over income after it had arisen, and could prevent its receipt by the life tenant. So far as the beneficiaries' right to receive income is concerned, the position is no different from that where a power of accumulation exists. Mr. Nourse accepts, I think, that on the Revenue's view a power such as that in clause 21 could have the effect of determining whether there was an interest in possession or not. That would be a curious consequence of powers which are really intended as aids to administration of the trust. One would get the same problem if there is simply a power to use income to pay the cost of improvements to land.
>
> Secondly, if a power such as that contained in clause 21 has the effect of determining whether an interest is in possession or not, the result in terms of liability to capital transfer tax may be startling. Suppose a power to pay capital taxes out of income; and suppose a period when no liability to the capital tax exists. A liability of large amount is then incurred (say to CGT). Consistently with the Revenue's view, what was previously a life interest in possession is determined (with a resulting charge to capital transfer tax). The CGT having been paid, the life interest in possession would then arise again, with a further charge to capital transfer tax, and so on. Similarly, if there is a power to effect improvements to land out of income, if a fund consisting of equities is sold and converted into land, the transposition of investments might result in a change to capital transfer tax.
>
> Another example of the operation of the principle as formulated by the Revenue is the case where property is held upon trust for A for life but the trustees have power to apply income for the benefit of his children. The birth of a child would determine A's life interest in possession with a resulting claim to capital transfer tax. The death of the child would restore it to possession with a similar claim.

Thirdly, the Revenue's proposition is that there is a life interest in possession in settled property if the holder of the interest is entitled to the net income (if any) of the property as it arises. But what is meant by 'net income?' The outgoings which are properly payable out of income must depend on the provisions of the settlement. The income receivable by a life tenant may be reduced or extinguished by any one or more of a number of powers—for example, a power of accumulation, a power to apply income in payment of capital improvements to land or premiums on a policy on the life tenant's life. If trustees are authorised to pay the cost of capital improvements to land out of income, there is no satisfactory distinction (so far as determining the 'net income' available for distribution is concerned) between the position arising under such a power and that arising under powers relating to payments which are more of an income nature; it is simply an incident of the life interest. It may be well after the end of the year before the trustees are in a position to decide whether to pay for improvements out of income or not. If they decide to do so, the cost may swallow up the whole or a large part of the income. Does such a power negative the existence of an interest in possession? If the answer is 'No,' what realistic difference is there between such a power and a power to accumulate? In both cases income is in effect being applied in augmentation of capital. If the answer is 'Yes,' one is faced with the problems, which I have mentioned, of intermittent powers which may cause interests in possession to arise and disappear again.

All these considerations lead me to doubt whether the test based upon the distinction between cases where the beneficiary is entitled to income as it arises and cases where the trustees have power to withhold income after it has arisen is satisfactory. The fact is that an income beneficiary's right to income is always a right to receive what remains after the trustees have exercised the powers which by the general law or by the settlement are conferred upon them in respect of that income. The trustees are always entitled to a reasonable time in which to exercise the powers. They can thus retain income as it arises and, depending upon the mode of exercise of the powers, divert it from the beneficiary altogether. Even in the simple case of charges of an income nature (for example, repairs), a period may well have to elapse after the end of the year before the trustees are able to decide whether to repair or not. The beneficiary's right to receive income is deferred and interfered with accordingly."

HMRC's attempt to rely on *Gartside* was also misfounded:

"It seems to me that the essential question is not whether a beneficiary can say of any income as it arises, 'that is mine.' In all but the simplest cases he will very often not be able to say that because the income will be subject to various administrative powers of the trustees. Nor, it seems to me, is the quantum of income which ultimately reaches the beneficiary a material matter. The fundamental question, I think, is whether his entitlement, whatever, if anything, it may turn out to be in terms of quantum, is a present entitlement in right of an interest in the trust property subject only to the proper exercise of the trustees' powers. And, an entitlement is a present entitlement notwithstanding that the trustees have, as they must have, a reasonable time in which to consider what course to adopt as to exercise of powers."

Fox J. concluded that, notwithstanding the trustees' power of accumulation, Fiona had an interest in possession in one-third of the trust fund.

The Court of Appeal

12–24   The argument before the Court of Appeal, who unanimously upheld Fox J., proceeded on slightly different lines, since HMRC no longer agreed that "interest in possession" had the same meaning as it did in the estate duty legislation. The Court of Appeal accepted HMRC's contention that the estate duty legislation was not relevant.

Buckley L.J. (with whom Bridge L.J. agreed)[23] concluded that Fiona had an interest in possession:

" . . . If one were to ask what interest one of the settlor's daughters had under the settlement as at the first day of a trust year of account next before March 26, 1976 in the unappointed part of the trust fund and its income during the ensuing year, the answer could, in my opinion, only be that she was then entitled to one-third of that income. True, one would have to go on to say that that interest was in certain respects defeasible, but it was a vested interest carrying the right to the enjoyment of the whole one-third of the income unless and until it was defeated, either by an appointment or by an exercise alone or more of the discretionary powers vested in the trustees. The description 'interest in possession' would, in my opinion fit it perfectly. The fact that the immediate enjoyment of the income might be postponed for a reasonable period to permit the trustees to consider whether to exercise any discretionary power vested in them in defeasance of the lady's vested right to the income is not, in my opinion, sufficient to deprive her interest of the character of an interest in possession. During that period she would be the person entitled to the income, although in the event her right to it might be partially or wholly defeated."

The House of Lords: majority views

HMRC appealed successfully (to the House of Lords, who decided in their favour by **12–25** a bare majority). Viscount Dilhorne and Lord Keith, with whom Lord Lane agreed, found for HMRC. Both Viscount Dilhorne and Lord Keith held that the meaning of "interest in possession" for estate duty purposes was irrelevant. Further, as the expression was not defined in any meaningful way, the words were to be given their ordinary and natural meaning. As to this, Viscount Dilhorne said:

"In Preston's 'Treatise on Estates' (1820) at p.89 an estate in possession is stated to be one which gives 'a present right of present enjoyment.' This was contrasted with an estate in remainder which it was said gave 'a right of future enjoyment.' In Fearne's 'Contingent Remainders' 10th Ed: (1844) Vol: 1 at p.2 it was said that an estate is vested when there is an immediate fixed right of present or future enjoyment; that an estate is vested in possession when there exists a right of present enjoyment; that an estate is vested in interest when there is a present fixed right of future enjoyment; and that an estate is contingent when a right of enjoyment is to accrue on an event which is dubious and uncertain.

In the light of these statements, it appears that in the nineteenth century the words 'an interest in possession' would have been interpreted as ordinarily meaning the possession of a right to the present enjoyment of something. The appellants in their Case contend that 'a beneficiary only has an interest in possession if his interest enables him to claim the whole or an ascertainable part of the net income, if any, of the property at the moment at which it is in the hands of the trustees.' The respondents in their Case contend that the phrase 'interest in possession' simply denotes an interest which is not in reversion—a present right of present enjoyment.'

So the parties agree that for there to be an interest in possession, there must be a present right to the present enjoyment of something, the Revenue contending that it must be to the enjoyment of the whole or part of the net income of the settled property. It is not the case—and in argument the respondents did not contend that it was—that if it is established that the interest is not in remainder or reversion or contingent, it must be concluded that it is in possession. In the present case Fox J. held ([1979] 2 W.L.R. 353 at 359) that 'There must be a present right of present enjoyment.' This was endorsed by Buckley L.J, and Templeman L.J. in the Court of Appeal ([1979] 3 W.L.R. 112 at pp.117, 120).

We were referred to a considerable number of statutes in which the expression 'interest in possession' is to be found. I did not find them of any assistance in relation to the meaning

---

[23] Templeman L.J. found for the taxpayer on slightly different grounds.

to be given to that phrase in the Finance Act 1975. It suffices to say that I saw nothing in them to indicate or suggest, and I see nothing in the Act itself, to suggest, that the phrase should be given any other meaning than that of a present right of present enjoyment. In my opinion that is its meaning in the Finance Act 1975.

The difficulty lies in its application to the facts of the present case. It is said by both parties to be one of fundamental importance. Whether or not that is the case, all we have to decide is whether on reaching twenty-one, Fiona and her sisters acquired interests in possession in settled property. In other words had they then a present right of present enjoyment of anything?

As to that, there are, it seems to me, two possible conclusions, The first is that the power of appointment under clause 2 not having been exercised, the three sisters on reaching that age acquired interests in possession defeasible should the trustees decide to exercise their power to accumulate income. They were then entitled absolutely to the capital and income of the trust fund in equal shares subject to the exercise of that power. The second is that they never secured an interest in possession for they never acquired on reaching that age the right to the enjoyment of anything, their enjoyment of any income from the trust fund depended on the trustees' decision as to the accumulation of income. They would only have a right to any income from the trust fund if the trustees decided it should not be accumulated or if they failed to agree that it should be or if they delayed a decision on this matter for so long that a decision then to accumulate and withhold income from the sisters would have been unreasonable."

Viscount Dilhorne noted that Fox J. had said that

" . . . the interest of a person who is entitled to the income of property subject only to a power in the trustees to accumulate is in possession . . . it is a present interest, giving a present right to *whatever income is not accumulated*."[24]

Having referred to Lord Reid's above-mentioned statement in *Gartside*, he said that Fiona's right to anything depended on what the trustees did or did not do. Her receipt of income was just as much at the discretion of the trustees as was the receipt of income by the beneficiaries in the *Gartside* case.

The trustees contended that a distinction was to be drawn between a trust to accumulate and a power to accumulate. The existence of a trust to accumulate precluded the existence of an interest in possession, but the existence of a power to accumulate did not do so. Viscount Dilhorne disagreed. No valid distinction was to be drawn in this context between a trust to accumulate and a power to accumulate. In what is the key passage in his judgment he said:

"A distinction has in my opinion to be drawn between the exercise of a power to terminate a present right to present enjoyment and the exercise of a power which prevents a present right of present enjoyment from arising."

Thus, although the exercise by the trustees of their overriding power of appointment might have the effect of terminating any interest in possession enjoyed by Fiona, the existence of such a power did not prevent such an interest from arising. The existence of the trustees' power of accumulation, on the other hand, did prevent her from having a present right of enjoyment. It is to be noted (Viscount Dilhorne may have been misquoted, or may not have said what he meant) that his statement makes much more sense if the relevant distinction is between the exercise of a power to terminate a present right of enjoyment and the *existence* of a power which prevents such a right from arising.

---

[24] Viscount Dilhorne's emphasis.

Lord Keith reached the same conclusion by a slightly different route. He had regard to paras 3(2) and 3(3) of Sch.5 to the Finance Act 1975, provisions which appeared to him:

> " . . . to contemplate that the entitlement to income which is spoken of is an entitlement which, for the time being at least, is absolute. If that is true of the part it must also be true of an interest which extends to the whole of the income of the property. In the present case Fiona certainly did not have an absolute right to any income of the property as it accrued. At that moment her entitlement was qualified by the existence of the trustees' power of accumulation, to the effect that she had no immediate right to anything, but only a right to later payment of such income as the trustees, either by deliberate decision or by inaction for more than a reasonable time, did not cause to be subjected to accumulation. In my opinion a right of that nature is not a present right of present enjoyment . . . "

Lord Keith noted that:

> "The primary contention for the trustees, which was accepted both by Fox J. and by the Court of Appeal, was that each daughter's interest was an interest in possession because it carried the present right to present enjoyment of one third of whatever part of the income of the settled property the trustees decided not to accumulate. The power of accumulation, like the overriding power of appointment, was properly to be regarded as one which might lead to defeasance of the vested right to income but which did not, by its mere existence, deprive the interest of the character of being in possession . . .
>
> It is to be observed that one problem arising from this point of view is that, logically pursued, it must lead to the conclusion that the interest goes in and out of possession according as the trustees refrain from accumulating or decide to do so, and to the further conclusion in the present case that, as the trustees did actually accumulate all the income up to the date of the relevant appointment, the interest was never in possession . . . "

He also said that:

> " . . . Further, I do not consider it to be a satisfactory state of affairs that the question whether a person has an interest in possession should turn on the distinction between the position where his interest derives from his being the object of a discretionary power and that where his interest results in a benefit only failing the exercise of such a power. The practical results as regards the person having the interest are unlikely to be materially different in either case, and I can see no good reason why the distinction should lead to a difference of treatment for purposes of capital transfer tax. The distinction between a trust and a power may be of importance for certain other purposes (see for example *McPhail v Doulton*) but none of the considerations leading to that result appear to me to be applicable here . . . "

The House of Lords: minority views

In his dissenting speech, Lord Russell (with whom Lord Salmon agreed) dealt with **12–26** the first of these latter two objections, as follows:

> "My noble and learned friend Lord Keith of Kinkel, in forming the opposite opinion, suggests that otherwise a conclusion follows that the interest goes in and out of possession according as the trustees refrain from accumulating or decide to do so, and to the further conclusion that as the trustees did actually accumulate all the income up to the date of the 1976 appointment, the interest was never in possession. I do not recall that this proposition was advanced for the Crown, who has already indicated agreed (as did the trustees) that the exercise or non exercise of the powers under cl 3 or cl 21 could make no difference to the outcome. I consider, with respect, that the conclusions stated above do not follow from the

view which I have, supporting the courts below, formed. The fact that an interest in possession is liable to defeasance by *subsequent* exercise of the power does not deny it that description when the benefit of it is thus subsequently taken away."

Furthermore, in his view the proper approach *was* to have regard to the traditional trust law distinction between a trust and a power:

" . . . The crucial question, in my opinion, lies in the well-known distinction between a trust and a power, a distinction recognised by this House in *In re Baden's Deed Trusts* (1971) A.C. 424, and there only regretted as a distinction which might lead in a given case to invalidity of the disposition. As I have already indicated this is clearly a case of a mere power to accumulate, as distinct from a trust to accumulate unless and to the extent to which the trustees exercised a power to pay allowances to the sisters or any of them. The sisters were able to say that as income accrued on the £16,000 they were then entitled to that income, subject to the possibility that the trustees might subsequently divert it from them by a decision to accumulate it."

Administrative vs dispositive powers

12–27   Viscount Dilhorne and Lord Keith both dealt with the point raised in the lower courts concerning the fact that although the administrative powers of trustees also entitled them to divert income from beneficiaries, those powers could hardly be regarded as depriving a beneficiary from having what would otherwise be an interest in possession. Viscount Dilhorne drew a distinction between "dispositive powers" and "administrative powers," and said that the possibility of the latter being exercised to divert income from a beneficiary was to be ignored in deciding whether that beneficiary had an interest in possession. In the past Parliament[25] had:

" . . . distinguished between the administration of a trust and the dispositive powers of trustees and in my opinion there is a very real distinction. A life tenant has an interest in possession but his interest only extends to the net income of the property, that is to say, after deduction from the gross income of expenses etc properly incurred in the management of the trust by the trustees in the exercise of their powers. A dispositive power is a power to dispose of the net income. Sometimes the line between an administrative and a dispositive power may be difficult to draw but that does not mean that there is not a valid distinction. In the present case the Revenue contended that the power given by clause 21 to apply income towards the payment of duties, taxes etc which but for the provisions of the clause would be payable out of or charged upon capital was a dispositive power and that this clause alone would prevent the sisters having an interest in possession on reaching twenty-one. I do not think that this is so. I think this clause falls on the administrative side of the line and merely elucidates the meaning to be given to clause 14."

Lord Keith drew a similar distinction:

"It is necessary to note a further argument for the respondents that Fiona's interest, subject as it was to the trustees' power of accumulation, did not differ on that account from the interest of an ordinary tenant for life, because that power was similar in principle to the ordinary administrative powers of trustees. Such powers might be exercised so as to absorb all the income received by the trustees in, for example, repairs and maintenance of the settled property, so that there was nothing left for the life tenant to enjoy. I am unable to accept this argument. I consider that a distinction is properly to be drawn between powers directed to the preservation of the trust estate for the benefit of life tenant and remainderman

[25] In FA 1969 s.36(6)(d) and in the Perpetuities and Accumulations Act 1964 s.8(1).

532

alike, and discretionary powers the exercise of which is intended to have an effect upon the actual benefits which the beneficiaries as such became entitled, by virtue of their several interests, to receive. It is not all appropriate, in my view, to equiparate a power to execute repairs with a power to distribute income at discretion among a class of beneficiaries, from the point of view of a person who is entitled to receive any income not dealt with under the power. And the considerations applicable in the case of a discretionary power to distribute income apply equally to a discretionary power of accumulation, the exercise of which in effect rolls up income for the benefit of a class of beneficiaries or objects contingently entitled."

Summary

As has been seen, in the *Pearson* case all the judges agreed that a person has an **12–28** interest in possession if he has a present right of present enjoyment. The point about which they disagreed was when a person has such a right. Six of the nine judges who heard the case took the view that the fact that trustees had a discretionary power of accumulation did not prevent a beneficiary from having a present right of present enjoyment. In the event, however, the three judges who felt that a beneficiary did not have a present right of present enjoyment in such circumstances carried the day.

The following points emerge from the *Pearson* case:

(1) *Power of accumulation*: where a beneficiary's right of enjoyment depends on trustees not exercising a power of accumulation that beneficiary does not have an interest in possession.[26]

(2) *Trust to accumulate*: no distinction is to be drawn in this context between a trust to accumulate and a power to accumulate.[27]

(3) *Actual accumulation*: the existence of an interest in possession does not depend on whether trustees have or have not in fact accumulated income.

(4) *Power of appointment or advancement*: the existence of an overriding power of appointment or power of advancement the exercise of which is capable of reducing or eliminating a beneficiary's interest in possession does not prevent that beneficiary from having such an interest, so long as that power cannot be used to affect the destination of income which has already arisen to the trust.

(5) *Defeasance/revocation*: the fact that an interest in possession is defeasible or revocable does not prevent it from being an interest in possession. It remains an interest in possession unless and until an event occurs by virtue of which it is defeated or revoked.

(6) *Traditional distinction*: the traditional distinction between interests in possession and interests in expectancy is not determinative in this context, nor is it exhaustive. A third kind of interest is capable of subsisting in settled property. Fiona's interest is a classic example of this kind of interest: it is not an interest in possession, but, equally, it can hardly be regarded as an interest in expectancy. Such interests are referred to in this book as "intermediate interests"; they are considered at para.11–65.

---

[26] The House of Lords was not assisted by an argument based on the Settled Land Act 1925 s.20(1)(viii) that the right to income from settled land may constitute an interest in possession even though that right is subject to a trust to accumulate.

[27] A power to insure against loss should not preclude the existence of an interest in possession. For the income tax consequences of a provision that insurance premiums shall be paid out of trust income see *Carver v Duncan* [1985] A.C. 1082.

(7) *Administrative versus dispositive powers*: this is a difficult and potentially contentious area. Both Viscount Dilhorne and Lord Keith drew a distinction between administrative and dispositive powers of trustees. Viscount Dilhorne's comment that "sometimes the line between an administrative and a dispositive power may be difficult to draw" is a masterly understatement, especially in view of his rather sparse comments on how that line is to be drawn.

The fineness of the line between the two kinds of powers is illustrated by *Miller v IRC*,[28] a Scottish case. The Scots law of trusts, of course, differs from the law of England and Wales both terminologically and conceptually. Scotland, for example, has no doctrine of concurrent legal and equitable interests; rather, a beneficiary has a right against the trustees to enforce their performance of the trust.

The facts in *Miller* were that the deceased was entitled under a marriage settlement which she made on alimentary liferent (non-assignable life interest) for herself; thereafter the trust fund was held on further alimentary trusts for her husband and children. There then followed a declaration empowering the trustees in:

> "striking the free income or produce of any year . . . , to appropriate such portion of revenue as they may think proper for meeting (1) depreciation of the capital value of any of the assets with regard to which they may think it prudent to provide for depreciation, and (2) for any other reason or purpose which the trustees may in their sole discretion deem to be advisable or necessary; and the trustees shall have power to decide what sums received by them fall to be treated as revenue and what as capital, and what payments made by them fall to be charged to revenue and what to capital."

The liferentrix died in 1982 and the trustees claimed that no tax was then payable on the basis that the effect of the aforesaid declaration was to prevent her from having an interest in possession in the trust fund. The Court of Session held unanimously that the trustees' power to apply income in the manner set out above was administrative, not dispositive, and that therefore the liferentrix did have an interest in possession. Lord Kincraig, giving the leading judgment, referred to Viscount Dilhorne's dicta in *Pearson* to the effect that a dispositive power has the effect of enabling income to be diverted so that it benefits others. The powers here were intended merely to preserve the trust capital for the benefit of the beneficiaries as a whole. In contrast to *Pearson*, the initial gift was the deceased's liferent, the powers being a burden on that gift. Their purpose was to maintain the land and buildings comprised in the trust fund for the benefit of all the beneficiaries, including the liferentrix, not to divert income away from her for the benefit of others. Furthermore, the powers were exercisable only in relation to the gross income of the trust before the free income was ascertained.

In practice, caution must be the advisor's watchword. The matter is normally dealt with by including a clause limiting the exercise of administrative powers so that the existence of those powers will not prevent an interest in possession from subsisting which would subsist if those powers did not exist. But this may give rise to other practical problems. Following the changes introduced by the Finance Act 2006, there is some concern about whether property added by the

---

[28] *Miller v IRC* [1987] S.T.C. 108. For a recent example where these questions were considered see *Trustees of the Fairburn or Douglas Trust v Revenue and Customs Commissioners* [2007] S.T.C. (S.C.D.) 338, where the power to apply income to pay insurance premiums was held not to be inconsistent with the existence of an interest in possession.

settlor to an existing interest in possession settlement will give rise to a new relevant property trust of the added property.[29] The consequence of limiting administrative powers is that trustees may not be able to use income to maintain capital assets of the trust (or to pay capital expenses such as capital gains tax or inheritance tax liabilities out of income). Prior to the changes introduced by the Finance Act 2006, this practical problem could be resolved by the settlor making payments to discharge expenditure for capital preservation which, if not exempt, would constitute PETs, and could therefore fall out of charge to IHT. Post-Finance Act 2006, caution should be exercised where the settlor (or any person) transfers assets to trustees—as these will be immediately chargeable if the Revenue's analysis is correct: any payment should, where possible, be one to which, for example, the exemption in s.21 (normal expenditure out of income) applies.

(8) *Anomalies*: both sides in *Pearson* said that the case put forward by the other side gave rise to various anomalies and injustices. Neither the House of Lords nor the Court of Appeal (where Buckley L.J. said that the ingenuity of counsel could almost always produce possible anomalies in either direction) found this helpful. One anomaly is worth noting. Fox J. noted that if the existence of the trustees' power of accumulation prevented Fiona from having an interest in possession then difficulties could arise in circumstances where property was held on trust for a childless person if the trustees had power to apply income for his children[30]: because the birth of his first child would determine his interest in possession.[31] It may be, however, that this is incorrect. Trustees have a "reasonable time"[32] to decide how to apply income which they have received, and it appears that they may exercise their discretion in favour of persons not yet born when that income arose. On this basis the person just mentioned would not have an interest in possession to begin with, because the trustees would be entitled to retain income for a period in case a child was born. If this approach is correct, the difficulties foreseen by Fox J. disappear.[33]

(9) *Free loans*: here there are two questions. First, will the existence of a power enabling trustees to loan trust property interest-free or at a reduced rate of interest preclude the existence of an interest in possession? Secondly, if the existence of such power does not preclude the existence of an interest in possession, will the exercise of such a power destroy an interest in possession? Although the exercise of a power to loan trust property interest-free may reduce or eliminate trust income it will not divert from a beneficiary income which may otherwise be his. Accordingly, the mere existence of such a power should not preclude the existence of an interest in possession. The position where such a power is exercised appears to vary according to whether the loan is of money or of property other than money.

When trustees lend money the money becomes the property of the borrower and thus ceases to be settled property, with the result that, by definition, no

---

[29] See para.12–17.

[30] So long as it is possible that he might have a child. No difficulties would arise if when the settlement was made A was incapable of having a child, but a problem would arise if he was capable of having a child when the settlement was made but, subsequently became incapable of having a child, because at that stage he would become entitled to an interest in possession in the property.

[31] If the child died there would be a further charge on the conversion of the discretionary trust back into an interest in possession trust.

[32] Some trust deeds specify a definite period in which case that is the appropriate period for the trustees to consider their position.

[33] See para.12–29.

535

interest in possession can subsist in it. The sums leaving the trust fund are replaced by a debt which forms part of the corpus of the trust fund together with the other trust assets.[34] The effect of such a loan is thus only to change the nature of the property in which the interest in possession subsists. Before the loan the interest subsists in property which yields income; after the loan the interest subsists in property which does not. The position is thus similar to that where trustees switch investments, and in the authors' view the making of an interest-free loan accordingly should not destroy an interest in possession. There may, however, be other consequences. The making of the loan will prima facie give rise to a charge under s.52(3) on the difference between the sum lent and the market value of the debt. The position will thus depend on the terms of the loan. If the arrangements are such that immediate repayment is virtually certain the trust fund will have sustained little, if any, diminution in value, and no charge should arise. To the extent that immediate repayment is not certain there will in theory be a charge, but provided repayment will take place within a reasonable period of time the amount brought into charge should be relatively small in comparison to the sum lent. If repayment within a reasonable time is unlikely, there may be a substantial charge.

The position where property other than money is lent is more difficult. It may be that such a loan creates an interest in possession in the borrower; this possibility is discussed at para.15–07. Even where the loan stops short of doing this, it still may result in the destruction of the subsisting interest in possession on the basis that even though the loan has not given the borrower effective enjoyment of the property it has taken that enjoyment away from the person who had the interest in possession in it. Accordingly, such loans must be approached with extreme caution.

Default entitlement

12–29   Circumstances may arise in which, e.g. property is held on discretionary trusts; the trustees have no power to accumulate income; and there is only one living member of the discretionary class in existence, with the result that the trustees must pay the trust income to that beneficiary. Does this mean that he has an interest in possession in the trust income? This question arose in *Re Trafford's Settlement*[35] in which Peter Gibson J. held, on the basis that the discretionary class was an open one, that the beneficiary did not have an interest in possession. The reason was that the entitlement of the beneficiary was only that the trustees should consider whether to pay the income to him. While the trustees were considering his claim another beneficiary might be born. That being the case, the sole existing beneficiary had no entitlement to the income as it arose, because the trustees might decide to pay it to a new beneficiary born while they were considering the existing beneficiary's claim to it. Where, on the other hand, the discretionary class was closed, then the last member of the class would have an interest in possession in the trust income. However, since the changes to the taxation of trusts introduced by the Finance Act 2006, a switch on or after March 22, 2006 from a

---

[34] See paras 15–05–15–08.
[35] *Re Trafford's Settlement* [1984] S.T.C. 236. And see *Re Locker's Settlement* [1977] 1 W.L.R. 1323; [1978] 1 All E.R. 216 and *Re Weir's Settlement* [1970] 1 All E.R. 297.

discretionary trust to an interest in possession trust will not be an occasion which gives rise to an exit charge: the trust will remain within the relevant property regime.

Standing orders

It may be that trustees of a discretionary trust anticipate that each year they will distribute the income to the same beneficiary and that they accordingly resolve that the trust income shall be paid direct to that beneficiary by a standing order on the trustees' bank account. HMRC argued in *Swales v IRC*[36] that such a situation was analogous to that which obtained in *Sansom v Peay*,[37] and that the beneficiary therefore had an interest in possession. Nicholls J., however, considered that no assistance was to be derived from *Sansom v Peay*, which was concerned with the construction of different statutory provisions. The correct analysis was that the standing order was no more than a convenient administrative arrangement for the trustees who, as a matter of general trust law, had no ability to fetter the exercise by them in the future of their discretion. The beneficiary had no more right than any other discretionary object to the trust income and this was so even though in practice the trustees would be unlikely to revoke the standing order without giving the beneficiary reasonable notice.

12–30

The *Lloyds Private Banking* case

In *Lloyds Private Banking v IRC*[38] the deceased left the half share in the matrimonial home owned with her husband on the following terms:

12–31

> "3(1) While my Husband Frederick Arthur Evans remains alive and desires to reside in the property and keeps the same in good repair and insured comprehensively to its full value with Insurers approved by my Trustee and pays and indemnifies my Trustee against all rates taxes and other outgoings in respect of the property my Trustee shall not make any objection to such residence and shall not disturb or restrict it in any way and shall not take any steps to enforce the trust for sale on which the property is held or to realise my share thereto or to obtain any rent or profit from the property.
>
> (2) On the death of my said Husband Frederick Arthur Evans I devise and bequeath the said property to my Daughter Kathleen Roberts-Hindle absolutely."

HMRC argued that Mr Evans had been given an interest in possession in the deceased's share. If this was correct, it meant that on Mrs Evans's death her IHT nil rate band was largely unused and on the husband's death IHT was chargeable on the entire property. The Special Commissioner[39] rejected this argument on the basis that the will did not create a settlement. Rather, there had been an absolute gift of the share to the daughter, subject only to a direction to the trustee to postpone sale.

On appeal, Lightman J. found for HMRC, noting that:

> "In consequence, if Lloyds is correct and cl 3(1) is not dispositive, the daughter is solely beneficially entitled and as such was, as soon as Mrs Evans died, entitled to bring an end to the trust, to require that the half-share be vested in her and to treat as totally ineffective the (in those circumstances) purely administrative provisions of cl 3(1). It would appear

[36] *Swales v IRC* [1984] S.T.C. 413.
[37] *Sansom v Peay* [1976] S.T.C. 494; see paras 15–07 and 12–35 and following.
[38] *Lloyds Private Banking v IRC* [1998] S.T.C. 559.
[39] *Lloyds Private Banking v IRC* [1997] S.T.C. (S.C.D.) 259.

improbable that this can have been the intention of Mrs Evans, involving as it does writing out of the will as devoid of legal effect elaborate directions in the will on their face designed to secure that Mr Evans could continue to occupy the property as his home for the rest of his life."[40]

Lightman J. took the view that the position laid down in cases such as *Bull v Bull*[41] was that a tenant in common under a trust for sale was entitled to occupy the entirety of the property and was not entitled to exclude any other tenant in common. Any co-owner could apply to the court for sale of the property. As a result, Mr Evans's occupation would have been precarious. He continued:

> "The regime designed by cl 3(1) is quite different. So long as Mr Evans fulfils the conditions there set out he is for the rest of his life elevated to the status of sole occupier and he is free from any possibility of a claim to pay for the right to exclude the daughter from occupation and from any risk of the daughter seeking an order for sale. A price is to be paid for these advantages. He is required as a condition of receiving these benefits so long as he receives them to pay all the outgoings (and this includes the insurance premiums). Mr Evans (as anticipated by Mrs Evans) took advantage of the provision."[42]

The result was that the will conferred upon Mr Evans a life interest in the half-share. His rights as tenant in common were not enough to exclude occupation for the rest of his life; to achieve that he also needed the rights conferred by the will. The fact that Mr Evans's right to occupy was "dressed up" as a set of administrative provisions was neither here nor there.

It is understood that HMRC take the view that a similar result will occur where the will provides that a sale of the property depends on the co-owner's consent, but it is thought that the position may not be analogous. Since the *Lloyds Private Banking* case the Trusts of Land and Appointment of Trustees Act 1996 has come into effect. Under s.13(7) a beneficiary in possession is given enhanced rights of occupation. In particular, trustees cannot impose conditions on his occupation which might have the effect of causing him to cease to occupy the property. As a result, testators may now feel that a surviving spouse has adequate protection without the need to include provisions like those in cl.3(1) in the *Lloyds Private Banking* case. It is not thought that s.13(7) of the Trusts of Land and Appointment of Trustees Act 1996 of itself gives the occupying beneficiary an interest in possession of IHT purposes.[43]

The *Walden* case

12–32   The opposite conclusion was reached in *Judge (personal representative of Walden Deceased) v RCC*,[44] where the personal representatives of Mrs Walden argued that she had not acquired an interest in possession in her husband's share of the matrimonial home. The Special Commissioner agreed.

Mr Walden had died in January 2000, leaving his residuary estate on trust for his wife and other members of his family. Clause 3 of his will provided as follows:

> "I GIVE free of tax and of any monies secured thereon by way of legal charge or otherwise to my Trustees ALL THAT my interest in the property known as and situate at 30

[40] *Lloyds Private Banking v IRC* [1998] S.T.C. 559 at 564.
[41] *Bull v Bull* [1955] 1 Q.B. 234.
[42] *Lloyds Private Banking v IRC* [1998] S.T.C. 559 at 564.
[43] See para.12–34.
[44] *Judge (personal representative of Walden Deceased) v RCC* [2005] S.T.C. (S.C.D.) 863.

Perrymead Street London SW6 OR the property in which I am at my death ordinarily resident or in which I have then last been ordinarily resident UPON TRUST with the consent in writing of my Wife during her lifetime to sell the same with full power to postpone sale for so long as they shall in their absolute discretion think fit and to hold the net proceeds of sale and other monies applicable as capital and the net rent and profits until upon the trusts and with and subject to the powers and provisions of my Residuary Fund (as hereinafter defined) as an accretion thereto AND I DECLARE my Trustees during the lifetime of my Wife to permit her to have the use and enjoyment of the said property for such period or periods as they shall in their absolute discretion think fit pending postponement of sale she paying the rates taxes and other outgoings and keeping the same in good repair and insured against fire to the full value thereof in some office of repute nominated by my Trustees in the names of my Trustees."

After Mr Walden's death, his trustees wrote to Mrs Walden in the following terms:

"I would confirm that under clause 3 of your late husband's will, 30 Perrymead Street is the sole asset of a Life Interest Trust and you will enjoy the occupancy of the property during your lifetime . . . you will be responsible for the actual payment of the premiums [for buildings insurance cover] as well as all the household bills etc including council tax.
. . .

Under Clause 4 of the will the residue of the estate is to be held on a discretionary trust for the benefit of yourself, your nephew and niece and also their children. As trustees we have the responsibility of exercising our discretionary powers under the terms of the will and also under trust law when considering making payment of capital and income to the discretionary beneficiaries. . . .

This discretionary trust is slightly different in as much that you, as the surviving spouse, is not nominated as the 'primary beneficiary'. . ."

The trustees completed Revenue account for inheritance tax on the basis that Mrs Walden had acquired an interest in possession in the property and Mrs Walden continued to reside there until her death. However, on her death—intestate—her personal representatives were advised that cl.3 of the will had created a discretionary trust and not an interest in possession in the property. HMRC issued a notice of determination stating that Mrs Walden had acquired an interest in possession in the property. Mrs Walden's personal representatives appealed, contending that the wording of cl.3 indicated that that Mrs Walden's occupation was at the discretion of the trustees; that cl.3 was not a direction to them; and that because Mrs Walden had no enforceable right to occupation, she had no interest in possession. HMRC contended, inter alia, that, if the appellants were right that cl.3 established a discretionary trust, then the trustee would have had to pay inheritance tax on the death of Mr Walden and that might have forced a sale of the property without the consent of Mrs Walden. It was unlikely that Mr Walden would have wished that the property would have to be sold to pay inheritance tax and that it was for that reason that the house was dealt with separately from the residue.

The Special Commissioner acknowledged that a right of occupation can be an interest in possession but that Mrs Walden had to have a right as against the trustees, in order for her to have obtained an interest in possession in the property. She would not have such right if the trustees had a discretion about whether or not to permit occupation. Acknowledging that *Lloyds Private Banking* makes it clear that a proper construction of the will is crucial to whether an interest in possession has been created, the Special Commissioner proceeded to construe the will. Although the drafting of cl.3 was defective, causing serious problems of construction, it was held that the final words dealing with occupation were clear and unambiguous. The words "for such period or periods as they shall in their absolute discretion think fit" did not give Mrs Walden a right to occupy the property: they gave the trustees a discretion as to whether to permit occupation. This was supported by the remaining language of cl.3.

539

This case is important because it confirms that occupation does not of itself give rise to an interest in possession. However, it does not provide an answer to the question of whether the exercise by trustees of the discretion to permit occupation will create an interest in possession: it was not argued by HMRC that the letter by the Trustees to Mrs Walden had the effect of giving her an interest in possession. In the authors' view, the letter in *Walden* could not in any event have had this effect, because it does not evidence the exercise by the Trustees of their discretion to permit occupation: it evidences their view that an interest in possession had already been created by Mr Walden's will.

12–33 But when an interest in possession arises in consequence of occupation of a matrimonial home is an important question in the context of debt or charge schemes[45] designed to utilise the nil-rate band of the first spouse or civil partner to die. Although the introduction of the transferable nil-rate band[46] reduces the need to enter into such schemes—there may still be good reasons to enter into them, for example, where the surviving spouse is likely to remarry as this may result in wasting the deceased spouse's unused nil-rate band if all his estate is left to his spouse. If the intention is to avoid the creation of an immediate post-death interest, then the trustees should not resolve or in any way indicate that they are permitting the surviving spouse to occupy the property,

HMRC have been known to argue that occupation by the surviving spouse of the matrimonial home in the following circumstances gives rise to an interest in possession: namely where—say—a half share of the matrimonial home is left by a spouse on discretionary trusts for a class of beneficiaries including the surviving spouse, and the surviving spouse continues to reside in the property in which she owns the other half share. This approach was followed even where the trustees have not purported to exercise their discretion to allow occupation of the deceased's half share. More recently, HMRC appear to have agreed that this cannot be the correct analysis. In the authors' view, an interest in possession cannot arise in these circumstances simply by virtue of the surviving spouse's occupation, because:

(1) even before the enactment of the Trusts of Land and Appointment of Trustees Act 1996 (see below), it was well established that a tenant in common has, by virtue of his undivided share in the property, a right to occupy the whole of the property; under that Act, the right of a tenant in common to occupy land is made express by virtue of s.12. Where the trustees have not exercised their discretion to permit the surviving spouse to occupy (what is now) their share of the property, it is difficult to see how the surviving spouse could be said to be occupying the property by virtue of a right derived from the trustees;

(2) if it is a trust to which the Trusts of Land and Appointment of Trustees Act 1996 applies, so that the persons with interests in the property are the two tenants in common, namely the surviving spouse and the trustees, it seems unlikely that a court would be persuaded to order the sale of the property or to force the payment of rent (ss.12 to 15 of that Act). In such circumstances, it is difficult to see how the surviving spouse's occupation can be analysed as a right of occupation derived from trustees.

Note that where the surviving spouse is a tenant in common, there may be CGT consequences arising from the fact that the deceased's share of the house now held by trustees is not occupied by the surviving spouse within the requirements of s.225 of the

---

[45] Described at paras 7–139 and 7–140.
[46] See paras 4–06 and following.

540

1992 Act, as interpreted in *Sansom v Peay*,[47] because the surviving spouse's occupation, first, is not of the trustees' half share but her own share and, second, is not "under the terms of the trust". In such circumstances, the availability of principal residence relief on gains realised on the sale by the trustees of their half share may be in doubt.

For the position where trustees *have* exercised a power to allow occupation, see paras 12–37 and following. For an example where the Special Commissioner held that an interest in possession in part of the property had arisen, see *Woodhall v IRC*,[48] discussed at para.12–42.

The Trusts of Land and Appointment of Trustees Act 1996

The possible impact of the Trusts of Land and Appointment of Trustees Act 1996 ("the 1996 Act") in relation to interests in possession is uncertain and controversial. HMRC have been asked for their views as to its effect in a variety of circumstances and have responded with (understandably) somewhat guarded answers.[49] The IHT impact of the 1996 Act has been judicially considered in *IRC v Eversden*,[50] but not in a way that gives any real guidance. Litigation in this area seems inevitable.   **12–34**

The 1996 Act, which came into force on January 1, 1997, applies to all trusts of land in England and Wales, including ones created before it came into force, apart from settlements already in existence before then which then contained land and were subject to the Settled Land Act 1925. Problems arise because of two provisions in the 1996 Act. First, s.12 confers on any "beneficiary who is beneficially entitled to an interest in possession[51] in land subject to a trust of land" a right of occupation of the land if certain conditions are satisfied, notably that the land should be available and suitable for occupation by the beneficiary. Secondly, where two or more beneficiaries have a right of occupation of the same land s.13 gives the trustees power to exclude or restrict the rights of occupation of one or more (but not all) of those beneficiaries, and to impose reasonable conditions on those beneficiaries whose rights are not so excluded or restricted, e.g. paying compensation to, or foregoing benefits under the trusts in favour of, those beneficiaries whose rights are so excluded or restricted.

Assume that under the terms of a settlement X and Y each have an interest in possession in land in circumstances such that ss.12 and 13 apply. The trustees exercise their s.13 power to allow X to occupy the land and to exclude Y from occupation. Has this exercise terminated Y's interest in possession and extended X's interest in possession to an interest in possession in the whole of the land? There is a real risk that this is the case. Where, on the other hand, the trustees do nothing and Y simply allows X to occupy the whole of the land, Y's interest would arguably be unaffected because he would retain his right to enjoy the land even though he chose for the time being to forego that enjoyment.[52]

Normally trustees would not exercise their s.13 power without also compensating Y. This they could do in a number of ways. If the trust fund also contained other assets

---

[47] *Sansom v Peay* [1976] S.T.C. 494.

[48] *Woodhall v IRC* [2000] S.T.C. (S.C.D.) 558.

[49] See *The Tax Journal*, February 6, 1997, p.19.

[50] *Eversden v IRC* [2002] S.T.C. 1109; see paras 7–35 and following. See also *Arkwright and Sellers v IRC* [2004] S.T.C. (SCD) 392, discussed at paras 25–55 and 25–65, for the impact of the 1996 Act in the context of valuation.

[51] "Interest in possession" in the 1996 Act does not necessarily have the same meaning as it does for IHT purposes.

[52] See *Woodhall v IRC* [2000] S.T.C. (S.C.D.) 558, discussed at para.12–42.

the income of which was sufficient to compensate Y, they might require X to forego the income from those investments. Or, if there were no such assets or the income from them was insufficient compensation, they might require X to pay Y an appropriate rent.

If Y is given an entitlement to the income from other assets, it is in the authors' view difficult to conclude otherwise than that he has acquired an interest in possession in those assets and that X's interest in those assets has come to an end. So long as the value of those assets is the same as the value of the land at the time the trustees exercise their s.13 power, neither X nor Y should make a transfer of value, because what has effectively happened is that the trustees have appropriated to their interests property of equal value. This appears to be HMRC's view so long as the arrangements can properly be viewed as purely administrative. Where, on the other hand, the trustees exercise their power but Y consents to or acquiesces in not being fully compensated, all or a part of his interest may come to an end. Even if the fact that the property in which X and Y's respective interests subsist has changed does not give rise to any immediate charge to IHT (for example, because the interest in possession is a pre-March 22, 2006 interest, a transitional serial interest or an immediate post-death interest),[53] it may be relevant in future, especially on their death, both in relation to IHT and CGT. This is one reason why litigation appears inevitable.

The 1996 Act caused particular problems where accumulation and maintenance trusts were concerned. Assume that land was held on such trusts for three beneficiaries in circumstances where the 1996 Act applied and that the eldest beneficiary attained an interest in possession in the land. Since he alone had an interest in possession, he alone had a right of occupation. Did he thereby have an interest in possession in whole of the land until the next beneficiary acquired an interest in possession? How could the trustees use their s.13 power to require him to compensate the other two beneficiaries given the fact that those beneficiaries were not at that stage entitled to any income and may have had defeasible shares in the trust fund (within the limits imposed by s.71) and what was the effect of their doing so?

Another area of difficulty concerns the common case where H and W own a house as tenants in common in equal shares and H dies, leaving his son a life interest in the house. Under the 1996 Act the trustees of the will trust, not the son, have an interest in possession in the house for purposes of the 1996 Act, with the result that W has the sole s.12 right of occupation.[54] Does this mean she has an interest in possession in the whole of the property, i.e. an immediate post-death interest?[55] If it does, how is the position affected if W is required under s.13 to pay the trustees of the will trust compensation?

One way of avoiding these problems may be expressly or by implication to exclude the operation of ss.12 and 13 in relation to the trust in question, though this is far from a complete answer. First, there is doubt as to whether express exclusion is possible. Secondly, where the purpose of the trust is to allow occupation of the land, exclusion by implication will not be possible.

Use or enjoyment of property generally: free loans

12–35   A difficult issue is whether a person who uses or enjoys property thereby acquires an interest in possession in it. For convenience in the following discussion such a

---

[53] See paras 11–51 and following.
[54] TLATA 1996 s.22(1) and (2).
[55] See paras 11–51 and following.

person will be regarded as having the benefit of a "free loan" and in the following discussion "free loan" means a loan repayable on demand and interest-free.

It is to be noted that under s.101 the participators are in certain circumstances deemed to be beneficially entitled to the company's interest in possession, namely where the company's interest is a pre-March 22, 2006 interest in possession, an immediate post-death interest, or a transitional serial interest.[56] In those circumstances although the legislation does not say so expressly, the corollary of this appears to be that the company is not beneficially entitled to the interest, so that in valuing the shares in the company the company's entitlement to the interest in possession is ignored.[57]

HMRC have at times suggested that such a loan creates an interest in possession, with the result that in relation to loans made pre-March 22, 2006, a charge to tax would have been imposed on the value of the property lent, not merely on the amount (often much smaller) by which the value of the trust fund was diminished by the loan.[58] In the authors' view, the correct position is as follows:

(1) that a loan of property other than money, e.g. where trustees allow a beneficiary to occupy a house, may, pre-March 22, 2006, have given rise to a charge to tax on the value of the property lent;

(2) but that a loan of money did not do so and would instead have given rise to a charge on only the amount by which the loan diminished the value of the trust fund.

The point is an important one. If the authors' view is correct an interest-free loan was and remains a relatively painless way of making funds available to a beneficiary.[59]

The authors' view is based on the fact that in law a distinction must be drawn between a loan of money and a loan of property other than money. Where money is lent, the money lent becomes the property of the borrower. Where, on the other hand, property other than money is lent that property continues to be owned by the lender. Thus, if a person lends a bicycle to a friend, he expects and is entitled to have that same bicycle returned to him; but if he lends his friend a five pound note, he does not expect to get the same five pound note back, nor is he entitled to do so. The significance of this is as follows.

Loans of money

Where trustees lend money to a beneficiary the money becomes the property of the **12–36** beneficiary and thus ceases to be settled property, with the result that, by definition, no interest in possession can subsist in it. The debt owed to the trustees replaces the money lent as a trust asset and falls to be held on whatever trusts subsisted in relation to the money.

Loans of other property

As was mentioned above, where property other than money is lent the property **12–37** remains that of the lender and thus continues to be settled property. The question of

---

[56] IHTA s.101(1) and (1A). For the definition of immediate post-death interest see paras 11–51 and following. For the definition of transitional serial interest, see paras 11–50 and following.
[57] See *Powell-Cotton v IRC* [1992] S.T.C. 625, discussed at para.2–102.
[58] See also paras 15–05–15–07.
[59] See also paras 11–19–11–20.

whether or not the borrower acquires an interest in possession in the property lent to him and of which he has the use and enjoyment is extremely difficult.

On the one hand, it is arguable that the position depends on the ability of the trustees to recover the asset lent. On this view, if the nature of the property and circumstances of the loan are such that the trustees can promptly and without difficulty recover the property, the loan should not create an interest in possession, because in such circumstances the borrower's position is so precarious that he cannot be said to have any real right to enjoy the property.[60] On the other hand, it is arguable that in such circumstances the borrower has an interest in possession, albeit one which can be revoked at any moment. The authors consider that although making a free loan may be analogous to appointing a revocable interest the two are not equivalent—in the latter case revocation is a mere possibility, while in the case of a loan it is expected. It is also arguable that in the case of a conventional appointment there is a definite point in time at which it can be said that the beneficiary is entitled as of right to the enjoyment of the appointed property, while in the case of a free loan expressed to be repayable on demand the borrower is not in quite the same position. The authors accordingly incline toward the view that a free loan does not create an interest in possession provided the trustees have the requisite powers of recovery.

A good example of the difficulties that can arise in practice occurs where trustees exercise a power to permit a beneficiary to occupy a dwelling-house. It will be instructive to consider HMRC's view. Initially HMRC took the view that the exercise by trustees of a power to permit a beneficiary to occupy a dwelling-house would not result in his becoming entitled to an interest in possession in the house. Following *Sansom v Peay*[61] HMRC changed their position and regarded such a beneficiary as having an interest in possession.[62] It was, of course, understandable that HMRC should be reluctant to see beneficiaries having the best of both worlds for CGT and CTT purposes. Nevertheless, *Sansom v Peay* does not appear to determine the position, since that decision was concerned with whether a beneficiary was "entitled to occupy" the house in question "under the terms of the settlement", not with whether he had an interest in possession in that house.

12–38   On August 15, 1979, HMRC issued the following Statement of Practice (SP10/79):

> **"Power for trustees to allow a beneficiary to occupy a dwelling-house.**
>
> Many wills and settlements contain a clause empowering the trustees to permit a beneficiary to occupy a dwelling-house which forms part of the trust property on such terms as they think fit. The Inland Revenue do not regard the existence of such power as excluding any interest in possession in the property.
>
> Where there is no interest in possession in the property in question the Inland Revenue do not regard the exercise of the power as creating one if the effect is merely to allow non-exclusive occupation or to create a contractual tenancy for full consideration. The Inland Revenue also take the view that no interest in possession arises on the creation of a lease for a term or a periodic tenancy for less than full consideration, though this will normally give rise to a charge for tax under F.A. 1975, Sch.5, para.6(3). On the other hand, if the power is drawn in terms wide enough to cover the creation of an exclusive or joint right of residence, albeit revocable, for a definite or indefinite period, and is exercised with the intention of providing a particular beneficiary with a permanent home, the Revenue will

---

[60] If the trustees do not have requisite powers of recovery it is more likely that the borrower will have acquired an interest in possession in the property lent since in such a case it is he who has the effective enjoyment of the asset.

[61] *Sansom v Peay* [1976] 1 W.L.R. 1073; [1976] S.T.C. 494.

[62] See paras 12–31 and following for the analysis where trustees have not exercised a power to allow occupation.

normally regard the exercise of the power as creating an interest in possession. And if the trustees in exercise of their powers grant a lease for life for less than full consideration, this will also be regarded as creating an interest in possession in view of Sch.5, paras 1(3) and 3(6).[63]

A similar view will be taken where the power is exercised over property in which another beneficiary had an interest in possession up to the time of the exercise."

This is not an easy statement to understand. The statement and its implications acquired increased significance in light of the enactment of Sch.20 to the Finance Act 2006, and in particular, where trustees wanted to secure transitional relief in the form of appointments of s.49C transitional serial interests.[64] Further guidance on SP10/79 came in the form of HMRC's response to questions raised by the CIOT and STEP in September 2007. HMRC's response is contained in a letter dated November 20, 2007.[65]

SP10/79 contains a number of assertions which, together with HMRC's clarification in November 2007 and the authors' views, may be summarised as follows:

1. *Existence of a power*: the mere existence of a power to allow a beneficiary to occupy a dwelling-house does not exclude any interest in possession in the property. Agreed.
2. *Leases:* there are three assertions:

(a) the grant of a lease for a term or a periodic tenancy for less than full consideration will not create an interest in possession;
(b) the grant of such a lease will normally give rise to a charge under para.6(3) of Sch.5 to the Finance Act 1975, now s.65(1)(b);
(c) the grant of a lease for life for less than full consideration will create an interest in possession under paras 1(3) and 3(6) of Sch.5 to the Finance Act 1975, now ss.43(3) and 50(6).

The authors agree with these assertions but would make the following comments:

(1) The presence or absence of full consideration where a lease is granted is relevant to the existence of an interest in possession only where a lease for life within the meaning of s.43(3) is concerned. All that matters where other leases are concerned is that a lease exists.
(2) Where a lease (other than a lease for life granted for less than full consideration) exists, the beneficiary/lessee is entitled to the use and enjoyment of property, i.e. the lease, which he owns outright, and which is therefore not settled property. The freehold remains settled property, encumbered now by the lease, but the beneficiary/lessee does not have an interest in possession in it.

3. *Contractual tenancies:* discretionary trustees will not create an interest in possession if they exercise a power to create a contractual tenancy for full consideration. The authors agree with this statement, but would again like to add a few comments. First, there is in law no distinction between a "lease" and a "contractual tenancy". The latter term is simply a colloquial term used to describe a lease which is granted without a

---

[63] Now IHTA 1984 s.49(1) and s.170 respectively.

[64] For the definition of a s.49C transitional serial interest, see para.11–56. Where a pre-March 22, 2006 interest in possession for A subsisted in property, transitional relief applied in that the first appointment during the period between March 22, 2006 and October 5, 2008 of an interest in possession in respect of the same property continued to be treated as a qualifying interest in possession. Where the new interest in possession, i.e. the transitional serial interest was not a new appointment to A, this was treated as a PET (and see paras 12–05 and following).

[65] This document can be accessed at *http://www.step.org/attach.pl/1979/3956/874668_1(PCL2).pdf.*

deed (as may be done where a lease for less than three years is granted). A contractual tenancy is thus simply a species of lease. The position where trustees grant a contractual tenancy is therefore exactly the same as where trustees grant a lease. In particular, the presence or absence of full consideration is irrelevant in determining whether the grant of the lease has created an interest in possession.

4. *Non-exclusive occupation:* discretionary trustees will not create an interest in possession if they exercise a power to allow a beneficiary to occupy a dwelling-house on terms such that his occupation is not exclusive. The authors agree. What is apparently envisaged here is that the trustees allow a beneficiary to occupy the house without giving him a lease as such. In such a case the beneficiary does not have a lease, but he may have a tenancy. What matters in such a case is whether the beneficiary has the right to exclusive possession of the premises. In particular, does he have the right to exclude the landlord? If he does, then normally he is a tenant and as such his enjoyment of the premises is sufficient to give him an interest in possession. If on the other hand, he does not have the right to exclusive occupation, he will not normally have a tenancy as a matter of general law and will consequently not be regarded as having an interest in possession.

5. *Tenancy:* the exercise by trustees of a power wide enough to cover the creation of an exclusive or a joint right of residence, albeit revocable, for a definite or indefinite period will "normally" be regarded as creating an interest in possession if the trustees intend to provide a particular beneficiary with a permanent home. The authors agree with this statement. The fourth edition of this book explains the authors' view that the vital factor is whether or not the beneficiary is given exclusive occupation. If he is, then, as a tenant, he will have effective enjoyment of the premises and accordingly will have an interest in possession in them. The authors were unable to see how the trustees' intention as such can be relevant, and noted that in the case of an irrevocable licence the licensee is entitled to reasonable notice—possibly of considerable duration—before he can be legally evicted (see *Vaughan v Vaughan*).[66] This, it was suggested, may be what HMRC had in mind, i.e. if the trustees' intention is to give the beneficiary a permanent home, the terms of his occupation may be such as to entitle him to notice sufficient to give him effective enjoyment of the property. HMRC were specifically asked to explain the use of the word "normally" in SP10/79 by STEP and the CIOT, as follows:

> "In what circumstances would HMRC *not* regard the exercise of the power by trustees which gives a beneficiary an exclusive right of occupation as *not* creating an interest in possession? [*Walden*] was a case where the trustees never positively exercised their powers because they did not know that she had, or they thought that she already had, an interest in possession."

HMRC's response was not inconsistent with the suggestion put forward by the authors. They responded as follows:

> "We imagine the instances where we would not regard the exercise of the power by trustees to give an exclusive right of occupation as creating an interest in possession would be rare. But such instances might be where there was no evidence of an intention by the trustees to provide a particular beneficiary with a permanent home or where significant doubt about the intentions of the trustees existed."

HMRC also agreed with the following statement put forward by STEP and the CIOT:

---

[66] *Vaughan v Vaughan* [1953] 1 Q.B. 762.

"It seems that the question of whether an interest in possession has been conferred comes down to whether the trustees have indeed exercised their powers in this way intending to confer exclusive occupation. While HMRC cannot give a definitive answer on a particular case without knowing the facts of that case, if there is evidence that the trustees have indeed *knowingly* exercised their powers so as to give a beneficiary exclusive occupation then we assume that, as a matter of principle, HMRC would consider an interest in possession has been created and, on the same basis, that the trustees could reasonably form a view themselves on this point if the relevant facts justified this conclusion."

6. *Subsisting interest in possession:* the position will be similar where the power is exercised over property in which another beneficiary had an interest in possession up to the time of the exercise. In the authors' view the position is more complicated. To begin with, where trustees loan property in which there is a subsisting interest in possession two questions arise. First, does the loan affect the existing interest in possession? Secondly, does the loan give the borrower an interest in possession in the property lent? Clearly, if the answer to the second question is in the affirmative, then so necessarily is the answer to the first, i.e. if the loan gives the borrower an interest in possession, then the subsisting interest will necessarily have come to an end. If this is the case the position is covered by the practice statement. It may be, however, that the loan destroys the existing interest while stopping short of giving the borrower an interest in possession.

The net effect of SP10/79 appears to be that no difficulties will arise where trustees **12–39** grant a lease (otherwise than for life) to a beneficiary or allow a beneficiary to occupy a dwelling-house on a non-exclusive basis. Furthermore, it is thought that in practice trustees can allow a beneficiary to occupy a house on an occasional basis, e.g. during holidays, even though this occupation may be exclusive, without creating an interest in possession; more permanent occupation may cause problems. Trustees wishing to allow a beneficiary to occupy a house on a more permanent basis might consider granting him a monthly tenancy at a nominal rent. This will have the same effect from a conceptual standpoint as a loan of money, i.e. instead of being entitled to the use and enjoyment of the house the beneficiary will be entitled to the use and enjoyment of the lease, which he owns and which, as was noted above, is therefore not settled property. So long as the annual rent is less than two-thirds of the 1973 rateable value of the house, the beneficiary will have no security of tenure.[67] That being the case, the grant of the tenancy will not depreciate the value of the trust property in any substantive way, and therefore no significant charge to IHT will arise.[68] The only disadvantage in adopting this approach will be that no CGT principal residence relief will be available.

SP10/79 and replacement property

A further issue that has been clarified by the above-mentioned correspondence **12–40** between STEP and the CIOT and HMRC, is the question of whether a beneficiary who acquires an interest in possession in line with SP10/79 merely acquires a present right of occupation, i.e. whether such a beneficiary acquires the right to occupy that particular property or whether he has acquired the right to occupy any house for the time being held by the trustees. The relevant parts of the exchange of views state as follows:

[67] Rent Act 1977 s.5.
[68] The authors are indebted to William Goodhart, Q.C. for this suggestion.

"In our view, and we understand that this is the view that HMRC have taken in practice in the past, the beneficiary acquires an interest in possession in the property when it is first occupied, and that interest continues even though the property is sold and a replacement property is then purchased and occupied by that same beneficiary. In such cases, there can be no question of the interest in possession coming to an end when the property is sold, and a new interest in possession commencing when the replacement property has been purchased and the beneficiary enters into occupation. If, therefore, the beneficiary began occupation on or before 21 March 2006 and the property is later replaced by another property using the proceeds of sale, the pre-March 2006 interest in possession continues unchanged. Do you agree?

HMRC response:

We agree that it is important to review the facts and the evidence of the trustees' intentions to identify the extent of the beneficiary's right of occupation. As far as Scenario 1 is concerned, we would agree with your proposition, on the basis that there is clear evidence that the trustees intended the beneficiary to have the right to occupy any property owned by the trustees for the purpose of providing a home for him."

HMRC also indicated that they agreed with the view that where the trustees intended only to provide a specific home for the beneficiary by granting him the right to occupy a named property owned by the trust, the beneficiary's interest in possession could be said to be restricted to that particular property so that, if that property were sold, even though it may be replaced in the future, the beneficiary's interest in possession would have come to an end.[69]

IV. SPECIAL STATUTORY PROVISIONS BEARING ON THE MEANING OF INTEREST IN POSSESSION

12–41   As was mentioned above, the legislation contains a number of provisions which bear on the meaning of interest in possession. The provisions are considered under the headings below.

Multiple user/enjoyment of property

12–42   The legislation contains an express provision dealing with the use or enjoyment of property by one or more persons jointly or in common. Section 50(5) provides that:

"Where the person referred to in s.49(1) above is not entitled to any income of the property but is entitled, jointly or in common with one or more other persons, to the use and enjoyment of the property, his interest shall be taken to subsist in such part of the property as corresponds to the proportion which the annual value of his interests bears to the aggregate of the annual values of his interest and that or those of the other or others."

It thus addresses the position of a person who, although not entitled to any income from settled property, nevertheless has an interest in possession in the property because he is entitled to the use and enjoyment of it jointly or in common with one or more other persons.

---

[69] These issues were raised in the context where trustees were looking to appoint s.49C transitional serial interests (see paras 11–56 and following) because it became relevant to know what trustees should have been doing in relation to SP10/79 type interests in possession.

Perhaps the first thing to note about s.50(5) is that it is wholly consistent with *Pearson* in regarding a person who has a present right of present enjoyment of property as having an interest in possession in that property. Assume, for example, that Blackacre is held in trust, and that A is entitled to occupy it rent-free. A has an interest in possession in the property, even though he is not entitled to the income from it. This is the effect of *Pearson*, not of s.50(5), which is not needed where only one person is entitled to the use and enjoyment of the property. For s.50(5) there must be a multiple entitlement.

When, then, does s.50(5) apply? The answer is, in fairly limited circumstances, i.e. the person in question:

(a) must be entitled to the use and enjoyment of the property, jointly or in common with other persons;
(b) must not be entitled to any income of the property.

The first requirement was considered by a Special Commissioner in *Woodhall v IRC*.[70] A deceased's will provided that no sale of the family home was to take place whilst any of his three children "shall desire to live there" and until the property was sold the executors and trustees were to permit the children "or each or [any] of them to occupy the same". The net proceeds of sale were to be divided among the three children equally. After the deceased died in 1957 one of the children left the family home in 1958 and died in 1971. A second, E, had apparently already left the family home in 1957. A third, A, lived there until he died in 1997. The fact that the property was settled property was not in dispute.

HMRC argued that by virtue of his sole occupation of the property A had an interest in possession in the entirety of the property, albeit it one which was defeasible by reason of the right of E, the surviving, non-occupying beneficiary, to occupy with A if he chose to do so. A's personal representative argued that A had no interest in possession at all or, if he did, under s.50(5) it subsisted in only half the house.

The Special Commissioner concluded that the terms of the will gave the children the right to occupy the property, the trustees having no power to choose between the children or to allow only one to occupy. A therefore had an interest in possession in the property. But, since E was also entitled to use and enjoy the property, s.50(5) applied. Accordingly, A had an interest in possession in only half the property.

The case is important because it confirms that what matters, at least for purposes of s.50(5), is *entitlement* to use and enjoyment, not actual use and enjoyment.[71]

It is to be noted that s.50(5) applies only if the person in question is not entitled to any of the income from the property. Use and enjoyment is thus not determinative: if A and B occupy property but can let it and keep the rent they are entitled to the income from the property and so s.50(5) will not apply.

An interesting question concerns what, if anything, s.50(5) implies in a case where the person is entitled to a small part of the income of property which he is entitled to use and enjoy in common with another. Assume that under the terms of a settlement X and Y are respectively entitled to 10 per cent and 90 per cent of the income of the trust fund, that any beneficiary entitled to any part of the income of the trust fund is entitled to occupy any residential property comprised in the trust fund, that the only trust asset is a residential property, Whiteacre, and that both X and Y live in Whiteacre. Section 50(5) does not operate, because X is entitled to some of the income from Whiteacre. Does the non-application of s.50(5) imply that for IHT purposes the only test for

---

[70] *Woodhall v IRC* [2000] S.T.C. (S.C.D.) 558.

[71] For the implications of the exercise by trustees of their powers under the Trust of Land and Appointment of Trustees Act 1996, see para.12–34 and *Private Client Business* (2001), p.134.

measuring X's interest in possession is his income entitlement? The authors incline to the view that that is the case on the basis that otherwise there would be no need for s.50(5).

Close companies

12–43   Where a close company is entitled to an interest in possession in settled property, the participators in the company are treated by s.101(1) as being beneficially entitled to that interest in possession according to their respective rights and interests in the company. Section 101(1A) provides that whether or not the company was a close company when it became entitled to the interest, where the interest was acquired on or after March 22, 2006, s.101(1) only applies in relation to the interest if the interest is an immediate post-death interest, or a transitional serial interest.[72] Note too that as drafted, s.101(1) does not apply to pre-March 22, 2006 interests acquired by a company on or after March 22, 2006. It is thought that this is an oversight which will be corrected by legislative amendment.

"Close company" has the meaning given to it by s.102(1).[73] The effect of s.101(1) is thus that if a person settles property on trusts such that a close company of which he is the sole owner has an interest in possession in the settled property which is either a pre-March 22, 2006 interest, an immediate post-death interest or a transitional serial interest, he will not make a transfer of value since the value of his estate will not have been diminished by his creating the settlement. Prior to April 20, 1978, it was thought possible to avoid tax by using certain schemes under which close companies incorporated (and therefore domiciled) abroad owned by UK domiciliaries were given interests in possession in exempt gilts.[74] The introduction of anti-avoidance legislation led to the recasting of these schemes: what is now s.101(1) was outflanked by the interposition of a settlement between the individual and the shares, so that he had an interest in possession in a close company which itself had an interest in possession in the exempt gilts. Section 101(2) renders this ineffective by treating as the individual's the interest to which the company is entitled.

It is to be noted that under s.101 the participators are deemed to be beneficially entitled to the company's interest. Although the legislation does not say so expressly, the corollary of this appears to be that the company is not beneficially entitled to the interest, so that in valuing the shares in the company the company's entitlement to the interest in possession is ignored.[75]

If an individual who owns shares in a company which has an interest in settled property gives away those shares the interest in possession which s.101 deems him to have is treated as having come to an end. The fact that he gave his shares to a charity does not mean that the charity exemption is available to the notional transfer of value he is treated as having made as a result of the termination of his interest.[76]

By virtue of s.101(1B) and (1C) introduced by the Finance Act 2006, a new rule applies which is designed to ensure that where a participator (the prior participator) disposes of any rights and interests in the company to another person (the later participator), s.101(1) does not treat the later participator as entitled to the interest in possession by virtue of the disposition to him of rights and interests by the prior

[72] For the definitions of immediate post-death interest and transitional serial interests, see paras 11–51 and 11–56—11–62 respectively.
[73] See paras 2–73 and 2–81.
[74] See para.9–19.
[75] *Powell-Cotton v IRC* [1992] S.T.C. 625, discussed at para.2–102.
[76] *Powell-Cotton v IRC* [1992] S.T.C. 625.

participator. He may already be a participator in the company so that s.101(1) applies to him in his own right—but the application of s.101(1) ceases in respect of those rights and interests which are disposed of to him by the prior participator. These provisions are expressed to be "without prejudice to the application of [IHTA 1984] in relation to the prior participator as the person making the disposal" which presumably means that if, for example, the disposal is made on death and the shares are gifted by the participator to his wife in his will, this will be an exempt transfer by virtue of s.18. Note that although this amendment is deemed to have come into force on March 22, 2006,[77] it is not limited to disposals after that date. It is thought that this too is a legislative oversight, and that it will be amended in due course.

Interests in unadministered estates

As a matter of general law, a person who has an interest in possession in the **12–44** residuary estate of a testator does not have an "interest" in the assets of the estate during the course of that estate being administered: see *Barnardo's Homes v IRC*.[78] All he has is a right to proceed against the executors if they fail to administer the assets properly; he thus has a chose in action, rather than any rights over the assets per se. Section 91 accordingly provides, in effect, that the residuary estate is to be treated as having been administered. The person who would have been entitled to the interest on the administration of the estate being completed is thus treated as being entitled to the interest from the date of the death in question. This is a "qualifying interest in possession" by virtue of being an immediate post-death interest. This means that if he disposes of his interest during the administration period or dies during that period a charge may arise under s.52(1) or s.4(1), notwithstanding the fact that as a matter of general law he is not entitled to an interest in possession in the residue. The charge will be based on the amount of the residue which has been ascertained plus the unascertained residue. The unascertained residue will be what remains of the estate after allowing for debts, specific bequests and charges or residue and before making any apportionments between income and capital; see s.91(2)(a).

It will be noted that s.91 applies only to a person entitled to an interest in the residue of a deceased person's estate. Where the entitlement is to a settled pecuniary legacy, s.91 will not operate to give the legatee an interest in possession, and if he dies before the legacy is paid no charge will arise under s.4(1).[79]

The s.91 statutory fiction prevents disputes arising as to when residue has been ascertained and ensures that, in appropriate cases, business or agricultural property relief will be available. It is understood that HMRC do not allow a discount in the valuation of an interest in such an estate for delay in concluding the administration of the estate and distributing the assets.

Survivorship clauses

It is common practice for a person making a gift by his will to include a clause under **12–45** which the gift takes effect only if the donee of the gift survives the donor for a specific period, e.g. 30 days. One reason for including such a clause is to prevent a double

[77] FA 2006 s.156 Sch.20 paras 7 and 26.
[78] *Barnardo's Homes v IRC* [1921] 2 A.C. 1.
[79] See *Re Harrison; Johnstone v Blackburn, etc., Infirmary* [1918] 2 Ch. 374.

charge from arising in respect of the same property if the donee dies within the specific period. In the absence of the clause, tax would have been charged both at the time of the first gift, and at the time of the donee's death. Section 92 takes account of such clauses. It provides that where under the terms of a will, or otherwise, property is held for any person on condition that he survives another for a specified period not exceeding six months, the legislation applies if the transferee survives the specified period as if the disposition which in fact takes effect at the end of the specified period took effect from the beginning of the specified period. In the same way, if the transferee does not survive for the specified period, the disposition which takes effect on the transferee's death is regarded as having taken effect from the beginning of the specified period. Thus, if A leaves property to B subject to B surviving A for 30 days, failing which the property goes to C, and B dies, the disposition to C is regarded as having taken place at the time of the gift by A, and no charge arises in respect of the gift on B's death. If, on the other hand, B survives until the end of the period, the gift to B which takes effect at the end of the 30 days is regarded as having taken effect at the time A first made the gift.

The typical clause contains an express or implied accumulation trust to avoid an interest in possession during the survivorship period. It will thus be appreciated that, in the absence of s.92, property held subject to a survivorship clause would be property in which no interest in possession subsisted during the survivorship period, with the result that on[80] the beneficiary surviving the specified period, a primary exit charge might arise on his becoming entitled to the property in question. Section 92 prevents this, since, on the expiry of the survivorship period, the beneficiary will be treated as having been entitled to the property as from the time of the gift, not as from the end of the survivorship period.

Exceptionally, property which is subject to a survivorship clause may be the subject of an overriding power of appointment. As was just mentioned, during the survivorship period property which is subject to a survivorship clause will be property in which no interest in possession subsists, with the result that the exercise of such an overriding power of appointment may give rise to an exit charge. Section 92(2) provides that the basic provisions just discussed do not affect the treatment of any such appointment. Thus, returning to the above example, if A left property by his will, and gave his executor a power to appoint the property during a specified period to such of E, D and F as the executor decided, the exercise by the executor of his power of appointment in favour of E, D and F could give rise to a charge under the relevant property regime notwithstanding the fact that at the end of the survivorship period B became entitled to such property as the executor had not appointed. It may be, of course, that s.144 will apply to relieve any distribution payment made in consequence of the exercise of such a power of appointment from being a capital distribution.[81]

It was previously the case that careful consideration had to be given to the effect of including a survivorship clause in a will. Assume, for example, that the husband's estate was worth £500,000, while his wife's estate was worth £65,000. Under the husband's will, his estate would pass to his wife, and vice versa. It made sense for the wife's will to include a survivorship clause, so that if her husband did not survive her by, say, three months, her estate passed to her children. On the other hand, it made sense for the husband's will to include a survivorship clause only in respect of part of the gift to his wife, so that at least some of his estate would pass to her even if she did not survive him by three months, thereby taking advantage of her nil rate band. The

---

[80] Subject to relief under IHTA 1984 s.65(4); see para.15–17.

[81] See paras 8–189 and following. In effect a two year survivorship provision can be obtained by the use of s.144.

introduction of the transferable nil-rate band[82] means that this is no longer an issue. For a case where a survivorship clause could be detrimental, see para.8–07.

Protective and disabled trusts

The legislation makes special provision to treat certain persons as having qualifying **12–46** interests in possession under trusts for disabled persons or protective trusts in circumstances where they would not otherwise have had such an interest. This is discussed at Chapters 21 and 22 respectively.

Scotland

There are various differences between the trust law of England and the trust law of **12–47** Scotland, and in order to ensure that the legislation operates with similar effect in England and Scotland s.46 provides that any reference to an interest in possession in settled property in so far as IHT applies to Scotland is a reference to an interest of any kind under a settlement by virtue of which the person "in right of that interest" is entitled to the enjoyment of the property or would be so entitled if the property were capable of enjoyment (including an interest of an assignee under an assignation of an interest of any kind of property subject to a proper liferent) and the person in right of such an interest at any time is deemed to be entitled to a corresponding interest in the whole or any part of the property comprised in the settlement. Thus, for all practical purposes, the definition of interest in possession should have the same meaning in Scotland as it does in England.

Qualifying interest in possession

Although, as was noted in Chapters 5, 11 and 12 the legislation does not define the **12–48** term "interest in possession" it does refer in a number of contexts to a "qualifying interest in possession". A "qualifying interest in possession" is defined for these purposes by s.59 as an interest in possession to which an individual is beneficially entitled and which if the individual became beneficially entitled to the interest in possession on or after March 22, 2006, is an immediate post death interest, a disabled person's interest or a transitional serial interest. Consequently, only pre-March 22, 2006 interests in possession, transitional serial interests, disabled person's interests and bereaved minors' interests will escape the relevant property regime. The definitions of each of the three new categories are considered in Chapter 11.

A "qualifying interest in possession" is also defined as an interest in possession to which, where certain conditions set out in s.59(2) are satisfied, a company is beneficially entitled and which, if the individual became beneficially entitled to the interest in possession on or after March 22, 2006, is an immediate post-death interest, a disabled person's interest within s.89B(1)(c) or (d)[83] or a transitional serial interest immediately before the company acquires it.

---

[82] See para.4–06.

[83] i.e. those disabled person's interests which are actual interests in possession as opposed to interests in discretionary trusts treated as qualifying interests in possession by virtue of the relevant provisions. For detailed discussion of disabled person's trusts, see Ch.21. Presumably this is because it is not possible to acquire discretionary interests.

The conditions of s.59(2) are that:

(1) the business of the company consists wholly or mainly in the acquisition of interests in settled property; and
(2) the company acquired the interest for a full consideration in money or money's worth from an individual who was beneficially entitled to the interest.

It is not clear whether the business of the company at the time it acquired the interest had to consist wholly or mainly in the acquisition of such interests. On a strict reading of the conditions this is not necessary.

The condition that the business of the company must consist wholly or mainly in the acquisition of interests in settled property is relaxed in two ways: first, the condition is treated as satisfied in relation to acquisitions made before March 14, 1975, provided the business of the company at the time of the acquisition consisted wholly or mainly in the acquisition of such interests; secondly, the condition need not be satisfied if the company is an insurance company[84] and has permission[85] to effect or carry out "contracts of long-term insurance".[86]

12–49 It is important to note that one of the effects of the definition of a "qualifying interest in possession" is that a kind of double taxation can arise where trustees of a discretionary trust have an interest in possession in another settlement. Assume, for example, that trustees of a discretionary trust, settlement A, are entitled to such income as may arise to the trustees of another settlement, settlement B. The trustees of settlement A are not, as trustees, capable of having a qualifying interest in possession in settlement B. This means that both settlements will be subject to the periodic charge. The trustees of settlement A will be subject to the charge because they hold the interest to which they are entitled on discretionary trusts. The trustees of settlement B will be subject to the periodic charge because no one has a qualifying interest in possession in the assets which they hold on trust. As regards settlement B, the charge will be levied on the value of the trust assets. As regards settlement A, the charge will be levied on the market value of the interest held by the trustees. The Consultative Document issued by HMRC in August 1980 drew attention to this, but the matter was not covered in the draft clauses pending further consideration. In a press release of March 26, 1982 HMRC stated that in the light of the judgment in *Thomas v IRC*[87] they took the view "that legislation may not be necessary in order to avoid a double charge". While the *Thomas* case may be helpful in certain circumstances, there must be some question as to how far it extends, and accordingly arrangements of the type just mentioned should generally be avoided where possible.

12–50 An interesting problem arises if, for example, a life tenant under one settlement ("Settlement 1") assigns his qualifying interest in possession to trustees of another settlement ("Settlement 2") under which that same beneficiary is a protected life tenant. Assume further that this happened before March 22, 2006 and that the instrument of assignment provided that the trustees of Settlement 2 must treat all monies received from Settlement 1 as income which will, therefore (unless and until the

---

[84] Within the meaning of ICTA1998 Pt XII Ch.I as amended by the Corporation Tax Act 2009; IHTA 1984 s.59(2)(b).

[85] Under either Pt 4 of the Financial Services and Markets Act 2000 or para.15 of Sch.3 to that Act (as a result of qualifying for authorisation under para.12(1) of Sch.3): IHTA 1984 s.59(2)(b).

[86] Being contracts which fall within the Financial Services and Markets Act 2000 (Regulated Activities) Order 2001 Sch.1 Pt II: IHTA 1984 s.59(4).

[87] *Thomas v IRC* [1981] S.T.C. 382. See para.22–04.

interest is forfeited) be paid to the protected life tenant. The IHT analysis is as follows:

(1) as a result of the assignment, Settlement 1 no longer contains a qualifying interest in possession since the life interest is now held by the trustees of Settlement 2;
(2) the assignment by the life tenant did not, however, constitute a transfer of value since there was no diminution in the value of his estate.

In practice, it is understood that HMRC did not seek to apply the special charging provisions to Settlement 1 despite the lack of qualifying interest in possession. Rather they looked through Settlement 2 and treated the protected life tenant as retaining his original interest. Presumably a similar result would have applied even if there was no provision in the assignment treating the monies received from Settlement 1 as income in the hands of the Settlement 2 trustees and even if the protected life interest was forfeited. A post-March 22, 2006 assignment of a qualifying interest in possession to a relevant property trust will not benefit from this treatment.

Corporation sole

Finally, for the purposes of s.59, but for no other purpose,[88] a person who is entitled **12–51** to an interest in possession as a corporation sole is treated as beneficially entitled to an interest in possession in that property. The property in which the corporation sole has an interest in possession will thus not be subject to the special charging provisions.

---

[88] See para.25–16.

CHAPTER 13

MAIN FEATURES OF RELEVANT PROPERTY REGIME

I. INTRODUCTION

13–01   As was seen in Chapter 10, under the inheritance tax legislation there are two separate and independent sets of charging provisions. The main set—that under which tax is charged on chargeable transfers, has already been discussed in Pt I of this book. Chapter 10 outlines the special set of charging provisions concerned with the treatment of settled property in which there is no "qualifying" interest in possession.[1]

Precisely what constitutes "settled property", an "interest in possession", and a "qualifying interest in possession" are matters of general importance dealt with separately in Chapters 11 and 12. For convenience, rather than using the unwieldy formula "settled property in which there is no qualifying interest in possession", we will refer simply to "relevant property" trusts. As noted in Chapter 10, since the changes introduced by the Finance Act 2006, the trusts that fall within the relevant property regime now include not only discretionary trusts, but also interest in possession trusts where the interest in possession is not a "qualifying" interest in possession. All other trusts with no qualifying interest in possession (e.g. *Pearson* trusts)[2] also fall to be taxed under the relevant property regime.

As explained in Chapter 10, all other property, be it (a) non-settled property, or (b) settled property in which there is a qualifying interest in possession, falls to be dealt with, if at all, under the main charging provisions. Settled property thus falls into two main categories—settled property in which there is a qualifying interest in possession and settled property in which there is no such interest. Special reliefs apply to certain categories of trusts referred to as "favoured trusts". Some of these trusts are accorded favoured treatment by falling to be treated as trusts with "qualifying interests in possession" and others are afforded favoured treatment, for example, by exemption from the periodic charge (see below) applicable to relevant property trusts.[3]

[1] See paras 11–50 and following.
[2] See paras 12–20 and following.
[3] The main features of favoured property trusts are considered in Ch.10, the charging provisions that apply to favoured trusts are considered in Ch.17, and the conditions for qualifying for favoured treatment are considered in Chs 18–26.

In earlier editions of this book, the short-hand "discretionary trusts" was used to describe all settlements which consisted of "settled property in which there is no qualifying interest in possession" because at the time of publication of those editions, no interest in possession settlement could fall within the relevant property regime. It was thus possible to sub-divide the tax treatment of discretionary trusts into two categories, those that fell to be taxed under the relevant property regime and those that received favoured treatment. It is now more convenient to think of the taxation of settled property as falling within three categories: (a) settled property in which there is a qualifying interest in possession, (b) settled property which falls to be taxed under the "relevant property regime", and (c) "favoured trusts".

This chapter introduces the main features of the relevant property regime. It is followed by detailed consideration of the charging provisions applicable to relevant property in Chapters 14 to 16. The provisions of general application to all settled property, for example, provisions as to the commencement of settlements are discussed in Chapter 10 at paras 10–11–10–22.

At the time of writing (as stated at para.10–09), HMRC have issued a consultative document with the aim of eliciting views on how to simplify the regime for taxing "relevant property" trusts, and, "if needed", introducing legislative change in the Finance Bill 2014. Changes to the regime outlined in this chapter and analysed in more detail in Chapters 14 to 16 are, therefore, probable.

Historical background

The special charging provisions were originally imposed by the Finance Act 1975, discussed in detail in Chs 7–12 of the first edition. The introduction in 1975 of the special charge and the combination of the periodic charge, which was relatively revolutionary, and exit charges which could in theory be imposed at 75 per cent on distributions between periodic charges made the use of (at that time) discretionary trusts,[4] unattractive.   **13–02**

However, the maximum rate at which tax can be charged on property held on relevant property trusts has now been reduced so much that it can no longer be regarded as very burdensome. The maximum rate in 1975 was 75 per cent. The introduction in 1982 of a new set of special charging provisions had the effect of reducing it to 15 per cent. The 1984 and 1988 Finance Acts further reduced it to 9 per cent and 6 per cent respectively and it has since remained at 6 per cent. The only real disincentive to holding property on relevant property trusts is that a transfer of property to a relevant property trust cannot be a PET: it is an immediately chargeable transfer.

The special set of charging provisions in force at present is the second set of special charging provisions which the legislation had imposed originally only on discretionary trusts, but now also on most new inter vivos interest in possession trusts.   **13–03**

The following discussion is concerned primarily with explaining how the second set of provisions work, not how these provisions differ from the old provisions. Nevertheless, it may be helpful to mention briefly some of the main features of the original provisions, both to put the new provisions in perspective and because some of the

---

[4] This expression is used as a term of convenience and not as a term of art. It is used to describe all settlements in which no interest in possession subsists.

features of the new provisions are more easily understood against the background of the original provisions. The original provisions had the following main features:

(1) A single code applied to all discretionary trusts. This code included various reliefs and exemptions, some of which were available to all discretionary trusts, and others of which were available only to certain kinds of discretionary trusts which qualified for favoured treatment.

(2) Tax was charged, broadly speaking, in two circumstances. First, an exit charge was imposed when property held on discretionary trusts ceased to be subject to the special charging provisions or, in certain fairly narrow circumstances, where the trustees entered into transactions which depreciated the value of property held on such trusts. Secondly, a periodic charge was imposed every 10 years and, where the trustees were resident outside the United Kingdom, annually in the first nine years of every 10-year period. The result was that property settled on discretionary trusts could be taxed three times—once, under the main charging provisions, on the creation of the settlement; again, under the periodic charge; and, finally, when the property ceased to be within the special charging provisions, e.g. because it ceased to be held on discretionary trusts.

(3) The provisions were based on two terms—"capital distributions" and "distribution payments". Tax was charged on capital distributions (which could be actual or notional), not on distribution payments (and not on chargeable transfers, which were brought into account only under the main charging provisions).

(4) The periodic charges were imposed on the value of the property in the trust fund at the time of the charge. Exit charges were normally imposed on the value of the property which ceased to be subject to the special charging provisions, and not, in contrast to the main charging provisions, according to the consequential loss principle, although there could in certain circumstances be a requirement to gross-up. No account was taken of how long the property by reference to which the charge was imposed had been held on discretionary trusts.

(5) The rate of tax depended on the cumulative total of distribution payments (which could be actual or deemed) made out of the settlement, not on the cumulative total of capital distributions made out of the settlement. In this respect the special charging provisions differed fundamentally from the main charging provisions. Under the main charging provisions both the charge to tax and the transferor's cumulative total are related to the chargeable transfers made by the individual in question. Under the special charging provisions, on the other hand, the charge to tax was based on capital distributions, while the cumulative total was based on distribution payments. The confusion that this caused was increased by the fact that it was possible to make a capital distribution without making a distribution payment, and vice versa, with the result that there could be a charge to tax without any increase in a settlement's cumulative total and, conversely, there could be an increase in a settlement's cumulative total without there being any charge to tax. Why the designers of the tax thought that the rate of tax should depend on the cumulative total of distribution payments rather than on the cumulative total of capital distributions was one of the unexplained mysteries of CTT.

(6) The 10-year periodic charge was levied at 30 per cent of the rate that would have otherwise applied, the annual charge at 3 per cent of that rate. Other charges were levied at the full rate of tax, subject to the availability of transitional relief. Any tax charged under the annual charge was allowed as a credit against capital distributions subsequently made out of the trust property.

Tax paid under the 10-year charge was applied to reduce the rate of tax on distributions made subsequent to the imposition of that charge.

As was mentioned at (2) above, under the original special charging provisions an **13–04** annual charge was imposed on a discretionary trust the trustees of which were not resident in the United Kingdom. This charge is not imposed by reference to any year ending after December 31, 1981. Furthermore, any tax charged under the annual charge (whether paid by the trustees or by the settlor) not already allowed as a credit against capital distributions subsequently made out of the trust property was allowed as a credit against any periodic or exit charges subsequently imposed.[5]

Not surprisingly, the original special charging provisions were subjected to consider- **13–05** able criticism, both because of their substance (in particular, the imposition of a full exit charge regardless of the time the property in question had been held on discretionary trusts) and their formal complexity. In August 1980, with a view to future reform, HMRC issued a consultative document on the CTT treatment of settled property generally. This document took as its starting point the principle adumbrated when CTT was originally formulated, namely that in general the charge to tax on settled property should be the same as that on property held absolutely, the so-called "parity principle". In December 1981, having considered various submissions made in response to the consultative document, HMRC issued a draft set of new special charging provisions, and these, in an extended and considerably, if rather hastily, modified form, were enacted in the Finance Act 1982, with effect from March 9, 1982. The new rules, which are now found in ss.58–85 of the Act, are generally thought to be fairer than the old; whether they are any simpler is questionable.

Elections for pre-CTT settlements

In order to take account of the fact that the introduction of the current rules might **13–06** prejudice certain taxpayers, who could not have anticipated the changes that were made by the Finance Act 1982, Pt II of Sch.15 to that Act provided that for a limited period—in most cases, until March 31, 1983, exceptionally until March 31, 1984—it was possible to elect for the old rules to apply to pre-CTT settlements. The provisions governing these elections are discussed at paras 12–08–12–16 of the second edition of this book.

Main features of relevant property regime

The special charging provisions have the following main features in relation to **13–07** relevant property:

(1) *Chargeable occasions*: the provisions impose two kinds of charge. First, they impose a charge every 10 years on relevant property. This is referred in the text as the "periodic charge". Secondly, they impose a charge when the value of the "relevant property" ceases to be subject to the "relevant property" regime. This may happen because the property in question ceases to be relevant property, e.g. where a beneficiary acquires a qualifying interest in possession in

[5] IHTA 1984 s.85.

559

the property, or because the property becomes held on favoured trusts. Alternatively, it may happen because the value of property which continues to be subject to the regime is reduced, e.g. where the trustees enter into a transaction which diminishes the value of the relevant property. This second kind of charge is referred to in the text as the "exit charge". The periodic charge is considered in detail in Chapter 14, and exit charges are considered in detail in Chapter 15.

(2) *The amount on which tax is charged*: where an exit charge is imposed, tax is charged on the amount by which the value of the trust fund is diminished as a result of the chargeable event in question. This is a major departure from the old legislation, under which tax was charged on the value of the property that left the trust fund; now the consequential loss rule applies. Grossing-up is necessary to the extent that trustees bear the tax due out of relevant property. Agricultural and/or business relief may be available to reduce the amount on which tax is chargeable; where such relief is available, it is given before any grossing-up. Where the periodic charge is imposed, tax is charged on the value of the relevant property then comprised in the settlement. Again, agricultural and/or business relief may be available to reduce this value.

(3) *The rate of tax*: the rules for determining the rate at which tax is charged on relevant property are somewhat complicated, and are discussed at Chapter 16. Some of the rules for determining the rate at which tax is charged are the subject of HMRC's recent consultative document (referred to at para.13–01 above). The approach of the legislation is to charge tax at a fraction of the "effective" rate of tax charged on the value transferred by a hypothetical chargeable transfer made by a transferor with a hypothetical cumulative total. The lifetime rates of tax are always used to find the effective rate of tax on this hypothetical transfer. Once the effective rate of tax has been determined, it is necessary to multiply that rate by a fraction specified by the legislation in order to determine the rate at which the tax is finally to be charged. The fraction varies according to whether an exit or a periodic charge is imposed, as follows:

(a) the position with regard to the periodic charge is simple—the fraction is always three-tenths; and

(b) in the case of exit charges, the appropriate fraction is three-tenths of, somewhat confusingly, another fraction, the denominator of which is 40 (i.e. x/40), and the numerator of which (x) is the number of complete successive quarters in the period beginning with the day on which the settlement commenced, or, if there has been a 10-year anniversary, with the day on which that anniversary fell, and ending with the day before that on which the exit charge was imposed. Assume, for example, that an exit charge is imposed in respect of property which has been comprised in a discretionary trust for two and a quarter years. The appropriate fraction would be:

$$\frac{3}{10} \times \frac{9}{40} = \frac{27}{400}$$

(4) *Reliefs*: certain reliefs are available to reduce or prevent an exit charge. These too are considered in Chapter 16.

CHAPTER 14

THE PERIODIC CHARGE

I. INTRODUCTION

Under the special charging provisions, a charge (the "periodic charge") is imposed, **14–01** broadly speaking, on relevant property every 10 years. No such charge is imposed on favoured property. As was mentioned above, the 1975 legislation imposed two periodic charges on property held on discretionary trusts—a general charge at 10-year intervals, and a special, annual charge imposed on non-resident trusts. The Finance Act 1982 abolished the annual charge as from January 1, 1982[1] and introduced a new 10-year charge which operates in relation to relevant property in much the same way as that imposed by the 1975 legislation. For the position with regard to credit for tax previously paid under the annual charge, see para.13–04.

There is some question as to the best way to refer to the periodic charge. The obvious name for it is the "10-year charge" or, for those with more sophisticated fiscal taste, the "decennial charge". However, both these terms are inappropriate, because in the remarks introducing the draft clauses it was stated that both the rate and the frequency of the charge were essentially a budgetary question, so that the possibility exists that the charge will be imposed other than at intervals of 10 years. So it is probably best to refer to the charge as the "periodic charge", i.e. the term used by HMRC in their introductory remarks in the 1980 consultative document.

II. THE CHARGE

The periodic charge is imposed by s.64, which provides that tax is to be charged **14–02**

[1] FA 1982 s.125.

where immediately before a settlement's 10-year anniversary[2] all or any of the property comprised in that settlement is relevant property.

III. THE CHARGEABLE AMOUNT

14–03   The general rule is that tax is charged immediately before each 10-year anniversary of a settlement on the value of the relevant property then comprised[3] in that settlement.[4] Value is not defined for the purpose of the periodic charge.

Section 160[5] provides that the value at any time of any property is its market value, and s.162(4) provides that a liability which is an encumbrance on any property reduces the value of that property. Nevertheless, it is not entirely clear what account, if any, is to be taken of liability for, inter alia:

(a) tax for past years which has not yet been assessed;
(b) CGT on unrealised gains;
(c) CGT on gains realised but not assessed; and
(d) costs incurred, e.g. in obtaining valuations.

It is thought that such liabilities, save, perhaps, those in respect of unrealised gains, should be taken into account in determining the "value" of the fund, with the result that the full periodic charge is levied on the "net" value of the fund.

Retained but unaccumulated income

14–04   Up to November 10, 1986, HMRC practice was to treat undistributed income of a discretionary trust, whether or not that income had been accumulated, as always forming part of the relevant property in the trust so that it was subject in full to the periodic charge. There were good reasons for doubting the correctness of this approach since the legislation appears to draw a distinction between property in a settlement on the one hand and income produced by that property on the other (see, for instance, s.43(2)). Such doubts eventually prompted HMRC to take further advice and as a result they published a Statement of Practice on November 10, 1986 (SP8/86) which modified their former views. The relevant portion of the Statement is as follows:

"4. In the light of that advice the Board of Inland Revenue now take the view—
(a) that *undistributed and unaccumulated income* should not be treated as a taxable trust asset, and
(b) that, *for the purpose of determining the rate of charge on accumulated income*, the income should be treated as becoming a taxable asset on the trust on the date when the accumulation is made.
5. This change in practice will be applied to all new cases and to existing cases where the tax liability has not been settled."

---

[2] See para.10–20.
[3] See para.10–12 for the special rules for determining when property becomes comprised in a settlement.
[4] IHTA 1984 s.64.
[5] For a more detailed discussion of IHTA 1984 s.160 generally, see paras 25–19 and following.

This approach involves determining when income is accumulated in the trust. Obviously when there is an express resolution to this effect by the trustees no problems will arise but often matters are not so simple and it must be remembered that income remains available for distribution for a reasonable time after it has arisen; see, for instance, *Re Locker*[6] where income which arose between 1965 and 1968 was still available for distribution in 1977. The Statement of Practice also leaves open the problem of whether payments of capital to a beneficiary are to be treated as comprising the property originally settled or subsequent accumulations of income.

Note, of course, that post-March 22, 2006 interest in possession settlements, although not "qualifying interests in possession"[7] for inheritance tax purposes, are nevertheless interest in possession settlements for general law purposes. Consequently income arising under such settlements belongs to the life tenant and the issue of retained but accumulated income does not arise.

HMRC's approach to calculations

The Statement of Practice does not assist in determining when undistributed income **14–05** retained in trustees' hands becomes accumulated, although the recent consultative document on the relevant property regime (referred to at para.13–01 above) suggests that this will be one of the areas of possible future legislative simplification. Until such time as any change takes effect, the question must therefore be answered on the basis of general trust principles. Basically, trustees have a reasonable time to distribute income after which it will be treated as accumulated. Needless to say, the imprecision generated by this rule is far from satisfactory since the computation of IHT charges depends upon the precise moment of accumulation. A further problem not addressed by the Statement of Practice is to identify the accumulated income once it has become part of the general fund. For instance, at the time of the periodic charge, which assets in the fund represent this income? Further, if distributions out of capital assets in the fund subsequently occur, do they come from the accumulated income and, if so, for which years?

In practice, HMRC calculate the annual value of the accumulations on the basis of an element of time basing, i.e. on the basis of a uniform growth rate which will reproduce the anniversary total assuming that income attributed to each year of the relevant decade is received at some time in that year and that each year's income is to be regarded as invested halfway through the year. This whole process can be represented algebraically as follows:

$$OC(1 + 1)^{10} + A1(1 + 1)^{9.5} + A2(1 + 1)^{8.5} + \ldots \; A10(1 + 1)^{0.5} = CC$$

where OC is the value of the opening capital, A1 is the first year's accumulation, A2 the second year's accumulation, and so on, and CC is the closing capital, i.e. the anniversary value of the whole trust fund. It may be noted that this approach does not depend upon the precise dates when income was accumulated: in cases where this date

---

[6] *Re Locker* [1977] 1 W.L.R. 1323.
[7] By virtue of IHTA s.59 (see para.11–50).

is known there is nothing to stop trustees from insisting on calculations based on that date in cases where a lesser charge would result.[8]

Agricultural relief and business relief

14–06   In some cases agricultural relief and/or business relief is available to trustees. Accordingly, where a periodic charge is imposed on an amount which is attributable to the agricultural value of agricultural property or the value of relevant business property,[9] the amount on which the periodic charge would otherwise be imposed is reduced by the appropriate percentage.

---

[8] HMRC's approach is discussed together with illustrations in *Capital Taxes News and Reports*, May 1989, Vol.8. For the position when an exit charge occurs before the first 10-year anniversary and there is accumulated income see *Private Client Business* (1996), p.75.

[9] By virtue of IHTA s.2(3) this occasion of charge is deemed to be a transfer of value.

CHAPTER 15

EXIT CHARGES

I. INTRODUCTION

This chapter is concerned with two subjects: the circumstances in which an exit **15–01** charge may be levied on relevant property, and the amount on which such a charge falls to be imposed. The legislation provides for the imposition of two alternative exit charges, which may be regarded as the price, in effect, of escaping from the periodic charge. The first is imposed when property ceases to be relevant property, e.g. when a qualifying interest in possession is appointed in such property. The second charge, which is expressed to apply only when the first does not, is imposed when the value of relevant property is reduced by a disposition made by the trustees of the settlement in which that property is comprised, e.g. where trustees grant a lease of land at an undervalue.

As was indicated above, largely identical charges are imposed on various kinds of favoured property. Unfortunately, as was also mentioned above, the draftsman has adopted a slightly unusual approach in imposing these charges—when he wishes to impose a charge he enumerates the circumstances in which that charge is imposed, but he does not provide that a fiscal event such as a transfer of value is to be regarded as having occurred when those circumstances are present. This has two unhappy effects. The first is that he is forced to enumerate the chargeable circumstances whenever he wishes to impose a charge to tax; the second, which follows from the first, is that this approach makes it difficult to write about the legislation without introducing some terminology of one's own. Accordingly, for convenience, the circumstances which can give rise to a charge to tax will be referred to as a "reduction in property" and a "reduction in value", and the charges which may arise where those circumstances are present will be referred to as "the primary exit charge" and "the secondary exit charge".

Although this chapter is concerned with the imposition of exit charges on relevant property, many of the comments made in relation, both to the circumstances in which a charge is imposed, and to the amount on which tax is charged, will apply equally to the exit charges imposed on favoured property.[1]

15–02 As mentioned above, the legislation imposes two exit charges, and each of these is considered in turn. All but one of the reliefs available to prevent a charge from being imposed are available to both charges, so it is appropriate to defer consideration of those reliefs until the discussion of the circumstances in which the charges may be imposed is complete. One relief, which applies only to the secondary exit charge, is dealt with in the discussion relating to that charge.

II. PRIMARY EXIT CHARGE

15–03 By s.65(1)(a), a charge is imposed where property comprised in a settlement ceases to be relevant property. Such a cessation may come about in three main ways:

(1) the property may cease to be settled property altogether, e.g. where a beneficiary becomes absolutely entitled to it;

(2) the property may become settled property in which there is a qualifying interest in possession, e.g. where an individual becomes beneficially entitled to a disabled person's interest in the property; and

(3) the property may become favoured property, e.g. where a non-bereaved minors' trust is replaced by a bereaved minors' trust by the exercise by the trustees of a power of appointment.

Changes in investments

15–04 It is to be noted that, subject to certain qualifications mentioned below, the manner in which the property in question ceases to be relevant property, i.e. whether under the terms of the trust, as the result of an appointment or advancement by the trustees, or by operation of law, is unimportant. All that matters is that property comprised in a settlement has ceased to be relevant property. This means that it is theoretically possible for a simple realisation of investments by the trustees to be the occasion of an exit charge, but this is not a cause for alarm since, as will be seen below, the amount on which tax is charged in such circumstances is nil—the value of the trust fund remains unaltered.

Free loans

15–05 In this discussion "free loan" means an interest-free loan expressed to be repayable on demand. In the pre-March 22, 2006 era, HMRC suggested that such a loan created an interest in possession,[2] with the result that a charge to tax was imposed on the value of the property lent, not merely on the amount (often much smaller) by which the value of the trust fund was diminished by the loan. Post-March 22, 2006, this issue remains

---

[1] As to which, see Ch.17.
[2] See para.12–35.

relevant where, for example, a free loan is made of a property settled in a will. Section 144 will normally prevent a charge arising, i.e. if a free loan which creates an interest in possession is made within two years of death,[3] but the question may be relevant to whether or not an immediate post-death interest[4] has arisen.

In the authors' view, the correct position is that while a loan of property other than money, e.g. where trustees allow a beneficiary to occupy a house, may give rise to a charge to tax on the value of the property lent, a loan of money will not do so, but will instead give rise to a charge on only the amount by which the loan diminishes the value of the trust fund. The point is an important one. If the authors' view is correct an interest-free loan may in appropriate circumstances be a relatively painless way of making funds available to a beneficiary.

The authors' view is based on the fact that, in law, a distinction must be drawn between a loan of money and a loan of property other than money. Where money is lent, the money lent becomes the property of the borrower. Where, on the other hand, property other than money is lent, that property continues to be owned by the lender. Thus, if a person lends a bicycle to a friend, he expects and is entitled to have that same bicycle returned to him; but if he lends his friend a five-pound note, he does not expect to get the same five-pound note back, nor is he entitled to do so. The significance of this is as follows.

Loans of money

Where trustees lend money to a beneficiary the money becomes the property of the **15–06** beneficiary and thus ceases to be settled property, with the result that, by definition, no interest in possession (qualifying or otherwise) can subsist in it. The sums leaving the trust fund are replaced by a debt which forms part of the corpus of the trust fund, together with the other trust assets. No interest in possession subsists in this debt, either. It is true that the making of a loan gives rise to a primary exit charge—property comprised in the settlement (the funds lent) cease to be relevant property—but the amount on which such a charge is imposed may be relatively small. The reasoning is as follows.

Under s.65(2)(a), the amount on which a primary exit charge is imposed is the amount by which the value of the relevant property comprised in the trust fund is reduced by the chargeable event. In the case of a loan this is the difference between the sum lent and the market value of the debt.[5] The value of the debt will depend on how the loan is secured. If the security is such that immediate repayment is virtually certain the trust fund will have sustained little, if any, diminution in value. To the extent that immediate repayment is not certain there will in theory be a charge, but provided repayment will take place within a reasonable period of time the amount brought into charge should be relatively small in comparison to the sum lent.

Loans of other property

As was mentioned above, where property other than money is lent the property **15–07** remains that of the lender. Thus, if a charge is to be imposed in respect of such a loan it can only be because the trustees have, by making the loan, diminished the value of the trust fund. The only other alternative is that the loan has created an interest in

---

[3] See para.15–28.
[4] See paras 11–51–11–55.
[5] Which will, it is assumed, be duly discharged, except to the extent that recovery is impossible/not reasonably practicable and has not become so by any act or omission of the lender: IHTA 1984 s.166.

possession in the property lent, which prior to March 22, 2006, would always have been an occasion when property ceased to be relevant property. Since March 22, 2006, this will only be an occasion when property ceases to be relevant property if the interest in possession created is a qualifying interest in possession. The first possibility is not worrying, since where it applies the charge will be only on such diminution in the value of the trust fund as the loan may occasion. Where, on the other hand, such a loan was made before March 22, 2006 and created an interest in possession, there was a danger that a charge would be imposed on the value of the property lent. However, post-March 22, 2006, the creation of an interest in possession in this way will not be a chargeable occasion: most post-March 22, 2006 interests in possession are unlikely to be a qualifying interest in possession and so property does not on that occasion cease to be relevant property.

The question as to whether or not a free loan of property other than money creates an interest in possession in the property lent is extremely difficult; for a full discussion, see paras 12–37 and following.

III. SECONDARY EXIT CHARGE

15–08 By s.65(1)(b), the secondary exit charge, which is expressed to apply only where the primary exit charge does not, is imposed where the trustees of a settlement make a disposition as a result of which the value of relevant property is less than it would be but for that disposition. A number of comments are in order concerning this charge.[6]

Meaning of "disposition" generally

15–09 There is no statutory definition of "disposition". The meaning of the term and the time at which a disposition is regarded as having been made as a matter of general law are discussed at paras 2–05 and following. As is noted there, it is clear that "disposition" is not a technical word, but an ordinary English word of very wide meaning.

Special statutory provisions

15–10 The already wide meaning of "disposition" is extended by the special charging provisions in the following ways.

Associated operations

15–11 Section 272 provides that a disposition includes a disposition "effected by associated operations". Precisely what this means is far from clear; for a full discussion, see paras 9–05 and following. It is to be noted that:

(a) for the purposes of the associated operations provisions an "operation" includes an omission[7];

---

[6] In the relatively rare case where trustees exercise their power to augment out of capital the income of a beneficiary HMRC regard the case as involving a distribution of capital and not the reduction of its value, so that the primary exit charge, not the secondary exit charge, applies; see Statement of Practice E6.

[7] IHTA 1984 s.268(1).

(b) operations effected before March 27, 1974, cannot be associated with operations effected on or after that date;

(c) the legislation contains no provision equivalent to s.268(3), which provides that where a transfer of value is made by associated operations carried out at different times that transfer is treated as having been made at the time of the last of those operations, the value transferred being reduced by that transferred by any earlier operations which constituted transfers of value in their own right. In the absence of such a provision, it appears that certain operations can in theory be brought into charge more than once. HMRC are, however, unlikely to attempt to do this.

Omission to exercise a right

Section 65(9) provides that for the purposes of the secondary exit charge trustees are **15–12** to be treated as making a disposition if they omit to exercise a right, unless it is shown that the omission was not deliberate. Such a notional disposition is treated as having been made at the time—or the latest time—when they could have exercised the right. At first glance it would seem that, given the fact that an operation is defined as including an omission, this provision is superfluous, but it must be borne in mind that it is necessary to establish that the trustees have made a disposition, and the legislation does not provide that an operation constitutes a disposition. It provides only that a disposition includes a disposition which is effected by an operation. Thus, without s.65(9), there might be some question as to whether or not the deliberate failure by trustees, e.g. to exercise their rights under a rent-review clause, could constitute a disposition, since that omission would constitute but one operation, with the result that it would not be said that there had been a disposition "effected by associated operations".

The main charging provisions contain, in s.3(3), a provision similar to s.65(9) though it is to be noted that s.65(9) is considerably wider than s.3(3), which applies only where a person deliberately omits to exercise a right with the result that both the value of his estate is decreased and the value of someone else's estate is increased. Perhaps the most obvious instance of trustees omitting to exercise a right is when they fail to exercise an option. Their deliberate failure to take up a rights issue would clearly be within s.65(9), as might be the deliberate non-exercise of voting rights. The trustees' intentions are irrelevant (though they may be relevant in determining if relief from a charge is available—see para.15–15), so that s.65(9) will prima facie apply even though the trustees omit to exercise a right with a view to protecting a trust asset, e.g. where trustees decide not to exercise a right to increase the rent from hitherto "good" lessees whose business is experiencing financial difficulties. "Right" is not defined, with the result that the right referred to could apply to a right in or over trust property which is not relevant property and even to a right given to the trustees under the trust deed, though it remains to be seen whether HMRC will press for such a wide interpretation. There is, of course, the further jurisprudential question of precisely what constitutes a "right" as a matter of general law.[8]

Close company transfers

Normally when a close company makes a transfer of value that transfer is treated as **15–13** having been made by the participators in that company according to their respective

[8] See para.2–22.

rights and interests.[9] It is possible, of course, for the trustees of a relevant property trust to be participators in a close company. Where this is the case there would be no point in the legislation merely attributing the transfer of value made by the company to the trustees, since the trustees, not being individuals, would not be chargeable to tax under the main charging provisions. Section 99(1) and (2) therefore provide that where any part of the value transferred by a close company is apportioned under s.94 to the trustees of a relevant property trust, the trustees are treated as if they had made a disposition as a result of which the value of the trust property at the time of the company's transfer had been reduced by an amount equal to the amount apportioned to the trustees. If the transfer increases the value of the trust property, as it might where, e.g. the company sells property at an undervalue to the trust, this amount is reduced by the amount of any such increase. In deciding whether the value of the trust property has been increased, there is left out of account the value of any rights or interests in the company possessed by the trust.[10] Assume a relevant property trust fund consists of a 60 per cent shareholding in X Ltd and that X Ltd makes a transfer of value of £10,000. Six-tenths of this (£6,000) will be apportioned to the trustees under s.94. The effect of s.99(1) and (2)(b) is to treat the value of the trust fund as having been reduced by this amount as the result of a disposition made by the trustees.[11]

Close company alterations

15–14   The original set of special charging provisions, not surprisingly, failed to envisage all the means by which value might be shifted out of trust property and into the hands of the beneficiary. In particular, no provision was made to catch two techniques for shifting value out of shares held by trustees. The first technique involved the company making a transfer of value. This was rendered ineffective by the Finance Act 1976, and, as was just seen, continues to be ineffective. The second technique was more sophisticated; it involved the trustees exercising their voting powers to alter the articles of the company, so that although the value of the totality of the shares in the company remained the same, value shifted out of the shares held by the trustees into those held by a beneficiary. The company was then wound-up, with the result that the company's assets[12] passed to the beneficiary. The Finance Act 1976 also rendered this technique ineffective; it provided that where an alteration was made in the share or loan capital of (or in any rights attaching to the shares in or debentures of) a company which was a close company for CTT purposes and not quoted on a recognised stock exchange which would otherwise be treated as a disposition made by the trustee-participators under s.39(5) of the Finance Act 1975, a capital distribution of an amount equal to the fall in value of the trust property was deemed to have been made at the time of the alteration. It is to be noted that the present special charging provisions,[13] do not contain a similar provision. In the Standing Committee debates, the Solicitor-General stated that no such provision was needed since "the charging structure of the new regime for discretionary trusts is such that there will now be an automatic tax charge in the

---

[9] IHTA 1984 s.94; see paras 2–73 and following.

[10] IHTA 1984 s.99(3); this prevents a charge from arising which in fairness ought not to arise.

[11] See also the discussion of s.99(1) and (2)(a) at paras 2–101 and following.

[12] These were often the original trust assets, which had been transferred to the company at some stage, perhaps in anticipation of the value-shifting scheme.

[13] Which since March 22, 2006 apply also to certain settlements in which interests in possession subsist, i.e. where the interest is not a qualifying interest in possession.

circumstances",[14] but did not indicate how that charge is to be imposed or state why, if such a charge was to be imposed automatically, it was necessary to make express provision to impose a charge where a close company the shares in which are held on relevant property trusts makes a transfer of value.

Special relief

As was mentioned above, the legislation provides one relief which is available to **15–15** prevent a charge from arising under the secondary exit charge only. By s.65(6), no tax is charged under the secondary exit charge if the disposition made by the trustees is such that, were the trustees beneficially entitled to the settled property in question, either s.10 (relief for essentially commercial transactions) or s.16 (relief on the grant of a tenancy of agricultural property) would prevent the disposition from being a transfer of value. For a full discussion of these reliefs, see paras 2–41 and following and 2–54.

In the second edition of this book it was suggested that the difficulties occasioned by the statutory hypothesis of beneficial ownership were likely to give rise to litigation and such litigation was subsequently forthcoming in *Macpherson v IRC*.[15] In that case the trustees of a discretionary trust intended to appoint the property on a protected life interest. Because this was pre-March 22, 2006, the appointment of a protected life-interest would have been an occasion for incurring a primary exit charge (the protected life-interest would have constituted a qualifying interest in possession). However, as a prelude to that appointment they agreed to revise an arrangement with a former beneficiary under which that beneficiary agreed to house pictures comprised in the trust fund. Looked at in isolation the agreement was commercial in nature although the case proceeded on the basis that its effect was to diminish the value of the property in the settlement. Accordingly, as the appointment on protected trusts took effect on the following day, it was that reduced value which would, prima facie, fall into charge. HMRC contended that the agreement and the subsequent appointment of the protected life interest were associated and that the appointment was therefore relevant in considering whether relief under s.10 was available to the trustees. It will be remembered that under that section the taxpayer must show that the disposition in question (the agreement in this case) was not made in a "transaction" intended to confer a gratuitous benefit on any person: for these purposes "transaction" includes a series of transactions and any associated operations. It follows from HMRC's argument that if the arrangement and the appointment were associated operations then the appointment, which was clearly designed to confer a gratuitous benefit on the appointee, would operate to deny relief under s.10. The trustees contended that:

(a) the appointment was not part of the transaction which fell to be tested by the statutory hypothesis; and
(b) the only way to avoid absurd results in applying that hypothesis was to exclude the extended definition of "transaction".

Unless this was done, for instance, no disposition could ever qualify for relief under s.65(6) because it could always be said that the disposition in question was associated

---

[14] *Hansard*, HC Vol.X, col.622 (June 10, 1982). In its application to post-March 22, 2006 settlements, the reference to "discretionary trusts" should read "relevant property" trusts.
[15] *Macpherson v IRC* [1987] S.T.C. 73.

with the making of the settlement, which was an operation intended to confer a gratuitous benefit.

The majority of the Court of Appeal found in favour of HMRC. They held that taking into account the extended definition of "transaction" did not necessarily prevent s.65(6) relief being available as it was always possible that the depreciatory transaction was not *made* in a series of transactions of which the original settlement was one. The majority also pointed out that, had the same facts arisen in the case of unsettled property, relief under s.10 would equally have been unavailable. Slade L.J. put matters[16] thus:

> "If an absolute owner of the pictures, for the purpose of facilitating a gift . . . had made an agreement, . . . in the terms of the 1977 agreement and had then proceeded to give the pictures . . . (subject to and with the benefit of the agreement) the next day, I cannot, for my part see how the agreement could possibly have attracted the exemption afforded by [s.(10)]. Even though the motive of the donor in entering into the agreement might not have been to save tax on the subsequent gift, its effect would have been to depreciate the value of the pictures; and that would have been just the kind of transaction which [s.3(1)] was designed to catch."

This decision was unanimously upheld in the House of Lords and Lord Jauncey (with whose speech the other Law Lords concurred) noted that an associated operation was only relevant if it was intended either per se or as part of a scheme to confer a gratuitous benefit. Accordingly, had the order of events in *Macpherson* been reversed so that the appointment was made before the agreement:

> "the agreement would undoubtedly have been associated with the appointment within the definition of [s.268] but it would not have been a relevant associated operation since it would have contributed nothing to the conferment of the gratuitous benefit which had already been effected by the appointment. It could alternatively be said that the transaction intended to confer gratuitous benefit had already been completed before the operation had been entered into, therefore although it was an associated operation it could not be said to have been made in that transaction."[17]

It is to be noted that trustees of a trust with qualifying interests in possession are treated more favourably—all the reliefs given to transfers of value are potentially available to them under s.52(3), as they were to trustees of a relevant property trust under the original special charging provisions. Of these reliefs, only that given by s.15 to waivers of dividends[18] is likely to be helpful to a relevant property trust, but it does seem that it would have been both simpler and more consistent for s.65(6) to have been drafted along the lines of s.52(3).

IV. GENERAL RELIEFS

15–16   The legislation includes a number of provisions the effect of which is to prevent an exit charge from arising. These are as follows:

Reduction within first quarter

15–17   Section 65(4) provides that no exit charge is imposed if the reduction in property or value occurs in a quarter beginning either with:

---

[16] *Inland Revenue Commissioners v Macpherson* [1987] S.T.C. 73 at 81e–f.
[17] *Inland Revenue Commissioners v Macpherson* [1988] S.T.C. 362 at 369d.
[18] See para.2–71.

(a) the day on which the settlement commenced[19]; or

(b) a 10-year anniversary.

Since, as will be seen in the next chapter, the rate at which an exit charge is imposed depends on how long the property in respect of which the charge is imposed has been relevant property, it might be thought that nothing much turns on whether a distribution is made within the "first quarter" or not, so long as it is made at a relatively early date, but this would overlook the full benefit to be gained from making a distribution within the "first quarter". This follows from the fact that since no exit charge is imposed on such a distribution, the cumulative total of the settlement is unaffected by it. Where, on the other hand, a distribution is made after the "first quarter", taper relief is given only in respect of the rate of tax, not the amount on which tax is charged. Thus the full amount of a distribution made after the "first quarter" cumulates, with the result that the rate at which future charges are imposed may be adversely affected.

Although s.65(4) is a relieving provision, it can result in IHT being charged because its effect can be to prevent other relieving provisions, the operation of which depend on the existence of an exit charge, from applying; see *Frankland v IRC*,[20] discussed at para.8–193.

Excepted payments

By s.65(5), tax is not charged in respect of certain payments, or in respect of a   **15–18** liability to make such a payment. For convenience, these payments will be referred to as "excepted payments", a term not used in the legislation.

Payments in respect of costs or expenses

Section 65(5)(a) provides that no tax shall be charged in respect of a payment of   **15–19** costs or expenses, so far as those costs or expenses are fairly attributable to relevant property, or in respect of a liability to make such a payment. It is thought that expenditure incurred in paying legal and accountancy fees falls under this head, so that, e.g. where trustees incur conveyancing costs in completing an appointment those costs should not be subject to tax. The position is less clear where trustees incur a charge to CGT in connection with an appointment, or have to make a payment under, e.g. ITTOIA 2005 s.646 but it is thought that such payments should constitute payments of "costs or expenses"; otherwise the payment by trustees of CGT would give rise to a primary exit charge, and this presumably is not intended. In the same way, a payment of IHT should also be a payment of "costs or expenses"; since if it is not there could be a double round of grossing-up.[21] If the trustees discharge out of capital expenses which are properly chargeable to income, protection may not be available under this head. It remains to be seen to what extent costs or expenses paid out of a mixed fund

---

[19] See paras 10–12 and following.
[20] *Frankland v IRC* [1996] S.T.C. 735.
[21] See para.15–50.

of relevant and non-relevant property are regarded as being "fairly attributable" to the relevant property.

Income payments

15–20   By s.65(5)(b), no tax is charged in respect of a payment which is or will be income of any person for any of the purposes of income tax, or in respect of a liability to make such a payment. As will be seen below, the meaning of the words "or will be" is far from clear. As a preliminary point, it is to be noted that no relief is available in respect of a payment which is or will be income for corporation tax purposes, even though a corporate body may be the object of a relevant property trust.

Payments which constitute income for the purposes of income tax fall into two categories: payments which as a matter of general law rank as income, and payments which are expressly deemed by statute to rank as income. Whether a payment has the quality of income as a matter of general law depends on the quality of the payment in the recipient's hands. The fact that it is made out of capital is not conclusive.[22]

Note, of course, that no charge arises when income is paid to beneficiaries with interests in possession, even where the interest is not a qualifying interest in possession and therefore within the relevant property regime.

School fees

15–21   The treatment for income tax purposes of capital advances made by trustees for the payment of school fees has been the subject of concern both to professional advisers and HMRC.[23] In the light of the decision of the Court of Appeal in *Stevenson v Wishart*,[24] it is believed that HMRC now accept that advances out of trust capital will generally be treated as capital in the hands of the recipient unless:

(1) The trust instrument provides that advances of capital shall be made each year to augment the income which that beneficiary receives in years when the income of the trust falls below a stated level (as in *Brodie's Will Trustees v IRC*).[25]

(2) The power to advance capital is to be exercised in order to maintain the beneficiary in the same degree of comfort as had been the case in the past (as in *Cunard's Trustees v IRC*).[26]

(3) The relevant capital payments amount to an annuity in the beneficiary's hands (as in *Jackson's Trustees v IRC*).[27]

---

[22] See *Brodie's Will Trustees* (1933) 17 T.C. 432; *Lindus and Hortin v IRC* (1933) 17 T.C. 442; *Cunard's Trustees v IRC* [1946] 1 All E.R. 159; *Stevenson v Wishart* [1987] S.T.C. 266. See also *Jackson's Trustees v IRC* (1942) 25 T.C. 13; *Postlethwaite v IRC* (1963) 41 T.C. 224; *Michelham's Executors and Trustees v IRC* (1930) 15 T.C. 737; *Williamson v Ough* [1936] A.C. 384; *Esdaile v IRC* [1936] 20 T.C. 700; *Peirse-Duncombe Trust Trustees v IRC* (1940) 23 T.C. 199; *Milne v IRC* [1956] 37 T.C. 10.

[23] See, for instance, the exchange of correspondence in *The Law Society Gazette*, June 2, 1982.

[24] *Stevenson v Wishart* [1987] S.T.C. 266.

[25] *Brodie's Will Trustees v IRC* [1933] 17 T.C. 432.

[26] *Cunard's Trustees v IRC* [1946] 1 All E.R. 159.

[27] *Jackson's Trustees v IRC* [1942] 25 T.C. 13.

Accordingly, unless the payments fall within any of the above situations they will not be taxed as income in the recipient's hands.

Foreign trusts

Where the trust is foreign, then, although the nature of the beneficiary's interest and rights fall to be determined according to the proper law of the trust, the quality of payments in the hands of the recipient must be determined in accordance with English law. This follows from the decision of Pennycuick J. in *Inchyra v Jennings*,[28] in which although payments to a UK beneficiary under a United States trust were capital in his hands under the relevant US law, they were held to be income for United Kingdom purposes and assessable as such.

15–22

Trustees' remuneration

Remuneration paid to a trustee resident in the United Kingdom will constitute income in his hands, and will consequently not be chargeable. Where remuneration is paid to a non-resident trustee, the remuneration will, as an income payment to a non-resident, be excluded from charge.

15–23

Payments deemed to be income by statute

Certain payments which as a matter of general law rank as capital payments are statutorily deemed to be income payments under the Income Tax Acts. In this context four[29] deeming provisions are particularly noteworthy, namely:

15–24

(1) ITTOIA 2005 s.654 under which income is treated as arising from a person's limited interest in residue in the whole or part of an estate's residue in cases A, B and C. Case A is where the interest has not ceased before the beginning of the tax year, and a sum is paid in respect of the interest in that year and before the administration period. Case B is where the tax year is the final tax year, the interest has not ceased before the beginning of that year and a sum remains payable in respect of the interest at the end of the administration period. Case C is where that tax year is a year before the final tax year, and a sum is paid

---

[28] *Inchyra v Jennings* [1966] Ch. 37. Contrast *Lawson v Rolfe* [1970] 1 Ch. 613 in which "stock dividends" were held to lack any element of recurrence and therefore not to have the quality of income in the recipient's hands.

[29] But see also ICTA 1988 s.249 and ITTOIA s.410(3) which together effectively provide that stock dividends paid to trustees which would to any extent have been accumulated or paid at the discretion of trustees are to be regarded as income in the trustees' hands for UK tax purposes. The tax treatment of stock dividends received by trustees of interest in possession trusts is discussed in the Revenue Statement of Practice SP4/94. In general, the trustees should consider whether, as a matter of trust law, the stock dividend should be regarded as income or capital, taking account of all the relevant facts and any specific provision in the trust deed. Provided that the facts support the trustees' decision HMRC will accept whichever of the three basic approaches—i.e. income, capital or capital with an adjustment payment made to the beneficiary with an interest in possession—the trustees decide to adopt. Stock dividends paid by a foreign company will normally rank as capital: see *Lawson v Rolfe* [1970] 1 Ch. 613; cf. *Rae v Lazard Investment Trust* [1963] 1 W.L.R. 555; 41 T.C. 1.

in respect of the interest in a later tax year but before the end of the administration period, or remains payable in respect of it at the end of that period.

(2) ITTOIA 2005 s.631, under which any payment whatsoever under a settlement to the settlor's infant unmarried child is deemed to be income to the extent that, in effect, the trustees have accumulated and not distributed income.

(3) ITTOIA 2005 s.633 under which payment of any capital sum to the settlor of a settlement by the trustees thereof or by a company connected[30] with the settlement may be treated as income, to the extent that, in effect, the trustees have accumulated and not distributed income.

(4) ITA 2007 s.731 under which the conferring of a benefit by non-resident trustees on a beneficiary may result in his being treated as having received an amount of income equal to the value of that benefit.

Particular difficulties may arise in connection with benefits deemed under ITA 2007 s.731 to be the income of a beneficiary under a non-resident trust. Where the trustees have received relevant income prior to conferring the benefit, an amount of relevant income equal to the value of the benefit is treated as the recipient's income. In these circumstances, it seems clear that part of the benefit treated under ITA 2007 s.731 as income will not be chargeable for IHT purposes, while the balance of the amount in question will be chargeable. If relevant income subsequently arises in relation to the recipient of the benefit, he will be subject to income tax on an appropriate amount, but there is no provision in the legislation which cancels out the original IHT assessment. It is understood that HMRC take the view that the words "or will be" in s.65(5)(b) operates to prevent a charge from arising when the benefit is conferred.

Consequences of payment being income

15–25   The fact that a payment is not a distribution payment because it is an income payment will often be cold comfort to the recipient, since it will mean that IHT has been avoided only because income tax has become payable. But in some circumstances the fact that the payment ranks as an income payment may be to the taxpayer's advantage. It may be that the rate of income tax is lower than that which applied for IHT, or, even better, that the taxpayer pays no income tax whatsoever, e.g. because the income is covered by his personal reliefs.

Where the trustees have already suffered income tax, it may be advantageous for them to make payments to a beneficiary which are income in his hands if, after taking into account his personal reliefs and any credit to which he is entitled, he will incur no further liability to income tax, since in that way he will have the use of the money in question. Even where the beneficiary's marginal rate of income tax is such that he will incur some further income tax liability, it still may be advantageous to make income payments if the IHT due on a capital payment of an equal amount would exceed the income tax due.

Income payments to non-residents

15–26   By s.65(5)(b), no tax is charged in respect of a payment which would for any of the purposes of income tax be income of a person not resident in the United Kingdom if

---

[30] See para.2–45.

he were so resident, or in respect of a liability to make such a payment. This provision derives from the fact that "income", which is not statutorily defined, has been held to mean "income subject to United Kingdom tax",[31] with the result that foreign income of a non-resident is not "income" within the meaning of the Income Tax Acts. This relief thus prevents what are in fact income payments made out of a foreign trust to a non-resident beneficiary from giving rise to a charge to IHT.

Excepted exits

Tax is not charged in respect of property which ceases to be relevant property in certain circumstances defined by reference to: **15–27**

- (a) when the property ceases to be relevant property; or
- (b) how the property ceases to be relevant property; or
- (c) what happens to the property on its ceasing to be relevant property.

For convenience, both linguistically and organisationally, these circumstances will be referred to collectively as "excepted exits", a term not used in the legislation.

Will trusts

By s.144, relief is available where, within two years after a person's death, an event occurs on which an exit charge would otherwise be imposed in respect of property: **15–28**

- (1) which was comprised in that deceased person's estate immediately before his death;
- (2) which was settled by his will; and
- (3) in which no interest in possession has subsisted since his death.

In such a case, no tax is charged, and the provisions apply as if the will had provided that on the testator's death the property should be held "as it is" held after the event. These trusts are discussed at paras 8–189 and following.

Court orders

By s.146(6), anything which is done in compliance with an order under the Inheritance (Provision for Family and Dependants) Act 1975[32] or which occurs on the coming into force of such an order does not constitute an occasion on which an exit charge may be imposed.   **15–29**

Charitable purposes

No exit charge is imposed in respect of property which ceases to be relevant property on becoming held for charitable purposes only without a limit of time (defined by a   **15–30**

---

[31] *Ormonde v Brown* (1932) 17 T.C. 333; *Astor v Perry* [1935] A.C. 398; *Becker v Wright* [1966] 1 W.L.R. 215; *Mapp v Oram* [1970] A.C. 362.
[32] See also paras 8–208 and following.

date or otherwise).[33] For the meaning of "charitable purposes", see paras 3–40 and following.

Political parties

15–31 No exit charge is imposed in respect of property which ceases to be relevant property on becoming the property of a political party qualifying for exemption under s.24.[34] For the definition of such a political party, see para.3–52.

National purposes

15–32 No exit charge is imposed in respect of property which ceases to be relevant property on becoming the property of a body mentioned in Sch.3.[35] The bodies so mentioned are listed at para.3–53.

Qualifications

15–33 The above exceptions are subject to certain qualitative and quantitative qualifications, as follows.

Qualitative qualifications

15–34 None of the exceptions cited at paras 15–30–15–32 above is available in relation to any property if *any* of the following qualifications apply:

(1) The disposition by which it becomes property of the relevant description is defeasible. For this purpose, a disposition which has not been defeated at a time 12 months after the property concerned became property of the relevant description and is not defeasible after that time is treated as not being defeasible, whether or not it was capable of being defeated before that time.[36]

(2) The property or any part of it may become applicable for purposes other than charitable purposes or purposes of a qualifying political party or a body mentioned in Sch.3.[37]

(3) At or before the time when the property becomes property of the relevant description, an interest under the settlement is or has been acquired for a consideration in money or money's worth by an excepted body of the kind mentioned above. For these purposes, a body is treated as acquiring an interest for a consideration in money or money's worth if it becomes entitled to the

---

[33] IHTA 1984 s.76(1)(a).
[34] IHTA 1984 s.76(1)(b).
[35] IHTA 1984 s.76(1)(c).
[36] IHTA 1984 s.76(5).
[37] IHTA 1984 s.76(6).

interest as a result of transactions which include a disposition for such consideration (whether to that body or to another person) of that interest or of other property.[38]

Quantitative qualification

It may be that if the above exceptions were not available the amount on which tax **15–35** would be charged (before agricultural and/or business relief and before any grossing-up)[39] would exceed the value of the property immediately after it becomes property of the body in question. In that case, no exception is available. Instead, tax is charged on that excess.[40]

This is an anti-avoidance provision, the aim of which is best explained by an example. Assume trustees own 51 per cent of the shares in an investment company (so that the shares do not qualify for business relief), and that they wish to appoint the shares absolutely to a beneficiary. In the absence of the quantitative qualifications, they might transfer 2 per cent of the shares free of tax to a charity, and then transfer the remaining 49 per cent of the shares (now valued on a minority basis) to the beneficiary, who, in turn, might repurchase the 2 per cent holding from the charity. The quantitative qualification frustrates this by ensuring that, in effect, relief is given only to the value of the 2 per cent holding (on a minority basis) which becomes the property of the charity. If in the above example the 51 per cent holding, 49 per cent holding and the 2 per cent holding were worth, for convenience, say, £51,000, £24,000 and £1,000 respectively, so that the appointment to the charity diminished the value of the trust fund by £27,000, an exit charge would have been imposed on £26,000.

It may be that the trustees receive consideration for transferring the property to the **15–36** body in question. In that case, in computing the excess the value of the property transferred to the body in question is reduced by the consideration received by the trustees.[41] Thus, if in the above example the charity had paid £1,000 for the shares, the amount to be brought into charge would have been £25,000. This is to be expected, since in effect no gift would have been made to the charity at all.

Excluded property

Since excluded property is not relevant property, in the absence of provision to the **15–37** contrary a charge would arise when trustees converted relevant property into excluded property. This would obviously be contrary to the spirit of the legislation, and provision is accordingly made to prevent the imposition of such a charge.

General exemption

Section 65(7) prevents an exit charge from arising by reason only that property **15–38** comprised in a settlement ceases to be situated in the United Kingdom and thereby

---

[38] This appears to be the net effect of IHTA 1984 s.76(7) and (8).
[39] IHTA 1984 s.76(4).
[40] IHTA 1984 s.76(3).
[41] IHTA 1984 s.76(3).

becomes excluded property by virtue of s.48(3)(a) (because the settlor of the settlement was domiciled outside the United Kingdom when he made the settlement).[42] The special rules in ss.80–82 are not relevant for this purpose.

Investment in exempt gilts

15–39   Section 65(8) prevents an exit charge from arising by reason only that property comprised in a settlement is "invested" in exempt gilts and thereby becomes excluded property by virtue of s.48(4)(b),[43] provided the settlor was not domiciled in the United Kingdom when he made the settlement. The use of the word "invested" causes concern insofar as it suggests that the relief may not be available where the trustees hold exempt gilts as excluded property for a short time for IHT purposes only, e.g. to shelter a ten year charge. It remains to be seen whether in a given case HMRC take this point, but to be safe trustees may wish to retain the gilts for a suitable period.

General rule

15–40   The general rule for determining whether s.65(8) applies to prevent a charge arising on a conversion of relevant property into exempt gilts is drafted by reference to s.48(4)(b). The position depends on whether the beneficiaries under the settlement satisfy the conditions attached to the exempt gilt in question. The domicile of the settlor is irrelevant.

Special rule: sections 80 and 82

15–41   A special rule for determining whether s.65(8) prevents an exit charge operates where s.80 or s.81 applies. The circumstances in which ss.80 and 81 can apply were discussed at paras 10–14 and following. It will be recalled that under s.80 a special rule applies where: (a) property becomes comprised in a settlement in circumstances such that the settlor, or his spouse or civil partner, widow or widower is beneficially entitled to a qualifying interest in possession immediately after it becomes so comprised; and (b) that property (or any part of it) subsequently becomes held on trusts under which none of those persons is beneficially entitled to a qualifying interest in possession (i.e. post-March 22, 2006, the rule only applies while the interest of the settlor, or his spouse or civil partner, widow or widower is a pre-March 22, 2006 interest in possession or a "postponing interest", namely an immediate post-death interest, or a disabled person's interest).[44] In such a case, the property in question is treated for the purposes of the special charging provisions as not having become comprised in the settlement when it was made but as instead having become comprised in a separate settlement at the time when the last of the persons just mentioned ceased to be beneficially entitled to an interest in possession in it. Section 82(3)(a) provides that in such cases s.65(8) will not

---

[42] See para.32–49.

[43] See para.32–35. The fact that FA 1998 converted certain gilts which were not capable of being excluded property into exempt gilts which were excluded property (see para.32–21) would in the absence of provision to the contrary have thus triggered an exit charge. FA 1998 s.161(3) prevents this from happening.

[44] IHTA s.80(4).

apply unless the settlor of the original settlement was domiciled abroad when he made the settlement.

Special rule: sections 81 and 82

As discussed at paras 10–14 and following, under s.81 where property ceases to be **15–42** comprised in one settlement and becomes comprised in another it is treated for the purposes of the special charging provisions as remaining comprised in the first settlement unless before it becomes comprised in the second settlement a person becomes beneficially entitled to the property. Section 82(3)(b) provides that in such a case s.65(8) will not apply unless the settlor of the transferee settlement was domiciled abroad when he made the transferee settlement. This is of increased significance post-March 22, 2006 as more trusts will fall within the relevant property regime. Resettlements from previously excluded property trusts should be avoided once the settlor has become domiciled or is deemed to be domiciled in the United Kingdom.

Exempt gilts and the deemed domicile rules

The application of the deemed domicile rules in deciding whether relief is available **15–43** under s.65(7) or s.65(8) is relatively straightforward. The rules always apply in determining the settlor's domicile in relation to property which became comprised in a settlement after December 9, 1974.[45] This is somewhat surprising and seems unfair because, in relation to both the basic rule in s.65(8) and to its extension where s.80 or s.81 operates, the deemed domicile rules normally do not apply in deciding whether exempt gilts are excluded property.[46] In addition, it appears that on a strict reading of the provisions the rules also apply without any limit of time in determining whether the special s.267(3) domicile test is satisfied for the purposes of s.65(7). This follows from the fact that the time limit for s.65(7) in the case of the single settlement is established by virtue of the fact that s.65(7) relief is defined by reference to s.48(3), which itself is subject to a time limit so far as the deemed domicile rules are concerned. Section 82, on the other hand, is not defined by reference to s.48(3). It remains to be seen whether HMRC take this point.

Tax traps: chargeable conversions

The relieving provisions in s.65(7) and (8) are by no means comprehensive. So far **15–44** as s.65(7) is concerned, consider the position where trustees convert relevant property into excluded property by selling investments and acquiring a reversionary interest, so that that interest itself becomes settled property. If that interest is situated outside the United Kingdom, then it may be excluded property under s.48(3)(a) so that s.65(7) applies.[47] If, on the other hand, it is situated in the United Kingdom, it can be excluded property only under s.48(1),[48] with the result that it is not within s.65(7).

---

[45] IHTA 1984 s.82(3).
[46] IHTA 1984 s.267(2).
[47] See para.32–49.
[48] See para.32–58.

Note too that s.65(7) does not prevent a charge from arising where trustees convert relevant property into excluded property by acquiring holdings in an authorised unit trust or a share in an open-ended investment company which satisfy the conditions of s.48(3A). However, this is an aspect which may soon be the subject of legislative amendment, being an aspect identified as requiring simplification in the recent consultative document issued by HMRC (referred to at para 13–01 above).

So far as s.65(8) is concerned, relevant property trustees who sell investments which are relevant property and purchase exempt gilts—with a view to converting the investment into excluded property—will precipitate an exit charge unless relief is available under s.65(8), applying inter alia the restrictive conditions concerning the settlor's domicile discussed above. Note also that s.65(8) is subtly restrictive: trustees who hold exempt gilts in circumstances where the gilts are not excluded property and who appoint a qualifying interest in possession in those gilts in circumstances such that the gilts become excluded property by virtue of s.48(4)(a) will trigger an exit charge because they will not be able to rely on s.65(8), which is framed by reference to s.48(4)(b) exclusively.[49]

Employee trusts

15–45   No exit charge is imposed in respect of shares in or securities of a company which cease to be relevant property on becoming held on trusts of the description specified in s.86, (as discussed at paras 24–02 and following), provided certain conditions are satisfied. The conditions are as follows:

(1) The person for whose benefit the trusts permit the settled property to be applied must include all or most of the persons employed by or holding office with the company.[50]

(2) At the date when the shares or securities cease to be relevant property or at a subsequent date not more than one year later the trustees must:

(a) own more than half of the ordinary shares in the company, and

(b) have powers of voting on all questions affecting the company as a whole which if exercised would yield a majority of the votes capable of being exercised thereon.

In addition, there must be no provisions in any agreement or instrument affecting the company's constitution or management or its shares or securities whereby this can cease to be the case without the trustees' consent.[51]

For these purposes, "ordinary shares" are shares which carry either:

(a) a right to dividends not restricted to dividends at a fixed rate, or

(b) a right to conversion into shares carrying such a right to dividends.

It may be that the articles of a company confer special voting rights on a class of shares in respect of one or more questions affecting the company as a whole. In the absence of provision to the contrary, trustees who had voting control on all other matters might be precluded by such class rights from having control. The legislation accordingly provides that where a company has shares or securities of any class giving powers of voting limited to:

(a) the question of winding up the company, and/or

(b) any question primarily affecting shares or securities of that class,

those questions are left out of account in determining whether the trustees have control.

---

[49] See para.32–35.

[50] IHTA 1984 s.75(1) and (2)(a).

[51] IHTA 1984 s.75(1) and (2)(b).

(3) The s.86 trusts must not permit any of the settled property to be applied at *any* time for the benefit of:

(a) the settlor; or

(b) a participator in the company in question; or

(c) any other person who is a participator in any close company that has made a disposition whereby property has become comprised in the settlement in question and which was relieved from being a transfer of value by s.13(1)[52]; or

(d) any other person who at any time after the property in question ceases to be relevant property or during the 10 years before that time has been a participator in either the company in question or a participator in a close company that has made a disposition of the kind mentioned in (c); or

(e) any person connected with any person mentioned in (a)–(d) above.[53]

For this purpose "close company" and "participator" have the meanings given in s.102,[54] and references to a participator in a company which is not a close company are construed as references to a person who would be a participator in the company if it were a close company.[55] It is important to note that there is ignored for this purpose any participator who (i) is not beneficially entitled to, or to rights entitling him to acquire at least 5 per cent of any class of the shares comprised in the issued share capital of the company in question, and (ii) who on a winding up of the company would not be entitled to at least 5 per cent of its assets.

Furthermore, in determining whether the trusts permit property to be applied in the prohibited manner, no account is taken of the following[56]:

(i) any power to make a payment which is the income of any person for any of the purposes of income tax, or which would be the income for any of those purposes of a non-resident if he were resident in the United Kingdom;

(ii) any power to appropriate shares in pursuance of a profit-sharing scheme approved under Sch.9 of the Taxes Act 1988, if the trusts are those of such a scheme; or

(iii) any power to appropriate shares to, or acquire shares on behalf of, individuals under a share incentive plan approved under Sch.2 of the Income Tax (Earnings and Pensions) Act 2003, if the trusts are those of such a plan.

Maintenance funds

15–46 The legislation provides that in two cases no exit charge is imposed in respect of property which becomes comprised in a maintenance fund.[57]

Capital gains tax holdover relief

15–47 Capital gains tax holdover relief is available under the Taxation of Chargeable Gains Act 1992 s.260, subject to various restrictions, where, per s.260(2)(a), a disposal is a

---

[52] See paras 2–68 and following.
[53] IHTA 1984 s.75(1), (2)(c) and (3).
[54] See para.2–72.
[55] IHTA 1984 ss.13(5), 75(1) and 75(2)(c).
[56] IHTA 1984 s.13(4).
[57] See para.27–73.

chargeable transfer. The occasion on which an exit charge is incurred is not a chargeable transfer: but any disposal which gives rise to a chargeable transfer will be within s.260(2)(a) because s.2(3) of the 1984 Act provides that references to chargeable transfers are to be construed as references to occasions on which tax is chargeable under inter alia the relevant property provisions. Accordingly, an exit charge ranks as a chargeable transfer for this purpose.[58] Note that if by operation of s.65(4),[59] s.144 or otherwise, the exit from a relevant property trust is not an occasion on which an exit charge is incurred, holdover relief will not apply.

V. THE CHARGEABLE AMOUNT

15–48   Where an exit charge is imposed, the general rule, laid down by s.65, is that tax is charged on that amount by which the value of the relevant property comprised in the settlement immediately after the chargeable event in question is less than it would be but for that event.[60] The legislation thus effectively imports into the special charging provisions the consequential loss rule that applies under the main charging provisions to actual transfer of value, and the comments made at para.6–13 in relation to that rule will apply.

Agricultural relief and business relief

15–49   It may be that agricultural relief and/or business relief is available to trustees under ss.103–124B. Where such relief is available, it is given at the appropriate percentage before any grossing-up.[61]

Grossing-up

15–50   If the trustees pay the tax out of relevant property comprised in the settlement immediately after the event in respect of which an exit charge is imposed, the amount on which tax would otherwise be charged must be grossed-up.[62] If the beneficiary pays the tax, no grossing-up is necessary. It may be that the trustees pay the tax out of favoured property, or out of property in which there is a subsisting qualifying interest in possession. If the trustees pay the tax out of favoured property on which an exit charge may be imposed, a primary exit charge will be imposed, and the relief available to payments in respect of costs or expenses will not prevent this charge from arising, since that relief is available only where the costs or expenses are fairly attributable to the property out of which the payment is made. If the payment is made out of property in which there is a qualifying interest in possession, the position varies according to whether or not the person entitled to that interest is also the person liable for the tax due in respect of the exit charge. If he is, tax will prima facie be chargeable under s.52(1), on the footing that his interest in possession in the amount paid by the trustees will have come to an end, but relief should be available under s.53(2) to prevent any charge from

[58] See para.10–37.
[59] See para.15–17.
[60] IHTA 1984 s.65(2)(a).
[61] IHTA 1984 ss.104(2) and 116(7).
[62] IHTA 1984 s.65(2)(b).

arising. If, on the other hand, the payment is made out of property in which the beneficiary under the relevant property trust does not have a qualifying interest in possession, a charge will arise under s.52(1) in respect of which relief under s.53(2) will be unavailable.

Relief for CGT paid by beneficiary

It may be that trustees incur an exit charge on an occasion on which a chargeable gain accrues to them, and that the CGT is borne by a person who becomes absolutely entitled to the settled property concerned.[63] In such a case, the amount on which the exit charge is imposed is reduced by the amount of CGT so borne.[64] It will be noted that the relief applies only where the trustees themselves make a gain, the relief is thus not available to gains made by trustees which are subsequently attributed to a beneficiary under the Taxation of Chargeable Gains Act 1992 s.87, unless the capital payment in respect of which the attribution is made itself results in the trustees making a gain under s.71 of that Act, the tax on which is borne by the beneficiary in question.

15–51

[63] IHTA 1984 s.65(2)(b).
[64] IHTA 1984 s.165(2).

CHAPTER 16

RATES OF TAX

PRE-CTT SETTLEMENTS

I. INTRODUCTION

16–01   The rules for determining the rate at which tax is charged on relevant property are crucial. Unfortunately, they are also somewhat complicated. Different rules apply according to whether the settlement commenced before March 27, 1974, or on or after that date, and different rules also apply according to whether the chargeable event in question takes place before, on the occasion of, or after the settlement's 10-year anniversary. This chapter is therefore divided into two main parts—one on settlements made on or after March 27, 1974, the other on settlements made before that date. For convenience, these kinds of settlements are referred to as "post-CTT" and "pre-CTT" settlements, respectively. A chronological approach is adopted in each of these parts, i.e. consideration is given first to charges occurring before the first 10-year anniversary, then to the charge on that anniversary, and then to subsequent charges.

Do note that, as regards post-CTT settlements, a recent consultative document issued by HMRC (and referred to at para.13–01 above) recognises that part of the complexity of the existing calculations of periodic and exit charges stems from the requirement to take into account transactions involving the settlor that took place before or at the same time as the trust was established, for example, gifts by the settlor in the seven years preceding the creation of the settlement, and other "related" settlements (see paras 16–11 and following below). The document acknowledges that reliance on historic data can result in problems in identifying and valuing transactions that took place decades before—particularly if there has been a change of trustees, or if the settlor is no longer alive or able to provide information. The document recognises that a calculation regime based only on data that was known to, or capable of being easily established by the current trustees might therefore be simpler to implement, but considers that there might be a risk of fragmentation of settlements across a number of trusts, each of which could benefit from its own nil-rate band. The consultative document elicits suggestions for how to simplify the regime. It remains to be seen what, if any, simplifications of the relevant property regime will follow.

The approach of the legislation is to charge tax at a fraction of the rate of tax **16–02** effectively charged on the value transferred by a hypothetical chargeable transfer made by a hypothetical transferor with a hypothetical cumulative total. The procedure is thus first to determine the tax that would be charged on this hypothetical chargeable transfer, and then to ascertain the effective rate at which that tax would be charged. Tax is then in fact charged at a fraction of that rate. The lifetime rates of tax are always used to find the effective rate of tax on the hypothetical transfer.[1] The following table sets out the basic rules.

Rate of tax: basic rules

Chargeable occasion	Pre-CTT settlements			Post-CTT settlements		
	Hypothetical value transferred	Hypothetical cumulative total	Fraction	Hypothetical value transferred	Hypothetical cumulative total	Fraction
Exit charges before first 10-year anniversary	The amount on which the exit charge is imposed	The distribution payments made and the amounts on which any exit charges have been imposed in the previous 10 years	3/10: before April 1, 1984 may have been 2/10	The value of all the property comprised in the settlement (and any related settlement) immediately after the commencement of the settlement, plus the value of any property which subsequently becomes comprised in the settlement whether or not it is still comprised in the settlement	The settlor's pre-settlement 7-year cumulative total	complete quarters $\frac{3/10 \times \text{since settlement commenced}}{40}$

[1] IHTA 1984 ss.66(3)(c) and 68(4)(c); see paras 6–42 and following.

Rate of tax: basic rules

Chargeable occasion	Pre-CTT settlements			Post-CTT settlements		
	Hypothetical value transferred	Hypothetical cumulative total	Fraction	Hypothetical value transferred	Hypothetical cumulative total	Fraction
First periodic charge	The amount on which the periodic charge is imposed	As for previous exit charge	3/10	The amount on which the periodic charge is imposed, plus (i) the value of all the property comprised in any related settlement immediately after that settlement commenced, and (ii) any property which has since become comprised in the settlement	The settlor's pre-settlement 7-year cumulative total, plus the amounts on which exit charges were imposed in the previous 10 years, plus in the case of settlements made between March 27, 1974 and March 8, 1982, distribution payments made in the previous 10 years	3/10
Subsequent periodic charge	The amount on which the periodic charge is imposed	The amounts on which any exit charges have been imposed in the previous 10 years	3/10	As for the first periodic charge		
Exit charges after a 10-year anniversary	The rate is the rate charged at the previous 10-year anniversary, adjusted to take account of any (i) reduction in the lifetime rates, and (ii) increase in the relevant property comprised in the settlement		complete quarters since $\frac{3/10 \times \text{last periodic charge}}{40}$	As for pre-CTT settlements		

The basic effect of the rules is as simple as the rules are complicated. It is that it is not expensive in IHT terms to hold property on relevant property trusts. The highest rate at which tax can be charged is at 30 per cent of the lifetime rates, i.e. under the regime at present in force at a rate of 6 per cent. As will be seen below, in many cases the rate of tax will be considerably lower, with the result that the price of holding property on relevant property trusts will often be outweighed by the advantages, fiscal and otherwise, of doing so. This treatment is of increasing importance post Finance Act 2006, given that new settlements which are not within the favoured property regime will be within the relevant property regime and this is so even if such new settlements contain interests in possession for beneficiaries, i.e. to the extent that such post-March 22, 2006 interests in possession are not qualifying interests in possession.[2]

Distribution payments

As will be seen below, in determining the hypothetical cumulative total, regard may have to be had to the amounts of certain distribution payments made between March 27, 1974, and March 8, 1982, out of the settlement in question. The rules for determining whether a distribution payment was made out of the settlement between these dates and the amount of any such distribution payment are discussed in Chapter 11 of the first edition of this book. It is to be noted that the legislation provides that only distribution payments "determined in accordance with the rules applicable before March 8, 1982 under para.11 of Sch.5 to the Finance Act 1975" fall to be brought into account.[3] Distribution payments made under s.118(4) of the Finance Act 1976 thus do not fall to be brought into account; this is presumably a drafting oversight.   **16–03**

The *Aird* case

In *IRC v Trustees of Sir John Aird (No.2)*,[4] Nourse J. dealt with a number of matters concerning distribution payments which had been the subject of considerable controversy and which, given, inter alia, the fact that in computing the rates of tax under the current rules regard may still have to be had to distribution payments made under the old rules, may in some cases still be relevant. These matters are discussed at paras 15–03–15–07 of the second edition of this book.   **16–04**

The facts of the case were simple. On May 9, 1974, trustees of a discretionary trust made an appointment in the following form: **16–05**

> "In exercise of the power for this purpose given to them . . . the Appointors hereby irrevocably appoint and declare that the sum of £38,000 shall forthwith be raised out of the capital of the Appointed Fund and held in trust for . . . Sir George John Aird absolutely."

HMRC accepted that since this appointment was made before March 13, 1975, it did not give rise to a charge to tax, but contended that the amount of the payment fell to be included in the trust's cumulative total. They argued first that the appointment constituted an actual distribution payment, in which case it clearly did cumulate within the terms of legislation (subject to an argument by the taxpayer concerning the amount which cumulated); second, if this was not the case, the appointment gave rise to an interest in possession in respect of which a distribution payment was deemed to have been made and which accordingly cumulated. Nourse J. agreed that the appointment gave rise to an interest in possession.

However, a transaction which passed an absolute equitable interest was not an actual distribution payment, which necessarily involved the passing of legal as well as beneficial title. In addition the following matters appear from the judgment: **16–06**

---

[2] See Ch.11 (Settled Property Definitions).
[3] FA 1982 s.110(7).
[4] *IRC v Trustees of Sir John Aird (No.2)* [1982] S.T.C. 544.

(1) Notional capital distributions cannot have been made before March 13, 1975, and therefore transactions made before that date which would have constituted notional capital distributions if made on or after that date cannot result in deemed distribution payments having been made for cumulation purposes.

(2) There is persuasive authority for the proposition that notional capital distributions made between March 13, 1975, and July 29, 1976, on the coming into effect of an interest in possession or of favoured accumulation and maintenance trusts did not have to be grossed-up.

(3) Given the circumstances in which an actual distribution will be regarded as having been made, many transactions which were thought to constitute actual distribution payments will not have done so but will instead have given rise to interests in possession. This will be important in two ways in relation to future transactions:

(a) the transaction will not affect the settlement's cumulative total if it was made before March 13, 1975; and

(b) the capital distributions treated as made between March 13, 1975, and July 29, 1976, will not have had to have been grossed-up, with the result that the trustees' cumulative total may be reduced accordingly.

Identification problems

16–07   As will be seen below, the rate at which tax is charged is in most cases determined partly by reference to how long the property in respect of which the charge in question is imposed has been relevant property. Where an exit charge is imposed, the rate of tax is determined partly by reference to the number of quarters during which the property has been relevant property since the settlement commenced or the last periodic charge was imposed, as the case may be.[5] A similar rule applies where the periodic charge is levied. It is thus vital to be able to identify the type of property in respect of which a charge is imposed.

Assume, for example, that X settles £100,000 and that four years later he adds a further £50,000 to the trust, with the result that the trustees hold £150,000 in a single bank account. One year later the trustees distribute £30,000 to a beneficiary. If this distribution is regarded as having been made out of the original £100,000 the rate of tax will be higher than if it is regarded as having been made out of the added £50,000. If it is regarded as having been made rateably out of the £100,000 and the £50,000, the position is somewhere in-between. Surprisingly, the legislation provides no rules of identification. Trustees will accordingly be well advised to segregate trust assets so that they can be readily identified, for two reasons. First, this may result in tax advantages. In the example just given, for instance, had the trustees deposited the added £50,000 in a separate account from which they made the distribution, the distribution would, it is thought, fall to be regarded as having been made out of that £50,000. Secondly, considerable difficulties may arise if such a policy is not adopted.[6]

16–08   It may be possible to exploit more actively the absence of any rules of identification. Assume, for example, that the trustees of a post-CTT settlement contemplating an appointment of £100,000 to a beneficiary hold shares worth £300,000. If they realise the shares and then appoint £100,000 in cash to the beneficiary it is arguable on a strict reading of the legislation that in determining the rate of tax regard is had only to the

---

[5] Except where the exit charge is imposed before the first 10-year anniversary of pre-CTT settlements.
[6] A similar policy should be pursued with accumulations of income: see para.14–04.

single quarter in which the trustees held the £100,000, with the result that the rate at which tax would otherwise have been charged is reduced. This follows from the fact that there is no provision under which references in the special charging provisions to any property are to be taken as including references to any property directly or indirectly representing that property, and, in the absence of such a provision, it is hard to see how HMRC are entitled to trace property. By way of contrast, though this is obviously not conclusive, such a provision is to be found elsewhere in the legislation—see ss.199(5), 200(4) and 201(6) (liability for tax) and s.237 (HMRC charge). Needless to say, it would be optimistic to think that a court would find that tax could be avoided so easily.

Charges arising on the same day

Special rules apply where more than one charge is imposed on the same day. First, **16–09** by s.266(1),[7] where the amount on which tax is charged depends on the order in which the charges are imposed, they are treated as having been imposed in the order which results in the smallest amount being brought into charge to tax. This means that if on the same day two exit charges are imposed, one of which requires grossing-up, and one of which does not, the one which requires grossing-up will (assuming it makes a difference) be treated as having occurred first, because that way the grossing-up will be done at a lower rate.

Secondly, s.266(2) makes provision to ensure that tax is borne rateably when more than one charge is imposed on the same day. The procedure is that tax is initially charged in the normal way (subject to any rearrangement under s.266(1) of the order in which the charges were imposed). The total amount subject to tax is then divided by the total tax chargeable to find the effective rate of tax. The amount on which tax is chargeable in respect of each distribution is then recharged at that effective rate to determine what part of the total tax chargeable is to be attributed to each chargeable occasion.

POST-CTT SETTLEMENTS

II. INTRODUCTION

This part of this chapter is concerned with the rules governing settlements which **16–10** commenced on or after March 27, 1974. It is worth repeating that a settlement is regarded as having commenced on the day that property first became comprised in it, and that there are special, vitally important rules for determining when, for the purposes of the special charging provisions, property becomes comprised in a settlement.[8]

Related settlements

As will be seen below, the rules governing post-CTT settlements are modified to the **16–11** taxpayers' disadvantage in the case of "related settlements", i.e. settlements made by

---

[7] As read in conjunction with IHTA 1984 ss.2(3) and 266(4).
[8] See paras 10–12 and following.

the same settlor and which commenced on the same day.[9] Two settlements are not related if all the property comprised in one or both of them, was, immediately after the settlement commenced, held indefinitely for charitable purposes only.[10]

It is important to note that a settlement is not a related settlement to the extent only that it consists of relevant property; indeed, a settlement can be a related settlement, somewhat anomalously, even though it is comprised wholly of favoured property or property in which there is a qualifying interest in possession.

16–12   The related settlement provisions are most likely to apply where will trusts are concerned—a settlor can easily avoid making related settlements where he makes settlements during his lifetime, by making settlements on different days.[11] Where a person anticipates making two or more settlements by his will the following points should be borne in mind. First, s.80 may prevent two settlements from being related which at first glance appear to be related. Assume, for example, that by his will X creates two settlements. The first gives his wife a life interest, while the second establishes discretionary trusts for his grandchildren. Although as a matter of general law those settlements are created on the same day, the effect of s.80 is that the first settlement will not commence for purposes of the special charging provisions until the widow's life interest comes to an end, with the result that the settlements are not related settlements. The corollary to this is that ostensibly unrelated settlements may in fact be related. If in the above example the widow on her death creates a discretionary will trust that settlement will be related to the settlement deemed by s.80 to have commenced on her death. Section 80 also means the corollary to this is that no advantage is to be gained by an individual's making an inter vivos settlement on himself for life, remainder on discretionary trusts, with a view towards preventing that settlement from being related to another settlement made by him on his death. Pre-March 22, 2006, the making of an inter vivos settlement for himself for life was not immediately chargeable, which might have made this a potentially attractive course to follow. However, even prior to the changes introduced by the Finance Act 2006, s.80 would have resulted in the lifetime settlement being treated as having commenced for the purposes of the special charging provisions on his death, which is also the time at which the discretionary trust would have been treated as commencing under s.83. The result would be that the settlements would be related.

Planning: pilot trusts

16–13   There does appear to be a fairly simple way of putting property into two or more settlements by will without those settlements being related settlements. Assume, for example, that by his will Z wishes to leave some property on interest in possession trusts for his children and other property on discretionary trusts for his grandchildren. He might consider settling a nominal sum during his life on trustees on the intended discretionary trusts. On his death he would add to this settlement the property destined for his grandchildren, The two settlements would be treated as having commenced on different days, and the addition by the will of property to the discretionary trust would not affect this—this follows from the fact that s.83, which provides that property which becomes comprised in a settlement in pursuance of a will is treated for the purposes of

---

[9] IHTA 1984 s.62(1).

[10] IHTA 1984 s.62(2).

[11] HMRC will be unlikely to be able to argue successfully that the settlements form a single composite settlement: see the Court of Appeal's decision in *Rysaffe Trustee Co (CI) v IRC* [2003] S.T.C 536, discussed at para.9–22.

the special charging provisions as having become comprised in it on the death of the testator, would not affect the date on which the discretionary trust is treated as having commenced, because s.60 provides that a settlement commences when property first becomes comprised in it.

The CCAB[12] in their "Memorandum on Taxation Anomalies and Practical Difficulties 1982" suggested that, in effect, a settlement should cease to be a related settlement to the extent that it has been wound up, converted into a permanent charity or become excluded property. It may be that the mischief caused by the existence of a related settlement can be brought to an end by bringing that settlement to an end. Assume that X settled £100,000 on discretionary trusts for his grandchildren and £200,000 on his son for life, remainder to a charity. The interest in possession settlement will come to an end on the son's death, because at that time the charity will become absolutely entitled to the trust property. Does this mean that the £200,000 settled on his son no longer falls to be taken into account in computing the rate at which tax is charged on the discretionary trusts for the grandchildren? **16–14**

The relevant provisions, ss.66(4)(c) and 68(5)(b), provide that in computing the rate of tax on a post-CTT settlement regard must be had to, inter alia, " ... the value, immediately after a related settlement commenced, of the property then comprised in it". In the authors' view, it would be anomalous for this value to be taken into account if the related settlement in question has ceased to exist, and this is so regardless of the fact that the value to which the legislation refers is the value of the property in question immediately after it became comprised in the related settlement, not the value of that property at the time at which the charge is imposed. If this is correct, then the mischief caused by the existence of a related settlement may be brought to an end by bringing that settlement to an end. This will have no adverse tax consequences so long as the person who becomes absolutely entitled to the trust property is resident or ordinarily resident and is the person entitled to a qualifying interest in possession. There will be no charge to IHT because there will have been no transfer of value: the person with the qualifying interest in possession will, by virtue of s.49 be treated as beneficially entitled to the property in which the interest subsists. The position will be more difficult where the trust is not a qualifying interest in possession trust, since in that case there may be a charge to IHT when the settlement is brought to an end. It is to be noted that it is not sufficient to appoint the property held in the related settlement on trusts such that the property is held indefinitely for charitable purposes—the existence of such trusts is relevant only in determining whether a settlement is a related settlement when it is made.

III. CHARGES BEFORE THE FIRST 10-YEAR ANNIVERSARY

It may be that an exit charge is imposed before the first 10-year anniversary of a post-CTT settlement, either because relevant property has ceased to be comprised in the settlement or the value of such property has been reduced. The general rule in such a case is that tax is charged at a fraction (known as the "appropriate fraction") of the "effective rate", i.e. the average rate at which tax would be charged on the value **16–15**

[12] Consultative Committee of Accountancy Bodies.

transferred by a hypothetical chargeable transfer made at the time of the charge to tax, with certain characteristics.[13]

Effective rate of tax

16–16   As matters stand, the first step in determining the rate at which tax is to be charged is to find the effective rate of tax on a hypothetical chargeable transfer made by a hypothetical transferor. This is done in the following way.

Hypothetical value transferred

16–17   The value transferred by the hypothetical transfer is taken to be:

(1) the value, immediately after the settlement commenced, of the property then comprised in it; plus
(2) the value, immediately after it became comprised in the settlement, of any property which subsequently became comprised in the settlement before the occasion of the exit charge in question, whether or not that property is still comprised in the settlement; plus
(3) the value, immediately after any related settlement commenced, of the property then comprised in it.[14]

It is to be noted that property which becomes settled on a death is regarded under s.83 as having become comprised in the settlement immediately before the death, with the result that its value at that time is the value to be taken into account. Thus, where a testator settles the whole or part of his residuary estate on discretionary trusts the value to be brought into account may well exceed the value of the trust fund when the administration of his estate is completed.

Tax traps

16–18   Three general points should be made about these rules. First, it is vital to note that the rules apply to any property coming within the above heads, not just to relevant property. This means that even excluded property, favoured property (particularly property held on qualifying accumulation and maintenance trusts, bereaved minors' trusts, age 18-to-25 trusts) and property in which there is a qualifying interest in possession must be brought into account, which seems unjustified. Secondly, what falls to be brought into account is the value, immediately after it became comprised in the settlement in question, of property falling within the specified categories. Subsequent changes in the value of that property are irrelevant, and this is so whether the changes are brought about by market forces or by the acts of the settlor, e.g. where he pays a premium on a life policy settled by him. Finally, it is also irrelevant that agricultural relief and/or business relief was available in respect of all or any of the property when

[13] IHTA 1984 s.68(1).
[14] IHTA 1984 s.68(1), (4)(a) and (5).

it was transferred to the settlement. This follows from the fact that the s.68(5) refers to the value of the property in question, and those reliefs, though given in respect of property, operate by way of reducing the amount on which tax is charged, not by way of reducing the value of property as such.[15]

Additions

A number of comments are also in order concerning the rule that it is necessary to **16–19** bring into account the value of any property which became comprised in the settlement after its commencement, whether or not that property (i) has remained comprised in the settlement, and (ii) was or is relevant property.[16] First, the rule seems fair in so far as it prevents a settlor from arranging to have an artificially low hypothetical value transferred by creating a small "pilot" settlement of, say, £100, as is often done, to which he then makes substantial additions. Secondly, the rule means that amounts on which previous exit charges have been imposed will be brought into account indirectly in computing the hypothetical value transferred. This follows from the fact that the value of any property which was comprised in the settlement but which has since ceased to be so comprised is brought into account. It would have been more logical to bring such amounts into the settlement's hypothetical cumulative total, as is done for purposes of the 10-year charge. Thirdly, it may be that the value of property comprised in the settlement was reduced in circumstances such that no exit charge was imposed, e.g. because one of the reliefs discussed at paras 15–16–15–47 was available. Such value will still be brought into account. This seems unfair, and compares unfavourably with the procedure in computing the effective rate for the purposes of the 10-year charge.[17]

Hypothetical cumulative total

The hypothetical cumulative total of the hypothetical transferor is taken to be equal **16–20** to the aggregate value transferred by the chargeable transfers made by the settlor in the seven-year period ending with the day on which the settlement commenced, disregarding any chargeable transfers made on that day.[18] The value transferred by any chargeable transfer made by the settlor on the creation of the settlement is left out of account

---

[15] See paras 26–16 and 26–114.

[16] For example, where a settlement qualified as an accumulation and maintenance settlement prior to the changes introduced by the FA 2006 and the trustees did not change the terms of the settlement so as to bring it within the more restrictive conditions of s.71 (as amended) and assuming that the settlement would not automatically have fallen within the bereaved minors' trust or age 18-to-25 trust regimes, then, on April 6, 2008, the settlement would have moved into the relevant property regime (see paras 18–33 and following). The legislation provided that there was to be no charge on that date. However, in calculating the rate of exit charges and periodic charges, the shift into the relevant property regime is treated as an addition under IHTA s.69(2)(b): the rates are calculated accordingly (see Ch.18, paras 18–42–18–44). See generally para. 16–35.

[17] See paras 16–25 and following.

[18] IHTA 1984 s.68(4)(b).

in the hypothetical cumulative total, having already been taken into account in the value of the chargeable transfer, as explained at para.16–17.

Example

16–21   The following example, to which reference will be made elsewhere in the following discussion, shows how the general rule operates.

On May 13, 1993, X, who then had a cumulative total of £250,000, settled £100,000 on trustees. Of this amount, £60,000 was held on wide discretionary trusts for such of A, B, C, and D as the trustees should appoint; the other £40,000 was held on trust for E for life, remainder on the discretionary trusts just mentioned. X thus made a chargeable transfer of £60,000, all of which was charged at 20 per cent and a PET of £40,000. The following events subsequently happened:

(1) On July 6, 1995, the trustees appointed an interest in possession in £20,000 to A, who undertook to bear any IHT that might be due.
(2) On October 15, 2002, the trustees appointed £30,000 outright to B, who undertook to bear any IHT that might be due.
(3) On May 13, 2003, the trust had its first 10-year anniversary; at the time the trustees held £30,000 on the said discretionary trusts.
(4) On July 23, 2008, E died, so that his interest in possession terminated, and the property in which his interest subsisted, which was worth £100,000, became held on discretionary trusts.

To find the rate of tax on, say, the £30,000 appointed to B, it is necessary first to find the effective rate of tax that would have been chargeable on a chargeable transfer of £100,000 made on the date of the distribution (October 15, 2002) by a hypothetical individual with a cumulative total of £250,000. The tax on such a transfer would have been £20,000 (20 per cent of £100,000).[19] The effective rate of tax would thus have been:

$$\frac{20,000}{100,000} = 20 \text{ per cent}$$

The appropriate fraction

16–22   Once the effective rate of tax has been determined, the next step is to multiply this effective rate by what the legislation refers to as the "appropriate fraction". This is three-tenths of the proportion of the first 10-year period that has passed (calculated in quarters) at the time of the chargeable occasion. This is expressed as a fraction, the numerator of which is the number of complete successive quarters in the period beginning with the commencement of the settlement and ending with the day before the chargeable occasion, and the denominator of which is 40 (being the total number of

---

[19] The nil-rate band for April 6, 2002 to April 5, 2003 was £250,000. For inheritance tax thresholds going back to March 18, 1986, see *http://www.hmrc.gov.uk/rates/iht-thresholds.htm* [Accessed October 5, 2012].

quarters in the 10-year period).[20] Thus, returning to the above example, by October 15, 2002, 33 complete successive quarters will have expired from the commencement of the settlement on May 13, 1993, so that the appropriate fraction is:

$$\frac{3}{10} \times \frac{33}{40} = \frac{99}{400}$$

The next step is to multiply the effective rate by this fraction:

$$\frac{99}{400} \times 20 \text{ per cent} = 4.95 \text{ per cent}$$

The tax payable in respect of the payment of £30,000 is thus:

$$£30,000 \times 4.95 \text{ per cent} = £1,485$$

Reduction of the fraction

Circumstances may arise in which all or part of the amount on which tax is charged **16–23** is attributable to property which was not relevant property throughout the period by reference to which the appropriate fraction is determined. In that case, any quarter which expired before the day on which the property became (or last became) relevant property is left out of the numerator, unless that day fell on the same quarter as that in which the period ends, in which case that quarter is counted even if it is incomplete.[21] Assume that in the above example an interest in possession had subsisted between February 1, 1994, and August 15, 1997, in the property by reference to which the charge arose. In that case, the 14 complete quarters prior to August 15, 1997 (the day on which the property last became relevant property) would be left out of the numerator, with the result that the fraction representing the quarters would be nineteen-fortieths (19/40).

IV. PERIODIC CHARGES

The general rule is that tax is charged on a 10-year anniversary of a post-CTT **16–24** settlement at 30 per cent of the "effective rate", i.e. the average rate at which tax would be charged on the value transferred by a hypothetical chargeable transfer made by a hypothetical transferor immediately before that 10-year anniversary.[22]

Hypothetical value transferred

The value transferred by the hypothetical chargeable transfer is taken to be equal **16–25** to:

[20] IHTA 1984 s.68(2).
[21] IHTA 1984 s.68(3).
[22] IHTA 1984 s.68(3).

(1) the value on which tax is charged under the periodic charge; plus
(2) the value immediately after it became comprised in the settlement of any property which was not then relevant property and which has not subsequently become relevant property while remaining comprised in the settlement in question; plus
(3) the value of any property comprised in any related settlement immediately after that settlement commenced.[23]

Hypothetical cumulative total

16–26 The cumulative total of the hypothetical transferor is taken to be equal to:

(1) the aggregate value transferred by the chargeable transfers made by the settlor in the seven years ending with the day on which the settlement commenced, disregarding any chargeable transfers made on that day (so that the value transferred by any chargeable transfer made by the settlor on the creation of the settlement is ignored); plus
(2) the aggregate amount on which any exit charges were imposed in respect of the settlement in the 10 years before the anniversary[24]; plus
(3) in the case of settlements made between March 27, 1974, and March 8, 1982, the amounts of any distribution payments made between March 27, 1974, and March 8, 1982, in the 10 years before the anniversary.[25]

Returning to the example given above at para.16–21, the settlement's first 10-year anniversary will have occurred on May 13, 2003, when £30,000 was held by the trustees on discretionary trusts. The nil-rate band at that time was £255,000. The position will be:

		£	
Hypothetical value transferred	=	30,000	value of trust fund
		40,000	value of commencement of settlement of property in which E's interest subsists
		_____	
		70,000	

Hypothetical cumulative total	=	250,000	settlor's pre-settlement cumulative total
		20,000	exit charge on July 6, 1995
		30,000	exit charge on October 15, 2002
		_____	
		300,000	

[23] IHTA 1984 s.66(3)(a) and (4).
[24] IHTA 1984 s.66(3)(b) and (5); see paras 27–71–27–103 for the position where the trustees have purchased heritage property.
[25] IHTA 1984 s.66(6).

The effective rate of tax will thus be 20 per cent, the nil-rate band having been used up by the hypothetical cumulative total. Tax will thus be charged at 30 per cent of this rate, i.e. at 6 per cent, with the result that the tax due is £30,000 × 6 per cent = £1,800.

Settlor's additions

It may be that, following the commencement of a settlement and after March 8, **16–27** 1982, but before the anniversary in question, the settlor makes a chargeable transfer which increases the value of the property comprised in the settlement. In that case, s.67 provides that in computing the hypothetical cumulative total regard is had to the value transferred by the chargeable transfers made by the settlor in the seven years ending with the day on which the increase occurs, if that amount exceeds the value transferred by the chargeable transfers made by him in the seven years prior to the commencement of the settlement,[26] and this is so regardless of whether the property the value of which is increased by the chargeable transfer is relevant property, favoured property or property in which there is a qualifying interest in possession. Such increases should thus normally be avoided.

Values left out of account

In determining the value transferred by the chargeable transfers made by the settlor **16–28** in the seven years ending with the addition, the following values are left out of account:

(1) Chargeable transfers made on the day the addition was made, so that the value transferred by the chargeable transfer by which the addition was made is left out of account.[27]
(2) Any value attributable to property the value of which is taken into account in determining the hypothetical value transferred by the hypothetical transfer[28] so as to prevent the same value being brought into account twice, once in computing the hypothetical value transferred and once in computing the hypothetical cumulative total.
(3) Any value attributable to property in respect of which an exit charge has previously been imposed and which forms part of the hypothetical cumulative total on the occasion of the charge in question,[29] so as to prevent the same value being brought into the hypothetical cumulative total twice.

If more than one increase is involved, it is necessary to compare the values transferred within the various seven-year periods in question, and to adopt that which provides the highest cumulative total.

Comments

Three comments are in order here. First, it is to be noted that s.67 applies only where **16–29** the value of the trust fund is increased by a chargeable transfer made by the settlor.

[26] IHTA 1984 s.67(1) and (2).
[27] IHTA 1984 s.67(3)(b).
[28] IHTA 1984 s.67(3) (b) and (4)(a).
[29] IHTA 1984 s.67(3)(b) and (4)(b).

Increases brought about by exempt transfers or by dispositions which are relieved from being transfers of value are thus left out of account. Thus, if a settlor adds property to a settlement in circumstances such that the additions are within the annual exemption and/or the normal expenditure out of income exemption, s.67 will not apply. In the same way, an increase brought about by a transfer of excluded property to trustees will not be within s.67. Secondly, it is immaterial for purposes of s.67 whether the amount of property comprised in the settlement is augmented; what matters is whether the value of such property is increased. Probably the best example of an increase in value only is the payment by the settlor of a premium on a life policy settled by him. Such an increase in value only could also happen where a settlor omits to exercise a right with the result that the value of property comprised in the settlement made by him is increased. Exceptionally, it might occur where, e.g. a settlor who controls a company, a substantial minority shareholding in which is held by trustees, transfers some of his shares to a third party with the result that the trustees holding is increased in value because they hold more shares than any other shareholder.

A chargeable transfer which increases only the value of property comprised in a settlement is disregarded for purposes of s.67 if it is shown that the transfer (a) was not primarily intended to increase the value of the property in question, and (b) did not result in that value being increased by more than 5 per cent immediately after the transfer,[30] and this is so however large that transfer might actually be.

Finally, it is possible to take advantage of the fact that no account is to be taken of chargeable transfers made on the day the addition was made. Assume, for example, that on successive days[31] a settlor sets up, say, three £100 discretionary trusts. On the fourth day he adds £100,000 to each trust, so that £100,100 is comprised in each settlement. The fact that no account is to be taken of other chargeable transfers made on that day appears to mean that the settlor's pre-addition cumulative total in relation to each trust will be only £300 and not £300 in relation to the first trust, £100,300 in relation to the second trust and £200,300 in relation to the third trust. In *Rysaffe Trustee Co (CI) v IRC*[32] a settlor, with a view to securing this advantage, on separate days made in sequence five separate discretionary settlements of five parcels of 6,900 shares each. HMRC successfully argued before the Special Commissioner that the making of all the settlements were associated operations and that therefore the settlor had made one composite settlement by an extended disposition but Park J. overturned her decision on the fundamental ground that all of the property comprised within the five settlements was already within the 10 yearly charge because each settlement was created by a "disposition" in the ordinary sense. Therefore, in order to bring the property within charge, it was not necessary or appropriate to consider whether the five settlements were created by associated operations. The Court of Appeal, adopting an even more robust approach, also found for the taxpayer trustees.[33]

Property previously charged

16–30   The legislation takes account of the fact that, during the 10 years preceding a 10-year anniversary, property may cease to be relevant property, with the result that an exit charge arises, and that by the time of that 10-year anniversary that property has again become relevant property comprised in the settlement in question, e.g. as where a

---

[30] IHTA 1984 s.67(2).
[31] So that the settlements are not related settlements.
[32] *Rysaffe Trustee Co (CI) v IRC* [2003] S.T.C. 536.
[33] See para.9–22 for a fuller discussion.

qualifying interest in possession vests and then terminates, leaving the property in which the interest subsisted subject once again to discretionary trusts. In such a case, the hypothetical cumulative total is reduced by the lesser of:

(1) the amount, before any grossing-up, on which the previous exit charge was imposed; and
(2) so much of the value on which the periodic charge is imposed as is attributable to the relevant property in question.[34]

Assume the facts are those stated in the example at para.16–21 but that on May 1, 1998, the trustees revoked half of A's interest in possession in £20,000 with the result that, of the £30,000 comprised in the settlement on May 13, 2003, £10,000 was attributable to the property in which that interest formerly subsisted.

In that case, the hypothetical cumulative total would be reduced by £10,000, i.e. from £300,000 to £290,000.

The relief seems incomplete in two ways. First, it is to be noted that the reduction **16–31** is made only in respect of property which has previously been subject to an exit charge. In fairness, the legislation should also provide for a reduction to be made where a distribution payment was made out of the settlement in circumstances where property ceased to be comprised in that settlement before March 9, 1982, and within the 10 years preceding the 10-year anniversary in question. Secondly, there appears to be no reason why the relief should not be available in respect of reductions in value as well as in respect of reductions in property.

Rate reduction

It may be that all or some of the value of the relevant property comprised in the **16–32** settlement immediately before a 10-year anniversary is attributable to property which throughout the immediately preceding 10 years either (i) was not relevant property or (ii) was not comprised in that settlement. Section 66(2) provides that in such a case the rate at which tax would otherwise be charged under the rules just discussed is reduced by one-fortieth for each of the successive quarters in the period which expired before the property became, or last became, relevant property comprised in the settlement.

Assume a settlement commenced for the purposes of the special charging provisions on January 10, 1991. On May 12, 1991, the trustees appointed a life interest in half the fund to one of the settlor's children (a qualifying interest in possession), but this child died on July 21, 1999 with the result that on January 10, 2001, the settlement's first ten-year anniversary, the whole of the settled property was relevant property worth, say, £200,000. Since the settlement's first 10-year anniversary falls on January 10, 2001 regard must be had to the quarters beginning on January 10, 1991. The first of these to expire at a time when relevant property comprised in the fund on January 10, 2001 was not relevant property was the quarter April 10–July 9, 1991. The last such quarter to expire was April 10–July 9, 1999, so that, in all, 33 quarters expired at a time when the property in question was not relevant property. The rate at which tax would otherwise

---

[34] IHTA 1984 s.67(5) and (6).

be charged on the half of the fund on which the qualifying interest in possession subsisted thus falls to be reduced by thirty-three fortieths.

V. RATE BETWEEN 10-YEAR ANNIVERSARIES

16–33   The rule for determining the rate of tax on an exit charge imposed between 10-year anniversaries is relatively simple, and, at least for taxpayers, quite helpful. This is because the rate is the appropriate fraction of the rate that was charged at the last 10-year anniversary, ignoring any previous rate reductions made under s.66(2).[35] In determining the appropriate fraction for this purpose, regard is had to the number of complete successive quarters in the period beginning with the most recent 10-year anniversary and ending with the day before the occasion of charge. This number is then reduced to take account of quarters during which the property by reference to which the charge is imposed was either not relevant property or not comprised in the settlement, in the usual way.[36] Thus, returning to the example at paras 16–21 and 16–26, the rate of tax on any exit charges imposed between May 13, 2003 and May 12, 2013 will be 6 per cent, and this is so regardless of how many exit charges are imposed during that period, and even though the value of the relevant property comprised in the settlement at the previous 10-year anniversary has increased.[37]

Reduction in rates of tax

16–34   It may be that there have been one or more reductions in the lifetime rates of tax since the previous 10-year anniversary. In that case, it is necessary to re-compute the effective rate of tax on that anniversary, using the rates in force at the time. Tax is then charged by reference to the recomputed effective rate.[38]

New or converted property

16–35   It may be that on or after the most recent 10-year anniversary and before the occasion of the exit charge in question either (a) property has become comprised in the settlement, or (b) property which was comprised in the settlement immediately before the anniversary but which was not then relevant property has become relevant property. This will normally occur as the result of either an addition by the settlor to the settlement, or because property already comprised in the settlement that was previously property in which there was a qualifying interest in possession or which was favoured property has become relevant property, be it as a result of an act of the trustee, by operation of law, or under the trust deed.

Where this occurs, s.69(2) provides that the rate at which tax is charged is the appropriate fraction of the rate at which it would have been charged at the previous

---

[35] IHTA 1984 s.69(1).

[36] IHTA 1984 ss.69(4) and 68(3).

[37] Decreases are, alas, similarly ignored. Trustees may thus have an incentive to make distributions or otherwise to remove property from the relevant property regime shortly before a settlement's second or subsequent 10-year anniversary if the effect of doing so will be to allow them to take greater advantage or the nil rate bands.

[38] IHTA 1984 Sch.2 para.3.

10-year anniversary (ignoring any s.66(2) reduction) if immediately before that anniversary that property had become relevant property. This means that the hypothetical value transferred at the previous 10-year anniversary must be adjusted so as to take into account the value of the property in question.

Special rules apply under s.69(3) for determining the value of the property in such a case. The general rule is that the value to be brought into account is the value of the property when it became (or last became) relevant property. This is subject to the qualification that where property has become comprised in the settlement the value to be attributed to it is the value immediately after it became comprised in the settlement if either the property (i) was relevant property immediately after it became comprised in the settlement, or (ii) was not relevant property immediately after it became comprised in the settlement and has not subsequently become relevant property while remaining comprised in the settlement.

As was noted at para.16–07, the legislation provides no rules of identification. This means that on a strict reading of the legislation s.69 could conceivably apply where trustees simply change investments,[39] but it is thought unlikely that HMRC will attempt to apply the legislation in this way.

[39] See para.15–04.

CHAPTER 17

PROPERTY HELD ON FAVOURED TRUSTS

I. INTRODUCTION

17–01   The rules governing property held on favoured trusts differ from those regulating relevant property in two main respects. First, such property is never subject to the periodic charge. Secondly, the rate at which tax is charged in the relatively rare case where an exit charge is imposed is generally determined in a much simpler way than that prescribed where an exit charge is imposed on relevant property. The exception is the rate at which tax is charged on the primary exit charge in relation to property leaving the age 18-to-25 trust regime: the mechanism for calculating the rate of this charge closely follows (but does not replicate) the mechanism for calculating the rate at which tax is charged under s.65, i.e. the exit charge on relevant property leaving a settlement before the ten-year anniversary.

The legislation provides a separate mini-code for each kind of property on which a charge is imposed. Fortunately, these mini-codes have a number of common features. The following discussion accordingly first considers these common features, and then goes on to discuss the features special to the particular kinds of property on which an exit charge may be imposed.

Before considering these various features, it will be helpful to note:

(1) the kinds of property which qualify for favoured treatment; and
(2) on which kinds of such property an exit charge may be imposed.

The legislation effectively divides property into two categories—that on which an exit charge may be imposed, and that which is not susceptible to such a charge, as follows:

Chargeable	Non-chargeable
Property held on accumulation and maintenance trusts	Excluded property
	Property held on permanent charitable trusts
Property held on trust for a bereaved minor	Property in a superannuation fund
	Property in a compensation fund
Property held on an age 18–25 trust	Property in a Lloyd's corporate trust fund
Property held on trust for a disabled person	
Property held on employee trusts	
Property held on temporary charitable trusts	
Property comprised in a maintenance fund	
Property held on protective trusts	

The terms of the trusts on which property must be held in order to come within each of these categories are discussed in Chapters 10–17. Note that since Finance Act 2006, it is no longer possible to create new accumulation and maintenance trusts. Note too that Finance Act 2006 introduced two new categories of favoured trusts—the age 18-to-25 trust and the trust for bereaved minors.

This chapter is concerned solely with the structure of the special charging provisions in relation to settled property to which favoured treatment is given. It is perhaps apposite to note that although exit charges may in theory be imposed on the property listed in the left-hand column above, in practice such charges seldom arise.

II. COMMON FEATURES

As already mentioned, a mini-code regulates the treatment of each kind of property on which an exit charge may be imposed. These mini-codes have in common certain rules governing the circumstances in which tax is charged, when relief is given from such a charge, and on what amount and at what rate tax is charged when no relief is available. These common features are as follows. **17–02**

Exit charges

As a general rule, the special charging provisions impose two kinds of exit charge —a primary charge, and a secondary charge; in one of the cases described below, a third charge is imposed.[1] The primary charge is similar to that imposed on relevant property, but varies slightly according to the particular kind of property concerned. The way it operates with respect to each kind of property is discussed below. The secondary exit charge, on the other hand, is not discussed below in relation to each kind of property, for two reasons. First, it is identical to that imposed on relevant property, i.e. **17–03**

---

[1] See para.17–30 in relation to Employee Trusts.

it is a residual charge imposed when trustees of property held on favoured trusts make a disposition as a result of which the value of the property in question is less than it would be but for that disposition. Secondly, the charge is imposed in exactly the same way on each kind of property, subject only to the modification of the length of the "relevant period" in certain cases.[2] Thus, reference should be made to the discussion at paras 15–08–15–15, which will apply to property held on favoured trusts in exactly the same way as it does to relevant property.

Reliefs

17–04   In the same way that the secondary exit charge is imposed in identical fashion on both relevant property and property held on favoured trusts, so certain reliefs available where a charge is imposed on relevant property, be it the primary exit charge or the secondary exit charge, are also available when a charge would in the absence of such relief be imposed on property held on favoured trusts. Reliefs which fall into this category are those given to excepted payments, excepted exits and excepted assets. For a full discussion of these reliefs, see paras 15–16–15–47.

The chargeable amount

17–05   The rules governing the amount on which tax is charged when a primary or secondary exit charge is imposed are exactly the same as those that apply in relation to relevant property, i.e. tax is charged on the amount by which the value of the property in question is diminished as a result of the chargeable event in question. Where the trustees pay the tax out of the same kind of property as that in respect of which the charge to tax arose, it is necessary to gross-up this amount. Agricultural relief and/or business relief may be available to reduce the amount on which tax is chargeable.[3]

The rate of tax

17–06   Save in the case of the primary charge imposed on certain exits from age 18-to-25 trusts (as to which see below), the rate of tax is calculated by multiplying each quarter of the "relevant period" by a fixed percentage[4] as indicated in the table set out below. In the case of the first 10 quarters, for instance, the rate of tax will be calculated as 10 quarters at a rate of 0.25 per cent per quarter thereby giving a total tax rate of 2.5 per cent. The maximum rate that can apply after 50 years is 30 per cent.

---

[2] See para.17–07.
[3] See para.15–49.
[4] IHTA 1984 s.70(6).

Per cent	Number of complete quarters in relevant period	
0.25	0–40	(first 10 years)
0.20	41–80	(10–20 years)
0.15	81–120	(20–30 years)
0.10	121–160	(30–40 years)
0.05	161–200	(40–50 years)
0.00	200–	(50 years +)

It will be noted that the rates under this regime are less favourable than under the relevant property regime. Under the latter the maximum rate of tax at present is six per cent, while under the favoured property regime that rate is exceeded once the "relevant period" reaches six and a quarter years. However, the advantage is the timing of the payment of the tax in that the periodic charge does not apply to favoured property. In most cases, IHT is only payable under the favoured property regime when the favoured trust is terminated.

The legislation takes account of the fact that the whole or part of the amount on which tax is chargeable may be attributable to property which was excluded property throughout, or at some time during, the relevant period by providing that any quarter throughout which the property was excluded property is to be ignored in determining the number of complete quarters in the relevant period.[5] The rules for identifying the "relevant period" vary according to whether the property in respect of which the tax is chargeable was converted from relevant property into favoured property, as set out below.

Property generally

The general rule, which always applies to property held on accumulation and maintenance trusts, is that the "relevant period" is the period ending with the day before the chargeable event in question[6] and beginning with the later of: **17–07**

    (1) the day on which the property being charged to tax became, or last became, the kind of favoured property in question; and

    (2) March 13, 1975.

Converted property

Exceptionally, the property in respect of which tax is chargeable may have been relevant property immediately before December 10, 1981, which between that date and March 8, 1982 became property held on favoured trusts of the kind in question. In that case, unless the property is held on accumulation and maintenance trusts, which fall always to be dealt with in accordance with the rules stated under the previous heading, the "relevant period" is the period beginning with the later of: **17–08**

    (1) the day on which the property became, or last became, relevant property before December 10, 1981; and

[5] IHTA 1984 s.70(7).
[6] IHTA 1984 s.70(8).

(2) March 13, 1975,

and ending with the day before the chargeable event in question.[7]

Special cases

17–09 The period during which the settled property is treated as having been subject to a particular favoured property regime may be extended by reference to a time when the settled property first became subject to another favoured property regime. For example, the rate of the primary or secondary exit charges imposed on an exit from a bereaved minors' trust under s.71B is calculated by reference to the extended "relevant period" which includes the periods during which the property was subject to accumulation and maintenance trusts or to age 18-to-25 trusts.[8] Similarly, the rate of the secondary exit charge imposed on an exit from an age 18-to-25 trust calculated under s.71G is calculated by reference to the extended "relevant period" which includes periods during which the property was subject to accumulation and maintenance trusts.[9]

EXAMPLES

17–10 The following examples show how the rules work:

(1) A settled property on accumulation and maintenance trusts on December 1, 1988. On October 13, 2003, the trustees entered into a depreciatory transaction with the result that an exit charge arose. The relevant period is December 1, 1988–October 12, 2003, with the result that 59 complete quarters fall to be brought into account, so that tax would be charged at 0.25 per cent for the first 40 quarters (10 per cent) and at 0.20 per cent for the next 19 quarters (3.8 per cent) = 13.8 per cent.

(2) B settled property on wide discretionary trusts on January 1, 1990. The trustees converted these trusts into accumulation and maintenance trusts on February 10, 1998. On November 14, 2003, the trustees entered into a depreciatory transaction giving rise to an exit charge. The relevant period is February 10, 1998–November 13, 2003.

(3) C settled property on June 1, 1976, on wide discretionary trusts. On December 25, 1981, the trustees made an appointment the effect of which was that the property became held on employee trusts. On June 1, 2002, the trustees made a chargeable payment out of the fund. Since the property was relevant property immediately before December 1981 and became favoured property between that date and March 8, 1982, the relevant period is June 1, 1976–May 31, 2002.

(4) D settled property on accumulation and maintenance trusts for Y on December 1, 2005. On January 25, 2007 the trustees made a settled advance to ensure that the trusts would fall within the age 18-to-25 trust regime. On April 6, 2008, the settled property did fall within the age 18-to-25 regime. The beneficiary of the settlement is a bereaved minor. On August 5, 2008, the trustees alter the terms

---

[7] IHTA 1984 s.70(9).
[8] IHTA 1984 s.71B(3).
[9] IHTA 1984 s.71G(3)(c).

of the trust to provide for Y to become absolutely entitled to all the income and capital of the settlement. On November 7, 2009 the trustees entered into a depreciatory transaction with the result that an exit charge arose. The relevant period is December 1, 2005–November 7, 2009.

III. SPECIAL FEATURES

Against the background of the rules that are common to each kind of property on which an exit charge may be imposed, let us now consider the treatment which is special to the various kinds of favoured trusts.

17–11

Accumulation and maintenance trusts

The changes introduced by Finance Act 2006 mean that no settlement created and no trust arising on or after March 22, 2006 can qualify for favoured treatment under s.71.[10] Post-March 22, 2006, s.71, as amended, does not apply to settlements which qualify for favoured treatment as trusts for bereaved minors (see below).[11] Subject to that, and up to April 6, 2008, favoured treatment under s.71 continued to apply to settlements which were already accumulation and maintenance settlements by virtue of having satisfied the conditions of (old) s.71 prior to March 22, 2006. From April 6, 2008, i.e. at the end of a transitional period, these trusts moved into the relevant property regime, unless the terms of settlement had been modified prior to that date so as to satisfy the more restrictive conditions of new s.71, introduced by Finance Act 2006.[12] The occasion when property moved into the relevant property regime by virtue of having ceased to qualify for favoured treatment as a result of failing to satisfy the condition of (new) s.71 was not an occasion of charge.[13]

17–12

For the taxation of accumulation and maintenance trusts before and after the Finance Act 2006 changes, see Chapter 18. In outline, the taxation of existing accumulation and maintenance settlements which satisfy the more restrictive post-Finance Act 2006 conditions is as set out below.

A primary exit charge is imposed when property held on accumulation and maintenance trusts ceases to be so held.[14] The secondary exit charge applies,[15] and the standard reliefs are available[16] in the usual way.

In addition, special relief is given by s.71(4), which provides that no exit charge is imposed in the following circumstances:

(1) On a beneficiary becoming beneficially entitled to, or to an interest in possession in, settled property on or before attaining the specified age at which he is to become beneficially entitled under the trusts (which cannot exceed 18 years of age).[17]

[10] IHTA 1984 s.71(1A).
[11] IHTA 1984 s.71(1B).
[12] FA 2006 Sch.20 para.3(1) and (2).
[13] FA 2006 Sch.20 para.3(3)
[14] IHTA 1984 s.71(3)(a).
[15] IHTA 1984 s.71(3)(b).
[16] IHTA 1984 ss.71(5) and 70(3) and (4). Note that unless the operation of the Trustee Act 1925 s.31 is excluded, there will never be an occasion when a beneficiary will become entitled to an interest in possession in the trust prior to attaining 18 years of age (see also *Stanley* v *IRC* [1944] 1 All E.R. 230).
[17] IHTA 1984 s.71(1)(a). Prior to the FA 2006 changes, the specified age could not exceed 25 years.

(2) On the death of a beneficiary before attaining the specified age, as a result of which property ceases to be held on favoured accumulation and maintenance trusts. This prevents a charge from arising where, e.g., a person who, by virtue of having acquired an interest in the trust fund, has ceased to be a beneficiary within the meaning of s.71 has his interest increased on the death of a beneficiary. Assume, for example, that A, B, and C are beneficiaries under an accumulation and maintenance trust, and that A, the eldest, attains 18, with the result that under the terms of the trust he acquires an interest in possession in one-third of the fund and so ceases to be a beneficiary for purposes of s.71. One year later B dies while still under the age of 18, with the result that A's interest is increased to an interest in possession in half the trust fund. The first relief afforded by s.71(4) would be unavailable, because A is no longer a "beneficiary" for purposes of s.71. A second relief is thus needed to prevent a primary exit charge from arising unfairly.

Rate of tax

17–13   Where a charge arises, the amount on which tax is charged is determined in the usual way, save that the starting date for determining the specified number of quarters by reference to which the date is fixed is always the later of March 13, 1975, and the day on which the property in respect of which tax is chargeable became held on accumulation and maintenance trusts.[18]

17–14   Note that the normal exit charges, including the rate at which tax is charged, are modified if at any time after March 22, 2006 but prior to April 6, 2008, or on the coming into force of the more restrictive conditions of (new) s.71, property ceased to satisfy the conditions of (old) s.71 without ceasing to be settled property, and the trust is no longer an accumulation and maintenance trust, is not a bereaved minors' trust, and is not a settlement with a qualifying interest in possession,[19] but satisfies the conditions set out in s.71D(6), i.e. if the trust property has moved into the age 18-to-25 regime (see paras 18–39–18–41). In those circumstances, the exit charges on age 18-to-25 trusts apply at the relevant rates[20] (see below).

Tax traps

17–15   Although property held on s.71 trusts is generally safe from primary and secondary charges, such charges can arise and given the rules for determining the rate of tax, can be disastrous.

Twenty-five year time bombs

17–16   Property held on s.71 trusts may have ceased to be held on such trusts 25 years after it became held on such trusts.[21] On the occasion of it ceasing to be held on s.71 trusts

---

[18] IHTA 1984 ss.71(5) and 70(8).
[19] IHTA 1984 s.71D(5).
[20] IHTA 1984 s.71D(4) and note that the settlement will fall within the 18-to-25 regime, although the settlement may not satisfy the condition of having been created by will or on intestacy, and although both the parents of beneficiaries of the settlement who are under the age of 25 may still be living.
[21] IHTA 1984 s.71(2)(a).

an exit charge would have been imposed at the staggering rate of 21 per cent. For a full discussion, see para.18–31.

Beneficiary deficit

When the class of beneficiaries remains open so that it is necessary to wait and see **17–17** whether or not a further beneficiary is born, the relieving provision in s.71(4)(b) will not operate in the event that no such beneficiary is born, with the result that the trust subsequently ends. Take the case of an accumulation and maintenance trust set up by Z in favour of his children. He has one child, A, who subsequently dies. At that moment, given that Z is still alive and capable of having more children, the accumulation and maintenance trust (assuming it is drafted to deal with this eventuality) remains in being. Were Z then to die without having produced further children the trust would end and an exit charge would therefore apply.

Bereaved minors' trusts

As of March 22, 2006, favoured treatment is afforded to settled property which is **17–18** held on trust for bereaved minors, so long as the conditions relating to bereavement of the minor beneficiary and to the creation of the trust are satisfied. The conditions relating to the creation of the trust are that the trust is held on statutory trusts for the benefit of a bereaved minor, are established under the will of a deceased parent of a bereaved minor, or are established under the Criminal Injuries Compensation Scheme.[22] The terms of the trust must provide that the bereaved minor will, on attaining the age of 18, become absolutely entitled to the settled property and the income arising from it, including any accumulated income. In addition to these conditions, the terms of the trust must be such that so long as the beneficiary is living and under 18, if any property is applied for the benefit of a beneficiary, it must be applied for the benefit of the bereaved minor, who must be entitled to all of the income arising from the property or the terms of the trust must provide that no income may be applied for the benefit of any other person.[23] The conditions for qualifying for favoured treatment as a bereaved minors' trust are considered in more detail in Chapter 19.

No exit charge arises where property ceases to be held on a bereaved minors' trust in three circumstances: (a) by virtue of the bereaved minor becoming absolutely entitled to the settled property on or before attaining the age of 18; (b) by virtue of the bereaved minor dying under the age of 18; or (c) by virtue of the property being paid or applied for the advancement or benefit of the bereaved minor.[24] By way of example of this last category, and depending on its terms, a settled advance out of a bereaved minor's trust before his 18th birthday which postpones absolute entitlement to the capital of the settlement to 25, will ensure that the settlement falls within the 18-to-25 trust regime without an exit charge arising at 18.[25]

In all other circumstances, primary and secondary exit charges may apply.[26] It will be noted that the terms of the bereaved minor's trust must ensure that the settled property and the income from the property cannot be paid to any person other than the bereaved minor, so it is difficult to envisage circumstances where a primary exit charge

---

[22] IHTA 1984 s.71A(1) and (2).
[23] IHTA 1984 s.71A.
[24] IHTA 1984 s.71B: see paras 19–14–19–16.
[25] See para.19–11.
[26] IHTA 1984 s.71B(1).

will in fact arise. In the rare cases when exit charges will apply, the charges follow the usual model for favoured property described above: provision is made for primary and secondary exit charges to apply; and the standard reliefs are available in the usual way.[27] The only modification to these rules is that the "relevant period" for calculating the rate of tax may be extended by reference to a period when the property was subject to one of two other favoured property regimes, or both, in the manner described in para.17–09 above.

Age 18-to-25 trusts

17–19   In addition to the bereaved minors' trust, as of March 22, 2006 a new category of favoured trusts came into being, namely the age 18-to-25 trusts,[28] the enactment of which was a concession to those who had made strong representations that 18 was too young an age for capital to vest outright. Despite the representations and calls for this to be changed, the age of vesting under the new restricted accumulation and maintenance settlements and the bereaved minor trusts was not changed. The position that now applies is that property previously subject to either the accumulation and maintenance trust regime or the bereaved minors' trust regime may become subject to the age 18-to-25 regime with the consequence that no exit charge arises at 18. Instead favoured treatment is afforded in that the rate of tax of the primary exit charge which is charged on exits from the age 18-to-25 trust (i.e., the charge which arises when property vests in a beneficiary between the ages of 18 and 25) reflects the fact that tax is charged only in respect of the period between 18 and 25 during which the property has remained settled.

A trust may also qualify for favoured treatment under this category if it was created by will or under the Criminal Injuries Compensation Scheme and at least one of the beneficiary's parents has died, provided that the following conditions are also satisfied, namely that the terms of the trust provide that the beneficiaries will on attaining the age of 25 become absolutely entitled to the settled property and to the income arising from it, including any accumulated income. In addition, the terms of the trust must be such that, so long as a beneficiary (B) is living and under 25, if any property is applied for the benefit of a beneficiary, it must be applied for the benefit of B, who must either be entitled to all of the income arising from the property or the terms of the trust must provide that no income may be applied for the benefit of any other person.[29] The conditions for qualifying for favoured treatment as an age 18-to-25 trust are considered in more detail in Chapter 20.

No exit charge arises where property ceases to be held on an age 18-to-25 trust (a) by virtue of the beneficiary becoming absolutely entitled to the settled property on or before attaining the age of 18, or (b) by virtue of the beneficiary dying under the age of 18, or (c) by virtue of the property being paid or applied for his advancement or benefit prior to or upon attaining the age of 18.[30] In all other circumstances, primary or secondary exit charges may apply.

Primary exit charge from 18-to-25 trust

17–20   A primary exit charge arises: (a) when a beneficiary becomes absolutely entitled to the settled property, any income arising from it and any accumulated income held for

[27] IHTA 1984 s.71B(3).
[28] IHTA 1984 s.71D.
[29] IHTA 1984 s.71D(5) and (6).
[30] IHTA 1984 s.71E(2).

his benefit on or before attaining the age of 25 but after attaining the age of 18; or (b) on the death of a beneficiary who has attained the age of 18; or (c) when property is paid or applied for the advancement or benefit of a beneficiary.[31]

In general terms, the method for calculating the rate of tax for the primary exit charge closely mirrors that used to calculate the rate on exits before the 10-year anniversary from the relevant property regime under s.68.[32] It is designed to ensure not only that tax is charged on application of capital for the benefit of beneficiaries between the ages of 18 and 25, but also that the rate of tax charged does not exceed the maximum rate for a full ten years under the s.68 charge (i.e. 6 per cent). The actual rate varies according to how long the property has remained in a settlement after the beneficiary's 18th birthday, the longest period being seven years, i.e. 28 quarters. At the time of writing, the primary exit charge from an age 18-to-25 trust cannot exceed 4.2 per cent.

Section 71F sets out the mechanism for calculating the rate of tax. The formula applied by s.71F(3) is: **17–21**

$$\text{Chargeable amount} \times \text{Relevant fraction} \times \text{Settlement rate}$$

Chargeable amount

The chargeable amount is the amount by which the value property comprised in the **17–22** settlement to which the age 18-to-25 regime applies is less immediately after the event giving rise to the charge than it would be but for the event. Grossing-up applies if tax is paid out of the 18-to-25 property.[33]

Relevant fraction

The relevant fraction is defined by s.71F(5). It is three-tenths (3/10) multiplied by so **17–23** many fortieths (1/40) as there are complete successive quarters in the period beginning with the day on which the beneficiary attained the age of 18, or, if later, the day on which the property became property to which the 18-to-25 regime applied, ending with the date of the occasion of the charge. No quarter throughout which property was excluded property is counted.[34]

Settlement rate

The "settlement rate" is defined as the effective rate (i.e. the rate found by express- **17–24** ing the tax chargeable as a percentage of the amount on which it is charged) at which tax would be charged on the value transferred by a chargeable transfer of the description specified in s.71F(8) and (9). That description closely mirrors the description contained in s.68(4) and (5). But note that the modification made for pre-CTT settlements in s.68(6) is not repeated. There is also no provision for disregarding the settlor's chargeable transfers made before March 27, 1974 as is provided for in s.68(4)(b). This, together with the absence of an equivalent provision to that contained in s.66(6),

[31] IHTA 1984 s.71F(2).
[32] See paras 15–03–15–07.
[33] IHTA 1984 s.71F(4).
[34] IHTA 1984 s.71F(6).

implies that it is possible for pre-CTT settlements made on the same date to be "related settlements" and for a settlor to have made chargeable transfers prior to March 27, 1974 which affect his cumulative total for the purposes of this exit charge. In practice, it is thought that HMRC will not take this point.

17–25   There are two further points to note:

(1) The s.71D qualifying conditions for an age 18-to-25 trust are expressed by reference to a single beneficiary and there is no equivalent provision to that contained in s.71(4)(b) (see para.17–12) which operates to eliminate an exit charge in the case where a beneficiary dies before attaining the specified age (i.e. 18). However for age 18-to-25 trusts, it is thought that no exit charge applies where the death of a beneficiary occurs before the age of 25 and that beneficiary's share accrues to other beneficiaries, on the ground that the conditions in s.71D continue to apply in respect of the property of the settlement. When an exit charge comes to be calculated in the case of a surviving beneficiary and for the purpose of calculating the relevant fraction, the number of complete quarters from the day on which the beneficiary attained the age of 18 will still be calculated by reference to the date when the surviving beneficiary attained the age of 18. Depending on whether the surviving beneficiary is older or younger than the deceased beneficiary, this may have a positive or negative impact on the quantum of the exit charge that might otherwise have applied to an exit charge on the share of the deceased beneficiary.

(2) Section 65(4) provides that for the purposes of the relevant property regime, no exit charge arises if the exit occurs in a quarter beginning with the day on which the settlement commenced. In relation to an age 18-to-25 trust, an exit in the first quarter after the beneficiary attained the age of 18 is chargeable—but the rate works out at 0 per cent (there are no complete quarters since attaining the age of 18). Accordingly, it is thought that holdover relief under TCGA 1992 s.260 applies to transfers of property out of the settlement made in that quarter.

Secondary exit charge from age 18-to-25 trust

17–26   The usual mechanism for calculating secondary exit charges applies, subject only to modification of the "relevant period" for calculating the rate of tax, which as in the case of exits from bereaved minors' trusts may be extended by reference to a period when the property was subject to the accumulation and maintenance trust regime, in the manner described in para.17–09 above. The mechanism for calculating the secondary exit charge means that in the case of age 18-to-25 trusts the rate of tax charged on a depreciatory transaction, i.e. under the secondary exit charge, can exceed the rate of the primary exit charge.

In relation to both primary and secondary exit charges, the usual reliefs for payments of costs, etc. apply, but they are expressly set out, and not incorporated by reference to s.70.[35]

Trusts for disabled persons

17–27   Prior to the Finance Act 2006, the legislation provided for favoured treatment to apply to settled property which, during the life of certain mentally disabled persons or

[35] IHTA 1984 s.71E(3) and (4).

persons in receipt of attendance allowances on discretionary trusts, secured that at least a proportion (specified by the legislation) of the settled property was applied during their lifetime, for their benefit. Under these rules, which applied to property transferred into such a settlement on or after March 10, 1981,[36] the disabled person was treated as being beneficially entitled to a qualifying interest in possession in the settled property. Any payments made out of such a settlement to a person other than the disabled person thus fell to be brought into charge, if at all, under s.52(1). The Finance Act 2006 has preserved and expanded this favoured treatment by introducing the following changes to these rules: (a) new categories of interests which now qualify for favoured treatment as disabled person's interests were introduced to afford favoured treatment to new interest in possession settlements for disabled beneficiaries arising on or after March 22, 2006, which would otherwise fall within the relevant property regime; (b) a new category of disabled trust was introduced, namely the self-settlement by a person with a condition expected to lead to a disability; and (c) the definition of a disabled person was expanded though this expanded definition applies only to property transferred into a settlement on or after March 22, 2006. These changes and the conditions which must be satisfied to qualify for relief are explained in Chapter 21. There are now four categories of settlement which either are, or fall to be treated as, interest in possession settlements, the interests in which are defined as "disabled person's interest".[37] The mechanism for affording favoured treatment is that disabled person's interests are treated as "qualifying interests in possession" they are thus outside the relevant property regime. Payments made out of such settlements to persons other than the disabled person fall to be brought into charge under s.52(1). Transfers of value into such settlements by a person other than the disabled person are PETs.[38]

Before 1981, the original rules applied, which like those originally regulating the treatment of protective trusts, lent themselves to abuse. Under those rules, where property held on trusts for a disabled person was transferred into settlement prior to March 10, 1981, the disabled person is not regarded as having an interest in possession, and some mechanism is accordingly necessary to impose a charge on payments made to anyone other than the disabled person. Section 74(2) accordingly imposes a primary exit charge where settled property ceases to be property comprised in such a settlement otherwise than by virtue of a payment made out of that property for the benefit of the disabled person.[39] The usual rules apply in imposing the secondary exit charge,[40] in determining what reliefs are available,[41] computing the amount on which tax is charged[42] and fixing the appropriate rate of tax.[43]

Protective trusts

The legislation recognises the special nature of protective trusts, which have long **17–28** been used to prevent profligate and otherwise unreliable beneficiaries from squandering trust assets. Under s.33(1) of the Trustee Act 1925, where any income is directed to be held on "protective trusts" for the benefit of a person (the "principal beneficiary") during a period (the "trust period") not exceeding his life, the income is held on trusts

[36] IHTA 1984 s.89.
[37] IHTA 1984 s.89B.
[38] See para.21–11.
[39] IHTA 1984 s.74(2)(a).
[40] IHTA 1984 s.74(2)(b).
[41] IHTA 1984 ss.74(3) and 70(3), (4) and (10).
[42] IHTA 1984 ss.74(3) and 70(5).
[43] IHTA 1984 ss.74(3) and 70(6)–(9).

under s.33(1)(i) such that during that period he has an interest in possession until he "does or attempts to do or suffers any act or thing or until any event happens, other than an advance under any statutory or express power" whereby he would be deprived of the right to receive the income. At that stage, his interest comes to an end, and the income is held under s.33(1)(ii) on discretionary trusts for the principal beneficiary, his spouse, and his children or remoter issue. If there is neither spouse nor issue, the income is held on discretionary trusts for the principal beneficiary and the persons who would be entitled to the trust property if he were dead.

The favoured treatment initially extended to property held on such trusts lent itself to tax avoidance, and in order to prevent abuses new rules were introduced by the Finance Act 1978 now contained in s.88, under which the principal beneficiary's interest is treated as continuing regardless of any failure or determination of that interest on or after April 12, 1978, with the result that a charge may arise under s.52(1), if any of the trust fund is distributed during his life to anyone other than himself or his spouse, and under s.4, on his death unless his spouse is next entitled under the trust on his death. Changes to s.88 introduced by the Finance Act 2006 mean that a failure or determination of a pre-March 22, 2006 protected life interest is disregarded: the deemed interest in possession is treated as being a pre-March 22, 2006 interests in possession.[44] A protected life interest created on or after March 22, 2006 will be excluded from the relevant property regime, only if the protected interest of the principal beneficiary is an immediate post-death interest, a disabled person's interest with an actual interest in possession in the settlement, or a transitional serial interest. In such cases and by virtue of s.88(4) the failure or determination of the protected life interest will be ignored.[45]

The enactment of what became s.88, of course, leaves open the position where a principal beneficiary's interest is determined before April 12, 1978. Section 73(2) accordingly imposes exit charges on property held on discretionary trusts to the like effect[46] as those specified in s.33(1)(ii) which became so held on the failure or determination before April 12, 1978, of trusts to the like effect[47] as those specified in s.33(1)(i). A primary exit charge is imposed when property held on such protective trusts ceases to be so held, otherwise than by virtue of a payment out of the settled property for the benefit of the principal beneficiary.[48] The usual rules apply in imposing the secondary exit charge,[49] determining what reliefs are available,[50] computing the amount on which tax is charged[51] and fixing the appropriate rate of tax.

Temporary charitable trusts

17–29   As was mentioned above, charitable trusts fall into two categories—those under which property is held indefinitely for charitable purposes only, and those under which property is held for such purposes only until the end of a period, whether defined by a date or in some other way, e.g. by reference to an event. For these purposes, settled property is regarded as held for charitable purposes when the trusts on which the property is held require the income from the property to be applied for charitable

[44] IHTA 1984 s.88(3).
[45] IHTA 1984 s.88(4).
[46] For the meaning of "trusts to the like effect", see para.22–01.
[47] IHTA 1984 s.88(4).
[48] IHTA 1984 s.73(2)(a).
[49] IHTA 1984 s.73(2)(b).
[50] IHTA 1984 ss.73(3) and 70(3), (4) and (10).
[51] IHTA 1984 ss.73(3) and 70(5).

purposes. If the trusts require part only of the income to be so applied, a corresponding part of the property is regarded as held for charitable purposes.[52]

Property held indefinitely for charitable purposes only is given favoured treatment in two ways. First, no periodic or exit charges are imposed on such property. Secondly, no exit charge is imposed in respect of property which ceases to be relevant property on becoming such property.[53] Property held on temporary charitable trusts, on the other hand, receives no such treatment. An exit charge may be imposed on such property, and there is nothing to prevent an exit charge being imposed when relevant property becomes such property.

A primary exit charge is imposed when property held on temporary charitable trusts ceases to be so held, otherwise than by virtue of an application for charitable purposes.[54] A secondary exit charge is imposed in the usual way, save that no such charge is imposed if the disposition made by the trustees constitutes an application of property for charitable purposes.[55] Subject to this qualification, the usual rules apply in determining what reliefs are available,[56] computing the amount on which tax is charged[57] and fixing the appropriate rate of tax.[58]

Employee trusts

The term "employee trusts" is used to describe a variety of trusts which satisfy the **17–30** requirements laid down by s.86. It may be that that no interest in possession in the settled property subsists in the settled property to which an individual is beneficially entitled, and that no company-purchased interest in possession[59] subsists in it. Where this applies, an exit charge may be imposed by s.72(2) in three circumstances, as follows:

(1) *Primary exit charge*: s.72(2)(a) provides that a primary exit charge is imposed where property held on employee trusts ceases to be so held, "otherwise than by virtue of a payment out of the settled property". What is envisaged is presumably a payment made under the rules of the trust in question.

(2) *Special exit charge*: a special exit charge[60] is imposed where a payment is made out of property held on employee trusts for the benefit of a person who is, or who is connected with:

(a) a person who has directly or indirectly provided any of the settled property otherwise than by additions not exceeding in value £1,000 in any one year[61]; or

---

[52] IHTA 1984 s.84. For the meaning of "charitable purposes", see para.3–40.

[53] IHTA 1984 s.76.

[54] IHTA 1984 s.70(2)(a).

[55] IHTA 1984 s.70(2)(b).

[56] See para.17–04.

[57] See para.17–05.

[58] See paras 17–06–17–10.

[59] IHTA 1984 s.72(1). For these purposes, IHTA 1984 s.72(1A) defines a company-purchased interest in possession as one which a company is beneficially entitled to, the business of the company consists wholly or mainly in the acquisition of interests in the settled property, and the company has acquired the interest in possession for full consideration in money or money's worth from an individual who was beneficially entitled to it. The latter requirement is relaxed by incorporating s.59(3) and (4), as to which see para.12–48.

[60] IHTA 1984 s.72(2), (3).

[61] "Year" for this purpose means March 26, 1974–April 5, 1974, and any year of assessment after 1973–1974; IHTA 1984 s.72(6)(b).

(b) a person who has acquired an interest in the settled property for a consideration in money or money's worth. For this purpose, a person is treated as acquiring an interest in this way if he becomes entitled to it as a result of transactions which include a disposition for such consideration (whether to him or another) of that interest or of other property; or

(c) in a case where the employment in question is employment by a close company within the meaning of s.94,[62] a person who is a participator (as defined in s.102) in relation to that company, and who either

    (i) is beneficially entitled to, or to rights entitling him to acquire, not less than 5 per cent of or of any class of the shares comprised in, its issued share capital, or

    (ii) would, on a winding-up of the company, be entitled to not less than 5 per cent of its assets.

It may be that the trusts governing the property out of which the payment is made are those of a profit-sharing scheme approved in accordance with Sch.9 of the Taxes Act 1988. In that case, no tax is chargeable under this head on an appropriation of shares in pursuance of the scheme.[63]

(3) *Secondary exit charge*: the usual secondary exit charge applies unless the disposition made by the trustees is by way of a payment out of the settled property.

Subject to what has been said above, the usual rules apply in determining what reliefs are available,[64] in computing the amount on which tax is charged,[65] and fixing the appropriate rate of tax.[66]

Employee trusts are considered in more detail at Chapter 24.

Maintenance funds

17–31   The rules regulating the treatment of maintenance funds are discussed at paras 27–70–27–103.

---

[62] IHTA 1984 s.72(6)(a).
[63] IHTA 1984 s.72(4).
[64] See para.17–04.
[65] See para.17–04.
[66] See paras 17–06–17–10.

CHAPTER 18

ACCUMULATION AND MAINTENANCE TRUSTS

This chapter is set out in two parts: Part I deals with the tax treatment of Accumulation and Maintenance trusts before the Finance Act 2006 changes and Part II deals with the tax treatment of such trusts after the Finance Act 2006 changes.[1]   **18–01**

I. ACCUMULATION AND MAINTENANCE TRUSTS BEFORE THE FINANCE ACT 2006

The rules regulating the treatment of accumulation and maintenance trusts were   **18–02** found in s.71 in its pre-Finance Act 2006 form. This part of this chapter is concerned with the conditions which a trust had to satisfy to be a favoured accumulation and maintenance trust within that section. The rules governing the imposition of charges on a trust which ceased to satisfy the s.71 requirements are discussed at paras 17–12–17–17.

The Perpetuities and Accumulations Act 2009 came into force on April 6, 2010 and, for trusts created after that date, replaced both the statutory 80-year perpetuity period and the common law lives in being plus 21-year period, with a 125-year perpetuity period. It also removed the limitation on accumulations so that they might continue for the life of the settlement (other than for charities where the period remains at 21 years). Neither change affects existing accumulation and maintenance trusts, since it is specifically stated that settlements in existence before that date (i.e. April 6, 2010) retain their perpetuity and accumulation periods,[2] and this is so, even where the execution of a special power of appointment or power of advancement after April 6, 2010, creates a

---

[1] For the pre-FA 2006 tax treatment of pre-March 22, 2006 interests in possession, see para.12–02.
[2] Perpetuities and Accumulations Act 2009 s.15.

new settlement.[3] Accumulation and maintenance trusts which would previously have enjoyed the benefit of s.71 treatment must of necessity continue to operate under the previous regime (see the discussion in this Part I, at paras 18–17–18–32, e.g. see para.18–24 as concerns the limits on accumulations).

The conditions which a trust needed to satisfy in order to qualify for favoured treatment were originally set out in para.15 of Sch.5 to the Finance Act 1975. The conditions established by s.71 were substantially identical to those in para.15, and Revenue and judicial statements made in relation to para.15 therefore applied equally to s.71.

Accumulation and maintenance trusts were treated favourably in a number of ways. The tax implications of creating the settlement are dealt with below. Once comprised in an accumulation and maintenance trust, property was treated favourably in four ways:

(1) the property was immune from the periodic charge;
(2) no exit charge was imposed on a beneficiary becoming beneficially entitled to, or to an interest in possession in, the property on or before attaining the age at which he was to become beneficially entitled under the trusts. Note that at the time all interests in possession were qualifying interests in possession;
(3) no exit charge was imposed on the property if a beneficiary died before attaining the specified age; and
(4) CGT hold-over relief was available in limited circumstances.

Creation of the trust

18–03   Section 71 trusts came into being in two ways: either they were created by a settlor, or an existing settlement (or part thereof) could be converted into a s.71 trust.

Where such a trust was created by a settlor during his lifetime by an outright transfer then that transfer would normally be a PET.[4]

If an existing trust was converted into an accumulation and maintenance trust the tax consequences would depend on the nature of the existing trust. If it was an interest in possession trust, its conversion into an accumulation and maintenance trust was normally a PET.[5] Where, on the other hand, the existing settlement was discretionary in form, an exit charge was imposed on its being converted into a s.71 trust.[6] If the trust was created on the settlor's death, so much of the value transferred on his death as was attributable to the gift into settlement was chargeable.

If trusts which could potentially fall within s.71 arose or were appointed before any member of the class of beneficiaries came into existence, there was a charge to IHT on the birth of the first member of the class as s.71 did not apply until there was or had been a "living beneficiary" in accordance with s.71(7).

Requirements

18–04   Prior to March 22, 2006, to receive favoured treatment under s.71 settled property generally needed to satisfy four requirements:

[3] Perpetuities and Accumulations Act 2009 s.15.
[4] For the more limited circumstances when a transfer will be a PET post-FA 2006, see paras 5–10–5–26.
[5] See para.18–34.
[6] See para.15–03, for instances when an exit charge would now be imposed.

(1) the property must have been held on discretionary trusts;

(2) there must have been at least one person, who, on or before attaining a specified age not exceeding 25, would have become entitled to, or to an interest in possession, in the property;

(3) it must have been mandatory that income from the property was to be accumulated so far as it was not applied for the maintenance, education or benefit of a beneficiary[7]; and

(4) the property must not have qualified for favoured treatment for an excessively long period.[8] This requirement was introduced by the Finance Act 1976.

These conditions are discussed in more detail below.

Discretionary trusts

Strictly speaking, the requirement was that there must have been no interest in possession in the settled property: for convenience, this will be referred to as the requirement that the property must have been held on discretionary trusts. In deciding whether this requirement was satisfied, s.31 of the Trustee Act 1925 was relevant.[9] **18–05**

Certainty of entitlement

There must have been at least one person, who, on or before attaining a specified age not exceeding 25, would have become entitled to, or to an interest in possession in, the property. This requirement had a number of aspects. The authors consider it is helpful to retain the discussion of these requirements in this edition of the book: accordingly, each of the conditions is considered below. **18–06**

Certainty of vesting

For property to qualify for favoured treatment under s.71, it must have been certain that someone would become entitled to at least an interest in possession in the property no later than on attaining a maximum age of 25. If at any time this requirement was not satisfied the property ceased at that time to qualify for favoured treatment. **18–07**

The fact that the trustees had a power to appoint the property or an interest therein in favour of a beneficiary before he attained a specified age not exceeding 25 was, of course, perfectly acceptable, because that could only accelerate the requisite vesting. What mattered was that, come what may, someone was sure to become entitled in the required manner no later than on attaining the age of 25. Where there was but one beneficiary the trustees therefore must not have had the power to revoke his interest or to appoint the property to which he was contingently entitled away from him. Where there was more than one beneficiary the trustees could have such powers so long as they were limited in an appropriate fashion.

---

[7] "Beneficiary" here has the meaning given to that term in IHTA 1984 s.71(1)(a).
[8] IHTA 1984 s.71(1) and (2); see para.18–31.
[9] See *Swales v IRC* [1984] S.T.C. 413.

621

This point was considered in the following extract of a letter from HMRC quoted in *The Law Society Gazette* of October 8, 1975:

> "The inclusion of issue as possible objects of a special power of appointment would exclude a settlement from the benefit of para.15 if the power would allow the trustees to prevent any interest in possession in the settled property from commencing before the beneficiary concerned attained the age specified. It would depend on the precise words of the settlement and the facts to which they had to be applied whether a particular settlement satisfied the conditions of para.15(1). In many cases the rules against perpetuity and accumulations would operate to prevent an effective appointment outside those conditions. Perhaps I should add that the application of para.15 is not a matter for a once-for-all decision. It is a question that needs to be kept in mind at all times when there is settled property in which no interest in possession subsists."

Limitations on certainty

18–08   It is clear that some limitations needed to be placed on the meaning of the word "will" for these purposes, and that, some uncertainties would have had to be disregarded. It could not be said, for instance, that a person who was alive on day 1 would be alive on day 2, and it was clear that if s.71 was to make any sense the possibility of disentitlement by death had to be disregarded, as did theoretical possibilities such as that of a beneficiary assigning his interest.

The position was reviewed generally by Vinelott J. and the Court of Appeal (the judgment of which was delivered by Fox L.J.) in *Inglewood v IRC*.[10] Trustees of a discretionary trust had in 1964 revocably appointed a trust fund on trusts such that on attaining the age of 21 a beneficiary acquired an interest in possession in the trust property. On May 5, 1975, the eldest beneficiary attained 21 and so became entitled to an interest in possession in part of the trust fund. On March 29, 1976, the trustees released their power of revocation. HMRC contended that two charges arose in respect of these events. The first occurred on the beneficiary attaining 21, the second under para.15(3) on the trustees releasing their power of revocation. The basis of HMRC's contention was that the existence of the power of revocation prevented the trust from being a favoured trust, since it meant that a beneficiary's entitlement was insufficiently certain. That being the case, no protection was available under para.15(2)(a) when the eldest beneficiary acquired her interest in possession on attaining 21. The release of the power of revocation in turn converted the remainder of the trust into a para.15 trust, so that a charge arose under para.15(3) on the date of the release.

18–09   The taxpayer argued that there was sufficient certainty of entitlement notwithstanding the existence of the power. Paragraph 15(1)(a), now s.71(1)(a), was merely:

> ". . . describing a state of affairs which will come about if the trusts of the settlement remain unchanged and if the beneficiaries live to obtain the vested interest. The possibility that the trusts affecting the settled property will be changed by the exercise of a power of revocation or appointment, or by an arrangement approved by the court under the Variation of Trusts Act 1958, and the possibility that a beneficiary with an interest contingent on attaining an age not exceeding 25 or on the happening of some earlier event such as marriage will die

---

[10] *Inglewood v IRC* [1983] 1 W.L.R. 866; [1983] S.T.C. 133.

before the contingency is satisfied, or will assign his interest or become bankrupt, must alike be disregarded."[11]

Vinelott J. thought this construction "impossible" and it also failed to find favour with the Court of Appeal, where Fox L.J. stated:

18–10

> "The paragraph is prescribing conditions for the applicability of a relief from taxation. One of those conditions is that 'one or more persons . . . will, on or before attaining a specified age not exceeding twenty-five, become entitled to, or to an interest in possession in, the settled property or part of it. It seems to us that the ordinary meaning of those words is that the condition will not be satisfied unless it can be said, if the person or persons attain an age not exceeding 25 they will be bound to become entitled. We do not think that involves stretching the meaning at all. And it does not involve reading in any words. The meaning is, to some extent, one of impression and we feel that as a matter of the ordinary use of English the word 'will', in the context, imports a degree of certainty. It suggests rigidity rather than flexibility. And it seems to us to be pushing the ordinary usage of English altogether too far to say that a person 'will' become entitled to property if he attains 21 or marries when his contingent interest can, at any time, be totally destroyed at the absolute discretion of the trustees and solely for the benefit of third parties. There is nothing in the language of para.15(1)(a) to suggest that possible future events may be disregarded. As a matter of language, therefore, our opinion of the meaning of para.15(1) coincides with that of the judge."

The Court of Appeal, however, found the taxpayer's construction to be a not impossible one and proceeded to analyse the position more thoroughly:

18–11

> "The trustees contend that the Crown's construction cannot be made to fit sensibly into the legal structure with which the paragraph must necessarily be dealing and is really destructive of para.15 altogether. If the Crown is right, it is said, how does one accommodate the provisions of para.15 to the facts that (a) a beneficiary's interest may be lawfully disposed of by him after he attains 18 and before it vests in possession, (b) his interest may be taken away from him on bankruptcy, (c) his interest may be prevented from vesting in him by reason of an order made under the Variation of Trusts Act 1958, or under the statutory jurisdiction of the Family Division on divorce or an order made by the Court of Protection in the event of his incapacity to manage his affairs, or (d) he may die before attaining a vested interest.
>
> As to the last of those, it seems to us that the contingency is inherent in the provisions of the paragraph itself. The paragraph applies where a person will on or before attaining a specified age not exceeding 25 become entitled to an interest in possession in settled property. The paragraph is dealing with contingent interests. A trust cannot be excluded from the operation of the paragraph because of the possible happening of an event inherent in the contingency which brings the trust within the paragraph in the first place. In our view, therefore, there is no substance in this point.
>
> As to the other matters ((a), (b) and (c)), we think that the answer is this. The paragraph provides that 'This paragraph applies to any settlement where . . . '. In our opinion 'where' means 'whereby'. Accordingly, we think the paragraph is concerned only with provisions which are contained in the settlement itself. That would include not only the express provisions of the settlement but also any which are incorporated by statutory provision. None of the matters to which we have referred in (a), (b) and (c) can be so described. They are the consequences, which cannot be avoided, of the operation of the general law on property interests. They are extraneous to the settlement and are not provisions of the settlement itself."

The test at this stage was thus, can it be said that the beneficiary will *under the terms of the settlement* attain the requisite entitlement? The trustees pointed out that at least

18–12

---

[11] See *British Tax Review* (1977), pp.65–67.

part and possibly the whole of the vast majority of trusts would not pass this test. This followed from the fact that most trusts contained a power of advancement. Powers of advancement come in basically two shapes and sizes. First, a settlor can confer on trustees an express power of advancement over such of the trust property as he specifies. Secondly, s.32 of the Trustee Act 1925 automatically gives trustees a power of advancement over half a beneficiary's putative share of capital. This statutory power can be excluded by the settlor under s.69(2) of the 1925 Act; it can also be enlarged by him. A power of advancement thus enables part or the whole of the capital to which it relates to be applied for the "benefit" of the person contingently entitled to the property. This meant, the trustees said, that such a power was capable of being exercised so that the property over which it was exercised ceased to be held on para.15 trusts:

> " . . . The word 'benefit' is very widely construed (see *Pilkington v IRC* [1964] AC 612, 40 TC 416). It will thus be possible by an exercise of the statutory power, to advance half the fund to the trustees of a new settlement under which the beneficiary's interest is postponed to an age later than 25 or, indeed, under which he took no interest at all (see *Hampden Settlement Trusts* [1977] TR 177). The sole criterion is the benefit of the beneficiary. It is for his benefit, for example for fiscal or family reasons, to make such an advance as I have mentioned there would be power to do so. Thus, in *re Hampden Settlement Trust* an advance was made on trusts under which the primary beneficiaries were the children of the advanced beneficiary. And in *Re Clore's Settlement Trust, Sainer v Clore* [1966] 1 WLR 955 capital was applied by making donations to charity, the beneficiary for whose benefit the advance was made being a young man of great wealth. Both cases were concerned with express power of advancement (and not the statutory power) but nothing turns on that."

18–13   Thus, the inclusion of a power of advancement—be it express or statutory—within a settlement meant that the settlement would not pass the test stated above. The trustees contended that Parliament could not have intended trusts to be disqualified from favourable treatment by such powers, because most trusts contained such powers. The Court of Appeal accepted this argument:

> "The result, in our opinion, is this. The word 'will' in para.15 does import a degree of certainty which is not satisfied if the trust can be revoked and the fund reappointed to some other person at an age exceeding 25. But a power of advancement has been for so long such a normal provision in a settlement for a person contingently on attaining a specified age, and since its sole purpose is to enable the trust property to be applied for that person's benefit before he attains the specified age, it would be artificial to regard the trust as not satisfying the provisions of the paragraph. A trust for A if he attains 25 is within the paragraph. It is impossible to see any rational ground why a trust for A if he attains 25 and with a power of advancement should not satisfy it also, more particularly since the exclusion of a power of advancement in such a case must be rare indeed . . . Our conclusion regarding the power of advancement is that while the prima facie meaning of para.15(1) *(a)* is clear it must be interpreted in the context of the practical application of the law of trusts. The statutory power of advancement is so commonly incorporated in trusts that para.15(1) *(a)* must be read so as to accommodate that and not so as to withdraw the benefit of the paragraph from a trust containing such a power. We could not regard the much used extension of the statutory power from a moiety to the whole as in any different position."[12]

The trustees then argued that a power of advancement was indistinguishable in relation to the property over which it existed from a special power of appointment which enabled the trustees to revoke the trusts on which property was held and to resettle that property on trusts which were outside para.15. This, however, the Court of Appeal was unwilling to accept:

[12] *British Tax Review* (1977), p.139.

"The trustees contend that the statutory power is, as to one moiety of the settled property, no different from a special power of appointment which enables the trustees to revoke the primary trusts and to resettle on trusts under which persons may take at ages in excess of 25. On the Crown's view it is said para.15 would be excluded as to one-half. It is no doubt true that for the purpose of the rule against perpetuities, the statutory power should be equated with a special power. But it is, in our opinion, quite unreal, in relation to para.15, to equate it to a power of revocation. A power of advancement is not given for the purposes of revoking the primary trust and resettling the trust property. Its purpose is auxiliary. It is given as an aid to enable the trust property to be used for the fullest benefit of the beneficiary and, as such, is a normal adjunct of any trust for a person contingently on attaining a specified age. We should observe that in cases of the *re Hampden* and *re Clore* type (which are rare anyway) it is a prerequisite to the transaction that the trustees should be satisfied that it is 'for the benefit' of the beneficiary who is advanced. To that extent it is similar to an administrative power. Its purpose, like an administrative power, is to aid the beneficial trusts and not to destroy them. Some administrative powers (e.g. the power conferred by s.55 of the Settled Land Act 1925 to give away small parts of the trust land for public purposes or a power to trustees to apply income for capital purposes) do affect beneficial interests but they are not truly dispositive in nature (see *Pearson v IRC* [1980] STC 318 at 333, [1981] AC 774 at 784)."[13]

The trustees, not surprisingly, were able to give a number of examples which might have been expected to be within para.15 but which on the Crown's construction were not, or which otherwise gave rise to practical difficulties. The Court of Appeal mentioned three. First, assume a trust under which assets were held for an infant beneficiary for life on protective trusts: the possibility of his becoming bankrupt while an infant meant that he might never become entitled to an interest in possession. Secondly, assume that A and B were twins, and that property was held on trust for A if he attained 18 and B was then alive: under the test posited above the possibility of A dying under 18 was disregarded, but the possibility of B's dying under that age was not disregarded, which seemed inconsistent. Thirdly, assume that if X had a child, property was to be held on trust for such of X's issue for the time being living as the trustees in their discretion thought fit during a perpetuity period, but that if X did not have a child, then the property was to be held in trust in equal shares for such children of Z who attained 21. In such a case the question whether the trust qualified for favoured treatment while X was childless and Z had infant children depended on whether X could be treated as incapable of having children, and it was unlikely that Parliament can have intended that favoured treatment should depend on this. The Court accepted that these were hard cases, but noted that illogicalities and hardships may occasionally result where a statute lays down conditions for the applicability of a section.

The *Inglewood* case was significant in that it established that the test of certainty was **18–14** whether the beneficiary would under the terms of the settlement (disregarding the existence of any power of advancement) achieve the required entitlement. Outside events such as the beneficiary disentitling himself by assigning his prospective interest after attaining his majority but before attaining the age specified by the settlement at which his interest was to vest, or of the court varying the trusts were thus to be ignored.

In the past, HMRC contended that the possibility of bankruptcy could not be ignored. The position was a controversial one.[14] It may be that there was a difference between the effect of bankruptcy as regards:

---

[13] *British Tax Review* (1977), pp.65–67, p.238.
[14] See para.22–05.

(1) a protected interest (which was dealt with by the Court of Appeal) where the bankruptcy was actually referred to in terms of the trust; and

(2) an ordinary interest vesting in possession at some future date where the bankruptcy operated outside the terms of the trust to vest an interest in the beneficiary's trustee in bankruptcy rather than in the beneficiary himself.

Whatever the position, the existence of a protective trust was to be ignored, because the provisions in s.88 dealing with protective trusts assumed that a person entitled to a protected interest remained so entitled notwithstanding the fact that he ceased to be so entitled as a matter of general law.[15]

Entitlement to the property or an interest in possession therein

18–15   It sufficed that a beneficiary acquired an interest in possession, and it was desirable to limit his interest to income. The fact that the trust deed empowered the trustees to revoke the beneficiary's interest in possession once it had vested did not of itself prevent the trust from qualifying for favoured treatment, though the cautious draftsman may have provided that the trustees could not exercise their power of revocation until, e.g. six months after the vesting in possession of the beneficiary's interest.

No holdover relief—CGT time bomb trusts

18–16   These trusts were important in practice. Unfortunately, explaining them is complicated slightly by the fact that some of the relevant sections—s.71(1) of the Taxation of Chargeable Gains Act 1992 and s.71 of the 1984 Act—have the same numbers. For convenience, we will refer to s.71(1) of the 1992 Act as "CGT s.71(1)".

The starting point in understanding the problem that arose in relation to such trusts was that if a beneficiary became absolutely entitled to trust assets the trustees would, for CGT purposes, be deemed by CGT s.71(1) to have disposed of and reacquired those assets for their then market value and so may have realised a gain for CGT purposes. Under s.260(2)(d) of the 1992 Act the trustees would normally have been able to elect for CGT holdover relief if, by virtue of s.71 of the 1984 Act, the disposal did not constitute an occasion on which IHT was chargeable.

Although this sounded comforting, it could easily result in a discomforting CGT–IHT mismatch. The reason was that many trusts which started as accumulation and maintenance trusts became interest in possession trusts by the time a beneficiary became absolutely entitled to assets so with the result that s.260(2)(d) holdover relief was not then available. Assume that under the terms of an English law trust X was to become absolutely entitled to the trust fund on attaining 25 and that until he attained that age the trustees held the trust income on trust to accumulate it so far as they did not apply it for his maintenance, education or benefit. If, as is often the case, the trust deed did not exclude the operation of s.31 of the Trustee Act 1925, the effect of s.31 would be to give X an interest in possession on attaining the age of 18 (maybe 21 if the trust was set up before January 1, 1970). His attainment of that age would not have given rise to a CGT s.71(1) deemed disposal, nor would his acquisition of an interest in possession have given rise to a charge to IHT, but it would have meant that the assets in which X's interest subsisted ceased to be held on accumulation and maintenance

---

[15] For the operation of IHTA 1984 s.88 pre- and post-FA 2006, see Ch.22.

trusts. When X attained 25 and became absolutely entitled to the trust assets, s.53(2) of the 1984 Act would have prevented any charge to IHT from arising, but s.71 of the 1984 Act would not have operated to do so, with the result that s.260(2)(d) holdover relief would have been unavailable in respect of any gain then arising.

Occasionally no action was required in respect of the potential liability to CGT because, notwithstanding the terms of the trust, the beneficiary would not have become absolutely entitled to the asset in question for CGT purposes.[16] Even if there was a problem, the trustees may have had sufficient power in the form of an overriding power conferred by the settlement or an enlarged statutory power of advancement under the Trustee Act 1925 s.32 to prevent (or defer) the vesting of the trust assets in the beneficiary.

One possible way out of the problem was to convert the trust back into an accumulation and maintenance trust. This is best explained by returning to the above example. X would direct the trustees of the settlement to hold the income to which he was entitled on trust to accumulate so much of the income as they did not apply for his maintenance education or benefit until he attained the age of 25. This would have had the effect of changing the trust from an interest in possession trust back into an accumulation and maintenance trust. X would have made a PET, but normally this would not be a concern (inexpensive term insurance could be taken out) and the result would be that on attaining 25 he would have become absolutely entitled to the trust fund in circumstances where s.71 of the 1984 Act would have prevented any charge to IHT arising, so that s.260(2)(d) holdover relief was available.[17]

Variation of shares

The fact that the beneficiaries' shares could be varied, whether by operation of the trust deed or by the trustees appointing a beneficiary's share away from him or revoking his interest, did not disqualify the trust so long as it remained certain that at least one of the beneficiaries would become entitled in the required manner on or before attaining the specified age. Such a variation would have occurred by operation of a trust deed, where, for example, there were two classes of children—say sons and daughters—the interests of the daughters to be defeated on the birth of a son. While it could not be said for certain that any of the daughters' interests would ever vest, the only event which could prevent such a vesting was the birth of a son, in which case it would be certain that the property would vest in him.   **18–17**

In the more common case where the trustees had power to appoint property away from a beneficiary (or to revoke his interest) the same result would have been obtained, provided, of course, that the power was exercisable only in favour of another beneficiary under the s.71 trust. HMRC accepted that this was the correct view.[18] The power to appoint away from a beneficiary (or to revoke his interest) would have had to be limited so that it was exercisable only while two or more beneficiaries were alive and under the specified age; otherwise it could have been said that the existence of the power infringed the certainty requirement. Thus, a power to transfer the share of a minor beneficiary to an older member of the class who had already attained the age of

---

[16] See *Stephenson v Barclays Bank* [1975] S.T.C. 151; *Crowe v Appleby* [1976] S.T.C. 301; *Lloyds Bank v Duker* [1987] 1 W.L.R. 1324; and *Jenkins v Brown* [1989] S.T.I. 436. Note that this defence is apparently not available in Scotland and that HMRC practice is not to accept *Duker* without query unless inter alia the trustees have a majority holding: see *Capital Gains Manual*, paras 37561–37562.

[17] If this approach was adopted and holdover relief secured any taper relief for which the assets in question qualified would have been forfeited.

[18] See Revenue Press Release of January 19, 1976.

627

25 would have infringed the rules; and any power to vary the shares of members of the class had to be restricted accordingly.

While the decision in *Bassil v Lister*[19] stated that the use of trust income in the payment of premiums on life policies would not be an accumulation within the meaning of the Accumulations Act 1800 (also known as the Thelluson Act) it was thought, as a result of s.71(1)(b) and the decision in *Inglewood*, that the mere existence of a power to pay life policy premiums out of income *may* have prevented a trust from satisfying the condition in s.71(1)(a) because it rendered it uncertain whether the beneficiary would acquire an interest in possession on or before attaining the specified age.[20]

Specified age

18–18   The beneficiary must have become entitled either:

    (1) on attaining a specified age not exceeding 25; or
    (2) before attaining such an age.

Strictly speaking, therefore, s.71 might not have applied[21] to a trust under which a beneficiary was to become entitled on the expiration of a period subsequent to his attaining a specified age. Fortunately, HMRC stated in a Press Release of September 2, 1977,[22] that (by concession) the requirements set out in the section were regarded as satisfied if it was clear that a beneficiary would attain the requisite entitlement by the age of 25. Some commentators queried why the specified age condition was not amended in the Finance Act 1982 s.114 or the pre-consolidation amendments prior to the 1984 Act to read "on or before the age of 25" instead of "on or before attaining a specific age not exceeding 25".

Unborn beneficiaries

18–19   Section 71 trusts could be created or appointed in favour of unborn persons so long as there was at least one living beneficiary at the time the trust was established. The subsequent death of that beneficiary before the birth of another beneficiary did not disqualify the trust from continuing to receive favoured treatment so long as the trust deed contained appropriate provisions to deal with such an eventuality, e.g. by providing that if there was no living beneficiary the trustees were to accumulate income accruing to them.[23] The reference to one or more persons in s.71(1) and the inclusion of unborn persons among "the beneficiaries" under s.71(7) made it clear that the condition as to becoming beneficially entitled to the settled property or to an interest

---

[19] *Bassil v Lister* [1851] 9 Hare 177.
[20] See HMRC Manual IHTM42810 (June 2007); see also the numbered points in para.12–38.
[21] See *White v Whitcher* [1928] 1 K.B. 453.
[22] Extra Statutory Concession F8.
[23] IHTA 1984 s.71(7).

in possession in it applied where it was satisfied by a class of individuals even if they would not individually have satisfied the requirement.[24]

Accrual on death

The possibility that the death of a beneficiary might be followed by the birth of a beneficiary needed to be dealt with since, in the absence of such provision, this could have had adverse consequences. **18–20**

Assume that trustees held property on s.71 trusts under which the income accruing to the trust was to be held for life in equal shares for such of the children of A who attained the age of 18, and that in the event of the death of a child under that age his share accrued to the surviving children in equal shares. A had three children, X, 26, Y, 19 and Z, 16. Z died on the eve of his 17th birthday. If at the time Z died the trustees' power to accumulate income derived from s.31 of the Trustee Act 1925 the property in which Z's contingent interest subsisted would have ceased to be held on s.71 trusts because in the absence of a living beneficiary the trustees would have lacked a power to accumulate. Instead, they would have had to pay the income to those entitled under the terms of the trust, i.e. to X and Y in equal shares. This would have meant that X and Y would have become entitled to interests in possession; since they would have done so on the death of a beneficiary who had not attained the specified age, relief would have been available under s.71(4)(b), and no exit charge would have been imposed. However, a charge could perhaps have arisen on the subsequent birth (or other addition, e.g. by adoption) of another beneficiary, since that would have operated to revive the s.71 trusts. Such a revival would have divested X and Y of the interests in possession to which they had become entitled on Z's death, and they would therefore have been treated as making PETs.

Normally the appearance of another beneficiary was unlikely, but in certain circumstances it was considered prudent to provide that in the event of there ceasing to be a living unmarried infant beneficiary the class of beneficiaries closed, with the result that there could be no such divesting.

Inadvertent divesting

If a trust provided that on attaining a specified age each beneficiary took an equal share in, or of, the trust fund, a beneficiary already entitled to an interest in possession could be divested of part of his interest. Assume that A settled property on terms that such of his children as attained the age of 18 became entitled to life interests in the property in equal shares. At the time the first child, X, attained 18 there was only one other child, Y. X therefore became entitled to an interest in possession in half the trust fund. One year later a third child Z was born to A, with the result that, in the absence of provision to the contrary in the trust deed, X's interest was reduced to take account of Z's putative entitlement, and X was left with an interest in only one-third of the fund. This, of course, meant that X had made a notional transfer under s.52(1) of one-third (36–16) of the property in which his interest had subsisted. **18–21**

Such an unhappy development was usually avoided for either of two reasons. First, if the entitlement was to capital the rule in *Andrews v Partington* would have applied **18–22**

---

[24] But note comments at para.18–31 in relation to potential tax charge.

unless excluded expressly or by necessary implication,[25] with the result that the class of beneficiaries would have closed on the occasion when the first beneficiary became entitled to his share of the capital. Thus, if in the above example A's children had become entitled to capital on attaining 18, Z would never have become a beneficiary at all, the class of beneficiaries having closed on A attaining his majority, with the result that although A's interest might have been enlarged (e.g. on Y's death under 18) it could not have been diminished. If, on the other hand, the entitlement was to income, the class closing rules did not operate as a matter of general trust law. It may thus have been desirable to close the class of beneficiaries; this could have been done in two ways. The first, and simpler, method was to provide in the trust deed for the class of beneficiaries to close on the occasion when the first beneficiary became entitled to an interest in possession. This was often done by including in the trust deed three related definitions. The first definition was that of the "Smith children",[26] who were defined to be all the children at present living or born in the future to the settlor by his wife. The second definition was that of the "class period", which was defined as the period ending on the twenty-fifth birthday of the first of the children to attain the age of 25 years. Finally, the "beneficiaries" under the trust were defined as the children living at the date the trust deed was entered into or born during the class period. If, on the other hand, it was desired to keep the class open, it would have been necessary to include a provision ensuring that a beneficiary's interest in possession was unaffected by any subsequent addition to the class of beneficiaries.

Mandatory accumulation

18–23   It was mandatory—whether under the terms of the trust instrument, or as a result of the operation of statute, or as a matter of general law—that income accruing to the trust was accumulated so far as it was not applied for the maintenance, education or benefit of a beneficiary. The simplest way to achieve this was to impose a trust to accumulate. This was done expressly or by allowing s.31 to impose the obligation. A mere power to accumulate would not have sufficed unless the trustees were obliged, in default of accumulation, to apply the trust income for maintenance, etc.

In the exceptional case where an unmarried infant had an interest in possession and the requirement to accumulate under s.31 was excluded by the trust instrument, the income had to be accumulated as a matter of general law since an unmarried infant could not give a good receipt, and this requirement was accordingly satisfied notwithstanding:

(1) the absence of any direction to accumulate in the trust instrument; and
(2) the exclusion of s.31.

The trust, however, did not receive favoured treatment, because the mere fact that the infant was unable to give a good receipt did not divest him of his interest in possession (if he died the accumulated income would have formed part of his estate), and therefore the requirement that the property was held on discretionary trusts would not have been satisfied. In such a case, an express direction to accumulate was therefore still necessary. The words "so far as not applied for the maintenance, education or benefit" in

---

[25] See *Re Wernher's Settlement Trusts* [1961] 1 W.L.R. 136; [1961] 1 All E.R. 184; *Re Edmondson's Will Trusts* [1972] 1 W.L.R. 183; [1972] 1 All E.R. 444; *Re Chapman's Settlement Trust* [1977] 1 W.L.R. 1163; *Re Clifford's Settlement Trusts* [1981] Ch. 63.

[26] The term "children" when used in isolation has certain legal implications which it may be desirable to avoid.

s.71(1)(b) was capable of being interpreted as meaning that a pure accumulation trust was outside s.71, but it was understood that HMRC accepted that such a trust could qualify for favoured treatment.

Limits on accumulation

A direction[27] to accumulate income for a period is effective under UK law[28] only in so far as that period does not exceed the lawful accumulation period under the Law of Property Act 1925 and the Perpetuities and Accumulations Act 1964,[29] a direction to accumulate beyond that period being void as regards the excess period.[30] The duration of a s.71 trust was thus limited to the lawful accumulation period. Section 31 of the Trustee Act 1925 was often crucial in determining this period.[31] **18–24**

There are six different lawful accumulation periods. Which one applies in a given case is a matter of construction of the instrument creating the settlement, the court "discovering" the settlor's intention where he did not expressly state it.

In relation to settlements made before July 16, 1964, there are four possible periods, namely:

(1) the settlor's life;
(2) 21 years from the settlor's death;
(3) the minority or respective minorities of any person or persons living or *en ventre sa mere* at the settlor's death; and
(4) the minority or respective minorities of any person or persons who under the limitations of the instrument directing the accumulation would for the time being, if of full age, be entitled to the income directed to be accumulated.[32]

So far as settlements made on or after July 16, 1964 are concerned, s.13 of the Perpetuities and Accumulations Act 1964 adds two further periods, namely:

(1) 21 years from the making of the settlement; and
(2) the minority or respective minorities of any person or persons in being on the date the settlement is made.

The age of majority in relation to trusts created or appointed before January 1, 1970, is 21; in relation to trusts created or appointed on or after that date the age is 18.

In each case only one of the above periods (i.e. not necessarily the longest) will be taken to have been intended by the settlor to apply: in relation to settlements made after July 15, 1964, the period will normally be 21 years from the making of the settlement.

Extension of permitted periods

Under s.165 of the Law of Property Act 1925, where under any statutory power (e.g. under s.31 of the Trustee Act 1925) or under the general law (i.e. because an infant **18–25**

---

[27] Or a power: see *Re Robb's Trusts* [1953] Ch. 459; and *Baird v Lord Advocate* [1979] A.C. 666.

[28] It may be possible to arrange matters so that the proper law of the settlement is a foreign law which does not have an accumulation period.

[29] In Scotland, the Trusts (Scotland) Act 1961. Both Acts apply only to natural persons and not, e.g., to a corporate settlor: see *Re Dodwell & Co's Trust Deed* [1979] Ch. 301.

[30] Law of Property Act 1925 s.164.

[31] As well as in determining the period during which income is in fact to be accumulated.

[32] Law of Property Act 1925 s.164.

cannot give a good receipt) income is accumulated during the period of a person's infancy, that period is ignored in deciding whether income has been accumulated beyond the period permitted by the 1925 and 1964 Acts. This is important, because it means that once the lawful period of accumulation has expired income can still be accumulated for a beneficiary so long as he is an unmarried infant, and this is so even if he is unborn when the lawful period expires, as the following example shows.

Assume that on January 1, 1955, X the father of three children, settled property in equal shares on such of his children as attained the age of 25, and that 22 years later a further child, Z, was born to X. The income generated by Z's share could be accumulated for a further 21 years,[33] notwithstanding the fact that Z was born one year after the end of the lawful accumulation period.

It should be noted that, although s.165 of the Law of Property Act 1925 operates where the income is accumulated under the general law as well as under a statutory power, for s.71 purposes the period of accumulation was effectively extended only where there was a statutory power of accumulation under s.31 or the child's interest was a contingent one. This followed from the fact that when income arising in respect of an interest in possession was being accumulated in consequence of the general law the infant had an interest in possession, with the result that the requirement that the property was to be held on discretionary trusts was not satisfied.

Settlements often directed income to be accumulated for a period of 21 years from the making of the settlement and in the event that an infant beneficiary was alive at the end of that period or was born thereafter his share of the income arising to the settlement was accumulated during his unmarried infancy in consequence of the combined effect of s.31 of the Trustee Act 1925 and s.165 of the Law of Property Act 1925. Exceptionally, where the settlor was young, it may have been desirable to direct that the income was accumulated during his lifetime. Such a direction had to be qualified, of course, so that the settlor's continued survival did not prevent the beneficiaries' interest vesting in the manner required by s.71. Where the settlor's lifetime was used as the period, the contrary possibility of the settlor's early demise also had to be catered for. This is because the stipulation of his life as the accumulation period would normally have been construed as operating to exclude s.31, with the result that if he died during the infancy of a beneficiary the infant's share of the property would have ceased to be held on s.71 trusts, the infant becoming entitled to an interest in possession notwithstanding the fact that the trustees were required to accumulate the income during his unmarried infancy as a matter of general law (because of his inability to give a good receipt). Therefore provision had to be made in the trust deed to ensure that s.31 applied in the event of the settlor dying during the unmarried infancy of any living beneficiary.

With regard to the requirement that trust income was to be accumulated, HMRC apparently took the view, that s.71(1)(b) was in effect a single requirement that income must be either accumulated or applied for the maintenance, education or benefit of a beneficiary.[34] It should be noted that the fund constituting the accumulations did not need to fall within the s.71 conditions so long as the main fund was within the section. This was satisfied by accumulations made under s.31.

Drafting

18–26 It was sometimes desirable to prolong for as long as possible the period during which income could be accumulated and during which the trust came within the terms of s.71.

---

[33] The age of majority in relation to trusts created before January 1, 1970.

[34] But see the income tax case *IRC v Berrill* [1981] S.T.C. 784, which supported the contention that the requirement meant that there must be a trust to accumulate.

In certain circumstances this might—at least at first glance—have appeared to involve somewhat complicated drafting.

Assume, for example, that a person wished to establish for his living and as yet unborn children[35] an accumulation and maintenance trust which came within the terms of s.71 for as long as possible. The first step was to provide that the children did not acquire interests in possession until attaining the age of 25. Account then had to be taken of the fact that in the circumstances it was possible for the beneficiaries to fall into three categories, namely:

(1) older children: one or more of these children could have attained 25 years of age before the end of the 21-year accumulation period;
(2) younger children: one or more of these children could have attained an age of between 18 and 25 years during the 21-year accumulation period; and
(3) unborn children: one or more of these children could have attained 18 years of age after the end of the 21-year accumulation period.

The problem in such circumstances was how best to integrate the provisions of s.31 of the Trustee Act 1925 into the trust deed. So far as the first two classes of children are concerned, it was desirable to exclude the vesting effect of s.31(1)(ii), since, if this was not done, the older and younger children would become entitled to interests in possession on attaining the age of 18, with the result that the income accruing in respect of their putative shares was no longer accumulated, notwithstanding the fact that the 21-year accumulation period had not expired. No such problem arose in respect of the unborn children, whose interests would vest on their attaining the age of 18, at which time they would become entitled to income from their respective shares either by virtue of the termination of the accumulation period (as extended under s.165 of the Law of Property Act 1925) or by virtue of s.31(1)(ii). The simplest solution was often to exclude s.31(1)(ii) of the Trustee Act 1925 until the end of the 21-year accumulation period. If this was done:

(1) the older children would not become entitled to interests in possession until attaining the age of 25;
(2) the younger children would not become entitled to interests in possession until the end of the 21-year accumulation period; and
(3) the unborn children would not become entitled to interests in possession until attaining the age of 18, i.e. until the end of the extended accumulation period.

An alternative approach was to provide that the trustees could during the 21-year accumulation period continue to exercise their statutory powers of maintenance and accumulation in favour of any beneficiary who attained 18 but not 25 years of age.

The rule in *Saunders v Vautier*

The rule in *Saunders v Vautier* was discussed above.[36] Under it one or more **18–27** beneficiaries may in certain circumstances terminate accumulation. Until they do so,

---

[35] Regard also should be had to the class closing rules: see paras 18–21, 18–22.
[36] See para.11–09.

however, accumulation continues. The possibility of their terminating accumulation by invoking the rule did not prevent the accumulation requirement from being satisfied.

Limited duration

18–28   The normal procedure before the introduction of the fourth requirement by the Finance Act 1976 was to provide for the beneficiaries to become entitled equally either to the trust property or to interests in possession therein on attaining the maximum possible specified age, having regard to the then lawful accumulation period. If the aim was to prolong the life of the accumulation and maintenance trust, the trustees were given power to appoint a beneficiary's share away from him; they exercised this power (at the latest) on the eve of a beneficiary's entitlement, with the result that the vesting was postponed and the remaining beneficiaries' presumptive shares were increased proportionately. The power to appoint away from a beneficiary (or to revoke his interest) was always limited so that it was exercisable only while there were two or more beneficiaries living and under the specified age, with the result that it could not be said that the existence of the power infringed the certainty requirement.

    In the event that no beneficiary was living at the time it was desired to create or appoint the trust an arbitrary beneficiary was selected, such as the first child to appear in the birth columns of a given newspaper. This, of course, did not involve any element of largesse, because (provided a bona fide beneficiary was born while the trust still qualified for favoured treatment) that child's share would be appointed away from him without any adverse consequences, his function having been merely to act as a "starter." Even if no bona fide beneficiary was ever born, with the result that the "starter" in fact became entitled to an interest in possession the situation was not irretrievable so long as the trustees had power to revoke his interest once it had vested, or if that interest was itself limited to a short period, e.g. one day. The drawback to this was, of course, that the termination of the starter's interest gave rise to a charge under s.52(1). In order to prevent the prolongation in this way of the life of an accumulation and maintenance trust, the Finance Act 1976 introduced a requirement that, in broad terms, the property comprised in the trust must not have qualified for favoured treatment for too long.

18–29   The requirement was stated in the alternative, it being sufficient that either of two tests—the one common grandparent test and the 25-year test—was satisfied.

The common grandparent test

18–30   Here the requirement was that all the beneficiaries and ex-beneficiaries (i.e. those beneficiaries who exceeded the specified age or died) were, or were before they died, grandchildren of a common grandparent. Special treatment was afforded to:

(1) the widow or widower; and
(2) the children of any ex-beneficiary who died before attaining the specified age,

in that they could be included in the class of beneficiaries—e.g. under the operation of a normal substitution clause, without the common grandparent requirement being infringed.[37]

---

[37] IHTA 1984 s.71(2)(b).

For this purpose, a person's children included his illegitimate children, his adopted children, and his stepchildren.[38] They did not, of course, include such children as may have appeared in the birth columns of any newspaper of his choosing. This, however, did not preclude such a child being used as the "starter" for a s.71 trust, because although the use of such a child would mean that the trust did not satisfy the common grandparent test, the trust would still receive favoured treatment for 25 years under the 25-year test.

The 25-year test: IHT time bomb trusts

This was straightforward. Not more than 25 years could elapse either: **18–31**

   (1) since the settlement was made; or
   (2) since the latest time when the trust otherwise qualified for s.71 treatment.

Where this test applied, a trust was disqualified after having received favoured treatment for 25 years.

Although this test was simple, it potentially gave rise to difficulties where on the expiry of 25 years there were still one or more infant beneficiaries whose interests had not vested, because after the expiration of 25 years the property to which they were contingently entitled would no longer have qualified for favoured treatment, but would instead have been subject to the special charging provisions.

This had two consequences. First, there was an immediate exit charge under s.71(3)(a) on the value of the property which ceased to be held on s.71 trusts at the staggering rate of 21 per cent (see para.17–06). Secondly, the property was within the relevant property regime and so was subject to exit and periodic charges. In particular, the property was subject to an exit charge if a beneficiary became entitled to it or to an interest in possession in it.

Given the fact that the 25-year test was introduced in 1976 no settlement could have failed it before April 15, 2001.[39] Since that date trusts relying on the 25-year test for their validity were at risk and trustees had to be certain whether or not reliance was placed on that test. In particular, careful analysis was required to be sure that what was thought of as "Grandfather X's Grandchildren's Settlement" really satisfied the common grandparent test. A recurrent trap was where although all the intended beneficiaries were grandchildren of a common grandparent but a child who was not such a grandchild was used as a "starter life".

The question arose as to what steps trustees could take to avoid the 25-year rule being infringed, with the disastrous consequences mentioned above. Depending on the powers available to them, trustees considered accelerating the beneficiaries' entitlements, either by bringing forward the vesting of their interests in possession or by vesting property in them absolutely.[40]

In view of the 25-year rule and the consequences mentioned above, where reliance was placed on the 25-year rule the draftsman needed to consider the vesting ages very

---

[38] IHTA 1984 s.71(8).

[39] A Revenue reminder was issued in relation to the April 15, 2001 date and its impact in *Inland Revenue Tax Bulletin*, Issue 50 (December 2000), p.813.

[40] The fact that the beneficiaries cannot give a good receipt should operate only to leave the trustees in an exposed position, not to invalidate the vesting. For a good discussion, see *Private Client Business* (2000), p.266.

carefully and needed to consider giving the trustees sufficient powers to allow them to accelerate entitlements.

Transitional provisions

18–32   Special provision had to be made for applying the 25-year test and the common grandparent test to s.71 trusts created or appointed before those tests came into force. The legislation accordingly provided that where such a trust satisfied the other requirements of a s.71 trust (i.e. conditions 1, 2 and 3 at para.18–04 above) the position was as follows:

(1) The 25-year test: this test ran from April 15, 1976, not from the date the trust first otherwise qualified for favoured treatment. Because of the transitional provision the 25-year condition only caused a loss of favoured trust status to any settled property (being settled property which did not satisfy the common grandparent condition) on April 15, 2001, or later.

(2) The common grandparent test was regarded as satisfied so long as:

(a) the common grandparent test was satisfied from April 15, 1976, even if it was not satisfied before then; or

(b) the common grandparent test was satisfied from April 1, 1977, and either there was a living beneficiary on that date, or all the beneficiaries had died or attained before April 15, 1976 the age specified by the terms of the settlement[41]; or

(c) there was no power under the terms of the settlement the exercise of which would result in the common grandparent test being satisfied, provided the trusts had not been varied after April 15, 1976.[42] Where the common grandparent test was satisfied the settlement could run for so long as requirements 1, 2 and 3 were satisfied.[43]

II. ACCUMULATION AND MAINTENANCE TRUSTS AFTER THE FINANCE ACT 2006

18–33   As indicated in Chapter 10, significant changes were made to the tax treatment of accumulation and maintenance trusts by the Finance Act 2006. Section 71(1A) of the IHTA 1984 (inserted by the Finance Act 2006) provides that no settlement which would otherwise qualify as an accumulation and maintenance settlement but which is created or arises after March 22, 2006 will attract the favourable tax regime set out in s.71 of the IHTA 1984. All such new settlements will need to qualify either as bereaved minors' trusts or age 18-to-25 trusts in order to attract any favourable treatment. In the absence of being able to attract favourable treatment, they will be subject to the relevant property regime in the usual way.

18–34   Until the Finance Act 2006 changes, property within accumulation and maintenance settlements was not regarded as "relevant property". As such, the relevant property

---

[41] The situation to which this is intended to apply is where a "starter" was used, a bona fide beneficiary born before April 1, 1977, and the starter was cut out of his entitlement by that date.
[42] IHTA 1984 s.71(6).
[43] See para.18–04.

regime did not apply: in other words there were no entry charges on the gift of assets into the accumulation and maintenance settlements (these gifts were usually PETs), there were no periodic charges on the value of the property within the settlement, and finally there were no exit charges where a beneficiary of the accumulation and maintenance settlement received assets from the settlement. Now, however, post-March 22, 2006 settlements, even if drafted in accordance with s.71 of the IHTA 1984, will not attract this favourable treatment.[44]

These new settlements will be chargeable under the relevant property regime (unless the conditions of bereaved minors' trusts or other provisions are satisfied).

The question that faced practitioners between 2006 and 2008 was what to do with **18–35** existing accumulation and maintenance trusts. As from April 6, 2008, para.3 of Sch.20 of the Finance Act 2006 provides:

"(1) In s.71(1)(i)(a) of IHTA 1984 (section applies to settled property only if one or more persons will become beneficially entitled on or before reaching a specified age not exceeding 25)—
    (a) for 'twenty-five' substitute 'eighteen', and
    (b) omit 'or to have an interest in possession in it'.
(2) Subparagraph 2(1) comes into force on 6 April 2008 but only for the purpose of determining whether, at a time, on or after that day, s.71 IHTA 1984 applies to settled property.
(3) There is no charge to tax under s.71 of IHTA 1984 in a case where—
    (a) settled property ceases, on the coming into force of subparagraph (1), to be property to which that section applies, but
    (b) that section would immediately after the coming into force of subparagraph (1) apply to the settled property but for the amendments made by subparagraph (1)."

The net effect of paras (3)(1) and (2) of Sch.20 of the Finance Act 2006 is that, as from April 6, 2008, in order for settled property to continue to qualify as property subject to the favourable accumulation and maintenance regime, the requirement is that one or more persons will, on or before attaining the specified age not exceeding 18 years, become beneficially entitled to it. Consequently, the vesting age is now 18 rather than 25 and it is no longer possible for a beneficiary to merely to attain an interest in possession in the settled property in order for the favoured treatment to apply: the beneficiary must, at the age of 18, become entitled to the capital of the settlement. This is consistent with the fact that, post the Finance Act 2006, such an interest in possession will rarely constitute a qualifying interest in possession. The remaining s.71 of the IHTA 1984 requirements (namely, the no interest in possession requirement and the 25 year longstop or common grandparent) were not amended by the Finance Act 2006 changes.

Before April 6, 2008 trustees were, therefore, faced with a number of choices of how **18–36** to deal with existing accumulation and maintenance settlements. If they did nothing, so that the beneficiary acquired an interest in possession at the age of 25, then from the April 6, 2008, the settlement would fall within the relevant property regime. There would be no entry charge on the occasion that the trust moved from the accumulation and maintenance trust regime to the relevant property regime (Finance Act 2006 Sch.20

---

[44] For an illustration of the difference of treatment between the pre- and post-FA 2006 treatment of transfers into accumulation and maintenance trusts, see *Marquess of Linlithhgow v HMRC* [2010] S.T.C. 1563. The issue in that case was whether the transfer of value into a pre-March 22, 2006 accumulation and maintenance settlement had occurred before or after March 22, 2006.

s.3(3)), but the assets within the settlement, which after April 6, 2008 became subject to the relevant property regime, would be subject to the periodic and exit charges.[45]

18–37   The second option, before April 6, 2008, was for the trustees to terminate the trusts and to advance the capital to the beneficiaries. However, this clearly had wider, non-tax, implications: for instance, it may have been thought imprudent to place a large amount of capital in the hands of relatively young beneficiaries. It was not, therefore, a step that trustees chose to take in many cases.

18–38   The third option was to amend the terms of the existing accumulation and maintenance settlement so that it complied with the stricter conditions that would apply from April 6, 2008 (and which were imposed by para.3(1), (2) of Sch.20 of the Finance Act 2006). In effect, the trustees had to alter the terms of the settlement so that a beneficiary became absolutely entitled to his share in the trust property at the age of 18. If this change was made before April 6, 2008, then as from the April 6, 2008 until such time as the beneficiary attained his entitlement to the capital at the age of 18, the existing accumulation and maintenance settlement would continue to attract the favourable tax regime that had applied to it before April 6, 2008. In other words, the settlement would have been free from the periodic and exit charges.

18–39   The fourth option was for the trustees to alter the terms of the settlement so that, although a beneficiary did not become absolutely entitled to trust property at the age of 18, he did become so entitled at the age of 25. Such a change would ensure that the property came within the age 18-to-25 trust provisions set out in s.71D of the IHTA 1984.
         Section 71D(6) provided:

"(a) that the [beneficiary] ('B') if he has not done so before attaining the age of 25, will on attaining that age become absolutely entitled to—
     (i) the settled property,
     (ii) any income arising from it, and
     (iii) any income that has arisen from the property held on the trusts for his benefit and being accumulated before that time, and
(b) that, for so long as B is living and under the age of 25, if any of the settled property is applied for the benefit of the beneficiary, it is applied for the benefit of B, and
(c) that, for so long as B is living and under the age of 25, either—
     (i) B is entitled to all of the income (if there is any) arising from any of the settled property, or
     (ii) no such income may be applied for the benefit of any other person."

In essence, s.71D(6) required: first, that a beneficiary who had not attained the age of 25 would at that age obtain an absolute right to the capital; second, that until he attained the age of 25 he was entitled to all the income of the settled property to which he would become entitled at 25 or that that income was applied or accumulated for the benefit of that beneficiary.

18–40   A degree of flexibility was provided by s.71D(7) of the IHTA 1984 in that the provisions of the age 18-to-25 trust applied even if the trustees had a wide power of advancement provided to them by s.32 of the Trustee Act 1925. It was, therefore, possible for trustees to enter into an age 18-to-25 trust before April 6, 2008 and, before

---

[45] HMRC's view is set out in HMRC Manuals IHTM42808.

the beneficiary attained the age of 25, to make a settled advance in favour of the beneficiary postponing the date of absolute entitlement beyond the age of 25.

However, it must be noted that the entry into the age 18-to-25 trust regime limited **18–41** the flexibility of the trustees in the matter of application of income arising from the settled property to which a beneficiary became entitled at the age of 25. Such income could only be applied to or for the benefit of the beneficiary who would become entitled to the settled property at the age of 25. Further, if the existing accumulation and maintenance trust provisions were altered before April 6, 2008 in order to comply with the provisions of s.71D of the IHTA 1984 (the age 18-to-25 trust), although they would avoid the periodic charge on the first 10-year anniversary of the settlement, there would be a primary exit charge on the exit of the property which occurred when the beneficiary attained the age of 25 (i.e. when the beneficiary became absolutely entitled to the property). In those circumstances, the maximum charge, at current rates, was limited to 4.2 per cent.[46]

Calculating the charges where the relevant property regime applies from April 6, 2008

As indicated above at para.18–36, if the settlement came within the relevant property **18–42** regime at April 6, 2008, it would be subject to the periodic charge and exit charges. The applicable principles are dealt with in Chapters 14–16. However, the following points are worth noting.

The periodic charge

The relevant commencement date for the purposes of calculating the periodic charge **18–43** is the commencement date of the settlement, i.e. the date that the settlement was first created.[47] So for a settlement created on April 6, 2003, the first 10-year anniversary would fall on April 6, 2013. It is immaterial for these purposes that the settlement did not contain relevant property at its inception.

However, the fact that the settlement did not contain relevant property throughout the period since its inception is dealt with by s.66(2) of the IHTA 1984: the rate at which tax is charged on that property is reduced by one-fortieth for each of the successive quarters in that period which expired before the property became relevant property comprised in the settlement. In effect, therefore, at a time before April 6, 2008, when the property was comprised in an accumulation and maintenance trust, the property was not relevant property and so would attract the reduction in tax rate set out at s.66(2).

Exit charges

Section 69 of the IHTA 1984 provides, inter alia, that where on or after the most **18–44** recent 10-year anniversary property which was comprised in the settlement but was not

---

[46] See para.20–14.
[47] IHTA 1984 s.61(1).

then relevant property later became relevant property, the value of the property for the purposes of calculating the exit charge is the value of that property at the time when it became relevant property. In effect, therefore, where property held on accumulation and maintenance trusts until April 6, 2008 became on that date relevant property, the value of that property at April 6, 2008 is the value to be taken into account for the purposes of calculating the exit charge.

Special rule for accumulation and maintenance trust containing pre-budget life policies

18–45 Special provision is made by s.46B of the IHTA 1984 to deal with trusts that existed before March 22, 2006 which contained life policies. The aim is to ensure that if any premium is paid on or after March 22, 2006 certain protective provisions are brought into play. The aim is to prevent the payment of premiums on or after March 22, 2006 creating new relevant property settlements.

18–46 Section 46B of the IHTA 1984 provides as follows:

"(1) Subsections (2) and (5) below apply where—
  (a) a settlement commenced before March 22, 2006,
  (b) a contract of life insurance was entered into before that day,
  (c) a premium payable under the contract is paid or an allowed variation is made to the contract, at a particular time on or after that day,
  (d) immediately before that day, and at all subsequent times up to the particular time, there were rights under the contract that—
    (i) were comprised in the settlement; and
    (ii) were settled property to which s.71 below applied
  (e) rights under the contract become, by reference to payment or the premium or as a result of the variation, comprised in the settlement, and
  (f) any variation of the contract on or after March 22, 2006 but before the particular time, so far as it was a variation that—
    (i) increased the benefits secured by the contract, or
    (ii) extended the term of the insurance provided by the contract
    was an allowed variation.
(2) If the rights mentioned in (1)(e) would, but for (1A) of s.71 below, become property to which that section applies, those rights shall become settled property to which that section applies when they become comprised in the estate.
(3) Subsection 5 below also applies where—
  (a) settlement commenced before March 22, 2006,
  (b) a contract of life insurance was entered into before that day,
  (c) a premium payable under the contract is paid, or an allowed variation is made to the contract, at a particular time on or after that day when there are rights under the contract—
    (i) that are comprised in the settlements and are settled property to which s.71A or s.71D applies.
    (ii) that immediately before that day were settled property to which s.71 below applied, and
    (iii) that on or after that day, but before the particular time, became property to which s.71A or s.71D below applies in circumstances falling within (4) below,
  (d) rights under the contract become, by reference to payment of the premium or as a result of the variation, comprised in the settlement, and

(e) any variation of the contract on or after March 22, 2006 but before the particular time, so far as it was a variation that—
    (i) increased the benefits secured by the contract, or
    (ii) extended the term of the insurance provided by the contract,
    was an allowed variation.
(4) The circumstances referred to in (3)(c)(iii) above are—
(a) in the case of property to which s.71D below applies, that the property on becoming property to which s.71D below applies ceased to be property to which s.71 applied without ceasing to be settled property;
(b) in the case of property to which s.71A below applies—
    (i) that the property on becoming property to which s.71A below applies ceased, by the operation of s.71(1B) to be property to which s.71 below applied, or
    (ii) that the property, having become property to which s.71D below applied in circumstances falling within paragraph (a) above, on becoming property to which s.71A below applies ceased, by the operation of s.71D(5)(a) below, to be property to which s.71D applied.
(5) If payment of the premium is a transfer of value made by an individual, the transfer of value is a potentially exempt transfer.
(6) In this section 'allowed variation', in relation to a contract, means a variation that takes place by operation of, or as a result of exercise of rights conferred by, provisions forming part of the contract immediately before 22 March 2006."

It is apparent that so long as the provisions of the accumulation and maintenance settlements under s.71 still applied as at March 22, 2006 to the policy held by such an accumulation and maintenance settlement, any rights under the policy that become comprised in the settlement by virtue of the payment of the further premium after March 22, 2006 will be subject to the favourable accumulation and maintenance trust rules that subsisted before March 22, 2006. What is also apparent is that, if the payment of the premium is a transfer of value, it is expressly treated as a potentially exempt transfer. Consequently, the payment of the premium will not give rise to a charge in the hands of the payer: either it is an exempt transfer (perhaps being normal expenditure out of income) or, provided the payer survives the payment of the premium by a period of seven years, payment becomes exempt at that point. Such a payment, being a transfer of value, is regarded as a potentially exempt transfer not only where the premium is paid into a settlement that is within the accumulation and maintenance trust regime, but also where it falls within the bereaved minors' trust regime or within the age 18-to-25 trust regime.[48]

It should, however, be noted that these favourable rules will be disapplied if there is **18–47** a variation of the trust other than a variation that falls within the definition of "allowed variation" in s.46B(6) of the IHTA 1984. An "allowed variation" is one which takes place by the operation of the terms of the policy as they existed immediately before March 22, 2006. For example, a provision within the terms of the life policy that actually increases or changes some of the requirements of the policy or a variation that occurs as a result of the exercise of the rights conferred by or provisions forming part of the contract immediately before March 22, 2006 is an "allowed variation". So if there are rights within the life policy which may be exercised, their exercise, post-March 22, 2006, will be regarded as "allowed variation" so as not to jeopardise the availability of the favourable PET treatment on the payment of premiums or the availability of favourable accumulation and maintenance settlement provisions to the

---

[48] See IHTA 1984 s.46B(3), (4), (5).

additional rights forming part of the contract as a result of the payment or a premium after March 22, 2006.

18–48   For those accumulation and maintenance settlements that ceased to come within s.71 of the IHTA 1984 on April 6, 2008, the position in relation to premium payments made after April 6, 2008 is that where a premium payment is made after that date to a settlement that is now within the relevant property regime, the payment is not a PET. However, a premium payment made after April 6, 2008 to a settlement that from that date qualifies as a bereaved minors' trust or age 18-to-25 trust will be a PET.

CHAPTER 19

BEREAVED MINORS' TRUSTS

I. INTRODUCTION

As was mentioned in Chapter 10, the Finance Act 2006 introduced two new **19–01** categories of favoured property trusts. This chapter is concerned with one of these two new categories, i.e. bereaved minors' trusts. The qualification requirements for bereaved minors' trusts are contained in the new s.71A, and are considered in Pt II of this chapter. The charging provisions are contained in s.71B and are considered in Pt III.

A "bereaved minor" is defined for the purposes of s.71A and s.71B of the IHTA **19–02** 1984 as:

"a person—
(a) who has not yet attained the age of 18, and
(b) at least one of whose parents has died".[1]

II. QUALIFICATION REQUIREMENTS

As mentioned above, s.71A contains the qualification requirements for bereaved **19–03** minors' trusts. It provides as follows:

"(1) This section applies to settled property (including property settled before 22 March 2006) if—

---

[1] IHTA 1984 s.71C.

643

(a) it is held on statutory trusts for the benefit of the bereaved minor under s.46 and s.47(1) of the Administration of Estates Act 1925 (succession on intestacy and statutory trusts in favour of issue of intestate), or

(b) it is held on trusts for the benefit of a bereaved minor and subsection (2) below applies to the trusts,

but this section does not apply to property in which a disabled person's interest subsists.

(2) This subsection applies to trusts—

(a) established under the will of a deceased parent of the bereaved minor, or

(b) established under the Criminal Injuries Compensation Scheme,

(c) established under the Victims of Overseas Terrorism Compensation Scheme,

which secure that the conditions in subsection (3) below are met.

(3) Those conditions are—

(a) that the bereaved minor, if he has not done so before the age of 18, will on attaining that age become absolutely entitled to—

(i) the settled property,

(ii) any income arising from it, and

(iii) any income that has arisen from the property held on the trusts for his benefit and been accumulated before that time,

(b) that, for so long as the bereaved minor is living and under the age of 18, if any of the settled property is applied for the benefit of a beneficiary, it is applied for the benefit of the bereaved minor, and

(c) that, so long as the bereaved minor is living and under the age of 18, either—

(i) the bereaved minor is entitled to all of the income (if there is any) arising from any of the settled property, or

(ii) no such income may be applied for the benefit of any other person.

(4) Trusts such as are mentioned in paragraph (a), (b) or (c) of subsection (2) above are not to be treated as failing to secure that the conditions in subsection (3) above are met by reason only of—

(a) the trustees' having the powers conferred by s.32 of the Trustee Act 1925 (powers of advancement), ... "

There are a few points to note in relation to these statutory qualification requirements in s.71A of the IHTA 1984.

Establishing a bereaved minors' trust

19–04 In order to qualify as a bereaved minors' trust, the trust must be held on trusts for the benefit of a "bereaved minor" and the requirements of s.71A(1)(a) or (b) must apply.

Intestacy

19–05 The reference in s.71A(1)(a) to the intestacy rules set out in the Administration of Estates Act 1925 ss.46 and 47(1) highlights the following issues:

(a) It appears that only settled property held on statutory trusts created by these intestacy provisions is capable of qualifying as settled property to which favoured treatment under this category applies. It does not, therefore, appear possible for a minor who benefits under foreign intestacy rules to be able to claim the benefit of bereaved minors' trust provisions in respect of such settled property.

(b) Sections 46 and 47(1) of the Administration of Estates Act 1925 do not stipulate that the bereaved minor must be the child of the intestate. It is, therefore, possible that a grandchild or a great grandchild could satisfy the requirement. "Issue" in this context is widely defined to include several generations of descendants, with the consequence that a bereaved minors' trust can arise on the intestacy of a grandparent with, however, the limitation that the grandchild who benefits must have lost at least one parent. In other words, the grandchild must still satisfy the requirement that he is a "bereaved minor" as defined in s.71C.[2]

Established under the will of the deceased, under the Criminal Injuries Compensation Scheme, or under the Victims of Terrorism Compensation Scheme

If s.71A(1)(a) does not apply, i.e. property is not held on the relevant statutory trusts **19–06** for the benefit of bereaved minors, then the provisions of s.71A(2) apply. Under subs.(2), a trust will be a bereaved minors' trust only if it is established under the will of a deceased parent of the bereaved minor, it is established under the Criminal Injuries Compensation Scheme, or it is established under the Victims of Terrorism Compensation Scheme, and in each case, the conditions of subs.(3) are met (as to which see paras 19–07–19–09).

As regards s.71A(2)(a):

(1) The definition of "parent" is found in s.71H. A parent includes a step-parent.[3] Further, a deceased individual is taken to be a parent of another individual if immediately before the deceased individual died he had parental responsibility for the other individual under the law of England and Wales, Scotland or Northern Ireland. The term "parental responsibility" has the same meaning as in the Children Act 1989. Similar provisions apply for the purposes of Scotland and Northern Ireland.

(2) The requirement that the bereaved minors' trust is established under the will of the deceased parent of the bereaved minor makes it possible for a bereaved minors' trust to be created by a deed of variation falling within s.142(1). A deed of variation falling within s.142(1) satisfies the "under the will" requirement because the trust that arises as a result of the deed of variation is deemed to have been created by the deceased under his will.[4]

(3) Further, trusts created in circumstances where s.144 applies (events occurring within two years of the death of the deceased), are also capable of qualifying as bereaved minors' trusts provided that the other conditions are met: s.144 deems these trusts to have been effected by the deceased.[5]

It is apparent also from the provisions of s.71A that it is not necessary for a bereaved minors' trust to arise immediately on the death of the deceased parent. Provided the trust arises under the will of a deceased parent of the bereaved minor, it can arise even

---

[2] For an illustration of this, see HMRC Manuals IHTM42815.
[3] IHTA 1984 s.71H(1).
[4] IHTA 1984 s.142(1).
[5] IHTA 1984 s.144(4).

after another interest has subsisted: contrast the position for immediate post-death interests.[6] The transition from an immediate post-death interest into a bereaved minors' trust will be a PET.[7]

Provided the conditions for qualification are satisfied, settled property will qualify for favoured treatment as a bereaved minors' trust whenever it is settled: it is not relevant whether it was settled before March 22, 2006 or after that date.

Certainty of entitlement

19–07 The bereaved minor must, at the latest at the age of 18, become absolutely entitled to the settled property and to the income arising from it and to any income that has arisen from the property held on trusts for his benefit and which has been accumulated before that time. In other words, if any other beneficiary is capable of benefiting from the income as it arises or from the accumulated income, then the settled property is not property to which the bereaved minors' trust provisions apply. It is also important to note that the bereaved minor must become absolutely entitled to the settled property at 18[8]: it is not sufficient that he becomes entitled to an interest in possession in the settled property.

A "bereaved minor" is defined in s.71C (see para.19–02 above). Trusts in favour of more than one bereaved minor should also qualify as bereaved minors' trusts. Where there are multiple bereaved minors, the legislation does not stipulate that they must be entitled to equal shares at the age of 18. Nor is there any prohibition on varying the presumptive shares of the bereaved minors while they are below the age of 18. However, once the shares have vested at the age of 18, the trust terms should not permit any possible variation to the bereaved minors' vested shares.

Income

19–08 There is a lack of flexibility in the manner in which the trustees can deal with the income of property which comes within the bereaved minors' trusts provisions: the bereaved minor must be entitled to all the income (if any) that arises from the settled property or alternatively no such income may be applied for the benefit of any other person. In other words, while it is not necessary for the income to be paid to the beneficiary while he is alive and under the age of 18 it is imperative, in order for the trust to qualify as a bereaved minors' trust, that no other person is capable of benefiting from that income.

This is in stark contrast to the flexibility that was permitted under the previous accumulation and maintenance trust provisions. Under those provisions, while the

---

[6] See para.11–53 in relation to immediate post-death interests.

[7] IHTA 1984 s.3A(1A)(c)(iii).

[8] IHTA 1984 s.71A(2) requires that the trusts created under the will of the deceased parent or established under the Criminal Injuries Compensation Board must "secure" that, inter alia, the bereaved minor becomes entitled to the settled property at 18. As a result, the possibility that the bereaved minor may die under the age of 18 will not prevent the trust from qualifying as a bereaved minors' trust.

beneficiary was alive and under the age of 18, the trustees had flexibility to determine for the benefit of which beneficiary the income of the settlement could be applied.[9]

Capital

While the beneficiary is under the age of 18 and alive, where settled property is applied for the benefit of a beneficiary it is only permissible to apply it for the benefit of that bereaved minor, or other bereaved minors of that trust. This again reduces flexibility because it means that the capital of the bereaved minors' trust may not be used to benefit any beneficiary other than the bereaved minors who will become absolutely entitled to the settled property at the age of 18.

19–09

Multiple beneficiaries, death before vesting age

Where the death of a minor beneficiary results in disentitlement under the age of 18 and in the increase of the presumptive shares of his siblings who are under the age of 18, no charge to inheritance tax arises.

19–10

Flexibility and the terms of the trust

It is not necessary for the terms of the bereaved minors' trust to be set out in the will of the deceased parent—provided that the trustees exercise a power of appointment, set out in the will, to create a bereaved minors' trust.

19–11

Some degree of flexibility is also retained in a bereaved minors' trust by the provisions of s.71A(4)(a) which provides that a trust will not fail to satisfy the conditions as to entitlement to income and settled property if the trustees have powers of advancement conferred on them by s.32 of the Trustee Act 1925.[10] This is so even if the maximum one-half distribution requirement is extended by the will.[11] It is, therefore, possible for the testator to create a will (or for the terms of the testator's will to be amended by a s.142 deed of variation) providing that the bereaved minor will become absolutely entitled at the age of 18 and for the trustees at a later date to employ their powers of advancement to create a settled advance deferring absolute entitlement to the capital until a later date. Depending upon the terms of the advancement, the amended trusts will either fall within the provisions of age 18-to-25 trusts[12] or will fall into the relevant property regime. In other words, if the trustees exercise the power of advancement in order to provide that the beneficiary becomes entitled to income at the age of 18 and to the capital at the age of 25, the settled advance will qualify as an age 18-to-25 trust. However, if there is no entitlement to the capital of the settled advance even at the age of 25, the settled advance will fall within the relevant property regime.

The fact that the bereaved minor may have an interest in possession from the age of 18 does not prevent the application of the relevant property regime given that such an

---

[9] See paras 18–06 and following.

[10] This is similar to the treatment of powers of advancement in the context of pre-March 22, 2006 accumulation and maintenance trusts—see paras 18–12–18–14 inclusive.

[11] IHTA 1984 s.71A(4)(b).

[12] As to which, see Ch.20.

interest in possession will not be a qualifying interest in possession. Further, such an interest cannot be an immediate post-death interest given that the bereaved minors' interest does not arise immediately on the death of the deceased parent but arises at a later stage on the occasion when the trustees of the bereaved minors' trust exercise the power of advancement conferred on them.[13]

Interaction with other settled property regimes

Interaction with other favoured property regimes

19–12   Property in which a disabled person's interest[14] subsists cannot qualify as a bereaved minors' trust.[15] An anomaly that arises as a consequence of death of a disabled person who is a bereaved minor under the age of 18 is discussed at para.21–27.

Interaction with certain interests in possession

19–13   By virtue of s.49A(4)(a), it is one of the qualifying conditions for immediate post-death interests, that s.71A does not apply to the settled property. Consequently, even where an interest in possession in the property is vested in the bereaved minor, favoured treatment as a bereaved minors' trust takes precedence over treatment as an immediate post-death interest.[16]

Where the conditions of s.71A are satisfied, the bereaved minors' interests will also not qualify as transitional serial interests.[17]

III. THE CHARGE TO TAX

19–14   Section 71B provides as follows:

> "(1) Subject to subsections (2) and (3) below there should be a charge to tax under this section—
> (a) where settled property ceases to be property to which s.71A above applies, and
> (b) in a case where paragraph (a) above does not apply, where the trustees make a disposition as a result of which the value of settled property to which s.71A applies is less than it would be but for the disposition.
>
> (2) Tax is not charged under this section where settled property ceases to be property to which s.71A applies as a result of—
> (a) the bereaved minor attaining the age of 18 or becoming, under that age, absolutely entitled as mentioned in s.71A(3)(a) above, or
> (b) the death under that age of the bereaved minor, or
> (c) being paid or applied for the advancement or benefit of the bereaved minor."

---

[13] Contrast para.11–53.
[14] See Ch.21.
[15] IHTA 1984 s.71(1)(A).
[16] See also para.11–55.
[17] See IHTA ss.49C(5)(a), 49D(6)(a), 49E(5)(a). For the qualification requirements for transitional serial interests, see paras 11–56–11–62.

The provisions of s.70(3)–(8) and (10) apply with amendments for the purposes of s.71A.[18]

The points to note in relation to the charge to tax under s.71B are as follows: **19–15**

(1) There is no charge to tax when the bereaved minor attains the age of 18 and on that occasion becomes absolutely entitled to the trust property, any income arising from it and any accumulated income that has arisen.
(2) There is no charge to tax if the bereaved minor dies under the age of 18.
(3) There is no charge to tax if the trustees pay or apply the settled property for the advancement or benefit of the bereaved minor, e.g. under a settled advance.

This appears to be a comprehensive list of occasions on which tax could arise on property ceasing to be part of the bereaved minors' trust. Consequently, it is unlikely that a charge to tax will arise in relation to a bereaved minors' trust. Note that even though there is no occasion of charge to inheritance tax, holdover relief from capital gains tax is available by virtue of s.260(2)(da) of the TCGA 1992.

Where, however, a charge does arise, the provisions of s.70(3)–(8) and (10)[19] apply to calculate the exit charge on property ceasing to form part of the bereaved minors' trust.

EXAMPLE 1

Ted dies leaving the residue of his estate under the terms of his will to his son **19–16**
Dougall absolutely contingent on Dougall attaining the age of 18. The terms of the will provide that only Dougall may benefit from the capital and income of his presumptive share, that should Dougall die under the age of 18, Ted's estate will pass to Jack and that the provisions of ss.31 and 32 of the Trustee Act 1925 are to apply with no limitation being placed on the amount of Dougall's presumptive share that may be advanced to him. At Ted's death Dougall is aged 12.

The following analysis applies:

(1) The requirements for the trust to be a bereaved minor's trust are satisfied: the terms of the trust secure that Dougall will become absolutely entitled to the trust property at the age of 18 (the existence of the power of advancement is disregarded) and that below that age all the income can only be used for his benefit.
(2) If Dougall dies under the age of 18, there will be no exit charge (s.71B(2)(b)).
(3) If Dougall lives to the age of 18 and becomes absolutely entitled to the trust property, there will be no exit charge (s.71B(2)(a)).

EXAMPLE 2

The same facts as above except that, before Dougall's 18th birthday, the trustees exercise the power of advancement vesed in them so that when he reaches the age of 18 he has an interest in possession with capital vesting at 25 absolutely.

[18] See paras 17–18 and following.
[19] See Ch.17.

The following analysis applies when Dougall reaches the age of 18:

(1) The bereaved minor's trust ends but there is no exit charge on that occasion because s.71B(2)(c) provides that no charge arises where settled property ceases to be property within a bereaved minors' trust as a result of being paid or applied for the advancement or benefit of the bereaved minor.
(2) The trust will come within the age 18-to-25 trusts regime.[20]

EXAMPLE 3

The same facts as in Example 1 except that before Dougall's 18th birthday the trustees exercise the power of advancement vested in them so that on Dougall's 18th birthday he becomes entitled to an interest in possession, the trustees retain the power to advance the capital for his benefit with remainders over for Jack.

The following analysis applies when Dougall reaches the age of 18:

(1) The bereaved minor's trust ends: there is no exit charge because s.71B(2)(c) provides that no charge arises where settled property ceases to be property within a bereaved minors' trust as a result of being paid or applied for the advancement or benefit of the bereaved minor.
(2) The trust will come within the relevant property regime. Although Dougall has an interest in possession in it, it is not a qualifying interest in possession[21]: the property within the trust will be subject to periodic and exit charges.

[20] See paras 19–11 and 20–10.
[21] For the meaning of qualifying interest in possession see para.11–50.

CHAPTER 20

AGE 18-TO-25 TRUSTS

I. INTRODUCTION

As stated at para.17–19, Finance Act 2006 introduced a new category of favoured **20–01** trusts: the age 18-to-25 trust. The enactment of the provisions discussed in this chapter was a concession to those who had made strong representations that 18 was too young an age for capital to vest outright, i.e. the age of vesting under the new restricted accumulation and maintenance settlements, and the bereaved minors' trusts. The introduction of favoured treatment that applies to age 18-to-25 trusts means that absolute vesting may be postponed to 25. While in the age 18-to-25 regime, the settled property benefits from a measure of favoured treatment, so that when property vests in a beneficiary between the ages of 18 and 25, the exit charge imposed reflects the fact that tax is charged in respect only of the period between 18 and 25 during which the property has remained settled. At current rates, this means a maximum rate of 4.2 per cent.[1]

There are three ways that an 18-to-25 trust can come into being:

(1) where property previously the subject of an accumulation and maintenance trust subsequently becomes subject to the age 18-to-25 trust regime.[2] This is discussed at para.18–39;

(2) where property previously the subject of a bereaved minors' trust subsequently becomes subject to the age 18-to-25 trust regime, see para.19–11; and

(3) where an age 18-to-25 trust has been created by will, or has been established under the Criminal Injuries Compensation Scheme, provided that the beneficiary has lost at least one parent.

The qualification requirements for age 18-to-25 trusts are contained in s.71D. The provisions imposing the primary exit charge, i.e. the charge on property vesting in a

---

[1] See para.17–19.
[2] IHTA s.71D(3), (4).

beneficiary between the ages of 18 and 25, are contained in s.71E. Section 71E also defines the circumstances in which an exit charge is not imposed at all. The provisions for calculating the rate of the primary exit charge are contained in s.71F, and the provisions for calculating the secondary exit charge are contained in s.71G.

The qualification requirements (s.71D) are discussed in Pt II below, and the charging provisions (ss.71E–71G) are considered in Pt III, by reference to paras 17–20–17–26.

II. QUALIFICATION REQUIREMENTS

20–02   Section 71D provides as follows:

"(1) This section applies to settled property (including property settled before 22nd March 2006) but subject to subsection (5) below, if—
  (a) the property is held on trusts for the benefit of a person who has not yet attained the age of 25,
  (b) at least one of the person's parents has died, and
  (c) subsection (2) below applies in relation to the trusts.
(2) This subsection applies to trusts—
  (a) established under the will of a deceased parent of the person mentioned in subsection 1(a) above, or
  (b) established under the Criminal Injuries Compensation Scheme
which secure that the conditions in subsection (6) below are met

. . .

(6) Those conditions are—
  (a) that the person mentioned in subsection (1)(a) or (3)(b)(i) above ('B'), if he has not done so before attaining the age of 25, will on attaining that age become absolutely entitled to—
     (i) the settled property
     (ii) the income arising from it
     (iii) any income that has arisen from the property held on the trusts for his benefit and been accumulated before that time,
  (b) that for so long as B is living and under the age of 25, if any of the settled property is applied for the benefit of the beneficiary, it is applied for the benefit of B, and
  (c) that, for so long as B is living and under the age of 25,
     (i) B is entitled to all of the income (if there is any) arising from any of the settled property, or
     (ii) no such income may be applied for the benefit of any other person.
(7) For the purposes of this section, trusts are not to be treated as failing to secure that the conditions of subsection (6) above are met by reason only of—
     (i) the trustees' having the powers conferred by section 32 of the Trustee Act 1925 (powers of advancement),
. . . "

There are a few points to note in relation to the statutory qualification requirements.

Establishing an age 18-to-25 trust

20–03   In order to qualify as an age 18-to-25 trust, the property must be held on trust for a beneficiary at least one of whose parents has died. The requirements for s.71D trusts are thus similar to those applying to trusts for bereaved minors save that the absolute vesting age is 25 instead of 18.[3]

Other than in the case where property was previously subject to accumulation and maintenance trusts, s.71D provides that the trust must be created by the will of the deceased parent, or it must be established under the Criminal Injuries Compensation Scheme. The definition of "parent" for these purposes is found in s.71H, and includes a step-parent.[4] A deceased individual is taken to be a parent of another individual if immediately before the deceased individual died he had parental responsibility for the other individual under the law of England and Wales, Scotland or Northern Ireland. The term "parental responsibility" has the same meaning as in the Children Act 1989. Similar provisions apply for the purposes of Scotland and Northern Ireland.

The requirement that the age 18-to-25 trust is established under the will of a deceased parent makes it possible for an age 18-to-25 trust to be created by a deed of variation falling within s.142(1) of the IHTA. The "under the will" requirement is satisfied because the trust that arises as a result of the deed of variation is deemed to have been created by the deceased under his will.[5] Trusts created in circumstances where IHTA 1984 s.144 applies (events occurring within two years of the death of the deceased) are also capable of qualifying as age 18-to-25 trusts provided that all other conditions are met: s.144 of the IHTA 1984 deems these trusts to have been effected by the deceased.[6]

Note that, unlike bereaved minors' trusts, age 18-to-25 trusts cannot arise under the intestacy rules of the Administration of Estates Act 1925 ss.46 and 47(1). This is because the statutory trusts on intestacy provide for absolute vesting at the age of 18. So it is not possible for an age 18-to-25 trust to arise in favour of a grandchild or great-grandchild (compare with the position under a bereaved minors' trust, see para.19–06).

It is apparent from the provisions of s.71D that, as with a bereaved minors' trust, it is not necessary for an age 18-to-25 trust to arise immediately on the death of the deceased parent. Provided the trust arises under the will of a deceased parent of the beneficiaries, it can arise even after another interest has subsisted, for example an immediate post-death interest.[7] However, the tax treatment of the transition will differ depending on whether it is a transition to an age 18-to-25 trust or a bereaved minors' trust. An inter vivos transition from an immediate post-death interest to a bereaved minors' trust will be a PET,[8] whereas the transition to an age 18-to-25 trust will be immediately chargeable.

Certainty of entitlement

The beneficiaries of an age 18-to-25 trust must, at the latest at the age of 25, but after the age of 18,[9] become absolutely entitled to the settled property and to the income arising from it and to any income that has arisen from the property held on trusts for their benefit and which has been accumulated before that time. In other words, if any beneficiary (other than a beneficiary within s.71D) is capable of benefiting from the **20–04**

---

[3] Note that this bereavement requirement does not prevent entry into the age 18-to-25 regime where property was previously subject to an accumulation and maintenance trust (IHTA s.71D(4)).

[4] IHTA 1984 s.71H(1).

[5] IHTA 1984 s.142(1).

[6] IHTA 1984 s.144(4).

[7] See para.19–06.

[8] IHTA 1984 s.3A(1A)(c)(iii). See para.19–06.

[9] Otherwise this would qualify as a bereaved minors' trust, as to which, see Ch.19.

income as it arises or from the accumulated income, then the settled property is not property to which the age 18-to-25 trust provisions apply.

Section 71D is drafted by reference to a single beneficiary ("B"), but it is thought that it is possible for an age 18-to-25 trust to have more than one beneficiary, so long as each of the beneficiaries (each one "B" for these purposes) satisfies the s.71D requirements and so long as it is not possible for any other person, i.e. other than a beneficiary who satisfies the requirements, to become entitled to the income or property of the trusts in the future.[10]

As with trusts for bereaved minors, where there are multiple beneficiaries, the legislation does not stipulate that they must each become entitled to equal shares at the age of 25. Nor, apparently, is there any prohibition on varying the presumptive shares (of income or capital) of the beneficiaries while they are below the age of 25: for instance, even where an interest in possession arises at the age of 18 by virtue of the operation of s.31 of the Trustee Act 1925.[11] However, once the shares have vested at the age of 25, the trust terms should not permit any possible variation to the beneficiaries' vested shares: it is not possible to appoint property away from a beneficiary who has reached vesting age, in order to avoid the exit charge.

Income

20–05   There is a lack of flexibility in the manner in which the trustees can deal with the income of property which comes within the age 18-to-25 trust provisions: the beneficiaries must be entitled to all the income (if any) that arises from the settled property or alternatively no such income may be applied for the benefit of any other person. In other words, while it is not necessary for the income to be paid to the beneficiary while he is alive and under the age of 25 it is imperative, in order for the trust to qualify as an age 18-to-25 trust, that no other person is capable of benefiting from that income.

As is the case with bereaved minors' trusts, this is in severe contrast to the flexibility that was permitted under the accumulation and maintenance trust provisions, where the trustees could determine for whose benefit the income of the settlement could be applied, while the beneficiary was alive and under the age of 18.

Capital

20–06   While the beneficiary is under the age of 25 and alive, where settled property is applied for the benefit of a beneficiary it is permissible to apply it for the benefit only of s.71D beneficiaries. This again reduces flexibility because it means that the capital of the age 18-to-25 trust may not be used to benefit any beneficiary other than the s.71D

---

[10] HMRC shares this view: see HMRC Manuals IHTM42816.

[11] This will not be a qualifying interest in possession, i.e. one which by virtue of IHTA s.49 would result in the beneficiary being deemed to be beneficially entitled to the property in which the interest subsists. Consequently, there will be no charge, under IHTA 1984 s.52, on the termination of the interest in possession.

beneficiaries who will become absolutely entitled to the settled property at the age of 25.

Multiple beneficiaries, death before vesting age

For the effect of disentitlement resulting from the death of a beneficiary, see para.17–25.

20–07

Flexibility and the terms of the trust

As with trusts for bereaved minors, it is not necessary for the terms of the age 18-to-25 trust to be set out in the will of the deceased parent. The requirement that the trust be created by will, will be satisfied if the trustees exercise a power of appointment set out in the will to create an age 18-to-25 trust (or a bereaved minors' trust, with a subsequent appointment into an age 18-to-25 trust).

20–08

Some degree of flexibility is retained by s.71D(7)(a) which provides that a trust will not fail to satisfy the conditions as to entitlement to income and settled property if the trustees have powers of advancement conferred on them by s.32 of the Trustee Act 1925.[12] This is so even if the maximum one-half distribution limitation contained in s.32 is extended by the will.[13] It is, therefore, possible for the testator to create a will (or for the terms of the testator's will to be amended by a s.142 deed of variation) which provides that a beneficiary, one of whose parents has died, will become absolutely entitled at the age of 25 and for the trustees at a later date to employ their powers of advancement to create a settled advance deferring absolute entitlement to the capital until a later date. Depending upon the terms of the advancement, the amended trusts either will fall within the provisions of the relevant property regime, or within another favoured property regime (for example, if the settled advance results in an appointment onto a s.89 disabled trust).[14]

Interaction with other settled property regimes

Section 71D(5) defines the circumstances when trusts which otherwise could qualify as age 18-to-25 trusts, will not qualify under this regime.

20–09

Interaction with other favoured property regimes

By virtue of s.71D(5)(a) any trust which is either a bereaved minors' trusts or an accumulation and maintenance trust, will not qualify as an age 18-to-25 trust. But where the trustees of a bereaved minors' trust exercise the statutory power of advancement vested in them prior to a beneficiary attaining the age of 18, to defer the vesting

20–10

---

[12] This is similar to the treatment of powers of advancement in the context of pre-March 22, 2006 accumulation and maintenance trusts—see paras 18–12–18–14 inclusive.

[13] IHTA 1984 s.71D(7)(b).

[14] See Ch.21.

of capital to the age of 25, the trust will then move into the age 18-to-25 trust regime.

20–11   The interaction of an age 18-to-25 trust with disabled person's interests is not clearly defined: contrast the interaction between age 18-to-25 trusts and the bereaved minors' trust regime where there is a blanket exclusion from qualification as a bereaved minors' trust in every case where there is a disabled person's interest.[15] Section 71D(5)(b) provides that a s.89 disabled trust will not qualify as an age 18-to-25 trust. But curiously,[16] it is only by virtue of s.89B(3) that property in which a disabled person's interest within s.89B(1)(c) subsists (i.e. an actual interest in possession rather than a deemed interest in possession[17] to which a disabled person becomes beneficially entitled on or after March 22, 2006) is prevented from falling within the age 18-to-25 regime. Furthermore, s.89B(3) does not exclude the other types of disabled person's interests covered by s.89B(1).

For instance, there is no express exclusion for self-settlements by persons with a condition expected to lead to a disability, i.e. settlements which are disabled person's interests within s.89(1)(b) or (d).[18] This appears to create a theoretical overlap. The absence of an express exclusion for self-settlements may arguably be explained by the fact that it will, in the case of a self-settlement, be difficult to satisfy the requirement in s.71D(2) that the trust is established either under the will of the deceased parent of the age 18-to-25 beneficiary or under the Criminal Injuries Compensation Scheme. In particular, trusts "established" under the Criminal Injuries Compensation Scheme be established by the Claims Officer rather than the person with a condition expected to lead to a disability.[19] Alternatively, age 18-to-25 trusts will be created by will and so by definition cannot be self-settlements falling within s.89B(1)(b) or (d). Note that although it is possible to create an age 18-to-25 trust by transition from an accumulation and maintenance trust, there can, in the authors' view, be no overlap with a settlement in which a disabled person's interest within s.89B(1)(b) or (d) subsists, because s.89B(1)(b) and (d) interests require that the settlor was, immediately before transferring the property into the settlement, beneficially entitled[20] to that property. In the context of conversion from an accumulation and maintenance settlement into an age 18-to-25 trust, this requirement cannot have been met because, by definition, no beneficiary of an accumulation and maintenance trust can have had a qualifying interest in possession in the settled property on or before April 6, 2008.[21]

20–12   Although it is not possible for property in which a s.89 disabled person's interest subsists to qualify as property to which s.71D applies, it is in theory possible that a disabled person may be a beneficiary under an age 18-to-25 trust. Interestingly, the death of a disabled person under the age of 18 will be treated differently depending on whether the disabled person has a disabled person's interest or is a beneficiary under an age 18-to-25 trust. The person holding a disabled person's interest is deemed beneficially to own the property in which the disabled person's interest subsists. As such, the death of that person under the age of 18 will trigger a transfer of value.

---

[15] See para.19–12.

[16] One would have thought the place for this should have been IHTA s.71D(5).

[17] See paras 21–13 and 21–15.

[18] See paras 21–13 and 21–14.

[19] However, note that the beneficiary could for IHT purposes be considered to be the "settler" having "indirectly provided funds for the purpose of or in connection with" the settlement (see IHTA 1984 s.44).

[20] It is not clear whether the settlor should be absolutely entitled to the property or whether a qualifying interest in possession will suffice.

[21] i.e. property in which an interest in possession subsisted at that date would have been outside the accumulation and maintenance trust regime.

However, s.71E(2)(b) provides that tax is not charged on the occasion that property ceases to fall within the provisions of s.71D as a result of the beneficiary's death under the age of 18. A similar anomaly arises in relation to a bereaved minors' trust and is considered at para.21–27. It is hoped that this anomaly will be dealt with by legislative amendment.

Interaction with certain interests in possession

20–13 Section 71D(5)(c) provides that settled property will not fall within the age 18-to-25 trust regime if a person is beneficially entitled to an interest in possession in the settled property, and:

(a) the person became beneficially entitled to the interest in possession before March 22, 2006; or
(b) the interest in possession is an immediate post-death interest,[22] or a transitional serial interest,[23] and the person became beneficially entitled to it on or after March 22, 2006.

In effect, where a beneficiary is treated as beneficially entitled to the property in which the interest in possession subsists (by virtue of s.49), the settled property will not qualify as an age 18-to-25 trust. On balance, this means that the beneficiary will receive the more beneficial tax treatment: there will be no exit charge imposed when property is applied for his benefit; property applied for the benefit of another will be a deemed PET by the beneficiary; and the risk of an increased inheritance tax charge on death can be insured against.

III. THE CHARGE TO TAX

20–14 Subject to certain reliefs,[24] s.71E imposes a charge to tax in all circumstances where settled property ceases to be property to which the age 18-to-25 regime applies except where this occurs:

(a) by virtue of a beneficiary becoming absolutely entitled to property (including any income from it, or accumulated income) at or under the age of 18;
(b) by virtue of the death of the beneficiary under the age of 18; or
(c) by virtue of property being paid or applied for the advancement or benefit of a beneficiary, at a time when the beneficiary is living and is age 18 or under.[25]

Note that even though there is no occasion of charge to inheritance tax in the three circumstances set out above, holdover relief from capital gains tax will apply by virtue of TCGA 1992 s.260(2)(db).

Different mechanisms are applied to determine the rate of tax for the primary exit charge, i.e. the charge that applies when property is either paid or applied for the benefit of a beneficiary who has attained the age of 18 but is not yet 25, or vests in the

---

[22] See paras 11–51–11–55.
[23] See paras 11–56–11–62.
[24] IHTA 1984 s.71E(3) and (4).
[25] IHTA 1984 s.71E(2).

beneficiary absolutely, and the secondary exit charge, i.e. the charge that applies in all other situations.

Section 71F defines the mechanism for calculating the primary exit charge. It is modelled on the exit charge from the relevant property regime, but because the charge is calculated by reference to the period during which the property remains settled after the beneficiary has attained the age of 18 (i.e. for a maximum of seven years, if the property vests at the age of 25) this charge can, at current rates, never exceed 4.2 per cent.

Section 71G defines the mechanism for calculating the secondary exit charge. The rate of the secondary exit charge is calculated by reference to the time during which property has been subject to 18-to-25 trusts (extended by reference to a time where the same property was subject to the bereaved minors' trust regime and/or the accumulation and maintenance trust regime). This can result in a much greater rate of tax than 4.2 per cent. Given the exemption for transfers of value which were not made with gratuitous intent,[26] secondary exit charges are in practice unlikely to arise.

The charging mechanisms for exits from age 18-to-25 trusts are described in detail at paras 17–20–17–26.

---

[26] IHTA 1984 s.71E(4).

CHAPTER 21

TRUSTS FOR DISABLED PERSONS

I. INTRODUCTION

Prior to the enactment of the Finance Act 2006, the legislation already accorded favoured treatment to settled property held during the life of "disabled persons"[1] (i.e. certain mentally disabled persons or persons in receipt of attendance allowances) on trusts in which no interest in possession in the settled property subsisted and which secured that at least a proportion (specified by the legislation) of the settled property was applied during their lifetime for their benefit. The original rules, like those originally regulating the treatment of protective trusts, lent themselves to abuse, and rules were introduced that applied in relation to property transferred into such a settlement on or after March 10, 1981.[2] Under these later rules, the disabled person was treated as being beneficially entitled to an interest in possession in the settled property, so that any payments made out of such a settlement to a person other than the disabled person thus fell to be brought into charge under s.52(1), if at all.   **21–01**

The beneficial treatment of trusts for disabled beneficiaries continues post Finance Act 2006. The Finance Act 2006 also introduced a new category of settlement which benefits from favoured treatment under this head, i.e. self-settlements by person with a condition expected to lead to a disability: s.89A. The remainder of this chapter is divided into two parts: Pt II deals with the inheritance tax treatment of pre-Finance Act 2006 trusts for disabled persons and Pt III deals with the post-Finance Act 2006 inheritance tax treatment of trusts for disabled beneficiaries.   **21–02**

---

[1] IHTA 1984 s.74(4).
[2] IHTA 1984 s.89.

On August 17, 2012, HMRC issued a consultative document on trusts for "vulnerable beneficiaries". The consultation closed on November 8, 2012.

The stated aims of the consultation include:

(i) Finding an effective definition of "vulnerable person" which ensures that the special tax treatment is applied to all vulnerable people; and

(ii) Finding how best to "align" the qualifying conditions that limit how trustees can use the trust capital and income.

As regards the definition of "vulnerable person", the document starts by explaining that in order to ensure certainty about when favoured tax treatment applies, it is applied to two easily defined and recognisable groups, i.e. orphaned minors,[3] and those with severe physical or mental disability. The latter group includes those in receipt of the highest or middle rate care component of disability living allowance, and those who struggle to administer or manage their affairs for reasons of mental incapacity (see para.21–16, below). Disability living allowance is being reformed to create a new benefit from 2013 which will be called the Personal Independence Payment. It is envisaged that there will be fewer claimants of this benefit, which is one reason why the Government is seeking views on whether other people should have access to the tax treatment afforded to vulnerable beneficiaries. Following the withdrawal of disability living allowance, a major route to qualifying as a vulnerable person may be via the "mental incapacity" test which is contained in the Mental Health Act 1983. The Government is also seeking views of whether detailed changes to this test are necessary.

As regards "alignment" of the qualifying conditions, the consultative document identifies:

(a) that there are two different conditions regarding the application of capital, depending upon which tax provision is in play which "adds complexity" to the legislation. For example, the terms of the trust must either secure that "not less than half" the property that is applied during the relevant person's lifetime is applied for that person's benefit (see e.g. s.89(1)(b)), alternatively, that "if any" of the settled property is applied whilst the relevant person is living (or, where applicable, under the relevant age) it is applied for the benefit of the relevant person (see e.g. s.89A(2)). The proposal is to require that the vulnerable beneficiary benefits from every application of the capital that is applied during their lifetime; and

(b) that there two different conditions as regards the application of income, again dependent on which tax provision is in play; this also adds unnecessary complexity to the legislation. As regards the application of income, note that there are no income conditions to qualify for the inheritance tax favoured treatment afforded to disabled persons' trusts, and none are proposed. Where otherwise tax provisions provide for income conditions in relation to other vulnerable beneficiary trusts or in relation to other taxes, the proposal is to harmonise these.

As with the other consultations which are ongoing at the time of writing, the outcome of this consultation and any legislative amendments proposed and enacted following

---

[3] See Ch.19.

the close of the consultation period will be considered in the next edition of this book.

II. PRE-FINANCE ACT 2006 TREATMENT OF TRUSTS FOR DISABLED PERSONS

Where property held on trusts for a disabled person was transferred into settlement **21–03** prior to March 10, 1981, the following rules apply. In outline: the disabled person is not regarded as having an interest in possession, and some mechanism is accordingly necessary to impose a charge on payments made to anyone other than the disabled person. Section 74(2) accordingly imposes a primary exit charge where settled property ceases to be property comprised in such a settlement otherwise than by virtue of a payment made out of that property for the benefit of the disabled person.[4] The usual rules which apply to favoured property apply in imposing the secondary exit charge,[5] in determining what reliefs are available,[6] in computing the amount on which tax is charged[7] and in fixing the appropriate rate of tax.[8]

Pre-1981 Disabled Trusts

Section 74 of the IHTA 1984 provides that favoured treatment is available to **21–04** property transferred into a settlement prior to March 10, 1981, if during the life of a disabled person it is held on trusts under which no interest in possession in the settled property subsist and which secure that any application of the property during his life is applied only or mainly for his benefit. Strictly speaking, if a trust is to qualify for favoured treatment it must exclude the statutory power of advancement in s.32 of the Trustee Act 1925, but in practice HMRC do not take this point. It is thought that the reference to "settled property" is to the capital of the trust fund,[9] and that a trust under which some or even all of the income could be applied for the benefit of a person or persons other than the disabled person still qualifies for favoured treatment. If this is not the case, it would be difficult, if not impossible, without giving the disabled beneficiary an interest in possession, to draft a settlement which secured that any application of the income during the disabled beneficiary's life after the expiry of the accumulation period was applied only or mainly for his benefit.

Under a s.74 trust, if the disabled person recovers, favoured treatment ceases to be available. The property will normally become "relevant property" and an exit charge will be imposed. For the principles which apply to calculate the charge to tax, see para.17–27.

The favoured treatment takes three forms: **21–05**

(1) first, if the person is the settlor, neither the making of the settlement nor any addition he makes to the settled property prior to March 10, 1981 is a chargeable transfer. Thus, although such a transfer is a transfer of value, it does

---

[4] IHTA 1984 s.74(2)(a).
[5] IHTA 1984 s.74(2)(b).
[6] IHTA 1984 ss.74(3) and 70(3) and (10).
[7] IHTA 1984 ss.74(3) and 70(5).
[8] IHTA 1984 ss.74(3) and 70(6)–(9) (see also Ch.17).
[9] See also para.14–04.

not give rise to a charge to tax, nor does it cumulate. It is also disregarded in determining what exemptions the disabled person has available to him in respect of subsequent transfers[10];

(2) secondly, the property is immune from the periodic charge because it is not "relevant property"[11]; and

(3) thirdly, s.74(2)(a) provides that no primary exit charge is imposed in respect of any payment made out of the settled property for the benefit of the afflicted person.[12]

21–06   The rules under the original special charging provisions were similar, and lent themselves to abuse. The fact that the afflicted person could make transfers into the settlement without making a chargeable transfer meant that he could make a modest settlement out of which property could be distributed after his death without any charge to tax arising. Given the absence of any cumulation, he could then have made a second, similar settlement on the following day, with the same result, and so on.

As will be seen below, s.89 was enacted to prevent this abuse.

Property settled on or after March 10, 1981, but before March 22, 2006

21–07   Favoured treatment is available under s.89 to property settled on or after March 10, 1981 which is held during the life of a disabled person on discretionary trusts which secure that at least half of the settled property applied during his lifetime is applied for his benefit. In deciding whether the trusts on which settled property is held satisfy this condition regard is had to whether the person was disabled when the property in question was transferred into the settlement, so that favoured treatment is not lost if the person recovers, and any powers of advancement conferred on the trustees by the Trustee Act 1925 s.32 or the Trustee (Northern Ireland) Act 1938 s.33 are ignored. As under the original rules, it is thought that the reference to "settled property" is to the capital of the trust fund, and that a trust under which some or even all the income could be applied for the benefit of a person or persons other than the disabled person would still qualify for favoured treatment.[13] Indeed, there appears to be no requirement that the disabled person should even be a member of the class of income beneficiaries. It is also to be noted that while half of the capital in fact applied during the life of the disabled person must be applied for his benefit there is no requirement that any capital need actually be so applied.

21–08   Under s.89, the disabled person is treated as being beneficially entitled to an interest in possession in the settled property with the result that the abuse mentioned above is prevented. Further, having an interest in possession therefore means that the property in which that interest in possession subsists is outside the relevant property regime. It is not therefore subject to periodic or exit charges. Additionally, gifts into a qualifying trust are PETs.

21–09   Strictly speaking, the fact that the disabled person is deemed to have an interest in possession may give rise to difficulties where trustees do not advance trust property to a beneficiary but instead apply it for his benefit. This follows from the fact that s.53(2)

---

[10] IHTA 1984 s.74(2)(a) in its original form.

[11] IHTA 1984 s. 58(1)(b).

[12] For a discussion of the rules governing the imposition of exit charges, see para.17–27.

[13] Cf. TCGA 1992 Sch.1 para.1(1)(b).

prevents a charge under s.52(1) from arising only where a beneficiary with a qualifying interest in possession becomes entitled either to the property in which his interest subsisted or to another qualifying interest in possession in that property, and not where the property is applied for his benefit. It remains to be seen whether HMRC will take this point, though for them to do so would be unfortunate given that s.89 expressly contemplates such applications. Payments made to or applications made for the benefit of a person other than the disabled person give rise to a transfer of value under s.52(1) by the disabled person and on his death a charge is imposed under s.4(1) in the usual way. There is no restriction on how the property is applied after his death. Since the disabled person is treated as beneficially entitled to an interest in possession in the property which is a qualifying interest in possession, if he creates the settlement no transfer of value will result. In other cases, i.e. where the settlor is not the beneficiary, the inter vivos creation of such a settlement will be a PET.

III. POST-FINANCE ACT 2006 TAX TREATMENT OF TRUSTS FOR DISABLED PERSONS

The Finance Act 2006 s.156 and Sch.20 para.6(1) and (3) introduced two new **21–10** provisions with effect from March 22, 2006, namely ss.89A and 89B of the IHTA 1984. Section 89A introduced provisions for dealing with a potentially disabled settlor and s.89B set out the extended definition of what interests amount to a "disabled person's interest".

Treatment of disabled person's interests

A "disabled person's interest" is given favourable treatment under the new inher- **21–11** itance tax regime. Section 49(1A) provides that, from March 22, 2006, s.49(1) applies to a disabled person's interest. As a result, a beneficiary with a disabled person's interest is deemed to be beneficially entitled to the property in which that interest subsists. One consequence is that the lifetime creation of a trust with a disabled person's interest will be a PET where the settlor is not the person with the disabled person's interest. If the settlor is the person with the disabled person's interest, the creation of the settlement will be a non-event—there being no reduction in the value of the disabled person's estate. Second, the termination of the disabled person's interest will be a transfer of value by the disabled person which may be a PET in appropriate circumstances. Third, the appointment of trust assets to the disabled person will be free of inheritance tax. Fourth, since a disabled person's interest is a qualifying interest in possession, the relevant property regime will not apply. Consequently, there will be no periodic or exit charges.

Section 89B sets out the definition of "disabled person's interest". It provides: **21–12**

"(1) In this Act 'disabled person's interest' means—
  (a) an interest in possession to which a person is under s.89(2) above treated as beneficially entitled,
  (b) an interest in possession to which a person is under s.89A(4) above treated as beneficially entitled,
  (c) an interest in possession in settled property (other than an interest within paragraph (a) or (b) above) to which a disabled person becomes beneficially entitled on or after 22 March 2006, or

(d) an interest in possession in settled property (other than an interest within paragraph (a) or (b) above) to which a person ('A') is beneficially entitled if—

    (i) A is the settlor,

    (ii) A was beneficially entitled to the property immediately before transferring it into the settlement,

    (iii) A satisfies [HMRC] as mentioned in s.89A(1)(b) above,

    (iv) The settled property was transferred into settlement on or after 22 March 2006, and

    (v) The trusts on which the settled property is held secure that, if any of the settled property is applied during A's life for the benefit of a beneficiary, it is applied for the benefit of A.

(2) Subsections (4) to (6) of section 89 above (meaning of 'disabled person' in subsection (1) of that section) have effect for the purposes of (1)(c) above as they have effect for the purposes of subsection (1) of that section."

21–13   There are therefore four categories of interest that qualify as a "disabled person's interest", namely:

(1) a deemed interest in possession in a trust for a disabled person under s.89(2) of the IHTA 1984;

(2) a deemed interest in possession in a self-settlement created by a potentially disabled person under s.89A of the IHTA 1984;

(3) an actual interest in possession in settled property[14] (other than an interest within (1) and (2) above) to which a disabled person has become entitled on or after March 22, 2006; and

(4) an actual interest in possession in a self-settled trust[15] (other than an interest within (1) and (2) above) into which settled property was transferred on or after March 22, 2006, which meets the requirements of potential disability set out in s.89A(1)(b), and which secures that if the capital is applied for any beneficiary's benefit it is applied only for the benefit of the settlor.

21–14   In relation to category 4, note that, unlike s.89A self-settlements, there is no restriction on the manner in which the power to terminate the trust may be exercised. For instance, there is no requirement that the power to terminate the trust should, when exercised, result in the settlor or another person becoming absolutely entitled to the settled property nor that a disabled person's interest within s.89B(1)(a) or (c) should subsist on termination.

21–15   In relation to category 3 above, it is only required that the entitlement to the interest in possession arises on or after March 22, 2006. In other words, the settlement in which the interest in possession arises may have existed before March 22, 2006. Further, it is worth noting that there are no conditions limiting the power to pay or apply the capital of the trust, nor any limitations relating to the termination of the trust.

21–16   For the purposes of category 3, a "disabled person" is defined as set out in s.89(4)–(6) of the IHTA 1984: a "disabled person" is a person who when the property is transferred into the settlement (s.89(4) of the IHTA 1984):

(a) is by reason of mental disorder (within the meaning of the Mental Health Act 1983) incapable of administering the property or managing his affairs; or

---

[14] This includes an interest which is deemed to continue by operation of IHTA 1984 s.88 despite forfeiture by the principal beneficiary of his life interest (see para.22–05).

[15] This too includes an interest which is deemed to continue by operation of IHTA 1984 s.88 (see fn.14 above).

(b) is in receipt of an attendance allowance under s.64 of the Social Security Contributions & Benefits Act 1992 or of the Social Security Contributions & Benefits (Northern Ireland) Act 1992; or

(c) is in receipt of a disability living allowance under s.71 of those Acts[16] by virtue of entitlement to the care component of the highest or middle rate. A person is entitled to the care component of the disability living allowance at the highest or middle rate if he satisfies prescribed conditions as to residence and presence in Great Britain or Northern Ireland and is so severely disabled mentally or physically that:

    (i) he requires frequent attention throughout the day or for a significant portion of the day in connection with his bodily functions; or

    (ii) he cannot prepare a cooked main meal for himself, e.g. he has difficulty reading recipes, chopping and peeling vegetables; or

    (iii) he requires continual supervision throughout the day in order to avoid substantial danger to himself or others.[17]

21–17 It is clear from the terms of subs.(4) that in order to satisfy that subsection the putative disabled person must actually be "in receipt of" the disability living allowance and the attendance allowance: it is not sufficient that that person would qualify if he applied. The position where a claim for the above allowances has been made but eligibility has not been formally determined at the time the property is transferred into the settlement is unclear. Strictly, the putative disabled person cannot be said to be "in receipt of" the allowances. If the strict position were adopted, hardship would result purely because the transfer of assets into the settlement was mistimed. The better view, it is suggested, is that if the applications for the attendance and disability living allowances are made before the transfer of assets into the settlement, and those applications are subsequently successful, the individual should be regarded retrospectively as satisfying the requirement that he is "in receipt of" those allowances.

21–18 Note that subs.(5) extends the definition of "disabled person" to include cases where the person in question would, when the property was transferred into the settlement, have been in receipt of attendance allowance or disability living allowance at the highest or middle rate in certain circumstances. Once again, the strict requirement is that the putative disabled person must have been in receipt of the above allowances. This may, however, cause difficulties where the claim for the allowances is made after the property is transferred into the settlement because SSCBA 1992 ss.69(4) and 76(1) provide that no allowance can be paid for periods that precede the claim for those allowances being made. It is suggested that the strict position may not be followed in order to ensure that the aim of subs.(5), namely to extend the meaning of "disabled person" to persons who may not in certain circumstances qualify, is fulfilled.

21–19 Subsection (6) extends the definition of "disabled persons" to persons who satisfy HMRC that they would have received the attendance allowance and the disability

---

[16] In relation to categories (b) and (c), it appears that a person who is in receipt only of foreign disability allowances cannot satisfy these requirements—this seems to follow from the fact that the only allowances that are considered relevant in determining whether a person is a "disabled person" are UK allowances. It is, however, possible that such a person may be able to satisfy HMRC that he is entitled to the UK disability allowances despite his non-residence (within s.89(6)) so as to qualify as a "disabled person".

[17] The eligibility requirements may change over time. Recourse should therefore be had to the latest leaflets issued by the relevant government agency.

living allowance at the appropriate rate had they met the conditions as to residence stipulated by the rules governing the availability of those allowances.

21–20   Subsections 89(4)–(6) of the IHTA 1984 all refer to the status of the person in question at the time when the property is transferred into the settlement. It is therefore essential that the putative disabled person satisfies the requirements of s.89(4)–(6) at that time, e.g. is in receipt of the attendance allowance and the disability living allowance at the time that the property is transferred into the settlement. A corollary is that if, after the property is transferred into the settlement, the disabled person ceases to receive these allowances, that person will nevertheless remain a "disabled person" so that the settlement in which his interest subsists will continue to qualify for favoured treatment.

21–21   Another issue that may cause difficulty is the position of assets that are transferred by an individual after March 22, 2006 into a settlement created by that same individual before March 22, 2006 in which a disabled person (as defined by s.89(4)) has an interest in possession. Strictly speaking, in the context of s.89B(1)(c) of the IHTA 1984, an interest can only be a disabled person's interest if the person became entitled to it on or after March 22, 2006 (required by s.89B(1)(c)). For trust law purposes the settlement is a single settlement with a single beneficiary having a single interest in possession. As such, the interest in possession in the property settled post-March 22, 2006 cannot, arguably, be said to be an interest to which the disabled person became entitled on or after March 22, 2006—it is not therefore a disabled person's interest. However, Budget Note BN 25 indicates that HMRC regard an addition to a settlement as creating a separate settlement. If that is correct (and opinion is divided on this issue),[18] it is arguable that the property added post-March 22, 2006 is a separate settlement and that the disabled person's interest in that newly settled property arises only after March 22, 2006 and is therefore a disabled person's interest (and, by extrapolation, the pre-March 22, 2006 interest held by the disabled person in the pre-March 22, 2006 settlement is not a disabled person's interest but is a pre-March 22, 2006 interest in possession). This result is intellectually unsatisfactory. It is hoped that guidance will be issued in due course to clarify the position.

Self-settlements

Section 89A of the IHTA 1984—self-settlements by potentially disabled individuals

21–22   The specific provision set out in s.89A is in addition to the provision for self-settlements for disabled settlors set out in s.89B(1)(d). In the latter, the settlor has an actual interest in possession in the settled property whereas in the former the settlor has a deemed interest in possession in the settled property.
The Finance Act 2006 s.156 Sch.20 para.6(1), (3) introduced a new s.89A. It provides:

> "(1) This section applies to property transferred by a person ("A") into settlement on or after March 22, 2006 if—
> (a) A was beneficially entitled to the property immediately before transferring it into settlement,

---

[18] See also paras 12–17–12–18.

(b) A satisfies [HMRC] that, when the property was transferred into settlement, A had a condition that it was at that time reasonable to expect would have such effects on A as to lead to A becoming—
   (i) a person falling within section 89(4)(a) above,
   (ii) in receipt of an attendance allowance mentioned in 89(4)(b) above, or
   (iii) in receipt of a disability living allowance mentioned in s89(4)(c) above by virtue of entitlement to the care component at the highest or middle rate, and
(c) The property is held on trusts—
   (i) under which, during the life of A, no interest in possession in the settled property subsists, and
   (ii) which secure that conditions (1) and (2) are met.

(2) Condition 1 is that if any of the settled property is applied during A's life for the benefit of a beneficiary, it is applied for the benefit of A.

(3) Condition 2 is that any power to bring the trusts mentioned in subsection (1)(c) above to an end during A's life is such that, in the event of power being exercised during A's life, either—
(a) A or another person will, on the trusts being brought to an end, be absolutely entitled to the settled property, or
(b) on the trusts being brought to an end, a disabled person's interest within s.89B(1)(a) or (c) will subsist in the settled property.

(4) If this section applies to settled property transferred into settlement by a person, the person shall be treated as beneficially entitled to an interest in possession in the settled property.
  . . . "

To summarise, s.89A requires that: **21–23**

(1) the settlor ("A") was beneficially entitled to the property immediately before it was settled by him;
(2) the property was settled on or after March 22, 2006;
(3) A satisfies HMRC that at the time the property was settled by A, A was suffering from a condition that it was reasonable to expect at that time would lead to A meeting one of the conditions in s.89(4)(a), (b) or (c);
(4) A has no actual interest in possession in the settled property;
(5) if any settled property is applied during A lifetime for the benefit of any beneficiary, it is applied only for the benefit of A; and
(6) any exercise of a power to bring the trusts to an end during A's lifetime results in either:
   (i) A or another person becoming absolutely entitled to the settled property; or
   (ii) a disabled person's interest within s.89B(1)(a) (a s.89(2) deemed interest in possession) or (c) (a post-March 22, 2006 actual interest in possession) subsists in the settled property.

The following points may be made in relation to the six requirements set out **21–24** above.

As concerns point (1)—It is not clear whether absolute ownership of the property to be settled is required or whether the requirement is satisfied if A has an interest in possession in it.

As concerns point (3)—First, it is important to note that provided that A can satisfy HMRC that his condition is reasonably likely to deteriorate so that he qualifies for, say, disability living allowance, it is not necessary that his condition does so deteriorate. In fact, a subsequent improvement in his condition will not alter the s.89A treatment. Second, for the purposes of determining whether A will be entitled to disability living allowance and attendance allowance, it is assumed that A will satisfy the requirements as to residence and that no provisions suspending the allowances apply.

As concerns point (5)—It appears possible for the terms of the settlement to permit the capital of the settlement to be applied for any of the beneficiaries. However, there is an absolute prohibition against any of the settled property actually being applied for the benefit of any beneficiary other than A.

As concerns point (6)—It appears to be possible for the terms of the settlement to permit the trustees to appoint/advance the trust assets away from A. However, they must not exercise their power in such a way as to fall foul of the requirements set out in (6) above.

Other qualifying self-settlements

21–25   Apart from s.89A self-settlements, an interest in a self-settlement falling within s.89B(1)(d) also qualifies as a "disabled person's interest". In order for the interest held by a person ("A") to qualify as a "disabled person's interest", the following requirements must be met:

(1) the settled property was transferred into the settlement on or after March 22, 2006;

(2) A is the settlor of the settlement;

(3) A was beneficially entitled to the property immediately before it was transferred into the settlement;

(4) A has an actual interest in possession in the settled property;

(5) A satisfies HMRC that at the time the property was settled by A, A was suffering from a condition that it was reasonable to expect at that time would lead to A meeting one of the conditions in s.89(4)(a), (b) or (c); and

(6) the trusts on which the settled property is held secure that if the capital is applied for any beneficiary's benefit it is applied only for the benefit of A.

21–26   There is a large degree of overlap between these requirements and those required by s.89A. Similar points may, therefore, be made in relation to many of the conditions (see para.21–23 above). Additionally, it is unclear what, if anything, is added by the stipulation that A not only must have been beneficially entitled to the property before it was transferred into the settlement but he must also be the settlor of the settlement. Clearly, if A was beneficially entitled to the property that was transferred into the settlement, the transfer of that property into the settlement will make him a settlor of the settlement. It is not clear whether the requirement that A is *the* settlor is aimed at ensuring that A, and no one else, is the settlor of the settlement.

Disabled person's interest vs. bereaved minors' trust

21–27   Although it is not possible for property in which a disabled person's interest subsists to qualify as property within a bereaved minors' trust,[19] it is in theory possible that a disabled person may be a beneficiary under a bereaved minors' trust.[20] Interestingly, the death of a disabled person under the age of 18 will be treated differently depending on whether the disabled person has a disabled person's interest or is a beneficiary under a bereaved minors' trust. The person holding a disabled person's interest is deemed

[19] IHTA 1984 s.71A.
[20] See Ch.19 on Bereaved Minors' Trusts.

beneficially to own the property in which the disabled person's interest subsists. As such, the death of that person under the age of 18 will trigger a transfer of value. However, s.71B(2) of the bereaved minors' trusts provisions states that tax is not charged on the occasion that property ceases to fall within the provisions of s.71A (bereaved minors' trusts) as a result of the beneficiary's death under the age of 18. This is probably a curious anomaly which will, it is hoped, be dealt with by legislative amendment.[21]

---

[21] A similar problem arises in the interaction between disabled person's interest and the age 18–25 trust regime: see para.20–12.

CHAPTER 22

PROTECTIVE TRUSTS

22–01   The legislation recognises the special nature of protective trusts, which have long been used to prevent profligate and otherwise unreliable beneficiaries from squandering trust assets. For trusts created after April 12, 1978, what is now s.88 affords a limited but very helpful form of favoured treatment. Consistent with the fact that most interest in possession trusts created post-March 22, 2006 will now fall to be taxed under the relevant property regime, for trusts created post-March 22, 2006, the s.88 relief applies only to those life interest trusts in which the protected life interest is either an immediate post-death interest, an interest in possession which qualifies as a disabled person's interest, or a transitional serial interest.[1] For protected life interest trusts created before March 22, 2006, s.88 continues to operate whether or not the forfeiture of the life interest occurs after March 22, 2006.[2] The references to the application of s.88 to protective trusts below should, as regards post-March 22, 2006 trusts, be read as references to its application to trusts in which an immediate post-death interest, an interest in possession which qualifies as a disabled person's interest, or a transitional serial interest.[3]

Section 88 applies to:

"... settled property held on ... trusts to the like effect as those specified in s.33(1) of the Trustee Act 1925."

Under s.33(1), where any income is directed[4] to be held on "protective trusts" for the benefit of a person (the "principal beneficiary") during a period (the "trust period") not exceeding his life, the income is held on trusts such that during that period he has an interest in possession until he "does or attempts to do or suffers any act or thing, or

---

[1] IHTA 1984 s.88(4).

[2] IHTA 1984 s.88(3). But note that a re-instatement of the interest in possession by trustees may bring the deemed interest in possession to an end. In most circumstances (but not, for example, in relation to a disabled person's interest), this will have the effect of moving the trust into the relevant property regime.

[3] Note that because IHTA 1984 s.71A(3)(c) (ii) (in respect of bereaved minors' trusts) and s.71D(6)(c)(ii) (in respect of age 18-to-25 trusts) require that no income may be applied for anyone other than the bereaved minor, or the beneficiary of the age 18-to-25 trust, it is not possible for a protected life interest trust to qualify for favoured treatment under these heads, as income may become payable to the spouse and issue of the principal beneficiary.

[4] See *Re Morris' Settlement* [1952] 2 All E.R. 528 and *Re Hunter* [1963] Ch. 372, for ineffective directions.

until any event happens, other than an advance under any express or statutory power" whereby he would be deprived of the right to receive the income. At that stage, his interest comes to an end, and the income is held on discretionary trusts for the principal beneficiary, his spouse, and his children or remoter issue. If there is neither spouse nor issue, the income is held on discretionary trusts for the principal beneficiary and the persons who would be entitled to the trust property if he were dead.

Precisely what will constitute "trusts to the like effect" is unclear.[5] HMRC gave their interpretation in *The Law Society Gazette* of March 3, 1976:

> "In our view trusts 'to the like effect' as those set out in s.33(1) of the Trustee Act are trusts which are not materially different in their tax consequences. We should not wish to distinguish a trust by reason of a minor variation or additional administrative power or duties. But in the first situation which you mention the extension of the list of potential beneficiaries to brothers and sisters of the principal beneficiary could be a means of giving relief to a trust primarily intended to benefit them. Such a trust would be regarded as outside the scope of para.18 of Sch.5 to the Finance Act 1975.
>
> On the other hand, it is clear from the existence of para.18(2)(b) that the insertion of a power to apply capital for the benefit of this primary beneficiary was contemplated as a possible feature of a settlement entitled to relief.
>
> You wrote to us again about the special exemptions from capital transfer tax for protective trusts.
>
> I appreciate that so long as the principal beneficiary has no spouse or issue the statutory trusts extend to the next of kin for the time being, who might well be brothers and sisters. But this is not at all the same thing as including them in the primary class of beneficiaries ab initio on an equal footing with the spouse and issue. In that event the brothers and sisters could receive the income of settled property to the entire exclusion of the principal beneficiary, his spouse and issue. I confirm that trusts which could produce the result would not be regarded as 'to the like effect' as those specified in s.33(1) of the Trustee Act 1925."

HMRC's view, in short, is that "to the like effect" means "to the like tax effect". This, of course, rather begs the question. It may well be that the tax effects of a protective trust will have to be taken into account in determining whether that trust is "to the like effect" as a s.33(1) trust; but that can hardly be the sole, or even the main criterion. Section 33 of the Trustee Act 1925 is not concerned with tax, and in determining whether trusts are to the like effect as those specified in s.33(1) regard must be had to all the effects of s.33(1), particularly those which s.33(1) is intended to achieve, not just to its (incidental) tax effects. The proper construction of the words "to the like effect" was considered by Vinelott J. in *Thomas v IRC*, discussed below.[6]

The normal position

In the absence of s.88 the treatment of a protective trust would be straightforward. **22–02**
On the termination of the principal beneficiary's (qualifying) interest in possession there would be a notional transfer under s.52(1), and, unless some relief or exemption applied, that transfer would constitute a chargeable transfer and be charged to tax accordingly. After that termination the property would be held on discretionary trusts and the relevant property regime would apply to it in the normal way. This could operate harshly—the trust would be subject to the periodic charge on each 10-year

---

[5] For a similar expression see the Variation of Trusts Act 1958 s.1(2) and *Re Wallace's Settlements* [1968] 1 W.L.R. 711; [1968] 2 All E.R. 209.
[6] See para.22–04.

anniversary during the lifetime of the principal beneficiary, and an exit charge would be imposed if anyone subsequently attained an interest in possession. For post-March 22, 2006 protective trusts which are taxed under the relevant property regime at the outset, the termination of the principal beneficiary's interest in possession (which is not a qualifying interest in possession) does not result in a notional transfer under s.52(1). There is thus no occasion of charge which s.88 is required to cure.

Treatment before April 12, 1978

22–03   Before April 12, 1978, the favoured treatment accorded by the Finance Act 1975 Sch.5 para.18 (the provisions originally regulating the treatment of protective trusts) to property held on protective trusts was such that, inter alia, tax was not charged on the termination of the principal beneficiary's interest in possession. This meant that it was in certain circumstances possible to use a protective trust to save tax. The procedure was that a person wishing to assign his interest in possession resettled his interest on protective trusts and then brought about a forfeiture so that the trust fund became held on discretionary trusts. The termination of the interest in possession on the forfeiture did not constitute a transfer of value, and the trustees could then distribute the trust property to the settlor's children or remoter issue. The distributions were charged to tax, but so long as the original settlement was made before March 27, 1974 (and assuming the beneficiaries were UK domiciliaries) transitional relief was available.

22–04   The efficacy of this technique was confirmed in *Thomas v IRC*.[7] The facts of the case were that Mrs Thomas had a life interest in a trust fund which on her death was to pass to her children in equal shares absolutely. On June 10, 1976, Mrs Thomas declared that the trustees should:

> "... hold her life interest in the Trust Fund upon protective trust under the Trustee Act 1925, section 33 upon trust for herself from the date hereof for the period of three weeks or her life whichever is the shorter subject thereto upon the trust applicable to the Trust Fund under the Settlement to the intent that any remainder of her life interest ... in the Trust Fund shall merge and be extinguished in the capital of the Trust Fund."

Two days later she purported to assign her life interest; the effect of this purported assignment was, of course, merely to determine her protected life interest, with the result that the trust fund became held on discretionary trusts until the end of the three-week period, at which time it vested in her children absolutely. The trustees contended that no charge arose under the predecessor to s.52(1), the Finance Act 1975 Sch.5 para.4(2) on the settlement by Mrs Thomas of her life interest since, although under para.4(1) that settlement terminated her interest, para.4(3) (now s.53(2)) provided that no charge arose on such a termination if the person who had the interest became on the same occasion beneficially entitled to another interest in the property in which the interest subsisted. Paragraph 18, in turn, prevented any charge from arising on the termination of Mrs Thomas's protected life interest, and, in the circumstances, no charge arose in respect of the distributions made to the children.

HMRC did not accept this, for two reasons. First, they contended that when Mrs Thomas assigned her life interest on protective trusts she created a sub-settlement of that interest, so that if para.18 applied at all, it applied only to her protected life interest and not to the trust fund itself. Vinelott J. rejected this argument:

[7] *Thomas v IRC* [1981] S.T.C. 382.

672

"In support counsel for the Crown referred me to the very wide definition of the word 'settlement' in para.1(2) of Sch.5, which includes 'any disposition . . . of property . . . whereby the property is for the time being (*a*) held in trust for persons in succession or for any person subject to a contingency'. He submitted, first, that those words are capable of applying to the declaration of trust, which was a disposition of Mrs Thomas's life interest in the trust fund whereby her income interest became held during the period of three weeks from the execution of the declaration of trust on trust for herself until the happening of some event apt to terminate the trust in para (i) of s.33(1) and thereafter on the discretionary trusts in para.(ii) of s.33(1); and, secondly, that para.18 is capable of applying to that sub-settlement if it is read as applying to 'settled property which or the income of which is held on the trusts specified in s.33(1) or on trusts to the like effect'.

It is, I think, clear that an assignment or declaration of trust of a life interest is a disposition of property within the definition of a 'settlement', and that a life interest may itself constitute 'settled property' to which the provisions of Sch.5 apply. For instance, if a life tenant were to assign his life interest to trustees on trust to invest each instalment of income when received and to pay the income to A during his life with remainders over, the assignment would constitute a settlement of the life interest and the provisions of Sch.5 would apply to the investments representing the income comprised in the assignment, which would constitute the 'property' settled by the settlement. The settled property from which that income arose would then be property in respect of which there would be no person beneficially entitled to an interest in possession. Indeed, it is possible to figure a case where the settled property in which the original life interest subsisted was excluded property within para.2 of Sch.5 while the sub-settlement of the income interest was not.

But these examples are far removed from the facts of the present case. In this case, the trust fund was property settled by the testator's will and, after the execution of the declaration of trust, it was property settled by the joint effect of the will and the declaration of trust. After the execution of the declaration of trust the trust fund was settled property the income of which was (subject to the second submission of counsel for the Crown) held on the trusts specified in s.33(1) or on trusts of the like effect. It is immaterial, if it be the case, that the income during Mrs. Thomas's lifetime or until the expiration of three weeks from the execution of the declaration of trust was also the subject of a 'settlement' falling within the definition in para.1(2). There is no separate fund which could be identified and treated as the 'settled property' subject to the trusts of that settlement.

That this is the correct approach to para.19 is I think confirmed by para.1(8) of Sch.5 which provides: 'Where more than one person is a settlor in relation to a settlement and the circumstances so require, this Schedule and s.25(3) (*d*) of this Act shall apply in relation to it as if the settled property were comprised in separate settlements.' Here, the circumstances do not so 'require', and indeed are inconsistent with 'the settled property' being treated as the subject of 'separate settlements'. Further, I find counsel's first submission for the Crown difficult to reconcile with his concession that, on the execution of the declaration of trust, the trust fund fell within para.4(3). If para.4(3) applied it applied only because on the execution of the declaration of trust Mrs Thomas became entitled to an interest in possession in the trust fund, and if that is right the trust fund continued to be settled property which was then held (subject to the second submission of counsel for the Crown) on the trusts specified in s.33(1)."

HMRC's second contention was that notwithstanding the fact that although Mrs Thomas had directed the trustees to hold her life interest "upon protective trusts under the Trustee Act 1925, Section 33" her interest was not held on such trusts or trusts to the like effect. This was because

" . . . where a settlor directs that the trustee of a settlement shall hold the income of property settled by him during his life on the statutory protective trusts, the provisions of s.33(1) similarly apply as if para.(i) had specifically provided that as between the settlor and the trustee in bankruptcy the bankruptcy should not be treated as an event terminating the trust for the payment of the income to the settlor, and that in consequence in such a case it cannot be said that the settled property is held on the trusts specified in s.33(1). He submitted also that the settled property cannot be said to be held on any 'like trusts' because, he said, one of the purposes of imposing protective trusts is to ensure that in the event of the bankruptcy of the principal beneficiary the income does not vest in his trustee but remains available for the support of him and his family."

Vinelott J. was unable to accept this argument:

" . . . The trustee in bankruptcy has the right under the general law to avoid the discretionary trust in para.(ii) and to receive, or to dispose of the right to receive, the income during the remainder of the trust period to the extent necessary to ensure that the claims of creditors are met in full . . . It is sufficient for the decision of this case to say that the practical effect of the bankruptcy is to terminate the trusts in para.(i) for the payment of the income to the principal beneficiary and to bring into operation the discretionary trust in para.(ii), but that the operation of the discretionary trust is in turn suspended unless and until the creditors are paid in full and may be destroyed altogether if the trustee sells the right to receive the income of the trust property during the remainder of the trust period.

Looked at in that light, it seems to me impossible to say that where a settlor settles property on trust to hold the income during a defined trust period on protective trusts for his own benefit, the income is not held on the trusts specified in s.33(1). The income is held on those trusts but the operation of those trusts may be restricted or avoided if the principal beneficiary becomes bankrupt by the operation of the rule of law which I have stated . . .

If it could be said that where a settlor settles a trust fund on trust to hold the income during a defined trust period on protective trusts for his own benefit the income is not held on the trusts specified in s.33(1) (because those trusts must be taken to be modified by the rule of public policy to which I have referred) it would none the less be the case, in my judgment, that the income is held on trusts to the like effect as those specified in s.33(1) . . .

Counsel for the Crown submitted that a protective trust of income for the benefit of a settlor could not operate in substantially the same way as a protective trust of income for the benefit of someone other than the settlor because it would not achieve the protection of the protected life tenant and his wife and family after bankruptcy of the protected life tenant, which as I have said, is one of the main objects achieved by the imposition of protective trusts. I do not agree. In my view the object can fairly be said to have been achieved, as nearly as the law permits, and with substantially the same effect."

Treatment on or after April 12, 1978

22–05   In order to stop taxpayers abusing the favoured treatment extended to protective trusts, the Finance Act 1978 s.71 substituted a new para.18(2), now s.88(2), so that as from April 11, 1978, the principal beneficiary's interest is treated as continuing regardless of any failure or determination of that interest, with the result that a charge may arise if any of the trust fund is distributed during his life to anyone other than himself or his spouse, and on his death unless his spouse is next entitled on his death under the trust. Interests which failed or determined after April 11, 1978, are regarded as having revived on that date, but no charge arises because of that revival. This means that the reliefs and exemptions normally available to all pre-March 22, 2006, and to some post-March 22, 2006 interests in possession will be available in respect of the protected life interest which is kept artificially alive by s.88(2)(a), so that normally no charge will arise if, e.g. the trustees make a payment to the principal beneficiary[8] or to his spouse.[9] Payment to any other beneficiary, on the other hand, will be the occasion of a transfer under s.52(1), which transfer will normally be a PET.

[8] FA 1975 Sch.5 para.4(3).
[9] FA 1975 Sch.6 para.1.

In *Cholmondeley v IRC*[10] the taxpayer tried to take advantage of what is now s.88(2) in a manner similar to that in which the taxpayer in the *Thomas* case took advantage of the legislation that originally applied to protective trusts. The facts, slightly simplified, were that S, who had a life interest in a trust fund, was empowered, together with the trustees, to appoint the trust fund as they thought fit. They appointed seven farms, forming part of the trust fund, to be held on protective trusts for X for life, remainder in tail male, with power to advance capital to remaindermen. On the following day three of the farms were advanced to one of the remaindermen absolutely, with the result that X's protected life interest in those farms terminated. The trustees contended that the advancement had caused a "failure or determination" of X's protected life interest in the farms within the meaning of what is now s.88(2), and that therefore the termination of his interest in possession in those farms should be disregarded. Scott J. held that this view could not be supported, stating that the reference to the "failure or determination" of the protected life interest is:

> " . . . in my view, a reference to the failure or determination of the protected life interest as such. It envisages an event which, under the limitations either contained in the trust instrument or imported therein by s.33, brings to an end the principal beneficiary's protected life interest. It does not envisage the removal from the settlement by the exercise of some overriding power therein contained of part or all of the property therein comprised. Such an event would in a real sense, I accept, cause the protective trusts to determine. But such an event would not cause the protected life interest either to fail or to determine under the limitations applicable to that life interest" (p.390c–d).

It will be recalled that in HMRC's view an accumulation and maintenance trust followed by a protective trust did not qualify for favoured treatment, because in HMRC's view it was insufficiently certain that the protected life interest would vest in possession within the required period.[11] As was mentioned above, the provision in s.88(2)(a) that any failure or determination of the protected interest is to be ignored meant that this element of uncertainty—if it ever existed—was removed, and such an accumulation and maintenance trust would qualify for favoured treatment. The substitution into the legislation of what is now s.88(2)(a) thus meant that existing trusts which would have been favoured accumulation and maintenance trusts had they not included a protective element were converted into favoured accumulation and maintenance trusts on April 11, 1978, with the result that, in the absence of provision to the contrary, a charge would have arisen under the Finance Act 1975 Sch.5 para.15(3). Section 71(2) accordingly provided that no capital distribution was to be treated as having been made under para.15(3), by reason only of the coming into force of s.71. Thus, trustees who before April 11, 1978 tried to convert a discretionary trust into an accumulation and maintenance trust but failed because the appointed trust contained a protective element could on the passing of the Finance Act 1978 pat themselves on the back since they had managed—with the draftsman's help—to convert the trust into a favoured trust without incurring a charge.

In *Egerton v IRC*[12] the opposite situation occurred—trustees of a discretionary trust had on July 19, 1978, made an appointment under which certain beneficiaries were given an entitlement such that the property became held on accumulation and maintenance trusts, subject to the fact that each beneficiary's share was to be held on protective trusts once his interest vested. HMRC contended that, given the provisions of s.71, a charge arose under the Finance Act 1975 Sch.5 para.15(3), on the appointment of the accumulation and maintenance trusts, and that the trustees could not shelter

[10] *Cholmondeley v IRC* [1986] S.T.C. 384.
[11] See paras 18–08–18–14.
[12] *Egerton v IRC* [1983] S.T.C. 531.

under the provision in s.71(2) that no capital distribution was to be treated as having been made under para.15(3) by reason only of the coming into force of s.71, since that provision was intended to prevent charges from arising in consequence of events which had occurred before April 11, 1978. The trustees contended that s.71 did not come into force until the Finance Act 1978 received the Royal Assent on July 31, 1978. The Court of Appeal held that s.71 applied as from April 11, 1978, with the result that the protection given by s.71(2) was not available.

Planning

22–06   It is easy to overlook the fact that quite different treatment is accorded for IHT and CGT to settled property held on those protective trusts to which s.88 applies in circumstances where there is a forfeiture within s.33(1)(i) of the Trustee Act 1925. The point is best brought out by an example. Assume that X has a pre-March 22, 2006 protected life interest in a trust fund and that, unmindful of s.33, he purports to assign his interest to his son. By virtue of s.33(1), the trust income will not be payable to the son. Instead, it will be held on discretionary trusts within s.33(1)(ii).

Fiscal dichotomy: the worst of both worlds

22–07   It would be easy to conclude from this that what was intended to be a PET to the son is converted by s.33(1) into an immediately chargeable transfer. In fact, this is not the case, because the combined effect of ss.88(2) and 88(3) is that the purported assignment is a non-event for IHT purposes, with the protected life tenant being treated as continuing to have a qualifying interest in possession in the settled property in question. This is not to say, however, that the purported assignment is a fiscal non-event. There is no provision in the CGT legislation affording any "life support" to the forfeited protected life interest. The result is a fiscal dichotomy; for IHT purposes the protected life tenant still has an interest in possession, and on his death he will be taxed accordingly. For CGT purposes, on the other hand, he has no interest at all, and so the assets in which his interest formerly subsisted will not have the benefit of a tax-free uplift on his death.[13] This is the worst of both worlds.

A side exit?

22–08   In such a case, it may be possible to rectify the position. In *Gibbon v Mitchell*[14] Millett J. set aside for mistake a deed under which a protected life tenant released his interest in order, as part of a tax planning exercise, to accelerate the interests under the trust of his children, on the basis that the transaction did not have the effect the protected life tenant intended. Accordingly, where the facts justify it, it may be possible to set aside a deed which accomplishes nothing for IHT and jeopardises the CGT

[13] This may have other tax consequences. For example, it may call into question the availability of relief from capital gains tax on the disposal of the beneficiary's principal private residence by trustees (see TCGA 1992 s.225) if the terms of the trust are drafted in such a way that they only permit occupation by the life tenant. In practice, other arguments may be available to the taxpayer, which make it unlikely that HMRC will take this point.

[14] *Gibbon v Mitchell* [1990] 3 All E.R. 338.

position. Note also that it is possible for a protected life tenant to make a PET. If the trustees exercise a power of advancement, that will not cause a s.33 forfeiture, and it will not activate s.88(2).[15]

Determination before April 12, 1978

The changes introduced by the Finance Act 1978 affected only the position where a **22–09** principal beneficiary's interest determined after April 11, 1978. Section 118(2) of the Finance Act 1982, now s.73, accordingly imposes exit charges on property held on discretionary trusts to the like effect as those specified in s.31(1)(ii) of the Trustee Act 1925 which became so held on the failure or determination before April 12, 1978, of trusts to the like effect as those specified in s.33(1)(i). A primary exit charge is imposed when property held on such protective trusts ceases to be so held, otherwise than by virtue of a payment out of the settled property for the benefit of the principal beneficiary. A secondary exit charge may also be imposed.[16]

---

[15] *Cholmondeley v IRC* [1986] S.T.C. 384.
[16] For a discussion, see para.17–28.

PENSION SCHEMES

23–01   Pension funds are among the largest funds in the country, the vast majority of pensions in the private sector in the United Kingdom being provided out of such funds. Both the income tax and the CGT legislation treat such funds favourably; were the IHT legislation not to make similar provision for pension funds the consequences would be dire indeed since such funds are settled properly for IHT purposes, and in the absence of special provision the normal rules relating to settled property would therefore apply to them. In so far as pre-March 22, 2006 interests in possession or transitional serial interests subsisted in the fund in the form of pensions or annuities they would be dealt with under the main charging provisions and brought into charge under s.52(1) during the pensioner's or annuitant's life and under s.4(1) on his death. So much of the fund as was held on discretionary trusts, or on most forms of lifetime trusts established after March 22, 2006, would be dealt with under the relevant property charging regime in the usual way.

The IHT treatment of pension schemes, in particular in relation to the treatment of death benefits, has been altered by the provisions of Finance Act 2004 and the Finance Act 2011. Many of the changes introduced by Finance Act 2004 came into effect on April 6, 2006, a date commonly known as "A-Day". From A-Day the various different regimes for approved pension schemes were consolidated into one set of rules, and approved schemes are now known as registered pension schemes. Further changes came into effect on April 6, 2011 when schemes previously described as unsecured pensions and alternatively secured pension provisions were replaced with the single type referred to as drawdown pensions and the IHT implications were simplified accordingly.

The effect of the 2011 changes was largely to reduce the different treatment of pension funds where the pensioner dies over or under the age of 75. However, the 75 threshold is still important in relation to income tax as where the pensioner dies before the age of 75 leaving an uncrystallised fund, the lump sum would be tax free. But if the pensioner dies over the age of 75 (or the fund is crystallised at any age) there will be an income tax charge of 55 per cent.

Note also that if the death benefits are (or are deemed to be) part of the deceased's estate they will be subject to IHT along with the rest of the estate. This may occur where, for example, the pensioner has a general power of nomination (see para. 23–10).

Favoured treatment generally

Section 151 applies to any registered pension scheme or fund which has an exemp-   **23–02**
tion for income tax (precisely which schemes and funds qualify for favoured treatment is considered below). In most cases s.151 operates primarily by:

(1) excluding the provisions relating to settled property in which there is a qualifying interest in possession; and
(2) excluding any charge on death.

Section 58(1)(d) provides that property held for the purposes of a registered pension scheme, a qualifying non-UK pension scheme or a s.615(3) scheme is not subject to the relevant property regime. The combined effect of ss.151 and 58(1)(d) is as follows:

- *Exit and periodic charges*: The special charging provisions are excluded entirely so that, so far as inheritance tax is concerned, distributions can be made with impunity and the scheme or fund is not subject to the periodic charge.
- *Interests in possession*: The exclusion of the normal rules relating to qualifying interests in possession means that such an interest is given the same treatment as any other item of property. Thus, if a person disposes of his interest during his lifetime he will make a transfer of value of the amount—having regard to the market value of the interest—by which that disposition diminishes the value of his estate, and both the reliefs and exemptions relating to actual transfers of value will be available to him.
- *Death*: The exclusion of the rule in s.49 under which a person entitled to a qualifying interest in possession is treated as beneficially entitled to the property in which his interest subsists would of itself normally preclude there being any charge in respect of such an interest on death. This follows from the fact that as a result of the exclusion, regard is had always to the market value of the interest, and the market value immediately before a person dies of an interest which comes to an end on the death of the person entitled to it is to be left out of account altogether. In the event that the interest continues after a person's death, e.g. where the deceased's pension becomes payable to his widow, the additional relief on death will not apply and the market value of the interest (not, as would normally be the case in the absence of s.151, the market value of the underlying property) will be brought into account. In the typical case a widow's pension would be a separate entitlement under the rules of the scheme, and not something of which the deceased was competent to dispose anyway. So, normally there would be no tax. But it would be otherwise in the case of a pension which is payable (as often

happens, to prevent hard cases) for the life of X or five years, whichever is the longer. If X died six months after his retirement, his estate will include as an asset, the right to four and a half years' pension, and this would be taxed at its market value.

23–03   To compensate HMRC, a person with a general power over property comprised in a s.151 trust is treated as owning that property, with the result that (i) if he exercises that power during his life he may make an actual transfer of value of that property, and (ii) if he dies without exercising that power, the property will form part of his estate immediately before he dies. The combined effect of ss.151(4) and 58(1)(d) means that it is desirable to ensure that an individual does not have a general power to dispose of the death benefits under s.151 schemes at a time when those benefits have value (i.e. on his death) and that the benefits are reinstated within the framework of the relevant property regime.

23–04   Section 151 does not affect the position where on a person's death a lump sum benefit accrues to his estate as of right: in such a case he will be assessed under s.4(1) on that benefit in the usual way. No charge is made, on the other hand, in respect of a sum paid by the trustees of the pension fund in exercise of their discretion (even if they are carrying out the expressed wishes of the deceased), since such a sum is not an addition which accrues to the deceased's estate by reason of his death, but by reason of the trustees' exercise of their discretion.[1]

Qualifying schemes and funds

23–05   From A-Day (April 6, 2006) s.151 only applies to the following schemes and funds:

(1) any registered pension scheme as defined in Finance Act 2004[2]; or
(2) any fund to which the Income and Corporation Taxes Act 1988 s.615(3) applies (pension funds for overseas employer).

Retirement annuity contracts, approved personal pension arrangements and other exempt approved or statutory schemes will qualify as registered pension schemes from A-Day. However, sponsored superannuation schemes which do not qualify as registered pension schemes or Income and Corporation Taxes Act 1988 s.615(3) schemes will not receive favoured treatment and will not receive the benefit of the reliefs given by s.151 or s.58(1)(d). This affects employers who have set up schemes for their employees (e.g. death in service schemes) where those schemes are not also registered pension schemes.

Favoured treatment in detail

23–06   The provisions concerning s.151 trusts have the following features and effects.

Relevant property charging regime

23–07   No charge to tax can arise under the special charging provisions in respect of

---

[1] See further para.23–11.
[2] Finance Act 2004 Pt 4 Ch.2.

property which is part of or held for the purposes of a s.151 scheme or fund.[3] This is subject to one qualification, namely that the relevant property regime does apply where a benefit which has become payable under the scheme or fund itself becomes settled. In such a case the normal rules apply, and the person who was entitled to the benefit is treated as the settlor even though someone else, e.g. the trustees of the fund, in fact made the settlement.[4] A typical example of this applying in practice would be where on a scheme member's death the trustees of a registered pension scheme apply £50,000 at their discretion for the benefit of his widow or surviving civil partner, children and dependants. The trustees pay £25,000 to the widow outright and £25,000 to trustees of an ad hoc trust for the deceased's children. This ad hoc trust will be taxed under the relevant property regime.

Interest in possession

An "interest" in or under a s.151 trust receives favoured treatment if, by s.151(2), **23–08** it:

> "(a) is, or is a right to, a pension or annuity; and
> (b) is not an interest resulting (whether by virtue of the instrument establishing the scheme or otherwise) from the application of any benefit provided under the scheme otherwise than by way of a pension or annuity."

The above wording is a little unusual, in two ways. First, the purpose of s.151(2) is to define the kind of interest which is to receive favoured treatment, and, as will be seen below, the treatment extended to such interests makes it clear that what the legislation is concerned with are certain kinds of interests in possession. Section 151(2), however, is a bit more circumspect—it refers only to an interest, not to an interest in possession. Secondly, while it is easy to see how an annuity or a pension can constitute an interest in possession, both involving an immediate entitlement to income, it is hard to see how a right to an annuity or pension can constitute an interest, much less an interest in possession. What the draftsman probably had in mind were certain estate duty cases[5] in which the House of Lords held that a life-tenant could have an interest in possession in a policy or other property notwithstanding the fact that that policy or property was incapable of producing income during his lifetime. Given those cases, it may have been thought that a person with, for example, a right to receive a pension on his retirement, would, by analogy with the estate duty case, have an interest in possession before he retired, with the result that if before retiring he disposed of that right or died he would have been assessable on the part of the fund allocated to support his pension on his retirement. There being some doubt whether or not this would in fact have been the case, the Parliamentary draftsman apparently hedged his bets by including a reference to such a right without going so far as to prejudge the issue by characterising such a right as a full-blown interest in possession. Section 151 thus refers only to an interest, not to an interest in possession, and in the following discussion the draftsman's lead will as a matter of convenience be followed, interest meaning any interest which qualifies for favourable treatment under s.151.

An example of an interest that would not qualify for such treatment occurs where a lump sum death benefit is settled on trusts creating an annuity; the resulting interest will not satisfy condition (b) of s.151(2), and the trusts will be taxed in the usual way. However, where there is an unexercised right to commute part of a pension the condition would not apply because the right would be one to which the scheme member

---

[3] IHTA 1984 s.58(1).
[4] IHTA 1984 s.58(2).
[5] See *Westminster Bank Ltd v IRC* [1958] A.C. 210.

was entitled under the rules and not one resulting from the application of the lump sum.

The favoured treatment afforded to any interest coming within s.151(2) has two aspects. First, s.151(3) provides that ss.49–53 do not apply to such an interest. Therefore it is clear that this provision applies only to qualifying interests in possession. This exclusion of ss.49–53 has a number of effects, the most important of which is that, in the event of a lifetime transfer or a transfer on death, tax will be charged on the value of the interest, and not, as would normally be the case, on the value of the underlying property. This follows from the exclusion of s.49. The exclusion of ss.51 and 52 affects only the position with regard to lifetime transfers, which is as follows:

(1) the exclusion of s.52(1) means that no charge will arise on the termination of the interest;
(2) the exclusion of s.51(1)(a) means that the disposal of the interest will not be relieved from being an actual transfer of value; and
(3) where the interest is disposed of the normal rules relating to dispositions will apply, and regard will be had to whether the disposition diminished the disponer's estate. The exclusion of s.49 means that in determining whether and to what extent there has been a diminution regard is to be had to the market value of the interest at the time of the disposition (i.e. the actuarial value of the interest), not to the market value of the underlying property.

These provisions should operate comparatively rarely because most pensions under registered pension schemes are expressly made non-assignable and non-commutable but it would apply to an annuity granted for a minimum period where the deceased died during the period, firstly on the death of the deceased and then on the subsequent termination of the interest. A widow's or surviving civil partner's pension might end inter vivos on remarriage or entering into a new civil partnership, but then its value would be nil.

The result is that if a person makes a gift of his pension he may be charged on the value of his pension, not on the value of that part of the pension fund supporting his pension. In the event that a person makes a chargeable transfer of his interest, s.210(1) relieves the trustees from liability for so much of the tax as is attributable to the value of the interest.

So far as transfers on death are concerned, there are two considerations. First, the exclusion of s.49 means that on a person's death the value to be brought into account immediately before his death is the value of the interest at that time, not the value of the underlying property. Thus, if the interest comes to an end on his death, no tax will be chargeable since the value of the interest immediately before he died would have been nil. If, on the other hand, the interest continues after his death, e.g. where it becomes payable to his personal representatives as of right, then it will have some value, and tax will be chargeable on that value under s.4(1). If the terms of the scheme are that a separate pension arises on a person's death, e.g. a pension in favour of his widow or surviving civil partner, no charge should arise in respect of that separate pension since neither it nor the right to it ever formed part of the deceased's estate.

Favoured treatment on death

23–09   Favoured treatment is afforded partly by the exclusion of s.49[6] and partly from the express provisions of s.51(2). The exclusion of s.49 will normally suffice to preclude

[6] See IHTA 1984 s.151(3).

any charge arising on death. As a long-stop, s.151(2) further provides that where an interest comes to an end on the death of the person entitled to it that interest is left out of account in determining the value of his estate immediately before his death. It is rather difficult to see what this adds to the exclusion of s.49, except for the technical difference that the effect of the exclusion of s.49 is that a nil value will be brought into account whereas under s.151(2) no value will be brought into account at all. The explanation may be that s.151(2) is dealing in plain terms with the common case (pension ceasing on death) and s.151(3) is dealing with less common cases in more technical language (e.g. rights disposed of inter vivos, pension terminating inter vivos, or guaranteed pension continuing after death as an asset of the estate), there being some overlap between s.151(2) and (3). Section 151 effectively continues the estate duty treatment of superannuation funds, and this provision is best seen as a vestige of the estate duty provisions rather than as being of substantive importance. Since s.151(2) applies only where the interest comes to an end on the death of the person entitled to it, it does not affect the treatment of an interest which continues after the death of that person; in such a case the market value of the interest will be brought into account, and the deceased's personal representatives, not the trustees of the pension fund, will be among the persons liable for tax.

General powers

It may be that under the rules of a scheme or fund a member has power to nominate **23–10** a benefit, e.g. a return of contributions or the lump sum payable on his death. It will be recalled that as a matter of general principle a power—not being a right or an interest—does not form part of a person's estate, but that s.5(2) provides that a person who has a general power over property other than settled property is treated as owning property over which that power subsists. In the absence of special provision, s.5(2) would thus not apply to such a power to nominate a benefit, such power being a power over settled property and therefore outside s.5(2).[7]

Section 151(4) alters the position so that s.5(2) applies to a general power to nominate benefits out of a s.151 trust. This means that if immediately before he dies a person possesses such a power he will be charged on his death under s.4(1) on the value of the property over which he had that power.

The consequences of his exercising such a power during his lifetime vary according to whether he exercised his power irrevocably, or only revocably. If the exercise is irrevocable, there will be an actual transfer of value of the amount by which the nomination diminishes the value of his estate. If the exercise is revocable, there will be:

(1) a free loan of the property nominated[8]; and
(2) a transfer of value in consequence of s.3(3) at the latest time the nomination could have been revoked.

It is important to remember that s.5(2) will apply only where there is a general power of nomination. Thus, if there is to be a power of nomination, it should either be a

---

[7] See para.25–07.
[8] *Westminster Bank Ltd v IRC* [1958] A.C. 210.

limited one, or one the exercise of which is left to the discretion of the pension fund trustees.[9]

Death benefits—death of scheme member under the age of 75

23–11   Please note that from A-Day, as well as potential IHT charges in relation to death benefits there is a potential additional charge known as the Lifetime Allowance Charge. An analysis of the Lifetime Allowance Charge is outside the scope of this book but in broad outline it is a pension scheme charge that applies when the value of an individual's aggregate pension fund on death is above the Lifetime Allowance (£1.5million from April 6, 2012). The Lifetime Allowance Charge applies in addition to IHT and there is no credit between these two taxes. Consequently, death benefits should be held on trust to avoid a potential double charge.

The favourable treatment under s.151 does not extend to benefits which accrue to a person's estate in consequence of his death, e.g. where his personal representatives are entitled as of right to a lump sum. Although such a sum will not be comprised in the deceased's estate on his death, the right to it will be, and the value of the benefit which is to accrue in consequence of it. Where, on the other hand, the trustees exercise their discretion in favour of the deceased's estate no charge will arise, because no right to the sum will have been comprised in the deceased's estate immediately before he died and the addition of the sum to his estate will have occurred by reason of the trustees exercising their discretion, not by reason of his death; consequently s.171 will not apply. Similarly, if the trustees make a payment to a person's estate in respect of a pension which ceased on his death the payment will not be brought into account since it will have accrued to his estate in respect of an interest qualifying for relief under s.151.

The Revenue, as it then was, issued the following statement on May 7, 1976:

> "This note has been prepared at the request of the National Association of Pension Funds primarily to enable the administrators of pension schemes to answer enquiries about the capital transfer tax liability of benefits payable under such schemes.
>
> No liability to capital transfer tax arises in respect of benefits payable on a person's death under a normal pension scheme except in the circumstances explained below. Such benefits are liable to capital transfer tax if:
>
> (a) they form part of his freely disposable property passing under his will or intestacy. (This applies only if his executors or administrators have a legally enforceable claim to the benefits: if they were payable to them only at the discretion of the trustees of the pension fund or some similar persons they are not liable to capital transfer tax.)
>
> or
>
> (b) he had the power, immediately before his death, to nominate or appoint the benefits to anyone he pleased.
>
> In these cases the benefits should be included in the personal representatives' account (schedule of the deceased's assets) which has to be completed when applying for a grant of probate or letters of administration. The capital transfer tax (if any) which is assessed on the personal representatives' account has to be paid before the grant can be obtained.
>
> On some events other than the death of a member information should be given to the appropriate Estate Duty Office. These are:

---

[9] See *Re J Bibby & Sons Ltd (Pension's Trust Deed)* [1952] 2 All E.R. 483; [1952] T.R. 321. It is thought that this would not result in the trustees being treated as beneficially entitled to the property over which the power existed.

(i) the payment of contributions to a scheme which has not been approved for income tax purposes;

(ii) the making of an irrevocable nomination of the disposal of a benefit by a member in his lifetime (otherwise than in favour of his spouse) which reduces the value of his estate (e.g. the surrender of part of his pension or his lump sum benefit in exchange for a pension for the life of another).

If capital transfer tax proves to be payable the Estate Duty Office will communicate with the persons liable to pay the tax."

Clarification of position of retirement annuities/personal pensions post A-Day

Prior to A-Day it was understood that where an individual took out a contract falling within the Income and Corporation Taxes Act 1988 s.630 and settled the death benefit payable thereunder on discretionary trusts the Revenue would treat the contract and settlement as a "scheme" for the purposes of s.151 and grant exemption on any payment made to a beneficiary within two years of the death of the settlor provided that the settlor retains no general power of appointment under the settlement.[10] Post A-Day approved retirement annuity contracts are treated as registered pension schemes to which the reliefs under s.151 apply.   **23–12**

Reservation of benefit and pre-owned assets tax

The Revenue, as it then was, confirmed in a Press Release of July 9, 1986 (SP10/86), that the reservation of benefit rules would not apply to such discretionary trusts of retirement annuity schemes.[11] It is thought that this existing HMRC practice will apply to all registered pension schemes. It is also thought that no pre-owned assets charge will arise to a scheme member even though the scheme member must as a matter of pensions law retain the absolute right to receive a cash lump sum, an annuity or enter into income drawdown.   **23–13**

Contributions to section 151 schemes

Section 151 deals with property already comprised in a pension scheme. Contributions to such schemes are governed by the normal rules. Contributions by participants to schemes under which they are the only beneficiaries will not normally diminish the value of the contributors' estate, and therefore will not constitute transfers of value. Contributions to schemes under which benefits are provided for others will be transfers of value: where the non-contributing beneficiary is the contributor's spouse or civil partner, the s.18 exemption will apply; where the non-contributing beneficiary is someone else there will normally be a charge to tax unless the contributions are exempt   **23–14**

[10] See *Inland Revenue Tax Bulletin* (February 1992), Issue 2, p.12.
[11] See para.7–96; see also the guidance notes at para.23–15.

under the annual exemption or as normal expenditure out of income. Contributions by employers will usually qualify for relief under s.12 or s.13.[12]

Pre-A-Day guidance notes on death of scheme member under the age of 75

23–15   Prior to A-Day, the Revenue, as it then was, issued the following guidance notes on the IHT treatment of benefits under pension schemes:

> "These notes replace those that were issued to explain the practice of the Capital Taxes Office regarding liability to Capital Transfer Tax on benefits payable under the rules of employees' retirement benefit schemes and superannuation funds and under retirement annuity contracts and trust schemes approved under s.226/226A of the Taxes Act 1987.
>
> They outline the effect on such benefits of Inheritance Tax (IHT) introduced by the Finance Act 1986 and refer in particular to s.151 of the Inheritance Tax Act 1984, as extended to approved personal pension arrangements by s.98(4) of the Finance (No.2) Act.

(A) *Payments to the deceased's legal personal representatives*

(1) Payments that are legally due to the legal personal representatives, and cannot be withheld from them at the discretion of any person exercisable after the death, form part of the deceased's estate and are taxable as such (subject to any spouse exemption under s.18 of the Inheritance Tax Act 1984 having regard to the devolution of the deceased's estate under his will or intestacy). Payment made to the legal personal representatives in exercise of a discretion exercisable after the death are not treated as part of the deceased's estate for tax purposes on his death.

(2) Payments which are taxable as at (1) above are not regarded as property comprised in a settlement and where they are paid over to duly constituted legal personal representatives, those representatives (not the trustees of the fund) are liable to tax. They should include the value of the payments in the personal representatives' account of the deceased's estate.

(3) Where payments are made to the duly constituted legal personal representatives, the person making them need not send a separate notification to the Capital Taxes Office.

(B) *Where the deceased had a general power of nomination*

(1) Where the deceased had a general power to nominate a benefit to anyone he wished and had not exercised his power irrevocably in his lifetime the benefit forms part of the estate for Inheritance Tax purposes and is taxable as such subject again to any 'spouse' exemption under s.18.

(2) The legal personal representatives are liable for any tax.

(3) Where the deceased's power of nomination is restricted to a specified class of persons which does not include himself, failure to exercise the power irrevocably in his lifetime will not give rise to a tax liability on death unless under the rules of the fund or scheme the benefit then forms part of his estate.

(4) Where the deceased had at the time of his death an option to have a sum of money paid to his legal personal representatives, that sum of money will normally be taxed as part of his estate. Where however an annuity is payable to the deceased's widow, widower or dependant under a contract or trust scheme approved under ss.226 or 226A of the Taxes Act or (before the commencement of that Act) under s.22 of the Finance Act 1956 or under Chapter II of Part I of the Finance (No.2) Act 1987 and

---

[12] See paras 2–64 and 2–67–2–69.

the deceased had an option to have a sum of money paid to his legal personal representative tax is not charged (s.152 of the Inheritance Tax Act 1984).

(C) *Annuities which continue to be payable after the deceased's death*

(1) Provided that the Scheme or Fund under which it is payable is one mentioned in ss.151(1) and 151(1A) of the Inheritance Tax Act 1984 a pension or annuity continuing after the deceased's death will not give rise to a tax liability in connection with his death unless the continuing pension or annuity results from the settlement or other application of a lump sum benefit (see s.151(2)(*b*)).

(2) If however the continuing pension or annuity is payable as of right to the deceased's legal personal representatives it will be taxable (see paragraph (A) above).

(D) *Gratuitous transfers of value*

(1) IHT is not considered to be chargeable under s.3(1) of the Inheritance Tax Act 1984, as a gratuitous transfer of value, on the contributions (made either directly or by a reduction in the remuneration which he would otherwise have received) by a member to provide any benefit to another person payable under retirement benefit or superannuation schemes, trusts, contracts or arrangements the main or substantial object of which is to make provision for a person on his own retirement. (As to the surrender of part of the benefit to which the member would himself have been entitled see (E) below.)

(2) The statement in paragraph 1 above does not extend to any *separate* provision made by a member for his dependants or otherwise, for example under a group life insurance scheme operated in conjunction with superannuation arrangements, even if the scheme or other provision is arranged and administered by or in co-operation with the employer. Nor does it extend to a contract under s.226A of the Taxes Act.

Premiums paid by the member on a policy on his life effected under a scheme of this kind or under such a contract may be chargeable to tax as gratuitous transfers of value although the transfers will commonly qualify for exemption under s.21 of the Inheritance Tax Act as normal expenditure out of income.

(3) In practice contributions (other than those provided as at (E)) payable under ordinary pension or superannuation schemes for members of the kind referred to in para.1 above will automatically be regarded as covered by the statement in this paragraph if the scheme is one to which s.151 applies (see ss.151(1) and 151(1A)). The tax position of contributions to and benefits arising from any other scheme will be considered individually when a transfer of value, which is not a potentially exempt transfer, occurs.

(E) *Disposition by nominations or surrender of benefits*

(1) Where
   (a) a member provides for a pension to another
      (i) by irrevocably surrendering part of his own pension, or
      (ii) by giving up a right to receive a lump sum (or part of it) payable to him on retirement or to his legal personal representatives on death
      or
   (b) he irrevocably nominates such a lump sum
   he will prima facie have made a potentially exempt transfer if his disposition is after March 17, 1986; (prior to that, between March 26, 1974 and March 17, 1986, a prima facie chargeable transfer would have arisen). If the potentially exempt transfer subsequently becomes a chargeable transfer the value transferred will be determined by the 'loss' to the member at the date the disposition is made and thereafter will normally be less than the value of the pension or lump sum ultimately paid to the beneficiary.

   A disposition of this nature could in appropriate circumstances be an exempt transfer under:

687

(a) s.18 (Transfers between spouses)

(b) s.19 (Values not exceeding £3,000)

(c) s.20 (Small gifts to same person)

(d) s.11 (Dispositions for maintenance of family)

(2) The revocable exercise of a power of nomination over a lump sum benefit will have the same Inheritance Tax consequences except that the disposition will be treated as taking effect at the latest time at which the member could have revoked his nomination (*e.g.* his retirement or his death).

(F) *Termination of a pension or annuity*

(1) Section 151 provides exemption on the termination on death or otherwise of a pension or annuity payable under a scheme or fund to which s.151(1) or 151(1A) applies. For this purpose a pension payable without proportion to the date of death is regarded as terminating on the death.

(2) Sections 151(2)(*b*) and 151(3) make it clear that the exemption does not apply to the termination of an interest under a trust of a *lump sum* benefit payable under a scheme or fund and s.58(2) and s.151(5) that it does not extend to a discretionary payment made out of a benefit which, having become payable, becomes comprised in a settlement. If a lump sum benefit is settled (for example, in the exercise of discretionary powers as to the disposal of a death benefit) claims for tax may arise on the termination of an interest in possession under the settlement or, if there are no interests in possession in the settled property, on the various chargeable events described in Chapter III, Part III of the Inheritance Tax Act 1984.

(3) Where a lump sum benefit is converted into a pension under the rules of the scheme or fund then normally neither the conversion nor the cesser of that pension will give rise to a tax charge. If however the lump sum benefit is surrendered to provide a pension for some other person then paragraph (E) above will apply.

(G) *Payments made in exercise of a discretion*

Where a lump sum benefit payable under a scheme or fund within ss.151(1) or 151(1A) is distributed or settled in exercise of a discretion neither such distribution nor the making of a settlement will give rise to a liability to tax.

(H) *Implications of the provisions on gifts with reservation*

As explained in the Press Release of July 9, 1986 (now Statement of Practice 10/86), the provisions introduced by s.102 of the Finance Act 1986 do not affect the former Estate Duty practice regarding gifts with reservation. Benefits under tax-approved superannuation arrangements that would have been exempt from capital transfer tax will also be exempt from Inheritance Tax even if they involve gifts with reservation."

Note that references in the above Revenue (as it then was) guidance to s.151(1) or s.151(IA) should be read as references to s.151(2). In addition, the s.18 exemption rule applies to a surviving civil partner. This guidance is no longer applicable. HMRC have now consolidated all their guidance into the Inheritance Tax Manual (IHTM) which can be viewed on the HMRC website (see IHTM17000 and onwards).

HMRC's view is that the irrevocable assignment of death benefits to a trust is a transfer of value within s.3(1) giving rise to an IHT charge, and from April 6, 2006 a lifetime chargeable transfer. However, HMRC has confirmed that the value of the gifted property on establishment of a trust (either in respect of an existing contract or at the inception of a new contract) will be treated as nominal if the policyholder concerned is in good health for a person of his or her age at the time the trusts are imposed. HMRC take the view that the bulk of the value of the pension policy, or the rights purchased by payment of premiums under the policy, relate to the ability of the policyholder to take pension benefits during his lifetime, and as such the transfer of value is treated as being of purely nominal value.

If a policyholder dies within two years of imposing the trust over death benefits, it may be necessary to demonstrate to HMRC that the policyholder was in normal good health at the time the trusts were imposed. Please note that this two-year period is not a fixed period and enquiries about death of the policyholder may be raised outside this period. If a policyholder is not in normal good health at the time of the assignment, there will be a potential charge to IHT under s.3(1). If, however, payment is made to the policyholder's spouse, civil partner or dependants, HMRC appear to accept that by virtue of s.11 (which provides that in certain circumstances a disposition is not a transfer of value), there will be no charge to IHT. If there is a charge it would be on the open market value of the death benefits less the value of the lump sum plus the open market value of the annuity element.

Section 3(3) provides that there will be a charge to IHT where a member dies before taking all available retirement benefits held on trust having attained the age when benefits could have been taken.[13] However, from April 6, 2011, s.3(3) is specifically disapplied by s.12(2ZA) where a member of a registered pension scheme, a s.615(3) scheme or qualifying non-UK pension scheme omits to exercise pension rights and s.12(2A)–(2E) were repealed from that date. Any lump sums taken are liable to income tax but not IHT. The Inland Revenue, as it then was, gave a concession that it would not raise a claim under s.3(3) if death benefits are paid to dependents of the policy-holder. This pre-A-Day concessionary approach was put on a statutory footing from A-Day.[14]

Pre A-Day it was agreed between the Inland Revenue, as it then was, and the Association of British Insurers[15] that in practice HMRC would not invoke s.3(3) where a member omitted to exercise his rights under an approved personal pension by taking a lump sum to purchase an annuity unless such an omission was a deliberate attempt to increase the value of another's estate rather than benefiting the member. The lump sum would have been liable to income tax at 35 per cent under s.206 of the Finance Act 2004. The Revenue's practice was to review the position of the survivor who could either continue in drawdown, purchase an annuity or elect for a lump sum within two years of the death of the policyholder. Again, this pre-A-Day concessionary approach was put on a statutory footing from A-Day.[16] Under SP10/86, IHT will not be payable on payments made by the trustees of registered pension scheme in exercise of a discretion to pay a lump sum benefit to any one or more of a member's dependants.

Other than by the application of s.3(1) and (3), no liability to IHT arises in respect of benefits payable on a person's death under a normal pension scheme except in the circumstances explained below.

Such benefits are liable to IHT if:

(a) they form part of his freely disposable property passing under his will or intestacy (this applies only if his personal representatives have a legally enforce-able claim to the benefits: if they were payable to them only at the discretion of the trustees of the pension fund or some similar persons they are not liable to IHT);
or

(b) he had the power, immediately before his death, to nominate or appoint the benefits to anyone he pleased.

---

[13] See para.2–23 and *Fryer v Revenue and Customs Commissioners* [2010] UKFTT 87 (TC).

[14] See para 23–48 for commentary on IHTA 1984 s.12(2A)–(2G).

[15] Joint paper dated June 20, 1999, "The Inheritance Tax Treatment of Deferral of Annuity Purchase and Income Withdrawal under Personal Pensions".

[16] See para 23–17 for commentary on IHTA 1984 s.12(2A)–(2G).

In these cases the benefits should be included in the personal representatives' account (schedule of the deceased's assets) which has to be completed when applying for a grant of probate or letters of administration. The IHT (if any) which is assessed on the personal representatives' account has to be paid before the grant can be obtained.

On some events other than the death of a member information should be given to HMRC. These are:

(a) the payment of contributions to a scheme which has not been registered for income tax purposes; and

(b) the making of an irrevocable nomination or the disposal of a benefit by a member in his lifetime (otherwise than in favour of his spouse or civil partner) which reduces the value of his estate (e.g. the surrender of part of his pension or his lump sum benefit in exchange for a pension for the life of another).

If IHT proves to be payable HMRC will communicate with the persons liable to pay the tax.

Replacement of unsecured pensions and alternatively secured pensions with drawdown pensions

23–16   With effect from April 6, 2011, the concept of the drawdown pension replaced the concepts of unsecured and alternatively secured pension provisions and ss.151A–151E and 12(2A)–(2E) of IHTA 1984 were repealed. A new s.12(2ZA) was inserted into IHTA 1984.

Death of scheme member under the age of 75

23–17   The pre-A-Day guidance continues to apply in relation to dispositions by scheme members who are not yet entitled to take pension benefits, i.e. the scheme member is under the relevant retirement age for the scheme. However, for scheme members who are capable of taking pension benefits because they have survived to the applicable pension age the concessionary approach adopted by HMRC before A-Day was replaced by s.12(2A)–(2G).[17] These amendments came into force from A-Day (April 6, 2006). However s.12(2A)–(2E) were repealed and replaced with a new s.12(2ZA) with effect from April 6, 2011 which disapplies s.3(3) where a member of a registered scheme, a qualifying non-UK scheme or s.615(3) scheme omits to exercise pension rights.

Prior to April 6, 2011, the mere failure to exercise any pensions rights by a scheme member (e.g. to take the whole or part of any lump sum, annuity or income drawdown entitlement under the scheme) at a time when he was entitled to exercise those pensions rights, did not trigger an IHT liability where s.10 prevented the disposition being a transfer of value.[18] However, the scheme member was deemed to have made a transfer of value under s.3(3) equal to the value of his unused pension rights on death if the following conditions were met[19]:

---

[17] IHTA 1985 s.12(2A)–(2G) inserted by Finance Act 2006 s.160 Sch.22 paras 1 and 2.
[18] IHTA 1985 s.12(2B).
[19] IHTA 1985 s.12(2B).

(a) the scheme member made an "actual pensions disposition"[20] which was not prevented from being a transfer of value by s.10 within the period of two years ending with the date of the scheme members death[21]; and

(b) when the above "actual pensions disposition" was made the scheme member had reason to believe that he would die within two years.[22]

An "actual pensions disposition" was defined in s.12(2F)(b) as a disposition within s.3(1) which arose by doing anything in relation to, or rights under, a registered pension scheme. Examples of an "actual pensions disposition" include assigning death benefits into trust, enhancing pension contributions to an existing policy held on trust or reducing the amount of income drawdown.

Consequently, if a scheme member under the age of 75 who was in good health had deferred taking pension benefits and continued to defer taking pension benefits after his health has deteriorated, so long as the intention behind the continuing deferral was not to confer a gratuitous benefit on another person, there was no transfer of value under s.3(3) of the remaining pension benefits on death.

Alternatively, if a scheme member under the age of 75 who knew that he was in poor health assigned his death benefits into trust, decreased the income benefits he took or increased his pension contributions, a transfer of value under s.3(3) arose on his death within two years of making such an "actual pensions disposition".

If the above conditions were met, and s.3(3) applied, there was no IHT charge if the death benefits were paid to the deceased scheme member's surviving spouse or civil partner, or someone who was financially dependent on the deceased scheme member at the time of his death.[23] In addition, no IHT applied if the death benefits were paid to a charity.[24]

Death of scheme member over the age of 75—drawdown pension fund rules

23–18

From April 6, 2011 the old rules for "alternatively secured pensions" that applied to over pensioners over 75 were abolished and replaced with the general concept of drawdown pensions. There are limits on how much pension can be drawn each year but there is no charge to IHT on any funds remaining under a registered pension scheme.

Death of a scheme member over the age of 75 prior to April 6, 2011—Alternatively Secured Pension (ASP) fund rules

23–19

Prior to April 6, 2011 different rules applied where the scheme member died after his 75th birthday and had an ASP fund. ASPs were introduced from A-Day and were a form of income drawdown for those over 75. The government's stated aim in introducing ASPs was to meet the needs of individuals with a principled religious objection to the pre-A-Day requirement of having to purchase an annuity with their pension funds (e.g. the Plymouth Brethren). Under an ASP a scheme member had the right to determine (subject to limits) the level of income they drewdown from their fund.

---

[20] Defined in IHTA 1985 s.12(2F)(b).
[21] IHTA 1985 s.12(2C)(a).
[22] IHTA 1985 s.12(2C)(b).
[23] IHTA 1985 s.12(2D)(a).
[24] IHTA 1985 s.12(2D)(b).

If a scheme member had not used all of his pension benefits (e.g. not bought an annuity or not exhausted his income drawdown fund) by his 75th birthday he automatically entered into the ASP regime. From April 6, 2007 on the death of a scheme member in ASP, the remaining capital of his ASP fund could not be transferred outright to the scheme member's surviving spouse, civil partner or dependents, or to the trustees of a trust set up during the scheme member's lifetime (unless it is a solely charitable trust), but instead had to be retained by the scheme administrator to provide retirement benefits.

In broad outline, ss.151A–151C[25] applied from April 6, 2007 to April 5, 2011 with effect that if a scheme member in ASP was not survived by a spouse, civil partner, financial dependent or the ASP fund was not paid to charity, there was an IHT charge as well as an unauthorised payment charge and potentially an unauthorised payment surcharge, etc., under Pt 4 of the Finance Act 2004.[26] Although an analysis of the unauthorised payment charge regime is outside the scope of this book, it is important to note that the aggregate rate of tax in the above circumstances could have been up to 82 per cent of the ASP fund.

On the death of a scheme member in ASP, in determining the value of his estate for IHT purposes, he was treated as if he had been entitled at death to property with a value equal to the "relevant amount".[27] The "relevant amount" was calculated as:

(a) the aggregate of the scheme member's ASP funds before his death; less
(b) the aggregate of the assets expended on "dependants' benefits" within the period of six months beginning with the end of the month in which the death occurs.[28]

"Dependants' benefits" were defined as ASP funds which were applied or designated by the scheme administrator to provide a "relevant dependant" with an annuity, scheme pension, unsecured income drawdown arrangement or ASP fund.[29] In addition, the definition of "dependants' benefits" also included ASP funds paid to charity.[30]

A "relevant dependant" was defined in relation to the deceased ASP scheme member as his surviving spouse or civil partner or someone who was financially dependant on him at his death.[31]

The "relevant amount" was taxed as the top slice of the deceased ASP scheme member's estate.[32]

Where there was an unauthorised payment charge and an IHT charge on the same ASP funds the aggregate of the two tax charges was the same in whichever order the two taxes are charged. Where the unauthorised payment charge was deducted by the scheme administrator before the IHT was due, then the aggregate of the scheme member's ASP fund before death was reduced by the amount of the unauthorised payment charge.[33] Conversely, where IHT was due before deduction of the unauthorised payment charge, then the amount due was calculated by reference to the gross

---

[25] Inserted by Finance Act 2007 s.69 and applies in relation to deaths of a scheme member in ASP where the scheme administrator becomes aware of the death or cessation of dependency occurring on or after April 6, 2007.

[26] An analysis of the regime for the taxation of pensions under Pt 4 of the Finance Act 2004 is outside the scope of this work.

[27] IHTA 1984 s.151A(2).

[28] IHTA 1984 s.151A(3).

[29] IHTA 1984 s.151A(4).

[30] IHTA 1984 s.151A(4).

[31] IHTA 1984 s.151A(5).

[32] IHTA 1984 s.151A(2).

[33] IHTA 1984 s.151A(4A).

value of the ASP funds with an adjustment to the unused nil-rate band to set against the ASP funds. The final result was an aggregate rate of tax on the ASP funds of up to 82 per cent.

Where a scheme member with an ASP fund died leaving property chargeable to IHT net of his chargeable ASP funds that was worth less than his nil-rate band, and the IHT charge arose before the unauthorised payment charge, the amount of the unused nil-rate band was grossed up.[34] In these circumstances the ASP funds were charged to IHT on the amount of the grossed up nil rate band, and this acknowledged that the gross ASP funds were subject to a subsequent unauthorised payment charge of up to 70 per cent.

The IHT treatment of a "relevant dependant" with "dependant's benefits" was outlined in s.151B. This section applied where a "relevant dependant" died a member of a registered pension scheme and had an unsecured income drawdown arrangement or a dependant's ASP arrangement which was funded with assets inherited from the original deceased ASP scheme member.[35] The section also applied where a "relevant dependant" with an unsecured income drawdown arrangement or a dependant's ASP arrangement ceased to be financially dependant on the original ASP scheme member.[36] In these circumstances there was a charge to IHT on the remaining inherited ASP funds,[37] other than in relation to assets paid to charity.[38] The calculation of the amount charged to IHT was the same as for s.151(A) but the remaining inherited ASP funds were treated as if they were an addition to the highest part of the value of the original deceased ASP scheme member's estate, but applying the nil rate band and rate of IHT in force at the date of death, or end of financial dependency, of the "relevant dependant".[39]

Where a dependant died in ASP but the ASP funds were not inherited from a scheme member who died over the age of 75 in ASP, s.151C applied. Section 151C operated in a similar way to the charge to IHT under s.151A, but unlike the treatment of inherited ASP funds under s.151B, the "relevant amount" in the charge under s.151C could be reduced, and consequently the IHT charge, by assets used by the scheme administrator to provide a dependant's unsecured income drawdown arrangement or dependant's ASP.[40]

With the introduction of transferable nil rate bands, if on the death of the original deceased ASP scheme member his or her nil rate band was not fully used, the same proportion that was unused was applied to the amount of the nil rate band in force at the date of death, or earlier cessation, of the dependant's benefits thus reducing the IHT charge.[41] Please note that a similar calculation in relation to the transferable nil rate band that applies for recapture charges on conditionally exempt property and woodlands occurring before or after the death of the surviving spouse or civil partner[42] also applied to IHT charges arising on inherited ASP funds under s.151B arising before or after the death of the surviving spouse or civil partner.[43]

---

[34] IHTA 1984 s.151A(4B) and (4C).
[35] IHTA 1984 s.151B(1).
[36] IHTA 1984 s.151B(1).
[37] IHTA 1984 s.151B(2) and (3).
[38] IHTA 1984 s.151B(4).
[39] IHTA 1984 s.151BA.
[40] IHTA 1984 s.151C(3D).
[41] IHTA 1984 s.151BA(6) and (7). For further details regarding the transferable nil rate band, please see Ch.4.
[42] See paras 4–18 and 4–19.
[43] IHTA 1984 s.151BA(8)–(12); HMRC guidance on the transferable nil rate band published on February 4, 2009, Inheritance Tax Manual, para.43047.

The scheme administrator was responsible for the payment of any IHT under ss.151A–151C and unauthorised payment charges in relation to ASP funds.

Death of scheme member or dependant over 75 with pension or annuity between 2008 and 2011

23–20   Finance Act 2008 introduced further potential IHT charges in relation to deaths of scheme members or dependants occurring on or after April 6, 2008. However, these potential charges were removed by Finance Act 2011, with effect from April 6, 2011, which repealed s.151D subject to transitional provisions. The following only applies to deaths between April 6, 2008 and April 5, 2011.

These reforms further underlined the age of 75 as an important threshold for the taxation of individuals with pension rights and the inability to pass capital held in pension funds down directly to successive generations after reaching that age. Section 151D applied where the following conditions were met:

(a) a member of a registered pension scheme, or a dependant[44] of such a member, died after reaching the age of 75;

(b) immediately before death the scheme member or dependant had under the registered pensions scheme an actual right to payments under a relevant pension (defined in s.151D(4) as a scheme pension or dependants' scheme pension) or relevant annuity (defined in s.151D(4) as a lifetime annuity or a dependants' annuity), or a prospective right to payments under a relevant pension; and

(c) at any time after the death a relevant unauthorised payment was made by the pension scheme.[45]

The definition of a relevant unauthorised payment (see s.151D(4)) was key in discerning whether there was a potential IHT charge. A relevant unauthorised payment was any unauthorised payment[46] which resulted in the payment of a lump sum in respect of the dead scheme member or dependant. For example, where a scheme member or dependant died over the age of 75 with an annuity and on his or her death a lump sum was paid s.151D applied and there is a potential IHT charge.

The definition of a relevant unauthorised payment also included an unauthorised payment[47] which was treated as made by virtue of the operation of Finance Act 2004 s.172B by reason of the relevant death. This section was an anti-avoidance provision which applied if on the death of a scheme member of a registered pension scheme there was an increase in the pension rights (e.g. rights to an annuity or pension) of another member of the same pension scheme which was attributable to the death, and the deceased scheme member and the other member whose pension rights were enhanced were connected persons for the purposes of Income Tax Act 2007 s.993. An important exemption was that the potential IHT charge under s.151D did not apply in relation to the operation of Finance Act 2004 s.172B if the registered pension scheme in question had more than 20 members and the benefits to which the other scheme members were

---

[44] As defined in Finance Act 2004 Sch.28 para.15 and included the spouse/civil partner at the date of death of a scheme member, children of the scheme member under the age of 23 and those financially dependant upon the scheme member.

[45] IHTA 1984 s.151D(1).

[46] As defined in Finance Act 2004 s.160(5).

[47] Finance Act 2004 s.160(5).

entitled under the pension scheme are increased at the same rate as a result of the relevant death.[48]

Where an IHT charge arose under s.151D the amount on which tax was charged was the difference between the amount of the relevant unauthorised payment and the amount of the liability due in relation to the unauthorised payment charge.[49] Therefore, as with other IHT charges in relation to pension schemes involving deaths over the age of 75 the IHT charged was net of the unauthorised payment charge.

IHT charged under s.151D was charged as if it was a transfer of value by the deceased scheme member or dependant as an addition to the highest part of the deceased scheme member or dependant's estate, but applying the nil rate band and rate of IHT in force at the time of the relevant unauthorised payment.[50] With the introduction of transferable nil rate bands, if on the death of the scheme member or dependant his or her nil rate band was not fully used, applying the rules in s.8A(2), the proportion that was unused could have been set against the s.151D charge.[51] Please note that a similar calculation in relation to the transferable nil rate band that applied for recapture charges on conditionally exempt property and woodlands occurring before or after the death of the surviving spouse or civil partner also applied to a s.151D IHT charge arising before or after the death of the surviving spouse or civil partner.[52]

It can be seen that the position has been simplified since the Finance Act 2011.

IHT issues arising out of holding pension death benefits on trust after death of scheme member

It is not possible to transfer pension death benefits to transferee trustees if the scheme member dies over the age of 75. However, under the age of 75 it is possible on the death of a scheme member for death benefits to be transferred to trustees of a separate trust set up during the scheme member's lifetime. Where an individual is a member of a number of different pension schemes, collecting the various death benefits together in one transferee trust can make ongoing administration of the death benefits easier.

23–21

As a result of Finance Act 2006 most lifetime trusts established to which death benefits can be assigned will be within the relevant property charging regime, the exception being certain trusts for disabled persons.[53] HMRC's previous concessionary practice was that where pension death benefits held on discretionary trusts are transferred to beneficiaries within two years of the scheme member's death no liability to IHT arises on the basis that s.58(1)(d) and s.151 continue to apply during this period so that the death benefits are not treated as relevant property.[54] This concessionary treatment is now enshrined post A-Day in s.58(2A)(a) which extends the s.58(1)(d) exemption from relevant property charges for settled property held for the purposes of a registered pension scheme, or a Taxes Act 1988 s.615(3) scheme, during the lifetime of the scheme member for the period from the death of the scheme member until their lump sum death benefit is paid out in accordance with the scheme rules.[55] In most cases, where Finance Act 2004 paras 13(c) and 15(1)(c) of Sch.29 apply, the relevant period will be within two years of the scheme member's death and the date when the

---

[48] Finance Act 2004 s.172B(7).
[49] IHTA 1984 s.151D(3).
[50] IHTA 1984, s151E(1)–(5).
[51] IHTA 1984 s.151E(6).
[52] IHTA 1984 s.151E(7)–(11).
[53] As to which, see Ch.21.
[54] Inheritance Tax Manual, para.17530.
[55] IHTA 1984 s.58(2A)(a).

scheme member first knew of the death. Section 58(2A)(b) extends this exemption on a statutory footing to Taxes Act 1988 s.615(3) schemes and to qualifying non-UK pension schemes (QROPs) provided the lump sum death benefit is paid within the two year period beginning with the earlier of the date of notification to the scheme administrator or the date on which the scheme administrator could reasonably have known about the scheme member's death.[56] Failure to meet these extended deadlines means that the death benefits will be treated as relevant property from the death of the scheme member, and the relevant property charging regime will apply as from the date of death.

However, where the pension trustees have discretion over whom they pay the death benefits to, HMRC take the view that although the two-year concessionary period above will apply to the exercise of their discretion, if they exercise that discretion to pay the death benefits to the trustees of a transferee trust, the transferee trustees will be subject to the relevant property regime. Consequently, any distributions from the transferee trustees may be subject to an exit charge even if the distribution is made within the period of two years of the scheme member's death. HMRC accept that where pension trustees have no discretion as to the recipient of death benefits on the death of a scheme member, e.g. they are under a direction to pay the death benefits to transferee trustees, the transferee trustees have the benefit of the two year concessionary period, calculated from the date of the scheme member's death, within which to make outright distributions to beneficiaries without any exit charges.

The scheme member is treated as the settlor of the transferee trust, which is important for the calculation of periodic and exit charges within the relevant property regime. If there is no discretionary trust under the original pension scheme the transferee trust is treated as having been established on the date of the transferee trust's creation and the ten yearly anniversary charge is calculated by reference to this date. If, however, the pension death benefits was held by the pension trustees on discretionary trusts, and on the death of the scheme member the death benefits are paid to a transferee trust created by the scheme member during his lifetime, the date of the transferee trust for the purposes of the 10-yearly anniversary charge is the date the scheme member first became a member of the original pension scheme. It is therefore possible that if the transferee trust contains death benefits assigned from various different pension schemes, if the deceased scheme member joined those schemes at different times there will be multiple incidences of periodic charges.

[56] IHTA 1984 s.58(2A)(b).

TRUSTS FOR THE BENEFIT OF EMPLOYEES

Section 86 applies to a variety of trusts. It is still of considerable practical significance since the trusts to which it applies may be very substantial. In particular, s.86 applies to profit-sharing schemes approved under the Taxes Act 1988 s.186 and to share incentive plans approved under ITEPA 2003 Sch.2. **24–01**

IHTA 1986 s.86 provides:

"86 Trusts for benefit of employees

(1) Where settled property is held on trusts which, either indefinitely or until the end of a period (whether defined by a date or in some other way) do not permit any of the settled property to be applied otherwise than for the benefit of—

(a) persons of a class defined by reference to employment in a particular trade or profession, or employment by, or office with, a body carrying on a trade, profession or undertaking, or

(b) persons of a class defined by reference to marriage [to or civil partnership with,] or relationship to, or dependence on, persons of a class defined as mentioned in paragraph (a) above,

then, subject to subsection (3) below, this section applies to that settled property or, as the case may be, applies to it during that period.

(2) Where settled property is held on trusts permitting the property to be applied for the benefit of persons within paragraph (a) or (b) of subsection (1) above, those trusts shall not be regarded as outside the description specified in that subsection by reason only that they also permit the settled property to be applied for charitable purposes.

(3) Where any class mentioned in subsection (1) above is defined by reference to employment by or office with a particular body, this section applies to the settled property only if—

(a) the class comprises all or most of the persons employed by or holding office with the body concerned, or

(b) the trusts on which the settled property is held are those of a profit sharing scheme approved in accordance with Schedule 9 to the Taxes Act 1988, or

(c) the trusts on which the settled property is held are those of a share incentive plan approved under Schedule 2 to the Income Tax (Earnings and Pensions) Act 2003.

(4) Where this section applies to any settled property—

(a) the property shall be treated as comprised in one settlement, whether or not it would fall to be so treated apart from this section, and

697

(b) an interest in possession in any part of the settled property shall be disregarded for the purposes of this Act (except section 55) if that part is less than 5 per cent of the whole.

(5) Where any property to which this section applies ceases to be comprised in a settlement and, either immediately or not more than one month later, the whole of it becomes comprised in another settlement, then, if this section again applies to it when it becomes comprised in the second settlement, it shall be treated for all the purposes of this Act as if it had remained comprised in the first settlement."

Qualifying property

24–02   After March 8, 1982 in order to benefit from IHTA s.86 treatment, two requirements must be satisfied. The first relates to the persons who may be benefited and the second requirement relates to the duration of the terms of the trust.

The first requirement

The settled property must be held on trusts which do not permit any of the property to be applied except for the benefit of:

(1) persons of a class defined by reference to employment in a particular trade or profession; or

(2) persons of a class defined by reference to marriage to or civil partnership with, or relationship to, or dependence on, persons within (1) above[1]; or

(3) persons of a class defined by reference to employment by, or office with, a body carrying on a trade, profession, or undertaking,[2] provided that either:

    (a) that class comprises all or most of the persons employed by or holding office with that body; or

    (b) the trusts on which the settled property is held are those of a profit sharing scheme approved in accordance with Sch.9 to the Taxes Act 1988; or

    (c) the trusts on which the settled property is held are those of a share incentive plan approved under Sch.2 to the Income Tax (Earnings and Pensions) Act 2003; or

(4) newspaper publishing companies,[3] provided that the only or principal property comprised in the settlement is shares in a newspaper public company or a newspaper holding company.[4]

24–03   Several points may be made in relation to these requirements.

First, it is arguable that in relation to the first three paragraphs above, the use of the disjunctive "or" at the end of s.86(1)(a) suggests that if it is possible to benefit persons falling within the descriptions at both s.86(1)(a) and (b), then the first requirement is failed. The better view is that this is too formalistic an interpretation and would arguably render ineligible most trusts for the benefit of employees: a main feature of such trusts being that they seek to benefit not only the employee/former employee but also that employee's/former employee's family.

[1] IHTA 1984 s.86(1)(b).
[2] IHTA 1984 s.86(1)(a).
[3] IHTA 1984 s.87(1).
[4] IHTA 1984 s.87(2).

Secondly, paras (1) and (2) above cover employees of the same trade or profession who have different employers while para.(3) covers employees of the same company although they may undertake different trades. It is thus not possible to benefit a small group of employees such as directors or higher paid employees.

Thirdly, in para.(2), neither "relationship to" nor "dependence on" is defined. Presumably the scope of these terms will be limited only in so far as it is necessary to prevent an abuse of the relief.

Fourthly, in para.(3), the term "body" is not statutorily defined by IHTA s.86 but in the light of *Customs and Excise Commissioners v Glassborrow*[5] it is unlikely to include a sole trader or (in England) a partnership. It is understood that HMRC have regarded a group of companies as forming a "body" for this purpose.

Fifthly, it is not uncommon for the terms of the trust to permit the settled property to be applied for charitable purposes: the fact that the trusts permit such an application will not prevent the trusts from satisfying the above requirement.[6]

Sixthly, in relation to para.(4), IHTA 1984 s.87 treats persons that satisfy the requirements of IHTA 1984 s.87 as if newspaper publishing companies were within the class of persons falling with s.86(1)(a) and (b). Section 87 provides that:

(a) "newspaper publishing company" means a company whose business consists wholly or mainly in the publication of newspapers in the United Kingdom[7];

(b) "newspaper holding company" means a company which:
(i) has as its only or principal asset shares in a newspaper publishing company, and
(ii) has powers of voting on all or most important questions affecting the publishing company as a whole which if exercised would yield a majority of votes capable of being exercised thereon[8]; and

(c) shares are treated as the principal property comprised in a settlement or the principal assets of a company if the remaining property comprised in the settlement or the remaining assets of the company are such as may be reasonably required to enable the trustees or the company to secure the operation of the newspaper publishing company concerned.[9]

The second requirement

The second requirement is that to come within s.86 the settled property must be held **24–04** on the trusts set out in the above paragraphs either:

(1) indefinitely; or
(2) until the end of a period, whether defined by a date or in some other way.[10]

Provided the requirements of s.86 are met, the relief will continue to be available to settled property regardless of whether the trustees have the power to vary the trusts and the fact that settled property may or will be applicable for the benefit of persons outside the specified classes set out in paras (1)–(3) above; but the relief would no longer be

---

[5] [1975] Q.B. 465.
[6] IHTA 1984 s.86(2).
[7] IHTA 1984 s.87(3).
[8] IHTA 1984 s.87(3).
[9] IHTA 1984 s.87(3).
[10] IHTA 1984 s.86(1).

available from such time as the settled property did become applicable for the benefit of some other persons.

It should also be noted that because many employee trusts are limited to certain employees only, s.86 will rarely be applicable. Even the so-called statutory ESOP —provided for in the Finance Act 1989 ss.67–74 and Sch.5 (as amended)—by limiting qualifying employees to all those who have been employed for a qualifying period whose length is 'not less than one year and not more than three years falls outside s.86.

Favoured treatment

24–05   Favoured treatment is given to property within s.86 in the following ways.

Periodic charge. Settled property in which there is no qualifying interest in possession to which s.86 applies will not be relevant property.[11] As a result, the property is immune from the periodic charge. However, if there is an interest in possession in the settled property which satisfies the requirements of s.58(1B) or (1C), the settled property will be "relevant property" to which the relevant property regime will apply.[12] Section 58(1B) of IHTA 1984 applies where an individual became entitled on or after March 22, 2006 to an interest in possession which was not an immediate post death interest, a disabled person's interest or a transitional serial interest.[13] Section 58(1C) of IHTA 1984 deals with any company that purchases an interest in possession from an individual who became entitled on or after March 22, 2006 to that interest in possession which was not an immediate post death interest, a disabled person's interest or a transitional serial interest in the hands of that individual.

Interests in possession. A person's interest in possession is disregarded provided his interest subsists in less than five per cent of the property to which s.86 applies.[14] The result is that such an interest falls to be disregarded under s.72(2)(a) during his lifetime, e.g. if he disposes of his interest. It will also be disregarded for the purposes of the relevant property regime. Further, an individual will not be treated as making a transfer of value under s.52(1) when his interest in possession terminates. No charge will arise under s.4(1) on death in respect of any such interest which may have been comprised in an individual's estate immediately before he died.

Payments. A payment out of a s.86 trust normally gives rise to an exit charge if it is made for the benefit of a person who is, or is connected with:

(1) a person who has directly or indirectly provided any of the settled property otherwise than by additions not exceeding in value £1,000 in any one year[15]; or

(2) a person who has acquired an interest in the settled property for a consideration in money or money's worth. For this purpose, a person is treated as acquiring an interest in this way if he becomes entitled to it as a result of transactions which include a disposition for such consideration (whether to him or another) of that interest or of other property; or

[11] IHTA 1984 s.58(1)(b).
[12] IHTA 1984 s.58(1A).
[13] See Ch.11–Settled Property Definitions.
[14] IHTA 1984 s.86(4)(b), except for purposes of s.55.
[15] "Year" for this purpose means March 26, 1974–April 5, 1974, and any subsequent year assessment after 1974–74; IHTA 1984 s.72(6)(b).

(3) in a case where the employment in question is employment by a close company within the meaning of s.94,[16] a person who is a participator (as defined in s.94) in relation to that company, and who either:

    (a) is beneficially entitled to, or to rights entitling him to acquire, not less than five per cent of, or of any class of the shares comprised in, its issued share capital, or

    (b) would, on a winding-up of the company, be entitled to not less than five per cent of its assets.

It may be that the trusts on which the property out of which the payment is made are held are those of a profit-sharing scheme approved in accordance with the Taxes Act 1988 Sch.9. They may also be for the appropriation of shares to, or acquisition of shares on behalf of an individual under an employee share ownership plan approved under the Finance Act 2000 Sch.8. In such cases, no tax is chargeable under this head of an appropriation of shares in pursuance of the scheme. If the trusts are those of a share incentive plan approved under Sch.2 of the Income Tax (Earnings and Pensions) Act 2003, no tax is charged on an appropriation of shares to, or acquisition of shares on behalf of, an individual.

Rate of tax. If an exit charge is imposed, the rate at which tax is charged is computed according to special rules.

Aggregation. Property to which s.86 applies is treated as comprised in one settlement even though it might not otherwise fall to be so treated. This is simply for convenience; were the property not so treated each contributor would be regarded as a separate settlor and his contribution would be regarded as constituting a separate trust fund. However, if the settled property ceases to satisfy the requirements of s.86 that property will no longer be treated as comprised in one settlement. HMRC have indicated that they do not consider sub trusts to be trusts falling within s.86 of IHTA 1984[17]: the result is that property within sub-trusts will be regarded by HMRC as being "relevant property giving rise to periodic and exit charges in accordance with the relevant property regime".

Furthermore, by s.86(5):

> "Where any property to which this section applies ceases to be comprised in a settlement and either immediately or not more than one month later, the whole of it becomes comprised in another settlement, then, if this section again applies to it when it becomes comprised in the second settlement, it shall be treated for all the purposes of this Act as if it had remained comprised in the first settlement."

This provision is important where, for instance, an employees' trust is wound up at the end of the trust's perpetuity period and the trust property is distributed to the participants in the scheme or returned to the settlor or settlors, the property then being resettled on new s.86 trusts. Provided the whole of the property is resettled within one month the termination and resettlement are ignored, with the result that the resettlement does not constitute a disposition or a transfer of value.

Aggregation

The first 10-year charge would become due on the first 10-year anniversary of the settlement but would be reduced from the maximum 6 per cent according to when revocable appointments were made to the sub-trusts.   **24–06**

---

[16] IHTA 1984 s.72(6)(a).
[17] See HMRC Brief 18/11 (April 2011), Pt 3.

HMRC are also understood to be of the view that because the appointed property would have left the protection of the s.86 exemption at the time of the revocable appointment to the sub-trust, a charge would also become due at the time of that revocable appointment under IHTA 1984 s.72. The s.72 charge requires a complex calculation but is approximately 1 per cent for each year that property was held in the trust within the scope of the s.86 exemption before the revocable appointment was made to the sub-trust.

It is arguable that HMRC's interpretation of s.86 is flawed. Section 86 applies to trust property which,

> "is held on trusts which . . . do not permit any of the settled property to be applied otherwise than for the benefit of . . . persons of a class defined by reference to . . . employment by . . . a body carrying on a trade."

The wording of s.86 therefore refers in the present tense ("is") to the terms of a trust that do not "permit" the property to be applied for the wider class (including persons not defined by reference to the relevant employment). It is arguable that provided that the sub-trusts are revocable at the discretion of the trustee, the class of persons who are permitted to benefit from the sub-trusts remains the same: the trustee retains the power to revoke the sub-trust appointments and reappoint the sub-trust property for the benefit of the wider class comprising all or most of the employees. However, where a trustee can only revoke sub-trusts with the consent of a protector the position is clearly weaker. In *Postlethwaite's Executors v HMRC,* it was held that although beneficiaries other than the relevant employee and his family could technically benefit from the sub-trust the probability was that they would not.

Many claims are known to be pending on this point so no doubt there will be greater clarity soon.

By revoking appointments to sub-trusts a line can hopefully be drawn under the possible future application of the relevant property regime changes. If HMRC's view is upheld in any future litigation, an exit charge would be triggered by the revocation, and a s.72 charge may already have become due upon the original appointments to the sub-trusts, but liability to future 10-year and exit charges should be capped. A consequence of the revocation of sub-trust appointments is that the security of those sub-trusts is lost. The funds are no longer ring fenced, albeit subject to the power of revocation, for the benefit of particular employees and their families.

Alternatively, a trustee could consider widening the class of beneficiaries of the sub-trusts so that the class specifically includes "all or most" of the employees. HMRC's view is that until such time as the sub-trust appointments are actually revoked, the funds which have been appointed are no longer being held for "all or most" of the employees and therefore no longer qualify for the s.86 exemption. Even if HMRC agree that widening the class of sub-trust beneficiaries in this manner brings the sub-trusts within the s.86 exemption, they may still argue that up until that point the sub-trusts fell outside the s.86 exemption and as such there is still a tax liability. If this view is correct, the widening of the class would arguably have the same impact as the revocation of the sub-trusts, thereby drawing a line under the future application of the relevant property regime. This may, however, be a difficult argument for HMRC to run since by specifically bringing all or most of the employees into the class of sub-trust beneficiaries the trustee is demonstrating that all or most of the employees were always permitted to benefit from the sub-trust.

It is arguable that what is achieved by widening the class of sub-trust beneficiaries is largely semantic. Whether all or most of the employees are primary beneficiaries, secondary beneficiaries or whether a sub-trust must be revoked in order for them to benefit, the fact remains that they are "permitted" to benefit and the s.86 exemption should continue to apply.

Consequences of creating a section 86 trust

The position with regard to the establishment of, and subsequent contribution to s.86 **24–07** trusts was discussed above at para.3–59. It will be recalled that, as a result of s.13, a disposition by a close company to a s.86 trust is not a transfer of value if certain conditions are satisfied: if they are not, the normal rules apply. Under s.28 a transfer of value by an individual to a s.86 trust may be an exempt transfer.

Disguised remuneration provisions: ITEPA 2003 Part 7A

The introduction of the disguised remuneration income tax rules by Finance Act **24–08** 2011 s.26 and Sch.2 with effect from April 6, 2011 has had a significant impact on the perceived attractiveness of trusts for the benefit of employees. A detailed discussion of these provisions is outside the scope of this work, however, the salient features are set out below.

The Gateway Provision

In order to come within the ambit of the disguised remuneration provisions, the **24–09** requirements of ITEPA s.554A must be satisfied. Section 554A(1) provides:

(a) there must be an employee ("A"), or a former employee or a prospective employee of another person ("B");
(b) there must be an arrangement ("relevant arrangement") to which A is a party or which otherwise wholly or partly covers or relates to A;
(c) it is reasonable to suppose that in essence (i) the relevant arrangement, or (ii) the relevant arrangement so far as it covers or relates to A, is (wholly or partly) a means of providing, or is concerned with providing, A with rewards, or recognition or loans in connection with A's current, former or prospective employment;
(d) a relevant step taken by a relevant third person ("P"); and
(e) it is reasonable to suppose that in essence the relevant step is taken wholly or partly in pursuance of the relevant arrangement or there is some connection (direct or indirect) between the relevant step and the relevant arrangement.

For the purposes of (s) and (c)(ii) above, A includes a person linked with A[18]: a "person linked with A" includes family, relatives, business partners, close companies of which A is participator and trusts of which A is a settlor.[19]

---

[18] ITEPA 2003 s.554A(5).
[19] ITEPA 2003 s.554Z1.

The relevant step must be taken by a relevant third person (defined as A or B acting as trustee of an arrangement, or any person other than A or B).

The relevant step

24–10   The legislation goes on to define the relevant steps in more detail in ss.554B and 554C of ITEPA 2003. Broadly, there is a relevant step under s.554B if:

(a)   a sum of money or asset held by or on behalf of P is earmarked (however informally) by P with a view to a later relevant step being taken by P or any other person in relation to that sum of money or any sum of money that may arise or derive (directly or indirectly) from it; or

(b)   a sum of money or asset otherwise starts being held by or on behalf of P, specifically with a view, so far as P is concerned, to a later relevant step being taken by P or any other person in relation to that sum of money or asset or any sum of money or asset which may arise or derive (directly or indirectly) from it,

Broadly, there is a relevant step under s.554C if P:

(a)   pays a sum of money to a relevant person[20];

(b)   transfers an asset to a relevant person;

(c)   takes a step by virtue of which a relevant person acquires securities, interests in securities or securities options[21];

(d)   makes available a sum of money or asset for use, or makes that sum of money or asset available under an arrangement which permits its use (i) as security for a loan made or to be made to a relevant person, or (ii) otherwise as security for the meeting a liability, or the performance of an undertaking, which a relevant person has or will have; or

(e)   grants to a relevant person a lease of any premises with an effective duration of at least 21 years.[22]

Broadly, there is a relevant step within s.554D if, without transferring the asset to the relevant person, P:

(a)   at, any time, makes an asset available for a relevant person to benefit from in a way that is substantially similar to the way in which that relevant person would have been able to benefit from the asset had the asset been transferred to that person; or

(b)   at or after the end of the period of two years starting with the day the day on which A's employment with B ceases, makes an asset available for a relevant person to benefit from.

24–11   Several points may be made about ss.554A–554C. First, the provisions are very broad in their ambit. Secondly, the gateway provision at ITEPA 2003 s.554A imports an objective assessment in determining two important elements of the test, namely:

---

[20] "Relevant person" is defined at para.554C(3) as A or any person chosen by A or within a class of persons chosen by A and includes any other person if P is taking a step on A's behalf or at A's direction or request.

[21] As defined for the purposes of Chs 1–5 Pt 7 and "acquires" is to be read in accordance with ITEPA 2003 s.421B(2)(a).

[22] The terms "lease" and "premises" have the same meanings as they have in Ch.4 Pt 3 of ITTOIA 2005.

(1) whether the arrangement is for the provision of employment related rewards, recognition or loans to A; and (2) whether the relevant step is connected with or in pursuance of the relevant arrangement.

Thirdly, the relevant step at s.554B(1)(a) is capable of applying even if the earmarking is very informal. Note: a general fund with no sub-funds in favour of specific employees should not be subject to an earmarking charge under this provision. HMRC agree—see Employment Income Manual EIM45110.

Fourthly, in relation to the words "with a view to a later relevant step being taken" in s.554B(1)(a), it appears that where the earmarking and the other relevant step, e.g. payment to A, are simultaneous, the requirements of s.554B(1)(a) are not met so that there is no earmarking under that provision. HMRC agree: see Employment Income Manual EIM45110.

Fifthly, the relevant step under s.554B(1)(b) is theoretically a concern whenever new assets or sums of money come to be held on the terms of the employee benefit trust. The scope for double or even multiple charging is great. It is arguable therefore that a sensible interpretation that does reduces the scope of such double or multiple charging should be adopted. For example, if assets replace assets already held by the employee benefit trust for the benefit a particular employee (whether those assets were held before December 9, 2010 or after that date), the receipt of such assets by the trust should arguably not trigger an earmarking charge under s.554B(1)(b) of ITEPA 2003.

Sixthly, in relation to a relevant step under s.554C, it is clear that loans, being payments of sums of money, will be caught.

Seventhly, in relation s.554C, the wide definition of a "relevant person" ensures that these provisions catch payments made to third parties at the request or direction of A.

Eighthly, s.554D is very broad in its scope and can apply where the asset is made available on a very informal basis and even where the relevant person does not actually benefit from the asset.[23]

Ninthly, if the asset is made available on or after two years after A's employment with B ceases, there is a relevant step even though A's benefit is similar to that which he would enjoy if he owned the asset.

The exemptions

There are several exclusions from the disguised remuneration provisions set out in ss.554E–554W of ITEPA 2003. There are exclusions for Approved Schemes (ITEPA 2003 s.554E) and for Employee share schemes (ITEPA 2003 ss.554I–554M). There is also useful exclusions for commercial transactions (ITEPA 2003 s.554F), for acquisitions out of sums or assets (ITEPA 2003 s.554R), for income arising from an earmarked sum or asset (s.554Q ITEPA 2003), for pension income and contributions (ITEPA ss.554S and 554T). **24–12**

The charge

Where A is charged under these provisions the value of the relevant step comprises employment income in his hands and is included in the year in which the relevant step is taken.[24] **24–13**

[23] ITEPA 2003 s.554D(3).
[24] ITEPA 2003 s.554Z2(1).

Where the relevant step is the payment of a sum of money, the value of the relevant step is equal to the sum of money.[25]

Where the relevant step is the transfer of an asset, the value to be charged is the higher of:

(a) the market value at the time of the relevant step of the asset which is the subject of the relevant step; and

(b) the cost of the relevant step (where "cost" is the expense incurred in connection with the relevant step).[26]

Section 554Z8 of ITEPA provides relief, in certain circumstances, if full consideration is paid by A. There is an anti-avoidance element to this relief because it is necessary that there is no connection between the transfer of the asset to A and a tax avoidance arrangement. "Tax avoidance arrangement" is an arrangement which has a tax avoidance purpose.[27] One is thrown back into the quagmire of determining "purpose" in order to demonstrate that the relief is available.

Summary

24–14 The disguised remuneration provisions are broad in their scope and potentially disproportionately harsh in their impact (given the scope for multiple taxation). They are likely to discourage the creation of tax motivated employee benefit trusts. Nevertheless, they will need to be tackled in the context of extracting funds/assets from existing employee benefit trusts, whether tax motivated or not.

---

[25] ITEPA 2003 s.554Z3.
[26] ITEPA 2003 s.554Z3(2), (6).
[27] ITEPA 2003 s.554Z(3), (13).

PART THREE

SPECIAL SUBJECTS

CHAPTER 25

ESTATE, VALUATION, LIABILITIES AND REVALUATION RELIEFS

I. INTRODUCTION

25–01 This chapter is concerned with the related topics of what property is comprised in a person's estate for IHT purposes, how property is valued for IHT purposes, how liabilities are taken into account and what revaluation reliefs are available.

ESTATE

II. THE GENERAL RULE

25–02 The general rule governing what property is comprised in a person's estate is found in s.5(1) which provides that a person's estate:

"is the aggregate of all the property to which he is beneficially entitled, except that the estate of a person immediately before his death does not include excluded property."

In applying this rule, five points should be borne in mind:

(1) "Property" is widely defined by s.272 to include "rights and interests of every description but does not include a settlement power".

(2) In determining whether or not a person is beneficially entitled to property as a matter of general law regard needs to be had to whether or not he actually holds in a fiduciary capacity property which he prima facie seems to own beneficially.

710

(3) The legislation provides that in three situations a person is to be treated as beneficially entitled to property to which he is not regarded as being entitled as a matter of general law.

(4) The legislation conversely provides that in four situations property is not comprised in a person's estate notwithstanding that he is beneficially entitled to it as a matter of general law.

(5) Excluded property to which an individual is beneficially entitled for IHT purposes is generally included in his estate, not excluded from it.

Each of these points will be considered in turn.

Definition of property

The definition of "property" at s.272 is extremely wide and will include all types of **25–03** real and personal property including amongst other things, money, securities, land, buildings, debts owed and partnership interests.[1] It should be noted that it does not include rights that cannot be legally enforced.

Is the owner a fiduciary?

In determining whether or not a person is beneficially entitled to property as a matter **25–04** of general law regard needs to be had to whether or not he actually holds in a fiduciary capacity property which prima facie seems to be his. In *Anand v IRC*,[2] the sons of a deceased Iranian man claimed that funds held in an English bank account in the deceased's sole name were held as trustee for the deceased and his sons. HMRC, finding that the requirements for a trust under English law had not been fulfilled, contended that the entire amount formed part of the deceased's estate. The Special Commissioner held that, taking into account the cultural circumstances of the family, the deceased was regarded instead as acting as "treasurer" for the family, with the effect that the sums held in his bank account were impressed with a trust and so not taxed as part of his death estate.

Property deemed comprised in a person's estate

The effect of the legislation is that in three situations a person is to be treated as **25–05** beneficially entitled to property to which he is not regarded as being entitled as a matter of general law.[3]

Interests in possession

By s.49(1), a person who is beneficially entitled to an interest in possession is treated **25–06** as being beneficially entitled to the property in which his interest subsists. This

---

[1] *Simon's Tax Directory*, I3.211.

[2] *Anand v IRC* [1997] S.T.C. (S.C.D.) 58. For consideration of bank accounts generally, see paras 25–08 and 25–60.

[3] See also *Wood Preservation Ltd v Prior* [1969] 1 W.L.R. 1077; [1968] T.R. 353 and *IRC v Ufitech Group Ltd* [1977] 3 All E.R. 924; [1977] S.T.C. 363 for the meaning of "beneficially entitled" in relation to conditional contracts.

provision is fundamental.[4] It means, for example, that where immediately before a person died he was beneficially entitled to an interest in possession the value to be brought into account is that of the property in which his interest subsisted, not the market value of the interest as such. Thus, if A dies owning a life interest in £100,000, the value to be brought into account is £100,000, not the value of his interest immediately before he died. The fact that the interest ceased on his death is irrelevant since he is treated as having made the transfer immediately before he died, and at that stage he was regarded as having been beneficially entitled to the property in question.[5]

General powers

25–07 The legislation makes special provision to deal with a person who has a general power over property. Section 5(2) provides that:

> "A person who has a general power which enables him, or would if he were sui juris enable him, to dispose of any property other than settled property, . . . shall be treated as beneficially entitled to the property or money; and for this purpose 'general power' means a power or authority enabling the person by whom it is exercisable to appoint or dispose of property as he thinks fit."

This provision is unusual. Although it means that the person with the power is to be treated as owning the property to which the power relates, no provision is made to ensure that the person beneficially entitled to that property ceases to be so entitled. The legislation thus clearly contemplates the same property being comprised in the estate of two (or more) different people. Normally this should not produce unfair results; this follows from the fact that the person in whose estate the property is in fact comprised will, given the fact that the property can be appointed away from him at any time, be regarded as owning property with a nil value.

General powers over bank accounts

25–08 General powers over bank accounts were considered in *O'Neill v IRC*,[6] in the Special Commissioner decision of *Sillars v IRC*,[7] and, more recently, in the Special Commissioner decision of *Taylor v Revenue and Customs Commissioners*.[8] In *O'Neill*, a father had opened joint bank accounts in joint names with his daughter. The existence of the accounts was not disclosed in the father's divorce proceedings, and the daughter was unaware of their existence until shortly before the father's death, when he gave her an envelope to take to the local bank manager "if anything happened to him." The Special Commissioner upheld HMRC's argument that the entire amount in the account formed part of the father's estate, finding, inter alia, that because the daughter's beneficial interest had been defeasible (the father being able to withdraw the entire

---

[4] See *Fetherstonaugh v IRC* [1984] S.T.C. 261 at 270a, discussed at para.26–20.

[5] IHTA 1984 s.171(2) does not apply: see para.8–17. On a lifetime transfer the method of valuation for shares comprised in a free estate may differ from that for shares in which an interest in possession exists: see para.5–17.

[6] *O'Neill v IRC* [1998] S.T.C. (S.C.D.) 110.

[7] *Sillars v IRC* (2004) S.T.C. (S.C.D.) 180. For the treatment of joint property generally (including bank accounts), see paras 25–58–25–62.

[8] *Taylor v RCC* [2008] S.T.C. (S.C.D.) 1159.

funds in the account at any stage), the father possessed a general power over the account within s.5(2).

The facts of *Sillars* were as follows. In March 1995, as part of a tax planning exercise, a mother had made gifts of £10,000 to each of her two daughters. A few days later, she transferred a bank account holding £43,701 into joint names with the daughters, again intending to make an immediate gift. Initially withdrawals were made only by the mother to cover her own expenses or gifts by her to other members of the family. In later years, withdrawals were made by the daughters on behalf of the mother. Payments into the account were only ever made by the mother. For income tax purposes, the interest on the account was returned by the mother and the two daughters equally and at all times the daughters regarded themselves as each owning one third of the balance in the account.

Following the mother's death, HMRC considered the whole account to be taxable as part of the mother's estate under s.5(2).[9] The Special Commissioner agreed with HMRC, finding that although the mother's power was not a general power in the ordinary sense, it did fall within the definition in s.5(2). The mother was able to dispose of the balance if she chose, the withdrawals were made for her benefit and no-one paid attention to whether she withdrew more than her one-third share. In short, the mother had a power to deal with the account as she saw fit, and it was not to be regarded as inconsistent that while the daughters saw themselves as owning a third of the balance from time to time, it was also understood that the mother was free to withdraw funds from the account for her own benefit. Furthermore, the Special Commissioner confirmed that the finding would not give rise to issues of double taxation since the daughters could not be regarded as having a general power over the account. On the basis of such confirmation, one can presume that the daughters' entitlements to the account were effectively valued at nil.

In *Taylor*, a wife was left two building society accounts by her husband on his death. The wife later put the accounts into the joint names of herself and her brother-in-law. The operating instructions of the accounts were that only one signature was required and that, on death, the whole account would pass to the survivor. It was mainly the wife who made withdrawals from the accounts to cover gifts to her sister's children and grandchildren. Income tax was deducted at source and only accrued interest was added to the accounts.

It was held that the wife was not a trustee of a trust established in favour of the brother-in-law. The wife had been left all the husband's property absolutely; there was no question of a formal or secret trust having been established, despite the husband expressing the view that he wanted to benefit the brother-in-law's children and grandchildren. Furthermore, s.5 provides that a person's estate is all the property to which he is beneficially entitled. If the brother-in-law was beneficially entitled to all the money in the building society accounts and if the wife was a trustee of the accounts for him, he would be treated as owning all the money in the accounts on the death of the deceased.

The Special Commissioner followed the principle established in *Sillars*, that the type of joint account should be analysed. The wife and brother-in-law each had a general power to dispose of the whole of the accounts. The operating instructions to the accounts clearly stated that the accounts were held by the wife and brother-in-law beneficially as joint tenants, rather than tenants in common. As the wife had a general

---

[9] HMRC also argued (and the Special Commissioner agreed) that the mother had made a gift with reservation of benefit, on the basis that there had been a gift of a chose in action consisting of the whole account. Possession and enjoyment had not been assumed by the daughters and the account had not been enjoyed to the entire exclusion of the mother. See Ch.7 for a full discussion of the rules on reservation of benefit.

power of disposal, at her death she was treated as having been beneficially entitled to the accounts under s.5(2).[10]

Other points

25–09   As demonstrated by *Sillars*, s.5(2) is widely drawn, and clearly includes powers that would not be regarded as "general powers" within the ordinary meaning of the term. It would, for instance, include a special or hybrid power if the donee of that power could exercise it in his own favour[11] unless, of course, as would normally be the case, the property in question was settled property.[12]

Nevertheless, s.5(2) should not extend to:

(1) a power of appointment under a discretionary trust, since s.5(2) does not extend to a power over settled property[13];

(2) a power of attorney, because since the donee of the power is a fiduciary to the donor of the power he is able to dispose of the property only as he thinks fit in the best interests of the donor; or

(3) a mortgagee's power of sale, since he owes a duty to the mortgagor to take reasonable care to obtain a proper price.

In addition, it is to be noted that the legislation provided that in one case a person with a general power over property was not treated as being beneficially entitled to that property. It was thought that under a contract or trust scheme approved by the Board of Inland Revenue under ss.619–621[14] of the Taxes Act 1988 or an approved personal pension arrangement within ss.630–655 of that Act an annuity became payable on a person's death to his widow/widower or to one of his dependants, and that under the terms of the contract or scheme a sum of money might at his option have instead become payable to his personal representatives. By s.152, in such a case that person is not treated as having been beneficially entitled to that sum by virtue of s.5(2). However, under the Finance Act 2004 s.326 Sch.42 Pt 3, ss.618–626 and ss.630–650 of the Taxes Act 1988 were repealed.

It has been held that where an individual has power under the terms of a life policy to designate who will receive the sum assured on his death he has a general power over the sum assured. In *Kempe v IRC*[15] the deceased was entitled under the terms of a policy funded by his employer to appoint anyone he wished to receive the sum assured when he died, failing which it passed to his estate. The Special Commissioner held that the moneys payable under the policy were property because they were payable as of right. The deceased had a general power over that property because he could appoint or dispose of the sum assured as he thought fit, could designate beneficiaries, alter a designation and could ensure that the sum was paid to his estate by not making a

---

[10] The Special Commissioner held that there had been a reservation of benefit; whilst the brother-in-law enjoyed the benefit of the accounts, the wife had not been entirely excluded under the meaning of s.102 of the Finance Act 1986 as she retained the right to deal with them.

[11] See *Re Penrose* [1933] Ch. 793.

[12] For the treatment of settlement powers, see para.25–12.

[13] See also para.11–08.

[14] Or, before the commencement of ICTA 1988, under ICTA 1970 s.226 or s.226A.

[15] *Simon's Tax Intelligence*, pp.1941–1942.

designation. The policy could benefit the deceased's next of kin only if the deceased designated them and he was under no obligation to do so.

Reservation of benefit

Under the Finance Act 1986 s.102(3) a person may immediately before his death be treated as being beneficially entitled to property which would not otherwise form part of his estate if, in effect, he previously made a gift of that property and reserved a benefit in respect of it. This is discussed at length in Chapter 7. **25–10**

Property deemed not comprised in a person's estate

The legislation provides that in four situations property is not comprised in a person's estate notwithstanding that he is beneficially entitled to it as a matter of general law. **25–11**

Settlement powers

The Finance Act 2002 introduced a new term, "settlement power", into the IHT legislation by inserting into the legislation a new section, s.47A. The introduction of this new section, together with a modification to the existing s.272 definition of "property", was in response to the Court of Appeal's decision in *Melville v IRC*.[16] **25–12**

This case concerned an issue which had been a subject of concern for some time, i.e. was a general power of appointment over settled property included in an individual's estate for IHT purposes? The facts of the case were that a settlor made a discretionary settlement under which, after the expiration of 90 days from the date of the settlement, he had a power in relation to the settlement which amounted to a general power of appointment. He later transferred assets to the settlement. The issue was whether, in determining the value transferred by that transfer, account was to be taken of his power to have the trust fund transferred to him at the end of the 90-day period. If it was, the value transferred was minimal; if it was not, the value transferred was substantial.

HMRC contended that the power was not "property" within the s.272 definition, under which, as we have seen, unless the context otherwise requires, "property" includes "rights and interests of any description". They argued that the scheme of the legislation was such that "property" was used in contradistinction to "powers" and the statutory context of the treatment of settled property did not allow a general power of appointment over settled property to be treated as "property".

The Court of Appeal found unanimously for the taxpayer on the basis that the power was a valuable right and there was no contextual requirement to conclude otherwise. Such a power was of a wholly different character from a reversionary interest. The reason why the provisions relating to settled property did not include any reference to powers was that those provisions were designed to apply to the beneficial interests in settled property as they existed at any given time and to the persons for the time being entitled to them.

---

[16] *Melville v IRC* [2001] S.T.C. 1271.

The taxpayer had previously succeeded on appeal before Lightman J.,[17] whose decision had spawned a host of "*Melville* schemes". This became a deluge after the Court of Appeal's decision. The purpose of these schemes was to overcome a tax planning dilemma. Assume X wishes to make a PET of some investments pregnant with substantial gain. If, e.g., before the provisions of the Finance Act 2006 came into effect he settled the assets on interest in possession or accumulation and maintenance trusts, he would have made a PET, but he would also have made a disposal for CGT purposes in respect of which a substantial chargeable gain would accrue. He could avoid this CGT result by settling the investments on discretionary trusts, so qualifying for holdover relief under s.260(2)(a) of the Taxation of Chargeable Gains Act 1992, but that would constitute an immediate chargeable transfer rather than a PET. "*Melville* schemes" offered a solution to this problem. By reserving to himself a general power of appointment the donor could minimise the value transferred by the chargeable transfer, while at the same time accessing s.260 holdover relief. It was, of course, essential to the claim for holdover relief that some value flowed out of his estate, and therefore the general power was normally not exercisable for a specified period, 90 days. Thereafter the trustees would appoint accumulation and maintenance or interest in possession trusts and the settlor made a PET by releasing his power of appointment.

The decision was not without its adverse implications. Consider what happens where a revocable trust confers an interest in possession on the settlor. In such a case the settlor is treated by s.49(1) as beneficially entitled to the trust property. But that does not displace the fact that he also owns the right to revoke the trust, which right is apparently, under *Melville*, a freestanding right with a value equal to the value of the property comprised in the trust fund. The result is that the settlor might stand to be taxed by reference to twice the value of the trust fund. The Court of Appeal acknowledged that this point favoured HMRC, but did not regard it as determinative.

There was also another dimension not considered in argument at any stage. Assume that in 1980 A, a foreign domiciliary, established a very substantial discretionary trust which he reserved the right to revoke and that in 2000 he died deemed domiciled in the United Kingdom for IHT purposes, at a time when all the property comprised in the trust fund was situated abroad and so excluded property and therefore outside the scope of IHT.[18] Under *Melville*, A's right to revoke the trust formed a very valuable asset in his estate. And, since A was deemed domiciled in the United Kingdom for IHT purposes, the fact that his right to revoke the trust may have been situated outside the United Kingdom would not have prevented that right from being chargeable on his death.

Furthermore, *Melville* was not relevant just to foreigners who had become domiciled in the United Kingdom for IHT purposes. It could have also affected foreigners who were not so domiciled but whose right to revoke a trust was situated in the United Kingdom. In such a case that right would be subject to IHT wherever the settlor might be domiciled.

Section 47A, which, together with the amendment to s.272, effectively repealed *Melville*, was a result of various representations made to HMRC on the above points. Section 47A defines "settlement power" as meaning "any power over, or exercisable (whether directly or indirectly) in relation to, settled property or a settlement." The amended s.272 definition of "property" provides that "property" does not include a settlement power.

The scope of the definition is open to question. In particular, the question arises as to whether a veto over one or more of the trustees' powers constitutes a "settlement

[17] *Melville v IRC* [2000] S.T.C. 628.
[18] See para.32–49.

power". Such a power is arguably a power over the trustees' powers rather than a power over settled property per se; the counter argument is, of course, that the veto is still nevertheless exercisable directly or indirectly in relation to the settlement. Against this, it can be argued that the wording of s.55A(2)(b)[19] implies that such a wide reading is inappropriate. Indeed, if such a reading was appropriate it would mean that an individual's right to prevent trustees exercising their statutory power of advancement under s.32 of the Trustee Act 1925 was a settlement power. The court has been reluctant to regard such powers as causing problems in the context of accumulation and maintenance trusts[20]; it remains to be seen what attitude they will adopt in the context of settlement powers.

These changes have effect in relation to transfers of value made after April 16, 2002.[21] This prevents "*Melville* schemes" based on the retention of a general power established after that date from achieving the desired IHT effect. The changes are also deemed always to have had effect (subject to and in accordance with the other provisions of the 1984 Act) for the purpose of determining the value, immediately before his death, of the estate of any person who died before April 17, 2002, for the purposes of the transfer of value which he was treated by s.4(1) as having made immediately before his death.[22] This retrospective effect prevents the decision in *Melville* from having had the adverse consequences to taxpayers discussed above.

The fact that a settlement power is not property comprised in a person's estate raises the question of whether it is therefore to be disregarded for all IHT purposes. It may be that it is relevant in applying the reservation of benefit provisions[23] and in certain valuation contexts.[24]

Purchased settlement powers

25–13 The draftsman foresaw that by excluding settlement powers from the property comprised in a person's estate he had created a potential device for tax savings because it opened the door to a person making IHT-free gifts for IHT by purchasing a non-asset for IHT purposes. He therefore introduced anti-avoidance provisions in new s.55A to counter such gambits (see para.2–138).

New *Melville* schemes

25–14 *Melville* schemes evolved which were not rendered ineffective by the introduction by the Finance Act 2002 of the anti-*Melville* provisions. One version involved a settlor settling property on trusts under which for a period of, 100 days, trust income was held on discretionary trusts following which the trust fund reverted to the settlor absolutely. The settlor's reversionary interest was property comprised in his estate, so that he made only a small chargeable transfer when he settled the property, at which time he claimed s.260 holdover relief. He subsequently settled his reversion on interest in possession or accumulation and maintenance trusts, thereby making a PET.

---

[19] See para.2–138.
[20] See para.18–25.
[21] FA 2002 s.119(6).
[22] FA 2002 s.119(7).
[23] See para.7–79.
[24] See para.25–66.

The restrictions on holdover relief announced on December 10, 2003, and introduced by the Finance Act 2004 meant that these *Melville* schemes ceased to be effective.

Acquired reversionary interest expectant on another interest

25–15 By s.55(1), where a person entitled to any interest (whether it is an interest in possession or otherwise) in settled property acquires a reversionary interest expectant (whether immediately or not) on that interest, the reversionary interest does not form part of his estate; this is an anti-avoidance provision the purpose of which is discussed at para.32–64.

Corporation sole

25–16 By s.271, a person is not regarded as being beneficially entitled to property to which he is entitled as a corporation sole.[25] A bishop of the Church of England is thus not regarded as being beneficially entitled to property which he owns by virtue of his office.

Excluded property

25–17 By s.5(1), immediately before a person dies his estate does not include excluded property.

III. EXCLUDED PROPERTY

25–18 It is common to assume that excluded property is "excluded" from a person's estate, or perhaps, from the scope of IHT altogether. That this is not the case (subject to exceptions) is shown by three provisions. First, as we have just seen, s.5(1) provides that a person's estate immediately before he dies does not include excluded property; this clearly implies that at all other times a person's estate does include any excluded property to which he is beneficially entitled.[26] Secondly, s.3(2) provides that in deciding whether a disposition has diminished the value of a person's estate no account is to be taken of any excluded property which ceases to form part of his estate; this virtually states in terms that a person's estate includes any excluded property to which he is beneficially entitled. Thirdly, reversionary interests are normally excluded property. As was discussed above, s.55(1), by providing that certain reversionary interests are not included in a person's estate, expressly excludes certain excluded property from becoming included in a person's estate. It follows from the foregoing that, subject to s.55(1), the purchase of excluded property will not diminish the purchaser's estate.

The fact that excluded property forms part of a person's estate at all times other than immediately before his death can be important. Assume, for example, that X owns outright 25 of the 100 issued shares in X Ltd, a company incorporated abroad, and that

---

[25] Except for the purposes of IHTA 1984 s.59: see para.12–51.
[26] See IHTA 1984 s.142(5) (discussed at para.8–128) in relation to variations and disclaimers.

some time ago his father, a foreign domiciliary, settled 30 shares in X Ltd on X for life. Given the domicile of X's father when he made the settlement, the 30 shares in which X has an interest in possession are excluded property.[27] X is nevertheless treated as owning 55 shares in X Ltd, and if he gives away, say, six of the shares which he owns outright he will be treated as having relinquished control of X Ltd, with all the invidious consequences that entails.[28] In much the same way, excluded property can also be related property.[29]

VALUATION

IV. INTRODUCTION

Two kinds of rule, general and special, govern valuation for IHT purposes. The general rule is what one would expect, namely that the value to be brought into account in the absence of provision to the contrary is the open market value of the property in question.[30] The special rules fall into two categories: those which deal with particular types of property, and those, notably the related property provisions, which have more general and novel effects.   **25–19**

Valuation in practice

In practice, valuation is a notoriously difficult and inexact process. HRMC recognises that competent valuers often differ as to what value is properly attributable to property: one result of this is that in many cases agreement between HMRC and the taxpayer is reached only after years of correspondence. At first sight, it would appear that it falls invariably to the taxpayer to contend for a low valuation, and to HMRC for a high one. In fact, this is not the case and will depend on the nature of the asset or rights being valued. See, for example, para.25–57. Taxpayers will also frequently seek to establish high base costs for CGT purposes, and it is understood that in establishing a reasonable value in other contexts HMRC sometimes attribute to property a lower value than that contended for by the taxpayer, even though this reduces the tax that would otherwise be payable with respect to the transaction in question. When arguing for a particular value, the taxpayer should bear in mind the potential penalties for inaccurate reporting—see para.29–168. It is also worth noting that taxable value will only be reviewed and agreed by HMRC where there is the prospect of an immediate liability.   **25–20**

The property to be valued

It is important to note that while the same general principles will usually be adopted for most taxes in determining how property is to be valued, a fundamentally different approach will often apply in deciding what property is to be valued for a given tax. For purposes of CGT, for instance, *what* will normally fall to be valued will be the property   **25–21**

[27] IHTA 1984 s.48(3); and see para.32–49.
[28] The transfer might qualify for business relief.
[29] See para.25–69.
[30] IHTA 1984 s.160.

disposed of. Where, on the other hand, there is an actual transfer of value for IHT purposes, the property disposed of will, in theory, not be valued at all. Assume, for example, that X owns 60 per cent of the shares in X Ltd., and that he makes an actual transfer of one-quarter of his shares. As tax is charged by reference to the fall in the value of his estate occasioned by the transfer, regard will have to be had to the value of a 60 per cent holding and a 45 per cent holding, not to the value of the 15 per cent holding in fact transferred.

This will be particularly important in connection with valuations of shareholdings in private companies. It is possible to secure favourable valuations for CGT by transferring shares in blocks of less than 10 per cent of the issued shares, so that any valuation is made on the best possible basis.[31] In theory this should not be effective for IHT, since regard is had to the value of the transferor's shareholding before and after the transfer. But in practice, the problems of valuations being what they are, HMRC may be content to value only the shares in fact transferred, so long as the transfer does not disproportionately diminish the value of the transferor's estate. This is most likely to be the case where transfers made by a sale at arm's length are effected before or contemporaneously with transfers made by gift, since in this way a prima facie value will be established for the shares which, provided no disproportionate diminution has occurred, obviates the need for further valuation. This is not to say that where a, say, 60 per cent shareholding is reduced to, say, a 57 per cent shareholding, regard will be had to the value of only a 3 per cent holding; rather, the value to be ascertained would be that of three-sixtieths of a 60 per cent holding. In some cases, the associated operations provisions may also be relevant in determining precisely what shares have been disposed of for IHT purposes.[32]

Appeals

25–22   It may be that the taxpayer and HMRC are unable to agree a valuation. In that case, HMRC will issue a notice of determination under s.221. By s.222(1), the person on whom the notice is served may appeal within 30 days by written notice to HMRC, specifying the grounds of appeal. The appeal itself will be before the Special Commissioners[33] or, provided certain conditions are met direct to the High Court,[34] or, in Scotland, to the Court of Session.[35] This is subject to the qualification that, by s.222(4), where land in the United Kingdom is being valued, the appeal is heard by the Lands Tribunal or, as the case may be, the Lands Tribunal for Scotland or Northern Ireland, not by the Special Commissioners, the High Court or Court of Session.[36] In the nature of things the first tier tribunal judge in a case not involving land is far more likely to be faced with problems of a valuation which neither he nor anyone can claim experience of and will, therefore, be very much dependent on the testimony of expert witnesses.

V. THE GENERAL RULE

25–23   The general rule governing valuation for IHT is found in s.160, which provides that:

---

[31] Subject to TCGA 1992 s.19.
[32] See paras 9–13–9–14.
[33] IHTA 1984 s.222(2).
[34] IHTA 1984 s.222(3).
[35] IHTA 1984 s.222(5).
[36] This is discussed more fully at paras 29–162 and following.

"... the value at any time of any property shall ... be the price which the property might reasonably be expected to fetch if sold in the open market at that time; but that price shall not be assumed to be reduced on the ground that the whole property is to be placed on the market at one and the same time."

This rule is virtually identical to the CGT[37] and estate duty[38] rules, and the CGT and estate duty cases on valuation will therefore be relevant for IHT purposes. The following comments are based largely on the decisions in those cases.

The hypothesis

It must be borne in mind that the sale referred to in s.160 is an entirely hypothetical **25–24** one. Plowman J. made this point in a telling fashion at first instance in the leading case of *Lynall v IRC*.[39] In a passage subsequently affirmed by the House of Lords, he said:

"... it is common ground that the shares must be valued on the basis of a hypothetical sale ... in a hypothetical open market between a hypothetical willing vendor ... and a hypothetical willing purchaser on the hypothesis that no-one is excluded from buying ..."

The fact that the sale is hypothetical has a number of consequences. First, it is irrelevant that in the circumstances the property cannot in fact be sold in the open market: see *IRC v Crossman*[40] and *Lynall*.[41] Thus, when the property to be sold consists of shares in a private company, the articles of which confer rights of pre-emption on other shareholders, those restrictions are ignored in ascertaining the price the shares would fetch in the open market; though, as will be seen below, such restrictions are taken into account in fixing that price.

As was noted by Plowman J., the parties to the sale are themselves hypothetical: in particular, the characteristics and circumstances of the person who actually owns or owned the property in question are to be ignored. The hypothetical vendor has two characteristics only, he is assumed to be willing to sell (but it is thought, not anxious to do so, i.e. he must be offered a price which will induce him to sell), and he is assumed to be honest. The purchaser has three attributes, he is able to make an offer, willing (but not anxious) to do so, and he is reasonably prudent. The fact that the property has a special value to him, because, for example, it consists of shares which would give him control of a company or enable him to prevent its being wound up, or is land which adjoins his own, does not preclude his presence in the open market from being taken into account.[42]

The so-called *Crossman* principle, which applies in valuing shares subject to transfer restrictions, has been applied in valuing a leasehold flat subject to a contingent liability. In *Alexander v IRC*,[43] a flat was purchased under the "right to buy" provisions of the (then) Housing Act 1980. All or part of the discount under that legislation must be repaid in the event of the flat being sold within five years of its purchase. The taxpayer,

---

[37] TCGA 1992 s.272(1) and (2).
[38] FA 1894 s.7(5).
[39] *Lynall v IRC* [1972] A.C. 680.
[40] *IRC v Crossman* [1937] A.C. 26.
[41] *Lynall v IRC* [1972] A.C. 680; see also para.25–37.
[42] *IRC v Crossman*, and, as will be seen below at para.25–30, his presence may affect the price the property would fetch.
[43] *Alexander v IRC* [1991] S.T.C. 112; see also para.25–52.

however, died in the first year. The Court of Appeal—following *Crossman*—held that for valuation purposes the open market value must be taken and the flat was to be valued on the basis of what a purchaser would pay to stand in the deceased's shoes, i.e. taking over the liability to repay the discount should he sell the property within the prescribed period.[44]

The market

25-25   Although s.160 refers to "the" open market, the fact that there is no one market in which all kinds of property are sold has led the courts to envisage a hypothetical market with certain characteristics. In particular, it is assumed that the sale will be well advertised to all prospective purchasers, who, where unquoted shares or securities are concerned, are assumed to be informed of all information that would have been available to a real purchaser on the day in question.[45]

It is clear from the recent cases of *Bower v HMRC* and *Watkins v HMRC*[46] that, whilst the courts will consider a hypothetical market, such a market must plainly exist for the product in real life. As Lord Hoffman reminds in *Grey v IRC*,

> "it cannot be too strongly emphasised that although the sale is hypothetical, there is nothing hypothetical about the open market in which it is supposed to have taken place."

In *Bower v HMRC*, Lewison J., reversing the earlier decision of the Special Commissioners, came close to saying that if there are no purchasers in the real world for an asset of the type under review, then that is the end of the matter. A proper enquiry as to this was required in all cases.[47]

In theory, in looking at the "hypothetical market" knowledge of subsequent events is ignored, but in practice HMRC are willing to take into account subsequent events which have occurred sufficiently soon after the date by reference to which the valuation of shares is made, provided the taxpayer can establish:

(1) that the events were predictable by the board of the company or by the prospective purchaser or vendor; and

(2) that the events would have been so predictable by the hypothetical prospective purchaser or vendor either because the size of the holding in question was such that the board of the company would have had to have confided the information to him or because the information was common knowledge (e.g. the gold price was high).

---

[44] Note that in the event of a sale of such property within four years of death valuation relief under IHTA 1984 s.190 would not be available. For the application of *Crossman* in the context of agricultural tenancies, see para.25-46.

[45] See IHTA 1984 s.168(1), discussed at para.25-37.

[46] *Bower v HMRC* [2008] EWHC 3105 (Ch); *Watkins v HMRC* [2011] UKFTT 745 (TC). See also para.25-27.

[47] Lewison J.: "Although the whole world is in theory free to bid, there must be an enquiry into who is in the market. This is an enquiry, not an assumption, and in my judgement, an enquiry is an enquiry on the facts . . . although the Special Commissioner was, in my judgement, entitled to consider potential purchasers, he was not entitled to invent them." (Lewison J. did not clarify exactly what he meant by "potential purchaser" other than to rule out a mere speculator.)

Needless to say, it is open to the taxpayer to contend that subsequent events should be ignored unless the above criteria are satisfied.

In *IRC v Stenhouse's Trustees*[48] the Court of Session considered what evidence may **25–26** be adduced in determining the open market value of unquoted shares under s.160. An expert witness for the trustees had estimated the value of the shares (which included a restriction on transfer) on the basis of company accounts and the general approach of stock market investors to investment trust companies and the level of yield that such investors might expect. The trustees argued that no account should be paid to actual transactions in or agreements on value relating to the shares. The Special Commissioner ruled that evidence of actual transactions was admissible only if the transactions were sales between parties at arm's length and that evidence of previous agreements was inadmissible. The trustees sought to defend this judgment before the Court of Session on the basis that the issue between the parties was hypothetical so that reliance on any transaction in the shares could be permitted only to the limited extent allowed by the Commissioner. Not surprisingly, HMRC's appeal was allowed, Lord President Clyde concluding that the true value of an asset may be found only after employing more measures than one and checking one result with another.[49] Accordingly, the first point argued for the trustees was "incomprehensible" whilst, on the second point, evidence of previous agreements had regularly been admitted as evidence of the value that would have been arrived at in hypothetical transactions in rating cases. Such evidence was therefore admissible in the present case. The conclusion is one of common sense: there may be many approaches to valuing property and the court has to weigh up the various alternatives suggested and determine how much weight is to be given to each.

The sale: "natural units"

Under estate duty, individual items of property were traditionally grouped in a **25–27** commonsense way for purposes of the hypothetical sale postulated by that legislation; elaborate subdivisions which artificially reduced or increased the value of property were to be ignored in favour of what was described as "the natural unit" (i.e. "any part of the estate which it is proper to treat as a unit for valuation purposes"). Thus, where individual items would have fetched a better price if sold as a group, the sale was assumed to be a collective one: see *Duke of Buccleuch v IRC*[50] and *Att Gen of Ceylon v Mackie*.[51]

For IHT purposes, the approach was re-addressed in the case of *Gray (surviving executor of Lady Fox, Deceased) v IRC*,[52] which looked again at the concept of the "natural unit" proposed in *Buccleuch*. Lady Fox owned the Croxton Estate in Huntingdonshire. The major part of the estate, some 3,000 acres, was let to a farming partnership in which she had a 92.5 per cent interest. She also had special rights of management and was obliged to provide all additional finance that might be required by the business. Although the other partners played a real commercial role in the management of the farming enterprise they subscribed only a small amount of capital, were not resident on the estate, and had their main business activities elsewhere. After

[48] *IRC v Stenhouse's Trustees* [1992] S.T.C. 103.
[49] *Duke of Portland v Woods Trustees* (1926) S.C. 640.
[50] *Duke of Buccleuch v IRC* [1967] 1 A.C. 506.
[51] *Att Gen of Ceylon v Mackie* [1952] 2 All E.R. 775.
[52] *Gray (surviving executor of Lady Fox, Deceased) v IRC* [1994] S.T.C. 360. For the implications of *Gray* on CGT valuations, see para.25–34.

Lady Fox's death in 1981, the partnership continued with the executors joining in the partnership until (an event not contemplated at the date of death) the estate was sold in 1984. The other partners received, for their interests in the tenancy, a sum arrived at by arm's length agreement.

The issue under consideration was how the freehold interest in the land should be valued. For these purposes, the following figures were agreed:

- Valuation of freehold interest in the land with vacant possession: £6,125,000.
- Value subject to tenancy: £2,751,000.

HMRC sought to increase the value of the freehold land by arguing that if the land and the partnership share were sold together they would fetch more than if both were sold separately. Their argument involved first establishing an overall value for the combined asset (being the partnership share and the land) and then deciding the "appropriate proportion" of this overall value to be attributed to the freehold land. To calculate the overall value it was necessary to start with the vacant possession value of the land, and to assume that the overall price for the freehold plus the partnership share would reflect this value, as reduced by the likely cost of buying out the minority partners and a discount to allow for the delay and complexity of obtaining vacant possession. The following elements were therefore brought into the calculation:

(1) Surrender value of the tenancy to be attributed to the partnership (approximately 45 per cent of the difference between vacant and tenanted values): £1,500,000.
(2) 7.5 per cent share attributable to partners other than Lady Fox: £100,000.
(3) Additional deduction attributed to delay, etc. in buying out other partners (being 7.5 per cent of vacant possession value): £460,000.

Accordingly, taking vacant possession value as £6,125,000 and deducting costs of £560,000 would produce a sum paid by the hypothetical purchaser of £5,565,000 of which the proportion attributable to the freehold land element of the package (as distinct to the partnership share) was £4,280,768.

The Lands Tribunal found at first instance that the freehold interest and the partnership share did not constitute a single unit under s.38 of the Finance Act 1975 (the equivalent of s.160) and that, as a matter of law, it had no power to aggregate the two distinct interests. Nor did the freehold interest and the partnership shares form a "natural" unit of property, so apportionment was inappropriate. However, it went on to suggest that if it could be judged appropriate to aggregate the two interests, HMRC were correct in their valuation.

On appeal, the Court of Appeal unanimously agreed that a unit of property within s.38 of the 1975 Act could comprise two or more component parts of any property, where one part comprised land and one part comprised something other than land, if that was the course that a prudent hypothetical vendor would have adopted. The court looked again at the finding in *Buccleuch* that items could only be lotted if they formed a "natural unit". Hoffman L.J., giving the main judgment, noted that while the "natural unit" had been a helpful term in that earlier case, it would be wrong to "elevate the term . . . to a universal touchstone for the application of the *Buccleuch* principle":

"The principle is that the hypothetical vendor must be supposed to have 'taken the course which would get the largest price' provided that this does not entail 'undue expenditure of time and effort'. In some cases this may involve the sale of an aggregate which could not reasonably be described as a 'natural unit'. Suppose, for example, there is evidence that at the relevant time a prudent seller would have discovered that a higher price could be obtained by the combined sale of two items which might otherwise have been thought entirely unrelated to each other. Such circumstances might arise from the peculiar demands of a small number of potential buyers or even those of a single one. In my view the hypothetical seller would in those circumstances have been, subject to the caveat I have mentioned, willing to sell the items together. The fact that no one would have described them as a 'natural unit' is irrelevant."[53]

In the absence of any other valuation, the value put forward by HMRC was accepted.

It will not, however, be the case that lotting will always be appropriate whenever the taxpayer has an interest both in the freehold and leasehold. On the particular facts of *Gray*—and especially the evidence that the livelihoods of the other parties were not bound up with a continuation of the partnership—a prudent purchaser could envisage that by the somewhat unusual route of acquiring the freehold reversion and a partnership interest he would eventually obtain vacant possession of the property. In the (perhaps more typical) case where the lease is to working members of the family and where its continuation is envisaged, *Gray* would not appear to justify lotting (the case of *Walton v IRC*,[54] discussed at para.25–46 below, may be taken as illustrative of such arrangements).

While the arrangement in *Gray* was common enough in the 1970s and 1980s, the current availability of 100 per cent agricultural relief means that such structures are less advantageous. In cases where lotting is not applicable, there may be relatively little to be gained from breaking existing structures; for instance, if it is assumed that property subject to a lease is worth 50 per cent of vacant possession value then, with agricultural property relief at 50 per cent, the tax charge (at 40 per cent) is at a rate of 10 per cent (on vacant possession value), which, paid by interest free instalments over 10 years, gives an annual charge of just over 1 per cent.[55]

In a case such as *Gray* where lotting is appropriate, although a near vacant possession value will be taken, agricultural relief, as a matter of strict law, would be limited to 50 per cent. Recognising the problem this could cause, HMRC confirmed in correspondence with the Country Landowners Association that, subject to close examination of the facts, 100 per cent relief will be given in three situations (albeit that on the strict wording of the legislation only the lesser (50 per cent) relief would be available). The three situations are:

(1) When the related property provisions apply to tenancies granted between spouses; for instance, where a husband grants a tenancy over his land to himself and his wife.
(2) In cases where the landowner has granted a *Gladstone v Bower* tenancy (i.e. a tenancy that must last for more than one year but less than two years).
(3) In cases such as *Gray* where lotting has occurred.

It seems that HMRC may give further consideration to other situations where the material interest in the land transferred is valued at near vacant possession value.[56] Furthermore, ESC F17 specifically provides that:

"On a transfer of tenanted agricultural land, the condition in I.H.T.A. 1984, s.116(2)(a) is regarded as satisfied where the transferor's interest in the property either:
(1) carries a right to vacant possession within 24 months of the date of transfer; or

---

[53] *Gray v IRC* [1994] S.T.C. 360 at 376–377.
[54] *Walton v IRC* [1996] S.T.C. 68.
[55] See *Private Client Business* (London: Sweet & Maxwell, 1994), pp.210–217.
[56] See *Private Client Business* (London: Sweet & Maxwell, 1995), p.10.

(2) is, notwithstanding the terms of the tenancy, valued at an amount broadly equivalent to the vacant possession value of the property."

25–28   On a similar note, HMRC has been known to contend that vacant possession values should be brought into account where a taxpayer makes a lifetime transfer of a freehold property encumbered by a lease owned by a company which he controls, on the basis that, by virtue of his control, he can secure vacant possession value. The authors have considerable reservations as to whether this argument is correct,[57] and indeed such an argument was rejected by the Court in the CGT case of *Henderson v Karmel's Executors*.[58] The case concerned the 1965 market value of land owned by the taxpayer which she let to a company that she controlled. The *Buccleuch* and *Mackie* cases referred to above were both considered by Nourse J., who concluded that:

> " . . . there would still have been two assets to be disposed of; first, the company's tenancy, which would either have had to be assigned to the purchaser or first surrendered to [the taxpayer] and, secondly, the reversion, which would have had to be conveyed to the purchaser. The first was an asset of the company and the second an asset of [the taxpayer]. I think it impossible to say that, because [the taxpayer] could in one way or another have extinguished the company's asset, therefore her asset was the unencumbered freehold and not the reversion expectant on the determination of the tenancy . . . In my view it is impossible to describe the procuring of the extinction of a tenancy as part of the arrangements preliminary to a sale of the freehold . . .
>
> Even if I were to assume that [the taxpayer] was the beneficial owner of all [the company's] shares and its sole director, I could not assume that a voluntary surrender or assignment of the company's tenancy would at any given time have been valid as a matter of company law. For all I know the company might have been in a parlous financial condition which would have enabled a liquidator to set the disposition aside."[59]

Section 10 to the rescue

25–29   As was seen above, s.160 expressly provides that the price which property might reasonably be expected to fetch if sold in the open market shall not be reduced on the ground that the whole property is placed on the market at the same time. The result is that a higher value may be attributed to property than would in fact be obtained from a sale in the open market. This may constitute a trap for the unwary. Assume, for example, that a father sells to his son 3,000 acres of land comprising six separate farming units. It could be that the market price for a single holding of 3,000 acres is less than the market price for a total of six farming units of 500 acres sold separately: in that case, the sale will diminish the value of the father's estate, and prima facie he will have made a transfer of value. Fortunately, a vendor in such circumstances should be relieved from making a transfer of value by s.10(1).[60]

The price

25–30   The assumed sale is hypothetical but if the asset being valued is of a type which is bought and sold in the real world the price realised by similar assets which have been

---

[57] See *Capital Taxes—A Quarterly Commentary* (1986), pp.2–7.
[58] *Henderson v Karmel's Executors* [1984] S.T.C. 572. The case primarily concerned the market value for CGT purposes. For the relationship between valuations for IHT and CGT, see para.25–34.
[59] *Henderson v Karmel's Executors* [1984] S.T.C. 572 at 577–578.
[60] See paras 2–41–2–52.

sold may be taken as to provide guidance of what might be realised in a hypothetical sale of a similar asset.

"Price" means the best possible price obtainable, but this does not mean that it is to be assumed that the hypothetical vendor would go to extremes to increase the price the property might otherwise fetch. Section 160 specifically provides that the price to be brought into account is the price that could *reasonably* be obtained in the open market: the sale is thus assumed to be on competitive, economic terms.[61] In determining the price, a number of factors may have to be brought into account, included among which are the following.

The special purchaser.[62] The extent to which the presence in the market of a special purchaser is to be taken into account in determining the price the property in question would fetch is not completely clear. In the early case of *IRC v Clay*[63] which was followed in *Glass v IRC*[64] the price the special purchaser, (an institution adjoining the deceased's former residence), was prepared to pay was the price brought into account. However, in the *Crossman* case the general view of the House of Lords appears to have been that the presence of a special purchaser was but one of the many factors to be taken into account; this is the view taken by most practitioners, and, it is understood, by HMRC, at least where the valuation of shares is concerned. The price he is willing to pay will normally increase the price that might otherwise be obtained, but will not be by itself conclusive. Any contention that members of the transferor's family would pay a special price for the property, where, e.g. shares in a family company are involved, needs in practice to be substantiated by specific and cogent evidence as to their intent and means before it will be accepted by HMRC. Where there is one possible purchaser only in the real market, there is persuasive (Privy Council) authority for the proposition that the presence of other purchasers must be assumed; otherwise the sale would be a forced rather than a voluntary one.[65]

Restrictions on sale. Where the property is subject to restrictions, the correct procedure is to assume that the property can be sold, but that any subsequent sale by the assumed purchaser will be subject to the same restrictions as at present affect the vendor.[66] The result is that the market price, although based on the assumption that the property is freely transferable, will be reduced to take the restrictions into account. This rule applies to restrictions such as the abovementioned rights of pre-emption on the sale of shares in a private company. Special rules apply where property is subject to a restriction for which consideration in money or money's worth was given, e.g. where the property is subject to a purchased (as opposed to a gifted) option.[67] In the case of jointly owned property, the co-owner's rights to the property will have a bearing on the price—see paras 25–58–25–62.

Costs of sale. Under estate duty, the open market price was the gross price before any deduction for the costs of sale. That this is also the case for IHT is implied by s.173, which provides that when foreign property passes on death an allowance is made for

---

[61] *Duke of Buccleuch v IRC* [1967] 1 A.C. 506—see, in particular, Lord Reid at 525: "We must take the estate as it was when the deceased died; often the price which a piece of property would fetch would be considerably enhanced by small expense in a minor repair or cleaning which would make the property more attractive to the eye of the buyer. But admittedly that cannot be supposed to have been done".

[62] For consideration of the special purchaser in the context of land valuations, see *Private Client Business* (London: Sweet & Maxwell, 2003), pp.283–291.

[63] *IRC v Clay* [1914] 3 K.B 466.

[64] *Glass v IRC* [1915] S.C. 449.

[65] See *Raja Vyricherla Narayana Gajapatiraju Bahadur Garbut v Revenue Divisional Officer, Vizagapatam* [1939] A.C. 302; *Walton v IRC* [1996] S.T.C. 68 (considered at para.25–46); and *Charkham v IRC* (1997) (a decision of the Lands Tribunal on May 6, 1997, considered in *Private Client Business* (London: Sweet & Maxwell, 1997), p.203); and see para.25–61.

[66] *IRC v Crossman* [1937] A.C. 26; *Lynall v IRC* [1972] A.C. 680.

[67] These rules are discussed at para.25–72.

additional expense which is shown to be attributable to the fact that the property is situated abroad.[68] By way of contrast, under the CGT legislation, costs of sale are expressly allowed as a deduction by s.38(1)(c) of the Taxation of Chargeable Gains Act 1992.

It is important to note that while costs of selling the property being valued are not to be taken into account, other costs may be relevant.[69] Assume, for example, that the property in question consists of shares which are valued on the basis that the best price would be obtained by winding up the company in question. In such a case the tax liability in respect of any balancing charges and any liability to CGT would in effect be brought into account, as may both the costs of the liquidation itself and of making redundancy payments due to employees.

Property situated abroad

25–31   The legislation does not lay down any special rule for the valuation of foreign property; it is understood that HMRC generally adopt the same approach to such valuations as they did for estate duty. This means that the value to be attributed to the property must be expressed in sterling, whether the hypothetical sale is assumed to take place in the United Kingdom or abroad. Where the sale is assumed to take place abroad, HMRC practice is first to value the property in local currency, and then to convert it into sterling according to the exchange rate on the date of valuation. Normally the London buying rate, which gives the lowest sterling equivalent, is adopted. The "best price" rule will usually mean that the hypothetical sale takes place in the country where the property is situated, although if there is an active market in the United Kingdom for the property, e.g. where shares in a foreign company are dealt in on the London exchange, the sale may be assumed to take place on the UK market.[70]

Blocked foreign assets

25–32   It may be that under the exchange control regulations of the country in which the property is situated neither the property nor the proceeds of sale can be taken out of the country. Where property is blocked in this way, account must be taken of the effect of this blocking on the value of the property. HMRC recognise this, and allow such discount from the official rate of exchange as they consider appropriate in the circumstances.

Rates of exchange

25–33   The normal practice is to adopt the London buying rate on the date of valuation. As this results in the lowest sterling value, this practice usually operates to the taxpayer's advantage, but it is open to him to show that some other rate is more appropriate.

[68] See paras 8–28 and 25–89. To compare sales of heritage property, see para.27–37.
[69] For the treatment of foreign expenses on sale of property, see para.25–89.
[70] Some shares, particularly in South African companies, are identifiable as being dealt with in London or Johannesburg as the case may be. Where such shares cannot be dealt with in London, they cannot be treated as being sold in London but must instead be treated as having been sold abroad, e.g. in Johannesburg.

Where currency is actually sold, the rate in fact obtained may apply. Where no rate is available, e.g. because of political factors, a rate must be estimated on the basis of available information. It may be, notably in the context of double tax relief, that it is necessary to convert foreign duty to sterling. In such cases, it is official practice to use the London selling rate on the day the foreign duty was paid, so as to give a larger credit.

Relationship with CGT

The relevance for CGT purposes of a valuation on death of an estate on which no **25–34** IHT is in fact payable was considered in the *Tax Bulletin* for April 1995 at p.210, which carried the following note under the heading "Inheritance Tax: Valuation of assets at the date of death":

"Where the value of an asset is ascertained for Inheritance Tax (IHT) purposes on the owner's death, this is also taken as the beneficiary's acquisition value for capital gains tax (CGT) purposes. We have been asked to say whether the Revenue [as it then was] will ascertain the value of the estate assets using the IHT principles, where either:
- the asset is wholly exempt or relieved from IHT; or
- no IHT is payable on the deceased's estate,

in order to provide a value for any other Revenue purpose, in particular the CGT acquisition value.

The value of an asset for IHT purposes is usually the price it would realise if sold in the open market. In certain circumstances special rules may apply to give a different value. For example, under the related property provisions of s.161 Inheritance Tax Act 1984, property held jointly by husband and wife is treated as a single unit in arriving at the value of their respective interests.

IHT is charged on the assets in a person's estate on death if their value together with the value of any chargeable lifetime gifts exceeds the IHT 'threshold' (£200,000 for deaths and other chargeable events occurring on or after April 6, 1996). There are various exemptions and reliefs. These include the exemption for assets given to a surviving spouse and up to 100 per cent relief for agricultural or business property.

If an asset is wholly exempt or relieved from IHT, neither the personal representatives of the deceased nor the Revenue can require the value of that asset to be ascertained for IHT purposes.

Where it is evident that any possible increase or decrease in the value of the chargeable assets of the estate, as included in an Inland Revenue Account, will leave the total value of the estate below the IHT threshold, it will not be necessary to ascertain the value of all the individual assets for IHT purposes. In some cases, particularly where the estate is close to the threshold, values may be considered but not necessarily 'ascertained'.

For example, the value included in the Inland Revenue Account for a holding of shares in an unquoted company might appear to the Revenue's Shares Valuation Division (SVD) to be too high. In this situation, as no IHT is at stake, SVD is unlikely to negotiate an ascertained value or IHT. On the other hand if the value included seems, on the face of it, too low, SVD may negotiate an ascertained value if the likely amount of IHT at stake warrants this.

If the value of an asset is not ascertained for IHT, the normal rules of s.272 of the Taxation of Chargeable Gains Act 1992 will apply to determine the CGT acquisition value of the beneficiary.

We have also been asked how the Revenue will approach the valuation of a holding of shares in an unquoted company where not all of the company's assets qualify for IHT business property relief, so that the shares are not wholly relieved. Again, SVD's approach will depend very much upon whether in any event IHT is payable and, if so, the amount of tax involved. SVD is unlikely to negotiate an ascertained value for the holding if very little or no tax is at stake."[71]

HMRC looked further at the relationship between IHT and CGT valuations in the August 1996 issue of *Tax Bulletin*, in the context of *Gray (surviving Executor of Lady Fox, Deceased) v IRC*.[72]

"We have been asked whether the decision of the Court of Appeal [. . .] has any implications for the valuation of assets for the purpose of capital gains tax.
The *Gray* case concerned the valuation of assets for what is now inheritance tax (IHT) but was at the material time capital transfer tax (CTT). Section 4 Inheritance Taxes Act (I.H.T.A.) 1984 deems a transfer of value to have been made for the purpose of CTT/IHT immediately before death equal to the value of the deceased's estate at that time. Section 5 I.H.T.A. 1984 defines a person's estate as 'the aggregate of all the property to which he is beneficially entitled'. Section 160 I.H.T.A. 1984 provides that [. . .] the value of any property at any time is [. . .] the price which the property might reasonably be expected to fetch if sold in the open market at that time [. . .]'. The main question in *Gray* was whether two items of property comprised in the deceased's estate must be taken separately or whether they could be treated as one unit for valuation under section 160 I.H.T.A. 1984.
The principle that emerged from *Gray* is that two or more different assets comprised in an estate can be treated as a single unit of property if disposal as one unit was the course that a prudent hypothetical vendor would have adopted in order to obtain the most favourable price without undue expenditure of time and effort.
This principle will be applicable to capital gains tax (CGT) valuations in which the statutory hypothesis on which the valuation is based deems two or more assets to be disposed of together. Examples will include:
- an acquisition by personal representatives or legatees under section 62 Taxation of Chargeable Gains Act (T.C.G.A.) 1992 of assets of which a deceased person was competent to dispose,
- an acquisition of settled property under section 71(1) T.C.G.A. 1992 on the occasion of a person becoming absolutely entitled to that settled property.
Where the principle established in *Gray* is followed, so as to value a number of assets collectively to produce a total valuation in excess of the value of the assets valued separately, an apportionment will be required in accordance with section 52(4) T.C.G.A. 1992. The apportionment is to be made on a just and reasonable basis and so must reflect the value of each of the assets. Commonly this will require an apportionment of the total value in proportion to the value of each asset.
Where the statutory hypothesis requiring a valuation proceeds on the assumption of a disposal of a single asset by itself the principle established in *Gray* cannot apply. For example, in *Henderson v Karmel's Executors* [1984] S.T.C. 572 the court held that even though at April 6, 1965 Mrs Karmel owned both the freehold interest in a farm and controlled the tenant company, so having the power one way or another to terminate the company's interest, that was insufficient to value the freehold interest on a vacant possession basis for CGT rebasing to April 6, 1965.
Other examples of valuation hypotheses for which assets will continue to be valued singly include:
- section 17 T.C.G.A. 1992 where there is a disposal of an asset for consideration deemed to be equal to its market value.
- section 35 T.C.G.A. 1992 when a valuation of an asset is required for the purpose of rebasing to March 31, 1982.
The single asset valuation for section 17 T.C.G.A. 1992 is modified by section 19 T.C.G.A. 1992 where there is a series of linked transactions between connected persons. Each

---

[71] See also *Private Client Business* (London: Sweet & Maxwell, 1995), p.219. See para.25–143 for the treatment of assets passing to an exempt beneficiary where revaluation relief will not be available for CGT purposes on a sale within the fourth year after death.
[72] *Gray (surviving Executor of Lady Fox, Deceased) v IRC* [1994] S.T.C. 360; see para.25–27.

disposal in the series may be treated as being made for consideration equal to a proportion of the aggregate value of all the assets in the series."

VI. APPLICATIONS OF THE GENERAL RULE

The application in practice of the market value rule gives rise to a number of considerations which vary according to the property which falls to be valued.[73] The following points should be borne in mind.

25-35

Unquoted shares and securities

The valuation of unquoted shares and securities is a subject in itself which is beyond the scope of this book. Bearing in mind the adage about the dangers to which a little knowledge may give rise, the authors have accordingly considered only the provisions in the legislation which are expressly concerned with this topic.[74]

25-36

Generally speaking, the normal market value rule applies, subject to one qualification, namely that by s.168(1) (the only provision in the legislation which expressly deals with the valuation of unquoted shares and securities):

25-37

> "In determining the price which unquoted shares or unquoted securities might reasonably be expected to fetch if sold in the open market it shall be assumed that in that market there is available to any prospective purchaser of the shares or securities all the information which a prudent prospective purchaser might reasonably require if he were proposing to purchase them from a willing vendor by private treaty and at arm's length."

This provision renders part of the decision in *Lynall v IRC*[75] irrelevant. In that case, one of the conclusions of the House of Lords was that unpublished information confidential to the directors of a company was not to be taken into account in valuing the shares in that company. This was so notwithstanding the fact that such information would often be available to a purchaser in a sale by private treaty, and, when available, would almost invariably affect the value of the shares. This aspect of the decision of the House of Lords has been rendered nugatory.

The legislation does not provide any guidance as to the kind of information a prudent prospective purchaser might "reasonably" require, and this will necessarily depend on the facts of each case. As a general rule, it is thought that a person with a controlling shareholding will normally be able to secure full disclosure of information, but will not be able to secure valuations. A person who holds between 25 per cent and 50 per cent of the issued shares should be able to require fairly full disclosure from the directors, including trading prospects, the nature of any investments held, and whether a listing, take-over or merger is imminent. Whether a person holding at least 5 per cent but less than 25 per cent of the issued shares is in a much weaker position than a person with a 25 per cent to 50 per cent shareholding may depend on the amount of money at stake. It is thought that if the amount is substantial their positions will be generally the same. If a smaller amount is involved, the smaller shareholder will probably be entitled to be

---

[73] For the treatment of property held by way of partnership, see Ch.28.

[74] As a starting point for further research, a basic summary of some of the key issues can be found in "Back to Basics—Share Valuation", *Tax Journal*, June 26, 2000.

[75] *Lynall v IRC* [1972] A.C. 680; see also para.25–24.

informed only of the general trends of the business. A person with a holding of less than 5 per cent will normally be in the position of an ordinary member of the public.

Quoted shares and securities

25–38   Section 272 defines quoted securities as "any shares or securities ... listed on a recognised stock exchange". HMRC accept as "recognised" a stock exchange recognised in the country in which it is situated and which provides a trading floor broadly comparable to that afforded by the Stock Exchange.[76]

There is no provision in the legislation for determining the market value of quoted shares and securities; in practice the so-called "quarter-up" rule provided for CGT purposes by s.272(3)(a) of the Taxation of Chargeable Gains Act 1992 is applied. Under this rule, the price to be brought into account is the lower limit of the shares for the day in question, plus one-quarter of the difference between the lower and higher limit of the quotation for that day, unless a price halfway between the highest and lowest bargains for that date is lower. Thus, if the quotation is 100–102, the price to be brought into account will be 100.5, unless the price halfway between the highest and lowest bargains for the day is lower, in which case that lower figure is the price of the shares. In the event that there is one bargain only, that price may be brought into account; bargains at special prices are left out of account.

Quotations are taken from the Stock Exchange Daily Official List.[77] Bargains for a given day are found in the listings of the day in question, unless the bargain occurs after 14.15, in which case it is found in the following day's list, where it is marked with a "F". It is important to note that quoted prices normally include any accrued dividends or interest. This is because where a company declares a dividend, it states that the dividend is to accrue to those persons listed as shareholders on its register at a certain date after the declaration of the dividend, but before the dividend is in fact due to be paid. This means that a person who sells his shares after that date, but before the dividend is in fact paid, is entitled to the dividend even though when it is paid he no longer owns the shares. The Official List takes account of this by noting, once the specified date has been passed, that the shares are to be sold "ex-dividend", i.e. without the dividend: such shares are marked "xd". It follows that in valuing shares (or securities) which are quoted ex-dividend, the agreed dividend (or interest) must be brought into account separately. It is to be noted that the Official List sometimes fails to include the "xd" marking a few days before the payment of the dividend or interest.

Where no quotation is available on the day on which the valuation falls to be made, because, for example, the Exchange is closed, regard may be had either to the last or next available quotation. Where more than one kind of share is being valued, each kind is valued separately, so that reference may be made to the last quotation for, say, ICI shares, but to the next available quotation for, say, shares in BP.

In the case of foreign stocks and shares quoted in the Stock Exchange Daily Official List, HMRC practice is to take the price quoted in the List rather than a foreign quotation, unless there is a dual register. The "quarter-up" rule is normally applied, although the price halfway between the highest and lowest bargains may also be

---

[76] Both tiers of the National Association of Securities Dealers Automated Quotations (or NASDAQ) were recognised by HMRC from March 10, 1992.

[77] Back copies of the Stock Exchange Daily Official List are available from the Stock Exchange. The Financial Times Business Research Centre also offers an historic price service.

accepted. If there is no List quotation, or there is a dual register, regard is had to the quotations on an appropriate local stock exchange.[78]

Exceptionally, regard will be had to some basis of valuation other than market quotations. This would be the case, where, for example, there have been no bargains for a substantial period, with the result that the quoted prices, whether on the London Exchange or abroad, were not an accurate guide to the true open market value of the shares.

Where British Government, local authority or public board stocks have less than five years to run they are marked with a reference "*1k*" to the back page. This indicates that the amount to be paid by the purchaser is the bargain price plus an amount equal to the gross interest which had accrued up to the date for which the bargain was done. It may be that the bargain is "ex-interest"; in that case the amount payable is the bargain price, less an amount equal to the gross interest accruing between the date for which the bargain was done and the date on which the interest is paid.

Where quoted shares or securities which were comprised in a person's estate immediately before his death are subsequently sold within one year of his death for a price less than the value attributed to the share immediately before his death, the revaluation rules discussed below at paras 25–131 and following may apply.

Securities on the Alternative Investment Market

The Alternative Investment Market ("AIM") was introduced in June 1995 as a **25–39** successor to the Unlisted Securities Market. Securities which are dealt on AIM do not fall within s.272 of the Taxation of Chargeable Gains Act 1992 and for IHT purposes are treated as unquoted shares.[79]

Unit trusts

The buying and selling prices of unit trusts are not always published. When they are **25–40** published, HMRC accept the lower price, i.e. the price at which the trust will buy back units from unit holders. Where no price is published on the day in question, the position is the same as with quoted shares, regard may be had to the last or next available price. Where price changes are not published daily, HMRC are usually prepared to accept the last published price as applying until a new price appears. Where units which were comprised in a person's estate immediately before his death are subsequently sold within 12 months of his death for a price less than the value attributed to the units on his death, the revaluation rules discussed at paras 25–109 and following may apply.

Mutual societies—take-overs and mergers

The position of members of a mutual society who become entitled to shares or cash **25–41** on completion of a merger, takeover or conversion of the business was commented on by the Capital Taxes Office in their newsletter of December 1997:

---

[78] See fn.68 above.
[79] IHTA 1984 s.105(1ZA).

"The qualifying members of a number of mutual societies have recently been receiving shares or cash on completion, take-over or conversion of the society business.

If a person died on or after the completion of vesting date, the shares or cash will of course form part of the estate. Additionally, we take the view that if a person died after the issue of a transfer document or prospectus but before the vesting date, the anticipated rights of the investor or borrower should be reflected in the open market value of that person's share in the society as at the date of death.

The value of the qualifying member's share is determined by what is due or received at the anticipated market price. This is generally disclosed in the transfer document or prospectus. The value will attract an appropriate discount to reflect uncertainty or delay in receiving the distributions due."[80]

The issue came before the courts in *Ward (Executors of Cook, Deceased) v IRC*.[81] The deceased in this case had several accounts with the Woolwich Building Society. On January 11, 1996, the Woolwich announced its proposal to convert to a public limited company, and a year later a transfer document containing details of the proposed conversion was made available. Members resolved to convert on February 11, 1997, and the deceased died on May 10, 1997. The flotation finally took place on July 7 of that year. HMRC contended that the deceased's building society accounts were at the time of death enhanced by a certain sum to reflect the anticipated benefit of the conversion to a plc. The executors argued that the deceased had only a hope of benefiting, which was valueless. The Special Commissioner upheld HMRC's contention, finding that, at the date of death, the "value" of the deceased's accounts included the rights conferred by the transfer document issued in January 1997, and that those rights "transcended the mere hope" that the deceased would obtain shares in the plc. In the absence of any other valuation, HMRC's formula for valuing the rights was adopted.

Businesses[82]

25–42   The valuation of a business is, apart from the valuation of any goodwill that may fall to be brought into account, a relatively straightforward process. A business is valued on one of two bases: either as a going concern, i.e. on a profit earning basis, or on the assumption that the business is to be discontinued and the tangible assets sold off; the basis which gives the greater value is the basis which is finally adopted.

Goodwill

25–43   Goodwill might be described as that part of the value of a business which does not derive from the market value of its tangible assets. Broadly speaking, the value of goodwill is found by comparing the profits the business is expected to make in the future with the profits a reasonably competent businessman would make in the same period using the assets (other than goodwill) and staff of the business in question, taking into account such matters as the rates of interest he would have to pay on any loans needed to finance the purchase of equipment of the kind used in the business. Where the transferor's participation in the business is terminated or reduced as a

---

[80] See Revenue *Tax Bulletin* for April 1998 for further and more detailed guidance from HMRC.
[81] *Ward (Executors of Cook, Deceased) v IRC* [1999] S.T.C. (S.C.D.) 1.
[82] Special rules apply in relation to business and instalment relief; see paras 26–82 and 29–115, respectively.

consequence of the transfer by reference to which the valuation falls to be made, the estimate of future profits must take this into account.

In practice, there are two traditionally accepted methods of valuing goodwill. In both cases, the first step is to estimate the level of profits the business can reasonably be expected to maintain without the participation of any individual, e.g. the proprietor, who may be leaving the business. In some cases, of course, the fact that the proprietor is leaving may be a cause for optimism; this would be the case where he was inefficient. Account will also have to be taken of the possibility of future competition—either from an individual leaving the business (unless he is bound by a restrictive covenant) or from outsiders.

The next step differs according to the method being used. The first method, which may be called the "capitalisation method", involves capitalising the estimated average annual yield for a number of years' purchase appropriate to the kind of business involved, and deducting from that sum the value of the tangible assets used in the business. The difference is the value of the goodwill attaching to the business.

Under the second method, which may be called the "super profit" method, there is deducted from the estimated annual yield so much of that yield as is attributable to the value of the tangible assets used in the business. The difference, the "super profit", is then capitalised by an appropriate number of years' purchase.

HMRC have advised that the capitalisation method will generally be the most appropriate for valuing the goodwill of a company, and that the super profit method is suitable only for small businesses.[83] However, the super profit method may in particular be inappropriate where the business is a small shop, which, once the value of the proprietor's services are deducted, will not make any super profit. Nevertheless, since such shops have traditionally been sought by individuals wishing to be in business on their own, some goodwill attaches to them. In the same way, persons may be willing to pay a premium for a brand name, even though the business in question is making no super profit or is even making a loss.

Special problems arise in valuing professional goodwill. Where the skills involved are personal to the practitioner, any goodwill he may have generated cannot be transmitted, and so, under the market value rule, will be left out of account in valuing his business. Where the profession is carried on in partnership, goodwill will normally exist in proportion to the size of the practice. When the practice is large, the departure of one or more of the partners, though of some effect, will be less likely to affect the firm's goodwill than where the partnership is small. Increasingly, firms, especially large firms, no longer require incoming partners to purchase goodwill; consequently such partners have no goodwill to dispose of, notwithstanding the fact that the firm as a whole has a goodwill. It nevertheless may be the case that the goodwill of the firm affects the value of a partner's share.

Land

25–44   The primary criterion for valuing freehold or leasehold property is the value of similar property in the same area.[84] The existence of any planning restrictions or

---

[83] Revenue *Share Valuation Manual,* SVM05030; see also *Findlay's Trustees v IRC* (1938) 22 A.T.C. 437.

[84] The Royal Institute of Chartered Surveyors, in consultation with the Valuation Office Agency, have given guidance to members on valuations of land in the context of s.160 and related case law—see UK GN3 of RICS Appraisal & Valuation Standards ("the Red Book"), revised July 31, 2003 and updated in January 2008. It is in the context of an earlier version of this guidance (GN21, published June 2002) that de Souza considers the concept of the "special purchaser" in *Private Client Business* (London: Sweet & Maxwell, 2003), pp.283–291. For the valuation of a "minority" interest in land, see para.25–61.

permissions must be brought into account, as must the possibility of restrictions being imposed, permissions being secured or compulsory purchase orders being made. When the property is situated in the United Kingdom, HMRC's valuation will be carried out by the District Valuer, who is normally well informed about values within the district for which he is responsible, and quite capable of presenting his views in a convincing manner should an appeal to the Lands Tribunal arise. There is thus a considerable incentive to the taxpayer to arrive at an agreed valuation. Once a valuation has been agreed, HMRC will not normally reopen the valuation if the land is in fact subsequently sold at a higher price, though it is open to the taxpayer to do so if the sale is for a price lower than the agreed value.

In valuing land, any rights which attach to or exist over the land must be brought into account. Thus, rights such as mining, mineral or sporting rights attaching to land will increase its value, while rights over land such as easements will decrease its value. The nature of a given right, and thus its effect on the valuation of the land in question, may vary according to the law which applies in the circumstances. This is well demonstrated by the laws applicable to different types of agricultural tenancies. A tenant of agricultural land in Scotland, for example, has almost perpetual security of tenure. South of the border, pre-1986 tenancies are usually limited to three generations, while tenancies under the Agricultural Holdings Act 1986 last for a single lifetime and those under the Agricultural Tenancies Act 1995 last for an agreed contractual term. Inevitably the nature of the tenancy concerned will have a significant bearing on the value of the underlying land.[85]

In general, land which can be sold with vacant possession will obviously be more valuable than it would be if it could be sold only on a tenanted basis. Property which is let is usually valued by capitalising the net annual value of the property by an appropriate number of years' purchase. The net annual value is the gross rental less such annual outgoings (other than income tax and management expenses), e.g. repairs, insurance premiums, etc. as are borne by the owner.

Where land which was comprised in a person's estate immediately before his death is subsequently sold within four years of his death for a price which is less than the value attributed to it immediately before he died, it may be that the revaluation rules discussed at paras 25–143 and following will apply, with the result that the lower value is brought into account, a refund being given or any outstanding liability being reduced, as may be appropriate.

Agricultural tenancies

25–45   In addition to having differing effects on the value of the underlying land, the various types of agricultural tenancies will inevitably themselves carry different values.

Tenancies granted pre-1995

25–46   These were traditionally thought to have no value attaching to them, being non-assignable, subject to a full rent which must be reviewed every three years and

---

[85] The valuation of agricultural land is, like the value of unquoted shares and securities, a subject in itself and beyond the scope of this book. For a general summary of the different methods of valuing agricultural tenancies, however, see paras 25–45 and following. See also paras 25–27 and 25–28 for lotting units of property where an individual owns both the freehold and leasehold.

requiring the tenant on pain of forfeiture to farm in accordance with the principles of good husbandry. Decisions of the Lands Tribunal for Scotland and the Court of Appeal in the cases of *Baird's Executors v IRC*[86] and *Walton v IRC*[87] respectively made it clear that they do in fact have value, and perhaps this is to be expected for tenancies granting lifelong security of tenure. Two key approaches for reaching a value have emerged from these two cases.[88]

In the Scottish case of *Baird*, the Lands Tribunal held that a valuation should be made under s.160, i.e. as though there was a hypothetical sale of the tenancy in the open market. On the basis that the tenancy was in fact non-assignable, the *Crossman* principle would apply, with the effect that the prohibition on assignment would be disregarded for the hypothetical sale but would be assumed to apply to the hypothetical purchaser.[89] As the taxpayer in *Baird* had not put forward a valuation for a tenancy he believed to be valueless, the District Valuer's valuation, which put the emphasis on the vacant possession premium, was adopted. The hypothetical purchase was deemed to be based on an equal division of the vacant possession value between the landlord and the tenant.

The vacant possession method established in *Baird* will be relevant to tenancies under English law where it can be demonstrated that there can be said to be a special purchaser. The valuation of the tenancy in such instances will be based on a vacant possession premium reflecting the interests of the landlord and tenant, and will usually amount to an equal split between the two parties (HMRC have suggested that while an equal split of the vacant possession premium would be the normal result, they acknowledge that this is open to negotiation).

In the minority of cases where no special purchaser exists (i.e. where it can be shown that the landlord is not a potential purchaser), the approach laid down in *Walton* is usually adopted. *Walton* concerned a freehold farm owned by the deceased and two sons as tenants in common in equal shares, where the land was let to a family farming partnership comprising the deceased and one of the sons. The Court of Appeal upheld the Land Tribunal's finding that, on the evidence that the landlords were in no position to purchase a surrender of the tenancy, a valuation of the tenancy based on the vacant possession premium was inappropriate. The correct approach was instead to value the tenancy as a going concern, to establish the price a purchaser would pay for the deceased's share of the tenancy with a view to continuing in business with the surviving partner. The value was decided as a capitalisation of the profit rent to be earned by the partnership, based on the current rent being below the market rate until the date of the next review.

In the leading judgment in *Walton*, Peter Gibson L.J. adopted the statements of Hoffmann L.J. in *Gray (surviving executor of Lady Fox, Deceased) v IRC*[90] that the willing buyer "reflects reality in that he embodies whatever was actually the demand for that property at the relevant time" and "the valuation is thus a retrospective exercise in probabilities, wholly derived from the real world but rarely committed to the proposition that a sale to a particular purchaser would definitely have happened". His own conclusion was as follows:

> "It is not necessary for the operation of the statutory hypothesis of a sale in the open market of an interest in a tenancy that the landlord should be treated as a hypothetical person, and

[86] *Baird's Executors v IRC* 1991 S.L.T. (Lands Tr.) 9.

[87] *Walton v IRC* [1996] S.T.C. 68.

[88] See Stanley's *Taxation of Farmers and Landowners,* Issue 13, ss.8.91 and following.

[89] See para.25–24.

[90] *Gray (surviving executor of Lady Fox, Deceased) v IRC* [1994] S.T.C. 360. The impact of *Gray* is discussed at para.25–27, and will be relevant to the valuation of freehold land where the owner of that land has a share in the partnership to which that land is let.

it is a question of fact to be established by the evidence before the Tribunal of fact whether the attributes of the actual landlord would be taken into account in the market. I would add that the same logic requires that in the case of a deceased partner owning an interest in a tenancy which is a partnership asset, regard should be had to the actual intention of the actual surviving partner and not to a hypothetical partner."[91]

The *Walton* method of valuation was subsequently followed in the 2001 case of *Greenbank v Pickles*,[92] a non tax-related case concerning a dispute between landlord and tenant.

Periodic tenancies with security of tenure under the Agricultural Holdings Act 1986 are, on the other hand, likely to be of little or no value on the death of the sole or surviving tenant. As the landlord will have a right under s.26 of the 1986 Act to terminate the tenancy on the tenant's death, s.171 (of the Inheritance Tax Act 1984)[93] should apply to take into account changes in value arising by reason of the death as though they had occurred prior to death. For these purposes, as the interest terminates not automatically on death but as a result of a landlord serving notice after death, the proviso in s.171(2) stating that the s.171 principle does not apply on the "termination on the death of any interest" should not apply.

Tenancies under the Agricultural Tenancies Act 1995

25–47   Very different considerations apply to tenancies under the 1995 Act (known as "Farm Business Tenancies") for which there is no security of tenure.[94] Tenancies of two years or less expire automatically at the end of the term, and tenancies fixed for more than two years can be terminated on notice of between 12 and 24 months. Questions of valuation are therefore only likely to arise in very limited circumstances, such as when the actual rent falls short of the open market rent (in which case a capitalised rental difference to the date of the next rent review may be appropriate).[95] Inevitably, the value of Farm Business Tenancies will be much lower than tenancies which benefit from security of tenure.

Farming subsidies

25–48   The European Commission's mid-term review of the Common Agricultural Policy has had a major impact on farming subsidies. The proposals published in October 2003 introduce a new single income payment (the "SIPE"), payable as from 2005, which is intended to consolidate various other arable and livestock subsidies paid to farmers previously. While it had been originally understood that, as with other subsidies, the payment would be linked to the land, it is now clear that the SIPE will be regarded as a personal entitlement based on the size of each farmer's holding, being the occupier

[91] *Gray (surviving executor of Lady Fox, Deceased) v IRC* [1996] S.T.C. 88. For further consideration of the two approaches laid down in *Baird* and *Walton*, see *Taxation* Vol.146 no.3790 and Vol.147 no.3805. Detailed guidance on the valuation of agricultural tenancies can also be found in the Valuation Office Agency *Inheritance Tax Manual*.
[92] *Greenbank v Pickles* [2001] 09 E.G. 230.
[93] Considered in detail at para.25–50.
[94] For a Farm Business Tenancy to exist certain conditions must be met, such as the land being farmed as a trade or business and the character of the tenancy being at least primarily agricultural—see the Agricultural Tenancies Act 1995 s.1.
[95] Stanley's *Taxation of Farmers and Landowners*, pp.468 and following.

of the land rather than the owner, of eligible land rather than the areas grown and the number of livestock kept.

SIPE is not agricultural property but is subject to the normal IHT rules. As SIPE is not agricultural property it cannot qualify for agricultural relief. However, it does appear that where the transferor is a farmer who has been farming for the requisite two years, SIPE will qualify for business relief when transferred with a business.[96] No doubt there will be much negotiation with HMRC on this subject.

Milk quota are similarly not regarded as interests in land per se, and can be transferred separately.[97] HMRC accept, however, that the quota can be regarded as attached to the land, and normally the value of the quota will be reflected in (and will enhance) the value of the land when transferred, and will attract agricultural relief if the requisite conditions are met.

When the quota (or the benefit derived from the quota) is transferred separately from the land a separate valuation will need to be carried out. In those circumstances, the quota will normally constitute an asset used in the business and so may attract business property relief under s.105(1)(a).[98]

Interests in settled property

In applying the market value rule to interests in settled property, the following points 25–49 should be borne in mind:

Interests in possession. By s.49(1), a person beneficially entitled to an interest in possession in settled property is treated as owning the property in which that interest subsists. In valuing such an interest, regard must thus be had to the market value of the underlying property, not to the market value of the interest. There are two exceptions to this rule. First, s.49(1) does not apply where a lessee entitled to occupy property for life is treated as having an interest in possession under s.43(3); the value of such a lessee's interest is discussed at para.32–59. Secondly, by s.49(2), where a person purchases an interest in possession for a consideration in money or money's worth he is not treated as having become entitled to the property in which the interest subsisted. This is an anti-avoidance provision, the purpose of which is best shown by an example. Assume that Jill is married to Joe, and that Jill's father wishes to give Jill £100,000 free of tax. Before June 14, 1978, this could have been arranged by (i) Joe settling £100,000 on Jill for, say, a week, remainder to himself, and (ii) the father purchasing Jill's interest for £100,000. The real value of the interest acquired by Jill's father would have been minimal, but under s.49(1) he would have been treated as having acquired £100,000, so that the purchase would not have diminished the value of his estate. At the end of the week his interest would have come to an end, but the reverter to settlor relief under s.53(3) would have prevented any charge from arising. What is now s.49(2) put an end to this very neat gambit as from June 14, 1978; now the father would make

[96] Stanley's *Taxation of Farmers and Landowners* Issue 22, ss.8.131 and *Tax Bulletin* June 2005, Special Edition.

[97] See *Cottle v Coldicott* [1995] S.T.C. (S.C.D.) 239. For further consideration of the tax treatment of milk quota see Stanley's *Taxation of Farmers and Landowners* Issue 22, ss.2.66 and following and 20.71 and following.

[98] See *Private Client Business* (London: Sweet & Maxwell, 2000), pp.139–144, however, where it is suggested that a milk quota owned by a land owner and used by a partnership does not qualify for relief under s.105(1)(d), not being "land or building, machinery or plant which . . . was used wholly or mainly for the purposes of business carried on by . . . a partnership of which he was then a partner".

a transfer of value of £100,000 on purchasing his daughter's "temporary" interest in possession.

Reversionary interests. Normally these will be excluded property,[99] with the result that no valuation will be necessary. If a valuation is necessary, the value to be brought into account will be the market value of the interest, calculated on an actuarial basis. It may be that a lessor is regarded as having a reversionary interest in property that is subject to a lease; in that case a special rule applies for determining the value of his interest.[100]

Intermediate interests. Exceptionally, an interest in settled property will be neither an interest in possession nor a reversionary interest, but will instead fall into a third category of interest for which the legislation makes no special provision. Such interests, which are rare, are referred to in this book as "intermediate interests", and are discussed at para.11–65. Since no special provision is made for them, it follows that the normal market value rule will apply in valuing them.

Valuation on death

25–50   It is tempting to assume—and it is often assumed—that one values a deceased person's estate with hindsight for IHT purposes, i.e. that in determining the value of the property comprised in a person's estate immediately before he died one assumes that his death was imminent. If, for example, Ernest, who is 70, purchases an annuity and, while struggling over the fine print of the policy, steps into traffic and is killed, what value is to be ascribed to the annuity?

Most advisors would probably say "None—immediately before his death no one would have paid anything for the annuity", presumably on the basis that any prospective purchaser would have foreseen Ernest's imminent demise. There may also be an unspoken assumption that Ernest was in any event old, without too long to live. But what if he was only, say, 30 years old? Would the answer be the same, that the annuity was valueless because of his impending death? Or would the correct approach be to say that Ernest's life expectancy was such that the annuity was relatively valuable?

We are now in a position to address the theoretical point—does one value a person's estate immediately before his death for IHT purposes in the knowledge that his death was imminent, or does one disregard this and assume that he would have lived for what constituted in his circumstances an actuarially normal period? Often, depending on the cause of death, and/or the nature of the property involved, it will not make a great deal of difference which approach is adopted. But the two approaches can yield dramatically different results when the death is completely unexpected and the asset is, e.g. an annuity, or shares which carry special rights during the shareholder's life.

The conventional view that one values with knowledge of the imminence of death is probably based on the fact that IHT on death is triggered by an actual death, following which the legislation directs one to jog backwards to the point immediately before the death. The relevant provision is s.4(1) which provides that:

> "On the death of any person tax shall be charged as if, immediately before his death, he had made a transfer of value and the value transferred by it had been equal to the value of his estate immediately before his death."

[99] See paras 32–58 and 32–59.
[100] See para.32–59.

740

While it is tempting to use this provision to justify the conventional method of valuing, it is clear from s.4(1) that the only reason one jogs backwards is to determine what property is to be valued, not how that property is to be valued. Why, in arriving at that value, should one assume that death was imminent? It is arguable that it would be inconsistent to have regard to the imminence of the settlor's death for the purpose of determining what property is comprised in his estate for IHT purposes, but not to have regard to the imminence of his death for the purpose of valuing that property.

The legislation itself provides grounds for arguing the contrary. Section 171(1)[101] provides that in determining the value of a person's estate immediately before his death certain changes in the value of his estate which have occurred by reason of the death are taken into account as if they had occurred before the death. Under s.171(2), a change prima facie falls within this category if it is an addition to the property comprised in the deceased's estate or "an increase or decrease" in the value of any property comprised in his estate, other than the termination on death of any interest or the passing of any interest by survivorship. Section 171 thus brings into charge, e.g. the proceeds of an insurance policy which matured on the deceased's death and which were payable to his estate: in the absence of s.171 the proceeds of the policy would not have been charged, because they were not comprised in the deceased's estate immediately before he died. More importantly, in this context, it brings in the aforesaid "increase and decrease". If one valued with hindsight, these changes would presumably have been taken into account anyway, without s.171.

Section 171 originally appeared as para.9 of Sch.10 to the Finance Act 1975, in which form it was subject to a qualification, namely that it did not apply either to the termination on death of any interest or to the passing of any interest by survivorship. This is still the case. Under the Finance Act 1975 it was possible to avoid tax by altering the articles of a company so that rights attached to shares only so long as the shareholder was alive, with the result that, either under the conventional view or s.171, immediately before his death the shares were worthless.[102] With a view to putting an end to this, the Finance Act 1976 amended para.9, so that a further qualification applied: as from May 28, 1976, no account was taken under para.9 of a decrease in the value of the property comprised in a deceased person's estate which resulted from such an alteration. This amendment, now found in s.171(2), appears to assume that the efficacy of the aforesaid technique depended on s.171 and that in valuing a person's estate immediately before he dies no regard is had to the imminence of his death. This follows from the fact that if one had regard to the imminence of the deceased's death the shares would be worthless immediately before his death, i.e. there would be no question of any decrease in their value resulting from his death. To put it the other way round, if the shares decreased in value as a result of his death, they must have been worth something immediately before his death, and that can have been the case only if regard was had to his life expectancy.

This amendment thus appears to strengthen the case that s.171 means that on death one values a person's estate on the basis that he would have continued to live on to the actuarial expectancy he had immediately before he died. It is possible, of course, to say (1) that this rule applies only for the special purposes of s.171, or (2) that the aforesaid amendment is misconceived and ineffective, but neither statement is convincing. And, if it is correct that one does not value with hindsight, then even 70-year-old Ernest's annuity will, unless he was literally on his deathbed, have some value and may even

---

[101] See paras 8–17 and following.
[102] The alteration in this way of rights attaching to shares might have given rise to a charge under FA 1975 s.39(5); even if it did, it was often a price worth paying in order to avoid a larger charge on death.

have a not inconsiderable value if, before meeting with his fatal accident, he was in good health for a man of his years.

Case law

25–51　The cases on the subject indicate that one values without foreknowledge of the imminence of death.

The Alexander *case*

25–52　*Alexander v IRC,*[103] discussed at para.25–24, does not provide any direct guidance, because the deceased's death had no effect on the value of the property. It is, however, not wholly without relevance, for two reasons. First, towards the end of his judgment, Ralph Gibson L.J. appears to suggest that if the discount had actually been clawed back on the deceased's death, then the full amount of the clawback would have been taken into account in valuing the property. Secondly, in the opening words of his judgment Nicholls L.J. said:

> "At first sight the executor's case is attractive: it cannot be right that, for capital transfer tax purposes, the lease should be valued in a sum greater than could have been obtained had the lease been sold at the time of the death. Had the lease been sold, the relevant repayment of discount would have become due and payable. Tax ought not to be payable on a greater amount than the net sum due which, in the event of such a sale, would have been received by the deceased's estate. Neither she nor her executor could have obtained more than the net sum. Unfortunately for the executor, this simple proposition does not accord with the basic scheme of this tax . . . "[104]

It is clear from this that there is no objection in theory to the s.160 test attributing to an asset a value which it could not be realised on an actual sale, but this does not necessarily preclude valuing with foreknowledge of the imminent death.

Powell v Osbourne

25–53　Some support for valuing with foreknowledge of the imminent death can be found in the case of *Powell v Osbourne.*[105] The facts of the case were that the deceased and the applicant, Patricia Powell, married in 1983 and subsequently separated. By the time the deceased died in October 1988 they had obtained a decree nisi but not a decree absolute. In August 1988 the deceased and his new partner, who was the respondent, purchased a property jointly for £91,000, of which £85,000 was provided by a joint mortgage on the property supported by a life policy which, in the event, on the deceased's death paid £85,000. The applicant commenced proceedings under the Inheritance (Provision for Family and Dependants) Act 1975 and, because the deceased's assets had been consumed in meeting his liabilities, claimed provision out of the house under s.9 of that Act.

[103] *Alexander v IRC* [1991] S.T.C. 112.
[104] *Alexander v IRC* [1991] S.T.C. 112 at 124f–h.
[105] Reported in the *Solicitor's Journal* of May 1993 at pp.287–288 and mentioned briefly in *The Times* of December 3, 1993.

The judge at first instance ruled that the value of the deceased's beneficial interest in the proceeds of the policy immediately before his death was effectively nil because the policy had been in force for only two months and immediately before his death had no sale or surrender value. The Court of Appeal allowed Patricia Powell's appeal on the basis that s.9, by providing that the value was to be determined immediately before death, meant that the court was to have regard to the imminence of death, with the result that where the value of the property in question depended upon death, as was the case with the life policy, the value immediately before death would be effectively the same as the value upon death.

The Fetherstonaugh *case*

In *Fetherstonaugh v IRC*[106] Oliver L.J. leant further weight to the view that the **25–54** imminence of death is disregarded when he said obiter:

> "The occasion of the deemed transfer of value is, it is true, related to the moment before the death of the deceased but there is nothing in the statute to suggest that the valuation is to be conducted on the basis that the impending demise of the deceased is a known factor which the hypothetical valuer is to take into account."[107]

The Arkwright *case*

The application of s.171 was considered more recently in the case of *Arkwright* **25–55** *(Williams Personal Representative) v IRC*,[108] the facts of which are set out at para.25–62. The first issue to be decided in the case was whether the value of the deceased husband's share of a property owned jointly with his wife should be reduced to reflect the wife's continuing right to occupy the property after the husband's death under the Trusts of Land and Appointment of Trustees Act 1996. Having found that it should, consideration was given as to whether a decrease in value occurred as a result of the death, which should also be taken into account when valuing the share.

HMRC argued that, on the facts, the proviso in s.171(2) applied, with the effect that the fact of death was not to be taken into account in determining the deceased's interest. The executors argued that s.171 did not apply on the basis that no change to the estate took place as a result of the husband's death; their argument centred on the fact that any change in value took place not as a result of the death but as a result of the imminence of death (which served to reduce the value of the interest by confirming that any purchaser of the interest would purchase subject to the surviving spouse's rights of occupation).

The Special Commissioner found that, on the facts, the s.171(2) proviso did not disapply the provisions of s.171(1). Furthermore, by virtue of the husband's death, there was a change (i.e. a decrease) in the value of the husband's share of the property. It was found that if the interest had been determined according to the normal rules (and valued immediately before death without regard to the fact that death was imminent), when that death subsequently occurred, a change in value would occur: it would become certain at that stage that the wife would survive her husband and that any

---

[106] *Fetherstonaugh v IRC* [1984] S.T.C. 261; see para.26–20.
[107] *Fetherstonaugh v IRC* [1984] S.T.C. 261 at 268.
[108] *Arkwright (Williams Personal Representative) v IRC* (2004) S.T.C. (S.C.D.) 89. See also para.25–65 for related property issues arising in the case.

hypothetical purchaser would therefore purchase subject to her rights of occupation. Such a change would be a decrease in value within s.171(2), with the effect that in addition to the wife's rights of occupation, the decrease in value that occurred by reason of the death was also to be taken into account when determining the value of the interest immediately before death.

The Special Commissioner's findings raise questions on several counts (see para.25–62) and, following an appeal by HMRC, the case was remitted to the Lands Tribunal for fresh consideration on the grounds that the Special Commissioner, though entitled to take a view on questions of law, was not entitled to rule on questions of fact in order to determine a valuation. As regards s.171, Gloster J. said that:

> "in circumstances where . . . the legal nature and incidents of the Deceased's interest as a tenant in common was not affected by his death or by the imminence of his death, it is essentially a question of fact . . . whether the imminence of his death, or his actual death, did, or did not, reduce the value of his interest to a notional purchaser . . . If either event did so, then that is a matter that can obviously be taken into account in the valuation and it is irrelevant whether such reduction falls to be considered under section 171 as occurring on death or prior to death."[109]

Clearly such a conclusion does not do much to resolve the application of s.171 and the question of whether one values with or without foreknowledge of death. Nevertheless, the Special Commissioner's interpretation of s.171 does add weight to the authorities suggesting that valuations should not be made with foreknowledge of imminent demise. After all, although the deceased in *Arkwright* was in fact seriously ill prior to his death, the Special Commissioner did not compare the decreased value on death with a slightly "less decreased" value immediately prior to death (reflecting the fact that death was imminent but not yet arrived). The pre-death value was expressed to be determined without regard to the fact of the impending death, at that stage taking it only to be a possibility (and not a significant one) that the husband would predecease his wife.

Position in practice

25–56 One of the authors espoused in an article[110] that the correct approach was to value without foreknowledge of the imminence of death. *Dymond*, which at the time was thought accurately to reflect HMRC's thinking, referred to this article and indicated that the basis espoused seemed contrary to *Powell v Osbourne* and was not that adopted by HMRC.[111]

In that author's experience HMRC have consistently valued with foreknowledge of the imminence of death and are understood to intend to continue doing so.

Annuities

25–57 The valuation of an annuity differs according to whether the annuity is payable out of settled property or not:

---

[109] *Arkwright (Williams Personal Representative) v IRC* [2004] EWHC 1720 (Ch) at [18].
[110] *British Tax Review* 1988, pp.431–433.
[111] *Dymond's Capital Taxes*, paras 23.153–159 and see also 24.500.

Settled property annuities. Where a person is entitled to a specified amount of income from settled property he is treated as having an interest in possession in the part of the property which is taken as producing that income. His position is thus that of a person with an interest in possession, with the result that the market value of the property in which his "interest" is taken to subsist must be brought into account. This may give rise to enormous practical difficulties.[112]

Similar difficulties exist in relation to the valuation of discounted gift trusts. This was considered in *Bower v Revenue and Customs Commissioners*.[113]

Mrs Bower, a lady of 90 years, had bought an estate-planning bond which she had settled on trusts for the benefit of her two sons having reserved rights to a fixed monthly payment of £300 based on an actuarial valuation of her life expectancy. She died shortly afterwards and the question arose as to the value of the transfer to the trust which was to be calculated by subtracting from the price paid for the bond the value of Mrs Bower's right to a monthly payment. The issue, therefore, was the price a purchaser might pay in the "open market" for the right to the monthly payments. HMRC had contended that as a result of Mrs Bower's age and health and the consequent inability of any potential purchaser to lay off the mortality risk by taking term insurance, the retained rights had only a nominal value of £250. In reversing the decision of the Special Commissioner, the High Court agreed.

In asking, as the Special Commissioner had, whether the sale in the open market contemplated that the sale must take place in "some conventional market manner" it was not clear to the High Court that the Special Commissioner had appreciated that the hypothetical sale must take place in the real world. Relying heavily on the judgment of Hoffman L.J. in *IRC v Gray*, Lewison J. stressed that an actual enquiry into the real market had to take place and that it was not correct to populate that real market with hypothetical speculators if, in reality, they did not share the characteristics of real buyers.[114] Having regard to that enquiry and based on the evidence presented to it, the court concluded that ascribing a nominal value to the retained rights in this case was the natural consequence of finding that the rights were not commercially, as opposed to legally, saleable (taking into account the inability to lay off the mortality risk) coupled with the assumption that a sale must have taken place.

The decision was followed in *Watkins v Revenue and Customs Commissioners*[115] which involved a similar discounted gift trust scheme. The tribunal found in this case that the income stream reserved by Mrs Watkins from a planning-bond purchased and settled in her 89th year and less than two years before her death should not be valued by hypothesising what the value would be in the "open market" as proposed by the appellant. It was common ground between the appellant and HMRC that term insurance could not be used to protect the value of Mrs Watkin's retained rights given her age. The appellants had tried to circumvent this difficulty through a series of creative propositions. Whilst the tribunal found that it is correct to look at what would happen in closely comparable situations for which there are accepted valuation techniques, it observed that "the evidence adduced by the appellant shows no existing market, let alone what could be described as an open market, for income streams to be

---

[112] See also para.2–127.

[113] [2008] EWHC 3105 (Ch).

[114] The failure of the Special Commissioner in this case to hear evidence as to the "real market" was much criticised. His decision, as he himself had described, was "little more than uninformed, but hopefully realistic guesswork". That said, it is difficult not to have some sympathy for him given that the actual yield on the retained rights was in the region of £1,500, Mrs Bower having survived the purchase of the plan by five months.

[115] [2011] UKFTT 745 (TC).

calculated, nor a market for any similar type of entitlement."[116] HMRC, in contrast, had produced evidence based on actual sales of life interests which demonstrated that such a sale would not take place at all unless a life policy had been put in place. On that basis it was again concluded that, in commercial terms, there was no real market in the income and that the value of the retained rights would be nominal.

Other annuities. The value to be brought into account in the case of any other annuity is the market value of the annuity, not the value of the underlying capital. If the annuity ceases on a deceased's death the value to be brought into account immediately before his death is normally thought to be nil, but in the authors' view the correct approach is to value the annuity on the basis that the deceased would have survived to his normal life expectancy. If the annuity continues to be payable after his death, the value to be brought into account will depend on the terms of the annuity contract.

Joint property

25–58   Jointly owned property gives rise to a number of subtle valuation points.

Joint tenants

25–59   The position is the same whether the tenancy is a joint one or a tenancy in common; in both cases the normal market value rule applies. On a joint tenant's death, his interest will pass as a matter of general law to the surviving joint tenant or tenants by virtue of the right of survivorship. Immediately before he dies, however, his joint interest will still form part of his estate, and therefore, unless the property is excluded property, the value of his interest must be brought into account. His position is thus effectively the same as that of tenant in common in equal shares.

Bank accounts[117]

25–60   Some of the difficulties arising in relation to valuing shares in bank accounts have been highlighted above, from which it is clear that much will depend on the facts of the particular circumstances and any evidence as to the intentions of the parties.[118] Generally, the main concern will be to identify the nature of the beneficial interests in the account; once this is achieved valuation should usually fall into place.[119] In identifying the beneficial interests there are some general principles to be borne in mind.

As a starting point, HMRC will, if possible, treat each party to a joint current account as being the beneficial owner of the money he has paid in and withdrawals by him will be deemed to be paid out of his own contributions so far as possible.[120] This was the

---

[116] It is interesting to compare the approach of the court here with the approach taken by the Lands Tribunal when dealing with valuation/market uncertainties—see for example *Prosser v IRC* [2000] EW Lands DETI.

[117] See also para.2–11.

[118] See paras 2–11, 25–04 and 25–08.

[119] For further examples of some typical situations when difficulties may arise in relation to joint bank accounts see *Dymond's Capital Taxes*, paras 10.430 and following.

[120] For HMRC guidance on joint property generally see HMRC Manuals IHTM15000 onwards.

approach adopted in *Sillars v IRC*[121] where, on the basis that the mother was the sole contributor to the account and all withdrawals were made either by her or by the daughters for her benefit, the whole of the money in the account was found to be within her estate. Similarly, as was demonstrated in *O'Neill v IRC*,[122] where an account is nominally in joint names but only one party has any control over its operation, the entire account will be included in the controlling party's estate.[123]

The 1965 case of *Re Bishop*[124] is authority for the fact that where (as in this case) a husband and wife individually purchase something with funds from a joint bank account into which they have both contributed, the new investment is regarded as belonging only to the individual making the purchase and not to them both jointly. This is presumably also the case where the joint account is held by parties other than spouses. However, in *Re Bishop* the husband and wife were regarded as drawing money not from the relevant proportion of the funds contributed by them but from a pool owned by them legally and beneficially as joint tenants. As to whether this would also apply in the case of account holders who are not spouses would depend on careful consideration of the particular facts. Where the owners of a joint account are unmarried and one party makes personal use of funds which the other has contributed, attention will have to be given as to whether a PET has occurred.[125]

On a practical level, in order to avoid some of the complications arising where the original contributions to a joint account are unequal, particularly where the parties are not husband and wife, the parties would be strongly advised to make a formal deed of gift and/or execute a declaration of trust confirming how the account is to be operated and, more importantly, what will happen to the balance of the account in the event of the death of one of the parties.

Minority interests

Subject to the related property rules applying (see paras 25–65 and following), where **25–61** a person's share in jointly owned property is to be valued, it is standard procedure to value that person's share in isolation rather than as a pro-rata share of the full amount. This ensures that the value reflects the fact that the co-owner does not have control of the asset.

HMRC's practice has generally been to allow a discount of 10 per cent from the pro-rata share of the open market value of the whole property (regardless of the size of the particular share). The issue has come before the authorities on numerous occasions (the discounts applied increasing each time). In *Charkham v IRC*[126] a valuation was sought for undivided shares in investment properties arising under a Will, ranging from 24.04 to 6.04 per cent, for which HMRC sought to make its usual discount of 10 per cent. The Lands Tribunal accepted the arguments of the taxpayer, looking instead at the ability of the minority owner to obtain an order for sale under the Law of Property Act 1925 s.30, and at whether the purpose of the trust for which the properties were held had come to an end. It found, on the basis of the authorities, that in selecting an appropriate

---

[121] *Sillars v IRC* [2004] S.T.C. (S.C.D.) 180; see para.25–08.
[122] *O'Neill v IRC* [1998] S.T.C. (S.C.D.) 110; see para.25–08. It would have been interesting to see what arguments HMRC might have raised had the daughter in this case predeceased her father.
[123] *O'Neill* is also interesting as an example of where an account will pass by survivorship where the surviving party had no interest during the joint lives.
[124] *Re Bishop* [1965] Ch. 450.
[125] See Ch.4. For transfers of value generally, see Ch.2.
[126] Unreported 1997 (Lands Tr). See also *Cust v IRC* (1917) 91 Estates Gazette 11 and *Wight v IRC* (1982) 264 Estates Gazette 935.

discount for the values of the different shares, no distinction should be made between the sizes of the various interests. The various interests in one property were discounted by 15 per cent, and the interests in the second property by 22.5 per cent for some years and 20 per cent for others.

The case clearly overturned HMRC's standard discount of 10 per cent, at least in relation to secondary retail and mixed tenure residential property (the Tribunal did not indicate what level of discount might be appropriate for other types of property).[127] *Charkham* was, however, subject to the trust for sale regime in place prior to the Trusts of Land and Appointment of Trustees Act 1996. As has now been demonstrated by the 2003 case of *Arkwright (Williams Personal Representative) v IRC*,[128] certain provisions of the 1996 Act could also have a significant bearing generally on the level of discount to be applied to different percentage interests in general[129]; see para.25–62.

This was reconsidered further in the case of *HSBC Trust Company (UK) Ltd v Twiddy*.[130] As discussed above prior to the Trusts of Land and Appointment of Trustees Act 1996 the previous policy of the Lands Tribunal had been to value the entirety of the property and then to apply a discount. However following the case of *Twiddy* this approach has been abandoned in favour of a valuation of the minority share in isolation. The deceased held a minority share in a mixed development portfolio. From the facts it appears that none of the other owners were inclined to buy the deceased's share. At the hearing it was put forward by both sides that the minority shareholding should be valued on a income generating basis. The only difference between the parties was whether the investment should be valued on a gross basis as is standard in the open market. The Lands Tribunal decided that a net approach was appropriate given the lack of control and inflexibility inherent in a minority shareholding.

Two particular aspects of the case are worth highlighting. Firstly following the abolition of the trust for sale under s.15(3) of the Trusts of Land and Appointment of Trustees Act 1996 it is in the court's discretion as to whether to order a sale. Secondly whilst this may appear to be a move away from the approach in *Charkham* the particular facts of the case may distinguish it. It should be noted that a restriction had been entered into by the owners of the property preventing a minority shareholder applying for an order to sale. It should be noted that without this restriction the Lands Tribunal may not have followed this path.

Rights of occupation

25–62   Section 12 of the 1996 Act gives rights of occupation to persons with an interest in possession in trust property, where the purposes of the trust include making the land available for occupation. This is also likely to have an impact on the value of an undivided share where a co-owner has the right to occupy. The issue came before the Special Commissioners in *Arkwright (Williams Personal Representative) v IRC*.[131] The deceased Mr Williams had owned a freehold property (worth £550,000) jointly with his wife as tenants in common in equal shares. On his death, his share of the property passed to his wife on life interest trusts, with remainder to his two daughters. By a subsequent deed of variation, the Will was varied to pass the de-

---

[127] See *Private Client Business* (London: Sweet & Maxwell, 1997), pp.203–209.

[128] *Arkwright (Williams Personal Representative) v IRC* [2004] S.T.C. (S.C.D.) 89.

[129] The Trusts of Land and Apportionment of Trustees Act 1996 is considered further at para.12–34 in the context of a beneficiary's right to occupy trust property in which he has an interest in possession.

[130] *HSBC Trust Company (UK) Ltd v Twiddy* Unreported August 24, 2006 (Lands Tribunal) and *Private Client Business* (2007), pp.11–14.

[131] *Arkwright (Williams Personal Representative) v IRC* (2004) S.T.C. (S.C.D.) 89; see also para.25–55.

ceased's share of the property to the daughters outright, at which point HMRC claimed IHT on a mathematical half of the value of the property, i.e. £275,000. Mr Williams's personal representatives appealed.

The Special Commissioner, allowing the appeal and finding that the value should be less than a mathematical half, made the following points:

> "1. Applying the principles of *Alexander v IRC*,[132] the relevant value was the sum which a purchaser in the open market might reasonably pay to be placed in the same position as the deceased. Immediately before his death, Mr Williams owned a half share in the property which he could dispose of subject to Mrs Williams's rights to occupy until her death under s.12 of the 1996 Act and, vice-versa, Mrs Williams owned a half share in the property which she could dispose of subject to Mr Williams's rights to occupy until his death under s.12 of the 1996 Act.
>
> 2. The question was whether those rights to occupy were of equal value. On the basis of *Lynall v IRC*[133] the hypothetical willing purchaser would be aware that each spouse enjoyed rights to occupy the property and those rights would reduce the open market value of the other's share. On the principle that the hypothetical sale is deemed to take place 'immediately' before death, the hypothetical purchaser would be aware that Mrs Williams was in better health and was younger than her husband: Mr Williams's share would therefore be discounted on the basis that the purchase was subject to Mrs Williams's continuing occupation and Mrs Williams's share, carrying a right to occupy following the likely death of her husband, would be regarded as worth more. Mr Williams's interest was therefore to be valued taking into account his wife's rights to occupation under the 1996 Act."

Consideration was also given as to the relevance of s.171(1) and the related property rules, for which see paras 25–55 and 25–65 respectively.

Although HMRC have now appealed (partly successfully) against the Special Commissioner's findings (see para.25–55), the High Court's findings have done little to clarify the effect of the 1996 Act on the value of jointly owned property and it is hoped the courts will have further opportunity to consider this issue in due course. The judgment of Gloster J. concludes simply that the Special Commissioner had no right to take decisions on a question of valuation, considering that "whether a notional purchaser of the Deceased's half share might take the existence of Mrs Williams' rights under the 1996 Act into account and, if so, how this would affect the value, was a valuation issue that should have been referred to the Lands Tribunal to decide on appropriate evidence".[134] The possible impact of the 1996 Act has therefore not been ruled out; nor has it been confirmed.

The Special Commissioner's findings in *Arkwright* clearly conflict with traditional views, and there are other questions that could helpfully be addressed.[135] For example, what or whose rights of occupation were to be regarded as attached to the deceased's share for the purposes of the hypothetical purchase—only those rights of the ailing deceased or would the hypothetical purchaser also have acquired a right to occupy? Would he have received any financial recompense for the occupation by the joint owner? Can the relevant sections of the 1996 Act even be said to apply to a situation of joint ownership such as this, where the trust structure is something of a conveyancing mechanism?

Furthermore, it could be said that the surviving spouse in *Arkwright* appears to have an interest in possession giving her a right of occupation of the entire property on terms which significantly reduces the value of the other joint interest. This raises the worrying

---

[132] *Alexander v IRC* [1991] S.T.C. 112; see para.25–24.
[133] *Lynall v IRC* [1937] A.C. 26; see para.25–24.
[134] *Arkwright (Williams Personal Representative) v IRC* [2004] EWHC 1720 (Ch) at [15].
[135] See *Trusts and Estates* March 2004, Vol.18, 3.

concern that she may be deemed to have an interest in possession. Where a matrimonial property is owned jointly by husband and wife, they could on this basis be regarded for IHT purposes as enjoying an interest in possession over the entire property, so that on death the entire value would be taxable in their estates. However, the definition of "settled property" in s.43 would presumably prevent such an argument in relation to property that is simply jointly owned, particularly where it is held, as in *Arkwright*, as tenants in common—see para.11–08.

The case of *Burden v UK*[136] has reconsidered these issues in the light of the Civil Partnership Act 2004. The case concerned whether two sisters who lived together for most of their lives should have the same inheritance tax relief as married couples and civil partners. As the couple were sisters they could not enter into a civil partnership under the Civil Partnership Act 2004. Their concern was that the survivor of the two would have to pay inheritance tax on the death of the first survivor. The s.18 exemption provides that property passing from a deceased to a spouse is exempt. With effect from December 5, 2005 this exemption was extended to a deceased civil partner, as introduced by the Civil Partnership Act 2004 for same sex couples but not family members living together. The sisters argued that it was unfair that they had to pay tax when couples defined as partners under the Civil Partnership Act did not. The sisters lost on the basis that the exemption promoted stable relationships by providing some financial security for the surviving partner or spouse.

Lloyd's underwriters

25–63   A Name's underwriting interest consists of his Member's Deposit, Reserve Funds, profits for open years, and, if the death occurs in the early part of the year, profits for the last closed year. The value of his interest is based on the Lloyd's solvency requirements. Because of the difficulty involved in estimating the profits of open years, by HMRC concession the valuation may be effected, provided the deceased Name's executors so elect within 12 months of obtaining probate, by reference to the actual profits of the open years when these are ascertained rather than on the statutory estimated basis. In both cases, a discount is allowed to take account of the fact that the accounts in question will be delayed in receipt. It is important to note that the collation of the information to be submitted to HMRC has a number of special facets and executors are well advised to seek expert guidance on this matter.

The case of *Hardcastle (the executors of Vernede, Deceased) v IRC*[137] has raised some interesting questions about the treatment of losses on underwriting contracts in the context of estate liabilities and business property relief—see para.25–87. The availability of business relief for underwriting interests generally is discussed at para.26–84.

It is HMRC practice to exclude from the valuation of an underwriter's "business" any assets situated abroad. For this purpose, any amount due in respect of the profits of the closed year is regarded in the case of a US member as a debt which has its situs in the United States, but the unascertained profits of open years are not so regarded. HMRC also exclude from the valuation certain government securities. It follows from this that it is open to a US member to arrange his affairs so as to limit any liability to

---

[136] *Burden v UK* [2008] S.T.C. 1305.
[137] *Hardcastle (the executors of Vernede, Deceased) v IRC* [2000] S.T.C. (S.C.D.) 532.

IHT by ensuring that his Deposit is represented by a letter of credit, and his reserves by United States or other foreign investments.

VII. SPECIAL RULES

Part VI contains a number of rules under which an artificial value is substituted for the open market value of property. As will be seen below, most of these rules are prejudicial to the taxpayer. **25–64**

Related property

The most interesting qualification to the general market value rule is found in s.161, which contains the provisions concerning related property. Section 161(1) provides that: **25–65**

> "where the value of any property comprised in a person's estate would be less than the appropriate portion of the value of the aggregate of that and any related property, it shall be the appropriate portion of the value of that aggregate."

The appropriate portion of the aggregate value of the property is determined under s.161(3), as being:

> "such portion . . . as would be attributable to the value of the first-mentioned property if the value of that aggregate were equal to the sums of the value of that and any related property, the value of each property being determined as if it did not form part of that aggregate",

one apportions the aggregate value to the various properties according to their individual values. Assume, for example, that Jim owns 35 shares in X Ltd, a company with 100 issued shares, which, taken together are worth £100,000, and that his wife Jane owns 30 shares in the same company. In the absence of the related property provisions, both shareholdings would be valued on a minority basis, with the result that Jim's shares would be worth, say, £17,500, and Jane's, say, £15,000. As will be seen below, under s.161(2) the property comprised in a husband's estate is related to the property comprised in his wife's estate, and vice versa. That being the case, the value to be attributed to each of the above shareholdings is the appropriate portion of the aggregate value of the two shareholdings. If the two shareholdings were one, the resulting shareholding of 65 shares would be valued on a majority basis, and would be worth, say, £65,000. The appropriate portion of this aggregate would be:

$$\text{Jim:} \ \frac{35}{65} \times £65,000 = £35,000$$

$$\text{Jane:} \ \frac{30}{65} \times £65,000 = £30,000$$

It may be that one parcel of shares is valued on a different basis than the parcel to which it is related. Assume, for instance, that in the above example Jane owned 30 shares and Jim owned 65 shares in X Ltd. In determining the appropriate portion of the aggregate value in such a case, no account is taken of the fact that on normal valuation principles Jim's holding is valued on a majority basis, while Jane's continues to be valued on a minority basis. This follows from s.161(4), which provides that in determining the appropriate portion of the aggregate value

> " . . . the proportion which the value of a smaller number of shares of any class bears to the value of a greater number thereof shall be taken to be that which the smaller number bears to the greater; and similarly with stock, debentures and units of any other description of property."

Thus, returning to Jim and Jane, if Jim owned 65 shares, the appropriate portions would be:

$$\text{Jim: } \frac{65}{95} \times £95,000 = £65,000$$

$$\text{Jane: } \frac{30}{95} \times £95,000 = £30,000$$

i.e. there would be no "weighting" to take account of the fact that Jim had a controlling shareholding.[138]

For the purposes of s.161(4), shares are not treated as being of the same class unless they are so treated by the practice of a recognised stock exchange or would be so treated if dealt with on such stock exchange.[139] It will be noted that the "unit-for-unit" basis of apportionment prescribed by s.161(4) is not confined to shares, however, but applies also to "units of any other description of property". The question of what might qualify as a "unit" for the purposes of this section was considered in *Arkwright (Williams Personal Representative) v IRC*[140] (for the facts of which see para.25–62), where it was found that half shares in a property owned as tenants in common did not constitute "units".

Both the executors and HMRC in *Arkwright* agreed that Mr and Mrs Williams's shares in the property were "related". It was also agreed, non-controversially, that the effect of s.161(1) and (3) was to find the aggregate value of the deceased Mr Williams's share and the related property, to which a ratio was to be applied based on the values of Mr Williams's shares and the related property when valued separately. If the value of the deceased's part of the aggregate was higher than the value of his property when valued separately, the value of the part of the aggregate would be used.

HMRC argued further, however, that Mr and Mrs Williams's shares of the property were "units of any other description of property" within the meaning of s.161(4), and consequently the ratio for the purposes of s.161(3) was half. The executors opposed such an argument on the basis that (relying both on the *Shorter Oxford English Dictionary* definition of the term and New Zealand case law)[141] in s.161(4) shares in land were not to be regarded as "units". Furthermore, the reference to "number" was in itself not relevant to percentage shares in land, and the references to "smaller

---

[138] The example assumes for the sake of convenience that the 95 per cent holding and the 65 per cent holding would be valued on the same basis, which might well not be the case.

[139] IHTA 1984 s.161(5). See TA 1988 s.841(1) and para.25–38 for what constitutes a recognised stock exchange.

[140] *Arkwright (Williams Personal Representative) v IRC* (2004) S.T.C. (S.C.D.) 89.

[141] *New Zealand Railways v Progressive Engineering Co Ltd* [1968] N.Z.L.R. 1053.

number" and "greater number" did not apply in the case of equal units. It was suggested that s.161(4) might apply to units in unit trusts or sets of furniture (for example a set of dining chairs) but not to incorporeal shares in land.

The Special Commissioner concurred with the executors' arguments and found that s.161(4) did not apply, and that the correct approach to valuation in this case was that in s.161(3).[142]

Whilst shares in property do not fall within s.161(4) they do come within the remit of s.161(3). The effect of that subsection was tested by the appellant in *Price v HMRC* which, following the death of the appellant's wife, involved the valuation of an undivided half share in the family home, which had been held as tenants in common.[143] The appellant's contention was straight forward. Whilst he accepted that the two parts had to be valued together, he claimed that such valuation had to be by reference to the inherent nature of each half share and that the aggregation of the two required by s.161 could not change result in their being treated as a single (and very different) item of property, i.e. the entire freehold rather than two half shares both subject to a market discount.

The appellant argued that the meaning of aggregate as found in s.161(1) simply meant "bringing together" or "total" as used in s.5(1) and that the "transformation" approach adopted by HMRC could only be used in relation to s.161(4) which had no application to land. He further noted that neither interest conferred on its owner any right to require the freehold of the property to be offered for sale in the market. Not surprisingly, the tribunal rejected the appellant's agreeing, effectively, with HMRC that s.161 had to be considered in the light of s.160 and "the price which the property might reasonably be expected to fetch if sold in the open market." Consequently, Mrs Price's interest in the property was 50 per cent of the value of the freehold interest the two half shares would represent to a purchaser if sold together.[144]

Definition

Having established the consequences of property being related property, the next **25–66** step is to consider what kind of property is regarded as being related property. By s.161(2), property is related to the property comprised in a person's estate if it:

(1) is comprised in his spouse's estate; or
(2) is, or has within the preceding five years been
    (a) the property of a charity, or held on trust for charitable purposes only, or
    (b) the property of a body mentioned in ss.24, 24A or 25,

and became such property or so held on a transfer of value made by him or his spouse after April 15, 1976, which was exempt to the extent that the value transferred was attributable to the property.

Note that property subject to a s.47 settlement power will not be "related" to property in the estate of the person entitled to exercise that power because the power will not be property for IHT purposes. It remains to be seen whether a settlement power

---

[142] In this respect the Special Commissioner's findings were upheld on appeal, the High Court concluding that the Special Commissioner was entitled to decide how IHTA 1984 s.161 should be construed and applied, being a question of law and not of fact.

[143] *Price v HMRC* [2010] UKFTT 474 (TC).

[144] The tribunal accepted the appellant's argument "would not deprive s.161 of all application" but stated that the purpose of the section was wider than the appellant suggested to prevent avoidance of IHT.

will be taken into account in valuing other property. If, e.g. A has a life interest subject to the exercise of a power of advancement and his consent is required to the exercise of that power, his ability to veto the exercise of the power would normally be taken into account in valuing his interest generally (as opposed to under the rule in s.49(1)). It may be that his veto is a settlement; see para.25–12. If it is, the question arises as to whether or not his interest should be valued in isolation from the veto. The position may turn on the terms of the settlement in question.

Spouses and Civil Partners[145]

25–67   It will be noted that in the case of spouses and civil partners the relationship is reciprocal; i.e. that property comprised in one spouse or civil partner is related to the property comprised in the spouse's or partner's estate, and vice versa. It is thought that the time for determining whether a person is a spouse or partner is the time of the event which occasioned the valuation. The reason for providing that such property is related is to prevent spouses or partners from reducing the value of their respective estates by means of exempt transfers between themselves, e.g. by a husband giving half of his controlling share holding to his wife. The related property provisions apply regardless of the domicile of the spouses or partners in question.

Charities, exempt bodies and discretionary trusts

25–68   The second category of related property was added to the original legislation to prevent individuals depreciating the value of their estates by making exempt transfers to charities and exempt bodies. At one stage it was common for a person with 51 per cent of the shares in a company to transfer 2 per cent of the shares to a charity, and then to transfer the remaining 49 per cent holding (now valued on a minority basis) to his son, who, in turn, might repurchase the 2 per cent holding from the charity. This will now be effective only if there is a gap of at least five years between the two transfers.

There is no reciprocal relationship where the second or third categories of related property are concerned, i.e. although the property in the trust or the exempt body is related to property in the estate of the settlor and that of the settlor's spouse, the property in their estates is not related to the property comprised in the trust or the exempt body.

Excluded property

25–69   It is important to bear in mind in connection with these provisions that excluded property is (except on death) comprised in a person's estate,[146] with the result that

---

[145] For the meaning of "spouse", see para.3–31.
[146] See para.25–18.

excluded property can be related property. Assume, for instance, that in the above example concerning Jane and Jim, Jim's shares were excluded property; e.g. because the company was incorporated abroad and Jim was domiciled abroad: despite this, Jim's shares would still be taken into account in valuing Jane's shares, and vice versa.

Revaluation

Under the revaluation rules, discussed below, where property to which immediately **25-70** before a person's death an artificially high value was attributed under the related property rules is sold within three years of his death for a lower price than that value, the property may be revalued; the price that property would have fetched on his death had the related property rules not applied is substituted for the value previously brought into account.

Planning

It is possible to draw the sting from the related property rules. Assume Dad owns 49 **25-71** per cent of the shares in Mum and Dad Ltd and Mum 12 per cent, that controlling shares are worth £100 each, minority shares £10 and that, because 100 shares have been issued, control resides in a block of 51 such shares. Under the related property rules the value of Dad and Mum's respective holdings is found by aggregating the two holdings together (thereby giving 61 per cent), which will have the effect of a controlling shareholding basis of valuation. Each share is therefore worth £100, so that Dad's 49 per cent holding becomes worth £4,900 and Mum's 12 per cent holding £1,200, giving a total value for the couple of £6,100.

What is the best way to transfer the entire 61 per cent holding to daughter Sue? As a rule of thumb it is the spouse with the smaller number of shares who should effect the transfer. Assume, therefore, that Mum transfers her 12 per cent shareholding. These shares must be valued at £100 each (as already noted) and therefore the fall in value of Mum's estate amounts to £1,200. The result of that transfer, however, is that Dad's 49 per cent holding becomes a minority holding, so that the value of his estate falls from £4,900 to £490 and, because Dad has not made a disposition, he has not made a transfer of value. If he subsequently transfers his own holding to Sue the total fall in value of the two estates is £1,690 (Mum—£1,200; Dad—£490). By contrast, had Dad transferred his holding first the result would have been that his 49 per cent holding had to be valued at £100 per share, thereby giving a transfer of value of £4,900. Mum's estate would then fall from £1,200 to £120 and, as a result of a later transfer by her, the combined transfers of value made by the couple could amount to £5,020.

Consider the position if the 12 per cent holding had been held on trust with Mum as life tenant and Sue as remainderman. If Mum were to surrender her life interest the transfer of value would be limited to the value of the property in the settlement, i.e. to a 12 per cent shareholding (see para.6–18). The related property provisions are inapplicable and so the total transfer amounts to £120. So far as Dad's estate is concerned, the knock-on effect will be a reduction in the value of his shareholding to £490. If both transfers go through the total value transferred would be a mere £610.

If Dad died leaving his shares to Mum, consider the advantage of a deed of variation redirecting 12 per cent of the shares to Sue. The result would be that Dad will make a transfer of value of £1,200 (a 12 per cent holding valued on controlling basis) and that Mum will be left with a minority shareholding of 49 per cent. If she, in turn, transfers that holding to Sue the combined transfer of value will be £1,690, significantly less than had the entire 61 per cent holding been transferred by Mum.

Restrictions on freedom to dispose of property

25–72   The legislation makes special provision to deal with the situation where a person's right to dispose of property is restricted or excluded by a contract, e.g. where a person has granted an option over property. Section 163 provides that in such a case the value of the property is reduced to the extent only that consideration in money or money's worth was given for the restriction or exclusion. Thus, to take a simple example, assume that George sells to trustees of a discretionary trust for full consideration of £3,750 an option to purchase George's house for £10,000 in one year's time. One year later, when the house is worth £15,000, the trustees exercise the option. Since they purchased the option for full consideration, the value of the house will be £10,000, with the result that George does not make a transfer of value even though he receives only £10,000 for property worth £15,000 in the open market.

Where the contract in question itself constituted a chargeable transfer,[147] e.g. where an option was granted for no consideration or for less than full consideration in money or money's worth, in computing the value of the property in question an allowance is made under s.163(1)(b) for so much of the value transferred (ignoring any grossing-up) by the previous chargeable transfer as is attributable to the exclusion or restriction. Thus, if in the above example George had by deed given the option to the trustees, the position would have been as follows. First, the gift would have constituted a transfer of value of £3,750 and a chargeable transfer, taking into account the annual exemption and assuming the trustees bore the tax, of £750. If the trustees exercised the option a year later, George would have transferred for £10,000 property worth in the open market £15,000; but, given the s.163(1)(b) allowance, the property would have been worth only £14,250 (£15,000 less £750). George would thus have made a transfer of value of £4,250 (£14,250 less £10,000 purchase price). It is important to note that even if George had borne the tax on the chargeable transfer he made on granting the option to the trustees, the value of the property would still have been £14,250, because the allowance under s.163(1)(b) is given to the value transferred before any grossing-up.

The position is slightly more complicated where the option is granted at an under-value. Assume, for example, that George grants to the trustees for £1,000 an option worth £4,750 to buy George's house in three years' time for £30,000. This will itself constitute a chargeable transfer of £750, taking into account the annual exemption (and assuming the trustees bear the tax). Just under three years later, when the house is worth £35,000, George dies. In valuing the house at that time, regard may be had to the option (the practical effect of which is to reduce the value to him of the house by £5,000), but only to the extent that the trustees gave consideration for it. The result is as follows:

---

[147] Or was part of associated operations which together constituted a chargeable transfer.

	£
market value of house	35,000
less part of reduction attributable to consideration $\dfrac{£1000}{£4750} \times £5,000$	1,053
	33,947
less allowance for previous chargeable transfer	750
	33,197

There are two qualifications to the above rules. First, by s.163(2), where the contract imposing the restriction or exclusion was made before March 27, 1974, the above rules apply only in relation to transfers made on death. Secondly, the above rules apply only to the first "relevant event" which occurs in relation to the property by reference to which the restriction or exclusion operates. By s.163(3), in relation to any property, "relevant event" means:

> "(a) a chargeable transfer in the case of which the whole or part of the value transferred is attributable to the value of the property; and
> (b) anything which would be such a chargeable transfer but for this section."

Thus, if after applying s.163 there is a chargeable transfer, or, if before applying s.163 there would have been a chargeable transfer, s.163 ceases to apply to the property in the future so far as the restriction or exclusion is concerned. But, if there would be no chargeable transfer in any event, as would be the case if, for instance, the parties in the above examples were spouses, s.163 does not apply to that transaction, and consequently will apply to the first subsequent transaction which is a "relevant event".

It is not entirely clear when, strictly speaking, s.163 will apply, i.e. in what circumstances a person's right to dispose of property will be regarded as having been restricted or excluded by a contract. A pedant might regard s.163 as missing the target at which it is clearly aimed. The intention is obviously to provide a rule for valuing property which is subject to, as the above examples indicate, an option or similar "restriction or exclusion". But, in strict law, such an option does not restrict or exclude a person's freedom to dispose of property. He remains free to do what he likes with the property; it is just that if he fails to honour the option he may be sued for breach of contract. It is likely, however, that in order to give effect to the intention behind s.163, the court would regard the possibility of such a claim being made as restricting or excluding a person's freedom to dispose of property.

A related area of uncertainty concerns when the restriction or exclusion is to be regarded as having been imposed. This question occurred to James MacLeod, who expressed his views in the following letter which appeared in the *CTT News* of September 1980:

> "In an effort to satisfy his curiosity, the writer got in touch with the Capital Taxes Office in Scotland. As a result of some probing, it seems that whilst the Inland Revenue accept that the memorandum and articles of association of a company constitute a contract, and that, in relation to a shareholder, the contract is made at the date when the shares are purchased, [what is now s.163] only comes into operation where a contract is made to exclude or restrict the right to dispose of property, that is, after the property has itself been acquired. This is so notwithstanding that [what is now s.163] relates to a contract made at any time. In other words, if the articles of a company impose restrictions on the transfer of shares, a purchaser of existing shares purchases the shares subject to these restrictions, so it cannot

be said that he has entered into a contract to restrict or exclude his right to dispose of the shares, because his right to dispose was restricted or excluded at the outset.

The writer is not entirely convinced of the Inland Revenue's argument, but if they are right then the 'privileged' position of pre-March 27, 1974 contracts might not be as privileged as one might think. For example, suppose a man with his wife entered into a partnership in 1960. The partnership deed provides that in the event of the death or retirement of one partner, the other is to succeed to the former partner's share at book value, without revaluation of assets. If, prior to March 27, 1974 two sons were taken into the firm as partners, and if the views expressed to the writer by the Capital Taxes Office in Scotland are correct, then it seems that neither of the sons has excluded or restricted his right to dispose of his property, in the context of [what is now s.163], because these restrictions existed at the time when the partnership interest was acquired. It would follow, therefore, that if one of the sons decided to retire, it might not be possible to rely on the position of pre-March 27, 1974 contracts, under [what is now s.163], to say that the value of the retiring partner's interest was to be fixed by reference to the terms of the partnership deed without regard to the true value of the underlying assets of the firm . . . "

Insurance policies

25–73   Section 167(1) provides a special rule for determining the value of a policy of insurance on a person's life or of a contract for annuity payable on a person's death in connection with a transfer of value or a charge under the special charging provisions.[148] Under this rule, the value of the policy or contract is taken to be at least the total of the premiums[149] paid or other consideration which, at any time before the chargeable event, has been paid under the policy or contract or any policy or contract for which it was directly or indirectly substituted. In arriving at this total, there is deducted any sum which at any time before the chargeable event has been paid under, or in consideration for, the surrender of any right conferred either by the policy or contract in question or by a policy or contract for which it was directly or indirectly substituted.

The broad effect of this rule is that the value of a policy is either its market value—commonly, but not always its surrender value[150]—or, under s.167(1), the total of the premiums paid in respect of the policy, if that total is greater. The reason s.167(1) makes express provision to bring in the value of any premiums paid is that in the few years immediately after a policy is taken out its surrender value, which, assuming the insured is in good health, will be its market value, will be low, since during those years the premiums will be used by the insurance company to defray its heavy initial costs (commissions, etc.). During that period the value to be brought into account will thus normally be the premiums or other consideration paid by the transferor, because that will represent the portion of his estate which the policy in effect represents at that time.

Unit-linked policies

25–74   It may be that the policy is one under which:

---

[148] Except where a charge is imposed because the value of the policy or contract is reduced apart from the rule: IHTA 1984 s.167(5).

[149] Since IHTA 1984 s.167(1) refers to "premiums" the amount to be brought into account is thought to be the amount of the premium disregarding any life assurance relief that may be available; cf. para.3–16.

[150] This may depend on whether the policy is "with profits" or "without profits".

(1) the benefit secured is expressed in units, the value of which is published and subject to fluctuation, and

(2) the payment of each premium secures the allocation to the policy of a specified number of such units.

If, in the case of such a unit-linked policy, the value at the time of the transfer (or exit charge or periodic charge) of the units allocated to the policy on the payment of premiums is less than the aggregate of what the respective value of those units was at the time of allocation, the value of the policy is taken to be its value under s.167(1), less the difference between the value of the units at that time and the value of the units at the time of allocation.[151]

Endowment policy linked to term policy: anti-avoidance

In two cases, the special rule in s.167(1) does not apply. First, by s.167(2), the **25-75** special rule does not apply either:

(1) in the case of a transfer of value which a person makes on his death, or

(2) in the case of any other transfer which does not result in the policy or contract ceasing to form part of the transferor's estate.

This is an anti-avoidance provision. Before it was enacted, it was possible to use s.167(1), itself an anti-avoidance provision of sorts, to avoid tax. The scheme by which this somewhat surprising result was achieved was both clever and complicated, and proceeded as follows. The first step was that the transferor, "the father", took out two related policies. The first was a pure endowment policy for which he paid a premium of, say, £50,000. Under this policy (i) he was to be paid a lump sum on attaining the age of, say, 100, and (ii) he had a right to surrender his policy and recover his premium, but this right lapsed in seven days. The second policy was a term policy under which the same benefit (the right to which vested ab initio in his son) was payable on his death; for this policy the father paid a small premium, say, £500. At this stage the father had thus made a transfer of value of £500. The second and crucial step was for the father to allow his right of surrender to lapse, at which stage s.167(1) became important. Under s.3(3) an omission to exercise a right can constitute a notional disposition and consequently a transfer of value if, inter alia, the omission decreases the value of the estate of the person who omitted to exercise the right in question. The father's allowing his right of surrender to lapse had this effect, since by virtue of that lapse the value shifted out of the endowment policy which he owned to the term policy owned by his son. Consequently, under s.3(3) there was a disposition since the value of the father's estate was decreased and the value of the son's estate was increased. Thus, prima facie, there was also a transfer of value by virtue of the provisions of s.3(1) and a chargeable transfer by virtue of s.2(1).

It then became necessary to determine the value transferred by the chargeable transfer. Section 167(1) provides that, in determining in connection with a transfer of value the value of a policy of insurance, it is necessary to bring into account at least the premiums paid on that policy. That being the case, the endowment policy had the same value both before and after the right to surrender lapsed, and consequently the value transferred by the chargeable transfer, i.e. the difference in the value of the pure endowment policy before and after the omission, was nil. Thus, there was no value transferred by the chargeable transfer when the value actually shifted.

[151] IHTA 1984 s.167(4).

The last step occurred on the father's death when the insurance company paid the son. In itself this had no effect on the father's estate—the policy was worthless (the special valuation rule did not apply on death once the right to surrender had lapsed)—and since death is not an associated operation, it could not be linked with the earlier parts of the scheme. This scheme was more subtle in that a right was built into the pure endowment policy at the outset so that the father, in addition to the right of total surrender within the first seven days, had the right to make partial surrenders during his lifetime. This enabled the father to derive an "income" from the policy, and this income was subject to little, if any, income tax.

In its original form, s.167(2) provided only that the special rule did not apply in the case of a transfer of value made on the death of the person whose life was insured, or on whose death the annuity was payable. As was seen above, this did not hinder the effectiveness of the scheme; on the contrary, it was essential to its effectiveness. As amended, s.167(2) provides that s.167(1) also does not apply in the case of a "transfer of value which does not result in the policy or contract ceasing to be part of the transferor's estate". This amendment effectively counteracts the scheme described above; the effect of the amendment is to provide that the value transferred by the chargeable transfer can be identified as the difference between the market value of the pure endowment policy before the right to surrender lapses, i.e. effectively the premiums paid, and the market value of the policy shorn of the right to surrender, i.e. a very low value.

Term policies

25–76   The second case in which s.167(1) does not apply is where certain term policies are concerned. By s.167(3), s.167(1) does not apply where the policy is one under which the sum assured becomes payable only if the person whose life is insured dies before the expiry of a specified term and during the life of a specified person. Where the specified term ends, or can, under the policy, be extended so as to end more than seven years after the making of the insurance, s.167(1) does not apply if, in the event that the person whose life is insured or the specified person dies before the expiry of the specified term, the policy is one under which:

(1) the premiums are payable during at least two-thirds of that term and at yearly or shorter intervals; and

(2) the premiums payable in any one period of 12 months are not more than twice the premiums payable in any other such period.

Section 167(3) is intended primarily to ensure that the normal market value rule applies in valuing policies which are taken out against the risk of a transferor dying within three years of making a chargeable transfer.

Amounts due

25–77   The valuation of debts owed to a person is dealt with by s.166, which provides that in determining the value to him of his right to receive any sum under any obligation, it is assumed that the obligation will be duly discharged. This assumption does not operate to the extent that the recovery of the sum is either impossible or not reasonably practicable, provided that it has not become so as a result of any act or omission by the creditor. It may be that recovery of the sum is impracticable only temporarily, e.g. where money abroad is prevented from being remitted to the United Kingdom by foreign exchange control regulations. In such a case the value of the right must be discounted as may be appropriate in the circumstances.

Farm cottages

The question of whether a particular farmhouse or cottage falls within "agricultural property" under s.115(2) is frequently before the courts.[152] Where cottages *are* found to meet the "character appropriate" test and are occupied solely by persons for agricultural purposes which are connected with the agricultural property concerned, special rules will apply in determining the value of the property including the cottage. Section 169 provides that in such a case the fact that the cottages are suitable for residential purposes of persons not so employed is to be ignored in valuing the cottages.

25–78

Furthermore, HMRC by concession regards s.169 as applying where the property is occupied by a retired farm employee or his or her widow (or widower), if the occupier is a statutorily protected tenant or the occupation is under a lease granted to the farm employee for his or her life (and that of any surviving spouse), as part of the employee's contract of employment by the landlord for agricultural purposes.[153]

Section 115(2) (and s.169(2)) specifically provide that the breeding and rearing of horses on a stud farm fall within "agricultural purposes" for the purposes of s.169(1). In *Earl of Normanton v Giles*,[154] however, the House of Lords held that a gamekeeper who was employed to keep and rear pheasants was not a person employed in agriculture for the purposes of s.1 of the Rent (Agriculture) Act 1976.

The question of valuing a farmhouse qualifying for agricultural property relief was considered in *Lloyds TSB (personal representative of Antrobus, Deceased) v IR Capital Taxes (Antrobus No.2)*.[155] HMRC argued that the requirement in s.115(3) to assume the property was subject to a perpetual covenant restricting its use to agricultural purposes was akin to a standard form covenant imposed for planning purposes, which would reduce the value of the farmhouse qualifying for APR. The PRs of the deceased argued for a less restrictive interpretation of s.115(3) in their proposal that the land could be farmed by a person whose main pursuits occurred else, someone they termed a "lifestyle farmer". The Lands Tribunal agreed with HMRC; it was not wrong, they held, to treat the perpetual covenant in s.115(3) as equivalent to a standard agricultural planning tie and as such not admitting for a "lifestyle farmer". The Lands Tribunal agreed that the agricultural value of the farmhouse in *Antrobus No.2* was established by applying a 30 per cent deduction from market value, and, if they were wrong about the "lifestyle farmer" point, a reduction of 15 per cent from market value would be appropriate.

LIABILITIES

VIII. INTRODUCTION

Under both CTT and IHT the basic rule is that in determining the value of a person's estate at any time the liabilities of that person are taken into account; see s.5(3). Not

25–79

---

[152] Agricultural relief is considered in Ch.26.

[153] Concession F16 dated February 13, 1995 (but embodying existing practice).

[154] *Earl of Normanton v Giles* [1980] 1 W.L.R. 28; [1980] All E.R. 106.

[155] *Lloyds TSB (personal representative of Antrobus, Deceased) v IR Capital Taxes (Antrobus No.2)* [2002] S.T.C. (S.C.D.) see para.26–131.

all liabilities, however, can be taken into account. Under CTT the basic rule was that a liability could be taken into account only if it satisfied one of two requirements. First, it could be taken into account if it was imposed by law,[156] e.g. where it was imposed by the tax code.[157] Secondly, where a liability was not imposed by law, it could be taken into account to the extent only that it was incurred for a consideration in money or money's worth. Assume X buys property worth £10,000 from Y for £12,500, which purchase price is left outstanding. The debt owed by X will be taken into account only as to £10,000. If A covenants to pay B £5,000 a year for seven years, A's liability to make the payments will not be taken into account, because it was not incurred for any consideration and was not imposed by law.

The Finance Act 1986 introduced further restrictions on what liabilities can be deducted in calculating a taxpayer's estate. These provisions apply only to debts or incumbrances created by dispositions made on or after March 18, 1986,[158] and are relevant only in determining the value of a person's estate immediately *before he died*. This section of the book will consider first the general rule derived from the CTT legislation and then the rules introduced by the Finance Act 1986.

IX. THE GENERAL RULE

25–80 The general rule that liabilities imposed by law or incurred for a consideration in money or money's worth are taken into account, although relatively easy to state, gives rise to a number of questions. For example, how are liabilities which crystallise after a person's death dealt with?

When a person dies he is treated as having made a transfer of value immediately before he died, but liabilities which arise after his death and which decrease the value of some specific property comprised in his estate will be brought into account under s.171 so long as they arise by reason of his death.[159] This would be the case, for example, where on the death of a partner there was no election for an income tax continuance. This would result in a cessation of the partnership and, therefore, an assessment to income tax for which, in the case of the deceased partner, his estate would be liable. Normally, provision would have been made by the partnership to deal with this contingency. On the crystallising of the contingency, the "contingency fund" set up by the partnership will cease to form part of the partnership assets with the result that the value of each partner's share in the partnership will be reduced proportionately. As specific property, the deceased partner's share, is affected, the reduction falls within s.171(2) and can thus be taken into account in valuing his estate.

A more difficult situation arises when the crystallisation on death of the liability does not decrease the value of specific property in the deceased's estate. This may be the case, for example, where a person has leased property and claimed capital allowances. If on his death the market value of the property exceeds its written-down value there will be a balancing charge,[160] but this liability will not fall within s.171, because it does not affect the value of specific property.

---

[156] A restriction in the articles of a company is not imposed by law; *Noble v Laygate Investments Ltd* [1978] S.T.C. 430.

[157] But see para.25–83 as to when tax is not a deductible liability.

[158] FA 1986 s.103(6).

[159] See para.8–17.

[160] See Capital Allowances Act 2001. The fact that the deceased's personal representatives can elect out of this charge is irrelevant since if they do so elect the liability remains, only its crystallisation is deferred.

In the authors' view, such a liability may be distinguished from a liability which is contingent on the happening of some event which may or may not happen, e.g. the contingent liability of a landlord to make payments to a tenant under the Rent Acts. It is true that a liability which is contingent on a person's death will not crystallise until he dies, and that therefore prima facie it does not fall to be taken into account in respect of the transfer he is treated as making immediately before he dies (unless it comes within s.171). But, unlike a liability contingent on an event which may or may not happen, the only thing contingent about a liability that depends on a person's death is when it will crystallise, not whether it will do so. In the authors' view, such "inevitable" liabilities may be better regarded as deferred rather than contingent liabilities, and should arguably be treated as existing liabilities which fall to be discharged in the future. They therefore should be brought into account and valued at the time of the transfer.

Liabilities incurred during administration of an estate

25–81 Under estate duty, debts which were actually paid in the due course of administering an estate were not disallowed solely on the ground that they had become statute-barred, and it is thought that such debts will be allowed as a deduction for IHT notwithstanding the fact that they are not legally enforceable, so long as they were imposed by law or incurred for a consideration in money or money's worth.

Liability for IHT

25–82 The legislation includes two provisions which deal with how liabilities to IHT are to be brought into account in determining the value of a person's estate. The first is s.5(4), which provides that in determining the value of a person's estate immediately after a transfer of value the transferor's liability, if any, to IHT is to be brought into account. It is this provision which gives rise to the requirement to "gross-up" certain transfers.[161] Section 5(4) raises some difficult questions in relation to actual chargeable transfers. Assume, for example, that a father makes a chargeable transfer to the trustees of a discretionary trust. Under s.199(1), the father will remain liable for the IHT due on the transfer until the tax is paid. If the trustees in fact pay the tax, then it seems clear that they need pay tax on the net transfer only and not on the transfer after any grossing-up. The situation is less clear where the transferee undertakes to bear the IHT on a transfer in circumstances where his undertaking constitutes a legally binding agreement on which the transferor could sue if the transferee failed to discharge his obligation. Returning to the above example, assume that notwithstanding their undertaking to pay the tax the trustees refused to do so, and HMRC sought to collect tax from the father. Given the fact that under s.5(4) the father's liability for IHT must be brought into account, it could be maintained that HMRC would be entitled to recover tax on a grossed-up basis from the father, who would, in turn, be entitled to recover from the trustees an amount equal to the tax paid to HMRC. Against this, it could be said that since the father's liability for tax was balanced by his right to receive from his son a sum equal to any tax he had to pay,[162] his liability to pay tax did not diminish the value of his estate, and therefore HMRC would be entitled to collect tax from him on only

---

[161] See paras 6–26 and following.
[162] IHTA 1984 s.166.

763

the chargeable transfer before any grossing-up. In this respect the drafting of s.5(4) appears to be defective.

It is also to be noted that the effect of s.5(4) appears to be that no regard is had to the nature of the property out of which a transferor satisfies his liability to tax. Thus, if, for example, Franco, a Spanish domiciliary, transfers property situated in the United Kingdom and pays the IHT due in respect of that transfer out of his bank account in Madrid, the fact that he has paid the tax out of excluded property appears to be irrelevant. This seems inconsistent with the general treatment of excluded property. The second provision which deals with how liabilities to IHT are to be brought into account in determining the value of a person's estate is s.174(2). This provides that any undischarged liability of a person to IHT is deductible from the value of his estate only if the tax is in fact paid out of his estate. Thus, if the deceased has an outstanding liability to IHT in respect of a lifetime gift, this liability will not be brought into account if it is in fact discharged by someone else.[163]

Liability to other taxes in connection with a transfer of value

25-83   A person's liability to any other tax in respect of which he may be chargeable in connection with a transfer of value is not brought into account in determining his liability to tax on that transfer.[164] Where CGT is chargeable as a result of a chargeable transfer or an exit charge, the value transferred will be reduced by that tax if it is borne by the donee.[165]

Valuation of liabilities

25-84   The general market value rule applies in determining the value of liabilities which fall to be brought into account. Thus, debts which bear interest at less than the market rate, or which bear no interest at all will have to be discounted unless they are repayable on demand. Where a debt bears interest at the market rate, no discounting is necessary. In the same way, by s.162(2), a liability which falls to be discharged after the time at which it is to be taken into account is valued as at the time at which it is to be taken into account, discounted as may be appropriate. Where a person is liable to IHT in connection with a transfer of value, no allowance is made for the fact that the tax owed is not due immediately.[166] Where there is a right to a reimbursement in respect of a liability, s.162(1) provides that the liability is taken into account only to the extent that reimbursement cannot reasonably be expected to be obtained.

The deceased's share of a liability attaching to a jointly owned asset is usually the same as the deceased's share of that asset. There may be cases where the deceased's share of the liability should be different from their share in the asset, in such cases it will be necessary to check the documentation evidencing the liability. For example where two unmarried partners, A and B, own a house jointly which is mortgaged for the purpose of financing A's business, it is possible that the debt may be solely that of

---

[163] Liability to IHT on a PET made by the deceased in the seven years before his death does not fall within s.174(2) even if that tax is paid out of the estate since the liability did not exist immediately before the death.

[164] IHTA 1984 s.5(4).

[165] IHTA 1984 s.165(1); see paras 6–37 and 15–50 respectively.

[166] IHTA 1984 s.162(3)(a).

A.[167] Where there is a right to reimbursement the same rules as above will apply to the valuation of that liability.

Transfers by instalments

In determining the value of a person's estate immediately before death, special rules apply for determining the amount of any liability he was under to make payments or transfer assets in consequence of a disposition to which s.262 applies. It will be recalled that s.262 applies, in effect, where an actual transfer of value is made by instalments. In such circumstances, the actual transfer of value occasioned by the initial disposition is effectively ignored and tax is instead charged as if each instalment made by the transferor was a separate disposition. It may be, of course, that the transferor dies before having finished making the instalments. In that case, s.175 makes provision for ascertaining how much of the transferor's outstanding liability to make instalments is to be brought into account. This is discussed at para.2–15.

25–85

Attribution of liabilities

The general rule, which is subject to a vital qualification discussed below, is that a liability which is an incumbrance on any property is taken, so far as is possible, to reduce the value of that property.[168]

25–86

Planning

It is clear from a planning standpoint that liabilities should not be secured on property which may qualify for business and/or agricultural relief. This follows from the fact that the liabilities will be taken as reducing the value of the property in question, with the result that the amount by reference to which the relief is given is also reduced. So far as is commercially possible, such property should thus be kept free of incumbrances; if it is necessary to secure a liability on such property, the liability should (again, in so far as it is commercially possible to do so) be secured first on property which does not qualify for such relief. In strict law, it appears that full business and/or agricultural relief will be available in respect of property so long as liabilities are not secured on that property, i.e. it suffices that the liabilities are not secured specifically on the property and they need not be secured specifically on property which does not qualify for such relief. If, for example, X dies with an estate worth £300,000, half of which is attributable to property qualifying for business relief, and, immediately before he died, he owed £100,000 to the bank which was secured on his estate generally, the correct analysis would appear to be that on his death he made

25–87

---

[167] HMRC Manuals IHTM15064.
[168] See IHTA 1984 s.162(4).

a transfer of value of £200,000, of which £150,000 was eligible for business relief. It is understood, however, that in practice HMRC may contend that a liability secured on a person's estate generally should be taken as reducing the value of the property comprised in that estate rateably. If this is correct, in the above example half of the outstanding liability would be taken to reduce the value of the business property to £100,000 with the result that one third less business relief was available. In order to prevent arguments with HMRC on this point from arising, it may thus be prudent—so far as it is commercially acceptable to do so—to secure liabilities specifically on assets not qualifying for business and/or agricultural relief.[169]

Free estate liabilities and settled property

25–88   Difficulties may arise where a person with an interest in possession in settled property has liabilities which exceed the value of his free estate. Assume, for example, that X dies leaving assets worth £50,000 and liabilities of £60,000, and that immediately before he died he had an interest in possession in £200,000. Obviously, no tax is due on his free estate, but (leaving aside any available nil rate band) is tax chargeable on the entire £200,000 in which his interest subsisted, or is that figure reduced by the £10,000 in liabilities which could not be set against his free estate? HMRC's view, as stated in IHTM, is as follows:

> "We take the view that a liability at any title may only be deducted against the assets at that title. This means that if there is an overall deficit on the free estate you cannot set this against the the value of settled property. This is derived from the judgements of Lawrence J and the Court of Appeal in *Re Barnes (Deceased)* (1938) 2 KB 684 in the first instance and (1939) 1 KB 316 CA. It is considered that these decisions, based on the relevant estate duty provisions in the 1894 Finance Act apply equally to the corresponding provisions in the inheritance tax legislation. However a contrary view is possible in view of IHTA 1984, s.5(1) and IHTA 1984, s.49(1)."[170]

The *Barnes* case concerned the application of an estate duty provision similar (though not identical) to s.5(3), to a deceased who had made gifts before his death which subsequently proved to be chargeable and whose liabilities on his death far exceeded the value of property then comprised in his estate. The Court of Appeal held that the excess liabilities did not reduce the value of the previous gifts.

It is debatable whether HMRC are in fact correct in their reliance on *Re Barnes*, being a case arising under the estate duty rather than IHT regime. And while it may make sense in principle for the approach taken in relation to estate duty to be taken in relation to IHT,[171] HMRC admit "a contrary view" is possible on the basis of the IHT legislation itself. Indeed, it seems that HMRC's position has been challenged a number of times on this point, unfortunately without ever having reached the courts, and it

---

[169] The question of whether underwriting losses constitute liabilities incurred "for the purposes of the business" which are to be deducted from the value of assets used in the business and for which business relief is available was addressed in *Hardcastle (the executors of Vernede, Deceased) v IRC* [2000] S.T.C. (S.C.D.) 532—see para.26–85.

[170] HMRC Manuals IHTM28397.

[171] A similar result is thought to follow when property subject to a reservation is included in a person's estate.

would be interesting to see how their approach stood up if it ever reached that stage.

Foreign element

Where a liability is to a person resident outside the United Kingdom and does not:

(1) fall to be discharged in the United Kingdom, and
(2) is not an incumbrance on property in the United Kingdom,

it is taken—so far as it is possible to do so—to reduce the value of property outside the United Kingdom.[172] HMRC's stated practice was to deduct debts arising in a particular foreign country primarily against the assets in that country, with any excess set proportionally against assets in other foreign countries.[173] There is, however, no statutory basis to this practice and it would therefore be open to challenge in appropriate circumstances.

In a case where an estate comprises UK debts and both United Kingdom and foreign property, HMRC's practice has been to deduct the debts primarily from UK assets and to deduct only the excess from assets abroad. Again there are no statutory grounds for this, but HMRC have maintained this approach despite conflicting case law.[174]

Where a debt is an incumbrance both on property situated in the United Kingdom and abroad, s.162(4) requires the debt to be apportioned between both such property.

As a general rule, taxes (other than those charged by reference to the transfer in hand) are to be deducted only from the value of property in the country by which the tax is imposed. There are exceptions: e.g. HMRC have agreed with the authorities in Ireland that where a person dies domiciled in England, Scotland or Wales owing taxes in Ireland but has no Irish assets, the taxes can be deducted from UK assets. Furthermore, the European Community Council Mutual Assistance Recovery Directive[175] requires HMRC, upon request by another European Member State, to enforce in the UK tax which is claimed in that state. It is likely that, as with taxes due in the United Kingdom, any foreign tax recovered under the Directive will be deductible from a deceased's UK estate.

Where expense is incurred to administer or realise property situated abroad, an allowance may be made against the value of that property under s.173 of up to 5 per cent of the value of that property in order to reduce the value of the estate subject to IHT.[176] The expense must for these purposes be additional to the expense which would have been incurred had the property been situated in the United Kingdom.

In practice, HMRC do not easily allow deductions for foreign expenses, and certainly not without detailed information and breakdowns of the expenses claimed. Estimates will also be required of what the likely expenses would have been had the

---

[172] IHTA 1984 s.162(5). Provided, of course, that the liability meets the requirements of IHTA 1984 s.5(5), being either imposed by law or incurred for consideration in money or money's worth. Section 162(5) provision may affect double taxation relief.

[173] HMRC Manuals IHTM28394.

[174] Introduced in the United Kingdom by FA 2002 s.134 and Sch.39.

[175] It is not clear whether the allowance should be available where property is locally situated in the United Kingdom but is shifted abroad as a result of a situs code operating under a double tax treaty. For further consideration of double tax treaties, see Ch.31.

[176] IHTA 1984 ss.5(1) and 3(3).

property concerned been situated in the United Kingdom. The types of expenses that would qualify for deduction include the more obvious examples such as fees for interpreters and translators and foreign legal costs, such as the fee for taking out a grant abroad. Legal costs incurred in the United Kingdom may also be deductible to the extent that they relate to activities arising only on account of the property being situate abroad. In line with HMRC's general practice of only deducting foreign taxes from foreign property, they have also been known to allow a deduction for a foreign liability to capital gains tax on the share of an un-crystallised gain attributable to a deceased's period of ownership.

No deduction for trustees' liabilities?

25–90   There appears to be a missing link in the legislation, the effect of which is that, at least in theory, no account will be taken of many liabilities incurred by trustees.

The point is best explained by an example. Assume that X dies and that immediately before his death property worth £500,000 is comprised in his free estate. At the time he has debts totalling £75,000, all of which were incurred for full consideration in money or money's worth, and none of which were rendered non-deductible by the Finance Act 1986 s.103. Thus, as matters stand, IHT is chargeable on £425,000. This follows from the fact that s.5(3) provides that "in determining the value of a person's estate at any time his liabilities at that time shall be taken into account . . . "; so, it is quite correct to take into account X's indebtedness.

Assume also that, immediately before he died, X had a life interest in settled property worth £700,000 and that, at that time, the trustees had outstanding debts of £100,000. One would reasonably assume that these debts should be taken into account in determining the amount on which tax is to be charged in respect of the trust fund. Unfortunately, this does not appear to be authorised by the legislation. The trustees do not have an "estate" within the meaning of s.5, because they are not beneficially entitled to any property.[177] Therefore, s.5(3) does not authorise the setting-off of their liabilities against the trust fund. It is true that under s.49(1) X is treated as having been beneficially entitled to the property in which his life interest subsisted, with the result that it formed part of his estate immediately before he died, but s.49(1) does not have the effect of deeming the trustees' liabilities to be his liabilities.

One way forward would be to rely on s.162(4), which provides that "a liability which is an incumbrance on any property shall, so far as possible, be taken to reduce the value of that property". The argument would be that s.162(4) applies because the trustees can have recourse to the trust fund to discharge liabilities which they have incurred in the due administration of the trust. Therefore the value of the property comprised in the trust fund is only £600,000. This, however, would involve ascribing to the term "incumbrance" a meaning that the term does not have, however benevolent a reading it may be given.

The net result in the above example is that on a strict reading of the legislation no account can be taken of the trustees' liabilities: X will pay tax on £100,000 more than he should do. This is plainly unacceptable, and indeed it is clear that in practice HMRC

---

[177] See, e.g. *Wise v Perpetual Trustee Co Ltd* (1903) A.C. 139; David J. Hayton, *Underhill and Hayton: Law Relating to Trustees* 15th edn (London: Butterworths, 1995), Ch.37 and *Halsbury's Laws of England*, edited by The Right Honourable Lord MacKay of Clashfern, 4th edn, re-issue Vol.28, para.701.

will allow such liabilities, possibly on the basis that the trustees have an equitable lien[178] against trust assets for debts they have incurred.

Business relief and instalment relief

As is discussed at paras 26–82 and following, special rules apply for determining the value of a business or an interest in a business for the purposes of business relief and instalment relief, and the effect of those rules may be that different values apply for those purposes than for other IHT purposes. The special rules do not apply for purposes of agricultural relief, which is given in priority to business relief.[179]   **25–91**

X. RESTRICTIONS ON LOANBACKS

Section 103 of the Finance Act 1986 changed in two ways the rules in relation to debts incurred and to incumbrances[180] created by a disposition made on or after March 18, 1986. It is important to note that these changes affect only the question of whether such debts and incumbrances can be taken into account in determining the value of a person's estate immediately before he died. First, the 1986 Act introduced a new anti-avoidance provision designed to render ineffective a ploy under which an individual took out a policy of life insurance for a premium payable on his death (which ranked as a charge against his estate) in return for which on his death the insurance company made a payment to a beneficiary chosen by the deceased. By s.103(7), in determining the value of a person's estate immediately after his death, no account is taken of any liability arising under or in connection with a policy of life insurance in respect of an insurance made on or after July 1, 1986, unless the whole of the sums insured under that policy form part of that person's estate immediately before his death. Secondly, it imported into the legislation a complicated estate duty restriction to the effect that no account is taken of a liability which represents a loanback to a donor of property which he has given away. The first of these changes is of limited interest and is largely self-explanatory. The second is far-reaching and deserves careful consideration.   **25–92**

Where a liability is a debt incurred or an incumbrance created by a disposition made by a person then, in determining the value of the estate, immediately before he died, of the person who incurred or created it, the liability may have to be abated in two cases in accordance with the complicated rules in the Finance Act 1986 s.103(1)–(6). These rules are similar to those found in the Finance Act 1939 s.31. Before considering them, it may be helpful to note the mischief at which they are aimed.   **25–93**

The mischief and the cure

Under the CTT legislation it was possible, to an extent, to have one's cake and eat it too. The basic technique involved a taxpayer making a gift of money which did not exceed his unused nil band, and then, after a decent interval, borrowing that money   **25–94**

---

[178] See para.26–192.
[179] See the inclusive definition in IHTA 1984 s.272.
[180] FA 1986 s.103(1)(a).

back, interest-free, from the donee. The original gift by the taxpayer was chargeable, but since it was within his nil band, no tax was actually payable. If he survived the gift by 10 years, it ceased to form part of his cumulative total, with the result that, assuming he made no chargeable transfers in the intervening 10 years, the gift was a non-event for CTT purposes. All this was unobjectionable. What was objectionable was the loanback. So long as the loan by the donee was expressed to be repayable on demand and was genuinely capable of being so repaid, the loan was regarded as not diminishing the value of the donee's estate, so that it did not constitute a chargeable gift. And, since the debt owed by the donor to the donee was deductible from the donor's estate, there was no question of the sum borrowed back being brought into charge in the donor's estate. The donor thus had his cake, in the form of the gift made with a view to surviving 10 years, and ate it too, i.e. but for a decent interval between the loan and loanback, he retained the use of the money.

To prevent this, the Finance Act 1986 s.103(1) provides:

> "Subject to subsection (2) below, if, in determining the value of a person's estate immediately before his death, account would be taken, apart from this subsection, of a liability consisting of a debt incurred by him or an encumbrance created by a disposition made by him, that liability shall be subject to abatement to an extent proportionate to the value of any of the consideration given for the debt or encumbrance which consisted of:
> (a) property derived from the deceased; or
> (b) consideration (not being property derived from the deceased) given by any person who was at any time entitled to, or amongst whose resources there was at any time included, any property derived from the deceased."

Consideration from property derived from the deceased

25–95   The first case where abatement is required is where the value of any of the consideration given for the debt or incumbrance consisted of property derived from the deceased.[181] The phrase "property derived from the deceased" means, subject to the let-out mentioned below, any property which was the subject matter of a disposition made by the deceased either by himself alone or in concert or by arrangement with any other person, or which represented any of the subject-matter of such a disposition, whether directly or indirectly, and whether by virtue of one or more intermediate dispositions.[182] "Subject-matter" includes for this purpose, in relation to any disposition, any annual or periodical payment made or payable under or by virtue of the disposition in question.[183] As has been noted, the word "disposition" includes a disposition effected by associated operations, with the result that the definition of "property derived from the deceased" is extraordinarily wide. In particular, there is no requirement that the deceased must have given the property in question to the person making the loan. Rather, it suffices that the property was at one time the subject-matter of a disposition by the deceased. The wide definition is, however, cut down by the statute, as is explained below.

The width of the definition can be illustrated by assuming that A makes a gift of his country cottage to his daughter. She sells the cottage and uses the proceeds to purchase quoted securities. The cottage, proceeds and quoted securities are all property derived

---

[181] FA 1986 s.103(3).
[182] FA 1986 s.103(3).
[183] FA 1986 s.103(6).

from the disposition made by A. It appears that the cottage will remain within the definition notwithstanding the purchase of the securities.

Let-out

The above rule is modified by s.103(4) if the disposition by the deceased of the property satisfies certain requirements. First, the disposition by the deceased must not have been a transfer of value. Thus, if the disposition was of excluded property, with the result that the disposition did not diminish the disponer's estate,[184] the rule will not apply. In the same way, the rule may not apply even if the disposition did not diminish the disponer's estate if one of the reliefs given to dispositions prevented it from being a transfer of value.[185] **25–96**

Secondly, it must be shown (i.e. the burden is on the taxpayer) that the disposition by the deceased of the property was not part of associated operations which included either:

(1) a disposition by the deceased, either alone or in concert or by arrangement with any other person, otherwise than for full consideration in money or money's worth paid to the deceased for his own use or benefit; or
(2) a disposition by any other person operating to reduce the value of the property of the deceased.

If both conditions are satisfied the relevant disposition is left out of account for the purposes of the provisions in s.103.

Home loan schemes

These schemes[186] came in various forms. Assume X owns a valuable house, Purple Acre. The following was the basic course of action under this kind of arrangement: **25–97**

(1) X established a UK resident trust ("the House Trust") under which X was entitled both to the trust income for his life and to occupy any dwelling-house owned by the House Trust;
(2) X sold Purple Acre to the House Trust for a purchase price left outstanding, interest-free and unsecured ("the Debt"). X continued to live in Purple Acre;
(3) X settled the debt on the trustees of an existing or a new accumulation and maintenance trust or interest in possession trust ("the Debt Trust") under which he was excluded from benefit.

The fact that X reserved a benefit in respect of Purple Acre was not worrying because, given his interest in possession in the House Trust, he would already be treated by s.49(1) as owning Purple Acre with the result that the clawback charge under s.102(3) of the Finance Act 1986 was displaced.[187]

---

[184] See paras 2–36–2–38.
[185] See paras 2–39–2–70.
[186] See paras 7–139 and 7–140.
[187] See para.7–139.

A major issue under these arrangements was whether s.103 prevented the Debt from being allowable against Purple Acre. Since s.103 disallows a liability "consisting of . . . an incumbrance created by a disposition" made by the person seeking to claim the liability as a deduction against his estate, such schemes normally involved an unsecured debt. This was not the end of the matter, however, because the debtor trustees had an equitable lien[188] against the property purchased in respect of their indebtedness to X and it was prudent to assume that this lien was an "incumbrance" for these purposes. There were, however, two further considerations.

First, was the lien/incumbrance "created by the disposition" made by X, as is required by s.103? The lien arguably arose by operation of law, not by the disposition made by X.[189]

Secondly, s.103 abated the amount of the debt allowable only "to an extent proportionate to the value of any of the consideration *given for* [authors' italics] the debt or incumbrance" which consisted inter alia of "property derived from the deceased". In the authors' view, Purple Acre was purchased by the trustees for the debt they owed to X, not for the lien enjoyed by the trustees of the House Trust. Against this, it might be said that X had a right of subrogation in respect of the trustees' lien, but the law in this area is not clear. Even if X had such a right, in the authors' view that right was not something given by the trustees.

Consideration from other resources

25–98   The second case where only the abated debt or incumbrance can be brought into account on a person's death is where the consideration given for the debt or incumbrance did not consist of property derived from the deceased, but was instead given by a person who was at any time entitled to, or amongst whose resources there was at any time included, any property derived from the deceased. The fact that the property was acquired prior to March 18, 1986, is apparently irrelevant. This test, which is laid down by s.103(1)(b) of the 1986 Act, is concerned with the case where the loanback is not out of property derived from the deceased as such, but is, as it were, enabled or facilitated by a disposition by the deceased of property, e.g. where X makes a gift to Y which enables Y to make a loan out of property which Y has owned all along.

25–99   It would also catch a loan by Y to X followed by a gift by X to Y. In *McDougal's Trustees v IRC*[190] the taxpayer borrowed money from the City of Edinburgh and bought an estate to be used as a public park for the City. It was held that since the City had the estate amongst its resources, s.31 of the Finance Act 1939 prevented the taxpayer's debt from being allowable.

First let-out

25–100   The second test is relevant only if the lender was a person who at some stage was entitled to, or amongst whose resources there was at some time included, any "property derived from the deceased". The phrase "property derived from the deceased" was

---

[188] See, e.g. *Wise v Perpetual Trustee Co Ltd* (1903) A.C. 139; David J. Hayton, *Underhill and Hayton: Law Relating to Trustees* 15th edn (London: Butterworths, 1995), Ch.37 and *Halsbury's Laws of England*, edited by The Right Honourable Lord MacKay of Clashfern, 4th edn, re-issue Vol.28, para.701.

[189] See *Davies v Powell* [1977] S.T.C. 32 and *Drummond v Austin Brown* [1984] S.T.C. 321.

[190] *McDougal's Trustees v IRC* [1952] T.R. 157.

considered in para.25–95. As was noted at para.25–96, there is a let-out if the disposition by the deceased of the property in question satisfies certain conditions. This let-out also applies under the second test.

Second let-out

Section 103(2) provides a second let-out where the "resource" test applies to all or **25–101** part of the consideration given. If it is shown that the value of the consideration given by the deceased exceeded that which could have been rendered available by an application of all the property derived from him, then no abatement is made in respect of the excess. Assume A gives property worth £10,000 to B. One year later B lends A £15,000. The loan is not wholly made out of property derived from A. No abatement is made in respect of the £5,000 by which the loan to A exceeds the resources of B, which includes the £10,000 given to him by A.

It is not immediately clear whether, in determining what property derived from the **25–102** deceased could have been applied in providing the consideration, regard is had only to property derived from the deceased which is amongst the resources of the person providing the consideration, or whether regard is to be had to property derived from the deceased regardless of by whom it is owned. It is thought that the former would be the preferable construction, if for no other reason than that the latter could cause insuperable practical difficulties in tracing all the property disposed of by the deceased. Even if this is wrong, s.103(2)(a), discussed below, should produce the same effect.

In determining how much of the property derived from the deceased falls to be taken **25–103** into account in abating the liability, no regard is to be had to two kinds of property. First, by s.103(2)(a), no regard is to be had to any property which is included in the consideration given. This restriction is obviously fair since, to the extent that such property is included in the consideration, the debt will be non deductible under s.103(1)(a).

Assume X gives shares worth £10,000 to Y. One year later Y sells half the shares back to X for £5,000, which is left outstanding. At the same time he lends X £11,000 out of property not derived from X. The £5,000 owed by X in respect of the sale will have been incurred for a consideration which consisted of property derived from himself, i.e. the shares. It will therefore be brought into account under s.103(1)(a) and accordingly eliminated by s.103(2)(a) in applying the resources test. The resources available to Y are thus £5,000, so that of the loan of £11,000, £6,000 (representing the "excess consideration") will not be abated.

Secondly, by s.103(2)(b), no regard is to be had to any property if it is shown that **25–104** the disposition of which it was the subject-matter was not made "with reference to, or with a view to enabling or facilitating" either:

(1) the giving by the deceased of the consideration in question, or
(2) the recoupment in any manner of the cost thereof.

It will thus fall to the taxpayer to show that, in determining what resources were available, certain property should be left out of account on the basis that, in effect, it was never intended to enable or facilitate a loan to the donor.

Assume that in 1976 X gave his daughter £10,000 as a marriage gift. In 1987 the daughter used the money as a down payment on a house. In 1988 the daughter lent

£2,000 to her father out of her own savings. In the circumstances, if HMRC are satisfied that X's marriage gift was not within s.103(2)(b), the £2,000 debt will not be abated.

25–105   The words "with reference to, or with a view to establish or facilitating" also appear in the associated operations provisions and will presumably be construed as referring to the subjective intent of the donor when he made the gift in question. Since the onus is on the taxpayer (in practice, the deceased's personal representatives) to show that he is not excluded from the let-out, it may be helpful if taxpayers record their intentions when making gifts.

Double or triple charges?

25–106   The new debt rules are capable of producing several charges to tax and in certain cases relief may be available under the Inheritance Tax (Double Charges Relief) Regulations 1987: see paras 8–36 and following. The fairness of these rules may be doubted. Take, for instance, a simple case involving the gift of a dwelling-house by A to his son B and the subsequent repurchase of the property by A for full market value, with that sum being left outstanding until A's death. Assume further that A dies within seven years of the original gift. The result of these transactions is as follows. First, the original gift, which was a PET when made, is brought into charge; secondly, the dwelling-house forms part of A's estate at death since it has been repurchased; and, finally, the outstanding purchase money is a non-allowable debt of A's estate. Accordingly, in this simple case the value of the house falls to be taxed three times; the aforesaid regulations provide no relief.

Planning

25–107   Various circumstances may arise in which it is thought desirable for trustees to make loans to a beneficiary resident in the United Kingdom who is also the settlor of the trust. In the authors' experience, it is often overlooked that the debt owed by the settlor-beneficiary will be a trust asset situated in the United Kingdom which s.103 will prevent from being a deductible liability in the settlor's estate.

In particular, it would be easy to think that where a foreign domiciliary creates a discretionary settlement of foreign situs property, no IHT problems can arise on the basis that such property, as excluded property, is effectively outside the scope of IHT. But this is not necessarily the case. Assume that, e.g. Xavier, a foreign domiciliary resident in the United Kingdom, borrows £300,000 from non-resident trustees of a discretionary settlement which he made in 1990 and acquires a cottage in the Lake District. The debt is secured on the cottage. This has two consequences. First, since Xavier is resident in the United Kingdom, the debt held by the trustees will be UK situs property (and so not excluded property) in respect of which Xavier has reserved a benefit. Secondly, the debt will be prevented by s.103 from reducing the value of the cottage. The net result is that Xavier is potentially liable to IHT on £600,000.

Although s.103(1) is of potentially wide application, it is possible to sidestep it in certain situations. Returning to the above example, assuming there were no non-tax inhibitions, the trustees could avoid the adverse effects of s.103 by lending the £300,000 to Xavier's wife. The fact that the trustees owned a UK situs asset in the form of the debt could be solved by their transferring the debt to an underlying company.[191]

Notional PET on discharge of debt

It may be that an individual who has incurred a debt or created an incumbrance which s.103(1) would prevent from being brought into account as a liability, pays or applies money or money's worth in or towards satisfying or reducing that debt or incumbrance. Section 103(5) provides that in such a case he is to be treated as having at that time made a PET equal in value to the money or money's worth so paid or applied. It will thus take such an individual seven years to convert his non-allowable liability into what amounts to a totally tax-free gift, but it may still be worth his while to attempt to do so since, if he survives the making of the PET by more than three years, he will pay less tax than if he had taken no action at all.

It is interesting that the draftsman has made use here of the concept of a PET. Since the new rules regarding liabilities apply only in valuing a person's estate immediately before he dies, the discharge during a person's lifetime of a liability precluded only by s.103 of the 1986 Act from being taken into account would not of itself constitute a transfer of value, because it would not diminish the value of his estate. The draftsman has, therefore, filled this gap by providing for a notional PET.

The application of this rule when a taxpayer purchases property which he had earlier given away is a matter of some uncertainty. Assume that A, having made a gift of a valuable chattel, subsequently decides that he cannot live without it. Accordingly, he purchases the chattel from the donee, paying full market value. Has A made a notional PET under s.103(5) at the time when he pays over the purchase price or, if the money is paid as part and parcel of the repurchase agreement, did A never incur any debt or encumbrance falling within s.103? Presumably the latter is the correct view.

REVALUATION RELIEFS

XI. INTRODUCTION

The legislation provides four kinds of revaluation relief, which fall into two categories. The first relief applies in relation to transfers made within seven years before a person's death. The remaining three reliefs apply where certain property comprised in a person's estate immediately before his death is sold within a prescribed period after his death for less than the value attributed to it immediately before he died. Both kinds of relief helpfully provide that it may be possible to substitute a more realistic value for the higher value previously attributed to the property. Each of the reliefs will be considered in turn.

XII. RELIEF FOR TRANSFERS MADE WITHIN SEVEN YEARS BEFORE DEATH

Sections 131–140 afford relief in certain circumstances where a person dies within seven years of making a transfer of value, IHT or additional IHT is payable and the

25–108

25–109

25–110

---

[191] Care would need to be taken that neither Xavier nor his wife were directors or shadow directors of the company for income tax purposes.

property he transferred has fallen in value between the transfer date and the date of his death. Provided certain conditions are satisfied the value transferred by the transfer is reduced for the purposes of calculating any tax due by any fall in the market value (as defined) of the property.[192] It should be noted that the relief can be claimed only where the IHT or additional IHT is payable on the transfer of value itself. The relief does not reduce the value of the chargeable transfer for the purposes of cumulation in calculating the tax on later transfers. The value to be set against the transferor's nil-rate band on death, for example, remains the value of the original transfer.[193] The relief must be claimed by a person liable to pay the whole or part of the tax.[194] For the persons who fall within this category, see para.29–64. By s.132(1), no relief is available if the transferred property is tangible movable property that is a wasting asset. For this purpose, property is a wasting asset if immediately before the transfer it had a predictable useful life, having regard to the purpose for which it was held by the transferor, of no more than 50 years.[195] By s.132(2), plant and machinery are regarded as always coming within this category.

The operation of these provisions can be far from straightforward. Section 131 looks at the market value of the assets at the date of the donor's death, i.e. their value in the hands of the donee rather than, as in s.3(1), the fall in value of the donor's estate. Where only part of the donor's interest is given away and thus a discount is applied both to the share remaining in the donor's hands and to the share received by the donee the result can be quite dramatic.

This can best be illustrated by way of an example:

A owns Blackacre worth £1 million. He gives 75 per cent to his daughter B and retains the remaining 25 per cent. A dies less than three years after the gift at which time Blackacre has fallen in value to £600,000.

If the customary 10 per cent discount[196] is applied to each of the respective shares, the value of the original gift would be:

Value of Blackacre at the date of the gift	£1,000,000
Less Value of share of Blackacre retained by A	
(£1,000,000 × 25 per cent) − 10 per cent	£225,000
Value of gift (loss to A's estate)	£775,000

In contrast the value of Blackacre in B's hands for the purposes of the relief under s.131 is calculated as follows:

Value of share of Blackacre at date of gift	
(£1,000,000 × 75 per cent) − 10 per cent	£675,000
Less Value of share of Blackacre at date of death	
(£600,000 × 75 per cent) − 10 per cent	£405,000
Section 131 relief	£270,000

---

[192] IHTA 1984 s.131(2)(a).
[193] HMRC Manuals IHTM14518.
[194] IHTA 1984 s.131(2)(b).
[195] IHTA 1984 s.132(2).
[196] See para.25–61 as to divergence from this custom.

Therefore the value of the gift after the relief is £775,000 – £270,000 = £505,000 and it is upon this figure that B will pay tax. In contrast the value of B's share of Blackacre is £405,000 (£600,000 × 75 per cent) – 10 per cent.

The difference is due to the 10 per cent discount which operates not only to increase the loss to the donor's estate but also reduces the value of the s.131 relief. The result would be even worse where shares in a family company were given away causing the donor to lose control or there is a gift of an undivided share in a chattel. In such instances the discount for a partial gift can be as high as 40 per cent.[197]

It should be noted that, where it is land or quoted or unquoted shares that were given away a claim may affect the value to be brought into account for CGT purposes under s.274 of the Taxation of Chargeable Gains Act 1992.

Agricultural relief and business relief

In the absence of provision to the contrary, the taxpayer would obtain a bonus when the original transfer qualified for agricultural and/or business relief. Assume that X gave to Y property worth £600,000, and that the value transferred qualified for 50 per cent business relief, so that the value transferred by the gift was only £300,000, and that X died two and a half years later, by which time the property had fallen in value to £400,000. The additional tax due because of X's death within three years of making the transfer would have been charged on only £100,000, i.e. the value transferred (£300,000) less the fall in market value (£200,000). Section 131(2A) accordingly provides that, with respect to transfers of value made, and other events occurring after March 17, 1986, the fall in market value will be reduced by the percentage by which the agricultural and/or business relief was given to the original transfer. Thus, in the example, the £200,000 fall in the market value would be reduced by 50 per cent, so that the adjusted value transferred was £200,000 (£300,000 less £100,000). **25–111**

Conditions for relief

By s.131(1), the relief is available where the transferred property either: **25–112**

(1) is, at the date of the transferor's death, the property of the transferee (the person whose property it became on the transfer), or of the transferee's spouse or civil partner, or
(2) has, before the date of the transferor's death, been sold by the transferee or his spouse or civil partner by a "qualifying sale".

The legislation uses the term "relevant date" to refer to the date on which the sale, or as the case may be, the death, occurs, and for the sake of convenience this term will also be used in the text.

What happens if not all the transferred property is sold at once? For example 1,000 shares in A plc are transferred to X who sells 500 on one date and the remaining 500 six months later (and, of course, both sales take place before the transferor's death and within seven years of the transfer). Can there be more than one "relevant date"? It is thought that the answer is "yes" and that the relief applies on each occasion transferred property is sold by a qualifying sale within the relevant period. The matter is not free

---

[197] See *Private Client Business* (London: Sweet & Maxwell, 1994), p.3.

from doubt however and clarification will only come through a decision of the courts or relevant legislation. However HMRC are believed to be likely to allow the relief for each sale and are understood to intend to include guidance to this effect in a forth-coming revision of the IHTM.

The position is even more unclear where the property was transferred to the donor in more than one tranche. For example D receives 500 shares in A plc on December 1, 2007 from B when the shares are worth £10 a share. D receives a further 500 shares in A plc on December 1, 2008 from B when the shares are worth £5 a share. D decides to sell 500 shares on January 31, 2009 when the shares are worth £4 a share and B subsequently dies in March 2009. It is unclear whether D can elect which shares are being sold, by stating he is selling the shares received in 2007, or whether the sale will be pro rated on D's entire holding in A plc. It is thought that if the shares can be readily identified, for example by a share certificate number, then D should be able to elect which shares he is selling. However, HMRC have not, to date, confirmed this view.

A further difficulty with s.131(1)(b) arises where property is held in a pre-March 2006 life interest trust, a transitional serial interest trust or a disabled persons trust that qualifies under s.89(2) as being treated as an interest in possession trust. Under s.49 in such circumstances it is the life tenant who is "the transferee". However if the transferred property is then sold it is the trustees who carry out the sale which can be done without reference to the beneficiary. The position can be distinguished from a "bare trust" where the trustees are selling at the direction of the beneficiary. On a strict interpretation s.131(1)(b) cannot therefore apply to a sale by trustees of a pre-2006 life interest trust, a transitional serial interest trust or a disabled trust because the sale is not by the transferee. However it is understood that HMRC accept that the relief would in practice apply.

Where transferred property is held by trustees of a number of sub-funds, perhaps as a result of several separate transfers, but the property itself is not sub-divided, for example where a large holding of shares is held for several funds, does the fact that each sub-fund cannot be said to hold particular shares but only a designated number out of the larger holding cause a further difficulty? Can the transferred property itself be said to have become the property of the trustees (who may only have a right to have a number of shares dealt with in accordance with the terms of the sub-fund) so that a subsequent sale by them qualifies for relief under s.131(1)(b)? Again the matter is not free from doubt but it is suggested that before selling any shares such trustees should identify the particular shares they are selling out of a specified sub-fund. HMRC should then accept in practice that the shares sold are the "transferred property" in respect of a particular transfer.

25–113 A sale is a qualifying sale for these purposes only if:

(1) it is at arm's length; and
(2) it is for a price freely negotiated[198] at the time of the sale; and
(3) no person concerned as vendor or as having an interest in the proceeds of the sale is the same as or connected[199] with any person concerned as purchaser or as having an interest in the purchase; and
(4) no provision is made, in or in connection with the agreement for the sale, that the vendor or any person having an interest in the proceeds of sale is to have any right to acquire some or all of the property sold or some interest in or created out of it.[200]

---

[198] For a discussion of the meaning of "sale" and "a freely negotiated price", see para.2–46.
[199] For the definition of connected persons, see para.2–45.
[200] IHTA 1984 s.131(3).

The relief will thus not be available in cases where the fall in value of the property has been engineered by an "artificial" sale at an undervalue.

Market value

As was mentioned above, the relief is given by reference to the fall in the market value of the property transferred by the transfer in question. For these purposes, market value is defined as the price the property might reasonably be expected to fetch if sold in the open market at the relevant date. This is subject to two qualifications, namely:

25–114

(1) that the price is not assumed to be reduced on the ground that the whole property is put on the market at the same time, and
(2) that in the case of unquoted shares it is assumed that in the open market there is available to any prospective purchaser all the information which a prudent prospective purchaser might reasonably require if he were proposing to purchase the shares or securities from a willing vendor by private treaty at arm's length.[201]

In addition, there are a number of special rules under which the value that would otherwise fall to be brought into account as the market value may be reduced or increased. The main purpose of these rules is to prevent a taxpayer from securing revaluation relief by artificially devaluing property before disposing of it in a qualifying sale, e.g. by altering the rights attaching to shares so as to depreciate the value of the shares prior to selling them. In such a case, the market value of the shares is increased to take account of the artificial reduction in value. Conversely, provision is also made to reduce the value of property, e.g. where a person sells with vacant possession property which, when it was transferred to him, was tenanted. In such a case, the value to be brought into account is, essentially, the value of the property on a tenanted basis. The rules are somewhat complicated; they become more understandable if one bears in mind that their purpose is to ensure that the value to be brought into account for purposes of the relief is the value that would have been brought into account if the only change since the transfer had been in the market itself and not, e.g. in the rights over or attaching to the property.

Shares and securities

Sections 133–140 make provision to increase or decrease the market value of shares in any of four cases, i.e. where before the relevant date:

25–115

(1) The transferee or his spouse or civil partner becomes entitled to a "capital payment" in respect of the shares.
(2) The transferee or his spouse or civil partner becomes liable to make a payment in pursuance of a call.
(3) There is a transaction, such as a reorganisation, in consequence of which the transferee or his spouse becomes liable to give any consideration for newly issued shares.

---

[201] IHTA 1984 s.140(2); see para.25–37 for a discussion of this rule.

(4) The shares are shares in a close company and the company makes a transfer of value or the share or loan capital of the company or the rights attaching thereto are altered. For this purpose, and throughout the following discussion, "shares" includes securities.[202]

Capital receipts

25–116   By s.133(1), if the transferee or his spouse or civil partner becomes entitled to a capital payment in respect of shares or securities, the market value of the shares or securities on that date is taken to be increased by an amount equal to the payment, unless the right to the payment is already reflected in the value of the shares. This prevents shares being "milked" of their value. Section 133(3) provides that for this purpose "capital payment" means any money or money's worth which does not constitute income for the income tax purposes. By s.133(2), if at any time before the relevant date the transferee or the spouse or civil partner receives or becomes entitled to receive in respect of the shares a provisional allotment of shares, and disposes of the rights, the amount of the consideration for the disposal is treated as a capital payment. This means that if shares are issued to a transferee or his spouse or civil partner on renounceable letters of allotment, any amount received by the transferee or his spouse or civil partner for disposing of the letters of allotment will be brought into account in valuing the shares. The amount to be brought into account is the amount received, not the value of the rights disposed of. It is thus possible to decrease the value of the property by giving away the rights or selling them at an undervalue. Such a gift or sale may itself give rise to a charge, but this would have been the position even if s.133 had provided that the value to be brought into account was the market value of the rights disposed of. Unfortunately, this does not appear to give much scope for planning, since a substantial benefit would normally accrue only where:

(1) a rights issue could be procured, and
(2) the value of the rights (and thus of the shares) was relatively high.

Payment of calls

25–117   By s.134, if the transferee or his spouse or civil partner becomes liable to make a payment in pursuance of a call in respect of the shares, the market value of the shares is taken to be reduced by an amount equal to the payment, unless the value of the shares already reflects that liability. This is the converse of the provisions in s.133 and ensures, in favour of the taxpayer, that increases in the value of shares deriving from such payment are left out of account.

Reorganisations, etc.

25–118   Section 135 takes account of the possibility of reorganisations, take-overs and similar transactions. By s.135(1), it applies where there is a transaction to which s.127 of the Taxation of Chargeable Gains Act 1992 applies, i.e. where there is:

---

[202] IHTA 1984 s.140(1).

(1) a reorganisation, within the meaning of s.126(1); or

(2) the conversion of securities within the meaning of s.132; or

(3) the issue by a company of shares in exchange for shares in another company in such circumstances that s.135 applies; or

(4) the issue by a company of shares under such an arrangement as is referred to in s.136.

Section 135 also applies:

(1) to any transaction corresponding to those mentioned above relating to a unit trust scheme to which s.127 applies by virtue of s.99, and

(2) where s.127 would apply in connection with shares compulsorily acquired in exchange for gilts if s.134 of the Taxation of Chargeable Gains Act 1992 had not been enacted.[203]

Where s.135 applies, there are two possible consequences, one relating to identification, the other to valuation. First, by s.135(3), the "new holding" and the "original shares", as defined in s.126(1) of the Taxation of Chargeable Gains Act 1992,[204] are treated as the same holding for purposes of the IHT revaluation relief.[205] Secondly, if, as part of the transaction in question, the transferor or his spouse or civil partner becomes liable to give any consideration for all or any part of the new holding, the market value of the shares is taken, in favour of the taxpayer, to be reduced by that consideration, unless the value of the shares already reflects that liability.[206] For this purpose:

(1) any surrender, cancellation or other alteration of any of the original shares or of the rights attached thereto, or

(2) any consideration consisting of any application, in paying up the new holding or any part of it, of the assets of the company concerned or of any dividend or other distribution declared out of those assets but not made

is not treated as consideration given for the new holding or any part of it.[207]

Close company shares

Section 136 lays down certain rules which apply only where the shares in question **25–119** are shares in a close company. For this purpose, "close company" has the same meaning as in s.102(1).[208] Under s.136(1), the market value of such shares may be increased or decreased where:

(1) the company makes a transfer of value, or

(2) there is an alteration in any of the company's unquoted[209] share or loan capital or to any rights attaching thereto[210] provided that no such increase or decrease is made under ss.133–135.

---

[203] cf. IHTA 1984 s.183.

[204] IHTA 1984 s.135(2).

[205] IHTA 1984 s.135(3).

[206] IHTA 1984 s.135(4).

[207] IHTA 1984 s.135(5).

[208] See para.2–74.

[209] See paras 25–36 and 25–37.

[210] See paras 2–18 and following.

In such a case, the market value of the shares is taken to be (again, to prevent the shares being "milked") increased by an amount equal to the difference between the market value of the shares at the time of the chargeable transfer and what their value would have been if the transfer or alteration had not been made.[211] This is subject to two qualifications. First, by s.136(3), where the increase is occasioned by the company making a transfer of value, the increase is reduced by any amount by which the estate of the individual (or of his spouse or civil partner) who made the chargeable transfer is increased by the company's transfer, provided the individual (or his spouse or civil partner) is domiciled in the United Kingdom at the time of the close company's transfer. In determining whether the person in question is so domiciled, the deemed domicile rules apply.[212] Secondly, by s.136(4), in the rare case where the transfer or the alteration increases the value of the shares, that increase is left out of account in determining the market value of the shares.

Interests in land

25–120   Section 137 makes provision to deal with the valuation of an interest in land where, at the relevant date:

(1) the interest is not the same in all respects and with the same incidents as it was at the time of the chargeable transfer, or
(2) the land in which the interest subsists is not in the same state and with the same incidents as it was at the time of the chargeable transfer.[213]

Regard is thus had both to any changes in the interest and to any changes in the land. An indication of the meaning of "incidents" is to be found in *Re Johnston's Application*[214] in which it was held that for purposes of s.12(3) of the War Damages Act 1943, "incident" was to be taken as meaning any factor connected with the interest in question which immediately before the damage affected the market value of the interest; the result in *Johnston's* case was that an option in a lease to purchase a freehold reversion fell to be taken into account.

Where either of the above conditions is satisfied, the market value of the land at the relevant date is taken to be increased by an amount equal to the difference between:

(1) the market value of the interest at the time of the chargeable transfer, and
(2) what that value would have been if the circumstances which prevailed on the relevant date and which result in either of the above conditions being satisfied had prevailed at the time of the chargeable transfer.[215]

A retrospective valuation of the interest will thus have to be made. The purpose of this adjustment in the sale price is to prevent a taxpayer from securing revaluation relief by artificially devaluing property before selling it, e.g. by granting a lease on less than commercial terms.

---

[211] IHTA 1984 s.136(2).
[212] IHTA 1984 s.267(1).
[213] IHTA 1984 s.137(2).
[214] *Re Johnston's Application* [1949] Ch. 524.
[215] IHTA 1984 s.137(1).

The above-mentioned rule, under which the market value of the land at the relevant date is taken to be increased, is subject to two qualifications. The first qualification operates where, after the date of the chargeable transfer, compensation becomes payable under any enactment to the transferee or his spouse either:

(1) because of the imposition of a restriction on the use or development of the land in which the interest subsists, or
(2) because the value of the interest is reduced for any other reason.

In that case, two results obtain: first, the imposition of the restriction or the other cause of the reduction in value is ignored; secondly, the market value of the interest is taken to be increased by an amount equal to the amount of the compensation.[216] The second qualification is that any increase in the value of the interest occasioned by changes in the interest or the incidents thereto, or in the land or the incidents thereto, is effectively ignored in valuing the interest in question[217]; this ensures that a person is not precluded from obtaining relief in respect of falls in the value of the property transferred to him.

Leases

Where the property is the interest of a lessee under a lease with less than 50 years **25–121** to run at the time of the chargeable transfer in question, the value of the lease may be adjusted in two ways. First, the lease, as an interest in land, is subject to the provisions of s.137. Secondly, by s.138(1), the market value of the interest on the relevant date is taken to be increased by an amount equal to the "appropriate fraction" of the market value of the interest at the time of the chargeable transfer. For this purpose, the appropriate fraction is:

$$\frac{P(1) - P(2)}{P(1)}$$

"P(1)" is the percentage that would be derived from the table in para.1 of Sch.8 to the Taxation of Chargeable Gains Act 1992 for the duration of the lease at the time of the chargeable transfer. "P(2)" is the percentage that would be derived from that table for the duration of the lease on the relevant date.[218] If the duration of the lease is not an exact number of years the percentage to be derived from the table is the percentage for the whole number of years plus one-twelfth of the difference between that and the percentage for the next higher number of years for each extra month, counting 14 days or more as one month.

Assume that on March 15, 1996, X transferred to Y a lease worth £300,000 which was due to expire on March 31, 2010, and that on December 1, 1998, X died at a time when the open market value of the lease was £100,000. The value of the lease would be computed as follows:

[216] IHTA 1984 s.137(3).
[217] IHTA 1984 s.137(4).
[218] IHTA 1984 s.138(2).

P(1): since the duration of the lease at the time of the chargeable transfer was 14 years and 17 days, the percentage from the table is:

$$58.971 + 1/12 \, (61.617 - 58.971) =$$

$$58.971 + 1/12 \text{ of } 2.646 =$$

$$58.971 + 0.2205 =$$

$$59.192$$

P(2): since the duration of the lease at the time of the death was 11 years and four months, the percentage from the table is:

$$50.038 + 4/12 \, (53.191 - 50.038) =$$

$$50.038 + 4/12 \text{ of } 3.153 =$$

$$50.038 + 1.051 =$$

$$51.089$$

The value of the lease at the time of the death is thus increased by:

$$\frac{59.192 - 51.089}{59.192} \times £300,000 = £41,068$$

with the result that the market value of the lease is:

$$£100,000 + £41,068 = £141,068$$

Property generally

25–122   Section 139(1) applies unless the property in question is shares, or an interest in land, or the property is the same in all respects at the relevant date as at the time of the chargeable transfer. Where s.139(1) applies, the market value of the property is taken to be increased by an amount equal to the difference, if any, between:

(1) the market value of the property at the time of the chargeable transfer, and
(2) what that value would have been if the circumstances which prevail at the relevant date and which result in the property being different in some respect had prevailed at the time of the chargeable transfer.[219]

A retrospective valuation will be necessary. In the event that the property has increased in value since the chargeable transfer because of such a change of circumstances, the increase is effectively ignored in computing the market value of the property for

---

[219] IHTA 1984 s.139(1) and (2).

784

purposes of relief[220]; this ensures that regard is had to the "real" value of the property in question.

Under s.139(4), two things happen where the property is neither shares nor an interest in land, and during the period between the time of the chargeable transfer and the relevant date benefits in money or money's worth are derived from the property which exceed a reasonable return on its market value at the time of the chargeable transfer. First, any effect of the benefits on the property is ignored for purposes of s.139(1). Secondly, the market value of the property is taken to be increased by an amount equal to the excess.[221] This prevents property from being "milked" of its value.

XIII. RELIEFS FOR TRANSFERS MADE ON DEATH

Property is often sold in the course of administering a deceased person's estate, and **25–123** sometimes the price obtained is less than the value attributed to the property immediately before the person dies. The legislation recognises that in certain cases where this happens it would be unfair to tax the deceased's estate on the higher value previously attributed to the property in question, and accordingly provides three reliefs. The effect of each relief is the same, namely to substitute a lower, more realistic, value for the value that had been attributed to the property on the deceased's death. The result is to reduce the value transferred by the notional transfer the deceased made immediately before he died, and any tax paid or owing in respect of that transfer is refunded or reduced.[222]

The first and second reliefs deal respectively with sales of certain "qualifying investments" and sales of land where the investments or land have fallen in value since the deceased's death. Under these reliefs the value substituted is, basically, the price in fact obtained for the investments or land in question. Investments are revalued only if sold within 12 months of the death; land is generally revalued only if sold within four years of the death. The third relief is concerned with sales of property to which an artificially high value was attributed on the deceased's death. The sale must occur within four years of the death. The value which is substituted is the value that would have been attributed to the property if the provisions which resulted in its being given an artificially high value had not applied and the property had instead been valued in accordance with the normal rules.

Planning

Note that in the case of land it is possible that the relief may apply where the subject **25–124** matter of the gift has *increased* in value. There is nothing in principle to prevent the sections applying in these circumstances and such a claim would be advantageous where no additional IHT is payable (where the transfer is covered by the donor's nil

---

[220] IHTA 1984 s.139(3).
[221] IHTA 1984 s.139(4)(b).
[222] The substituted value will also apply for CGT purposes; TCGA 1992 s.274.

rate band even if the relief increases the value) or where the additional IHT is outweighed by a saving in CGT.[223]

Sales of qualifying investments and sales of land: common terms and features

25–125   As was mentioned above, relief is provided for transfers on death where the whole or part of the value transferred was attributable either to certain qualifying investments or to land where either has changed in value since the death. Before discussing these reliefs in detail, it will be convenient to consider certain terms and features common to both reliefs so as to avoid unnecessary duplication in the discussion below.

The appropriate person

25–126   By ss.178(1) and 190(1), the appropriate person in relation to qualifying investments or any interest in land comprised in a person's estate immediately before his death is the person liable for tax attributable to the value of those investments, or, as the case may be, that interest in land. If there is more than one such person and one of them is in fact paying the tax, he is the appropriate person.[224]

As the appropriate person is defined as the person liable for the IHT, it must follow that if no IHT is payable in respect of the relevant property (e.g. because of the spouse or charity exemptions) there is no one who can satisfy the definition of an appropriate person. Thus, in the case where property comprised in a deceased's estate passed to his widow and is sold within three years of death for a value in excess of the probate value, HMRC will not accept a claim to substitute the greater sale proceeds for that value for both IHT and (more significantly) CGT purposes. This was affirmed in the *Stonor* case[225] where the Special Commissioner stated that, in her view, the whole scheme of Pt VII of the Act is that there is liability only for tax which is actually payable. A "person liable" for the tax is the person who has actually paid it or is under an obligation to pay. Where no such liability or obligation exists there is no such person. This is supported by s.190(1) which states that where there is more than one person liable to pay the tax and one of them actually pays it then the one who pays is the "appropriate person".

In cases where *Stonor* does not apply, e.g. where the donor's nil rate band is available to shelter most of the increase in value, the case appears to establish that there is nothing in principle to prevent a claim under s.191 applying to increases in value. The Special Commissioner noted that "the section does not state in terms that it cannot apply where values increase on death". However, HMRC advanced further arguments, which were not considered by the Special Commissioner, based on the heading of s.191 ("The Relief") and on parliamentary papers, that the relief was not intended to permit the substitution of higher values for the purposes of CGT and such a claim may therefore be resisted.

Personal representatives and trustees

25–127   By ss.178(4) and 190(3), the personal representatives of the deceased and the trustees of a settlement are each treated as a single continuing body of persons (distinct

---

[223] See paras 25–34 and 25–126.
[224] For the persons so liable, see para.29–55.
[225] *Stonor v IRC* [2001] S.T.C. (S.C.D.) 199.

from the persons who may from time to time be the personal representatives or trustees).

Claims

By ss.179(1) and (3) and 191(1)(b), the appropriate person must claim the relief, **25–128** stating the capacity in which he makes the claim.

Valuation

By ss.178(5) and 190(4), in any case where it is necessary to determine the price at **25–129** which any investments or any interest in land was purchased or sold, or it is necessary to determine the best consideration that could reasonably have been obtained on the sale of any investments or any interest in land, no account is taken of expenses (whether by way of commission, stamp duty, stamp duty land tax or otherwise) which are incidental to the sale or purchase.

Date of sale

Various provisions govern the date on which investments or an interest in land are **25–130** regarded as having been sold, as follows:

(1) *Date of contract.* By ss.189(1) and 198(1), where any investments or any interest in land are sold or purchased by the appropriate person, the date on which they are sold or purchased is taken to be the date on which he entered into a contract to sell or purchase the investments. The date on which a sale is made pursuant to a contract is thus irrelevant, and a sale completed, e.g. more than a year after the death will be brought into account if the contract for the sale was made within 12 months of the death.
(2) *Options.* By ss.189(2) and 198(2), where the sale or purchase of any investments or any interest in land by the appropriate person results from the exercise (whether by him or any other person) of an option, the date of sale is taken to be the date on which the option was granted.

Against this background, it is now possible to consider the reliefs in detail.

XIV. REVALUATION OF QUALIFYING INVESTMENTS SOLD WITHIN ONE YEAR OF DEATH

The broad effect of ss.178 and 179 is that where "qualifying investments" are sold **25–131** within one year of a death for less than the value attributed to them on death the value of the investments is reduced by an amount equal to the "loss on sale". Both "qualifying investments" and "loss on sale" are terms of art. By s.178(1) "qualifying investments" means:

" . . . shares or securities which are quoted at the date of the death in question, holdings in a unit trust which at that date is an authorised unit trust [as defined in ICTA 1988 s.468] and shares in any common investment fund established under s.42 of the Administration of Justice Act 1982."

Section 272 provides that shares or securities are "quoted" if they are listed on a recognised stock exchange. Shares quoted on the NASDAQ Stock Market based in the United States may qualify where the date of death was on or after March 10, 1992. Shares traded on the Alternative Investment Market, which replaced the Unlisted Securities Market at the end of 1995 do not qualify for relief (see para.25–39).

Section 178(2) provides that where shares or securities in respect of which quotation on a recognised stock exchange[226] were suspended at the date of the death are sold[227] within one year of the death they are qualifying investments if they are again quoted at the time of the sale.

The "loss on sale" is the difference between the "value on death" and the "sale value". By ss.178(1) and 179(1)(a), "value on death" means:

" . . . the aggregate of the values which, apart from this Chapter, would be the values for the purposes of tax of all the qualifying investments comprised in a person's estate immediately before his death which are sold by the appropriate person within the period of twelve months immediately following the date of the death."

and by ss.178(1) and 179(1)(b), "sale value" means:

" . . . the aggregate of the values of those investments at the time they were so sold, taking the value of any particular investments for this purpose as the price for which they were so sold or, if it is greater, the best consideration which could reasonably have been obtained for them at the time of the sale."

An appropriation to satisfy a pecuniary legacy, which requires consent under the terms of the Will (or where the executors powers to appropriate are not extended so as not to require consent) is regarded by HMRC as constituting a sale for this purpose.

In essence, the relief is thus quite straightforward. One simply compares the total value on death of all the qualifying investments which have been sold with the price in fact received for those investments, and reduces the value attributable to those investments at the time the deceased died by the difference.

Unfortunately, as was seen above in connection with the revaluation relief given in respect of transfers made within seven years before death, revaluation reliefs are never simple, and the legislation includes a number of detailed qualifications to the above rules. Some of these qualifications are similar to those found in the revaluation relief given in respect of transfers made within seven years before death, while others are peculiar to this relief.

Relief for cancelled and suspended investments

25–132   Events in the late 1980s pointed to a weakness in the revaluation rules. The collapse in value of shares did not lead to any alteration of their probate value: it was necessary for there to be a qualifying sale of the security so that executors had to sell the securities—albeit that the consideration was merely 1p—in order to fall within the precise scope of s.179. Failure to obtain revaluation relief could have left the executors

---

[226] For what constitutes a "recognised stock exchange," see para.25–38.
[227] Or exchanged: see para.25–139.

with a substantial IHT bill on an investment having no value. In extreme cases the entire value of the estate could have been exhausted. The IHT position contrasted with CGT legislation which provided for an election to be made in cases where a chargeable asset had become of "negligible" value (see s.24 of the Taxation of Chargeable Gains Act 1992).

Section 198 of the Finance Act 1993 inserted new ss.186A and 186B into the 1984 Act which have effect in relation to deaths occurring on or after March 16, 1992, and afford relief in two further situations. These changes enable relief to be claimed even though the securities have not actually been sold:

(1) *Cancelled investments* (s.186A): if qualifying investments owned at death are cancelled (without being replaced by other shares or securities) they are treated as having been sold for a nominal consideration of £1 immediately before cancellation.

(2) *Suspended investments* (s.186B): if the quotation on the stock exchange is suspended at the end of the period of 12 months immediately following the death, then if the value at death of the investments exceeded their value at the end of the 12-month period, they are treated as then being sold by the appropriate person for a price equal to their value at that time. Relief can therefore be claimed without a sale having taken place.

Agricultural relief and business relief

25–133 The fact that the shares qualified for agricultural or business relief should not be relevant to this revaluation relief because those reliefs operate by reducing the value transferred by a transfer of value, not by reducing the value of any property; see paras 26–16 and 26–114. Neither s.179(1)(a), which refers to "the values for the purposes of tax" nor s.179(1)(b), which in effect refers to their value on sale as their actual sale price, contemplates any such reduction. Furthermore, if business or agricultural relief were to be taken into account one would expect to find an express mechanism for doing so such as that provided in relation to the revaluation relief given in respect of transfers made within seven years of death; see para.25–111. The effect of reducing the value of the shares by business or agricultural relief would, of course, be catastrophic: were such a reduction to operate then where 100 per cent relief was available there never would be a loss on sale.

Anti-avoidance

25–134 The relief is intended to assist people who are, in effect, forced by circumstances, notably the requirement to pay IHT, to sell qualifying investments which have fallen in value since the death in question. It is not intended to assist people who sell qualifying investments only or mainly in order to take advantage of the relief and who, having done so, reinvest in qualifying investments shortly thereafter. Section 180(1) accordingly provides that where at any time during the period beginning with the death in question and ending two months after the date of the last sale which qualifies for relief, the person making the claim purchases any qualifying investments in the same capacity as that in which he makes the claim, the loss on sale of the investments to which the claim relates is to be reduced by a fraction. The fraction is:

$$\frac{\text{Aggregate purchase price of purchased qualifying investments}}{\text{Value of all qualifying investments sold}}$$

Assume, for example, that X's estate included qualifying investments worth £150,000, and that his executor sold these investments for £100,000 within one year of X's death. With the proceeds of sale he purchased £60,000 in qualifying investments and £25,000 in unquoted investments. The £50,000 loss on sale would be reduced by:

$$\frac{£60,000}{£100,000} \times £50,000 = £30,000$$

with the result that the value of the qualifying investments would be reduced by £30,000 to £120,000. The loss on sale is extinguished if the aggregate purchase price of the purchased qualifying investments exceeds the aggregate sale value of the qualifying investments sold.

By s.180(2), if the person who makes the claim does so in a capacity other than that of personal representative or trustee (e.g. as a surviving joint tenant), the above-mentioned restriction in s.180(1) has effect only in relation to assets purchased otherwise than in the capacity of personal representative or trustee. Furthermore, no account is taken of any qualifying investments purchased by him unless they are of the same description as one of the qualifying investments to which the claim relates.

This means that if, e.g. a surviving joint tenant makes a claim, account is taken of qualifying investments purchased by him in that capacity only if they are of the same description as one of the qualifying investments to which his claim relates. Section 180(3) provides that for this purpose:

(1) two investments which are not investments in an authorised unit trust or common investment fund are not treated as being of the same description if they are separately listed on a recognised stock exchange, and

(2) an investment in one authorised unit trust or common investment fund is not treated as being of the same description as an investment in another authorised unit trust or common investment fund.

Assume, for example, that X dies leaving quoted ordinary shares in A plc worth £100,000. His executor, Y, is also a legatee under X's will, and, as executor, he sells half of the A plc shares for £40,000, making a loss on sale of £10,000. He uses £30,000 of the proceeds of sale to purchase other qualifying investments. As legatee, he receives £16,000, representing shares in B plc which were worth £20,000 on death. He reinvests £6,000 of it in B plc shares, £5,000 in C plc shares, and £5,000 in a common investment fund. This will have two effects. First, under s.180(1), his reinvestment as executor will mean that the £10,000 loss on sale will be reduced by:

$$\frac{£30,000}{£40,000} \times £10,000 = £7,500$$

to £2,500. Secondly, his reinvestment as legatee will mean that under s.180(2) the £4,000 (£20,000 − £16,000) loss on sale will be reduced by:

$$\frac{£6,000}{£16,000} \times £4,000 = £1,500$$

It follows from the above that it may be of the utmost importance to establish the time at which the administration of an estate is completed. This would be the case where, for example, a sole executrix also inherits the whole of the deceased's estate. Unless she reinvests the sale proceeds as executrix, no account will be taken of any qualifying investments purchased by her unless they are of the same description as one of the qualifying investments to which the claim relates.

Capital receipts

Section 181 makes provision to bring into account any capital receipts in determin- **25–135** ing the sale value. It provides that where at any time after the death in question the appropriate person receives any capital payment which is attributable to any qualifying investments comprised in the deceased's estate immediately before his death and he sells those investments within one year of the death, the price for which the investments were sold or, as the case may be, the best consideration which could have reasonably been obtained for them at the time of the sale, is taken to be increased by an amount equal to the capital payment. It is to be noted that any such capital payment is to be taken into account regardless of whether it was received during the 12 months immediately following the death or thereafter. For this purpose "capital payment" does not include the price paid on the sale of the investments but does include any money or money's worth which does not constitute income for the purposes of income tax. By s.181(2), if the appropriate person receives or becomes entitled to receive in respect of any qualifying investments a provisional allotment of shares in or debentures of a company and he disposes of his right to do so, the amount of the consideration for the disposal is treated as a capital payment attributable to those investments.

Payment of calls

Conversely, s.182 makes provision to bring into account any payment of calls in **25–136** determining the value on death. Section 182 states that if at any time after the death in question the appropriate person pays an amount in pursuance of a call in respect of any qualifying investments comprised in the deceased's estate immediately before his death, and those investments are sold by the appropriate person within one year of the death, the value on death of those investments is the amount so paid plus the value of the investments before any revaluation relief.

Reorganisations, etc.

Section 183 takes account of the possibility of reorganisations, take-overs and **25–137** similar transactions. It applies where there is a transaction to which s.127 of the Taxation of Chargeable Gains Act 1992 applies, where there is:

(1) a reorganisation, within the meaning of s.126(1); or

(2) the conversion of securities within the meaning of s.132; or

(3) the issue by a company of shares or debentures in exchange for shares in or debentures of another company in such circumstances that s.135 applies; or

(4) the issue by a company of shares or debentures under such arrangement as is referred to in s.136.

Section 183 also applies to any transaction corresponding to those mentioned above relating to a unit trust scheme to which s.127 applies by virtue of s.99.[228]

Where s.183 applies, there are two possible consequences, one relating to identification, the other to valuation. First, by s.183(2), the "new holding" and the "original holding", as defined in s.126(1), are treated as the same holding for purposes of the revaluation relief. Secondly, by s.183(3), if, as part of the transaction in question, the appropriate person gives or becomes liable to give any consideration for all or any part of the new holding, the value on death of the new holding is taken to be the aggregate of:

(1) the value on death of the original holding, and

(2) an amount equal to that consideration.

In any other case, the value of the new holding is taken to be the same as the value on death of the original holding. Section 183(4) provides that for these purposes:

(1) any surrender, cancellation or other alteration of any of the original shares or of the rights attached thereto, or

(2) any consideration consisting of any application, in paying up the new holding or any part of it, of assets of the company concerned, or of any dividend or other distribution declared out of those assets but not made,

is not treated as consideration given for the new holding or any part of it.

By s.183(5), if within one year of the death the appropriate person sells any investments comprised in the new holding, the value on death of those investments is determined by the following formula:

$$\frac{Vs(H-S)}{(Vs+Vr)}$$

For this purpose:

Vs is the sale value of the investments;

Vr is the market value at the time of the sale of any investments remaining in the new holding after the sale;

H is the value on death of the new holding;

S is the value on death of any investments which were originally comprised in the new holding but which have been sold on a previous occasion or occasions. In this context, the market value of any investments at any time means the value which, before any

[228] Compare IHTA 1984 s.135.

revaluation relief, they would have for IHT[229] purposes if they were comprised in the estate of a person who died at that time.[230]

Assume A dies owning 2,000 shares in B plc, which are quoted at £1.50 each, and that shortly after A's death B plc, makes a one-for-two rights issue at 50p each, which A's executor takes up, paying £500 for 1,000 new shares. Within one year of A's death the executor sells 1,000 shares for £1,250 (£1.25 per share). The calculation for finding the value on death of the shares sold is:

$$Vs = £1,250$$

$$Vr = £2,500 \ (2000 \text{ shares at } £1.25)$$

$$H = £3,500 \ (£3,000 \text{ plus } £500)$$

$$S = \text{nil}$$

$$= £1,167$$

$$\frac{£1,250 \ (£3,500 - \text{nil})}{£1,250 + £2,500} = £1,167$$

The value on death for IHT purposes is thus £1,167, with the result that there is no loss on sale; on the contrary, there is a profit of £83 (£1,250 − £1,167).

Later but still within one year of A's death, the executor sells 500 shares for 90p each. The calculation would then be:

$$\frac{450 \ (3,500 - 1,167)}{450 + 1,350 \ (1500 \text{ shares} \times 90p)} = £583$$

The value on death of the 500 shares is thus £583, with the result that there is a loss on sale of £133 (£583 − £450). The result of the two sales is thus a net loss on sale of £50.

Effect of purchase, etc. of investments of the same description

Section 185(1) makes provision to deal with the situation where, within one year of **25–138** the death in question, the appropriate person sells any investments which form part of a holding of investments which are all of the same description and which consist of (i) investments comprised in the deceased's estate immediately before his death, and (ii) investments acquired by the appropriate person, by purchase or otherwise, after the death but not in circumstances in which s.183 above applies. In such a case, the investments sold are treated as having been sold out of the "old" and "new" holdings in proportion to the size of those holdings. Assume, for example, that on Y's death 500

[229] IHTA 1984 s.160.
[230] IHTA 1984 s.183(6).

shares in A plc devolve on X and that six months later X purchases a further 250 shares in A plc. He then sells 300 shares; 200(300 × 500/750) of these shares will be regarded as having been sold out of the 500 shares comprised in Y's estate on his death, and 100(300 × 250/750) will be regarded as having been sold out of the new holding.

By s.185(2), if the appropriate person holds investments of any description in the capacity of personal representative or trustee, the investments are not treated as forming part of the same holding as investments which, though of the same description, he holds otherwise than in that capacity.

Exchanges of qualifying investments

25–139   As was noted above, in determining the value on death regard must be had to the value of all qualifying investments sold within one year of the death. It may be that qualifying investments are exchanged rather than sold. In that case, they may be treated as having been sold, by s.184(1), if within one year of the death in question the appropriate person exchanges (with or without any payment by way of equality of exchange) any qualifying investments comprised in the deceased's estate immediately before his death, then, regardless of the nature of the property taken in exchange, the investments are treated as having been sold at the date of the exchange for a price equal to their market value. If their market value is at the date of the exchange greater than their value on death, s.187(2) provides that for these purposes the market value of any investments is the value they would have prior to the application of this revaluation relief. Section 184 is intended to prevent taxpayers from abusing the revaluation relief by selling investments which have fallen in price and exchanging investments which have risen in value. Two comments are in order here. First, by s.184(2), s.184 does not apply in any case where the exchange falls within s.183(1), above. Secondly, s.184 treats an exchange as a sale only if the qualifying investments have appreciated in value. The exchange of a qualifying investment which has fallen in value may thus be positively disadvantageous since no relief will be available in respect of the fallen value of the qualifying investment in question.

Value of part of a fund

25–140   Section 186(1) deals with the case where only part of a holding of qualifying investments is comprised in a person's estate and investments included in that holding are sold by the appropriate person within one year of the death in question. In that case the entirety of the holding is treated as being comprised in the estate, and the value of the investments comprised in the estate is taken to be the "taxable fraction" of the value of the investments to which the claim relates. For this purpose the "taxable fraction" is:

$$\frac{\text{Value (before revaluation relief) of the part of the holding comprised in the deceased's estate}}{\text{Value (after revaluation relief) of entire holding}}$$

This is intended to deal with the situation where a person dies entitled to an interest in part of a settled fund. The effect of s.186 is simply that the deceased's share of any loss on sale is proportional to his interest in the trust fund.

Attribution of values to specific investments

Section 187 makes provision for determining the value of any particular investment, **25–141** referred to as a "specific investment", which is included among the qualifying investments taken into account in determining the loss on sale. By s.187(2), the general rule is that the value of a specific investment is its sale value. This is subject to three increasingly complicated qualifications. Firstly, by s.187(4), the sale value of a specific investment must be reduced by any amount paid in pursuance of a call.

Secondly, by s.187(5), the sale value of a specific investment must be reduced where under s.183(3) the value on death of a "new holding" includes the consideration for the new holding the appropriate person gave (or became liable to give) in connection with the reorganisation, etc. The amount by which the sale value must be reduced is:

" . . . an amount which bears to that consideration the like proportion as the value on death of the specific investment sold bears to the value on death of the whole of the new holding."

Assume, for example, that on X's death his estate included various qualifying investments, all of which were sold within 12 months of his death. One of the investments was 2,000 shares in A plc which on his death were worth £4,000. A plc subsequently made a one-for-one rights issue at £1.25 for each new share. This was taken up by X's executor at a cost of £2,500 with the result that under s.183(3) the value on death of the shares in A plc was increased to £6,500 (£4,000 + £2,500). The executor later sold 3,000 A plc shares for £4,500. Applying s.187(5) the sale value of the 3,000 shares, worth £4,500, would be reduced by:

$$\frac{£3,000}{£4,000} \times £2,500 = £1,875$$

with the result that the sale value of the 3,000 shares was £2,625 (£4,500 − £1,875).

The third qualification applies where the calculation of the loss on sale is affected by the anti-avoidance provisions under s.180(1), which, it will be recalled, apply where at any time during the period beginning with the death in question and ending two months after the date of the last sale which qualifies for relief, the person making the claim purchases any qualifying investments in the same capacity as that in which he makes the claim. In such a case the loss on sale of the investments to which the claim relates must be reduced, as was outlined above at para.25–134. Where this occurs, s.187(3) applies, the position varying according to whether on death the value of a specific investment exceeds its sale price or the sale price of a specific investment exceeds its value on death. By s.187(3)(b), if on death the value of a specific investment exceeds its sale price, the value of the investment is the aggregate of its sale value and an amount equal to the "relevant proportion" of the difference between its sale price and its value on death. By s.187(3)(b), if the sale price of a specific investment exceeds its value on death, the value of the investment is its sale value less an amount equal to the "relevant proportion" of the difference between its value on death and its sale price.

Before examining the consequences of s.187(3), certain points are worth noting. Firstly, a new term, "sale price", is introduced. This is defined by s.187(6) to be the price for which the investment was sold by the appropriate person or, if it is greater, the best consideration which could reasonably have been obtained for the specific investment at the time of the sale. For this purpose, any capital payments must be brought into account.

Secondly, s.187(3) refers to the "relevant proportion" of the difference between the sale price and the value on death of the investment in question. Section 187 does not define "relevant proportion"; instead, this expression is defined in s.178(1), which provides that "relevant proportion" means the proportion by which the loss on sale is reduced under s.180, i.e. it is the

$$\frac{\text{Aggregate purchase price of purchased qualifying investments}}{\text{Value of all qualifying investments sold}}$$

Thirdly, in determining the "value" of an investment for purposes of s.180, the above-mentioned qualifications to the general rule laid down by s.187(2) apply, i.e. the value is reduced by any amount paid in pursuance of a call or by any consideration given for a new holding. Against this background, it is now possible to consider how s.187(3) operates.

Assume that X died, and that his estate included qualifying investments as follows:

Qualifying investments	Value on death	Sale value	Gain/loss
2,000 shares in A plc	£4,000	£2,800	(£1,200)
1,000 shares in B plc	£1,000	£1,200	£200
3,000 shares in C plc	£6,000	£6,000	nil
	£11,000	£10,000	(£1,000)

During the period between X's death and two months after the date of the last sale made within 12 months after X's death, X's executor purchased £6,000 worth of qualifying investments. Applying s.180, the £1,000 loss on sale thus fell to be reduced by £600 as follows:

$$\frac{£6,000}{£10,000} \times (£1,000) = (£600)$$

The value of the qualifying investments on death was thus reduced from £11,000 to £10,600 (£11,000 − £400 loss on sale).

It is now possible to attribute values to the shares in A plc, B plc and C plc. The sale value of the shares in A plc was £2,800. It therefore follows that s.187(3)(a) applies, since the value on death of the shares in A plc exceeded their sale value by £1,200. The value of the shares in A plc is thus their sale value, £2,800, plus an amount equal to the "relevant proportion" (£6,000/£10,000) of the difference between their value on death and their sale price, i.e.

$$\frac{£6,000}{£10,000} \times £1,200 = £720$$

The value of the shares in A plc is thus £3,520 (£2,800 + £720). Given the fact that the sale price of the B plc shares exceeds their value on death by £200, s.187(3)(b) governs the valuation of the shares in B plc. Their value will be their sale value, £1,200, less an amount equal to the "relevant proportion" (£6,000/£10,000) of the difference between their value on death and their sale price, i.e.

$$\frac{£6,000}{£10,000} \times £200 = £120$$

The result is that the value of the shares in B plc is £1,080 (£1,200 − £120). Finally, as there is no difference between the value on death of the shares in C plc and their sale price, s.187(3) does not apply, and therefore the value of those investments, as one would expect, remains unchanged.

Limitation of loss on sale

It will be recalled that revaluation relief is given by reducing the value immediately **25–142** before the death in question of the investments to which the claim relates by an amount equal to the "loss on sale". In the absence of provision to the contrary, it might be possible for the loss on sale to exceed the value of the investments to which a claim relates immediately before death, with the result that a negative value was attributed to the investments in question. As will be seen from the example below, this could occur where an amount has been paid in pursuance of a call as mentioned in s.182, or where investments are sold following a reorganisation, etc., as mentioned in s.183(5). Section 188 accordingly provides that in any case where the loss on sale of any investments would exceed their value, as determined before any revaluation relief under Ch.III, their sale value is to be increased so that the loss on sale would be equal to their value after revaluation relief under Ch.III.

Assume that on X's death his estate included 1,000 £1 shares (30p paid) in A plc and that immediately before his death these shares were worth £300. X's executor subsequently pays a call of £450, so that under s.182 the value on death of the shares was £750. Subsequently, within 12 months of X's death, X's executor sold the shares for £400. In the absence of s.188, the loss on sale, £350, would exceed the value of the investments, £300, before revaluation relief. That being the case, under s.188 the sale value of the investments is increased to £350, with the result that the loss on sale is restricted to £300, and the value of the qualifying investments after revaluation relief under Ch.III is nil (rather than −£50).

XV. REVALUATION OF INTERESTS IN LAND SOLD WITHIN FOUR YEARS OF DEATH

Chapter IV of Pt VI originally provided relief where an interest in land comprised **25–143** in a person's estate immediately before he dies was sold by the appropriate person[231] within three years of the date of death.[232]

---

[231] See para.25–126.
[232] See para.25–130 for the date on which a sale was regarded as having taken place.

The Finance Act 1993 s.199 inserted a new s.197A into the 1984 Act entitled "Sales in fourth year after death". This provision has effect as regards deaths occurring on or after March 16, 1990, and extends the relief to sales taking place in the fourth year from the death. This is achieved by treating a sale in the fourth year as having occurred within three years of the death, and this can have some subtle results:

(1) A fourth year sale at a profit will not be taken into account if the appropriate person sold other interests in land within three years of death at a loss on which relief was claimed (i.e. that relief will not be reduced by the later profit).

(2) Fourth year sales will not be relevant in determining the period during which a purchase of further land by the appropriate person will restrict or exclude the relief under s.192. Further, if the only relief claimed is for a fourth year sale there is no adjustment for subsequent purchases under s.192.

(3) A fourth year sale at a profit to a beneficiary, etc. will not restrict the relief on other sales at a loss as provided for under s.196.

Relief may also be available where an interest in land is compulsorily acquired after the expiry of a period of three years; this is discussed below.

"Interest in land" is defined negatively; by s.190(1), it does not include any estate, interest or right by way of mortgage or other security. In practice the term is given a wide meaning. An interest in an unadministered estate is not an interest in land since it is a chose in action, not an interest in any specific property, but it may be treated as an interest in land by virtue of s.91 (see para.25–145).

The appropriate person must claim the relief, stating the capacity in which he makes the claim. Under the relief, the value

(1) of the interest in question, and

(2) of any other interest comprised in the deceased's estate immediately before he died which is sold during the three-year period by the person making the claim acting in the same capacity as that in which he makes the claim

is the "sale value" (as defined below) of the interest in question. Relief should thus normally be claimed only where, having regard to all the sales, there is a net loss; once made, a claim cannot be withdrawn. Furthermore the terms of s.191 are such that if the relief is claimed and the aggregate of all sales within three years after the death results in a gain not only will the relief be lost but additional IHT will be due. Say, for example, PRs sell Whiteacre in year 1 for a loss of £10,000 and make a claim under s.191. In year 3 after the market has picked up they sell Blackacre at a profit of £20,000. Not only will they lose the relief under s.191 but they will pay additional IHT on £10,000. Extreme care must therefore be taken whether a claim should be made and, if so, its timing, where there is more than one interest in land which may be disposed of.

In addition, it must be borne in mind that a claim may affect the value to be brought into account for CGT purposes under s.274 of the Taxation of Chargeable Gains Act 1992. Exceptionally, and having regard to HMRC's opposition to such a claim in the *Stonor* case,[233] it may thus be possible to claim the revaluation relief even where, having regard to all the sales, there is a net gain. This would be the case where no adverse IHT consequences would arise from the making of such a claim (e.g. where the transfer on death was wholly or partly within the testator's nil rate band even after the relief) but where the making of such a claim would result in a higher base value for

---

[233] See para.25–126.

CGT purposes.[234] However, a claim cannot be made where the estate is exempt, e.g. where spouse or charity relief is applicable, see para.25–126. A claim to substitute a higher value may be made only in respect of sales within three years of the date of death.

The position where a person has an interest in land which is part of a larger interest which may be sold by someone else deserves special attention. This follows from the fact that under s.191(1) a claim can be made only by someone who has sold an interest in land. This could work both to the taxpayer's advantage and to his detriment. If the interest has fallen in value, it will be to his disadvantage not to be party to the sale, since he will not be able to claim relief. He could remedy this, of course, by arranging to be a party to the sale. If, on the other hand, the interest has risen in value, it will be to his advantage not to have the sale brought into account.

Definitions

"Sale value" is a term of art as are two other terms, "sale price" and "value on death". They are defined by s.190(1) as follows: **25–144**

Sale value. This is the sale price of an interest in land, as increased or reduced by the provisions in Pt VI Ch.IV.[235]

Sale price. This means the price for which an interest in land is sold, or, if it is greater, the best consideration, disregarding incidental expenses (see para.25–129), that could reasonably have been obtained for it at the time of the sale.

Value on death. This means, in relation to any interest in land comprised in a person's estate immediately before his death, the value which before any revaluation relief[236] would be its value as part of the estate for IHT purposes.

Inapplicability of the relief

Sales of certain interests are left out of account, as follows: **25–145**

(1) By s.191(2), the sale of an interest is left out of account if the sale value of the interest differs from its value on death by less than the lower of
(a) £1,000, and
(b) 5 per cent of its value on death.
   Note that it is not possible to combine in one sale several pieces of land forming "natural units"[237] in order to exceed the 5 per cent/£1,000 restriction.

(2) By s.191(3), the sale of an interest is left out of account if the sale is a sale by a personal representative or trustee to:
(a) a person who, at any time between the death and the sale, has been beneficially entitled to, or to an interest in possession in, property comprising the interest sold; or

---

[234] Compare the relief given to qualifying investments sold within one year of death, where the value of the investments can be reduced but never increased: see para.25–131.
[235] See paras 25–147 and following.
[236] Either under IHTA 1984 Ch.IV or under s.176 (see paras 25–154–25–156).
[237] See para.25–27.

(b) the spouse or civil partner or a child (which HMRC does not consider to include an illegitimate child or a step-child) or remoter descendant of a person within (a) above; or

(c) trustees of a settlement under which a person within (a) or (b) above has an interest in possession in property comprising the interest sold. It may be that following a successful claim for relief a deed of variation is entered into such that, say, condition (a) would have been infringed had the deed been executed before the sale. It is not clear whether entering into such a deed will result in the relief being withdrawn retrospectively, on the footing that under s.142(1) the variation in question would be treated as having been effected by the deceased.

(3) By s.191(3), the sale of an interest is left out of account if it is a sale in connection with which the vendor or any person within (a), (b) or (c) above obtained a right to acquire the interest sold or any other interest in the same land.

(4) The exclusions at (a) and (b) apply only where the entitlement of the purchaser is in "property *comprising* the interest sold". HMRC is believed to interpret "comprising" liberally so that if the purchaser's entitlement is only to a share in the property sold it will not be excluded from relief.

For the purposes of s.191(3) where property is comprised in an unadministered estate within the meaning of s.91(2),[238] a person is treated as having in that property the same interest as he would have if the administration of the estate had been completed.

Interest to which a claim relates: conundrum

25–146   Section 190(2) provides that in Ch.IV any references to the interest to which a claim relates is a reference to the interest which falls to be brought into account after applying the excluding provisions in s.191. The difficulty arises that in order to determine whether an interest falls to be excluded by s.191, it is necessary to know the sale price of the interest, and in some circumstances that will be ascertained only after applying ss.192–196. But, before it is possible to apply ss.192–196, it is necessary to determine if the interest is one to which the claim relates, i.e. if the interest is one which has not been excluded by s.191. Needless to say, the effect of this conundrum is unclear.

Adjustments for changes between death and sale

25–147   Section 193 makes special provision to deal with the valuation of an interest in land where at the date of the sale:

(1) the interest is not the same in all respects with the same incidents as it was at the date of the death; or

(2) the land in which the interest subsists is not in the same state and with the same incidents as it was at the date of the death. Regard is thus had both to any changes in the interest and to any changes in the land.[239] The meaning of "incidents" is discussed at para.25–120.

---

[238] See para.12–44.
[239] IHTA 1984 s.193(2).

Where either of the above conditions is satisfied, the sale price of the land is taken to be increased by an amount equal to the difference between:

(1) the value on death of the interest, and
(2) what that value would have been if the circumstances which prevailed on the dates of the sale and which result in either of the above conditions being satisfied had prevailed immediately before the death.[240] A retrospective valuation of the interest may thus be necessary. The purpose of this adjustment in the sale price is to prevent a taxpayer from securing revaluation relief by artificially devaluing property before selling it, e.g. by granting a lease on less than commercial terms.

The above rule is subject to two qualifications. The first occurs under s.193(3) where after the date of the death but before the date of the sale compensation becomes payable under any enactment to the appropriate person[241] or any other person liable[242] for tax attributable to the value of the interest either:

(1) because of the imposition of a restriction on the use or development of the land in which the interest subsists, or
(2) because the value of the interest is reduced for any other reason.

In that case, two results obtain: first, the imposition of the restriction or the other cause of the reduction in value is ignored; secondly, the sale price of the interest is increased by an amount equal to the amount of compensation. The second qualification is that by s.193(4) any increase in the value of the interest occasioned by changes in the interest or the incidents thereto, or in the land or the incidents thereto, is effectively ignored in valuing the interest in question; this ensures that a person is not precluded from obtaining relief by artificial increases in the value of property, e.g. where a person sells with vacant possession property which, when it was transferred to him, was tenanted.

Leases

Where the claim relates to an interest which is the interest of a lessee under a lease **25–148** with less than 50 years to run at the date of the death in question, the sale price of the interest may be increased under s.194. The increase is of an amount equal to the "appropriate fraction" of the value on death of the interest. For this purpose, the "appropriate fraction" is the same as that which applies for purposes of s.138; see para.25–121, where an example is given.

Adjustments for other interests

Section 195 provides that the sale price of an interest to which a claim relates must **25–149** be increased if in determining its value on death any other interests, whether in the same or in some other land, are taken into account. The increase is equal to the

---

[240] IHTA 1984 s.193(1).
[241] See para.25–126.
[242] See para.29–55.

difference between the value on death of the interest and the value which would have been the value on death if no other interests had been taken into account. This provision is apparently intended to deal with circumstances in which the value on death of an interest derives partly from the fact that the deceased held other interests, so that the value of the interests if they were sold together would exceed the aggregate value of the interests if they were sold separately. In the absence of s.195 it might have been possible to take advantage of the relief by selling separately a "related" interest for a lower price than the interest would have fetched if sold together with the other interests to which it related. Section 195 prevents this by providing that the sale price is increased by, in effect, the amount the interest would have fetched if sold on death with the other interest. This is anti-avoidance with a vengeance: it would have been fairer to provide that the amount by which the sale price should be increased is the amount the interest would have fetched if sold with the other interest at the time the interest was sold, not at the time of death.

Adjustment for sales and exchanges

25–150   As was noted above, all sales within the three-year period must be brought into account except for sales falling within s.191(2) (the £1,000/5 per cent rule) or s.191(3) (sales to connected persons). In the absence of provision to the contrary, this would mean that sales which came within s.191(3) and which were made for a price exceeding the value on death would not be brought into account, with the result that the claimant had the best of both worlds: sales on which a loss was made would qualify for relief, while sales on which a profit was made would be left out of account. An alternative means of taking unfair advantage of the relief would be to sell interests which had fallen in value and to exchange interests which had increased in value: since only sales are brought into account, no account would be taken of the exchanges. Section 196 prevents this by providing that an addition is made to the sale price where a claimant acting in the same capacity as that in which he makes the claim:

(1) sells an interest which is prevented from being brought into account only by s.191(3), or
(2) exchanges (with or without any payment by way of equality of exchange) within the period of three years immediately following the date of the death any interest in land which was comprised in the deceased's estate immediately before his death,

and the sale price of the interest, or, in the case of an exchange, its market value at the date of the exchange, exceeds its value on death. The amount of the addition varies according to whether the claim relates to one interest or to more than one interest. If the claim relates only to one interest, the addition is equal to the excess of the sale price (or, in the case of an exchange, the market value at the date of the exchange) over the value on death. If the claim relates to more than one interest, the addition is equal to the "appropriate fraction" of the excess of the sale price (or, in the case of an exchange, the market value at the date of the exchange) over the value on death. The "appropriate fraction" is:

$$\frac{\text{Difference between value on death of the interest and its sale price as adjusted under ss.193–195}}{\text{Numerator + corresponding differences for all other interests to which the claim relates}}$$

Assume that four interests—A, B, C and D—are comprised in X's estate, and that each is worth £50,000. A, B and C are sold on the open market for £55,000, £46,000 and £44,000 respectively, D is sold to a beneficiary under X's will for £40,000 at a time when it is, in fact, worth £58,000 which amount is its "sale price" and therefore the figure to be brought into account. The results are thus:

	A	B	C	D
Value on death	£50,000	£50,000	£50,000	£50,000
Sale price	£55,000	£46,000	£44,000	£58,000
Difference	+ £5,000	− £4,000	− £6,000	+ £8,000

The sale prices of A, B and C must be increased by the appropriate fraction of £8,000, the excess of the "sale price" received for D over the value on death as follows:

addition to sale price of $\quad A = £8,000 \times \dfrac{£5,000}{£5,000+£4,000+£6,000} = £2,667$

addition to sale price of $\quad B = £8,000 \times \dfrac{£4,000}{£4,000+£5,000+£6,000} = £2,133$

addition to sale price of $\quad C = £8,000 \times \dfrac{£6,000}{£6,000+£5,000+£4,000} = \underline{\underline{£3,200}}$

$$£8,000$$

The sale of D thus has the effect of converting the net loss of £5,000 made on the sale of A, B and C to a net gain of £3,000—exactly what one would expect.

Adjustment for purchases

Section 192 applies where a person who has made a claim has, acting in the same **25–151** capacity as that in which he made the claim, purchased any interest in land within four months after the last of the sales to which the claim related. In such a case there is a "claw-back" of sorts. No revaluation relief under Chap.IV is available at all if the aggregate of all the purchase prices[243] of all the interests so purchased exceeds the aggregate of the sale prices as adjusted under ss.193–195 of all the interests in respect of which relief is claimed. Otherwise the sale price of every interest to which the claim relates is increased or decreased. Where the sale price of the interest in question exceeds the value on death the sale price is increased by the "appropriate fraction" of the difference between the value on death of the interest in question and its sale price as adjusted under ss.193–196. Where, on the other hand, the sale price of the interest in question is less than the value on death of that interest, the sale price is reduced by the "appropriate fraction" of the difference between the value on death of the interest in question and the sale price as adjusted under ss.193–196. The appropriate fraction is:

---

[243] Disregarding incidental expenses: see para.25–129.

$$\frac{\text{The aggregate of the purchase prices of the interests purchased}}{\text{The aggregate of the sale prices of the interests sold}}$$

Assume, for example, that X's estate includes three interests—A, B and C—worth £50,000 each on his death, and that after selling these properties for £29,000, £32,000 and £59,000 respectively, his executor reinvests £80,000 in land and £40,000 in quoted securities. The respective sale price of interests A and B will be increased and the sale price of interest C will be decreased, as follows:

	A	B	C
Value on death	£50,000	£50,000	£50,000
Sale price	£29,000	£32,000	£59,000
Difference	− £21,000	− £18,000	+ £9,000

Interest	Difference		Appropriate Fraction		Increase/ decrease to sale price
A	£21,000	×	$\dfrac{£80,000}{£120,000}$	=	+ £14,000
B	£18,000	×	$\dfrac{£80,000}{£120,000}$	=	+ £12,000
C	£9,000	×	$\dfrac{£80,000}{£120,000}$	=	− £6,000

The effect is thus very different from that which obtains under s.196, where the whole of the excess of the sale price or market value of the interests sold or exchanged is apportioned among the interests concerned. Under s.192 only part of the consideration applied to purchases may be brought into account: in the above example, for instance, only £20,000 of the £80,000 was brought into account in adjusting the sale prices. This, of course, is not surprising, since the adjustments are concerned with entirely different problems.

Compulsory acquisition more than three years after death

25–152   By s.197, relief may be available in respect of an interest:

(1) if after the end of the period of three years immediately following the date of the death the interest is acquired from the appropriate person in pursuance of a notice to treat served before the death or within that period by any authority possessing powers of compulsory acquisition, and

(2) if, after applying Ch.IV, the sale value of the interest is less than its value on death.

In determining whether the sale value of the interest is less than its value on death it may be necessary to apply s.192. If the claim relates solely to interests compulsorily acquired, s.197(3) provides that in determining for purposes of s.192(1) whether a purchase has been made within four months of the sale to which the claim relates, s.192 is ignored.

It should be noted that s.197A (see para.25–143) has no effect in relation to s.197(1) **25–153** and the relevant period remains three years immediately following the death. Section 198(3) provides that if an interest is acquired from an appropriate person in pursuance of a notice to treat served by an authority possessing powers of compulsory acquisition, the date on which the interest is sold is taken to be the date on which compensation for the acquisition is agreed or otherwise determined (variations on appeal being disregarded for this purpose) or, if earlier, the date when the authority enter on the land in pursuance of their powers. This is expressed to be subject to s.198(4), which provides that if an interest in land is acquired from the appropriate person (a) in England, Scotland or Wales by virtue of a general vesting declaration within the meaning of the Compulsory Purchase (Vesting Declarations) Act 1981 or, in Scotland, Sch.24 to the Town and Country Planning (Scotland) Act 1972, or (b) in Northern Ireland, by way of a vesting order, the date on which the interest is sold by the appropriate person is taken to be the last date of the periods specified in the declaration or, in Northern Ireland, the date on which the vesting order becomes operative.

A case concerning development land tax, *IRC v Metrolands (Property Finance) Ltd*[244] suggests that s.197 may be wider than it appears. The facts of the case were that Metrolands owned land in respect of which it served a purchase notice on the local council under s.180(1) of the Town and Country Planning Act 1971, requiring the council to buy the land. On December 20, 1974, the council agreed to buy the land by serving a compliance notice under s.181(1)(a) of the Act, but the cash settlement was not agreed until August 11, 1976. The question for the House of Lords was whether the disposal took place before August 1, 1976, the date on which the Development Land Tax Act 1976 came into effect. The relevant provision in the 1976 Act was s.45(4), which provided that:

> "where an interest in land is acquired compulsorily by an authority possessing compulsory powers, the time at which the disposal . . . is made is the time at which the compensation for the acquisition is agreed . . . "

The House of Lords held that a reverse compulsory acquisition is within s.45(4), with the result that the date of the disposal was August 11; development land tax was therefore payable. Although the wording of s.45(4) is similar to that in ss.197 and 198(3), it remains to be seen if an interest is acquired from the appropriate person "in pursuance of a notice to treat" (as is required by those paragraphs) in the case of a reverse compulsory acquisition.

XVI. SALES OF ARTIFICIALLY VALUED PROPERTY

Under s.176, provided certain conditions are satisfied, revaluation relief is available **25–154** in two cases where, because of certain rules under which property is specially aggregated for purposes of valuation, an artificially high value has been attributed to property

---

[244] *IRC v Metrolands (Property Finance) Ltd* [1982] 1 W.L.R. 341; [1982] 2 All E.R. 557.

comprised in a person's estate immediately before he died. The first case where such relief may be available is where property valued in accordance with the related property rules is subsequently sold for a price lower than the value previously attributed to it under those rules. The second case is where property which ceased to be comprised in a person's estate on his death has been taken into account in valuing property which continued to form part of his estate after his death. This usually happens as a result of s.49(1), under which a person who is entitled to an interest in possession in settled property is treated as being beneficially entitled to the property in which his interest subsists.

In either of these cases, it may happen that the deceased's personal representatives sell the property which vested in them on the deceased's death and receive for it less than the value previously attributed to it under the legislation. Where this happens, the artificially high value initially attributed to the property may be replaced by the value which would have been attributed to the property had the provisions as to aggregation not applied. This is not to say that the property in question is revalued by itself: regard must still be had to any other property which is or has been vested in the vendors since the death. All that is undone is the artificial aggregation. Once determined, the "disaggregated value" is then reduced by any other reliefs such as business relief which were originally given to the "aggregated value" of the property in question, assuming, of course, that those reliefs are still available: the possibility of their being lost as a result of revaluation relief is discussed below. The last step is to recompute the value transferred by the notional transfer made by the deceased immediately before he died. Tax paid or owing is then refunded or reduced as may be appropriate. The relief must be claimed within the general six-year time limit specified by s.241.

Conditions for relief

25–155   The relief is hedged around with a number of conditions intended to prevent it being given where sales are made with a view towards securing the relief rather than because of genuine commercial considerations. The conditions are as follows:

(1) The property must have been valued on the deceased's death either:
   (a) in accordance with the related property rules, or
   (b) in conjunction with property which was also comprised in the deceased's estate; but which has not at any time since that death been vested in the vendors.[245]
(2) The sale must have been made within three years of the deceased's death.[246]
(3) The persons concerned with the sale must satisfy certain requirements. These are that:
   (a) the vendors must have been either,
      (i) the deceased's personal representatives, or
      (ii) the persons in whom the property vested immediately after the deceased's death.[247]
      A sale by a residuary legatee will thus not qualify. It is understood that HMRC will regard property which was vested in the vendors prior to the death as satisfying (ii), e.g. where the deceased's executors were the

---

[245] IHTA 1984 s.176(1).
[246] IHTA 1984 s.176(1).
[247] IHTA 1984 s.176(3)(a).

trustees of a settlement in which the deceased had an interest in possession.

(b) the vendor must not be the same as and must not be connected[248] with any person concerned either as:
  (i) a purchaser, or
  (ii) having an interest in a purchase.[249]
This means, e.g. that the sale cannot be by an executor to himself acting privately. Nor can the sale be to a trust under which a vendor, or, e.g. his wife has an interest in possession, since the vendor would then be connected with a person having an interest in the purchase.

(c) the vendors must not obtain in connection with the sale either:
  (i) a right to acquire the property sold, or
  (ii) any interest in or created out of the property.[250]
This means, e.g. that the vendors cannot as part of the sale acquire a call option over the property.

(d) No person having an interest in the proceeds of sale can obtain in connection with the sale either:
  (i) a right to acquire the property sold, or
  (ii) any interest in or created out of the property.[251]
This means that, e.g. a residuary legatee cannot acquire as part of the sale a call option over the property.

(e) No person having an interest in the proceeds of sale can be the same as or can be connected with any person concerned either as:
  (i) purchaser, or
  (ii) having an interest in the purchase.[252]
This means that, e.g. the wife of a residuary legatee cannot be the purchaser.

(4) The sale must itself satisfy certain requirements. It:
  (a) must have been made at arm's length; and
  (b) must have been for a price freely negotiated at the time of sale; and
  (c) must not have been made in conjunction with any other property valued artificially as mentioned above.[253]
It will be noted that it is insufficient that, as is the case under s.10(1), the sale was equivalent to one made at arm's length or that the price was equivalent to a freely negotiated one. For the relief to apply the sale must have been made at arm's length and the price must have been freely negotiated.

(5) The price obtained on the sale, adjusted as needs be to take into account any difference in the circumstances at the date of the death and the sale, must be less than the value attributed to the property on the deceased's death before either this relief or the relief given in respect of land[254] sold within three years of death is taken into account.[255] Comparison is thus made between the sale price (adjusted as needs be) and the aggregate value attributed to the property on the deceased's death.

(6) Where the property sold is shares in or securities of a close company, between the death and the sale their value must not have been reduced by more than 5

[248] See para.2–45.
[249] IHTA 1984 s.176(3)(c).
[250] IHTA 1984 s.176(3)(d).
[251] IHTA 1984 s.176(3)(d).
[252] IHTA 1984 s.176(3)(c).
[253] IHTA 1984 s.176(3)(b).
[254] See paras 25–143 et seq.
[255] IHTA 1984 s.176(4).

per cent as a result of an alteration in the company's share or loan capital or in any rights attaching to the shares in or securities of the company.[256]

Disadvantageous claims: business relief and agricultural relief

25–156   Claiming revaluation relief may be disadvantageous in certain circumstances, since it may result in the loss of the business relief and/or agricultural relief which was available to the transfer made on the transferor's death. In certain circumstances, these reliefs are available to shares or debentures only if they gave the transferor control of the company in question. Where on a person's death business or agricultural relief was given to shares or debentures on the basis that they gave the transferor control, and the shares are revalued under s.176, the relief previously given is withdrawn unless the revalued shares or debentures would by themselves have given the transferor control of the company; see ss.105(2) and 122(2). This prevents a taxpayer from having the best of both worlds—control for the purposes of securing reliefs, but a minority holding for purposes of valuation. It is to be noted that once a claim is made under s.176 it cannot be withdrawn. It follows from this that the consequences of making a successful claim should be considered carefully, as should the manner of realising the shares in question. If the shares or debentures which have devolved on the vendors carry control, the shares or debentures should, so far as it is possible to do so, be sold in blocks such that agricultural and/or business relief is not lost.

---

[256] IHTA 1984 s.176(5). The definition of "close company" is that in s.102(1); see para.2–74. "Alteration" includes extinguishment.

CHAPTER 26

CONTROL, BUSINESS, AGRICULTURAL AND WOODLANDS RELIEF

I. INTRODUCTION

26–01   This chapter is concerned with three vital reliefs: business relief, agricultural relief and woodlands relief. Each is considered in turn. The interaction of the reliefs is also discussed. As will be seen, the question of whether a person controls a company may be important in deciding if business relief or agricultural relief is available, and the chapter therefore begins by considering the definition of control, which, as will be seen in Chapter 29, may also be important in determining whether tax can be paid by instalments.

CONTROL

II. OVERVIEW

26–02   The legislation provides three vital reliefs—business relief, agricultural relief and instalment relief—the availability of which depends to a large part on whether or not the person seeking the relief had control of a company in the manner specified by the legislation. One would therefore expect to be able to determine in any given set of circumstances whether a person had sufficient control to qualify for the relief or reliefs (e.g. business relief and instalment relief) sought. This, however, is not the case. Instead, one finds that even in fairly straightforward cases one's advice must be hedged about with qualifications. The circumstances in which a person is to be regarded as having the requisite control are, in short, far from clear. The importance of control in relation to these reliefs is as follows:

(1) *Business relief.* Control is important in two ways for the purposes of business relief. First, quoted shares or securities qualify for 50 per cent relief, and unquoted securities for 100 per cent relief, if in each case they gave the

transferor control of the company immediately prior to the transfer.[1] Secondly, any land, building, machinery or plant used by a company qualifies for relief only if, inter alia, the transferor controlled the company immediately before the transfer.[2]

(2) *Agricultural relief.* Control is also important in two ways for the purposes of agricultural relief. First, where the value transferred by a transfer of value is determined by reference to the value of shares in or securities of a company,[3] agricultural relief is available only if the shares or securities gave the transferor control of the company immediately before the transfer.[4] Relief is available in respect of shares or securities of a company if the company or someone else has occupied agricultural property for certain specified periods. In deciding whether it has been in such occupation, the company is treated as having occupied the property at any time when it was occupied by a person who subsequently controls the company.[5] Secondly, in determining whether a person other than the company has occupied property sufficiently long to qualify for relief, regard is had to any occupation by a company controlled by him.[6]

(3) *Instalment relief.* It may be possible to pay by instalments tax that is attributable to the value of shares or securities[7] which gave the transferor control of the company immediately before the chargeable event.[8]

It is vitally important to note that the legislation provides two different tests. In some cases the relevant test is whether the transferor had control of a company, while in other cases, the relevant test is whether *shares or securities* gave him control. Where business, agricultural or instalment relief is sought in respect of shares or securities on the basis of control, the relief will be available only if those shares or securities gave the transferor control of the company in question. Where, on the other hand, a transferor either seeks business relief in respect of land, a building, machinery or plant used by a company he controls (or wishes, with a view to demonstrating occupation for purposes of agricultural relief, to maintain that he controls a company) there appears to be no requirement that he controlled the company by virtue of shares or securities per se; instead, it suffices that he had control within the special IHT meaning, regardless of how he may have derived that control.

Before turning to the special definition of control, two points concerning style need to be made. First, all three reliefs are available to trustees of relevant property trusts. The words "transferor" and "transfer" should accordingly be read below as referring where appropriate to trustees and to periodic and exit charges. Secondly, where a transfer of value is made on death, the reliefs are, strictly speaking, available in the circumstances mentioned above only if the deceased had the requisite control immediately before he died, not immediately before the transfer in question. Since it would be cumbersome to refer constantly to a transferor who "controlled the company immediately before the transfer or the death, as the case may be," it was thought that

---

[1] IHTA 1984 ss.104(1) and 105(1).

[2] IHTA 1984 ss.105(1), 105(6) and 269.

[3] It is thought that agricultural relief and instalment relief will be available where the transferor derived control partly from shares and partly from securities; this is now also the case for 100 per cent business relief in the context of unquoted shares and securities: see IHTA 1984 s.105(1).

[4] IHTA 1984 s.122(1).

[5] IHTA 1984 s.123(5).

[6] IHTA 1984 s.123(5).

[7] See fn.3, above.

[8] IHTA 1984 ss.227(1), (3), (5) and 269 or, in the case of a transfer made on death, immediately before his death.

811

reference to the death could be omitted from the text without distorting the legislation, and this has been done.

III. DEFINITION OF "CONTROL"

The general rule

26–03   The special definition of control, which applies for the purposes of business, agricultural and instalment relief, is found in s.269 which begins by laying down a general rule to which there are then added three important qualifications. The general rule is that a person has control of a company at any time:

> ". . . if he then has the control of powers of voting on all questions affecting the company as a whole which if exercised would yield a majority of the votes capable of being exercised thereon . . . "

In its original form the legislation provided that a person also had control of a company if he had voting control "on any particular question" affecting the company as a whole. This was virtually identical to the estate duty definition of control found in s.55 of the Finance Act 1940. Under estate duty, of course, it was generally inimical to a taxpayer's interests to have control of a company, since if he had control his shares stood to be valued on a net assets basis which almost inevitably produced a higher value than if some other basis had been used. For CTT purposes, on the other hand, it could be to a taxpayer's advantage to have control. For the parliamentary draftsman to have adopted the wide estate duty definition thus evidenced a measure of unexpected, if inadvertent, largesse on his part.

26–04   Given the availability of the above mentioned reliefs, the articles of many companies were altered so that voting control on various relatively inconsequential questions, e.g. the site of the registered office of the company, attached to a particular block of shares with the result that, for the purposes of the above reliefs, any number of individuals had control of the same company. This simple tax saving device was brought to an end in relation to transfers of value made after April 19, 1978. As from that date, the general rule is that a person has control of a company at any time only if he has voting control on all questions affecting the company as a whole.

26–05   It is to be noted that the test of whether or not a person has control in relation to a given question is whether he controls the majority of the votes on that question: it is not whether, for example, he can carry that question. Thus, he need not, for example, be able to pass a special resolution so as to secure the winding up of the company. What matters is that he controls over 50 per cent of the votes on such a question.

Qualifications to the general rule

26–06   In three cases, a person is regarded as having control of a company even though he in fact does not have voting control on all questions affecting the company as a whole, as follows:

> (1) *Related property.* By s.269(2), shares or securities are deemed to give a person control of a company, if, taken together with any shares or securities which are

related property, they would suffice to give him voting control on all questions affecting the company as a whole. Thus, if X owns shares giving him 40 per cent of the votes in a company and a further 20 per cent of the votes attach to shares held by his wife, both X and his wife will be deemed to have voting control of the company. If, on the other hand, the shares carrying 20 per cent of the votes were not held by X's wife, but were instead related property by virtue of being owned by a charity, X would be deemed to have control of the company, but the charity would not.[9] If X, his wife and the charity each held 20 per cent of the votes, both X and his wife would have control of the company, but the charity would not.

(2) *Interests in possession.* By s.269(3), where a person is beneficially entitled to an interest in possession which satisfies s.49(1A) in shares or securities comprised in a settlement, he is deemed to have any powers of voting which the shares or securities give to the trustees of the settlement. For the purposes of s.49(1A), the interest in possession must be one in existence before March 22, 2006, an immediate post death interest, a disabled person's interest or a transitional serial interest. This is referred to in the remainder of this chapter as a non relevant property interest in possession. Thus, if Y owns shares giving him 30 per cent of the votes in a company and he is entitled to a non relevant property interest in possession in shares which carry 25 per cent of the votes in the company he will be regarded as controlling 55 per cent of the votes in the company. The changes introduced by the Finance Act 2006 mean that the circumstances in which s.269(3) can apply have now been severely restricted. Unless a beneficiary has a non relevant property interest in possession then he will not be deemed to have any powers of voting which the shares or securities give to the trustees of the settlement.

(3) *Special powers.* The articles of a company may confer special voting rights on a class of shares in respect of one or more questions affecting the company as a whole. In the absence of provision to the contrary, a person who had voting control on all other matters might be precluded by such class rights from having control. The legislation accordingly makes special provision to deal with a company in which a class of shares or securities gives voting powers on either or both of two questions, i.e.:

(a) the question of winding up the company;
(b) any question primarily affecting that class of shares or securities.

By s.269(4), in such circumstances, these two questions are left out of account in determining whether a person has voting control on all questions affecting the company as a whole. It is to be noted that the exclusion under s.269(4) operates only where the special voting rights are limited to questions of winding up and/or class rights. If the shares in question give voting power on any other question, s.269(4) does not apply, and the person in question will have control only if he has voting control on all questions affecting the company as a whole, including, for example, the question of winding up.

This used to be a particularly important point. Before 1996, someone who had effective control of a company and whose shares were valued on that basis may have discovered that because another person had control on one question he was deprived of 50 per cent business relief. The particular area where this used to cause problems was in relation to *Bushell v Faith*[10] clauses designed to prevent a director from being

---

[9] The charity's property is related to X's property, but X's property is not related to the charity's property; see para.25–65.

[10] *Bushell v Faith* [1970] A.C. 1099. These are clauses designed to circumvent Companies Act 2006 s.168.

removed by ordinary resolution. For IHT purposes such clauses may mean that no shareholder can have control of that company since no one will control all questions affecting the company as a whole. Take, for instance, the case of A who owns 90 per cent of the ordinary shares and B who owns 10 per cent. B's position as director is protected by a *Bushell v Faith* clause giving him a multiple of 10 votes per share on any resolution to dismiss him as director (and on any resolution to change this article). From the point of view of A, although he owns 90 per cent of the company, he no longer controls all questions affecting that company, since he cannot dismiss B by ordinary resolution. Accordingly, he will not be entitled to business relief based upon the control test being satisfied. However, given that *Bushell v Faith* clauses are commonly employed in unquoted rather than quoted companies, the position has obviously been substantially alleviated by the introduction of 100 per cent relief for minority unquoted shareholdings, which has effectively removed the problem that could arise when company articles include *Bushell v Faith* clauses.[11] The relevance of this point is now therefore only for unquoted securities and the rare cases where quoted companies have *Bushell v Faith* clauses in their articles of association.

IV. COMMENTARY

26–07   The fact that the legislation appears to provide two different tests where the reliefs relating to control are concerned raises three interesting questions:

(1) Where relief is sought in respect of a transfer of shares or securities, need the transfer of the shares or securities cause the transferor to lose control of the company?

(2) In deciding whether a person controls a company, can regard be had to votes he controls which attach to shares which he does not own beneficially (e.g. where shares are registered in the name of a trustee of a relevant property trust)?

(3) In relation to agricultural relief and business relief, in deciding whether a person controls a company, can regard be had to votes which he controls which do not attach to shares at all?

Is loss of control necessary?

26–08   The first question concerns what the legislation means when it provides that shares or securities qualify for relief if they gave the transferor control prior to the transfer in question.

At first sight it seems possible to read the legislation as meaning that when a person transfers shares or securities those shares or securities will qualify for relief only if the transfer causes the transferor to lose control of the company. This follows from the use of the phrase "shares or securities . . . which gave the transferor control of the company immediately before the transfer". Under this reading, if X had a 60 per cent holding in X plc and gave a 9 per cent holding to his daughter, the 9 per cent holding would not qualify for relief because X retained 51 per cent of the shares, i.e. a controlling shareholding: the 9 per cent, therefore, did not of itself give him control immediately before the transfer.

[11] See para.26–24.

Fortunately, this is thought not to be the case. The correct view is thought to be that it suffices that the shares formed part of a controlling shareholding before the transfer. The 9 per cent holding would thus come within the definition of a controlling shareholding for these purposes. This view is based on two considerations—one, equitable, the other, technical. The "equitable" consideration is that it would be anomalous if shares which were valued on a control basis, as the 9 per cent holding in the above example would have been, did not qualify for the various reliefs clearly intended for such shares.

The technical consideration arises in connection with business relief, in respect of which two points are relevant. First, s.105(1)(cc) expressly provides that shares or securities of a quoted company qualify for the 50 per cent relief if, inter alia, they:

" . . . (either by themselves or together with other such shares or securities owned by the transferor) gave the transferor control of the company immediately before the transfer."

A similar provision applies in the case of securities of an unquoted company in the context of 100 per cent relief. As will be seen below, the words in brackets raise certain difficult questions as to the proper construction of some of the business relief provisions, but at least they seem to make it clear beyond doubt that a transfer of securities may qualify for business relief even though that transfer does not cause the transferor to lose control of the company.

Secondly, if it were correct that the 9 per cent holding in the above example did not qualify for relief, then the same shares could be "relevant business property" within the meaning of s.105(1)(cc) for one purpose but not for another. This follows from the fact that, by s.105(1)(d), (read in conjunction with s.105(6)), a transfer of land, a building, machinery or plant owned by the transferor and used by a company controlled by him does not qualify for relief unless the shares or securities of the company in question were themselves relevant business property of the transferor immediately before the transfer in question. This means that if the narrow, "loss of control" test applies the same shares could be relevant business property within s.105(1)(cc) for one purpose but not for another. Assume that X in the above example owned a factory which he let to X plc, and that the day before X transferred the 9 per cent holding to his daughter he gave the factory to his son. Under s.105(6), it would have been necessary in relation to the gift to the son to see if X owned a controlling shareholding, i.e. shares which ranked as relevant business property within s.105(1)(cc), and for this purpose the 9 per cent holding, regarded prior to the gift to the daughter as an integral part of the 60 per cent holding, would have been relevant business property within s.105(1)(cc). It would thus seem strange to say that when X gave the 9 per cent holding to his daughter the shares no longer ranked as relevant business property within s.105(1)(cc). These technical points arise, it is true, only in connection with business relief for quoted shareholdings, but they are thought to lend support to the general proposition that the relevant test for all those reliefs—business, agricultural and instalment relief—is whether the shares or securities in question formed part of a controlling holding prior to the transfer in question. HMRC are thought to regard this as the correct test.

Is beneficial ownership necessary?

The question as to whether account can be taken only of votes attaching to shares owned beneficially by the transferor is somewhat more difficult, and the answer may depend on the context in which the question arises. **26–09**

The first context in which the question may arise is where business, agricultural or instalment relief is sought in respect of shares or securities. Subject to one important qualification concerning business relief (see below) there seems to be a good argument that regard can be had to whatever votes the transferor controls which attach to shares or securities, and not just to votes attaching to shares or securities which he owns (or is treated as owning) beneficially. This follows from the fact that all three reliefs refer simply to shares or securities which gave the transferor control; in particular, no reference is made to shares or securities owned beneficially by the transferor which gave him control. That being the case, the question arises as to whether as a matter of general law the transferor controlled a majority of the votes attaching to shares or securities of the company in question. In particular, there is nothing to suggest that votes held by a person in one capacity are not to be aggregated with votes held by him in some other capacity. Section 269(3) is inconclusive on this point. On the one hand, in so far as it aligns the position as regards the votes to be attributed to a person who owns shares outright and those to be attributed to a person who is beneficially entitled to a non relevant property interest in possession in shares, it implies—and this would be consistent with the reliefs by reference to which control is important—that what matters is beneficial entitlement and beneficial entitlement alone. On the other hand, in so far as it indicates that in its absence a person beneficially entitled to an interest in possession in shares would not be regarded as controlling the votes attaching thereto, it suggests that, in the absence of provision to the contrary, regard is to be had to the general law in deciding who controls votes attaching to shares or securities.[12]

As was mentioned above, this view is subject to one important qualification, namely that there is some ground for saying that where business relief is concerned regard is to be had only to votes attaching to shares owned beneficially by the transferor. This follows from s.105(1)(cc) which, as was mentioned above, provides somewhat ambiguously that 50 per cent relief is available in respect of,

> "shares or securities of a company which are quoted and which (either by themselves or together with other such shares or securities owned by the transferor) gave the transferor control of the company immediately before the transfer."

The effect of this provision is far from clear. To begin with, the use of the word "owned" is somewhat surprising. Presumably, it is intended to mean beneficial ownership, since a reference to mere legal ownership would be pointless. But, if this is the case, one would have expected the draftsman to adopt language consistent with the rest of the legislation and to refer to, e.g. "shares or securities comprised in the transferor's estate", or "shares or securities to which the transferor was beneficially entitled".

Stylistic considerations aside, there are at least two other reasons for regarding the word "owned" as referring to legal and/or beneficial ownership. First, as was mentioned above, business relief is available to trustees of relevant property trusts, the word "transferor" in ss.103–114 being taken to mean "trustees" where appropriate.[13] Trustees, of course, are never beneficially entitled to the property vested in them as trustees. Therefore, at least in relation to such trustees, "owned" presumably means legal ownership.

Secondly, if the narrow construction of "owned" is correct, a transferor might control a company for some purposes of business relief, but not for others, and this would be inconsistent. As was mentioned above, 50 per cent business relief on business assets owned directly by the transferor is available only if, inter alia, two conditions are satisfied, as follows:

[12] See *IRC v Harlon Coal Co Ltd* [1960] Ch. 563.
[13] IHTA 1984 s.103(1).

(1) by s.105(1)(d), the land, building, plant or machinery in question must have been used by a company controlled by the transferor, and

(2) by s.105(6), in so far as the transferor owned shares or securities in the company, those shares or securities must themselves have been relevant business property.

Now, assume that X transfers plant which X plc has used, and that X is the first named trustee of a relevant property trust which owns shares giving the trust control of X plc, so that it is his name that appears on the share register. In the circumstances, it seems clear that as a matter of general law X controls X plc[14] and that the first of the above conditions is thus satisfied. The next step is therefore to determine whether the shares are relevant business property. To be relevant business property they must come within s.105(1)(cc), but they will not do so if the narrow construction of "owned" applies because X does not own the securities beneficially. X will thus control X plc for some purposes of business relief, but not for others, with the result that the legislation appears inconsistent.

Two comments are in order about this point. First, the Finance Act 1978 introduced a new category of relevant business property—non-controlling shares in an unquoted company, (which, per the Finance Act 1996, now qualify for 100 per cent business relief), but did not amend s.105(6) to take account of this change. This means that 100 per cent business relief is now available in respect of land, etc. owned by an unquoted company, even though the shares the transferor "owns" do not give him control, with the result that the inconsistency mentioned above does not arise unless the transferor owns non-controlling securities. Prior to the Finance Act 1978, the inconsistency was thus more marked. Secondly, and perhaps more importantly, the "inconsistency" argument may prove rather too much. This is because even if it is correct that votes attaching to shares or securities not owned beneficially by the transferor may be taken into account in deciding whether the transferor had control, it still might be possible for a person to have control within s.105(1)(d) but not within s.105(1)(b). This follows from the fact that it appears that in deciding whether a person controls a company for purposes of s.105(1)(d) it may be possible to take account of any votes he controls in law, whether those votes attach to shares or not. This, of course, brings us to the last of the three questions originally posed above.

Votes not attaching to shares

As was noted above, one of the relevant tests in determining whether agricultural **26–10** relief and 50 per cent business relief in respect of land, etc. are available is whether the transferor controlled the company which used the land, etc. or carried on the business in question. In relation to these reliefs the test appears simply to be whether or not as a matter of general law a person controls a majority of the votes. In particular, there is nothing to suggest that votes must attach to shares held by the transferor beneficially, or that votes held by a person in one capacity are not to be aggregated with votes held by him in some other capacity (as was noted above s.269(3) is inconclusive on this point). Indeed, it appears that the transferor's control need not derive from shares or securities at all but could, for example, result from his holding a casting vote as a

---

[14] See para.26–11.

director or chairman of the board. This, of course, makes matters even more interesting and necessitates a reference to the general law.

The general law

26–11   Assuming that, as was the case for estate duty (except where statute provided otherwise), regard is to be had in some circumstances to what votes a person controls as a matter of general law, the various cases decided on this point for other taxes become relevant. There is, of course, a nice irony here, since in the past the arguments of HMRC have always been intended to establish that the taxpayer had control; it seems that now the shoe is on the other foot, and that those arguments may be deployed against them. The effect of the decided cases may be summarised as follows:

(1) *Chairman of the board.* It is common for the chairman of a board of directors to hold a casting vote at general meetings of the company by virtue of express provisions in the company's articles of association. Following the case of *Walker's Executors v IRC*,[15] it is now clear that a casting vote of this kind will be relevant in determining whether the chairman has control of the company for the purposes of s.105(1)(d).

In *Walker's Executors*, the Chairman, Mrs Walker, held exactly 50 per cent of the votes in the company in question and in addition a casting vote in her capacity as Chairman of the Board of Directors. Her executors claimed 50 per cent business relief on the land owned in her own name which was used wholly or mainly for the purposes of the company's business. They submitted that Mrs Walker had had control of the company by reason of the aggregate of her 50 per cent shareholding and her casting vote. The Revenue, as it then was, denied that Mrs Walker had control, on the basis that when exercising her casting vote as Chairman, she had owed a fiduciary duty to the company as an officer of the company, which would have prevented her from using the casting vote in her own interests in the event of any conflict between her personal interest as shareholder and that of the company.

The Special Commissioner rejected this argument, referring specifically to s.269(3), which provides, as noted above, that a person with an interest in possession (now a non-relevant property interest in possession) in shares or securities of a company is to be treated as entitled to their voting rights, irrespective of whether such person might himself be a trustee with fiduciary duties.

(2) *Votes not attaching to shares.* It follows from *Walker's Executors* that the votes which give a person control need not attach to shares at all, but may instead be vested in him for some other reason, e.g. because of the position he holds.

(3) *Directors.* It appears that if a company holds shares in another company, and the board of directors determines that those votes are to be exercised by one of its directors, that director controls the votes attaching to the shares, and this is so notwithstanding the fact that he holds the votes in a fiduciary capacity. Although there is no decided case law authority on this point, the decision in *Walker's Executors* appears by analogy to confirm this analysis.

(4) *Trustees.* By s.360 of the Companies Act 1985, a company registered in England is prohibited from entering on its register notice of any trust. A person whose name is on such a company's register is thus registered qua shareholder,

---

[15] *Walker's Executors v IRC* [2001] S.T.C. (S.C.D.) 86.

not qua trustee. Where there is only one active trustee, he controls the votes attaching to the shares registered in his name; *Re Perkins, Ex p. Mexican Santa Barbara Mining Co.*[16] Where there are two or more active trustees the trustee whose name is on the register normally controls the votes: the fact that he cannot act without the concurrence of one or more of his fellow trustees is irrelevant. This follows from the leading case of *Barclays Bank Ltd v IRC (Shipside's Executor)*,[17] in which the House of Lords held that in deciding whether for the purposes of estate duty the deceased Mr Shipside had voting control, regard was to be had both (i) to the votes attaching to shares owned by him beneficially, and (ii) given the fact that the articles of the company in question gave the person in whose name shares were registered the right to vote those shares, to the votes attaching to shares registered in his name as one of four trustees of a settlement: see also *J Bibby & Sons Ltd v IRC*.[18] If a trustee is a bare trustee, it may be that the beneficiary controls the votes attaching to the shares on the footing that the trustee must act according to the beneficiary's desires. This was the view of the Court of Appeal in the *Bibby* case, though the House of Lords regarded it as an open question. In the *Shipside* case, Lord Denning thought the beneficiary controlled the votes, as did, in effect, Lord Reid.[19] It follows from the above that an individual may for purposes of some of the reliefs be able to arrange to have control of a company in which he owns a minority shareholding without altering the basis on which his shareholding is valued. The most obvious example of circumstances in which this might be done is where an individual with a majority shareholding settles shares on, say, a discretionary trust for his children, with the result that his shareholding is reduced to a minority shareholding: so long as he is a trustee of the settlement and the trust shares are registered in his name, it is arguable, on the basis of the *Shipside* case, that the votes attaching to the trust shares (assuming that under the company's articles the person in whose name shares are registered controls the votes attaching thereto) should be taken into account in deciding whether he controls the company.[20] This analysis now seems to have been confirmed by the *Walker's Executors* case in the context of a chairman's casting vote. It should be mentioned that this may put the shareholder/trustee in a difficult position in equity, since his duties as trustee might well conflict with his interests as a shareholder.

(5) *Beneficial joint holders.* If A and B jointly own shares registered in A's name, it appears that A controls the votes. (It is always open to joint holders to have their holding split and registered in their names separately: see *Burns v Siemen's Bros Dynamo Works.*[21])

(6) *Mortgagee.* A mortgagee of shares controls the votes attaching thereto; *Burns v Siemen's Bros Dynamo Works: Wise v Lansdell.*[22]

(7) *Unpaid vendor.* A vendor who has not been paid or who has been paid only partly for shares may control the votes attaching to the shares; *Musselwhite v CH Musselwhite & Son Ltd.*[23]

---

[16] *Re Perkins, Ex p. Mexican Santa Barbara Mining Co* [1890] 24 Q.B.D. 613.

[17] *Barclays Bank Ltd v IRC (Shipside's Executor)* [1961] A.C. 509.

[18] *J Bibby & Sons Ltd v IRC* [1945] 1 All E.R. 667; 29 T.C. 167.

[19] See also *IRC v Silverts Ltd* [1951] Ch. 521; *John Shields & Co (Perth) Ltd v IRC* [1950] S.C. 441; 29 T.C. 475.

[20] Subject to the above-mentioned qualifications concerning business relief.

[21] *Burns v Siemen's Bros Dynamo Works* [1919] 1 Ch. 225.

[22] *Burns v Siemen's Bros Dynamo Works: Wise v Lansdell* [1921] 1 Ch. 420.

[23] *Musselwhite v CH Musselwhite & Son Ltd* [1962] Ch. 964.

(8) *Nominees*. Where shares are registered in the name of a nominee, the principal, not the nominee, controls the votes attaching to the shares (*Kirby v Wilkins*[24]), unless, of course, the nominee agreement states to the contrary.

(9) *Indirect control*. It appears that where a person controls company A, which, in turn, controls company B, he also controls company B; see *British-American Tobacco Co Ltd v IRC*,[25] *IRC v FA Clark & Son Ltd*,[26] and *S Berendsen Ltd v IRC*.[27] The question may arise as to whether his control derived from the shares in company A, company B, or both. It is to be noted that if the board of company A had determined that the votes exercisable by company A in respect of the shares in company B were to be exercisable by one of the directors of company A, that director (and not the person who controlled company A) would probably be regarded as controlling company B.

(10) *Capacity*. *Walding (Executors of Walding, Deceased) v IRC*[28] has established that the capacity of a shareholder to exercise their votes is not to be taken into account. In the *Walding* case, the deceased owned 45 per cent of the share capital in a private company with a further 24 per cent being held in the name of her grandson who, at the relevant time, was four years old. Did the deceased have control of the company within s.269? For the executors it was argued that, as the section referred to "votes capable of being exercised", the capacity of shareholders was relevant and, given that the grandson was not, in reality, capable of exercising the voting rights attached to his shareholding, the deceased had in fact controlled the company. Knox J., unsurprisingly, rejected this analysis holding that the words in s.269 referred to the category of voting rights concerning all questions affecting the company as a whole (as opposed to votes on matters not affecting the company as a whole). The ability of shareholders to exercise those votes was irrelevant.

BUSINESS RELIEF

V. INTRODUCTION

26–12   One of the most important reliefs is that afforded to transfers of business property: its effect may be to eliminate completely the tax that would otherwise be payable. The complicated provisions governing this relief therefore deserve careful study.

The relief is available to actual and notional transfers of value alike.[29] It is available also to periodic and exit charges, and in the following discussion "transferor" should, where appropriate, be read as "trustees", and "transfer of value" as "periodic charge" or "exit charge", as the case may be.[30] The availability of business relief for periodic and exit charges will make it an increasingly important aspect of estate planning following the changes to the taxation of trusts as introduced by the Finance Act 2006. The relief may be claimed, but need not be. Where it is not claimed, HMRC practice

---

[24] *Kirby v Wilkins* [1929] 2 Ch. 444; see also the bare trustee cases cited above.
[25] *British-American Tobacco Co Ltd v IRC* [1943] A.C. 335.
[26] *IRC v FA Clark & Son Ltd* [1941] 2 K.B. 270.
[27] *S Berendsen Ltd v IRC* [1958] Ch. 1.
[28] *Walding (Executors of Walding, Deceased) v IRC* [1996] S.T.C. 13.
[29] IHTA 1984 s.3(4).
[30] IHTA 1984 s.103(1).

is to give the relief on a provisional basis. The relief, once given, may be clawed-back.[31]

Following a successful trial period, HMRC have agreed that non-statutory clearances will be provided to "business owners" on the availability of business relief. Clearances will be provided as to the tax position following a specific business transaction or event where, regardless of the age of the legislation, it can be demonstrated that there is material uncertainty over the application of the law and that the issue is commercially significant to the business itself. A non-statutory clearance can be sought both pre-transaction (where evidence is supplied that the transaction is genuinely contemplated) or post-transaction. In either instance HMRC will aim to provide a response within 28 days of an application being received.

Where relief is available it is given by reducing by a percentage so much of the value transferred by a transfer of value as is attributable to the value of certain kinds of business property called "relevant business property". It is *not* given by reducing the value of such property. The approach of the legislation in relation to this formulation is multilayered and highly technical. It operates as follows:

(1) *categories of relevant business property:* it establishes a number of categories of relevant business property and the percentage relief that is available in respect of each of these categories;

(2) *qualitative limitations on relevant business property:* it provides three rules under which, even if the property comes within one of the specified categories, it is nevertheless prevented from being relevant business property because it infringes certain requirements designed to ensure that the relief is available only, in effect, to deserving cases;

(3) *quantitative limitations on the value of relevant business property:* these limitations operate in two ways:
    (a) they limit in some cases the value of relevant business property to which the value transferred by the transfer in question is attributable; and
    (b) they limit in some cases the amount of value transferred which qualifies for relief; and

(4) *clawback of relief:* in certain cases relief previously given may be clawed back retrospectively.

The relief has been extended a number of times since it was first introduced. It now covers three kinds of property and is given at two rates in respect of "transfers of value made and other events occurring on or after March 10, 1992"[32]—100 per cent and 50 per cent, depending on the kind of property involved, as follows:

	Relevant Business Property	*Relief*
1.	A business or an interest in a business	100%
2.	Shares in or securities of a company	100/50%
3.	Certain land, buildings, plant or machinery	50%

HMRC have confirmed that the phrase "other events occurring" will be applicable in the following situation. In 1987 Sam gave away business property then qualifying for 50 per cent relief to his daughter (a PET) and in the following year transferred

---

[31] See paras 26–101–26–112.
[32] F(No.2)A 1992 Sch.14 para.8.

similar property into a discretionary trust (a chargeable transfer). He died on March 11, 1992. In both cases the original transferees retained the property. Both transfers qualify for 100 per cent relief at the date of death so that, in the case of the 1987 transfer, no tax is payable; in the case of the 1988 transfer, no further tax is payable. Although HMRC have confirmed that this is their interpretation of the position,[33] this is a little surprising as, on a strict reading of the legislation, the death of Sam in 1992 should not affect the rate of relief applicable to the transfers made in 1987 and 1988. Instead, the significance of Sam's death in 1992 should be to trigger the clawback provisions so that the tax payable on the transfers in 1987 and 1988 is recalculated on the basis of the reliefs applying on those dates.[34]

In relation to cumulations, HMRC have also confirmed that, where there has been an immediately chargeable transfer, it is the rate of relief that applied at the time of the transfer that is relevant for determining the cumulative total of previous chargeable transfers.[35] The fact that the transfer would now qualify for a higher rate of relief is not relevant. This contrasts with the position in relation to PETs where it is the rate of relief applicable at the date that the transfer becomes chargeable that is relevant for the purposes of determining the cumulative total of previous chargeable transfers.[36]

Avoidance of double relief

26–13   A person cannot claim business relief on so much of the value transferred by the transfer in question as has been reduced by agricultural property relief[37] or woodlands relief.[38]

Conditions for the relief

26–14   The fact that business relief is available only in respect of so much of the value transferred by a transfer of value as is attributable to the value of any relevant business property raises three questions:

What is relevant business property?

What is the value of such property?

When is the value transferred by a transfer of value attributable to the value of such property?

Identifying the property transferred

26–15   Exceptionally, a question may arise as to the nature of the property to which the value transferred is attributable. In *Reynaud v IRC*[39] four brothers each transferred shares qualifying for business relief into four separate discretionary settlements. On the following day the company in which the shares were held bought back from the

[33] HMRC Manuals IHTM25264.
[34] See paras 26–101–26–112.
[35] HMRC Manuals IHTM25262.
[36] HMRC Manuals IHTM25262.
[37] IHTA 1984 s.114(1).
[38] IHTA 1984 s.114(2).
[39] *Reynaud v IRC* [1999] S.T.C. (S.C.D) 185; for a full discussion, see para.9–21.

trustees some of the shares; the trustees then sold the remaining shares to a third party purchaser. The Revenue, as it then was, contended that the purchase by the company of the shares was an operation associated with the transfer of the shares into the settlements and that therefore there had been an extended disposition the effect of which was that the brothers had transferred cash to the trustees rather than the shares that had been purchased by the company from the trustees, with the result that no business relief was available.

The Special Commissioner agreed that the transfers into the settlements and the purchases were associated operations. But in his view in the context of s.268(3) an operation was relevant

" . . . only if it is part of the scheme contributing to the reduction of the estate . . . Here the value of the estates of the brothers were diminished as a result of gift into settlement alone. The purchase of own shares contributed nothing to the diminution which had already occurred and was not therefore a relevant associated operation."[40]

The value transferred was attributable to the shares, not the cash.

VI. HOW THE RELIEF IS GIVEN

Before examining the complicated provisions which regulate the availability of **26–16** business relief, it will be helpful to consider how the relief is given when it is available. The relief is *not* given by reducing the value of any property. Rather, so much of the value transferred by the transfer in question as is attributable to relevant business property is reduced by the percentage appropriate to the property in question. If part only of the value transferred is attributable to qualifying property that part only is eligible to be reduced.[41] It follows from the fact that the amount to be reduced is the value transferred by a transfer of value that the relief is to be given in the following way:

(1) The value transferred is reduced by the appropriate percentage.[42] Thus, if on January 1, 2004, X settled on a relevant property trust his controlling share-holding in a quoted company in circumstances where the value transferred by the transfer of value made by X was £400,000, the £400,000 would first have been reduced by 50 per cent to £200,000.

(2) Any available exemptions are then taken into account. Assuming X's annual exemption was available to him and he had not used his previous year's annual exemption,[43] X would thus, before grossing up, have made a chargeable transfer of £194,000.

(3) The value transferred is reduced by any CGT borne by the donee.[44]

(4) The resulting figure is then grossed up at the appropriate rate, as may be necessary.

[40] *Reynaud v IRC* [1999] S.T.C. (S.C.D) 185 at 190g and 191e.
[41] IHTA 1984 s.104(1).
[42] IHTA 1984 s.104(1) and (2).
[43] IHTA 1984 s.19(2).
[44] IHTA 1984 s.165.

The result is that the relief is even more beneficial than at first sight it might appear, both because it is given before exemptions and grossing up, and because the reduction is made to the top slice of the transfer, tax at the higher rate possibly being avoided accordingly.

VII. CATEGORIES OF RELEVANT BUSINESS PROPERTY

Categories of property capable of qualifying for relief

26–17 There are seven designated categories of property. These are set out below, together with the appropriate rate of relief for each category.

26–18 It will be helpful to begin by listing the seven categories and the rates of relief.[45] Following changes made by the Finance Act 1996, the basic position regarding transfers of value made on or after April 6, 1996, is as follows:

(1) A business or an interest in a business qualifies for 100 per cent relief.[46]

(2) Unquoted shareholdings (including shares dealt with on AIM and USM) qualify for 100 per cent relief whatever the size of the shareholding.[47]

(3) Unquoted securities qualify for 100 per cent relief if the taxpayer owns a controlling interest in the company (note that unquoted means not listed on a recognised stock exchange; securities dealt with on AIM and USM are treated as unquoted).[48]

(4) Quoted voting shareholdings qualify for 50 per cent relief if the taxpayer owns a controlling interest in the company (note that quoted means listed on a recognised stock exchange; shares dealt with on AIM and USM are treated as unquoted).[49]

(5) Quoted securities qualify for 50 per cent relief if the taxpayer owns a controlling interest in the company.[50]

(6) Land, buildings, machinery or plant owned outside a business qualify for 50 per cent relief if they are used wholly or mainly for the purposes of a business carried on by a company of which the transferor had a controlling interest or by a partnership of which the transferor was a partner.[51]

(7) Land, buildings, machinery or plant owned outside a business qualify for 50 per cent relief if the transferor had an interest in possession in the land etc. and

---

[45] The provisions concerning holding companies, which are somewhat complicated, are summarised towards the end of the discussion. The special rules that apply where property to which the reservation of benefit rules apply are discussed at paras 26–189–26–193. For the position where there is a partly exempt transfer, see paras 8–58–8–113.

[46] IHTA 1984 ss.104(1)(a) and 105(1)(a).

[47] IHTA 1984 ss.104(1)(a), 105(1)(bb) and 105(1ZA). Prior to April 6, 1996, unquoted shares only qualified for 100 per cent relief if the transferor held more than 25 per cent of the voting shares in the company.

[48] IHTA 1984 ss.104(1)(a), 105(1)(b), 105(1ZA) and 269.

[49] IHTA 1984 ss.104(1)(b), 105(1)(cc), 105(1ZA) and 269.

[50] IHTA 1984 ss.104(1)(b), 105(1)(cc), 105(1ZA) and 269.

[51] IHTA 1984 ss.104(1)(b), 105(1)(d) and 269.

they were used wholly or mainly for the purposes of a business carried on by him.[52]

Category 1: a business or an interest in a business (100 per cent)[53]

This category includes property such as a sole trader's business. Woodlands man- **26–19** aged on a commercial basis come within this category. "Business" is the subject of a definition at once inclusive and exclusive—it includes a business carried on in the exercise of a profession or vocation, but excludes a business carried on otherwise than for gain.[54] The business of a "hobby farmer" is unlikely to qualify for relief. There is persuasive authority for the proposition that "business" is a word of wide import which must be given its ordinary meaning unless the context requires otherwise.[55] In partic- ular, it is much wider than "trade". Section 105(3), by referring to "the business of . . . making or holding investments", makes it clear that business in this context extends to non-trading activities, e.g. that of a landlord who lets property. "Investment busi- nesses" thus prima facie qualify but, as will be seen at para.26–32, s.105(3) prevents any relief from being available in respect of a business which consists wholly or mainly of "investments". It is possible for a business to be multifaceted or hybrid, i.e. it may consist of a variety of activities, e.g. trading, making investments and letting prop- erty.

Not all activities will constitute a business: note in this connection the comments of Park J. in *Jowett v O'Neill & Brennan Construction*,[56] a corporation tax case, that a company is not carrying on a business merely because it holds a bank account and receives interest. Similarly, in *HMRC v Salaried Persons Postal Loans Ltd*[57] another corporation tax case, Lawrence J. held that in circumstances where a company ceased to trade but let the property it owned to tenants, the company should not be deemed to be "carrying on a business".

The business (except in the case of a market maker or a discount house) need not be carried on in the United Kingdom.[58]

An interest in a business will include a partner's share in a partnership carrying on a business, and this is so whether the share is that of a full-time, part-time, sleeping or limited partner. Where trustees of a settlement carry on a business it is understood that HMRC will regard beneficiaries who have non-relevant property interests in possession as having interests in the business, but will regard beneficiaries who have reversionary interests as not qualifying for relief. Where an estate is in the course of administration, and included among the assets of the estate is a business, beneficiaries of the estate who would be entitled to an immediate post death interest had the administration been

[52] IHTA 1984 ss.104(1)(b) and 105(1)(e).

[53] IHTA 1984 ss.104(1)(a) and 105(1)(a). The rate was 30 per cent for transfers after April 6, 1976, and before October 27, 1977, 50 per cent for transfers after October 26, 1977, and before March 10, 1992, and 100 per cent for transfers after March 9, 1992.

[54] IHTA 1984 s.103(3).

[55] See *Commissioner of Income Tax v Hanover Agencies Ltd* [1967] 1 A.C. 681. See also the VAT cases: *Customs and Excise Commissioners v Morrison's Academy Boarding Houses Association* [1978] S.T.C. 1; *National Water Council v Customs and Excise Commissioners* [1979] S.T.C. 157; *Church of Scientology of California v Customs and Excise Commissioners* [1979] S.T.C. 297; and the *Excess Profits Duty cases*: *IRC v The Marine Steam Turbine Co Ltd* [1920] 1 K.B. 193; *IRC v The Korean Syndicate* [1921] 3 K.B. 258; and *Town Investments v Department of the Environment* [1978] A.C. 359.

[56] *Jowett v O'Neill & Brennan Construction* [1998] S.T.C. 482.

[57] *HMRC v Salaried Persons Postal Loans Ltd* [2006] EWCH 763 (Ch).

[58] IHTA 1984 s.105(4)(a).

completed will have an interest in the business.[59] A creditor of a business does not have an interest in the business.[60]

Prior to the Special Commissioner's decision in *Trustees of the Nelson Dance Family Settlement v HMRC*[61] it was widely accepted that the individual assets of a business were not within this category; therefore where individual assets of a business were transferred it was thought that it was not possible to secure relief under this head. The position was thus very similar to what it was under CGT retirement relief per ss.163–164 of the Taxation of Chargeable Gains Act 1992 (now repealed), and the unhappy experience of the farmer in *McGregor v Adcock*.[62] Adcock owned and farmed 35 acres of land. He sold 4.2 of these acres, and claimed retirement relief on his gain. His claim was rejected by Fox J. on the ground that the sale of part of the land did not constitute a disposal of his farming business as was required by what became s.163.[63] Had the disposal been a transfer of value for IHT purposes, no business relief would have been available, for the same reason. Agricultural relief, on the other hand, might have been available.[64]

To the surprise of many commentators, the decision in *Nelson Dance* altered the long held analysis that the assets of a business do not constitute "a business or an interest in a business". The case involved the transfer of farming land to a discretionary settlement. The land qualified for agricultural relief, but since it had development potential, the trustees also claimed business relief in relation to the excess value. The trustees' claim was based on the fact that there had been a reduction of "relevant business property" in the deceased's estate. HMRC rejected the claim but, on appeal, the Special Commissioner found that business relief was applicable on the basis that "all that is required is that the value transferred by the transfer of value is attributable to the net value of the business." This decision was upheld following HMRC's unsuccessful appeal to the High Court.[65] Mr Justice Sales held that the Special Commissioner's approach had the benefit of simplicity and certainty and was consistent with the general "loss to donor" principle governing the operation of IHT rules. For business relief to be available there is no requirement that the property transferred should be a business which retains its character as a business in the hands of the transferee, or even that the property transferred should itself have the character of a business.

Therefore, provided that the assets transferred are used in a business and are attributable to that business' net value, then there is now scope for business relief to apply. The case highlights that when considering the availability of business relief it is myopic to simply focus attention on identifying whether or not a transfer falls within one of the categories of "relevant business property" identified in s.105(1). Instead, the proper approach is to identify the transfer of value that has resulted in a reduction in the value of "relevant business property" in the transferor's estate, irrespective of whether an actual transfer of the "relevant business property" takes place.

In light of this new analysis, there are likely to be many instances where tax has been paid following the transfer of assets on the understanding that business relief was not

---

[59] IHTA 1984 s.91.

[60] See para.26–21.

[61] *Trustees of the Nelson Dance Family Settlement v HMRC* [2008] S.T.C. 792. This was affirmed in the appeal to the Chancery Division [2009] EWHC 71 (Ch).

[62] *McGregor v Adcock* [1977] 1 W.L.R. 864; [1977] S.T.C. 206.

[63] For decisions on the meaning of "part of a business" see *Pepper v Daffurn* [1993] S.T.C. 466, *Jarmin v Rawlins* [1994] S.T.C. 1005 and *Plumbly (personal representatives of the estate of Harbour (Deceased)) v Spencer* [1999] S.T.C. 677 and for the meaning of an "associated business", see *Clarke v Mayo* [1994] S.T.C. 570. It may be noted that the CGT legislation referred to "part of a business" whereas s.105(1)(a) concerns an "interest in a business".

[64] See *Melon v Hector Powe Ltd* [1981] 1 All E.R. 313.

[65] *Trustees of the Nelson Dance Family Settlement v HMRC* [2009] EWHC 71 (Ch).

available. In circumstances where tax has been assessed and paid then there is no scope to claim overpaid sums or interest. If tax has not yet been paid (because the transfer was a PET or within the transferor's nil rate band) then cumulative totals can be recalculated to take into account the revised understanding of the law.

There is another advantage in giving business assets to a trust rather than outright: if the donor makes a gift to a trust within his available nil rate band (before the deduction of BPR) and then dies within seven years, the clawback provisions of s.113A(2) will not apply: the nil rate band will be calculated as though business relief was available at the time of the gift. By contrast, if the gift was outright to an individual, the full value of the gift will eat into the donor's nil rate band.

The "rule" in Fetherstonaugh

Somewhat surprisingly, where an individual has an interest in possession in an asset that he uses in his business the asset may fall within this category, and so qualify for 100 per cent relief. It is assumed that this rule will only apply following the Finance Act 2006 where an individual has a non relevant property interest in possession. In the pre Finance Act 2006 case of *Fetherstonaugh v IRC*,[66] the majority of the Court of Appeal held that on the death of a sole trader who carried on his business on land held on the trusts of a settlement under which he had an interest in possession both the business and the land fell within this category, so qualifying for full relief,[67] the land doing so on the basis that, by virtue of what is now s.49(1), the deceased owned the land, which he had used in his business within the meaning of what is now s.110(b). The then Financial Secretary to the Treasury confirmed in a published letter of October 1985 that full relief is available "where the circumstances accord with" those in *Fetherstonaugh*. It is not clear precisely what this means but relief under this head will arguably be available not only on the kind of transfer on death that occurred in *Fetherstonaugh*, but also in the somewhat rare case where during an individual's lifetime he makes on the same occasion an actual transfer of value of his business and his interest in possession in the asset terminates. There also appears to be no justification for confining the decision to land. Where, on the other hand, the individual's interest in possession terminates but he continues to carry on his business the asset will qualify as relevant business property only if it is land, buildings, machinery or plant falling within the seventh category in which case relief will be available at only 50 per cent.

26–20

Retiring from a partnership

Care should be taken when a partner retires from a partnership. Any funds that continue to be held on a former partner's capital account will not qualify for business relief. In *Beckman v IRC*,[68] it was held that a retired partner simply becomes a creditor of the partnership and no longer has an interest in a business for the purposes of business relief. A partner should therefore consider whether his partnership interest should be gifted before he retires so as to secure 100 per cent business relief. The alternative would be to continue as a partner with reduced responsibilities, but given that this is likely to mean that a partner will continue to have unlimited liability without full involvement on a day to day basis, this alternative might not be attractive. A more

26–21

[66] *Fetherstonaugh v IRC* [1984] S.T.C. 261.
[67] At the rate of 50 per cent at that time.
[68] *Beckman v IRC* [2000] S.T.C. (S.C.D.) 59.

radical alternative might be for a retiring partner's share in the partnership to be taken over by a corporate vehicle now that unquoted shareholdings qualify for 100 per cent relief whatever the size of the shareholding.

Lloyd's names

26–22   Under s.105(1)(a), a Lloyd's name's interest prima facie qualifies for business relief at the rate of 100 per cent. This will apply in relation to profits and losses for closed years that have not been declared, his Lloyd's deposit, his personal reserve fund and his special reserve fund. If the assets in question are not immediately available, the interest may be discounted, as appropriate, to take account of this fact.[69]

Profits and losses for closed years that have been declared will not be relievable. This means that where there are losses, these will be relievable against the deceased's chargeable estate. Where, however, there are profits, these will not be relievable and will be subject to IHT. Following the decision in *Hardcastle (executors of Vernede, Deceased) v IRC*,[70] profits and losses for open years (whether or not declared) should not be taken into account for the purposes of calculating business relief for a Lloyd's name. As with profits and losses for closed years which have been declared, this means that losses for open years will be relievable against the deceased's chargeable estate but profits will be subject to IHT.

The availability of business relief to Lloyd's names is subject to two qualifications. First, relief will not be available to the extent that the size of the deposits and reserves at the date of the death exceed the name's requirements, given his premium limit, since in such a case the "excess" deposits and reserves could not justifiably be regarded as assets which were used in the business.[71] This is so notwithstanding the fact that a Lloyd's name would be advised to retain substantial reserves given the significant historic losses. Secondly, if the name has entered into an insurance policy the effect of which is to make his Lloyd's assets immediately available to his personal representatives on his death, the discount mentioned above will not be available.[72]

Where Lloyd's have accepted bank guarantees and letters of credit in lieu of assets, HMRC practice has been to accept that the collateral security taken by the bank will also qualify for business relief to the extent of the smaller of the value of the guarantee and the asset upon which it is secured, provided, of course, that the asset itself satisfies the normal ownership conditions for business property relief. The position has changed following the decision in *IRC v Mallender (executors of Drury-Lowe, Deceased)*.[73] In this case, it was held that the assets used to secure a loan or guarantee used for the purposes of a business are not themselves used for the purposes of the business. Accordingly, following this decision, business relief will not be available in relation to assets charged in respect of a loan or guarantee taken out for the purposes of a business.

Single Farm Payment

26–23   The "single farm payment" was introduced in 2005 as a consequence of the Mid Term Review of the Common Agricultural Policy. Entitlement is allocated to the

---

[69] See para.25–63.

[70] *Hardcastle (executors of Vernede, Deceased) v IRC* [2000] S.T.C. (S.C.D.) 532; see also para.26–85.

[71] See para.26–85.

[72] The policy should not affect the *availability* of business relief; see also *Private Client Business* (London: Sweet & Maxwell, 2001), pp.191–196.

[73] *IRC v Mallender (executors of Drury-Lowe, Deceased)* [2001] S.T.C. 514; see also para.26–84.

occupier rather than the owner of farmland and is capable of sale without land. It is characterised as an asset which is separate from land rather than as an interest in land and therefore cannot qualify for agricultural relief. However, business relief may be available.

Where the transferor is a farmer who has been farming for at least two years, the single farm payment will qualify for 100 per cent business relief as an asset of the business, assuming it has been used in the business or is required for future use in the business. Entitlement will qualify for business relief where the owner has put farmland out of production in order to receive the single farm payment, provided the farmer is still carrying on a business on a commercial basis, and provided the nature of the business remains essentially that of a trading concern rather than one that consists wholly or mainly of dealing in land or making or holding investments. It follows that the transfer of entitlement by someone who is not carrying on a trading business will not qualify for business relief. Similarly, the transfer of entitlement as an individual asset, rather than the business itself, or an interest in business, will not qualify for business relief unless it can be shown that the transfer of entitlement is attributable to the net value of the business as per *Nelson Dance*.[74]

Category 2: unquoted shareholdings (100 per cent)[75]

This category consists of unquoted shares (but not securities) in a company, includ- **26–24** ing shares dealt with on USM and AIM.[76] Any unquoted shares are covered by this category irrespective of the size of the holding or any voting rights (if any) attached to them.

Category 3: control holdings of unquoted securities of a company (100 per cent)[77]

This category consists of unquoted voting securities of a company (including **26–25** securities dealt with on USM and AIM)[78] which either by themselves or together with

---

[74] See para.26–19.

[75] IHTA 1984 ss.104(1)(a) and 105(1)(bb). For controlling unquoted shareholdings the rate was 30 per cent for transfers after April 6, 1976 and before October 27, 1977, 50 per cent for transfers after October 26, 1977, and before March 10, 1992, and 100 per cent for transfers after March 9, 1992. For non-controlling unquoted shareholdings the position is more complicated. The rate was 20 per cent for transfers after October 26, 1977 (the date this category was introduced) and before March 15, 1983, and 30 per cent for transfers after March 14, 1983, and before March 17, 1987. After March 16, 1987, the category was split into two. For unquoted shareholdings which were non-voting or owned by persons controlling 25 per cent or less of the votes the rate was 30 per cent for transfers after March 16, 1987, and before March 10, 1992, 50 per cent for transfers after March 9, 1992, and before April 6, 1996, and 100 per cent for transfers after April 5, 1996 (subject to transitional provisions). For unquoted shareholdings which were voting and owned by persons controlling more than 25 per cent of the votes for at least two years the rate was 50 per cent for transfers after March 16, 1987, and before March 10, 1992, and 100 per cent for transfers after March 9, 1992. From April 6, 1996, all unquoted shareholdings were brought together in the same category under IHTA 1984 s.104(1)(a).

[76] IHTA 1984 ss.105(1ZA) and 269.

[77] IHTA 1984 ss.104(1)(a) and 105(1)(b). The rate was 30 per cent for transfers after April 6, 1976, and before October 27, 1977, 50 per cent for transfers after October 26, 1977, and before March 10, 1992, and 100 per cent for transfers after March 9, 1992.

[78] IHTA 1984 ss.105(1ZA) and 269. Securities and shares dealt with on the Unlisted Securities Market were treated as quoted shares between March 17, 1987, and March 9, 1992 (inclusive) under IHTA 1984 s.272 as amended by FA 1987 Sch.8 para.17. This was reversed in relation to business relief by IHTA 1984 s.105(1ZA) inserted by F(No.2)A 1992 Sch.14 para.2.

other such securities and any unquoted shares owned by the transferor gave the transferor control of the company immediately before the transfer.

It is important to note that, as with control holdings of quoted voting shares, unquoted securities are within this category only if they carry votes. Non-voting securities will thus never come within this category—even though they are owned by a person who controls the company—and consequently will never qualify for the 100 per cent relief. This contrasts with unquoted shares which do not carry votes which, following the changes made in 1996, qualify for 100 per cent relief under s.105(1)(bb). Where a person has control of a company through unquoted shares notwithstanding any securities within s.105(1)(b) then the securities will not be business property because they do not give the person control. It is the shares that give the person control. It also appears that relief is not available under this head where the control derives partly from one class of securities and partly from another, since in such a case the securities of the first class do not give the transferor control by themselves or together with "other *such* securities". Nevertheless, it is understood that where a transferor controls a company HMRC practice is to give relief to any unquoted securities which contribute to his control.

In this context, it is perhaps worth noting that although it is common for securities to carry negative voting rights on certain limited issues (usually issues affecting the value of the security itself) it is unusual for securities to be capable of carrying voting rights on all issues affecting the company as a whole, because this would make the securities in practice akin to shares. It is, however, possible that the articles of association of the company might provide that where a shareholder also owns securities in the company, the votes attaching to his shares will be given extra weight. If by virtue of these weighted votes, the shareholder has control of the company, then the securities will have contributed to giving him control as required by s.105(1)(b). Another example of a security which could give control might be a convertible loan note which is capable of being converted into a controlling shareholding.

Category 4: control holdings of quoted voting shareholdings (50 per cent)[79]

26–26   This category consists of quoted shares in a company which either by themselves or together with other such quoted shares or securities owned by the transferor gave the transferor control of the company immediately before the transfer. Shares dealt with on USM and AIM are treated as unquoted.[80] As discussed at para.26–08, it suffices that the transferor had control of the company before the transfer. It should also be noted that, as with control holdings of unquoted or quoted securities, quoted shares are within this category only if they carry votes.

Category 5: control holdings of quoted securities (50 per cent)[81]

26–27   This category consists of quoted securities in a company which either by themselves or together with other such quoted securities or shares owned by the transferor gave the

---

[79] IHTA 1984 ss.104(1)(b) and 105(1)(cc). The rate was 30 per cent for transfers after April 6, 1976, and before October 27, 1977, 50 per cent for transfers after October 26, 1977, and before March 10, 1992, and continued at 50 per cent for transfers after March 9, 1992.

[80] IHTA 1984 ss.105(1ZA) and 269; and see fn.76 above.

[81] IHTA 1984 ss.104(1)(b) and 105(1)(cc). The rate was 30 per cent for transfers after April 6, 1976, and before October 27, 1977, 50 per cent for transfers after October 26, 1977, and before March 10, 1992, and continued at 50 per cent for transfers after March 9, 1992.

transferor control of the company immediately before the transfer. As with control holdings of quoted shares and unquoted securities, quoted securities are within this category only if they carry votes.[82]

Non-qualifying shares or securities: windings up and revaluations

Shares in or securities of a company do not come within categories 2, 3, 4 or 5 in two cases: **26–28**

(1) Winding up: shares in or securities of a company do not come within categories 2, 3, 4 or 5 if at the time of the transfer:
  (a) a winding up order has been made in respect of the company; or
  (b) the company has passed a resolution for a voluntary winding up; or
  (c) the company is otherwise in the process of liquidation.[83]
  But shares in or securities of a company may qualify for relief notwithstanding the presence of any of the above three circumstances if:
  (a) the company's business is to continue to be carried on after a reconstruction or amalgamation; and
  (b) the reconstruction or amalgamation either:
    (i) is the purpose of the liquidation; or
    (ii) takes place not later than one year after the transfer of value in relation to which the shares were relevant business property.[84]
(2) Revaluations: shares or securities of a company do not come within categories 2, 3, 4 or 5 if after the transferor's death they are subsequently sold on a minority basis by the deceased's personal representatives and revaluation relief is claimed under s.176. In such a case business relief given previously is retrospectively withdrawn, and the tax charged on death recomputed.[85]

Category 6: certain land, buildings, machinery or plant (50 per cent)[86]

Land, buildings, machinery or plant are within this category if they are used wholly **26–29** or mainly for the purposes of a business carried on either (i) by a company which the transferor controlled immediately before the transfer, or (ii) by a partnership of which he was a partner immediately before the transfer.[87] This is subject to the qualification that if the transferor owned shares or securities in the company, those shares or securities must themselves have been relevant business property[88] while if the transferor was a partner, his partnership interest must itself have been relevant business property.[89] This means, inter alia, that the transferor must have owned[90] the shares/

[82] See para.26–26.
[83] IHTA 1984 s.105(5); the position where a company is to be wound up and carried on as an unincorporated business is not entirely clear, but it seems business relief would not be available.
[84] IHTA 1984 s.105(5).
[85] IHTA 1984 s.105(2)(b); see para.25–156.
[86] IHTA 1984 s.104(1)(b). The rate was 30 per cent for transfers after April 6, 1976, and before March 10, 1992, and 50 per cent for transfers after March 9, 1992.
[87] IHTA 1984 ss.104(1)(b) and 105(1)(d).
[88] IHTA 1984 s.105(6).
[89] IHTA 1984 s.105(6).
[90] Compare agricultural relief.

securities or partnership interest for at least two years prior to the transfer of the land, buildings, plant or machinery. This qualification is discussed at paras 26–59–26–71.

"Land" will include an interest in land such as a lease. "Business" is defined as for the first category. Assets used in a business carried on by the transferor as a sole trader will not come within this category but may fall within the first category.

Neither "machinery" nor "plant" is defined; reference must accordingly be made to the decided cases. For the purposes of estate duty, the Revenue, as it then was, took the view that "working animals" and "production livestock" came within this category notwithstanding the fact that certain decisions tended against this view[91] and it is understood that the same view is taken for IHT purposes. "Working animals" include, e.g. draught horses and working sheepdogs. "Production livestock" are livestock permanently employed in farming whose function is the production of products for sale such as milk, calves, etc. Animals which are to be slaughtered or sold will thus not qualify for relief. Accordingly, dairy, but not beef cattle will qualify. An animal which is to be so permanently employed but at the time of transfer has not yet been so employed, e.g. because of youth or infirmity, is not regarded by HMRC as qualifying.

In the context of partnerships, many partners have historically been reluctant to transfer assets into the name of the partnership simply to ensure 100 per cent relief (under the head of a "business" or an "interest in a business" under s.105(1)(d)). This reluctance principally stems from the financial disadvantages of surrendering the entire beneficial interest of the asset to the partnership. However, in the case of *Brander v HMRC*[92] it appears to have been accepted that partners can enter into arrangements between themselves such that partners effectively remain the beneficial owners of assets contributed to the partnership. In the *Brander* case it was accepted that land which was effectively still owned by an individual partner, but used by the partnership, was a partnership asset and therefore within the value of the business qualifying for 100 per cent relief. In order to achieve this outcome, it must be made clear that the relevant asset forms part of the contributing partner's capital account. The partnership agreement will also need very careful drafting in order to ensure that in the event of a winding-up of the partnership or a sale of the asset then the value will be credited to the original owner's capital entitlement with an adjustment for any profit or loss realised. This brings such transfers into line with the existing capital gains tax analysis, as HMRC accept that if a partner contributes property to a partnership but retains a 100 per cent beneficial ownership then there is not a disposal for capital gains tax purposes. It should be noted, however, that irrespective of the arrangements made by the partners, an asset of the partnership will be available to claims from creditors and to third parties.

Category 7: certain land, buildings, machinery or plant in which the transferor had an interest in possession (50 per cent)[93]

26–30 Any land, buildings, plant or machinery which immediately before the transfer was comprised in a settlement in which the transferor was beneficially entitled to an interest

---

[91] See *Yarmouth v France* (1887) I.R. 19 Q.B.D 647; *Earl of Derby v Aylmer* (1915) 6.T.C. 665.
[92] See *Brander v HMRC* [2010] UKUT 300 (TCC).
[93] IHTA 1984 s.104(1)(b). The rate was 30 per cent for transfers after March 9, 1981 (when the category was introduced) and before March 10, 1992, and 50 per cent for transfers after March 9, 1992.

in possession is within this category if at that time it was used wholly or mainly for the purposes of a business carried on by the transferor[94] which was itself relevant business property in relation to that transfer.[95] There does not appear to be a requirement that the interest in possession is a non relevant property interest in possession. However, in order for this category of relief to apply, the ownership conditions described in para.26–61 must be satisfied and so, in practice, the interest must be a non relevant property interest in possession. For this purpose "land" includes, as it does for purposes of the sixth category of approved property, an interest in land such as a lease; "business" is defined as for purposes of the first category,[96] and machinery or plant as for the sixth category. If the transferor used the land, etc. in his business and made a transfer of both his interest and his business, relief may be available at 100 per cent under the first category.[97]

Somewhat curiously, where an individual carries on his business on land or in a building held on the trusts of a settlement in which he has a non relevant property interest in possession or uses in his business machinery or plant held on such trusts the land, etc. may qualify for 100 per cent relief; see *Fetherstonaugh v IRC*, discussed at para.26–20.

Where trustees carry on business in partnership but do not hold the land, etc. as a partnership asset then the land, etc. will fall within this category only if the individual entitled to the non relevant property interest in possession is a partner; otherwise the land, etc. will not be used for the purposes of a business carried on by a partnership of which he is a partner. If, on the other hand, the land, etc. is held on relevant property trusts, the land, etc. will come within the sixth category of relevant business property —the trustees will be "the transferor"[98]—and potentially qualify for 50 per cent relief. The position can be improved in both cases if the land, etc. is brought into the partnership as a partnership asset because the relevant asset for business relief purposes will then be the business which will fall within the first category of relevant business property and so be capable of qualifying for 100 per cent relief.

VIII. QUALITATIVE LIMITATIONS ON AVAILABILITY OF RELIEF

There are three qualitative limitations which may prevent property which prima facie **26–31** falls within one of the specified categories of relevant business property from qualifying as relevant business property:

(1) *investment businesses and companies*: a business or an interest in a business will not be relevant business property if it is "an investment business" and shares or securities in a company will not be relevant business property if the company is an "investment company";

(2) *ownership and user*: depending on the kind of property concerned, unless certain ownership and user requirements are satisfied the property will not be relevant business property; and

---

[94] IHTA 1984 s.105(1)(e).
[95] IHTA 1984 s.105(6).
[96] IHTA 1984 s.105(1).
[97] See para.26–19.
[98] IHTA 1984 s.103(1)(b).

(3) *binding contract for sale*: property will not be relevant business property if at the time of the transfer of value that property is subject to a binding contract for sale.

Each of these limitations will be considered in turn.

Limitation 1: investment businesses and companies

26–32   The first general limitation on the availability of relief is found in s.105(3) which operates by providing, in effect, that notwithstanding that a business, an interest in a business or shares in a company prima facie fall within one of the specified categories of relevant business property it is nevertheless prevented from being relevant business property.

26–33   Section 105(3) provides that no relief is available where the business concerned is one of "investments", i.e. where the business carried on consists wholly or mainly of:

(1) dealing in securities, stocks or shares; or
(2) dealing in land or buildings; or
(3) making or holding investments.

For the sake of convenience, a business within s.105(3) will be called an "investment business" and a company within s.105(3) will be called an "investment company".

Three vital points are worth repeating concerning the meaning of "business": first, the comments at para.26–19 concerning the wide meaning of "business" apply; secondly, "business" extends to the business of making or holding investments; thirdly, it is possible for a business to be multifaceted or hybrid, i.e. it may consist of a variety of activities, e.g. trading, making investments and letting property.

All or nothing test

26–34   It is vital to note that s.105(3) involves an all or nothing test: either property is relevant business property or it is not. Where s.105(3) applies to shares in a company, for example, the shares are entirely disqualified notwithstanding that some of their value derives from trading activities. Conversely, once it is established that a business is not wholly or mainly an investment business, investments which it owns may well qualify for relief; see para.26–100.

The case law

26–35   It is therefore not surprising that the question of whether a business is wholly or mainly an investment business has led to more case law than any other single IHT issue. Furthermore, that case law has tended more to underline than to resolve the difficulties involved in applying the wholly or mainly test. However, the case of *IRC v George (executors of Stedman, Deceased)*[99]—the only case to reach the Court of

---

[99] *IRC v George (executors of Stedman, Deceased)* [2004] S.T.C. 147.

Appeal and commonly referred to as the *"Stedman* case"—appears at last to provide sensible guidance.

Before considering the Court of Appeal's decision in *Stedman*, it will be instructive **26–36** to review the various approaches that were adopted by different Special Commissioners and judges at first instance prior to that decision.[100] As will be seen, a number of cases, including *Stedman*, involved caravan parks with significantly varying fact patterns.

Martin (executors of Moore, Deceased) v IRC[101]

Martin concerned the business of owning and letting industrial units on three-year **26–37** leases at fixed rents. The Special Commissioner, S Oliver Q.C., commented that the business activities fell into one of the three following categories:

(1) those directed at making the investments, i.e. finding tenants, negotiating rents and granting and accepting surrenders of leases;
(2) compliance activities carried out as landlords, e.g. keeping the exterior painted and in good repair; and
(3) management activities, i.e. keeping the property tidy, secure and in good repair and generally keeping up the standards of the investment activity.

He held that the first two categories were of or attributable to making or holding investments and that the third category covered activities that were incidents of the business of holding investments:

> "The activities which a landlord carries out because he is obliged to under the lease are incidental to the tenancy and so fall on the 'holding investments' side of the equation. The business activities, if any, carried out by the landlord for gain and which are not required by the lease fall on the other side of the equation. The activities carried on by the landlord which are not required under the lease and for which he receives no separate consideration will fall on the 'holding investments' side of the equation if they are connected with and incidental to the holding of the property as an investment.
> . . . active though Mrs Moore's business was, none of the activities that had anything to do with the property were concerned with anything other than the making or holding of investments. To express the point positively, they were all part and parcel of the business of making or holding investments."[102]

In reaching this conclusion, Mr Oliver firmly rejected the suggestion that a line could be drawn between "passive" property investment and "active" management. To do so would give an unnaturally restricted meaning to the words of exclusion found in s.105(3) and would result in activities being left out of the investment holding side of the equation that could reasonably be described as incidents of investment holding.[103] However, he acknowledged that:

[100] An unreported Special Commissioner case involving a commercial landlord who maintained a high quality of service to his professional tenants (the services embracing primarily cleaning operations, maintenance and decoration) was held entitled to business relief. The taxpayer was considered to be acting as managing agent: his daily activities and his obligations far exceeded those which would normally be placed on the holder of an investment; see *Taxation*, May 3, 1990, p.126. The Special Commissioner, THK Everett, has since commented that the facts of this case were "exceptional". See also *Powell v IRC* [1997] S.T.C. (S.C.D.) 186, discussed at para.26–40.
[101] *Martin (executors of Moore, Deceased) v IRC* [1995] S.T.C. (S.C.D.) 5.
[102] *Martin (executors of Moore, Deceased) v IRC* [1995] S.T.C. (S.C.D.) 5 at 10.
[103] *Martin (executors of Moore, Deceased) v IRC* [1995] S.T.C. (S.C.D.) 5 at 9.

"Had there been activities of producing income distinct from the rents, such as fees for cleaning or security services provided quite separately from the landlord's obligations, those would not have been part of the investment holding activities and might have tipped the balance in determining whether the business in question consisted wholly or mainly of the making or holding of investments. But that was not the case here."[104]

It is important to note that if there had been such activities that were separate from the landowning part of the business, they would need to have constituted more than 50 per cent of the business to fall outside the restriction in s.105(3).[105]

Burkinyoung (executor of Burkinyoung, Deceased) v IRC[106]

26–38　The Special Commissioner in the subsequent case of *Burkinyoung* was also S. Oliver QC. *Burkinyoung* also concerned the business of owning and letting properties, i.e. furnished flats on assured shorthold tenancies. Here the whole profit derived by Mrs Burkinyoung from the property came to her as rent. As in *Martin*, there were no activities that were not included as part of the lease or separate from the landowning part of the business and which could outweigh the activities attributable to making or holding investments and so no business relief was given.

In denying business relief, Mr Oliver applied his decision in *Martin* and held that the activities carried out in complying with the landlord's covenants under the lease or leases of the investment property were:

" . . . activities of 'holding investments' in determining whether the business was one that consisted wholly or mainly of the making or holding of investments: that would be the case however onerous the landlord's obligations might be and however much the landlord had been involved in the control or management of the property letting business."[107]

Mr Oliver therefore affirmed his concept of "incidental activities" included as part of a lease or licence and went on to reiterate that a line could not be drawn between "passive" property investment on the one hand and "active" management. He commented that:

"The construction sought by the taxpayer which seeks to distinguish between the operations of the active and of the passive landlord is too vague and too dependant on degrees of involvement to have been what Parliament contemplated when the relief was designed. Were there any doubt on this score it is, I think, removed by the statements of the Right Hon Joel Barnett MP."[108]

Hall (executor of Hall, Deceased) v IRC[109]

26–39　*Hall* was the first of a number of cases which considered whether owners/managers of caravan parks qualify for business relief. The business at Tanat Caravan Park

---

[104] *Martin (executors of Moore, Deceased) v IRC* [1995] S.T.C. (S.C.D.) 5.
[105] See para.26–34.
[106] *Burkinyoung (executor of Burkinyoung, Deceased) v IRC* [1995] S.T.C. (S.C.D.) 29.
[107] *Burkinyoung (executor of Burkinyoung, Deceased) v IRC* [1995] S.T.C. (S.C.D.) 29 at 33.
[108] *Burkinyoung (executor of Burkinyoung, Deceased) v IRC* [1995] S.T.C. (S.C.D.) 29. The statements of the Right Hon Joel Barnett MP are set out in 911 HC Official Report (5th series), Col.11.25–11.26 and are fully quoted in the *Martin* decision.
[109] *Hall (executor of Hall, Deceased) v IRC* [1997] S.T.C. (S.C.D.) 126.

consisted of almost 100 static caravans and 11 wooden chalets let on 45 year leases. Caravan owners were not permitted to occupy their caravans for four months during winter and were not permitted to buy or sell their caravans except through the agency of Tanat Caravan Park. Facilities were supplied in accordance with the terms of the site licence granted by the local authority. The Special Commissioners, T.H.K. Everett and D.A. Shirley, held that business relief was not available because the business mainly involved making or holding investments.

The Special Commissioners were referred to the case of *Minister of Agriculture, Fisheries and Food v Mason*[110] in which it was held that an employee was to be regarded as employed wholly or mainly in connection with activities carried on by way of business if he spent more than 50 per cent of his time on the commercial part of the activity. In *Hall*, of the total income of the business the greatest component (amounting to either 84 per cent or 65 per cent depending on how the calculation was performed) was attributable to rents and standing charges. In reaching their decision Commissioners Everett and Shirley considered the concept of "incidental activities" included as part of a lease or licence formulated in *Martin* and *Burkinyoung* before concluding that:

> "In such circumstances we have come to the conclusion that the activities of the business carried on at Tanat Caravan Park consisted mainly of the making or holding of investments. Although the receipt of commissions on the sale of caravans forms part of the business we find that it was ancillary to the main business of receiving rents from owners of caravans and lessees of chalets. The business was preponderantly one of the receipt of rents."[111]

The approach in *Mason*, which was followed in *Hall*, contrasts with the "substantial" test that used to apply to business asset taper relief for CGT purposes before it was abolished (with effect from April 6, 2008) where HMRC applied a more stringent test under which relief at the business asset rate was available only if 20 per cent or less of the activities of a trading company were activities other than trading activities.[112]

Powell (personal representatives of Pearce, Deceased) v IRC[113]

Powell was the second of the caravan park cases and was also heard by Mr Everett. **26–40** The business consisted of the hiring out of caravan pitches on long and short term lettings and providing ancillary utilities and services and of related amenities.

The facts of the case were broadly on all fours with *Hall* except that in *Powell* there was no evidence of business activity over and above the mere receipt of income from caravan rents. Mr Everett therefore endorsed the concept of "incidental activities" included as part of a lease or licence. In denying business relief Mr Everett followed the decision in *Hall* and commented that:

> " . . . the whole of Mrs Pearce's income falls on the 'holding investments' side of the line. Most of the activities which she carried out were either required under the terms of the lettings or pursuant to the terms of the caravan licence which governed the lettings. The only activities not so covered such as, for example social visits and organising medical call outs etc. received no financial reward. No doubt such activities served to enhance the

---

[110] *Minister of Agriculture, Fisheries and Food v Mason* [1969] 1 Q.B. 399.
[111] *Hall (executor of Hall, Deceased) v IRC* [1997] S.T.C. (S.C.D.) 126 at 131.
[112] Inland Revenue, *Tax Bulletin* 62.
[113] *Powell (personal representatives of Pearce, Deceased) v IRC* [1997] S.T.C. (S.C.D.) 181.

goodwill of the business but they seem to fall once again on the 'holding investments' side of the line."[114]

It is worth noting that Mr Everett also held that the assessment of the profits of the business to income tax under Case I of Sch.D is irrelevant in the context of IHT.[115]

Furness v IRC[116]

26–41   Mr Everett was also the Special Commissioner in *Furness*, the third of the caravan park cases. In *Furness*, the business had a licence for 218 static caravans and held a number of caravan rallies during the summer months. Permanent residence of the park was not permitted nor was occupation of the caravans during the month of February. The site provided a club house (which included a bar), a shop and a fishing club and bowling club operated from the park. As in *Hall*, static caravans could only be purchased from or sold to Mr Furness.

Mr Everett considered the income and profit figures produced by the rentals from the static caravan sites and compared these with the income and profit figures arising from caravan sales and the other activities. He was not asked to consider a comparison of income and profits in *Hall* or *Powell*, although in *Powell* the only income arising was from caravan rents. Accountancy evidence was produced to show that, in the years 1993 to 1996 inclusive, the income arising from caravan sales, sundry sales and tours and rally charges exceeded the income from the rental of static caravan sites, both before and after deductions and expenses. It is worth noting that, in contrast to the subsequent decision in *Weston (executor of Weston, Deceased) v IRC*,[117] the manner in which the accounts were presented was considered helpful and shows that good record keeping can be important.

Having considered the accounting evidence, Mr Everett distinguished his earlier decisions in *Hall* and *Powell* and held that there were a number of activities that were separate from the landowning part of the business and which were not making or holding investments. Having looked at the business and the activities in the round, he concluded that these separate activities outweighed the investment activities, i.e. the lettings. It is also worth noting that, in taking account of the considerable amount of work undertaken by Mr Furness and three employees in looking after the welfare of the residents and maintaining the park, he appeared to be trying to re-draw a distinction in respect of "active" management which had been so firmly rejected by S. Oliver Q.C. in *Martin* and *Burkinyoung*. Mr Everett concluded that:

> "Such very considerable activity does not in my view correspond to what one would normally expect to find in a business concerned wholly or mainly with the making or holding of investments."[118]

Farmer (executors of Farmer, Deceased) v IRC[119]

26–42   *Farmer* concerned the availability of business relief in the context of a farming business where properties that no longer had an agricultural use were let on shorthold

---

[114] *Powell (personal representatives of Pearce, Deceased) v IRC* [1997] S.T.C. (S.C.D.) 181 at 186.
[115] *Powell (personal representatives of Pearce, Deceased) v IRC* [1997] S.T.C. (S.C.D.) 181 at 185.
[116] *Furness v IRC* [1999] S.T.C. (S.C.D.) 232.
[117] *Weston (executor of Weston, Deceased) v IRC* [2000] S.T.C. 1064; see para.26–43.
[118] *Weston (executor of Weston, Deceased) v IRC* [2000] S.T.C. 1064 at 237.
[119] *Farmer (executors of Farmer, Deceased) v IRC* [1999] S.T.C. (S.C.D.) 321.

tenancies. The Special Commissioner, Dr A. N. Brice, derived from the *Furness* case the principle, which she then went on to apply, that it is necessary to look at the business and it activities in the round and to consider all the relevant factors including the net profits and work undertaken by the owner and his employees. In *Farmer*, the following factors were considered:

(1) the overall context of the business;
(2) the value of the capital employed in the respective parts of the business;
(3) the time spent by the employees and consultants;
(4) the levels of turnover of the respective parts of the business; and
(5) the net profit figures for the respective parts of the business.

Having looked at the business and its activities in the round and considered the above factors (without giving predominance to any one factor), Dr Brice held that the business consisted mainly of farming and not of making or holding investments. Business relief was therefore allowed even though the lettings were more profitable than the farm because the other factors supported the conclusion that the business consisted mainly of farming.[120]

It is interesting to note that when analysing the overall context of the business, Dr Brice appeared to be influenced by the fact that most of the let properties were buildings formerly used by the farm and that they were located towards the centre of the land comprising the estate. Most of the buildings would not have existed had it not been for their previous connection with the farm.

It is also worth noting that the farming and letting activities were presented as a single business in the accounts. If the letting activities had been presented as a separate business in the accounts, rather than a subsidiary part of the farming business, then the letting activities would prima facie not have been relievable.[121] Where the "wholly or mainly" test cannot be satisfied, it would be important for the investment activities to be presented as a separate business so as not to prejudice the availability of business relief in respect of the non-investment activities.

Weston (executor of Weston, Deceased) v IRC[122]

The "wholly or mainly" test was considered, this time by the court, in *Weston*, the fourth of the caravan park cases. Lawrence Collins J. held that the Special Commissioner, again Mr Everett, had been correct in following the approach in *Farmer* in concluding that the business of the caravan company in *Weston* consisted mainly of making or holding investments. Mr Everett had looked at the time spent by employees on various parts of the business, the capital employed in the business, the income from investment activities and the profits generated by the respective parts of the business before standing back and looking at the matter in the round. But Mr Everett was more sceptical of accountancy evidence and the amount of time spent by employees than in his earlier decision in *Furness*. In denying business relief in *Weston*, Mr Everett commented that:

26–43

---

[120] The approach in *Farmer* is remarkably similar to that previously used when considering whether a company was a trading company and thus qualified for business asset taper relief treatment for CGT purposes. CGT taper relief was abolished with effect from April 6, 2008.
[121] IHTA 1984 s.105(3).
[122] *Weston (executor of Weston, Deceased) v IRC* [2000] S.T.C. 1064.

" . . . schedules based on re-allocating profit figures according to the amount of time spent by employees on maintenance as against the amount of time spent in realising caravan sales cannot, in my view, be relied upon . . . [and] . . . pitch fees exceeded in amount the sums realised by caravan sales in four out of six years from 1989 to 1994."[123]

This seemed to reaffirm the position set out by Stephen Oliver Q.C. in *Martin* and *Burkinyoung* that a distinction cannot be drawn between "passive" property investment and "active" management.

IRC v George (executors of Stedman, Deceased)[124]*: Laddie J.'s "investment bag" approach*

26–44   The question as to whether the nature of the activities carried on by a business was "wholly" or "mainly" making or holding investments also arose in *Stedman*, the fifth and final of the caravan cases. In *Stedman*, the company owned a caravan site and carried on the following business activities:

(1) a residential homes park consisting of 167 mobile caravans owned by the residents;
(2) a club and bar for residents and non residents;
(3) storage of touring caravans when not in use;
(4) the office from which the administration was run;
(5) a separately let warehouse and shop;
(6) fields let on grazing licences;
(7) an insurance agency from which the company received commission.

In relation to the residential homes park, all residents paid site fees and received connections to services. The company made a profit on the supply of water, electricity and gas, which it resold to residents. The company also took a commission on the sales of caravans on the site and received interest on cash balances.

The Special Commissioner, Dr J.F. Avery Jones, had looked at each of the activities separately and decided whether or not that activity was the making or holding of investments before considering the business in the round, as in *Farmer*. On the basis that the caravan storage business plus the rental income were investment activities and 40 per cent of the turnover, 20 per cent of the gross profit and 16 per cent of the net profit before the payment of director's fees was referable to holding investments, Dr Avery Jones then looked at the business in the round before allowing business relief and concluding that the business was not mainly that of making or holding investments.

On appeal, Laddie J. reversed the decision of Dr Avery Jones and held that:

" . . . what falls within the investment business 'bag' is not only the core holding of the land and the receipt of fees or rent in respect of its use, but also all those activities which, viewed through the eyes of an average businessman would be regarded as 'incidental' to that core activity . . . activities which are incidental to the letting of land are not severable from it and take on the investment character of the letting . . . an activity which is incidental to, say, an investment business does not cease to be so because the landlord decides to make an additional profit on it."[125]

[123] *Weston (executor of Weston, Deceased) v IRC* [2000] S.T.C. (S.C.D.) 30 at 37.
[124] *IRC v George (executors of Stedman, Deceased)* [2004] S.T.C. 147.
[125] *IRC v George (executors of Stedman, Deceased)* [2003] S.T.C. 468 at 483.

In reviving the concept of "incidental activities" applied by Stephen Oliver Q.C. in *Martin* and *Burkinyoung* and followed by Everett in *Hall* and *Powell*, Laddie J. held that the business of the company was the holding of investments and accordingly did not qualify for business relief.

IRC v George (executors of Stedman, Deceased)[126]: active family business triumphs in the Court of Appeal

The Court of Appeal, on the only occasion in which it has considered the question **26–45** of whether or not a business consisted wholly or mainly of making or holding investments, unanimously reversed the first instance decision in *Stedman* and restored the decision of the Special Commissioner, Dr Avery Jones. This decision of the Court of Appeal now represents the law in this crucial area relating to the availability of business relief.

In his judgment, Carnwath L.J., with whom Hale L.J. (the only other judge sitting in the Court of Appeal) agreed, considered in detail the status of services provided by the company and in particular the comments made by Stephen Oliver Q.C. in *Martin*.[127] Although he agreed that in general terms property "management" is part of the business of holding property as an investment, Carnwath L.J. commented:

"I would not extend that term to additional services or facilities provided to the occupants . . . whether or not they are included in the lease and covered by the rent. . . . in my view, the characterisation of such services depends on the nature and purpose of the activity, not on the terms of the lease (or, where relevant, a site licence). . . . There is nothing in [the] judgment [of *Fry*[128]] to support the view that, merely because services or facilities are required by the lease, and their cost is included in the rent, they lose their character as services, and become part of the 'holding' of the investment."[129]

This is important. Carnwath L.J. went on to hold that it was wrong to consider the matter as requiring

"the opening of an investment 'bag', into which are placed all the activities linked to the caravan park, including even the supply of water, electricity, and gas, simply on the basis that they are 'ancillary' to that investment business."[130]

Carnwath L.J. recognised that looking at the matter in terms of a concept of "incidental activities" does not give sufficient weight to the hybrid nature of a caravan site business where the holding of the property as an investment is only one component of the business. The approach of Carnwath L.J. shows a welcome return to considering a business in the round when deciding whether it consists wholly or mainly of making or holding investments. This will offer considerable comfort to owners of landowning businesses that carry on significant activities that can be severed from the landowning part of the business, particularly in the light of Carnwath L.J.'s concluding comment:

"I find it difficult to see any reason why an active family business of this kind should be excluded from business relief, merely because a necessary component of its profit-making activity is the use of land."[131]

---

[126] *IRC v George (executors of Stedman, Deceased)* [2004] S.T.C. 147.
[127] These are set out in para.26–37.
[128] *Fry v Salisbury House Estate Ltd* [1930] 1 K.B. 304.
[129] *IRC v George (executors of Stedman, Deceased)* [2004] S.T.C. 147 at 155.
[130] *IRC v George (executors of Stedman, Deceased)* [2004] S.T.C. 147 at 162.
[131] *IRC v George (executors of Stedman, Deceased)* [2004] S.T.C. 147 at 163.

It should be noted however, that although HMRC have described *Stedman* as "helpful" their IHTM[132] indicates that caravan park cases will be considered carefully, with cases being referred to their technical group.

Since *Stedman*, the volume of cases relating to the wholly or mainly test going through the courts has settled down. However, there are still five cases worthy of note.

(1) *Clark v Revenue and Customs Commissioners*[133]

This case concerned a company which owned a large number of properties from which it received rent together with income from over 100 properties that it managed on behalf of family members and for which it charged a fee of 7.5 per cent of the rent. The company had its own workforce to manage, renovate and refurbish the properties. The Special Commissioner carefully analysed the company accounts in an attempt to distinguish the level of profit attributable to each activity. He found that the level of profits relating to investment activities was £208,488, whilst the level associated with non-investment activities, was £147,617. Despite the greater proportion of company profitability favouring investment activities, the executors maintained that, in terms of time spent by staff and directors, the non-investment activities were dominant. However, the Special Commissioner was of the opinion that the emphasis on management and staff time produced such a large loss that it could not be justified. Therefore, looking at the business in the round, it consisted wholly or mainly of investment activity and did not qualify for business relief. The maintenance of the properties was insufficient to constitute the separate provision of services but was instead inherent in the property ownership. The in depth study of accounting evidence differed somewhat to the approach taken in *Farmer*. In that case the non-investment trade was carried out at a loss but the Commissioner did not seem to feel that this should lessen its importance in the overall context of activities.

(2) *Phillips v Revenue and Customs Commissioners*[134]

Phillips was the first time that the Court has been asked to consider whether or not the making of loans constituted the making or holding of investments for business relief purposes.

On the date of Mrs Phillips' death, the deceased owned shares in an unquoted company. The Memorandum and Articles of Association defined the company as a "property investment company" but during the deceased's lifetime the company had not actually held any investment properties. Instead, the company made loans to other family companies the majority of which, in turn, invested in properties. The Special Commissioner found that although the loans were mainly used to make investments, this did not automatically make the loans themselves investments. The fact that the company did not extract any profits from the investments made by the companies to which loans were made was indicative of this. Ultimately, the Commissioners decided that the company did not consist wholly or mainly of making or holding investments and therefore qualified for business relief. The case emphasised that for business relief

---

[132] HMRC Manuals IHTM25279.
[133] *Clark v Revenue and Customs Commissioners* [2005] S.T.C. (S.C.D.) 823.
[134] *Phillips v Revenue and Customs Commissioners* [2006] S.T.C. (S.C.D.) 639.

purposes, it is important to look at the activity of the business at the date of death and two years before and not the activity undertaken by the business prior to that.

(3) *Piercy's Executors v Revenue and Customs Commissioners*[135]

The *Piercy* case is an interesting comparison to the decision in *Phillips*. In *Piercy*, the Special Commissioner was asked to consider whether a property development company, which was in receipt of proportionately more rental monies than other trading profits, was wholly or mainly an investment company. The company had a history of property development and it was accepted that all the properties on its books had been originally acquired as trading stock for subsequent development and resale. However, the company showed a growing trend of receiving disproportionate amounts of rent from these properties. Unsurprisingly, HMRC argued that, on a balance of activities test, the company was clearly of an investment nature. The executors of the deceased rejected these arguments and maintained that the properties were retained with a development motivation at all times. For example, a proposed development in Islington had been blighted by various rail link proposals with the result that a decision had been made to postpone development and rent the properties for five years. The Commissioner found that, notwithstanding the long delays and resultant slow level of trading, the company did trade at all times. In some respects therefore, the case contradicts the findings in *Phillips* that it is necessary to focus on the activities of the business during the last two years before the deceased's death.

(4) *McCall v Revenue and Customs Commissioners*[136]

The personal representatives of Mrs McClean claimed the fields adjoining her house should attract business relief so that the whole value (as opposed to just the agricultural value) would fall out of charge for IHT purposes. The deceased's mental condition deteriorated so that, by 1995, she no longer had any understanding of the nature of her interest in the land or any arrangement entered into in relation to the fields. As a result of Mrs McClean's condition, her son in law became responsible for the fields. With the assistance of a local contractor he tended to the fields and let them to local farmers. It is worth noting that there is no requirement for the landowner to be actively involved in the business for relief to be available, although in other cases it may be unhelpful as it may indicate that there is not a single business. It was estimated that the contractor and son in law combined spent approximately 100 hours a year seriously tending the land. Tasks included weed control, fence maintenance, litter and damage control and drainage and water works.

At first instance, the Special Commissioner found without difficulty that the business was one that consisted wholly or mainly of the making of investments. The land was being used not to make a living *on* it, but instead, to make a living *from* it. The activities surrounding the land were not so substantial as to constitute themselves a part of the business distinct from holding the land and so, looking at the business in the round, there was little else than the business of holding an investment. The Court of Appeal in Northern Ireland upheld the decision finding that the test to be applied was that of an intelligent businessman who would be concerned with the use to which the asset was

[135] *Piercy's Executors v Revenue and Customs Commissioners* [2008] S.T.C. (S.C.D.) 858.
[136] *McCall v Revenue and Customs Commissioners* [2009] S.T.C. 990.

being put and the way it was being turned to account. The appeal judges were in full agreement that the activities of the deceased were nothing more than maintenance work necessary to enable the deceased to let the land for grazing and that the deceased's business consisted of earning a return from grassland the real and effective value of which lay in its grazing potential. The tax payer's work was deemed to be akin to a landlord maintaining a let property to achieve a better rent.

This case reinforces the point that in instances where land has been let and there is value in excess of the agricultural value, enhanced value will be taxed unless the maintenance activities of the owners is sufficient to prevent the land from being considered an investment. What will be important is whether the landowner is responsible for cultivating the grass by fertilising the land rather than merely maintaining it. If the latter can be demonstrated, relief should be available.[137] The Court of Appeal decision also illustrates that the retention of a right by the owner to enter the land during the period of agistment and the absence of full and exclusive rights of occupation in favour of the grazier does not automatically prevent the business from being regarded as an investment business.

(5) Brander v Revenue and Customs Commissioners[138]

Following the death of the Fourth Earl of Balfour, the courts were asked to decide whether business property relief should apply to a mixed agricultural estate in Scotland. The Estate consisted of various farms with associated buildings, cottages, grazing, woodlands and sporting rights. The case related to an interest in a partnership which carried on estate management and farming activities. The land, which was a partnership asset has at one time been held in trust for the deceased with him enjoying an interest in possession. The partnership was formed less than two years before death. At first instance, the First Tier Tribunal was asked to decide whether the estate was a single composite trading business or whether the cottage lettings were a separate business. In the event that there was a composite business, it also had to be decided whether the cottage lettings meant the business was wholly or mainly investments and therefore not qualifying for business property relief. The First Tier Tribunal decided that the whole estate had been run by the deceased for his own benefit—the role of the trustees was passive and the deceased regarded himself as carrying on a single enterprise. It was concluded that although the trust was a separate entity, there were not two separate businesses. With regard to whether the composite business was an investment business, it was necessary to look at activities "in the round." Relevant factors include turnover, profit, expenditure and time spent by everyone in various activities. The judgment noted that it was important to look at "where the preponderance of activity and effort lies." Taking these factors into account, the tribunal was satisfied that the business should qualify for relief. The facts were complicated in this case but the approach in *Farmer* was endorsed and followed.

On appeal by HMRC to the Upper Tribunal, these findings were upheld. It was felt that,

> "to suggest that the activities carried on at Whittingehame Estate comprised wholly or mainly the making or holding of investments is to belittle the efforts required properly and profitably to manage the various components of an estate of this nature."

---

[137] HMRC Manuals IHTM24124 which describes when conacre and agistment licenses in Northern Ireland will qualify for relief.
[138] *Brander v Revenue and Customs Commissioners* [2009] UKFTT 101.

The decision should give comfort to landed estates that are run using a composite business model that includes a mixture of in-hand farming, sporting activities, farm letting and residential letting. Provided care is taken to ensure that investment activities remain ancillary to trading aspects of the business then these activities within a single composite business should not prejudice the availability of business relief. It is also worth noting that as in *Farmer*, the judgment emphasised the historic connection between the cottage lettings and the farming activities of the estate. It was felt that the cottages were an important component in the overall business as they were historically part of the overall farming enterprises or housed full time estate workers.

Limited Liability Partnerships (LLPs)

A point about investment business should also be made with specific reference to **26–46** LLPs[139] that hold the shares of trading companies.

While an LLP has a legal persona, s.267A[140] indicates that an LLP is entirely transparent for IHT purposes. This transparency means that when considering whether the business carried on by the LLP is wholly or mainly making or holding investments for the purposes of s.105(3), it should be possible to look through to the assets themselves and not simply consider the business they support.

However, where an LLP is investing in unquoted shares in trading companies, the IHTM[141] suggests a different approach such that you should "look at the nature of the business underpinned by those assets, rather than the nature of the assets themselves, to see whether s.105(3) is in point. Thus, in the case of an LLP investing in unquoted shares in trading companies, it would be inappropriate to allow relief on the basis that the underlying assets constitute business property: the true position is that the nature of the business conducted by the LLP falls within s.105(3) so that relief is not available."

This position has been re-iterated by Graeme Blair writing in the *Tax Journal*,[142] who states:

> "It is not uncommon for LLPs to own the share capital of unquoted trading subsidiaries which provide services to them . . . Business property relief is not available under IHTA 1984, s.105(1) as the property (deemed to be owned by the members directly) is not a business or an interest in a business. However, there is an argument that business property relief is potentially available on the interest in these trading companies, as they are deemed to be an interest in the share capital of unquoted trading companies which, since 10 March 1992, have attracted 100 per cent relief."

Unfortunately, Blair gives no basis for his assertion that relief may be available, and so we are left with the unsatisfactory position of HMRC's view apparently being at odds with the interpretation of s.267(A) and in conflict with more generalised discussions of other commentators[143] as to the treatment of LLPs for the purposes of s.105(1).

---

[139] See also para.28–04.

[140] Inserted by Limited Liability Partnerships Act 2000 s.11.

[141] HMRC Manuals IHTM25094.

[142] *Tax Journal* (January 14, 2008), Issue 916, 15.

[143] For example, *Simons Direct Tax Service*, (London: LexisNexis), Ch.17.111 states "The partnership share of a member of a limited liability partnership also falls within the business relief category. Although a limited liability partnership has corporate status with legal personality separate from that of its members, it is expressly treated for IHT purposes as if it were an ordinary partnership".

Given this inconsistency, it would be prudent when considering business holding structures involving LLPs, to bear in mind the risk that relief under s.105(1) may not automatically be available where an LLP holds shares in a trading company.

Summary

The nature of the s.105(3) "all or nothing" test is likely to mean that the question of whether a business is wholly or mainly an investment business will continue to lead to disputes with HMRC. The following points can be drawn from the cases just discussed:

(1) Business relief will not be available where the only business activity is the receipt of income from rents.
(2) Good record keeping and accountancy evidence can be helpful and should be regularly reviewed. An owner can then take an informed view as to whether, on a subsequent transfer of value, business relief is likely to be available or whether it would be denied because the business consists wholly or mainly of making or holding investments. If business relief is unlikely to be available, an owner might be in a position to take steps to improve the position by managing activities that can be severed from the landowning part of the business as a separate business so that business relief is available in respect of that part of his business activities.
(3) The nature of services will depend on the nature and purpose of the activity, not whether they are included as part of a lease or licence and covered by rent.
(4) Where there is a hybrid business, even if more than 50 per cent of the turnover and profits of the business are attributable to holding investments, relief may nevertheless be available if, having looked at the business in the round, there are other factors which support the view that the business does not consist wholly or mainly of making or holding investments.

Temporary investments

26–47   If the assets of a business have been sold and are awaiting investment, business relief might still be available depending on the activities of the company and the intention of the deceased. In *Brown's Executors v IRC*[144] the deceased owned 99 of the 100 shares in an unquoted company which carried on business as the operator of a nightclub. The nightclub was sold in January 1985 and the proceeds placed in an interest bearing account. It was not intended that the company should cease trading and the proceeds were available at short notice. The company considered acquiring other nightclubs. The deceased suffered a heart attack in the autumn of 1985 and died suddenly in November. The Revenue, as it then was, considered that the shareholding did not attract business relief since at the time of death the business of the company consisted wholly or mainly of the making or holding of investments. Disagreeing, the Special Commissioner held that the question depended on the activities of the company combined with the intentions of the directors. Given that:

(1) there was an intention to replace the nightclub;

---

[144] *Brown's Executors v IRC* [1996] S.T.C. (S.C.D.) 277.

(2) the money was available on short notice; and

(3) the office of the company dealing with administration and marketing continued to operate as before;

he concluded that there had been no change in the nature of the business. This shows that the fact that all assets with which a business is carried on have been sold is not necessarily inconsistent with the company continuing to carry on its business.

Businesses outside s.105(3)

A number of businesses fall outside s.105(3) by reason of either express statutory exclusion, Parliamentary statements or HMRC practice. **26–48**

Market makers and discount houses

For the purposes of s.105(3), a business is not an "investment business" if it is **26–49** wholly that of a market maker or of a discount house, provided it is carried on in the United Kingdom.[145] "Market maker" means a person who:

(1) holds himself out at all normal times in compliance with the rules of The Stock Exchange as willing to buy and sell securities, stocks or shares at a price specified by him; and

(2) is recognised as doing so by the Council of The Stock Exchange.[146]

Following the formation of The London International Financial Futures and Options Exchange by the merger of the London International Financial Futures Exchange and the London Traded Options Market, regulations[147] were introduced with effect from March 23, 1993, extending business and interest free instalment relief to traders performing functions similar to market makers (in relation to financial futures and options on the London International Financial Futures and Options Exchange).

HMRC have published draft legislation which (once implemented) will extend business relief to businesses carrying out the business of a market maker, within the definition given by the Markets in Financial Instruments Directive (2004/39/EC), in a regulated market of a European Economic Area Member State. The new legislation is due to come into force on December 31, 2012.

Property dealing and property holding companies

In Standing Committee debates[148] the Chief Secretary to the Treasury said that a **26–50** property dealing or property holding company would not be within s.105(3) if it included building, construction or land development. He also gave an assurance that housing stocks would be regarded as stock in trade. The Revenue, as it then was, have

---

[145] IHTA 1984 s.105(4)(a).

[146] IHTA 1984 s.105(7).

[147] The Inheritance Tax (Market Makers) Regulations 1992 (SI 1992/3181).

[148] *Hansard*, cols 1268, 1269 (June 30, 1976).

confirmed that this is their interpretation of the position and it is assumed that HMRC would take the same view.[149]

Holiday lettings

26–51   Furnished holiday homes may qualify for business relief provided the owner plays an active role in the management of tenancies. To meet the requirements of a furnished holiday home and be eligible for certain tax reliefs, the pattern of lettings must satisfy the conditions in Income Tax (Trading and Other Income) Act 2005 Pt 3 Ch.6. These requirements were made more stringent following changes to the legislation with effect from April 6, 2012. The requirements are now that:

(1) The property must be available for commercial letting as holiday accommodation for at least 210 days a year (previously 140 days a year);

(2) it must actually be let as holiday accommodation for at least 105 days a year (previously 70 days a year); and

(3) it must not normally be let for continuous periods of more than 31 days to the same tenant in seven months of the year.

HMRC have agreed that the distinction between a business of furnished holiday lettings and a business of running an hotel may be minimal and in such circumstances the business should not be denied business relief on the grounds that it consists wholly or mainly of holding investments. HMRC have previously stated that relief should normally be allowed where:

(1) the lettings are short term (for example, weekly or fortnightly); and

(2) the owner—either himself or through an agent such as a relative or house-keeper—was substantially involved with the holidaymaker(s) in terms of their activities on and from the premises even if the lettings were for part of the year only.

HMRC indicated that following advice from the Solicitor's Office they were reconsidering their approach to furnished holiday homes and it may well be that some cases that might have previously qualified for relief should not have done so.[150] In particular, HMRC said that they would be looking closely at the level and type of services rather than who provided them. Taxpayers were also warned that, until further notice, any claim for relief on a holiday home will be referred to HMRC's Technical Team at an early stage.

This more robust stance has inevitably seen HMRC challenge a growing number of business relief claims in the context of furnished holiday lettings. Against this background the case of *Nicolette Vivian Pawson (Deceased) v Revenue & Customs*[151] was an important test case in assessing the validity of HMRC's approach. Mrs Pawson died on June 20, 2006 owning a 25 per cent interest in a holiday let property known as Fairhaven in Thorpeness, Suffolk. Her executors claimed that her interest in the property attracted business relief. There were two points in dispute that needed to be overcome by Mrs Pawson's executors in order for their claim to be successful. HMRC's contention was that (i) Fairhaven was not being used for the purposes of a business and/or that the activities were not being carried on for a gain, and (ii) even if

---

[149] HMRC Manuals IHTM25264.
[150] HMRC Manuals IHTM25278.
[151] *Nicolette Vivian Pawson (Deceased) v Revenue & Customs* [2012] UKFTT 51 (TC).

the use to which Fairhaven was being put did amount to the operation of a business or an interest in a business then the use to which it was being put consisted wholly or mainly of "holding investments" and therefore automatically took it outside the scope of relief by virtue of s.105(3).

The Commissioners found without difficulty that the activities at Fairhaven amounted to the operation of a serious business carried out for a gain. Similarly, the Commissioners found that Fairhaven did not amount to wholly or mainly the holding of an investment. In reaching their decision the Commissioners considered how an intelligent businessman would categorise the use to which a given business asset is put and how it is turned to account. In their mind there was,

> "no doubt that an intelligent businessman would not regard the ownership of holiday letting property as an investment as such and would regard it as involving far too active an operation for it to come under that heading".

It was concluded that this would be the view of an intelligent businessman because of "the need to constantly find new occupants and to provide services unconnected with and over and above those needed for the bare upkeep of the property as a property." This analysis was somewhat surprising given that the business consisted of only one property and the amount of work involved in managing the business was not onerous. Mrs Pawson did not use modern advertising (such as the internet) and the range of services were restricted to laundry, cleaning, television and telephone. The findings are obviously helpful to taxpayers in that it sets a relatively low threshold for relief. However, it is understood that HMRC will be appealing the decision and so it would be unwise to place too much reliance on this First Tier Tribunal decision until the position becomes clearer. The advice remains that the more services it is possible to demonstrate are being provided, the greater the likelihood of business relief being available.

Shares in holding companies

The main business of many holding companies consists in holding the shares of their **26–52** subsidiaries. Accordingly, in the absence of a limitation to s.105(3), none of the shares in such a company could be relevant business property. Section 105(4)(b) accordingly provides that s.105(3) does not apply to shares in or securities of a company if the business of the company consists wholly or mainly in being a holding company of one or more companies whose business falls within s.105(3), i.e. whose business is not "investments".

This requirement is presumably intended to ensure that shares in a holding company **26–53** qualify for relief only if the business of the group *as a whole* is not "investment". Whether the legislation always has the intended effect remains to be seen. Assume, e.g. that a holding company has three small but expanding trading subsidiaries and one large investment subsidiary, the assets and income of which slightly exceed the aggregate assets and income of the trading companies; does the business of the holding company consist mainly in being the holding company of the trading subsidiaries or the investment company, or, perhaps, neither?

Meaning of "holding company" and "subsidiary"

What is meant by "holding company" is obviously crucial in this context. By **26–54** s.103(2), "holding company" and "subsidiary" have the same meanings as in s.1159 of and Sch.6 to the Companies Act 2006. Under these statutory provisions, the relationship of holding company and subsidiary exists between two companies if:

(1) the first company is a member of the second company and controls the composition of the board of directors of the second company; or

(2) the first company holds more than half in nominal value of the second company's equity share capital; or

(3) the second company is a subsidiary of a subsidiary of the first company.

For these purposes, a holding company and all its subsidiaries are members of a group, and a company's equity share capital means its issued share capital other than any part of that capital which carries no right to participate in dividends or capital beyond a specified amount in a distribution.[152] Participating preference shares thus rank as equity share capital for these purposes.

Tax trap

26–55   Assume that trustees of a relevant property trust hold all the shares in a holding company which in turn owns a 40 per cent shareholding in an unquoted trading company. The ten year anniversary of the trust is looming. If the trust owned the shares in the trading company directly, 100 per cent business relief would be available. But since the holding company is not a "holding company" for the purposes of business relief the s.105(4)(b) let-out from s.105(3) does not apply, and no relief at all is available.

Sub-holding companies

26–56   On a strict reading of the legislation arguably no relief is available in respect of shares in a holding company which has sub-holding companies but HMRC are understood to accept that this would be unfair and will normally not preclude the relief from being available solely on this ground.

Investment subsidiaries

26–57   Where shares in or securities of a company are transferred and the business of that company is not an investment business but the company owns a subsidiary the business of which is an investment company then, although relief is available in respect of the shares transferred, under s.111 no relief is given in respect of so much of the value transferred by the transfer as is attributable to the value of the shares in the subsidiary. As this restriction is a quantitative restriction whereas the restriction in s.105(3) is a qualitative restriction, discussion of the s.111 restriction is deferred to para.26–87.

Excepted assets

26–58   Provision is also made to preclude the relief from being given either directly or indirectly in respect of assets which are not genuinely part of the business in question.

---

[152] IHTA 1984 s.103(2).

This restriction, also quantitative, is discussed in detail at paras 26–88–26–100 (where it will be seen that it is less worrying than might be thought).

Limitation 2: user and ownership

Failure to satisfy the conditions as to ownership and user will often be the reason **26–59** why property does not qualify for business relief. The condition as to ownership applies to all seven categories of property; the condition as to user applies only to the sixth and seventh categories of property. Under these conditions, throughout the two years immediately preceding the transfer in question the property transferred must have been:

(1) owned by the transferor[153]; and
(2) where the sixth category of land, buildings, plant or machinery is concerned, used wholly or mainly for the purposes of a business carried on by either:
  (a) a company of which the transferor then had control, provided that if the transferor owned shares or securities in the company those shares or securities were themselves relevant business property in relation to that transfer[154]; or
  (b) a partnership of which he was then a partner, provided that his interest in the partnership was itself relevant business property in relation to that transfer[155]; or
(3) where the seventh category of land, buildings, plant or machinery comprising settled property in which the transferor is beneficially entitled to an interest in possession is concerned, used wholly or mainly for the purposes of a business carried on by the transferor.

Category 6 property

The situation envisaged with regard to land, etc. within the sixth category, is, e.g. **26–60** that of a person who owns a building which he leases to a company which he controls. So long as (i) his shareholding is itself relevant business property immediately before he transfers the building, and (ii) he has owned the building for the last two years,[156] and (iii) the company has used the building wholly or mainly for its business during the last two years, the building will be relevant business property.[157]

It is important to note that where the property is land, buildings, plant or machinery used by a company in which the transferor has a controlling shareholding, the transferor must have owned his shareholding throughout the two years immediately preceding the transfer (although in the case of an unquoted company the holding would not need to have conferred control throughout this entire period so long as it existed by the time of the transfer; control could arise, e.g. by another shareholder's interest being repurchased by the company).

Where, on the other hand, the property transferred is shares that form part of a controlling shareholding, the transferor need not have owned all the shares from which

[153] IHTA 1984 s.106.
[154] IHTA 1984 ss.105(1)(d), (6) and 112(3)(a).
[155] IHTA 1984 ss.105(1)(d), (6) and 112(3)(a).
[156] IHTA 1984 s.106.
[157] IHTA 1984 s.112(3)(a).

he derives control throughout the preceding two years; it suffices that he owned the shares transferred throughout those two years. Where transfers of property used by a company and shares in the company are contemplated careful record keeping will thus be in order.

In theory, difficulties may arise where a person who as a sole trader uses land, buildings, plant or machinery which qualifies for 100 per cent business relief in his business:

(1) transfers his business to a partnership of which he is a partner or a company which he controls; and
(2) allows the partnership or company to use the land, etc.

This is because, strictly speaking, even though prior to the transfer the land, etc., qualified for 100 per cent relief, it will not qualify for any relief after the transfer until it has been used by the partnership or company for two years. This follows from s.112(3), which provides that land, etc., is not relevant business property unless it has been used "as mentioned in" s.105(1)(d) throughout the two years immediately preceding the transfer of value in question. Nevertheless, it is understood that in practice HMRC are prepared to allow relief in such circumstances. More importantly, however, the property would only qualify for 50 per cent relief going forward once held by a company or partnership.

Category 7 property

26–61   While property will come within the sixth category of qualifying property only if it has been used wholly or mainly for business purposes throughout the two years immediately preceding the transfer in question, property can come within the seventh category of approved property even if it does not satisfy this requirement. This legislative anomaly historically gave rise to the opportunity for tax planning involving the use of trusts in which the settlor retained an interest in possession. Following the Finance Act 2006 however, there are almost no circumstances in which this type of planning will be appropriate. The only circumstance in which tax planning of this nature may still be applicable is where there is potential to create an interest in possession trust for a disabled person under s.74. In all other instances, tax planning in this context is obsolete since it is not possible to create a lifetime non relevant property interest in possession trust. The two approaches outlined below are included for completeness only and it is recognised that their application has historic relevance only save where a disabled person's trust is being created.

Firstly, the legislation imposes certain quantitative limitations on the relief where an asset is not used in a business; see paras 26–88–26–100. Where a person intended to give a business or shares (or securities) in a company to someone in circumstances where these limitations were relevant, it was possible to consider extracting from the business or the company the "offending" assets and settling them on trusts under which he retained an interest in possession, remainder to the transferee. So long as the asset continued to be used in the business, 50 per cent relief would prima facie be available on the termination of the interest in possession notwithstanding that that occurred within two years of his making the settlement. This approach was less attractive where the transfer was to be of shares or securities, both because the extraction of the assets from the company may have caused corporation tax problems and because the transferor may have lacked a business in which the assets could be used so as to bring them within the seventh category of qualifying property.

Secondly, circumstances may have arisen in which a person who carried on a business as a sole trader and also carried on business in a partnership owned an asset used by the partnership which he wished to gift, but which had not been used by the partnership throughout the preceding two years, so that the asset did not satisfy the sixth category user test. If he withdrew the asset from the use of the partnership, settled it on trusts under which he retained for a period with remainder to the intended transferee and used the asset in the business he carried on as a sole trader, 50 per cent relief would prima facie be available on the termination of his interest in possession notwithstanding that that occurred within two years of his making the settlement.

In both the cases just considered regard would have to be had to the CGT consequences of settling the asset and the possible availability of holdover relief under s.165 of the Taxation of Chargeable Gains Act 1992.

Notional ownership

A transferor is treated as having owned property in two cases.   **26–62**

Firstly, where the transferor became entitled to the property on the death of another person he is treated as having owned it from the date of the other's death.[158] He is thus credited with ownership during the administration of the deceased's estate. This will apparently apply where property is redirected to a person as a result of a variation under s.142 with the result that the person to whom the property is redirected is treated as having owned the property from the date of death, not merely from the date on which the variation was affected. Strictly speaking, a person does not on the death of another become entitled to property which forms part of the deceased's unadministered residuary estate and which is liable to realisation in the administration of the estate, see *Sudeley v Att Gen*[159] but in practice HMRC are thought not to take this point.[160]

Secondly, if the deceased was his spouse or civil partner he is treated as having owned the property during any period during which his spouse or civil partner owned it, irrespective of how long they have been married or in a civil partnership.[161] The fact that he has owned the property for less than two years, therefore, does not necessarily debar him from securing relief.

It is important to note that there is no general provision aggregating the ownership of husband and wife or civil partners.[162] Thus, if during his lifetime a husband transfers to his wife property qualifying for business relief and within two years the wife transfers the property to, e.g. her daughter, no business relief will be available in respect of the wife's transfer, even though relief was available (when it was not needed) on the husband's transfer.

Partial user

It may be that a small part only of land or a building is used for business purposes,   **26–63**
e.g. where a doctor uses part of his house for a surgery. In the absence of provision to the contrary, the part so used would not qualify for relief since the land or building as

---

[158] IHTA 1984 s.108(a).
[159] *Sudeley v Att Gen* [1896] 1 Q.B. 354.
[160] HMRC Manuals IHTM25302.
[161] IHTA 1984 s.108(b).
[162] Such as previously existed in a CGT taper relief context before it was abolished with effect from April 6, 2008.

a whole would fail the "wholly or mainly" test.[163] This would compare unfavourably with the CGT relief given to principal private residences under which if part of the premises in question is used exclusively for business purposes, relief is lost only in relation to that part.[164] Fortunately, s.112(4) provides that if part of the land or building was used exclusively for business purposes, that part and the remainder are treated as separate assets, with the result that the part so used is not precluded from qualifying for the relief. The value of the part so used is taken to be such proportion of the value of the land or building "as may be just" in the circumstances. However, this position should be compared against the case of *Seymour (Ninth Marquess of Hertford) v Inland Revenue Commissioners*.[165]

Personal use

26–64 By s.112(6), an asset which at any time is used wholly or mainly for the personal benefit of the transferor or of a person connected with him is deemed not to have been used wholly or mainly for the purposes of the business concerned at that time. Any such use during the requisite period of user is thus fatal.

Relaxation of ownership and user conditions

26–65 There are two cases in which the conditions relating to ownership and user need not be satisfied.

Quick succession relief

26–66 The first exception involves a kind of quick succession relief. It may be that a person transfers property which does not satisfy the minimum ownership and user requirement, e.g. because he dies within two years of acquiring the property. If that property was eligible for business relief when it was transferred to him, relief for the present transfer may still be available. If either the earlier transfer or the present transfer was on death, the two year ownership requirement does not apply,[166] and the user requirement is treated as satisfied so long as there was appropriate user between the two transfers.[167] This exception applies where the earlier transfer would have been eligible for business relief if such relief had been capable of being given at that time.[168]

Replacements

26–67 The second exception is concerned with extending relief to property which was eligible for relief or which would have been eligible had it not been replaced. Even though property has not been owned and used for the required two years it will still satisfy the ownership and user conditions if it replaced other property and:

[163] IHTA 1984 s.105(1)(d).
[164] TCGA 1992 s.224(1).
[165] *Seymour (Ninth Marquess of Hertford) v Inland Revenue Commissioners* [2005] S.T.C. (S.C.D.) 177, see para.26–84.
[166] IHTA 1984 s.109.
[167] IHTA 1984 s.112(3).
[168] IHTA 1984 s.109(1)(a).

(1) the property in question—the "new property"; and

(2) the property it replaced—the "old property"; and

(3) any property directly or indirectly replaced by the old property which was itself replaced by the new property

was owned[169] and, in the case of land, etc. used[170] by the transferor for periods which together comprised at least two years falling within the five years immediately preceding the transfer. It is thus possible to have gaps in ownership and user, provided that contained within the five years before the transfer are periods totalling two years during which the property and property it replaced were owned by the transferor and used in the required manner.

Where one is considering shares held by a transferor in an unquoted company (i.e. shares falling within s.105(1)(bb)), if they are identified with other shares previously held by the transferor for CGT purposes under the provisions of ss.126–136 of the Taxation of Chargeable Gains Act 1992 (e.g. because they were acquired pursuant to a bonus or rights issue or as part of a share for share exchange) then his period of ownership is regarded as including his period of ownership of those other shares.[171] This rule does not apply, however, in the case of shares falling within ss.105(1)(b) or 105(1)(cc). The Special Commissioner was asked to interpret the share identification rules in *Vinton v Revenue and Customs Commissioners*[172] following the purported reorganisation of a company in which Mrs Dugan-Chapman owned shares on her death. In that case, two days before her death, Mrs Dugan-Chapman was allotted one million ordinary shares in the company. Her executors argued that these shares should attract business relief on the grounds that they could be identified with other shares in the company which Mrs Dugan-Chapman held for a period of more than two years prior to her death. They maintained that the allotment of one million shares followed on from the reorganisation of the company's share capital within s.126 Taxation of Chargeable Gains Act 1992 and therefore fell within s.107(4) and qualified for business relief. In particular, they claimed that the reorganisation was either (i) a larger reorganisation of the share capital and the issue of one million shares was part of it; or, (ii) there was a rights issue totalling one million shares all of which were taken up by Mrs Dugan-Chapman, a substantial proportion of which were acquired by reference to an existing shareholding. The executors also contended that the company exercised its affairs with relative informality so that the *Duomatic*[173] principle (which broadly deems certain formalities to have been satisfied) had to be considered when interpreting events. The Revenue, as it then was, on the other hand, regarded the one million shares as a simple subscription. The Special Commissioner found that there was insufficient evidence to support the executors' claims that a reorganisation had taken place and the *Duomatic* principle could not be applied. There was no real evidence that the members were aware of the relevant facts so that the one million shares could not be identified with any of the deceased's pre-existing shares.

As can be seen from the above case, the meaning of "replaced" is not entirely clear. It is understood that HMRC take the view that one business can replace another for these purposes even though they are entirely dissimilar, e.g. where a greengrocer sells his business and goes into hairdressing. It is not entirely clear whether one kind of business property will be regarded as replacing a different kind of business property, e.g. where with the proceeds of a sale of shares a person purchases a business; where a person transfers his business to a company in exchange for shares; or where a sole

---

[169] IHTA 1984 s.107(1).

[170] IHTA 1984 s.112(3)(b).

[171] IHTA 1984 s.107(4).

[172] [2008] S.T.C. 592.

[173] *Re Duomatic Ltd* [1969] 2 Ch. 365.

trader begins to trade in partnership, so that he owns a share in the partnership rather than his business. But there seems to be no reason in principle why business relief should not be available to the "new" property in such cases.

26–68   There are two qualifications to this exception. The first concerns the property in (2) and (3) above, i.e. the "replaced property". The qualification is that the replaced property itself must have been relevant business property immediately before it was replaced. In determining whether it was relevant business property the "two years out of five years" exception does not apply.[174]

The second qualification concerns the amount of business relief available. Even if a replacement, i.e. the "new property" is relevant business property, the relief is limited to the relief which would have been available on the replaced property.[175] It is therefore impossible to get relief on any additional value which is peculiar to the new property, or at a higher rate, e.g. on the replacement of a controlling quoted shareholding by an unquoted shareholding. For these purposes changes resulting from the formation, alteration or dissolution of a partnership or from the acquisition of a business by a company controlled by the former owner of the business are disregarded.[176]

26–69   It is to be noted that a problem may arise where a partner dies owning land and buildings used by the partnership, but which the surviving partners are unable to purchase. If, as will often be the case, the property in question passes to the deceased partner's widow, no business relief—the user condition will not be satisfied—will be available to the widow going forward, even though relief would have been available to her husband. In such a case, the relief is thus of no value: it is available when it is not needed (the spouse or civil partner exemption will normally prevent any charge arising on the partner's death), but when it is needed, e.g. on the widow's death, it is not available. The Law Society included among their 1980 Budget submissions a recommendation that business relief should be available in respect of such a subsequent transfer by a surviving spouse, but so far the legislation has not been amended to give effect to this recommendation. A similar difficulty may arise where the original transfer by the partner is a lifetime transfer.

26–70   Finally, it is also worth noting that if one replaces assets qualifying for agricultural relief with business assets (or vice versa), then Revenue Interpretation 95 states that one may adopt the combined holding period when considering whether the minimum ownership condition has been satisfied in relation to the replacement property.

Missives of sale in Scotland[177]

26–71   Under Scots law the sale of heritable property is normally effected by missives of sale under which the vendor delivers the disposition against payment of the purchase price. The missives form a binding contract; but the vendor is not divested of his rights until delivery of the disposition. Occasionally the purchaser pays over the purchase price on condition that the disposition is delivered within a specified period. In such circumstances, the question arises as to whom agricultural and/or business relief is due. Under estate duty and initially for CTT, HMRC practice was, fairly, to regard the purchaser rather than the vendor as qualifying for any reliefs due. This practice ceased as from June 8, 1978, when HMRC issued the following press release:

---

[174] IHTA 1984 s.107(1).
[175] IHTA 1984 ss.107(2) and 109(2).
[176] IHTA 1984 s.107(3).
[177] See *British Tax Review* (1978), p.271; and see IHTA 1984 s.113.

"Where a person sells heritable property situated in Scotland, the sale is effected by way of missives of sale followed, usually sometime later, by the delivery of a disposition of the property. The question has arisen as to whether the purchaser or the seller is entitled to any Capital Transfer Tax reliefs which may be attributable to heritable property if a transfer of value, e.g. on the occasion of a death, occurs during the period between completion of the missives of sale and delivery of the disposition of the property. Hitherto, it has been the practice both for Estate Duty and Capital Transfer Tax to give reliefs attributable to heritable property to the purchaser's estate.

In a recent non tax case (*Gibson v Hunter Home Designs Ltd (in liquidation)* 1976 S.L.T. 94) the Court of Session ruled that, between the date of completion of the missives and the date of delivery of the disposition of the property, the seller is not divested of any part of his right of property in the subjects of sale. The Board of Inland Revenue have accordingly been advised that any Capital Transfer Tax or Estate Duty reliefs which are attributable to heritable property fall to be given to the seller. Where, for example, the seller of agricultural property dies between completion of the missives and delivery of the disposition of the property, any Capital Transfer Tax agricultural or business reliefs due will be given to his estate. If the purchaser dies between these two dates these reliefs will not be available.

This view of the law will be applied to existing cases, subject to the statutory provisions which restrict the reopening of settled cases, in particular for Capital Transfer Tax para.26 of Sch.4 to the Finance Act 1975 (Determination of questions on previous view of the law) and for Estate Duty s.35 of the Finance Act 1951 (Restriction on reopening cases on the ground of legal mistake)."

This statement seems misconceived since, given the fact that no business relief is available to a transferor in respect of property with regard to which he has entered into a binding contract for sale,[178] the vendor will not be eligible for business relief.

Limitation 3: no binding contract for sale

26-72   The legislation is designed to give relief to business property, not to the proceeds of sale of such property, and s.113 accordingly provides that property is not relevant business property if at the time of the transfer a binding contract for the sale of the property has been entered into. This is subject to two qualifications, namely that this restriction will not apply if:

(1) the property is a business or an interest in a business and the sale is to a company which is to carry on the business and is made in consideration wholly or mainly of shares in or securities of that company; or
(2) the property is shares or securities and the sale is made for the purpose of reconstruction or amalgamation.[179]

It is understood that if parties enter into a contract for sale of relevant business property subject to a condition outside of the control of the parties being satisfied, then HMRC will not regard that contract as being a binding contract for sale until the condition is satisfied.

Put and call options, cross options and accruer arrangements

26-73   HMRC have always accepted that, although put and call options leave the respective parties in essentially the same commercial position as a buy and sell agreement, they

---

[178] See para.26-72.
[179] IHTA 1984 ss.113(a) and (b).

do not of themselves constitute binding contracts for sale, with the result that s.113 does not apply.

HMRC have also, over a series of statements set out below, eventually made it clear that they accept that accruer arrangements also do not constitute binding contracts for sale for the purposes of s.113. HMRC are thought to maintain this view. As will be seen below, their position has not always been clear with regards to accruer arrangements (although it has always been the authors' view that such arrangements did not infringe s.113). The history of the matter is as follows.

Revenue Statement of Practice SP12/80

26–74   The first Revenue statement was Statement of Practice SP12/80 dated October 13, 1980, as follows:

> "The Board understand that it is sometimes the practice for partners or shareholder directors of companies to enter into an agreement (known as a 'Buy & Sell' Agreement) whereby, in the event of the death before retirement of one of them, the deceased's personal representatives are obliged to sell and the survivors are obliged to purchase the deceased's business interest or shares, funds for the purchase being frequently provided by means of appropriate life assurance policies.
>
> In the Board's view such an agreement, requiring as it does a sale and purchase and not merely conferring an option to sell or buy, is a binding contract for sale within I.H.T.A. 1984, s.113. As a result the IHT business relief will not be due on the business interest or shares. (I.H.T.A. 1984, s.113 provides that where any property would be relevant business property for the purpose of business relief in relation to a transfer of value but a binding contract for its sale has been entered into at the time of the transfer, it is not relevant business property in relation to that transfer.)"

This statement, by indicating that accruer arrangements were binding contracts for sale within s.113, caused considerable concern.

The Law Society Gazette 1981 statement

26–75   In response to this statement, the following statement appeared in *The Law Society Gazette* of May 6, 1981:

> **"Capital transfer tax—buy and sell agreements**
> The Revenue published on 13 October 1980 a statement of practice (SP12/80) entitled 'Capital Transfer Tax—Business Relief from Capital Transfer Tax: "Buy and Sell" Agreements'. The publication has caused a considerable amount of concern, but it is hoped that the following table will indicate the problem is in fact far more limited than has been feared. It is hoped that practitioners will find that, in most cases, they will be able to obtain both business relief and take advantage of the instalment options for C.T.T. purposes without any significant disadvantage being caused to the partner either giving away his interest or dying. It should also be mentioned that in those cases where business relief and the instalment option are not available according to the drafting of the deed, it would be sensible to review the position as quickly as possible as it is thought that only in exceptional cases could there by any fear that the redrawing of the documents would, of itself, give rise to any charge and the business relief and instalment option availability are quite likely to be of significant benefit."

Event	C.T.T. payable on	Business relief available	Instalment option available
1. Partnership determines on death. Partnership assets realised and estate entitled to deceased's share of proceeds.	Value of partnership interest.	Yes	Yes, until business sold.
2. Partnership continues with estate entitled to represent deceased.	Value of partnership interest.	Yes	Yes.
3. Partnership continues with partnership share falling into deceased's estate but with option for other partners to acquire either on valuation or formula.	Value of partnership interest (normally calculated in accordance with valuation or formula).		Yes, until option exercised.
4. Partnership continues with share of deceased partner accruing to surviving partners with estate entitled to payment either on valuation or formula.	Value of partnership interest (normally calculated in accordance with valuation or formula).	Yes	Yes, until sums actually received from surviving partners.
5. Partnership continues and partnership share falls into deceased's estate but partnership agreement provides obligation for executors to sell and for surviving partners to buy partnership share either at valuation or in accordance with formula.	Value of partnership interest (normally calculated in accordance with valuation or formula).	No	Yes.

CCAB letter

It was not clear whether the statement had been agreed with the Revenue, as it then **26–76** was, or was accepted by the Revenue, but Revenue, as it then was, practice seemed to be consistent with the Law Society statement.

The availability of business relief on death in respect of property which was subject to a binding contract for sale was subsequently raised by the CCAB in the following letter of May 10, 1982:

"The Inland Revenue Statement of Practice SP12/80 dated October 13, 1980 sets out the views of the Board as to the effect of paragraph 3(4), Schedule 10 to the Finance Act 1976 on agreements between partners or shareholder directors whereby, in the event of death before retirement, the deceased's personal representatives must sell, and the survivors must buy, the deceased's interest in the business.

Paragraph 3(4) denies relief where business property is the subject of a binding contract of sale which has been entered into at the time of transfer, and the Statement of Practice states that agreements of the type referred to above, commonly known as 'buy and sell' agreements, fall within this definition.

It has generally been assumed that paragraph 3(4) was intended to deny relief where the transferor had decided to cease trading, had entered into a binding contract for the sale of his business, and had subsequently died or given away his interest before completion of the sale. In the words of *Dymond's Capital Transfer Tax*, page 298, 'There is no point in giving business relief where the property is, in effect, cash realised on the sale of a business'.

However, the Statement of Practice extends the application of paragraph 3(4) to situations where the sale is to take place only in the event of death before retirement. By inference it is assumed that business relief will also be denied in such circumstances to lifetime transfers, even though there was no intention to cease trading and the sale on death might be expected to be many years away. We consider this practice to be contrary to the intention of the legislation and to give rise to many anomalies because business relief will depend upon the form of words used rather than the substance. The following are examples of various forms of partnership provisions and the apparent effect on the availability of business relief.

	Partnership provision	**Apparent effect**
(a)	On the death in service or retirement of a partner the surviving partners shall purchase his share in the partnership for £X.	If a partner gives away part of his partnership share in his lifetime, or dies in service, business relief will presumably not be available.
(b)	On the death in service or retirement of a partner the surviving partners have an option to buy and the retiring partner (or his personal representatives) have an option to sell his share in the partnership.	If a partner gives away part of his partnership share in his lifetime, or dies in service, 50 per cent business relief will be available as an option is not a binding contract for sale.
(c)	There is no provision for the purchase of a partner's share. By his will a partner directs that if he dies in service his partnership interest is to be sold.	If he gives away part of his partnership share in his lifetime or dies in service, 50 per cent business relief will be available as there is no binding contract for sale.
(d)	On the death in service or retirement of a partner his share is to accrue to the surviving partners who shall pay an annuity to the partner or his widow as appropriate.	If a partner gives away part of his partnership share in his lifetime, or dies in service, is this to be construed as a binding contract for sale?

We are aware that an article appeared on this subject in *The Law Society Gazette* of May 6, 1981, a copy of which is attached for ease of reference, but it is not clear whether this interpretation has the approval of the Revenue."

Revenue 1982 reply

26–77   The Revenue replied, in a letter dated July 5, 1982, in the following terms:

"The purpose of para.3(4) of Sch.10 to the Finance Act 1976 was to limit business relief to transfers of business property. To that end para.3(4) denies relief when—because of a binding contract for sale—what the transferor passes to the transferee is in effect an entitlement to the sale consideration rather than the right to a continuing business interest. While in principle therefore relief is not available on a transfer of business property which is bound by a contract for sale, the decision in any case involving the transfer of an interest in a partnership will depend on the terms of the partnership agreement. It was this situation which our Statement of Practice 12/80 was designed to illuminate (its purpose was not—nor, of course, could it—extend the scope of para.3(4)).

In your examples (b) and (c) business relief will be available, but taking example (a) against this background it is clear that business relief will not be available on a partner's death in service or retirement. But if the contract for sale is not operative in his lifetime so that he can give his interest away—and it continues as a business interest in the hands of the recipient—then business relief will be available. Similarly in example (d) business relief will be available on a lifetime transfer of a partner's interest if the accrual clause and annuity provision does not then come into operation; but if it does, spouse exemption may be due to the extent of the value of the annuity. On death in service there would again be no business relief, but exemption would be due on the widow's annuity. In the case of example (d) the CGT Statement of Practice of January 17, 1975 may also be in point. Any chargeable gains accruing to a retired partner would be computed by comparing the consideration received (including the capitalised value of the annuity) with the CGT 'cost', or the market value at the date of death for the personal representatives of a deceased partner.

While I accept that this is not a straightforward area, the effect does not seem to me to be contrary to the intention of the legislation, nor would there appear to be anomalies. The substance of the agreement is different in the different examples so it is not surprising that the tax consequences are also different.

Finally, for the sake of completeness, the article in the *Law Society Gazette* for May 6, 1981 correctly states the general position since it is only in the final case that a binding contract for sale exists before the death of the partner."

Commentary

A number of points came out of this correspondence. Firstly, the Revenue, as it then was, letter states that business relief is available only if the gifted business "continues as a business interest in the hands of the recipient". This is plainly wrong, though, interestingly, it does foreshadow the clawback of business (and agricultural) relief introduced by the Finance Act 1986 (discussed below at paras 26–101–26–112 and paras 26–157–26–166). Secondly, it was helpful to have Revenue confirmation that they agreed with the statement in *The Law Society Gazette*. There was, however, a problem, namely that the Revenue analysis of the example in (d) of the CCAB letter appeared to be at odds with the *Gazette* statement. The latter, in example 4, says that business relief is available where there is an automatic accruer clause. The Revenue letter says in relation to example (d) that it is not. The authors agree with the *Gazette* statement, for the following reasons.

To begin with, there is judicial authority for the proposition that, except where the statutory context otherwise requires, "contract for sale" means a transfer for a consideration in money and does not extend to a transfer for a consideration in other than money, e.g. in money's worth.[180] Where partners enter into an accrual agreement on

26–78

---

[180] See *Coats (J&P) v IRC* [1897] 1 Q.B. 778; *Kirkness v Hudson (John) Co Ltd* [1955] A.C. 696; *Robshaw v Mayer* [1957] Ch. 125; *Littlewoods Mail Order Stores Ltd v IRC* [1963] A.C. 135; In *Re Westminster Property Group Plc*, *Times Law Reports*, January 30, 1985.

forming a partnership[181] there is no contract for sale at the time the partner leaves the firm, because the accrual at that time of the rights and monies to the continuing partners and the outgoing partner respectively is not a transfer of his rights under the partnership agreement in exchange for moneys due to him from the continuing partners. Nor is the partnership agreement itself a contract for sale, because the only consideration given by the parties to it was consideration in money's worth, namely their reciprocal entering into of the partnership agreement when the partnership was formed. Where, on the other hand, para.5 of the Law Society's statement applies, there is a contract for sale, because the deceased partner's executors and the continuing partners are respectively obliged to sell and buy his share, and this contract is binding because the parties to it are bound by the partnership agreement to go ahead with this sale.

Notwithstanding their reply, the Revenue appeared to accept in practice that accruer arrangements did not infringe s.113.

Revenue 1996 Statement

26–79   The Revenue, as it then was, in a statement published in *The Law Society Gazette* of September 4, 1996, at p.35 and set out below, subsequently confirmed that they agreed with the 1981 Statement in the *Gazette* and also allayed fears that their practice concerning options had changed.

> "The Inheritance Tax Act 1984, s.105, provides that property consisting of a business or interest in a business, e.g. a share in a partnership, is relevant business property for the purposes of pt. V c.1 of that Act and would be eligible for relief from IHT at the rate of 100 per cent.
>
> Section 113 of the Act provides that property will not qualify for relief if, at the time of the transfer of the property, whether during lifetime or on death, it is subject to a binding contract for sale.
>
> Statement of Practice 12/80 gives the view of the board of the Revenue on 'buy and sell' agreements. If a partnership agreement provides that in the event of death before retirement of a partner, the deceased's personal representatives are obliged to sell, and the surviving partners are obliged to purchase the deceased's partnership share, the Revenue's view is that this will require a sale and purchase rather than merely conferring an option to buy or sell. The arrangement would constitute a binding contract for sale within s.113 so that business relief would not be available on the partnership share. An article appeared in the *Gazette*, May 6, 1981, giving examples of various types of partnership agreements dealing with the devolution of a partnership share on death, and how these would be treated for IHT purposes, i.e. whether or not business relief would be available. The article indicated that where, on the death of a partner, the partnership continued with the share of the deceased partner accruing to surviving partners and the estate being entitled to payment, either on valuation or using a formula, the provisions of s.113 would not apply and there would be no preclusion of business relief.
>
> There has recently been concern that the Revenue's attitude on this point had changed, and that where an agreement provided for an accruer of a partnership share on death as outlined above, relief would not be available. There was also concern that in some circumstances, the decision in *Spiro v Glencrown* [1991] 1 All E.R. 680 was being interpreted as providing authority for an option to constitute a binding contract for sale, so that where a partnership agreement provided for continuation on death, with the partnership share falling into the deceased's estate but with the option for other partners to acquire the share, business relief would not be available. At a recent meeting, Revenue representatives were able to confirm that there had been no change in their view on buy and sell agreements

---

[181] The position where the original partnership agreement contains no provisions about accruer and a subsequent agreement concerning accruer is entered into is more complicated; see para.28–20.

and that the *Gazette* article could still be relied upon. Business relief would be available on a partnership share passing under the type of accruer provision described above. It was also confirmed that the *Spiro v Glencrown* decision would not be cited as authority for an option constituting a binding contract for sale unless the option had been exercised at the time of death, or other transfer where material."

Sales of assets other than relevant business property

It is important to note that this limitation applies only in respect of binding contracts **26–80** for sale of property which, but for this limitation, would be relevant business property. If, e.g. a sole trader has contracted to sell some of the assets in his business, but not the business itself, this limitation will not apply.[182]

IX. QUANTITATIVE LIMITATIONS ON THE AVAILABILITY OF THE RELIEF

As was mentioned above, business relief is given by reducing by a specified **26–81** percentage so much of the value transferred by a transfer of value as is attributable to the value of relevant business property. At this stage in the discussion it is assumed that there is relevant business property. There are thus two remaining issues:

(1) What is the value of relevant business property for the purposes of business relief?
(2) How much of the value transferred is attributable to that value?

It is in relation to these issues that the legislation imposes two quantitative limitations on the availability of business relief.

Limitation 1: value of relevant business property

The starting point is that the normal market value rule applies, subject to two vital **26–82** qualifications.

The value of a business or an interest in a business

The general rules for valuing property are modified in three very important ways for **26–83** the purpose of determining the value of a business or an interest in a business for the purposes of business relief. The basic modifications are that:

(a) by s.110(a), the value of a business is taken to be its net value;
(b) by s.110(b), the net value of a business is the value of the assets used in the business (including goodwill) reduced by the aggregate of any liabilities incurred for the purposes of the business.

---

[182] For guidance, see the CGT cases of e.g. *Pepper v Daffurn* [1993] S.T.C. 466; *Jarmin v Rawlins* [1994] S.T.C. 1005 and *Clarke v Mayo* [1994] S.T.C. 570. Contrast the position for agricultural relief under IHTA 1984 s.124.

The same modifications apply for the purpose of determining the ability to pay IHT by instalments, but not for the purpose of agricultural relief.[183]

Assets used in the business

26–84   Two questions arise in this context; the first concerns the meaning of "business", the second the meaning of "assets used in the business".

It was explained previously[184] that "business" has a wide meaning which is not limited to trading but which extends to making or holding investments and to hybrid businesses consisting of both trading and making or holding investments. Although a business which consists wholly or mainly of making or holding investments cannot qualify for business relief[185] a hybrid business which does not consist wholly or mainly of making or holding investments can do so and in such a case the investments should normally be assets used in the hybrid business.[186]

The meaning of "assets used in the business" has been considered judicially in three cases, with some surprising results.

In *Fetherstonaugh v IRC*[187] a majority of the Court of Appeal held that "assets used in the business" should be given their natural and ordinary meaning, so that land used by the taxpayer in his business qualified for relief even though it was comprised in a settlement in which he had an interest in possession and not in his business per se. The relevant words were thus, in the circumstances of that case, to be given what amounted to a wide reading. Following the Finance Act 2006, this analysis would only apply where the assets are held within a settlement with a non relevant property interest in possession.

A narrower reading, on a different point, was adopted in *IRC v Mallender (executors of Drury-Lowe, Deceased)*.[188] The case concerned the position of a deceased Lloyd's name who, in order to fulfil Lloyd's requirements, had secured a bank guarantee which formed part of his Lloyd's deposit. In order to provide the bank with an indemnity for giving the guarantee the Lloyd's name had given the bank a charge over a freehold commercial property he owned. Following the name's death the issue arose as to how much, if any, of the commercial property qualified for business relief. Revenue, as it then was, practice was to give business relief on the value of property charged in this way up to the amount of the guarantee, but no more. The personal representatives were not satisfied with this. The value of the property far exceeded the amount of the guarantee and they argued that since the name's business would have been seriously affected had he not given the indemnity the whole of the commercial property on which the indemnity was secured qualified for business relief.

The Special Commissioner found for the deceased's personal representatives, but Jacob J. held that the only asset "used in the business" was the guarantee. The business was concerned only with getting the guarantee in place; how it was obtained was immaterial to the business, i.e. there was no actual nexus between the underwriting business and the indemnity. Thus, not only was business relief not available on the

---

[183] IHTA 1984 s.227(7)(a)–(c); see paras 25–86 and 26–33.
[184] See para.26–19.
[185] See paras 26–32–26–58.
[186] See paras 26–32–26–58 and para.26–100.
[187] *Fetherstonaugh v IRC* [1984] S.T.C. 261; see para.26–20.
[188] *IRC v Mallender (executors of Drury-Lowe, Deceased)* [2001] S.T.C. 514.

whole of the property, it was not available even up to the amount of the guarantee.[189]

The most recent decision on the meaning of "assets used in the business" can be found in *Ninth Marquess of Hertford (executors of Eighth Marquees of Hertford, Deceased) v IRC*.[190] In this case, the Special Commissioner returned to a wider interpretation of the legislation. Prior to the Eighth Marquess of Hertford's death, he made a gift of his freehold interest in Ragley Hall, its contents and the goodwill of the Ragley Hall public opening business, to his son. The public opening business meant that the whole of the exterior of Ragley Hall was accessible to viewing by the public and 78 per cent of the interior (by volume) was open. The remaining 22 per cent of the interior was leased back to, and occupied by the Eighth Marquess and his family and was closed to the public. The Eighth Marquess of Hertford died within seven years of making the gift and so the potentially exempt transfer became chargeable other than to the extent business relief applied. It was agreed between the parties that the public opening business was 'relevant business property' and, to the extent that the gift by the Eighth Marquess comprised the business, business relief was applicable. The dispute was as to whether the whole of Ragley Hall should be regarded as a single asset (despite the lease to the Eighth Marquess) and eligible for business relief or, as contended by the Revenue, whether business relief should be restricted to take into account the 22 per cent of Ragley Hall which was privately occupied. The Special Commissioner found that that it was not possible to divide Ragley Hall in any sensible way. The public could see the whole of the exterior of the building and the whole of the building was a vital backdrop to the business carried on. Whilst accepting that it was not inevitably the case that whatever interest one might have in a single building was one single asset, given the nature of the business, on balance, the freehold of Ragley Hall should be considered as a single asset and business relief should therefore be available on the whole.

Liabilities incurred for the purposes of the business

The next issue is what liabilities are "incurred for the purposes of the business". **26–85** Here there are two areas of concern. First, can "purposes of the business" be given a wide reading so that liabilities either not charged on any assets or, conceivably, charged on assets not qualifying for relief, nevertheless reduce the value of assets qualifying for business relief? Assume, e.g. that X borrows on overdraft to fund his business. Will the borrowing reduce the value of his business for the purposes of business relief? More difficult is the situation where X borrows, secures his borrowing on a non-business asset and introduces the borrowed funds into his business. It is clear that for IHT purposes generally the borrowing reduces the value of the asset on which it is secured.[191] What, then, is the position if it also reduces the value of his business for the purpose of giving business relief?

The answer may be found in *Mallender*. One would expect that the rule concerning liabilities would mirror that concerning assets and that, accordingly, liabilities incurred outside the business would be disregarded. The fact that the legislation refers to

---

[189] The charge would have reduced the value of the commercial property; IHTA 1984 s.162(4). What the personal representatives had hoped to achieve was to take the whole of the property out of charge to IHT. See also Matthew Hutton & Barry D. McCutcheon, *Private Client Business* (London: Sweet & Maxwell, 2001), pp.191–196.

[190] *Ninth Marquess of Hertford (executors of Eighth Marquees of Hertford, Deceased) v IRC* [2005] S.T.C. 177.

[191] IHTA 1984 s.162(4).

liabilities "incurred for the purpose of the business" would support such a reading. And, in *Mallender* itself there was no suggestion that the indemnity reduced the value of the deceased Lloyd's name's interest.

The second concern is that, paradoxically, "incurred for the purpose of the business", may be given too narrow a reading. This concern arises as a result of the Special Commissioner's decision in *Hardcastle (the executors of Vernede, Deceased) v IRC*[192] which considered whether Lloyd's underwriting losses from the open and run-off years constituted liabilities incurred "for the purposes of the business" within s.110(b). In what many saw as a surprising decision, the Special Commissioner held that such losses did not comprise liabilities of the business and therefore could instead be claimed as a deduction against the value of the rest of the estate for IHT purposes.

Prior to *Hardcastle* the practice of the Revenue, as it then was, had always been to regard trading contracts as business assets, being the means by which the underwriting business was carried on. Contracts with a negative value were regarded as liabilities incurred in the course of the business and therefore deductible from the assets for which relief was available.

The deceased's executors in *Hardcastle* argued that such a practice was wrong on the basis that, inter alia, the assets used in the business were those funds deposited at Lloyd's and that liabilities incurred for the purposes of the business included sums borrowed to fund those deposits; trading profits were not, on the other hand, assets of a business and trading losses were, accordingly, not liabilities incurred for the purposes of the business. It was also submitted that a trading contract constituted property to be included in a deceased's estate for the purposes of s.5(1), which had to be valued. It was argued that if such a contract had a positive value then it would not comprise "an asset used in the business" because it would form part of the very business itself. For the same reason, if the contract had a negative value then it was argued that it would not constitute a liability incurred "for the purposes of the business".

The Special Commissioner upheld the executors' appeal, making the following observations:

(1) The definition of property in s.5 is not confined to property that is capital in nature. The liabilities to be taken into account in determining an estate should therefore include all debts, both of a capital and income nature. Applying this to an underwriting business, the assets of the property within s.5(1) would include the assets of the business as well as trading profits. The liabilities to be taken into account under s.5(3) would similarly include liabilities of the business as well as trading losses.

(2) It was in this context that business relief had to be considered. Citing the remarks of Oliver L.J. in *Fetherstonaugh*, a distinction was drawn between the way in which the net value of a business is calculated for the purposes of business relief and the valuation of a business for the general purposes of IHT. It was noted that for the purposes of IHT generally, not only assets and liabilities of a business would be brought into account but also any trading profits or losses. However, s.110 prescribes a different method of valuation that incorporates only two elements, namely the assets used in the business and the liabilities incurred for the purposes of the business. Section 110 provides that, for the purposes of business relief, "the net value of a business is the value of the assets used in the business . . . reduced by the aggregate amount of any liabilities incurred for the purposes of the business".

---

[192] *Hardcastle (the executors of Vernede, Deceased) v IRC* [2000] S.T.C. (S.C.D.) 532.

(3) In the absence of direct authority on the meaning of the words "assets used in the business" in the IHT legislation, the Special Commissioner made a distinction (applying the income tax principles laid down in *Van den Berghs Ltd v Clark*)[193] between expenditure which brought an asset into existence on the one hand and ordinary commercial contracts on the other. The former were said to be "assets used in the business" but not the latter. Applying these principles to the facts of the case, the Special Commissioner found that the insurance contracts in respect of which the results had not been notified to the deceased at the date of death were ordinary commercial contracts made in the course of the deceased carrying on his business as an underwriter. The Special Commissioner said that "they were contracts for the disposal of his product which was the assumption of risk in return for a premium". Therefore, for the purposes of business relief, it was held that if such contracts gave rise to a profit they should not be regarded as assets used in his business. The corollary of this was that if the contracts gave rise to a loss, they did not constitute liabilities incurred "for the purposes of the business".

The decision in *Hardcastle* clearly conflicts with the approach of the Revenue, as it then was, to liabilities relating to underwriting contracts, with the result that in the past contracts at a profit will have been regarded as business property (causing an underpayment of IHT), and contracts at a loss will have been deducted from business property causing an overpayment of IHT in respect of the rest of the estate.[194]

The Revenue's failure to appeal against the decision may have been that they perceived a potential long-term benefit to excluding profitable contracts from the value of relievable property, but the authors understand that it was more likely to have been as the result of an administrative oversight.

The full consequences of *Hardcastle* remain to be seen. It has been suggested[195] that the drafting of s.110(b) is deliberately restrictive in its definition of "net value" and that had Parliament wished business relief to attach to a "balance sheet value", this could easily have been specified. On the basis of such a view, the case may have wider implications for liabilities incurred in the day-to-day running of businesses, which post-*Hardcastle* should perhaps not be deducted from business property, but rather from the non-business assets of an estate. Both creditors and debtors referred to in a company balance sheet would frequently have no place in the valuation of the company in question.

By contrast, others see the case as having less impact and the view has also been expressed[196] that the Special Commissioner was wrong to rely on the distinction between income and capital expenditure, and that the only condition in s.110(b) for assets and/or liabilities to be included in the valuation of a business should be that they are "used in the business".

It does seem that HMRC have so far continued to operate according to their old practice and they have indicated that they do not anticipate any change in the future as a result of the decision in *Hardcastle*. This will be particularly fortunate for owners of businesses with a large part of their value comprising stock in trade as such assets may not, on a strict interpretation of *Hardcastle,* be eligible for relief. On the other hand,

---

[193] *Van den Berghs Ltd v Clark* [1935] A.C. 431.
[194] See *Trusts and Estates Tax Journal*, April 2001, p.7.
[195] See *Trusts and Estates Tax Journal*, April 2001, p.9.
[196] See *Trusts and Estates Tax Journal*, May 2001, p.6. This article suggests that the s.110(b) draftsman did in fact have a balance sheet in mind, with the assets to be taken into account including both fixed assets as well as stock in trade and the liabilities to be deducted including long term borrowings (such as may be used to purchase premises) as well as short-term debts such as unpaid rent or wages.

some taxpayers may wish to invoke *Hardcastle* to maximise business relief by restricting the liabilities to be taken into account in valuing their business. In the authors' experience HMRC are likely to respond to such attempts by seeking to confine (not always convincingly) *Hardcastle* to its facts. It remains to be seen how the courts will regard *Hardcastle* on a future analysis of s.110(b). As matters stand, draftsmen of wills should certainly be careful to focus on the difference between the definition of the underwriting business itself and the relievable value of the business as defined by s.110(b): a legacy of "all my Lloyd's business" could now potentially carry with it non-relievable property.

The value of an interest in a business

26–86   Sections 110(a) and (b) apply for determining the value of an interest in a business but, by s.110(c), in ascertaining the net value of an interest in a business, no regard is had to assets or liabilities other than those by reference to which the net value of the entire business would be ascertained. Rights and interests of partners inter se, e.g. to receive or pay annuities, will thus be left out of account.

Groups of companies

26–87   The normal rules apply, except that, by s.111, where a company is a member of a group, and the business of one of the members is "investments",[197] the value of the shares is what it would be if the member carrying on the "investment" business were not a member of the group. The value of shares in an "investment" company is thus precluded from qualifying for the relief, with the result that if the shares in a holding company are transferred, so much of the value of those shares as is attributable to any "investment" subsidiary will be left out of account in determining how much of the value transferred qualifies for business relief.[198] The restriction specified by s.111 does not apply if the business of the "investment company" consists wholly or mainly in the holding of land or buildings wholly or mainly occupied by members of the group whose business is not "investments".[199]

Assume that X has for many years owned shares in X Ltd, a holding company of two trading companies, A Ltd and B Ltd and one company, C Ltd, which holds investments and carries on trading and which is an investment company. The shares in the investment company are worth £20,000 and the shares in the trading companies are worth £50,000 and £30,000 respectively. X transfers shares in X Ltd, his circumstances being such that the value transferred by this transfer is £50,000.

As X Ltd's main business is being a holding company of two trading companies, relief will be available, but in computing this relief the value of the shares in the investment company must be left out of account. Relief is thus prima facie available on £40,000, representing 80 per cent of the value transferred that qualifies for business relief (£80,000/£100,000).

It might be possible to arrange matters so that s.111 did not operate to restrict the relief by reference to the shares in C Ltd. This would be the case if sufficient of C Ltd's investments could be transferred to one of the other companies, e.g. the holding

---

[197] See paras 26–33 and following for the meaning of "investments"; see paras 26–181 and following for planning.
[198] See also para.26–57.
[199] IHTA 1984 s.111(b).

company, so that C Ltd lost its character as an investment company: see paras 26–181 and following.

Limitation 2: excepted assets

It will be recalled that business relief is available only in respect of so much of the value transferred by a transfer of value as is attributable to the value of any relevant business property. Hitherto we have been concerned with the nature and value of the relevant business property. The final, more subtle consideration is the determination of how much of the value transferred is attributable to the value of the relevant business property. In making this determination, so much of the value of the relevant business property as is attributable to any "excepted assets" is left out of account. **26–88**

The reason for this restriction is that, in the absence of provision to the contrary, it would be tempting for a taxpayer to use his business or company as a vehicle for transferring his private assets. Just before transferring his business, e.g. to his son, he could "park" some of his private assets in the business. On transferring his business he would secure business relief on the value of the business. Provided the private assets had been used[200] in the business to some extent, they would be taken into account in valuing the business notwithstanding the fact that, in reality, they had very little to do with the business. The transferor would thus have succeeded in securing business relief for what were, in reality, his private assets. Similarly, a person could transfer his private assets to his own company and then transfer the shares in the company, with the result that business relief would also be secured indirectly for the private assets.

The legislation accordingly makes provision to deny relief in respect of assets which in reality are not used in the business, including excessive cash reserves. It does so by providing that the value of "excepted assets" is to be left out of account in determining what part of the value transferred by a transfer of value is attributable to the value of the relevant business property in question.[201] The result is that although the assets form part of the business, or belong to the company, their value is ignored in determining how much of the value transferred by the transfer in question qualifies for business relief.

Assume X owns all 100 shares in X Ltd, and that all the shares are relevant business property. X Ltd owns assets worth £100,000, £20,000 of which are excepted assets. X gives 25 shares to his son: the value transferred is, say, £25,000. Of this £25,000, 80 per cent is attributable to the value of relevant business property. The remaining 20 per cent is attributable to the value of the excepted assets. Business relief will thus be given only in respect of £20,000 (80 per cent of £25,000).

If X had given 51 shares to his son the effect would have been more subtle. Assume that after the transfer X's remaining 49 shares are worth, say, £24,500, with the result that the value transferred is £75,500. Of this, £60,400 (80 per cent of £75,500) is attributable to relevant business property. The remaining 20 per cent, £15,100, is attributable to the value of the excepted assets. Thus, it is not simply a question of leaving the value of excepted assets out of account; what must be left out of account is so much of the value transferred as is *attributable* to those assets.

Definition of "excepted assets"

An asset is not an excepted asset if it satisfies either of two tests, i.e. if: **26–89**

[200] IHTA 1984 ss.110(b) and 227(7)(b); see para.26–84.
[201] IHTA 1984 s.112.

(1) it was used wholly or mainly for the purposes of the business concerned throughout the whole of the last two years or such lesser period as the transferor owned the asset (or a corresponding interest in the asset in the case of an interest in a business) immediately preceding the transfer of value[202] ("past user"); or

(2) it is required at the time of the transfer for future use for the purposes of the business in question ("future user").[203]

Each of these tests will be considered in turn.

Past user

26–90   The provisions concerning past user are somewhat complicated and it will be best to consider how they apply to each kind of business property in turn. In each case below, any condition stated is the condition which must be fulfilled if the asset in question is not to be an excepted asset.

A business

26–91   The asset must have been used wholly or mainly for the purposes of the business:

(a) throughout the last two years immediately preceding the transfer of value during which the transferor owned the asset; or

(b) throughout the whole of the period (if less than two years) immediately preceding the transfer of value during which the transferor owned the asset.[204]

An interest in a business

26–92   The asset must have been used wholly or mainly for the purposes of the business:

(a) throughout the last two years immediately preceding the transfer of value during which the transferor owned an interest in the asset; or

(b) throughout the whole of the period (if less than two years) immediately preceding the transfer of value during which the transferor owned an interest in the asset.[205]

Shares in or securities of a company

26–93   The asset must have been used wholly or mainly for the purposes of the company's business:

---

[202] IHTA 1984 ss.112(2)(a) and (5).
[203] IHTA 1984 s.112(2)(b).
[204] IHTA 1984 ss.112(2)(a) and (5).
[205] IHTA 1984 ss.112(2) and (5).

(a) throughout the last two years immediately preceding the transfer of value during which the company (or any other company which immediately preceding the transfer of value was a member of the same group) owned the asset; or

(b) throughout the whole of the period (if less than two years) immediately preceding the transfer of value during which the company (or any other company which immediately preceding the transfer of value was a member of the same group) owned the asset.[206]

HMRC have made it clear that the test will not be satisfied if the asset was used for the purposes of a previous business during the period in question.[207]

It is to be noted that, under the above tests, it suffices that the asset in question was used wholly or mainly for the purposes of the business throughout the whole of the relevant period, i.e. the two years immediately preceding the transfer or the whole period (if less than two years). This is extremely helpful. It means that an asset will not be an excepted asset even though it was purchased shortly before the transfer of the business, provided, of course, that it was used wholly or mainly for the purposes of the business throughout the period in question. A transferor with spare cash who is contemplating a transfer of his business may thus wish to acquire business equipment a few months before the anticipated transfer.

Group user

Special provision is made to aggregate user by group companies. In deciding whether an asset satisfies the past user requirement periods of user by other group companies will be brought into account.[208] Thus, it is not possible to prevent an asset which has been used for non-business purposes in one company from being an excepted asset by transferring it to another company where it is used for business purposes for a short time before the shares are transferred. Use by a group company which is an investment company is not aggregated for these purposes.[209]

26-94

Deemed non-business user and asset splitting

In applying the above tests, two further points must be borne in mind. Firstly, by s.112(6), where an asset is used wholly or mainly for the personal benefit of the transferor or a person connected with him the asset is deemed to have not been used wholly or mainly for the purposes of the business in question. Any such use during the requisite period of use is thus fatal. Secondly, by s.112(4), when part only of any land or building which would otherwise be an excepted asset is used exclusively for the purposes of a business, the part so used is treated as a separate asset, a "just"

26-95

[206] IHTA 1984 ss.112(2) and (5). For the definition of "group", see IHTA 1984 s.103(2) and para.26–54.
[207] HMRC Manuals IHTM25351.
[208] HMRC Manuals IHTM25351.
[209] IHTA 1984 s.112(2).

proportion of the value of the whole being attributed to it. The excepted assets test therefore is not an all or nothing test like the "wholly or mainly" test.[210]

Future user

26–96 By s.112(2)(b), an asset is not an excepted asset if at the time of the transfer it is required for future use for the purposes of the business in question. This future user test does not apply in deciding whether land or buildings, machinery or plant, which is relevant business property by virtue only of being used by a company or a partnership is an excepted asset[211]; only the past user test can apply in relation to such property.

"Cash mountains" and future user

26–97 The future user test, though simple to state, may give rise to problems in practice. In particular, where the asset in question is cash or investments, disputes may arise as to how much of the cash or investments is required for the purposes of the business in question. It is understood that HMRC will not challenge reasonable claims for relief, but that they are wary of businesses and companies being used as "pocketbooks" so as to secure relief for cash or investments which would not qualify for business relief if held privately.

The future user test was considered in *Barclays Bank Trust Co Ltd v IRC*.[212] The deceased owned 50 per cent of the issued shares in a company which sold bathroom and kitchen fittings. At the date of his death in 1990, the company held more than £450,000 in cash deposits which were invested for periods of up to 30 days. Just before his death, the company had approached X Ltd with a view to purchasing its assets but no reply was received and X Ltd was liquidated. In 1997 the company spent in excess of £335,000 on a venture, which involved the import of goods from China.

The Revenue, as it then was, accepted that the company needed some £150,000 cash at the time of the deceased's death but considered that the balance of £300,000 was not required at the time of the transfer for future use for the purposes of the business and so constituted an excepted asset. The appellant argued that the cash was needed to purchase the properties of X Ltd and pointed out that it had used over £300,000 in 1997. However, the Special Commissioner held that it was not sufficient to say that, because an asset might be required at some time in the future, it was required "for future use" for the purposes of the business within s.112(2)(b):

> "Was the £300,000 cash held by the company required on 23 November 1990 for future use for the purposes of the business? This is a question of fact and on the evidence before me I cannot find that it was so required. I do not accept that 'future' means at any time in the future nor that 'was required' includes the possibility that the money might be required should an opportunity arise to make use of the money in two, three or seven years' time for the purposes of the business. In my opinion and I so hold that 'required' implies some imperative that the money will fall to be used upon a given project or for some palpable business purpose. For example, if the company had negotiated for the properties at Leigh on Sea in 1990 and there was a realistic possibility that it would buy the properties early in 1991, then it could fairly be said that the money was 'required' on 23 November 1990 for

---

[210] See para.26–34.
[211] IHTA 1984 s.112(3).
[212] *Barclays Bank Trust Co Ltd v IRC* [1998] S.T.C. (S.C.D.) 125.

that purchase even if, let it be supposed, the proposed purchase in fact later fell through, because, for example, the vendor could not show a good title or the vendor withdrew the property from the market. As it is, on the facts, there is no evidence before me that the company was to be the purchaser or that Mr and Mrs Wilkins or either of them was to be the purchaser."[213]

Two further points may be noted: first, that the decision as to whether assets are needed for the business must, in the first instance, be one for the managers of the business (albeit that any such decision may be reviewed by the courts to see that it accords with the requirements for the relief); second, that the directors of a company carrying a cash reserve will be advised each year to indicate, when considering the accounts, the purposes for which that reserve is needed.

The case of *Barclays Trust Co Ltd* should be compared to the position in *Brown's Executors v IRC*.[214] In that case, it was found that the intentions of the deceased are an important consideration and secondly, the fact that the assets of a company have been sold pending further investment does not necessarily make it inconsistent with the company continuing to carry on business.

Unincorporated businesses vs companies

The way the legislation restricts the availability of relief by reference to the use to **26–98** which assets are put is slightly puzzling. Firstly, it imposes a restriction by providing that in determining the value of a business regard is had to "assets used in the business": see paras 26–83–26–86. Secondly, it imposes a restriction with regard to excepted assets, which are also defined by reference to business user. In the *Mallender* case,[215] Jacob J. said that he provisionally preferred the argument of the Revenue, as it then was, that the excepted assets rules were concerned not so much with legal title as with what was happening as a matter of fact, but it remains to be seen whether that is the correct approach.

One thing that is clear is that there is a mismatch between the rules governing incorporated and unincorporated businesses. As was discussed, under s.110 the value of a business or an interest in a business for IHT purposes extends only to assets *used* in the business. Thus, if an asset is not used at the time in the business, the value of the business for business relief is reduced by the value of that asset. Section 110 is silent as to the time of the use; presumably the relevant time is the time of the transfer of value in question.

Where shares in a company are concerned, s.110 is irrelevant, non-business user **26–99** being attacked under the s.112 excepted assets provisions. But the s.112 user requirements differ from the s.110 requirements in two significant ways. Firstly, there is no simple present user test as such; rather there is a past user test which extends back two years from the time of the transfer or, if the asset was acquired within those two years, to the time when the asset was acquired. Secondly, there is a future user test. This test apparently extends to both (i) assets which are being used at the time of the transfer and are required for future use and (ii) assets which are not being used at the time of the transfer but which are required for future use. In practice the net result appears to be that a business which owns an asset which it does not use at the time of the transfer but

---

[213] *Barclays Bank Trust Co Ltd v IRC* [1998] S.T.C. (S.C.D.) 125 at 128.
[214] See para.26–47.
[215] See para.26–84.

which it requires for future use will not obtain relief on the value of that asset while a company may do so.

Planning: treatment of investments held in hybrid businesses

26–100   "Excepted assets" are defined by reference to business user. It is vital to note that although the excepted assets rules might seem to be a considerable source of concern where a business or a company owns investments, this concern is often misplaced. "Business" is a very wide term[216] and HMRC accept that a business can be multi-faceted or hybrid. Where, e.g. a company which trades also owns investments the key question HMRC will normally ask is "whether the company has a hybrid business embracing trading and investment components or has a purely trading business accompanied by one or more non-business assets".[217] HMRC will normally investigate this matter carefully and it is important that it is clear from the conduct of the parties concerned that they regard the investments as an integral part of a hybrid business, in which case the investments should not be excluded assets. On this basis the ownership of, e.g. quoted investments or let property need not result in the value transferred that would otherwise qualify for business relief being reduced because of the presence of excepted assets.

X. CLAWBACK OF RELIEF ON LIFETIME TRANSFERS

26–101   The Finance Act 1986 introduced into the legislation provisions which may operate to clawback business relief previously given to a chargeable transfer made after March 17, 1986 and within seven years of the transferor's death.[218] Similar provisions apply in relation to the relief available to a PET which proves to be a chargeable transfer because it was made within seven years of the transferor's death.[219] In the case of a transfer which was chargeable when it was made this may result in additional tax being charged on the basis that the value transferred is what it would have been had no relief been given.[220] It will not, however, and this seems anomalous, affect the value transferred by the transfer for purposes of cumulation. Where, on the other hand, a failed PET is concerned, the value transferred is for all purposes taken to be what it would have been had no relief been available, with the result that both the tax due and the transferor's cumulative total may be affected.[221]

The thinking behind the clawback is presumably that since the purpose of business relief is to prevent charges to IHT from breaking up businesses the relief should not be available if the business is not retained by the person to whom it is transferred. This is fair enough, but why does the clawback operate with regard only to lifetime transfers? Given that it does and with the potential retrospectively to lose business relief at 100 per cent, the lifetime clawback rules are an important factor which may encourage the transfer of business property to be postponed until death.

---

[216] It is in this context unlikely to extend to an activity carried on otherwise than for gain.
[217] Inland Revenue *Shares Valuation Manual*, 27170; see para.26–19 and *Taxation*, July 1, 2004, pp.358–360.
[218] IHTA 1984 s.113A(2).
[219] IHTA 1984 s.113A(1).
[220] IHTA 1984 s.113A(2).
[221] IHTA 1984 s.113A(1).

The legislation operates by assuming that where the transferor dies within seven years of a transfer no relief is available unless, generally speaking, two conditions are satisfied, as explained below. It may be that the conditions are satisfied with respect to part only of the property originally transferred. In such a case, only a proportionate part of so much of the value transferred as is attributable to the original property is protected from the clawback.[222]

As discussed at para.26–109, there was an argument that because clawback depended upon there having been either a potentially exempt or chargeable transfer, the clawback rules could not apply when one was dealing with 100 per cent relievable property. Whilst the existence of this "loophole" was never accepted by the Revenue, the legislation was amended by the Finance Act 1996 with effect from November 28, 1995, to put the matter beyond doubt.[223]

First condition—transferee's ownership

Section 113A(3)(a) provides that the property which was relevant business property **26–102** in relation to the transfer of value in question must have been owned by the transferee throughout the period beginning with the date of that transfer and ending with the date of the transferor's death or the transferee's death, whichever is earlier.[224] The following illustrates how the rules work in relation to a transfer which is chargeable when it is made. Assume that on June 1, 2003, X settled property on a discretionary trust, thereby making a transfer of value, before business relief, of £540,000. The transfer qualified for business relief at 50 per cent, and this reduced the value transferred to £270,000. The trustees paid the tax due of £1,400. If X dies, say, five-and-a-half years later and the trustees have by then sold the property the extra tax due will be computed on the basis that the value transferred was £540,000. If X had a nil cumulative total when he made the transfer the tax due would prima facie be £110,800 (based on a nil rate band of £263,000), and 40 per cent of that amount[225] = £44,320 would be due in additional tax. Against this could be set the tax previously paid of £1,400, so that additional tax of £42,920 was in fact due. X's cumulative total would be unaffected.

Now consider the position where there has been a failed PET. Assume that X gives Y shares qualifying for business relief. Two years later Y sells the shares. Eighteen months after the sale X dies. The transfer to Y will be a PET which proves to have been a chargeable transfer. Although business relief will initially have been available, it will be clawed-back because Y did not own the shares throughout the period beginning with the date of the transfer and ending with X's death. Accordingly, all of the value transferred at the date of the gift that qualified for business relief will be subject to charge *and* that value transferred will be included in X's cumulative total.[226]

Settled property trap

Although the requirement as to ownership seems straightforward, it can give rise to **26–103** problems where settled property is concerned. Before the changes included in the Finance Act 2006, this was of particular concern in respect of accumulation and

[222] IHTA 1984 s.113A(5).
[223] IHTA 1984 s124A(7A).
[224] IHTA 1984 ss.113A(3)(a) and (4).
[225] Because of 60 per cent taper relief.
[226] See para.6–11.

maintenance trusts (as they were) before April 6, 2008. Thus if X settled property qualifying for business relief on accumulation and maintenance trusts and e.g. his son became entitled to the trust income within seven years, relief would have been lost retrospectively if X died within seven years of making the PET which established the trust, because the transferee—the trustees—will have ceased to own the property. The Finance Act 2006 has effectively eliminated this trap, since under the relevant property regime, beneficiaries are not deemed to be the beneficial owners of trust property with effect from March 22, 2006. There will not, therefore, be any deemed change of ownership if a beneficiary subsequently becomes entitled to an income interest under the terms of a settlement.

Second condition—availability of relief

26–104   The second condition is concerned with whether, broadly speaking, the property transferred to the transferee has continued to qualify for business relief. Before considering this condition it may be helpful to note that it need not be satisfied in one case.

Let-out

26–105   There is no need to fulfil the second condition where the property was transferred after March 16, 1987,[227] and was:

(1) shares or securities which were quoted at the time of the transfer; or
(2) unquoted securities of a company where the control test was satisfied; or
(3) unquoted shares in a company.[228]

In relation to (2) and (3) above, the securities/shares must have been unquoted throughout the whole period beginning with the date of the transfer and ending with the earlier of the death of the transferor and the transferee.[229] In all other cases the second condition is relevant, and varies according to whether or not the transferor predeceased the transferee.

Second condition—relief for transferee

26–106   If the transferor predeceases the transferee the legislation posits that on the death in question[230] the transferee made a notional transfer of value immediately before the death of the transferor and then provides that the value transferred by the transferor will remain reduced only if, in relation to the transferee's "ghost" transfer of value, the property in question would have been relevant business property in the hands of the transferee.[231] It should be noted that s.113A(3)(b) provides that in determining whether the property in question is relevant business property in relation to the "ghost" transfer

[227] FA 1987 s.58(3).
[228] IHTA 1984 ss.113A(3)(b) and (3A).
[229] IHTA 1984 s.113A(3)(a).
[230] IHTA 1984 s.113A(4).
[231] IHTA 1984 s.113A(3)(b).

of value made by the transferee no regard is had to the two year ownership requirement imposed by s.106.

Changes in categories and attribution of value

In determining whether business relief remains available the sole consideration **26–107** where the second condition is concerned is whether or not the property in question was "relevant business property", i.e. the fact that it falls within a different category of relevant business property qualifying for a different percentage relief does not matter. Nor does it matter that part of the value transferred by the "ghost" transfer of value deemed to be made by the transferee is not attributable to the value of the relevant business property in question, e.g. because it is attributable to the value of excepted assets within s.112.

Share acquisitions

A special rule applies where shares owned by the transferee immediately before the **26–108** death in question (a) would be identified with the original property (or part of it) under ss.126–136 of the Taxation of Chargeable Gains Act 1992,[232] or (b) were issued to the transferee in consideration of the transfer of a business or an interest in a business consisting of the original property (or part of it). In such a case the shares are treated as if they were the original property (or part of it).[233]

Interaction with 100 per cent relief

When the rates of business relief were increased with effect from March 10, 1992, **26–109** it was contended that the clawback rules could not apply in respect of property qualifying for 100 per cent relief when one was dealing with 100 per cent relievable property. The argument put was that clawback depends upon there having been either a PET or chargeable transfer and that, in the case of gifts of business property qualifying for 100 per cent relief the value transferred is nil and therefore there is no chargeable transfer. The Revenue (as it then was) did not accept this and in the authors' understanding took the view that there was a chargeable transfer albeit one of a nil value transferred. This was important for CGT purposes because it meant that, e.g. where an individual transferred to a discretionary trust property qualifying for 100 per cent business relief (or agricultural relief) the disposal could qualify for CGT holdover relief under s.260(2)(a).[234] The Finance Act 1996 s.184(5) removed such doubt as existed on the clawback position by providing that in applying the clawback rules no account should be taken of business or agricultural relief available in respect of the

---

[232] Formerly CGTA 1979 ss.77–86.
[233] IHTA 1984 s.113A(6).
[234] See *Private Client Business* (1993), p.138. The Revenue (as it then was) were referred to this article and confirmed in writing that in their view a transfer of value, the value transferred by which was reduced to nil by 100 per cent relief, was nevertheless a chargeable transfer.

original transfer. It is not thought that this affects the ability to claim holdover relief under s.260(2)(a).

Replacements

26–110   It may be that the transferee has disposed of all or part of the original property before his own death or the death of the transferor. In such a case, s.113B provides that the conditions as to ownership and the continuing status of the original property as relevant business property (as discussed above in paras 26–102 and 26–104) will be taken to be satisfied in relation to the original property if the following conditions are satisfied[235]:

(1) the whole of the consideration received by the transferee for the disposal has been applied by him in acquiring other property (the "replacement property")[236];

(2) the replacement property is acquired, or a binding contract for its acquisition is entered into, within three years or such longer period as the Board may allow after the disposal of the original property (or a binding contract for the disposal of that property is entered into, if that is earlier and the disposal subsequently takes place)[237];

(3) the disposal and acquisition are both made in transactions at arm's length or on terms such as might be expected to be included in a transaction at arm's length[238];

(4) the replacement property is owned by the transferee at the time of the death in question[239];

(5) throughout the period beginning with the date of the chargeable transfer and ending with the death in question (disregarding any period between the disposal and acquisition), either the original property or the replacement property was owned by the transferee[240];

(6) in relation to a notional transfer of value made by the transferee immediately before the death in question, the replacement property would be relevant business property (ignoring the two year ownership requirement imposed by s.106).[241]

The rules are modified to cover the case where the transferor predeceases the transferee[242] and either:

(a) the transferee has disposed of all or part of the original property before the transferor's death; or

(b) has entered into a binding contract for sale of the property so that it is not relevant business property in relation to the "ghost" transfer of value mentioned at para.26–106 which is made by the transferee on the transferor's death.[243]

[235] IHTA 1984 s.113B(1)(a), (3), (4) and (8).
[236] IHTA 1984 s.113B(1)(b); it is thought that "consideration" here means the consideration net of the expenses of sale.
[237] IHTA 1984 ss.113B(2)(a) and (7) as amended by FA 1994 s.247.
[238] IHTA 1984 s.113B(2)(b).
[239] IHTA 1984 ss.113B(3)(a) and (4).
[240] IHTA 1984 ss.113B(3)(b) and (4).
[241] IHTA 1984 ss.113B(3)(c) and (4).
[242] IHTA 1984 s.113B(5)(a).
[243] IHTA 1984 s.113B(5)(c).

In such a case, if the replacement property is acquired, or a binding contract for its acquisition is entered into, after the death of the transferor, but within three years of the disposal of the original property or part[244] (or a binding contract for the disposal of that property is entered into, if that is earlier, and the disposal subsequently takes place),[245] then the requirement in (4) above that the replacement property is owned by the transferee at the time of the death in question is dispensed with and the relevant time in relation to the other conditions, instead of being the death in question or the time immediately therebefore is instead the time when the replacement property was acquired.[246] However, there remains no possibility of a backwards rollover for IHT and, even where a replacement is made within three years after the disposal, replacement relief will be available only if *all* the proceeds of sale are reinvested.

Share acquisitions

A special rule applies to shares owned by the transferee immediately before the 26–111 death in question: where shares satisfy the conditions mentioned in para.26–108 the shares are treated as if they were the replacement property (or part of it).[247]

Commentary

Six points need noting about the replacement property provisions. Firstly, they apply 26–112 only where the whole of the consideration from the disposal of the original property is applied in acquiring the replacement property. Why this should be the case is hard to understand. The CGT legislation deals specifically with the situation where the consideration for the disposal of a business asset is used only partly in acquiring other assets (see s.153 of the Taxation of Chargeable Gains Act 1992). Secondly, the replacement property provisions do not apply if the replacement property was acquired before the disposal of the original property. Again, this is to be contrasted with the CGT position. Roll-over relief under s.152 of the Taxation of Chargeable Gains Act 1992 is available if the replacement asset is acquired up to 12 months before or three years after the disposal of the original asset. Thirdly, except where a share acquisition[248] is concerned, the provisions apply only to the first replacement, i.e. if X is given property, replaces it and then sells the replacement property and replaces it, the provisions will not apply to the second replacement property. Again, why this should be the case is hard to understand. Fourthly, it does not matter into what category of relevant business property the replacement property falls.[249] Next, it appears that where the replacement property qualifies for both agricultural and business relief the replacement property provisions will not apply because s.114 provides that where agricultural relief and business relief are both available in respect of a transfer agricultural relief takes precedence with the result that the replacement property would not, as replacement property, satisfy the second condition mentioned at para.26–104. Finally, it should be

[244] IHTA 1984 s.113(5)(b) as amended by FA 1994 s.247.
[245] IHTA 1984 s.113(7).
[246] IHTA 1984 s.113(5).
[247] IHTA 1984 s.113B(6).
[248] See para.26–108.
[249] See para.26–107. Note also that the qualification provided by the FA 1987 s.58(3) in relation to s.113A, discussed at para.26–105, applies equally for purposes of s.113B.

noted that HMRC have published guidance[250] on the position when agricultural property is replaced by business property (or vice versa) shortly before the owner's death and, on the donor's death, where the donee of a PET of agricultural property has sold it and reinvested the proceeds in a non-agricultural business (or vice versa) as follows:

"In the Revenue's view, where agricultural property which is a farming business is replaced by non-agricultural business property, the period of ownership of the original property will be relevant for applying the minimum ownership condition to the replacement property. Business property relief will be available on the replacement if all the conditions for that relief are satisfied. Where non-agricultural business property is replaced by a farming business, and the latter is not eligible for agricultural property relief, section 114(1) does not exclude business property relief if the conditions for that relief are satisfied.

There could be cases where, agricultural land is not part of a farming business, so any replacement could only qualify for business property relief if it satisfied the minimum ownership conditions in its own right. However, our experience suggests such cases are likely to be exceptional.

Where the donee of a PET of a farming business sells the business, and replaces it with a non-agricultural business, the effect of section 124A(1) is to deny agricultural property relief on the value transferred by the PET. Consequently, section 114(1) does not exclude business property relief if the conditions for that relief are satisfied; and, in the reverse situation, the farming business acquired by the donee can be 'relevant business property' for the purposes of section 113B(3)(c)."

AGRICULTURAL RELIEF

XI. INTRODUCTION

26–113   The legislation contains, in effect, two versions of agricultural relief. The agricultural relief given by the Act was introduced, with effect from March 10, 1981, by the Finance Act 1981 and is discussed at paras 26–114 and following. This relief replaced the original relief, which was found in Sch.8 to the Finance Act 1975. The rules governing the availability of the old relief can, however, still be relevant, since in certain cases 100 per cent relief is available if the taxpayer satisfies the requirements for the old relief. A full discussion of the old relief can be found in the third edition of this work at paras 14–110 and following.

26–114   Sections 115 to 124C afford relief where the value transferred by a transfer of value is attributable to agricultural property situated in the United Kingdom, the Channel Islands or the Isle of Man.[251] Under s.122(3)(b) of the Finance Act 2009, inheritance tax relief was extended to agricultural property in the European Economic Area on transfers of value on or after April 22, 2009. This extended relief has retrospective effect.[252] This followed a request from the European Commission. For other agricultural land farmed outside the EEA, it may be that business relief will be available.

Like business relief, the relief is available to actual and notional transfers alike, and extends to periodic and exit charges.[253] Throughout this discussion "transferor" should accordingly be read, where appropriate, as "trustees", "transfer of value" as "periodic

[250] See RI 95.
[251] IHTA 1984 s.115(5).
[252] Finance Act 2009 s.122(7).
[253] IHTA 1984 s.115(1).

charge" or "exit charge" and "value transferred" as "the amount on which tax is charged on the occasion of a periodic or an exit charge".

The relief is given by reducing by 100 or 50 per cent so much of the value transferred by a transfer of value as is attributable to the agricultural value of agricultural property. It is not given by reducing the value of property as such.[254] One hundred per cent relief is available in relation to property carrying the right to vacant possession (or the right to obtain it within the next 24 months) or if the transferor's interest in the property is valued at an amount broadly equivalent to its vacant possession value. One hundred per cent relief is also available if the property is let on a post August 31, 1995, tenancy or, under the transitional provisions, if the transferor would have qualified for relief under Sch.8 to the Finance Act 1975. Fifty per cent relief is available in relation to all other agricultural property. The availability of 100 per cent relief is discussed at paras 26–134–26–166.

The 100 and 50 per cent rates of relief apply in relation to transfers of value made and other events occurring on or after March 10, 1992. The previous rates of relief were 50 and 30 per cent. The transitional problems caused by the change in the rates of relief are considered at para.26–12.

The relief need not be claimed; it cannot be disclaimed.

The terms "agricultural property" and "agricultural value" are specially defined for the purposes of the relief. Since they are central to the relief, it will be helpful to consider them at the outset.

XII. DEFINITIONS

Definition of "agricultural property"

"Agricultural property" is defined, in somewhat bewildering fashion, in s.115(2). **26–115** The definition is best divided into three parts (each of which is considered below separately) as follows:

> "agricultural land or pasture (*part 1*) and includes woodland and any building used in connection with the intensive rearing of livestock or fish if the woodland or building is occupied with agricultural land or pasture and the occupation is ancillary to that of the agricultural land or pasture (*part 2*); and also includes such cottages, farm buildings and farmhouses, together with the land occupied with them, as are of a character appropriate to the property (*part 3*)."

Preliminary matters

Before considering each of these parts in detail, a few preliminary points fall to be **26–116** made.

Agriculture

Although the definition of "agricultural property" does not refer to "agriculture", **26–117** the meaning of "agriculture" is nevertheless relevant because the meaning of "agricultural" depends on it. Furthermore, as will be seen below, relief is available in respect of certain property only if it is occupied "for the purposes of agriculture".

[254] This can be important; see para.16–18 and, in relation to TCGA 1992 s.274, para.25–34.

There is no definition of "agriculture" or "agricultural" in the Act. In *Dixon v IRC*[255] the Special Commissioner referred to the definition contained in s.96 of the Agricultural Holdings Act 1986 (which is also used in s.38 of the Agricultural Tenancies Act 1995). The IHTM[256] refers to "agriculture" as being defined by reference to s.96 which provides that:

> "'agriculture' includes horticulture, fruit growing, seed growing, dairy farming and livestock breeding and keeping, the use of land as grazing land, meadow land, osier land, market gardens and nursery grounds, and the use of land for woodlands where that use is ancillary to the farming of land for other agricultural purposes and 'agricultural' shall be construed accordingly."

The issue in *Dixon* was whether fruit growing and the use of land as grazing land constituted agriculture. The deceased died owning a 60 per cent interest in 0.6 acres comprising an overgrown orchard and garden, having made a gift of the balancing 40 per cent interest approximately four years prior to her death. The damsons in the orchard were picked by a neighbouring commercial fruit grower and sold together with his own fruit. On occasion ewes, lambs and calves grazed in the orchard. The Special Commissioner held that, in light of the definition in the Agricultural Holdings Act 1986, it was clear that fruit growing and the use of land as grazing land could be agriculture but added that:

> "it seems to me that whether these activities are or are not agriculture for the purposes of the 1984 Act is a matter of fact and degree to be determined in the light of the purposes of the 1984 Act. The purposes of the 1984 Act are not to give relief for a private residence and garden but to give relief for land and pasture used for agriculture. In this appeal, although there was some sale of surplus fruit, and there was some grazing of sheep in return for household duties, these activities are consistent with the conclusion that the property was used as a residence and a garden and not for agriculture".[257]

Whilst there is no comprehensive definition of "agriculture" for IHT purposes, s.115(4) of the 1984 Act provides that the breeding and rearing of horses on a stud farm and the grazing of horses in connection with those activities shall be taken to be agriculture. "Stud farm" is not defined; HMRC take the view that there must be an element of horse breeding and that the number of horses held at the date of death together with the breeding record in recent years will be important factors.[258] However, land used for grazing leisure horses does not satisfy the "occupied for the purposes of agriculture" test (see para.26–129) and so cannot qualify for agricultural relief.[259]

Cultivated crops

HMRC accept that the cultivation of a crop for purposes other than as food for human consumption may be included in the definition of "agriculture".[260] Examples

[255] *Dixon v IRC* [2002] S.T.C. (S.C.D.) 53.
[256] HMRC Manuals IHTM24220.
[257] *Dixon v IRC* [2002] S.T.C. (S.C.D.) 53 at 58.
[258] HMRC Manuals IHTM24068.
[259] *Hemens v Whitsbury Farm & Stud Ltd* [1988] 2 W.L.R. 72 and *Wheatley's Executors v CIR* (SpC 149) [1998] S.T.I. 559.
[260] HMRC Manuals IHTM24062.

given are reeds for thatching, nurseries growing seeds, tree nurseries and the growing of grass for turf.

Livestock, deadstock, harvested crops, plant and machinery

26–118 Livestock, deadstock, harvested crops and plant and machinery are clearly not within the definition; they may, however, qualify for business relief.

Sporting rights

26–119 HMRC has directed that the value of fishing rights does not form part of the agricultural value of agricultural land.[261] Other sporting rights may qualify for agricultural relief but only if they are exercised for normal agricultural purposes (e.g. shooting game that damages crops) as opposed to commercial purposes. The exploitation of sporting rights such as commercial shoots may qualify for business relief if agricultural relief does not apply.

Short rotation coppice land and buildings

26–120 The definition of "agricultural property" was extended by the Finance Act 1995 (in the case of transfers of value made and other events occurring on or after April 6, 1995) so that land on which short rotation coppice is cultivated shall be regarded as agricultural land and buildings used in connection with the cultivation of short rotation coppice shall be regarded as farm buildings.[262] Short rotation coppice is defined as "a perennial crop of tree species planted at high density, the stems of which are harvested above ground level at intervals of less than 10 years".[263] Cultivating short rotation coppice is a way of producing renewable fuel for bio-mass-fed power stations. In simple terms, willow or other cuttings are planted on farmland and, after the first year, are harvested every three years or so and then made into chips which are used as fuel.

Habitat schemes

26–121 The definition of "agricultural property" was further extended by the Finance Act 1997. In relation to transfers of value made and other events occurring on or after November 26, 1996, land in a habitat scheme was regarded as agricultural land and buildings used in connection with the management of land in accordance with the requirements of a habitat scheme were regarded as farm buildings.[264] Land was in a habitat scheme if an application for aid under one of the enactments listed in s.124C(3) had been accepted in respect of the land and the undertakings to which the acceptance

---

[261] HMRC Manuals IHTM24039.
[262] FA 1995 s.154(2)(a) and (b).
[263] FA 1995 s.154(3).
[264] IHTA 1984 s.124C(1).

related had neither been terminated by the expiry of the period to which they related nor been treated as terminated. In general terms the owner or occupier undertook to keep the land out of agricultural production for 20 years and manage it for the purpose of improving or maintaining it as a wildlife habitat.

From January 2000, the habitat scheme ceased in England and in effect it became subsumed into the existing Countryside Stewardship Scheme. This scheme does not ban agricultural activity and it does not include any specific option for taking land out of agricultural production. However, the scheme is not limited to agricultural land and therefore someone accepted into the scheme would not automatically qualify for agricultural relief.[265] In Scotland, the habitat scheme ceased on December 31, 1996 and was subsumed into the Countryside Premium Scheme.

There are many other agricultural schemes that can apply to agricultural land. The Farm Woodland Premium Scheme (administered by DEFRA) promotes the establishment of woodland by offering annual payments to compensate for the agricultural income foregone. The scheme is only open to farmers who, either personally or through a manager, run an agricultural business that includes the land to be converted to woodland. Agricultural relief is not available as the purpose of the scheme is to take the land out of agriculture.[266]

Appeals

26–122   Appeals on whether property is agricultural property are to the First-Tier Tribunal.[267]

Part 1 of the definition: agricultural land or pasture

26–123   The question has arisen as to whether "land" is to be given a wide meaning under the Interpretation Act 1978 to include buildings situated on that land. If so, it would mean that there was no need to address the more difficult question of whether a building comes within Pt 3. Thus, in *Starke (executors of Brown, Deceased) v IRC*[268] the taxpayers contended on this basis that a six bedroomed farmhouse set on 150 acres of land (and which would clearly not have satisfied the "character appropriate" requirement in Pt 3 of the definition) qualified for agricultural relief as "agricultural land" within Pt 1 of the definition. Not surprisingly, the Court of Appeal accepted the argument of the Revenue, as it then was, that the expression "agricultural land or pasture" meant bare land and should not be given the wider meaning adopted in the Interpretation Act (which applies "unless the contrary intention appears"), so making sense of Pts 2 and 3 of the definition.

In determining whether land is "agricultural" it is necessary to establish whether the principal purpose for which the land is used is agriculture; see para.26–117 concerning the definition of agriculture. HMRC accept that occasional use of agricultural land for purposes other than agriculture does not prevent the land from constituting agricultural property.[269] The example given is of farmland over which an annual point-to-point

[265] HMRC Manuals IHTM24066.
[266] HMRC Manuals ARTG 2050.
[267] IHTA 1984 s.222(2).
[268] *Starke (executors of Brown, Deceased) v IRC* [1995] S.T.C. 689.
[269] HMRC Manuals IHTM24061.

horse race is run. In *Dixon v IRC*[270] (see para.26–117), when considering whether the orchard and garden were agricultural land or pasture, the Special Commissioner said that there was a question as to whether the definition in s.115(2) required there to be some element of commerciality. This was not a question which she had to answer for the purpose of the appeal. However, she did comment that there is no mention of commerciality in s.115.[271]

HMRC take the view that land cultivated for the growing of energy crops is agricultural land and such use qualifies as occupation for agricultural purposes (see para.26–143). Cultivation of the land to produce the crop is a key requirement in enabling land to qualify for agricultural relief. HMRC has referred to a case[272] concerning reed beds that grow naturally and were then cut for thatching. There was no tilling, sowing or cultivating of the land and all the taxpayers did was to cut the reeds. The absence of tillage meant that the reed beds could not be classed as agricultural land. The generally accepted view is that land under cultivation will be regarded as being used for the purposes of agriculture.

Part 2 of the definition: woodlands and buildings connected with intensive rearing

26–124 The meaning of "woodlands" is discussed at para.26–196. See para.26–142 concerning whether woodlands are "occupied".

In deciding whether the occupation of woodlands is "ancillary" to the occupation of agricultural land or pasture, a practical approach is taken. A decision is made as to how much of the woodland is required to service all the agricultural needs of the occupier's holding. This might include woodland shelter belts, game coverts, fox coverts, coppices grown for fencing materials to be used on the farm and clumps of amenity trees or spinneys. Woodlands occupied other than for agricultural purposes such as amenity parkland or woodlands used for production of commercial timber will not be agricultural but may qualify for business relief (see paras 26–12–26–112) or woodlands relief (see paras 26–194–26–206).[273]

The inclusion in the definition of buildings used in connection with the intensive rearing of livestock or fish largely gives statutory effect to ESC J2, which applied for the purposes of CTT relief. The difference is that under that concession there was no requirement that the occupation had to be ancillary to that of agricultural land or pasture. Where buildings are used for intensive rearing but the occupation is not ancillary (e.g. because there are a large number of buildings and there is little or no agricultural land or pasture) business relief should be available. The rate of relief will be 100 per cent if the building is owned either by the transferor, and he is farming as a sole trader, or is an underlying asset of a farming partnership of which the transferor is a partner. Fifty per cent business relief will be available if the building is owned by the transferor and used for intensive rearing either by a partnership of which the transferor is a partner or by a company which he controls; this relief may be available against the tenanted value of the building.

It is understood that a fish breeding tank or pond may be regarded as a building used in connection with the intensive rearing of fish but that a stream or other flowing water

[270] *Dixon v IRC* [2002] S.T.C. (S.C.D.) 53.
[271] *Dixon v IRC* [2002] S.T.C. (S.C.D.) 53 at 59.
[272] *Tayside Region v Reedways Ltd* Unreported 1982.
[273] HMRC Manuals IHTM24032.

will not be.[274] A fish farm will not be treated as agricultural property if the fish are reared for sport. Oyster beds are not regarded as agricultural property.[275]

Under estate duty, a concession was extended to buildings used for intensive cultivation of mushrooms and to tomato glasshouses, and it is understood that this extension also applies for IHT.[276]

Definition of "occupied with"

The meaning of "occupied with" was reviewed by the House of Lords in the case of *Hambleton DC v Buxted Poultry Ltd*.[277] In order to succeed with their claim that a poultry processing factory was an agricultural building, Buxted Poultry Ltd had to show that the factory was "occupied together with" buildings used for the keeping or breeding of poultry. The House of Lords held that the factory was not an agricultural building and they indicated that for one building to be "occupied together with" another, both must be:

(1) in the same occupation and jointly controlled or managed at the same time; and

(2) occupied together so as to form a single agricultural unit.

As mentioned above, woodland and buildings used for the intensive rearing of live-stock or fish qualify for agricultural relief only if they are occupied with agricultural land and the occupation is ancillary to that of the land. Therefore, agricultural relief may not be available where there are buildings used for intensive farming activities such as egg production or breeding pigs and there is little or no land. However, business relief may be available if a business owns and occupies the buildings and land.

The case of *Williams (personal representative of Williams, Deceased) v RCC*[278] provides some helpful guidance on the issue. The deceased owned a poultry farm, comprising three broiler houses used for the intensive rearing of chickens and around seven acres of land.

On the deceased's death, the Special Commissioner had to decide whether the broiler houses attracted relief. He decided that they were properly described as farm buildings but that they would only pass the test in s.115(2) if they were occupied as a subsidiary part of the larger agricultural operation carried out on the other land with which they were occupied. The Special Commissioner's view was that the broiler houses domi-nated the land they occupied and there was no evidence of a wider agricultural operation on the remainder of the occupied land. The occupation of the broiler houses could not, therefore, be regarded as ancillary to that of the agricultural land.

It will be rare for an intensive building to satisfy Pt 2 as it is likely to be occupied for its own purposes and not ancillary to other land. If the intensive buildings are occupied by the transferor they will normally qualify for business relief if agricultural relief is not available. One exception may be if an intensive building was part of an

---

[274] *Hansard*, col.785 (June 18, 1981). See also HMRC Manuals IHTM24033.
[275] *Gunter v Newtown Oyster Fishery* (1977) 244 E.G. 140.
[276] *Shares Valuation Manual*, 27850.
[277] *Hambleton DC v Buxted Poultry Ltd* (1993) 2 W.L.R. 34.
[278] *Williams (personal representative of Williams, Deceased) v RCC* (2005) SpC 00500.

intensive and extensive mixed farming operation and was just a small part of that operation.

Part 3 of the definition: property of a character appropriate

This is the most difficult part of the definition of "agricultural property", largely **26–125** because of the character appropriate requirement. Before considering that requirement it may be helpful to make a few points about the various kinds of property mentioned in Pt 3 of the definition.

Cottages

Whilst HMRC has stated that agricultural relief is primarily intended to apply to **26–126** "cottages occupied by persons employed solely for agricultural purposes in connection with the agricultural property concerned",[279] there is scope for a cottage occupied by a retired farm employee or his surviving spouse or civil partner to qualify for relief. The questions of whether a cottage occupied by a retired farm employee or his surviving spouse or civil partner is occupied for the purposes of agriculture and whether it is of a character appropriate are considered at paras 26–129 and 26–131 respectively.

The circumstances in which 100 per cent agricultural relief is available are discussed generally at paras 26–134–26–139. HMRC's view has been that 100 per cent relief is available in respect of farm cottages if:

(1) the agricultural worker's occupation of the cottage was protected and the benefit of the transitional provisions[280] is available to the transferor;
(2) the agricultural worker occupied the cottage under an unprotected service tenancy; or
(3) the worker's occupation arose under a tenancy which began on or after September 1, 1995.

In all other circumstances HMRC's view has been that the rate is 50 per cent.[281]

This means that where a farm cottage is occupied by an agricultural worker under a pre-September 1, 1995, tenancy, which offers protection under the Rent (Agriculture) Act 1976, and the transferor does not benefit from the transitional provisions, only the lower rate of relief is available. The authors doubt the correctness of HMRC's approach.[282] It seems somewhat incongruous that an agricultural worker's occupation of a farm cottage can constitute occupation by the transferor for the purposes of s.117 (see para.26–144) but that the same "representative occupier" concept does not mean that 100 per cent relief is available under s.116(2)(a).

Farm buildings

Section 115(4) provides that any buildings used in connection with the breeding and **26–127** rearing of horses on a stud farm are to be taken to be farm buildings; see para.26–117.

---

[279] HMRC Manuals IHTM24034.
[280] IHTA 1984 ss.116(2) and 116(3).
[281] HMRC Manuals IHTM24034.
[282] See also *Private Client Business* (1998), pp.4 and 171.

Buildings used in connection with the cultivation of short rotation coppice also constitute farm buildings[283] (see para.26–120) as do buildings used in connection with the management of land in accordance with the requirements of a habitat scheme,[284] see para.26–121.

Farmhouses

26–128   There is no statutory definition of the term "farmhouse" but it is taken to be "a dwelling for the farmer from which the farm is managed".[285] Accordingly, there will usually only be one farmhouse per agricultural holding. In *Higginson's Executors v IRC*[286] a former hunting lodge on an estate comprising 63 acres of agricultural land, which the deceased had farmed and subsequently let on conacre terms, was held not to be a farmhouse within the meaning of s.115(2). This was despite the fact that the Revenue, as it then was, had conceded the land constituted a farm and the Special Commissioner stated that "where there is a farm one would ordinarily expect to find a farmhouse ancillary to the land".[287] The "single most significant fact" which went against the taxpayer (although arguably one which should not have been relevant) was the high price for which the estate was sold shortly after the transferor's death and which meant that, as a farm, the estate would represent "an appalling investment" in terms of yield. The Special Commissioner seems also to have been influenced by the "very attractive" nature of the residence, with its "fine rooms", in concluding there was a house with farmland, the house predominating the agricultural unit, and not vice versa. Interestingly, the Special Commissioner considered that the business plan and financial forecast drawn up to test the economic viability of the venture was "not deemed to be unsatisfactory". Indeed in *Lloyds TSB Bank Plc (Personal Representative of Antrobus (Deceased)) v Inland Revenue Commissioners*[288] the accounts showed that the farming business in question had been running at a loss from 1995, but the profitability of the farming activities was not deemed to be conclusive.[289]

Similar comments were echoed in *Golding v Revenue and Customs Commissioners*,[290] where it was held that the lack of a substantial profit was not "detrimental" to a decision that the farmhouse is "character appropriate".

In *Rosser v IRC*[291] the activities carried out at the property were important to the finding that it did not constitute a farmhouse. The Special Commissioner said that, despite a "proud history" as a farmhouse, immediately before the transferor's death the building had become a retirement home. The farm business was managed from elsewhere and the only activities being carried on at the building (provision of early morning refreshments and the midday meal and the storage of agricultural equipment and pesticides) were insufficient to characterise it as a farmhouse.

The subject of what is necessary for a house to qualify as a farmhouse for tax purposes was raised again in *Arnander (Executors of McKenna) v HMRC*.[292] The house

---

[283] FA 1995 s.154(2).
[284] IHTA 1984 s.124C(1)(c).
[285] *Rosser v IRC* [2003] S.T.C. (S.C.D.) 311 at 322.
[286] *Higginson's Executors v IRC* [2002] S.T.C. (S.C.D.) 483.
[287] *Higginson's Executors v IRC* [2002] S.T.C. (S.C.D.) 483 at 486.
[288] [2002] S.T.C. (S.C.D.) 468.
[289] *Private Client Business* (2003), p.2.
[290] [2011] UKFTT 351 (TC).
[291] *Rosser v IRC* [2003] S.T.C. (S.C.D.) 311.
[292] *Arnander (Executors of McKenna) v HMRC* (2006) S.P.C. 565.

(Rosteague House) was an Elizabethan manor house with seven bedrooms and 8,000 sq ft of accommodation. A separate farmhouse had been built in the early 1900s from which point the main house was separated from the farming. From 1984 Mr McKenna and his wife took on the farming and sold off the farmhouse. They were then 73 and 74 years old respectively and farmed through a contractor. Clearly, Rosteague House was not the farmhouse from the provision of the new farmhouse in 1908 until 1984. The question was whether Mr and Mrs McKenna had brought the farming in hand. The Special Commissioner said "if the farmer of the land is the person who farms it on a day-to-day basis rather than the person who is in over all control of the agricultural business conducted on the land then Mr McKenna was not the farmer. The purpose of the occupation at Rosteague House was not to undertake the day-to-day farming activities". As a result, the house was not a farmhouse.

As a result of the *Arnander* case, it will no longer be enough to show that the house is of a character appropriate to the land (see para.26–131) and that it is occupied for agriculture (see para.26–129) to secure agricultural relief on a farmhouse. It will also be necessary to show that the house was occupied in order to farm the land and, most importantly, the occupier farmed the land on a day-to-day basis. Being in overall control of the agricultural business is not sufficient. Contracting agreements should be reviewed carefully to ensure that day-to-day decision making is reserved by the occupier so that a farmhouse will qualify for relief.

HMRC make it clear that careful attention should be paid to claims for 100 per cent relief for farmhouses and, in particular, they will investigate whether the farmhouse was the centre of the farming operations conducted on the land.[293]

Occupation for agriculture

Derelict buildings are not occupied for the purposes of agriculture nor are buildings **26–129** used as a tack room as the livery of horses is not an agricultural purpose.[294] In either case relief will not be available.

The requirements of s.117 are discussed at paras 26–140–26–150, including the requirement that the property must have been occupied for the purposes of agriculture. Two specific points fall to be made about whether cottages and farmhouses have been occupied for the purposes of agriculture:

(1) ESC F16 provides that a cottage occupied by a retired farm employee or his surviving spouse shall be regarded as occupied for the purposes of agriculture provided that either the occupier is a statutorily protected tenant or the occupation is under a lease granted to the farm employee for his life and that of any surviving spouse as part of his contract of employment by the landlord for agricultural purposes. Presumably this will now apply to a surviving civil partner as well as a surviving spouse.
(2) A problem will arise if, e.g. a landed estate is farmed through a partnership and the transferor who resides in the farmhouse retires from the partnership—the farmhouse will cease to be occupied for the purposes of agriculture.

---

[293] HMRC Manuals IHTM24036.
[294] *Arnander (Executors of McKenna) v HMRC* (2006) S.P.C. 565.

In the case of *Arnander*,[295] the house could not be regarded as being "occupied for the purposes of agriculture" as required by s.117 as the owners were unable to attend personally to farming matters as they were elderly and infirm.

Character appropriate to the property: identifying the property

26–130 As indicated above, the requirement that the cottage, farm building or farmhouse must be of a character appropriate to the property is the most controversial and difficult requirement. The "character appropriate" issue normally arises in relation to renovated farmhouses of significant value, many of which bear little resemblance to the relatively humble abodes of the working farmers who originally occupied them.

In applying the character appropriate test it is first necessary to determine the "property" to which regard should be had. HMRC's view has always been that regard is had to the agricultural property within the transferor's estate immediately before the transfer. This includes land subject to grazing or mowing licences (however, it should be noted that lettings of more than one year may destroy the lessor's occupation of the land),[296] the transferor's interest in an agricultural tenancy (even though the tenancy may be of negligible value in his estate) or a farm business tenancy.[297] Land owned by a company controlled by the transferor or held as an underlying asset of a partnership of which he was then a member should also be taken into consideration. Where the transferor was a partner in a partnership, any land which is farmed by the partnership as tenant will also be taken into account. HMRC guidance indicates that where the interest amounts to less than a protected tenancy or a farm business tenancy, advice should be obtained from their Technical Group.[298]

In *Starke v IRC*.[299] Morritt L.J., whilst acknowledging that the "official view" was that there had to be a nexus derived from common ownership between the property claimed to fall within Pt 3 and other agricultural land or pasture, stated that "the alternative view might be that the nexus, which must surely be required, may be provided by common occupation without common ownership".[300] The Special Commissioner in *Rosser v IRC*[301] gave consideration to Morritt L.J.'s comments but agreed with the Revenue, as it then was, that the nexus must be derived from common ownership rather than common occupation—regard is to be had to the agricultural property in the transferor's estate when making the transfer.[302] He went on to emphasise the wide definition of property under the Act, giving as an example a person who at his death legally owned farm buildings and had a right of profit in agricultural property to which the character of the farm buildings was appropriate; both the farm buildings and the property would, he said, be part of the deceased's estate.[303]

HMRC suggest that in addition to there being unity of identity of ownership between the cottage, farm building or farmhouse and the property to which regard is had in applying the character appropriate test, there must also be unity of identity of occupation. The Special Commissioner in *Rosser* did not comment on whether there had to be common occupation in addition to common ownership in order for property to be taken

[295] *Arnander (Executors of McKenna) v HMRC* (2006) S.P.C. 565.
[296] HMRC Manuals IHTM24091.
[297] HMRC Manuals IHTM24074.
[298] HMRC Manuals IHTM24074.
[299] *Starke v IRC* [1995] S.T.C. 689.
[300] *Starke v IRC* [1995] S.T.C. 689 at 695.
[301] *Rosser v IRC* [2003] S.T.C. (S.C.D.) 311.
[302] *Rosser v IRC* [2003] S.T.C. (S.C.D.) 311 at 322.
[303] HMRC Manuals IHTM24033.

into account in applying the character appropriate test. However, it is important to have regard to land let away when identifying the total extent of agricultural property. If part of the land is let away, this will be a negative factor in determining whether the farmhouse, for example, is of a character appropriate to the agricultural land in the estate. However, there remains a degree of uncertainty over the relevant "nexus"; contrary to HMRC guidance, in the First-Tier Tribunal case of *Hanson v Revenue and Customs Commissioners*,[304] it was held that common occupation was the essential nexus, rather than common ownership. The main issue in this case was the connection between the agricultural land, most of which was not owned by the deceased but by his son, and the farmhouse on which inheritance tax relief was being claimed. The farmhouse was, at the time of Mr Hanson's death, owned by a trust of which he was the life tenant. It was occupied by his son who also owned and farmed 128 acres of land, together with some 28 acres owned by his father and some additional rented land. The tribunal held:

> "it seems to us that the purpose of the relief is to reduce the tax burden on agricultural property, including farmhouses, which have been occupied for the required period(s) for the purposes of agriculture 85 This statutory purpose does not seem to us to require that such a farmhouse must be part of a larger agricultural estate whose value is being charged to IHT at the same time and by reference to the same transfer."

The tribunal held that there was only a requirement for common occupation of the farmhouse and agricultural land, and not common ownership. It seems likely that HMRC will appeal this decision.

HMRC are understood to accept that agricultural property can be taken into account in applying the character appropriate test whether it falls within Pt 1 (agricultural land or pasture) or Pt 2 (woodlands and buildings used for intensive rearing of livestock or fish) of the definition contained in s.115(2) and even if it has not been occupied for the relevant period under s.117.

The appropriateness of the character

Having established the property to which regard should be had, it is then necessary **26–131** to assess whether, in relation to that property, the cottage, farm building or farmhouse is of a character appropriate. There is no single conclusive test. Consideration has been given to the appropriate tests to be applied in a number of cases:

(1) In *Starke v IRC*,[305] Blackburne J. on the initial appeal from the Special Commissioners commented (obiter) that for a cottage, farm building or farmhouse to be of a character appropriate it had to be "proportionate in size and nature to the requirements of the farming activities conducted on the agricultural land or pasture in question".[306]

(2) In *Dixon v IRC*[307] the Special Commissioner applied three tests[308]:

    (a) The elephant test—although you cannot describe a farmhouse which satisfies the character appropriate test you will know one when you see it.

    (b) Man on the (rural) Clapham omnibus—would the educated rural layman regard the property as a house with land or a farm?

---

[304] [2012] UKFTT 95 (TC).
[305] *Starke v IRC* [1994] S.T.C. 295; see para.26–130.
[306] *Starke v IRC* [1994] S.T.C. 295, at 299.
[307] *Dixon v IRC* [2002] S.T.C. (S.C.D.) 53; see para.26–117.
[308] *Dixon v IRC* [2002] S.T.C. (S.C.D.) 53 at 59.

(c) Historical dimension—how long has the house in question been associated with the agricultural property and is there a history of agricultural production?

She concluded that the deceased's cottage was not of a character appropriate to the 0.6 acres of garden and orchard in the deceased's estate at the date of her death (though, strictly speaking, it was not necessary for her to consider this issue having already concluded that the garden and orchard did not constitute agricultural land).

(3) In *Lloyds TSB (personal representative of Antrobus, Deceased) v IRC*[309] *(Antrobus No.1)* the Special Commissioner, in determining whether a farmhouse was of a character appropriate, referred to both the *Starke* and *Dixon* cases and summarised the relevant principles to be applied as follows[310]:

(a) Is the house appropriate, by reference to its size, content and layout, to the farm buildings and area of farmland being farmed?

This principle was derived from the House of Lord's decision in *IRC v Korner*,[311] an income tax case concerning the deductibility of expenditure on repairs and maintenance of a farmhouse. The issue of whether the property in question was a farmhouse had been conceded by the time the case reached the House of Lords but Lord Upjohn commented (obiter) that "to be the farmhouse for the purposes of [s.526 of the Income Tax Act 1952] it must be judged in accordance with ordinary ideas of what is appropriate in size, content and layout taken in conjunction with the farm buildings, and the particular area of farm land being farmed, and not part of a rich man's considerable residence".[312] The Special Commissioner said that, whilst Lord Upjohn's comments were relevant to the definition of a farmhouse rather than the question of whether a farmhouse was of a character appropriate, what he had said did encapsulate the idea that a farmhouse had to be of a character appropriate.[313]

(b) Is the house proportionate in size and nature to the requirements of the farming activities?—see *Starke* above.

(c) The so-called "elephant test"—see *Dixon* above.

(d) The so-called "man on the (rural) Clapham omnibus test"—see *Dixon* above.

(e) The so-called "historical dimension test"—see *Dixon* above.

(4) In *Antrobus No.1* the farmhouse was held to be of a character appropriate. Reference was made to the fact that the house had once been a family home of some distinction but had fallen into a poor state of repair and, at the transferor's death, was being used as any other farm building. Evidence showing the house was comparable, in size and layout, to 27 other farmhouses within the area was also influential; although, as has been pointed out, "why should all 27 properties be of a character appropriate?"[314]

Comparing the *Antrobus No.1* decision with the decision in *Higginson's Executors v IRC*[315] raises the concern that a house which has been kept in a good state of repair is less likely to qualify as a farmhouse which is of a character

[309] *Lloyds TSB (personal representative of Antrobus, Deceased) v IRC* [2002] S.T.C. (S.C.D.) 468.
[310] *Lloyds TSB (personal representative of Antrobus, Deceased) v IRC* [2002] S.T.C. (S.C.D.) 468 at 480.
[311] *IRC v Korner* [1969] 45 T.C. 287.
[312] *IRC v Korner* [1969] 45 T.C. 287 at 297.
[313] *Lloyds TSB (personal representative of Antrobus, Deceased) v IRC* [2002] S.T.C. (S.C.D.) 468 at 479.
[314] *Lloyds TSB (personal representative of Antrobus, Deceased) v IRC* [2002] S.T.C. (S.C.D.) 468 at 481.
[315] *Higginson's Executors v IRC* [2002] S.T.C. (S.C.D.) 483.

appropriate than one which has been allowed to fall into disrepair. This is echoed in *Golding*[316] where the poor condition of a property, Blue Gate Farm, appeared important in the determination that it was of a "character appropriate". Indeed, the tribunal considered that "the state and condition of the farm is such that it would only be acceptable as a farmhouse" and this meant that they were "satisfied that the educated rural layman would also agree that the house was a farmhouse".

(5) The principles enunciated in *Antrobus No.1* were applied in *Rosser v IRC*[317] to a barn, which it was held was of a character appropriate to the two acres of land comprised within the deceased's estate. The barn was also used to support the farming activities on 39 acres of land which the deceased had gifted to her daughter some years before her death. The Special Commissioner said that the fact that the barn had an association with the 39 acres as well as the two acres was "the more difficult aspect of this Appeal" but that s.115(2) did not require him to make a finding that the barn was used exclusively for the two acres. The question was whether the barn was of a character appropriate to the two acres. The association of the barn with the 39 acres was though a "material fact" which had to be weighed against the facts supporting the proposition that the barn was of a character appropriate to the two acres.[318]

(6) In the case of *Arnander* (see para.26–128), the size of the house was entirely disproportionate to the land being farmed and it was held that a rural layman would view it as a country house rather than a farmhouse.

It was noted at para.26–126 that special treatment applies to certain cottages occupied by a retired farm employee or his surviving spouse or civil partner. In a situation covered by ESC F16, HMRC is understood not to apply the character appropriate test unless any of the following circumstances apply:

(a) A physical characteristic of the cottage, e.g. its size, makes it inappropriate for occupation by a farm employee.

(b) There are more cottages occupied by retired farm employees than by active farm employees on the estate.

(c) When the retired farm employee was employed it was not on property in the transferor's estate at the date of the transfer, e.g. at the time the retired farm employee was employed the estate was considerably larger but a substantial part no longer belongs to the transferor.

HMRC provides guidance[319] on the factors that it will take into account when considering the character appropriate test, which reflects the decisions of the Special Commissioners in the above cases.

Definition of "agricultural value"

It will be recalled that only so much of the value transferred by a transfer of value **26–132** as is attributable to the agricultural value of agricultural property qualifies for relief. By s.115(3), the agricultural value of any agricultural property is taken to be:

---

[316] [2002] S.T.C. (S.C.D.) 483.
[317] *Rosser v IRC* [2003] S.T.C. (S.C.D.) 311.
[318] *Rosser v IRC* [2003] S.T.C. (S.C.D.) 311 at 325.
[319] HMRC Manuals IHTM24051.

" . . . the value which would be the value of the property if the property were subject to a perpetual covenant prohibiting its use otherwise than as agricultural property."

The effect of this definition is to exclude from the agricultural value of agricultural property any additional value arising from development or hope value[320] and any non agricultural use. Such value may qualify for business relief.

HMRC is known to contend that the agricultural value of farmhouses is approximately 30 per cent less than the open market value (even if there is no development potential) by drawing an analogy between the perpetual covenant of s.115(3) and an agricultural planning tie. Interestingly, in *Higginson's Executors v IRC*[321] the Special Commissioner stated (obiter) that where a house has "vanity value on account of its site, style or the like" this should not create a significant difference between the agricultural value and the open market value.[322] However, the approach of the Revenue, as it then was, was confirmed as being correct in *Lloyds TSB (personal representative of Antrobus, Deceased) v IR Capital Taxes*[323] (*Antrobus No.2*). *Antrobus No.1* had determined that the house qualified as a farmhouse; the question in *Antrobus No.2* was how far an assumed covenant against use other than as agriculture limited the value qualifying for agricultural relief.

HMRC argued that the requirement in s.115(3) to assume that the property was subject to a perpetual covenant prohibiting its use otherwise than as agricultural property was equivalent to a covenant in the standard form imposed for planning purposes. The PRs of the deceased argued that a farmhouse subject to a s.115(3) covenant could be occupied by any person who farms the surrounding farmland from the farmhouse whether or not he was solely or mainly employed in agriculture.

They further argued that this meant that the agricultural value of the farmhouse should reflect the amount that a "lifestyle" farmer might pay for it. The definition of "lifestyle" farmer (which was accepted by the Lands Tribunal) was a farmer who might spend 95 per cent or more of his time working elsewhere and still uses the property as agricultural property in compliance with the perpetual covenant.

The Lands Tribunal held that in order for a house to be a farmhouse for the purposes of the definition of agricultural property it should be the house of the person who lives in it in order to farm the land comprised in the farm and who farms the land on a day-to-day basis (see para.26–128). Therefore, the agricultural value of a property should be determined on the basis that the s.115(3) perpetual covenant would prevent its use other than in this way, thereby excluding the "lifestyle" farmer (whose principal reason for living in the house is the amenity afforded by it and by the land) and the additional amount he would be prepared to pay.

The Lands Tribunal stated that they did not think it was wrong to treat the s.115(3) perpetual covenant as equivalent to a standard agricultural planning tie. They considered such a condition as less restrictive as there was a prospect of release; it included occupiers who were employed in agriculture in the locality and it included occupiers "last working" in agriculture and their widows and widowers. The Lands Tribunal went a step further by saying that they did not think a farmhouse would automatically cease to be a farmhouse for the purposes of s.115(2) if a farmer who had lived there for many years retired but continued to live in the house or if he died and his widow continued to live there (see para.26–129).

The Lands Tribunal agreed that the agricultural value of the farmhouse in *Antrobus No.2* was established by applying a 30 per cent deduction from market value. In

[320] *Pissaridou v Rosser* (2005) Ew Lands TMA/40/2005.
[321] *Higginson's Executors v IRC* [2002] S.T.C. (S.C.D.) 483; see para.26–128.
[322] *Higginson's Executors v IRC* [2002] S.T.C. (S.C.D.) 483 at 487.
[323] *Lloyds TSB (personal representative of Antrobus, Deceased) v IR Capital Taxes* (2005) Ew Lands DET/47/2004.

reaching a decision, the Lands Tribunal looked at evidence of the sale of three properties subject to a standard agricultural planning tie and made limited external inspections of two farmhouses in respect of which agricultural values had been agreed between the taxpayer and HMRC. They also took into account the marketing and offers that were made for the deceased's property.

The Lands Tribunal decided that if they were incorrect about the "lifestyle" farmer point (such that the demand from a lifestyle farmer *may* be taken into account in calculating agricultural value), then the agricultural value would be 15 per cent less than market value. This is because, although the bids of lifestyle farmers are often above those of working farmers, a lifestyle farmer subject to an agricultural planning tie would not be prepared to pay as much for a property as someone who was not subject to the covenant.

Antrobus No.2, together with the case of *Pissaridou*,[324] is likely to have wide implications for purchasers and owners of agricultural property. Much farming is now done by contract farming arrangements and other methods, which may not be sufficient to qualify for the day-to-day farming basis that *Antrobus No.2* states. Equally, it may still be possible to show that, in different circumstances, the discount applied may be lower or even non-existent.

The definition of "agricultural value" also means that in determining the agricultural value of agricultural property there is no requirement to bring into account liabilities which have been incurred for the purposes of the farming business but which have been secured on property which is not agricultural property. The position thus compares favourably with that which obtains where business relief is available,[325] and makes investment in agricultural property that much more attractive from a planning standpoint.

Planning: switching liabilities

Advantages may be obtained by switching liabilities charged over agricultural **26–133** property to other assets owned by the taxpayer. Assume, e.g. that A dies leaving a farm worth £1,000,000 which is eligible for 100 per cent relief together with investments worth £500,000. The farm is subject to a mortgage of £500,000. The mortgage reduces the value of the farm for IHT purposes to £500,000. The value of the farm will qualify for 100 per cent agricultural relief (if its value is all agricultural value). If the charge was over the investments, the value of the investments would be reduced to nil for IHT purposes and the value of the farm would still qualify for 100 per cent agricultural relief, so that there was no IHT to pay.

XIII. NATURE OF THE RELIEF

As was mentioned above, the relief is given by way of a percentage reduction of so **26–134** much of the value transferred by a transfer of value as is attributable to the agricultural

---

[324] *Pissaridou v Rosser* (2005) Ew Lands TMA/40/2005.
[325] See para.25–79 and IHTA 1984 s.110(b).

value of the agricultural property.[326] One hundred per cent relief is available in the following three cases. In all other cases, the rate of relief is 50 per cent.

Vacant possession land

26–135 One hundred per cent relief is available if immediately before the transfer the transferor's interest in the property:

(1) carries the right to vacant possession; or
(2) carries the right to obtain vacant possession within the next 24 months; or
(3) is, notwithstanding the terms of the tenancy, valued at an amount broadly equivalent to the vacant possession value of the property.[327]

Section 116(2)(a) provides that 100 per cent relief is available only if there is vacant possession or the right to obtain it within the next 12 months. The extension to 24 months (and the inclusion of property valued at an amount broadly equivalent to its vacant possession value) came by virtue of an ESC (ESC F17) dated February 13, 1995. There had previously been difficulties with *Gladstone v Bower* tenancies since traditionally these were of 23 months' duration. With the passage of the Agricultural Tenancies Act 1995 such arrangements will in any event disappear. The current trend is in favour of share farming and contract farming agreements. Provided care is taken in the drafting of these agreements, the transferor should be entitled to 100 per cent relief under the "vacant possession" heading.

Section 116(6) provides that for the purposes of establishing whether there is a right to vacant possession or a right to obtain it within the period specified, the interest of one of two or more joint tenants or tenants in common (or in Scotland, joint owners or owners in common) is taken to carry this kind of right if the interests of all of them together carry this right.

The vacant possession requirement raises certain questions. Firstly, the position is not clear where a person lets land to a partnership of which he is a partner. It would seem strange for him to be regarded as having vacant possession on the basis of his two (freehold and leasehold) interests. Rather it is thought that 100 per cent relief will be available if the partnership has a post-August 31, 1995, tenancy[328] but only 50 per cent relief in the case of an older tenancy (unless the transitional provisions apply).[329] If no tenancy has arisen, whether the transferor's interest carries the right to obtain vacant possession within 24 months will depend upon the provisions as regards dissolution contained in the partnership agreement. Secondly, although as a matter of law a tenant for life under a Settled Land Act 1925 settlement could be regarded as having vacant possession, a tenant for life under a trust of land could not, even if he had a right to occupy the land. Nevertheless, it is thought that in practice a person with an interest in possession in settled property will be regarded by HMRC as having the right to vacant possession if the trustees have that right subject only to that person's entitlement under

---

[326] IHTA 1984 s.116(1). IHTA 1984 s.116(7) provides that for this purpose "the value transferred by a transfer of value shall be calculated as a value on which no tax is chargeable." Since tax is charged on chargeable transfers and not on transfers of value this provision is pointless; it is probably a hold over from the original relief found in Sch.8 to the FA 1975.

[327] IHTA 1984 s.116(2) and ESC F17.

[328] See para.26–138.

[329] See para.26–137.

the terms of the settlement to occupy the property in question.[330] Finally, it seems that where a person owns a freehold tenanted by a company which he controls he will satisfy the vacant possession requirement.[331]

Planning: disturbing existing structures

Whether it will be advantageous to disturb an existing structure in order to achieve **26–136**
100 per cent relief (under s.116(2)(a) or (c)) is questionable and each case must turn on its own facts. If it is assumed that tenanted land has a value equal to 50 per cent of vacant possession value, then the tax position of the owner is that 50 per cent of his tenanted value is relieved leaving 25 per cent of the freehold value subject to the IHT charge. At a top rate of 40 per cent, that works out at an average tax rate of 10 per cent which, payable annually by instalments, equals a tax charge of 1 per cent per annum —not enough, it may be thought, to disturb complex existing arrangements given the possibility that 100 per cent relief may be withdrawn in the future.

The position may be easier following the Regulatory Reform (Agricultural Tenancies) (England and Wales) Order 2006, which has amended s.4 of the Agricultural Tenancies Act 1995. This now enables a new tenancy agreement to be granted to an existing tenant under which the tenant continues to enjoy the rights given to him under the Agricultural Holding Act 1986. HMRC accept that agricultural relief is available at a rate of 100 per cent provided the tenancy is granted after August 31, 1995.[332] In valuation terms, the tenant is disposing of one tenancy in exchange for another of equal value and so there should be no transfer of value for inheritance tax purposes. There should also be no chargeable gain for capital gains tax purposes unless HMRC argue that the tenancy has a capital value (see comments at para.26–138).[333]

Tenanted land: transitional provisions

It may be that a transferor does not qualify for 100 per cent relief on the basis of **26–137**
vacant possession. In that case, provided he has been beneficially entitled to his interest since before March 10, 1981, 100 per cent relief may still be available under the transitional provisions of ss.116(2)(b) and (3) in respect of so much of the value transferred as would have qualified for agricultural relief under the Finance Act 1975 had he disposed of his interest by a transfer of value at midnight on March 9, 1981, and claimed that relief.[334] If the £250,000/1,000 acre limit that applied under the Finance Act 1975 is exceeded, the excess qualifies for only 50 per cent relief.[335]

Three comments are in order concerning the transitional provisions governing tenanted land. Firstly, the relief is not intended to assist those who since the introduction of the new relief have ceased, be it by an act of commission or omission, to enjoy vacant possession. Accordingly, the legislation provides that 100 per cent relief will not

---

[330] See note of a meeting between The Law Society and the Revenue; *Simon's Tax Intelligence*, August 21, 1981, p.436.

[331] ESC F17.

[332] HMRC Manuals IHTM24243.

[333] If there were a gain, roll-over relief should be available under TCGA 1992 s.152. Care should be taken if the new tenancy is considered a wasting asset as a gain might become chargeable under TCGA 1992 s.154(2).

[334] See 3rd edn of *McCutcheon*, paras 26–110 and following for a full discussion of agricultural relief under the FA 1975.

[335] IHTA 1984 s.116(4).

be available under this head if since March 10, 1981, the transferor's interest has either carried the right to vacant possession or the right to obtain that right within the next 12 months, or failed to do so by reason of his deliberate act or omission.[336] Secondly, it may be that a transferor became entitled to his interest on the death of his spouse or civil partner on or after March 10, 1981. In that case, s.120(2) deems him to have been entitled to his interest for any period for which his spouse or civil partner was entitled to it, but 100 per cent relief is available only if:

(1) the deceased spouse or civil partner would have qualified for agricultural relief under the Finance Act 1975 if he/she had disposed of his/her interest by a transfer of value at midnight on March 9, 1981, and claimed that relief; and
(2) neither the transferor's interest nor that of the deceased spouse or civil partner carried the right to vacant possession or the right to obtain that right within the next 12 months, or failed to do so by reason of the deliberate act or omission of the person in question.

Finally, the extension of 100 per cent relief to qualifying tenanted land is intended to prevent a transferor whose land was tenanted before March 10, 1981, and who qualified for agricultural relief, from being prejudiced by the introduction of the new legislation. Section 116(5) accordingly provides that in deciding whether the £250,000/1,000 acre limit is exceeded there must be brought into account transfers of value made on or after March 10, 1981, only if relief has been claimed in respect of them under the transitional provisions. A transferor approaching the limit thus does not have to worry about transferring land in respect of which 100 per cent relief is sought under these provisions before transferring any other land.

Tenancies

26–138   With the passage of the Agricultural Tenancies Act 1995, and in order to encourage the creation of new farm tenancies, the Finance Act 1995 extended 100 per cent relief to landlords in cases where property is let on tenancies beginning on or after September 1, 1995.

In order to qualify as a farm business tenancy for the purposes of the Agricultural Tenancies Act 1995, the tenancy must satisfy the following conditions:

(1) the business condition—all or part of the land must be farmed for the purposes of a trade or a business and must have been since the commencement of the tenancy; and one of either,
(2) the agriculture condition—having regard to the use of the land, the nature of any commercial activities and any other relevant circumstances the nature of the tenancy must be wholly or primarily agriculture; or
(3) the notice condition—the parties have served notice on each other specifying that the tenancy can remain an agricultural tenancy even if the predominant use of the land and/or buildings becomes non-agricultural.

Two points are worth highlighting. Firstly, if the notice condition is satisfied agricultural relief will not be available to the extent that the land is occupied for non

---

[336] IHTA 1984 s.116(3)(b).

agricultural purposes even if it remains a farm business tenancy. Secondly, if the agriculture condition is satisfied and the owner of the land allows non agricultural business activities there is a concern that the tenant will have security of tenure under the Landlord and Tenant Act 1954 unless this is specifically excluded.

HMRC has confirmed in Revenue Interpretation 121 that 100 per cent relief applies in the case of all tenancies beginning on or after September 1, 1995: i.e. the relevant tenancy does not have to be a new style farm business tenancy under the 1995 legislation but would include, for instance, successor tenancies under the previous legislation.

The Finance Act 1996 extended 100 per cent relief where one tenant succeeds another after August 31, 1995, by adding three new categories to s.116 as follows:

(1) After August 31, 1995, a tenant dies and the tenancy becomes vested in another person (as a result of him being beneficially entitled under the deceased tenant's will or his intestacy) and is binding on the landlord and that person as landlord and tenant respectively (i.e. without any grant of a new tenancy). The deemed new tenancy is treated as arising on the death of the tenant.[337]

(2) Where there is a statutory succession to a tenancy as a result of the death of the tenant after August 31, 1995, the successor's tenancy is treated as beginning at the date of death, not as from the date of the grant (so that if the landlord died between those dates 100 per cent relief would be available).[338] This provision does not apply in relation to property in Scotland.[339]

(3) Where the transferor dies after August 31, 1995, the tenant having previously given notice of intention to retire in favour of a new tenant, then provided such retirement occurs within 30 months of the notice, the tenancy thereupon granted or assigned to the new tenant is treated as commencing immediately before the death of the owner of the land.[340]

In terms of the tenancy itself, traditionally a tenancy granted at a rack rent was thought not to have any capital value, but it is understood that HMRC sometimes challenge this view and attempt to ascribe a capital value to a tenancy granted at a rack rent, on the basis that the landlord would be prepared to buy the tenant out in order to secure vacant possession. Whether a given tenancy can be regarded as having a capital value will depend on the terms of that tenancy and the circumstances of the landlord and the tenant.[341] Tenants are known to have received up to half the difference of the value of the land with vacant possession and the value of the land tenanted, and HMRC is well aware of this. A tenancy to which a capital value is ascribed should itself qualify for 100 per cent agricultural relief unless there has been a sub-letting, in which case the sub-lease may qualify for 100 per cent relief while the head-lease will qualify for at most 50 per cent relief.

One point worth highlighting is that where there is a farm business tenancy, a landowner will only qualify for agricultural relief on the agricultural value of the land. There will be no business relief for any development or hope value or any other non agricultural value such as amenity value. Business relief might be available if instead of a farm business tenancy the land is farmed under a suitable contract farming or other

[337] IHTA 1984 s.116(5A).
[338] IHTA 1984 s.116(5B).
[339] IHTA 1984 s.116(5C).
[340] IHTA 1984 s.116(5D).
[341] See paras 25–45–25–47.

in hand arrangement. If a farmhouse is involved note comments at para.26–128 in respect of day to day decision making.

Reverse double discounting

26–139   Prior to the extension of 100 per cent relief to cases where property is let on tenancies beginning on or after September 1, 1995, there was a danger of reverse double discounting, i.e. tax being charged on a vacant possession basis with only 30/50 per cent relief being given. Assume, e.g. that in 1994 X, who had farmed his land for the past eight years, granted a tenancy over his land to his son in circumstances such that s.16[342] applied, and that two years later he gave the freehold to his son. It appears that it would have been open to the Revenue, as it then was, to argue that:

(1) the grant of the tenancy and the gift of the freehold were associated operations which effected a transfer of value of the freehold land valued on a vacant possession basis; and

(2) at the time of the transfer the land was tenanted, with the result that only 30/50 per cent relief was available.

Difficulties may also have arisen where (prior to September 1, 1995) a farmer let his farm to himself and his wife, perhaps as partners. The tenancy, given the related property rules, would not have devalued the farm, but would have meant that only 30/50 per cent relief was available.

XIV. CONDITIONS FOR RELIEF

26–140   Relief will be available, so long as the property is not subject to a binding contract for sale, if either of two tests is satisfied with regard to the agricultural property to which the value transferred by the transfer of value in question is attributable. These tests are as follows:

(1) two-year test: throughout the two years ending with the date of the transfer the transferor must have occupied the property for the purposes of agriculture[343]; or

(2) seven-year test: throughout the seven years ending with the date of the transfer:
   (a) the transferor must have owned the property; and
   (b) the transferor or someone else must have occupied the property for the purposes of agriculture.[344]

It is important to note that under the two-year test the only requirement is one of occupation, i.e. there is no requirement that the transferor owned the property in question throughout the two years, or any lesser period, preceding the transfer. Thus, if X, having farmed Y's land for two years, buys the land and immediately gives it to his son he will qualify for relief under the two-year test even though he owned the land

---

[342] See para.2–54.
[343] IHTA 1984 s.117(a).
[344] IHTA 1984 s.117(b).

only momentarily and in circumstances where no business relief would be available. Under the seven-year test, on the other hand, the transferor must have owned the property throughout the preceding seven years, but he need not have himself occupied it at all during that period. All that matters is that it was occupied for agricultural purposes *throughout* that period by someone, be it an individual, trustees or a company, or by a combination of two or more such occupants.

Two traps in particular are worth noting. First, under both tests the requirements must be satisfied *throughout* the period in question, so that a vacancy, however short, will render the relief unavailable. Secondly, an individual may qualify for 100 per cent relief under the two-year test; if he then lets his land, he will qualify for relief only under the seven-year test, with the result that he may have to wait for as long as five years before he qualifies for any agricultural relief at all.

Occupation test

"Occupation" is a crucial requirement, not only for the purposes of the tests discussed at para.26–140 above but also, for instance, for the purposes of s.115(2) which provides that woodlands and any building used in connection with the intensive rearing of livestock or fish constitute agricultural property "if the woodland or building is occupied with agricultural land or pasture". **26–141**

Characteristics of occupation

Consideration was given in *Harrold's Executors v IRC*[345] to the characteristics of occupation. The case involved a dilapidated farmhouse situated on land farmed by the deceased and his son in partnership. The house had been unoccupied and in the process of renovation from July 1983, when the vendor moved out, until February 1986 when the deceased gave his share in the house to his son; the father died in August 1990. Between July 1983 and February 1986 the house was unfurnished apart from normal fixtures and some carpets. The son went into the house three or four times a week to carry out minor running repairs. The major works of renovation were commenced in mid-1985, with a view to the son eventually moving in. The Special Commissioner referred to a number of cases concerning the meaning of "occupied": **26–142**

(1) *Graysim Holdings Ltd v P&O Property Holdings Ltd*[346] a case concerning Pt II of the Landlord and Tenant Act 1954. Lord Nicholls stated:

> "the concept of occupation is not a legal term of art, with one single and precise legal meaning applicable in all circumstances . . . In many factual situations questions of occupation will attract the same answer, whatever the context . . . But the answer in situations which are not so clear cut is affected by the purpose for which the concept of occupation is being used. In such situations the purpose for which the distinction between occupation and non-occupation is being drawn, and the consequences flowing from the presence or absence of occupation, will throw light on what sort of activities are or are not to be regarded as occupation in the particular context."[347]

---

[345] *Harrold's Executors v IRC* [1996] S.T.C. (S.C.D.) 195.
[346] *Graysim Holdings Ltd v P&O Property Holdings Ltd* [1996] A.C. 329.
[347] *Graysim Holdings Ltd v P&O Property Holdings Ltd* [1996] A.C. 329 at 334.

(2) *Associated Cinema Properties Ltd v Hampstead BC*,[348] a rating case. Du Parcq L.J. stated:

> "It is significant that no case could be cited in which occupation had been held to be established without proof of some overt act amounting to evidence of user . . . a mere intention to occupy premises on the happening of a future uncertain event cannot, without more, be regarded as evidence of occupation."[349]

(3) *Arbuckle Smith & Co Ltd v Greenock Corp*,[350] another rating case. Lord Reid stated:

> "I think that it would accord with the ordinary use of language to say that the owner who in some way enjoys the accommodation is occupying the premises, but that the owner who merely maintains, repairs or improves his premises is not thereby occupying them."[351]

With Lord Nicholls' comments in the *Graysim* case in mind, the Special Commissioner in the *Harrold* case then considered the characteristics of occupation of various types of agricultural property, which he said differed according to the use to which they are put:

> "Arable land is usually sown with seed, the harvest is taken and carried and the land is ploughed. Pasture is typically used for grazing sheep and cattle. Woodland on the other hand may require little or no attention depending on the state of the crop of trees grown thereon. In early years after it has been planted up, it requires far more attention than in later years as the trees grow towards maturity. The characteristics of occupation of woodland differ markedly from those relating to arable land and to pasture. So too does the occupation of farm cottages which characteristically are physically occupied by farm employees and therefore are occupied by the employer. The occupation of woodland might be said to border on what Lord Nicholls called 'non-occupation'. Nevertheless on that woodland or in that woodland a crop (of timber, typically) is growing and thereby it can be said to be occupied by the farmer for that purpose."[352]

The Special Commissioner went on to hold that the farmhouse had not been occupied by the partners (i.e. the father and son) for the two years prior to the date of the transfer to the son.

In the not uncommon case of dilapidated (and therefore unused) farm buildings the *Harrold* case confirms that agricultural relief will not typically be available. However, HMRC has accepted that certain periods of non-occupation of a property are unavoidable. They should, therefore, normally disregard a necessary absence whilst a building is cleared of rot and re-roofed provided that the works are carried out in a business-like manner.[353] However, the absence of four years whilst the supposed occupant was living in a care home was found in *Atkinson v Revenue and Customs Commissioners*,[354] on appeal to the Upper Tax Tribunal, to be too significant for this to qualify as occupation for the purposes of the occupation test.

The facts of the case were as follows. The deceased, Mr Atkinson, had been a partner in a farming partnership conducted on land let to the partners under a tenancy agreement. Mr Atkinson lived in a bungalow built on the farm holding for a number of

---

[348] *Associated Cinema Properties Ltd v Hampstead BC* [1944] K.B. 412.
[349] *Associated Cinema Properties Ltd v Hampstead BC* [1944] K.B. 412 at 416.
[350] *Arbuckle Smith & Co Ltd v Greenock Corp* [1960] A.C. 813.
[351] *Arbuckle Smith & Co Ltd v Greenock Corp* [1960] A.C. 813 at 824.
[352] *Harrold's Executors v IRC* [1996] S.T.C. (S.C.D.) 195 at 202.
[353] HMRC Manuals IHTM24114.
[354] [2011] UKUT 506 (TCC).

years until he became ill in 2002. Following a period in hospital, he went to live in a care home until his death four years later. Prior to his death, he made occasional visits to the bungalow which remained furnished and contained his belongings, and he continued as a partner in the farming business. The Upper Tax Tribunal held that there must be a sufficient objective connection between occupation and agricultural activity. This would not necessarily be met by identifying continuing links with the property in question or an agricultural business. The only time that the bungalow had been occupied for the purposes of agriculture was through Mr Atkinson using it as a dwelling prior to his living in the care home. Once Mr Atkinson stopped living in the bungalow, its primary purpose for agriculture was no longer satisfied. Moreover, the Upper Tax Tribunal held that the fact that Mr Atkinson remained as a partner did not mean that the bungalow continued to be occupied for the purpose of agriculture by the partnership. In this case an important factor was that it was clear that Mr Atkinson would never be able to return to the property.

Occupation for the purposes of agriculture

26–143 HMRC has accepted that the following land uses are occupation for the purposes of agriculture[355]:

(1) Cultivation to produce food for human consumption.
(2) Use to support livestock kept to produce food for human consumption, such as meat or other products, such as wool.
(3) The keeping of such other animals as may be found on an ordinary farm, e.g. horses kept for farm work.
(4) The breeding and grazing of racehorses on a stud farm.
(5) Land set aside for permanent or rotational fallow.

Land grazed by horses which are not racehorses on a stud farm or kept for farm work is not occupied for the purposes of agriculture. In *Wheatley v IRC*[356] the deceased had owned, throughout the seven years prior to his death, a meadow which had been subject to a grazing agreement. The grazier used the land for feeding horses, not for rearing or breeding them. It was agreed that the meadow was pasture within s.115(2) but also that the horses were not in any way connected with use for agriculture or any business purpose. The Special Commissioner agreed with the Revenue, as it then was, that for land used solely for grazing horses to be "occupied for the purposes of agriculture" the horses had to have a connection with agriculture. In this case, this was not so; they were neither livestock nor part of a stud farming business. Consequently, agricultural relief was not available.

Actual, representative and notional occupation

26–144 It appears that, for the purposes of s.117, occupation falls into three general categories—actual, representative and notional. It is clear that where a person actually occupies land physically he is an occupier for these purposes, and this is so regardless

---

[355] HMRC Manuals IHTM24102. See para.26–129 concerning the occupation of farm cottages and farmhouses for the purposes of agriculture.
[356] *Wheatley v IRC* [1998] S.T.C. (S.C.D.) 60.

of his status as an occupier, be it as owner, tenant or licensee. In addition, representative, as opposed to actual occupation, may also suffice, so that tied cottages occupied by employees may qualify for relief under the two year test, as may a house occupied by a farm manager. Where land is farmed by a partnership, each partner is as a matter of law in occupation of all the land.[357] This is accepted by HMRC.[358] However, this should be considered in light of *Atkinson* (see para.26–142 above). Once Mr Atkinson ceased living in the property, the partnership ceased to have a connection with that property. Lastly, in certain cases a person may qualify for relief even though he has not been in actual or legal occupation for the requisite period. This is because the legislation provides that in certain cases a person is to be treated as having occupied property.

What is also clear is that trustees who employ a farm manager and who take the benefit of the farm profits and the burden of the farm losses are in occupation.

Ordinarily, a person will not be in occupation where he lets a farm to a third party who himself carries on the trade of farming. An owner might like to consider alternative arrangements, for example, a suitably drafted contract farming arrangement if he wants to be in occupation.

Grazing licences through farm business tenancies will normally give the tenant the right to occupy the land. This will usually mean that the owner will have to satisfy the seven year ownership requirement to secure agricultural relief rather than the two year occupation test. Care should therefore be taken in respect of licences to graze animals or take grass from land. Provided a grazing licence is for less than one year and the owner retains responsibility for hedging, ditching or fertilizing the land and periodically inspects the grazier's animals he should continue to be regarded as occupying the land. Similarly, where there is a licence for the sale of grass, the owner should retain responsibility for preparing the land for agricultural use so that he continues to be regarded as occupying the land.[359]

Notional occupation

26–145   In seven cases, a person is treated as occupying land, as follows:

(1) *Death.* By s.120(1)(a), where a transferor becomes entitled to agricultural property on the death of a person and subsequently occupies the property his occupation is deemed to have begun on that person's death. Strictly speaking, a person does not on the death of another become entitled to property which forms part of the deceased's unadministered residuary estate and which is liable to realisation in the administration of the estate,[360] but HMRC is thought not to take this point in practice.[361]

(2) *Death of spouse or civil partner.* By s.120(1)(b), if the deceased was the transferor's spouse or civil partner, the transferor is deemed to have occupied the property for any period for which the spouse or civil partner actually, legally or notionally occupied it. Where, on the other hand, the transfer is inter

[357] HMRC Manuals IHTM24072. Except in Scots law, which is varied for this purpose, but see para.26–145, para.5. For a consideration of whether a limited partner under the Limited Partnerships Act 1907 occupies agricultural property, see *Private Client Business* 1997, p.67, and for the position in Scotland, *Private Client Business* 1997, p.248.
[358] HMRC Manuals IHTM24072.
[359] HMRC Manuals IHTM24073 and 24074.
[360] *Sudeley v AG* [1896] 1 Q.B. 354.
[361] HMRC Manuals IHTM24121.

vivos, the donee spouse or civil partner gets no credit for the donor spouse's or civil partner's occupation.

(3) *Replaced property.* It may be that the property occupied by the transferor at the time of the transfer replaced other agricultural property he occupied for agricultural purposes. In that case s.118(1) (in order to allow for sales and purchases) provides for the two-year occupation test to be satisfied if the respective periods of occupation together total at least two years out of the five years immediately preceding the transfer. Section 118(3) prevents a person from obtaining extra relief by replacing property with more valuable property by providing that the relief given is limited to that which would have been given if no replacement had been made. For this purpose, changes resulting from the formation, alteration or dissolution of a partnership are ignored.[362]

(4) *Company occupation.* By s.119(1), a transferor is treated as occupying property which a company he controls[363] occupies.

(5) *Partnerships.* Occupation by a partnership constitutes occupation by all the partners. Similarly, members of a limited liability partnership are treated as occupying any property which the limited liability partnership occupies.[364] Although see *Atkinson* at paras 26–142 and 26–144 above.

(6) *Scottish partnerships.* By s.119(2), occupation by a Scottish partnership is treated as occupation of it by the partners notwithstanding s.4(2) of the Partnership Act 1890.

(7) *Successions.* See para.26–148.

There may be a difficulty with the notional occupation rules in the following situation. Assume that Mr Smith acquired a farm in January 2000 which he farmed himself until his death in June 2002. Under the terms of his will the farm passed on a life interest trust to his surviving spouse and the trustees took over the farming of the land. If Mrs Smith were to die in June 2004 the IHT position is that:

(a) she is treated as having owned the land from the date of her husband's acquisition in 2000 (see para.26–147, para.2); and

(b) her interest in the farm carries the right to vacant possession,

but is she in occupation? HMRC's approach to such situations is not known. There is a risk that she will not be regarded as having been in occupation and, because the total ownership period is less than seven years, agricultural relief will not be available on her death.

Ownership test

The rules governing agricultural relief present semantic difficulties[365] in that in some places reference is made to ownership, whereas in others reference is made to beneficial entitlement. A question thus arises as to whether a person beneficially entitled to an interest in possession in agricultural property is regarded as owning that property for these purposes. Strictly, a tenant for life under a Settled Land Act settlement and not the trustees thereof can be said to "own" the property in question. A tenant for life   **26–146**

---

[362] IHTA 1984 s.118(4).

[363] See para.26–08.

[364] HMRC Manuals IHTM24072. IHTA 1984 s.267A(a) as inserted by the Limited Liability Partnership Act 2000 s.11 with effect from April 6, 2001.

[365] Compare the discussion at para.26–09.

under a trust of land, on the other hand, cannot be said to "own" the trust property: the trustees own it. It is understood that HMRC regard s.49(1) as sufficient to impute ownership to any individual with an interest in possession in settled property, so that these difficulties should not cause practical problems.[366] Following the Finance Act 2006, a person will only be imputed with ownership if he has an interest in possession that satisfies s.49(1A). For the purposes of s.49(1A) the interest in possession must be one in existence before March 22, 2006, an immediate post death interest, a disabled person's interest or a transitional serial interest.[367] This is referred to in the remainder of this chapter as a non relevant property interest in possession. The ownership requirement is, of course, relevant only under the seven-year test.

Notional ownership

26–147   In six cases, a person is treated as owning agricultural property, as follows:

(1) *Death.* By s.120(1)(a), where a transferor became entitled to the property on the death of a person, his ownership is deemed to have begun on that person's death. He is thus credited with ownership during the administration of the deceased's estate. This will apparently apply where property is redirected to a person under a variation within s.142, with the result that the person to whom the property is redirected is treated as having owned the property from the date of death, not merely from the date on which the variation was effected. As stated at para.26–145, para.1, HMRC are not thought to take the point that, strictly speaking, a person does not on the death of another become entitled to property which forms part of the deceased's unadministered residuary estate.

(2) *Death of spouse or civil partner.* By s.120(1)(b), if the deceased was the transferor's spouse or civil partner, the transferor is deemed to have owned the property for any period for which his spouse or civil partner owned it. This does not apply on an inter vivos spouse or civil partner transfer.

(3) *Replacements.* It may be that the property owned by the transferor at the time of the transfer replaced other agricultural property he owned some time during the 10 years immediately preceding the transfer. In that case, s.118(2) provides that the seven-year ownership (and occupation) condition is satisfied if the respective periods of ownership together totalled at least seven of the 10 years and throughout this combined period of ownership the property was occupied by the transferor or another for the purposes of agriculture. Section 118(3) limits the relief available in such circumstances, as mentioned in para.26–145, para.3.

(4) *Limited liability partnership.* Members of a limited liability partnership are treated as being entitled to any property to which the limited liability partnership is entitled.[368]

(5) *Transitional provisions.* See para.26–137.

---

[366] See note of a meeting between The Law Society and the Revenue; *Simon's Tax Intelligence,* August 21, 1981, p.436.

[367] IHTA 1984 s.49 (1A).

[368] IHTA 1984 s.267A(a) as inserted by the Limited Liability Partnership Act 2000 s.11 with effect from April 6, 2001.

(6) *Successions*. See below.

Successions

As a kind of quick succession relief, s.121 provides that the conditions as to **26–148** occupation and ownership are deemed to be satisfied in respect of a transfer where the following conditions are satisfied:

(1) There must have been an earlier transfer of value which qualified for Ch.II relief or which would have qualified for such relief if the relief had then been available to transfers of value.

(2) Either the earlier transfer or the current transfer must have been made on death.

(3) The property which in relation to the earlier transfer qualified (or would have qualified) for relief must have become through that transfer the property of either the current transferor or the current transferor's spouse.

(4) At the time of the current transfer the property in question must be occupied for agricultural purposes by:
   (a) the current transferor; or
   (b) the personal representatives of the earlier transferor.

(5) Apart from the ownership and/or occupation requirements, the property in question would have been eligible for relief in relation to the current transfer.

It may be that the property which satisfies the above requirements directly or indirectly replaces property which would have been eligible for relief. In that case, s.121(2) prevents a person from obtaining extra relief by replacing property with more valuable property by providing that the relief is limited to that which would have been given if no replacement had been made. For this purpose, changes resulting from the formation, alteration or dissolution of a partnership are ignored.

The legislation makes special provision to deal with the case where the value transferred by the earlier transfer was not wholly attributable to the agricultural value of the agricultural property in question. In such circumstances, only a proportion of the amount of the agricultural value of the agricultural property by reference to which the value transferred by the current transfer is determined is brought into account. Assume, for example, that only one-third of the earlier transfer was attributable to the agricultural value of agricultural property. In that case, the agricultural value of the agricultural property by reference to which the current transfer is calculated will be reduced by two-thirds.[369]

Settled property[370]

Applying the provisions to settled property can be difficult. In particular, questions **26–149** may arise as to whether a person entitled to an interest in possession in land can be said (a) to enjoy vacant possession of the land, and (b) to own land within the meaning of Ch.II. As noted in para.26–135 and at para.26–146 above, in practice HMRC will

---

[369] IHTA 1984 s.121(3).
[370] See also "Agricultural Tenancies of Settled Property" (1983) 80, *The Law Society Gazette* 2109.

regard a person with a non relevant property interest in possession as having vacant possession if the trustees, subject to his entitlement, have vacant possession, and, will regard a person entitled to such an interest in possession in land as owning that land. Where the property is held in a trust where a beneficiary does not have a non relevant property interest in possession the trustees will be treated as owning the land. The general rule is that relief is most likely to be available under the seven-year test, because under that test there is no requirement that the transferor occupied the land. Relief will be available under the two-year occupation test as follows:

(1) Non relevant property interest in possession trust:
    (a) 100 per cent relief: available if the person entitled to the interest is in occupation under the terms of the settlement, in which case he is regarded as having vacant possession.
    (b) 50 per cent relief: may only be available if the person entitled to the interest is in occupation other than under the settlement, e.g. under a pre-September 1, 1995, lease, since in such circumstances he may not be regarded as having vacant possession. HMRC's position on this point is not known.
(2) Discretionary trust:
    (a) 100 per cent relief: available only if the trustees (the transferor in such a case) are in occupation, e.g. because they carry on a business.
    (b) 50 per cent relief: unlikely to be applicable, since trustees rarely, as trustees, occupy as tenants. However, it may be relevant if trustees are members of a farming partnership and a pre-September 1, 1995, tenancy has been granted to the partnership.

It is understood that it is HMRC practice to regard the value transferred by a transfer of a reversionary interest in settled property which is agricultural property (or an interest in an unadministered estate which contains agricultural property) as being attributable to that property.

Binding contracts for sale

26–150   The relief is never available if at the time of the transfer the transferor has entered into a binding contract for the sale of the property in question.[371] For this purpose, a sale to a company is disregarded if it is wholly or mainly in consideration of shares in or securities of the company which will give the transferor control of the company.[372]

It may be that a person signs a contract to sell his agricultural land, enters into a contract to buy other agricultural land, but dies before either sale is completed. It is thought that in practice HMRC will allow agricultural relief in such cases, though whether relief is restricted to the agricultural value of the smaller property, if the values are not equal, is not clear. For the position with regard to missives of sale in Scotland, see para.26–71.

If a person contracts to sell agricultural property subject to a pre-condition being satisfied which is outside the control of the parties, e.g. a sale subject to planning permission being obtained, and then dies before the pre-condition has been satisfied, it

---

[371] See paras 26–72–26–80.
[372] IHTA 1984 s.124(1).

is understood that HMRC will not regard there as being a binding contract for sale. The binding contract for sale will arise only when the pre-condition has been satisfied.

As noted in para.26–73, HMRC accept that put and call options, cross options and accruer arrangements do not constitute binding contracts for sale.

XV. COMPANIES

The legislation lays down special rules for determining whether shares in or securities of a company qualify for relief. These rules are concerned with three questions: **26–151**

(1) Is the value transferred by the transfer of the shares or securities attributable to the agricultural value of agricultural property?
(2) Are the conditions for relief satisfied?
(3) How much relief is available?

Attribution

By s.122(1), in order for the value transferred by a transfer of shares in or securities of a company to be taken to be attributable to the agricultural value of agricultural property three requirements have to be satisfied: **26–152**

(1) The agricultural property to which the value transferred is attributable must form part of the company's assets.[373]
(2) Part of the value of the shares or securities must be capable of being attributed to the agricultural value of the agricultural property in question.
(3) The shares or securities must have given the transferor control[374] of the company immediately before the transfer (see paras 26–02–26–11).

Conditions for relief

Relief is available if either of two tests is satisfied: **26–153**

(1) Two-year test: throughout the two years ending with the date of transfer:
 (a) the company must have occupied the property in question for the purposes of agriculture; and
 (b) the transferor must have owned the shares or securities;
 or
(2) Seven-year test: throughout the seven years ending with the date of the transfer:
 (a) the company must have owned the property in question; and
 (b) the transferor must have owned the shares or securities; and

---

[373] Strictly, shares in a holding company which has a farming subsidiary thus do not qualify for relief, but it is understood that in practice HMRC are prepared to attribute the value transferred to the underlying agricultural property.
[374] IHTA 1984 s.122(2).

(c) the company or one or more other persons (whether concurrently or consecutively) must have occupied the property in question for the purposes of agriculture.[375]

For the above purposes, a company is treated as having occupied the property in question at any time when it was occupied by a person who subsequently controls the company[376]; there is no similar provision with regard to ownership. This will be of assistance in relation to the two-year test; under the seven-year test the identity of the occupier is unimportant. The situation which is envisaged is when a transferor incorporates a previously unincorporated farming business and transfers the farming assets, including the land, to the company. HMRC take the view that, strictly speaking, s.123(5) does not apply to the transferor's occupation of agricultural property in the period between his acquiring control of the company and subsequently transferring the property to the company.[377]

The requirement that the transferor must have owned the shares or securities throughout the two or seven years ending with the date of the transfer could be problematic in the case of a widow who inherits from her late husband shares in a company, part of the value of which is attributable to the agricultural value of agricultural property, and who dies before herself having owned the shares or securities for the prescribed number of years. There is no provision in the Act for the widow to be credited with her late husband's period of ownership; as discussed at para.26–147, para.2, the position would have been different if the deceased husband had owned the agricultural property itself and left it to his widow. It is understood that HMRC accept that this situation is anomalous and that concessionary relief should be given. However, even if concessionary relief is not available, surviving spouses or civil partners who cannot satisfy the requirements in s.123(1)(b) should be eligible for business relief in respect of the shares by virtue of s.108(b).

Replacements

26–154   Section 123 contains a number of provisions governing replaced property. Firstly, it may be that agricultural property owned and/or occupied by the company at the time of the transfer replaced other agricultural property it owned and/or occupied for agricultural purposes some time during the 10 years immediately preceding the transfer. In that case s.123(2) provides as follows concerning the *company's* ownership and occupation requirements:

(1) Two-year test: this is satisfied if during the five years immediately preceding the transfer its respective periods of occupation together totalled at least two years.
(2) Seven-year test: this is satisfied if during the 10 years immediately preceding the transfer its respective periods of ownership and occupation (by the company or another) totalled at least seven years.

Secondly, the shares or securities transferred may have replaced other agricultural property or other shares or securities the value of which is wholly or partly attributable

[375] IHTA 1984 s.123(1).
[376] IHTA 1984 s.123(5) and see paras 26–02–26–11.
[377] *Shares Valuation Manual*, 112070.

to the value of agricultural property. In that case, s.123(3) provides as follows concerning the *transferor's* ownership requirements:

(1) Two-year test: this is satisfied if during the five years ending with the date of the transfer his respective periods of ownership totalled at least two years.
(2) Seven-year test: this is satisfied if during the 10 years ending with the date of the transfer his respective periods of ownership totalled at least seven years.

Finally, s.123(4) prevents extra relief from being obtained by replacing property with more valuable property by providing that the relief is limited to that which would have been given had no replacement been made. For this purpose, changes resulting from the formation, alteration or dissolution of a partnership are ignored. However, there remains no possibility of a backwards roll-over for IHT and, even where a replacement is made within three years after the disposal, replacement relief will be available only if *all* the proceeds of sale are reinvested.

Non-qualifying shares and securities

Shares or securities which might otherwise qualify for relief are prevented from doing so in two cases. Firstly, shares and securities will not qualify for relief if at the time of the transfer the transferor has entered into a binding contract to sell them, unless the sale is made for the purpose of reconstruction or amalgamation.[378] A similar restriction operates for the purposes of business relief.[379] Secondly, it may be that the transfer is made on death, and that within three years there is a "qualifying sale" of the shares which results in a lower value being retrospectively substituted for the shares under s.176. In that event, any agricultural relief previously given will be retrospectively withdrawn at the time the revaluation relief is given under s.176 unless the shares in question would themselves have given the transferor control.[380] This is to prevent the transferor from having the best of both worlds, agricultural relief on the basis that he had a controlling shareholding, and revaluation relief on the basis that he had a minority shareholding. Where agricultural relief is withdrawn business relief at 100 per cent should be available if the shares are unquoted.

26–155

Amount of relief

One hundred per cent relief is available if any of the following three tests are satisfied; in all other cases the rate of relief is 50 per cent:

26–156

(1) *Vacant possession*: this test is satisfied if immediately before the transfer the company's interest carried either the right to vacant possession or the right to obtain vacant possession within the next 24 months or if the company's interest was valued on a vacant possession basis.[381]

---

[378] IHTA 1984 s.124(2).
[379] See paras 26–72–26–80.
[380] IHTA 1984 s.122(2); see para.26–28 for a similar restriction on business relief.
[381] IHTA 1984 ss.116(2) and 122(3) and ESC F17.

(2) *Transitional relief*: whilst the Revenue's *Shares Valuation Manual*[382] states that transitional relief does not apply to agricultural property belonging to a company, it is understood that HMRC recognise that the transitional provisions can exceptionally apply on the transfer of a controlling shareholding in a company owning agricultural property. The situation which the legislation is intended to cover is the relatively rare one where the transferor owned shares in a company which owned agricultural land let to a partnership of which it was itself a partner. In such a case, provided the transferor satisfied the "working farmer" requirement, e.g. by being a director of the company, he would have qualified for the maximum rate of agricultural relief (then 50 per cent) under Sch.8 to the Finance Act 1975. Accordingly, the legislation attempts to preserve his position and it would seem that 100 per cent relief will be available if:

(a) the transferor has owned the shares in the company since before March 10, 1981[383]; and

(b) the company satisfies the vacant possession test[384]; and

(c) had the transferor disposed of his shares by a transfer of value at midnight on March 9, 1981, and claimed agricultural relief he would have qualified for it.[385]

It is believed to be the case that the company must have owned the agricultural property since before March 10, 1981 although the drafting of this part of the legislation seems to be defective. The basic drafting difficulty is that s.122(3)(a) provides that references in ss.116(2)(a) and (3)(b) to the transferor's interest are to be construed as references to the company's interest but does not deal with the question as to how s.116(2)(b) links up, as one would expect it should do, with s.116(3).

(3) *Tenancy*: the land is let by the company on a post-August 31, 1995, tenancy. The availability of 100 per cent relief in this situation is not immediately obvious from the wording of the legislation—s.122(3)(a) makes no provision for the reference in s.116(2)(c) to the transferor's interest to be construed as a reference to the company's interest. However, Revenue's *Shares Valuation Manual*[386] states that 100 per cent relief is available if the land was let on a tenancy beginning on or after September 1, 1995.

XVI. CLAWBACK OF RELIEF ON LIFETIME TRANSFERS

26–157   The Finance Act 1986 introduced into the legislation provisions which may operate to clawback agricultural relief previously given to a chargeable transfer made after March 17, 1986, and within seven years of the transferor's death.[387] Similar provisions apply in relation to the relief available to a PET which proves to be a chargeable transfer because it was made within seven years of the transferor's death.[388] In the case of a transfer which was chargeable when it was made this may result in additional tax being charged on the basis that the value transferred is what it would have been had no relief been given.[389] It will not, however, and this seems anomalous, affect the value

[382] At 112030.
[383] IHTA 1984 s.116(2).
[384] IHTA 1984 ss.116(2), (3) and 122(3)a.
[385] IHTA 1984 ss.116(2) and (3).
[386] At 112030.
[387] IHTA 1984 s.124A(2).
[388] IHTA 1984 s.124A(1).
[389] IHTA 1984 s.124A(2).

transferred by the transfer for purposes of cumulation. Where, on the other hand, a failed PET is concerned, the value transferred is for all purposes taken to be what it would have been had no relief been available, with the result that both the tax due and the transferor's cumulative total may be affected.[390]

The thinking behind the clawback is presumably that since the purpose of agricultural relief is to prevent charges to IHT from breaking up farming businesses the relief should not be available if the business is not retained by the person to whom it is transferred. This is fair enough, but the legislation is hardly a model of consistency: why, e.g. does the clawback operate with regard only to lifetime transfers? Given that it does, and with the potential retrospectively to lose agricultural relief at 100 per cent, the lifetime clawback rules are an important factor which may encourage the transfer of agricultural property to be postponed until death.

Agricultural relief could have been given either because the property was agricultural property to which s.116 applied or was shares or securities of a company owning agricultural property, in which case the value transferred would have been treated by s.122(1) as being attributable to the value of the underlying property. The legislation refers to such s.116 property and to such shares or securities as "the original property".[391]

The legislation operates by assuming that where the transferor dies within seven years of a transfer no relief is available unless, generally speaking, three conditions are satisfied, as explained below. It may be that the conditions are satisfied with respect to part only of the property originally transferred. In such a case, only a proportionate part of so much of the value transferred as is attributable to the original property is protected from the clawback.[392]

As discussed at para.26–109, there was an argument that because clawback depended upon there having been either a potentially exempt or chargeable transfer, the clawback rules could not apply when one was dealing with 100 per cent relievable property. Whilst the existence of this "loophole" was never accepted by HMRC the legislation was amended by the Finance Act 1996 with effect from November 28, 1995, by providing that in applying the clawback rules no account should be taken of business and agricultural relief. Hence in deciding whether the transfer is chargeable or potentially exempt no reduction in the value transferred is made.[393]

First condition—transferee's ownership

Section 124A(3)(a) provides that the original property must have been owned by the **26–158** transferee throughout the period beginning with the date of the chargeable transfer and ending with the date of the transferor's death or the transferee's death, whichever is earlier.[394] The following example illustrates how the rules work in relation to a transfer which is chargeable when it is made. Assume that on June 1, 2003, X settled agricultural property on discretionary trusts, thereby making a transfer of value, before agricultural relief, of £540,000. The transfer qualified for agricultural relief at 50 per cent and this reduced the value transferred to £270,000. The trustees paid the tax due of £3,000. If X dies, say, five-and-a-half years later and the trustees have by then sold the property the extra tax due will be computed on the basis that the value transferred was £540,000. If X had a nil cumulative total when he made the transfer the tax due

---

[390] IHTA 1984 s.124A(1).
[391] IHTA 1984 s.124A(8).
[392] IHTA 1984 s.124A(5).
[393] IHTA 1984 s.124A(7A).
[394] IHTA 1984 ss.124A(3) and (4).

would prima facie be £110,800 (based on a nil rate band of £263,000), and 40 per cent of that amount (because of 60 per cent taper relief) = £44,320 would be due in additional tax. Against this could be set the tax previously paid of £3,000, so that additional tax of £41,320 was in fact due. X's cumulative total would be unaffected.[395]

Now consider the position where there has been a failed PET. Assume that X gives Y shares qualifying for agricultural relief. Two years later Y sells the shares. Eighteen months after the sale X dies. The transfer to Y will be a PET which proves to have been a chargeable transfer. Although agricultural relief will initially have been available, it will be clawed-back because Y did not own the shares throughout the period beginning with the date of the transfer and ending with X's death. Accordingly, all of the value transferred at the date of the gift that qualified for agricultural relief will be subject to charge *and* that value transferred will be included in X's cumulative total.[396]

Settled property trap

26–159   Although the requirement as to ownership seems straightforward, it can give rise to problems where settled property is concerned. Before the changes included in Finance Act 2006, this was of particular concern in respect of accumulation and maintenance trusts. This was because, given s.49(1), there was a change of ownership when a beneficiary became entitled to an interest in possession in settled property in which no such interest previously subsisted. Thus, if X settled property qualifying for agricultural relief on accumulation and maintenance trusts and, e.g. his son became entitled to the trust income within seven years, relief would have been lost retrospectively if X died within seven years of making the PET which established the trust, because the transferee—the trustees—would have ceased to own the property. As indicated above, following the Finance Act 2006, a beneficiary will only be treated as owning the property if their interest qualifies as a pre-March 22, 2006 interest in possession, an immediate post death interest, a disabled person's interest or a transitional serial interest. This concern will therefore only apply in very limited circumstances and, in due course, not at all.

It is worth noting that if a beneficiary is treated as owning the trust property, there should be continuity of ownership for the purposes of agricultural relief if that property is advanced to him.[397]

Second condition—no binding contract for sale

26–160   The original property must not be subject to a binding contract for sale at the earlier of the death of the transferor and the transferee.[398]

Third condition generally—occupation of agricultural property

26–161   Where the original property was agricultural property the third condition is in two parts:

[395] See para.6–21.
[396] See para.6–21.
[397] IHTA 1984 ss.49(1) and 124A(8).
[398] IHTA 1984 ss.124A(3) and (4); see paras 26–72–26–80; cf. the rules governing the clawback of business relief, which impose no such restriction.

(1) immediately before the earlier of the death of the transferor and the transferee the property must have been agricultural property; and

(2) throughout the period beginning with the chargeable transfer and ending with the earlier death of the transferor and the transferee the property must have been occupied by either the transferee or another for the purposes of agriculture.[399]

Third condition for companies—ownership and occupation

Where the original property consisted of shares in or securities of a company the third condition is also two-fold, i.e. throughout the period beginning with the chargeable transfer and ending with the earlier of the death of the transferor and the transferee: **26–162**

(1) the company must have owned the underlying agricultural property; and

(2) the underlying property must have been occupied by the company or another for the purposes of agriculture.[400]

Share acquisitions

It may be that shares owned by the transferee immediately before the death in question (i) would be identified with the property originally transferred (or part of it) under ss.126–136 of the Taxation of Chargeable Gains Act 1992, or (ii) were issued to the transferee in consideration of the transfer of agricultural property consisting of the replacement property (or part of it). In such a case, the transferee's period of ownership of the original property is treated as including his ownership of the shares.[401] **26–163**

Replacements

It may be that the transferee has disposed of all or part of the original property before his own death or the death of the transferor.[402] In such a case, s.124B provides that the conditions as to ownership and the continuing status of the original property (as discussed above in paras 26–158, 26–161 and 26–162) will be taken to be satisfied in relation to the original property if the following conditions are satisfied: **26–164**

(1) the whole of the consideration received by the transferee for the disposal has been applied by him in acquiring other property (the "replacement property")[403];

(2) the replacement property is acquired, or a binding contract for its acquisition is entered into, within the period of three years (or such longer period as HMRC may allow) after the disposal of the original property (or the binding contract for the disposal of that property being entered into, if that is earlier and the

---

[399] IHTA 1984 ss.124A(3) and (4) and see para.26–143.
[400] IHTA 1984 ss.124A(3)(c) and (4) and see para.26–143.
[401] IHTA 1984 s.124A(6).
[402] IHTA 1984 ss.124B(1) and (4).
[403] IHTA 1984 s.124B(1): it is thought that "consideration" here means the net proceeds of sale.

disposal subsequently takes place)[404] (the "allowed period" was previously 12 months (with no discretion to extend) but was changed to three years (or such longer period as HMRC may allow) by the Finance Act 1994 in relation to transfers of value made and other events occurring after November 29, 1993);

(3) the disposal and acquisition are both made in transactions at arm's length or on terms such as might be expected to be included in a transaction at arm's length[405];

(4) at the time of the death in question the replacement property is owned by the transferee and is not subject to a binding contract for sale[406];

(5) throughout the period beginning with the date of the chargeable transfer and ending with the disposal, the original property was owned by the transferee and occupied by him or another for the purposes of agriculture[407];

(6) throughout the period beginning with the date when the transferee acquired the replacement property and ending with the death in question, the replacement property was owned by the transferee and occupied by him or another for the purposes of agriculture[408]; and

(7) the replacement property is agricultural property immediately before the death in question.[409]

Condition (5) suggests that reliance cannot be placed on s.124B where the original property consists of shares in or securities of a company owning agricultural property and the original property is disposed of other than in a situation to which s.124A(6)(a) applies. In addition, conditions (6) and (7) suggest that shares in "agricultural companies" cannot qualify as s.124B replacement property.

The rules are modified to cover the case where the transferor predeceases the transferee[410] and the transferee has either:

(1) disposed of all or part of the original property before the transferor's death; or

(2) entered into a binding contract for sale of the property.[411]

In such a case, if the replacement property is acquired, or a binding contract for its acquisition is entered into, after the death of the transferor, but within three years (or such longer period as HMRC may allow) of the disposal of the original property or part[412] (or the binding contract being entered into, if that is earlier, and the disposal subsequently takes place)[413] then the requirements in (4) and (6) above are dispensed with and any reference to a time immediately before the death in question is taken to be the time when the replacement property was acquired.[414] However, there remains no possibility of a backwards roll-over for IHT and, even where a replacement is made

[404] IHTA 1984 ss.124B(2), (7) and (8).
[405] IHTA 1984 s.124B(2).
[406] IHTA 1984 ss.124B(3) and (4).
[407] IHTA 1984 s.124B(3).
[408] IHTA 1984 ss.124B(3)(c) and (4).
[409] IHTA 1984 ss.124B(3)(d) and (4).
[410] IHTA 1984 s.124B(5)(c).
[411] IHTA 1984 s.124B(5).
[412] IHTA 1984 s.124B(5). As stated at para.26–164, para.2, the "allowed period" was previously 12 months but was changed to three years (or such longer period as HMRC may allow) by the FA 1994 in relation to transfers of value made and other events occurring after November 29, 1993.
[413] IHTA 1984 s.124B(7).
[414] IHTA 1984 s.124B(5).

within three years after the disposal, replacement relief will be available only if *all* the proceeds of sale are reinvested.

Share acquisitions

It may be that a transferee acquires shares which (i) would be identified with the **26–165** replacement property (or part of it) under ss.126–136 of the Taxation of Chargeable Gains Act 1992, or (ii) were issued to the transferee in consideration of the transfer of agricultural property consisting of the replacement property (or part of it). In such a case, the transferee's period of ownership of the replacement property is treated as including his ownership of the shares[415] but it is not clear whether this will actually be of assistance to the transferee given the occupation requirement contained in s.124B(3)(c) and the requirement contained in s.124B(3)(d) that the replacement property constitutes agricultural property immediately before the death. There is an apparent inconsistency between s.124B(6) and the requirements of s.124B(3).

Commentary

Three points need noting about the replacement property provisions. Firstly, they **26–166** apply only where the *whole* of the consideration from the disposal of the original property is applied in acquiring the replacement property. Why this should be the case is hard to understand. The CGT legislation deals specifically with the situation where the consideration for the disposal of a business asset is only partly used in acquiring other assets (s.153 of the Taxation of Chargeable Gains Act 1992). Secondly, the replacement property provisions do not apply if the replacement property was acquired before the disposal of the original property. Again, this is to be contrasted with the CGT position. Roll-over relief under s.152 of the Taxation of Chargeable Gains Act 1992 is available if the replacement asset is acquired up to 12 months before or three years after the disposal of the original asset. Thirdly, the provisions apply only to the first replacement, i.e. if X is given property, replaces it, and then sells the replacement property and acquires other property, the provisions will not apply to the last acquired property, except perhaps where a share acquisition is concerned and s.124B(6) applies (although see para.26–165). Again, why this should be the case is hard to understand.

XVII. SCOTTISH AGRICULTURAL LEASES

The legislation deals with an inequity which had arisen regarding the treatment of **26–167** agricultural tenancies in Scotland. In Scotland, unlike in the rest of the United Kingdom, such a tenancy is not regarded under the agricultural tenancy law as necessarily terminating on death. Instead, it is treated as a single tenancy which may, subject to certain restrictions, be bequeathed and which continues with the new tenant. If it terminated before death (as it does elsewhere in the United Kingdom) then the value immediately on death would be nil, and no problems would arise. Since it continues, HMRC rightly or wrongly took the view that such a tenancy could have

[415] IHTA 1984 s.124B(6).

some ascertainable value immediately before death, even though it could generally be neither assigned nor sublet to third parties. In valuing such tenancies, HMRC had regard to, inter alia, the unexhausted manurial value of the land and the possibility of a buy-out by the landlord. In practice tax was charged on values approaching 25 per cent of the vacant possession value of the land.

This practice was capable of causing hardship, mainly because the inheriting tenant could be left with a tax charge in respect of an asset, the lease, which he could neither sell nor borrow against. The effect might be to drive him out of farming. The legislation accordingly introduced an element of fiscal equity into the treatment of fixed-term leases and leases by tacit relocation (i.e. on a year-to-year basis), in two ways.

Firstly, s.177(1) provides that where any part of the value of a person's estate immediately before his death is attributable to the interest of a tenant in an unexpired portion of a lease for a fixed term of agricultural property in Scotland and the deceased either:

(1) had been a tenant of that property continuously for a period of at least two years immediately preceding his death; or
(2) had become a tenant of that property by succession,

any value associated with any prospect of renewal of the lease by tacit relocation is left out of account in determining the value transferred on the death. The words "associated with" are thought to be equivalent to the more normal expression in the legislation of "attributable to".

Secondly, s.177(2) provides that where any part of the value of a person's estate immediately before his death is attributable to the value of the interest of a tenant of agricultural property in Scotland which is an interest held by virtue of tacit relocation, the value of the interest is left out of account in determining the value transferred on his death if two conditions are satisfied, namely:

(1) he was a tenant of the property continuously for a period of at least two years immediately preceding his death (or he had become tenant of the property by succession); and
(2) the interest in question was acquired on his death by a new tenant.

The value which is left out of account by virtue of s.177(2) does not include the value of any rights to compensation in respect of tenant's improvements; see s.177(4).

XVIII. PROCEDURE WHERE BOTH RELIEFS ARE AVAILABLE

26–168   It may be that the value transferred by a transfer of value qualifies for both agricultural relief and business relief. This could happen in one of two ways. Firstly, it might be that part of the value transferred is attributable to agricultural property and part to business property. Alternatively, it might be that the whole of the value transferred is attributable to property which is both agricultural property and business property, e.g. where agricultural land is let to a partnership of which the transferor is a partner.

The procedure where part of the value transferred is attributable to agricultural property and part to business property is best explained by way of an example.

Assume that on July 1, 2003, A settled on trustees of a discretionary trust (i) a farm worth £750,000, of which £650,000 was attributable to the agricultural value of agricultural property and which qualified for 50 per cent relief, and (ii) plant worth

£300,000 of which £200,000 was attributable to the value of relevant business property and which also qualified for 50 per cent relief. A bore the IHT and the trustees paid the CGT, which amounted to £120,000. The procedure would be as follows:

(1) Find how much of the value transferred is attributable to agricultural property:

$$£1,050,000 \times \frac{£750,000}{£1,050,000} = £750,000$$

(2) Find how much of this value is attributable to the agricultural value of that property:

$$£750,000 \times \frac{£650,000}{£750,000} = £650,000$$

(3) Take 50 per cent of the part of the value transferred which is eligible for agricultural relief:

$$50\% \times £650,000 = £325,000$$

(4) Find how much of the value transferred is attributable to business property:

$$£1,050,000 \times \frac{£300,000}{£1,050,000} = £300,000$$

(5) Find how much of this value is attributable to relevant business property:

$$£300,000 \times \frac{£200,000}{£300,000} = £200,000$$

(6) Take 50 per cent of this sum:

$$50\% \times £200,000 = £100,000$$

(7) Add the agricultural relief and the business relief:

£
325,000
100,000
425,000

(8) Subtract this figure from the value transferred:

£
1,050,000
− 425,000
625,000

(9) Bring into account any exemptions:

£
625,00
− 3,000
622,000

919

(10) Deduct any CGT borne by the transferee:

$$
\begin{array}{r}
£ \\
622{,}000 \\
-\ 120{,}000 \\
\hline
502{,}000
\end{array}
$$

This is the value transferred by the chargeable transfer after all reliefs and exemptions but before grossing-up.

26–169   When the same property qualifies for both business relief and agricultural relief, s.114(1) provides that agricultural relief is to be given in preference to business relief.

XIX. COMPARISON OF BUSINESS RELIEF AND AGRICULTURAL RELIEF

26–170   The following points should be borne in mind concerning the availability of agricultural relief and business relief:

(1) Limitation: business relief is available without limit; agricultural relief may rarely not be, because of the limitation under the old rules.[416]

(2) There are express rules governing the treatment of liabilities in determining the availability of business relief, but not in determining the availability of agricultural relief.[417]

(3) Development value: business relief is available on the development value of land; agricultural relief is restricted to agricultural value.

(4) Woodlands: agricultural relief is limited to woodlands occupied with agricultural land or pasture where the occupation is ancillary to that of the agricultural land or pasture; business relief is not so limited.

(5) Territorial scope: agricultural relief is limited to agricultural property in the United Kingdom, Channel Islands, the Isle of Man or the European Economic Area; business relief is not so limited (see comments at para.26–114).

(6) Crops: agricultural relief is limited to growing crops; business relief extends to harvested crops.

(7) Livestock, deadstock, plant and machinery: business relief is available; agricultural relief is not.

(8) Farmhouses, farm buildings and cottages: business relief is available only if the building is used wholly or mainly for business purposes; where part only of the building is used exclusively for business purposes, an apportionment will be made. Whether agricultural relief is available, on the other hand, depends on whether the building is of a character appropriate to the property, and there is no question of any apportionment.

(9) Binding contracts for sale: a binding contract to sell a particular asset out of an unincorporated business should not affect the availability of business relief but it will affect the availability of agricultural relief.

(10) Agricultural relief must be given in priority to business relief.

---

[416] See para.26–137.
[417] See para.26–85.

It follows from the above that, generally speaking, business relief is more widely available than agricultural relief. In two cases, agricultural relief may be available at 100 per cent while business relief may be available at only 50 per cent or not at all:

(a) Where a person makes land available to a partnership of which he is a partner or to a company which he controls the maximum business relief that will be available to him is 50 per cent;

(b) A person who has been farming and who transfers part of the land but who continues to farm may not qualify for any business relief, because he has not transferred his business. However, see comments at para.26–19 in relation to the case of the *Nelson Dance Family Settlement v RCC*.[418]

XX. PLANNING FOR BUSINESS RELIEF AND AGRICULTURAL RELIEF

The legislation lends itself to planning in various ways. It also contains traps for the uninformed. The following are among the points, some of which have been referred to previously but are worth reiterating, to be borne in mind. We will consider first points relevant to both reliefs, then points particular to business relief, and last points particular to agricultural relief.   **26–171**

Planning points for both reliefs

The following points are relevant in relation to both reliefs.   **26–172**

Wait and win on CGT

It seems an obvious point, but think twice about giving or selling shortly before death property which qualifies for business or agricultural relief. The reason is that the relief will still be available on death, but a sale or gift will forfeit the CGT free uplift that would otherwise have been available on death. If, for commercial reasons, it is important to tie up a sale before a death, consider entering into cross options which do not constitute binding contracts for sale.   **26–173**

Wait and win on clawbacks

The clawback provisions can operate only in respect of lifetime gifts. If there is a likelihood that property is to be sold, postpone the gift, if possible, until after the intending donor's death. If, for commercial reasons, it is important to tie up a sale before a death, consider entering into cross options which, as above, do not constitute binding contracts for sale.   **26–174**

Investing to secure relief: "sickbed" arrangements

Assume that X is somewhat elderly or infirm and that her son wishes to embark on a business which will qualify for 100 per cent business relief or 100 per cent   **26–175**

---

[418] *Nelson Dance Family Settlement v RCC* [2009] EWHC 71 (Ch).

agricultural relief and that X is willing to fund this business by giving him £500,000. Instead of giving him the £500,000 she could go into partnership with him. If she simply gives him the £500,000 she must survive seven years to avoid any charge to IHT. If she dies within three years, IHT will be due in full on the £500,000. If, on the other hand, she invests the £500,000 in acquiring a partnership interest (X, as the active partner would manage the £500,000 in the partnership business) she could qualify for 100 per cent relief after two years. This amounts to "sickbed" (as opposed to "deathbed") planning under which the relevant survival period is reduced to two years.

Recycling relief

26–176 Mr X owns a business worth £2,000,000 qualifying for 100 per cent business relief or 100 per cent agricultural relief and investments worth £2,500,000. Mrs X will run the business on Mr X's death. If Mr X leaves the business to his children and the investments to Mrs X, 100 per cent relief will be available on Mr X's death and the investments will pass free of IHT to Mrs X under the spouse exemption. Mrs X could then use £2,000,000 of the investments to buy the business from the children. Since the transfer of the business by Mr X occurred on his death this will not be an occasion for the clawback of business relief or agricultural relief. If Mrs X survives the purchase by two years, 100 per cent business relief or 100 per cent agricultural relief could be available on her death. If Mr X does not leave Mrs X sufficient funds to purchase the business, all or part of the purchase price could be left outstanding by the children.[419]

Testamentary gifts of business assets or agricultural property

26–177 When drafting a will for an individual who owns assets which qualify for 100 per cent business relief or 100 per cent agricultural relief a draftsman may wish to include a specific legacy of those assets to a non-exempt beneficiary so as not to waste the relief by leaving the assets to the surviving spouse or civil partner. The risks with including such a legacy is that, at the date of the testator's death, the assets may no longer qualify for 100 per cent relief: in the case of business relief there may, e.g. be excepted assets such that the value transferred that is attributable to the value of relevant business property is less than the open market value; in the case of agricultural relief HMRC may succeed in establishing that the agricultural value of the assets is less than their open market value.

A sensible alternative to a specific legacy is a legacy of all property which qualifies for relief (whether at the rate of 50 per cent or 100 per cent) upon discretionary trusts for a class including non-exempt beneficiaries, but also the surviving spouse or civil partner. To the extent that there is an IHT liability (because the value transferred that is attributable to the value of property is less than the open market value or the value of the property that qualifies for 50 per cent relief exceeds the unused nil rate band), it can be appointed by the legacy trustees to the surviving spouse or civil partner within two years of the testator's death, so neutralising the IHT liability.[420] Another option is

---

[419] The possible application of FA1986 s.103 would have to be considered; see paras 8–57 and following. If land is involved consider the stamp duty land tax implications of the purchase of the land by Mrs X.

[420] IHTA 1984 s.144; see paras 8–189–8–205.

to include a legacy upon discretionary trusts of all assets which qualify for 100 per cent relief together with assets qualifying for relief at less than 100 per cent but in the latter case only up to the amount of the testator's unused nil rate band. With this option there is no need to include the surviving spouse or civil partner within the class of discretionary beneficiaries. The disadvantages are that the business or farming enterprise may become split between the legacy fund and residue and difficult valuation issues will be involved in establishing which assets pass into the legacy fund.[421]

Encumbrances on business property or agricultural property

Last, bear in mind that where a liability is an encumbrance on property it reduces the value of the property for IHT purposes; s.162(4).[422] Liabilities secured on assets which qualify for business relief or agricultural relief should be avoided where possible because they reduce the value of that property for IHT purposes and so effectively reduce or eliminate the availability of the relief. Where possible such liabilities should be secured on non-qualifying property; see paras 26–85 and 26–133. **26–178**

Planning points for business relief

A variety of opportunities and traps exist in relation to business relief. **26–179**

Two "all or nothing" rules

Remember that there are two "all or nothing" rules. Firstly, business relief operates to reduce so much of the value transferred by a transfer of value as is attributable to the value of relevant business property. So, to obtain business relief, you must first have "relevant business property". Section 105(3) provides that shares in a company the business of which consists wholly or mainly of making or holding investments are not relevant business property, and that is so even though some of the value of the shares is attributable to trading assets. Either property is relevant business property or it is not. The relief does not operate on a proportional basis. Secondly, it may be that shares in the holding company of a group are relevant business property, but that included in the group are one or more companies the business of which consists wholly or mainly of making or holding investments. In that case, by s.111, the value of the shares in the investment subsidiary are ignored in valuing the holding company shares and this is so even though some of the value of the shares is attributable to trading assets. **26–180**

How to obtain 100 per cent relief by repositioning investments within a group of companies

"Business" is defined for CGT holdover relief under s.165 of the Taxation of Chargeable Gains Act 1992 as being confined to a trade, profession or vocation. There is no such definition for IHT purposes. It may be that a company carries on a hybrid **26–181**

[421] See Matthew Hutton & Barry D. McCutcheon, *Private Client Business* (London: Sweet & Maxwell, 2003), p.305.
[422] See paras 25–86–25–91.

business consisting of both trading and holding investments. In that case, so long as the business of the company does not fall within s.105(3), the investments will not be excepted assets. Assume that you act for X, who owns all the shares worth £2,000,000 in a family company, Parent Trading Ltd, which has a wholly owned subsidiary, S Ltd, worth £500,000. The value of Parent Trading Ltd on its own comfortably exceeds the value of S Ltd. X wants to settle some of the shares on a trust for her children, under which neither she nor her husband can benefit. S Ltd trades, but also owns quoted investments which it actively manages and which the directors regard as being an intrinsic part of the business carried on by S Ltd. The value of the quoted investments is such that S Ltd is an investment company for the purposes of ss.105(3) and (4) but S Ltd would be mainly a trading company if it did not own some of the quoted investments. Even if Parent Trading Ltd owned all S Ltd's investments Parent Trading Ltd would still not be an investment company.

The problems

26–182   As matters stand, there are two interrelated problems. First, since S Ltd is an investment company, s.111 will operate to deny relief on so much of the value of X's shares in Parent Trading Ltd as is attributable to the value of its shares in S Ltd. Secondly, s.165 holdover relief will be restricted by reason of the existence of S Ltd's non-trading assets.[423] X could solve the s.165 problem if she settled the shares in Parent Trading Ltd on non-settlor interested[424] discretionary trusts, because holdover relief would then be available under s.260, which takes priority over s.165[425] and does not contain the same restriction as s.165. Unfortunately, as matters stand, this will give rise to a chargeable transfer of so much of the value transferred as is attributable to the shares in S Ltd, i.e. £500,000.

Improving the position

26–183   The position would be considerably improved if sufficient of S Ltd's quoted investments were transferred to Parent Trading Ltd to change the status of S Ltd from an investment business to a non-investment business for IHT purposes because in that case Parent Trading Ltd would still not be an investment company, S Ltd would cease to be an investment company and none of the investments owned by either company, each of which will be carrying on a hybrid business, should be s.112 excepted assets. Full business relief would thus be available, so that if the shares were settled on discretionary trusts full holdover relief would be available under s.260 without X incurring a charge to IHT.

Relief on injected investments[426]

26–184   A partner or a shareholder may be able to secure business relief on the value of investments by transferring them into a partnership or company[427] where his interest or

---

[423] TCGA 1992 s.165(6).
[424] The definition of a "settlor interested" trust was amended from April 6, 2006 and is now defined as a trust under which the settlor, the settlor's spouse or the settlor's minor children can benefit.
[425] TCGA 1992, s.165(3)(d).
[426] See also para.26–100.
[427] If the transferor does not own all the shares in the company the company's share capital will have to be re-organised to avoid the transferor making a gift to the other shareholders.

shares qualify for business relief. The investments themselves do not qualify for relief but they increase the value of the partner's interest or the shares in the company, which does qualify for relief. The investments should not be excepted assets.[428] So long as the business of the company becomes a hybrid of trading and managing investments, the fact that the partnership or company has not owned the assets for two years prior to any transfer of the interest or shares is neither here nor there because the two year ownership requirement applies only in relation to the partnership interest or shares. Transferring the assets might, of course, trigger a charge to CGT in the case of a transfer to a company. Normally it is possible to avoid a charge to CGT on a transfer to a partnership by amending the partnership agreement so that the transferor effectively remains entitled to all the value of the investments, i.e. a separate capital account is set up for the transferor partner. Merely injecting cash which is not invested will probably not suffice. HMRC take the view that a degree of activity is needed for a business to exist and that merely holding cash on deposit is not a business activity.[429]

Wait and win with *Fetherstonaugh*

26–185 Assume X carries on a business and has a life interest under a non relevant property settlement which owns land (or buildings, plant or machinery) used in the business. X, who is getting on a bit, asks your advice as to whether there is any advantage in surrendering his life interest in the land so as to make a PET.

It is clear that if he surrenders his interest, 50 per cent business relief will be available under s.105(1)(e). But what is the position if he retains his interest and dies? Although it might be thought that s.105(1)(e) governs the position so that only 50 per cent relief is available, 100 per cent relief will be available by virtue of the Court of Appeal's decision in the *Fetherstonaugh* case.[430] X may therefore be well advised to be patient and allow his interest to pass on his death, which may have the added advantages of securing a CGT free uplift on his death and avoiding any IHT clawback issues.

Planning points for agricultural relief

26–186 It remains to mention two points concerning agricultural relief.

Planning for retirement

26–187 The *Rosser*[431] case illustrates the dangers of transferring agricultural property to the next generation whilst continuing to live in what has been the farmhouse. The risks are

---

[428] Care would be needed to ensure that s.105(3) was not infringed; see also the comments at para.26–84 concerning the *IRC v Mallender (executors of Drury-Lowe, Deceased)* [2001] S.T.C. 514.

[429] Note in this connection the comments of Park J. in *Jowett v O'Neill & Brennan Construction* [1998] S.T.C. 482, a corporation tax case, that a company is not carrying on a business merely because it holds a bank account and receives interest.

[430] *Fetherstonaugh v IRC* [1984] S.T.C. 261; there is some doubt as to whether *Fetherstonaugh* can apply otherwise than on a transfer on death though it is possible to read the case as meaning that 100 per cent relief is available in respect of a lifetime transfer if the transfer includes both the business and the interest under the settlement; see para.26–20.

[431] *Rosser v IRC* [2003] S.T.C. (S.C.D.) 311.

that either the residence will cease to constitute a farmhouse or that even if it continues to be classified as a farmhouse it will not be regarded as of a character appropriate to the retained agricultural property. Farmers wishing to take a less active role whilst still involving the next generation might consider keeping all of their agricultural property until death and entering into a suitably drawn contract farming agreement with their children. See comments in relation to the *Arnander*[432] case at para.26–129.

Replacing pre-September 1, 1995, tenancies

26–188   See para.26–136 concerning the replacement of a pre-September 1, 1995, tenancy so as to secure 100 per cent relief.

XXI. RESERVATION OF BENEFIT—PIGGY-BACK TRANSFERS

26–189   The Finance Act 1986 Sch.20 para.8 deals, in a somewhat novel way, with a donor who has given away property in respect of which agricultural and/or business relief is relevant. Assume that X gives to Y property, which in X's hands qualifies for agricultural or business relief, and that X retains a benefit in respect of the property so that, in relation to him, it is "property subject to a reservation".[433] Sometime later the property ceases to be subject to a reservation, so that X then makes a notional PET of the property or, failing that, X dies, with the result that the property is at that stage clawed back into his estate. In such a case, in the absence of provision to the contrary, agricultural and business relief might well have not been available in respect of the property brought into charge by virtue of s.102(3) or (4) of the Finance Act 1986, and this would have been unfair given the fact that if X had retained the property, relief would have been available. Paragraph 8 deals with this problem in three different ways, depending on the kind of property involved.

Business relief: shares or securities

26–190   In determining whether the property clawed back into charge is shares or securities that are capable of attracting business relief they are assumed to be owned by the donor at the time of the clawback charge and to have been owned by him since the disposal by way of gift. He is thus treated, in effect, as never having made the gift. Relief is then given accordingly.[434] Assume that W owns the shares in W Ltd and gives 20 per cent of those shares to T subject to a reserved benefit. W dies, having still reserved a benefit, so that the shares are treated as forming part of his estate. It is assumed that the shares had been retained by W from the date of the gift until the date of his death. One hundred per cent relief will therefore be available under s.105(1)(bb). If business relief is being claimed on the basis of s.105(1)(b) or (cc) the shares given away, but subject

[432] *Arnander (Executors of McKenna) v HMRC* (2006) S.P.C. 565.
[433] See generally Ch.7.
[434] FA 1986 Sch.20, paras 8(1) and (1A).

to a reservation, are aggregated with shares retained by the transferor in determining whether he had control of the company.

Shares or securities in farming companies

Where the property clawed-back into charge is shares or securities falling within **26–191** s.122(1)[435] relief is available only if:

(1) the value transferred by the donor's disposal qualified for relief at the time of the disposal; and
(2) throughout the period beginning with the disposal and ending with the date of the clawback the donee owned the shares or securities.[436]

Assuming these conditions are satisfied, the notional transfer made by the donor on the occasion of the clawback is assumed to have been made by the donee.[437] There is thus, in effect, a notional transfer made by one person (the donee) in respect of a notional transfer made by someone else (the donor), a "piggy-back" transfer, as it were, by the donee.

In determining whether the value transferred by this piggy-back transfer would have qualified for relief had the donee actually made it, it is assumed that the requirements in s.123(1)(b) as to the ownership of the shares or securities are satisfied.[438] Relief is then given to the donor's transfer at the rate at which the donee's transfer would have qualified.[439] This means that there appears to be a discrepancy with the rules regulating the availability of business relief on shares or securities. Under the business relief provisions regard is had solely to the donor's position. Under the agricultural relief provisions, on the other hand, what matters is the donee's position. If he would have qualified for only 50 per cent relief, then that is all that the donor is entitled to, and that is so even if the donor would have been entitled to 100 per cent relief had he retained the shares. Conversely, if the donee would have qualified for 100 per cent relief, the donor gets the benefit of that relief even though he would have qualified for only 50 per cent relief had he retained the shares.

All other property

The position with regard to all other property is that in determining whether business **26–192** or agricultural relief is available and, if so, in the case of agricultural relief, at what percentage, the donee is assumed to have made a "piggy-back" transfer of the property clawed-back, relief being given to the donor at the rate at which the donee would have qualified for it.[440] In determining whether the donee would have qualified for relief, ownership by the donor prior to the disposal by way of gift is treated as the donee's ownership and occupation by the donor prior to the disposal and thereafter is treated as occupation by the donee.[441]

---

[435] See paras 26–151–26–156.
[436] FA 1986 Sch.20, paras 8(1)(c) and (3).
[437] FA 1986 Sch.20, para.8(1A).
[438] FA 1986 Sch.20, para.8(3).
[439] FA 1986 Sch.20, para.8(1A).
[440] FA 1986 Sch.20 paras 8(1) and (b) and (1A)(b).
[441] FA 1986 Sch.20 para.8(2).

Assume X gives his ironmonger business to his daughter Z and it is agreed that he shall be paid one half of the net profits from the business each year. He retains this benefit until the date of his death. Whether business relief is available is decided by treating the transfer of value as made by the donee, Z. Accordingly, Z must satisfy the conditions for relief although she can include the period of ownership of X before the gift.

Donee's premature death

26–193   If the donee predeceases the donor he can be called back from the grave to make, where needed, his "piggy-back" transfer but, of course, only in a notional form. In such a case, regard is had to his personal representatives or, as the case may require, the person (if any) by whom the property, shares or securities concerned were taken under a testamentary disposition made by the donee or under his intestacy (or partial intestacy).[442]

WOODLANDS RELIEF

Introduction

26–194   The legislation recognises that it would be unfair to tax growing trees—which might take several generations to mature—in the same way as other crops. In addition, such taxation could easily discourage afforestation. Chapter III of Pt V accordingly provides a special deferral relief, available only in respect of chargeable transfers made on death, where the value of any part of a person's estate immediately before he dies is attributable partly to the value of land in the United Kingdom on which trees or underwood are growing. In such a case, it may be possible for the deceased's personal representatives or any other person liable for the whole or part of the tax to elect to leave the value of the growing trees (but not the land itself) out of account in determining the value transferred on the deceased's death, and instead to pay tax when the trees are actually disposed of. If there is no disposal, tax is charged on the next death in the usual way unless, of course, another election is made to defer tax. Any election to defer tax must be made in writing to the Board within two years of the death or such longer time as the Board may allow. See paras 5–14–5–16 for a discussion of the problems which have arisen when a PET was made of woodlands which had qualified for estate duty deferral. The restriction on the availability of the relief to the United Kingdom has come under pressure from the European Commission. In 2009, woodlands relief was extended to woodlands in the European Economic Area.[443]

Availability of the relief

26–195   The relief is available only if the following conditions are satisfied:

[442] FA 1986 Sch.20 para.8(5).
[443] FA 2009 s.122.

928

(1) The value of a person's estate immediately before he died must have been partly attributable to the value of the land:
  (a) on which trees or underwood are growing;
  (b) which is situated in the United Kingdom or the European Economic Area; and
  (c) which is not agricultural property.
  By s.115(2), "agricultural property" is defined for these purposes to include woodland if the woodland is occupied with agricultural land or pasture, and the occupation is ancillary to the occupation of the agricultural land or pasture. If the land in question is agricultural property the woodlands relief will not be available but agricultural relief or business relief may be available. However, it will, of course, normally be preferable to claim agricultural relief first if possible, since this would give the opportunity of an outright reduction in the charge to tax, rather than a mere deferral.
(2) The deceased must either (i) have been beneficially entitled to the land throughout the five years immediately preceding his death, or (ii) have become beneficially entitled to the land otherwise than for a consideration in money or money's worth.[444] Where the deceased had a non relevant property interest in possession in the land for the required period this condition will be met since, by s.49(1), he will be treated as having been entitled to the land. The condition will not be met by a shareholder in a company the assets of which consist of or include woodlands, since as a matter of company law shareholders are not beneficially entitled to the assets of a company in which they hold shares.[445] Nor will the conditions be met by a partner of a partnership even if the entire partnership business is that of woodland ownership and management. It also follows that the condition will not be met if before his death the deceased contracted to sell the land, since in that case he will hold the land on trust for the purchaser.[446] Under estate duty, deathbed purchases of woodlands were used to avoid tax; such purchases are clearly ineffective for IHT purposes.
(3) A person liable for the whole or part of the tax must elect in writing for relief within two years of the death or such longer time as the Board allows.[447]

Definition of "woodland"

Some care needs to be taken in defining "woodland". In the past, this had not been a contentious issue, and the *New Shorter Oxford English Dictionary* definition ("land covered with wood, i.e. with trees; a wooded region or piece of ground") appeared to deal with the issue with admirable clarity, and indeed no other statutory or judicial definition of the word had previously been attempted. However, *Jaggers v Ellis*[448] has cast some doubt as to whether the term may be applied to any area of land covered with trees. Although decided in the context of s.53 of the Taxes Act 1988 (which deals with the trading status of farming and commercial occupation of land, except in the case of woodlands), in the absence of any other legal definition of woodland, this must be a decisive interpretive development.

26–196

---

[444] IHTA 1984 s.125(1).
[445] *Short v Treasury Commissioners* [1948] A.C. 534; *Macaura v Northern Assurance Co* [1925] A.C. 619.
[446] For the position where there are missives of sale in Scotland, see para.26–71.
[447] IHTA 1984 s.125(3).
[448] *Jaggers (trading as Shide Trees) v Ellis* 1997 S.T.C. 1417.

The judgment of Lightman J. in *Jaggers* attempted to add a number of indicative factors as potential tests to define woodland. The case concerned a Christmas tree plantation on approximately nine acres of land on the Isle of Wight, and the Court of Appeal clearly took exception to the term "woodland" being applied to the plantation given that many of the Christmas trees were small in size and maturity and, according to the inspector, resembled bushes rather than trees. Lightman J.'s key definition was as follows:

> "The term 'woodland' connotes a wood, a sizeable area of land to a significant extent covered by growing trees of some maturity, height and size."[449]

He went on to suggest the following additional tests to qualify his definition:

(1) There is no mathematical or scientific formula for deciding the area of land, the density of trees or maturity, height or size required for this purpose.[450]

(2) As to the maturity, height and size of the trees there is something to be said for the rule of thumb that their wood should be capable of being used as timber, for woodlands are frequently used and cultivated for timber production, and this is the size of trees ordinarily associated in the mind's eye with a wood.[451]

Although Lightman J. is clearly correct that woodlands are usually used for timber production, and it is in the context of timber production that woodlands relief from IHT is most commonly claimed, it is far from clear that as a necessary consequence of this the term should be statutorily interpreted to exclude areas of land covered with trees (which in this case were used for commercial purposes), mainly on the grounds that the purpose of their use was not for the production of timber.

Apart from this non-sequitur in the reasoning of the judgment, there are arguably two key limitations on the definition of "woodland" used by Lightman J. when applied in the context of the IHT relief. The first is that it was used in the context of s.53 of the Taxes Act 1988. The relevant reference in s.53(4) is to " . . . land which comprises woodlands or is being prepared for forestry purposes". It is entirely possible that Lightman J.'s interpretation was governed by the juxtaposition of the reference to forestry purposes with the word "woodlands" in this sub-section, and indeed some commentators[452] have cast doubt on this departure from the dictionary definition. The second limitation is that s.125 refers to "the value of trees or *underwood*". The *New Shorter Oxford English Dictionary* definition of "underwood" is: "small trees, shrubs etc., growing beneath higher timber trees—a quantity, kind or particular area of this undergrowth".[453] It is strongly postulated that the case for the plantation in *Jaggers* qualifying as woodland would have been even stronger for IHT purposes because of this extra qualification.

The submission of the authors is that the judgment in *Jaggers* does not provide a logical or helpful definition of woodland, and should not carry any weight in the context of ss.125 and 126. There are also further arguments that it should not apply at all to the IHT relief. However, until further judicial comment is given (particularly in the context of the IHT relief), taxpayers should bear in mind the possibility that claims for woodland relief on wooded areas of land not cultivated for the purpose of timber

---

[449] *Jaggers (trading as Shide Trees) v Ellis* 1997 S.T.C. 1417. at 1422.
[450] *Jaggers (trading as Shide Trees) v Ellis* 1997 S.T.C. 1417. at 1423.
[451] *Jaggers (trading as Shide Trees) v Ellis* 1997 S.T.C. 1417.at 1423.
[452] See, e.g. *The Personal Tax Planning Review* (1999), Vol.6, Issue 3.
[453] *The New Shorter Oxford English Dictionary*, 4th edn, (Oxford: Oxford University Press, 1993).

production may well be open to challenge by HMRC on the strength of the judgment in *Jaggers*.

Deferral of liability

Where the relief is available s.125(2)(a) provides that, if an election is made, the **26–197** value of the trees or underwood (but not of the underlying land) is left out of account in determining the value transferred by the deceased on his death. Although the land itself cannot, by definition, qualify for agricultural relief, where the woodlands are commercially managed the underlying land may qualify for business relief.

Subsequent charges to tax: under main charging provisions

Once the relief has been given a charge can arise in two ways. First, it can arise **26–198** under the main charging provisions in the usual way. Thus, if on the deceased's death his son became entitled to an immediate post death interest in possession in the woodlands, tax will be charged under s.52(1) if the son's interest comes to an end during his lifetime. If the son still possesses the interest when he dies there will be a charge under s.4, unless, of course, a further election to defer tax is made.

Subsequent charges to tax: crystallisation of deferred charge

The second way in which a charge can arise is by crystallisation of the deferred **26–199** charge. This will happen where all or part of the trees or underwood[454] or any interest in the trees or underwood is disposed of, whether with the underlying land or not. This is subject to the qualification that no charge will arise:

(1) if deferred tax has already been paid on the trees or underwood in question because of a previous disposal[455];
(2) if the disposal is to the disposer's spouse or civil partner[456];
(3) if there has been an intervening death on which tax was charged on the land in question. This is best explained by way of example.

Assume A dies leaving woodlands to B, that an election is made, and that B dies leaving woodlands to C without an election being made. If C disposes of the woodlands there will not be a deferred charge, because tax was charged on the woodlands on B's death. If B's death had not been the occasion of a chargeable transfer of the woodlands, e.g. because an election was made, there would be a deferred charge on the disposal, and, as will be seen below, it would be made by reference to A's death, not to B's.

---

[454] IHTA 1984 s.130(1)(c).
[455] IHTA 1984 s.126(3).
[456] IHTA 1984 s.126(2).

931

It should be noted that the fact that the disposal is to an exempt body such as a charity does not prevent the deferred charge from crystallising.

The amount on which tax is charged

26–200   The amount on which tax is charged depends on whether or not the disposal is a sale for full consideration in money or money's worth. If it is, the amount on which tax is charged is the net proceeds of sale. In any other case, e.g. a gift, or a sale at an undervalue, the amount is the net value of the trees or underwood at the time of the disposal. For this purpose, the "proceeds of sale" and the "net value" are the amount left after deduction of expenses incurred in:

(1) disposing of the trees or underwood;
(2) replanting, within three years of a disposal, in order to replace the trees or underwood disposed of;
(3) replanting to replace trees or underwood previously disposed of, so far as the expense was not allowable on a previous disposal.[457]

The above is subject to the qualification that an expense is allowable only insofar as it is not allowable for income tax.[458]

Quasi-business relief

26–201   In the absence of special provision there would be an anomaly concerning business relief, the source of which would be that s.126(1) is a separate charging provision which is predicated on the existence of a disposal, not on the existence of a transfer of value. This would mean that although the trees or underwood might have qualified for business relief on the deceased's death, that relief, which applies only to transfers of value, would be unavailable to reduce the amount on which tax was charged under s.126(1) on a disposal. Section 127(2) prevents this by providing that where the trees or underwood in question would have been taken into account in determining the value of any relevant business property in relation to the transfer of value made on the death by reference to which the deferred charge is made, the amount on which tax is chargeable under s.126 on a disposal is reduced by 50 per cent. In the event that the deceased died before April 6, 1976, the date on which business relief became available under the Finance Act 1976, the 50 per cent reduction is still available if the trees or underwood would have been so taken into account had business relief been available at that time.

Rate of tax

26–202   To find the rate or rates at which tax is chargeable regard is had to the rate of tax that would have applied if the amount on which tax is chargeable had been taxed at the top slice of the transfer by reference to which the deferred charge is made. That transfer

---

[457] IHTA 1984 s.130(2).
[458] IHTA 1984 s.130(1)(b). See the changes made in the FA 1988 to the treatment of woodlands.

will be the last chargeable transfer on which an election was made. Thus, if A dies leaving woodlands to B, who makes an election on A's death, and B dies, leaving the woodlands to C, his widow, on C's disposing of the woodlands regard will be had to A's rate of tax, not to B's. By s.127(1), in finding the top slice any amount on which tax was charged on a previous disposal must be brought into account; see the example below. It may be that since the death there has been a change in the death rates. In such a case, by para.4 of Sch.2, the deferred charge is levied at the death rates in force at the time the deferred charge crystallises, not at the rates in force at the time of the death in respect of which the relief was given.

Relief for tax paid

As was noted above, it may be that the disposal also constitutes a chargeable transfer. **26–203** In such a case, by s.129, the value transferred by the chargeable transfer is calculated as if it has been reduced by the tax chargeable under s.126.

Interaction with business relief

The legislation prevents both business and woodlands relief from being given in **26–204** certain circumstances. It may be that woodlands are disposed of so that two charges arise—one under s.126 because the deferred charge is crystallised, and one because the disposal is itself a chargeable transfer, with the result that, as was just noted, the value transferred by the chargeable transfer is reduced by the tax chargeable under s.126. Business relief may be available in respect of the disposal, but by s.114(2) in giving the relief the value transferred by the transfer of value made on the disposal must first be reduced by the tax chargeable under s.126.

EXAMPLE

X died in August 1978, having made no previous chargeable transfers, and leaving, **26–205** inter alia, woodlands worth £100,000 to his son Y. His personal representatives elected to leave the woodlands out of account, with the result that on his death X made a chargeable transfer of £50,000. X's affairs were such that business relief (at 50 per cent) would have been available on the woodlands. In 1979 Y sold some of the woodlands for a full consideration of £40,000. This triggered a deferred charge, but as 50 per cent business relief would have been available on X's death, the amount to be brought into account was only £20,000. This was taxed at the death rates that applied in 1979 on transfers between £50,000 and £70,000 as follows:

$$£10,000 \times 30\% = £3,000$$

$$£10,000 \times 35\% = \underline{£3,500}$$

£6,500 deferred tax due

933

In February 1996 Y gave his spouse Z some of the woodlands worth £45,000.[459] This would not have given rise to a deferred charge, nor would it have constituted a chargeable transfer.[460]

In June 1997 Z settled some of the woodlands, worth £40,000, on discretionary trusts. This would have resulted in both a deferred charge and a chargeable transfer. As business relief would have been available on X's death the £40,000 would have been reduced to £20,000 and taxed at the rates that apply between £70,000 and £90,000 in June 1997 as follows:

$$£20,000 \times 0\% = \text{nil deferred tax due}$$

Assuming Z had made previous chargeable transfers totalling £200,000, that she has already used her available exemptions, and that business relief is available, tax would have been charged under the main charging provisions as follows:

	£
Valued transferred	40,000
less deferred tax	Nil
	40,000
less 50% business relief	20,000
	20,000

20,000 (to be brought into account and taxed at the rates that applied on transfers between £200,000 and £220,000 in June 1997 (nil rate band = £215,000))

$$£15,000 \times 0\% = \text{Nil}$$

$$£5,000 \times 20\% = \frac{£1,000}{£1,000} \text{ tax due}$$

Since deferred tax had been charged on the woodlands, subsequent disposals of the woodlands by the trustees will not be subject to the deferred charge. Notice that if deferred tax had been triggered in the above example then even though no tax had been charged on the transfer from Z (e.g. because it fell within Z's nil rate band) there would be no question of any refund of the deferred tax, which arises on a separate chargeable occasion.

In September 2002 Y died. His personal representatives paid the tax on the woodlands comprised in his estate, which Y left to his son. Subsequent disposals of the woodlands by the son will not be subject to the deferred charge.

Administration

26–206   Note the following administrative points:

[459] IHTA 1984 s.126(2).
[460] IHTA 1984 s.18(1).

(1) *Deferred charge*. The person liable for deferred tax where the disposal is by way of sale is the person who is entitled to the proceeds of the sale. Where the disposal is made otherwise than by way of a sale the person liable is the person who would be entitled to the proceeds of the sale if the disposal were a sale.[461] The person liable must deliver a return or account within six months from the end of the month in which the disposal takes place.[462] Tax is due six months after the end of the month in which the disposal occurs.[463]

(2) *Chargeable transfer*. Where the transfer is made during the transferor's lifetime an election can be made to pay tax by 10 yearly instalments, the first of which is due six months after the end of the month in which the transfer is made, interest running on each instalment only after it falls due.

---

[461] IHTA 1984 s.208.
[462] IHTA 1984 s.216(7).
[463] IHTA 1984 s.226(4).

CHAPTER 27

HERITAGE PROPERTY

I. INTRODUCTION

27–01   This chapter is concerned with three related subjects—conditionally exempt transfers, periodic and exit charges in respect of which a conditional exemption or deferral is given, and maintenance funds for historic buildings. As was discussed in Chapters 3 and 8, certain transfers made to charities or to various specified public bodies are exempted from being chargeable transfers under the main charging provisions and do not give rise to exit charges under the special charging provisions. In addition, the legislation makes provision—in a rather complicated fashion—to extend favoured treatment to transfers of certain property (realty and chattels) important to the national heritage, but which remain in private ownership. Transfers of such property are afforded special treatment only so long as certain conditions remain satisfied with respect to the property in question. The essence of these conditions is that the public must have reasonable access to the property, and the property must be maintained to an acceptable standard. The test of what is "reasonable access" and the quality test of the property concerned were materially altered by the Finance Act 1998. A transfer of value which qualifies for such favoured treatment is known as a "conditionally exempt transfer"; an occasion on which an exit charge would otherwise arise which qualifies for such treatment is known as a "conditionally exempt occasion". In the event that a condition attaching to such a transfer or occasion is infringed, the favoured treatment is withdrawn, and tax becomes payable. It is to be noted that the favoured treatment given to heritage property does not extend to shares in a company which owns such property.

Other reference material

Until the Finance Act 1998, the principal reference document in respect of heritage **27–02** property was the Revenue (as it then was) booklet IR67 "Capital Taxation and the National Heritage". The booklet is no longer available from HMRC but following consultations between HMRC and various professional bodies (Heritage Group of Lawyers, Historic Houses Association and the Museums, Libraries and Archives Council ("MLA")[1] a revised edition of HMRC's comprehensive memorandum "Capital Taxation and the National Heritage" was published on September 15, 2011 ("the Memorandum"). The Memorandum supersedes booklet IR67 and other Revenue publications since then and covers legislative and other changes up until 2009. The new Memorandum follows the familiar format of IR67 though it is not in booklet form). IR67 is still relevant for transfers of heritage property not affected by the Finance Act 1998 and for all transfers before March 17, 1998. Other useful reference documents include the "Capital Taxes—Relief for Heritage Assets: Notes on the changes made by the Finance Act 1998" issued by the Revenue in January 1999, the MLA Acceptance in Lieu Report published annually up until 2009/10 and *The Goodison Review*.[2]

Extra-statutory concession: foreign-owned works of art and decorations and awards

Before turning to the various provisions, it is to be noted that the Enactment of Extra- **27–03** Statutory Concessions Order 2009 amended ss.5(1)(b) and 64(2) of the 1984 Act such that foreign-owned works of art situated in the United Kingdom solely for the purpose of public display, cleaning or restoration will not become liable to inheritance tax on the owner's death and are not to be regarded as relevant property for the purposes of calculating the charge to tax arising under s.64.[3]

The 2009 Order also amended s.6 of the 1984 Act such that decorations awarded for valour are excluded property if they have never been disposed of for money or money's worth[4] to enable beneficiaries who wish to retain them for sentimental reasons from being liable to a potentially significant inheritance tax charge.[5]

II. CONDITIONALLY EXEMPT TRANSFERS

The provisions relating to conditionally exempt transfers fall into three categories. **27–04** The original provisions, i.e. those found in Sch.5 to the 1984 Act, were regarded as an interim measure pending the recommendations of the Select Committee on a Wealth Tax. Under these provisions, exemption was given only to transfers made on death. Although exemption is no longer given under those provisions, they can still be

---

[1] On July 26, 2010 it was announced that the MLA would be abolished. Its functions were transferred on October 1, 2011 to the Arts Council England and the National Archives.

[2] Nicholas Goodison, The Goodison Review, *Securing the Best for our Museums: Private Giving and Government Support* (January 2004).

[3] SI 2009/730 art.13 superseded the extra-statutory concession previously published by the Revenue in relation to foreign-owned works of art.

[4] SI 2009/730 art.14 superseded the extra-statutory concession previously published by the Revenue in relation to decorations for valour or gallant conduct.

[5] HMRC memorandum, *Capital Taxation and National Heritage*, para.4.11.

relevant where conditions attaching to an exemption given under those sections cease to be satisfied so that a charge arises. The provisions in Sch.5 were then superseded effectively by ss.30–34, which apply to transfers made after April 6, 1976. The provisions in ss.30–34 apply to lifetime transfers as well as to transfers made on death, but for periodic and exit charges, see ss.78–79. In relation to certain property ("works of art") a further set of provisions was added by the Finance Act 1998 Sch.25 paras 4 and 5 introducing a new test for "reasonable access" for the general public and limiting the quality test to that of pre-eminence. All three sets of provisions are considered; emphasis is given to the rules governing a transfer or death on or after March 17, 1998, which are considered first. The relationship of these provisions to estate duty is also discussed.

Spouses and charities

27–05   The exemptions given for:

> (1) transfers between spouses; and
> (2) transfers to charities

take precedence over the conditional exemption given to heritage property in ss.30–34 and the Finance Act 1998 s.142 and Sch.25, which therefore apply only in so far as neither the spouse nor the charity exemption applies to the transfer in question.[6] Nevertheless, on a transfer of ownership, legal or beneficial, HMRC will require the transferee to join in the undertakings (see para.27–10 below).

PETs

27–06   It is important to understand the interaction of the PET and conditional exemption regimes. The availability of the conditional exemption is disregarded in deciding whether or not a transfer of value can be a PET. If the transfer is in fact a PET and the transferor dies within seven years of making it then it is possible, following his death, to claim conditional exemption. This is explained below, at para.27–23.[7]

The requirements for conditional exemption

27–07   A transfer of value is a conditionally exempt transfer to the extent that the following requirements are satisfied:

> (1) The value transferred must be attributable to property which was:
>> (a) transferred by a notional transfer made on death[8]; or
>> (b) acquired by the transferor on a death and on that death either (i) the property had been transferred to him by a notional transfer under s.4, which was itself a conditionally exempt transfer, or (ii) the value of the

---

[6] IHTA 1984 s.30(4).
[7] Contrast the position on maintenance funds: see para.27–76.
[8] IHTA 1984 s.30(3).

938

property was left out of account for purposes of CTT or estate duty because of the equivalent estate duty exemption[9]; or

   (c) owned beneficially by the transferor, his spouse, or by the two of them throughout the six years ending with the transfer.[10]

(2) The property in question must be designated by the Treasury under s.31.[11]

(3) A person the Board[12] think appropriate must give the undertaking required for that kind of property.[13] The undertaking is usually given by the new owner. Where property is held in trust the "owner" includes the trustees and any beneficiary having the use and enjoyment of the property from time to time.

(4) It should be noted that a claim must be made in advance of the charge where the occasion of charge is the anniversary charge to IHT for discretionary trusts[14] or the approval of a proposed maintenance fund. In this regard, it should be noted that following the Finance Act 2006, a number of trusts are now subject to the relevant property regime and it is likely that more trusts will become subject to the relevant property regime in time (see Chapter 10). The result of this is a number of works of art or items of heritage property which did not previously need to be conditionally exempt (say because they were held in an old-style life interest or accumulation and maintenance trust) will be subject to 10-yearly anniversary charges going forward. It is important to note that if a ten year anniversary falls before conditional exemption is granted, then the IHT will have to be paid and cannot be claimed back at a later stage.[15]

The conditional exemption may therefore be claimed: **27–08**

   (a) for transfers made on death;

   (b) for lifetime transfers into a discretionary trust or to a company;

   (c) for a lifetime transfer which was a PET when made if the donor dies within the following seven years; and

   (d) where the donor has reserved a benefit which subsists until or is given up within seven years of his death.

The position in relation to a failed PET, be it an actual PET under (c) or a notional PET under (d) above, is discussed at para.27–24. Note that the six year ownership requirement in 1(c) in para.27–07 above is relevant only if the conditional exemption is claimed for a lifetime transfer or on a conditionally exempt occasion under s.78 (e.g. a s.65 exit charge).

Interests in possession

It suffices that the transferor[16] has an interest in possession in the property; he need   **27–09**
not own the property outright. Since the Finance Act 2006, an interest in possession would primarily refer to a pre-March 22, 2006 interest in possession, though will also

---

[9] IHTA 1984 s.30(3).

[10] IHTA 1984 s.30(3), e.g. for four years, by the wife, and two years by the husband.

[11] IHTA 1984 s.30(1).

[12] The functions of the Treasury were transferred to the then Commissioners of the Inland Revenue ("the Board") on July 25, 1985.

[13] IHTA 1984 s.30(1).

[14] IHTA 1984 s.79(3).

[15] HMRC memorandum, *Capital Taxation and the National Heritage*, Appendix 2, para.21.

[16] Or as the case may be, the transferor's spouse, or the person from whom the transferor acquired the property.

include immediate post death interests, disabled person's interests and transitional serial interests.[17] This follows from the fact that the exemption is given to the extent that the value transferred is attributable to property which satisfies the above criteria, i.e. the exemption is given by reference to property, not to property as such. As has been noted previously, under the legislation a person beneficially entitled to an interest in possession (being either a pre-March 22, 2006 interest in possession, an immediate post death interest, a disabled person's interest or a transitional serial interest) in property is treated as owning the property in which his interest subsists.[18] The value transferred by any transfer involving an interest in possession in property will therefore be attributable to the property in which that interest subsists, with the result that for the purposes of the conditional exemption there is no difference between property which a person owns outright and property in which he has an interest in possession. Any life interest trusts created on or after March 22, 2006 will not give rise to an interest in possession (as they are subject to the relevant property regime) and so the life tenant in such a case could not be the transferor in this capacity.

Designation and undertaking

27–10   The Board may designate property falling within any one of five categories as qualifying for conditional exemption. These, as well as the undertaking which is required to be given in each case, are set out below. In all cases an undertaking must be given that, until the person beneficially entitled to the property dies or the property is disposed of, reasonable steps will be taken for securing reasonable access to the public.[19] In the case of land in Items 2 and 4 the undertaking will include strict adherence to agreed best practice for sound ecological management. Items 3, 4 and 5 in the Table are referred to as "associated properties" and, in the event of a charge to tax arising, are subject to special rules: see paras 27–32 and following.

Kind of property	Basic undertaking
1. *Works of art, etc:* any works of art, pictures, prints, books, manuscripts, scientific collections or other things not yielding income which appear to the Board to be of national,[20] scientific, historic or artistic interest and are of pre-eminent quality (see para. 27–19).[21]	The property will be kept permanently in the United Kingdom and will not leave it even temporarily except for a purpose and a period approved by the Board,[22] and such steps as agreed between the Board and the person giving this undertaking, as are set out in the undertaking, will be taken for the preservation of the property and for securing reasonable access to the public.[23]

---

[17] IHTA 1984 s.49(1A).

[18] IHTA 1984 s.49(1) and s.49(1A).

[19] IHTA 1984 ss.31(2) and (4).

[20] IHTA 1984 s.31(1), "national interest" includes interest within any part of the United Kingdom; IHTA 1984 s.31(5).

[21] IHTA 1984 s.31 and (aa) inserted by FA 1998 Sch.25 para.4.

[22] IHTA 1984 s.31(2).

[23] IHTA 1984 s.31(2).

Kind of property	Basic undertaking

Note that what is "reasonable access" is a different test for undertakings given after July 30, 1998, from that which applies to undertakings given on or before that date, as is discussed below at para.27–12. In addition, undertakings given before the Finance Act 1998 can be varied to secure public access which is not confined to access only where a prior appointment has been made.[24]

If it appears to the Board that any documents contain information which for personal or other reasons ought to be treated as confidential they may exclude those documents as they think fit from so much of the above undertaking as relates to public access.[25]

2.	*Land:* any land which in the Board's opinion is of outstanding scenic, historic or scientific interest.[26]	Such steps as are agreed between the Board and the person giving this undertaking, are set out in the undertaking and will be taken for the maintenance of the land and the preservation of its character.[27]
3.	*Buildings:* any building for the preservation of which special steps should in the Board's opinion be taken by reason of its outstanding historic or architectural interest.[28]	Such steps as agreed between the Board and the person giving this undertaking are set out in the undertaking and will be taken for the maintenance, repair and preservation of the property.[29]
4.	*Related land:* any land which in the Board's opinion is essential for the protection of the character and amenities of that building.[30]	See Item 3 above. An additional undertaking must be given[31]; see para.27–17 below.

---

[24] IHTA 1984 s.35A, as amended by FA 1998 Sch.25 paras 8(1) and (10).

[25] IHTA 1984 s.31(3).

[26] IHTA 1984 s.31(1); a site of special scientific interest can be expected to qualify: see *Hansard*, Vol.417, col.318.

[27] IHTA 1984 s.31(4).

[28] IHTA 1984 s.31(1). It seems that the land and the relevant building need not be owned by the same person.

[29] IHTA 1984 s.31(4).

[30] IHTA 1984 s.31(1). Before March 17, 1985, the land had to adjoin the building; FA 1985 s.94; and see para.27–17.

[31] IHTA 1984 s.31(4A).

5.   *Associated objects:* any object which in the Board's opinion is historically associated with such a building.[32]

Such steps as are agreed between the Board and the person giving this undertaking are set out in the undertaking and will be taken for the maintenance, repair and preservation of the object and for keeping it associated with that building.[33]

27–11 Included among the Law Society's 1979 Budget submissions was the following:

> "Treasury Form 700A states the requirements laid down as to fulfilment of the undertaking to take reasonable steps to secure reasonable access to the public for conditionally exempt objects. Conditions (i) and (ii) approved by the Treasury involve the Owner of the object either also owning a house suitable to be opened to the public, or in lending the object to a public collection on a long-term basis. The basic premises of exemption are therefore either that the owner of a heritage object is also the possessor of a house of a nature appropriate to be opened to the public, or is prepared to forego personal enjoyment of the object. Other methods of access are only permissible if the claimant can conclusively show both alternatives are unreasonable.
>
> The system therefore virtually precludes the ownership and enjoyment of a heritage object by persons of ordinary means and restricts the ownership of our heritage to those who are either otherwise well endowed, or who regard the object as an investment to be stored elsewhere rather than something which they wish to care for personally.
>
> The requirement of a conclusive burden of proof on the claimant is unreasonable and The Law Society has received representations from firms of solicitors pointing out the difficulties and the alternatives that are available even where the test has been satisfied. It is difficult to persuade a museum or gallery to accommodate an object for a possibly limited period of a few months at a time, as this interferes with the permanent collection and it is known that, for example, the Tate Gallery has declined an object on the ground that the removal to and from the owner's residence would contribute to the deterioration of the object itself. The alternative of a view by appointment system with public notice has been described as 'a burglar's charter' as it gives public notice that a possibly valuable object is in a private house.
>
> *It is recommended* that the Treasury review their public access requirements, particularly in cases where the claimant may be seeking a conditional exemption for only a small number of objects perfectly capable of being displayed in a normal dwelling house. It is suggested that possibly access should be restricted in these circumstances to persons able to show they are bona fide representatives of learned bodies who need to view the object for study purposes."

On July 30, 1982, the Revenue (as it then was) issued a press release announcing that they had revised Form 700A. Accompanying guidance notes listed three ways in which the public access undertaking may thenceforth be fulfilled. An owner who did not live in a house which was open to the public could now choose between:

(1) lending his objects for display in a privately owned house or room regularly open to the public;

(2) lending his objects (anonymously, if he chose) on a long term basis to a public collection be it national, local authority or university, or a museum, gallery or

---

[32] IHTA 1984 s.31(1)(e). It seems that the object and the relevant building need not be owned by the same person.

[33] IHTA 1984 s.31(4).

historic house run by a charitable trust. If he wanted an indemnity against loss or damage he could apply to the Museums and Galleries Commission, which was responsible for the indemnity scheme operated by the Minister for the Arts; or

(3) agreeing to allow viewing by appointment and to lend (again, anonymously, if he chose), where it could be done without physical risk to the object, on request by a public collection, for special exhibitions that were properly organised and met sufficient security standards. Publication of the availability of an object for viewing by appointment was by an entry on the registry of heritage property in the National Art Library of the Victoria and Albert Museum and elsewhere. Owners were required—if requested—to lend the object for special exhibitions for up to six months in a two year period, and to make arrangements for members of the public to view the object.

It was clear from the revised form that the owner need only register the name and address of someone acting on his own behalf—he need not identify himself or the address at which the object was held, with the result that the so called "burglar's charter" was done away with.

The position from July 31, 1998

Since July 31, 1998, it has not been possible to provide public access to conditionally **27–12** exempt property solely by prior appointment. Instead, HMRC require open access on a certain number of days a year and for the terms of the undertaking to be published. Guidance as to the extent of open access that will need to be provided to the public was first issued by HMRC in the form of an Annex to the IHTM (this was compiled with help from the National Archives and following comments from the Heritage Lawyers' Group and Historic Houses Association[34]). The Annex was withdrawn following the publication of the Memorandum which incorporates the guidance previously contained in the Annex. HMRC note that the guidance on public access requirements is just that; it is not exhaustive nor binding and will evolve over time in line with the cases that are seen. However, it provides a useful starting point when considering the post July 30, 1998 requirements of open access.

HMRC's approach to the demands of open access is neatly encapsulated in the Memorandum:

> "Other than for the statutory need for open access, we do not follow a prescriptive approach. Instead, we interpret the legislation broadly as normally requiring an acceptable quality and quantity of access on an annual basis, in the context of an undertaking sufficiently robust for its purpose and period."[35]

The Government objective in requiring open access, when coupled with the more rigid pre-eminence test (for which, see para.27–19 below), is to ensure that all conditionally exempt works are, or will be (in due course), regularly available for access in public museums and galleries, etc. or more prominent private and other houses and buildings (e.g. National Trust properties) regularly open to the public. To this end, HMRC's responsibility is to agree the steps for preservation of the heritage property and for

---

[34] HMRC, *Changes to Procedures for Conditional Exemption and National Heritage Matters*, November 2007.

[35] HMRC memorandum, *Capital Taxation and the National Heritage*, Appendix 1A, para.6.

securing reasonable access, whilst the Arts Council England will consider pre-eminence. The Guidance Notes make it clear that HMRC do not want owners to have to produce an undue amount of detail initially but that they do, however, need demonstrative evidence of an owner's serious intention to enter into and be bound by a suitable access arrangement before public money is devoted to testing the claim for exemption.[36] In other words, HMRC will no longer allow a claim to be made for conditional exemption and for there then to be prolonged correspondence and negotiations as to a) whether the object is pre-eminent or not (the taxpayer is expected to have already determined this to a large degree himself) and b) what the access requirements should be. To this end, HMRC notes that it is expected that a great many of the points concerning open access should be resolved **before** an application for conditional exemption is made.

Where a claimant has works of art which are already in galleries or historic houses open to the public or are the subject of suitable loan arrangements with museums or galleries, then HMRC see no reason why owners with the help of the guidance should not be able to make acceptable proposals for open access at the time of the claim. In the case of owners claiming exemption for a range or large number of items not presently on display in a historic house open to the public or in a public museum or gallery, HMRC consider that such owners should have decided whether they intend to display the items at their homes on terms acceptable to them or to arrange for display elsewhere. Any proposals for display elsewhere should be well-formulated, with the borrowing organisations prepared to take the items on terms acceptable to HMRC, even if the detail remains to be finalised. In the case of owners claiming exemption for just one or a handful of probably disparate items neither normally kept nor presently on display in a historic house open to the public or in a public museum or gallery, HMRC's preference is for these items to be displayed long term or on a regular basis in a public museum, gallery or historic house open to the public. Such an owner when claiming exemption will have to demonstrate interest from a museum, gallery or from the owner of a historic house to display the items on a long term or regular basis before HMRC are willing to refer it to the Arts Council England for a decision on pre-eminence. Alternatively, owners whose homes are not the sort of buildings that open to the public might want to offer open access at home. This might be because they do not want routinely to part with their works of art or are having difficulty in finding museums or galleries willing to commit themselves to such arrangements. HMRC state they would need to be satisfied that the at-home arrangements and the steps the owner intends to take to seek out exhibitions on an ongoing basis, would properly deliver the access requirements.[37]

With HMRC clear that the above principles are, to an extent, requirements before any applications for conditional exemption are even entertained, it is necessary to be aware of what open access will entail. In general, a conditionally exempt item should be available to the public for viewing at the owner's home (if already open to the public or it would be suitable for displaying the items), at another suitable building that opens to the public or at a suitable public museum, gallery or other similar institution. The access should be for a suitable period and time each year and without the need for a prior appointment. Although strict guidelines as to what a suitable period would be are not given, HMRC notes that they "would not expect this annual period to be less than a month or so (or, where it suited an owner and an institutional borrower, a corresponding triennial arrangement)".[38] However, the Guidance does concede that "only in very

---

[36] HMRC memorandum, *Capital Taxation and the National Heritage*, Appendix 1A, para.8.
[37] HMRC memorandum, *Capital Taxation and the National Heritage*, Appendix 1A, para.8.
[38] HMRC memorandum, *Capital Taxation and the National Heritage*, Appendix 1A, para.9.

exceptional circumstances" could HMRC "accept that gaps of three or more years are reasonable".[39]

Although each owner will put forward and agree different access proposals, in practise many owners meet such requirements for open access by means of participating in Heritage Open Days (and indeed HMRC encourage such owners to do so). The Heritage Open Days programme was established in 1994 and is currently funded by English Heritage and operates under the management of the Heritage Open Days National Partnership; a consortium of organisations including the National Trust, The Heritage Alliance, and Civic Voice. The programme ensures that for four days in September each year a large number of private houses and buildings across the UK are open to any member of the public who wishes to visit them for free.[40] HMRC can and will agree that participation in this (even on a reduced scale, say on two of the four days and with a limited number of visitors), combined with access by appointment throughout the rest of the year is sufficient to meet the open access requirements.

Further to the actual requirements for access as detailed above, HMRC also make it clear that this should be supplemented with access with prior arrangement at other times (i.e. as is the case for most items conditionally exempted pre-July 31, 1998), a willingness to make loans to public collections for special exhibitions and a willingness to provide curators with images to help them in mounting exhibitions.[41]

A number of objects do not necessarily fit into the requirements for open access as detailed above and there are a number of qualifications. It is acceptable to display, say, a representative sample of a dinner service or silver set, so long as the remainder can be accessed by appointment. A full catalogue of any conditionally exempt archive should be deposited with The National Archives, thereby making it available for public access, whilst other manuscripts and drawings (or a representative sample of them) should be displayed for short periods (where conservation considerations permit) or loaned to a suitable institution. As far as printed books are concerned, the requirements are normally met if the public can see the books' spines on library shelves or in a house open to public access. To widen the publicity for these works, HMRC now ask owners to allow publication of their titles in either the English Short Title Catalogue (for all books printed mainly, but not exclusively, in English between 1473 and 1800) or the Incunabula Short Title Catalogue (all books, pamphlets or broadsides printed before 1501), both of which are run by the British Library. Finally, any items in a house open to the public but not on the public route should be accessible by rotation onto the public route, arrangements for special tours or by secure access on request on days when the house is open.[42]

HMRC agree that an owner may charge a reasonable amount for access and images and leave it to the owner to determine what is reasonable.[43] HMRC's position is that any charges should normally be along the lines of those made by locally comparable sources, such as the National Trust. HMRC do not think that with open access an owner should seek proof of a vistor's identity, though in cases of access by prior arrangement they consider that it is acceptable to seek both proof of identity (i.e. a passport) and proof of address (i.e. a utility bill), much as are required under money laundering regulations.[44] There is also further guidance concerning insurance of items loaned to public collections, open access to items in remote or distant locations (which is not

---

[39] HMRC memorandum, *Capital Taxation and the National Heritage*, Appendix 1A, para.9.
[40] See *http://www.heritageopendays.org.uk* [Accessed October 10, 2012] for further details.
[41] HMRC memorandum, *Capital Taxation and the National Heritage*, Appendix 1A, para.9.
[42] HMRC memorandum, *Capital Taxation and the National Heritage*, Appendix 1A, para.10.
[43] HMRC memorandum, *Capital Taxation and the National Heritage*, Appendix 1A, para.11.
[44] HMRC memorandum, *Capital Taxation and the National Heritage*, Appendix 1A, para.11.

encouraged) and the use of electronic images on websites to complement (rather than replace) open access.[45]

The Memorandum also provides an indication of best practice for access by prior appointment, both pre-July 31, 1998 and post-July 30, 1998. Again, there should be a suitable entry on the HMRC website giving sufficient information as to allow the public the opportunity to decide whether or not to make an appointment. The public can then make contact with the contact point so as to make an appointment as soon as reasonably practicable.[46] The Memorandum states, perhaps unrealistically, that Owners

> "should normally allow viewing on the day requested by the prospective viewer or offer a choice of viewing between 10.00 and 16.00 on any one of at least three weekdays and two Saturdays or Sundays within the following four weeks".[47]

A number of points are made as to holidays, the breaking of appointments etc and the Memorandum concludes by inviting the public to inform HMRC "if they feel short-changed" or find fault with the system. The Memorandum also notes that the owners and their advisers should approach HMRC if they are unsure how best to proceed in any particular circumstance.[48]

In practice, and in the authors' experience, the above guidelines for open access can cover a multitude of different access plans and each case is very much determined on its own merits. What is an acceptable proposal for open access in one case will be unacceptable in another. The Heritage Team of HMRC are always willing to discuss proposed arrangements with the intention that the competing demands of the need for public access and the proportionate way in which an owner is expected to provide this can be balanced out.

Although there is provision that if there is a failure to agree what is "reasonable access" in all the circumstances, then this will lead to HMRC stating their view unilaterally which is then tested at a hearing before a Special Commissioner, as will be seen above, HMRC's view is that they will not entertain applications for conditional exemption without there having been a great deal of thought put into the proposals for open access which are expected to accompany the initial application. It is likely therefore that HMRC will not entertain too many failures to agree reasonable open access.

27–13   As well as the requirements for open access detailed above, the Finance Act 1998 introduced legislation whereby in certain cases HMRC can seek to vary any agreed undertakings before the next chargeable event. From July 31, 1998, under s.35A any undertaking (including those made before this date) may be varied from time to time by agreement between the Board and the person bound by the undertaking.[49] The main purpose of this section is to provide increased access to those items exempted before the new rules were introduced in 1998 and where access is available only "by appointment". In certain circumstances, the Special Commissioner may direct that the varied undertaking is to have effect from a date specified by him if he is satisfied that:

(1) the Board have made a proposal for the variation of the undertaking to the person bound by it;

---

[45] HMRC memorandum "Capital Taxation and the National Heritage", Appendix 1A, para.11.
[46] HMRC memorandum, *Capital Taxation and the National Heritage*, Appendix 1A, paras 18–21.
[47] HMRC memorandum, *Capital Taxation and the National Heritage*, Appendix 1A, para.23.
[48] HMRC memorandum, *Capital Taxation and the National Heritage*, Appendix 1A, paras 25–26.
[49] IHTA 1984 s.35A as inserted by FA 1998 Sch.25 para.8.

(2) that person has failed to agree the proposed variation within six months after the date on which the proposal was made; and

(3) it is just and reasonable in all the circumstances to require the proposed variation to be made.[50]

The date specified by the Special Commissioner must not be less than sixty days after the date of his direction. It should also be noted that this section will not take effect if, before the date specified, a variation different from that to which the direction relates is agreed between the Board and the person bound by the undertaking.[51]

There is a right to appeal to the Special Commissioners, and against the determination of that appeal, to the High Court if the appellant is dissatisfied with the determination on point of law.[52]

The position from July 31, 1998 for works of art conditionally exempt from March 9, 1982

Re an application to vary the undertakings of A and B

Many items conditionally exempted between March 9, 1982 and July 30, 1998 **27–14** satisfied the reasonable access test if they were available for view only "by appointment". There is provision in the Finance Act 1998 for such undertakings to be reviewed so they include open access as described above.[53]

HMRC's ability to vary existing undertakings was considered by the Special Commissioners (Stephen Oliver QC) in *Re An Application to Vary Undertakings*.[54] The Special Commissioners were invited by the Revenue (as it then was) to determine whether a proposed revision of two sets of undertakings (relating to chattels owned by A and B respectively) should be enforced under the procedure in s.35A as set out in para.27–13 above. The two taxpayers contended that, firstly, the Revenue was not competent retrospectively and unilaterally to renegotiate agreements for "by appointment" only access and secondly and in any event, the revised proposals were not just and reasonable in all the proposed circumstances and so did not meet the criteria set out in s.35A(2).

The Special Commissioner held that the Revenue had no discretion as to whether or not they could renegotiate the undertakings as this was a matter for Parliament and Parliament had legislated for such renegotiations. He commented that:

> "it is clear from a reading of the heritage provisions in the 1998 Act that Parliament has introduced a package of measures designed to secure enhanced public access to conditionally exempt assets. The procedures are different depending upon whether conditional exemption is obtained by reason of existing undertakings or subsequent undertakings. Nonetheless Parliament, and not the Inland Revenue, has determined what the public interest is and how it is to be served. Consequently, whatever force there may be in any particular criticisms to the policy, the Proposals cannot be faulted on the grounds that there is no overriding public interest behind them."[55]

---

[50] IHTA 1984 s.35A(2).
[51] IHTA 1984 ss.35A(3) and (4).
[52] IHTA 1984 ss.221–225.
[53] IHTA 1984 s.35A as amended by FA 1998 Sch.25 paras 8(1) and 10.
[54] *Re An Application to Vary Undertakings* (2004) UKSC SpC00439.
[55] *Re An Application to Vary Undertakings* (2004) UKSC SpC00439 at 56.

It follows from this that to challenge HMRC's authority under the 1998 Act to seek to implement the variation of existing agreements is probably a matter for judicial review, thereby meaning, in the absence of any such judicial review or a change in the legislation by Parliament, HMRC are prima facie authorised by the legislation to look to implement such variations. However, for such variations to be implemented by the Special Commissioner, any proposals should be just and reasonable in all of the circumstances and so will depend upon the individual facts of each case.

The Special Commissioner considered the facts of each case before him. Both taxpayers lived in country houses which were not conditionally exempt and IHT had been paid when both of them inherited their property. In accordance with their agreed undertakings, both had made the conditionally exempt chattels available for inspection by the public on a "by appointment" basis but HMRC were now looking for open access without prior arrangement on at least 15 days a year for A and 10 days a year for B, as well as imposing a requirement for four daily tours of up to 10–25 people for each taxpayer.

The Special Commissioner found that the proposals put forward by HMRC in both matters were so "as to make it neither just nor reasonable ... to direct that the Proposals take effect".[56] He cited a number of reasons for his decision, making clear that all of them should be applied strictly on a case by case basis. One of his prime considerations was that the homes concerned were clearly private family homes (on which there was no conditional exemption and IHT had been paid) and that it would have been a major intrusion into their family lives so as to re-organise their homes to receive the public on such a scale. Further, due to the large number of conditionally exempt items in each case, it would have been unreasonable to suggest, as an alternative, that they be transported to a place of general public access and, in any event, local museums were only interest in specific items for specific events rather than displaying the collection as a whole on a continuing basis. The Special Commissioner also considered the security ramifications of the Proposals and found that it was not a problem to be ignored (despite what HMRC had previously argued), noting that:

> "I think the Proposals fail to recognize the already burdensome position of the Owners and the security implications tend to the unreasonable side of the equation".[57]

The Special Commissioner commented in conclusion that:

> "Access to the Part I objects calls for a serious intrusion into the family lives of the Owners. The increased risks of theft and damage to the Owners' possessions occasioned by the Proposals are ... beyond what Parliament had in mind when empowering the inclusion of extended access requirements and publication requirements. The retroactive effect of the Proposals is such as to impose on the Owners a state of affairs that they would not have adopted had all the options been open to them when they entered into the existing undertakings. The consequence is that they may now be required to pay the IHT, if they reject or breach the varied conditions, at a possibly greater rate than that applicable when the transfers from the previous owners took place; and they will have to pay the tax on a different and possibly increased value ... the disadvantages that would be imposed on them were the Proposals to be enforced are disproportionate to the aim of achieving greater public access to the Part I objects."[58]

In summary therefore, the Special Commissioner was very careful to ensure that he did not rule against HMRC's ability to vary pre-July 31, 1998 undertakings (which he upheld) but equally was careful to ensure that both decisions were made on the

---

[56] *Re An Application to Vary Undertakings* (2004) UKSC SpC00439 at 177.
[57] *Re An Application to Vary Undertakings* (2004) UKSC SpC00439 at 153.
[58] *Re An Application to Vary Undertakings* (2004) UKSC SpC00439 at 177.

particular facts and indeed every situation will depend on its own facts (much as shown in the closing remarks of the judgment noted above). To this end, the decision could be utilised by both HMRC and taxpayers in support of any claims they bring either to vary any existing undertakings or to prevent any such variation, though, of course, it will become less important over time as the provisions become redundant and pre-July 31, 1998 undertakings come to be renewed on the next transfer of value.

Publicity from July 31, 1998

Another key part of the open access requirement is the need for publicity to be **27–15** given to all conditionally exempt items. Central to this is the HMRC website (*http://www.hmrc.gov.uk/heritage*) which consists of a database, divided into three sections (Works of Art, Land, Buildings and their Contents and Collections of works of Art and other objects) and which replaces the former "V&A" List. The details to be included in each entry are set out in the revised Memorandumand consist of, inter alia, a full description of the object, group or collection, the county in which it can be seen (though not the full address), a contact point for information and viewing details. Where collections of works of art are concerned, generic descriptions which seek to draw attention to the best or most attractive works of art or pieces are acceptable.[59] In practice, the details required for the website are not as intrusive as were initially feared and it does not seem to have served as a "burglar's charter" as many homeowners were greatly concerned that it would. HMRC's practice is to agree the terms of publicity at the same time as agreeing the undertakings and so it is possible, on a case by case basis, to try and limit the full extent of the information provided.

Where there are items which are displayed in a house not normally open to the public, HMRC also require the owner to provide more publicity than the entry on the website. In such instances an owner is also expected to provide further publicity in the local press or at the local tourist information centre as well as in a national publication or guide.[60] For those who have undertaken to do so, images shall also be provided to museum and gallery curators, students etc at a reasonable charge.

Administration

Hitherto, the conditional exemption procedure has been administered by HMRC **27–16** with the benefit of specialist advice from other bodies such as the Countryside Agency (now Natural England) and others as appropriate. The Goodison Review recommended that administration be transferred to the Department of Culture, Media and Sport, specifically the MLA. On July 26, 2010 it was announced the MLA would be abolished under new proposals to cut the number of public bodies funded by the Government. Its functions were transferred on October 1, 2011 to the Arts Council England and the National Archives. HMRC continue to administer the procedure, whilst the Arts

---

[59] HMRC memorandum, *Capital Taxation and the National Heritage*, Appendix 1A, para.15.
[60] HMRC memorandum, *Capital Taxation and the National Heritage*, Appendix 1A, para.17.

Council England now considers the pre-eminence or otherwise of the various objects.

Additional undertaking

27–17   There is an additional undertaking required in the case of related land[61] which stems from the fact that such land only receives conditional exemption because it is essential for the protection of the character and amenities of an outstanding building which is itself eligible for exemption. Accordingly, if exemption is to be granted for such land not only must suitable undertakings be given in respect of the land itself but, in addition, corresponding "supportive undertakings" must be given in respect of the outstanding building whose character and amenities the land protects; other qualifying essential amenity land lying between the building and the area of land in question; and any other essential amenity land which HMRC consider to be "physically closely connected" with either the land in question or the outstanding building. It is for the person seeking the designation of related land to secure that any undertaking required is given.[62]

27–18   A typical illustration where such undertakings are required would be where an outstanding building is owned by A, and two other taxpayers (B and C) own qualifying land adjoining the outstanding building. A claim for exemption by C will, in such a case, depend upon supportive undertakings being given by both A and B. The requirement for supportive undertakings is mandatory in the case of the outstanding building and any intervening land: in the case of other land "physically closely connected" the matter is one for the discretion of HMRC. Where such supportive undertakings are required in the case of property which has already been conditionally exempted, the original undertakings must be renewed. Thus, in the case of the owner of the outstanding building, it will be necessary for him to agree that a wider area embracing the related land is to be covered by inter-dependent undertakings.

Designation—the quality test

27–19   For works of art, the Finance Act 1998 introduced radical change. Before July 31, 1998 the required standard was known as "museum quality", i.e. of a "sufficiently high quality to be displayed in a public collection, whether national, local authority or university".[63] Over time, this had become an undemanding test. In relation to the making of designation on a claim made from July 31, 1998 the requisite standard is now "of pre-eminent" quality.[64] This is the well established test used in Acceptance in Lieu (see paras 27–20 and 29–144) cases as administered previously by the MLA and henceforth by the Arts Council England. It connotes an object that is of central, rather than of merely marginal, significance in the context of display in a public collection or important historic building. The requisite standard has to be established under one or more of the following heads:

[61] IHTA 1984 s.31(4A).
[62] IHTA 1984 s.31(4F).
[63] IR 67, Ch.4.
[64] IHTA 1984 s.31(1)(a) and (aa).

(i) Does the object have an especially close association with our national life and history?

(ii) Is the object of especial artistic or art—historical interest?

(iii) Is the object of especial importance for the study of some aspect of art, learning or history?

(iv) Does the object have an especially close association with a particular historic setting?[65]

This is a much tighter test and only a small fraction of works of art previously eligible for designation will be eligible henceforth. In short, as stated above, the conditional exemption rules for works of art are, over time, likely to be satisfied only by a relatively small number of items kept permanently, or nearly so, in places with substantial access for the general public.

Acceptance in lieu of tax

If a work of art meets the pre-eminent quality standard, the Acceptance in Lieu Panel **27–20** at the Arts Council England can agree that, following the owner's death, the item may be accepted by the Treasury in lieu of or on account of the IHT payable by the estate. Agreement has to be reached on value and location for display. The IHT liability is calculated and, typically but not invariably, 25 per cent of the tax is credited back to the estate (the "douceur") which, added to the value net of tax, gives a net credit towards the estate's total IHT liability.[66] (See the MLA annual Acceptance in Lieu Reports for greater detail and a description of items accepted up until 2009/2010.) Since 1998 it is relevant to note that the lack of an Acceptance in Lieu agreement does not mean an item does not satisfy the pre-eminent quality test. A similar arrangement exists for designated land but the douceur is, generally, only 10 per cent: the vendor does not have the option of taking it abroad! There is a corresponding provision in relation to CGT payable on the disposal.[67] The Goodison Review included recommendations for extending the Acceptance in Lieu process, e.g. to taxes other than IHT payable by an estate After much campaigning by galleries and museums, the Government announced proposals to incentivise taxpayers to donate pre-eminent objects and works of art to the nation during their lifetime in return for a reduction in the donor's liability to income tax and capital gains tax. HMRC and the Department for Culture, Media and Sport launched a joint consultation in June 2011 and HMRC subsequently published draft legislation outlining the new Cultural Gifts Scheme in December 2011 which was included in the Finance Act 2012 under the heading "Gifts to the Nation".[68]

Gifts to the Nation

The scheme operates alongside the existing Acceptance in Lieu (AIL) scheme and **27–21** will share a £30,000,000 annual limit. Under the scheme, a donor may offer a pre-

---

[65] Acceptance in Lieu Report 2005/06, p.8.
[66] IHTA 1984 s.32(4)(b).
[67] TCGA 1992 s.258(2)(b).
[68] Finance Act 2012—Sch.14 "Gifts to the Nation".

eminent object to the nation and if that object is accepted, the donor will receive a tax reduction equal to a fixed percentage of the object's agreed value. The scheme is open to individuals acting in a private capacity and corporate bodies but excludes trustees, personal representatives and joint owners. The tax reduction available to an individual tax payer will be 30 per cent of the donated object's value and 20 per cent for corporate donors. Individuals may apply the tax-reduction against their income tax and/or capital gains tax liabilities and corporate bodies against their corporation tax liabilities.

The scheme applies to any object, any collection or group of objects, or any object with a particular association to a significant building, that is "pre-eminent"[69] (the same criteria apply as for the Acceptance in Lieu scheme) but by contrast to the Acceptance in Lieu scheme it does not apply to gifts of land or buildings. Donated objects will be allocated to any museum, art gallery or library which would preserve the object for the public benefit.

The Finance Act 2012 also contains amendments to other tax provisions.[70] For example, conditionally exempt objects will become wholly exempt from inheritance tax if donated under the scheme, thereby avoiding the recapture charge that would otherwise be triggered by the donation.

Works of art "attached" to buildings

27–22   Property lawyers debate endlessly whether an object such as a garden statue is or is not part of a building. If it is a fixture, it may be designated as part of the building. If not, then either it will now have to satisfy the pre-eminent test or the associated object test for designation. It will readily be seen that the outcome will have a material impact on the tax status of the object both for IHT and CGT purposes. In the recent case of *Brudenell-Bruce v Moore*,[71] framed paintings were held not to constitute fixtures despite being secured by "large heavy-duty hooks drilled into the walls". However, the case brought by Harborough County Council against Lord Hazelrigg illustrates the bizarre conclusions that can be reached.[72] As a result items previously treated and taxed as chattels may in fact be part of a building and vice versa. If "chattels" and the building are ostensibly in separate ownership the result can be quite alarming.[73]

Claims

27–23   The exemption must be claimed.[74] Claims should be made to the Heritage Team (which is part of Charity Assets & Residence, Inheritance Tax Department) of HMRC, and should provide full details of the property in question, a statement as to why the asset is considered to qualify for exemption, confirmation that proposals to provide public access will be made, and confirmation there is no present intention to sell the assets.[75] Failure to provide full details may delay the processing of the claim. Claims

---

[69] Finance Act 2012 s.22 Pt 4 Sch.14.

[70] Finance Act 2012 Pt 5 Sch.14.

[71] [2012] EWHC 1024 (Ch).

[72] This case is unreported. For an account of the facts, see N.E. Palmer and A.H. Hudson, *Art Antiquity and Law* (2000), p.37.

[73] For a full analysis, see J. LeM. Scott, "Classification of Fixtures Under English Law: An Inspector's Whim?" in *Art Antiquity and Law* (2000), p.319.

[74] IHTA 1984 s.30(1)(a).

[75] HMRC memorandum, *Capital Taxation and the National Heritage*, para.3.5.

for exemption must be made within two years of the date of the transfer or in the case of a failed PET (see para.5–08), the relevant death, or within such longer period as the Revenue may allow.[76] In relation to periodic and exit charges the claim must be made in advance of the transfer (see para.27–07).

Retrospective exemption on failed PETs

It may be that a person who has made an actual PET under s.3A or a notional PET **27–24** under s.102(4) of the Finance Act 1986 dies within seven years of making the PET. In that case, it is possible, following his death to make a claim for the property to be designated.[77] The question whether the property is appropriate for designation is determined by reference to the circumstances existing after the death of the transferor.[78] No claim can be made to the extent that the value transferred by the failed PET is attributable to heritage property which was disposed of by a sale during the period beginning with the date of the transfer and ending with the death of the transferor,[79] unless the special exemption discussed at para.27–25 is available. If at the time of the transferor's death an undertaking is given by such person as the Board think appropriate in the circumstances of the case or is in force under s.258 of the Taxation of Chargeable Gains Act 1992 with respect to any property concerned, then that undertaking is treated as an undertaking given under s.30.[80]

Special exemption

It may be that a transferor makes a failed PET, and that the transferee in the period **27–25** between the making of the PET and the death of the transferor disposes of the property. Section 26A provides that if the property which is the subject matter of the PET has been or could be designated by the Board under s.31(1) and, during the period beginning with the date of the PET and ending with the death of the transferor, that property has been disposed of either:

(1) to the Board in satisfaction of tax[81]; or
(2) by sale by private treaty to a body mentioned in Sch.3 to the 1984 Act, e.g. the British Museum, the National Gallery, etc or otherwise than by way of sale to such a body,

the PET is deemed to be an exempt transfer.

Subsequent charges generally

As its name implies, a conditionally exempt transfer remains exempt only so long as **27–26** certain conditions remain satisfied. Once those conditions cease to be satisfied there

---

[76] IHTA 1984 s.30(3BA).
[77] Such claim cannot be made at the time of the transfer: see para.27–06. On maintenance funds, see para.27–71.
[78] IHTA 1984 s.31(1A).
[79] IHTA 1984 s.30(3C).
[80] IHTA 1984 ss.30(3B), 31(A) and (4G).
[81] See paras 29–144–29–149.

will be a "chargeable event". By s.32(1), tax is chargeable the first time after the conditionally exempt transfer (or if conditional exemption has been given to a failed PET, the death of the transferor[82]) that a "chargeable event" occurs with respect to property in respect of which a conditional exemption has been given. It is important to realise:

(1) that s.32(1) is an independent charging section under which tax is charged on "chargeable events", not on chargeable transfers; and
(2) that the grant of a conditional exemption only prevents a charge being made on the transfer to which the exemption is given.

Thereafter the normal rules apply, so that if the property is the subject of a further chargeable transfer, tax will be charged under the main charging provisions in the usual way. The same transaction may thus constitute both a chargeable transfer and a chargeable event, in which case there will be two charges to tax—one under the main charging provisions, and one under s.32. Alternatively, a transaction may constitute a chargeable transfer but not a chargeable event, and vice versa: then there will be a charge only under the main charging provisions or under s.32 as the case may be. There are special rules for "associated property": see paras 27–32–27–47.

Tax credit

27–27   Provision is made so that any tax charged under the main charging provisions may be set off against any tax charged under s.32. By s.33(7), where there has been a conditionally exempt transfer of property, then, in so far as the value transferred by a subsequent chargeable transfer is attributable to that property, the tax charged under the main charging provisions is allowed as a credit against any tax charged under s.32. If the chargeable transfer is also a chargeable event, the tax charged under the main charging provisions is allowed as a credit at once. If the chargeable transfer is not also a chargeable event, the credit is given against the first charge to tax to arise under s.32(1) in the future. It may be that after a conditionally exempt transfer of any property there is a PET, the value transferred by which is wholly or partly attributable to that property. If the PET is a chargeable event with respect to the property or, after the PET, but before the death of the person who is the transferor of the PET, a chargeable event occurs with respect to the property, the tax charged by reference to that event is allowed as a credit against any tax which may become chargeable, by reason of the failure of the PET, on so much of the value transferred by the failed PET as is attributable to the property. In such a case, s.33(7) does not apply with respect to any tax becoming chargeable on the failed PET.[83]

Chargeable events

27–28   Under s.32 there are three chargeable events. As was noted above, tax is charged under s.32 on the first one to occur.[84] The three events are as follows:

---

[82] IHTA 1984 s.32(1).
[83] IHTA 1984 s.32(5A).
[84] IHTA 1984 s.32(1).

(1) *The failure to observe an undertaking.* The first case in which there is a chargeable event is the failure to observe in a material respect an undertaking[85] given with respect to the property.[86] Usually the Board will give the person concerned due notice of the failure and an opportunity to remedy it before taking steps to withdraw the exemption. Where an undertaking varied by a Special Commissioner under s.35A is ignored, there will be a chargeable event if there is a failure in a material respect to observe the varied undertaking after 60 days.[87]

Normally such a failure, although constituting a chargeable event, will not result in a charge also being made under the main charging provisions. A breach of the undertaking will give rise to a deemed disposal for CGT under the Taxation of Chargeable Gains Act 1992 s.258(5).

(2) *The disposal of the property in question, whether by sale, gift, or otherwise.*[88] The second case in which there is a chargeable event is where the property is disposed of. The disposal of an interest in possession in settled property will amount to a disposal of the property in which that interest subsists[89] and thus will constitute a chargeable event. It is unlikely that HMRC would regard the loss or destruction of property as a disposal unless, of course, the loss or destruction were deliberate,[90] or, what is more probable, the loss or destruction implied that there had been a breach of an undertaking. Such a breach would constitute a chargeable event, whether or not insurance moneys were available. Again, a charge to CGT may also arise. There is a vulnerable period after the transfer and before conditional exemption is agreed during which loss or destruction for any reason will ensure a charge to either IHT or CGT or both on the transfer.

(3) *The death of the person beneficially entitled to the property.*[91] The third case in which there is a chargeable event is where the person beneficially entitled to the property dies. He will also be treated under s.4(1) as having made a transfer of value immediately before he died, with the result that tax may also be charged under the main charging provisions on the value of the whole of his estate, including the value of the property in question. It should be noted that where the property is owned jointly by two or more persons in undivided shares the death of one co-owner will trigger a chargeable event.

Excepted events[92]

The legislation provides that, generally speaking, a disposal or a death is not a **27–29** chargeable event in cases where the disposal or death leaves the status of the property

[85] Being either an undertaking given under IHTA 1984 s.30 or an undertaking given under IHTA 1984 s.32(5)(b) which replaced either an undertaking given under IHTA 1984 s.30 or an undertaking given under IHTA 1984 s.32(5)(b).

[86] IHTA 1984 s.32(2). The Treasury must be satisfied that there has been such a failure. The time of the event is the time when the failure occurred, not the time when the Treasury becomes satisfied that there has been a failure.

[87] IHTA 1984 s.35A(3), as inserted by FA 1998 Sch.25 para.8.

[88] IHTA 1984 s.32(3)(b).

[89] IHTA 1984 s.49(1).

[90] See para.2–06.

[91] IHTA 1984 s.32(3)(a).

[92] The term "excepted events" is used by the authors as a matter of convenience; it does not appear in the legislation.

effectively unchanged. To begin with, the legislation provides that a disposal (other-wise than by way of sale) or a death is not a chargeable event if that disposal or death constitutes a transfer of value which is itself conditionally exempt.[93] Assume that a father inherits a Picasso painting via a conditionally exempt transfer and subsequently gives or leaves it to his son, who in turn gives the requisite undertaking to the Treasury on the basis that the Picasso is of pre-eminent quality (see para.27–19). The result is that the Picasso passes to the son via a conditionally exempt transfer, so that the father's death/disposal is not a chargeable event. From a CGT standpoint, there will be no CGT consequences on the father's death. A lifetime gift to the son will be free from CGT so long as the property has been designated and the disposal is by way of a gift.[94] As an undertaking has been given under s.31, there is relief under the Taxation of Chargeable Gains Act 1992 s.258, and the disposal is deemed to have been made for a consideration such that neither a gain nor loss arises.[95] Similarly, where there is a death or a disposal otherwise than by way of sale, and the requisite undertaking under s.31 is given with respect to the property by such person as the Treasury think appropriate in the circumstances, the disposal or death is not a chargeable event.[96] This covers the case where on a disposal or a death there is a transfer of value which is exempt under the spouse or charity exemptions. Such a transfer would not be condi-tionally exempt[97] and therefore, but for this provision, the disposal or death would be a chargeable event.

27–30   These reliefs raise the question of what constitutes a disposal "otherwise than by sale". The meaning of "sale" was considered briefly at para.2–46 where it was noted that in the absence of express statutory provision an exchange should not constitute a sale. HMRC are unlikely to contend that where a landowner lets parkland to a tenant at a rack rent for grazing purposes there has been a disposal by way of sale provided the terms of the tenancy require the tenant to comply with the management agreement in the undertaking which may include, for example, a restriction on what type of chemicals can be applied. The position where there is a lease is more difficult.[98] The Leasehold Reform, Housing and Urban Development Act 1993 and the Leasehold Reform Act 1967 empower leaseholders of long lease flats and houses respectively to purchase the freehold of their buildings in certain circumstances. If the property is conditionally exempt from IHT, any disposal by the freeholder would have led to a charge to IHT. In relation to a building comprising flats, the leaseholders' initial notice is of no effect if the freehold interest has previously been designated under s.31(1)(b), (c) or (d). However, there is no parallel provision in the 1993 Act in relation to the individual leaseholder's right to acquire a new, extended lease of a flat.

In relation to a house, there are additional factors to consider. A leaseholder's notice of claim is of no effect if the house has been designated under s.31(1)(b), (c) or (d) *and* the lease was either granted before November 1, 1993 (or was granted before that date but the leaseholder has to rely on ss.1A or 1B of the 1967 Act) *or* (where the lease was granted before November 1, 1993) the leaseholder has to rely on the extended rights to enfranchisement introduced by ss.1A, 1AA and 1B of the 1967 Act. Again, there is no parallel provision in relation to the leaseholder's right to acquire a new, extended lease of the house.

---

[93] IHTA 1984 s.32(5)(a), as substituted by FA 1998 Sch.25 para.7 in relation to any undertaking on or after July 31, 1998.
[94] TCGA 1992 s.258(3)(a).
[95] TCGA 1992 s.258(4).
[96] IHTA 1984 s.32(5)(b).
[97] IHTA 1984 s.30(4).
[98] See *Young v Markworth Properties* [1965] Ch. 475.

Stephen Dorrell, the Financial Secretary to the Treasury announced in the written reply to a parliamentary question on May 7, 1993, that the Government was proposing that where as a consequence of the exercise of the right to enfranchise a house or acquire an extended lease of a house or flat there was a disposal of part of the designated property, the IHT charge would be limited to the interest sold. For these purposes, "designated" includes circumstances where the application to HMRC is pending. However, any legislation concerning this proposal is still outstanding.

The legislation also provides that a disposal to the National Gallery, the British Museum, or some other body mentioned in Sch.3, or to HMRC in satisfaction of tax[99] is not a chargeable event.[100] In the same way, if within three years of a person's death his personal representatives, or, in the case of settled property, the trustees thereof (or the person next entitled) make such a disposal his death is not a chargeable event.[101] The above is subject to the qualification that where the disposal is to the National Gallery, etc. the disposal must be either:

27–31

(1) by sale by private treaty, and not, e.g., by auction; or
(2) be otherwise than by sale.[102]

Subsequent charges on associated properties

Section 32A establishes a separate mini code for associated properties, i.e.:

27–32

(1) buildings of outstanding historical or architectural interest;
(2) related land; and
(3) associated objects.[103]

Tax is charged in respect of the property (or a part) in question on the first occurrence after the conditionally exempt transfer of that property (or, if the transfer was a failed PET, after the death of the transferor) of a relevant chargeable event.[104] The effect of the special rules is that any event which breaks up the entity (i.e. a disposal of the whole, or a part or of an associated property or any breach of the undertakings) will give rise to a charge on the whole of each associated property which has been conditionally exempted unless a specific exception applies.

Associated properties—chargeable events

There are for this purpose three kinds of chargeable events, as follows:

27–33

---

[99] IHTA 1984 s.32(4) as substituted by FA 1998 Sch.25 para.7 in relation to any undertaking on or after July 31, 1998.

[100] See paras 20–128 and following.

[101] See paras 20–128 and following. A disposal of property made after an excepted disposal is not a chargeable event with respect to the property unless there has again been a conditionally exempt transfer of it after that disposal. Thus, if there has been an excepted disposal to the British Museum and the Museum disposes of the property that disposal will not be a chargeable event.

[102] IHTA 1984 s.32(4)(a).

[103] IHTA 1984 s.32A(1), and see para.27–10.

[104] IHTA 1984 s.32A(2).

(1) *Breach of undertaking*: if the Board are satisfied that an undertaking given for the maintenance, repair, preservation, access or keeping with regard to property (hereinafter referred to simply as "an undertaking") has not been observed in a material respect the failure to observe the undertaking is a chargeable event with respect to the whole of each of the associated properties of which there has been a conditionally exempt transfer.[105]

(2) *Death*: if the person beneficially entitled to one of the associated properties dies and an undertaking has been given, the death is a chargeable event with respect to the whole of each of the associated properties of which there has been a conditionally exempt transfer.[106]

(3) *Disposal*: if an associated property (or part of it) is disposed of, whether by sale, gift or otherwise and an undertaking has been given in respect of it, the disposal is a chargeable event with respect to the whole of each of the associated properties of which there has been a conditionally exempt transfer.[107]

Associated properties—excepted events[108]

27–34   The legislation provides that certain events which would otherwise be chargeable events under the above mentioned heads are relieved from being such events. To begin with, a death or a disposal is not a chargeable event if the personal representatives of the deceased (or, in the case of settled property, the trustees or the person next entitled) within three years of the death make or, as the case may be, the disposal is:

(1) a disposal of the property (or part) concerned by sale by private treaty to a body mentioned in Sch.3 to the 1984 Act, or to such a body otherwise than by sale; or

(2) a disposal of the property (or part) concerned in satisfaction of the tax.[109]

This is subject to the qualification that where such disposal is a part disposal, the event is not an excepted event with respect to property other than that disposed of unless any undertaking previously given with regard to the property (or part) concerned is replaced by a corresponding undertaking given by such person as the Board think appropriate in the circumstances of the case. For this purpose, "part disposal" means a disposal of property which does not consist of or include the whole of each property which is one of the associated properties and of which there has been a conditionally exempt transfer.[110]

27–35   It is also provided that the death or disposal of property otherwise than by sale is not a chargeable event if:

(1) the transfer of value made on the death or the disposal is itself a conditionally exempt transfer; or

---

[105] IHTA 1984 s.32A.
[106] IHTA 1984 s.32A(4)(a).
[107] IHTA 1984 s.32A(4)(b).
[108] The term "excepted event" is used by the authors as a matter of convenience; it does not appear in the legislation.
[109] IHTA 1984 s.32A(5); see paras 29–144–29–149.
[110] IHTA 1984 s.32A(6).

(2) the requisite undertaking (as described in s.31) is given with respect to the property by such person as the Board think appropriate in the circumstances in the case or, where the property is related land, the requisite undertakings described in s.31 are given by such person as the Board think appropriate in the circumstances of the case.[111]

A special rule applies where the whole or part of any property is disposed of by sale. In that case the disposal is a chargeable event only with respect to the whole or part actually disposed of if the requisite undertaking or undertakings (as described in s.31) are given by such person as the Board think appropriate in the circumstances of the case.[112]

Finally, in the event that, notwithstanding the foregoing qualifications, an event remains chargeable, that event may be partly relieved from being a chargeable event if either: **27–36**

(1) the Board are satisfied that there has been a failure to observe, as to one of the associated properties or part of it, an undertaking for the property's maintenance, repair, preservation, access or keeping; or
(2) there has been a disposal of one of the associated properties or part of it and it appears to the Board that the entity consisting of the associated properties has not been materially affected by the failure or disposal.

In that case the Board may direct that the event will be chargeable only with respect to the property or part as to which there has been a failure or disposal.[113]

The chargeable amount

Where there is a chargeable event, be it under s.32 or s.32A, then subject to two qualifications, the amount on which tax is charged is equal to the market value of the property in question at the time of the chargeable event.[114] The first qualification is that where the chargeable event is a disposal on sale, the value of the property is taken to be equal to the proceeds of the sale provided that two conditions are satisfied, namely that the sale: **27–37**

(1) was not intended to confer any gratuitous benefit on any person; and
(2) was either an arm's length transaction between unconnected persons or an equivalent transaction.[115]

The second qualification is that if the occasion of the charge is also the occasion of a charge to CGT under the Taxation of Chargeable Gains Act 1992 s.258, then the value of the asset for IHT purposes is reduced by the amount of CGT payable.[116] It is to be

---

[111] IHTA 1984 s.32A(8) as substituted by and (8A) inserted by FA 1998 Sch.25 para.7.
[112] IHTA 1984 s.32A(9) as substituted by FA 1998 Sch.25 para.7.
[113] IHTA 1984 s.32A(10).
[114] IHTA 1984 ss.33(1)(a) and 160.
[115] IHTA 1984 s.33(3). For similar conditions, see IHTA 1984 s.10, discussed at paras 2–41 and following. The Chief Secretary to the Treasury said in the Standing Committee debates on the 1976 Finance Bill that the estate duty practice of ignoring that part of the sale proceeds which are referable to improvements and additions to the property would continue for CTT (and, therefore, presumably for IHT); *Hansard*, June 29, 1976.
[116] See TCGA 1992 s.258(8).

noted that the way the legislation is formulated it is not possible to claim business or agricultural relief.[117] This may be important since conditionally exempt land will often be farmland and some of the buildings may be used for public opening as a business.

"Proceeds of sale" was held for the purposes of the equivalent estate duty provision to mean the net proceeds of sale after payment of such proper expenses of sale as commissions.[118] Presumably this will also be the position for IHT. It may be that part of the property was unconditionally exempt under the spouse or charity exemption, and that the remainder was conditionally exempt. In that case the amount on which tax is charged is reduced, proportionately.[119]

The rate of tax

27–38   When a tax charge arises on a chargeable event, it is calculated by reference to the circumstances of a person who has in the past made a conditionally exempt transfer of the property. He is referred to as the "relevant person". Accordingly, in determining the rate of tax, three main factors are relevant:

    (1) the identity of the "relevant person";

    (2) whether at the time of the chargeable event the relevant person is alive or dead; and

    (3) if the relevant person is dead, when he died.

27–39   1. *The relevant person.* The relevant person is defined by reference to the "last transaction" which has taken place in respect of the property by reference to which the chargeable event in question has occurred. The transactions which fall to be taken into account for this purpose are conditionally exempt transfers and conditionally exempt occasions (i.e. as discussed below at para.27–50, this refers to occasions which have been conditionally exempted from the imposition of an exit charge), and the "last transaction" means:

    (1) if there has been only one transaction regarding the property before the event, that transaction[120];

    (2) if there have been two or more transactions regarding the property before the event and the last transaction was before the period of 30 years ending with that event, the last of those transactions[121];

    (3) if there have been two or more transactions regarding the property before the event and only one of them was within the period of 30 years ending with that event, the last of those transactions[122]; or

    (4) if there have been two or more transactions regarding the property within the period of 30 years ending with that event, whichever transaction HMRC may select.[123] HMRC is given this discretion so that they can prevent the rate of tax being determined by reference to the cumulative total of a "man of straw" who

---

[117] Compare the deferred charge on woodlands; see para.26–199.
[118] See *Tyser v Att Gen* [1938] Ch. 426.
[119] IHTA 1984 s.33(4)
[120] IHTA 1984 s.33(5)(a).
[121] IHTA 1984 s.33(5)(a).
[122] IHTA 1984 s.33(5)(b).
[123] IHTA 1984 s.33(5)(c).

was interposed into a series of conditionally exempt transfers in order to secure that a low rate of tax was charged.

The position then depends on whether the last transaction was a conditionally exempt transfer or a conditionally exempt occasion. If the last transaction was a conditionally exempt transfer, the relevant person is the person who made the transfer. If, on the other hand, the last transaction was a conditionally exempt occasion, the relevant person is the person who is the settlor in relation to the settlement in question (if there is more than one such person, the relevant person is the person HMRC selects).

Two types of transaction are left out of account in determining the identity of the relevant person. They are:

(1) transactions made or occurring before any previous chargeable event in respect of the property in question; and
(2) transactions made or occurring before any event which would have been a chargeable event had it not been an excepted event by virtue of being:
   (a) a disposal to the National Gallery, etc., or to HMRC in satisfaction of tax, or
   (b) a death followed within three years by such a disposal.[124]

27–40 2. *Relevant person alive*. If the relevant person is alive, the rate/rates are those which would apply if at the time of the chargeable event he had made a chargeable transfer and the value transferred thereby had been equal to the amount on which tax is chargeable under s.32 (see para.27–37). For this purpose, the lifetime rates always apply and this is so even if the relevant person dies within seven years of the chargeable event.[125]

27–41 3. *Relevant person died on or after March 13, 1975*. In such a case, the chargeable amount is added to the value transferred on his death and treated as the highest part of that value.[126] If the relevant person is that person because he made a conditionally exempt transfer, the position varies according to whether that transfer was made during his lifetime or on his death. If it was made during his lifetime, the lifetime rates apply and this is so even though he died within seven years of making the transfer. If the transfer was made on his death, the death rates apply. If, on the other hand, the relevant person is the person who is the settlor in relation to the settlement, tax is charged at the lifetime rates if he created the settlement in his lifetime, and at the death rates if he created it on his death.[127]

27–42 4. *Relevant person died before March 13, 1975*. In such a case, the position is slightly complicated, since account must be taken of what the position would have been under estate duty. The rule is that it is assumed that:

(1) the relevant person died when the chargeable event occurred;

---

[124] IHTA 1984 s.33(1)(b)(i) and (2A).

[125] IHTA 1984 s.33(1)(b)(i) and (2A). Note that any earlier PETs made by him are left out of account for cumulation purposes. Further, the charge is not revised if the PETs subsequently fail because of the death of the relevant person within seven years.

[126] IHTA 1984 s.33(1)(b)(ii). The relevant rates are, prima facie, those in force at the date when the relevant person died: however, by Sch.2 para.5 if the rates were reduced before the chargeable event those lower rates will apply.

[127] IHTA 1984 ss.78(4) and 33(2). If the transfer was made on death because the property was clawed-back into the transferor's estate under the reservation of benefit rules in FA 1986 s.102(3) the lifetime rates apply: see s.33(2)(a).

(2) the value transferred on his death was equal to the amount on which estate duty was chargeable when he in fact died; and

(3) the amount now brought into charge had been added to that value and had formed the highest part of it.[128]

The same rules apply for determining whether the lifetime or death rates are appropriate as where the relevant person died on or after March 13, 1975.[129]

27–43   The general effect is thus to enable HMRC to impose the charge that would have been imposed had the conditional exemption not been given in the first place. This is achieved by charging the person liable for tax as though he were standing in the shoes of the relevant person at the time when the latter made the conditionally exempt transfer. In two cases less tax may be charged in respect of the transfer which was given conditional exemption. The first case is, if the conditionally exempt transfer was an actual transfer which occasioned a disproportionate diminution in the value of the relevant person's estate, the disproportionate element will escape charge, because the amount on which tax is charged is calculated without reference to the consequential loss provisions. Given the nature of the property by reference to which the exemption is given, such disproportionate diminutions will be rare. More significant is the second case since the legislation means that advantage can be taken of the rates of tax prevailing at the rate of the chargeable event in question rather than at the time of the conditionally exempt transfer. Furthermore, if the relevant person was alive at the time of that transfer, tax (charged at the lifetime rates) will not be increased in the event of his dying within seven years. A disadvantage of the rules is that the charge is levied not on the value of the property at the time of the conditionally exempt transfer but on its value at the time of the chargeable event: accordingly increases in value will commonly be brought into charge.

Re-instatement of transferor's cumulative total

27–44   If matters are to be arranged so that tax is to be charged as if, in effect, the conditional exemption had never been given, the relevant person's cumulative total must also be increased to what it would have been had he in fact been charged on the transfer which was granted conditional exemption. To this end, s.34(1), provides that:

> "Where tax has become chargeable under ss.32 or 32A above by reference to a chargeable event in respect of any property ('the relevant event') the rate or rates of tax applicable to any subsequent chargeable transfer made by the person who made the last conditionally exempt transfer of the property before the relevant event shall be determined as if the amount on which tax has become chargeable as aforesaid were value transferred by a chargeable transfer made by him at the time of the relevant event."

The general effect of s.34(1) is thus to add the amount on which tax is charged to the relevant person's cumulative total. Here a number of comments are in order. First, by s.78(6), where the last conditionally exempt transaction regarding property by reference to which a chargeable event has occurred was a conditionally exempt occasion in respect of that property (as opposed to a conditionally exempt transfer of that property)

---

[128] IHTA 1984 s.78(5).
[129] IHTA 1984 s.78(6).

the amount on which tax is charged is not added to the relevant person's cumulative total.

Secondly, s.34 affects the cumulative total of "the person who made the last conditionally exempt transfer of the property" before the chargeable event in question. Although that person will normally be the relevant person, this will not always be the case. As was noted above, where within 30 years of the chargeable event in question there has been more than one chargeable event HMRC may select the relevant person. If they select the transferor of other than the most recent conditionally exempt transfer he will be the relevant person, but it will be the person who makes the most recent conditionally exempt transfer whose cumulative total will suffer.

Thirdly, s.34(1) affects only the rate/rates applicable to chargeable transfers made after the chargeable event in question. Chargeable transfers made before the chargeable event are unaffected. This, however, might leave a gap in the legislation. If the person who made the last conditionally exempt transfer had died by the time of the chargeable event in question, by definition he would not have made any further chargeable transfers, with the result that, if he were the relevant person in relation to a subsequent chargeable event in respect of which tax was chargeable under ss.32 or 32A, the rate of tax applicable to that event would be the same as that applicable to the previous chargeable event.

Assume that on his death A, who has made no previous chargeable transfers, made **27–45** a conditionally exempt transfer to his son B of two pictures worth £60,000 and £70,000 respectively. The remainder of A's estate, worth £180,000, was charged to IHT. Five years later B sells the first picture, now worth £65,000. Under s.33 the £65,000 will, for the purpose of ascertaining the correct rate of tax, be added to the £180,000, and taxed as the top slice of £245,000; but the £65,000 would not form part of his cumulative total. Therefore, in the absence of provision to the contrary, if B were to sell the second painting for, say, £75,000, the £75,000 would, for purposes of ascertaining the correct rate of tax, be added to the £180,000, not to the £245,000. HMRC would thus go short.

Section 34(2) therefore provides that if the person who made the last conditionally exempt transfer of the property in question is dead and is the relevant person in relation to a subsequent chargeable event (the sale of the first picture) the amount on which tax is chargeable under s.33 on that chargeable event (£65,000) is added to that person's cumulative total. The result is that for purposes of ascertaining the correct rate of tax on the subsequent chargeable event (i.e. the sale of the second picture) the £75,000 would be added to £245,000.

Finally, there is a special rule where:

(1) the person who made the last conditionally exempt transfer of the property is not the relevant person; and
(2) at or within five years of the time of the chargeable event in question the property is or has been comprised in a settlement made not more than 30 years before that event; and
(3) the settlor has made a conditionally exempt transfer[130] of the property within those 30 years

---

[130] For this purpose conditionally exempt transfers made before (a) any previous chargeable event in respect of the same property, or (b) any event which would have been a chargeable event had it not been an excepted event by virtue of being (i) a disposal to the National Gallery, etc. or to HMRC in satisfaction of tax, or (ii) a death followed within three years by such a disposal are left out of account: IHTA 1984 s.34(4).

In this case the above provisions operate to uplift the settlor's cumulative total, not that of the person who made the last conditionally exempt transfer before the chargeable event in question.[131] This provision is an anti-avoidance provision aimed at settlements of heritage property in favour of persons with low cumulative totals.

EXAMPLE

27–46   The following example based on one from the HMRC booklet IR67 (which is now out of print—see para.27–02 above) but reworked with up to date figures and tax rates illustrates the calculation of the tax on a chargeable event.

The facts

   June 1972—A buys a Francis Bacon.

   May 1979—A dies, bequeathing the Bacon to B. The Treasury[132] designate the painting. B gives the necessary undertakings, and conditional exemption is given on A's death. A's estate, apart from the Bacon, is worth £400,000; he had previously made chargeable lifetime transfers of £80,000.

   June 1983—B gives the Bacon to his son C. Although B has not owned the Bacon for six years, his transfer to C is eligible for conditional exemption because he inherited the painting on A's death, on which it was conditionally exempted.[133] On B's transfer to C the painting is again designated by the Treasury, the necessary undertakings are given and the transfer is conditionally exempted.

   June 2000—C sells the Bacon to D for £2 million.
   The sale is a chargeable event[134] and tax is payable by C on the £2 million gross sale proceeds.[135]

Application of statutory rules

Either A or B may be selected as the relevant person[136] for the purpose of calculating the tax:

---

[131] IHTA 1984 s.34(3).
[132] Prior to the transfer of responsibilities to the then Inland Revenue on July 25, 1985.
[133] See para.27–07
[134] See para.27–28.
[135] See para.27–37.
[136] See para.27–39.

(a)   If A was selected as the relevant person, the tax would be calculated as follows:

A's total of chargeable transfers	£280,000
(£80,000 + £400,000)	
Sale proceeds	£2,000,000
	£2,280,000
Tax on £2,280,000 at date of sale at the death rates	£992,000
Less: Tax on £280,000 at date of sale	£192,000
Tax on chargeable event	£800,000

(b)   If B was selected as the relevant person, the tax would be calculated as follows:

B's cumulative total of chargeable transfers up to June 2000 (say)	£200,000
Sale proceeds	£2,000,000
	£2,200.000
Tax on £2,200,000 at half death rates in force at the date of death (less £325,000 nil rate band)	£375,000
Less: Tax on £200,000 at half death rates in force at the date of death	NIL
Tax on chargeable event	£375,000

A would be selected as the relevant person in this case, as the tax on the chargeable event will then be higher than if B had been selected. But as B made the last conditionally exempt transfer of the Bacon, the £2 million sale proceeds will be included in B's cumulative total of chargeable transfers for the purpose of calculating the tax on his future transfers in the following seven years.[137]

Liability for tax

27–47   Liability for tax varies according to the nature of the chargeable event in respect of which a charge arises. Where the event is the failure to observe an undertaking or a death, the person liable for the tax chargeable under ss.32 or 32A is the person who, if the property were sold at the time of the failure or death, would be entitled to receive (whether for his benefit or not) the proceeds of sale or any income arising from those proceeds.[138] Where the chargeable event is the disposal of the property, the person so liable is the person by whom or for whose benefit the property is disposed of.[139] Any

[137] See para.27–44.
[138] IHTA 1984 s.207(1).
[139] IHTA 1984 s.207(1)

person liable is required to deliver an account[140] and to pay the tax due[141] within six months of the end of the month in which the chargeable event occurs.

Exemption under the old rules

27–48   As was mentioned above, the Finance Act 1975 also contains provisions under which certain transfers made on death used to qualify for conditional exemption. Those provisions no longer operate to confer such exemption but they may still be relevant where there is a breach of a condition attaching to an exemption given under those provisions before the provisions in the Finance Act 1976 came into effect on April 7, 1976.

The provisions in the Finance Act 1975 differ from those in the Finance Act 1976 in two main respects. First, the Finance Act 1975 exempted only transfers made on death. Secondly, exemption was given under two different sections, according to the nature of the property in question. Exemption was given under s.31 to transfers of the first kind of property which until 1998 qualified for exemption under the Finance Act 1976, i.e. to transfers of works of art, books, scientific collections, etc.; exemption was given under s.34 to transfers of the other four kinds of property dealt with under the 1976 Act. The requisite undertakings were the same except that in the case of works of art, etc. there was no requirement that reasonable steps be taken for securing reasonable access to the public, only that reasonable facilities for examining the object in question for the purpose of (a) research, or (b) seeing the steps taken for the preservation of the object, would be allowed to any person the Treasury authorised to make such examination.[142]

Where the exemption was given, the value of the property was left out of account in determining the value transferred by the transfer in question. So far as subsequent charges were concerned, the Finance Act 1975 did not include any provision concerning "chargeable events" as such. Instead, it provided for a charge on the happening of certain events which amounted to what subsequently became chargeable events under the Finance Act 1976 and are now chargeable events under the Inheritance Tax Act 1984. Tax became chargeable if:

(1) there was non-observance in a material respect of an undertaking[143]; or
(2) the object was disposed of by sale or otherwise.[144] Disposals did not attract a charge if they were either:
    (a) by sale by private treaty or otherwise than by sale to the National Gallery, etc., or
    (b) otherwise than by sale where another undertaking was given, or
    (c) to HMRC in satisfaction of tax.[145]

If the exemption had been given on more than one death, e.g. where it was given on A's bequest of his Gauguin painting to B, and on B's bequest of the Gauguin to C, the exemption was withdrawn in respect only of the transfer by B.[146]

---

[140] IHTA 1984 s.216(7).
[141] IHTA 1984 s.226(4).
[142] See now IHTA 1984.
[143] IHTA 1984 Sch.5 paras 1(1) and 3(1).
[144] IHTA 1984 Sch.5 para.5(1)(c).
[145] IHTA 1984 Sch.5 paras 1(3) and (4), 3(6).
[146] IHTA 1984 Sch.5 paras 1(2) and 3(2).

In certain circumstances the Finance Act 1975 will still apply in determining the consequences of a breach of a condition attaching to an exemption given under s.31 or s.34. This will depend on two factors, namely:

(1) whether an intervening conditionally exempt transfer has been made under the Finance Act 1976; and
(2) if such a transfer has been made, whether the intervening transfer was made during the transferor's life or on his death.

The position is as follows:

(1) *No intervening transfer.* If conditional exemption was given under the old rules and there is a disposal or a non-observance thereunder before any conditionally exempt transfer of the property is made under the new rules, the old rules apply.[147]
(2) *Intervening lifetime transfer.* If conditional exemption was given under the old rules and before any disposal or non-observance thereunder a conditionally exempt lifetime transfer is made or a conditionally exempt occasion occurs under the new rules, then, on the first occurrence of either a disposal/non-observance under the old rules or a chargeable event under the new rules, HMRC may elect to apply the old rules or the new rules as they see fit.[148]
(3) *Intervening transfer on death.* If conditional exemption was given under the old rules and before any disposal or non-observance thereunder a conditionally exempt transfer is made on death or a conditionally exempt occasion occurs under the new rules, then, on the first occurrence of either a disposal/non-observance under the old rules or a chargeable event under the new rules, tax is chargeable under the new rules, not under the old rules.[149]

Withdrawal of exemption under the old rules

The procedure when an exemption is withdrawn under the old rules differs according **27–49** to whether or not the precipitating non-observance or disposal occurred within three years of the death to which the claim related (i.e. prior to April 6, 1979).

(1) *Within three years.* In this case the market value of the property in question at the time of the death was added back to the estate. Tax was then charged on the new total. This had two effects. First, tax was charged on the exempted property. Secondly, the average rate applicable to the whole estate was increased, with the result that the revised total tax on the estate had to be apportioned between the exempt part and the rest of the estate.[150]

Assume A died in June 1975 owning a Picasso painting worth £50,000 which he left to his son, and to which conditional exemption was granted. The rest of A's estate was worth £600,000. The tax due on his death was therefore £329,750. In July 1976 his son disposed of the painting for £200,000. Tax was then charged as if the exemption had never been given, i.e. on £650,000 =

---

[147] This follows from the fact that FA 1976 makes no provision to deal with this situation; therefore the FA 1975 provisions apply.
[148] IHTA 1984 s.35(2)(a).
[149] IHTA 1984 s.35(2)(b).
[150] FA 1975 ss.33(2)(a) and 34(7)(a).

£362,250. The tax would then have been attributed to the exempted property and to the rest of the estate as follows:

$$\text{On } £50,000 = £362,250 \times \frac{50,000}{650,000} = £27,865$$

$$\text{On } £600,000 = £362,250 \times \frac{600,000}{650,000} = £334,385$$

less £329,750 already paid = £4,635

The persons liable for the additional tax (£4,635) payable on the rest of the estate were always the persons who were liable for tax at the time of the death in respect of which the conditional exemption was granted.[151] They had to deliver an account and pay the tax due within the normal time limits.[152] For the persons liable and accountable for the tax attributable to the exempt property (£27,865), see para.27–50.

(2) *After three years.* The procedure is the same except that (a) no additional tax is due on the rest of the estate, and (b) the amount to be brought into account is the market value of the object at the time the exemption is withdrawn, unless the withdrawal is because of sale, in which case the sale proceeds[153] (after payment of CGT) are brought into account.[154]

Assume the same facts as in the previous example, but that the sale was in August 1979 and was for £100,000. Tax would have been charged as if the exemption had never been given, but on £700,000 (£600,000 + £100,000) = £340,000.[155] Tax would then have been attributed to the exempted property:

$$\text{tax on } £100,000 = £340,000 \times \frac{100,000}{700,000} = £48,571$$

No additional tax is payable on the rest of the estate. For the persons liable for the tax attributed to the exempt property (£48,571), see para.27–50.

Liability for tax

27–50   Where conditional exemption under the old rules is lost and tax charged under Sch.5 para.1(2) or para.3(2) in respect of a disposal of an object or property, the person liable for the tax is the person by whom or for whose benefit the object or property in question was disposed of.[156] Where, on the other hand, a charge arises under paras 1(1) or 3(1) because an undertaking given in respect of an object or property has not been observed in a material respect, the person liable for the tax is the person who, if the object or

[151] See para.29–78(4).
[152] See paras 29–07(8) and 29–104(4).
[153] That is, the net proceeds: see para.27–37.
[154] IHTA 1984 Sch.5 para.2(2) and para.20–62.
[155] Applying the pre-October 27, 1977, rates.
[156] IHTA 1984 s.207(4).

property in question was sold at the time IHT becomes chargeable, would be entitled to receive (whether for his benefit or not) the proceeds of the sale or any income arising from those proceeds.[157] Any person liable is required to deliver an account[158] and to pay the tax due[159] within six months of the end of the month in which the chargeable event occurs.

No tax credit

The old rules contain no provision equivalent to s.33(7). It will be recalled that under s.33(7) where a chargeable event also constitutes a chargeable transfer the tax charged under the main charging provisions is allowed as a tax credit against tax charged under s.32. There is no such provision in the old rules. The result is that if the disposal or non-observance constitutes a chargeable transfer, tax will be payable in full under the main charging provisions and under Sch.5 para.1(2) or para.3(2), as the case may be.

27–51

Estate duty tie-in

There was a similar exemption for estate duty under the Finance Act 1930 s.40,[160] and the estate duty legislation contained various provisions which dealt with a subsequent disposal or non-observance of an undertaking in much the same way that the IHT legislation deals with such events. The estate duty legislation remains in force in relation to exemptions given under s.40, and in the event of a disposal or non-observance those provisions will apply, unless there has been a conditionally exempt transfer of the property under the 1976 or later rules (the "1976 rules"), i.e. new rules prior to that disposal or non-observance. In that case, the rules relating to the interaction of the old rules and the 1976 rules discussed above apply, with the result that the position depends on whether the intervening conditionally exempt transfer was made during lifetime or on death:

27–52

(1) *Intervening lifetime transfer*

If exemption was given under s.40 and before any disposal or non-observance under the estate duty legislation a conditionally exempt transfer is made under the 1976 rules during the transferor's lifetime, then, on the first occurrence of either a disposal/non-observance under the estate duty legislation or a chargeable event under the 1976 rules, HMRC may elect to apply the estate duty legislation or the new rules as they see fit.[161]

(2) *Intervening transfer on death*

If exemption was given under s.40 and before any disposal or non-observance under the estate duty legislation a conditionally exempt transfer is made under the 1976 rules on the transferor's death, then, on the first occurrence of either a disposal/non-observance under the estate duty legislation or a chargeable event under the 1976 rules, tax is chargeable under the 1976 rules, not under the estate duty legislation.[162]

---

[157] IHTA 1984 s.207(5).
[158] IHTA 1984 s.216(7).
[159] IHTA 1984 s.226(4).
[160] IHTA 1984 Sch.6 para.4.
[161] IHTA 1984 s.35(2)(a); Sch.6 paras 4(2) and (3).
[162] IHTA 1984 s.35(2)(b); Sch.6 paras 4(2) and (3).

It should also be noted that for many items exempted in the estate duty era, conditional exemption will no longer be available and especially since the Finance Act 1998. As a result the estate duty charge will not be wiped out on the next death so that it may apply when the asset is sold. When a transfer is made and no new exemption can be obtained in respect of the transfer (due to lack of pre-eminence or inability to provide suitable open access) the old estate duty liability will survive the transfer with the "Estate Duty Undertakings" continuing to apply.

HMRC has confirmed in the Memorandum that where an object is exempt under Finance Act 1930 s.40, estate duty is payable only on sale or (for deaths in and after 1950) on the failure to observe undertakings to preserve it in the United Kingdom and allow access for specified purposes or (for occasions in and after 1965) where the donee fails to renew the donor's undertakings. The law does not allow owners to opt out of these conditions by paying the estate duty based on current values; the exemption can only be brought to an end by the means detailed above.[163]

Conditional exemption on death before April 7, 1976

27–53   It may be that there has been a transfer of value after April 6, 1976, be it a lifetime transfer or a transfer made on death, of property:

(1) which was conditionally exempted from estate duty under the Finance Act 1930 s.40; and

(2) in respect of which IHT is payable, because no exemption (conditional or otherwise) is available.

If estate duty becomes payable, e.g. because the property is sold, the IHT paid is allowed as a credit against the estate duty due.[164]

It is to be noted that estate duty applied not only to property passing on death but also to property which a person gave away within a certain period before his death. As a general rule, the duty charged on his death in respect of such gifts could be reduced by a taper relief under the Finance Act 1960 s.64. HMRC for some time applied this taper relief to reduce the amount liable to an estate duty clawback where conditional exemption had been given in respect of any inter vivos gift. In a press statement of May 3, 1984, HMRC announced that they had been advised that this procedure was incorrect, and that taper relief under s.64 was in fact not available to reduce the amount liable to a clawback charge. They also, however, stated that assessments under which the taper relief had previously been given would not be reopened.

III. CONDITIONAL EXEMPTION/DEFERRAL OF EXIT AND PERIODIC CHARGES

27–54   The legislation makes provision to exempt conditionally or to defer conditionally certain occasions on which an exit or a periodic charge would otherwise be imposed. The relevant provisions are ss.78 and 79, which are modelled on and linked to the new rules enacted in the Finance Act 1998. Section 78 deals with exit charges, and provides

---

[163] See HMRC's memorandum, *Capital Taxation and the National Heritage*, Appendix 3, for further details.

[164] FA 1976 ss.79(7) and 83(4), (7) and (8).

for a conditional exemption only. Section 79 is concerned with periodic charges, and provides for both a conditional exemption and a conditional deferral.[165] The claim for deferral must be made before the transfer under ss.78 or 79: see para.27–07. This applies even if trusts are only liable to a periodic charge by reason of the impact of Finance Act 2006 (see para.27–09 for details).

It is interesting to note the consequences for periodic and exit charges where **27–55** conditional exemption was granted either for estate duty under the Finance Act 1930 s.40 or for CGT under the Finance Act 1965 s.31(4), the Capital Gains Tax Act 1979 s.147(4), or the Taxation of Chargeable Gains Act 1992 s.258(4) on or before relevant assets were transferred to a discretionary settlement. By virtue of s.79(3) of the 1984 Act, s.79(1) is not in point so there is no periodic charge in respect of which conditional exemption has to be claimed. Furthermore, as an exit charge under s.78 of the 1984 Act is based on the tax payable on the prior periodic charge it means the tax on such a transfer is nil. The three Acts regulating the CGT treatment are all intended for this purpose (and see para.27–65).

Exemption from exit charges

By s.78(1) a transfer of property or other event (such as the creation of an interest **27–56** in possession in the property) does not give rise to an exit charge, provided that the following conditions are satisfied:

(1) the property by reference to which the charge falls to be made must have been comprised in the settlement throughout the six years ending with the transfer or event in question[166];
(2) the property in question must be designated under s.31 by the Board[167]; and
(3) a person[168] the Board think appropriate must give the undertaking required for that kind of property.[169] Under s.31 the Board may designate five kinds of property.[170] The undertakings required under s.78 are those required where a transfer of value is made of heritage property.[171] As is the case under s.30, the conditional exemption must be claimed (see para.27–23 above). Claims should be made to the Heritage Team (Charity Assets & Residence, Inheritance Tax) of HMRC and should include full details of the property in question.[172] Claims should be made no more than two years after the date of the transfer or within such longer period as the Board may allow.[173]

Subsequent charges

An occasion on which an exit charge would otherwise be imposed which qualifies **27–57** for conditional exemption under s.78 is known as a "conditionally exempt occasion",

---

[165] See paras 27–64–27–70.
[166] IHTA 1984 s.78(1).
[167] IHTA 1984 s.78(1)(a).
[168] In the case of land, such persons as may be required to give undertakings: IHTA 1984 s.78(1)(b).
[169] IHTA 1984 s.78(1)(b).
[170] This was discussed above at para.27–10.
[171] See para.27–10.
[172] See para.27–23.
[173] IHTA 1984 s.78(1A) as inserted by FA 1988 Sch.25 para.3.

and the rules which apply to it are similar to those which apply to conditionally exempt transfers. To begin with, tax is charged on the first occurrence of a chargeable event in respect of the property. The same events that are excepted from being chargeable events where conditionally exempt transfers are concerned are also exempted from being chargeable events for these purposes. In addition, by s.78(3)(b), references to a disposal otherwise than by sale in s.32(5) include references to any occasion on which an exit charge is imposed.[174] It may be that conditional exemption was given to a capital distribution under the rules originally laid down by the Finance Act 1976. The legislation accordingly provides that references to a conditionally exempt occasion are also references to a conditionally exempt distribution as it was defined under those rules,[175] with the result that the same charges are imposed in respect of distributions which qualified for conditional exemption under those rules as are imposed in respect of occasions which are conditionally exempted under the current rules.

Associated property

27–58   Where tax is chargeable with respect to any of the last three kinds of property which the Board may designate for conditional exemption tax is also chargeable with respect to any property associated with that property, as under s.32.[176]

The chargeable amount

27–59   Where tax is chargeable with respect to any property, the amount on which tax is charged is the market value of the property at the time of the chargeable event.[177]

The rate of tax

27–60   The rate of tax is determined in two steps. The first step is to apply the rules that apply on the first occurrence of a chargeable event after a conditionally exempt transfer.[178] The relevant person by reference to whose circumstances the tax is calculated is the settlor of the settlement; when more than one person is the settlor HMRC can select any one of them.[179] If the settlement was made under a will the tax charge is calculated by reference to the death rate scale; otherwise it is calculated at half the death rate scale. The scales used will normally be those in force at the time of the chargeable event.[180] Section 78(4) provides transitional relief for discretionary trusts in that tax is, in appropriate circumstances, charged at only a percentage of the rates that would otherwise apply. The percentage is 30 per cent if the conditionally exempt occasion preceding the chargeable event occurred before the first 10-year anniversary falling after the property became comprised in the settlement concerned. If the occasion

---

[174] IHTA 1984 s.78(2) and (3).
[175] IHTA 1984 s.78(2).
[176] IHTA 1984 ss.78(3)(a) and 32A(3).
[177] IHTA 1984 ss.78(3)(a) and 33(1)(a).
[178] IHTA 1984 s.78(3)(a). See paras 27–38–27–43.
[179] IHTA 1984 s.78(3).
[180] IHTA 1984 Sch.2 para.5.

occurred after the first but before the second 10-year anniversary to fall after the property became so comprised, the percentage is 60 per cent.[181]

It is to be noted that the aforesaid system introduces an element of unfairness where **27–61** before April 1, 1983, conditional exemption is granted to an event giving rise to an exit charge and a chargeable event occurs on or after that date, since tax in respect of that event will be charged without taking account of the fact that had conditional exemption not been granted transitional relief might have been available to the event to which the conditional exemption had been granted.

Administration

The usual rules apply.[182] **27–62**

Reinstatement of the trust's cumulative total

As was noted above, the cumulative total of an individual who makes a conditionally **27–63** exempt transfer in respect of which a chargeable event arises must be recalculated. Under the rules previously in force the cumulative total of trustees who made a conditionally exempt distribution in respect of which a chargeable event arose also had to be recalculated, but under the rules in force since 1984 the cumulative total of trustees of a discretionary trust to which a conditional exemption has been given need not be recalculated if a chargeable event occurs.[183]

Exemption/deferral from periodic charges

As was mentioned previously, under s.79 special rules apply where the periodic **27–64** charge is concerned. Under these rules the 10-year charge may be exempted or deferred, depending on the circumstances in which the charge arises.

Exemption from charge

If a discretionary settlement contains property which on or before the occasion on **27–65** which it became comprised in that settlement was the subject of either (i) a conditionally exempt transfer,[184] or (ii) an "exempt" disposal for CGT purposes under the Taxation of Chargeable Gains Act 1992 s.258[185] the property is conditionally exempted from the periodic charge. Where the exemption derives from a previous conditionally exempt transfer, the exemption continues until the first time a chargeable event occurs

---

[181] IHTA 1984 ss.61(1) and 78(4).
[182] See paras 29–07, 29–62 and 29–103 for accountability, liability and due date for payment, respectively.
[183] IHTA 1984 s.78(b).
[184] IHTA 1984 s.79(1); see paras 27–07–27–23.
[185] IHTA 1984 s.79(2).

with respect to the property.[186] Where the exemption derives from the previous "exempt" disposal, the exemption continues until the first time an event happens on which the property is treated as sold under the Taxation of Chargeable Gains Act 1992 s.258(5).[187] Once the exemption has ceased to apply the periodic charge is imposed in the usual way, i.e. a charge is made on the next 10-year anniversary on the basis of the trust's cumulative total at the time of that anniversary: losing the exemption has no retrospective effect.

Deferral of charge

27-66 Where there has been no such conditionally exempt transfer or "exempt" disposal, e.g. where the trustees have purchased the property, the periodic charge is deferred if:

(1) the property by reference to which the charge arises is designated under s.31 by the Board; and
(2) a person the Board think appropriate gives the undertaking required for the kind of property in question.[188]

It should be noted that the property does not have to have been held in the settlement for six years.

As was the case under ss.32 and 78, a claim must be made. If the charge is deferred, the charge that would otherwise have arisen is deferred until the first event in respect of which, if there had been a conditionally exempt transfer of the property when the claim was made, a chargeable event would have taken place. This is subject to the qualification that the deferral continues if after the property became comprised in the settlement and before any such notional chargeable event takes place there has been a conditionally exempt occasion in respect of the property in question.[189]

Effect of loss of deferral

27-67 Where a deferred charge crystallises (but not where there has been a s.79(1) conditionally exempt transfer or a s.79(2) "exempt disposal"), tax is charged on an amount equal to the value of the property in question at the time of the precipitating chargeable event.[190] The rate at which tax is charged is found by multiplying one or more percentages, ranging from 0.25 per cent down to 0.05 per cent, by a specified number of quarters.[191] In order to find the specified number of quarters, it is necessary first to determine how many complete quarters are contained in the "relevant period". Once this has been done, tax is charged at the following rates:

---

[186] IHTA 1984 s.79(1).
[187] IHTA 1984 s.79(2).
[188] IHTA 1984 s.79(3). Note that the property must have been designated by HMRC and the requisite undertakings given *before* the date of the periodic charge. It is therefore important to claim in advance so that the formalities can be completed in time.
[189] IHTA 1984 s.79(4).
[190] IHTA 1984 s.79(5).
[191] IHTA 1984 s.79(6).

Per cent	Number of complete quarters in relevant period
0.25	0–40
0.20	41–80
0.15	81–120
0.10	121–160
0.05	161–200
0.0	200–

For this purpose, the "relevant period" means the period beginning with the latest of:

(1) the day on which the settlement commenced;
(2) the date of the last 10 year anniversary of the settlement to fall before the day on which the property became comprised in the settlement; and
(3) March 13, 1975,

and ending with the day before the event giving rise to the charge.[192]

Liability for tax

27–68   The persons liable for any tax in respect of a deferred charge are (a) the trustees of the settlement, and (b) any person for whose benefit any of the property or income from it is applied at or after the time of the event occasioning the charge.[193] For accountability and due date for payment, see paras 29–06 and 29–69(4) respectively.

Where the loss of deferral arises by virtue of a transfer out of the settlement and therefore on the occasion of an exit charge, there is a credit for tax payable on the loss of deferral against the tax on the exit charge.[194]

Hybrid settlements

27–69   It is possible, of course, for a periodic charge to be deferred with respect to part only of the property comprised in the settlement. This would occur where part of the settled property is heritage property and part is not. In such a case the question arises as to whether the value of the heritage property is taken into account in determining the rate of tax charged on the non-heritage property, since, if it is, the average rate of tax charged on the non-heritage property may be greater than if the heritage property was left out of account altogether. It seems safe to assume that the value of the heritage

---

[192] IHTA 1984 s.79(7).
[193] IHTA 1984 s.207(3); it is unclear whether this includes persons who were trustees at the time of the deferral but not at the time tax is charged.
[194] IHTA 1984 s.33(7).

property is not intended to be brought into account, but it is not clear from the wording of s.82(1)[195] that this is in fact the way s.82 operates.

A special rule applies where trustees purchase[196] property, and then make a claim and give an undertaking, with the result that the periodic charge which would otherwise have been imposed on the first 10-year anniversary after their doing so is deferred, if on that anniversary a periodic charge falls to be imposed on other property comprised in the settlement. In that case, in calculating the rate at which the periodic charge is imposed on that other property, the value of the consideration given by the trustees for the heritage property which they acquired is brought into the hypothetical cumulative total by reference to which the rate of the periodic charge is fixed as if that value were an amount on which an exit charge had been imposed at the time the property was acquired.[197]

Adjustments to settlement's cumulative total

27–70   Amounts on which the periodic charge is imposed do not cumulate, and accordingly no adjustment is made to take account of any charge arising on the withdrawal of a conditional exemption or conditional deferral.

IV. MAINTENANCE FUNDS FOR HISTORIC BUILDINGS[198]

27–71   The treatment of maintenance funds for historic buildings is dealt with by s.27 and Sch.4, the purpose of which is to encourage owners to set aside funds both to maintain their property and to provide for a reasonable measure of public access to it. These provisions replace (as from March 9, 1982) s.84 of the Finance Act 1976, the provision which originally regulated maintenance funds, and ss.88–90 of and Sch.16 to the Finance Act 1980 which both modified s.84 and introduced a number of new rules. All subsequent statutory references are to the post-1982 provisions, unless otherwise indicated. It will be convenient to consider the rules under three main headings —property becoming comprised in a maintenance fund, property comprised in a maintenance fund, and property ceasing to be comprised in a maintenance fund. Until 1998 there were provisions for one-estate elections (for deductions for rent) under s.27 of the Taxes Act 1988.[199]

27–72   As a preliminary matter, two points of general trust law should be noted. First, a maintenance fund is ostensibly a purpose trust, and as a matter of trust law a purpose trust is invalid. This is subject to the qualification that where it can be shown that the benefits arising under the trust are sufficiently direct and tangible to give to someone locus standi to apply to the court to enforce the trust, the trust will be valid notwithstanding that it is expressed to be for a purpose.[200] Thus, so long as the object of the

---

[195] See paras 10–23–10–35.
[196] Strictly speaking, the rule applies whenever trustees have given consideration for property.
[197] IHTA 1984 s.79(8) and (9).
[198] See "Aspects of Maintenance Funds", *The Law Society Gazette* (1984), p.1661.
[199] ICTA 1988 s.27, repealed by FA 1998, with effect for income tax purposes after April 5, 2001, and for corporation tax for accounting periods beginning on or after April 1, 2001.
[200] See *Re Denley's Trust Deed* [1969] 1 Ch. 373; *McPhail v Doulton* [1971] A.C. 424; *Re Lipinski's Will Trusts* [1976] Ch. 235.

976

trust is to benefit individuals—e.g. those living in the house—in a tangible way the fund should not fail on this ground.

Secondly, regard must also be had to the rule against perpetuities. The Perpetuities Act 2009 came into force on April 6, 2010. All post-commencement trusts now have a 125-year perpetuity period, even if the trust deed refers to a different period. However, the law as it was prior to the Perpetuities Act 2009 continues to apply to pre-commencement trusts. Therefore, if the trust was framed by reference to a life in being, the perpetuity period, by the end of which the property must vest, is that life plus 21 years. If the trust is not framed by reference to a life in being the perpetuity period cannot exceed 80 years.[201]

For the sake of completeness, it should be noted that a maintenance fund can be established by a lifetime transfer, on death, and even by a deed of variation.[202]

Property becoming comprised in a maintenance fund

The legislation provides that favoured treatment is extended to property becoming comprised in a maintenance fund in two ways.[203] First, certain transfers of value of such property are exempt transfers. Secondly, relief is given from exit charges that would otherwise be imposed in respect of relevant property which becomes such property. The Finance Act 1998 s.144 introduces a two year time limit for transfers of assets to approved maintenance funds in respect of transfers of value made on or after March 17, 1998 (subject to extension by the Board).[204] **27–73**

Exempt transfer

By s.27, a transfer of value is an exempt transfer to the extent that: **27–74**

(1) the value transferred by it is attributable to property which by virtue of the transfer becomes, or immediately after the transfer remains, comprised in a settlement;

(2) it is not prevented from being an exempt transfer by the provisions of ss.18, 23, 24, 25, 26 or 56[205]; and

(3) a Board direction in respect of the property is already in force at the time of the transfer, or the Board subsequently give such a direction.[206]

The inclusion in (1) of the words "immediately after the transfer remains" means that the exemption is available to property already comprised in a settlement in which

---

[201] The rule against purpose trusts and the rule against perpetuities do not apply to charitable trusts.

[202] For the powers of trustees to transfer property into a maintenance fund under s.64 of the Settled Land Act 1925, see *Raikes v Lygon* [1988] 1 W.L.R. 281; [1988] 1 All E.R. 884; (1988) *The Law Society Gazette* (1988), p.34.

[203] For the treatment of property moving from one maintenance fund to another or rejoining a maintenance fund, see paras 27–88 and following.

[204] IHTA 1984 s.27(1A), inserted by FA 1988 s.144.

[205] IHTA 1984 s.56(1), (3) and (4). For purposes of s.56(3) and (4), the trustees of a settlement in respect of which a direction has effect are treated as a body within s.26, so that the restriction in s.56(3) on acquisitions of interests applies even if the acquisition is from, e.g., a charity: see para.3–59.

[206] IHTA 1984 s.27 and Sch.4 para.1(2).

there is an interest in possession if on the termination of that interest the Board give a direction.

Retrospectively exempt transfers

27–75   Exemption may be retrospectively available to a transfer of value on a person's death of settled property in which he had an interest in possession if a direction is subsequently given in respect of that property within a specified period. Section 57A provides that this occurs where, after March 16, 1987:

> (1) a person dies who immediately before his death was beneficially entitled to an interest in possession in property comprised in a settlement; and
> (2) within two years after his death the property becomes held on trusts by virtue of which a Board direction is given in respect of the property.[207]

The trusts can be either of the settlement in which the property was comprised on the relevant death or the trusts of another settlement.[208] Where the property became held on the trusts as the result of court proceedings, the stipulated period is extended to three years if the property could not have become so held without those proceedings.[209]

Following the Finance Act 1998, the application for exemption must be made within two years of the date of the transfer (where the transfer is after March 16, 1998) or within such longer period as the Board may allow.[210]

The PET problem

27–76   As discussed in para.27–24 above, it is possible to claim retrospectively conditional exemption for heritage property transferred by a failed PET. This position does not, however, apply to supporting property which might otherwise have been put into a maintenance fund. Accordingly, this raises real problems for the owner of heritage property. He is given the choice between simply giving the heritage property away, e.g. to his heir, together with supporting property (i.e. property which on his death would otherwise go into a maintenance fund) in the knowledge that if he does not then survive for seven years conditional exemption cannot be claimed retrospectively on the supporting property. Alternatively, he can give away the potentially designated property, hoping that if he dies within seven years conditional exemption terms will be agreed following his death and by will leave the maintenance fund property to the maintenance fund. After seven years surviving the gift he will then alter his will to leave the property, away from the maintenance fund which is then redundant.

Favoured treatment

27–77   Subject to what is said below, where the above conditions are satisfied the property is treated as having on the relevant death become subject to the aforesaid trusts, with

[207] IHTA 1984 s.57A(1) and (2).
[208] IHTA 1984 s.57A(1).
[209] IHTA 1984 s.57A(3), inserted by FA 1987 Sch.9 paras 1 and 4.
[210] IHTA 1984 s.27(1A), inserted by FA 1998 s.144.

the result that exemption under s.27 becomes retrospectively available. Furthermore, no disposition or other event occurring between the date of the death and the date on which the property becomes subject to the aforesaid trusts, so far as it relates to the property, is a transfer or value or otherwise a chargeable[211] occasion. It may be that the value of the property when it becomes held on the aforesaid trusts is lower than so much of the value transferred on the relevant death as is attributable to the property. In that case, retrospective exemption is given only to the extent of the lower value.[212]

Qualifications

Retrospective exemption is not available if any of the following conditions are infringed: **27–78**

(1) the disposition by which the property becomes held on the aforesaid trusts is defeasible[213];
(2) the property which becomes held on those trusts was itself an interest in settled property[214];
(3) the trustees who hold the property on those trusts have, for a consideration in money or money's worth, acquired an interest under a settlement in which the property was comprised immediately before the relevant death or at any time thereafter[215]; or
(4) the property which becomes held on the aforesaid trusts does so for a consideration in money or money's worth, or is acquired by the trustees for such a consideration, or has at any time since the relevant death been acquired by any other person for such a consideration.[216]

For this purpose, a person is treated as acquiring property for a consideration in money or money's worth if he becomes entitled to it as a result of transactions which include a disposition for such consideration, whether to him or another, of that or other property. For the kind of mischief which (3) and (4) above are aimed at preventing, see para.27–81.[217]

Relief from exit charges

The legislation provides that in two cases no exit charge is imposed in respect of property which becomes comprised in a maintenance fund. First, no exit charge is imposed in respect of property which ceases to be relevant property on becoming property in respect of which the Board has given a direction under Sch.4.[218] This relief is subject to two restrictions. First, it does not apply in relation to any property if, at or before the time when it becomes property in respect of which the direction has effect, an interest under the settlement in which it was comprised immediately before it ceased   **27–79**

---

[211] IHTA 1984 s.57A(2).
[212] IHTA 1984 s.57A(5).
[213] IHTA 1984 s.57A(4)(a).
[214] IHTA 1984 s.57A(4)(b).
[215] IHTA 1984 s.57A(4)(c).
[216] IHTA 1984 s.57A(4)(d).
[217] IHTA 1984 s.57A(6).
[218] IHTA 1984 Sch.4 para.16(1).

to be relevant property is or has been acquired for a consideration in money or money's worth by the trustees of the settlement in which it becomes comprised on ceasing to be relevant property. For these purposes, trustees are treated as acquiring an interest for such a consideration if they become entitled to that interest as a result of transactions which include a disposition for such a consideration (whether to them or to another person) of that interest or of other property.[219] Secondly, it may be that if the relief was not available the amount on which tax would be charged (before agricultural and/or business relief and before any grossing-up)[220] would exceed the value of the property immediately after it becomes property in respect of which the direction has effect. In that case, the relief is not available, and tax is charged instead on that excess. If the trustees receive a consideration for transferring the property then in computing the excess the value of the property transferred to the body in question is reduced by the consideration received by the trustees.[221] This is an anti-avoidance provision, the general purpose of which is to prevent trustees from entering into depreciatory transactions which would otherwise have the effect of reducing the value of relevant property which they retained in circumstances such that, thanks to para.9(1), no charge to tax would arise.[222] For convenience, this restriction—which, as will be seen below, is referred to frequently in the legislation—will be called the "restriction on disproportionate diminutions".

27–80   Secondly, by para.17(1), no exit charge is imposed where after the property in question ceases to be relevant property an individual makes a transfer of value which satisfies the following conditions:

(1) the transfer of value is exempt under s.27[223];
(2) the value transferred by the transfer of value is attributable to the property in question; and
(3) the transfer of value is made within 30 days after the occasion which would otherwise have given rise to an exit charge, unless that occasion is the death of the settlor, in which case the period is two years.[224]

Restrictions

27–81   This relief is subject to restrictions similar to those stated above. First, it is subject to the restriction on disproportionate diminutions.[225] Secondly, the relief is not available if the individual has acquired the property for a consideration in money or money's worth. For this purpose, a person is treated as acquiring property for a consideration in money or money's worth if he becomes entitled to it as a result of transactions which include a disposition for such consideration (whether to him or another) of that or other property.[226] This prevents tax being avoided in the following way. Assume that X is a beneficiary under a trust which owns an historic building worth, say, £1 million. His father wishes to transfer to him £1 million free of IHT. The trustees could transfer the house to X, who would then sell it to his father for £1 million. So long as the father

[219] IHTA 1984 Sch.4 para.16(3) and (4).
[220] IHTA 1984 Sch.4 para.18
[221] IHTA 1984 Sch.4 para.16(2).
[222] See para.15–35 for an example of how this restriction works in a different context.
[223] See para.27–74.
[224] IHTA 1984 Sch.4 para.17(1) and (2).
[225] IHTA 1984 Sch.4 paras 17(4) and 18.
[226] IHTA 1984 Sch.4 para.17(3).

transferred the house to a maintenance fund within 30 days, he would—in the absence of provision to the contrary—have succeeded in transferring £1 million to his son free of IHT. No charge would have arisen in respect of the transfer of the property to the son by the trustees since, given the father's transfer of the property to the maintenance fund, the above-mentioned relief would have been available. The purchase by the father of the house would not have constituted a transfer of value by him to the son, because the purchase would not have diminished the value of the father's estate. Nor would the transfer of the property by the father to the maintenance fund have given rise to a charge to tax, since that transfer would have been exempt under s.27. The legislation prevents this technique from being effective by ensuring that in such circumstances no relief is available in respect of the original distribution by the trustees to the son.

Board directions

27–82 The special provisions only apply to a transfer to a maintenance fund if the Board give the appropriate direction. In certain circumstances, the Board must give a direction; in other cases, they may do so. The Board must give a direction if they are satisfied that three requirements and two conditions are fulfilled. The three requirements are:

(1) The trusts on which the property is held must be such that throughout the period of six years beginning with the date on which the property became so comprised the property and the income therefrom can be applied only for:

  (a) the maintenance, repair or preservation of, or making provision for public access to "qualifying property" which is defined in Sch.4 para.3(2) as (i) a building which has been designated under the Finance Act 1975 or the Finance Act 1976 or s.31(1)(b), (c), (d) or (e),[227] or (ii) land which adjoins such a building and which itself has been so designated,[228] or (iii) any object which in the Board's opinion is historically associated with such a building[229]; or

  (b) the maintenance, repair or preservation of property which has itself been put into the maintenance fund; or

  (c) such improvement of property held in the fund as is reasonable having regard to the purpose of the trusts; or

  (d) defraying the expenses of the trustees in relation to the property held on the trusts.[230]

  In so far as income is not applied in these ways and is not accumulated, it must be capable of being applied for the benefit only of a body mentioned in Sch.3, i.e. museums, etc.[231] or for the benefit of a "qualifying charity".[232] For this purpose, a charity is a qualifying charity if it exists wholly or mainly for maintaining, repairing or preserving for the public benefit buildings of historic

---

[227] See paras 27–10 and 27–48.

[228] The property will not be within this category if since the last occasion on which an undertaking was given under FA 1975 s.34 or FA 1976: ss.76, 78(5)(b) or 82(3) tax has become chargeable under s.34 or under ss.78 or 82(3) of FA 1976: see IHTA 1984 Sch.4 para.3(2)(c).

[229] It will be noted that pictures, prints, books, manuscripts, works of art, scientific collections and other things not yielding income are not capable of being supported out of a maintenance fund unless they are in the Treasury's opinion historically associated with the building in question.

[230] IHTA 1984 Sch.4 paras 1(1), 2(1)(a), 3(1)(a)(i) and 3(2).

[231] See para.3–53.

[232] IHTA 1984 Sch.4 paras 1(1), 2(1)(a) and 3(1)(a)(ii).

or architectural interest, land of scenic, historic or scientific interest or objects of national, scientific, historic or artistic interest, "national interest" including interest within any part of the United Kingdom.[233]

(2) The trusts on which the property is held must be such that if any of the settled property ceases to be held on those trusts within the above-mentioned six-year period or, if the settlor (or the life tenant) dies in that period, at any time before his death, the property must be capable of devolving only on a Sch.3 body or a qualifying charity.[234]

(3) After the expiry of the above-mentioned six-year period income arising from the property held on the trusts must be capable of being applied only for the maintenance, repair or preservation of, or making provision for public access to, the land, building, object or objects mentioned above or for the benefit of a Sch.3 body or a qualifying charity.[235] It will be noted that this requirement applies only to income arising to the trust (including accumulations of income) but not to the capital of the fund.

The two conditions which must be satisfied are:

(a) the property transferred into the maintenance fund must be of a character and amount appropriate for the purpose of the trusts.[236] Property which produces no income will normally not be appropriate for such purposes, especially if its own maintenance might make excessive demands on the fund's resources. HMRC might also regard property which would be related property if transferred to a charity as being of a character inappropriate to the maintenance fund. Settlements of excessive amounts might be regarded as being inappropriate in amount; equally, pilot funds (i.e. a small initial transfer into the fund) would not be acceptable unless there was a reasonable prospect of substantial additions although several have been approved; and

(b) the trustees must be approved by the Board and, at the time the direction is given, be resident in the United Kingdom.[237] In addition, they must include either a solicitor, an accountant, i.e. a member of an incorporated society of accountants,[238] or a member of such other professional body as the Board may allow in the case of the property concerned, e.g. a land agent or a trust corporation.[239] "Trust corporation" for this purpose means a person that is a trust corporation for the purposes of the Law of Property Act 1925.[240] The IHT rules for determining residence apply,[241] save that where the trustee is a trust corporation, the corporation tax rules apply, so that the trust corporation will be regarded as resident where its central management and control abides, or from March 15, 1988, if it was incorporated in the United Kingdom.[242]

The general effect of the first requirement is that a fund would not qualify for exemption unless the property for the maintenance of which it was established had itself previously been the subject of a conditionally exempt transfer. In order to ease

[233] IHTA 1984 Sch.4 para.3(4).
[234] IHTA 1984 Sch.4 paras 1(1), 2(1)(a) and 3(1)(b), and 3(5A).
[235] IHTA 1984 Sch.4 paras 1(1), 2(1)(a) and 3(1)(c).
[236] IHTA 1984 Sch.4 para.2(1)(a)(ii).
[237] IHTA 1984 Sch.4 para.2(1)(b)(iii).
[238] IHTA 1984 Sch.4 para.2(3).
[239] IHTA 1984 Sch.4 para.2(1)(b)(ii).
[240] IHTA 1984 Sch.4 para.2(3).
[241] See para.11–47.
[242] IHTA 1984 Sch.4 para.2(2); *De Beers Consolidated Gold Mines v Howe* [1906] A.C. 455; FA 1988 s.66.

this restriction, para.3(3) provides that where it appears to the Board that provision is made or is to be made by a settlement for the maintenance, repair or preservation of an historic house and/or land adjoining such a house, they may: (i) designate the property under para.3(3); and (ii) accept the required undertaking with respect to the property. The effect of such designation and acceptance is that, provided the above conditions are satisfied, para.3 will apply to the transfer.

By Sch.4 para.7, where the Board has given a direction in respect of property, the trusts on which that property is held are enforceable at the suit of the Board and the Board have the rights and powers of a beneficiary as respects the appointment, removal and retirement of the trustees.

Claims

Claims in relation to maintenance funds should be sent, with details similar to those **27–83** that would accompany a claim for a conditional exemption, to the Heritage Team of Charity Assets & Residence, Inheritance Tax of HMRC.[243] It is important to note that while a claim for a conditional exemption can be made only where a transfer of value has taken place, this is not now the case where maintenance funds are concerned, and the Board may, following a claim, give a direction[244] so that the person intending to set up the fund knows where he stands before actually transferring any property. HMRC has confirmed in the Memorandum that it will not be necessary to involve HMRC's Solicitors' Office in deciding whether a draft trust instrument complies with Sch.4 where the trust instrument follows the form of one which has been previously agreed.[245]

Previous directions

It may be that property became comprised in a settlement by virtue of a transfer of **27–84** value made before March 9, 1982, which was exempt under the Finance Act 1976 s.84. Such property is treated as property in respect of which a Sch.4 direction has been given.[246] In the same way, designations, undertakings, and acceptances made under the Finance Act 1976 s.84(6) are treated as made under Sch.4 and, in relation to them, para.3(3) are treated as having been in force when those designations, undertakings, and acceptances were made.[247] Paragraph 3(3A) refers to s.35A which provides for the right for undertakings given before July 31, 1998, to be varied by the Board (for which, see paras 27–13–27–14 above).

Withdrawal of direction

It is vital to bear in mind that if in the Board's opinion the facts concerning any **27–85** property or its administration cease to warrant a direction continuing in effect they may

[243] HMRC memorandum, *Capital Taxation and the National Heritage*, para.8.5 for further details of the conditions to be satisfied for the arrangements to apply.
[244] IHTA 1984 Sch.4 para.1(2).
[245] HMRC memorandum, *Capital Taxation and the National Heritage*, para.8.5(c)(iv).
[246] IHTA 1984 Sch.4 para.1(3).
[247] IHTA 1984 Sch.4 para.3(5).

at any time by notice in writing to the trustees withdraw that direction on such grounds, and from such date, as the notice may specify,[248] in which case charges to tax will be imposed.[249]

Property comprised in a maintenance fund

27–86   Property comprised in a maintenance fund receives favoured treatment in that it is not subject to the periodic charge.[250] An exit charge may be imposed on such property in certain circumstances; this is discussed below. By Sch.4 para.6, where a direction has effect in respect of property, the trustees shall from time to time furnish the Board with such accounts and other information relating to the property as the Board may reasonably require. HMRC's Memorandum sets out the amount of detail they require about maintenance funds in the accounts; a distinction is drawn between those funds with gross annual income of over £25,000 and those with gross annual income of under £25,000.[251]

Property ceasing to be comprised in a maintenance fund

27–87   As was mentioned above, after the initial six-year period the property comprised in the settlement may be applied or devolve otherwise than for "approved purposes". The price of such an application may, however, be a charge to tax, as follows.

Exit charges generally

27–88   Exit charges may be imposed by para.8 of Sch.4 on settled property held on trusts which comply with the requirements set out at para.27–82 and in respect of which a Sch.4 direction has effect. For convenience, such property will be referred to as "property comprised in maintenance fund". Special rules apply where property became comprised in a fund on the termination of an interest in possession: see para.27–75. So far as the general rules are concerned, a primary exit charge may be imposed if such property (including accumulated income) ceases to be such property otherwise than:

(1)   by virtue of an application for the approved purposes mentioned in the first requirement discussed at para.27–82 above; or

(2)   by devolving on a Sch.3 body or a qualifying charity.[252]

A primary exit charge may thus be imposed if the Board withdraw a direction or if there is an "unapproved" application or devolution. The circumstances in which property and/or accumulated income will be regarded as having been applied otherwise

---

[248] IHTA 1984 Sch.4 para.5.
[249] See para.27–88.
[250] IHTA 1984 s.58(1)(c).
[251] HMRC memorandum, *Capital Taxation and the National Heritage*, Appendix 6, for further details.
[252] IHTA 1984 Sch.4 paras 8(2)(a) and (3).

than for approved purposes are far from clear, and trustees may have to tread cautiously to avoid triggering a potentially disastrous charge to tax.[253]

Even where a devolution on a Sch.3 body or a qualifying charity is prima facie an "approved" one, a charge will still arise if at or before the time the property devolves an interest in the property is or has been acquired for a consideration in money or money's worth by that or another such body or charity. This is subject to the qualification that no regard is had to any acquisition from another such body or charity. For these purposes, a body or a charity is treated as acquiring an interest for a consideration in money or money's worth if it becomes entitled to the interest as a result of transactions which include a disposition for such consideration (whether to that body or charity or to another person) of that interest or other property.[254] A secondary exit charge is imposed in the usual way[255] unless the disposition made by the trustees is by way of an "approved" application.[256]

Relief from exit charges

The legislation provides two reliefs from exit charges imposed by para.8. First, by para.9, no charge is levied in respect of property which within 30 days after the occasion on which tax would otherwise be chargeable under para.8 (unless that occasion is the death of the settlor, in which case the permitted period is two years)[257] becomes comprised in another settlement as, the result of a transfer of value which is exempt under s.27. The legislation makes special provision to relax the criteria which must be satisfied before the Board are required to give a direction in respect of the settlement to which the property is transferred in such circumstances. By Sch.4 para.4, the Board must give a direction if the two conditions and the third requirement (which is modified to apply as from the time the property becomes comprised in the settlement) stated at para.27–82 are satisfied.[258] This is subject to the qualification that if the unapproved devolution by virtue of which the property ceased to be comprised in the first settlement fell before the expiry of the six-year period the usual requirements apply, save that the six-year period of the second settlement is regarded as having begun at the time the six-year period of the first settlement began.[259] **27–89**

Secondly, by para.10, tax is not charged under para.8 in respect of the property which ceases to comply with the requirements set out at para.27–82 and in respect of which Sch.4 direction has effect if it does so on becoming property to which either: **27–90**

(1) the settlor or his spouse is beneficially entitled; or
(2) the settlor's widow or widower is beneficially entitled if the settlor has died in the two years preceding the time when it becomes such property.[260]

---

[253] For a useful discussion on the difficulties that may arise, see "What charge for admission?" in *The Law Society Gazette*, November 11, 1981. The tax charged in such cases is considered at para.27–93.
[254] IHTA 1984 Sch.4 paras 17(1) and (2).
[255] See para.10–10.
[256] IHTA 1984 Sch.4 para.8(2)(b) and (3).
[257] IHTA 1984 Sch.4 para.9(1) and (2).
[258] The relaxed criteria also apply where relief would have been available but for the restriction on disproportionate diminutions.
[259] IHTA 1984 Sch.4 para.4(2).
[260] IHTA 1984 Sch.4 para.10(1).

The position of maintenance funds thus differs from that of other discretionary trusts, to which the "reverter to settlor" exemption is unavailable.

Restrictions on reliefs

27–91   The availability of relief under paras 9 and 10 is subject to a number of restrictions, Both reliefs are subject to two restrictions identical to those stated at para.27–81.[261] In addition, para.10 relief is subject to three further restrictions. First, it is not available unless the person who becomes beneficially entitled to the property is domiciled (applying the deemed domicile rules) in the United Kingdom when he becomes so entitled.[262] Secondly, relief is not available in respect of property which ceased to be relevant property and became comprised in a maintenance fund in circumstances such that para.9(1) or (4) prevented an exit charge from being imposed (or would have prevented the imposition of such a charge in the absence of the restriction on disproportionate diminution).[263] Finally, no relief is available in respect of property which ceased to be comprised in a maintenance fund and subsequently became comprised in a maintenance fund in circumstances such that para.9(1) prevented an exit charge from being imposed (or would have prevented the imposition of such a charge in the absence of the restriction on disproportionate diminution).[264]

The amount on which tax is charged

27–92   Where a charge is imposed under para.8, the amount on which tax is charged is the amount by which the value of the property comprised in the settlement immediately after the chargeable event is less than it would be but for that event. If the trustees pay the tax out of the maintenance fund the amount on which tax would otherwise be charged must be grossed-up.[265] It should be noted that agricultural property relief or business property relief is capable of applying to reduce the chargeable amount,[266] as references to chargeable transfers include references to occasions on which tax is chargeable under Sch.4.[267]

Rate of tax—previously relieved property

27–93   The rules for determining the rate of tax vary according to whether or not the property in respect of which the exit charge in question is imposed is, in effect, property which was previously relevant property which became comprised in the maintenance fund in circumstances such that the reliefs mentioned at para.27–75 applied (or would have applied but for the restriction there mentioned on disproportionate diminutions). For convenience, such property will be referred to as "previously relieved property". (It may be that property became comprised in a settlement by virtue of a transfer of

---

[261] IHTA 1984 Sch.4 paras 9(3)–(5) and 10(2)–(5).
[262] IHTA 1984 Sch.4 para.10(8).
[263] IHTA 1984 Sch.4 para.10(6); see paras 27–79–29–81.
[264] IHTA 1984 Sch.4 para.10(7); see para.27–89.
[265] IHTA 1984 Sch.4 para.8(3).
[266] HMRC memorandum, *Capital Taxation and the National Heritage*, Appendix 5, para.6.
[267] IHTA 1984 s.2(3).

value made before March 9, 1982 which was exempt under the Finance Act 1976 s.84, and that such property is treated as property in respect of which a s.27 direction has been given.[268] Such property is treated for the purposes of determining the rate of tax as having become property comprised in a maintenance fund when that transfer was made.)[269] Where previously relieved property is concerned the rate of tax is found by multiplying one or more percentages, ranging from 0.25 per cent down to 0.05 per cent, by a specified number of quarters. In order to find the specified number of quarters, it is necessary to determine how many complete quarters are contained in the "relevant period". Once this has been done, tax is charged at the following rates.[270]

Per cent	Number of complete quarters in relevant period
0.25	000–40
0.20	041–80
0.15	081–120
0.10	121–160
0.05	161–200
0.00	200–

For this purpose, the relevant period is the period ending with the date before the event giving rise to the charge to tax and beginning with the latest of:

(1) the date of the last 10-year anniversary of the settlement in which the property was comprised before it ceased (or last ceased) to be relevant property;
(2) the date on which the property became (or last became) relevant property before it ceased (or last ceased) to be such property; and
(3) March 13, 1975.[271]

It may be that the property in respect of which tax is chargeable has exited from a maintenance fund and subsequently become comprised in a maintenance fund—be it for the same maintenance fund or a different one—in circumstances such that para.9 prevented an exit charge from arising (or would have done so but for the qualification relating to disproportionate diminutions mentioned at para.27–81). In such case, the property is treated as never having ceased to be comprised in a maintenance fund.[272]

The rate of tax—other property

Where property other than previously relieved property is concerned, the position is **27–94** much more complicated. In such a case, a comparison must be made between two rates

[268] See para.27–84.
[269] IHTA 1984 Sch.4 para.15.
[270] IHTA 1984 Sch.4 para.11(1) and (2).
[271] IHTA 1984 Sch.4 para.11(3).
[272] IHTA 1984 Sch.4 para.11(4).

of tax, with the charge being imposed at whichever rate proves higher.[273] The first rate of tax is found in much the same way as where previously relieved property is concerned, i.e. by multiplying the percentages given above by a specified number of quarters. In order to find the specified number of quarters, it is necessary first to determine how many complete quarters are contained in the "relevant period". For this purpose, the relevant period is the period (i) beginning with the day on which the property in respect of which tax is chargeable became (or first became) property comprised in a maintenance fund, and (ii) ending with the day before the event giving rise to the charge.[274] In determining the relevant period there is disregarded any occasion on which property became property comprised in a maintenance fund which occurred before the imposition of an exit charge under para.8.[275] The rules for determining the second rate of tax vary according to whether, inter alia, (a) the settlor is alive or dead, (b) the property in respect of which the charge is imposed was previously comprised in a maintenance fund, and (c) any previous charge has been imposed.

27–95   *Settlor alive.* If the settlor is alive, the second rate is the effective rate—i.e. the average rate[276] at which tax would be charged at the lifetime rates if at the time the exit charge is imposed the settlor had made a chargeable transfer of the amount subject to that charge.[277]

27–96   *Settlor died on or after March 13, 1975.* If the settlor died on or after March 13, 1975, the second rate is the effective rate at which tax would have been charged if the amount on which the exit charge is imposed had been added to the value transferred on the settlor's death and formed the highest part of that value transferred. The death rates apply if the settlement was made on his death, while the lifetime rates apply if the settlement was made during his life, even if he died within seven years of having made the settlement.[278]

27–97   *Settlor died before March 13, 1975.* If the settlor died before March 13, 1975, the second rate is the effective rate at which tax would have been charged if:

(1) the settlor had died on the date occasioning the exit charge;
(2) the value transferred on his death had been equal to the amount on which estate duty was chargeable when he in fact died; and
(3) the amount on which the exit charge is imposed had been added to that value and had formed the highest part of it.

The death rates apply if the settlement was made on the settlor's death, while the lifetime rates apply if the settlement was made during his life, even if he died within seven years of having made the settlement.[279]

27–98   *Special rules.* Special rules apply in certain circumstances:

---

[273] IHTA 1984 Sch.4 para.12(1) and (2).
[274] IHTA 1984 Sch.4 para.13(1) and (2).
[275] IHTA 1984 Sch.4 para.13(3). For this purpose, the exit charge by reference to which the rate is being determined and any exit charge which would have been relieved under para.9 had it not involved a disproportionate diminution are ignored: para.13(4).
[276] IHTA 1984 Sch.4 para.14(8).
[277] IHTA 1984 Sch.4 para.14(8) and (9).
[278] IHTA 1984 Sch.4 para.14(2) and (9).
[279] IHTA 1984 Sch.4 para.14(3) and (9).

(1) for determining the identity of the settlor for the above purposes;

(2) bringing into account amounts previously subjected to exit charges under para.8; and

(3) where there has been a reduction in the tax rates, as follows:

1. *Property previously comprised in a maintenance fund.* It may be that tax is chargeable in respect of property which was previously comprised in another maintenance fund but which ceased to be so comprised and became comprised in the current fund in circumstances such that para.3 relief was available (or would have been available but for a disproportionate diminution). In such a case, the settlor for the above purposes is the person who was the settlor of the first settlement unless HMRC determine that the settlor of the current settlement should be the settlor for purposes of determining the rate of tax. If there has been a string of such settlements, the settlor is the settlor of the first settlement, subject to any determination by HMRC that he should be taken to be the settlor of any of the other settlements.[280] HMRC is given the ability to make these determinations so that they can prevent the rate of tax being determined by reference to the cumulative total of a "man of straw" who was interposed in a series of transfers between maintenance funds.

2. *Previous charges.* It may be that in the 10 years preceding the current charge another charge was imposed in respect of which tax was charged at the second rate. In such a case, a special rule applies if the person who is the settlor (as determined, where appropriate, by HMRC) for purposes of the current charge is the same person as the settlor for purposes of the previous charge (whether or not the settlements are the same and, if the settlor is dead, whether or not he has died since the previous charge). In such a case, account must be taken of the amount on which the previous exit charge was imposed. If the settlor is alive, that amount is for purposes of calculating the rate of the current charge taken to be the value transferred by a chargeable transfer made by the settlor immediately before the occasion of the current charge. If the settlor is dead, that amount is for purposes of calculating the rate of the current charge taken to increase the value transferred (or taken as transferred, as the case may be) on the settlor's death. If more than one charge was previously imposed, the aggregate of the amounts on which tax was previously charged must be brought into account.[281]

3. *Reduction in rates.* It may be that tax is chargeable under para.8 after a reduction in the rates and the rate at which it is charged falls to be determined by reference to a death which occurred before that change. In that case, the relevant rates are those in effect at the time the charge is made so that advantage is taken of the reduced rates of tax.[282]

Special exit charge—interests in possession

It may be that property became comprised in a maintenance fund on the occasion of **27–99** a transfer of value which was made by a person beneficially entitled to an interest in possession in the property. In that case, so far as the value transferred by the transfer

---

[280] IHTA 1984 Sch.4 para.14(4) and (5).
[281] IHTA 1984 Sch.4 para.14(6) and (7).
[282] IHTA 1984 Sch.2 para.6.

of value was attributable to the property, a special regime, set out in para.15A; applies if the transfer was an exempt transfer by virtue of the combined effect of s.27 and s.57(5) or s.57A or would, but for those sections, have been a chargeable transfer.[283] For the purpose of this discussion, the person who made the transfer of value will be called "the relevant person".

27–100   In such a case, no charge is levied in respect of property which within 30 days after the occasion on which tax would otherwise be chargeable under para.8, unless that occasion is the death of the settlor or the relevant person, in which case the permitted period is two years.[284]

27–101   The relief given by para.10[285] is not available if the relevant person died at or before the time when the property became property to which para.8 applies.[286] In any other case para.10 has effect as if the requirements relating to the settlor, his spouse and widow/widower were replaced by a provision framed by reference to property to which the relevant person's spouse is beneficially entitled or property to which that person's widow or widower is beneficially entitled if that person has died in the two years preceding the time when it becomes property to which para.8 applies. This is subject to the qualification that this rule applies only if a spouse, widow or widower would have become beneficially entitled to the property on the termination of the interest in possession had the property not then become property to which para.8 applies.[287]

27–102   The rules set out in para.27–93 for determining the rate of tax do not apply. The relevant rules are those found in paras 27–94 and following, subject to certain modifications. First, under the special rules in para.27–98, in relation to property previously comprised in a maintenance fund, the rules stated at paras 27–98–27–99 apply only in respect of property which was, in relation to either of the settlements therein mentioned, property to which para.15A applied. In that case, the Board may elect to substitute the relevant person for the settlor.[288] If there has been a string of such settlements, then the rules stated in paras 27–98–27–99 apply only if the property was, in relation to any of those settlements, property to which para.15A applied. Again, the Board can substitute the relevant person or any person selected by them as a settlor in relation to any of the previous settlements or the current settlement.[289] Where the Board make a substitution, that substitution has effect for purposes of applying the rules discussed at para.27–88 in relation, to previous charges.[290] If the relevant person died at or before the time when the property became property to which para.8 applies the relevant rates are the death rates.[291]

Liability for tax

27–103   The persons liable for tax charged under para.8 are the trustees of the settlement, and, as respects tax on the value of property which devolves on any person, the person

---

[283] IHTA 1984 Sch.4 para.15A(1) and (2).
[284] IHTA 1984 Sch.4 para.15A(3); see para.27–78.
[285] See para.27–90.
[286] IHTA 1984 Sch.4 para.15A(4).
[287] IHTA 1984 Sch.4 para.15A(4).
[288] IHTA 1984 Sch.4 para.15A(7).
[289] IHTA 1984 Sch.4 para.15A(8).
[290] IHTA 1984 Sch.4 para.15A(9).
[291] IHTA 1984 Sch.4 para.15A(10).

on whom that property devolves.[292] Any person liable must deliver an account before six months have expired from the end of the month in which the event by reason of which tax became chargeable occurred[293]; tax falls due at the end of this six month period.[294] Tax which remains outstanding after the due date carries interest as from that date at such rate as the Board may from time to time prescribe.[295]

[292] IHTA 1984 s.207(3).
[293] IHTA 1984 s.216(7).
[294] IHTA 1984 s.226(4).
[295] IHTA 1984 s.233(1)(c).

CHAPTER 28

PARTNERSHIPS

I. INTRODUCTION

28–01   Unlike the estate duty legislation, which in the Finance Act 1969 made special provision for charging duty on partnership interests, the legislation is largely silent regarding partnerships (and this remains so despite the advent of limited liability partnerships).[1] Accordingly, the liability of a partner in respect of:

(1) his share in the partnership; and
(2) the activities of the partnership,

is governed by the legislation generally in the same way as the liability of any other person.

The purpose of this chapter is to consider how these principles apply to partnerships, those entities treated as partnerships and those entities which may be partnerships but are not treated as such for tax purposes. As will be seen, the application in theory of these principles raises a considerable number of complex questions.

The application of the reservation of benefit rules to partnerships is discussed at paras 7–141 and following.

---

[1] Limited Liability Partnership Act 2000 with effect from April 6, 2001 (by virtue of SI 2001/3316).

Since April 6, 2001, three types of partnership have existed in English law: a **28–02** partnership formed in accordance with the Partnership Act 1890 (an "ordinary partnership"); a limited partnership, introduced under the Limited Partnership Act of 1907, in which the liability of one or more of the partners could be limited whilst also retaining general partners with unlimited liability; and a partnership formed by incorporation under the Limited Liability Partnership Act 2000 (a "limited liability partnership").

Ordinary partnerships

An ordinary partnership is not a legal entity distinct from the partners; instead, under **28–03** s.1(1) of the Partnership Act 1890, it is "the relation which subsists between the persons carrying on a business in common with a view of profit". It follows from the fact that the firm is not a distinct legal entity that the firm cannot itself act, nor can it own any property. Rather, the partners act as mutual agents and property is owned either by one or more of the partners in their own right, in which case they permit the firm to use it under a lease or license, or by the partners in common as partners, in which case the property is usually referred to as "partnership property". In the case of partnership property, each member of the partnership has an interest in the whole of the property, but no partner has a right to any particular portion of the property What he has a right to is his share of so much of the proceeds of sale of the property as remains after payment of all partnership debts and liabilities. In addition, he may be entitled to a share of the profits produced by the partnership property. In the case of property owned by an individual partner, on the other hand, that partner owns the property and any other partner is at most entitled only to a share of the profits produced by the property. It follows from this that a distinction is to be drawn between:

(1) a partner's share in a firm; and
(2) his interest in the property which he owns as an individual.

His share is usually comprised of three rights:

(a) his right on any surplus arising from the sale of partnership property on a dissolution,
(b) his right to his share of the firm's profits, and
(c) his right on the dissolution of the partnership to the working capital he has contributed.

Seen this way, his share may be regarded as a tripartite chose in action,[2] which, depending on the partnership agreement, he is free to deal with as he may choose. His interest in property which he owns as an individual partner is a beneficial interest in the property itself. His interest in partnership property is one of the three rights of which his partnership interest is comprised.

Although there is no doubt that the key to analysing the nature of a partnership lies in the proprietary nature of a partner's interest in the underlying property of the particular partnership, the difficulty is that there may arguably be some uncertainty

---

[2] This analysis of the nature of a partnership share is important when considering the effect of the reservation of benefit rules in this area: see para.7–141.

about the precise nature of a partnership share in the context of the Inheritance Tax Act 1984. Although a partnership interest may only entitle a partner to a share of the surplus assets on dissolution,[3] in *IRC v Gray* [1994] S.T.C. 360, Hoffman L.J. (as he then was) identified and drew a distinction between an internal and external perspective. At 377, he stated as follows:

> "As between themselves, partners are not entitled individually to exercise proprietary rights over any of the partnership assets. This is because they have subjected their proprietary interests to the terms of the partnership deed which provides that the assets shall be employed in the partnership business, and on dissolution realised for the purposes of paying debts and distributing any surplus. **As regards the outside world, however, the partnership deed is irrelevant. The partners are collectively entitled to each and every asset of the partnership, in which each of them therefore has an undivided share.**"[4]

From the external perspective, therefore, a partnership is, at least for some purposes, transparent and partnerships have already been treated as transparent in *some* IHT contexts.[5]

There is no HMRC published guidance on this difficult issue. In the context of inheritance tax, it does seem to be HMRC's consistent approach to treat an interest in traditional partnerships as a single "chose in action", and it is thought that this must be the correct analysis.

Limited liability partnerships

28–04   The Limited Liability Partnership Act 2000 (which came into force on April 6, 2001) created a new legal entity: the limited liability partnership or "LLP", a body corporate with unlimited capacity whose members are those persons registered at Companies House. An LLP has a legal personality separate from that of its members and can therefore enter into contracts and sue and be sued in its own name. The law relating to partnerships is expressly excluded from applying to LLPs[6] which are therefore gov-

---

[3] This seems to have been the basis for treating a partnership share as personalty rather than realty, whatever the nature of underlying partnership assets But note that the distinction in English law between real property and personal property is not the same as the conflict of laws distinction for between immovable property and moveable property. In this context, the relevant distinction is between movable and immovable property; some property treated as personalty under English law includes some important interests in immovables. There is no clear English authority on whether a partner's interest in partnership land is an interest in a movable or in an immovable (see Dicey, Morris, and Collins, *The Conflict of Laws*, 14th edn (2006), para.22–013).

[4] The distinction has also been drawn in the High Court in the earlier case of *Re Fuller's Contract* [1933] Ch. 652, per Luxmoore J. at 656.

[5] See also *Burdett-Coutts v IRC* [1960] 1 W.L.R. 1027, where the deceased's partnership interest was held to be eligible pro tanto for the reduced-rate relief under FA 1954 s.28 in respect of plant and machinery. Note that in the decided cases on situs of partnership interests, albeit cases which turned on the fact that partners did not have direct interests in underlying property of the partnership, no distinction was drawn between the situs of the asset consisting of a "share" in the partnership and the situs of the underlying property of the partnership (see e.g. per Lord Herschell in *Laidlay* at 483: "My Lords, it has been said that the point to be determined is, what is to be regarded as the locality in which the partnership is situate? I think it would be more accurate to state the question thus: What is to be regarded as the locality in which the property of the partnership is situate?"; and at 490: "My Lords . . . I think that this asset was a share in partnership property consisting of a business and property locally situated in India, and that the share, therefore, must equally be regarded as an asset situated in India"). The outcome of the application of this rule is therefore not at odds with treatment of partnerships as transparent. As regards nature of a partner's interests in the underlying partnership property, see also *Mackinlay (Inspector of Taxes) v Arthur Young McClelland Moores & Co* [1990] 2 A.C. 239 at 249A: "[a partner] is, with his partners an owner of the undertaking in which he is engaged and he is entitled, with his partners, to an undivided share in all the assets of the undertaking".

[6] Limited Liability Partnership Act 2000 s.1(5).

erned by the terms of their members' agreement, or by default the Limited Liability Partnership Act 2000.

Whilst LLPs have a legal persona, they are tax transparent.[7] Section 267A expressly provides that:

(a) property to which a LLP is entitled, or which it occupies or uses, shall be treated as property to which its members are entitled, or which they occupy or use, as partners;

(b) any business carried on by a LLP shall be treated as carried on in partnership by its members;

(c) incorporation, changes in membership or dissolution of a LLP shall be treated as the formation, alteration or dissolution of a partnership; and

(d) any transfer of value made by or to a LLP shall be treated as made by or to its members in partnership (and not by or to the LLP as such).

This tax transparency means that the normal reliefs and exemptions available to partners in an ordinary partnership are equally available to members of an LLP. In particular, because s.267A(d) deems transfers of value to be made by the members of the LLP and not by the LLP itself, liability under s.94 (under which a transfer made by a close company may be apportioned to the participators in that company) cannot arise even if the LLP might otherwise be a close company.

By virtue of s.267A the introduction of the LLP has not resulted in any substantive change to the way in which the IHT legislation is applied to partnerships.

The IHT concerns on the conversion of an ordinary partnership to a LLP are therefore essentially the same as those that apply to any formation, variation or dissolution of an ordinary partnership.[8] Any changes to the arrangements made as a result of the conversion will usually be commercial in nature (and thus relievable under s.10(1)[9] regardless of whether or not a transfer of value has actually arisen). However, the practitioner dealing with family partnerships should take particular care to ensure that the terms of the members' agreement of the new LLP do not confer any gratuitous benefit on partners.

A further word of caution is perhaps necessary. There was some concern that LLPs might be adopted by investment businesses for tax reasons in addition to their primary purpose for use by the professions. During the Standing Committee debate, it was stated that extra-statutory concessions and statements of practice which affected LLPs might be amended when the statutory provisions had been settled, but IHTMs[10] do now refer to the treatment of certain investment interests held by LLPs, in particular, where an LLP passively holds shares in a trading company. There is uncertainty as to whether such an interest will be eligible for relief under s.105(1) given that HMRC does not appear to accept that relief is available, although that would seem to be at odds with HMRC's interpretation of s.267A.[11]

Situs of a partner's share

The Act does not contain any rules to determine the situs of a share in a general or limited partnership. That being the case, the common law rules apply. **28–05**

---

[7] For the purposes of the Tax Act, an LLP will only be tax transparent if it carries on a trade, profession or business.

[8] See paras 28–15 and following.

[9] See paras 2–41 and following.

[10] HMRC Manuals IHTM25094.

[11] See para.26–46.

The situs of a chose in action is generally situate where it is enforceable. An interest in a partnership business governed by English law or law similar to English law will therefore be situate in the country where the business is carried on. More difficult problems arise where multi-national partnerships are concerned. It seems that if in the firm's accounts and in the partnership agreement, the business which the firm carries on in different countries is treated as a separate business carried on in each of the countries involved, the partner's share is divided into separate parts for each notional separate business.[12] The divided part of each partner's share is situate in the country in which that part of the business is carried on. It has also been suggested that the partner's share is situate where the headquarters of a business carried on in more than one country is located.[13] This must necessarily be a question of fact. There is limited guidance in the case law about the appropriate weight to give to particular facts. But the country in which the partners reside is thought to be irrelevant.[14]

There is greater uncertainty about the situs of interests in foreign partnerships where the partnership owns land in the UK. There are two possible answers to the question of the situs of the partner's share in the partnership, so far as it relates to UK land: (a) the partner's "share" of the land might be situate where the land is situate; or (b) it might be situate where the firm carries on its business (i.e. as in the analysis in the preceding paragraph). There is no authority precisely on point, but the accepted approach based on principle (i.e. by reference to the place of enforceability of a *chose in action*), seems to be:

(a) first to ascertain the proper law of the partnership agreement which governs the partnership owning the land;

(b) then to construe the partnership agreement in accordance with the proper law and, in the light of that agreement so construed, to determine whether the partner has a direct interest in land, or only an interest in the surplus assets[15];

(c) if the partner has a direct interest in the land, that interest must be situate where the land is situate, so that if the land is in the UK, situs of the partnership share cannot be outside the UK. If, on the other hand, the partner does not have a direct interest in land, his share is arguably a moveable asset and its situs should be determined in accordance with the rules for determining the situs in a firm owning only moveables—situs will be the place where the firm carries on its business; and

(d) where a partnership owns both land and moveables and, by the proper law of the partnership agreement, the partners have a direct interest in the land, a partner's share should arguably be divided into the part relating to moveable property and the part relating to land, each part having a different situs.

However, the chose in action analysis is in contrast with what is expressed to be the position as regards LLPs. As set out above, IHTA 1984 s.267A deems LLPs to be transparent entities for inheritance tax purposes. It does so in part by providing at IHTA 1984 s.267A(a) that property to which an LLP is entitled or which it occupies or uses is to be treated as property to which its members are entitled, or which they occupy or use, as partners. Arguably, the result of this fiction is that, as stated in HMRC's Inheritance Tax Manual IHTM at 25094:

---

[12] *Beaver v Master in Equity of Victoria* [1895] A.C. 251 (PC); see *Lindley & Banks on Partnership*, para.36–66.

[13] See Dicey, Morris, and Collins, *The Conflict of Laws,* 14th edn (2006), para.22–049; see also Lawton, Goldberg and Fraser, *The Law of Partnership Taxation,* 2nd edn (1979), paras 13–087 and following.

[14] *Commissioner of Stamp Duties v Salting* [1907] A.C. 449.

[15] See *Boyd v Attorney General for British Columbia* (1916) 54 S.C.R. 532; and *Haque v Haque* (No.2) (1965) 114 C.L.R. 98.

"... an interest in a LLP is deemed to be an interest in each and every asset of the partnership, while an interest in a traditional partnership is a 'chose in action', valued by reference to the net underlying assets of the business. This may require you to consider issues of situs of property"

It follows from HMRC's approach that looking through a UK LLP to the situs of each underlying asset can have the consequence that if a non-UK domiciled individual is a member of a UK LLP which owns land both within the UK and outside the UK, the value attributable to his share of land outside the UK should be treated as non-UK situate property, notwithstanding that his interest as a member of the LLP would itself constitute a UK situated asset.

The deeming provision in s.267A, while ostensibly designed to ensure that UK LLPs are taxed in the same way as traditional partnerships, would not necessarily seem to have that effect. However, the external perspective of the nature of partnership interests, identified by Hoffman L.J. (as he then was) and applied in a different IHT context in *Gray* (see para.28–03, above), means that effectively a conventional partnership is or can be treated as transparent. If this is the correct approach to apply to determining situs for inheritance tax purposes, the treatment of conventional partnerships would be consistent with the deemed position for UK LLPs (as understood by HMRC). Of course, by no means does this imply that this is the correct approach. But the point to note here is that there is at the very least a risk that interests in conventional partnerships too might be transparent for IHT purposes, with the consequence that one would look through to the underlying property of the partnership to determine the situs of the partnership interest. In addition to doubts about situs of partnership interests when the partnership holds UK land, it is for this reason that the use by foreign domiciliaries of foreign partnerships or other similar foreign entities to invest in UK land for UK estate planning purposes is generally considered to be inadvisable.

An interest in a partnership that is not governed by English law, or by a proper law that is similar to English law, will need to be considered by reference to the laws of that jurisdiction. As regards foreign LLPs, it should be noted that while the s.267A provisions apply to an interest in a LLP established under the Limited Liability Partnership Act 2000, they do not apply to LLPs established in other jurisdictions which, depending on their governing legislation, may be treated as bodies corporate for IHT purposes despite being regarded as transparent for direct tax purposes,[16] or by virtue of the provisions of para.1 Sch.15 of the Finance Act 2003, i.e. the provision that determines which entities should be classified as partnerships for SDLT purposes.

Transactions affecting a partner

Broadly speaking, transactions affecting a person as a partner may be regarded as falling within two categories: **28–06**

(1) transactions involving partnership property and in respect of which the partner has some rights by virtue of his share in the partnership; and
(2) transactions involving his partnership share per se;

or, to put it another way, transactions which affect only the *value* of the rights of which a partner's share is comprised and transactions which affect the *nature* of those rights.

[16] A list of entities regarded by HMRC as transparent for direct tax purposes can be found at HMRC Manuals INTM180030.

Before considering the different types of transactions affecting a person as a partner, a word should be said about partnerships in Scotland.

III. SCOTTISH PARTNERSHIPS

28–07   Under Scots law, a partnership is a legal entity distinct from the partners.[17] The Limited Partnership Act of 1907 introduced the concept of a partnership where certain partners had limited liability provided those partners took no part in the management of the business. These have proved popular in Scotland for use in agricultural tenancies for many years and, more recently, as vehicles for investments in Lloyd's or as holding vehicles for non-UK domiciliaries. There are no special provisions in the legislation for dealing with Scottish partnerships equivalent to the provisions in ss.267A and 94.[18] A Scottish partnership has been held to be a collection of individuals recognised as a separate legal entity[19] and as such it cannot be an "individual" for the purposes of s.2(1) and so cannot make a chargeable transfer. It therefore appears to follow that where a Scottish partnership makes a transfer of value the partners can be assessed only on the footing that, in failing to exercise their rights to prevent the transfer, they have made a notional disposition under s.3(3) which has diminished the value of their shares in the partnership.[20] In the event of their being assessed on this footing, the partners may be able to claim relief under s.10(1)[21] if they can show that, in effect, there were good commercial reasons for their failure to prevent the transfer. A Scottish limited partnership is likely to have a UK situs for IHT purposes.[22] The awkward way that Scots partnerships fit into the scheme of the legislation provides a foretaste of the difficulties that arise in analysing the treatment of their English counterparts (if counterparts they be).

IV. PROPERTY TRANSACTIONS

28–08   As was mentioned above, the first kind of transaction which may affect a partner is a transaction which involves either:

(1) partnership property, i.e. property which is owned by the partners together and in respect of which each partner normally has some rights by virtue of his share in the partnership; or

(2) property which is owned beneficially by an individual partner.

Partnership property

28–09   Where a firm disposes of partnership property, each partner, as agent of the other partners,[23] makes a disposition of the property concerned, and if that disposition

---

[17] Partnership Act 1890 s.4(2).

[18] Although this is the subject of review: the Law Commissions of Scotland, England and Wales have prepared a draft Bill replacing both the Partnership Act 1890 and the Limited Partnership Act 1907 which is currently the subject of further consultation.

[19] *Douglas v Phoenix Motors* 1970 S.L.T. (Sh Ct) 57 and for more general discussion of the Scots position, see *Major v Brodie* [1998] S.T.C. 491.

[20] This view was confirmed in HMRC Manuals IHTM04052 and IHTM04053.

[21] See paras 2–41 and following.

[22] If this is undesirable for non-UK domiciliaries, conversion to a foreign entity such as a US Limited Liability Company may be attractive. See paras 34–66 and following.

[23] Partnership Act 1890 s.5 and Limited Liability Partnership Act 2000 s.6.

diminishes the value of his share in the partnership, he prima facie makes a transfer of the value. In the same way, if the firm omits to exercise a right, each partner may be regarded as making a notional disposition under s.3(3)[24]; if that notional disposition reduces the value of his share, he will be regarded as having prima facie made a transfer of value in the usual fashion (subject to any argument that any individual partner was not in himself able to prevent the omission and therefore could not be said to have failed to act). In the same way, a partner who has made such a transfer may rely on the reliefs and exemptions available to any person who has made such a transfer of value.

Foreign element

It is important to note that although the property disposed of is partnership property, **28–10** the property by reference to which any charge arises is normally the partner's share in the firm. This is because of the nature of a partner's share in a partnership (described above) and is particularly important where the partner is a foreign domiciliary, since in that case it may be that, under s.3(2), the disposition did not diminish the value of the partner's estate. Section 3(2) provides that in determining whether a transfer of value has been made:

> " . . . no account shall be taken of the value of excluded property which ceases to form part of a person's estate as a result of a disposition."

At first glance, the position of a non-domiciled partner in a firm which has disposed of partnership property situated abroad at, e.g. at undervalue, would appear to be unenviable, since the property which the firm has disposed of would not have formed part of his estate, and therefore s.3(2) would not come into operation. It is thought, however, that this need not be the case, for two reasons. First, it may be possible to contend that under the proper law of the partnership agreement (which is simply a contract between the partners) the partner in fact has an interest in the property disposed of, not just a right to receive the profits arising from that property. This would not be the case under English law, but it may be the case if the proper law of the contract is other than English law. Alternatively, it might (just!) be arguable that although the partner's share has not ceased to form part of his estate, one of the constituent elements of that share—his right to receive a share of the profits generated by the property in question—has done so, and that therefore he can rely on s.3(2), provided, of course, that the right was situated abroad (which it probably would be on the footing that it shared the situs of the property to which it attached). Both these approaches involve complicated and largely uncharted areas which it is beyond the scope of this book to explore.[25]

Property owned by an individual partner

Here there are two considerations, the position of the individual partner, and the **28–11** position of the other partners in the firm. So far as the individual partner is concerned, any actual or notional disposition by him of the property in question which diminishes the value if his estate will be available. Normally the disposition will be his alone, with

---

[24] See paras 2–17 and following.
[25] Which approach, if either, is to be adopted will depend on where the property or right in question is situated.

the result that the other partners will not have made a transfer of value notwithstanding any diminution in the value of their estates occasioned by his disposition. In the unlikely event that they have the right to prevent him from making the disposition, they may be regarded as having made a notional disposition under s.3(3) in which case they, too, will have made a transfer of value, unless, of course, they can rely on s.10(1).

Foreign element

28–12   So far as the individual partner is concerned, the property disposed of will cease to form part of his estate, with the result that, if it is excluded property, s.3(2) will normally ensure that the value of his estate is not diminished by the disposition. In the unlikely event that his disposition results in his partners making a transfer of value by virtue of their being treated as having made a disposition under s.3(3), they will be able to rely on s.3(2) only if they show that any rights they formerly enjoyed in respect of the property in question:

> (1) were excluded property; and
> (2) ceased to form part of their estates as a result of the disposition they were treated as having made under s.3(3).

Free loans

28–13   For the sake of completeness, some comment should be made as to the position of a partner who allows his firm to use property free of charge or for less than what he might have received if he had placed the property on the open market. His position will vary according to whether he is entitled to require the property to be returned to him immediately or only after the expiry of a given period. So long as he is entitled to require the property to be returned to him on demand, the loan will not constitute a transfer of value by him, but in any other case it may do so.[26]

V. TRANSACTIONS AFFECTING A PARTNER'S SHARE

28–14   It will be convenient to consider the various ways in which a partner may incur a charge as a result of a transaction which affects the nature of his share in a firm, starting with the formation of a firm and working through to the partner's death.

Formation of a firm

28–15   On forming a firm, some or all of the partners will contribute capital and will agree to share assets and profits in a certain way. Even if the ratio is in direct proportion to the value of the capital introduced, in theory each contributor could be said to diminish the value of his estate, because he will cease to be entitled to the immediate enjoyment of the property, which he can reclaim only with the agreement of the other partners.

---

[26] See para.2–07.

Even if it could be argued that there were any actual diminution in value, this diminution would normally be relieved from being a transfer of value by s.10(1), as will virtually any other diminution in the value of his estate occasioned by the formation of the partnership, so long as the terms according to which the partners enter into partnership are of an essentially commercial nature (although regard must be had to the fact that if HMRC regards partners as connected persons at the moment that they form the partnership, it must be shown that the disposition was such as might be expected to be made in a transaction at arm's length between persons not connected with each other—see below).[27] In particular, the fact that one partner puts up the capital while another, in effect, contributes energy and/or know-how, will not preclude the relief from being available.[28] The introduction of a new partner into a firm means, of course, that in law the old partnership ceases and a new one begins. The above mentioned considerations apply in the same way on the introduction of a new partner or, for that matter, to any change in partnership shares, as they do on the formation of the "original" partnership.

Partners as connected persons

It is to be noted that in relation to their dealings with their partnership shares, **28–16** partners are connected persons for purposes of IHT generally, and for purposes of s.10(1) in particular. This follows from the fact that a partner is connected with any person with whom he is in partnership and with the spouse or civil partner or relative of the individual with whom he is in partnership. It is true that partners are not connected persons in relation to acquisitions or disposals of partnership assets pursuant to bona fide commercial arrangements,[29] but, since partnership shares are not partnership assets, this exception does not apply to partners in relation to their dealings with their shares. It would also seem that partners are connected with each other at the point of creation of the partnership if one adopts HMRC's stated view that for CGT purposes, trustees and settlors are connected at the moment when property is put into the settlement.[30] This means that in order not to be a transfer of value, not only must the disposition lack gratuitous intent (a subjective test) but it must also be made on such terms as might be expected in a transaction at arm's length between unconnected persons (an objective test).[31]

Accruer arrangements

Partnership agreements may provide that a partner's share will, on his death or **28–17** retirement, accrue to the continuing partners, normally for a price, namely the repayment of the balance on his capital account. As was noted above, on entering into a partnership agreement, a partner disposes of his right to the immediate enjoyment of any property he contributes to the partnership, and where there are accruer arrangements the question thus arises as to whether, in view of the accruer arrangements, this disposition diminishes the value of his estate. This will depend on a number of factors

---

[27] IHTA s.10(1)(b).
[28] See *Att Gen v Boden* [1912] 1 K.B. 539, discussed below.
[29] TCGA s.286(4). See para.2–45.
[30] See CG14590.
[31] If there is a transfer of value on the formation of a partnership, business or agricultural relief may be available.

including inter alia, the profits he expects to receive from the business of the partner-ship and the amount he is to receive on his death or retirement, and, where the other partners enter into a similar agreement, the likelihood of his surviving his fellow partners. Even if his entering into the arrangement has occasioned a diminution in the value of his estate, the relief under s.10(1) will normally be available if the terms of the arrangement are essentially commercial.

The case of *Att Gen v Boden*[32] may be particularly useful in establishing whether such an arrangement is essentially commercial in nature. The facts of the case were that Henry Boden entered into a deed with his two sons under which the sons agreed:

(1) to devote so much time and attention to the business of the partnership as the proper conduct of its affairs required; and
(2) not to engage, without their father's consent, in any other trade or business except upon the account of and for the benefit of the partnership.

Their father, on the other hand, was bound only to give as much time and attention to the business as he thought fit. On his death or retirement his share was to accrue to his sons in equal shares on their paying to his personal representatives its value, excluding any valuation or allowance for goodwill, which was to accrue equally to the sons free of payment. Henry Boden died, and HMRC claimed estate duty on the value of the goodwill on the ground that the goodwill did not pass "by reason only of the bona fide purchase . . . for full consideration in money or money's worth . . ." as was required by s.3(1) of the 1894 Act.

Hamilton J. held that the goodwill was not dutiable:

"the question whether full consideration was given or not may no doubt be solved by putting a value on the property which passed on the one side, and weighing against it the money value of the obligations assumed on the other; but that is not the only method of solving the question. Another method is by looking at the nature of the transaction and considering whether what is given is a fair equivalent for what is received; and that is the way in which the question should be approached in this case."[33]

Whether or not the purchase came within s.3(1) was a question of fact, not of law, and the intention of the parties at the time, while evidence of the facts, was not conclusive. The partnership deed provided that the partnership was to continue for at least as long as the father's life, that he was to have the final say in the management of the partnership, and that although his capital was to be employed in the business, the partnership profits were in substance to be earned by the sons. He had therefore received full consideration in money or money's worth.

A few comments are in order about this decision. First, it is not entirely clear whether on the true construction of the partnership deed there was an automatic accruer to the sons, or whether they had an option to purchase their father's share on the exercise of which the goodwill accrued to them. Secondly, the goodwill was assumed by Hamilton J. to be "of very little value"; how much reliance can be placed on the decision where a substantial value is involved thus remains to be seen. It is also important to note that the decision is not authority for the proposition that a transferor who procures that his partners will undertake greater obligations than his own will automatically be able to rely on s.10(1). Rather, regard will have to be had to all the facts in question[34]; in particular, given the terms of s.10(1), account will have to be taken of the transferor's intention.

---

[32] *Att Gen v Boden* [1912] 1 K.B. 539.
[33] *Att Gen v Boden* [1912] 1 K.B. 539 at 561.
[34] See the Irish case of *Re Clark* (1906) 40 I.L.T. 117; and *Brown v Att Gen* (1898) 79 L.T. 572, a succession duty case.

A second case which is helpful in this context is *Att Gen v Ralli*[35] in which the nature of the partnership business was such that large reserves were necessary. Each partner agreed that on his death or retirement his shares would pass to the surviving partner free of payment. The eldest of the partners retired and died shortly thereafter. Lawrence J. held for a variety of reasons that the deceased's share of the reserves was not dutiable. In particular, he found as a fact that the business needed large reserves which should not be disturbed on the death or retirement of a partner. The arrangement:

> " . . . was an ordinary business arrangement, and it applied equally to all the partners. The consideration moving from one partner to the others was the undertaking of each partner to be a partner on those terms, one of which was that his interest in the reserves should pass to his partners if he retired or died."[36]

Options

As an alternative to the accruer, the partners may give each other an option to purchase the share of an out-going partner on his death or retirement. The exact legal effect of a partner granting such an option is not entirely clear. Two analyses appear possible, as follows: **28–18**

(1) the partner has disposed of his rights to deal freely with his partnership share[37]; or

(2) the partner has incurred a contingent contractual liability to transfer his share on dying or retiring.

If the correct analysis is that the partner has disposed of his right to deal freely with his partnership share, the next consideration is whether that disposition has diminished the value of his estate. In determining whether there has been such a diminution, regard will be had to factors such as those mentioned above in connection with automatic accruer provisions. If there is such a diminution, relief may still be available under s.10(1) if the terms on which the option is granted are essentially commercial. If the partners to whom the option is granted agree to pay an annuity to the widow or surviving civil partner of the partner granting the option as part of the price paid for the option or to be paid for the partner's share on the exercise of the option, the availability of relief under s.10(1) may be jeopardised as discussed below.

If the correct analysis is that the partner has not disposed of any of his rights, but has instead merely incurred a contingent contractual liability to transfer his share on dying or retiring, the position is somewhat more complicated. The first question that arises is whether a person who incurs a contingent liability makes a disposition.

The effect of a person incurring a liability was discussed at para.2–16. It is thought that he does not make a disposition: if this is correct, the grant of the option will not constitute a transfer of value. If, on the other hand, this is incorrect and the partner has made a disposition, the question arises as to whether that disposition has diminished the value of the estate.

---

[35] *Att Gen v Ralli* [1936] 15 A.T.C. 523.

[36] *Att Gen v Ralli* [1936] 15 A.T.C. 523 at 526.

[37] HMRC consider (see HMRC Manuals IHTM25120) that if the surviving partners have the option to purchase the deceased's share in the business for a fixed price or a balance sheet figure, this restricts the deceased's ability to dispose of his partnership interest and amounts to a fetter such that if the fetter was not granted for full consideration then the open market value of the deceased's interest will be taxable (IHTA s.163(1)(a)).

Under s.5(3) and (5) a liability is taken into account in valuing a person's estate, but only to the extent that it is imposed by law or incurred for a consideration in money or money's worth. It is not clear whether a contingent liability falls to be taken into account.[38] If it does not fall to be taken into account, the partner will not have made a transfer of value at this stage, but he may make a transfer of value when he subsequently transfers his share under the option agreement; see below. If the liability does fall to be taken into account, the question remains as to whether partners who enter into reciprocal agreements give a consideration in money or money's worth. It is thought on the basis of the *Boden* case that they do, and in such circumstances HMRC will probably accept that the liability falls to be taken into account, with the result that regard will have to be had as to whether the grant of the option has diminished the value of the grantor's estate. If there is a diminution:

(a) relief will normally be available under s.10(1) if the terms on which the option is granted are essentially commercial; and
(b) no charge will normally arise when the partner subsequently transfers his share pursuant to the option agreement.

Where, on the other hand, the partner grants the option gratuitously, the liability he incurs will not come within the terms of s.5. His estate will therefore have sustained no diminution in value, and consequently he will not have made a transfer of value at this stage; but a charge may arise later when he transfers his share under the option agreement.[39]

Annuities

28–19   As was mentioned above, provision may be made to pay an annuity to one or more of a deceased partner's dependants. Such a provision may prove somewhat awkward, and needs to be analysed from two standpoints:

(1) that of the partner to whose dependant(s) the annuity is to be paid; and
(2) that of the partners who undertake to pay the annuity.

Where a partner agrees that his partnership share will accrue to the surviving partners in return partly for their paying one or more of his dependants an annuity, he will inevitably manifest some gratuitous intent towards the dependant(s) in question at the time the agreement is entered into, with the result that the relief under s.10(1) will not be available. There does not appear to be a simple way around this problem. If, for example, it was agreed that an annuity was to be paid to the partner himself, and he subsequently assigned the right to that annuity to the dependant(s) in question, the original agreement and subsequent assignments could be regarded as associated operations, with the result that the s.10(1) relief would still be in jeopardy. It thus appears that where a partner enters into an accruer arrangement partly in exchange for the other partners agreeing to pay an annuity to one or more of his dependants, he makes a transfer of value of the amount by which his estate is diminished by his entering into that agreement. The position then varies according to whether the dependant is his spouse or civil partner or some other person.

---

[38] See para.25–80.
[39] See below.

Where the dependant is the partner's spouse or civil partner the position is eased by the fact that in practice HMRC will regard the transfer as exempt under the s.18 exemption up to the value of the annuity at the time the agreement is entered into, on the footing that the transfer increased the value of the spouse or civil partner's estate by that amount.[40]

Where, on the other hand, the dependant is someone other than the partner's spouse or civil partner, it appears that the whole of the partner's transfer will normally be a PET.

So far as the position of the partners granting the annuity is concerned, normally in practice they will not be regarded as making a chargeable transfer. It is thought that the grant of such an annuity can be distinguished from the grant of an option, in that the former does not affect property to which the partners granting the annuity are beneficially entitled, while the latter affects the share in the partnership of each partner granting the option. Thus, whatever the proper analysis of the grant of an option, it seems that the grant of an annuity involves merely the incurring of a contractual liability. Accordingly, it should not constitute a disposition, or, therefore, a transfer of value.[41] In the unlikely event that it does constitute a disposition, questions arise, as they did above, as to:

(a) whether it is possible in theory to take the liability, which is contingent, into account; and, if it is,
(b) whether the liability was incurred for a consideration in money or money's worth.

As to whether a contingent liability can be taken into account in valuing a person's estate; see para.25–80. As to whether an annuity in such circumstances is entered into for a consideration in money or money's worth, it is thought that where reciprocal agreements are entered into this test should be satisfied, on the basis of the *Boden* case. The question will then be whether the grantor has diminished the value of his estate by granting the annuity, and, if he has, whether s.10(1) will relieve him from having made a transfer of value. If there has been no such diminution, there will be no adverse consequences on the grant or the payment of the annuity. If there has been a diminution, and relief is not available under s.10(1), then s.262 will apply,[42] with the result that there will be no immediate charge. Instead, a charge will arise on the gift element of any such annuity as is in fact subsequently paid. Fortunately, in the normal case, s.10(1) relief should be available, as is shown by the following extract from a Revenue (as it then was) letter which appeared in *The Law Society Gazette* of July 2, 1975:

> "You also referred to annuities becoming payable on the death of a partner. In the normal case, where the partnership agreement can itself be regarded as a commercial transaction the agreement to pay the annuity would itself be covered by the provision of s.20(4) Finance

---

[40] Since the widow or surviving civil partner might not be able to enforce the annuity (*Re Miller's Agreement* [1947] Ch. 615; cf. *Beswick v Beswick* [1967] 2 All E.R. 1197) in strict law her estate is not increased by the value of the annuity. In practice HMRC have allowed the exemption so long as the annuity is in fact subsequently paid; see HMRC Manuals IHTM11076.

In HMRC Manuals IHTM25120, HMRC say that where the Articles of Partnership provide that the deceased's share in the partnership is to pass to the surviving partners in return for the payment of an annuity to the deceased's widow or surviving civil partner and the arrangement was made for full consideration, the deceased's partnership interest will be exempt under IHTA s.18. HMRC go on to say that if the arrangement was not made for full consideration, the open market value will be taxable on death but a deduction will be given against that figure for the capital value of the annuity to the spouse or civil partner which is spouse or civil partner exempt.

[41] See para.2–16.
[42] See paras 2–15 and 25–85.

Act 1975[43] as would the actual payments as and when they came due. The commencement of the annuity on the death of the partner would not in itself be an occasion for charge although his share of the partnership would normally be part of his estate."

Subsequent agreements

28–20   It may be that the original partnership agreement contains no provisions regarding accruers, options or annuities, and that agreements on one or more such matters are subsequently entered into. Alternatively, provisions relating to the matters which are contained in the original agreement (or entered into subsequently) may be varied. Where this happens, the considerations mentioned above in relation to provisions regarding accruers, options or annuities will apply, subject to two qualifications. First, the partners at this stage will be connected persons. Secondly, it may be that where an existing partner enters into an accruer arrangement or grants an option in respect of his share, he ceases to be beneficially entitled to his share. If that is so, regard will be had in the usual way to whether his so ceasing to be beneficially entitled diminishes the value of his estate, and, if it does, whether relief is available under s.10(1).

Retirement and dissolution

28–21   When a partner retires, his share in the partnership normally passes to the continuing partners, either by accruer, or because the continuing partners exercise an option to purchase his share, or, exceptionally, by a sale on terms negotiated at the time. Where the share passes by accruer, no charge should arise, for two, or possibly three, reasons. First, it may be that the share ceased to form part of the outgoing partner's estate at the time he entered into the accruer agreement, in which case neither of the ingredients necessary for the transfer of value, a disposition and a diminution, will be present. Secondly, even if his share is comprised in his estate at the time he retires, the outgoing partner cannot be regarded as having made a disposition of his share; rather, his share accrues by operation of law, in a fashion similar to that by which the interest of a joint tenant passes on his death to the surviving tenant or tenants. Finally, in the unlikely event that the transfer of his share to the continuing partners is regarded as a disposition, the question will arise as to whether that disposition has diminished the value of his estate. This will depend, in turn, on the value of his interest. The general valuation rule is, of course, that the amount to be brought into account is the price the property might reasonably be expected to fetch in a sale in the open market.[44] In the absence of any special provision to the contrary, the position would thus be that the amount to be brought into account in respect of the interest would be nil, since a purchaser would be unwilling to pay anything for an interest which was destined to accrue immediately to someone else. This raises the question as to whether there is any special valuation provision. The position here is not entirely clear. Section 163 lays down a special rule where by a contract made on or after March 27, 1974 "the right to dispose of property has been excluded or restricted". In such circumstances, in valuing the property the exclusion or restriction is taken into account only to the extent that consideration in money or money's worth was given for it. This raises two questions. First, does s.163 apply to accruer clauses? Secondly, what is its effect if it does so apply?

[43] Now IHTA 1984 s.10.
[44] IHTA 1984 s.160.

So far as the first question is concerned, it is thought that an accruer provision does not restrict or exclude a partner's right to dispose of his share: all that it affects is the ultimate destination of his share. Even if this is not the case, it is thought that s.163 should not apply to an accruer provision contained in a partnership agreement from the outset, since as a matter of general law it is thought that it cannot be said that such a provision excludes or restricts the partner's right to dispose of his interest, i.e. the interest is defined partly in terms of that provision. The position is different where an accruer provision is added subsequently to the partnership agreement, since in such a case the provision is not an integral part of the interest but rather an attachment, as it were, thereto. The IHTM suggested that s.163 could apply to an accruer clause but made no distinction between an accruer provision that exists from the inception of the partnership and one introduced at a later stage.[45]

If s.163 is given a wider construction than that which in the authors' view is warranted so that it applies in valuing an interest which is subject to an accruer arrangement, the question will arise as to what extent consideration was given in money or money's worth to the partner in return for his entering into the arrangement. Here the above mentioned estate duty cases will be relevant.

The position where the continuing partners exercise an option to purchase a retiring **28–22** (as distinct from a deceased) partner's share is similar to that where the share passes by accrual, except that where the share passes by a sale pursuant to the exercise of such an option it is clear that the outgoing partner makes a disposition where he sells his share. The first question that arises in respect of such a sale is therefore whether or not that sale has diminished the value of his estate. In answering this, regard will have to be had to the valuation considerations, notably the effect of s.163 just canvassed in relation to accruer arrangements. In the event that the sale did diminish the value of the retiring partner's estate, he will prima facie have made a transfer of value. The question will then arise as to whether he can rely on s.10 on the footing that the grant of the option and the subsequent sale pursuant thereto are, as associated operations, a transaction which is of an essentially commercial nature. In the event that relief under s.10 is not available, allowance will be made under s.163 for the value previously transferred by the retiring partner at the time he granted the option (assuming s.163 in fact applies in the circumstances).

In the unlikely event that the partner's share is unfettered by any accruer arrangements or options (or the partners choose not to exercise their options), so that the transfer of the retiring partner's share is by a straightforward sale, the normal rules will apply, regard being had to whether the sale diminishes the value of the outgoing partner's estate, and, if it does, whether, which will normally be unlikely, relief is available under s.10.

The position where an annuity previously granted by partners is paid to a partner on his retirement was discussed above. Where the annuity is granted to him on his retirement, the position is the same as where the annuity is granted to him prior to his

---

[45] HMRC Manuals IHTM09771: "Restrictions or a fetter on an individual's freedom to dispose of certain assets can reduce the value of an estate. For example it may be agreed that a partnership interest shall on death pass to the continuing partners either without payment or at a favourable price, or a friend or relative might be granted an option to purchase a property for less than the market price. IHTA 1984 s.163 deals with this sort of situation by ignoring the restriction and valuing property on the normal valuation basis unless certain conditions are met." See also HMRC Manuals IHTM25120 which provides that HMRC consider that where articles of partnership provide that a deceased partner's interest in the partnership should pass to the surviving partners, either at a book figure (i.e. the figure at which the capital account stood in the last published balance sheet prior to death) or for no payment at all or for a fixed sum, or the surviving partners have the option to purchase the deceased's share in the business for a fixed price or a balance sheet figure, this is a restriction of the deceased's ability to dispose of his partnership interest as he wishes, and such restrictions amount to a fetter.

retirement (i.e. it is thought that a charge will arise only, if at all, on the payment of the annuity). It should be noted that if a retiring partner's share is unfettered by accruer or option arrangements and he voluntarily transfers his capital account to the continuing partners in exchange for an annuity which actuarially proves to be worth less than the value of his capital account, a gift with reservation of benefit can result as the transaction will be treated as a sale of the retiring partner's share for less than full consideration.[46]

On a dissolution, partners will be regarded as having disposed of their shares, but normally no charge will arise as a result.

Death

28–23   The position on death differs from that on retirement in two ways. First, on death the question of whether or not the partner has made a disposition is irrelevant, because he is treated by s.4(1) as having made a transfer of value immediately before he died. Secondly, given the fact that the transfer is a notional one which does not depend on the presence of a disposition, there is no possibility of relief being available under s.10(1). This being the case, at most only two questions arise. The first is whether or not the partner's share was comprised in his estate immediately before he died; as was noted above, it is thought this question will arise only where an accruer agreement or option was entered into some time after the partner joined the firm or as part of a variation of the original partnership agreement. If his share did not comprise part of his estate then, obviously, no charge can arise in respect of it. A charge will arise, however, on any money payable in respect of the share under the accruer or option agreement. Assuming his share did form part of his estate immediately before he died, the second question arises, namely, what value is to be attributed to his share? This raises the same issues as were discussed above in connection with accruer arrangements, i.e. does the normal market value rule apply, or must account be taken of s.163 (which applies in relation to transfers made on death whenever the contract by which the partner's right to dispose of his interest was excluded or restricted). If s.163 does not apply the general market value rule will determine the issue, and the value to be brought into account will be nil. If s.163 does apply, the position will depend on whether the deceased partner received a consideration in money or money's worth for entering into the accruer or option agreement.

28–24   For the sake of completeness, reference must also be made to s.171. Under this provision, a decrease in the value of a person's estate which has occurred by reason of his death is taken into account as if it had occurred before his death unless it is caused by:

(1) the termination on his death of an interest; or
(2) the passing of an interest by survivorship.

These provisions raise two questions. First, do they apply where a partnership interest passes under an accruer agreement? Secondly, what is their effect if they do apply?

It is thought that the reference in s.171(2) to "the passing of any interest by survivorship" is a reference to the passing of the interest of a joint tenant, and that therefore the only question that arises in relation to accruer arrangements is whether on

---

[46] HMRC Manuals IHTM14316. The position would probably turn on whether the retiring partner was aware that he was transferring his capital for less than it was worth. See paras 7–147 and following.

a partner's death his interest can be regarded as terminating. There is some judicial authority on the point, Lord Cohen in *Perpetual Executors & Trustees Association of Australia Ltd v The Commissioner of Taxes*[47] having stated that in a case like *Boden* a deceased partner's interest in goodwill must pass, along with his interest in the other assets, to his personal representatives. This clearly implies that in such a case a partner's share does not terminate. In practice, of course, the position will normally turn on the drafting of the partnership agreement in question.

If s.171 does apply, the position may vary according to whether or not the special valuation rule in s.163 applies. If that rule does not apply, s.171 would not appear to affect the position. This follows from the fact that in the absence of s.171 the amount to be brought into account would be nil, while applying s.171 the amount to be brought into account would also be nil. The position where s.163 applies is more interesting. In that case the question arises as to whether or not s.171 overrides s.163. As was just seen, where s.171 applies the amount to be brought into account is nil, while, as was seen above, where s.163 applies, a substantial amount may fall to be brought into account. The interaction of ss.163 and 171 is far from clear, but, in the authors' view, s.163 overrides s.171. Otherwise s.163, which is clearly intended to apply in relation to transfers made on death in the same way as it applies to lifetime transfers, would be deprived of much of its effect. A further distinction between transfers made during the partner's life and that made on his death, is, of course, that certain exemptions available to the former may not be available to the latter.

Foreign element

Circumstances may arise in which a partner who is neither domiciled nor ordinarily **28–25** resident in the United Kingdom transfers his partnership share at a time when the partnership assets include exempt gilts which qualify as excluded property for IHT purposes.[48] It may well be that those gilts are s.112 excepted assets for purposes of business relief, so that so much of the value transferred by the transfer as is attributable to the gilts does not qualify for business relief.[49] In that case, HMRC have excluded from the value transferred the value attributable to the gilts according to the following formula[50]:

$$\text{Value of exempt gilts} \times \frac{\text{value of partner's share}}{\text{total value of partnership}}$$

Presumably similar treatment will be accorded on a partner's death and extend in relation to both lifetime and death transfers to other partnership property which would be excluded property if owned by the transferor partner directly.

VI. BUSINESS/AGRICULTURAL RELIEF AND INSTALMENT OPTION

Business relief may be available in respect of a partnership share or in respect of **28–26** assets owned by a partner which are used by a partnership of which he is a partner, and

[47] [1954] A.C. 114.
[48] See para.32–31. Bear in mind that the deemed domicile rules do not apply for this purpose.
[49] See paras 26–88 and following.
[50] HMRC Manuals IHTM27264.

agricultural relief may be available to a person who carries on farming as a trade in partnership. Section 113 provides that property does not qualify for business relief if at the time of the transfer in question a binding contract for the sale of property has been entered into. HMRC's stated view is that where partners enter into agreements between themselves to the effect that the surviving partners may purchase the partnership interest of the partner who has died, only exceptionally will such an agreement fall within s.113.[51] Notwithstanding the views expressed by HMRC as to the possible application of s.113, it is thought that a partnership agreement containing an accruer provision or giving partners options to purchase the shares of other partners is not in any event a "contract for sale" of a partnership interest, but is instead an agreement from which the share derives its nature (at least where the provisions in question are contained in the partnership agreement from the outset—the position is less clear where the provisions are added to the agreement subsequently).

A problem arises where a partner dies owning land or buildings used by the partnership (so that the property qualifies for business relief under s.105(1)(e)), but which the surviving partners are unable or unwilling to purchase. Often the property in question will pass to the deceased partner's widow or surviving civil partner, but although business relief would have been available to the deceased partner in respect of the property no relief would have been available in respect of the property in his widow or surviving civil partner's hands. In such a case the relief is thus of no value: it is available when it is not needed (the s.18 exemption will normally prevent any charge arising on the partner's death), but when it is needed, e.g. on the widow or surviving civil partner's death, it is not available.

Tax on a partnership interest may in appropriate cases be paid by interest-free instalments over 10 years; see paras 29–91 and following. In the event that an option to purchase such a partnership interest is subsequently exercised by the surviving partners, the instalment option will cease to be available.[52]

For particular issues relating to the availability of business relief on interests in LLPs, see paras 26–46 and 28–04.

VII. INSURANCE POLICIES

28–27   It is common practice for a partner to effect a policy on his own life in terms either that the policy is held in trust for other persons generally or that the policy monies are payable to X if he survives the partner, or to the partner's personal representative if he survives X. In the former case it is clear that the policy is settled property; in the latter case it may be so. Such arrangements are usually commercial, and HMRC accordingly issued an explanatory statement in September 1976 that is now encapsulated in Extra-Statutory Concession F10.

---

[51] HMRC Manuals IHTM25292 stated that for the agreement to come within s.113 it has to provide "for the interest of the deceased partner to pass to his or her personal representatives, that the personal representatives are required to sell the interest to the surviving partners or shareholders who are in terms obliged to buy it. These requirements are rarely satisfied".

[52] IHTA 1984 s.227(4).

CHAPTER 29

ADMINISTRATION

I. INTRODUCTION

29–01   The administration of the tax is under the care and management of the Commissioners of Inland Revenue,[1] hereafter referred to as "the Board". The following discussion adopts a more or less chronological approach; it begins by considering the accounts and other information which a taxpayer may be required to submit to HMRC, then moves on to who may be liable for tax, when and how tax must be paid, and so on. Although the legislation often refers only to chargeable transfers, that term includes periodic and exit charges for this purpose. This follows from s.2(3) which provides that:

> " . . . except where the context otherwise requires, references in this Act to chargeable transfers to their making or to the values transferred by them shall be construed as including references to occasions on which tax is chargeable under Chapter III of Part III of this Act (apart from section 79), to their occurrence or to the amounts on which tax is then chargeable."

Accordingly, statutory provisions which refer only to chargeable transfers are in the text generally referred to as applying both to chargeable transfers and to periodic and exit charges.

Definitions

29–02   Various terms that appear in this chapter are defined in other chapters, as follows: "estate"—Chapter 10; "control"—Chapter 14; "settlement", "settlor", "trustee" and "interest in possession"—Chapter 11. The terms "personal representatives" and "purchaser" also appear frequently in this chapter. These have the meaning given to them by s.272:

> "'personal representatives' includes
> (a) any person by whom or on whose behalf an application for a grant of administration or for the resealing of a grant made outside the United Kingdom is made;

---

[1] IHTA 1984 ss.215 and 272.

(b) any person who takes possession of or intermeddles with, or otherwise acts in relation to property so as to become liable as executor or trustee[2] (or, in Scotland, any person who intromits with property or has become liable as a vitious intromitter);

(c) any person to whom the management of property is entrusted on behalf of a person not of full legal capacity,

'purchaser' means a purchaser in good faith for consideration in money or money's worth other than a nominal consideration and includes a lessee, mortgagee or other person who for such consideration acquires an interest in the property in question.[3]

'mortgage' includes a heritable security and a security constituted over any interest in moveable property."

Scotland and Northern Ireland

References in this chapter to the Court of Session should be construed as references, where appropriate, to that court as the Court of Exchequer in Scotland[4]; references to the High Court should be construed in relation to Northern Ireland as references to the Court of Appeal in Northern Ireland, except where the context otherwise requires.[5]   **29–03**

Pence

The value of assets and liabilities included in the body of the HMRC Accounts, whether as individual items or as totals carried forward from separate schedules, may be rounded down to the nearest £ but the figures for tax and interest must include pence.[6]   **29–04**

Enquiries

Enquiries should be addressed in England, Scotland and Northern Ireland respectively to: **29–05**

HM Revenue and Customs
Ferrers House
PO Box 38
Castle Meadow Road
Nottingham NG2 1BB
England
DX 701201 Nottingham 4

---

[2] See *IRC v Stype Investments (Jersey) Ltd* [1982] S.T.C. 625, discussed at para.29–64.

[3] For the meaning of "a purchaser in good faith", see *Peffer v Rigg* [1977] 1 W.L.R 285; [1978] 3 All E.R 745.

[4] IHTA 1984 s.249(5).

[5] IHTA 1984 s.225(3).

[6] See *The Law Society Gazette*, November 3, 1976.

HM Revenue and Customs
Meldrum House
15 Drumsheugh Gardens
Edinburgh EH3 7UG
Scotland
DX ED 542001 Edinburgh 14

HM Revenue and Customs
Level 3
Dorchester House
52–58 Great Victoria Street
Belfast BT2 7
Northern Ireland
DX 2001 NR Belfast 2

Probate & Inheritance Tax Helpline: 0845 3020900

II. ACCOUNTS

29–06   Section 216 provides that certain persons must deliver to the Board accounts of certain transactions and events, though the Board may make regulations dispensing with the delivery of accounts. As will be seen below, any person who in the absence of such a dispensation fails to deliver an account may incur penalties. By s.216(5), no one but a personal representative has to deliver an account with respect to any property if a full and proper account of the property specifying its value has already been delivered by someone else:

(1) who is or would be liable for the tax attributable to the value of the property; and

(2) who is not or would not be liable with him jointly as trustee.

The general rule is that an account must be delivered before the expiration of 12 months from the end of the month in which the transaction or event occurred or, in certain cases, if it expires later, the period of three months beginning with the date on which the person in question becomes liable for tax.[7]

The form and content of accounts is prescribed by the Board. Accounts must be supported by such books, papers and other documents as the Board may require and, if the Board so require, must be verified on oath or otherwise as they may stipulate. An account delivered to a probate registry pursuant to arrangements made between the Board and the President of the Family Division or the Lord Chancellor is treated as an account delivered to the Board.[8] By s.217, if a person who has delivered an original account under s.216 discovers that that account is defective in a material respect by reason of anything contained in or omitted from it, he must within six months of his

[7] IHTA 1984 s.216(6)(a)–(c).
[8] IHTA 1984 s.257(3).

1014

discovery deliver a further account containing such information as may be necessary to remedy the defect.

The legislation lays down special rules where personal representatives are concerned (see para.29–08 below), but otherwise proceeds on the basis of the chargeable event in question. It does not provide that an account must be delivered in respect of a transfer of value made by a close company or in respect of a notional chargeable transfer made by a participator as a result of such a transfer of value. This, of course, does not mean that such individuals need not pay tax on such transfers; they, and the company, are liable for tax (see below) and interest will run from the due date if the tax is not paid.

Chargeable events

There are nine categories of chargeable event for purposes of accountability, as **29–07** follows.

(1) *Chargeable transfers generally.* Every person who is liable as transferor for tax on a chargeable transfer (or who would be liable if tax were chargeable on that transfer) is accountable.[9] Since exempt transfers (and PETs, which are assumed to be exempt when they are made)[10] are not chargeable transfers, the transferor need not account for them. The reference to a transferor who would be liable if tax were chargeable means that a transfer within the transferor's nil rate band must be accounted for.

(2) *Notional transfers of value.* Every trustee liable for tax on a notional transfer of value (or who would be liable if tax were chargeable on that transfer) is accountable.[11] Again, the fact that the transfer is within the transferor's nil rate band does not remove the trustee's accountability. The fact that trustees must account for notional transfers means that they must account both for lifetime transfers made under s.52 on the termination of an interest in possession and for transfers made on the death of a person who immediately before he died was beneficially entitled to an interest in possession in the trust property. This is subject to the qualification that the trustees need not submit an account if the deceased's personal representatives have already delivered a full and proper account.[12]

(3) *Failed actual PETs.* Every person whose estate was increased in value by an actual transfer of value which proved to be a failed PET is accountable for that failed PET and this is so even though the failed PET fell within the transferor's unused nil rate band.[13]

(4) *Failed notional PETs.* Where a transfer of value is made under s.52 and that transfer is a PET which subsequently fails any person entitled, whether beneficially or not, to an interest in possession in the settled property in question and any person for whose benefit any of that property or the income from it is

[9] IHTA 1984 s.216(1)(a).
[10] IHTA 1984 s.3A(6).
[11] IHTA 1984 s.216(1)(b).
[12] IHTA 1984 s.216(5).
[13] IHTA 1984 ss.199(1)(b) and 216(1)(bb).

applied at or after the transfer is accountable. The settlor may also be accountable if the trustees are non-resident.[14] The fact that the failed PET fell within the transferor's unused nil rate band does not remove accountability.

(5) *Failed deemed PETs.* The legislation provides that a person is deemed to have made a PET in two cases—where he ceases to reserve a benefit in respect of property which was subject to a reservation and where during his lifetime he discharges a debt which would not have been allowable against his estate for IHT purposes had it still been outstanding when he died.[15] In both cases, the position will be the same as where an actual PET has failed. This follows from the fact that in both cases the deemed PET will have been made by a disposition—where a benefit ceases to be reserved the person who previously reserved it is deemed by the Finance Act 1986 s.102(4) to have made a PET by a disposition, and the discharge of a non-allowable debt will itself constitute a disposition as a matter of general law.

(6) *Reservation of benefit clawback on death.* Where under the reservation of benefit rules property is clawed back into a person's estate on his death any person in whom the property is vested, whether beneficially or otherwise, at any time after the death or who at any such time is beneficially entitled to an interest in possession in the property is accountable, and this is so even though the transfer made on the death was within the deceased's unused nil rate band.[16]

(7) *Exit and periodic charges.* Every trustee liable for tax on an exit or periodic charge or who would be liable if tax were chargeable (e.g. at other than a nil rate) is accountable.[17]

(8) *Loss of conditional exemption.* Where conditional exemption on a transfer of value or capital distribution is lost so that a charge arises under ss.207 or 79, any person liable for the tax due must deliver an account within six months from the end of the month in which the charge arose.[18]

(9) *Woodlands.* Where a deferred charge on woodlands crystallises, any person liable for the tax due must deliver an account within six months of the end of the month in which the charge arises.[19]

Personal representatives

29–08 Section 216(1) requires that the personal representatives of a deceased person must deliver an account. For this purpose, by s.261, in relation to Scotland, references to an account are construed as references to such an inventory or additional inventory as is mentioned in s.38 of the Probate and Legacy Duties Act 1808, which has been duly exhibited as required by s.38. It may be that there are no personal representatives in respect of all or some of the property comprised in a deceased person's estate because the property is such that no grant of representation or confirmation is required in the United Kingdom for it. In that case, by s.216(2), every person in whom any of the property vested (whether beneficially or otherwise) on or at any time after the deceased's death or who at any such time is beneficially entitled to an interest in possession

---

[14] IHTA 1984 ss.201(1)(b)–(d) and 216(1)(bd).
[15] See paras 5–37 and following.
[16] IHTA 1984 ss.200(1)(c) and 216(1)(bc).
[17] IHTA 1984 s.216(1)(c), except where the charge arises under s.79.
[18] IHTA 1984 s.216(7).
[19] IHTA 1984 s.216(7).

in any such property must deliver an account. Where any of the property which formed part of the deceased's estate is at any time after his death comprised in a settlement and there is no person such as that just mentioned, every person for whose benefit any of that property (or income from it) is applied at any such time must deliver an account.[20] While the need for such a provision is understandable, its effect may in certain circumstances be to require persons to submit accounts who could not reasonably be expected to know that they must do so.

The general rule is that a person required to deliver an account must specify to the best of his knowledge and belief all the property (and the value thereof) which formed part of the deceased's estate immediately before his death.[21] This means that besides specifying property to which the deceased was in fact beneficially entitled, the account must also specify:

  (1) property in which the deceased was beneficially entitled to an interest in possession; and

  (2) property over which he had a general power.[22]

By s.216(3)(b), for all deaths occurring on or after March 9, 1999, such an account must also include details of any chargeable transfers made by the deceased within seven years of death (excluding accounts which are delivered only in respect of settled land in England and Wales).

The general rule is subject to four qualifications. First, if after making the fullest enquiries[23] that are reasonably practical in the circumstances, the personal representatives are unable to ascertain the exact value of any particular property, their account will as regards that property be sufficient in the first instance if it contains:

  (1) a statement to that effect;

  (2) a provisional estimate of the value of the property; and

  (3) an undertaking to deliver a further account of the property as soon as its value is ascertained.

Secondly, the Board may from time to time give general or special directions for restricting the property to be specified by any class of personal representatives. Thirdly, where the account is to be delivered by a person who is an executor of the deceased in respect only of settled land in England and Wales the account need specify to the best of his knowledge and belief only the land and the value of that land. Finally, where an account must be delivered by a person under s.216(2), it also suffices if he satisfies the Board that an account will in due course be delivered by the personal representatives of the deceased. As a general rule, personal representatives must deliver an account within 12 months of the end of the month in which the deceased died. This is subject to the qualification that the personal representatives may, if it gives them more time, deliver the account within three months of the date on which they first began to act as personal representatives.[24] Where a person is required by s.216(2) to deliver an account, he must do so before the end of three months from the time when he first has

---

[20] IHTA 1984 s.216(2), unless the estate is an excepted estate; see para.29–10.
[21] IHTA 1984 s.216(1) and (2).
[22] See paras 25–07 and 25–08.
[23] See paras 29–168 and following regarding penalties.
[24] IHTA 1984 s.216(6)(a).

reason to believe that he is required to deliver such an account. As will be seen below, interest on unpaid tax will start to run before an account must be delivered.

Small lifetime chargeable transfers

29–09   With a view to simplifying administration where a charge is unlikely to arise, HMRC, in exercising the powers conferred upon them by s.256(1), introduced regulations[25] eliminating the need to submit accounts in respect of certain lifetime chargeable transfers. These regulations have two effects. First, no account need be submitted in respect of an "excepted transfer", which is defined as a chargeable transfer made on or after April 1, 1981, which is an actual disposition by an individual who:

(1) has made chargeable transfers in that year of assessment, including the transfer in question, the values transferred by which do not exceed £10,000; and
(2) has a cumulative total for over the last 10 years, including the transfer in question, which does not exceed £40,000.

The second effect of the regulations is to eliminate the need to submit accounts in respect of certain transfers made on the lifetime termination of an interest in possession. Under the regulations, no account need be submitted in respect of an "excepted termination", which is defined as a termination where:

(1) the transferor has, in connection with the termination, given to the trustees of the settlement a notice under s.57(3) informing them of the availability of the annual and/or the marriage gifts exemption; and
(2) the value transferred does not exceed the amount of the exemption(s) specified in the notice.

In certain circumstances, notwithstanding the above, it still may be necessary to submit an account. First, HMRC may require by notice in writing that an account be submitted. In this connection, trustees receive special treatment: if within the period of six months beginning with the date of an excepted termination the Board do not issue a notice requiring an account of the property in which the interest in question subsisted, the trustees are discharged from any claim for tax attributable to the value of that property unless, of course, the case involves fraud or failure to disclose material facts. The fact that the trustees are so discharged does not affect the liability to tax of any person other than the trustees, nor does it affect the tax on any property other than that in which the interest subsisted. It may be that a person who has relied on the regulations and not delivered an account discovers that the transfer or termination is not an excepted one. In that case, he will discharge his obligations if he delivers an account within six months of his discovery. For the position where an earlier transfer is discovered after an excepted transfer, see para.6–56.

Excepted estates

29–10   Regulation 4 of the Capital Transfer Tax (Delivery of Accounts) Regulations 1981 (SI 1981/880) provides that a person is not required to deliver an account of property

[25] Inheritance Tax (Delivery of Accounts) (Excepted Transfers and Excepted Terminations) Regulations 2002 (SI 2002/1731).

comprised in an "excepted estate" for IHT purposes. An "excepted estate" is defined in reg.3 as an estate where (subject to various other conditions being satisfied) the total gross value of the estate immediately before death does not exceed a specified amount. Subsequent amending Regulations have raised that specified amount from time to time and introduced changes to the original rules.

Changes to the Regulations

Various changes have been made to the rules governing excepted estates. The most **29–11** recent are set out below, followed by a summary of the present position.

1996 changes

The Inheritance Tax (Delivery of Accounts) Regulations 1996 (SI 1996/1470) **29–12** introduced changes to the rules in relation to deaths after April 5, 1996. Details of the changes made by this SI are set out in the following Statement by HMRC:

"Estates qualifying
Executors or administrators of straightforward smaller estates ('excepted estates') will not have to deliver an account to the Inland Revenue. An estate will qualify as an excepted estate only where the following conditions are met:
- the deceased died domiciled in the United Kingdom;
- the total gross value of the estate before deduction of any debts, together with the value of any gifts as mentioned below, does not exceed £180,000;
- the estate consists only of property which has passed under the deceased's will or intestacy, or by nomination, or beneficially by survivorship. (Where any of the value of an estate relates to joint property passing by survivorship, it is the value of the deceased's beneficial interest in that property which counts for the purposes of the £180,000 limit);
- any estate assets situated outside the United Kingdom have a total value of not more than £30,000 (previously £15,000); and
- any taxable lifetime transfers made within seven years of the deceased's death consist only of cash, quoted shares or quoted securities ('specified transfers') with a total gross value not exceeding £50,000 (previously such transfers would have ruled out the excepted estates procedure).

Estates not qualifying
The excepted estates procedure does not apply where the deceased had:
- within seven years of the death made a chargeable or potentially exempt transfer other than specified transfers;
- made a gift with reservation of benefit which either continued until death or ceased within seven years before the death;
- enjoyed an interest in possession in settled property at, or within seven years before, the death."

1998 changes

The rules were further amended from July 1, 1998, in relation to deaths on or after **29–13** April 6, 1998, by SI 1998/1431 (for estates in England and Wales); by SI 1998/1430 (in relation to Scotland); and SI 1998/1429 (for Northern Ireland). There were three changes:

    (i) the limit of the value of property situated outside the United Kingdom which may form part of the deceased's estate was raised from £30,000 to £50,000;

    (ii) the limit on the aggregate value of chargeable transfers which are "specified transfers" was raised from £50,000 to £75,000; and

    (iii) the limit on the aggregate of the gross value of the deceased's estate and the value of specified transfers was raised from £180,000 to £200,000.

2000 changes

29–14   By SI 2000/967 (for estates in England and Wales); by SI 2000/966 (in relation to Scotland); and SI 2000/965 (for Northern Ireland), the limit on the aggregate of the gross value of the deceased's estate and the value of specified transfers was further increased from £200,000 to £210,000 for deaths on or after April 6, 2000, with effect from May 1, 2000.

2002 changes

29–15   By SI 2002/1733 for deaths on or after April 6, 2002, the rules were further amended with effect from August 1, 2002. There were six changes:

    (i) the limit on the value of property situated outside the United Kingdom which may form part of the deceased's estate was increased from £50,000 to £75,000;

    (ii) the limit on the aggregate value of chargeable transfers which are "specified transfers" (as newly defined) was increased from £75,000 to £100,000;

    (iii) the limit on the aggregate of the gross value of the deceased's estate and the value of any "specified transfers" (as above) was increased from £210,000 to £220,000;

    (iv) of (iii) above, a limit of £100,000 could be attributable to settled property in which the deceased was entitled to an interest in possession;

    (v) the definition of "specified transfers" was extended to include a transfer of an interest in land, and furnishings and chattels disposed of at the same time and to the same person, intended to be enjoyed with the land, save that any property transferred was subject to a reservation to which s.102 of the Finance Act 1986 applied or became settled property; and

    (vi) a new category of excepted estates was introduced to cover those individuals who had never been domiciled or treated as domiciled in the United Kingdom where the value of such a person's estate situated in the United Kingdom was wholly attributable to cash or quoted shares or securities with a gross value not in excess of £100,000.

It is to be noted that before April 6, 2002, there was no provision for the excepted estates provisions to apply where *any* settled property was aggregated with the estate, nor where there was a lifetime chargeable transfer of anything other than cash or quoted shares.

2003 changes

By SI 2003/1658, for deaths on or after April 6, 2003, with effect from August 1, **29–16** 2003, the limit on the aggregate of the gross value of the deceased's estate and the value of any "specified transfers" was increased from £220,000 to £240,000.

2004 changes

With effect from November 1, 2004, the Inheritance Tax (Delivery of Accounts) **29–17** (Excepted Estates) Regulations 2004 came into force. For deaths occurring after April 5, 2004 the new regime extended the existing rules for excepted estates in two ways. The extension brought within the excepted estates definition all estates where the gross value of the estate for IHT purposes, plus the chargeable value of any transfers in the seven years prior to death, does not exceed:

(1) the nil rate band; or
(2) £1 million and the net chargeable estate after deduction of the s.18 and/or charity exemption *only* is less than the nil rate band, subject to the additional limitations specified below.

The limits imposed as to the value of any foreign property, any "specified transfers", any settled property or any non-domiciled individual's estate situated in the United Kingdom, as previously amended by SI 2002/1733 (stated at para.29–15(i), (ii), (iv) and (vi), above) remained in effect. However changes to these limits were subsequently brought in by the amending 2006 regulations, SI 2006/2141, and so for all deaths on or after September 1, 2006, the current position for the limits on the values of these types of property is as follows:

(i) the limit for the value of foreign property is £100,000;
(ii) the limit for the value of "specified transfers" is £150,000;
(iii) the limit for the value of settled property is £150,000; and
(iv) the limit for the value of a non-domiciled individual's UK estate is £150,000.

The Inheritance Tax (Delivery of Accounts) (Excepted Estates) (Amendment) Reg- **29–18** ulations 2011 (SI 2011/214) further amended the 2004 regulations. These came into force on March 1, 2011 and apply to deaths occurring on or after April 6, 2010 (but see below with regard to normal expenditure out of income claims). These regulations:

(1) allow for the first time an excepted estates return to be submitted when the personal representatives of an estate claim the benefit of a transferable nil rate band but only where the entirety of the first deceased's nil rate band was unused, for example where their whole estate was transferred to their spouse or civil partner. The first deceased must have died:
(a) on or after November 13, 1974 where the deceased was the spouse of the first deceased; or
(b) on or after December 5, 2005 where the deceased was the civil partner of the first deceased.

In addition the following criteria must also be met:

(c) the first deceased must have been domiciled in the UK when they died;
(d) their estate must have consisted only of
  (i) property passing under their will or intestacy, and
  (ii) jointly owned assets;
(e) if their estate included foreign assets, their gross value must not have exceeded £100,000 (as above); and
(f) agricultural and business relief did not apply; and

(2) require, with regard to any person who has died on or after March 1, 2011, that any gifts in excess of £3,000 per tax year and which are considered to be exempt as normal expenditure out of income, are nevertheless treated as chargeable transfers and must be included as specified transfers in determining whether or not an estate qualifies as an excepted estate.

For all excepted estates the IHT205 (or Form IHT207 where the deceased was domiciled abroad) (Form C5 in Scotland) are required to be delivered, whether by a practitioner or personal applicant, direct to the relevant probate registry (or, Sheriff Clerk).

Commentary

29–19   It is to be noted that forms IHT205 and IHT207 do not constitute an "account" for IHT purposes but the information contained in them will be deemed to be information delivered to HMRC. Consequently, where that information is delivered fraudulently or negligently and a liability to tax arises as a result, the IHT penalty regime[26] will apply. HMRC will continue to undertake the spot checks already made under the current excepted estates regime by reviewing a random number of such estates from across the country. The automatic discharge will continue to apply so that unless HMRC make a request for more detailed information within the 35-day period (60 in Scotland),[27] the persons liable will be discharged from any further claims to tax. If, however, it is later discovered that the estate does not in fact qualify as an excepted estate, the personal representatives have six months from the date of the discovery to deliver a corrective account Form C4 to HMRC. It is to be noted that, in these circumstances, a full IHT400[28] will not then be required. In deciding whether or not an estate is excepted, the personal representatives must be satisfied as to the individual values of the assets and liabilities in the estate. In coming to such a decision, they must have made the fullest enquiries that are reasonably practicable.[29] Where there is any doubt as to values, so that the estate is a border-line case, the personal representatives would be well-advised to submit a full account.

These changes were anticipated to have brought a further 30,000 estates within the excepted estates regime.

Accounts and discharges

29–20   As mentioned in para.29–19 above, HMRC retain the right to call for an account by issuing to the personal representatives a notice in writing within 35 days of the issue

[26] See para.29–168.
[27] See para.29–20.
[28] See para.29–45.
[29] See para.29–37.

of the grant of probate (in Scotland, within 60 days of the issue of confirmation). If HMRC do not issue a notice calling for an account, personal representatives are automatically discharged from any further claims for IHT in respect of the property comprised in the estate in question, and any charge on that property is extinguished at the end of 35 or 60 days, as the case may be. If, on the other hand, a notice is issued by HMRC, the automatic discharge does not apply. In such cases, discharge from any liability to IHT will only automatically take effect following the issue of HMRC's closure letter which from April 30, 2007 has replaced the formal clearance certificate issued previously: see para.29–92. However, automatic discharge is not given in cases of fraud or failure to disclose material facts, nor does it affect the tax position where it is later discovered that there is further property in the estate and as a result the estate is no longer an excepted one. It may be that a person has obtained a grant of representation without delivery of an account and that he later discovers that the estate is not in fact an excepted one. Currently, he must then deliver an account of all the property comprised in the estate within six months of his discovery. For the position where an earlier transfer is discovered after the death of a transferor whose estate was an excepted estate, see para.6–56.

Excepted terminations and chargeable events

New regulations, which apply for terminations or chargeable events arising under **29–21** relevant property trusts made on or after April 6, 2007, have been made that excuse trustees from delivering an IHT100 in respect of those occasions of charge.[30]

Pre-March 22, 2006 life interest trusts

Qualifying trusts

The new regulations only apply to the termination of a life interest in a trust: **29–22**

- for a bereaved minor[31];
- for a disabled person[32];
- in which there is an immediate post-death interest[33];
- in which there is a transitional serial interest[34]; or
- of settled property where the person became beneficially entitled to an interest in possession before March 22, 2006.

Termination of a pre-March 22, 2006 life interest that does not exceed available exemptions

Where trustees bring a pre-March 22, 2006 life tenant's interest in settled property to   **29–23** an end, the life tenant is treated as making a transfer of value. If the life tenant has not

---

[30] Inheritance Tax (Delivery of Accounts) (Excepted Transfers and Excepted Terminations) Regulations 2008 (SI 2008/605 & 2008/606).
[31] As defined in IHTA 1984 s.71A.
[32] As defined in IHTA 1984 s.89, s.89A or s.89B.
[33] As defined in IHTA 1984 s.49A.
[34] As defined by IHTA 1984 ss.49B–49E.

made any chargeable transfers personally, they can give notice to the trustees that the exemptions they are entitled to are available for use against the property in which their life interest is being terminated. Where the value transferred is covered by the exemptions available, the termination is an excepted termination.

Relevant property trusts including post-March 22, 2006 life interest trusts

Qualifying occasions of charge

29–24   The regulations apply to four occasions of charge:

- all charges in connection with pilot trusts;
- a periodic, or 10-year, charge;
- a proportionate, or exit, charge; and
- a charge on an 18–25 trust.[35]

Pilot trusts

29–25   Regulations first made in 2002 provided exclusion for pilot trusts. The new regulations extended the exclusion to other trusts so that where:

- the chargeable event is on or after April 6, 2007;
- the settlor provided no further property which became comprised in the settlement after its commencement;
- there are no related settlements;
- the trustees of the settlement are resident in the United Kingdom and remain so for the life of the trust;
- the gross value of the settled property throughout the existence of the settlement does not exceed £1,000; and
- the only property comprised in the settlement throughout the existence of the settlement is cash,

then the trustees do not need to deliver an account. The new regulations do not revoke the 2002 regulations, which apply from April 6, 2002, for charges up to and including April 5, 2007. The 2002 regulations are in same form as above with the exception that requirements in the last two points that the settled property was cash and did not exceed £1,000 in value applied at the time of the chargeable event and not throughout the existence of the settlement. This change ensures that this part of the new regulations only applies to pilot trusts.

General conditions

29–26   For all relevant property trusts other than pilot trusts there are three general conditions that have to be met before considering whether an occasion of charge is one that falls within the excepted settlement regulations. These conditions are that:

[35] IHTA 1984 s.71E.

1024

- the settlor is domiciled in the UK at the time the settlement was set up and has remained so domiciled throughout the existence of the settlement until either the occasion of charge or the settlor's death, if earlier;
- there are no related settlements; and
- the trustees of the settlement are resident in the UK throughout the life of the settlement.

Should the settlement fail any one of these initial conditions, it cannot qualify as an excepted settlement.

10-year charge

Where a 10-year charge has arisen and the settlement passes the general conditions, **29–27** it will qualify as an excepted settlement where the value of the notional aggregate chargeable transfer specified in s.66(3) does not exceed 80 per cent of the nil rate band.

Proportionate, or exit, charges

Before first 10-year charge

Where a proportionate charge has arisen before the first ten-year charge and the **29–28** settlement passes the general conditions it will qualify as an excepted settlement where the value of the notional aggregate chargeable transfer specified in s.68(4) does not exceed 80 per cent of the nil rate band.

Between 10-year anniversaries

Where a proportionate charge has arisen between 10-year anniversaries and the **29–29** settlement passes the general conditions it will qualify as an excepted settlement where the value of the notional aggregate chargeable transfer specified in s.66(3), taking account of s.69, does not exceed 80 per cent of the nil rate band.

18–25 Settlements

Where a charge arises in respect of an 18–25 trust and the settlement passes the **29–30** general conditions it will qualify as an excepted settlement where the value of the notional aggregate chargeable transfer[36] does not exceed 80 per cent of the nil rate band.

Value of notional chargeable transfers for 10-year and proportionate charges, post-March 22, 2006 life interest trusts and 18–25 settlements

To calculate the value of the notional chargeable transfer, no relief that might be due **29–31** should be deducted and any liabilities that may be deductible from assets in charge

---

[36] As adjusted in accordance with IHTA 1984 s.71F(8).

should also be ignored. In addition, in arriving at the notional aggregate chargeable transfer, if the total of previous cumulative transfers includes proportionate charges that were themselves excepted from delivering an account, the values to be used in arriving at the total of previous cumulative transfers must also be before deduction of any relief or liabilities.

Statutory clearance

29–32   There is generally no statutory clearance for an excepted settlement because the death of the settlor with seven years of making the transfer may affect the rate at which tax is charged on a settlement as any potentially exempt transfers fail and cumulate with other chargeable transfers. The only exceptions are for terminations of life interest trusts and pilot trusts where unless HMRC issue a notice to the trustees to deliver an account within six months of the date of the occasion of charge, the trustees are discharged from any claim to tax. The discharge does not apply in the case of fraud or failure to disclose material facts, and only applies to the trustees' liability for tax.

Requirement to deliver an account

29–33   Where a trustee has not delivered an account in reliance on the new regulations, and it is subsequently discovered that the transfer or termination was not excepted from the requirement to deliver an account, then provided an account is delivered within six months of that discovery, the trustees are treated as if they had delivered their account in time.

Death of the transferor

29–34   Where a settlor dies and relevant property charges have arisen, the trustees will need to ascertain whether or not the settlor had made any potentially exempt transfers within seven years of the creation of the settlement. Where these fail by reason of the death of the settlor, this may alter the notional aggregate of chargeable transfers that was used to establish whether or not the relevant property charge was excepted from delivering an account.

Obtaining probate

29–35   The effect of s.109 of the Supreme Court Act 1981 is that personal representatives cannot obtain probate until they have produced an account showing either that tax due in respect of a deceased person's estate has been paid or that no such tax is payable. The Non-Contentious Probate Fees Order 2004 (SI 2004/3120), provides for the collection of probate fees for the first grants of estates. Currently, a flat fee of £40 is payable if the net value of the estate passing under the grant exceeds £5,000. An application for a grant made through the Personal Application Section requires payment of a fee of £50 in addition to any other fee which may apply.[37] Applications are

[37] Non-Contentious Probate Fees Order 2004 (SI 2004/3120).

submitted by completion of HMRC Form IHT400, together with form IHT421, see para.29–50. Personal applicants are required to complete form PA1 and form IHT205. On receipt of the completed form PA1 and ancillary documents by the Probate Registry, the applicant will be invited to attend at least one appointment following which the oath, prepared in the registry, may be sworn (or affirmed). No changes have been made to the rules governing applications in Scotland for confirmation to an estate. The inventory must therefore be completed and presented to the Sheriff Clerk in the normal way.

Excepted estates

Where all the conditions for qualifying as an excepted estate are satisfied, IHT205 **29–36** or IHT207 is required to be completed and sent direct to the probate registry. In such circumstances, however, there is no requirement for the completion of an IHT421. Where the application is being made by a personal applicant, as stated above, Forms PA1 and IHT205 are required to be delivered. The fees payable are those payable on a personal application, as set out above. An applicant for probate of an excepted estate is now required to swear to one of the three alternative IHT certificates in the Oath as to the value of the estate and care should be taken that the correct one is used.

Problems with values

Section 216(3A) sets out the circumstances where provisional estimates of the value **29–37** of any property may be given and practitioners should be aware of the particular wording of that section which provides that, subject to a couple of provisos, estimated values may be given if, "after making the fullest enquiries that are reasonably practicable", the personal representatives are unable to ascertain the exact value of any property (see para.29–08 above). If they have gone through that process and can still not establish an exact value, a provisional estimate may be given. However, the estimate should nevertheless be a realistic one, based on the best information enquiries have revealed. Nominal values therefore will not be accepted. Whilst that seems perfectly clear, practitioners should be wary. There are increasingly more instances where HMRC are imposing penalties by reference to this section, under s.247 for negligence in delivering an account.

The Robertson *case*

The Scottish case of *Robertson v IRC*[38] illustrates HMRC's hard line. An account **29–38** was delivered to HMRC and tax of £400,000 paid within two months of death (due to some pressure from a beneficiary for the sale of a property in the estate). Under the legislation, the account was not due until twelve months after the death and interest was not due to run until at the earliest six months from the month of death. The executor, and local solicitor, submitted an amount of £60,000 for the deceased's house (which was put on the market within two months of death), £5,000 for the contents and an estimated value of £50,000 for a small cottage in Hertfordshire, subject to a protected

---

[38] *Robertson v IRC* [2002] S.T.C. (S.C.D.) 182.

tenancy, pending the outcome of professional valuations for the latter two assets. Subsequently, the house sold for £82,000, the contents were valued at a surprising £24,845 (it turned out there were various antiques amongst them) and the cottage in Hertfordshire at £315,000 (it transpired that it came with five acres of agricultural land). The valuations had been produced within three months of death and were submitted to HMRC seven days after the second valuation was received, duly notifying HMRC of the increased value of the cottage, although omitting, by oversight, to mention the contents valuation. (This was however remedied in correspondence shortly afterwards and was not an issue raised by HMRC later.)

HMRC sought to impose a penalty under s.247 which was not agreed and brought the case before the Special Commissioners. HMRC applied s.216(3A) and contended that the account delivered did not comply with that section, arguing that the executor had not made any enquiries let alone the fullest of enquiries and had, HMRC contended, simply returned estimated figures in haste in order to obtain the grant of probate.

The Special Commissioner found for the executor. He noted that the enquiries required by statue were those that were "reasonably practicable in the circumstances". HMRC made no submissions as to what it considered to be reasonably practicable. The Commissioner found that the executor had made a thorough examination of the deceased's home and appreciating that valuations would be required, had taken steps to obtain them, returning in the meantime, in accordance with accepted practice, estimated values, which had been duly marked up as such. He stated that he could not therefore accept that the executor's actions amounted to the negligent delivery of an account and that HMRC had failed on the facts to establish this either beyond reasonable doubt or on the balance of probabilities. Moreover, the Commissioner stated that it had been perfectly in order for the executor to deliver estimated values and to put in hand immediate steps to obtain professional valuations.

Whilst this case sets no precedent, it may give courage to others not to simply accept or settle their cases but to challenge the aggressive approach[39] being taken by HMRC who, it is to be noted, made no public announcement of a change of practice in this area prior to a reference to it in the August 2000 HMRC newsletter. In this, some examples of penalty cases were given but they provided only the barest of details whereas in reality there will always be additional facts to account for the circumstances of any particular situation.

The objective of HMRC in strengthening the penalty legislation[40] and their approach to it must be to encourage the accuracy and reliability of accounts. The old, some would say casual, approach of practitioners providing provisional figures in accounts is clearly no longer acceptable, nor is the omission from or undervalue of an asset in an account.

Urgent cases

29–39   The December 2000 newsletter from HMRC mentions a specific concession to s.216(3A) in cases where the personal representatives need to obtain the grant of probate urgently. Here, HMRC permit the use of estimated figures where no enquiries at all have been made. HMRC suggest that any practitioner requiring a grant urgently contact them in the first instance to discuss their requirements. It would seem that if practitioners can obtain HMRC's confirmation that their case falls within this category,

---

[39] See para.29–179.
[40] See paras 29–168 and following.

there should at least be some protection for executors who need to act quickly, but whether HMRC will give the requisite confirmation that the matter is "urgent" will depend on the circumstances of each case and will no doubt not be lightly given.

National Savings and Investments

Repayments in respect of a deceased's holding of National Savings Certificates, **29–40** Stock or a deposit with the National Savings Bank may be made by the Director of Savings without his requiring a grant of probate or letters of administration.[41] However, this general rule does vary from product to product and practitioners should therefore consult NS&I with regard to the actual products with which they are dealing. At the time of going to press, NS&I[42] current practice is generally to make such repayments up to a value of £15,000.

Additionally, where the aggregate value of certain National Savings products (including National Savings certificates, stock, deposits in the National Savings Bank and premium savings bonds), held in the name of the deceased jointly with another (not being the deceased's spouse or civil partner), is in excess of £50,000, repayments or transfers will be made only on the production to NS&I of a statement from HMRC to the effect that either no IHT is payable as a result of the death or that any IHT so payable has been paid. By implication, the HMRC statement is not required where the aggregate value of the assets for such holdings is less than £50,000.[43]

Loans to pay IHT

Personal representatives often found themselves in a difficult position: until they **29–41** paid the tax due on an estate they could not obtain probate, and until they obtained probate their power to deal with the estate was very limited. The result was that it was often necessary for them to borrow at high interest rates in order to pay the tax due. This problem was often solved by the personal representatives either borrowing the necessary funds from the relevant beneficiaries; obtaining an advance of monies from certain banks and building societies who were happy to pay HMRC direct; or by the personal representatives exercising the instalment option even though the intention was to pay off the tax in one sum. What happened in such cases was that as soon as the grant had been obtained the personal representatives then simply paid off the whole of the tax on the instalment option property. The Law Society repeatedly suggested to HMRC that the problem should be eased and although the Keith Committee has rejected suggestions that tax should generally be made payable after a grant has been obtained, HMRC, in conjunction with the British Bankers' Association and the Building Societies Association, has at last now acted to take steps to assist with this problem.

First, since March 31, 2003, voluntary participating institutions under the "Inher- **29–42** itance Tax Direct Payment Scheme" accept instructions from personal representatives to make the initial payment of tax by electronic transfer from the deceased's account,

[41] See the National Savings Stock Register Regulations 1976 (SI 1976/2012) para.41, as amended by SI 1984/600 reg.2; the Savings Certificates Regulations 1991 (SI 1991/1031) para.15; and the National Savings Bank Regulations 1972 (SI 1972/764) para.40, as amended by SI 1984/602 reg.2.

[42] National Savings and Investments.

[43] See the Regulations cited at fn.41 above.

provided certain conditions are met. In such circumstances, HMRC form IHT423 should be completed and submitted to HMRC prior to the submission of the IHT400.[44] Practitioners can access more details about the scheme, including the combined process of obtaining an IHT reference in such cases, and the relevant form and notes accompanying the IHT423 from HMRC's website *http://www.hmrc.gov.uk* [Accessed October 10, 2012].

Secondly, and in addition to the above, personal representatives may also use qualifying National Savings investments or British Government Stock on the Bank of England register to pay the tax. Details of the investments to be used and official statements of value giving the value of those should be supplied to HMRC with the IHT400[45] and the IHT421. Please note that payment by this method may take up to four weeks to process and so should not be used in urgent cases. For more information, practitioners should refer to HMRC's website.

Where loans for the payment of tax are still taken out, however, the position is alleviated somewhat by the Income Tax Act 2007 s.403, under which interest on a loan (but not on an overdraft) to personal representatives qualifies for income tax relief provided that the loan is used:

(a) in paying IHT where the personal representatives are obliged to pay the tax under s.226(2) (i.e. where the personal representatives are obliged to pay tax on delivery of their account); or

(b) in repaying another loan to which s.403 applies.

References to IHT in s.403 include interest payable on that tax.

The Income Tax Act 2007 s.404 states that:

"interest on a loan within s.403(1) is eligible for relief only insofar as it is paid in repect of a period ending within 12 months from the making of the loan used by the personal representatives to pay IHT under s.226(2)."

Forms

29–43   Various forms, set out below, are used to deliver accounts. The forms, which vary according to the chargeable occasion, may be downloaded from HMRC's website *http://www.hmrc.gov.uk*, or obtained by post direct; see para.29–05 for the relevant addresses.

Lifetime chargeable transfers

29–44   Since November 1, 2003, all non-death events giving rise to a charge to IHT should be reported on new form IHT100, replacing old forms IHT100 and IHT101. The forms for chargeable events are as follows:

---

[44] See para.29–45.
[45] See para.29–45.

Chargeable events	IHT100 and Schedules
Gifts or other transfers of value	IHT100a
Termination of an interest in possession	IHT100b
Assets ceasing to be held in discretionary trusts—proportionate, or exit, charge	IHT100c
Non-interest in possession settlements principal, or 10-year anniversary, charge	IHT100d
Charge on special trusts	IHT100e
Cessation of conditional exemption— disposal of timber or underwood	IHT100f

Account leading to grant of representation in England, Wales and Northern Ireland

29–45 On February 14, 2000, new HMRC form IHT200 was introduced. This replaced (except for Scotland) the former account forms used on death, notably forms 200, 201 (non-domiciliaries) and 202 (short form). On November 17, 2008 a revised account, form IHT400, was introduced. Taking effect on June 9, 2009 it replaced the IHT200 to report the transfer of an estate for inheritance tax, for deaths on or after April 18, 1986, where a full account was required. For excepted estates, IHT205 or IHT207 should be completed: see para.29–36. The IHT400 comprises a single form with separate schedules (IHT401 to IHT423) to be completed according to the circumstances. Although it is generally agreed by practitioners that completing the new composite form takes longer as more information is required up-front by HMRC, it is also acknowledged that it does save on the number of requisitions raised by HMRC in correspondence later. The IHT400 is evidence of a tougher approach being taken by HMRC which in turn is part of the new self-assessment regime whereby the onus of providing the correct information to HMRC is placed firmly on the taxpayer, here the executors, with penalties imposed for incorrect information and unnecessary delay; see paras 29–168 and following.[46]

The IHT400 provided a variety of new supplementary forms for, inter alia, listing bank and building society accounts (IHT406) and for notifying HMRC of an intention to claim conditional exemption for heritage assets (IHT420). It also included a new form IHT402 for claiming the transfer of any unused nil rate band. This followed the 2007 Pre-Budget Report on October 9, which proposed changes to IHT whereby spouses and civil partners were able to transfer any part of the unused nil rate band, not used on the death of the first spouse or civil partner, to the survivor. The effect of this was that the survivor's estate could benefit from an increased nil rate band on their death. Legislation was introduced in the 2008 Finance Bill but the change took immediate effect, i.e. where the survivor died on or after October 9, 2007. All claims to transfer the unused nil rate band are required to be supported by the production of certain documents including a death certificate of the first spouse/civil partner to die, the marriage or civil partnership certificate for the couple, the Will of the first spouse

[46] For assistance in completing IHT200, see the Revenue's leaflets IHT215 and IHT210 which provide guidance for the practitioner.

or civil partner, a copy of the grant of probate or Confirmation obtained on the death of the first spouse or civil partner to die and a copy of any relevant deed of variation or similar document.

Reduced account

29–46   It is no longer possible to complete a reduced account[47] but where the conditions are met short form IHT205 or IHT207 may be completed.

Other forms

29–47   Additional related forms are as follows:

Account to lead to double probate, grant *de bonis non* or cessate grant	A–5C
Loss relief on sale of shares	IHT35
Loss relief on sale of land	IHT38
Corrective Account[48]	C4
Application for Certificate of Clearance	IHT30
Application to transfer funds to pay IHT	D20

For personal applications, form PA1 and either IHT205 or IHT207 should be completed: see paras 29–35 and 29–36 above.

Scotland

29–48   Applications leading to Confirmation in Scotland require the completion of inventory form C1 in all cases and HMRC form IHT400 together with any necessary supplementary schedules (see above) unless the estate is excepted in which case only form C1 is required. Any corrective account information should be reported on form C4.

Inheritance Tax Toolkit

29–49   The Inheritance Tax toolkit was introduced to assist and support tax agents and advisers for whom the completion of inheritance tax accounts does not make up a significant part of their work. HMRC recognise that the toolkit may also be helpful to

[47] See former Revenue leaflet IHT19.
[48] Although this is more often than not dispensed with and the information reported in correspondence by the practitioner.

other agents, more familiar with such work, in validating their approach to this particular type of work and to trustees and personal representatives in completing the IHT400 (or even the IHT205), as many of the considerations, such as valuation, apply to these.

The toolkit applies to all deaths occurring on or after April 6, 2010 and whilst it may assist with dealing with earlier deaths, reference to earlier legislation, in force at the relevant time, will need to be made in such a case.

HMRC are aware that personal representatives will have to review and gather together a substantial amount of information in order to complete an IHT400. Consequently the "fact find" is of utmost importance and will undoubtedly be useful to those practitioners less familiar with such work.

The content of the toolkit reflects HMRC's view of how tax law should be applied and is intended to provide guidance on common areas of error which HMRC frequently see in the majority of returns which they receive and sets out helpful steps the practitioner can take to help reduce those errors. The main areas of error fall into four main categories: omissions, valuations, applying the correct legislation, rules and practices and record keeping. It is to be noted, however, that risks arising in relation to business and agricultural property relief and reliefs associated with works of art and other National Heritage Assets, are not specifically dealt with, as, says HMRC, such issues are not involved in the majority of forms IHT400.

Application procedure

Prior to the 2004 changes to the excepted estates regime, if there was no tax to be **29–50** paid, and the deceased died domiciled in the United Kingdom, a self-receipted D18 showing no tax was payable could be sent direct to the probate registry with the papers for the grant without the need to submit the D18 to HMRC, whilst the IHT200[49] could *at the same time* be submitted separately to HMRC at the appropriate office: see para.29–05.

Where:

(1) there was tax to pay; or
(2) there was an application to settle the tax from National Savings or British Government Stock on the Bank of England Register; or
(3) it was claimed that the deceased died domiciled outside the United Kingdom; or
(4) the grant was required only in respect of settled land,

the D18 had to be sent to HMRC, along with the tax, and the IHT200.[50] In the case of the latter three situations above, the papers had first be "cleared" by HMRC at their "pre-grant" section before the receipted D18 was returned to enable the grant application to proceed. Following the 2004 changes to the excepted estates regime, with effect from November 1, 2004, for an estate that did not qualify as an excepted estate, the D18 with Form IHT200 was required to be sent to HMRC in every case. From this date, the Court Service would no longer issue a grant where the D18 had not been authorised by HMRC. This remains the case with regard to the IHT400 which has to be sent with the IHT421 to HMRC in all cases and where the IHT421 has not been authorised by HMRC, the Court Service will not issue a grant. For excepted estates, the IHT205 or

---

[49] See para.29–45.
[50] See para.29–45.

the IHT207 may be sent direct to the probate registry. Additionally, since November 5, 2007, all payments of IHT now require an IHT reference to be obtained before submission of the IHT400[51] to HMRC. From October 22, 2007, applications may be made online via the HMRC website, although postal applications are also possible. This change has therefore extended the process of applying for an IHT reference where the Direct Payment Scheme was being used for all IHT paying estates.

III. INFORMATION AND INSPECTIONS

29–51   The legislation specifies that in various circumstances a person may be required to provide information to HMRC or to allow inspections by authorised persons.

Settlements with non-resident trustees

29–52   Under s.218, any person who in the course of his trade or profession has been concerned with the making of a settlement may be required to make a return to HMRC. The only qualification to this is that a barrister is never required to make a return of a settlement with the making of which he has been concerned in the course of his profession. Foreign lawyers working in the United Kingdom sometimes take the view that they are not obliged to make a return but the legal basis for this is uncertain. The requirement arises where the following conditions are satisfied:

(1) the settlement is inter vivos;
(2) the person knows or has reason to believe both
   (a) that the settlor was a UK domiciliary when he made the settlement,[52] and
   (b) that the trustees of the settlement are not or will not be resident in the United Kingdom[53]; and
(3) no other person has made such a return or delivered an original account in relation to the settlement.

The return must show the names and addresses of the settlor and of the trustees of the settlement. It must be made within three months of the making of the settlement.

Instruments varying dispositions on death

29–53   It may be that persons concerned with an instrument of variation[54] need to satisfy certain reporting requirements. If an instrument of variation within s.142 is effected which results in additional IHT being payable the election that s.142 is to apply will have to be made not only by the persons making the instrument but also, under s.142(2), by the deceased personal representatives (such persons and personal representatives being called by s.142(2A) "the relevant persons"). By s.218A in such a case,

---

[51] IHT 402.
[52] Applying the deemed domicile provisions; see IHTA 1984 s.267.
[53] For the special rules concerning the residence of trustees, see IHTA 1984 s.201(5) and paras 11–47 and following.
[54] See paras 8–115 and following.

1034

as from July 31, 2002, the relevant persons or one of them must within six months of the day on which the instrument was made:

(a) deliver a copy of the instrument to the Board; and
(b) notify the Board of the amount of the additional tax.

Information gathering

The legislation empowers HMRC to obtain information in a number of ways, as set out below.

29–54

Section 219 information requests

Section 219 gives the Board power to require any person, by notice, to furnish them with such information as they may require. The notice, which may be combined with one related to income tax, must:

29–55

(1) be in writing;
(2) specify the information required;
(3) allow the recipient at least 30 days to respond; and
(4) only be given with the consent of a Tax Tribunal who must be satisfied that, in all the circumstances, the issue of such a notice is justified.[55]

By s.219(3), a barrister or solicitor is not obliged to disclose without his client's consent any information with respect to which professional privilege could be claimed. This is subject to two qualifications. First, a solicitor may be obliged to disclose the name and address of his client. Secondly, a solicitor with a client who is resident outside the United Kingdom and who carries on outside the United Kingdom a business which includes the provision for persons within the United Kingdom of services or facilities relating to:

(1) the formation of companies outside the United Kingdom;
(2) the making of settlements outside the United Kingdom; or
(3) the securing of control over or the management or administration of companies or settlements outside the United Kingdom,

may be obliged to disclose the names and addresses of persons in the United Kingdom for whom such services or facilities have been provided in the course of his client's business.

Section 219A document requests

Under s.219A, inserted by the Finance Act 1999 s.106 with effect from July 27, 1999, the Board has additional and more extensive power to call for documents. This

29–56

---

[55] IHTA 1984 s.219(1A) introduced by FA 1990 s.124 with effect to all such notices given after July 25, 1990; see also TMA 1970 s.20, amended by the Transfer of Tribunal Functions and Revenue and Customs Appeal Order 2009/56.

must be by notice in writing and is only applicable to a person who has delivered, or is liable to deliver, an account. The notice should specify the time limit, which cannot be less than thirty days, within which the documents called for must be delivered to the Board.

A person in receipt of such a notice may be required by an officer of the Board to produce such documents as are in his possession or power and to furnish such accounts or particulars as may be reasonably required. Such documents, accounts or particulars however may be required only for:

(1) enquiring into an account (including any claim or election included in it);
(2) determining whether such an account is incorrect or incomplete and, if so, to what extent; and
(3) making a determination for the purposes of a notice of determination of a person's tax liability.

In compliance with the above, the Board will accept photocopies or facsimiles of original documents but the original must be available for inspection within such a time as may be specified within the notice. An officer may take copies of any such documents produced to him. These provisions are subject to one specific exception, namely that there is no obligation under such a notice for a person to produce such documents, accounts or particulars relating to the conduct of any pending appeal by that person.

Sections 219 and 219A compared

29–57   It is worth noting that there are distinct differences in the provisions set out in ss.219 and 219A. First, unlike s.219, there is no general exception in s.219A for documents covered by professional privilege. Accordingly a professional executor must have regard to any information in his possession even though he would consider such information to be privileged. Secondly, s.219 refers to "information" whereas s.219A is specifically limited to the documents, etc. specified above. Thirdly, powers under s.219A may be exercised without the consent of a Tax Tribunal, unlike the powers contained in s.219. There is, however, a right of appeal under s.219B to a Tax Tribunal within 30 days of such a notice being issued under s.219A. The Tax Tribunal may if the Board's request in the notice appears to be reasonably required confirm the notice or, if not, set it aside. The usual rules applying to appeals to the Tax Tribunal apply equally in these circumstances (see para.29–162 on "Appeals") except that there is no right of further appeal against the Tax Tribunal's decision.

Exchange of information with other countries

29–58   Section 173 Finance Act 2006[56] allows HMRC to exchange information with other countries but only on conditions that preserve confidentiality. Such an arrangement may be made with the government of any territory outside the United Kingdom by an Order in Council, approved by a resolution of the House of Commons.

Provided the Board are satisfied that the government of the foreign territory is bound by or has undertaken to observe rules of confidentiality which are not less strict than

---

[56] As inserted by FA 2000 s.147(1) with effect from July 10, 2003.

those applying in the United Kingdom, no obligation of secrecy is to prevent them from disclosing to any authorised officer of the government of the foreign territory such information as is required to be disclosed in accordance with the arrangements.

Exchange of information within the European Community

Various Finance Acts[57] introduced provisions to increase the powers of HMRC to **29–59** obtain information. The intention was to ensure that adequate powers were available to satisfy the European Community Mutual Assistance Recovery Directive[58] which requires HMRC to obtain information needed by the revenue authority of another Member State. In support of these provisions no obligation of secrecy imposed by statute or otherwise precludes HMRC from disclosing information to a competent revenue authority in another Member State. In this way information can be passed to other EEC member countries.

Valuation inspections

Section 220 provides that if the Board authorise any person to inspect any property **29–60** in order to ascertain its value, the person having custody or possession of the property must permit him to inspect it at such reasonable times as HMRC may consider necessary. Any person who wilfully delays or obstructs such an inspection is liable on summary conviction to a fine not exceeding level 1 on the standard scale (within the meaning of s.37 of the Criminal Justice Act 1982 (as amended by the Criminal Justice Act 1991)).

Inspection of public records

The effect of s.259 is that persons authorised by the Board may without payment **29–61** inspect documents in the custody of "public officers"[59] if such inspection may result in tax being paid, and may take notes and abstracts. A fine of £300 may be payable if inspection is refused.

IV. LIABILITY

The provisions governing liability to tax are somewhat complicated. We begin by **29–62** establishing who can be liable for charges which arise under the main charging provisions—adopting the normal distinction between actual and notional transfers —and the special charging provisions. The next consideration is the various limitations

---

[57] Principally FA 2000, as extended by FA 2002 s.134 and Sch.39.

[58] Directive 77/799 of December 19, 1977, enacted in the United Kingdom by FA 1978 s.77, as extended by the Recovery of Duties and Taxes Etc Due in Other Member States (Corresponding UK Claims, Procedure and Supplementary) (Amendment) Regulations 2005 (SI 2005/1709).

[59] For the meaning of public officer, see *Henly v Lyme Corp* [1828] 5 Bing 91 at 107; *R v Whitaker* [1914] 2 K.B. 1283; *Re Racal Communications* [1981] 2 A.C. 374; and *Graham v White* [1972] 1 All E.R. 1159.

which are placed on the liability of certain persons, following which attention is given to a number of special cases. It is important to note from the outset that where two or more persons are liable for the same tax each of them is liable for the whole of it.[60] In the following discussion references to property will normally include references to any property directly or indirectly representing it.[61]

Actual transfers

29–63　Liability for tax chargeable on actual chargeable transfers is governed by ss.199(1) and 203. Section 199(1) is expressed to apply where a chargeable transfer is

> "... made by a disposition (including any omission treated as a disposition under s.3(3) of this Act) of the transferor".

It is thought that the reference to s.3(3) is illustrative rather than definitive, and that s.199(1) also applies where the chargeable transfer is made by a disposition treated as made otherwise than under s.3(3), e.g. where the disposition is treated as made under s.98(1); otherwise no liability would arise in respect of such transfers.

　　The legislation then draws a distinction between the persons who are liable for tax due on an actual transfer which is chargeable when it is made, e.g. where the transfer is to trustees of a discretionary trust, and the persons who are liable for tax due because a transferor fails to survive a transfer by seven years, e.g. where there is a failed PET or where additional tax proves to be payable on a transfer which was chargeable when it was made.

Up-front liability

29–64　Five categories of persons are liable for the tax due on an actual transfer of value which is chargeable when it is made, as follows:

(1) *Transferor.* By s.199(1)(a), the transferor is liable for any tax due on an actual transfer. If he bears the tax, he is liable on the value transferred after grossing-up.[62] As was mentioned above his liability is unaffected by any arrangement made privately between him and the transferee, e.g. that the latter is to bear some or all of the tax. Such arrangement would affect the incidence of tax only, and if the tax were not forthcoming from the transferee HMRC could still have recourse to the transferor, whose liability would remain intact. If the transferee pays the tax, then the transferor ceases to be liable for it.

(2) *Transferor's spouse or civil partner.* In certain circumstances, the transferor's spouse/civil partner or ex-spouse/ex-civil partner has a liability identical to that of the transferor. By s.203(1), this occurs when the transferor is liable for any tax, and, by another transfer made by him after March 26, 1974, any property became the property of someone who at the time of both transfers was his spouse/civil partner. In such a case, the spouse is liable for so much of the tax as does not exceed the value (applying the related property rules) of the property at the time it was transferred to him or her. This applies whether the

---

[60] IHTA 1984 s.205.
[61] IHTA 1984 ss.199(5), 200(4) and 201(6).
[62] IHTA 1984 s.204(6).

transfer of value to the spouse/civil partner was made before or after the chargeable transfer in respect of which the transferor's liability arose. This ensures that HMRC is not short-changed by a transferor who, having made a chargeable transfer, then transfers his remaining worldly goods to his spouse/civil partner and pleads poverty to HMRC. Such a transferor may not have to pay the tax, but his spouse/civil partner will. By s.203(2), such a spouse/civil partner will have a reduced liability if:

(a) the chargeable transfer is made after the transfer to the spouse/civil partner;

(b) the property transferred to the spouse/civil partner either is still the property of the spouse/civil partner when the chargeable transfer occurs or, if it is not, was previously sold by the spouse/civil partner by a "qualifying sale"[63];

(c) the property transferred to the spouse/civil partner had a lower market value on the date of the chargeable transfer or "qualifying sale" than it had at the time it was transferred to the spouse/civil partner; and

(d) the property transferred to the spouse/civil partner is not tangible moveable property.

If the above conditions are satisfied, the spouse/civil partner's liability is limited to the lower market value mentioned in (c) above. It appears that for the purposes of s.203(2) "property" does not include property directly or indirectly representing it, and that, given the reference to "market value," the related property rules do not apply in valuing the property.

(3) *Transferee.* By s.199(1)(b), any person whose estate is increased in value by the chargeable transfer in question is liable for the tax due on that transfer. A person could thus be a transferee even though he was not the recipient of the property transferred.

(4) *Beneficiaries.* By s.199(1)(d), where by a chargeable transfer any property becomes comprised in a settlement, any person for whose benefit any of the property or the income therefrom is applied is liable for the tax due on the chargeable transfer in question.

(5) *Others.* By s.199(1)(c), the following persons are also liable:

(a) any person who at any time after the transfer is beneficially entitled to an interest in the property to which the tax in question is attributable; and

(b) any person in whom is vested (whether beneficially or otherwise) at any time after the transfer the property to which the tax in question is attributable. Section 199(4) provides that for this purpose property is treated as being vested in two kinds of persons: first, any person who takes possession of, intermeddles with, or otherwise acts in relation to, property so as to become liable as executor or trustee (or, in Scotland, any person who intromits with property or has become liable as a vitious intromitter); secondly, any person in whom management of property is entrusted on behalf of a person not of full legal capacity.

In *IRC v Stype Investments (Jersey) Ltd*[64] the question arose as to whether a person was said to have intermeddled by removing to his place of residence funds which he held as a nominee. The facts of the case were that Stype, which was resident in Jersey, held land—Guy's Estate—in the United Kingdom as nominee for Sir Charles Clore, at

---

[63] "Qualifying sale" has the same meaning as in s.131. Sections 133–140 have effect as if: (1) references to the chargeable transfer were references to the spouse transfer; (2) references to the transferee's spouse were omitted; and (3) references to s.131 were references to ss.203, 203(3) and (4).

[64] *IRC v Stype Investments (Jersey) Ltd* [1982] S.T.C. 625.

whose request it sold the land to a United Kingdom purchaser, the Prudential. The completion of the sale was effected after Sir Charles died, but before a grant of representation had been obtained in respect of his estate, with the result that Stype had to hold the net proceeds of sale on behalf of the estate. This it did by transferring the proceeds to its bank account in Jersey. When, nearly two years after Sir Charles's death, personal representatives had still not been appointed, HMRC sought, inter alia, the delivery of an account from Stype, on the grounds that it had intermeddled with the proceeds of sale.

The Court of Appeal accepted that a person does not intermeddle with the proceeds of a sale merely by lawfully receiving them, but that was not the end of the matter. Stype had intermeddled with the proceeds of sale, because, in the words of Templeman, L.J.:

> "It seems to us that if a stranger so deals with proceeds of sale of English property belonging to a deceased in such manner as to submit the proceeds of sale to another jurisdiction and is unable to pay and account for the proceeds of sale to the English representatives when constituted in England, the stranger has intermeddled with the estate and constituted himself an *executor de son tort*, liable to pay capital transfer tax in England."

It is to be noted that the point in issue in the case was a procedural one, namely whether HMRC had established a "good arguable case" so as to obtain leave under Order 11[65] of the Rules of the Supreme Court to serve an originating summons on Stype in Jersey. Thus, strictly speaking, the Court of Appeal's decision does not establish that Stype intermeddled, but only that HMRC established that they had a "good arguable case" that Stype had intermeddled. Nevertheless the tenor of the judgment is such that the case is in fact strong authority for the proposition that Stype had intermeddled.

It is also to be noted that the Court of Appeal said that there was a grave possibility that the object of directing the payment of the proceeds to Jersey had been to evade tax, and that if this was the case it may have been the product of a criminal conspiracy to defraud HMRC. The court accordingly felt strongly that HMRC should ask the Director of Public Prosecutions to investigate.

The *Stype* case is perhaps now of less relevance as, at the time, HMRC needed to show that the nominee company had intermeddled with the United Kingdom estate. Now it can more easily rely on s.200(1)[66] which provides that, as far as the IHT on a transfer on death is attributable to the value of any property, liability is imposed on any person in whom the property is vested, whether beneficially or otherwise, at any time after the death.

Stype is a fairly extreme case and it is perhaps unlikely that HMRC would bring a claim against a Jersey nominee company in anything other than a similarly extreme case. HMRC has stated,[67] with regard to nominees:

> "The Board have said that it would not be in accordance with their normal practice to seek to make the nominee company of a clearing or merchant bank, or a Lloyd's underwriting agent, liable for tax on the property vested in it where the company or agent has parted with the property without notice of the facts giving rise to the tax liability."

Liability caused by transferor's death

29–65   Where a transferor dies within seven years of making a transfer with the result that tax is due on a failed PET or additional tax is due on a transfer which was chargeable

---

[65] Replaced by the Civil Procedure Rules 1998: see r.6.21.
[66] See para.29–63.
[67] HMRC Manuals IHTM30036.

when it was made, the persons liable for that tax are those set out in para.29–64, but with the substitution of the transferor's personal representatives for the transferor.[68]

Notional transfers

There are three situations in which a person is treated as having made a transfer of value, i.e.: **29–66**

    (1) when a close company in which he is a participator makes a transfer of value;

    (2) when he is beneficially entitled to an interest in possession in settled property and that interest comes to an end during his lifetime; and

    (3) when he dies.

Unless such a transfer is exempt or, in the case of (2), potentially exempt, a charge will arise and tax may be due. The persons liable for such tax are as follows.

Transfer of value by a close company

Liability is governed exclusively[69] by s.202(1) under which three categories of person may be liable, as follows: **29–67**

    (1) The company itself, which is liable for the tax as from the date of the chargeable transfer in question.

    (2) Any person to whom any amounts have been apportioned under s.94, but only in so far as the tax remains unpaid after it ought to have been paid. Such a person can be liable for only that part of the tax corresponding proportionately to the part of the transfer apportioned to him. A person to whom no more than 5 per cent. of the value transferred is apportioned is not liable as a person within this category for any of the tax.[70]

    (3) Any individual the value of whose estate is increased by the company's transfer (such an individual may also be the relevant person in category 2). An individual in this category is liable only in so far as the tax remains unpaid after the due date, and cannot under this head ever be liable for an amount greater than the amount by which his estate was increased in value by the transfer in question.[71]

The legislation does not make any express provision as to liability for additional tax that falls due by reason of the transferor's death within seven years of making the transfer, but this does not mean that no one is liable for such tax. Rather, the same

---

[68] IHTA 1984 s.199(2).
[69] IHTA 1984 s.202(4).
[70] IHTA 1984 s.202(2).
[71] IHTA 1984 s.202(3).

persons are liable for the tax initially due on the transfer and for any additional tax which subsequently proves chargeable.

Termination of an interest in possession

29–68   Where a charge arises under s.52(1) by reason of the termination of an interest in possession the position is similar to that which arises in respect of actual transfers, i.e. there can be three different kinds of liability—liability for tax due at the time the interest terminated, liability for tax subsequently due because the transfer proved to be a failed PET and liability for additional tax due on a transfer which was chargeable when it was made but which the transferor failed to survive by seven years. The position is as follows.

Up-front liability

29–69   Where a charge arises under s.52(1) at the time the transfer is made, under s.201(1) and (3), four categories of persons may be liable (subject to the general limitations mentioned previously) for the tax due, as follows:

(1) *Trustees.* A trustee is liable for such tax, except that trustees of a super-annuation scheme or fund are not liable under this head.[72]

(2) *A person entitled to an interest in possession.* Any person entitled to an interest in possession in the settled property after the transfer is made is liable under this head. The interest need not be beneficial, so that trustees who themselves hold an interest in possession on trust will be liable under this head. Assume, for example, that X, as trustee, holds a trust fund worth £100,000 on trust for A, for life, and that A assigns his interest to Y to hold it on discretionary trusts, so that A makes a chargeable transfer under s.51. If X does not pay the tax by the due date, Y will be liable, but only up to the value of A's life interest.

(3) *Beneficiaries.* Any person for whose benefit any of the settled property or the income therefrom is applied at or after the time of the transfer comes within this category.

(4) *Settlor.* The settlor is liable if the chargeable transfer is made during his lifetime and the trustees are not resident in the United Kingdom for the time being unless:

   (a) the settlement[73] was made before December 11, 1974; and

   (b) the trustees were resident in the United Kingdom when the settlement was made; and

   (c) in the case of a chargeable transfer made after December 10, 1974, the trustees had not been resident in the United Kingdom at any time during

---

[72] IHTA 1984 s.210.

[73] See IHTA 1984 s.201(4) where more than one person is a settlor in relation to a settlement; and see paras 15–42 and 16–18.

the period between December 10, 1974, and the time of the transfer in question.[74]

Liability caused by the transferor's death

Where a transferor dies within seven years of making a transfer with the result that **29–70** tax is due on a failed PET or additional tax is due on a transfer which was chargeable when it was made, the persons liable are those set out in para.29–69, subject to two qualifications. First, s.201(2) provides that the settlor can never be liable for any additional tax due as the result of the transferor's death. Secondly, so far as failed PETs are concerned, s.201(3A) provides that the settlor cannot be liable for the tax due on such a PET if:

(1) the settlement was made before March 17, 1987; and
(2) the trustees were resident[75] in the United Kingdom when the settlement was made, but have not been resident there at any time between March 16, 1987, and the transferor's death.

Death

Under s.200 five categories of person may be liable for the tax on a chargeable **29–71** transfer made on death, as follows:

(1) *Personal representatives*. Section 200(1)(a) provides that the deceased's personal representatives are liable for so much of the tax as is attributable to the value of property in the deceased's estate at death which either:
  (a) was not immediately before the death comprised in a settlement; or
  (b) was comprised in a settlement and consists of land in the United Kingdom which devolves upon or vests in the deceased's personal representatives.
  By s.209(1), a personal representative is not liable under this head for tax attributable to the value of any heritable property in Scotland which is vested in him as executor in the circumstances and for the purposes mentioned in s.18(1) or (2) of the Succession (Scotland) Act 1964. Nor, by s.209(3) is he liable where tax is charged under s.147(4) on a death as a result of a person claiming legitim.
(2) *Trustees*. Trustees of a settlement are liable for so much of the tax as is attributable to the value of any property comprised in a settlement of which they are trustees and in which the deceased had an interest in possession.[76]
(3) *Persons in whom property is vested*. Where property is vested in a person (whether beneficially or otherwise) and the tax in question is attributable to the value of that property, he is liable for that tax.[77] Normally this will catch those who take under the deceased's will or intestacy. Property may be treated as vested in a person if, e.g. he intermeddles with it.[78]

---

[74] IHTA 1984 s.201(3).
[75] See paras 32–02 and following for the rules governing residence.
[76] IHTA 1984 s.200(1)(b).
[77] IHTA 1984 s.200(1)(c).
[78] IHTA 1984 ss.199(4) and 200(4); see para.29–64.

(4) *Persons beneficially entitled.* Where a person is beneficially entitled to an interest in possession in the settled property and tax is attributable to the value of that property, he is liable for that tax.[79] This covers the situation where the deceased had an interest in possession and on his death someone else has such an interest. For this purpose, a person entitled to part only of the income of the property is deemed to be entitled to an interest in the whole of the property.[80]

(5) *Beneficiaries.* Where immediately before the death property was comprised in a settlement, any person for whose benefit any of the property or income therefrom is applied after the death is liable for so much of the tax as is attributable to the value of the property which was comprised in the settlement immediately before the death.

Discretionary trusts—the special charging provisions

29–72   Liability for tax under the special charging provisions is governed by s.201, under which the persons liable are precisely the same persons who are liable for the tax on a notional chargeable transfer made under s.52. If the amount on which tax is chargeable had to be ascertained by grossing-up, they are liable on the tax due after grossing-up.[81] So far as the settlor's liability is concerned, it may be the case that trustees of a non-resident discretionary trust are unwilling to discharge their liability with the result that HMRC recover from the settlor the tax due. If the settlor pays the tax, he will be entitled under s.212(1) (see below) to a charge on the trust property, albeit that he may find it difficult to enforce the charge against foreign situs trust assets.

Limitations on liability

29–73   There are various important limits on the liability of persons, both as to how much tax a person can be called on to pay and when he may be called on to pay it. It will be helpful to divide the limits as to quantum into two categories—main limitations and secondary limitations.

Main limitations

29–74   The main limitations as regards quantum are as follows:

(1) *Personal representatives.* By s.204(1), a person is liable under s.200(1)(a) for any tax[82] as a personal representative of a deceased person to the extent only:

(a)   so far as the tax is attributable to property, which, immediately before the death, was comprised in a settlement and consists of land in the United

---

[79] IHTA 1984 s.200(1)(c).
[80] IHTA 1984 s.200(3).
[81] IHTA 1984 s.204(6).
[82] Including tax due on property clawed back into the estate under the reservation of benefit rules (IHTA 1984 s.204(9)) and extra tax due because the deceased died within seven years of an earlier transfer.

Kingdom, or so much of that property as is at any time available in his hands for the payment of the tax, or might have been so available for his own neglect or default; and

(b) so far as the tax is attributable to the value of any other property, of the assets (other than such land) which he received as personal representative or might have so received but for his own neglect or default.

(2) *Trustees.* By s.204(2), a trustee is liable in relation to any property to the extent only of:

(a) so much of the property as he has actually received or disposed of, or as he has become liable to account for to the persons beneficially entitled thereto; and

(b) so much of any other property is for the time being available in his hands as trustee for the payment of the tax, or might have been so available but for his own neglect or default.

(3) *Persons in whom property is vested.* By s.204(3), a person in whom property is vested, whether beneficially or not, who is liable otherwise than as a personal representative under s.200(1) or as a trustee is liable to the extent only of the property vested in him.

(4) *Persons with beneficial interests in possession.* By s.204(3), a person liable for tax as a person beneficially entitled to an interest in possession in settled property is liable to the extent only of the property in which his interest subsists.

(5) *Beneficiaries.* By s.204(5), a person liable for tax as a person for whose benefit settled property or the income therefrom is applied is liable to the extent only of the amount of the property or income, reduced in the case of income by the amount of any income tax borne by him in respect of it, and, in the case of other property in respect of which he has borne income tax under the Income Tax Act 2007 ss.720 and 731 by the amount of that tax.

Secondary limitations

The secondary limitations as regards quantum are as follows: **29–75**

(1) *Bona fide purchaser.* A purchaser of property and a person deriving title from or under such a purchaser is not liable for tax due on an actual lifetime transfer or a notional transfer on death as a person in whom property is vested or as a person having an interest in possession in property unless the property is subject to an HMRC charge.[83] "Purchaser" for this purpose means a purchaser in good faith for consideration in money or money's worth other than a nominal consideration. It includes a lessee, mortgagee or other person who for such a consideration acquires an interest in the property in question.[84]

(2) *Grossing-up.* Where the amount on which tax is charged on an actual transfer or an exit charge is arrived at by grossing-up, only the transferor, in the case of an actual transfer, or, if the tax is outstanding on his death, his personal representatives and, in the case of an exit charge, the trustee of the settlement

---

[83] IHTA 1984 ss.199(3) and 200(2); and see paras 29–81 and following.
[84] IHTA 1984 s.272; see also para.29–02.

in question, are liable for so much of the tax due as is attributable to that part of the chargeable amount which derives from the grossing-up.[85]

Nature of liability

29–76   In the absence of authority to the contrary it might be argued that a non-resident cannot be liable for IHT and/or that a personal representative can be liable only in a representative and not in a personal capacity. These issues arose in *IRC v Stannard*.[86] The facts were that a testator died on September 19, 1976, resident and domiciled in England. The defendant was his executor, who was resident in Jersey. The defendant received a notice of determination to CTT. Since he did not appeal within the 30-day prescribed time limit the notice became conclusive against him, and proceedings were initiated by HMRC to enforce payment.

The defendant claimed immunity as a Jersey resident. Scott J. rejected that defence. He regarded that issue as settled against the defendant by the Court of Appeal in *IRC v Stype Investments (Jersey) Ltd*.[87] In that case a Jersey Corporation had pleaded immunity from process in England. The Court of Appeal held that the cause of action arose in England; the corporation representative had voluntarily come to England, accepted a conveyance of English land as nominee for the deceased and incurred personal liabilities to the Crown for English tax. The exercise by the English Courts of its powers in those circumstances would not cause any affront to the Courts or inhabitants of Jersey. Likewise in *Stannard* the cause of action arose in England; the occasion of the charge to tax was the death of a person domiciled and resident in England.

Scott J. also rejected the second argument that the defendant was not personally liable for the outstanding CTT. He held that liability to CTT on death could not, logically, be a personal liability of the deceased for which an executor was responsible in only a representative capacity. As was the case for estate duty, it was an original and personal liability of the executor. It was clearly imposed by what is now s.200(1) but was limited[88] to the value of the assets which the personal representative received or would have received but for his own neglect or default from the deceased's estate. That limitation went to the extent of the liability, not its character. It followed then that the Crown could enforce payment by a court order in the *de bonis propriis* form, i.e. enforceable by execution against the personal assets of the personal representative. An order in the *de bonis testatoris* form would have been appropriate if liability had been representative and execution would have been restricted to the assets in the deceased's estate.

That form of execution would be appropriate where there was an outstanding liability of the deceased as a result of a transfer before death, which the personal representative takes over, since his liability then is clearly representative.

Priority of liability

29–77   Although, as was mentioned above, where two or more persons are liable for the same tax each of them is liable for all of it,[89] s.204(6)–(9) establish certain rules the

---

[85] IHTA 1984 s.204(6).
[86] *IRC v Stannard* [1984] S.T.C. 245.
[87] *IRC v Stype Investments (Jersey) Ltd* [1982] S.T.C. 625; see para.29–64.
[88] See para.29–74.
[89] IHTA 1984 s.205.

effect of which is that some persons may be called on to pay the tax before others, as follows.

(1) *Transferor of actual transfer (and his personal representatives).* The transferor of an actual transfer[90] which was chargeable when it was made (and which therefore was not a PET) is liable as from the date of that transfer for such tax as was chargeable when the transfer was actually made (but not for any additional tax chargeable because he dies within seven years of making the transfer),[91] and so are his personal representatives should that tax be outstanding when he dies. All other persons are liable only if the tax remains unpaid after it ought to have been paid.[92] The transferor and, where appropriate, his personal representatives, are thus primarily liable.

(2) *Recipient of actual transfer.* It may be that an actual transfer turns out to be a failed PET or that the transferor of an actual transfer which was chargeable when it was made dies within seven years of making it with the result that tax or additional tax is chargeable. In that case, the personal representatives of the transferor are liable for the tax due as a result of the transferor's death within seven years of making the transfer in question to the extent only that:

(a) it remains unpaid 12 months after the end of the month in which the transferor died; or

(b) in consequence of the main limitations mentioned at para.29–74 none of the persons mentioned at para.29–64(3)–(5) is liable for the tax.[93]

The net effect of this rule is that the primary liability for the tax falls, broadly speaking, on the persons who were on the receiving end of the transfer.

(3) *Lifetime charges on settled property.* Where there is a notional transfer under s.52(1) or an exit or periodic charge under the special charging provisions the trustees of the settlement in question are liable as from the date of the chargeable event or, where there is a failed PET or additional tax due because the transferor has died within seven years of the transfer, the transferor's death. All other persons are liable only if the tax remains unpaid after it ought to have been paid.[94] The trustees are thus primarily liable.

(4) *Reservation of benefit death clawback.* Where property is clawed back into a person's estate immediately before his death under the reservation of benefit rules, a person liable under s.200(1)(a) as a personal representative for tax attributable to the value of the property is liable only if the tax remains unpaid 12 months after the end of the month in which the death occurs.[95] Thus, in relation to liability arising under such a clawback, the persons primarily liable are those mentioned at para.29–71(3) and (5), i.e. the persons, broadly speaking, in whom the property is vested or who can benefit from the property.

Special cases

In certain cases, special rules apply, as follows: **29–78**

---

[90] See para.2–03.
[91] IHTA 1984 s.204(7).
[92] IHTA 1984 s.204(6).
[93] IHTA 1984 s.204(8).
[94] IHTA 1984 s.204(6).
[95] IHTA 1984 s.204(9).

(1) *Legitim.* Where tax is charged under s.147(4) on a death as a result of a person claiming legitim[96] the persons liable are the person who claims legitim and any person in whom the property is vested (whether beneficially or otherwise) at any time after the death, or who at any such time is beneficially entitled to an interest in possession in such property.[97] Section 200(1)(a) does not apply in relation to the tax, but the limitation under s.204(1) on the liability of personal representatives applies to the person who claims legitim.[98]

(2) *Pension rights.* Where tax is attributable to the value of an interest coming within s.151(2)(a) and (b), the personal representatives of the deceased, not the trustees of the superannuation fund, are liable.[99]

(3) *Woodlands.* Where a deferred charge crystallises under s.126, the person liable is the person who is entitled to the proceeds of the sale or who would be so entitled if the disposal were a sale.[100]

(4) *Conditionally exempt transfers and distributions.* By s.207, the persons liable for tax chargeable under Sch.5, or under s.32, in respect of loss of a conditional exemption are as follows:

(a) charge under para.1(1) of Sch.5—the person who if the object was sold at the time the tax became chargeable, would be entitled to receive (whether for his benefit or not) the proceeds of sale or any income arising therefrom;

(b) charge under para.1(2) of Sch.5—the person by whom or for whose benefit the object is disposed of;

(c) charge under para.3(1) of Sch.5—the person who, if the property was sold at the time the tax became chargeable, would be entitled to receive (whether for his benefit or not) the proceeds of sale or any income arising therefrom;

(d) charge under para.3(2) of Sch.5—the person by whom or for whose benefit the property was disposed of; and

(e) charge under s.32—where the charge arises on death or on a failure to observe an undertaking the person who, if the property were sold immediately after the death, would be entitled to receive (whether for his own benefit or not) the proceeds of sale or any income arising therefrom; in any other case, the person by whom or for whose benefit the property is disposed of.

Overseas electors

29–79   By the Finance Act 1996 s.200(4), in determining for the purposes of liability to tax of an overseas elector[101] or the liability of any other person to tax the person whose liability is being ascertained can decide that regard is to be had to any relevant action[102] taken by the overseas elector in connection with electoral rights. This effectively displaces the basic rule in the Finance Act 1996 s.200 that such actions are to be

---

[96] In Scotland, the surviving spouse and descendants of the deceased are entitled to claim a fixed share of the estate, called legal rights. The children's share is known as *legitim*; see paras 8–216 and following.

[97] IHTA 1984 s.209(2); see ss.199(4) and 200(4) for the extended meaning of vested, discussed at para.29–64(5). And see s.200(3) for the rule extending the property in which a person is regarded as having an interest.

[98] IHTA 1984 s.209(3).

[99] IHTA 1984 s.210.

[100] IHTA 1984 s.208.

[101] See para.32–22.

[102] See para.32–22.

disregarded in determining a person's domicile.[103] Where such a decision is taken the overseas elector's domicile is determined by reference to such rights for the purposes only of ascertaining the liability in question.[104] Normally it is not advantageous for a taxpayer to be domiciled in the United Kingdom. Such a decision might be taken where, e.g., X has died leaving his estate to his spouse/civil partner in circumstances where it is clear that X was domiciled in the United Kingdom, but the domicile of his spouse/civil partner—and, therefore, the availability of the unlimited s.18 exemption—is in doubt. X's personal representatives could invoke s.204 if they thought it helpful to tip the balance in establishing that the spouse/civil partner was domiciled in the United Kingdom.

Tax and settlements

A settlor may settle property on trustees on terms that the trustees are to pay any IHT **29–80** that may arise as a result of the creation of the settlement. At one stage HMRC were quick to charge the settlor to income tax under what was the Taxes Act 1988 Pt XV, now the Income Tax (Trading and Other Income) Act 2005 Pt 5 Ch.5, on income accruing to the settlement during the period in which any of the tax remained unpaid, on the footing that the settlor had retained an interest under the settlement. It was questionable whether this practice was correct, and on April 6, 1982, HMRC issued a Statement of Practice (SP 1/82) that they would no longer seek to attribute income arising after April 5, 1982, to a settlor in this way.

V. INLAND REVENUE CHARGE

Under s.237(1)(a), there is a general rule that where the tax due under the main or **29–81** special charging provisions is "for the time being unpaid", a charge, known as the "Inland Revenue charge", is imposed on any property[105] to the value of which the amount on which tax is charged is wholly or partly attributable. For this purpose, references to property include references to any property directly or indirectly representing it. The words "for the time being" suggest that the Inland Revenue charge is imposed from the time of the chargeable occasion and not from the date when the payment falls due.[106] In addition, by s.237(1)(b), in three cases an Inland Revenue charge may also be imposed on any property comprised in a settlement where the tax is due in respect of:

(1) the chargeable transfer by which the settlement was made; or
(2) a chargeable transfer made under s.51, on the termination of an interest in possession in property comprised in the settlement; or
(3) an exit charge imposed on settled property.

---

[103] See para.32–22.

[104] Since by FA 1996 s.200(1)(a) and (4)(a) "tax" for this purpose includes income tax and CGT, the election is for all purposes of liability to IHT.

[105] IHTA 1984 s.237(1).

[106] This is supported by the fact that otherwise IHTA 1984 s.211(3), which gives personal representatives a right to recover tax where an Inland Revenue charge has been imposed, would be meaningless: but s.211(3) may be meaningless in any event; see para.29–86.

Section 237(3A) makes special provision to deal with a failed PET. In such a case property to the value of which the value transferred by the PET is wholly or partly attributable, or an interest in such property, is not subject to the Inland Revenue charge if it has been disposed of to a purchaser before the transferor's death, but if the property has been otherwise disposed of before the death the property and any interest in it is subject to the charge.

Two kinds of property are never subject to the charge. First, by s.237(3), where the chargeable transfer is made on death, personal or moveable property is not subject to the charge if:

(1) it is situated in the United Kingdom;
(2) it was owned beneficially by the deceased (disregarding s.49(1)); and
(3) it vests in his personal representative.

For this purpose, and for deaths on or after March 9, 1999, "personal property" excludes leaseholds which are therefore brought within the scope of the charge.[107] Prior to January 1, 1997, the expression "personal property" also included jointly owned shares in land so that the charge did not apply to such property. However, following the abolition of the statutory trust for sale of undivided shares in land, and of the doctrine of conversion, and the subsequent repeal of the reference to such jointly owned land by the Trusts of Land and Appointment of Trustees Act 1996, the scope of the charge was extended to include such jointly-owned land.

The scope of the charge was further extended in 1999[108] when new provisions were introduced applying the charge to chargeable events relating to conditionally exempt property. Under these provisions, where any tax charged on the value transferred by a chargeable event remains unpaid, a charge is imposed in favour of the Board either:

(1) on the property or object in question; or
(2) where the event giving rise to the charge was a disposal of the property or object to a purchaser, on any property for the time being representing that property or object.

The inter-play of the 1999 provisions with the remainder of s.237 is significant when one considers that a chargeable event may or may not occur on the occasion of something which is itself a chargeable transfer. Without s.237(3B) and s.237(3C) there would be no charge in circumstances where the chargeable event is not a chargeable transfer. Conversely, where the chargeable event is a chargeable transfer, the charge which attaches to real property will take effect on death and, in addition, a charge on movable objects will take effect under s.237(3B) and s.237(3C) which would not be the case under s.237(1).

By s.237(4), heritable property situated in Scotland is not subject to the charge, but where such property is disposed of, any other property representing it is subject to the charge to which the heritable property would otherwise have been subject. Thus, the replacement of heritable property may create a charge which would not have otherwise been present. Since "property" includes property representing property, it is not possible to avoid the charge by exchanging property for heritable property. It is also to be noted that under Scots law leases are heritable in nature and therefore the 1999 amendments to the definition of "personal property" referred to above has had no effect in Scotland. However, the introduction in 1999 of the provisions applying the

---

[107] FA 1999 s.107(1).
[108] By the insertion of IHTA 1984 s.237(3B) and (3C) by FA 1999 s.107(2).

charge to chargeable events relating to conditionally exempt property, has finally extended the charge to Scotland.

There is no obligation on HMRC to register their charge and failure to do so does not amount to negligence.[109]

How the charge takes effect

By s.237(5), where the charge is imposed on property, it takes effect subject to any **29–82** incumbrance thereon which is allowable as a deduction in valuing that property. Section 237(6) then provides that any disposition of property subject to the charge takes effect subject to that charge (unless a certificate of discharge has been obtained).[110] This has the important effect of extending liability for the tax from the person liable on general statutory principles to the person for the time being owning the property. This is subject to the qualification that, by s.238, in certain cases where property (or an interest in property) which is subject to the charge is disposed of to a purchaser, the property or interest ceases to be subject to the charge, but the property for the time being representing it becomes subject to the charge. This occurs where:

(1) in the case of land in England and Wales, the charge was not registered as a land charge, or, in the case of registered land, was not protected by notice on the register;

(2) in the case of land in Northern Ireland, the title to which is registered under the Land Registration Act (Northern Ireland) 1970,[111] the charge was not entered as a burden on the appropriate register maintained under that Act, or was not protected by a caution or inhibition under that Act, or, in the case of other land in Northern Ireland, the purchaser had no notice of the facts giving rise to the charge;

(3) in the case of personal property situated in the United Kingdom other than such property as is mentioned in (1) or (2) above, and of any property situated outside the United Kingdom, the purchaser had no notice of the fact giving rise to the charge; or

(4) in the case of any property, if a certificate of discharge has been given by HMRC under s.239 and the purchaser has no notice of any fact invalidating the certificate.

For these purposes, by s.238(3), "the time of disposition" means (1) in relation to registered land, the time of registration of the disposition, and (2) in relation to any other property, the time of completion.

Expiry of charge

Section 238(2) provides that where property subject to a charge or an interest in such **29–83** property is disposed of to a purchaser in circumstances where the charge continues over the property, it will cease to be so subject on the expiration of the period of six years beginning with the later of:

---

[109] *Howarth's Executors v IRC* [1997] S.T.C. (S.C.D.) 162.
[110] See paras 29–155 and 29–156.
[111] IHTA 1984 s.238(1)(b).

(1) the date on which the tax became due; and

(2) the date on which a full and proper account of the property was first delivered to HMRC in connection with the chargeable event in question.

By s.256(1), the Board may make regulations discharging property from an Inland Revenue charge, subject to such restrictions as may be specified in those regulations. The Board may also make regulations discharging persons from further claims for tax. This is subject to the qualification that the regulations may not discharge any person from tax in case of fraud or failure to disclose material facts and may not affect any further tax that may subsequently be shown to be payable by virtue of ss.93, 142, 143, 144 or 145,[112] or that may be payable if any further property is afterwards shown to be included in the estate of a deceased person immediately before his death.

VI. BURDEN OF TAX

29–84 As was noted above, a number of persons may be liable for tax due, and HMRC are entitled to collect the tax from any of them. The question thus arises as to whether a taxpayer who is liable for or has in fact paid tax must raise or bear that tax out of his own resources or whether he is entitled to raise or recover the tax from some other source or person. This will depend on:

(1) whether any agreement has been entered into or directive given in respect of how the tax is to be borne; and

(2) whether the legislation makes any provision as to how the tax is ultimately to be borne.

Agreements and directions

29–85 Where a legally binding agreement or direction has been entered into or given, that agreement or direction must be taken into account in determining who must ultimately bear the tax in question. If, for example, the transferor and transferee have agreed that the transferee will bear the tax in circumstances such that a legally binding contract (which need not be in writing) to that effect exists between them, and the transferor pays the tax to HMRC, he will be entitled to sue on the contract to recover the tax from the transferee if the transferee does not reimburse him.[113] In the absence of such an agreement, the transferor will be unable to recover from the transferee. The same rule applies where the transferor has agreed to bear the tax: if the tax is in fact collected from the transferee he will be entitled to recover it from the transferor only if there is a contract which legally binds the transferor to pay the tax or reimburse the transferee. The position is the same in relation to tax on a chargeable transfer or an exit charge in connection with settled property, i.e. regard is had first of all to any directions given by the settlor and to any agreements which may exist between the transferor and transferee or the trustees and beneficiaries, as the case may be. So far as wills are concerned, testators often specify how tax payable in respect of their wills is to be borne, e.g. by directing that tax is to be paid out of a particular fund, or that certain gifts are to bear

---

[112] See paras 8–114 and following.

[113] Grossing-up would in the authors' view be required to the extent only that the transferor was unable to recover the tax from the transferee.

their own tax. The effect of such a direction will depend on the proper construction of the will. This, in turn, will depend on the established rules of construction generally, and, where they are relevant, the various estate duty, legacy duty and succession duty cases concerned with similar directions.[114] In this connection, it is to be noted that the effect of para.1 of Sch.6 to the 1984 Act and s.100 of the Finance Act 1986 is that references in documents (whenever executed) to estate duty or death duties have effect, so far as may be, as if they included a reference to IHT chargeable on death.

Statutory provisions

The legislation in this area lays down four rules giving a person the right to raise or recover tax he has paid.[115] "Tax" for this purpose includes both interest on tax and costs properly incurred in respect of tax.[116] The first three of these rules are: **29–86**

(1) *Generally*: by s.212(1), the general rule is that a person who is liable for the tax attributable to the value of any property has the power (whether or not the property is vested in him), for the purpose of paying the tax or raising the amount of tax he has paid, to raise the tax by a terminable charge on, or a sale or mortgage of, that property or any part of that property. The only persons who do not have such a power are the transferor and his spouse.
(2) *Limited interest*: by s.212(2), a person who has a limited interest in any property and who pays the tax attributable to that property is entitled to the same charge to which he would be entitled if the tax had been raised by means of a mortgage of the property to him.
(3) *Partly exempt transfers*: s.41 provides special rules for PETs.[117]

As the fourth rule, which is of more general application, was the subject of controversy sufficiently intense to prompt an amendment to the original legislation, it may be helpful to begin by considering the background to this amendment before setting out the relevant statutory provisions.

The position originally

The fourth rule concerns the burden of tax on gifts made on death. Under estate duty   **29–87** the rule was that real property, wherever situated, and personal property situated outside the United Kingdom bore its own tax, while personal property situated in the United Kingdom did not. The basis of this rule is not clear. UK personalty was said not to bear its own tax because such tax was a testamentary expense (*Re Clemow*).[118] The position with regard to UK personalty thus appears to have been based on the general law, not on the estate duty legislation. The position with regard to how tax on other property was to be borne was more complicated. There were a number of authorities to the effect that such property bore its own tax because it was subject to an Inland Revenue charge, but the real basis for the rule might also have been the general law.[119]

---

[114] See R. Dymond, *Dymond's Death Duties*, 15th edn (1973).

[115] By IHTA 1984 s.212(3), any money held on the trusts of a settlement may be used to pay the IHT on any property comprised in the settlement which is held on the same trusts.

[116] IHTA 1984 s.212(4); see also para.8–107.

[117] See para.8–107.

[118] *Re Clemow* [1900] 2 Ch. 182.

[119] See "The Incidence of Capital Transfer Tax on Death" in *The Journal of the Law Society of Scotland* (October 1982).

Not surprisingly, the legislation contained provisions similar to that found in the estate duty legislation. The key provision was s.28(1) of the Finance Act. 1975,[120] which, prior to being amended in 1983, provided that:

"Where personal representatives have paid an amount of tax and
    (a) the tax is tax on the value transferred by a chargeable transfer made on death; and
    (b) an Inland Revenue charge for that amount is imposed on any property under paragraph 20 of Schedule 4 to this Act or would be so imposed but for sub-paragraph (4) of that paragraph;
the amount shall, where occasion requires, be repaid to them by the person in whom the property is vested."

Since para.20[121] imposed an Inland Revenue charge on personal property situated outside the United Kingdom and on real property[122] (wherever situated) which was beneficially owned by the deceased, it was thought, as was the case under estate duty, that this meant that personal representatives who had paid tax on such property were, "where occasion requires", to be repaid by the person in whom the property was vested so that "where occasion required" real property and foreign UK personalty bore its own tax.

It is to be noted that s.28(1) contained an inherent inconsistency, i.e. the personal representatives' right arose only where (i) they had paid the CTT, and (ii) an Inland Revenue charge was imposed on the property; but if the personal representatives had paid the tax, no charge could be imposed on the property. Thus, if s.28(1) was read literally it was meaningless; accordingly, it probably fell to be construed as if it read "an Inland Revenue charge for that amount was previously imposed . . .".

Assuming that personal representatives could have a right to be repaid under s.28(1), the next question was, when did occasion require such repayment?

It was thought, on the basis of the estate duty case of *Christie's Trustees v Christie's Trustees*,[123] that occasion required unless (a) the deceased directed that his executor should bear the tax, or (b) where trust property was concerned, the beneficiaries under the will were not identical with or did not have interests identical to those of the beneficiaries under the trust, so that normally real property and foreign personalty bore its own tax. The Scottish case of *Re Dougal*[124] cast doubt on this.

Re Dougal

29–88   *Dougal*, put simply, involved a will which the Court of Session construed as giving:

    (1) a specific legacy of a house to the testatrix's granddaughter; and
    (2) a life-rent in residue to the testatrix's son, remainder to her other grandchildren.

The question for the court was whether the CTT attributable to the legacy fell to be borne by the legacy or by the residue. This question had been a live issue in Scotland for some time. Indeed, on June 8, 1978, the then Inland Revenue issued a statement to

[120] Now, in amended form, IHTA 1984 s.211.
[121] Now IHTA 1984 s.237.
[122] In Scotland the distinction is between moveable and heritable property.
[123] *Christie's Trustees v Christie's Trustees* [1943] S.C. 97.
[124] *Re Dougal* [1981] S.T.C. 514. The case is known in Scotland as *Cowie's Trustees* [1981] S.T.C. 514.

the effect that they had taken the advice of Scottish Counsel, who had advised that where there was a specific bequest of an item of heritable (i.e. real) property in respect of which the will was silent as to the burden of tax, the tax attributable to the value of the property was a debt to be paid out of the property which fell to be borne, by the legatees, while CTT attributable to the value transferred by a specific bequest of moveable (i.e. personal) property was a testamentary expense the burden of which fell to be borne by the residuary estate subject to any contrary direction in the will. The position, advised Counsel, was the same as for estate duty, but not everyone agreed with this and, in the event the Court of Session thought otherwise.

Of the judgments given by the court, that of the Lord President is the most helpful. He assumed that s.28(1) did apply, but that in the circumstances it made no difference, because the occasion did not "require" the granddaughter to repay the personal representatives:

> "By itself s.28(1) does not answer the critical question. It merely provides a right to recover tax paid from the person in whom relevant property is vested 'where occasion requires.' Lord President Normand's explanation of this expression in *Christie's Trustees v. Christie's Trustees* 1943 SC 97 at 104 is of no real assistance for it applies to a situation in which—under the law prior to 1964 and, perhaps, down to 1975—the property in question did not pass to the executor as such, and to the former law in which the deceased's failure to direct that estate duty on that property shall be borne by the executor was of importance. The words 'where occasion requires' must, I think, in the context of capital transfer tax legislation, mean where, in the case of particular property comprised within an estate on which capital transfer tax has been paid, that property is liable to bear its proportion of that tax. There is nothing in the testamentary provisions here to show that the specific legacy of the house was to bear its proportion of the capital transfer tax paid. There is, further, so far as I can discover, nothing in the provisions of the Finance Act 1975 on the subject of capital transfer tax which places heritage, which is the subject of a specific bequest under such liability."

The Lord President's judgment thus gave simple meaning to the relatively obscure words "where occasion requires". An occasion required repayment where the will—or, exceptionally, the statute[125]—directed how the tax was to be borne. In the absence of such a direction, s.28(1) had no application, with the result that the gift was effectively free of tax.

While *Dougal* may have resolved the position in Scotland, it caused widespread concern elsewhere in the United Kingdom as to how tax on real property fell to be borne.

Subsequent legislation

29–89 Section 11 of the Finance (No.2) Act 1983 eliminated any doubts as to how tax chargeable on deaths after 1983 on UK property which vested in personal representatives and which was not, immediately before the death, comprised in a settlement, was to be borne by substituting a new s.28(1), now s.211(1) and (2).

Chargeable transfers made on death: the present position

29–90 We are now in a position to consider the fourth rule. By s.211(1) and (2),[126] where personal representatives are liable for tax chargeable on death on UK property which

---

[125] See IHTA 1984 s.41.
[126] Introduced by the FA (No.2) 1983 s.11.

vests in them and which was not, immediately before the death, comprised in a settlement, such tax is to be treated as part of the general testamentary and administration expenses of the estate, subject to any contrary direction shown by the deceased in his will. Accordingly, applying *Clemow*, such property will not bear its own tax unless the testator so directs.

Additionally, by s.211(3), personal representatives who have paid tax on any property following a death, which does not fall to be borne as part of the estate's general testamentary and administration expenses, have a right to be repaid by the person in whom the property to the value of which the tax is attributable is vested, provided that "occasion requires" such repayment. Thus, for s.211(3) to apply two conditions must be satisfied. First, the tax in question must not fall to be borne as part of the general testamentary and administration expenses of the estate. Secondly, occasion must require the personal representatives to be repaid. It appears that in applying s.211(3), property falls into two categories; United Kingdom and foreign property.

The position where UK property is concerned appears fairly straightforward. The first condition will be satisfied only where the testator has directed that tax on the property is not to be borne as part of the estate's general testamentary and administration expenses (otherwise s.211(1) will apply). The second condition is seemingly also satisfied, assuming that *Dougal* establishes that "occasion requires" personal representatives to be repaid where, inter alia, the testator has directed that property is to bear its own tax. The net effect thus appears to be that UK property bears its own tax only if the testator so directs.

The position where foreign property is concerned is more difficult. It is not clear whether as a matter of general law tax on such property falls to be borne as a general testamentary and administration expense. The implication of the wording of s.211(1) is that it does not, unless the will shows a clear intention that it should. If tax on foreign property does not constitute a general testamentary and administration expense then, assuming again that *Dougal* establishes the correct approach, regard will presumably have to be had to the testator's directions and the law generally in deciding whether "occasion requires" such property to bear its own tax. If, on the other hand, tax on foreign property does constitute a general testamentary and administration expense then, applying *Clemow*, and by s.211(3), such property will not bear its own tax unless the testator so directs. If the implication of the statutory rule mentioned above is indeed correct, this confirms what was previously thought to be the law on the basis of estate duty cases.[127]

Instruments

29–91   It may be that a person who has paid tax by instalments or who might have done so is entitled to recover all of that tax from someone else. In that case, by s.213, the person from whom he is entitled to make such recovery is entitled to refund the tax by the same instalments (with interest) unless, of course, he waives his right to do so. If personal representatives choose to discharge all the tax on property qualifying for the instalment option in one payment they may then find, when they come to reclaim that tax from a beneficiary made specifically liable to pay it, that he decides that he will only repay them in instalments. Accordingly, it will be prudent for personal representatives always to exercise the instalment option, or at the very least only not to exercise it if

---

[127] The leading case is *Re Scull, Scott v Morris* (1917) 87 L.J. Ch. 59.

they have the prior agreement of the relevant beneficiary to the payment of the tax in a single instalment.

Certificates

By s.214(1), the Board must grant to a person who has paid or borne tax[128] which **29–92** is attributable to the value of any property, and for which he is not ultimately liable, a certificate (on his applying by any such form as they may prescribe), specifying the tax paid and the debts and incumbrances allowed in valuing the property. By s.214(2), such a certificate is, except to the extent of any repayment which may be or become due from the Board, conclusive as between any person by whom the tax specified in the certificate falls to be borne and the person seeking to recover the tax from him. Moreover, any repayment of the tax falling to be made by the Board shall be regarded as having been duly made if made to the person producing the certificate.

In practice now, however, when HMRC is satisfied that all tax and interest due has been paid, they will now write to confirm that. In order to use their resources more effectively, HMRC have stated that, with effect from April 30, 2007, they would be changing the effect that their closure letter will have. Therefore, current practice is that HMRC will write to confirm when their enquiries are complete and that they are closing their files. This letter therefore now provides the necessary confirmations conferred previously by the issue of a certificate of clearance but does away with the necessity of practitioners having to apply formally for it or of HMRC having to issue them. HMRC have confirmed that such a closure letter will have exactly the same effect as the formal certificate.

Practical administration problems

The above rules give rise to a number of serious practical problems faced by **29–93** personal representatives of deceased transferors, by personal representatives of deceased transferees and by trustees.

Practical problems for personal representatives of deceased transferors

In three cases personal representatives may be liable for IHT if persons primarily **29–94** liable (the donees of the property) have reached the limits of their liability to pay or if the tax remains unpaid for 12 months after the end of the month of death. These occasions are, first, if a PET is brought into charge because of the death; secondly, when a lifetime chargeable transfer is subject to additional IHT because of the death; and, finally, if the estate of the deceased includes property subject to a reservation.

---

[128] Or interest on tax: IHTA 1984 s.214(3).

These contingent liabilities present major problems for personal representatives and the following should be noted.

Exposure to extra tax

29–95   Under the reservation of benefit rules in the Finance Act 1986 s.102, property in which a donor has reserved a benefit may be treated as comprised in his estate at death. In such cases the donee of the property is made primarily liable for the resulting tax but, should he fail to pay that tax by 12 months after the end of the month of death, the deceased's personal representatives are then made liable. In these cases it is thought that personal representatives are given a right of recovery from that donee under s.211(3). By contrast, the subsection gives no such right to personal representatives made liable for tax on a failed PET or for extra tax on a chargeable lifetime transfer made within seven years of death, because it is limited to the recovery of tax paid on the value transferred by chargeable transfers made on death.[129] Presumably, there would be a right of recovery based on general equitable principles but, in these cases, the personal representatives have the power to raise tax under s.212(1), as has been mentioned, although this is not likely to help them if the gift was cash or the property has been sold or taken out of the jurisdiction.

The personal representatives' liability may arise long after the estate has been fully administered and distributed (e.g. a PET may be discovered which is not only itself taxable but which also affects the charge on subsequent lifetime chargeable transfers and on the death estate). Even if tax has been paid on the estate and a certificate of discharge obtained, the personal representatives remain liable to pay any further tax that may arise in these situations. Assume X dies and his personal representatives, unaware of any lifetime gifts, pay tax and distribute the remainder of the estate. Consider the following:

(a) After some years a lifetime gift by Mort made six years before his death and which was potentially exempt when made is discovered. Although no tax is chargeable on that gift, it affects the rate of tax charged on a death estate and the personal representatives are held accountable for extra tax on the death estate.

(b) A gift made one year before Mort's death is discovered. In this case not only will the personal representatives be accountable for extra tax as above but in addition, if the donee fails to pay tax on the gift within 12 months of the death, the personal representatives will then be liable to pay that tax.[130]

Indemnities

29–96   There is, of course, nothing to stop a donor taking an indemnity from his donee to pay any future IHT as a condition of making the lifetime gift. Such an arrangement would be expressed as an indemnity in favour of the donor's estate and would not

---

[129] See *Private Client Business* (1998), p.58 for the arguments that personal representatives have, first, a right of indemnity against the donee of a failed PET for recovery of tax paid by them under compulsion of law twelve months after the donor's death and, secondly, a common law right to go against the residuary beneficiaries where the failed PET comes to light after distribution of the estate.

[130] Their liability is limited to the net assets in the estate which have passed through their hands.

involve a reservation of benefit in the gifted property.[131] Such personal indemnities are, however, vulnerable in the event of the bankruptcy or emigration of the donee. As the personal representatives have power to obtain security for such an indemnity[132] they should insist on it, thus safeguarding their position as far as possible.

Insurance

One possibility is for the personal representatives to take out insurance (up to the **29–97** limit of their liability) against the risk of a failed PET subsequently being discovered, bearing in mind that there is no time limit applicable to prevent this discovery from leading to a tax charge on both the failed PET and an increased charge on the estate. Insurance can be arranged on a case by case basis and, for the peace of mind of the personal representatives and to assure beneficiaries that the estate will be distributed promptly without their requiring either indemnities or a retention of assets, such insurance comes at a relatively modest cost. What remains uncertain, however, is whether as a matter of trust law the personal representatives have implied power to take out such indemnity cover. To guard against the possibility that they do not, and rather than leaving the matter therefore to be specifically agreed by the beneficiaries, it would be better for testators to give express powers of insurance in such cases to their personal representatives.

Retention of assets

It will not be satisfactory for personal representatives to retain estate assets to cover **29–98** the danger of a future tax liability. Apart from being unpopular with beneficiaries, there is no guarantee that personal representatives will retain an adequate sum to cover the tax liability on a possible PET the execution of which they are unaware—only by retaining all the assets in the estate would they be wholly protected.

Renunciation of probate

If, having made the fullest of enquiries, the personal representatives have any doubts, **29–99** they can always consider renouncing probate.

Some comfort

Limited comfort to personal representatives is afforded by a letter from HMRC to **29–100** the Law Society dated February 11, 1991,[133] which states:

"The Revenue will not usually pursue for IHT personal representatives who
  • after making the fullest enquiries that are reasonably practicable in the circumstances to discover lifetime transfers, and so

---

[131] See para.7–98.
[132] Administration of Estates Act 1925 s.36(10).
[133] Published in *The Law Society Gazette* on March 13, 1991.

- having done all in their power to make full disclosure of them to the Board of Inland Revenue
- have obtained a certificate of discharge and distributed the estate before a chargeable lifetime transfer comes to light.

This statement . . . is made without prejudice to the application in an appropriate case of s.199(2) *Inheritance Tax Act* 1984."

Practical problems for personal representatives of deceased transferees

29–101   Personal representatives also face potential problems where the transferee of a PET dies. The personal representatives are responsible for the deceased's debts and other liabilities and, where the transferor of the PET has already died, they will be responsible for discharging the tax liability arising as a result of the transferor's death. In such a situation, there should be no problem in calculating the liability. However, if the transferor is still alive on the death of the transferee, the difficulty for the transferee's personal representatives is that the tax liability is only a potential one. Accordingly, the transferee's personal representatives might consider making some provision for the potential liability arising as a result of the death of the transferor within seven years. The difficulty is knowing what level of provision to make.

In the above scenario, the personal representatives should investigate if there were any gifts inter vivos made to the deceased in the seven years prior to death and, if so, what other transfers the transferor had made before each transfer in question as this will affect the transferor's cumulative total and therefore the rate of tax payable by the transferee.

The beneficiaries of the deceased transferee's estate will wish for the estate to be distributed in full and the personal representatives may find themselves in a difficult position. As discussed above, the issues of keeping back a reserve, obtaining an indemnity or insurance cover in theses situations arises and although insurance might be the better solution of the three, the trustees may have a problem if they have no express authority to do so under the provisions of the will.

Practical problems for trustees

29–102   Trustees face problems of a similar nature. Assume, for instance, that A is the life tenant of a trust fund and that he surrenders his interest inter vivos as a result of which the settlement comes to an end and the property passes to the remainderman, B. A has made a PET and, accordingly, if he dies within seven years, IHT will be payable. The trustees will be liable for that tax and may therefore face difficulties of recovery if they have distributed the fund to B.[134]

A separate problem may also arise in the following situation. Assume that A was the life tenant of a trust fund and that on his death his free estate was left to his surviving spouse/civil partner with the result that his nil rate band was available to reduce the tax charge on the trust assets. Within two years of A's death, however, a deed of variation is entered into as a result of which A's free estate now passes to a chargeable person

---

[134] It will also be important for trustees in such cases to ensure that a beneficiary such as A makes an election to set his annual and/or gifts in consideration of marriage exemption against a future tax liability. The appropriate notice utilising this election should be made at the time when the PET occurs: see paras 3–04 and 3–20.

(e.g. to A's daughter). As a result, the tax liability of the trustees is increased so that, again, difficulties may arise if they have already distributed the trust fund.[135]

VII. DUE DATE FOR PAYMENT

The general rule is found in s.226(1),[136] under which the due date for payment of tax **29-103** is determined by reference to the date on which the charge in question arises, as follows:

> (1) If the charge is made after April 5 but before October 1, tax is due at the end of April in the following year.[137]
> (2) In any other case, tax is due six months after the end of the month in which the charge is made.

It follows that any charge falling in (1) must always give at least as long to pay as a charge falling in (2), and will normally give a much longer time to pay. The best time to incur a charge from this standpoint is shortly after the beginning of the tax year. Payment of tax can now be made direct to HMRC under the Inheritance Tax Direct Payment Scheme which came into effect on March 31, 2003; see para.29–34 above.

Special cases

The general rule stated above is subject to a number of qualifications, as follows: **29-104**

> (1) *Transfers made on death.* By s.226(1), tax due on a chargeable transfer made on death is always due six months after the end of the month in which the transfer was made. On delivery of their account, the deceased's personal representatives must under s.226(2) pay all the tax for which they are liable; in addition, they may also pay any part of the tax chargeable for which they are not liable if the persons who are liable request them to do so. The fact that the personal representatives must on delivery of their account pay all the tax for which they are liable is important, because normally they will obtain a grant of probate or letters of administration authorising them to act only by submitting the account and making such a payment.[138] Tax will thus normally be paid before the due date.
> (2) *Transfers made within seven years of death.* Where excess tax becomes chargeable as a result of a transferor dying within seven years of making a transfer, any excess tax is due six months after the end of the month in which he died.[139] Since the personal representatives of the deceased are not initially liable for such tax, they may obtain their grant of representation before the excess tax is paid. Where the tax on the transfer was payable by instalments, without interest, the additional tax is also payable in 10 annual instalments,

---

[135] See paras 8–114 and following. Note that the trustees' consent is not required to any such instrument of variation.

[136] And see IHTA 1984 s.2(3).

[137] The legislation refers to October 1, but this is its practical effect. Tax on a transfer made on, e.g., October 15 will be due at the end of April in the following year.

[138] See para.29–27.

[139] IHTA 1984 s.226(3)(a) and (3A).

without interest, the first such instalment falling due six months after the date of the death. This leaves two series of instalments to be paid.

(3) *Exit and periodic charges—additional charges.* It may be that an individual makes a PET and then settles property on trust or adds property to a settlement of which he is the settlor, the trustees incur an exit or periodic charge and that individual dies within seven years of making the PET with the result that further tax is due in respect of the exit or periodic charge. While any tax on the failed PET is due six months after the end of the month in which that individual died,[140] the legislation does not specifically deal with any extra tax due from the trustees.

(4) *Conditional exemptions.* By ss.226(4), tax chargeable under ss.32, 32A or Sch.5 on the loss of conditional exemption is due six months after the end of the month in which the event which precipitated the charge occurred.

(5) *Woodlands.* Section 226(4) also provides that where tax is chargeable under s.126 on the loss of the woodlands deferral relief, the tax in question is due six months after the end of the month in which the precipitating disposal occurred.

HMRC may accept or demand payment of tax by reference to the value entered in an original or a supplementary account which has been delivered to them. This in no way prejudices their right to recovery of any additional tax which they discover to be due. They are not authorised to recover tax from or require the payment of tax by any person in excess of his liability therefore.

Blocked foreign assets

29–105   Blocked foreign assets are dealt with by an extra statutory concession F6 in the following terms:

"Where, because of restrictions imposed by the foreign government, executors cannot immediately transfer to this country sufficient of the deceased's foreign assets for the payment of [IHT] attributable to them, they are given the option of deferring payment until the transfer can be effected. If the amount in sterling that the executors finally succeed in bringing to this country is less than this tax, the balance is waived."

VIII. INTEREST

29–106   Section 233(1) provides, in effect, that interest on unpaid tax runs from the date on which the tax fell due. The charge to interest is not precluded under the Convention for the Protection of Human Rights and Fundamental Freedoms 1950 and it has been held that charging interest on outstanding tax falls within the first Protocol to the Convention as securing the payment of taxes. The European Convention on Human Rights therefore does not provide the taxpayer with a good defence to a claim by HMRC for interest on unpaid IHT.[141] By s.236(2), tax unpaid in consequence of the operation of s.146 in conjunction with an order made under the Inheritance (Provision for Family

---

[140] IHTA 1984 s.226(3B).
[141] *Prosser v IRC* [2003] S.T.C. (S.C.D.) 250. For a general discussion on human rights and inheritance tax, see Ch.31.

and Dependants) Act 1975 does not carry interest for any period before the order.[142] Where a chargeable event which is reported late must be treated as made after another chargeable event in fact made after it, interest on any tax that is due because the transferor's cumulative total at the time the first event is treated as having been made exceeds his total at the time of the earlier event does not run until six months after the date on which the event in fact occurred was discovered.[143] For property accepted in lieu of tax (or interest), the general rule is that interest on unpaid tax stops running as at the date when the offer in lieu is accepted but see para.29–144 for details of the provisions set out in s.233(1)(A).

Under estate duty it was HMRC's practice not to charge interest on unpaid duty while an account or a corrective affidavit was working in the Estate Duty Office. In a statement of September 30, 1975, HMRC made it clear that, while this practice continued to apply for estate duty, it did not apply for CTT.[144]

Rate of interest

Section 233(2) formerly provided that the rate of interest varied according to the nature of the chargeable event but since December 16, 1986 interest has been payable at a single rate regardless of the type of transfer. In July 1986 the Revenue announced that interest rates would in future follow more closely movements in commercial rates of interest. However, in the case of IHT, although it was recognised that the interest rate would be kept broadly in line with the rates appropriate to other taxes, it was not likely to change as often as those other rates. Very frequent changes in the IHT rates of interest would obviously cause extra work in the administration of the tax especially in cases where it is being paid by instalments spread over 10 years. **29–107**

The Finance Act 1989 s.178 brings together in one place the authority for making variations in the rates of interest and for the first time sets out the wide range of options available. Changes in rates are to be made by the Treasury by regulations in the form of statutory instruments: such regulations may, for instance, vary the specified rate for different purposes; specify a rate or provide for the rate to be linked to some other rate; make variations to a rate fixed by a formula; provide for rounding up or rounding down of average rates; provide for circumstances in which an alteration is or is not to take place; and allow alterations of rates to have effect from an earlier or later date. The first such order is the Taxes (Interest Rate) Regulations 1989 (Sl 1989/1297). Under reg.4 the interest rate applicable in relation to capital taxes is set out and provision for changes in the applicable rate by reference to a formula. For details of current and historical rates of interest see HMRC's website, *http://www.hmrc.gov.uk*.

In the *Tax Bulletin* for April 1997 at p.422 the following changes were announced:

> "Interest on unpaid IHT is charged at an annual rate and the Revenue calculates a daily rate from this using a 365 day year. It has been drawn to our attention that our system of calculation is not completely in line with that adopted elsewhere in the Inland Revenue.
>
> We have therefore amended our computerised assessing system and the interest factor tables we use. This change takes effect on April 6, 1997. Any interest accruing on or after that date is calculated as if every year is a leap year. This will give a small advantage to the taxpayer in three out of every four years.

---

[142] See paras 8–207 and following.
[143] See paras 6–53 and following.
[144] See also para.29–144 for non-payment on certain heritage property accepted in lieu of tax.

The repayment supplement paid by the Revenue on overpayments of IHT and interest will continue to be calculated using a 365 day year. Again, this will give the taxpayer a small advantage where the period includes February 29."

Non-deductibility of interest

29–108   Section 233(3) provides that interest payments are not deductible in computing any income, profits or losses for any tax purposes. HMRC takes the view that interest is not deductible under s.697(1) of the Taxes Act 1988 in calculating the income of a person with an absolute interest in an estate in the course of administration, but will tax a person with a limited interest in property by reference only to the income he in fact receives, so that such a person in effect obtains a deduction for higher rate tax purposes in respect of interest repayments.[145]

Repayments

29–109   It may be that a taxpayer pays too much tax or interest, and that HMRC make a repayment to him. In that case, s.235 provides that the amount in question carries interest from the date on which it was paid to HMRC at the same rate as that at which the tax, if outstanding, would have carried interest. Here three points concerning HMRC practice should be noted. First, HMRC are understood to pay interest from the date the tax was paid to them even though had the tax been outstanding it would not have carried interest. Secondly, difficulties may arise where there is an election to pay tax by instalments, and, in order to prevent interest running while a valuation is being agreed, a payment on account in respect of the first instalment is made which is well in excess of the expected amount of the instalment. HMRC takes the view that in such circumstances interest runs in favour of the taxpayer on the difference only between the total liability and the payment on account, not on the difference between the instalment and the payment on account. HMRC are understood to base this practice on the exact wording of s.235. Finally, an awkward situation may arise where a taxpayer has made a payment on account and HMRC has subsequently agreed that no tax is in fact due because, for example, the transfer is not chargeable or is entirely within the nil rate band. In such cases, HMRC has been known to resist the payment of interest on the footing that s.235 provides that interest falls to be paid only on "any repayment of an amount paid in excess of a *liability* for tax". HMRC's argument in such cases is that since there is no liability therefore there can also be no interest due. Where it is anticipated that this difficulty may arise, it may be helpful to include in the letter that accompanies the payment a statement to the effect that the payment is made only on the condition that if no tax subsequently proves payable the payment made on account will be repaid with interest at the appropriate rate under s.235.

Tax which is repayable on a claim made under s.236(3)[146] carries interest from the date on which the claim is made. Interest on repayment because a transfer has been set aside under s.150 runs from the date of the claim.

[145] CCAB Guidance Note, February 3, 1978, STI February 10, 1978, pp.49–50.
[146] See paras 3–62 and 7–205.

Interest on a repayment is not income of the person to whom the repayment is made for tax purposes.[147]

IX. PAYMENT OF TAX BY INSTALMENTS

In certain circumstances it is possible to pay by instalments the tax due on a **29–110** chargeable transfer, a periodic charge or an exit charge. Broadly speaking, the tax due must have been attributable to land, certain shares, a business or woodlands. The instalments[148] on chargeable events occurring after March 14, 1983 may be paid over 10 years by equal annual instalments. Tax on chargeable events occurring on or before that date may be paid over eight years, either by eight equal annual or 16 equal biannual payments. In addition, and this is particularly important, the outstanding tax subject to certain qualifications carries interest only from the date on which any given instalment is due. This is thus an extremely valuable relief.

To obtain a grantor representation personal representatives will, in appropriate cases, first have to pay IHT. To reduce the amount of tax that would otherwise become payable at this stage it is now standard practice for personal representatives to exercise the instalment option in all cases where this facility is available. Once a grant has been obtained the personal representatives may then decide to pay off all the outstanding IHT (see s.227(4)). The case of *Howarth v IRC*[149] provides a salutary reminder for personal representatives of the difficulties that these arrangements may produce. Three personal representatives were involved (the deceased's son and his wife together with an employee of the firm of solicitors which dealt with the administration of the estate). The estate included land and the option to pay tax by instalments was duly exercised. With the conclusion of the administration period the executors then vested all the assets in the names of the relevant beneficiaries (apparently the son and wife). At first outstanding instalments on the land were duly paid by the son but after he was declared bankrupt arrears built up and eventually HMRC issued notices of determination against each of the executors. Given the bankruptcy of the testator's son the liability—amounting to some £8,084—inevitably fell on the "professional executor" (i.e. the employee of the firm of solicitors). The executors appealed against the notices of determination although only the professional was represented at the subsequent hearing. Arguments on his behalf were:

(i) that he was already suffering from ill health which would be adversely affected by the enforcement proceedings; and

(ii) that HMRC had delayed unduly in raising the notices of determination (evidenced by the fact that the notice was raised almost two years after he had retired from his employment on grounds of ill health).

These arguments were summarily rejected. A final contention, that HMRC had been negligent in not registering a charge against the property was also dismissed on the basis that although s.237 imposes such a charge in favour of HMRC, the legislation does not impose any obligation to register that charge.

The legislation governing the payment of tax by instalments is complicated. The following discussion, at the risk of appearing repetitious, seeks to make it understandable by spelling out precisely what conditions relate to each kind of property to

---

[147] IHTA 1984 ss.235(2) and 236(3).
[148] IHTA 1984 s.227.
[149] *Howarth v IRC* [1997] S.T.C. (S.C.D.) 162.

which the relief is available. As was mentioned above, the relief is available to periodic/exit charges as well as to chargeable transfers, and references to a transferor below should be read as including references to trustees where appropriate.[150]

Election

29–111   Section 227(1) provides that the election to pay by instalments must be made in writing. No time limit is specified, but it will normally be desirable to make the election before tax falls due, which in the case of a transfer made on death, is six months after the end of the month in which the death occurred,[151] and in other cases varies according to when the charge arose.[152] Even if an election is made, there is nothing to prevent the taxpayer from paying the outstanding tax, together with any interest due, at any time.[153]

Qualifying property and related conditions

29–112   Instalment relief is available where:

(1) the amount on which tax is chargeable is attributable to the value of property falling within one of a number of specified categories of property; and
(2) certain related conditions are satisfied.

Each of the categories and the related conditions are discussed in turn.

Land

29–113   By s.227(2), land qualifies for instalment relief, wherever it is situated, and whatever its description; a leasehold property in, e.g., Spain will thus qualify.

Related conditions

29–114   The general rule is that, by s.227(1)(b), relief is available only if the tax is borne by the person benefiting from the chargeable event. This is subject to two qualifications. First, this rule does not apply to transfers made on death. Secondly, by s.227(1)(c), where tax is due as a result of:

(a) a transfer made on the termination of an interest in possession under s.52(1); or
(b) a periodic or an exit charge,

---

[150] IHTA 1984 ss.3(2) and 227(1)(c).
[151] IHTA 1984 s.226(1).
[152] See para.29–103.
[153] IHTA 1984 s.227(4).

relief is available only so long as the land continues to be comprised in the settlement in question.

Shares

By s.228, instalment relief is available in respect of shares falling within one of the following categories. **29–115**

Controlling shares

By s.228(1)(a), shares or securities come within this category if they gave the transferor control of the company immediately before the chargeable event in question. Control for this purpose has the special meaning given to it in the legislation.[154] **29–116**

Related conditions

The general rule is that, by s.227(1)(b), relief is available only if the tax is borne by the person benefiting from the chargeable event. This is subject to two qualifications. First, this rule does not apply to transfers made on death. Secondly, by s.227(1)(c), where tax is due as a result of: **29–117**

   (a) a transfer made on the termination of an interest in possession under s.52(1); or
   (b) a periodic or an exit charge,

relief is available only so long as the shares continue to be comprised in the settlement in question.

Minority unquoted "hardship" shareholdings

By s.228(1)(b), shares or securities come within this category if they satisfy the following conditions: **29–118**

   (1) They did not give the transferor control of the company immediately before the chargeable event in question. The use of the term "minority" is thus slightly misleading, since a majority holding would come within this category if the shares in question did not carry voting control, e.g. because extra votes attached to another class of shares.
   (2) They are not quoted.[155] Shares listed on the Alternative Investment Market (previously the Unlisted Securities Market) fall within this category.

Related conditions

There are two general rules, both of which must be satisfied: **29–119**

---

[154] See Ch.26.
[155] IHTA 1984 s.228(5).

(a) *Transferee bears tax.* The first general rule is that, by s.227(1)(b), relief is available only if the tax is borne by the person benefiting from the chargeable event. This is subject to two qualifications. First, this rule does not apply to transfers made on death. Secondly, by s.227(1)(c), where tax is due as a result of:

    (i) a transfer made on the termination of an interest in possession under s.52(1); or

    (ii) a periodic or an exit charge,

relief is also due so long as the shares continue to be comprised in the settlement in question.

(b) *Hardship.* The second general rule is that, by s.228(1), HMRC must be satisfied that the tax attributable to the shares or securities cannot be paid in one sum without *undue* hardship. For this purpose, it is assumed that the shares or securities concerned would be retained by the persons liable to pay the tax.[156] The meaning of "undue hardship" is unclear. The phrase was discussed in the parliamentary debates[157] on the CGT instalment option contained in s.40 of the CGTA 1979 (now the Taxation of Chargeable Gains Act 1992 s.280), some suggestion being made that it may be necessary to look only to the resources available to the taxpayer as a result of the chargeable event.[158] As was noted, HMRC's decision in this matter is final. This rule is subject to the qualification that in the case of a transfer made on death it suffices for purposes of this rule that the tax on the shares or securities in question and the tax on any other property qualifying for instalment relief for which the person paying the tax is liable in a given capacity comprises at least 20 per cent of the total tax for which he is liable in that capacity. Given this 20 per cent test, a person should take care to set charges against property which does not qualify for instalment relief, so that the amount of tax due from his personal representatives in respect of property which does qualify for relief may be maximised.[159]

Other minority holdings

29–120   By s.228(1)(d) and (3), shares (but not securities) come within this category if they satisfy the following conditions:

    (1) they did not give the transferor control of the company immediately before the chargeable event in question;

    (2) they are not quoted;

    (3) the amount of the value transferred which is attributable to the shares before any grossing up exceeds £20,000[160]; and

    (4) either:

        (a) their nominal value is at least 10 per cent of the nominal value of all the shares of company at the time of the chargeable event; or

        (b) the shares are ordinary shares and their nominal value is at least 10 per cent of the nominal value of all ordinary shares in the company at the time

---

[156] IHTA 1984 s.228(1)(c).
[157] *Hansard* Standing Committee E col.1544 (June 27, 1972).
[158] See para.29–137.
[159] IHTA 1984 s.228(2).
[160] IHTA 1984 s.228(3); the figure of £20,000 (£5,000 in relation to chargeable events before March 15, 1983) appears to be arrived at after any business relief.

of the chargeable event in question. "Ordinary shares" for this purpose are shares which carry either

(i) a right to dividends not restricted to dividends at a fixed rate, or
(ii) a right to conversion into shares carrying such a right.[161]

Related conditions

The general rule is that, by s.227(1)(b), relief is available only if the tax is borne by **29–121** the person benefiting from the chargeable event. This is subject to two qualifications. First, this rule does not apply to transfers made on death. Secondly, by s.227(1)(c), where tax is due as a result of:

(a) a transfer made on the termination of an interest in possession under s.52(1); or
(b) a periodic/exit charge,

relief is also due so long as the shares continue to be comprised in the settlement in question.

Businesses

By s.227(2)(c) and (7), it may be possible to pay by instalments so much of the tax **29–122** due on a chargeable transfer or a periodic/exit charge as is attributable to the "net value" of a business or an interest in a business. "Business" is the subject of a definition at once inclusive and exclusive: by s.227(7)(d), it includes a business carried on in the exercise of a profession or vocation, but excludes a business carried on otherwise than for gain. It must therefore be open to doubt whether the "business" of a hobby farmer whose principal goal is tax mitigation will qualify for relief. There is persuasive authority for the proposition that "business" is a word of wide import which must be given its ordinary meaning unless the context requires otherwise.[162] There is some authority for the view that a landlord who lets property with a view to making a profit from the rentals carries on a business for these purposes.[163] The business need not be carried on in the United Kingdom. HMRC accepts that tax payable in respect of a Lloyd's underwriting interest may be paid by instalments under this head.

For this purpose the value of a business is taken to be its net value,[164] which is the value of the assets used in the business (including goodwill) reduced by the aggregate amount of any liabilities incurred for the purposes of the business.[165] In ascertaining the net value of a business no regard is had to assets or liabilities other than those by reference to which the net value of the business would have falled to be ascertained if

[161] IHTA 1984 s.228(3) and (4); cf. the definition in ICTA 1988 s.832(1) of "ordinary share capital".
[162] See para.26–19.
[163] See para.26–19.
[164] IHTA 1984 s.227(7).
[165] IHTA 1984 s.227(7). In *Fetherstonaugh v IRC* [1984] S.T.C. 261 discussed at para.26–20, the majority of the Court of Appeal held that on the death of a sole trader who carried on his business on land held on the trusts of a settlement under which he had an interest in possession 50 per cent business relief was available on the land as well as the business on the basis that, by virtue of what is now s.49(1), the deceased owned the land, which he used in his business within the meaning of what is now s.110, the wording of which is identical to that in s.227(7). It is thought that the *Fetherstonaugh* case is not in point where the ability to pay tax by interest free instalments is concerned.

the tax had been attributable to the entire business.[166] These are important limitations on the ability to pay IHT by instalments in respect of a business or an interest in a business. Precisely the same rules apply for the purposes of determining the extent to which business relief is available in respect of a business and the reader is referred to the discussion at paras 26–81 and following.

Related conditions

29–123   The general rule is that, by s.227(1)(b), relief is available only if the tax is borne by the person benefiting from the chargeable event. This is subject to two qualifications. First, this rule does not apply to transfers made on death. Secondly, by s.227(1)(c), where tax is due as a result of:

(a) a transfer made on the termination of an interest in possession under s.52(1); or
(b) a periodic or an exit charge,

relief is available only so long as the business or interest continues to be comprised in the settlement in question.

Tax tip

29–124   It is interesting to note that while the rules governing the availability of business relief contain anti-avoidance provisions framed by reference to "excepted assets",[167] the rules governing the ability to pay IHT by instalments contain no such provisions. Accordingly, while instalment relief is usually available if business relief is available, in some cases—usually concerning shares in companies—instalment relief may be available even if business relief is not; see also Chapter 26.

Woodlands

29–125   It may be that tax due in respect of woodlands which has been deferred under s.125 becomes payable as a result of a disposal of the woodlands. Section 229 provides that if the disposal is itself a chargeable transfer the person paying the tax due in respect of that transfer may elect (in writing) to pay that tax by instalments: there are no related conditions. The deferred tax must in any event be paid six months after the end of the month in which the disposal was made.[168]

Due date for instalments

29–126   The first instalment is due in the case of a transfer made on death within six months after the end of the month in which the transfer was made.[169] An election to pay by

---

[166] IHTA 1984 s.227(7).
[167] See paras 26–58 and 26–88.
[168] IHTA 1984 s.229.
[169] IHTA 1984 s.227(3)(a).

instalments the tax due in respect of a death may be used to postpone the date when that tax would otherwise be paid and to relieve the personal representatives from the need to obtain loan finance in order to fund the tax. This is because a grant of probate will only be obtained when the relevant tax has been paid[170] and, accordingly, as the grant is usually obtained well within six months of the date of death, payment of tax is therefore accelerated. Further, a loan will often be required to fund that tax. By exercising the election to pay by instalments less tax (or, in appropriate cases, no tax) will need to be paid to obtain the grant.[171] The first instalment in any other case is due when the tax is normally due.[172] A person who has a right to recover the tax from someone else liable for the tax should bear in mind that he can recover it only in instalments, unless, of course, the other person agrees otherwise.[173]

Interest on instalments

Where tax can be paid by instalments the general rule is that the instalments are interest-free, i.e. that they carry interest only from the date on which any given instalment is due.[174] This rule always applies where the tax is attributable to property which qualifies for agricultural relief under s.116; to the extent that such tax can be paid by instalments, the instalments are always interest free.[175] The general rule does not apply to certain categories of land and shares, in which case the interest on the whole of the unpaid tax runs from the original due date for payment, the effect of the legislation being merely to legitimate late payment of tax. The fact that the taxpayer is entitled to pay by instalments in these cases is thus of relatively little benefit to him. The two cases in which the general rule does not apply are as follows.

29–127

Land

The general rule does not apply where the tax due is attributable to land, except in two cases. First, if instalment relief is available, the instalments will be interest-free if the land qualifies for agricultural relief. Secondly, if the land is a business asset, the tax will be attributable to the business; not the land, in which case the general rule will apply. Subject to these two qualifications, the position with regard to land is as follows. To begin with, s.227(3) provides that:

29–128

> "interest under s.233 below on the unpaid portion of the tax shall be added to each instalment and paid accordingly . . .",

but this does not indicate from what date the interest accrues. It is therefore thought that the governing provision is s.233, which provides that if an amount of tax is unpaid after the end of certain specified periods (mentioned below), that amount carries interest as from that date, with the result that instalment relief ceases to be so advantageous. Two periods are specified:

---

[170] See paras 29–27 and 29–33.
[171] See para.29–91 for a further reason why personal representatives should at least consider exercising the instalment option.
[172] IHTA 1984 s.227(3)(b); see paras 29–103 and 29–104.
[173] IHTA 1984 s.213.
[174] IHTA 1984 s.234(1)(a).
[175] IHTA 1984 s.234(1)(a) and (2).

(1) if the chargeable transfer was made after April 5 and before October 1, the period ends with April 30 of the next year; and

(2) in any other case, the period ends six months after the end of the month in which the transfer is made.

It appears to follow that in certain cases the first instalment will fall due before any interest has accrued. Once interest begins to accrue on the unpaid portion of the tax, it is added to each instalment and is payable accordingly.[176]

Shares in "investment" companies

29–129 By s.234(2) and (3), the general rule does not apply where the tax due is attributable to shares or securities of a company whose business consists wholly or mainly of:

(1) dealing in securities, stocks and shares;

(2) dealing in land or buildings; or

(3) the making or holding of investments.[177]

Similar rules apply for the purposes of business relief and many of the considerations that apply in relation to business relief[178] will also apply for purposes of instalment relief.[179] The question of whether or not a business consists wholly or mainly of making or holding investments has been considered in a number of cases concerning business relief; see paras 26–31 and following.

29–130 By s.234(2) and (3)(b) and (c), any company whose business (i) is wholly that of a market maker[180] or discount house and is carried on in the United Kingdom, or (ii) consists wholly or mainly in being a holding company (within the meaning of s.736 of the Companies Act 1985)[181] of one or more companies which are not investment companies is not an investment company for this purpose.

Requirement (ii) is presumably intended to ensure that shares in a holding company qualify for relief only if the business of the group *as a whole* is not investments. Whether the legislation always has this effect remains to be seen. Assume, for example, that a holding company has three small but expanding trading subsidiaries and one large investment subsidiary, the assets and income of which slightly exceed the aggregate assets and income of the trading companies; does the business of the holding company consist mainly in being the holding company of the trading subsidiaries or the investment company?

So far as the s.736 meaning of a holding company is concerned, that section provides that the relationship of a holding company and subsidiary exists between two companies if:

(1) the first company is a member of the second company and controls the composition of the Board of Directors of the second company; or

---

[176] IHTA 1984 s.227(3).

[177] Interest will accrue only from the date on which any given instalment is due to the extent that the share/securities qualified for agricultural relief.

[178] IHTA 1984 ss.105(3) and (4), and 112(2).

[179] See paras 26–31 and 26–81 and following.

[180] As defined in IHTA 1984 s.234(4); see para.14–49.

[181] Substituted by the Companies Act 2006 s.1159.

(2) the first company holds more than half in nominal value of the second company's equity share capital; or

(3) the second company is a subsidiary of a subsidiary of the first company.

For this purpose, a company's equity share capital means its issued share capital other than any part of that capital which carries no right to participate in dividends or capital beyond a specified amount in a distribution.[182] Participating preference shares thus rank in equity share capital for these purposes.

Some areas of difficulty

The rules governing the payment of tax by instalments are not free from difficulty. **29–131**
Note the following.

Agricultural land as a business asset

Where agricultural land is a business asset the question arises as to whether **29–132**
instalment relief is available only in respect of the transferor's business (of which the land is an asset), or whether it is also available, independently, in respect of the land. The point is an important one where, e.g. the land was purchased with borrowed money. If relief is available in respect of the business only, the restriction in s.227(7)(b) will apply, with the result that the borrowing will be taken into account in determining the value of the business. This will reduce the amount of tax which can be paid by instalments and thus by interest-free instalments. If, on the other hand, the relief is available in respect of the land, there will be no such restriction, and all the tax attributable to the land will qualify for interest-free instalment relief.

Assume for example, that X is a sole trader who farms land which he owns and which is shown in his accounts as a business asset. He borrows £500,000 on the security of non-business assets, e.g. quoted securities, and with this £500,000 he purchases additional land which he farms and which is also shown in his accounts as a business asset. Three years later he dies, with the borrowing still outstanding. At the time of his death his business is worth £1,300,000, of which £600,000 is attributable to the land which he purchased with the borrowed £500,000, £400,000 is attributable to the land which he originally owned, and £300,000 is attributable to stock, plant and machinery, etc. The £1 million attributable to the land qualifies for 50 per cent agricultural relief; the £300,000 attributable to stock, etc. qualifies for 50 per cent. business relief. The question arises as to how much of the tax attributable to the assets comprised in X's business will be payable by interest-free instalments.

It is clear that so much of the tax as is payable by instalments will be payable by interest-free instalments, either because the tax is attributable to the value of a business or because the tax is attributable to value reduced by agricultural relief. What is not clear, however, is how much of the tax will be payable by instalments in the first place. It is at this point that the key question emerges—where a sole trader dies owning land used in his business and shown in his accounts as a business asset can tax be paid by instalments only on the footing that the tax is attributable solely to the value of a business, or can some of it also be paid by instalments on the footing that it is attributable to the value of land?

[182] Companies Act 1985 s.744.

In the above example, given the £500,000 borrowing, the net value of the business will be only £800,000 with the result that, if tax is payable by instalments in respect of the business alone, only eight-thirteenths (800,000/1,300,000) of the tax will be payable by instalments. If, on the other hand, the land is relevant, then all of the tax payable in respect of the land will be payable by instalments. The net result will then be the 10/13ths of the tax will be payable by instalments. This follows from the fact that the entire value of the land will be brought into account, while the value of the other business assets (£300,000) will be extinguished by the £500,000 borrowing.

It was put to HMRC that the intention of the legislation was that tax which is attributable to value transferred which has been reduced by agricultural relief should be payable by interest-free instalments, and that where a sole trader owns as a business asset land qualifying for agricultural relief tax attributable to that land should, be capable of being paid by instalments on the basis of the business or the land. Unfortunately, they disagreed with this view, stating that this result was not intended. Relief, in their view, was given in respect of the business alone.

Lifetime transfers into trusts

29–133   Certain aspects of the rules regulating the payment of tax by instalments where property is transferred into trust need special attention. Section 227(1) provides that tax on a lifetime chargeable transfer can be paid by instalments only if either the tax on the transfer is borne by "the person benefiting from the transfer" or the transfer is made on the termination of an interest in possession and the property concerned continues to be comprised in the settlement. Three kinds of problems arise in relation to this requirement.

Transfers to discretionary trusts

29–134   The first problem concerns transfers to discretionary trusts. Assume, e.g. that X settles on discretionary trusts shares in circumstances such that if the transfer was made to an individual who bore the tax on it the tax would be payable by instalments. There appears to be no reason why the position should be any different if the tax is borne by the trustees of a discretionary trust, but as a matter of strict law there must be some doubt as to whether such trustees can be regarded as the "person benefiting from the transfer". One way of resolving this problem is to read the words "person benefiting from the transfer" as being synonymous with the words "the transferee of the transfer" so that instalment relief is available in respect of transfers to discretionary trustees in the same way as it is available to transfers to individuals. HMRC has indicated that they agree that the legislation should be read this way, and in practice they appear to apply it in this way.

Transfers to interest in possession trusts

29–135   The second problem concerns lifetime transfers to trusts in which there is an interest in possession. Who, if anyone, is the "person benefiting" from such a transfer? Even if the liberal statutory construction just suggested is adopted, it remains unclear whether the trustees or the person or persons with the interest or interests in possession under the trust are the person or persons benefiting from the transfer. The trustees and beneficiaries are both liable for the tax under s.199. In practice, the settlor normally makes the transfer on condition that the trustees, not the beneficiaries, bear any IHT due. It would thus appear reasonable, as a practical matter, to regard the trustees as the persons "benefiting" from the transfer, with the result that instalment relief will be available (assuming all the other relevant requirements are satisfied). If, on the other hand, the person with the interest in possession is regarded as the person benefiting from the transfer, it will be necessary for the transferor, the trustees and beneficiaries to enter into a novel, complicated and in practice probably unsatisfactory agreement if the relief is to be available. HMRC has indicated that they regard the trustees as the persons benefiting from the transfer whether the trust is discretionary or one in which there is an interest in possession, or, for that matter, hybrid, i.e. a trust under which some of the trust property is held on discretionary trusts and the rest on interest in possession trusts.

The £20,000/10 per cent requirement

The third problem concerns the conditions in s.228 establishing the kind of property **29–136** to which tax must be attributable if tax is to be payable by instalments. Section 228(1)(d) provides that tax attributable to the value of shares which (i) do not give the transferor control of the company immediately before the transfer, and (ii) were not quoted can be paid by instalments if, inter alia, two conditions stated in s.228(3) are satisfied. The first is that so much of the value transferred by the transfer as is attributable to the shares must exceed £20,000. The second is that either (i) the nominal value of the shares must be not less than 10 per cent of the nominal value of all the shares of the company at the time of the death, or (ii) the shares must be ordinary shares the nominal value of which is not less than 10 per cent of the nominal value of all the ordinary shares of the company at the time of the transfer. It is to be noted that the conditions set out in s.228(3) are framed by reference to the value transferred by the chargeable transfer in question. Where property is transferred to a trust in which there is more than one subsisting interest in possession the question accordingly arises as to whether the transferor has made one transfer to the trustees or one transfer to each of the persons having an interest in possession. Assume, for example, that X transfers shares to trustees of a trust fund under which A and B each have an interest in possession in half the trust fund. If the value transferred is £30,000, the question arises as to whether X has made two chargeable transfers of £15,000 each, in which case the first condition in s.228(3) will not be satisfied, or one chargeable transfer of £30,000, in which case that condition will be satisfied. The problem is solved (in the taxpayer's favour) if s.228(3) is construed in a manner consistent with the construction which it was suggested s.227(1) should be given, i.e. if X is regarded as having made one chargeable transfer to the trustees. HMRC has indicated that they agree that s.228(3) should be construed in this way.

It follows from this that it might be useful to interpose a trust when an individual wishes to make transfers to two or more individuals in circumstances such that the £20,000/10 per cent requirement:

(1) would be satisfied in relation to the shares transferred by all the transfers; but
(2) would not be satisfied in relation to any single transfer.

Assume, for instance, that in the example just given no trust fund was in existence and that X wished to transfer the shares to A and B. Gifts made directly to them would not qualify for instalment relief. If, on the other hand, X interposed a trust, the single transfer to the trustees would satisfy the conditions in s.228(3), and the trustees could subsequently advance the shares to A and B.[183] The interposition of the trust might in theory be disregarded under the *Ramsay* principle, depending on how long the property was retained in the trust.

Undue hardship

29–137   Section 228(1)(c) provides that tax on certain shares or securities of a company can be paid by instalments provided, inter alia, that the shares or securities are not quoted on a recognised stock exchange and that the tax attributable to their value cannot be paid in one sum without "undue hardship". Section 228(1)(c) provides that for this purpose the question whether the tax could be paid in one sum without undue hardship falls to be determined on the assumption that the shares or securities concerned would be retained by the persons liable to pay the tax. Given this statutory assumption, can it be argued successfully that where assets are transferred to trustees who have no other assets on condition that the trustees pay any IHT due it would be impossible for the trustees to pay the tax without undue hardship? Unfortunately, HMRC think not. On the subject of undue hardship, they have stated in a letter that:

> "... 'Hardship' in the context of a taxing statute plainly imports something more than liability to pay the tax, and the further requirement that the hardship should be 'undue' reinforces the view that it shall go substantially beyond the ordinary and indeed inevitable consequence of the taxable disposition under which the transferor intends to effect a net-of-tax gift. In those circumstances, the tax must ultimately be provided out of all or part of any gifted property comprised in the disposition and/or out of the transferee's other resources. The fact that a particular transferee's expectation of gratuitous benefit is diminished or conceivably extinguished does not ... necessarily constitute 'hardship,' much less 'undue hardship.'
>
> It follows that where the transferor and the *trustees*, with clear perception of all the fiscal and financial implications, set up a transfer under which the trustees deliberately and under professional advice commit themselves to a tax consequence which they can only meet by a sale or other dealing with the property transferred, this office would see no grounds on which it could recommend to the board that it should exercise its discretion to facilitate payment of the tax by instalments."

Limitations on availability of the relief

29–138   The legislation provides that tax which might otherwise be payable by instalments may not be so payable or may cease to be so payable if certain conditions are infringed. There are three separate rules, as follows.

Excess tax

29–139   It may be that the tax on a failed PET or the additional tax due on a transfer which was chargeable when it was made and which the transferor failed to survive by seven

---

[183] After making provision for the payment of the tax due.

years is prima facie payable by instalments. In that case, regard must be had to s.227(1A)–(1C), under which the ability to pay such tax is restricted unless at least one and, in certain cases, two conditions are satisfied.

The first condition is that the transferee owned the property in question throughout the period beginning with the transfer and ending with the earlier of the death of the transferor and the transferee.[184] Thus, if the transferee gives the property away or sells it, this condition will be infringed. This is subject to two comments. First, if the transferee sells the property and applies the whole of the consideration towards the purchase of replacement property which comes within s.113B or s.124B the relief will still be available.[185] This is rather lazy drafting: the draftsman should have included a new section dealing with replacements rather than relying on ss.113B and 124B. A proper provision would stipulate that the replacement property should qualify for instalment relief; why should it have to qualify for business or agricultural relief? Secondly, the definition of transferee[186] is such that difficulties identical to those mentioned at paras 26–106 and 26–107 may arise.

Unquoted shares and securities

29–140 Where the property is unquoted shares or unquoted securities, there is a further condition, namely that the shares or securities must remain unquoted throughout the period beginning with the date of the transfer and ending with the earlier of the death of the transferor and the transferee. This condition applies only in relation to transfers made after March 17, 1987.[187]

Commentary

29–141 Note that under the above limitation difficulties can arise only during the period while both the transferor and the transferee are alive. Thus, if, e.g. the transferor dies and the transferee sells the property, the above limitation will not apply. But the next limitation will.

Tax generally

29–142 By s.227(4), if any part of the property (other than woodlands) in relation to which an election has been made is sold, a proportionate part of the unpaid tax, together with any interest accrued, becomes payable "forthwith". This is so even if the sale occurs within the six months preceding the due date for the first instalment, except that in that case the unpaid tax is not due until the expiry of the six months. By s.227(6)(a), where the property is a business or an interest in a business, the sale of an interest or part of an interest in the business is treated as a sale of a corresponding part of the business. In certain cases, a transaction or event is treated as a sale. First, by s.227(6)(b), the payment under a partnership agreement or otherwise of any sum in satisfaction of the

[184] IHTA 1984 s.227(1C)(a).
[185] IHTA 1984 s.227(1C)(b).
[186] IHTA 1984 s.227(1B).
[187] IHTA 1984 ss.227(1A) and 228(3A); see the discussion at para.26–105.

whole or any part of an interest in a business, even if not on a sale, is treated as a sale of that part of the interest at the time of payment. Secondly, by s.227(5), where instalment relief has been given in respect of property on the footing that the tax is borne by the person benefiting from the transfer, any chargeable transfer (other than one made on death) or periodic/exit charge the value transferred by which is wholly or partly attributable to the value of the land, shares, securities or business is treated as a sale for these purposes. Where instalment relief has been given on the footing that the property continued to be comprised in a settlement, the property is treated as having been sold when it ceases to be so comprised. While the word "forthwith" has been given a stringent judicial construction in some contexts, it is thought that in practice it will suffice if tax due is paid within a reasonable time.

Commentary

29–143   It is understood that HMRC takes the view that relief under ss.227(1)(b) and (1)(c) are not mutually exclusive. This can be important in relation to losing or keeping the ability to pay tax by instalments. Assume that X dies and at the time of his death he owns, inter alia, a farm which he has for some time been farming in partnership with his widow. By his will he leaves the farm to his widow for life, remainder absolutely to his son, provided the son survives the widow. If he does not, the farm passes absolutely to X's nephew. This is a common state of affairs and a common testamentary provision.

Next, assume the widow assigns her life interest to her son, so that he has an absolute but defeasible interest in the farm. The widow makes a PET, and if she dies within seven years the son can elect to pay the IHT due by interest free instalments over 10 years as a result of the combined effect of ss.227(1) and (2)(c) and 234(1)(a), on the assumption that agricultural relief is available to the PET.

Four years later the widow dies, with the result that the property vests indefeasibly in the son, so that it ceases to be comprised in the settlement created by X's will. Again, an unexceptional event, and certainly not one which would reasonably be expected to have any adverse IHT consequences. Unfortunately, one reading of s.227 would result in the son being unable to pay by instalments the tax due in respect of the assignment by his mother of her life interest. This follows from s.227(4) and (5). Section 227(4) provides, inter alia, that if at any time all or any part of the property is sold, the tax outstanding at that time becomes payable forthwith. This provision is not in itself a cause for concern, but s.227(5)(b) provides that in a case within s.227(1)(c) property which ceases to be comprised in the settlement in question is to be treated as having been sold. The result, if s.227(1)(c) is the provision enabling the son to pay the tax due by instalments, is that he is deemed to have made a sale as a result of his becoming indefeasibly entitled on his mother's death, and so must pay "forthwith" the tax which would have otherwise been payable by instalments. It is understood that HMRC takes the view that in such a case it is permissible to read s.227(1)(b) as being the operative provision, with the result that the ability to pay the tax by instalments is not lost.

X. ACCEPTANCE OF PROPERTY IN SATISFACTION OF TAX

29–144   Section 230 provides that, on the application of any person liable to pay tax the Board may, if they think fit, and the Secretary of State[188] (hereafter referred to as "the

---

[188] The term covers all the Secretaries of State in the UK Government (used in s.230 of the National Heritage Act 1980).

Ministers") agree to accept in satisfaction of the whole or any part of the tax due (or the interest thereon) property[189] falling within one of the following four categories:

(1) *Land*. Land for this purpose includes buildings and other structures as well as land covered by water. The land need not have been the subject of a chargeable transfer or a periodic/exit charge, and may be accepted regardless of whether the liability in question arises in respect of real or personal property.

(2) *Associated objects*. Objects come within this category if they are or have in the past been kept in a building with which it appears to the ministers desirable for the object to remain associated if:

(a) HMRC have determined to accept or have accepted the building in satisfaction or part satisfaction of the tax or estate duty; or

(b) the building or any interest therein belongs to the Crown, the Duchy of Lancaster or The Duchy of Cornwall; or

(c) the building belongs to or is held for the purposes of a government department; or

(d) the building is one of which the Secretary of State is guardian under the Ancient Monuments and Archaeological Areas Act 1979; or

(e) the building is one of which the Department of the Environment for Northern Ireland is guardian under the Historic Monuments and Archaeological Objects (Northern Ireland) Order 1995; or

(f) the building belongs to any of the heritage bodies specified in Sch.3.[190]

(3) *Pre-eminent objects*. This category is comprised of any picture, print, book, manuscript, work of art, scientific object or other thing which the Ministers are satisfied is pre-eminent for its national, scientific, historic or artistic interest. For this purpose, "national interest" includes interest in any part of the United Kingdom and in determining whether an object or collection or a group of objects is pre-eminent, regard is had to any significant association of the object, collection or group with a particular place. Among the objects which have been accepted is the bulk of the manuscripts left by Henry Williamson, the author best known for his story *Tarka the Otter*; it is unusual for a modern author's manuscripts to be accepted, since only rarely will they be regarded as being of pre-eminent interest. Details of property accepted in lieu of tax were, up until 2009/10, published annually by the Museums, Libraries and Archives Council (MLA)[191] in their periodic report.

(4) *Collections*. This category is comprised of any collection or group of pictures, prints, manuscripts, works of art, scientific objects or other things if the Ministers are satisfied that the collection or group, taken as a whole, is pre-eminent for its national, scientific, historic, or artistic interest, "national interest" again including interest in any part of the United Kingdom.

The acquisition price is a matter for negotiation between HMRC and the taxpayer in question and although previously this used not to exceed the amount due, that is no longer the case (see para.27–20 for more details). The acceptance price can be based on the value of the property at the date of the offer or at the date of acceptance. If the offer date valuation is adopted HMRC may arrest the accrual of interest on any unpaid inheritance tax or estate duty from that date.[192] To calculate the acceptance price, the

---

[189] The property need not form part of the estate of the transferor or transferee.

[190] See para.3–53.

[191] On July 26, 2010 it was announced that the MLA would be abolished. Its functions were transferred on October 1, 2011 to the Arts Council England and the National Archives.

[192] IHTA 1984 s.233(1A)—HMRC's practice is to assume offers are made on the offer date bases, with attendant remission of interests, unless the offeror gives notice to the contrary.

normal practice is to deduct from the price that would otherwise have been payable, 75 per cent of the CGT and/or IHT that would have been payable on the sale, i.e. the vendor is offered an amount corresponding to the net amount after IHT of the object plus a "douceur" of his tax saving. The douceur for chattels has generally but not invariably been 25 per cent but for land, provided the land in question is of outstanding interest, 10 per cent. There is no douceur, however, if the land does not fall within this category. It is worth noting that these rates were introduced when tax levels were significantly higher than they are now and the benefits of taking up offers in lieu were therefore also greater. If the douceur were to be increased by, say, 20–30 per cent, vendors would have a greater incentive to make offers in lieu, thus potentially providing a greater number of acquisitions, but whether our museums and galleries would benefit from this, with higher acquisition costs, is arguable. However, recent guidance contained in para.11.27 of HMRC's memorandum, *Capital Taxation and the Naitonal Heritage* confirms that the douceur is now fixed at 25 per cent of the notional tax for chattels and 10 per cent for land.

Acceptance in lieu often yields the same financial advantage for the vendor as a private treaty sale. It may be more desirable, especially where objects which have a particularly close association with an historic building are concerned, since if such objects are accepted in lieu they may be allowed to remain in situ.

Procedure

29–145   Offers in lieu of tax should be made to HMRC. All such offers should be accompanied by full details of the property including an indication of its current market value. Normally three colour photographs (prints or transparencies) will be required. HMRC will consult with the Arts Council England[193] in respect of offers of chattels. Advice on the quality and valuation of the chattels is then obtained from experts so that Ministers can be advised on whether the offer should be accepted or not. For further details of the procedures for seeking advice and the criteria applied see the annual MLA Acceptance in Lieu Reports (up until 2009/10), the revised edition of HMRC's memorandum entitled *Capital Taxation and the National Heritage*[194] (previously IR67) (and paras 27–02 and 29–146 below). Offers of land or buildings are considered separately by the Department for Culture, Media and Sport in consultation with English Heritage, the Countryside Agency and English Nature, as well as the corresponding bodies in Scotland and Wales where appropriate. There will be no acceptance in lieu if the proposed recipient is wholly or almost entirely financed by central government. In such cases, the vendor would be invited to pursue a private treaty sale. Land and buildings will normally only be accepted if the offeror nominates a suitable and willing recipient such as the national park authorities or the local nature conservation trusts.

Once the above procedure has been completed, HMRC will be authorised to negotiate acceptance of the property in question up to a certain figure or instructed to reject the offer. Once agreement on value has been reached, the tax satisfied by the acceptance of the property is calculated. No relief is allowed for the taxpayer's costs.

Allocation of moveable objects will be decided by the Ministers who will consult with the Arts Council England on appropriate recipients. Applications are also invited from public museums or galleries and should be sent to the Acceptance in Lieu Panel

---

[193] Previously Resource: Museums, Libraries and Archives Council, The Council for Museums, Archives and Libraries and formerly the Museums & Galleries Commission.
[194] See Ch.11.

Secretariat at the Arts Council England (see the website for further details[195]). In the case of archives, the Historical Manuscripts Commissioner and Chief Executive of the National Archives advises on allocation. Some offers of property may be made conditional upon the property passing to a particular institution or remaining in situ where it has a significant association in a particular setting. In such cases, undertakings as to the care, maintenance and preservation of the object for the public benefit and sufficiency of public access will be required.

Treasury booklet

The Inland Revenue booklet IR67 (first published in December 1986) used to be the principal reference document in respect of Heritage Property. This is now out of print and following consultations between HMRC and various professional bodies (Heritage Group of Lawyers, Historic Houses Association and, prior to its abolition, the MLA) a revised edition of HMRC's comprehensive memorandum *Capital Taxation and the National Heritage*, was published on September 15, 2011. The memorandum supersedes booklet IR67 and other publications since then and covers legislative changes up until 2009. Other useful reference documents are the annual MLA Acceptance in Lieu Reports (the final report published was for the year 2009/10). Copies of the Acceptance in Lieu Reports can be found on the Arts Council England website.[196]

29–146

Property subject to conditional exemption

It may be that the property offered in satisfaction of tax is itself the subject of conditional exemption. In that case by Sch.5 paras 1(4) and 3(4), and s.32(4)(b), the disposal of the property to HMRC will not result in the loss of conditional exemption. Instead, the property will cease to be vulnerable to IHT.

29–147

Prior to 1998, the standard of objects which qualified as being of pre-eminent national, scientific, historic or artistic interest and which therefore could be accepted in lieu of tax, was very much higher than the standard applicable for conditional exemption. The same standard now applies to both (although it should be noted that the criteria for acceptance in lieu of tax are not always the same as those which apply for conditional exemption under s.30, for which see Chapter 21 and especially paras 27–04 and following). The pre-eminence test for objects must satisfy the test of pre-eminence in the context of a national, local authority or university collection (or through association, above).

Power to sell property

Under s.231, a person who has power to sell property in order to raise money for the payment of tax may agree with the Board for the property to be accepted in satisfaction of tax or interest on tax. Aside from the nature of the consideration and its receipt and application, such an agreement is treated for all purposes as a sale under that power. The fact that a person has only a power to sell property thus does not debar him from

29–148

[195] *http://www.artscouncil.org.uk* [Accessed October 10, 2012].
[196] See fn.94.

transferring property to the Board in satisfaction of tax or interest thereon. Again, such a transfer will not result in loss of conditional exemption.

Interest

29–149   As already noted, the transferor is offered a "douceur" of 25 per cent of the tax exemption (i.e. the item will be valued net of IHT plus 25 per cent of that IHT saved). Under such arrangements the offeror obtains the benefit of any rise in the value of the property between the date of the offer and its acceptance by HMRC but he has to pay interest on the unpaid IHT until that offer is accepted. Section 233(1A) provides that from March 18, 1987, taxpayers can continue on this basis *or* can elect for the value of the property to be taken at the date of the offer (thereby avoiding the payment of any interest but foregoing the benefit of any subsequent rise in the value of the property).

XI. RECOVERY OF TAX

29–150   Here six topics are relevant—notices of determination, the position where a question has been determined on the basis of a previous view of the law, legal proceedings, administrative action, certificates of discharge, and adjustments where there has been an underpayment or overpayment of tax. Each will be considered in turn.

Notices of determination

29–151   Once it appears to the Board that a transfer of value has been made, or a charge has arisen under the special charging provisions, they have power under s.221(1) to issue a written notice stating that they have determined certain matters relevant to the transfer or charge. Such a notice may also be issued where a claim is made by a taxpayer. The notice, which is given to any person who appears to be the transferor or the claimant or to be liable for any of the tax chargeable, must state the time within which and the manner in which appeal against a determination may be made. By s.258, a notice may be served by being:

(1) delivered to the person;
(2) left at his usual or last known place of residence; or
(3) posted to him at his usual or last known place of residence or business or employment.

Section 221(2) provides that the matters which may be stated in such a notice are all or any of the following:

(1) the date of the transfer or charge;
(2) the value transferred and the value of any property to which the value transferred is wholly or partly attributable;
(3) the transferor;
(4) the tax chargeable, if any, and the persons who are liable for the whole or part of it;

(5) the amount of any payment made in excess of the tax for which a person is liable and the date from which and rate at which tax or any repayment of tax overpaid carries interest; and

(6) any other matter that the Board think relevant for purposes of the tax.

The Board are entitled to determine these matters to the best of their judgment, unless the fact has been stated in an account or return, and the Board are satisfied that the account or return is correct, in which case the determination must be made in accordance with it.

Under s.221(5), a determination may be conclusive in either of two ways. First, unless there is an appeal it is conclusive against the person on whom it is served. If he lodges an appeal it may be varied by written agreement with the Board, or it may be varied or quashed on appeal. Secondly, where a notice has been served on the transferor specifying a determination of the amount chargeable on an occasion or a previous occasion, that determination is conclusive against the transferor who was notified of it and against any other person but only in so far as it is relevant to tax chargeable in respect of subsequent occasions. This is subject to any adjustment for any under/overpayment of tax on previous occasions. In addition it is to be noted that s.254(1) provides that a notice specifying a determination which can no longer be varied or quashed on appeal is sufficient evidence of the matters determined.

Determination of questions on previous view of the law

Under s.255, where a payment has been made and accepted in satisfaction of liability **29–152** for tax on a view of the law which at the time was generally received or adopted in practice, any question as to whether too little or too much tax has been paid or as to what was the right amount payable falls to be determined on the same view, and this is so notwithstanding the fact that, in the light of a subsequent legal decision or otherwise, the view on the basis of which the payment was made and accepted was or may have been wrong. This protects taxpayers and HMRC alike from the effects of court decisions or changes in practice which may transpire after a taxpayer's liability has been settled and discharged. It will be noted that s.255 applies only if the tax in question has been paid, and only where the view on which the payment was made and accepted was generally received or adopted in practice.[197] While the latter requirement is understandable, the requirement that tax must have been paid before s.255 can be invoked is unduly restrictive, and s.255 should be amended to provide that matters settled on an existing view of the law should not be capable of being reopened, regardless of whether or not tax has been paid. As matters stand, a taxpayer who has agreed with HMRC that he has no tax liability at all cannot rely on s.255 if HMRC subsequently changes their mind.

Legal proceedings

Section 242 provides that the Board cannot take any legal proceedings for the **29–153** recovery of any amount of tax or interest thereon which is due from a person unless:

(1) he and the Board have agreed the amount in writing; or

---

[197] See *Murray's Trustees v Lord Advocate* [1959] S.C. 400; T.R. 255; 38 A.T.C. 247.

(2) the amount has been specified in a notice of determination.

When an appeal under s.222 (see below) is pending against such a notice, the Board cannot take legal proceedings to recover the amount so specified other than such part of it as may be agreed in writing or specified in a further notice of determination as not being in dispute. If the taxpayer does not agree with the amount specified in the further notice he may, under s.242(3), appeal to the Special Commissioners, and this is so even though the principal appeal is about the value of land (where appeal lies to the Land Tribunal). Once an appeal under s.222 has been decided tax must be paid, whether or not a further appeal is made.

In *Powell v IRC*,[198] an appeal by personal representatives against notices of determination issued by HMRC in respect of a transfer of value which failed deemed to have been made on a death so that the notices of determination were upheld, the Special Commissioner commented[199]:

> "Finally I must record that Mr Grierson pointed to the unfairness to his clients of the statutory provisions requiring payment of tax on the failure of an appeal to this tribunal. I record that Mr Tidmarsh made it plain that it was the practice of the Revenue not to enforce payment in such circumstances where a notice of an appeal to the High Court was received. I assume that the Revenue will abide by that indication in the instant case should the personal representatives decide to appeal to the High Court."

Proceedings in Great Britain are governed by the Crown Proceedings Act 1947 (which applies in Northern Ireland as amended by the Northern Ireland (Crown Proceedings) Order 1981),[200] and, in England and Wales, the Civil Procedure Rules 1998, as amended. IHT proceedings will normally be brought in the High Court by the Board; they may be initiated, subject to the usual jurisdictional limits, in the county court by either party.

Under s.243, without prejudice to any other remedy, tax and interest can in Scotland be sued for and recovered in the sheriff court so long as the amount of tax and interest does not exceed the sum for the time being specified in s.35(1)(a) of the Sheriff Courts (Scotland) Act 1971. Secondly, under s.244 an officer of the Board authorised by the Board to do so can address the court in any proceedings for the recovery of tax or interest.

Administrative actions

29–154   The legislation makes special provision for property which is the subject of an administration action pending in the courts. By s.232, where proceedings are pending in any court for the administration of any property to the value of which any tax charged on a chargeable transfer or periodic/exit charge is attributable, the court is required to make provision out of any property in its possession or control for the payment of any of the tax (or interest thereon) which is attributable to the property and which remains unpaid.

Certificates of discharge

29–155   Section 239 provides for two kinds of certificate of discharge, each of which is considered below. By s.239(4), neither kind of certificate discharges any person from

[198] *Powell v IRC* [1997] S.T.C. (S.C.D.) 181.
[199] *Powell v IRC* [1997] S.T.C. (S.C.D.) 181 at 188.
[200] SI 1981/233.

tax in the case of fraud or failure to disclose material facts, nor does it affect any further tax that may be payable if any further property is later shown to have been included in the estate of a deceased person immediately before his death, any further tax that may be payable as a result of a deed of variation or a disclaimer,[201] or any further tax that may be payable by reason of too great an increase having been made under s.8A (transfer of unused nil rate band between spouses or civil partners) where the nil rate band maximum at the time of the survivor's death is to be treated as increased by the percentage in s.4. This is subject to the qualification that in so far as a certificate shows any tax to be attributable to the value of any property, it remains valid in favour of a purchaser (as defined in s.272) of that property who is without notice of any fact invalidating the certificate.

Certificates discharging property

By s.239(1), where a person liable for any tax on a chargeable transfer (or a periodic/ **29–156** exit charge) applies to the Board, the Board, if satisfied that the tax attributable to the value of property specified in the application has been or will be paid, *must* give a certificate to that effect if either:

(1) the chargeable transfer was made on death; or
(2) the transferor has died.

In any other case (HMRC practice is to consider only applications from trustees) the Board *may* give such a certificate, but need not do so. Section 239(3)(a) provides that a certificate, if granted, discharges the property in question from the Inland Revenue charge on its acquisition by a purchaser. It does not discharge the person liable, and it is not available to any person other than a person who is liable; a certificate is not available where no tax is chargeable and thus cannot be obtained to secure confirmation from HMRC that no charge has arisen, e.g. because a transfer is exempt. The certificate does not rank as a determination of value, either for lHT purposes or for purposes of s.274 of the Taxation of Chargeable Gains Act 1992. As might be expected, a certificate will not be issued lightly on the footing that tax *will* be paid. The most usual application of s.239(1) is to enable property subject to an Inland Revenue charge to be disposed of; in such cases where the property is registered land and notice of the Inland Revenue charge has been entered in the register, the appropriate form is now Form 31/61. Special forms are available in Scotland.

Certificates discharging property and persons

Section 239(2) provides that where tax is or may be chargeable on a transfer of value **29–157** or a periodic/exit charge,[202] any person who is or might be liable for the whole or part of the tax may apply to the Board for a certificate which certifies the amount of tax due or that no tax is chargeable. By s.239(3)(b), the certificate extinguishes any Inland Revenue charge for the tax in question and discharges all persons from any further

---

[201] The certificate therefore does not protect personal representatives against their contingent liability when tax is unpaid on a failed PET, additional tax remains unpaid on a chargeable lifetime transfer or when, as the result of a failed PET being discovered, extra tax becomes payable on the estate of a deceased.
[202] IHTA 1984 s.239(5).

claim for that tax. An application should normally be made on Form 30 (but see para.29–92 for comments on current practice). Two years must normally lapse from the chargeable event before an application can be made, though if the Board thinks fit to entertain earlier applications they may do so. In practice, early applications are entertained if the applicant believes that the amount of tax in question will not need to be adjusted. In the case of a transfer made on death, the applicant must deliver a full statement to the best of his knowledge and belief of all property included in the deceased's estate immediately before he died; in any other case, a full and proper account is required. As under s.239(1), the Board must give a certificate if the transfer was made on death or if the transferor has died; otherwise the issue of a certificate is at their discretion. The fact that s.239(2) refers to the liability of a person in connection with a transfer of value is anomalous, since liability arises in respect of chargeable transfers, not transfers of value. It does, however, perhaps inadvertently, underline the fact that under s.239(2) it is possible to secure confirmation that a transfer is partly or wholly exempt. This follows from the fact that it is possible to apply for confirmation that no tax is chargeable.

Failed PETs

29–158   The general principle is that a certificate under s.239(2) may be applied for at the end of two years from the relevant transfer of value (or earlier if the Board allow) by a person who is or might be liable for the whole or part of the tax. Obviously this provision needs amendment in the case of PETs, since, as has already been noted, they are presumed to be exempt at the time when they are made and are clawed into charge only if the transferor dies within seven years. Accordingly, s.239(2A) provides that a certificate in respect of a PET may not be applied for until two years after the transferor has died unless the Board allow an application at an earlier time after the death.

Adjustments

29–159   It may be that too little or too much tax has been paid under the main or the special charging provisions. In that case, the position is as follows:

Underpayment

29–160   Where too little tax has been paid, s.240(1) provides that the tax under-paid is payable with interest, regardless of whether or not the amount already paid was stated in a notice of determination. This is subject to the qualification that where tax attributable to the value of any property is paid in accordance with an account delivered to the Board, and the payment is made and accepted in full satisfaction of the tax in question, no proceedings can be brought for the recovery of any additional tax attributable to the value of that property after the expiry of certain time limits, as follows:

(1) in the case of fraud, wilful neglect or default, proceedings cannot be brought more than six years later than the fraud, wilful neglect or default comes to the knowledge of the Board[203];

[203] IHTA 1984 s.240(3).

(2) in any other case, proceedings cannot be brought more than six years from the later of:
  (a) the date on which payment (in the case of tax paid by instalments, the last payment) was made and accepted; or
  (b) the date on which the tax or the last instalment fell due.

On the expiry of the above periods both liability for any additional tax and the Inland Revenue charge are therefore extinguished.[204]

The rule concerning fraud, wilful neglect or default applies not only to the fraud, wilful neglect or default of a person liable for the tax but also, in the case of discretionary trusts, to that of a person who is the settlor in relation to the settlement in question.

Overpayment

Section 241 provides that where a taxpayer proves to the Board's satisfaction that **29–161** too much tax or interest has been paid in respect of a chargeable transfer or a periodic/exit charge, the Board must repay the excess unless the claim for repayment was made more than six years after the date on which the payment or last payment was made. By s.235, any such repayment carries interest from the date on which the payment was made. Assessments which lead to repayments of overpaid tax are not initiated automatically by HMRC if the amount involved is £25 or less.[205] This, of course, is an administrative practice only and does not prevent a taxpayer from claiming back any overpaid tax to which he may be entitled.

XII. APPEALS

Section 222 provides that a person on whom a notice of determination has been **29–162** served may appeal against any determination specified in the notice. He must do so in writing within 30 days of being served, and must specify the grounds of his appeal. Under s.223, an appeal may be brought out of time with the consent of either HMRC or, under the new tax appeals system introduced on April 1, 2009, the Tax Tribunal (to whom an appeal now lies, see below). Consent must be given where an application is made and HMRC are satisfied that:

  (1) there was a reasonable excuse for not appealing within 30 days; and
  (2) the application to bring a late appeal was made without reasonable delay.

If HMRC are not satisfied, they must refer the application to the tribunal for determination.

It has been argued that an appeal under s.222 amounts to a determination of civil rights and obligations within the meaning of art.6(1) of the Convention for the Protection of Human Rights and Fundamental Freedoms 1950 in Pt 1 of Sch.1 to the Human Rights Act 1998 but it has been held that this is not the case and accordingly The European Convention on Human Rights does not provide the taxpayer with grounds to attack such appeals under s.222 on the basis of procedural issues such as,

---

[204] IHTA 1984 s.240(1) and (2).
[205] SP6/95.

e.g. whether the hearing is conducted within a reasonable time and by an independent and impartial tribunal.[206]

Venues

29–163   As stated above, from April 1, 2009, appeals must be made to the Tax Tribunal. The Tax Tribunal was established by the Transfer of Tribunal Functions and Revenue and Costs Appeals Order 2009, and replaces the Special Commissioners who previously heard appeals on tax matters. The Tax Tribunal has two tiers. The First-Tier Tribunal hears appeals against any decision of HMRC and the second tier, or the Upper Tribunal, hears appeals from decisions of the First Tier Tribunal. These tribunals (unlike the Special Commissioners) are entirely independent of HMRC and are part of the Ministry of Justice.

All appeals must now be made to the First Tier Tribunal. However, this is subject to three qualifications as set out in s.222(3)(a) and (b) which allow appeals to be made elsewhere. First, if the appellant and the HMRC agree, then the appeal may be heard by the High Court instead. Secondly, the appellant may apply to the High Court to have his case heard by that court rather than the First Tier Tribunal, in which case it must be so heard if the court is satisfied that the matters to be decided on the appeal are likely to be substantially confined to questions of law, and gives leave for that purpose. However, in *Bennett v IRC*[207] the taxpayer appealed against the Notice of Determination to the High Court under the procedure set out in s.222(3)(b). Whilst not agreeing with this HMRC left it to the Court to decide the matter and Lightman J. identified two factors to be considered in such cases:

(1) the need for special circumstances if an appeal to the Special Commissioners [now the First Tier tribunal] were to be bypassed. He confirmed that it was not enough for the appeal to be substantially confined to questions of law; and

(2) there will be cases where the interests of justice require that leave to be given, notably where the issue because of its novelty or importance or otherwise should go to the High Court.

He commented:

"This appeal is an exceptional case meriting the grant of leave. This issue is a short but important one of law. There is no authority on the meaning of s.21 which is a section of far reaching application. Neither party would leave the matter at the stage of decision of the Special Commissioners. A leap-frog to the High Court saves the time of the Special Commissioners and delay to the parties and the costs of the hearing before the Special Commissioners which in relation to the sums involved must be substantial. A hearing before the Special Commissioners would serve no useful purpose and the issue of law merits the immediate attention of the High Court."[208]

Conversely, in *Starke v IRC*,[209] Blackburne J. appears to have regarded it as sufficient that he was satisfied that the issue was substantially confined to a question of law.

Thirdly, s.222(4) and (4B) provide that an appeal on any question as to the value of land must be made to the Upper Tribunal if the land is in England and Wales, or to the

---

[206] *Taylor v IRC* [2003] S.T.C. (S.C.D.) 254. For a general discussion on human rights and inheritance tax, see Ch.31.
[207] *Bennett v IRC* [1995] S.T.C. 54; see para.3–14.
[208] *Bennett v IRC* [1995] S.T.C. 54 at 57.
[209] *Starke v IRC* [1995] 1 W.L.R. 1439.

Lands Tribunal for Scotland or Northern Ireland if the land is in Scotland or Northern Ireland. The Transfer of Tribunal Functions Order 2009 transferred the role from the Land Tribunal of England to the Upper Tribunal as of April 1, 2009.

The purpose of referring questions of the valuation of land to a separate tribunal is to avoid the need to submit a fresh appeal against the determination of the First Tier Tribunal on the basis of a disputed land valuation. This problem arose in *Gray v IRC*[210] where the question was in part one of law (was it possible to lot together land and personalty?) and in part a valuation of land. In the result, the Lands Tribunal of England (now the Upper Tribunal) assumed jurisdiction, although the correctness of this was open to question. Accordingly, it will be sensible in cases where a valuation of land is involved (albeit not as the only issue in the appeal) to proceed by way of appeal to the First Tier Tribunal who can then, as appropriate, refer matters to the Upper Tribunal or the Lands Tribunal of Scotland or Northern Ireland. An appeal from a decision of the Lands Tribunal lies by way of case stated to the Court of Appeal.[211]

Procedure before the Tax Tribunal

This is governed by the First Tier Tribunal (Tax) Rules 2009. These regulations are **29–164** in turn supplemented by an 'explanatory leaflet' issued by the Ministry of Justice. The content of these regulations is not reproduced in full here, and therefore it is recommended to anyone appearing before the First Tier Tribunal to consult these regulations as these now largely supersede the case law on procedure which had accumulated under the Special Commissioner's procedure. For procedure on statutory appeals generally, see s.2 of the practice direction to Pt 52 of Civil Procedure Rules 1998, as amended.

In order to begin proceedings a Notice of Appeal must be completed. Once the appeal is submitted it will be placed into one of four categories—Default Paper, Basic, Standard or Complex. There is a different procedure for each category. Default Paper cases will be decided by the tribunal after reading the Notice of Appeal and any supporting written material submitted by the applicant or HMRC. Such cases are usually dealt with without a hearing although applicants, or HMRC, may request one and the tribunal has the discretion to grant this request. The tribunal will notify HMRC that an appeal has been made. HMRC then has 42 days to submit a Statement of Case to the tribunal. The applicant may then provide a written response to the HMRC's Statement of Case within 30 days. The tribunal will then send a written response with their final decision.

In the Basic category, cases are dealt with by way of an informal hearing. In such cases there is no requirement for HMRC to produce a Statement of Case. Both the appellant and HMRC are expected to attend the hearing and will be given the opportunity to put forward their case to the tribunal. The tribunal make their decision at the end of the hearing.

The majority of appeals fall within the Standard or Complex categories. In such cases, once the Notice of Appeal has been submitted to the tribunal, HMRC has 60 days to provide a Statement of Case. The applicant will then have 42 days from receipt of the Statement of Case to provide the tribunal and HMRC with the list of documents upon which they intend to rely. HMRC must produce a similar list of documents. The tribunal may make other case management directions prior to the hearing. The hearing

---

[210] *Gray v IRC* [1994] S.T.C. 360; see para.25–27.
[211] Following *CIR v Arkwright and Sellars* [2004] EWHC 1720 (Ch) points on interpretation of the law should be brought before the Special Commissioners rather than the Lands Tribunal.

will take place at the most local tax tribunal for the appellant, and the tribunal will then make their order at the hearing.

In most appeals, the burden of proof is on the appellant. As such it is up to the appellant to show why HMRC are incorrect; however, in cases involving penalties, the burden of proof is on HMRC who must satisfy the tribunal that the penalty has been correctly imposed.

Appeals to the Upper Tribunal can only be made where leave to appeal has been granted. Leave is only granted where there are grounds to believe that an error of law has been made. This includes the incorrect application of procedural rules as well as of the substantive law. Such applications must be made within 56 days of the date the tribunal made the order.

A judge of the First Tier Tribunal will consider an application for permission to appeal. If the judge refuses permission to appeal then the appellant can apply directly to the Upper Tribunal for permission. Alternatively, if an applicant believes that there has been an irregularity in the arrangements for dealing with an appeal, they may apply to the First Tier Tribunal for the decision to be set aside. Such applications must be made within 28 days. Such irregularities could be procedural or relate to the admissibility of evidence.

Procedure before the High Court

29–165   Where an appeal lies directly to the High Court, procedure is governed by the Civil Procedure Rules 1998, as amended and, in particular, s.II of the practice direction to Pt 52 (previously O.91, r.2 of the Rules of the Supreme Court). The appellant's notice of appeal in the prescribed form must be served within 30 days of the date on which the appellant gave notice of appeal (or on which leave to appeal out of time was given). An appeal from a decision of the High Court lies to the Court of Appeal and then to the House of Lords.

Procedure before the Lands Tribunals

29–166   This is governed by rules of the respective Lands Tribunals, under the Lands Tribunal Act 1949, which have their own particular rules which should therefore be consulted as necessary.

Internal review procedure

29–167   HMRC introduced a new internal review process on April 1, 2009. This aims to give taxpayers a fast and efficient way to request HMRC to reconsider their appealable tax decisions without incurring the cost of the tax tribunal. HMRC's aim is to make it as easy as possible for taxpayers, particularly those without an accountant or other agent, to challenge an appealable decision and thus it is one of the most important tools available to a taxpayer. Reviews are optional and are undertaken by a trained review officer who has not previously been involved with the decision of the particular case and who in the majority of cases, HMRC advises, will be outside the immediate management chain of the decision maker. Reviews have to be completed within 45 days (unless a different period is agreed with the taxpayer). If the taxpayer does not want a review, or rejects the result of the review, they can appeal to the relevant tax tribunal for a decision.

XIII. PENALTIES

In order to ensure the effective collection of tax the legislation imposes a number of penalties to encourage prompt and accurate reporting. Under ss.245–248, a penalty may be incurred in six cases.

29–168

At the risk of appearing repetitious, the following discussion is divided up into several parts, on the basis of the statutory provisions, so as to spell out exactly the way penalties apply in particular circumstances.

Failure to deliver accounts, provide information or documentation

By s.245, a person who fails to deliver an account under s.216 or s.217 is liable:

29–169

(1) to a penalty of £100[212];
(2) to a further penalty not exceeding £60 a day if the failure continues after it has been declared by a court or the Tax Tribunal, the period ceasing the day before the account is delivered;
(3) to a further penalty of £100[213] if the proceedings in which the failure could be declared are not commenced within six months of the end of the period given by s.216(6) or (7) or 217,[214] whichever is applicable, and the account is not delivered by the end of that period; and
(4) to a further penalty not exceeding £3,000[215] if the failure to deliver the account continues after the anniversary of the end of the period given by s.216(6) or (7), whichever is applicable, and there would have been a liability to tax shown in the account.

The above is subject to three restrictions:

(a) the total penalty under (1) and (3) above shall not exceed the maximum tax liability proved by the taxpayer;
(b) a taxpayer who delivers the required amount before commencement of proceedings is not liable to a penalty under (2) above; and
(c) a person who has a reasonable excuse for failing to deliver an account shall not be liable to any penalty above unless he fails to deliver the account without unreasonable delay after the excuse has ceased.

---

[212] IHTA 1984 s.245(2)(a) as amended by FA 2004, where the relevant period under ss.216(6) or (7) or 217 expires after six months from July 22, 2004.
[213] IHTA 1984 s.245(3) as amended by FA 2004, where the relevant period under ss.216(6) or (7) or 217 expires after six months from July 22, 2004.
[214] See paras 29–06 and 29–08.
[215] IHTA 1984 s.245(4A) as inserted by FA 2004, where the relevant period under s.216(6) or (7) expires after July 22, 2004; where the relevant period expires on or before July 22, 2004, the penalty does not apply until 12 months after July 22, 2004.

Previously, the penalties listed at (1) and (2) above were of a maximum of £50 and £10 respectively and, more recently, the fixed penalties under (1) and (3) above were of an amount not exceeding, rather than a fixed amount of, £100.

Failure to make a section 218 return or comply with a section 219 notice

29–170   By s.245A(1) and (2), a person who fails to make a return under s.218 (see para.29–62, regarding the provision of information as to the making of an overseas trust) or fails to comply with a notice under s.219 (see paras 29–54 and following, regarding the provision of general information to HMRC) shall be liable:

    (1) to a penalty of up to £300; and
    (2) to a further penalty not exceeding £60 a day if the failure continues after it has been declared by a court or the Tax Tribunal, the period ceasing the day before the return is made or the notice is complied with.

The above is subject to two restrictions:

    (a) a taxpayer who makes the return or complies with the notice above before commencement of proceedings is not liable to a penalty under (2) above; and
    (b) a person who has a reasonable excuse for failing to make a return or comply with a notice shall not be liable to any penalty above unless he fails to make the return or comply with the notice without unreasonable delay after the excuse has ceased.

Previously, the penalties listed at (1) and (2) above were of a maximum of £50 and £10 respectively.

Failure to comply with a section 219A notice

29–171   By s.245A(3), a person who fails to comply with a notice under s.219A(1) or (4) (regarding the provision to produce documents or copy documents to HMRC—see para.29–56) shall be liable:

    (1) to a penalty of up to £50; and
    (2) to a further penalty not exceeding £30 a day if the failure continues after it has been declared by a court or the Tax Tribunal, the period ceasing the day before the notice is complied with.

The above is subject to two restrictions:

    (a) a taxpayer who complies with the notice above before commencement of proceedings is not liable to a penalty under (2) above; and
    (b) a person who has a reasonable excuse for failing to comply with a notice shall not be liable to any penalty above unless he fails to comply with the notice without unreasonable delay after the excuse has ceased.

Failure to deliver instrument of variation and notify additional tax

29–172   By s.245A(1A) (inserted by the Finance Act 2002 s.120(3), (4) with effect for instruments made after July 31, 2002) and (1B), a person who fails to comply with the requirements of s.218(A) (inserted by the Finance Act 2002 s.102(2), (4) with effect for instruments made after July 31, 2002) (information to be reported regarding instruments varying dispositions on death—see para.29–53) shall be liable:

(1) to a penalty of up to £100;
(2) to a further penalty not exceeding £60 a day if the failure continues after it has been declared by a court or the Tax Tribunal, the period ceasing the day before the requirements are complied with; and
(3) to a further penalty not exceeding £3,000 if the failure to comply with the requirements of s.218A continues after the anniversary of the end of the period of six months referred to in s. 218A(1).[216]

The above is subject to two restrictions:

(a) a taxpayer who complies with the requirements before commencement of proceedings is not liable to a penalty under (2) above; and
(b) a person who has a reasonable excuse for failing to comply with the requirements of s.218A shall not be liable to any penalty above unless he fails to comply with those requirements without unreasonable delay after the excuse has ceased.[217]

Fraudulent or negligent delivery by a person liable for tax

Under s.247, a person liable for any tax on a chargeable transfer or a periodic or exit charge who fraudulently or negligently[218] delivers, furnishes or produces to the Board any incorrect account, information or document, is liable to a penalty not exceeding the difference between the amount of tax for which he is actually liable, and any other person is liable by virtue of the operation of s.8A (transfer of nil rate band between spouses or civil partners), and the amount of tax for which he would be liable if the information supplied by him were correct.[219]   **29–173**

Fraudulent or negligent delivery by a person not liable for tax

By s.247(3), a person not liable for any tax on a chargeable transfer or a periodic/exit charge who negligently or fraudulently delivers, furnishes or produces to the Board any incorrect account, information or document is liable to a penalty not exceeding   **29–174**

---

[216] IHTA 1984 s.245A(1B) inserted by FA 2004, where the period of six months referred to in s.218A(1) expires after July 22, 2004; where the said period expires on or before July 22, 2004, the penalty does not apply until 12 months after July 22, 2004.

[217] IHTA 1984 s.245A(5), as amended by FA 2004, where the period of six months referred to in s.218A(1) expires after July 22, 2004.

[218] For these purposes, "negligence" is given an extended meaning: s.248(1) provides that if after any account, information or document has been delivered, furnished or produced by any person without fraud or negligence it comes to his notice that it was incorrect in any material respect, it shall be treated for these purposes as having been negligently delivered, furnished or produced, unless the error is remedied without unreasonable delay.

[219] As amended by FA 2004, with effect for accounts, information and documents delivered as from July 23, 2004.

£3,000.[220] The differentation between negligence and fraud under this head has now been removed so that there is now the single penalty only.

Assisting

29–175   By s.247(4), any person who assists in or who induces the delivery, furnishing or production of any account, information or document which he knows to be incorrect is liable to a penalty of up to £3,000 (formerly £500).

Failure of third party to inform HMRC of error

29–176   By s.248(2), if after any account, information or document has been delivered, furnished or produced by any person it comes to the notice of any other person that it contains an error whereby tax for which the latter is liable has been or might be underpaid, he must inform HMRC of the error; if he fails to do so without unreasonable delay, he is liable to a penalty as if he had himself delivered, furnished or produced the account, information or document and had done so negligently.

Failure to appear or respond before the Tax Tribunal

29–177   By s.7(3) of the Tribunal Procedure (First-Tier Tribunal) Rules 2009, the First Tier Tribunal has power to refer matters to the Upper Tribunal, and ask the Upper Tribunal to exercise its powers under s.25 of the Tribunals, Courts and Enforcement Act 2007. The Upper Tribunal has all the powers of the High Court in respect of the attendance and examination of witnesses and the production and inspection of documents. A failure to comply with an order of the Upper Tribunal will be contempt of court and as such the tribunal has a wide discretion to impose a fine and even, although unlikely, to commit the offender to prison.

Mitigating factors

29–178   The Revenue leaflet IHT13 "Inheritance Tax Penalties" which was withdrawn on March 31, 2006, and has now been replaced by the "Customer Guide to Inheritance Tax" on the HMRC wesbite, made reference to various mitigating factors to which the Revenue may still have regard, such as disclosure, co-operation and gravity, which may lead to substantial discounts. For example, the following reductions on penalties may be given:

- for disclosure—up to 20 per cent (or up to 30 per cent for full and voluntary disclosure);
- for co-operation—up to 40 per cent; and

[220] As above.

1094

- for gravity—up to 40 per cent.

Practitioners should consult the HMRC website for information on these points.

A wake up call

The new penalty increases are substantial and, in fraud cases, such increases must be **29–179** welcomed. However, the new approach being taken by HMRC must cause all practitioners to follow published HMRC guidance as closely as possible by submitting their accounts only after careful and thorough investigation, to minimise the risks of having penalties imposed. The HMRC website referred to above provides guidance generally in this area and practitioners should consult it if only to alert themselves to the possible pitfalls.

HMRC has admitted[221] that their compliance teams are now taking a more assertive approach where fraud and negligence are concerned since the legislation introduced tougher provisions in 1999. HMRC's aim is, on their own admission, to concentrate on serious negligence or fraud. Thus, whilst penalties in individual cases may be higher, HMRC may be seeking to impose them on fewer occasions. Additionally, the consequences of the Human Rights Act are such that HMRC are now required to advise taxpayers about the penalty process as soon as possible after they consider that a penalty might be an issue. HMRC has therefore standardised their initial letter to make it clear that it is a letter of enquiry only and not a notification of an immediate claim to a penalty.[222]

A section of the HMRC IHT & Trusts Newsletter of April 2008 on penalties is to be noted. It states:

> "FA 2007 legislated a new single penalty regime for incorrect returns for income tax, capital gains tax and other taxes. The Finance Bill 2008 contains legislation to extend those provisions and create a single penalty regime for all incorrect returns across all the taxes, levies and duties administered by HMRC—and this includes IHT.
>
> The proposals include a provision enabling HMRC to levy a penalty on a third party who deliberately provides false information to, or deliberately witholds information from, the taxpayer. In an IHT context, an example may be where the donee of a lifetime gift from someone who has died, deliberately witholds information about the gift from the personal representative, causing them to deliver an incorrect account that understates the amount of IHT due. The amount of the penalty would be calculated in the same way as if payable by the taxpayer.
>
> The new provisions will have effect from a date to be appointed by Treasury Order. It is expected that the new provisions will cover errors on returns for periods commencing on or after 1 April 2009 where the return is due to be filed on or after 1 April 2010."

Award of penalties

Under s.249, the responsibility for commencing proceedings for the recovery of **29–180** penalties lies with the Board, except that in Scotland it lies with the Board or the Lord Advocate. (Exceptionally, as mentioned above, penalties may be awarded summarily

---

[221] See Inland Revenue IHT Newsletter, August 2004.
[222] For a general discussion of human rights in the context of inheritance tax, see Ch.31.

by the Tax Tribunal.) Section 250 provides that the limitation period for such proceedings is three years from the date on which the amount of tax properly payable in respect of the chargeable transfer or periodic/exit charge was notified by the Board to the person or anyone of the persons liable for the tax or any part of it. Where a person who has incurred a penalty has died, any proceedings for its recovery which have been or could have been commenced against him may be continued or commenced against his personal representatives; any penalty awarded in proceedings so continued or commenced is a debt due from him and payable out of his estate. The Board are not bound to institute proceedings to recover a penalty,[223] and s.253 gives the Board a discretion to mitigate any penalty, or to stay or compound any proceedings for the recovery of the penalty, or, after the judgment, to mitigate further or remit entirely the penalty in question.

Proceedings may be commenced before the Tax Tribunal or in the High Court. For details of the procedure before the Tax Tribunal see para.29–164. By s.252, any penalty awarded by the tribunal is recoverable as a debt due to the Crown. An appeal lies from a decision of the First Tier Tribunal to the Upper Tribunal and then to the High Court. Either party to the proceedings can appeal on a point of law; only the defendant/defender may appeal against the amount of any penalty awarded. An appeal against the amount of penalty should not be made lightly: the court has power to increase the amount of the penalty (up to the statutory limit) as well as to reduce or confirm it. Where proceedings are brought in the High Court, they are deemed to be civil proceedings by the Crown within the meaning of Pt II of the Crown Proceedings Act 1947 (or that part of the 1947 Act as may be for the time being be in force in Northern Ireland).

---

[223] IHTA 1984 s.260.

NEW ANTI-AVOIDANCE MEASURES

PART A

DISCLOSURE OF TAX AVOIDANCE SCHEMES FOR INHERITANCE TAX

I. INTRODUCTION: THE DOTAS FRAMEWORK

Provisions for the disclosure of tax avoidance schemes ("DOTAS") first became a **30–01** feature of our tax system by enactment in 2004. The DOTAS code, i.e. the rules and framework by which DOTAS is applied are contained in FA 2004 ss.306–319. These provisions set out the definitions for terms used in DOTAS as well as the framework within which the DOTAS operates. The framework provisions are supplemented by regulations contained in secondary legislation and by detailed guidance entitled: *Guidance: Disclosure of Tax Avoidance Schemes* ("the Guidance"). At the time of writing, the Guidance was last updated in February 2012 and is stated as having effect from April 6, 2011.

The purpose of the DOTAS provisions is to ensure that HMRC receive detailed information about tax avoidance schemes which take advantage of loopholes in legislation almost as soon as steps are taken to implement schemes, or shortly after schemes are proposed. This enables HMRC and the Treasury either to challenge the schemes by technical argument and assessment where they do not consider the scheme to be technically sound, or more often than not, to enact legislation to block loopholes and to do so much sooner than would otherwise be the case: there can be a delay of up to two years (or more in the case of inheritance tax), between the implementation of a scheme and the filing of a tax return which may, depending on the quality of the disclosure, put HMRC on notice.

30–02   Although a detailed discussion of the general DOTAS rules and their application is outside the scope of this work, the salient features are outlined here in brief. Broadly, the regime imposes a duty to disclose "notifiable arrangements" (i.e. arrangements which fall within any description prescribed by the Treasury by regulations which enable tax advantages to be obtained).[1] It sets out what information must be disclosed and by whom it must be disclosed, and it also sets out the consequences of failure to comply with the requirements of the regime.

30–03   (1) **The duty to disclose**—in general this falls on the "promoter" (which is defined to include introducers),[2] but may also fall on others, including the client in limited circumstances.[3] It is only necessary to disclose the same scheme once.[4]

(2) **Time limit for disclosure**—the arrangement must be notified within five days beginning with the day after the promoter: (i) makes a firm approach to another person to make the scheme available for implementation; (ii) makes a scheme available for implementation by another person; or (iii) become aware of a transaction forming part of the scheme.[5]

(3) **Form of disclosure**—detailed provisions set out what information must be disclosed. There are four prescribed forms available for this purpose,[6] which one is used will depend on whether there is a promoter or an offshore promoter or no promoter.

(4) **HMRC information powers**—by an application to the First-tier Tribunal, HMRC are able to apply for an order that: (i) an arrangement must be disclosed under the DOTAS rules[7]; (ii) a promoter provides further information or documents[8]; (iii) the promoter explains why he considers the scheme to be non-disclosable[9]; and (iv) the arrangement be disclosed.[10]

(5) **Sanctions for non-disclosure**—penalties governed by TMA 1970 s.98C (as amended by FA 2007 and FA 2010) apply if there is a failure to disclose an arrangement.

30–04   DOTAS was introduced in FA 2004 in respect of direct taxes only, but was subsequently extended to VAT, SDLT and NICs, and most recently has been extended to Inheritance Tax, with effect from April 6, 2011. At the time of writing, the rules governing DOTAS as it applies to inheritance tax are contained in secondary legislation introduced under FA 2004 s.306, namely:

(1) the Inheritance Tax Avoidance Schemes (Prescribed Descriptions of Arrangements) Regulations 2011[11]; and

---

[1] Whether a scheme was notifiable was considered in *Commissioners of Revenue and Customs v Mercury Tax* [2009] S.T.C. (S.C.D.) 743.

[2] FA 2004 s.308. "Promoter" is defined in FA 2004 s.307.

[3] FA 2004 ss.309, 310.

[4] FA 2004 s.308(5).

[5] FA 2004 s.308(2).

[6] Go to *http://www.hmrc.gov.uk* [Accessed October 10, 2012]; and see para.17.4 of the Guidance.

[7] FA 2004 s.306A.

[8] FA 2004 s.308A.

[9] FA 2004 s.313A.

[10] FA 2004 s.314A.

[11] SI 2011/170.

(2) the Inheritance Tax Avoidance Schemes (Information) (Amendment) Regulations 2011.[12]

II. THE IHT DOTAS RULES

Regulation 2 of The Inheritance Tax Avoidance Schemes (Prescribed Descriptions of Arrangements) Regulations 2011 provides: **30–05**

"(1) For the purposes of Part 7 of the Finance Act 2004 (disclosure of tax avoidance schemes) the arrangements specified in paragraph (2) are prescribed in relation to inheritance tax.
(2) Arrangements are prescribed if —
(a) as a result of any element of the arrangements property becomes relevant property; and
(b) a main benefit of the arrangements is that an advantage is obtained in relation to a relevant property entry charge.
(3) In this regulation—
'property' shall be construed in accordance with section 272 of the Inheritance Tax Act 1984(1);
'relevant property' has the meaning given by section 58(1) of the Inheritance Tax Act 1984 (2);
'relevant property entry charge' means the charge to inheritance tax which arises on a transfer of value made by an individual during that individual's life as a result of which property becomes relevant property;
'transfer of value' has the meaning given by section 3(1) of the Inheritance Tax Act 1984."

Regulation 3 provides the important exception to arrangements that may come within reg.2, and is discussed in para.30–13 below. **30–06**

For these purposes, the definitions provided by FA 2004 s.318 apply: **30–07**

(1) "Arrangements" includes any scheme, transaction or series of transactions.
(2) "Advantage" in relation to any tax means:

"(a) relief or increased relief from, or repayment or increased repayment of, that tax, or the avoidance or reduction of a charge to that tax or an assessment to that tax or the avoidance of a possible assessment to that tax,
(b) the deferral of any payment of tax or the advancement of any repayment of tax, or
(c) the avoidance of any obligation to deduct or account for any tax".

III. ANALYSIS

It is readily apparent that the scope of DOTAS as applied to inheritance tax is limited to arrangements as a result of which property becomes relevant property. Some transfers are therefore entirely outside the operation of the regime. **30–08**

Further, for many advisers, a key question will be to determine the extent of the limitation contained in the second limb of reg.2(2) namely that a *main benefit* of the

[12] SI 2011/171.

arrangements is that a tax advantage is obtained in relation to a relevant property entry charge.

These two aspects are considered below.

Becomes relevant property

30–09   It follows that if the arrangements do not involve property becoming subject to the "relevant property" regime, the DOTAS rules are not engaged. The use of the word "becomes" indicates that property already within the relevant property regime, whether or not its introduction to the regime was tax advantaged, is outside the provisions.

The usual definition of "relevant property" applies here.[13] Consequently, the creation of excluded property settlements[14] is not within the scope of DOTAS. Neither is the creation of any settlement which is not "relevant property", i.e. by virtue of falling within the definition of a qualifying interest in possession[15] or by virtue of being subject to a favoured property regime.[16]

It is also clear that as currently enacted, the DOTAS regime will not be engaged in situations which do not involve transfers to or transfers between settlements: such transfers being outside the relevant property regime altogether: where no "relevant property" trust is envisaged, transfers between individuals and companies will be outside the ambit of these rules.

The main benefit is an advantage in relation to the relevant property entry charge

30–10   A tax "advantage" is broadly defined to capture any avoidance, reduction, relief from or deferral of the relevant tax. Consequently, any avoidance, relief from or reduction or deferral of the relevant property entry charge will be an "advantage" for these purposes. HMRC's Guidance suggests[17] that where there are:

(1) arrangements which result in property becoming relevant property;
(2) there is no transfer of value; but
(3) in the absence of other intervening steps in the arrangements there would have been a transfer of value,

the DOTAS rules may be engaged so that disclosure is required.

One concern arising from this statement is that innocent historic transactions (e.g. converting property within the charge to inheritance tax into excluded property) that occurred sometime before the arrangements as a result of which that property became settled property may fall within this HMRC example. This is due to the combined effect (i) of the absence of any time limit beyond which transactions may be left out of account and (ii) the breadth of the term "arrangements". It is arguable however that

---

[13] See Ch.11—Settled Property Definitions.
[14] See para.11–15.
[15] See para.11–50.
[16] See Ch.17—Property Held on Favoured Trusts.
[17] Guidance para.11.4.3.

the better view is that prior transactions effected independently and without reference to the transactions in issue must be disregarded.

"Main benefit"

The rules have been drafted to import objectivity: the enquiry is not as to the purpose **30–11** of any person implementing or promoting the arrangement but as to the *main benefit* that will accrue. The use of the term "main benefit" alone, as opposed to an extended formulation (i.e. "the main benefit, or one of the main benefits") opens up scope for arguments along the lines that there are multiple benefits, all of which are main benefits and only one of which is a tax advantage, the result being that, since it cannot be said that the tax advantage was the main benefit, the DOTAS rules will not be engaged. Doubtless, this obvious weakness will be remedied by further secondary legislation in due course, although currently, HMRC's view as embodied in the Guidance is that it will be "obvious" what the relationship is between the tax advantage and any other benefits of the tax product that a client is buying.[18]

"An advantage in relation to the relevant property entry charge"

Further, if the advantage produced by arrangements is not *in relation to* the relevant **30–12** property entry charge, or if the arrangements include the obtaining of an advantage in relation to the relevant property entry charge, but that part of the relevant arrangements is grandfathered (see below), it would appear that there is no obligation to make a disclosure to HMRC under DOTAS. So for example, if a settlor settles property into trust but retains a valuable reversionary interest in order not to incur a substantial relevant property entry charge, it would appear that there is no obligation to disclose the arrangement,[19] even if the main benefit of the arrangements would ultimately be to make a gift of the valuable reversion (and perhaps ultimately the property originally settled) to avoid inheritance tax altogether.

The authors recognise that depending on the facts, such arrangements may be susceptible to attack inter alia along the *Ramsay*[20] lines or under the new GAAR.[21] The only point made here is that there does not presently appear to be an obligation to disclose such arrangements under DOTAS.

Grandfathering

Regulation 3 of the Inheritance Tax Avoidance Schemes (Prescribed Descriptions of **30–13** Arrangements) Regulations 2011[22] seeks to exclude from the scope of IHT DOTAS

[18] Guidance para.11.5.
[19] See para.25–14 and Guidance para.11.7Q.
[20] See para.9–30.
[21] See Pt B of Ch.30.
[22] SI 2011/170.

arrangements that are "substantially the same" as those that were available before April 6, 2011: the aim is to apply the rules only to new and innovative arrangements. It provides as follows:

> "Arrangements are excepted from disclosure under these Regulations if they are of the same, or substantially the same, description as arrangements—
> (a) which were first made available for implementation before 6th April 2011; or
> (b) in relation to which the date of any transaction forming part of the arrangements falls before 6th April 2011; or
> (c) in relation to which a promoter first made a firm approach to another person before 6th April 2011."

The unhappy drafting raises questions such as:

> (i) What does "substantially the same" mean in this context?
> (ii) How minor must the differences in implementation be in order for the successor scheme to be regarded as not being substantially the same as the predecessor scheme?
> (iii) What criteria are to be used to determine whether a post-April 6, 2011 arrangement is substantially the same to a pre-April 6, 2011 arrangement?

"Substantially the same"

30–14　As regards the meaning of "substantially the same", the Guidance provides as follows[23]:

> "A promoter is required to disclose the same scheme only once. Minor changes, for example to suit the requirements of different clients, need not be separately disclosed providing the revised proposal remains substantially the same.
> What constitutes a change in a scheme or arrangement so that it is no longer substantially the same is a matter which will need to be considered on each occasion.
> In our view a scheme is no longer substantially the same if the effect of any change would be to make any previous disclosure misleading in relation to the second (or subsequent) client.
> In general provided the tax analysis is substantially the same we will regard schemes as 'substantially the same' where the only change is a different client including a different company in the same group.
> We will not regard schemes as substantially the same where there are changes to deal with changes in the law or accounting treatment, changes in the tax attributes for example, schemes creating income losses instead of capital losses or other legal and commercial issues.
> However, special care must be taken where an existing tax product is used as part of an otherwise bespoke scheme. This has been described to us as 'the use of existing toolkit'.
> Where a piece of 'existing toolkit' is used as part of a separate scheme for the same or different client then it may be that the resulting scheme is so different from the earlier planning idea that the disclosure position needs to be considered afresh. In some situations this might involve the client being given two or more numbers, for example where the

[23] At para.12.2.3.

scheme involves a combination of ideas that were themselves disclosed and allocated a number."

"Makes available for implementation" and "firm approach to another person"

These expressions take the meaning given to them in FA 2004 s.308. Paragraph 12.3 of the Guidance sets out HMRC's view in this respect in some detail, and is not repeated here.

30–15

Finally, para.11.7 of the Guidance contains a list of "grandfathered" arrangements, as follows:

30–16

"**A : Arrangements where property does not become relevant property**
If arrangements do not result in any property becoming relevant property at any stage then the arrangements are not disclosable as the Regulations will not apply.
B : Arrangements that qualify for relief/exemptions
(**a**) A single step that qualifies for a relief or exemption (where there are no other steps in order to gain an advantage) will not require disclosure.
(**b**) Where the arrangements lead to qualification for:
- multiple reliefs or exemptions;
- more than one application of the same relief or exemption;
- a single relief or exemption where there are further steps in order to gain an advantage;

then disclosure will not be required where the arrangements can be shown to be covered by the grandfathering rule.
When considering whether arrangements which qualify for a relief or exemption require disclosure, it is important to remember that the arrangements must result in property becoming relevant property for the Regulations to apply.
C : The purchase of business assets[24] **with a view to transferring the assets into a relevant property trust after two years.**
The purchase of business assets (whether or not they are insurance backed) with a view to holding them for two years prior to transferring them into a trust (and therefore qualifying for relief under s.105) is not disclosable provided that there are no further steps in the arrangements as the grandfathering rules will apply.
D : The purchase of agricultural assets[25] **with a view to transferring the assets into a relevant property trust after the appropriate period.**
The purchase of agricultural assets (whether or not they are insurance backed) with a view to holding them for two years prior to transferring them into a trust (and therefore qualifying for relief under s.117(a)) or seven years prior to transferring them into trust (and therefore qualifying for relief under s.117(b)) is not disclosable provided that there are no further steps in the arrangements as the grandfathering rules will apply.
E : Pilot settlements[26]
The establishment of pilot settlements with a nominal sum (regardless of the number of settlements and whether they are created on successive days) would not require disclosure where there is no advantage obtained in relation to the relevant property entry charge. An advantage in respect of the ten year anniversary and exit charges is not disclosable under the Regulations.
F : Discounted Gift Trusts/Schemes[27]
Discounted gift schemes/trusts where the residual trust is a bare trust would not require disclosure as there is no property becoming relevant property.

---

[24] For a discussion on the circumstances when business assets qualify for relief from inheritance tax, see Ch.26 from para.26–12.

[25] For a discussion on agricultural property relief, see Ch.26 from para.26–113.

[26] See para.16–19.

[27] See para.7–150.

Where, in relation to a discounted gift trust/scheme, property becomes relevant property then disclosure will not be required where the grandfathering provisions apply.

G : Excluded property trusts[28]; disabled trusts[29]; employee benefit trusts which satisfy s.86[30] and a qualifying interest in possession trust[31]

Property which is transferred into the above trusts does not become relevant property and is therefore not disclosable under the Regulations unless, as a further element of the arrangements, property does become relevant property and an advantage is obtained in respect of the relevant property entry charge. This will be subject to the grandfathering rules applying.

H : Transfers on death into relevant property trusts

A transfer into a relevant property trust made under the terms of a person's Will or paid into a relevant property trust on a person's death will not require disclosure.

I : Changes in distribution of deceased's estates

S.17 prevents there from being a transfer of value where there is:

  (i) a variation or disclaimer to which s.142(1)[32] applies;

 (ii) a transfer to which s.143[33] applies;

(iii) an election by a surviving spouse or civil partner under s.47A of the Administration of Estates Act 1925;

(iv) the renunciation of a claim to legitim or rights under s.131 of the Civil Partnership Act 2004 within the period mentioned in s.147(6).

Where property becomes relevant property but s.17 applies to the transaction then disclosure will not be required.

In addition, where distributions are made from property settled by Will to which s.144[34] applies then disclosure will not be required.

J : Transfers of the Nil Rate Band every seven years

The transfer of the settlor's nil rate band into a relevant property trust every seven years (provided there is no other step or steps to the arrangements which enable an advantage to be obtained in respect of the relevant property entry charge) will not be disclosable as the grandfathering provisions will apply.

K : Loan into trust[35]

A transfer into a relevant property trust by way of loan where, other than the establishment of the trust, it is a single step transaction, will not be disclosable as the grandfathering provisions will apply.

L : Insurance policy trusts

A transfer of the rights to the benefits payable on death into a relevant property trust will not be disclosable even where other benefits, for example, critical illness benefits are payable to the settlor as the grandfathering provisions will apply.

The payment of premiums on a policy settled into a relevant property trust paid by the settlor or other person will not be disclosable as the grandfathering provisions will apply.

M : Making a chargeable transfer followed by a potentially exempt transfer

Where a settlor makes a chargeable transfer prior to a potentially exempt transfer so as to ensure that their full nil rate band is available for the chargeable transfer, the arrangements are not disclosable unless there are further arrangements so as to allow an advantage to be obtained in respect of the relevant property entry charge as the grandfathering provisions will apply.

N : Deferred shares

The transfer of deferred shares into a relevant property trust in itself is not disclosable. However, where the transfer is part of arrangements which enable an advantage to be

---

[28] See para.11–15.
[29] See para.12–46 and Ch.21.
[30] See para.2–50 and Ch.24.
[31] See para.11–50.
[32] See paras 8–115 and 8–176.
[33] See para.8–206.
[34] See para.8–189.
[35] See paras 12–35 and following.

obtained in respect of the relevant property entry charge then disclosure may be required. This will depend on whether it can be shown that the grandfathering provisions will apply.

O : Items of national importance

Where a transfer of value is exempt under the following provisions then the transfer does not result in property becoming relevant property:

    (i) s.27 (Maintenance funds for historic buildings etc.)[36];

    (ii) s.30 (Conditionally exempt transfers)[37];

    (iii) s.57A (Relief where property enters maintenance fund).[38]

Where property does not become relevant property then the Regulations will not apply.

P : Pension death benefits[39]

The transfer of pension scheme death benefits into a relevant property trust where the scheme member retains the retirement benefits will not in itself require disclosure. However, where the transfer is part of arrangements which enable an advantage to be obtained in respect of the relevant property entry charge then disclosure may be required. This will depend on whether it can be shown that the arrangements are within the exceptions to disclosure outlined in Regulation 3.

Q : Reversionary Interests

Where property is transferred into a relevant property trust and the settlor retains a reversionary interest then the transfer will not require disclosure as long as it can be shown that the grandfathering rule applies.

R : Transfers of value

A disposition is not disclosable where:

- it is not a transfer of value, and
- it does not form part of wider arrangements, of which one of the main purposes is to avoid an entry charge.
- This would include dispositions which are not transfers of value under the following sections:

    (i) s.10 (dispositions not intended to confer gratuitous benefit)[40];

    (ii) s.11 (dispositions for maintenance of family)[41];

    (iii) s.12 (dispositions allowable for Income Tax or conferring benefits under a pension scheme)[42];

    (iv) s.13 (dispositions by close companies for the benefit of employees)[43];

    (v) s.14 (waiver of remuneration)[44];

    (vi) s.15 (waiver of dividends)[45];

    (vii) s.16 (Grant of tenancies of agricultural property).[46]

Where there are:

- arrangements which result in property becoming relevant property;
- there is no transfer of value; but
- in the absence of other intervening steps in the arrangements there would have been a transfer of value,

disclosure will be required unless it can be shown that the grandfathering rules will apply.

S : Gifts to companies[47]

Gifts to companies whilst being chargeable transfers do not result in property becoming relevant property and so will not require disclosure under the Regulations."[48]

---

[36] See paras 27–71 and following.
[37] See paras 27–04 and following.
[38] See paras 27–73–27–81.
[39] See para.23–21.
[40] See para.9–18.
[41] See para.23–15.
[42] See Ch.23.
[43] See Ch.15.
[44] See para.2–70.
[45] See para.2–71.
[46] See para.2–54.
[47] See para.7–50.
[48] Guidance para.11.7.

30–17   It appears from published figures that there has been a reduction in the number of inheritance tax arrangements disclosed under DOTAS. It is not clear whether this reduction is due to the effectiveness as a deterrent or whether the unremitting ingenuity of tax practitioners in developing arrangements has succeeded in avoiding the need for disclosure under these provisions.

The DOTAS regime is relatively new in the context of inheritance tax so that it is somewhat difficult to assess its impact on estate planning. Clarity obtained on issues such as the effect of legal professional privilege on the operation of DOTAS in the context of other taxes will doubtless inform the approach of practitioners and HMRC alike in relation to DOTAS in the context of inheritance tax.

PART B

GENERAL ANTI-ABUSE RULE

I. INTRODUCTION

30–18   The purpose of this Part of Chapter 30 is to introduce the proposal for a general anti-abuse rule ("GAAR"). Later editions of this book will include analysis of the final version of the GAAR as will be enacted in so far as it affects inheritance tax. Inheritance tax has always had specific provisions to counter tax planning opportunities,[49] and has also been thought to be subject to the *Ramsay* doctrine and its developments.[50] It is now also one of the taxes that will be included under a GAAR announced in the June 2012 budget.

30–19   The GAAR was announced in November 2011 following the publication of a report by an independent study group recommending the enactment of a GAAR ("the Report").[51] A consultative document on the GAAR, which included draft legislation, was published on June 12, 2012.[52] Although the GAAR was said to be in response to the Report, a number of the recommendations that were made in the Report did not find their way into the draft legislation. The consultation ran until September 14, 2012 and a response document was published on December 11, 2012 summarising the responses to the consultation, noting the various amendments to the draft legislation and explaining why some changes and not others had been made to the draft. It would appear that a number of the respondents considered that inheritance tax should be excluded from the taxes covered by the GAAR because of the long-term planning that may be involved, and the indicators of abuse in the draft legislation were inappropriate for inheritance tax. Revised legislation and draft

---

[49] See Ch.9.

[50] See para.9–30.

[51] G. Aaronson QC, "GAAR Study: A study to consider whether a general anti-avoidance rule should be introduced into the UK tax system", November 11, 2011, available at *http://www.hm-treasury.gov.uk/d/gaar_final_report_111111.pdf* [Accessed November 12, 2012].

[52] Issued September 14, 2012: *http://customs.hmrc.gov.uk/channelsPortalWebApp/channelsPortalWebApp.portal?_nfpb=true&_pageLabel=pageLibrary_ConsultationDocuments&id=HMCE_PROD1_032113&propertyType=document* [Accessed November 12, 2012].

guidance were also published on December 11, 2012 for technical consultation. The key changes incorporated in the latest draft relate to the "double reasonableness" test; the wording of which has "been clarified to ensure that the GAAR operates as intended". The provisions dealing with counteraction notices and consequential adjustments have been expanded. The updated draft legislation sets out the procedural requirements relevant to the application of the GAAR by HMRC, including details of the role of the GAAR Advisory Panel.

The GAAR is intended to have effect in relation to any arrangements entered into on or after the date of Royal Assent to the Finance Bill 2013.

II. PURPOSE OF THE GAAR

The GAAR is intended as a targeted rule, rather than a broad spectrum one, and is **30–20** intended to catch "artificial and abusive arrangements" rather than "the centre ground of tax planning".

To achieve this targeted approach, the GAAR co-opts the test of whether the "obtaining of a tax advantage was the main purpose, or one of the main purposes" of an arrangement,[53] a test which is familiar in the non-inheritance tax context. But while this is set-up as a filter, any business or individual who does not consider the incidence of taxation in making arrangements is likely to be overlooking a fundamental consideration. Indeed, this is a problem frequently encountered by some current anti-avoidance rules, where taking tax advice can mean that tax avoidance is treated as being a main element of planning. Consequently one might question the usefulness of this filter. The Government's response to this concern was to refine the second filter, i.e. the "double reasonableness" test.

The second proposed filter is that arrangements will be considered as "abusive" if **30–21** they "cannot reasonably be regarded as a reasonable course of action".[54] We are told[55] that this does not require the judge to give his view on whether tax arrangements are a reasonable course of action but instead requires the judge to consider what the range of reasonably held views is. Therefore, the GAAR will not apply if, even though the judge does not himself regard an arrangement as a reasonable course of action, he nonetheless considers, in all the circumstances, that such a view may reasonably be held. The proposed indicia of such "abusive" arrangements can be summarised as ones where the tax effect of an arrangement is out of proportion to the economic purposes, so including, for example, schemes such at that recently examined in the *Eclipse 35* case.[56] In response to concerns that inheritance tax planning often does not have a commercial context, the draft legislation has been amended, and transactions or agreements that include non-commercial terms are no longer highlighted as indicators of abusiveness.

Where an abusive arrangement is identified, it will be counteracted on a "just and reasonable" basis.[57] On the basis that anything other than just and reasonable action

---

[53] Clause 2(1) of the consultation draft published on December 11, 2012.
[54] Clause 2(2) of the consultation draft published on December 11, 2012.
[55] See "HMRC's GAAR Guidance – Consultation Draft Part A – Scope of the GAAR legislation (as at 11 December 2012)" at para.5.2.2.1.
[56] *Eclipse Film Partners No.35 LLP v Revenue and Customs Commissioners* [2012] UKFTT 270 (TC).
[57] Clause 4 of the consultation draft published on December 11, 2012.

must necessarily be unjust and unreasonable, this would seem to be impossible to object to. However, such a test can only be applied subjectively and therefore gives no certainty as to what an outcome may be. Counteraction will be subject to existing appeal provisions. There is also provision for making a claim for consequential adjustments to be made by the taxpayer subject to the counteraction notice or any other persons.[58] Under the current draft, such adjustments can only have a relieving effect on a "just and reasonable" basis. Concerns about taxpayer confidentiality have not been addressed and it is not clear how a third party, who is not aware of a counteraction notice, will know to make a claim for a "just and reasonable" adjustment to its tax returns.

For the GAAR to be invoked, the burden is on HMRC to demonstrate to a Tribunal that the arrangements are abusive and the counteraction just and reasonable.[59] The GAAR also incorporates the Advisory Panel proposed by the author of the Report, which will issue opinions on whether the GAAR should be applied in a particular case. However, the opinions issued by the Advisory Panel will not be binding. This also raises the prospect of possible judicial review proceedings against HMRC if HMRC proceed with the application of GAAR despite a ruling from the Advisory Panel that such a step would not be reasonable in the circumstances.

Regrettably, it seems no account has been taken of suggestions for a pre-transaction clearance procedure, which would do much to mitigate the uncertainty which ironically may be exacerbated, at least initially, by a GAAR. If this is simply because there is insufficient HMRC manpower to operate such a procedure, this is a great shame, but there is no evidence that this suggestion is going to be taken on board.

30–22   It is the role of guidance and non-statutory material that distinguishes the GAAR from the approach taken by conventional targeted anti-avoidance legislation. In determining whether or not an arrangement is abusive in the context of existing legislation, a Court or Tribunal will have regard to all the circumstances including:

(i) whether the substantive results of the arrangements are consistent with any principles on which those principles are based (whether express or implied), and the policy objectives of those provisions,

(ii) whether the means of achieving those results involves one or more contrived or abnormal steps, and

(iii) whether the arrangements are intended to exploit any shortcomings in those provisions.[60]

Forcing a purposive interpretation of tax legislation on Courts and Tribunals, in all circumstances, would seem to be an attempt to incorporate in statute HMRC's previously expressed view of tax avoidance being "a situation where less tax is paid than Parliament intended". The normal approach to purposive construction is to look for policy objectives in the language of the legislation itself, but the reference both to policy objectives and shortcomings in the provisions makes it clear that the GAAR is intended to address what HMRC might regard as the flaw in the *Ramsay* doctrine, in that a purposive interpretation cannot be applied to re-characterise an arrangement in circumstances where the legislation is sufficiently prescriptive. Note that the court or Tribunal is obliged to take HMRC's guidance about the GAAR that was approved by the Advisory Panel, and any opinion of the Advisory Panel about the arrangements,

[58] Clause 5 of the consultation draft published on December 11, 2012.
[59] Clause 6 of the consultation draft published on December 11, 2012.
[60] Clause 2(2) of the consultation draft published on December 11, 2012.

into account.[61] It *may* also take into account guidance, statements or other material (whether of HMRC, a Minister of the Crown or anyone else) that was in the public domain at the time that the arrangements were entered into,[62] as well as evidence of established practice, but only if HMRC had indicated its acceptance of that practice at the time the arrangements were entered into.[63]

What form of indication of acceptance by HMRC will be adequate? For example, is the list of grandfathered arrangements for the purposes of IHT DOTAS (see para.30-16 above) indicative of HMRC's acceptance of the practice of settling property while retaining a valuable reversionary interest in it to avoid the relevant property entry charge? It seems not, given the statement that "the scope of the schemes covered by DOTAS is also different from the scope of tax arrangements which are caught by the GAAR".[64] On the other hand, commonly implemented schemes, such as reversionary lease schemes, are expressly listed as an example which HMRC considers the GAAR will apply to, inter alia on the basis that "HMRC has not indicated that these arrangements give rise to the claimed tax result".[65] There have already been calls for a "white list" in which HMRC will expressly indicate which schemes are not going to be subject to the GAAR.[66]

While the initial consultative document and the draft legislation both reaffirm the importance of guidance in determining the scope of a GAAR, the step proposed in the Report of making that guidance binding, and of publishing the opinions issued by the Advisory Panel, has not been adopted "due to the risk of breaching taxpayer confidentiality". However, at the time of writing, the proposal is for the Advisory Panel to publish a summary of anonymised key principles emerging from cases that are referred to it.

While the revised draft legislation has put more flesh on the skeletal outline of a GAAR and its operation, more questions remain unanswered than answered. In particular: **30–23**

(i) How can taxpayers rely on guidance which is non-binding—and how can certainty be introduced in such shifting sands?

(ii) How is the GAAR to interact with the existing, and significant, range of anti-avoidance provisions in the UK tax code, both practically and conceptually—are they to be phased out, and, if so, when?

(iii) How is the GAAR to achieve taxpayer confidence? As the CBI support[67] indicated, a GAAR may well be a good thing if properly drafted. In this respect while clear and comprehensive guidance will undoubtedly be helpful, it is regrettable that the Government has proposed that this should be prepared by HMRC and has not supported the proposal for the Advisory Panel itself to

---

[61] Clause 6(2) of the consultation draft published on December 11, 2012.

[62] The examples of such materials given in: "HMRC's GAAR Guidance—Consultation Draft Part B—Examples of how the GAAR applies to tax arrangements (as at 11 December 2012)" at para.1.2 include: Hansard, Explanatory Notes, Written Ministerial Statements, academic literature, external practice, etc.

[63] Clause 6(3) of the consultation draft published on December 11, 2012.

[64] See "HMRC's GAAR Guidance—Consultation Draft Part A—Scope of the GAAR legislation (as at 11 December 2012)" at para.1.5.3.

[65] See "HMRC's GAAR Guidance—Consultation Draft Part B—Examples of how the GAAR applies to tax arrangements (as at 11 December 2012)" at para 4.1. In the author's view, there is much to be criticised in HMRC's analysis in this section; the analysis in para.4.2 is marginally better.

[66] One such example is given in "HMRC's GAAR Guidance—Consultation Draft Part B—Examples of how the GAAR applies to tax arrangements (as at 11 December 2012)" at para.8.

[67] CBI letter to HMRC on GAAR consultation, September 16, 2012, available at *http://www.cbi.org.uk/ media-centre/press-releases/2012/09/cbi-responds-to-government-consultation-on-the-gaar* [Accessed November 12, 2012].

produce guidance, independently from taxpayers and HMRC. This may well serve to undermine taxpayer confidence in the GAAR and lead to it being treated as a sword for HMRC to attack legitimate tax planning (e.g. arguably, reversionary lease schemes), rather than simply the shield against tax abuse proposed by the Report. Confirmation that there will be no HMRC representative on the Advisory Panel has been welcomed.

III. CONCLUSION

30–24   In constructing a GAAR, the difficult task is not to ensure that is will catch "morally repugnant" tax avoidance, but to ensure that legitimate commercial and family arrangements are not caught and that taxpayers and HMRC alike will be able to determine with certainty where the line is drawn. However, as proposed, it seems that it will be many years before a comprehensive body of guidance and judicial decisions emerge and this certainty is achieved. This is regrettable as the main purpose of a GAAR should be to increase certainty for Parliament, HMRC and taxpayers alike. On the basis of the consultative document and the more recent draft legislation, it seems unlikely that this will be achieved and an opportunity will have been missed.

CHAPTER 31

HUMAN RIGHTS

I. INTRODUCTION

The purpose of this chapter is to introduce and to describe in outline the impact, on inheritance tax, of the European Convention for the protection of Human Rights and Fundamental Freedoms ("the Convention") which came into force in 1953. There have to date been three decided cases in the area of inheritance tax and human rights, one at the level of the Special Commissioners (the predecessor to the First-tier Tribunal (Tax Chamber)) and two at the level of the European Court of Human Rights, each on the availability of the spouse exemption.[1] Although these cases have been mentioned in previous editions of this book, the authors now feel that this subject merits consideration in a separate and self-contained chapter by way of introduction to the context in which human rights arguments can be, and have been, raised: particularly so given that this is likely to be an area of further development.

31–01

The Convention

The Convention contains guarantees in respect of a number of specific human rights. The rights are stated to be inherent (as they derive from our humanity), inalienable and universal.[2] The substantive rights in the Convention have been supplemented by additional protocols. Broadly, these protocols either amend the framework of the Convention system, or they expand the categories of rights that are protected. So far as relevant for present purposes, the UK has ratified art.1 of Protocol 1 which provides

31–02

---

[1] IHTA 1984 s.18. See para.3–29.
[2] See the Preamble to the United Nations Universal Declaration of Human Rights.

additional rights, and which is the only article in the Convention which makes express reference to taxation (see para.31–09, below).

Legal machinery

31–03   Two legal entities were created to supervise the operation of the Conventions: the European Commission on Human Rights and the European Court of Human Rights. Before November 1998, one of roles of the European Commission on Human Rights was to determine whether applications were admissible in light of the requirements set out in arts 24–27 of the Convention.[3] It was only if the European Commission on Human Rights considered that the complaint was admissible that the matter would pass to the European Court for a decision. But on November 1, 1998, the 11th Protocol to the Convention was introduced with the aim of simplifying and speeding up the system. The previous European Commission and European Court of Human Rights were replaced with a full time European Court of Human Rights that determines admissibility and decides cases.

A discussion of the approach that is taken to the interpretation of rights under the Convention, and the relationship between the law of European Union and the Convention are outside the scope of this work.

Human Rights Act 1998

31–04   The specific legal rights guaranteed by the Convention were indirectly part of UK law prior to the introduction of the Human Rights Act 1998, but they were enforceable only by means of direct application to the European Court of Human Rights. Under the Human Rights Act 1998, the majority of the Convention rights have been incorporated into UK law. The rights that have been incorporated are those set out at arts 2–12 and art.14 of the Convention; arts 1–3 of the 1st Protocol and arts 1–2 of the 6th Protocol.

As a result of the enactment of the Human Rights Act 1998:

- all "public authorities" are required to act in a way that is compatible with the Convention rights, except if prohibited from so doing by legislation. Failure to act in accordance with Convention rights renders the acts of public authorities unlawful. "Public authority" is defined to include all courts and tribunals and all bodies whose functions are of a public nature.[4] This includes HMRC and the Tax Tribunals, but not Parliament;
- all UK legislation, whenever made, must be read and given effect to in such a way, so far as possible, as to be compatible with the Convention rights.[5] However, the task is still one of interpretation i.e. the ascertainment of what, taking into account the presumption created by s.3 of the Human Rights Act 1998, Parliament would reasonably have intended. It has been held that this was not intended to have the effect of requiring the courts to give the language of statutes "acontextual" meanings[6]; and

---

[3] These contain criteria for admissibility, a discussion of which is outside the scope of this chapter.
[4] HRA 1998 s.6.
[5] HRA 1998 s.3(1).
[6] *R. (on the application of Wilkinson) v Inland Revenue Commissioners* [2006] S.T.C. 270 per Lord Hoffman at para.[16]. In that case, the House of Lord declined to interpret the word "widow" in TA 1988 s.262 as including "widower".

- in the event that a compatible interpretation is not possible, the higher courts (i.e. in the tax context, this means only the Court of Appeal and the Supreme Court) are empowered to declare that that provision of UK law is incompatible with the Convention rights.[7] In a case before the Tribunal, if the Tribunal is not able to find a Convention-compatible interpretation, it will have to decide the case in a "non-compatible" way, and can do no more that draw attention to the incompatibility in its decision.

When interpreting UK legislation, the UK courts are required to have regard to the relevant judgments, decisions, declarations and opinions of the European Court of Human Rights, the European Commission on Human Rights and the Committee of Ministers for the Council of Europe.[8] Although, this means that the value of such precedent is persuasive and not binding, it has been held that in the absence of some special circumstances, the UK courts should follow the jurisprudence of the European Court of Human Rights.[9]

Mechanism for enforcing Convention Rights

Under the Human Rights Act 1998, the Minister in charge of a Bill must make one of two statements before the second reading in each House.[10] This will either be a statement that, in the Minister's view, the provisions of the Bill are compatible with Convention rights, or that the Government wishes nonetheless to proceed with the Bill. This provision has the effect of requiring Ministers (and their respective departments) to consider the potential impact on Convention rights of each new Bill and to obtain legal advice, and therefore affords indirect protection, at least to the extent that the Minister does not want to breach a Convention right. **31–05**

Otherwise, only a person who is a "victim" may bring proceedings under the Human Rights Act 1998.[11] Any person who wishes to claim that a public authority has acted, or proposes to act, in a way which is incompatible with a Convention right must either: **31–06**

(1) bring proceedings against the authority under the Human Rights Act 1998 in the appropriate court or tribunal (i.e. almost always by means of judicial review); or

(2) rely on the Convention right (or rights) concerned in any legal proceedings (i.e. by asserting the breach of the right as a ground of appeal in a normal appeal, e.g. to the First-tier Tax Tribunal).

Remedies

Apart from a declaration of incompatibility (see para.31–05) and the summary power of amendment contained in s.10 of the Human Rights Act 1998 (in so far as these may **31–07**

---

[7] HRA 1998 s.4.
[8] HRA 1998 s.2.
[9] *R. (on the application of Alconbury Development Ltd) v Secretary of State for the Environment, Transport and the Regions)* [2001] 2 W.L.R. 1389.
[10] HRA 1998 s.19.
[11] HRA 1998 s.7.

be described as remedies)[12] no new remedies are created by the Human Rights Act 1998: a court or tribunal may grant such relief or remedy within its powers that it considers just and appropriate.[13] Damages are awarded on a discretionary basis and may be awarded only by a court that has power to award damages (or other form of compensation) in civil proceedings. The First-tier Tax Tribunal has no power to award damages, and so it has no power to award damages for breach of a Convention right to taxpayers. The power to extend the remedial powers of Tribunals[14] has not been exercised in relation to the First-tier Tribunal (nor its predecessors, i.e. the General or Special Commissioners, or the VAT Tribunal).

The Upper Tribunal does have power to award damages only when it is exercising its judicial review function and may make such an award only if it is satisfied that this result would have followed from High Court proceedings begun at the time of the application.[15]

II. MAIN ARTICLES OF THE CONVENTION RELEVANT TO TAX

31–08   The Convention articles which have most often been relied upon in the tax context are set out below and are followed by a necessarily brief explanation of some of the important issues arising in connection with their application and interpretation.[16]

31–09   In terms of relevance to this work, this list begins with art.1 of Protocol 1 because it is the only article which makes express reference to taxation.

Article 1 of Protocol 1—Protection of Property

> "Every natural or legal person is entitled to the peaceful enjoyment of his possessions. No one shall be deprived of his possession except in the public interest and subject to the conditions provided for by law and by the general principles of international law.
>
>   The preceding provisions shall not, however, in any way impair the right of a State to enforce such laws as it deems necessary to control the use of property in accordance with the general interest or to secure the payment of taxes or other contributions or penalties".

As is immediately apparent, art.1 of Protocol 1 affords protection to individuals, companies and other legal entities. The term "possessions" is widely construed to include legal rights, money, and tangible and intangible property. Thus, tax is an

---

[12] See, for example, *Burden v UK* [2008] S.T.C. 1305, in which the UK Government argued that a declaration of incompatibility coupled with the s.10 power provided a mechanism for speedily correcting a defect in legislation. Referring to previous decisions to the same effect, the argument was rejected on the basis that the Human Rights Act 1998 does not place any legal obligation on the executive or the legislature to amend the law following a declaration of incompatibility, so it cannot be regarded as an effective remedy. However, the Grand Chamber did not exclude the possibility that the practice of giving effect to the national courts' declarations of incompatibility may in the future be so certain as to indicate that s.4 imposes an obligation on the state.

[13] HRA 1998 s.8(1).

[14] Afforded by HRA 1998 s.7(11).

[15] TCEA 2007 ss.15 and 16.

[16] For a comprehensive overview of the early case-law on subject, see Philip Baker, "Taxation and the European Convention on Human Rights" (2000) BTR 4. There have been some important developments since the article was written, but the article remains a useful resource as regards the pre-2000 Strasburg jurisprudence in this area.

interference with enjoyment of possession because it deprives the person of the money with which he discharges his liability to pay tax. However, the intention was not to deprive states of their taxing powers, and the second paragraph preserves an exception for taxation.

As an exception to a fundamental right, however, the decided cases illustrate that it **31–10** is accepted that all taxation must satisfy the principles underlying the Convention: it must be imposed according to law, it must serve a valid purpose in the public or general interest, and the provisions adopted must be a reasonable and proportionate means to achieve that end. Taxation may adversely affect the right to enjoyment of possessions if it places an excessive burden on the person or fundamentally interferes with his or its financial position. But it is for national authorities to decide on the form of taxes to be collected in the light of local political, social and economic conditions and States therefore enjoy a wide "margin of appreciation" (discretion) in this area.[17] As regards the margin of appreciation, the following guidelines have emerged from the case-law:

(1) although the margin of appreciation available to the national legislature under art.1 is a wide one, the measure imposed must have a legitimate aim, in the sense of not being manifestly without reasonable foundation;

(2) where the measure has a legitimate aim, there must be a reasonable relationship of proportionality between the means employed and the aim sought to be realised; and

(3) a fair balance must be struck between the demands of the general interest of the community and the requirements of the protection of the individual's fundamental rights, and this balance will not be struck if the measure results in a person or a section of the public having an individual and excessive burden.[18]

The requirement that, for a tax to be justified, it must be "subject to the conditions provided for by law" brings into play the principle of legal certainty which is inherent throughout the Convention. This broadly means that a tax measure must be accessible to the persons concerned, precise and foreseeable in its application.[19] And it should be noted that there is no general principle against the retrospective application of tax legislation, so long as the interference with the Convention right is proportionate and does not go beyond what is necessary to be effective.[20]

The approach of UK courts to art.1 of Protocol 1 has been very similar to the approach of the European Court of Human Rights. There has, to date, been no case where a substantive UK tax measure has been held to be unlawful.[21] Based on the outcome of the cases taken to date, it is thought that provided that the measure in question can be shown to be discriminatory, arguments based on the right under art.1

[17] For a summary of these principles, see for example *Kaira v Finland*, Application No.27109/95.

[18] See for example, *Wasa Liv v Sweden*, Application No.13013/87.

[19] For two recent cases where the European Court of Human Rights has held that the tax measures were not lawful for the purposes of art.1 of Protocol 1, see *Shchokin v Ukraine* [2011] S.T.C. 401 and *OAO Neftyanaya Kompaniya Yukos v Russia* [2011] S.T.C. 1988.

[20] See for example, *A, B, C, D v UK*, Application No.8531/79; *National and Provincial Building Society v UK*, Application Nos 21319/93, 21449/93 and 21675/93; *Nap Holdings UK Ltd v UK*, Application No.27721/95.

[21] For two recent decisions in which the retrospective effect of the relevant provisions was held not to be a breach of art.1 of Protocol 1, see *R. (on the application of Huitson) v Revenue and Customs Commissioners* [2011] EWCA Civ 893, CA; and *R. (on the application of Shiner) v Revenue and Customs Commissioners* [2011] S.T.C. 1878.

of Protocol 1, in conjunction with art.14 (see para.31–16) are more likely to succeed.

Article 6—Right to a Fair Trial

31–11   "1. In the determination of his civil rights and obligations or of any criminal charge against him, everyone is entitled to a fair and public hearing within a reasonable time by an independent and impartial tribunal established by law. Judgment shall be pronounced publicly but the press and public may be excluded from all or part of the trial in the interests of morals, public order or national security in a democratic society, where the interests of juveniles or the protection of the private life of the parties so require, or to the extent strictly necessary in the opinion of the court in special circumstances where publicity would prejudice the interests of justice.

2. Everyone charged with a criminal offence shall be presumed innocent until proved guilty according to the law

3. Everyone charged with a criminal offence has the following minimum rights:
   (a) to be informed promptly, in a language which he understands and in detail, of the nature and cause of the accusation against him;
   (b) to have adequate time and facilities for the preparation of his defence;
   (c) to defend himself in person or through legal assistance of his own choosing or, if he has not sufficient means to pay for legal assistance, to be given it free when the interests of justice so require;
   (d) to examine or have examined witnesses against him and to obtain the attendance and examination of witnesses on his behalf under the same conditions as witnesses against him; and
   (e) to have the free assistance of an interpreter if he cannot understand or speak the language used in court."

The purpose of art.6 is to ensure procedural fairness in the determination of both criminal charges and civil rights and obligations. There is no definition of "civil rights and obligations". The focus is on the character of the right and whether the dispute is determinative of "private" rights and obligations. However, certain matters that would be classified as justiciable public law matters in the UK have for these purposes been classified as matters to which art.6 might apply, on the ground that such matters involve rights of a "pecuniary" nature.

31–12   Tax is the exception to the evolving rule that public law matters of a pecuniary nature are "civil".[22] In *Ferrazzini v Italy*,[23] the European Court of Human Rights considered whether, due to changed attitudes in society with regard to the legal protection that falls to be accorded to individuals in their relations with the state, the scope of art.6(1) should be extended to cover disputes between citizens and public authorities as to the lawfulness under domestic law of the tax authorities' decisions. It held, by a majority of 12 to 6 that it should not.

Nonetheless, not all tax disputes are outside the ambit of art.6:

(1) In limited circumstances, a claim that has its genesis in an administrative matter (e.g. tax) may be transformed into a claim that involves the determination of civil rights. In at least one UK case, it has been held that the claim

---

[22] See *Ferrazzini v Italy* [2001] S.T.C. 1314, where the European Court of Human Rights held that simply indicating that a matter is pecuniary in nature was not sufficient for it to be classified as a civil right and thereby to fall within the parameters of art.6(1).

[23] *Ferrazzini v Italy* [2001] S.T.C. 1314.

involved a determination of "civil rights and obligations".[24] Although the complaint was ultimately unsuccessful, it was held that the rights at issue in both the restitution proceedings and the judicial review proceedings were "civil" in nature.

(2) Article 6 is applicable to tax proceedings if they involve the determination of a "criminal charge". As well as tax matters that are treated a criminal in the UK, the imposition of a fiscal penalty may also be characterised as "criminal" for the purposes of art.6(1). Three criteria are applied to determine whether a penalty is a "criminal charge", namely: (a) the classification of the penalty in domestic law; (b) the nature of the offence; and (c) the nature and degree of severity of the penalty that the person concerned risked incurring. As regards the last criterion, the penalty is likely to be treated as a criminal charge if it is substantial, has a deterrent purpose and is punitive. The size of the penalty therefore is only one relevant factor, but the Strasbourg jurisprudence suggests that the liability to penalties of as low as 10 per cent may be regarded as involving the determination of a criminal charge.[25]

Relevance of art.6 to penalty cases

To date, there have been a number of cases where the legitimacy of the default **31–13** surcharge regime (under the Value Added Tax Act 1994) has been considered by the Tribunal. Challenges are based on the disproportional nature of the penalty imposed and the penalty is usually challenged under art.1 of Protocol 1. In *Greengate Furniture Ltd*,[26] the VAT Tribunal held that the lack of any mitigation provision indicated that the default surcharge regime went beyond that which was strictly necessary. However, the regime was not "devoid of reasonable foundation" and the test established in *Roth International Transport Roth GmbH v Home Secretary*[27] that it could be regarded as "not merely harsh but plainly unfair" was not met. But the VAT Tribunal did go on to say that there may be cases where a surcharge does meet the test in *Roth*.

A number of cases since have been decided on the basis that the *Roth* test was not met, but *Enersys Holdings UK Ltd v HMRC*[28] is a recent case that is an exception to the general rule. In addition to the feature identified in *Greengate* that rendered the surcharge regime susceptible to unfairness (i.e. the lack of power to mitigate the penalty), the First-tier Tribunal held that two further features had the potential to undermine its proportionality, namely (a) the fact that the penalty was the same whatever the delay, and (b) the absence of any upper limit.[29] It is to be noted that in *Enersys*, a penalty of £131,881 was imposed because the Appellant company's VAT return was a day late.

With regard to art.6, counsel for the Appellant company referred to *Jussila v Finland*,[30] arguing that the penalty imposed on the appellant company was a "criminal charge" and that accordingly, a court or tribunal dealing with a penalty to which art.6 applied must have the power to quash the decision of the body below.[31] Since the law

[24] *National and Provincial Building Society v UK*, Application Nos 21319/93, 21449/93 and 21675/93. Cf. *Taylor v IRC* [2003] S.T.C. (S.C.D.) 254, and see para.29–163.
[25] See, for example, *Jussila v Finland* [2009] S.T.C. 29.
[26] *Greengate Furniture Ltd v Customs and Excise Commissioners* [2003] V. & D.R. 178.
[27] *Roth International Transport Roth GmbH v Home Secretary* [2003] Q.B. 728.
[28] *Enersys Holdings UK Ltd v HMRC* [2010] SFTD 387.
[29] *Enersys Holdings UK Ltd v HMRC* [2010] SFTD 387 at 404f.
[30] See fn.24.
[31] See *Taddei v France*, Application No.36118/97.

did not permit reduction of the penalty, the penalty should be discharged if found to be disproportionate. The First-tier Tribunal did not consider it necessary to decide whether art.6 was in point, since it considered that it had ample authority[32] to disapply the penalty, if it held it to be disproportionate and that accordingly, the appellant did not need to invoke art.6. But it does give an indication of how art.6 might be relied upon in appropriate cases.

Penalties and Inheritance Tax

31–14   Although the authors are not aware of any case where a taxpayer has expressly sought to rely on the protections afforded by art.6 in the context of UK inheritance tax (but see below for a case where art.6 was referred to), it is apprehended that an appeal against penalties may provide the opportunity for art.6 to be explored in the context of the imposition and collection of inheritance tax, hence the inclusion here of comment on art.6 of the Convention. HMRC appears increasingly to be seeking to impose penalties on executors. If this trend continues, this may soon become an area where human rights arguments are successfully invoked.

Robertson v IRC[33] is an example of the Revenue (as it then was) seeking unsuccessfully to impose penalties on an executor, namely Mr Robertson. Mr Robertson, a local solicitor had completed the account and put in estimated values for the assets in Mrs Stanley (the deceased's) estate, at the same time instructing professional valuers. It transpired that Mrs Stanley's furniture included some antiques and the valuation figure for these came out at almost five times the amount that Mr Robertson had entered. Further, a rental property owned by Mrs Stanley included five acres of agricultural land, so the value originally used for this property had been underestimated. Both of the professional valuations were available within two months or so, and Mr Robertson sent a corrective account to the Revenue (as it then was). Unfortunately, he omitted to mention the revaluation of the house contents. On February 2, 2000, the CTO wrote to Mr Robertson asking about the basis on which the household and personal effects had been valued. By letter dated February 7, 2000, it was explained that the original valuation had been provisional, enclosing the valuation report that had been obtained thereafter. The Revenue made enquiries into the reason why the original values had been entered, and Mr Robertson explained that in the circumstances of the case, "time was of the essence", and that the estimates contained in the original account were felt to be reasonable at the time.

His explanation notwithstanding, the CTO considered that the executors had not fulfilled their obligations under s.216 of the Inheritance Tax Act 1984, and that consequently, a penalty was due under s.247 of that Act. The CTO later advised that a penalty of £10,000 would be charged (calculated by reference to 10 per cent of the tax found to be payable in excess of the amount initially estimated, having taken into account the fact that the executors has voluntarily disclosed the relevant information and co-operated fully with the CTO). The penalty was later reduced to £9,000.

Mr Robertson considered that amount was excessive, and on hearing the "summons" (under the procedure provided for by s.249 of the Inheritance Tax Act 1984), the Special Commissioner agreed. He was unimpressed with the Revenue's submission that the executor had acted with undue haste. Although the decision turned on whether the executor had negligently delivered an incorrect account, the report seems to suggest

[32] Referring to *Garage Molenheide BVBA v Belgium* (C-286/94) [1998] S.T.C. 126.
[33] *Robertson v IRC* [2001] SpC 309, Unreported. HMRC's approach to this case is not unique, see Colin Lever, "Executor on trial" in *Taxation* (2010), Vol.165, Issue 4239.

that, although art.6 was not cited or relied on by the taxpayer, the Special Commissioner did note art.6(2) and the decision in *King v Walden*[34] in passing. That decision was to the effect that the imposition of penalties for fraudulent or negligent delivery of incorrect accounts or returns was "criminal" for the purposes of art.6(2), and therefore would shift to HMRC the burden of proof in penalty appeals.

Article 8—Right to Respect for Private and Family Life

"1. Everyone has the right to respect for his private and family life, his home and his correspondence.
2. there shall be no interference by a public authority with the exercise of this right except such as is in accordance with the law and is necessary in a democratic society in the interest of national security, public safety or the economic well-being of the country, for the prevention of disorder or crime, for the protection of health or morals, or for the protection of the rights and freedoms of others."

31–15

Article 8(1) protects the following:

1. the person's private life (held to include protection of professional life and not just domestic life)[35]:
2. the person's family life (held to include the relationship of cohabiting couples where there is financial dependence)[36]:
3. the person's home (held to include his office)[37]: and
4. the person's correspondence (including letters, telephone calls on personal as well as business lines, faxes and possibly, by analogy, emails).

Claims that art.8 rights have been infringed may occur in the context of an investigation by HMRC during the course of which HMRC have required disclosure of information or documents. Whether there has been an incursion into the person's life, home or correspondence may be easily established. It is then for HMRC to demonstrate that its incursion is justified under art.8(2).

HMRC's justification must demonstrate that:

(a) its actions are in accordance with the law. This requirement is satisfied where abuse of the measure used by HMRC is prevented by the existence of appropriate safeguards[38];
(b) its actions are necessary in a democratic society. This requirement is satisfied where, on balance, the individual's right to respect for private life is outweighed by the general need to interfere with the individual's rights; and
(c) its actions are in the interests of any of the following:
   (i) national security,
   (ii) public safety,
   (iii) the economic wellbeing of the country,
   (iv) for the prevention of disorder or crime,
   (v) for the protection of health or morals, or
   (vi) for the protection of rights and freedom of others.

[34] *King v Walden* [2001] S.T.C. 822.
[35] *Funcke v France* [1993] 16 EHRR 297.
[36] *X v Switzerland* [1978] 13 DR 248.
[37] *Niemietz v German* [1992] 16 EHRR 97.
[38] *Huvig v France* [1990] 12 EHRR 528; *Kruslin v France* [1990] 12 EHR 547.

This list of interests is exhaustive.[39]

Article 8 was unsuccessfully invoked in *Holland v IRC*.[40]

Article 14—Prohibition of Discrimination

31–16
"The enjoyment of the rights and freedoms set forth in this Convention shall be secured without discrimination on any ground such as sex, race, colour, language, religion, political or other opinion, national or social origin, association with a national minority, property, birth or other status."

Article 14 is not a free-standing non-discrimination rule: it does not prohibit discrimination as such, but only prohibits discrimination in the enjoyment of the rights and freedoms contained in the Convention. A complaint must therefore point to the right or freedom in respect of which discrimination is alleged. Article 14 alone cannot be the basis of a complaint where none of the other rights or freedoms contained in the Convention is engaged. However, it is not necessary to show that the other article has actually been breached, merely that the other Convention right is protected in a discriminatory fashion.[41]

Not every difference in treatment will engage art.14. In order for art.14 to be engaged there must be a difference in treatment of persons in an analogous or in a relevantly similar situation,[42] and the difference in treatment must have no objective or reasonable justification i.e. there is no legitimate aim or there is no relationship of proportionality between the means employed and the aims sought to be achieved. Member States have a wide margin of appreciation in deciding whether the differential treatment is justified.[43]

In the tax context, art.14 is most often raised in conjunction with art.1 of Protocol 1 on the basis that the right to enjoyment of possessions has been infringed by tax rules which operate in an unjustified and discriminatory way.

III. INHERITANCE TAX CASES

31–17
In the Inheritance Tax context, it is exclusively s.18 of the Inheritance Tax Act 1984 (the spouse exemption) that has been the subject of now three attempts to apply the Convention to extend the scope of the exemption to:

(1) a co-habiting heterosexual partner: *Holland (Executor or Holland, Deceased) v IRC*[44];

(2) co-habiting sisters: see *Burden v UK*[45]; and

[39] *R. v IRC ex parte Banque Internationale a Luxembourg SA* [2000] S.T.C. 708.
[40] See below at para.31–18.
[41] *Belgian Linguistic (Nos 1 & 2) (No.1)* (1967) Series A, No.5 (1979–80) 1 EHRR 241; *(No.2)* (1968) Series A, No.6 (1979–80) 1 EHRR 252.
[42] *DH v Czech Republic* [2007] 175 ECHR.
[43] *Stec v UK* [GC] Nos 65371/01 and 65900/01.
[44] *Holland (Executor or Holland, Deceased) v IRC* [2003] S.T.C. (S.C.D.) 43.
[45] *Burden v UK* [2007] S.T.C. 252 (Fourth Section); [2008] S.T.C. 1305 (Grand Chamber).

(3) a co-habiting homosexual couple: see *Courten v UK*.[46]

So far, these attempts have been unsuccessful. The decisions are discussed below.

Holland (Executor of Holland, Deceased) v IRC

The taxpayer was not married to the deceased, but had lived with him as husband and **31–18** wife for 31 years before his death on April 17, 2000. Her claim that the property which passed to her on his death should be exempt from inheritance tax under s.18 of the Inheritance Tax Act 1984 was refused by the Revenue (as it then was) by a decision dated May 11, 2001, on the ground that the taxpayer was not married to the deceased. The taxpayer appealed contending:

(1) that the word "spouse" in s.18 was not restricted to those who were legally married but also included those who had lived together as husband and wife;
(2) alternatively, that her rights to respect for private and family life pursuant to art.8 of the Convention and to peaceful enjoyment of her possessions pursuant to art.1 of Protocol 1 of the Convention were being infringed on the grounds of discrimination based on status within art.14 of the Convention; and
(3) that s.3 of the Human Rights Act 1998 required s.18 to be read in a way which would remove the discrimination. She claimed that she was entitled to the protection afforded by the Human Rights Act 1998 because it took effect before the notice of determination had been given.

As regards the first contention, it was held that the meaning of the word "spouse" had to accord with the understanding of the ordinary man using the work in its popular sense at the relevant time. The ordinary man in the year 2000, or indeed the year 2002, would certainly say that the word "spouse" meant a man and a woman who were legally married. That view was consistent with the other provisions of the 1984 Act and with the provisions of the tax code generally. Specific reference was made to the spouse exemption contained in s.58 of the Taxation of Chargeable Gains Act 1992, which was stated to be "mirrored by s.18 of the 1984 Act which exempts from inheritance tax such transfers during life or on death."[47]

Note there does not appear to have been any consideration of the fact that the spouse exemption for capital gains tax purposes applies only where an individual "is living with"[48] his or her spouse (and now civil partner). However, it was noted that other statutes have used the phrase "living together as man and wife" and if that phrase appeared in the taxing acts, the Special Commissioners would give effect to it. At para.[46] of the decision the Special Commissioners recorded:

> "The fact is, however, that although the phrase does appear in other statutes, it does not appear in the 1984 Act which also indicates to us that it is the intention of Parliament that the 1984 Act should apply only to spouses, that is persons who are legally married".

As regards the second contention, it was held that the European Court of Human Rights had established the principle that married persons were not in an analogous situation with non-married persons. In the absence of special circumstances, the UK

[46] *Courten v UK* [2008] ECHR 1546.
[47] At para.[43].
[48] TCGA 1992 s.58(1)(a).

had to follow the clear and constant jurisprudence of the European Court of Human Rights.

As regards the last issue, the Special Commissioners held that they were obliged to look at the law as it was at the date of death of Mr Holland, irrespective of the fact that the notice of determination as issued after the Human Rights Act 1998 came into force.

Burden v UK

31-19   In *Burden*, the applicants were two elderly cohabiting sisters. Neither had married nor borne any children. They had lived together all their lives in a stable, committed and mutually supportive relationship, and for the last 30 years, they had occupied a property built on land inherited from their parents. The property was jointly held by the two sisters and the value of each sister's half share in the property exceeded her nil-rate amount (£300,000 at the time of the application).[49] Tax would therefore have been payable on the death of one of the sisters, and the sisters feared that upon the first death, the survivor would have to sell the family home to pay the tax. The sisters maintained that their relationship was analogous to a civil partnership and they submitted that to deny them the s.18 relief would be in breach of art.14 in conjunction with art.1 of Protocol 1, because, although it applied to married persons and to those in a civil partnership, it did not apply to them.

The UK maintained that the application was inadmissible on various grounds that were ultimately rejected. As regards the substantive arguments, the European Court of Human Rights (Fourth Section—it was subsequently referred to the Grand Chamber, see further below) held by four votes to three that there had been no violation of art.14 read in conjunction with art.1 of Protocol 1.

It held as follows:

(1) That it was for national authorities to make the initial assessment, in the field of taxation, of the aims to be followed and means to be used and the state enjoyed a wide margin of appreciation where it was assessing whether and to what extent, differences in otherwise similar situations, justified different treatment.

(2) The court would generally respect the legislature's policy choice unless it was manifestly without reasonable foundation and subject to the proviso that, in creating and implementing a scheme of taxation, the state was not to discriminate between taxpayers in a manner which was inconsistent with art.14.

(3) In assessing whether it was objectively and reasonably justifiable to deny cohabiting siblings the inheritance tax exemptions allowed to survivors or marriages and civil partnerships, both the legitimacy of the social policy aims underlying the exemption and the wide margin of appreciation had to be considered.

(4) A government might often have to strike a balance between the need to raise revenue and the need to reflect other social objectives in its taxation policies and because of the direct knowledge of their society and its needs, the national authorities were in principle better placed that the international judge to appreciate what was in the public interest on social and economic grounds.

(5) Any system of taxation, to be workable, had to create marginal situations and individual cases of apparent hardship or injustice.

[49] Both sisters also held other property and investments totalling £150,000.

(6) The UK could not be said to have exceeded the wide margin of appreciation, and the difference of treatment was reasonably and objectively justified.

The dissenting opinions of Judges Bonello, Garlicki and Pavlovschi are worth **31–20** noting. In particular:

- Judges Bonello and Garlicki objected to the way in which the doctrine of margin of appreciation was applied in this case. The margin of appreciation is an imprecise and often controversial doctrine, and some academics have noted that the European Court of Human Rights relies too heavily on it. The question is whether it is necessary at all in relation to the resolution of conditional rights, and whether allowing a prima facie breach to go unpunished has the effect of devaluing Convention rights.[50]
- Judges Bonello and Garlicki were prepared to agree that with regard to tax matters, there may be some kind of presumption that the solutions adopted by the national legislature remain within this margin of appreciation, and that it would be for the applicant to demonstrate that the application of the tax legislation in his or her case exceeded the state's margin of appreciation. However, they considered that this "burden of proof" is not unlimited; that once an applicant demonstrates that the way in which the tax legislation was applied created a situation of apparent hardship or injustice, the onus shifts towards the government who must then show that there was good reason for their actions.
- Further, they considered that if the court were to decide that a situation of apparent hardship or injustice remains compatible with the Convention standards, it must give a full explanation as to how it applied the "margin of appreciation" concept. They added:

> "The national legislature is, generally speaking, free to adopt any reasonable policy of inheritance tax exemptions. As long as the United Kingdom confined the exemptions to married couples, such categorisation might have been justified under Article 12 of the Convention. However, once the UK legislature decided to extend the exemption to permanently cohabiting same-sex couples, the problem left the specific sphere of Article 12. Thus, any further categorisation in the area of inheritance tax exemptions has to satisfy general standards of reasonableness and non arbitrariness resulting from Article 14. Of course, we do not want to cast doubt upon the reasonableness of extending exemptions to those same sex couples choosing to form a civil partnership and denying such exemption to mixed-sex couples preferring not to enter into any form of official union. But once the legislature decides that a permanent union of two persons could or should enjoy tax privileges, it must be able to justify why such a possibility has been offered to some unions while continuing to be denied to others. The problem of siblings living together permanently did not escape the attention of the UK legislators and an appropriate amendment was proposed by the House of Lords. It was, however, rejected in the House of Commons on the basis of widespread agreement that the Civil Partnership Bill 'is not the appropriate legislative base on which to deal with [the problem]' (see paragraph 19 of the judgment). Such an approach may have been correct from the perspective of parliamentary technique, but it could not absolve the legislature from providing an equitable solution to the problem at a later stage.
>
> 3. The situation of permanently cohabiting siblings is in many respects emotional as well as economical—not entirely different from the situation of other unions, particularly as regards old or very old people. The bonds of mutual affection form the ethical basis for such unions and the bonds of mutual dependency form the social

---

[50] T.H. Jones, "The devaluation of Human Rights under the European Convention" (1995) P.L. 430 at 449.

basis for them. It is very important to protect such unions, like any other union of two persons, from financial disaster resulting from the death of one of the partners.

The national legislature may establish a very high threshold for such unions to be recognised under tax exemption laws; it may also provide for particular requirements to avoid fraud and abuse. But unless some compelling reasons can be shown, the legislature cannot simply ignore that such unions also exist.

The situation of permanently cohabiting siblings under the UK legislation has also been negatively affected by the fact that—being within the prohibited degrees of relationship—they cannot form a civil partnership. In other words, they have been deprived of the possibility of choice offered to other couples. That is why the present case cannot be determined by reference to the *Shackell v the United Kingdom* decision (see paragraph 46 of the judgment), since the latter was based on the fact that the persons affected were generally free to choose whether or not to enter into a formal union."

- They concluded by alluding to the fact that the manner in which the sisters were to be taxed "may raise problems under art.8 if the extent of her tax obligations compels the surviving sister to leave her house or otherwise to sacrifice the lifestyle to which she has been accustomed".
- Judge Pavlovschi too had an interesting perspective. He considered that the decisive element in the case was the nature of the property (i.e. the family home) and the applicant's personal attitude to it. In his opinion:

"Had assets purchased by the applicants during their co-habitation been at stake, I would have had no difficulty in accepting the majority's approach and, moreover, I would have readily agreed that part of such shared assets, inherited by a surviving sibling, could and should be considered as taxable property. In the case before us, however, we are faced with a qualitatively different situation. The case concerns the applicants' family house, in which they have spent all their lives and which they built on land inherited from their late parents. This house is not simply a piece of property—this house is something with which they have a special emotional bond, this house is their home.

It strikes me as absolutely awful that, once one of the two sisters dies, the surviving sister's sufferings on account of her closest relative's death should be multiplied by the risk of losing her family home because she cannot afford to pay inheritance tax in respect of the deceased sister's share of it.

I find such a situation fundamentally unfair and unjust. It is impossible for me to agree with the majority that, as a matter of principle, such treatment can be considered reasonable and objectively justified. I am firmly convinced that in modern society there is no 'pressing need' to cause people all this additional suffering."

31–21   At the applicant's request, the matter was referred to the Grand Chamber of the European Court of Justice. The Fourth Section had left open the question whether the applicants, as siblings, could claim to be in an analogous position to a married couple or to those in a civil partnership, holding that any difference in treatment was in any event reasonably and objectively justified, regard having been had to the wide margin of appreciation enjoyed by states in the area of taxation.

The Grand Chamber reached the same conclusion as the Fourth Section (this time by 15 votes to 2), i.e. there had been no violation of art.14, taken together with art.1 of Protocol 1. However The Grand Chamber preferred to found its decision on the lack of analogy between those who have entered into a legally binding marriage or civil partnership agreement, on the one hand, and on the other hand, those, such as the applicants, who are in a long-term relationship of cohabitation.

31–22   The Grand Chamber held:

"[62] The Grand Chamber commences by remarking that the relationship between siblings is qualitatively if a different nature to that between married couples and homosexual civil partners under the United Kingdom's Civil Partnership Act. The very essence of the connection between siblings is consanguinity, whereas one of the defining characteristics of a marriage or Civil Partnership Act union is that it is forbidden to close family members . . . the fact that the applicants have chosen to live together all their adult lives, as do many married and Civil Partnership Act couples, does not alter this essential difference between the two types of relationship.

[63] Moreover, the Grand Chamber notes that it has already held that marriage confers a special status on those who enter into it. The exercise of the right to marry is protected by Art 12 of the Convention and gives rise to social, personal and legal consequences . . .). In *Shackell* (cited above), the court found that the situations of married and unmarried heterosexual cohabiting couples were not analogous for the purposes of survivors' benefits, since 'marriage remains an institution which is widely accepted as conferring particular status to those who enter it'. The Grand Chamber considers that this view still holds true.

. . .

[65] As with marriage, the Grand Chamber considers that the legal consequences of civil partnership under the 2004 Act, which couples expressly and deliberately decide to incur, set these types of relationship apart from other forms of co-habitation. Rather than the length or supportive nature of the relationship, what is determinative is the existence of a public undertaking, carrying with it a body of rights and obligations of a contractual nature. Just as there can be no analogy between married and Civil Partnership Act couples, on the one hand, and heterosexual and homosexual couples who choose to live together but not to become husband and wife or civil partners, on the other hand (see *Shackell*, cited above), the absence of such a legally binding agreement between the applicants renders their relationship of cohabitation, despite its long duration fundamentally different to that of a married or civil partnership couple . . . "

Judges Bratza and Björvinsson delivered concurring opinions, but preferred the reasoning of the Fourth Section, i.e. that the difference of treatment was within the margin of appreciation of the respondent state. The principal reason for preferring the analysis of the Fourth Section was that in Judge Björvinsson's opinion, the majority of the Grand Chamber chose to compare factors which were not comparable to reach their conclusion that the relationship of consanguinity was fundamentally different to that of marriage. As regards what he considered to be the comparable nature of the sisters' relationship to marriage or civil partnership, Judge Björvinsson stated as follows: **31–23**

"I believe that in these circumstances any comparison of the relationship between the applicants, on the one hand, and the relationship between married couples and civil partnership couples, on the other, should be made without specific reference to the different legal framework applicable, and should focus only on the substantive or material differences in the nature of the relationship as such. Despite important differences, mainly as concerns the sexual nature of the relationship between married couples and civil partner couples, when it comes to the decision to live together, closeness of the personal attachment and for most practical purposes of daily life and financial matters, the relationship between the applicants in this case has, in general and for the alleged purposes of the relevant inheritance tax exemptions in particular, more in common with the relationship between married or civil partnership couples, than there are differences between them. Despite this fact, the law prohibits them from entering into an agreement similar to marriage or civil partnership and thus take advantage of the applicable rules, including the inheritance tax rules. That being so, I am not convinced that the relationship between the applicants as cohabiting sisters cannot be compared with married or civil partner couples for the purposes of art.14 of the convention. On the contrary there is in this case a difference in treatment of persons in situations which are, as a matter of fact, to a large extent similar and analogous."[51]

In his dissenting opinion, Judge Zupanic also took issue in strong terms with the failure (as he perceived it) properly to explain why consanguinity should be singled out

[51] *Burden v UK* [2008] S.T.C. 1305 at 1323.

as the characteristic which made the sisters' relationship not analogous to that of a married couple or of civil partners. He described the failure of the Grand Chamber to give a reply to the applicants on this issue as filling him with shame.[52]

31–24   The following passage from the dissenting opinion is quoted below as a matter of general interest, because it comes close to suggesting that inheritance taxation is inherently questionable:

> "Of course, it is always possible to say that a government has a legitimate interest in collecting money from taxes paid by the taxpayers. The same goes for the inheritance tax payable upon the death of the person whose estate becomes taxable when transferred through inheritance to another person. What is the legitimate government interest behind this kind of taxation?
>
> It is difficult to maintain that there is anything inherently legitimate about taxing the transfer of wealth upon the death of an individual. For example, one might argue that the state adds insult to injury when taxing an estate left to the survivors of a close relationship. In this sense, one might imagine a scale of taxation that would be progressive in positive correlation with the relational distance between the deceased and the surviving relative. But this is just one aspect of inheritance taxation, an example perhaps of how inherently questionable the inheritance taxation is in principle.
>
> When it comes, therefore, to the differentiation between different classes as regards inheritance taxation it is inherently difficult to maintain that the treatment of one class in preference to another class is rationally related to any legitimate government interest. Yet, once we accept inheritance taxation as something normal, the differentiation between different classes for inheritance taxation purposes become decisive".

The authors do note, however, that the judge did not go that far.

Courten v UK

31–25   In *Courten*, the applicant was the survivor of a homosexual co-habiting couple who had acquired a property which they owned as joint tenants. HMRC sought tax on the share of the property to which the deceased partner had been entitled, also refusing a request that the spouse exemption should apply by concession on the basis that prior to the enactment of the Civil Partnership Act 2004, Mr Courten had not been able to enter into a civil partnership with his partner. Mr Courten applied to the European Court of Human Rights, complaining that s.18 IHTA 1984 contravened art.14 of the Convention, read together with art.1 of Protocol 1. The Court rejected the claim. It held that this was not a civil partnership where the parties had undertaken public and binding obligations towards each other. The applicant could not therefore claim to have been in an analogous situation to married couples. Further, the fact that Civil Partnership Act 2004 had not been enacted at the time that the facts giving rise to application arose did not change the analysis: member states enjoyed a margin of appreciation in the timing of the introduction of legislative changes so that the UK was not to be criticised for not having introduced the Civil Partnership Act at an earlier date.

IV. CONCLUSION

31–26   It remains to be seen whether, despite the unfavourable (for the applicants) outcome of these cases, UK taxpayers will seek to mount challenges to other provisions of the

[52] *Burden v UK* [2008] S.T.C. 1305 at 1326.

Inheritance Tax Act 1984 based on the Human Rights Act 1998 and the Convention rights.

As regards the spouse exemption, and bearing in mind that one of the reasons given **31–27** in *Holland* for deciding that "spouse" in s.18 cannot refer to unmarried couples, was that tax legislation in general does not include those who live together as husband and wife, it will be interesting to see if the introduction e.g. of s.809M(3)(a) and (b) of the Income Tax Act 2007 will change anything. In the context the remittance basis of taxation, s.809M(3)(a) and (b) provides that for the purposes of determining whether a remittance has been made to a "relevant person", a man and a woman living together as husband and wife are treated as husband and wife, and two people of the same sex living together as if they were civil partners of each other are treated as civil partners: tax legislation has started now to follow taxpayers into their bedrooms.

The introduction of ITA 2007 s.809M(3) looks set to be the beginning of a pattern: in the consultative documents on the introduction of a statutory test for residence,[53] it is proposed that a "relevant relationship" for the purposes of determining the number of relevant connections an individual has with the UK, in order to determine whether they are resident here for tax purposes, should include the relationship where "P and another person are living together as husband and wife, or if they are of the same sex, as civil partners".[54] At para.3.119 of the document headed "Statutory Definition of Tax Residence and Reform of Ordinary Residence: a summary of responses" (dated June 2012) it is recorded that many respondents to the original consultation considered the inclusion of "common-law" partners within the definition of a UK resident family as unfair, as such partnerships are not normally recognised for tax relief purposes and expressed concern about how such relationships would be identified and how it was intended to differentiate between committed partnerships and more casual relationships. The Government response was as follows[55]:

> "3.124 Many common-law partnerships are long-lasting stable relationships that are very similar to marriage. Excluding common-law partners as a connection to the UK could be seen to give some unmarried couples a tax advantage as they could find it easier to remain non-resident than an equivalent married couple. Although there can be some difficulty in determining when a relationship becomes a 'common-law' equivalent to a marriage, with the introduction of tax credits there are existing legal definition of common-law partners and HMRC have significant experience of making such determinations. The Government therefore believes that common-law partnerships should continue to be included in the definition of a family connection."

Could all this mean that if the scope of the spouse exemption is challenged in the future, an applicant taxpayer will be able to persuade a court that the scheme under examination is the tax code as a whole, and that in light of tax legislation enacted since *Burden*—which (in certain circumstances) does not differentiate between persons living together as husband and wife or as civil partners—the scope of the exemption should be extended?[56] Further, bearing in mind the inherently intrusive investigation

[53] See Ch.32.
[54] See para.20(2) of Sch.1 to the document headed "Statutory Definition of Tax Residence and reform of Ordinary Residence: a summary of responses", dated June 2012.
[55] See paras 3.122–3.124 of the document referred to in the previous footnote.
[56] Note the decision in *Morrison's (Debbie) Application* [2010] NIQB 51 which concerned the a benefit which treated unmarried partners of deceased police officers less favourably than widows, widowers or bereaved civil partners. The applicant's principal ground of challenge was art.1 of Protocol 1 when read together with art.14. Referring inter alia to *Burden v UK* [2008] S.T.C. 1305, the respondent submitted that the applicant was not in an analogous position to a bereaved spouse or civil partner, and did not succeed, because the relevant legislative scheme under examination did not permit such discrimination.

required to ascertain if individuals are living together as husband and wife or civil partners, one wonders whether discrimination between those that are married or civil partners and those that are not will in the long term continue to be held to be justified, especially if claims are made of breaches of art.8: the margin of appreciation afforded to states seems narrower in connection with art.8 than that afforded in connection with art.1 of Protocol 1.

31–28   As a final note, it will be interesting to consider whether the General Anti-Abuse Rule (GAAR), as enacted,[57] will be "subject to the conditions provided for by law" for the purposes of art.1 of Protocol 1, which, as noted at para.31–10 above, brings into play the principle of legal certainty and which means that it must be accessible to the persons concerned, precise and foreseeable in its application.[58]

---

[57] See Pt B of Ch.30.
[58] For discussion of the political background which has given rise to the UK Government's desire to introduce a GAAR and a lucid outline of some of the possible consequences for trustees, see C. Gothard and J. Austen, "'Abusive' tax avoidance: what are the implications of HMRC's draft GAAR?", *Trusts and Trustees* (Oxford Law, September 2012).

PART FOUR

THE INTERNATIONAL DIMENSION

CHAPTER 32

TERRITORIAL SCOPE: DOMICILE, EXCLUDED PROPERTY, SITUS

I. INTRODUCTION

Inheritance tax is, at root, a tax on property, and it is in terms of property that the **32–01** territorial scope of the tax is defined. Generally speaking, the territorial scope is governed by two broad principles:

(1) tax is chargeable on all property situated in the United Kingdom, regardless of where the person who owns the property is domiciled; and

(2) tax is chargeable on all the property of a person domiciled in the United Kingdom, wherever his property may be situated.

The tax is thus essentially a worldwide tax, which, broadly speaking, extends to all property other than property which is both:

(a) situated outside the United Kingdom; and

(b) owned by a person domiciled outside the United Kingdom.

This, however, is only the general principle, the application of which is modified in various ways. First, special rules apply to settled property. Secondly, certain kinds of property situated in the United Kingdom may be outside the scope of the tax. Finally, the position may be affected by double tax treaties.

The United Kingdom is comprised of Great Britain (England, Scotland and Wales) and Northern Ireland. It does not extend to the Isle of Man or any of the Channel Islands (although in certain cases the IHT legislation takes account of those jurisdictions).

In so far as property falls outside the territorial scope of the tax, it normally does so because it is "excluded property". Whether or not property is excluded property depends on three factors—the nature of the property, where it is situated, and the domicile of certain persons specified by the legislation. This chapter is accordingly concerned[1] with three topics: the definition of excluded property and the consequences of property being excluded property, situs, and domicile. It will be convenient to consider domicile first.

32–02   As was mentioned above, whether or not property is excluded property depends in part on the domicile of certain persons specified by the legislation.[2] A person's domicile can also be important in a number of other IHT contexts, and may be significant for CGT and income tax. The question of where an individual is domiciled as a matter of general law is a subject in itself, and readers interested in this question should consult *Dicey, Morris and Collins on the Conflict of Laws*. One of the special features of the legislation is that certain individuals not domiciled in the United Kingdom as a matter of general law are deemed to be domiciled here for many IHT purposes, and it is with the deemed domicile provisions that the following discussion is primarily concerned. However, as these provisions make sense only if the basic treatment of domicile under the general law is understood, the discussion commences with a few introductory remarks about domicile generally.

II. DOMICILE GENERALLY

Domicile generally

32–03   Strictly, no one is domiciled in the United Kingdom per se. Rather, they are domiciled in one of the constituent jurisdictions in the United Kingdom, the law of England and Wales, Scotland or Northern Ireland being the relevant law in relation to those jurisdictions. References in the IHT legislation to a person domiciled or not domiciled in the United Kingdom are accordingly taken as references to a person domiciled or not domiciled in one of the four jurisdictions comprised within the United Kingdom.[3] For convenience, reference in the following discussion is made to the law of England and Wales ("English Law"), Scottish and Northern Irish law in this area being largely the same for all practical purposes.

The basic position under English law is that every individual has a domicile, and he can have only one domicile at a time. An existing domicile is presumed to continue until a change of domicile has been proved (the burden of proof lies on the party

---

[1] The chapter also considers quasi-excluded property: see para.32–43.

[2] HMRC have demonstrated an appetite for litigation in this area in relation to IHT: see *Anderson v IRC* [1998] S.T.C. (S.C.D.) 43; *F v IRC* [2000] S.T.C. (S.C.D.) 1; *Civil Engineer v IRC* [2002] S.T.C. (S.C.D.) 72; *Moore's Executors v IRC* [2002] S.T.C. (S.C.D.) 463; *Surveyor v IRC* [2002] S.T.C. 501; *Allen and Hately (executors of Winifred Johnson, Deceased) v HMRC* [2005] S.T.C. (S.C.D.) 614; and the early stages of the *Gaines-Cooper* litigation—*Gaines-Cooper v HMRC* [2007] S.T.C. (S.C.D.) 23 and [2007] EWHC 2617 (Ch).

[3] The same applies mutatis mutandis to the Channel Islands.

asserting the change[4] and the standard of proof for these purposes is the balance of probabilities).[5] Domicile is in a territory which is subject to a single system of law.[6] An individual is not domiciled in the United States, for example; rather, he is domiciled in one of those states, e.g. New York.[7] Furthermore, what matters in proceedings before an English court is where the individual in question is domiciled as a matter of English law,[8] not where he is domiciled by virtue of the law of some other state.[9] Under English law there are three kinds of domicile[10]: domicile of origin, domicile of choice and domicile of dependence. Each will be considered in turn.

Domicile of origin

When an individual is born he acquires a domicile of origin. Normally this will be **32–04** his father's domicile at the time of the child's birth.[11]

If a child is illegitimate[12] he will take his mother's domicile.[13]

If a child is born after his father's death he will take his mother's domicile.[14]

These rules mean that a person may be domiciled in a country[15] in which he never sets foot: in particular, his domicile is not to be confused with his nationality; still less with his residence.

An individual never loses his domicile of origin (although, exceptionally, an adopted child acquires a new domicile of origin from his adoptive parent upon adoption).[16] His domicile of origin may be superseded,[17] however, either by a domicile of choice or by a domicile of dependence. In both cases his domicile of origin then falls into abeyance, but will revive on the lapsing of his domicile of dependence or the abandonment of his

[4] *Moorhouse v Lord* (1863) 10 H.L. Cas. 272.

[5] *Henwood v Barlow Clowes International Ltd* [2008] EWCA Civ 577; *Holliday v Musa* [2010] EWCA Civ 335. Some cases suggest that the proof should be "beyond reasonable doubt" (e.g. in *Henderson v Henderson* [1967] P. 77 it was said that the standard of proof "goes beyond a mere balance of probabilities") but, as *Dicey* notes (at 6–019): "It is clear that the standard is . . . proof on the balance of probabilities".

[6] *Re Fuld's Estate (No.3)* [1968] P. 675.

[7] Other federal jurisdictions include Australia, Canada and Switzerland.

[8] "The domicile . . . must be determined . . . according to those legal principles applicable to domicil which are recognised in this country and are part of its law": Lindley M.R. in *Re Martin* [1900] P. 211.

[9] His domicile under foreign law may be important under the doctrine of *renvoi*.

[10] The 1987 Law Commission Report on domicile recommended substantial changes to the law of domicile, including the abolition of the domicile of origin; to date, those changes have not been implemented. For a discussion of the proposals see *Private Client Business* (1993), p.19.

[11] *Udny v Udny* (1869) L.R. 1 Sc. & Div. 441.

[12] In Scotland, the status of illegitimacy was abolished by s.21 of the Family Law (Scotland) Act 2006 and therefore ceased to be a relevant factor in determining domicile. That Act introduced a different method of determining domicile for individuals under the age of 16—where a child's parents share the same domicile and the child has a home with either or both of them, the child will take his parents' domicile; where the child's parents have different domiciles, or the child has a home with neither parent, the child's domicile will be that of the jurisdiction with which he has the closest connection.

[13] An illegitimate child whose parents subsequently marry will take his father's domicile (as a domicile of dependence) from the date of the marriage but his domicile of origin will remain unchanged.

[14] Special rules apply to children born to parents living apart. See *Dicey, Morris & Collins on the Conflict of Laws*, L. Collins, A. Briggs, J. Harris, J.D. McClean, C. McLachlan, C.G.J. Morse (eds), 14th edn (London: Sweet & Maxwell, 2010), p.6–028.

[15] Strictly, the reference should be to a "state" but readers may find the word "country" more familiar.

[16] This will normally be the domicile of his adoptive father or, if there is no adoptive father, that of his adoptive mother, at the time of the child's adoption.

[17] Although, as has often been observed, a domicile of origin has a particularly adhesive quality. See *Douglas v Douglas* (1871) L.R. 12 Eq. 617; *Winans v Att Gen* [1904] A.C. 287; and *Ramsay v Liverpool Royal Infirmary* [1930] A.C. 588. Note that a domicile of origin, in contrast to a domicile of choice, cannot be lost by abandonment unless a replacement domicile is acquired (*Re Clore Deceased (No.2)* [1984] S.T.C. 609 Ch. D.).

domicile of choice[18] unless his abandoned domicile of choice is immediately replaced by a new domicile of choice.[19]

Domicile of choice

32–05   An individual becomes capable of acquiring a domicile of choice when he attains 16 or marries under that age.[20] It is not easy to acquire a domicile of choice.[21] To do so an individual must be:

(1) physically present in another country[22]; and
(2) have a settled intention to reside permanently or indefinitely in that country.[23]

In practice this means minimising[24] all direct permanent ties with the country in which one is currently domiciled and establishing permanent ties with the country in which the domicile of choice is sought to be established. Mere residence in the country is insufficient, and this is so even though the person in question has no intention of residing elsewhere.[25] The fact that the individual has expressed a determination never to return to the country in which he was previously domiciled and has arranged to be buried in the new country is also insufficient.[26]

For two contrasting cases, see *IRC v Bullock*[27] in which a Canadian who lived in the United Kingdom out of deference to his wife's wishes but who intended to return to Canada on his wife's death was held not to have acquired a UK domicile of choice, and *Furse v IRC*[28] in which an American who under no such constraint lived in England and planned to continue to do so until he was unable to continue an active physical life

---

[18] *Henwood v Barlow Clowes International Ltd* [2008] EWCA Civ 577.

[19] *Udny v Udny* (1869) L.R. 1 Sc. & Div 441.

[20] Since January 1, 1974, see Domicile and Matrimonial Proceedings Act 1973 s.3. Individuals born before December 31, 1957 will have become capable of acquiring a domicile of choice on their twenty-first or eighteenth birthdays or on January 1, 1974, in line with changes to the age of legal capacity (different rules applied in Scotland). Note also that, although it is not possible to marry under the age of 16 in the United Kingdom, it is possible to do so in some other jurisdictions.

[21] " . . . the acquisition of a domicile of choice is a serious matter not to be lightly inferred from slight indications or casual words"—Scarman J in *Re Fuld's Estate (No.3)* [1968] Ch. D. 675.

[22] Purely temporary residence will not fulfil this condition and nor will residence of a secondary character (*Plummer v IRC* [1987] S.T.C. 698). However, the fact that the individual's residence in a jurisdiction may be illegal is irrelevant (*Mark v Mark* [2006] 1 A.C. 98).

[23] It is the intention to reside permanently/indefinitely in a country that is relevant, not the individual's intention as to acquiring a domicile there.

[24] Ideally, all direct links should be severed. Where such links remain, it must be possible to demonstrate clear reasons for their retention that do not suggest continuing links with the domicile the individual is seeking to abandon. In this context, note that, although maintaining accommodation in a country is not conclusive in determining whether a domicile there has been abandoned (particularly where the individual may have houses in a number of different countries (see *Henwood v Barlow Clowes International Ltd* [2008] EWCA Civ 577), it will be a factor to which HMRC is likely to attach significance, and this is particularly so where the accommodation is the individual's former main home and it continues to be occupied by the individual's family (*Re Shaffer, Morgan v Cilento* [2004] EWHC 188 (Ch); *Gaines-Cooper v HMRC* [2007] EWHC 2617 (Ch)).

[25] *Bell v Kennedy* (1868) L.R. 1 Sc. & Div 307.

[26] *Ramsay v Liverpool Royal Infirmary* [1930] A.C. 588.

[27] *IRC v Bullock* [1976] 1 W.L.R. 1178; [1976] S.T.C. 409.

[28] *Furse v IRC* [1980] 3 All E.R. 838; [1980] S.T.C. 596. See also *Cramer v Cramer* (1986) 16 Fam. Law 333 and *Plummer v IRC* [1987] S.T.C. 698.

here was held to have acquired a UK domicile of choice on the footing that his intention to leave was not even a hope or aspiration.

A person who has acquired a domicile of choice will lose that domicile when: **32–06**

(1) he ceases to reside in the country of his domicile of choice; and
(2) ceases to intend to reside in that country.[29]

He need not, however, have a positive intention never to return to that country.[30]

Where a person, having acquired a domicile of choice in Country X, returns to the country of his domicile of origin with only a vague and indefinite intention of returning to Country X, his domicile of origin may revive.[31]

Furthermore, even when a person abandons a domicile of choice without returning to the country of his domicile of origin, his domicile of origin may nonetheless revive. Thus, if Mr B has an English domicile of origin and travels to France with the clear intention of settling there permanently he will acquire a French domicile of choice the moment he sets foot on French soil. If he subsequently decides he no longer wishes to remain in France and leaves, but without forming an intention as to where he will settle, his English domicile of origin will revive. Similarly, if Mr B were to leave France with the intention of settling permanently in the American State of Colorado he will retain his French domicile of choice until he departs from France. At that moment his English domicile of origin will revive and will remain in force until he arrives in Colorado, the state in which he intends to settle permanently, at which time he will acquire a Colorado domicile of choice. This revival of his English domicile of origin could have extremely important consequences for Mr B were he to die en route to Colorado or under the deemed domicile rules.[32]

Domicile of dependence

Various kinds of person can have a domicile of dependence. Of these the most   **32–07** important are infants and (in respect of marriages taking place before January 1, 1974) married women.

Infants

Since January 1, 1974,[33] a child has a domicile of dependence, normally his father's   **32–08** domicile, until he attains the age of 16[34] or marries under that age, at which time he

---

[29] *Udny v Udny* (1869) L.R. 1 Sc. & Div 441; *Agulian v Cyganik* [2006] EWCA Civ 129.

[30] *Qureshi v Qureshi* [1972] Fam. 173.

[31] *Re Fuld* [1968] P. 675; *Fielder v IRC* [1965] T.R. 221. It is, of course, perfectly possible for an individual who has acquired a domicile of choice in a country to move elsewhere (e.g. to take up employment) while retaining the intention to return; in those circumstances the domicile of choice will not be lost.

[32] See paras 32–14 and following.

[33] Domicile and Matrimonial Proceedings Act 1973; the Act does not apply in Scotland.

[34] In Scotland the relevant respective ages are 14 for a boy and 12 for a girl.

becomes capable of acquiring a domicile of choice.[35] Thus, if A is born when his father is domiciled in England and, when A is five, his father emigrates with his family to New Zealand with the intention of making New Zealand his permanent home, A will have an English domicile of origin and dependence until his father reaches New Zealand. At that time A's father will acquire a New Zealand domicile of choice, and A will have an English domicile of origin which has been temporarily superseded by a New Zealand domicile of dependence. It is thought that A will retain this domicile of dependence until he acts in such a way that his domicile of origin revives (e.g. he leaves New Zealand intending to settle elsewhere), or he acquires a domicile of choice (e.g. he settles in, say, France, with the intention of residing there permanently).[36] It is usually easier to establish that a person has abandoned a domicile of dependence than it is to prove that he has abandoned a domicile of choice.[37]

Married women

32–09   At common law, a married woman could not acquire a domicile of choice by her own act. She had a domicile of dependence, which she acquired on becoming married and which was the same as her husband's domicile, her domicile changing with his. Now, by s.1 of the Domicile and Matrimonial Proceedings Act 1973, a married woman's domicile after December 31, 1973, is ascertained by reference to the same factors as in the case of any other individual capable of having an independent domicile, so that the dependent domicile of a married woman is abolished.[38] This is subject to the qualification that, by s.1(2), a woman married before January 1, 1974, who acquired her husband's domicile on marrying him will retain that domicile as a domicile of choice[39] unless she changes it by abandoning that domicile so that either her domicile of origin revives or she acquires a new domicile of choice.[40]

Domicile and nationality

32–10   Nationality, especially the acquisition of nationality in a jurisdiction in which a domicile of choice is claimed, is relevant, but not conclusive, in determining domicile. A distinction is to be drawn between an individual who wishes merely to obtain a travel document and an individual who wishes to cement his relationship with a country.[41] Nationality may, however, be significant in the context of double taxation relief.[42]

A foreign domicile is not necessarily inconsistent with an application for, or the grant of, a UK passport. Applicants for UK nationality should bear in mind that the Home Office may regard someone whose tax affairs are not in order as being of an

---

[35] See para.32–05 above.
[36] See *Re Macreight* (1885) 30 Ch. D. 165; *Gulbenkian v Gulbenkian* (1937) 158 L.T. 46.
[37] See *Harrison v Harrison* [1953] 1 W.L.R. 865; *Henderson v Henderson* [1967] P. 77.
[38] *Puttick v Att Gen* [1980] Fam. 1.
[39] Unless her husband's domicile was the same as her domicile of origin (in which case no change is needed).
[40] *IRC v Duchess of Portland* [1982] Ch. 314.
[41] *Bheekhun v Williams* [1999] 2 F.L.R 229; *F v IRC* [2000] S.T.C. (S.C.D.) 3.
[42] See, e.g., paras 33–144 and following.

inappropriate character to become a UK citizen and accordingly may seek information on that point from HMRC.

Domicile of a company

It has been held for income tax purposes that a company is domiciled in the country in which it is registered.[43] It is thought that this will apply for IHT purposes. **32–11**

Evidence

HMRC no longer provide rulings on an individual's domicile status.[44] **32–12**
Domicile often arises in the context of a deceased person and this can prove a major stumbling block because the deceased is no longer available to give evidence as to his intentions.[45] It is therefore often advisable to obtain from an individual a formal statement of his intentions for future reference. A person's declaration of intent, which is admissible as evidence under the Civil Evidence Act 1995, will of course be persuasive only in so far as it is supported by his conduct.

In this context, it is helpful to bear in mind the information HMRC may request in connection with an individual's domicile.[46] **32–13**

III. DEEMED DOMICILE RULES

Let us now consider the deemed domicile rules. These are found in s.267,[47] which provides that in certain circumstances a person not domiciled in the United Kingdom as a matter of general law[48] is deemed to be domiciled in the United Kingdom. There are two rules; under the first, a person who has ceased to be domiciled in the United Kingdom as a matter of general law may still be regarded as domiciled in the United Kingdom. Under the second a person may be regarded as domiciled in **32–14**

---

[43] *Gasque v IRC* [1940] 2 K.B. 80.

[44] Revenue and Customs Brief 34/10 states that: "HMRC will consider opening an enquiry where domicile could be an issue, or making a determination of Inheritance Tax in such cases, only where there is a significant risk of loss of UK tax . . . HMRC does not consider it appropriate to state an amount of tax that would be considered significant".

[45] See, e.g. *Anderson v IRC* [1998] S.T.C. (S.C.D.) 43.

[46] Revenue and Customs Brief 34/10 states that, in relation to enquiries into domicile: "Individuals should also bear in mind that enquiries into domicile involve a detailed inquiry into all of the relevant facts and HMRC is likely to require considerable personal information and extensive documentary evidence about the taxpayer and the taxpayer's close family." See also, e.g., the extensive nature of the items set out in the Schedule of Useful Information and Documents at HMRC Residence, Domicile and Remittance Basis Manual at RDRM23080 and the details requested about both the deceased and the deceased's spouse in Sch.IHT401 to Form IHT400.

[47] For s.41 Constitutional Reform and Governance Act 2010, see para.32–24 below.

[48] FA 1975 s.51(3) made express provision to this effect, but s.51(3) was not included in the 1984 consolidating legislation. It is not thought that a deemed domicile would be taken into account in determining how s.267 applied.

the United Kingdom notwithstanding the fact that he has never been domiciled in the United Kingdom.

The three-year rule

32–15   By s.267(1)(a), a person who was domiciled in the United Kingdom on or after December 10, 1974, as a matter of general law remains a UK domiciliary for three years[49] after he ceased to be so domiciled under the general law. Thus, if Mr M, a UK domiciliary, left the United Kingdom on December 31, 2011, to live permanently in Italy he will retain his UK domicile under this head until January 1, 2015.[50]

The 17-year rule

32–16   By s.267(1)(b), a person is deemed to be a UK domiciliary on a given date if (a) he was resident in the United Kingdom on or after December 10, 1974, and (b) he has been resident in the United Kingdom in not less than 17 of the 20 years of assessment ending with that in which that date falls.

32–17   The question of whether a person is resident for these purposes is determined as for income tax.[51] The effect of this provision is both to treat persons who have never been domiciled in the United Kingdom as UK domiciliaries, provided that they have been resident in the United Kingdom for a sufficiently long period, and to treat as still domiciled in the UK persons who have ceased to be domiciled in the United Kingdom as a matter of general law, provided they have been resident in the United Kingdom for a sufficiently long period. It is important to note that under s.267(1)(b) a person may be deemed to be domiciled in the United Kingdom for more than three years after he ceases to be domiciled here as a matter of general law.

32–18   The residence test does not require that the taxpayer must have been resident for a complete period of 17 years. This is because the legislation is concerned with a person who is resident in a tax year and such residence may be acquired if the individual concerned comes to the United Kingdom at the very end of the tax year (e.g. on April 1) with the intention of remaining indefinitely in the United Kingdom. In such a case the individual will be resident in the United Kingdom for that tax year (which is about to end) and that year will count as the first year of residence for the purpose of the 17-year test. Similarly, were he to leave the United Kingdom soon after the commencement of a tax year, then he may be treated as resident in the United Kingdom in that final tax year. Accordingly, in an extreme case an individual could arrive in the United Kingdom on April 1 in one year, remain for the next 15 years and then leave on April 10 in year 17 and yet be caught by the 17-year test even though he was only physically resident in the United Kingdom for a little over 15 years.

Care needs to be taken in the case of the long-term UK resident non-domiciliary who leaves the United Kingdom after becoming deemed domiciled but subsequently returns. Assume Mr C, who is domiciled in Rubovia, comes to the United Kingdom to

---

[49] The reference in s.267(1)(a) is to "years" (i.e., a period of 12 months) while that in s.267(1)(b) is to "years of assessment".

[50] Mr M may have to wait until April 6, 2015, to escape entirely from the deemed domiciled rules; see para.32–19.

[51] IHTA 1984 s.267(4). For years of assessment up to 1992–93 this was the position but subject to the qualification that no regard was to be had to the availability for the individual's use of any dwelling-house in the United Kingdom. As this became the position for income tax for years of assessment after 1992–93 (see FA 1993 s.208), this qualification ceased to be necessary.

study, marries and remains here for 20 years; following a divorce he returns to Rubovia in August 2011 and takes up a new job there. Mr C is subsequently asked by his employers to accept a two-year post in their London office and he therefore resumes residence in the United Kingdom in January 2016; a few weeks later Mr C has a cycling accident on his way to work and dies from his injuries. Although he has only recently returned to the United Kingdom, and his stay was expected to be a relatively short one, Mr C remains deemed domiciled in the United Kingdom because he has still been resident in the UK in 17 out of the last 20 years; his worldwide estate is therefore subject to IHT on his death. Had Mr C's return to the United Kingdom been delayed until April 6, 2016 he would have been non-resident for four complete tax years, his previous period of UK residence would have fallen out of account for the purpose of calculating the 17 years and only his UK situs assets would have been subject to IHT on his death.

Two tier test

It is important to bear in mind that it is necessary to apply both the three-year rule **32–19** and the 17-year rule to a UK domiciliary emigrating from this country if he has been a longstanding resident here. Assume that Mr R, who has been domiciled and resident all his life in the United Kingdom, emigrated permanently to Monaco on December 31, 2011. Under the three-year rule he will retain his UK domicile until January 1, 2015. It might be tempting to suggest that he can therefore establish an "excluded property" settlement after December 31, 2014. This, however, would be incorrect because under the 17-year rule Mr R was still UK resident in the 2011/12 tax year and not until he has been non-resident for three complete tax years will he fall outside the 17-year rule; he will therefore retain his UK domicile until April 6, 2015.[52]

Special cases

The legislation makes special provision for dealing with three categories of per- **32–20** son.

Diplomats

A serving diplomat is not deemed by s.267(1)(b) to be domiciled in the United **32–21** Kingdom by virtue of longstanding residence, but a former diplomat who remains in the United Kingdom after retirement is subject to s.267(1)(b) and his earlier residence while serving as a diplomat is taken into account.[53]

Overseas electors

Special provision is made to avoid the domicile of registered overseas electors[54] **32–22** from being prejudiced by their actions in that capacity. In determining his domicile under general law at any time after April 5, 1996 or for the purposes of the 3-year deemed domicile rule in s.267(1)(a) after April 5, 1993, the following actions of such an elector are disregarded if taken in connection with electoral rights[55]:

[52] It is, of course, important that Mr R does not resume UK residence in the 2015/16 tax year.
[53] See also Diplomatic Privileges Act 1964, for tax exemptions generally.
[54] A person is registered as an overseas elector if he is registered in any register of parliamentary electors in pursuance of such a declaration as is mentioned in the Representation of the People Act 1985 s.1(1)(a) or registered under s.3 of that Act; FA 1996 s.200(3).
[55] FA 1996 s.200(1).

(a) the individual does anything with a view to, or in connection with, being registered as an overseas elector; or

(b) the individual, when registered as an overseas elector, votes in any election at which he is entitled to vote by virtue of being so registered.[56]

If the overseas elector so wishes[57] these rules do not apply in determining his domicile at any time if at that time it falls to be determined for the purpose of ascertaining his or any other person's liability to IHT. If his liability is so determined it is taken to be so determined for the purpose only of ascertaining the liability in question.[58]

Visiting forces

32–23   A period during which any member of a visiting force[59] (or of a civilian component of such a force)[60] of a designated country who is not a British citizen, a British Dependent Territories citizen, a British Overseas National or a British Overseas citizen is in the United Kingdom by reason solely of his being such a member is not treated as a period of residence in the United Kingdom or as creating a change of his residence or domicile.[61]

Members of the House of Commons or the House of Lords

32–24   Section 41 Constitutional Reform and Governance Act 2010 introduced a new provision relating to a form of "deemed" domicile. Under that section, an individual who is, for any part of a tax year, a Member of the House of Commons or a Member of the House of Lords is to be treated as resident, ordinarily resident and domiciled in the United Kingdom for the whole of that tax year for the purposes of income tax, capital gains tax and inheritance tax.[62] The provision does not apply to bishops, judges or Members of the European Parliament.

IV. WHEN THE DEEMED DOMICILE RULES APPLY

32–25   It is important to note that the deemed domicile rules apply only in certain contexts. Frequently s.267(1) is overridden by express statutory provision (see ss.267(2)[63] and 267(3)[64]). In particular its application may be affected by double taxation treaties.[65]

---

[56] FA 1996 s.200(2).

[57] FA 1996 s.200(4)(b).

[58] FA 1996 s.200(4); see para.29–71.

[59] The rule applies equally to any members of the armed forces of a designated country (and of any civilian component thereof) attached to any designated allied headquarters and in relation to certain persons of any category for the time being agreed between the United Kingdom government and the other members of the North Atlantic Council; IHTA 1984 s.155(4) and (5).

[60] IHTA 1984 s.155(3).

[61] IHTA 1984 s.155(1) and (2).

[62] See also the Residence, Domicile and Remittance Basis Manual at RDRM10565: "The deemed status will apply to the whole of each tax year in which a person is a member of either House, starting with the 2010–2011 tax year, even if that person is a member for only part of the tax year and regardless of whether or not they are on a leave of absence. This does not affect their residence or domicile status for other purposes."

[63] Subs.267(2) provides that the deemed domicile rules shall not apply in relation to exempt gilts (see para.32–31 below).

[64] Subs.267(3) provides that the deemed domicile rules shall not apply in relation to specific UK Government securities, savings bonds and deposits where the person beneficially entitled to them is domiciled in the Channel Islands or the Isle of Man.

[65] See paras 33–29, 33–35.

There are six contexts in which s.267(1) is important:

(1) *Excluded property and quasi-excluded property.* The section applies in determining whether certain kinds of property are excluded property or quasi-excluded property.

(2) *Spouse/civil partner exemption.* The section applies in determining whether a person's spouse is a UK domiciliary for purposes of deciding whether the limited spouse exemption applies.[66]

(3) *Close companies.* The section applies in determining whether an amount is to be apportioned to a person under s.94(1).[67]

(4) *Revaluation relief.* The section applies in determining whether revaluation relief is available under ss.131–140.[68]

(5) *Exit charges.* The section applies in determining whether a settlor was domiciled in the United Kingdom so as to prevent an exit charge from being imposed in respect of property which ceased to be relevant property on becoming excluded property.[69]

(6) *Maintenance funds.* The section applies in determining whether in certain circumstances a charge to tax arises in respect of a maintenance fund.[70]

V. EXCLUDED PROPERTY GENERALLY

A great deal of tax planning turns on the fact that property is either excluded **32–26** property or can be turned into excluded property. The reader will do well to bear in mind in this connection that "excluded property" is something of a misnomer. Although it is common to assume that excluded property is "excluded" from a person's estate or, indeed, from the scope of IHT altogether, that is incorrect[71] and there is no substitute for understanding exactly how favoured treatment is afforded to excluded property. Although this matter has been discussed at length elsewhere it is worth reviewing briefly. It will be recalled that the following provisions are relevant:

(1) *Section 3(2)—dispositions of excluded property.* Normally a disposition of excluded property will not have any adverse consequences, because such a disposition will not be regarded as diminishing the disponer's estate. This follows from s.3(2), which provides that no account is to be taken of the value of excluded property which ceases to form part of a person's estate.[72] Consequently one of the essential ingredients in an actual transfer of value, a diminution, will be missing, and no charge will arise.

(2) *Section 5(1)—transfers on death.* On a person's death he is treated as having made a transfer of value immediately before he died, and tax is charged on the value of his estate at the time of that notional transfer. But no tax will be charged on the value of any excluded property that the deceased may have owned when he died, because by s.5(1) the estate of a person immediately before his death does not include excluded property.[73]

---

[66] See para.3–35.
[67] See para.2–82.
[68] See paras 25–109 and following.
[69] See para.10–35.
[70] See para.27–71.
[71] See para.1–12.
[72] See paras 2–36 and following.
[73] See para.25–18.

(3) *Section 53(1)—termination of certain interests in possession.* Under s.52(1), a person who is beneficially entitled to a qualifying interest in possession in settled property is treated as having made a transfer of value if at any time during his life that interest comes to an end, tax being charged accordingly. But, by s.53(1), no tax is chargeable under s.52(1) if the settled property in which the interest subsisted was excluded property immediately before the interest terminated.[74]

(4) *Section 58(1)—definition of relevant property.* By s.58(1) excluded property is not relevant property, with the result that it is not subject to periodic charges nor, as a general rule, exit charges.[75]

(5) *Section 65(7) and (8)—Conversion of relevant property into excluded property.* Provided certain conditions are satisfied, no exit charge is imposed in respect of property which ceases to be relevant property on becoming excluded property.[76]

(6) *Sections 80 and 82—Conversion of excluded property into relevant property.* In certain circumstances, changes in the beneficial entitlement under a trust may result in excluded property being converted into relevant property.[77]

It should also be borne in mind that excluded property can be robbed of its value to the extent that liabilities are set against it, either because they are an incumbrance on that property or because the liability is to a person resident outside the United Kingdom.[78]

Partnerships

32–27   The analysis of the treatment of excluded property which is partnership property can be subtle; see paras 28–10, 28–12 and 28–25.

Reservation of benefit

32–28   The position where an individual has reserved a benefit in respect of excluded property or ceases to reserve a benefit in respect of such property requires careful consideration; see paras 7–10 and following and 5–38 and following respectively.

VI. DEFINITION OF EXCLUDED PROPERTY

32–29   Excluded property can be classified in a number of ways. Probably the simplest approach is to divide it into three categories—property situated in the United Kingdom, property situated abroad and reversionary interests.

Property situated in the United Kingdom

32–30   Five kinds of property situated in the United Kingdom are excluded property, as follows:

[74] See para.2–114.
[75] See paras 10–23 and following.
[76] See para.10–35.
[77] See paras 10–23 and following.
[78] See para.25–89.

(1) exempt gilts[79] which satisfy certain conditions;

(2) a holding in an authorised unit trust if certain conditions are satisfied;

(3) a share in an open-ended investment company if certain conditions are satisfied;

(4) certain rights owned by a person domiciled in the Channel Islands or the Isle of Man; and

(5) certain emoluments paid to, and certain tangible moveable property owned by, an individual in a visiting force (and certain other individuals).

In addition, certain foreign currency accounts qualify as quasi-excluded property. Each of these categories will be considered in turn.

Exempt gilts

"Gilt" is a shorthand term for a security issued by the Treasury. The Treasury can **32–31** issue a gilt with the condition that the security, and the interest on it, is exempt from UK taxation so long as it is held beneficially by or on behalf of persons who satisfy certain conditions. "Exempt gilts" is shorthand for such securities. Traditionally, one of the conditions was that the person in question was domiciled and ordinarily resident outside the United Kingdom, and the IHT legislation reflected that. The traditional position has changed in two ways.

First, as a result of s.154 of the Finance Act 1996 and certain amendments to the Treasury's powers, the Treasury has since April 1996 had power to issue securities that are exempt gilts regardless of the owner's domicile and ordinary residence, and the IHT legislation was modified accordingly, so that as from April 29, 1996,[80] what matters is whether the conditions attaching to a particular gilt were satisfied.

Secondly, the effect of the Finance Act 1998 has been that since April 6, 1998, all gilts (with one exception)[81] issued before that date without any conditions for exemption from taxation[82] are treated as having been issued with the benefit of tax exemption, including IHT exemption, where the relevant persons are not ordinarily resident in the United Kingdom, wherever they may be domiciled.[83] This change substantially increased the number of exempt gilts where the test for exemption was ordinary residence. Since this change was effective only as from April 6, 1998, gilts falling within this category have been capable of qualifying as excluded property only from that date.[84] As proposals presently stand, the concept of "ordinary residence" will cease to exist with effect from April 6, 2013 so that the condition to be fulfilled for securities issued thereafter,[85] or for existing securities where there is a change of

[79] Also referred to as "FOTRA" (Free of Tax to Residents Abroad) securities.

[80] IHTA 1984 ss.6(2) and 48(4) as amended by FA 1996 Sch.28 paras 7 and 8; April 29, 1998, was the date on which FA 1996 received the Royal Assent.

[81] Aside from 3 1/2 per cent War Loan 1952 or after, issued with a condition authorised by F(No.2)A 1915 s.47; FA 1998 s.161(7).

[82] This change has no effect on securities issued before April 6, 1998 which had conditions as to domicile and/or ordinary residence attaching to them.

[83] FA 1998 s.161(1) and (5).

[84] Where investments are relevant property the conversion of those investments into exempt gilts which qualify as excluded property will be the occasion of an exit charge under s.65(1)(a) unless the restrictive conditions in s.65(8) apply; see paras 15–39 and following and 32–38. The fact that FA 1998 converted certain gilts which were not capable of being excluded property into exempt gilts which were excluded property would in the absence of provision to the contrary thus have triggered such an exit charge. FA 1998 s.161(3) prevents this from happening.

[85] As the proposals stand, the change will not apply to securities issued before that date unless there is a change in beneficial ownership.

beneficial ownership after that date, will be that the relevant persons are not *resident* in the United Kingdom.

Summing up, the result of these changes is that what matters as from April 29, 1996, for IHT purposes in determining whether or not a gilt is excluded property is whether the persons beneficially entitled to them or, in the case of settled property, by or on whose behalf the exempt gilts are held, satisfy the conditions attaching to the particular gilt in question. All exempt gilts issued before April 1996 will have foreign domicile as a condition, and so will most of the exempt gilts issued since then. The same test applies to non-exempt gilts which were converted to exempt gilts by the Finance Act 1998, but that test applies to such gilts only from April 6, 1998, the date of the conversion. Readers should bear in mind that where domicile is a relevant condition it is determined without regard to the IHT deemed domicile rules.[86]

Since the list of exempt gilts changes regularly as a result of certain issues maturing and new issues being made, the authors have not included a list of gilts capable of being excluded property.[87]

Relevant time for determining status of gilts

32–32   Under estate duty where A transferred exempt gilts to B what mattered was whether the relevant conditions were satisfied after the transfer, i.e. whether transferee B satisfied the relevant conditions. For IHT, the relevant time is the time immediately before the chargeable event, i.e. regard is had to whether A satisfied the relevant conditions. There is no authority directly on the point in relation to exempt gilts owned beneficially, but in the authors' view it follows irrefutably from the Court of Appeal's decision in *Von Ernst Et Cie SA v IRC*.[88]

Scope of favoured treatment

32–33   Where an exempt gilt qualifies as excluded property so do warrants received in respect of it but not encashed, as does apportioned interest due up to, but receivable after the relevant IHT chargeable event. Income tax repayments on such interest payments will also qualify as excluded property.

Beneficially owned exempt gilts

32–34   Exempt gilts owned beneficially by a person—be it an individual or a company—are excluded property if that person satisfies the conditions attached to the gilts. As noted, in most cases the conditions are that the person is domiciled and ordinarily resident[89] outside the United Kingdom, but in some cases the condition may be only that the person is ordinarily resident outside the United Kingdom. HMRC regard it as essential that on the date of the transfer the gilts must in fact be registered in the name of the

---

[86] IHTA 1984 s.267(2).

[87] A list of exempt gilts as at April 5, 1998 appears in the IHT Manual (IHTM04306) but the authors would advise readers to check the position by telephoning HMRC's Probate and IHT helpline on 0845 3020 900.

[88] *Von Ernst Et Cie SA v IRC* [1980] W.L.R. 468; [1980] S.T.C. 111; see paras 32–35 and 32–36.

[89] See para.32–31 above as to the likely abolition of "ordinary residence".

transferor, and where large sums of IHT are at stake, they will check on this.[90] Having noted that, there seems to be no reason why exempt gilts held by a bare trustee or a nominee for a person who satisfies the conditions attached to the gilts should be prevented from qualifying as excluded property.

Settled exempt gilts

An exempt gilt which is settled property is excluded property in two cases, i.e.:   **32–35**

(1) under s.48(4)(a), if a person of a description specified in the condition attached to the exempt gilt has a qualifying interest in possession[91] in the exempt gilt; and

(2) under s.48(4)(b), if no person has a qualifying interest in possession in the exempt gilt it is shown that all known persons[92] for whose benefit the settled property (and not just the gilt) or income from it has been or might be applied,[93] or who might become beneficially entitled to an interest in possession in it, are persons of a description specified in the condition attached to the gilt.

In *Von Ernst Et Cie SA v IRC*[94] the Court of Appeal confirmed that where an interest in possession is appointed in exempt gilts the time for determining whether the gilts are excluded property is immediately before the appointment[95] and that the reference to "persons for whose benefit the settled property . . . might be applied" is a reference to persons who could in law become beneficially entitled to property; trustees of a charity are not persons for this purpose (a payment to a charity for its charitable purposes not being for the "benefit" of the charity) and so the inclusion of charities in the beneficial class will not prevent the gilts being excluded property.

Regard needs to be had to all the property comprised in the settlement. The fact that there are two or more settlors is irrelevant for this purpose because the normal rule[96] in s.44(2) for treating property provided by separate settlors as comprised in separate settlements is disapplied by s.44(2) in this context.

Since the reference in s.48(4)(b) is to "known" persons regard need not be had to unborns or future spouses/civil partners of a beneficiary.[97] Where the trustees have

---

[90] HMRC Manuals IHTM4294.

[91] If a close company has a qualifying interest in possession in the gilts regard will be had under IHTA 1984 s.101(1) to the circumstances of the participators in that company; see para.12–43. Normally a non-close company will not have a qualifying interest in possession; s.59. If it does, regard will be had to whether the company satisfies the relevant conditions. If it does not, the test in s.48(4)(b) will apply.

[92] HMRC accept that the reference to "known persons" excludes unborns and future spouses or civil partners: HMRC Manuals IHTM4298. See below for the position of charities.

[93] For older settlements the phrase "has been or might be applied" in s.48(4)(b) may raise the question of how far back it is necessary to trace applications; HMRC are likely to use a cut-off date of March 27, 1974 but it is arguable that it should in fact be March 13, 1975 as the date on which the Finance Act 1975 (introducing Capital Transfer Tax) received the Royal Assent. It is, of course, within Parliament's power to legislate retrospectively. Equally, it is an established principle of statutory construction that Parliament is presumed to have intended legislation to apply prospectively only, and compelling evidence is needed to displace this presumption (see *R v Wallington General Commissioners, Ex p. Fysh* [1962] T.R. 393; cf. *Customs and Excise Commissioners v Thorn Electrical Industries Ltd* [1975] 1 W.L.R. 1661; [1975] S.T.C. 617).

[94] *Von Ernst Et Cie SA v IRC* [1980] W.L.R. 468; [1980] S.T.C. 111.

[95] Compare *Re Smith* [1951] Ch. 360.

[96] See para.11–43.

[97] Confirmed in IHT Manual IHTM27248.

power to add beneficiaries or have a power of appointment which they can exercise in favour of virtually anyone the condition in s.48(4)(b) will not be satisfied unless the trustees can and do restrict the exercise of the power in an appropriate fashion.

The reference in s.48(4)(b) to "the settled property" suggests that the fact that prior to the event in question settled property or income has been applied to benefit a person who did not satisfy the relevant condition but who at the time of that event can no longer benefit from the settled property should not prevent the condition from being satisfied. The point is not clear where at that event that beneficiary is still alive. If they are dead, the application to them should arguably be ignored on the basis that s.48(4)(b) contemplates only applications to a person capable of being, e.g. domiciled or ordinarily resident. It is not clear whether "application" in this context would extend to the vesting of capital in a beneficiary under the terms of a trust rather than pursuant to the exercise of a power.

Difficulties may also arise where trustees pay income to a "non-qualifying" person who has an interest in possession in the settlement if the settlement subsequently becomes discretionary. In such a case it could be argued that the trust property was incapable of being excluded property under s.48(4)(b). The counter arguments would be that applications made when there is an interest in possession should be ignored and that the payment of income to a person entitled to it is not in any event an application of income within the meaning of the section.

Trustees may hold on discretionary trusts some exempt gilts where the relevant condition is domicile and ordinary residence[98] outside the United Kingdom and others where the relevant condition is ordinary residence outside the United Kingdom only. If all the "known persons" are ordinarily resident outside the United Kingdom but one or more are domiciled in the United Kingdom only the latter gilts will be excluded property.

Anti-avoidance

32–36   The legislation contains anti-avoidance provisions designed to prevent exempt gilts being used to avoid tax. The main way in which exempt gilts were so used was to break up discretionary trusts where some but not all of the beneficiaries under the trust were foreign domiciliaries. In such a case, the trust property was advanced into a settlement under which (unlike the head settlement) the only beneficiaries were neither domiciled nor ordinarily resident in the United Kingdom. This sub-settlement was regarded as a separate settlement. The trustees of the sub-settlement then:

(1) borrowed a sum of money equal to the value of the advanced property;
(2) charged the money on that property; and
(3) used the borrowed money to purchase exempt gilts.

The effect of these operations was that the value of the advanced property was reduced to nil, with the result that the only value to be brought into account in the event of a distribution was the value of the gilts, and they were excluded property.[99] That being the case, outright appointments could be made with impunity to the non-domiciled and non-resident beneficiaries of the sub-settlement.[100] Once the appointments were made,

---

[98] See para.32–31 above as to the likely abolition of "ordinary residence".

[99] The scheme described in the text is only one version of a number of essentially similar schemes commonly in use between 1975 and 1978. Although the other schemes may have varied in detail, the principle was always the same.

[100] See FA 1975 Sch.5 para.11(11).

the advanced property ceased to be settled property, and the gilts, having served their prophylactic purpose, were sold. This technique is now rendered ineffective by s.48(5).

In the *Von Ernst* case, property was resettled and interests in possession appointed along the lines just mentioned, but, notwithstanding the resettlement, on a failure of the sub-trusts (e.g. if all the beneficiaries thereof were killed) the gilts would have been held on discretionary trusts for two UK charities; one corporate, the other unincorporated. That being the case, the taxpayer at first instance (but not before the Court of Appeal) apparently felt himself unable to rely on the gilts being excluded property under the "all known beneficiaries" test stated above, and consequently contended that where interests in possession were appointed in favour of non-domiciliaries in gilts held on discretionary trusts, the correct time for deciding whether the gilts were excluded property was immediately after the interests in possession were appointed to the non-domiciliaries. As was mentioned above, this argument failed, both at first instance and before the Court of Appeal. Before the Court of Appeal, however, the taxpayer successfully took the point that in the circumstances the charities were not persons for "whose benefit" settled property could be applied or who might become "beneficially" entitled to an interest in possession. They were "mere conduit pipes," with the result that the scheme was effective after all.[101] This, at any rate, was the reasoning of Buckley L.J. and Templeman L.J. who agreed with him.[102]

Another, more sophisticated avoidance technique exploited a discrepancy between Sch.5 and Sch.7 to the Finance Act 1975. Paragraph 24(5) of Sch.5 contains a "look-through" provision under which the participators in a close company which has an interest in possession are regarded as being entitled to that interest according to their respective rights and interests in the company. Schedule 7 contains no such provision. The scheme exploited this discrepancy as follows. Assume A wished to transfer £100,000 free of CTT to B. A would:

(1) purchase £100,000 worth of exempt gilts;
(2) form A Ltd, a company incorporated, registered and resident abroad in which A was the sole shareholder; and
(3) settle the gilts on A Ltd for one week, remainder to B.

The creation of the settlement would not give rise to any charge to CTT since, by virtue of paras 24(5) and 3(1) of Sch.5, A would still be treated as beneficially entitled to the gilts. But, since para.24(5) did not apply to Sch.7, A Ltd—a foreign domiciliary not ordinarily resident in the United Kingdom—had an interest in possession in the gilts for purposes of para.3 of Sch.7, with the result that the trust property was excluded property. That being the case, no charge arose on the termination of the interest in possession and the vesting of the property absolutely in B,[103] at which stage the property ceased to be settled property. The position is now covered by s.101(2) of the 1984 Act.[104]

---

[101] It is thus arguable that the Court of Appeal's finding that the correct time for deciding whether the gilts were excluded property was immediately before the interests were created is, at least technically, obiter. Obviously, such an argument is of little comfort.

[102] Bridge L.J. held that the decisive factor with regard to the incorporated charity was that a payment out of a discretionary trust in favour of a charity attracted no CTT and, that being the case, it would be paradoxical that the mere possibility of such a payment being made out of a discretionary trust should deprive that trust of immunity under what is now s.48(4). Buckley L.J. expressly agreed with Bridge L.J., but it is questionable how far the reasoning of Bridge L.J. with regard to the incorporated charity can be relied on.

[103] FA 1975 Sch.5 para.4(1).

[104] *IRC v Brandenburg* [1982] S.T.C. 555 suggests that the scheme did not work in the first place; see para.9–17.

Section 101(1) would be insufficient to counter a more sophisticated structure interposing a settlement between the shares in the company and the ultimate beneficiary, i.e. a structure under which the UK domiciliary had an interest in possession in shares in a close company domiciled outside the United Kingdom which itself had interest in possession in settled property consisting of exempt gilts. Section 101(2) accordingly provides that such a person is effectively regarded as having the interest which the trustees have, with the result that the more sophisticated scheme is also rendered ineffective.

Planning

32–37   Notwithstanding the above anti-avoidance provisions, exempt gilts can still be used to advantage in certain circumstances, notably where a person emigrates from the United Kingdom. During the first three years following the acquisition of a foreign domicile, such an emigré will be deemed to be domiciled in the United Kingdom for most IHT purposes. But the deemed domicile provisions do not apply for the purposes of s.48(4), and therefore such an individual can render his estate largely immune from IHT by borrowing as large a sum as possible on the security of his estate and investing that sum in exempt gilts. So long as the borrowed sum is charged on his estate (other than gilts) most of the value to be brought into account will be attributable to the gilts, and they will be excluded property. In the same way, trustees of a trust under which a non-UK domiciliary has an interest in possession can convert most of the trust property into excluded property by investing in exempt gilts.

The fact that exempt gilts may be excluded property if the person who owns them or has an interest in possession in them if that person, though domiciled in the United Kingdom, is not ordinarily resident[105] here, opens up further possibilities.

Traps for trustees

32–38   Two kinds of traps await trustees of relevant property trusts in relation to exempt gilts.

First, trustees of a relevant property trust all the beneficiaries of which pass the "known persons" test in s.48(4)(b) and the trust fund of which consists of investments other than exempt gilts might regard themselves as derelict in their duty for failing to convert those investments into excluded property by purchasing exempt gilts. Such a conversion needs, however, to be approached cautiously. The investments will be relevant property and their conversion into excluded property will mean that they will have ceased to be relevant property so that prima facie an exit charge arises under s.65(1)(a).[106] A relief exists under s.65(8) to displace this charge, but the conditions for it to apply are more stringent than one might expect.[107]

A worse problem could arise where trustees who held exempt gilts on relevant property trusts in circumstances where the gilts are not excluded property because one or more individuals satisfy the relevant conditions in relation to the gilts but others do

---

[105] See para.32–31 above as to the likely abolition of "ordinary residence".

[106] See paras 15–04 and following.

[107] IHTA 1984 s.65(8); see paras 15–37 and following. Similar difficulties do not arise where a qualifying interest in possession subsists in the investments because the existence of the interest in possession is unaffected by the change in investments.

not, so that the s.48(4)(b) "known persons" test was not satisfied. Trustees in such circumstances might have been tempted, e.g. to appoint an interest in possession to an individual who satisfied the relevant condition with a view to converting the exempt gilts into excluded property. Again, this would give rise to an exit charge, but in this case without the possibility of any relief under s.65(8).

Authorised unit trusts and open-ended investment companies

In order to avoid discouraging foreign investors, the legislation provides that both a **32–39** holding in an authorised unit trust and a share in an open-ended investment company are excluded property in relation to transfers of value or other events occurring after October 15, 2002,[108] if either:

(a) the person beneficially entitled to the holding or share is an individual domiciled outside the United Kingdom for IHT purposes[109]; or

(b) the holding or share is comprised in a settlement unless the settlor was domiciled in the United Kingdom for IHT purposes when the settlement was made.[110]

For IHT purposes:

(a) "authorised unit trust" means a scheme which is a unit trust scheme for the purposes of the Income Taxes Acts (see s.1007 Income Tax Act 2007) and in the case of which an order under s.243 of the Financial Services and Markets Act 2000 is in force[111]; and

(b) "open-ended investment company" means an opened investment company within the meaning given by s.236 of the Financial Services and Markets Act 2000 which is incorporated in the United Kingdom.[112]

Trap for trustees

Trustees of an excluded property settlement that holds UK situs assets (including cash **32–40** in a UK situs account) should not then directly reinvest in an authorised unit trust or an open-ended investment company. If they do, they will trigger an exit charge, as the exemption in s.65(7) that applies where non-excluded property is reinvested in foreign situs property does not apply where the reinvestment is into an authorised unit trust or open-ended investment company. Although it seems likely that the failure to extend the exemption to authorised unit trusts and open-ended investment companies was an

---

[108] FA 2003 s.185(8).
[109] IHTA 1984 s.6(1A).
[110] IHTA 1984 s.48(3A)(a).
[111] IHTA s.272, as amended by FA 2003 s.186(5)–(8).
[112] FA 2003 s.186(5)–(8).

oversight, HMRC are known to take this point.[113] Trustees holding UK situs assets and wishing to invest in authorised unit trusts or open-ended investment companies should ensure that the proceeds of sale of their UK investments, or cash held in the United Kingdom, is first changed into non-relevant property by moving it out of the United Kingdom before the investment is made.

Islands' rights

32–41   By s.6(3), certain rights to which a person domiciled in the Channel Islands or the Isle of Man is beneficially entitled are excluded property. By s.267(2), in deciding whether the person in question is so domiciled the deemed domicile provisions are disregarded. The rights in question are those conferred by:

(1) war savings certificates;
(2) national savings certificates (including Ulster savings certificates);
(3) premium savings bonds;
(4) deposits with the National Savings Bank or with a trustee savings bank; and
(5) deposits with a savings bank with respect to which a certificate of the Treasury under s.326 of the Taxes Act 1988 is in force.

Strictly speaking, a person cannot be domiciled in "the Channel Islands" because each of those Islands has a separate system of law. It is, however, safe to assume that the court would read the reference to domicile in the Channel Islands as a reference to domicile in a particular island.[114]

Visiting forces

32–42   By s.155, two kinds of relief are given to visiting forces and other qualifying persons.[115] First, the emoluments paid by the government of any designated country to such a person are excluded property. Secondly, any tangible moveable property the presence of which in the United Kingdom is due solely to the presence in the United Kingdom of any such person while serving in the requisite capacity is also excluded property.

Quasi-excluded property

32–43   In certain instances, the Act provides for certain types of property to have a kind of

---

[113] And see IHT Manual IHTM04262.
[114] See para.32–03.
[115] See para.32–23 for the persons who qualify for this relief.

quasi-excluded status by excluding such types of property from the value of an estate. These are described below.

Foreign currency accounts

Section 157 excludes from the value of the estates of certain foreign domiciliaries the **32–44** balance of certain foreign currency accounts. Although such accounts are not excluded property, the treatment given to them and the tests which must be satisfied for that treatment to be available have certain features in common with excluded property, and such foreign currency accounts are accordingly considered in this chapter.

Under estate duty, HMRC took the view that if a foreign currency account maintained in the UK branch of a foreign bank was subject to certain specified restrictions the debt was not primarily repayable in the United Kingdom, with the result that the debt was not regarded as situated in the United Kingdom. With the introduction of CTT, HMRC's view changed, and each case was judged on its own particular facts. This was obviously prejudicial to UK banks, and s.96 of the Finance Act 1982 introduced a relief (available in relation to deaths after March 8, 1982) designed to remedy this.

Now, under s.157, in determining the value immediately before he died of the estate of a person who was at that time domiciled, resident and ordinarily resident[116] outside the United Kingdom, there is left out of account the balance of any "qualifying foreign currency account" of his. It may be that immediately before he died he was beneficially entitled to an interest in possession under a settlement:

(1) the settlor of which was domiciled outside the United Kingdom when he made the settlement; and
(2) the trustees of which were not domiciled, resident and ordinarily resident in the United Kingdom immediately before the death in question.[117]

In that case, the balance of that account is also left out of account. For this purpose, a "qualifying foreign currency account" means any non-sterling account with a bank.[118] Foreign domiciliaries and non-resident trustees who could maintain accounts within s.157 may thus still be well advised to maintain such bank accounts outside the United Kingdom.

Whether an individual is resident or ordinarily resident[119] in the United Kingdom is determined as for income tax purposes. The residence of trustees is determined according to the usual IHT rules.[120] As was noted above, s.157 refers to the "domicile" of trustees, and withholds the relief if the trustees are domiciled in the United Kingdom. To the authors' knowledge, this is the first and only time that trustees have been regarded as having a domicile. Given the fact that the relief is available unless the trustees are domiciled in the United Kingdom, this does not give much cause for alarm,

---

[116] Under present proposals the concept of "ordinary residence" will be abolished with effect from April 6, 2013 so that, for deaths on or after April 6, 2013 the test will be whether the deceased was domiciled and resident outside the United Kingdom.

[117] See fn.116—for deaths on or after April 6, 2013 the test will be whether the trustees were domiciled and resident outside the United Kingdom.

[118] "Bank" has the meaning given by the Income Tax Act 2007 s.991; IHTA 1984 s.157(6). For deaths occurring before April 30, 1996, the account had to be with the Bank of England, the Post Office or a "recognised bank" or "licensed institution", which terms had the same meanings as in the Banking Act 1979.

[119] See fn.116 above as to the likely abolition of "ordinary residence".

[120] See para.11–47.

since the onus will be on HMRC to establish both that the trustees had a domicile as a matter of law generally and that the trustees in question are domiciled in the United Kingdom.

It is vital to bear in mind that (i) s.157 provides relief in relation only to a death, and (ii) accounts within s.157 are not excluded property. This means that lifetime gifts made out of such accounts may give rise to a charge.

Overseas pensions

32–45   As discussed in Chapter 8, s.153 provides that certain overseas pensions are left out of account in determining the value of a person's estate immediately before his death.[121]

Foreign-owned works of art

32–46   Sub-sections 5(1)(b) and 64(2)[122] provide for relief from IHT on foreign-owned works of art on, respectively, death (where the work of art is property to which a person is beneficially entitled) and ten-year anniversaries (where the work of art is held by a settlement to which the relevant property provisions would apply) and where the work of art is physically situated in the United Kingdom solely for the purpose of public display, cleaning or restoration. "Foreign-owned" is defined in s.272 as property to which a person domiciled outside the United Kingdom is beneficially entitled, or if the property is comprised in a settlement, where the settlor was domiciled outside the United Kingdom when the property became comprised in the settlement.

Property situated abroad

32–47   Property situated abroad falls into two main sub-categories—property generally, and settled property.

Property generally

32–48   By s.6(1), non-settled property which is situated abroad is excluded property if an individual domiciled outside the United Kingdom is beneficially entitled to it. The deemed domicile provisions apply. Section 6(1) is the key territorial provision: it means, in effect, that foreign domiciliaries are not normally liable in respect of so much of their property as is situated outside the United Kingdom.[123]

Settled property

32–49   By s.48(3), settled property situated abroad is excluded property if the settlor was domiciled outside the United Kingdom for IHT purposes when he made the settlement.

---

[121] See para.8–24.

[122] With effect in relation to deaths and 10-year anniversaries occurring on or after April 6, 2009. For deaths and 10-year anniversaries before that date ESC F7 allowed for the same (though concessionary) reliefs.

[123] See para.2–14 for the correct approach where a gift is made by cheque.

It is important to note that there are two distinct time references, i.e. what matters is:

(1) the situs of the property at the time of the purported charge; and
(2) the domicile of the settlor at the time he made the settlement.[124]

The residence (except for the purpose of determining whether the settlor is deemed domiciled in the United Kingdom for IHT purposes) and ordinary residence of the settlor is thus irrelevant under this rule, as is the domicile,[125] residence and ordinary residence of the beneficiaries. Nor does the position turn in any way on the proper law of the settlement or the residence of the trustees.

Additions

Although in general the rule seems simple, it does raise two interesting questions. **32–50**

First, what is the position where a UK domiciliary adds property to a settlement he made when he was domiciled abroad? HMRC's view is that, given the s.43 definitions of "settlement" and "settled property", a settlement in relation to any particular asset is made when that asset is transferred to the settlement trustees to be held upon the trusts of the settlement.[126] On this basis, the answer to the question posited above is that the added assets will not be excluded property.

While the authors have some sympathy with HMRC's attempt to prevent individuals who have become domiciled in the United Kingdom from converting non-excluded property to excluded property by adding it to a settlement made when they were not so domiciled, they are far from convinced that HMRC's approach, which would seem strange to the mind of a Chancery lawyer, is correct.

The corollary to HMRC's view is presumably that property added by a person to a settlement when he is not domiciled in the United Kingdom is excluded property even though he was domiciled in the United Kingdom when he created the settlement. Since the authors are not convinced that HMRC's view is correct they would strongly advise emigrants from the United Kingdom to create new settlements rather than add property to existing settlements.

Multiple settlors

Secondly, what is the position where several persons, one or more of whom is **32–51** domiciled abroad, and one or more of whom are domiciled in the United Kingdom, contribute property to a settlement? HMRC have stated that, in light of Chadwick J.'s decision in *Hatton v IRC*,[127] their practice in applying the excluded property rules to settlements to which more than one person has contributed is that the determination of the extent to which non-UK situs settled assets are excluded property by reason of the

---

[124] By s.267(3), for purposes of determining the settlor's domicile when he made the settlement, the deemed domicile provisions apply only if the property in question became comprised in the settlement on or after December 10, 1974.

[125] Note, however, the anti-avoidance provisions referred to at para.32–56 below.

[126] Revenue Interpretation RI 166. See also IHT Manual IHTM04030: "You should proceed on the basis that, for any given item of property . . . held in a settlement, the settlement was made when that property was put in the settlement."

[127] *Hatton v IRC* [1992] S.T.C.140; see paras 11–13 and following.

settlor's domicile is a relevant "required circumstance" within s.44(2) and that where a clear, or reasonably sensible, attribution of settled property between the contributions made by several settlors is possible, there will be a separate settlement, with its own attributed assets, for each settlor. If, on the other hand, no such attribution is feasible, each of the settlors will be regarded as having made a separate settlement comprised of all the assets in the actual settlement.[128]

Special added requirement

32–52   A special rule in ss.80 and 82, imposing an additional test, applies for the purpose of the special charging provisions that apply to relevant property trusts; see paras 10–25 and following.

Planning

32–53   It follows from the above that trustees of a settlement made by a person who was a foreign domiciliary when he made the settlement who hold assets situated in the United Kingdom should endeavour to reinvest in assets situated abroad so that the property becomes excluded property. If this is not possible, e.g. because the trustees wish to retain the assets, they should consider transferring the assets to a non-resident holding company incorporated abroad in which they hold the shares. The effect of such a transfer will be that the property comprised in the settlement will be shares in a foreign company which, provided the company's register is kept abroad, will be property which is situated abroad.[129]

It also follows that if a non-UK domiciliary creates a foreign settlement all the property comprised in that settlement will, provided the property is situated abroad generally,[130] be completely outside the IHT net as long as the settlement exists. Thus, if Mr B, a German domiciliary who is resident and ordinarily resident in the United Kingdom, creates a discretionary trust of property which at the material time is situated abroad the trustees can make distributions without any charge, and this is so even if the fund grows far beyond its original size. Moreover, the trust will also be immune from the periodic charge. If, on the other hand, the trust is one in which there is a subsisting qualifying interest in possession, there will be no charge to tax on the termination of that interest during the life of the person who is beneficially entitled to it, nor, if he retains his interest, on his death[131] although, as noted above, account needs to be taken of the effect of ss.80 and 82.

Deeds of variation

32–54   Last, an excluded property settlement may, in appropriate circumstances, be established under a posthumous instrument of variation notwithstanding that the individuals

---

[128] Revenue Interpretation RI 166.
[129] See para.32–66.
[130] See para.32–49.
[131] IHTA 1984 ss.53(1) and 5(1), respectively. The interaction with the reservation of benefit rules are discussed at paras 5–38 and following and 7–16 and following.

effecting the instrument are themselves domiciled in the United Kingdom; see para.8–120. Unfortunately, such an effect cannot be achieved for CGT purposes.[132]

Interests in possession

Under s.49(1), a person beneficially entitled to a qualifying interest in possession is treated as being beneficially entitled to the property in which his interest subsists. This does not mean, however, that the property ceases to be settled property. The property remains settled property, and in deciding whether it is excluded property regard is had under the special rules governing settled property to the domicile of the settlor when he made the settlement, not, under the general rule laid down by s.6(1), to the domicile of the person who is treated as being beneficially entitled to the property by virtue of s.49(1). This follows from the fact that it is s.48 and not s.6 which establishes the test where the property in question is settled property.

32–55

Anti-avoidance: purchased interests in excluded property settlements[133]

Until December 5, 2005 UK domiciliaries could look to mitigate IHT by purchasing interests in existing excluded property settlements. With effect from that date,[134] however, s.48(3B) was introduced into the Act. The effect of section is to deny excluded property status to any property in a settlement that has been the subject to an interest in possession[135] held at any time by a UK domiciliary where that interest arose from a disposition for consideration in money or money's worth. The interest does not have to be held by the person providing the consideration and may have been acquired indirectly (e.g. by Mr M who gives it to Mr G).

32–56

As s.48(3B) refers specifically to entitlement to an "interest in possession" it did not catch arrangements where a different interest was acquired. Finance Act 2012, however, introduced a further new anti-avoidance provision, s.74A. Under s.74A, where a UK domiciliary acquires, or becomes able to acquire, an interest in settled property and there is, as a result of the arrangements, a reduction (or series of reductions) in the UK domiciliary's estate, each reduction will be subject to IHT as an immediately chargeable transfer and the assets held in the settlement will cease to be excluded property and instead become subject to the relevant property regime.

Reversionary interests

The rules regarding reversionary interests are complicated, and it will be convenient to consider them under six sub-headings—the general rule, exceptions to the general rule, the foreign element, settled reversionary interests, the special case, and the CGT position. It is important to note that for IHT purposes the term "reversionary interest" has a wider meaning than that normally attributed to it as a matter of general law. By s.47, "reversionary interest" means "a future interest under a settlement, whether it is

32–57

---

[132] *Marshall v Kerr* [1994] S.T.C. 638.
[133] See also para.32–59 below as to purchased reversionary interests.
[134] Section 48(3B) did not affect interests acquired before that date.
[135] The effect of the section is not confined to qualifying interests in possession.

vested or contingent". Thus, any future interest, not only an ultimate reversion, is a reversionary interest for IHT purposes.

The general rule

32–58   By s.48(1), the general rule is that a reversionary interest, wherever it may be situated, is excluded property. The reason the legislation provides that such interests are excluded property derives from the original basic aim of the legislation, which was, in effect, to tax capital once a generation. This aim is given effect in two ways where settled property is concerned: where there is a subsisting qualifying interest in possession in the property the person beneficially entitled to that interest is treated as being beneficially entitled to the property itself; where there is no such interest the special charging provisions operate so that in theory the tax yield is the same as it would have been had someone been beneficially entitled to the property. That being the case, to tax someone else on any *future* interest he had in the same property would amount to double taxation of that interest. The legislation accordingly provides that reversionary interests are excluded property, with the result that such interests are effectively immune from IHT.

Exceptions to the general rule

32–59   A reversionary interest is not excluded property, in the following three circumstances:

(1) *Consideration.* By s.48(1), a reversionary interest is not excluded property if it was acquired at any time (i.e. whether by the person entitled to it or by a person previously entitled to it) for a consideration in money or money's worth. This is an anti-avoidance provision, in the absence of which it would be easy to make tax-free gifts. If, for example, B owned a reversionary interest worth £5,000, and A wished to make B a gift of £5,000, A could do so by means of a simple two-step transaction. First, he would buy B's reversion for £5,000. This would not amount to a transfer of value by A, because his estate would have suffered no diminution as a result of his purchase. Then A would give the reversion back to B. This would not amount to a transfer of value either, because, being a disposition of excluded property, it would not[136] have diminished the value of A's estate.[137] The net result would thus have been that A transferred £5,000 free of tax to B. Section 48(1)(a) prevents this by providing that in A's hands the reversion is not excluded property.

Further anti-avoidance provisions in s.81A were introduced[138] to counter certain types of IHT planning arrangements that took advantage of the fact that, following the changes made to the IHT treatment of settled property in FA 2006 s.5(1) and (1A), a (non-qualifying) interest in possession no longer formed part of a person's estate. For instance, an individual, Mr Q, might therefore acquire, for consideration, a future (i.e. reversionary) life interest in a trust. There was no charge to IHT when the initial trusts terminated and the

---

[136] Unless the courts gave a quite unjustifiable scope to the doctrine of associated operations.
[137] IHTA 1984 s.3(2).
[138] By Finance Act 2010 s.52(1).

reversionary interest became an interest in possession and, as the interest in possession did not form part of Mr Q's estate, Mr Q could assign it on trust for others without a charge to IHT. However, with effect from December 9, 2009, where a reversionary interest, acquired by a person for consideration, comes to an end upon that person becoming entitled to an interest in possession, he is treated as making a disposition of the reversionary interest at that time and that disposition cannot be a PET.

(2) *Settlor/Spouse*. By ss.48(1)(b) and (2) a reversionary interest in a settlement made on or after April 16, 1976, is not excluded property if it is, or, in some cases, has been, one to which either the settlor or his spouse is beneficially entitled. This, too, is an anti-avoidance provision. In its absence it would be a relatively simple matter for a father who wished to transfer property free of tax to, say, his son, to do so. First, the father would create a settlement by selling his son an interest in possession in the property for a short period, say, six months. The sale itself would not give rise to a charge to tax; the son would give full consideration. The father's remainder would, as a reversionary interest, be excluded property, and he could thus give it free of IHT to the son. The legislation prevents this by providing that the reversion in the father's hands (or those of his spouse) is not excluded property.

The reason the legislation refers to a reversionary interest to which the settlor's spouse has (at any time) been entitled is twofold. First, it deals with the case where the settlor has died. Assume the settlor's spouse owned a reversion and the settlor died. The spouse would at that stage have ceased to have been a spouse, because a widow is not a spouse.[139] Secondly, the extension of the prohibition was necessary to counter an avoidance scheme which took advantage of the since repealed mutual transfer provisions. By s.48(2), in deciding whether a reversionary interest is excluded property no account is taken of the fact that the settlor or his spouse has been beneficially entitled to it if the interest arose under a settlement made after April 15, 1976, and he or she acquired the interest before March 10, 1981.

Following the changes made to the IHT treatment of settled property in FA 2006, it was possible for a time to take steps to avoid IHT by establishing a trust in which a settlor, Mr S (or his spouse/civil partner), retained a future (i.e. reversionary) life interest subject to initial trusts for the benefit of others; as the reversionary interest formed part of Mr S's estate, its retention reduced the overall transfer of value made on establishing the trust. In the absence of anti-avoidance provisions, there was no charge to IHT when the initial trusts terminated and the reversionary interest became an interest in possession; under s.5(1) and (1A) the interest in possession did not then form part of Mr S's estate and Mr S could then assign it on trust for others without a charge to IHT. Alternatively, Mr S could make an outright gift of the interest when it was still in reversion; provided the gift was to another individual it would constitute a PET. The anti-avoidance provisions in s.81A were introduced[140] to counter these types of arrangements. With effect from December 9, 2009, where a settlor or a settlor's spouse/civil partner (a "relevant reversioner") becomes entitled to a reversionary interest, first, any disposition of that reversionary interest cannot be a PET and, secondly, if the reversionary interest comes to an end by virtue of the relevant reversioner becoming entitled to an interest in

---

[139] *Vestey's Executors v IRC* [1949] 1 All E.R. 1108; (1949) 31 T.C. 1.
[140] By Finance Act 2010 s.52(1).

possession, he is treated as making a disposition of the reversionary interest at that time and, again, that disposition cannot be a PET.

(3) *Leases.* Where a lease is created, otherwise than for a full consideration in money or money's worth, for a life or lives, or terminable on, or by reference to death, this is treated as creating a settlement, even though no settlement would be regarded as subsisting under the general law. By s.47, the lessor's future interest expectant on the termination of the lease is a reversionary interest but, by s.48(1)(c), such a reversionary interest is not excluded property. The reason for this lies in the special valuation rules that apply to leases which are treated as settlements. Under these rules, the value of the lessor's interest is fixed from the outset as a proportion of the value of the underlying property, determined according to the amount of consideration given for lease; that proportion does not thereafter change, however long the lease has to run; the lessee's interest is treated as subsisting in the proportion of the underlying property which is not treated as the value of the lessor's interest. The rules derive from two provisions.

First, s.50(6) provides that:

"Where, under s.43(3) above, a lease of property is to be treated as a settlement, the lessee's interest in the property shall be taken to subsist in the whole of the property less such part of it as corresponds to the proportion which the value of the lessor's interest (as determined under Part VI of this Act) bears to the value of the property."

Secondly, s.170 provides that:

"Where, under s.43(3) above, a lease of property is to be treated as a settlement, the value of the lessor's interest in the property shall be taken to be such part of the value of the property as bears to it the same proportion as the value of the consideration, at the time the lease was granted, bore to what would then have been the value of a full consideration in money or money's worth."

The effect of these provisions is that if, e.g. A grants a lease to B for two-thirds of the consideration that B should have paid, B is treated as having an interest in one-third of the property, while A is treated as owning the remaining two-thirds of the property.

Authorised unit trusts and open-ended investment companies

32–60   A reversionary interest in a holding in an authorised unit trust[141] or in a share in an open-ended investment company[142] is excluded property in relation to a transfer of value or other event occurring after October 15, 2002[143] if the person beneficially entitled to it is an individual domiciled outside the United Kingdom.[144] In relation to interests in possession arising on or after December 5, 2005, these provisions are

---

[141] See para.32–39.
[142] See para.32–39.
[143] FA 1986 s.186(8).
[144] IHTA 1986 ss.6(1A) and 48(3A)(a) and (b).

1158

subject to the anti-avoidance provisions relating to purchased trust interests in s.48(3B) and (3C).

The foreign element

Although some controversy existed under the original IHT legislation[145] as to the treatment of reversionary interests as excluded property, the position can now be confidently stated to be as follows:

    32–61

(1) where the settled property in which the reversionary interest subsists is situated in the United Kingdom, the general rule in s.48(1) (and the three exceptions thereto) apply; and

(2) where the settled property in which the reversionary interest subsists is situated outside the United Kingdom, the general rule in s.48(1) (and the three exceptions thereto) apply but even if that rule is not satisfied the interest will still be excluded property under s.6(1) if an individual domiciled outside the United Kingdom for IHT purposes is beneficially entitled to it.[146]

Situs of reversionary interests

The courts have never clearly ruled as to whether a reversionary interest is an interest in trust assets in specie or a chose in action; if it is the former it would be situated where the trust assets are situated; if it is the latter, it would normally be regarded as situated in the country where it is properly recoverable.[147] HMRC take the view that a reversionary interest will normally be situated where the trustees of the property to which the interest relates reside.[148]

    32–62

Settled reversionary interests

Where a person settles a reversionary interest (so that the interest itself becomes settled property, as opposed to being merely an interest in settled property), it is thought that the position varies according to whether the interest is situated in the United Kingdom or abroad. If the interest is situated in the United Kingdom, the general rule under s.48(1) applies, and the interest (and thus the settled property it comprises) will be excluded property unless the interest falls within one of the three exceptions to the general rule.[149] If the interest is situated outside the United Kingdom, the governing provision is s.48(3)(a), so that the interest (and thus the settled property it comprises)

    32–63

---

[145] See para.15–31 of the third edition of this book.
[146] HMRC Manuals IHTM4286.
[147] See *New York Life Insurance Co v Public Trustee* [1924] 2 Ch. 101; *Swiss Bank Corp v Boehmische Industrial Bank* [1923] 1 K.B. 673; *Sutherland v Administrator of German Property* [1934] 1 K.B. 423.
[148] HMRC Manuals IHTM27230.
[149] It is thought that the limitation in IHTA 1984 s.98(1)(b) applies only where the reversionary interest arose under a settlement made by the settlor.

is excluded property only if the person who settled the interest was an individual domiciled outside the United Kingdom at the time he made the settlement.

Special case: acquisition of reversionary interest by beneficiary with prior interest

32–64   As a general rule[150] a person's estate is the aggregate of all the property to which he is beneficially entitled. This is, however, subject to a qualification found in s.55(1) which provides that where a person beneficially entitled to an interest (whether or not an interest in possession) in any settled property acquires a reversionary interest expectant on that interest, the reversionary interest which he acquired is not part of his estate. The reason for this provision is as follows. Assume A has a qualifying interest in possession in settled property; A is treated as owning the property in which his interest subsists. If he were to acquire a reversionary interest in the same property he would therefore be regarded as acquiring something which he already owned. If he paid money to acquire the interest the value of his estate would have been diminished, but he probably would have been able to rely on s.10(1), with the result that he would not have made a transfer of value notwithstanding that diminution. The fact that the reversion was excluded property would have been irrelevant, since the excluded property provisions apply only to property leaving one's estate, not to property entering it. Accordingly, s.55(1) provides that in such circumstances the reversionary interest never becomes comprised in the purchaser's estate,[151] and s.55(2) provides that in such circumstances the relief under s.10(1) is unavailable. The net result is that such a purchaser is regarded as having made a gift of the purchase price.

32–65   In the absence of provision to the contrary it would be possible to avoid tax notwithstanding s.55(1). Assume that, as in the example above, A has a qualifying interest in possession in settled property with his son (B) entitled to the remainder interest. Instead of A purchasing the reversion, that reversion is purchased instead by C (who could be, for example, A's spouse or a friendly charity). C then sells the reversion to A; under s.55(1) the purchase price paid by A is a transfer of value but would qualify for either the spouse or charity exemption. The net result would thus be that B ended up with the sale price free of IHT. Section 56(1) prevents this by providing that the exemptions available under ss.18 and 23–27 do not apply in relation to property which is given in consideration of the transfer of a reversionary interest in circumstances where, thanks to s.55(1), that interest does not form part of the estate of the person acquiring it.

VII. THE SITUS RULES

32–66   While there are special rules for determining a person's domicile, there are no such rules, except where a double taxation treaty applies, for determining the situs of property. That being the case, the normal common law rules apply. This contrasts with the CGT legislation, which contains special rules for determining the situs of property, but which lacks any provision for determining a person's domicile. The result is that

---

[150] See para.2–04.

[151] This seems unnecessary since, given the fact that the purchaser is already treated as owning the property, the payment of the purchase price would diminish the value of his estate even though the reversion was incorporated into the purchaser's estate.

a person can be domiciled in the United Kingdom for IHT purposes, but not for CGT purposes, and the same property can be situated in different places for purposes of IHT and CGT. (So far as income tax is concerned the normal common law rules apply for determining both domicile and situs.)

Under common law every asset has a situs and that situs can only be in one jurisdiction at any particular time.[152]

Situs, like domicile, is a subject in itself, and the reader is again referred to *Dicey, Morris and Collins on the Conflict of Laws*.[153] An overview of the main rules appears below:

(1) Bank and building society accounts:
    (a) As to bank accounts, see below under "Debts".
    (b) A building society account[154] is an interest in the society and, if the account is with a UK building society, it will have a UK situs.[155]

(2) Bare trusts:
The nature and situs of the interest of a beneficiary under a bare trust raises difficult questions which were considered, if not resolved, by the Court of Appeal in *IRC v Stype Investments (Jersey) Ltd*.[156] The facts of the case are set out at para.29–64. At the time when the Court of Appeal heard the case the domicile of Sir Charles Clore had not been finally determined, and HMRC accordingly wished to establish that his interest under the bare trust was situated in the United Kingdom. This turned on whether Sir Charles could be regarded as having:
    (a) rights under the contract of sale which, since they were enforceable in the United Kingdom would have been regarded as being situated in the United Kingdom, or
    (b) only rights as a beneficiary against the trustee for due performance of the trust, which would have been situated in Jersey, where the trustee was resident.

In argument before the court it was suggested that this turned on whether Sir Charles's interests after entering into the contract of sale were moveable or immoveable, but the Court of Appeal held that this was not critical:

> "Immediately after the contract for sale had been entered into by Stype Investments with the Prudential, Sir Charles was entitled in equity to the Guy's Estate in fee simple subject to, and with the benefit of, the contract. He was entitled in equity to the purchase price payable by the Prudential and to the benefit of the rights of Stype Investments to enforce in England the obligations of the Prudential and to be paid damages for breach of those obligations. Whether those interests of Sir Charles ought to be classified as immovables, as the Inland Revenue assert, or as movables, as Stype Investments claims, is immaterial. Those interests were property situate in England. The Guy's Estate was land in England, the rights to specific performance and damages were enforceable, and only enforceable, in England, and the purchase price was an obligation or debt which would fall to be performed and paid by the Prudential, an English company, and this obligation or debt was therefore also situate in England."

(3) Bearer shares and securities:

---

[152] *R v Williams* [1942] A.C. 541.
[153] See also the IHT Manual at IHTM27071 and following.
[154] Note that a number of former UK building societies are now banks, following demutualisation.
[155] See IHT Manual IHTM27151.
[156] *IRC v Stype Investments (Jersey) Ltd* [1982] Ch. 456.

Bearer shares and securities are situated where the share certificate is physically located.[157]

(4) Chattels:

Chattels are situated wherever they happen to be physically at the relevant time, even if the location is of a temporary nature.[158] Special rules apply to ships and aircraft (see below).

(5) Debts:

Debts fall into four categories, as follows:

(a) Generally: debts are normally situated where the debtor resides.[159]

(b) Bank debts (bank accounts): a debt owed by a bank in respect of a bank account is situated at the branch where the debt is primarily repayable.[160] In practice, this is normally the branch where the account is maintained.

(c) Specialty debts: a debt due under a deed is situated where the deed is kept.[161] As Scottish law does not recognise a specialty debt, in Scotland the debtor's residence will determine the situs.

(d) Judgment debts: a judgment debt is situated where the judgment is recorded.

(6) Land:

An interest in land: this is situated where the land itself is situated. This rule applies equally where an interest in land[162] is treated under the doctrine of conversion as an interest in personalty, e.g. where there is a trust for sale.

(7) Partnership share: see para.28–05.

(8) Policies of life assurance:

Generally, a policy is situated where the proceeds are payable under the terms of the policy. Where the policy is silent (and subject to the circumstances noted below) the situs will be where the life assurance company is resident (normally where the company has its head office):

(a) Where the policy provides for payment at a place other than the company's residence, the policy will be situate at the place of payment.

(b) Where the policy is issued by a branch in a different jurisdiction and either provides for payment at head office or a branch, or does not provide for a place of payment, the policy may be situate at that branch provided the whole course of business in relation to the policy was transacted in the country where the branch is located. To satisfy the requirement as to the "whole course of business", the policy must have been issued to a person who is, and remains, resident in the same country as the branch, that person must retain the policy there and pay the premiums to that branch and representation to the person's estate must be taken, and the policy monies collected, there.

(c) Policies issued under seal (i.e. by deed)[163] are specialty debts and the policy is situated where the policy deed is held at the relevant time.

(9) Registered shares and securities[164]:

---

[157] *Winans v Att Gen (No.2)* [1978] S.T.C. 272.
[158] See para.32–46 above for the special rules that apply to foreign-owned works of art.
[159] *New York Life Insurance Co v Public Trustee* [1924] 2 Ch. 101.
[160] *Martin v Nadel* [1906] 2 K.B. 26; *R v Lovitt* [1912] A.C. 212.
[161] *Gurney v Rawlins* (1836) 2 M. & W. 87; *Royal Trust Co v Att Gen For Alberta* [1930] A.C. 144; *Kwok Chi Leung Karl v Commissioner of Estate Duty* [1988] S.T.C. 728.
[162] Other jurisdictions may regard certain interests in, or relating to, land as movable property.
[163] Note the comment at IHTM27104 regarding Lloyd's policies: "Most Lloyds policies are embossed with a seal but they are not specialties unless additionally they bear the witnessed personal signature of the General Manager of Lloyds Policy Signing Office."
[164] See above for the treatment of bearer shares and securities.

In general, shares are situated where they can "effectively be dealt with".[165]
More specifically:

(a) Registered shares and securities are situated where they are registered.[166] In some cases, there is more than one register. Where (as is the case for UK companies) the shares or securities can only legally be dealt with on one (main) register, situs of the shares and securities is determined by the location of that main register; other shares or securities which are transferable upon more than one register are situated where they would normally be dealt with in the ordinary course of business.[167]

(b) Registered government securities: these are situated at the place of registration.

(10) Reversionary interests: see para.32–62.

(11) Securities issued by international organisations:
Certain securities issued by international organisations are deemed to have a non-UK situs. Examples are securities issued by the OECD support fund and the European Bank for Reconstruction and Development. The Inheritance Tax Manual provides details at IHTM27141, IHTM27142 and IHTM27143.

(12) Ships and aircraft:
A ship's situs depends on whether she is within national/territorial waters or on the high seas. When in national/territorial waters she is situated where she is physically located; but when she is on the high seas her situs is determined by her port of registration.[168] The same rules apply by implication to aircraft[169] so that an aircraft in flight in international airspace will have a situs in its country of registration but where it is on the ground in, or in the airspace of, a particular jurisdiction, it will have a situs in that jurisdiction.

(13) Unadministered estates:
Under s.91 of the Act an interest (whether limited or absolute) in the whole or part of the residue of an unadministered estate is treated as a direct interest in the underlying assets and it is therefore the situs of each underlying asset that is relevant for IHT rather than the situs of the estate itself.[170]

Planning

It is often possible to change the situs of the relevant asset. For example, assume that **32–67** trustees of a settlement created by a foreign domiciliary own a debt situated in the United Kingdom and which is therefore not excluded property. As matters stand, the relevant asset is the UK situs debt. The trustees could alter the situs of the relevant asset by transferring the debt to a company[171] whose shares are registered abroad in exchange for shares in that company, in which case the relevant asset would be the non-UK situs shares.

---

[165] Per Lord Dunedin in *Brassard v Smith* [1925] A.C. 371 at 376, explained in *R v Williams* [1942] A.C. 541 as meaning "effectively dealt with as between the shareholder and the company".

[166] The fact that the business of the company may be administered entirely outside the country where the register is kept is irrelevant: see *Baelz v Public Trustee* [1926] Ch. 863.

[167] *Treasurer of Ontario v Aberdein* [1947] A.C. 24. See also *Standard Chartered Bank v IRC* [1978] 1 W.L.R. 1160; [1978] S.T.C. 272.

[168] *Trustees Executors and Agency Co Ltd v IRC* [1973] Ch. 254.

[169] Per Tomlinson J. in *Dornoch v Westminster International BV* [2009] EWHC 889 (Admlty) at 103.

[170] This is in contrast to the general rule that the interest is a chose in action enforceable against the personal representatives.

[171] If the nature of the asset is such that a director or shadow director of the company benefits from it, regard will have to be had to the ITEPA 2003 implications of the arrangement.

There is no better example of the dramatic effect such an approach can produce than *Kwok Chi Leung Karl v Commissioner of Estate Duty*[172] which involved the successful avoidance of Hong Kong estate duty. The facts were that the Hong Kong resident testator owned shares which on his death would be liable to Hong Kong estate duty because they were "property situate" in Hong Kong. In order to convert the property into property not so situate a Liberian company was formed with a registered agent in Monrovia for service of process on it there. The directors were three of the testator's sons; all the issued shares were bearer shares held by the testator's wife and his four sons. The company resolved to acquire from the testator his share in consideration of a non-negotiable promissory note, payable on demand in Monrovia after 60 days. Eight days later the contract for the sale of shares was executed. The very next day the testator died.

The Hong Kong Revenue refused to accept that no duty was payable and succeeded before the Hong Kong Court of Appeal. The Privy Council found for the taxpayer, holding that since it had not been suggested in any of the previous proceedings that the transactions were a sham the Privy Council was bound to proceed on the basis that the transactions genuinely transformed the testator's shares into the promissory note. The only issue was therefore where that note was situated. The Hong Kong Court of Appeal had approached the matter on the footing that the only "property" of the testator on his death was his present right to assign the future right to present the promissory note and to receive payment and that whether the situs of that right was represented by the presence of the testator himself or by the note as a physical chattel, both were situated in Hong Kong.

The Privy Council found this approach misconceived. The promissory note was a chose in action and the fact that it was not immediately recoverable did not affect its status. The basic rule was that a chose in action was situated in the country in which it could be recovered or enforced. As a matter of general law this fell to be determined in the case of a corporate debtor according to the whereabouts of the company for purposes of service, not according to where it was resident for tax purposes. Even if service could be performed in both Monrovia and Hong Kong, since the contract provided for the debt to be discharged in Monrovia that was where the note was situate.

The Privy Council arrived at this conclusion "without any feeling of satisfaction", but noted that there would have been nothing startling about such a conclusion in the context of an arm's length transaction. The Privy Council did, however, leave a marker for other tax planning gymnastics of a similar ilk:

> "As has already been stated, no challenge has been raised to the bona fides of the transaction, so that their Lordships have been compelled, as were the courts below, to treat it in the same way as an arm's length transaction. Lest, however, it should be thought that the door has been opened to making estate duty in Hong Kong a voluntary imposition, their Lordships would add that it would be unwise to assume that the genuineness of similar transactions in the future will necessarily be beyond challenge."[173]

---

[172] *Kwok Chi Leung Karl v Commissioner of Estate Duty* [1988] S.T.C. 728.
[173] *Kwok Chi Leung Karl v Commissioner of Estate Duty* [1988] S.T.C. 728 at 732–733.

CHAPTER 33

DOUBLE TAXATION RELIEF

I. INTRODUCTION

IHT is a worldwide tax, and there will often be occasions on which there is both a **33–01**
charge to IHT and a charge to one or more similar foreign taxes. This is particularly

likely to happen on death. The legislation accordingly makes provision in ss.158 and 159 to give two kinds of relief where such a dual (or multiple) charge arises. The first kind of relief, unilateral relief, is available whether or not a double taxation treaty[1] is in force with the other country or countries charging tax. The second kind of relief, bilateral relief, is available only where a treaty is in force. In the event that both kinds of relief are available only one relief is in fact given—that which gives the greater benefit to the taxpayer.[2] Where the relief given is the same under both unilateral and bilateral relief, it will be treated as given under the relevant treaty.[3]

33–02   The main aim of double taxation treaties is to limit the tax jurisdiction of the contracting states to avoid double taxation. The treaties seek to prevent or resolve situations of double taxation which arise where the tax claims of two countries (the country where the deceased was domiciled and the country where an asset is located) overlap (co-existence) or where two or more countries regard the deceased as "domiciled" in their territory (dual domicile cases) or a certain asset as situated in their territory (dual situs cases).

Older treaties usually do not alter the fundamental principle contained in most domestic laws that a state should have a right to tax all the assets (wherever situated) of individuals who are domiciled in their territory and that the state in which the deceased was not domiciled but in which he left assets should have a taxing right in relation to these assets. Instead, they provide for a relief in the form of a tax credit to be given by the country of domicile for tax paid in the country of the asset's situs (see e.g. the Treaty with France of 1963).

33–03   The OECD Models[4] departed from the principle of co-existence of tax jurisdictions coupled with a relief mechanism; they instead introduced the idea that the taxing right of the domicile state should have precedence over the taxing right of the situs state. Accordingly, the OECD provides that "other property", i.e. property other than immovables and business property, is taxed primarily by the country of domicile, with the other state reserving a secondary taxing right, but only in limited circumstances. Most modern treaties concluded by the United Kingdom, such as those with Ireland and South Africa (1978), the Netherlands (1979), Sweden (1980) and the United States (1978), are substantially founded on this principle.

33–04   A separate question is whether the contracting states may apply a treaty to extend their tax jurisdiction. This question arises when the treaty allocates taxing rights to one of the contracting states in a situation in which it would not have any tax jurisdiction under its own domestic rules. In such circumstances, the code contained in the treaty should operate only to allocate the tax jurisdiction when both states claim a right to tax the property and both states would impose duty under their domestic laws. Therefore, one should start with the domestic laws—if a country does not impose a charge to tax under its domestic law, then the treaty does not apply. Conversely, if both countries impose a charge to tax (or one does and the other does not as a result of a specific exemption), the potential double taxation that arises is to be resolved in accordance with the treaty.

---

[1] The word "treaty" has been used throughout this chapter in preference to "double tax agreement", "double tax convention" and "double tax arrangement".

[2] IHTA 1984 s.159(7).

[3] HMRC Manuals IHTM27189.

[4] The 1966 and 1982 Model Double Taxation Conventions on Estates and Inheritances and on Gifts.

Double tax relief normally assumes three forms, each of which is best shown by an   **33–05**
example.

Tax credit

First, provision may be made to give a tax credit. Assume Alex, a UK domiciliary,   **33–06**
dies owning property situated in the United Kingdom and property situated abroad in
a country—"Arcadia" (not Utopia, where, of course, taxes do not exist)—which
imposes a tax similar to IHT. Under UK law[5] lHT is charged on both the United
Kingdom and the Arcadian property, and under Arcadian law Arcadian tax is charged,
by virtue of the property being situated in Arcadia, on the Arcadian property. The first
way in which double tax relief could be given would be for the tax paid in Arcadia to
be allowed as a credit[6] against the IHT due on the Arcadian property. This would
effectively prevent a dual charge on the same property.

Scope of charge restricted

Secondly, provision may be made by treaty to restrict the scope of the charge.   **33–07**
Assume the facts are as above, but that under Arcadian law Alex is an Arcadian
domiciliary, and that under the IHT deemed domicile rules he is a UK domiciliary. In
such a case provision may be made so that IHT is not chargeable on the Arcadian
property. Both IHT and Arcadian tax will be charged on the UK property, but Alex will
be given a credit for the IHT paid on that property against the Arcadian tax due on
it.

Situs rules

Thirdly, situs rules may be prescribed by treaty. These will prevent the same property   **33–08**
being regarded as situated in more than one place. Assume the facts are as above, but
that Arcadian law regards the property as situated in the United Kingdom while under
UK law the property is situated in Arcadia. If situs rules are prescribed the property will
be regarded as situated in but one place, be it the United Kingdom, Arcadia, or,
perhaps, a third country.

Unilateral v bilateral relief

Unilateral relief provides only the first kind of relief. Where bilateral relief applies   **33–09**
all three kinds of relief will normally be available; exceptionally, some of the estate

---

[5] Strictly speaking there is no such thing as "UK law", but it is thought that this expression, which is used
in the text to comprehend the law of England and Wales, the law of Northern Ireland and the law of Scotland
is not misleading or improper.

[6] See para.25–33 for the helpful official practice regarding the conversion of foreign duty to sterling.

duty treaties (e.g. the 1956 Treaty with Switzerland) provided only for the latter two kinds of relief, and not for a tax credit. Bilateral relief may also result in the deemed domicile provisions being overridden.[7] Where bilateral relief is available by virtue of an estate duty treaty the relief is available only on death, while unilateral relief is available on lifetime transfers as well as on transfers on death; indeed, where appropriate, it is also available on capital distributions.

33–10   Given the fact that unilateral relief is always available and operates only by providing for a tax credit, it will be easier to consider it first. Before doing so, however, two minor points deserve mention.

Further points

33–11   First, neither the legislation nor any of the double tax treaties refers to "countries". Instead, reference is made to "territories". Under estate duty, "territory" included territorial subdivisions of a country, such as Swiss cantons and the states in the United States where those subdivisions impose death duties of their own, even though those duties may have been imposed in addition to "federal" duty.[8] The position is the same for IHT.[9]

Secondly, for double taxation purposes "tax" in ss.158 and 159 does not include interest on tax or any other payment or penalty for late payment of tax—a good reason for paying taxes promptly.

Concessionary relief

33–12   In addition to unilateral relief and bilateral relief, both discussed is more detail below, certain foreign taxes may be allowed as a deduction against the value of estate on death, or the value of particular assets.

1. *Canadian income tax*
In 1978 the 1946 Canadian Death Duties Agreement was terminated with effect from October 1, 1978, but concessionary treatment is granted with regard to the Canadian income tax charge which arises on the death of an individual. Under Canadian income tax law the estate of an individual is deemed to have been disposed of immediately before his death, and income tax is charged on any resulting capital gains. For IHT purposes, a person's outstanding debts are deducted in arriving at the value of his estate but, as the Canadian income tax charge arises after the death, this would not strictly be an allowable debt for IHT. However, a deduction is allowed by concession ESC F18 which reads as follows:

"1. Under 5(3) of the IHT Act 1984 a person's liabilities at the time of death are taken into account in arriving at the value of their estate for the purposes of IHT. The Board

---

[7] See para.33–28.
[8] Although there are currently no federal duties in the Swiss cantons (see para.33–122), there are proposals to introduce a federal gift and estate tax. If the proposals are implemented, the tax would most likely be introduced as from January 1, 2016, although it is anticipated that certain of its provisions relating to lifetime gifts would have retrospective effect to January 1, 2012.
[9] See HMRC Manuals IHTM27181.

of Inland Revenue will by concession regard this provision as applying to income tax in Canada charged on a deemed disposal immediately before death, even though the liability may not in strictness have arisen until the person had died.

2. Where there is an IHT charge on a deceased person's world-wide estate, and income tax in Canada is charged on deemed gains which are attributable to assets forming part of that estate, the Canadian tax will rank as a deduction in arriving at the value of the estate for IHT purposes. The Canadian tax will normally be treated as reducing the value of assets outside the United Kingdom whether those assets are liable to IHT or not; but if the Canadian Tax exceeds the value of those assets, the excess will be set off against the value of the United Kingdom assets."

The effect of the concession is that the Canadian income tax will be allowable as a deduction in arriving at the value of the estate for IHT purposes.

2. *Shares*

Where shares that are regarded as having a UK situs for IHT purposes are also subject to tax in another country, the foreign tax is, by concession, allowable as a deduction in valuing the shares for IHT purposes. This concessionary treatment does not apply to cases falling within ss.158 and 159 of the Act nor to circumstances where the liability to foreign tax arises under the terms of a double tax treaty to which the United Kingdom is not a party.[10]

III. UNILATERAL RELIEF

Unilateral relief is provided for under s.159. Assuming the conditions outlined below are met, relief against IHT will be given by the United Kingdom in respect of foreign taxes whether or not the other jurisdiction affords similar relief. Unilateral relief also differs from bilateral relief in that it provides only for a tax credit for overseas tax. It does not affect:　　**33–13**

(1) the property on which tax is charged[11]; or
(2) the situs of property.

Furthermore, where unilateral relief is given the deemed domicile rules operate　　**33–14**
without restriction.[12] This means that when a person dies he may be taxed on his worldwide assets in more than one territory. As was mentioned above, where both unilateral and bilateral relief are available, only one type of relief, the one that helps the taxpayer more, is given.[13]

Conditions for relief

Unilateral relief will be available if the following four conditions are satisfied:　　**33–15**

---

[10] See IHTM27201. The IHT Manual notes that the concession "applies in the same way where the obligation to pay the foreign tax on death falls upon the company and the company has the right to be reimbursed by the personal representatives of the deceased shareholder before it registers a transfer of the shares."

[11] The fact that unilateral relief does not remove an asset from the charge to tax is relevant in determining the availability of a deceased spouse/civil partner's unused nil rate band on the death of the surviving spouse/ civil partner—see IHTM43025.

[12] Compare where bilateral relief is given; see para.33–28.

[13] IHTA 1984 s.159(7).

(1) HMRC must be satisfied that any amount of tax chargeable in any overseas territory under the law of that territory is attributable to[14] the value of property.

(2) The overseas tax must be:
(a) of a character similar to that of IHT; or
(b) chargeable on or by reference to death or gifts inter vivos.

(3) The overseas tax have been paid by the person liable to pay it.

(4) The IHT chargeable by reference to the disposition or event in question must also be at least partly attributable to the value of the property in question.[15]

Tax credit

33–16   The relief takes the form of a tax credit against the IHT attributable to the value of the property in question. This credit varies with the situs of the property in question in the following way.

Property situated in the overseas territory

33–17   By s.159(2), where the property is situated in the overseas territory and not in the United Kingdom, credit is given for all the overseas tax (up to the amount of IHT which is attributable to the value of the property).

Property situated in the United Kingdom

33–18   The legislation makes no provision for property situated in the United Kingdom but not in the overseas territory charging tax, and therefore as a matter of law no credit is given for any of the tax charged by that territory.[16]

Property not situated in the United Kingdom or the overseas territory

33–19   It may be that the property is not situated in either the United Kingdom or the overseas territory. This could happen, e.g. where a person domiciled in New Zealand under New Zealand law and domiciled in the United Kingdom under UK general law or the deemed domicile provisions died owning property situated in the Bahamas, where there are no death duties. New Zealand duty and UK IHT would both be charged on a worldwide basis, with the result that the Bahamian property would be subject to a dual charge. In such a case the credit is calculated under s.159(3) according to the formula:

---

[14] For meaning of "attributable to" see para.3–39.

[15] IHTA 1984 s.159(1) and (6).

[16] By concession, where shares are situated in the United Kingdom under UK law, and the overseas territory imposes tax for some reason other than the situs of the shares HMRC allow the foreign tax to be deducted from the value of the shares. See para.33–12 above.

$$\frac{\text{IHT}}{\text{IHT} + \text{overseas tax}} \times \text{smaller of IHT and overseas tax} = \text{credit}$$

Thus, if the facts are as above and the IHT is £100,000 and the New Zealand duty £50,000, the tax credit is:

$$\frac{£100,000}{£100,000 + £50,000} \times £50,000 = £33,333$$

It may be that tax is charged in the United Kingdom and in two overseas territories, in one of which the property is situated, and in the other of which it is not. In that case, by s.159(5), the above calculation is made after the IHT has been reduced by the unilateral (or, where appropriate, the bilateral) credit given against the IHT for the tax paid in the territory in which the property is situated.

For example, assume that the property in the above example was situated in Germany, not the Bahamas, so that in addition to the IHT of £100,000 and the New Zealand tax of £50,000, German tax of £25,000 was also payable. In that case there would have been two tax credits, one of £25,000 under s. 159(2) for the German tax, and one of:

$$\frac{£75,000}{£75,000 + £50,000} \times £50,000 = £30,000$$

for the New Zealand tax.[17]

Property situated both in the United Kingdom and in the overseas territory

This exceptional case is envisaged by s.159(3)(b) and (4)(b). It could arise either because: **33–20**

(1) under English law it is possible in certain circumstances for the same property to be situated in two different places (e.g. where a bill of exchange is transferable in the United Kingdom and the debtor is resident abroad the bill itself is situated in the United Kingdom but the debt is situated at the debtor's residence); or

(2) because of a conflict between a law of the United Kingdom (which would regard the property as situated here) and that of an overseas territory charging tax that the property is situated there.[18] While there is no express provision in s.159 to suggest that reference is to be made to other than UK law, so that as

---

[17] If New Zealand gave credit for the German tax, the result would be £75,000/£75,000 − £25,000 X £25,000 = £18,750.

[18] There could also be circumstances where there is a conflict between English law and Scots law e.g. as regards a specialty debt which English law regards as situated where the deed is kept, while Scots law regards the same debt as situated where the debtor resides (in such a case the position is the same as under para.33–19 above).

a matter of statutory construction prima facie no reference to foreign law can be made, a second rule of statutory construction allows such a reference where the context requires it, and in the circumstances the context requires such a reference.

IV. BILATERAL RELIEF

33–21 Far fewer double taxation treaties apply for IHT purposes than for income tax and capital gains tax purposes. Ten treaties are currently relevant for IHT purposes (although, as will be explained, the effect of some of these treaties is now limited.) Each is commented on below.

In considering how far references in a treaty to a "spouse" includes a civil partner, the IHTM notes, at IHTM27161,

> "that not all the countries with which we have Double Taxation Conventions will necessarily have civil partnership legislation ... As a result, please do not automatically assume that civil partners will have the same rights as spouses."

Current treaties

33–22 The current[19] treaties are:

France—Double Taxation Relief (Estate Duty) Order 1963
India—Double Taxation Relief (Estate Duty) Order 1956
Ireland—Double Taxation Relief (Taxes on Estates of Deceased Persons and Inheritances and on Gifts) Order 1978
Italy—Double Taxation Relief (Estate Duty) Order 1968
Netherlands—Double Taxation Relief (Taxes on Estates of Deceased Persons and Inheritances and on Gifts) Orders 1980 and 1996
Pakistan—Double Taxation Relief (Estate Duty) Order 1957
South Africa—Double Taxation Relief (Taxes on Estates of Deceased Persons and on Gifts) Order 1979
Sweden—Double Taxation Relief (Taxes on Estates of Deceased Persons and Inheritances and on Gifts) Orders 1981 and 1989
Switzerland—Double Taxation Relief (Taxes on Estates of Deceased Persons and Inheritances) 1994
USA—Double Taxation Relief (Taxes on Estates of Deceased Persons and on Gifts) Order 1979

How the treaties operate

33–23 Bilateral relief takes two forms. First, relief is available under the four surviving estate duty treaties (with France, India, Italy and Pakistan), which continue to operate, and have effect for IHT as they did for estate duty. These treaties apply only where the

---

[19] The treaty with Canada was terminated with effect from October 1, 1978. For the concessionary treatment now applicable see para.33–12 above.

charge arises on death. Secondly, relief is available under treaties made with the government of any foreign territory to afford relief from double taxation in relation to IHT and any "foreign IHT" imposed by the laws of that territory. The only such treaties in force at the time of writing are those with Ireland, South Africa, the United States, the Netherlands, Switzerland and Sweden. Inheritance tax treaties may have retrospective effect.[20]

Most countries base their succession tax jurisdiction on "domicile" and situs. **33–24** Whenever an individual dies leaving assets in various countries, the tax claims of the state where the deceased was domiciled are likely to overlap, in part, with the tax claims of the state where the assets are situated (if different). One of the aims of double tax treaties is to allocate the tax jurisdiction between the state of domicile and the state of situs.

Most modern treaties concluded by the United Kingdom, such as those with Ireland, **33–25** the Netherlands, South Africa, Sweden and the United States are based on the solution adopted by the OECD Models[21] that the taxing right of the state of domicile should, in most circumstances, have precedence over the taxing right of the situs state. Accordingly, "other property", i.e. property other than immovables and business property, is taxed primarily by the country of domicile, with the other state reserving a secondary taxing right, but only in limited circumstances. By contrast, the Treaty with France, for example (which was concluded before the 1966 OECD Model was published), maintains the traditional model of coexistence between the taxing rights of the state of domicile and of the state of situs, coupled with a relief from double taxation provided by way of a credit given by the state of domicile for tax paid in the state of situs.

In addition to the situations mentioned above of overlapping tax claims between two **33–26** countries (the country of domicile and the country of situs)—which can often be resolved using unilateral relief provisions, without the need for a treaty—there might be instances of conflicting claims if two (or more) states assert that the deceased was domiciled in their territory, or where the country of the deceased's domicile does not recognise that a certain asset (e.g. a debt) was situated in the state which claims tax jurisdiction based on situs. In these circumstances, any unilateral relief provision may not help. To avoid these so-called "characterisation" conflicts, various treaties contain an agreed situs code to avoid a dispute over the location of an asset, and a tie-breaker provision to deal with dual domicile cases.

Estate duty treaties

The legislation contains two provisions with regard to existing estate duty treaties. **33–27** First, s.158(6) provides:

> "Where arrangements with the government of any territory outside the United Kingdom are specified under any Order in Council which—
> (a) was made, or has effect as made, under s.54 of the Finance (No.2) Act 1945 or s.2 of the Finance Act (Northern Ireland) 1946 and
> (b) had effect immediately before the passing of this Act,
> the Order shall, notwithstanding the repeal of that section by the Finance Act 1975, remain in force and have effect as if any provision made by those arrangements in relation to estate duty extended to capital transfer tax chargeable by virtue of section 4 above . . ."

[20] IHTA 1984 s.158(2). The Irish treaty is retrospective to the start of CTT; see para.33–54.
[21] See para.33–03.

This ensures that the surviving estate duty arrangements may continue to apply for IHT purposes where a charge arises on death. Moreover, as discussed below, even where the surviving treaties have limited application (because, for instance, estate duty (or its equivalent) has been abolished in the other treaty territory) these arrangements can still have significant effects on IHT liability because of the effect of their terms on the UK's rules on deemed domicile.

Deemed domicile rules overridden

33–28   Under s.267(1) an individual is treated as domiciled in the United Kingdom if he was domiciled in the United Kingdom at any time within the previous three years or was resident in the United Kingdom for seventeen out of the previous 20 tax years.[22] However, s.267(2) provides that the deeming provisions in s.267(1) shall not affect the interpretation of any subsisting double tax treaty referred to in s.158(6) (that is, concluded before 1975).

Territorial restriction

33–29   The first effect of the treaties is that where a person dies domiciled outside the United Kingdom, IHT is charged only on so much of his property as is situated in the United Kingdom. The treaties achieve this effect by providing that, in such a case, in determining the amount or rate of British tax[23] no account is taken of property situated outside the United Kingdom.

It is at this stage that the importance of ignoring the deemed domicile rules in interpreting the treaties can be appreciated. Assume Pierre is domiciled in France under the general laws of the United Kingdom and France but in the United Kingdom under the deemed domicile rules. He owns property situated in the United Kingdom and property situated on the Continent. He dies and, given his "dual domicile", he is subject to both French estate duty and IHT. Under s.267(2) Pierre's deemed United Kingdom domicile is ignored for the purpose of interpreting the Anglo-French Treaty. He can therefore rely on art.V of the Treaty to ensure that IHT is charged only on his United Kingdom assets; see paras 33–44 and following. If s.267(2) did not displace the deemed domicile rules the protection afforded by art.V of the Treaty would not have been available, and Pierre, a deemed UK domiciliary, would have been liable to both IHT and French estate duty on his worldwide assets.

The above is subject to the qualification that art.V does not apply where the disposition giving rise to the charge to tax is governed by British law.[24] This restriction originates from the fact that the law governing the succession was relevant under the estate duty rules at the time.[25]

---

[22] For a detailed discussion on s.267, see paras 32–14 and following.

[23] Estate duty applied to Great Britain; IHT applies to the United Kingdom.

[24] For a detailed discussion of this point see Michael Parkinson, "'A disposition or devolution regulated by the law of some part of Great Britain': the proviso to the limitation of taxing rights in the inheritance tax treaties with France, India and Pakistan", *Private Client Business* (2011) 126. Note also, that the terms of the treaty with Italy on this point are rather different—see paras 33–73 and following.

[25] For example, see Stamp J. *In Re Weston's Settlements*: "Under section 28 of the Finance Act, 1949, exemption is conferred from estate duty in respect of property passing on the death if the property is not situate in the United Kingdom and it is shown that the proper law regulating the devolution of property or the disposition under or by reason of which it passes is the law neither of England nor of Scotland, and one of the conditions following is satisfied. Among those conditions is the condition that the property passes under or by reason of a disposition made by a person who, at the date at which the disposition took effect, was domiciled elsewhere than in some part of Great Britain." [1969] 1 Ch. 223 at 231–32.

It follows that, if a deceased's will is governed by British law, or if a charge to IHT arises on the termination of a qualifying interest in possession in a settlement[26] governed by "British" law, the treaty exemption will not be available, except, if the property situated abroad is land, in which case it would appear from the decision of the House of Lords in *Philipson-Snow v IRC*[27] that the law governing the disposition would be the *lex situs*.

Situs rules

The situs rules are important in two obvious ways. First, it follows from what was **33–30** just said concerning the operation of provisions such as art.V of the French[28] Treaty (and the limitation by s.267(2) of the deemed domicile rules) that a non-UK domiciliary's liability to IHT on property to which he is beneficially entitled will depend on where the property is situated. This, in turn, may depend on the situs rules in the treaty in question. Secondly, the rules may be important in the case of a person who at the time he died was beneficially entitled to a qualifying interest in possession under a settlement made by a settlor who was not a UK domiciliary[29] when he made the settlement. In such a case no charge will arise if the property in which the deceased's interest subsisted was situated outside the United Kingdom at the time of his death, since under s.48(3) the property will be excluded property.[30]

Tax credit

It may be that a person domiciled in the United Kingdom under the general law dies **33–31** owning property situated in the United Kingdom and property situated abroad. In that case the UK tax on the property situated abroad is charged to the extent only that it exceeds the foreign tax on that property, i.e. the taxpayer in effect gets a tax "credit" for foreign tax paid on the property in question. Conversely, a person who dies domiciled outside the United Kingdom owning property situated in the United Kingdom may be entitled to a "credit" for the UK tax paid against any foreign tax on the property situated in the United Kingdom.

IHT treaties

Section 158(1) provides that where arrangements have been made with the govern- **33–32** ment of any territory outside the United Kingdom with a view to affording relief from double taxation in relation to IHT and any tax imposed by the laws of that territory which is either:

(1) of a similar character to IHT; or

---

[26] No charge to IHT will arise, of course, is the settlement is an excluded property settlement.

[27] *Philipson-Snow v IRC* [1961] A.C. 727.

[28] Note that the French treaty contains more detailed situs rules than the other Estate Duty treaties.

[29] In deciding whether the settlor was a UK domiciliary, the deemed domicile rules will not apply if the settlement was made before December 10, 1974: IHTA 1984 s.267(3).

[30] For less obvious, and more complicated, ways in which the situs rules may be important see "Timeo Danaos" (by nine authors) in *British Tax Review* (1977), p.115.

(2) is chargeable by reference to death or gifts made inter vivos,

then those arrangements shall override the IHT provisions as regards relief from IHT and the determination of the situs of property for IHT purposes.

Fiscal domicile

33–33   The IHT treaties take account of the fact that an individual may under the domestic laws of the states which are party to the treaty in question be domiciled in both those states (e.g. as a result of the IHT deemed domicile rules), and accordingly provide a system of rules for establishing in which of the states in question the individual is to be regarded as domiciled for purposes of the treaty. The system used in the treaties is based on the OECD Model. It is to be noted that an individual's treaty domicile applies for purposes of the treaty in question only. Thus, if an individual who is domiciled in the United Kingdom for IHT purposes but who is domiciled abroad for the purposes of the treaty in question makes a settlement of foreign property, that property will not be excluded property for IHT purposes; it may, of course, receive favoured treatment under a specific provision of the treaty in question.[31]

Treaty quirks

33–34   Some specific treaty provisions are worth highlighting.

Effect of deemed domicile rules overridden

33–35   The treaties with France, Italy, India and Pakistan restrict the operation of the deemed domicile rules.[32]

Spouse exemption

33–36   As explained at para.3–35, where property passes from a UK domiciled spouse to a non-domiciled spouse, the usual spouse exemption is restricted.[33] However, further relief for gifts between spouses may be afforded by the terms of any relevant treaty. The treaties with the Netherlands, Switzerland, Sweden and the United States provide for an exemption of 50 per cent of the value transferred in these circumstances, subject to the specific conditions set out in each treaty.

Settled property

33–37   Under the treaties with the Netherlands, South Africa and Sweden, the United Kingdom cannot tax settled property if at the time of the making of the settlement the

---

[31] See para.33–37 below and, e.g., art.5(4) of the Treaty with the United States, discussed at para.33–149.

[32] See para.33–28 above and HMRC Manuals IHTM13024.

[33] Currently to £55,000. The 2012 Budget included proposed changes that would, inter alia, tag the exemption for non-UK domiciled spouses to the nil rate band.

settlor had a domicile in the other state (under the terms of the treaty) and was not a United Kingdom national who had been domiciled in the United Kingdom (again, under the treaty) in the preceding 10 years.

V. TREATY WITH FRANCE

The Double Taxation Treaty between the United Kingdom and France was con-   **33–38** cluded on June 21, 1963 and came into force on June 21, 1963 (see Double Taxation Relief (Estate Duty) (France) Order (SI 1963/1319)).

French tax jurisdiction

A detailed explanation of the French domestic tax system is outside the scope of this   **33–39** book. However, as the potential for double taxation is a pre-requisite for the application of the Treaty, it may be useful to outline the basic conditions which may give rise to a French tax claim in the context of a succession.

French succession tax is levied on a worldwide basis if the deceased was "domiciled" ("*domicilié*") in France (see paras 33–42 and following for a definition of "domicile"), though credit is given for foreign taxes paid (see s.784 of the *Code Général des Impôts* ("CGI")). If the deceased was not "domiciled" in France, succession tax is levied in respect of any immovables or movables situated there[34] which he owned directly or indirectly. In addition, France subjects any immovables or movables (wherever situated) received by a beneficiary who is domiciled in France to succession tax, though unilateral relief in the form of a tax credit is given in respect of foreign taxes.

The general definition of "domicile" under French law is contained in art.102 of the French Civil Code (an individual is "domiciled" in the place where he has his "principal establishment" ("*son principal établissement*")); art.4B of the CGI contains a special definition of "domicile" for tax purposes. Accordingly, an individual is "domiciled" in France for tax purposes, if he:

(1) has his "*foyer*" (literally: "hearth") or his primary place of residence ("*lieu de séjour principal*") in France (the "*foyer*" test is a subjective one that seeks to establish the place which an individual considers to be his home);
(2) carries out a professional activity (whether as an employee or not) in France, unless he can show that this activity has an ancillary character; or
(3) has the centre of his economic interests in France.

The Treaty applies to French succession duty, to UK estate duty and to any other   **33–40** duties of a similar character imposed in either state on death. The therefore Treaty covers IHT payable on death and so includes IHT payable on the death of a beneficiary with a qualifying interest in possession and in respect of property subject to a reservation of benefit as at the death (but not on lifetime gifts or, therefore, failed PETs)

---

[34] The *Code Général des Impôts* contains a situs code—see para.33–46.

and "*droits de mutation à titre gratuit*" (see s.750ter of the CGI) on deaths in France.

Avoidance of double taxation

33–41   The basic approach of the Treaty is to avoid double taxation:

(1) by treating a deceased as having been domiciled in only one of the states for Treaty purposes; and
(2) by giving the state in which property is situated the primary right to tax that property, the country in which the deceased was domiciled giving credit for that tax.

Fiscal domicile

33–42   There are two related issues. The first is where the taxpayer is domiciled under the domestic law of each of the countries. The second, if he is domiciled in France under French law and the United Kingdom under UK law, is where he is domiciled for purposes of the Treaty.

Domestic domicile

33–43   Domicile for UK IHT purposes is determined under the general law. By virtue of ss.158(5) and 267(2), the deemed domicile rules do not apply in a situation where the deceased was domiciled in France under its general law and in the United Kingdom under its general law. They do, however, apply where there is no domicile "mis-match" under the Treaty, i.e. where the deceased was domiciled in the United Kingdom under French general law and in the United Kingdom under UK general law (including the deemed domicile rules).

Treaty domicile

33–44   The respective domestic rules of France and the United Kingdom apply, save that by ss.158(6) and 267(2) the IHT deemed domicile rules are prevented from applying where, under French domestic law, the individual is domiciled in France.

33–45   Dual domicile cases arise easily under the French Treaty, because of the wide definition of French domicile and the tenacious nature of domicile in the United Kingdom (even taking account of the limitation on the application of the "deemed domicile" rules referred to above). Where an individual is domiciled in both countries art.II(3)(b) provides for the application of tie-breaker tests based on permanent home, centre of vital interests, habitual abode, nationality and mutual agreement.

Treaty situs

33–46   The Treaty provides in art.IV detailed rules for determining the treaty situs of an asset. By art.III(1), these rules, which apply for the purposes of the imposition of tax and of any tax credit, operate only where on a person's death he was domiciled in one of the states and duty would be imposed in both states or in one state but not the other but for some "specific exemption" in the latter state. The rules will thus apply where IHT is prevented from being charged by, e.g., the spouse exemption.

The situs code in art.IV deals specifically with immovables (see art.IV(a); it is **33–47** understood that in France immovables are defined in arts 527–536 of the *Code Civil*), tangible movable property and rights and interests therein (art.IV(b)); debts, secured or unsecured, including debentures and debenture stock, bills of exchange, promissory notes and cheques (art.IV(c)); securities issued by any government, county council, *département*, municipality or other public authority (art.IV(d)); shares or stock in a company (art.IV(e)); moneys payable under a policy of assurance (art.IV(f)); an interest in a partnership, including a *société en nom collectif, a société en commandite simple* and a *société civile* under French law (art.IV(g)); goodwill (art.IV(h)); ships and aircraft (art.IV(i)); patents, trademarks, designs copyrights (art.IV(j)); rights or causes of action *ex delicto* (art.IV(k)); judgement debts (art.IV(l)); and "any other right or interest" (art.IV(m)).

Taxing rights

The Treaty establishes two kinds of taxing rights: **33–48**

(1) *Exclusive taxing rights*: in two cases, it assigns exclusive taxing rights to one country.
(2) *Dual taxing rights and tax credits*: aside from the two cases just mentioned, where the taxpayer is treaty domiciled in one country and the asset is situated in the other country the country in which the taxpayer is domiciled has a domicile taxing right and the situs country retains a situs taxing right.

Exclusive taxing rights

Subject to one qualification, the country in which the deceased was Treaty domiciled **33–49** has the exclusive right to tax property which is Treaty situated outside the other country:

(1) under art.V(1) if the deceased died Treaty domiciled in France then France has the exclusive right to tax property outside Great Britain and such property is disregarded in determining the amount or rate of IHT. This is subject to the qualification that if the property passes under a disposition or devolution regulated by some part of Great Britain,[35] the United Kingdom retains its right to tax on the basis of domicile and the property is relevant in determining the amount or rate of IHT; and
(2) under art.V(2), if the deceased died Treaty-domiciled in Great Britain the United Kingdom has the exclusive right to tax property Treaty-situated outside

[35] See para.33–29.

1179

France, and this is so regardless of whether the passing of the property was regulated by French law.

Great Britain does not include Northern Ireland; the position with regard to Northern Ireland is discussed below.

Dual taxing rights

33–50 Save as just discussed, where the taxpayer is Treaty domiciled in one country and the asset is situated in the other country the country in which the taxpayer is domiciled retains its taxing rights and the country retains its situs taxing right. Under art.V(3), the situs country must allow any "exemption, allowance or relief, or any remission or reduction of duty" which would have been applicable if the deceased had been domiciled in its territory.

Tax credit

33–51 By art.VI, the state which imposes tax under its domicile right must give credit for the tax imposed by the other state on property situated in its territory. Note that this does not avoid all double taxation: if X dies domiciled in the United Kingdom for IHT purposes but Treaty-domiciled in France and owns property in a third state which passes under a disposition or devolution regulated by some part of Great Britain both France and the United Kingdom will be able to impose tax and, since the property is not situated in either state, art.VI will not apply, so that no credit is available.

Northern Ireland

33–52 The position with regard to Northern Ireland is rather curious. As a matter of general law "Great Britain" does not extend to Northern Ireland. Article II of the treaty contains a separate definition of the United Kingdom and Great Britain and, while art.X extends the treaty to Northern Ireland, on a strict reading the extension relates only to the definition of "duty" in art.II(1)(e) and not to the definition of "territory" in art.II(1)(d). If this is correct then it appears to produce some interesting results:

(1) where the deceased dies domiciled in France the United Kingdom cannot impose IHT on property situated in Northern Ireland because in such a case France has an exclusive taxing right; and

(2) where the deceased dies Treaty domiciled in Northern Ireland, there is nothing in the Treaty to prevent both France and the United Kingdom from imposing tax on so much of the individual's estate as is situated outside Great Britain. No tax credit would be available in respect of property so situated; in particular, France would not give credit for IHT paid on property situated in Northern Ireland because it would not be situated in the territory of the United Kingdom.

The authors have not come across this situation but expect that in practice the Revenue authorities in both states do not adopt such a strict approach. See also the position under the Treaty with Pakistan, discussed at para.33–91.

VI. TREATY WITH INDIA

The Double Taxation Treaty with India was concluded in relation to estate duty. **33–53** India abolished estate duty in 1985. However, because of the effect of s.158(6), the Treaty with India continues to be of significance where an individual dies domiciled in India under the general law of both the United Kingdom and India in circumstances where he would, but for the Treaty, be deemed domiciled in the United Kingdom; note that the domicile position must be established under the laws of both jurisdictions and not just that of the United Kingdom.

The effect of ss.158(6) and 267(2) and the proviso to art.III(3) is to restrict the application of the IHT deemed domicile rules in relation to estates passing on death to property either situated in Great Britain or passing under a disposition or devolution governed by British law. See paras 33–27 and following for further commentary on these issues.

The Treaty is relevant when considering whether IHT is payable on death, including in relation to a qualifying interest in possession or in respect of property subject to a reservation. It does apply in relation to lifetime transfers (including failed PETs).

VII. TREATY WITH IRELAND

The Double Taxation Treaty between the United Kingdom and the Republic of **33–54** Ireland (the "Contracting States") was concluded on December 7, 1977. It takes effect retrospectively as follows:

(1) In the Republic:
  (a) in respect of gift tax, from February 28, 1974; and
  (b) in respect of inheritance tax, from April 1, 1975.
(2) In the United Kingdom:
  (a) in respect of CTT on a death, from March 13, 1975; and
  (b) otherwise, from March 27, 1974.

The taxes which are the subject of the Treaty are CTT, Irish gift tax, Irish inheritance **33–55** tax and any tax imposed by either state in addition to, or in place of, these taxes, which is identical or substantially similar to them. IHT and Irish capital acquisitions tax ("CAT")[36] are thus included.[37] The Treaty applies:

(1) to any person who is within the scope of the above taxes; and
(2) to any property by reference to which there is a charge to such a tax.

---

[36] In Ireland gift tax and inheritance tax are constituent taxes of CAT.
[37] Note, however, that Irish Probate Tax is not covered by the Treaty—see IHTM28101.

The stated purpose of the Treaty is twofold, to avoid double taxation, and to prevent fiscal evasion.

33–56 At the time the Treaty was negotiated both Ireland and the United Kingdom imposed the taxes covered by the treaty by reference to domicile.[38] That has since changed; Ireland now levies CAT on the basis of the residence[39] of the transferor or beneficiary of a gift or inheritance, although the old CAT domicile rules have been preserved for benefits received from trusts created prior to December 1, 1999, and gifts and inheritances prior to that date.

33–57 The Treaty is still workable in most cases as it recognises the right of each country to levy tax and to determine situs according to its own law. Moreover, the fact that the basis of charge in Ireland has been changed from domicile to residence does not affect the operation of the Treaty where the assets are situate in either Ireland or the United Kingdom, as the domicile/residence basis of charge in neither country is relevant in determining whether, or to what extent, credit relief is available in these circumstances. However, domicile is relevant in determining which state gives a credit to relieve double taxation in respect of assets situate in a third country, and the change in the basis of charge in Ireland could have an effect on the operation of the Treaty in these circumstances.

Avoidance of double taxation

33–58 In contrast to many of the other treaties, the Treaty makes no attempt to avoid a double charge being imposed on the same property: under art.5 each state retains the right to charge tax under its own laws. Double taxation is avoided through a system of tax credits.

33–59 Assume, for example, that an Irish resident domiciliary, dies owning property which under both United Kingdom and Irish law is situated in the United Kingdom. Irish inheritance tax will be charged on his worldwide assets and IHT on the property situated in the United Kingdom. Article 8(1) avoids double taxation in such circumstances by providing that, in such a case, the taxpayer is entitled to a credit for so much of the tax paid in the state in which the property is situated as is attributable to that property. This credit is applied against (and cannot exceed) so much of the tax paid in the other state (Ireland, in this case) as is attributable to the property situated in the first state (the United Kingdom).

Assets in a third country

33–60 Article 8(2) provides that, where both jurisdictions seek to charge tax by reference to domicile on property which is not situated in either jurisdiction the position is to be

[38] The general law on domicile is virtually identical in both jurisdictions, although Ireland has no equivalent of the Domicile and Matrimonial Proceedings Act 1973 and no deemed domicile rules.

[39] Domicile continues to be relevant for non-Irish domiciliaries. A non-Irish domiciliary is not considered to be resident or ordinarily resident in Ireland for CAT purposes unless:
    (a) the date of the disposition occurs on or after December 1, 2004; and
    (b) that person has been resident in Ireland for the five consecutive years of assessment immediately preceding the year of assessment in which that date falls; and
    (c) that person is either resident or ordinarily resident in Ireland on that date.

resolved by apportioning the tax between the states. It avoids double taxation by providing that the state which has "subsidiary taxing rights" (see below) must give a tax credit for so much of the tax paid in the other state as is attributable to the property in question. As under art.8(1) the credit cannot exceed so much of the tax payable in the state giving the credit as is attributable to the property in question.

However, where the issue is not one of double domicile (because, for example, a deceased Irish resident is regarded by both Ireland and the United Kingdom as domiciled in the United Kingdom) the position is more difficult. The tie-breaker clause in art.4(2) will not be relevant as both jurisdictions regard the deceased as UK domiciled; Ireland's basis for imposing tax is the deceased's residence. It seems that the Treaty does not provide in this situation for either country to have subsidiary taxing rights. Article 5(2) does not have any application to this scenario as the words in art.5(2)(a) refer to "where a person's domicile has been determined under paragraph (2) of Article 4 . . . ". Here the deceased's domicile has not been determined under art.5(2) and so art.5(2) cannot apply in determining which country's taxing rights are subsidiary.

33–61

It is thought that it is most likely that the United Kingdom have primary taxing rights because the deceased is UK domiciled and domicile was the basis of the tax charge in both countries when the Treaty was negotiated.

It may be open to the competent authorities to exercise the wide powers granted to them under art.11 to interpret the Treaty to apply art.5(2)(a) to cases where domicile is determined under art.4(1) in the same way as it is applied to cases where domicile is determined under art.4(2). If this approach were to be taken then, in the circumstances suggested above, Ireland, as the state of non-domicile, would have subsidiary taxing rights.

Limit on grossing-up where IHT paid from non-UK situs property

Article 6(1) of the Treaty provides that:

33–62

> "For the purposes of this Treaty, the of any property shall be determined by each Contracting State under its own law, except that, where part of the value by reference to which tax is imposed in the United Kingdom is represented by a liability to tax which is satisfied out of property situated outside the United Kingdom, then that part of the value shall be deemed to be attributable to that property."

The effect of art.6(1) is that, where a charge to IHT depends upon the property transferred having a UK situs, and the transferor making the transfer of UK property, pays the IHT out of property situated outside the United Kingdom, the value of the non-UK property used to pay IHT is not grossed-up.

Situs

Article 6(1) of the Treaty provides that for the purposes of the Treaty the situs of any property is to be determined by each state under its own law. In theory, therefore, property could be situated in one place under UK law and in another under Irish law. In practice such conflicts should be rare since United Kingdom and Irish law are virtually identical in this area. Article 6(2) provides that where such a conflict does arise so as to affect the credit given under art.8(1) or art.8(2), the situs is determined

33–63

exclusively under the law of the state with subsidiary taxing rights. If neither state has such rights, the situs is determined by mutual agreement.

Fiscal domicile

33–64   Article 4 lays down the rules for establishing a person's domicile. The purpose of these rules is not to give a state exclusive taxing rights (as under the Treaty both states retain their right to tax on a global basis) but to which state has primary or subsidiary taxing rights.

33–65   Article 4 begins by stating that the question of whether a person is, or was at any material time, domiciled in a contracting state is determined in accordance with the law of that state, including any deeming provisions (so the IHT deemed domicile rules apply in determining domicile in the United Kingdom). Where there is a double domicile, the fiscal domicile under the Treaty of the individual concerned is determined in accordance with the following rules:

(1) *Permanent home.* He is deemed to be domiciled in the state in which he has, or had at the material time, a permanent home available to him.

(2) *Centre of vital interests.* If he has or had a permanent home available to him in both[40] states, his domicile is deemed to be in the state with which his personal and economic relations are, or were at the material time, closer, that state being regarded as the "centre of his vital interests".

(3) *Habitual abode.* If the state in which he has or had his centre of vital interests cannot be determined, or if he has not or had not a permanent home available to him in either state, his domicile is deemed to be in the contracting state in which he has, or had at the material time, a habitual abode.

(4) *Nationality.* If he has or had an habitual abode in both or neither of the states, his domicile is deemed to be in the state of which he is, or was at the material time, a national.[41]

(5) *Mutual agreement.* If he is or was a national of both or neither of the states, the question is to be settled by mutual agreement between the authorities.

Subsidiary taxing rights

33–66   The state which has subsidiary taxing rights is determined under art.5 as follows:

(1) *Non-settled property.* Where property is not comprised in a settlement, and a person's domicile has been determined under the fiscal domicile rules, the state with subsidiary taxing rights is the state in which the person is not domiciled.

---

[40] This test does not apply if he had a home in neither state.

[41] Art.1(a). For this purpose "national" means:

(1) in relation to the Republic, any citizen of Ireland, any legal person, association or other entity deriving its status as such from the law in force in the Republic; and

(2) in relation to the United Kingdom any citizen of the United Kingdom and colonies, any British subject under s.2 of the British Nationality Act 1948 whose notice given under that section has been acknowledged before December 7, 1977, any British subject by virtue of s.13(1) or s.16 of the British Nationality Act 1948; and any legal person, association or other entity deriving its status as such from the law in force in the United Kingdom.

For this purpose, "person" means, in the Republic, the disponer, and in the United Kingdom, the transferor.

(2) *Settled property.* Where the property is settled property the position is more complicated.

    (a) Where:

        (i) the proper law[42] of the settlement as regards that property at the time when the settlement was made was the law of the Republic, and

        (ii) the settlor has been determined other than under the fiscal domicile rules to have been a United Kingdom domiciliary when he made the settlement,

    the United Kingdom has subsidiary taxing rights.

    (b) Where:

        (i) the proper law of the settlement as regards that property at the time when the settlement was made was not the law of the Republic, and

        (ii) the settlor has been determined other than under the fiscal domicile rules to have been a United Kingdom domiciliary, but

        (iii) under its own law the Republic would impose tax on property outside its territory because at some later time either the proper law of the settlement as regards that property was the law of the Republic *or* because at some later time the settlor's domicile has been determined under the fiscal domicile rules to have been in the Republic,

    the Republic has subsidiary taxing rights.

    (c) Where:

        (i) the proper law of the settlement as regards that property at the time when the settlement was made was not the law of the Republic, and

        (ii) the settlor's domicile has been determined under the fiscal domicile rules, and

        (iii) the conditions in (b) above are not satisfied,

    the state in which he was not domiciled at that time has subsidiary taxing rights.

For the above purposes, "settlement" has the meaning which it has under UK law relating to IHT, and a settlement is made when property first becomes comprised in it.

Time limit

Article 9 provides that any claim for a credit or for a repayment of tax must be made within six years from the date of the event in which the claim is made. **33–67**

Prevention of fiscal evasion

Article 12 makes provision for the United Kingdom and the Republic to exchange such information as is necessary for carrying out (i) the provisions of the Treaty, and **33–68**

---

[42] When the Treaty was introduced, CAT was charged on settled property wherever situated if the proper law of the settlement was Irish law. Ireland no longer imposes CAT on the basis of proper law.

(ii) the domestic laws of the states concerning taxes covered by the Treaty in so far as the taxation thereunder is in accordance with the Treaty. Any information so exchanged is treated as secret and is not to be disclosed to unauthorised persons.

VIII. TREATY WITH ITALY

33–69   The Double Taxation Treaty between the United Kingdom and Italy (SI 1968/304) was concluded on February 15, 1966 and came into force on February 9, 1968.

Italian tax jurisdiction

33–70   Italy reintroduced succession duty in 2006. A detailed explanation of the Italian domestic tax system is outside the scope of this book. However, as the situs code contained in the Treaty as the potential for double taxation is a prerequisite for the application of the Treaty, it may be useful to outline the basic conditions which give rise to an Italian tax claim in the context of a succession.

Italian succession tax is levied on a worldwide basis if the deceased was resident in Italy, though credit will be given for foreign taxes paid. If the deceased was not resident in Italy, succession duty is levied in respect of any movables and immovables situated in Italy (Law 262/2006 contains a situs code). If the deceased was not resident in Italy and there were no assets situated in Italy, there will be no Italian succession duty payable, irrespective of whether or not there was an Italian resident beneficiary.

Under art.2(2) of the Italian income tax code, an individual is deemed to be resident in Italy if, for the greater part of the tax year (i.e. 183 days or more), he is: (a) registered in the Italian Civil Registry of the resident population; (b) resident in Italy according to the Italian Civil Code; or (c) domiciled in Italy according to the Italian civil code.

Article 43(1) of the Italian Civil code provides that the domicile of an individual is the place where he has established the principle centre of his business and interests (*sede principale dei suoi affari e interessi*).

Article 43(2) of the Italian Civil Code provides that the residence of an individual is the place where he has his habitual abode (*luogo di dimora abituale*). Case law has provided that residence is determined by two factors: the objective circumstance of being permanently in a certain place; and the clear intention to remain there permanently. This can be ascertained based on the individual's habits—for example if he maintains his home and centre of personal relationships in Italy.

The Treaty applies to Italian succession duty, to UK inheritance tax and to any other duties of a similar character imposed in either state on death. The Treaty therefore includes IHT payable on the death of a beneficiary with a qualifying interest in possession and in respect of property subject to a reservation of benefit as at the death (but not on lifetime gifts or, therefore, failed PETs).

Avoidance of double taxation

33–71   The basic approach of the Treaty with Italy, like that with France, is to avoid double taxation by treating a deceased as having been domiciled in only one of the states for Treaty purposes; and by giving the state in which property is situated the primary right to tax that property, the country in which the deceased was domiciled giving credit for that tax.

The situs rules of the Treaty do not apply where the result of their application would be to bring them within the taxing net of one of the states which would not otherwise have imposed any duty on them.

Fiscal domicile

There are two related issues. The first is where the taxpayer is domiciled under the **33–72** domestic law of both countries. The second, if he is domiciled in Italy under Italian law and the United Kingdom under UK law, is where he is domiciled for the purposes of the Treaty.

Domestic and treaty domicile

Domicile for UK IHT purposes is determined under the general law. By virtue of **33–73** ss.158(5) and 267(2), the deemed domicile rules do not apply in a situation where the deceased was domiciled in Italy under its general law and in the UK under its general law.

Article V provides that the rights of the United Kingdom to impose tax on an individual domiciled in the other contracting state are limited to UK situs property and property "passing under a settlement governed by its law". This wording is more limited than that in the other Estate Duty treaties which refer to "a disposition or devolution" rather than a "settlement".

The deemed domicile rules do, however, apply where there is no domicile "mismatch" under the Treaty, i.e. where the deceased was domiciled in the United Kingdom under Italian general law and in the United Kingdom under UK general law (including the deemed domicile rules).

Domestic domicile for Italian tax purposes is determined according to Italian law, as explained at para.33–70 above.

The Treaty applies the respective domestic rules of Italy and the United Kingdom to determine the domicile of the deceased.

As in the Treaty with France, dual domicile cases arise easily under the Italian Treaty. Where an individual is domiciled in both countries (i.e. in Italy under Italian law and in the United Kingdom under UK law), art.II(2)(b) provides for the application of the standard tie breaker tests based on permanent home, centre of vital interests, habitual abode, nationality and mutual agreement.

Treaty situs

The Treaty provides in art.IV detailed rules for determining the treaty situs of an **33–74** asset. By art.III(1), these rules, which apply for the purposes of the imposition of tax and of any tax credit, operate only where on a person's death he was domiciled in one of the states and duty would be imposed in both states or in one state but not the other but for some "specific exemption" in the latter state. The rules will thus apply where IHT is prevented from being charged by, e.g. the spouse exemption.

The situs code in art.IV deals specifically with immovables (see art.IV(1); tangible movable property and rights and interests therein (art.IV(2)); debts, secured or unsecured, (art.IV(3)); bank accounts (art.IV(4)); securities issued by any government, county council, commune, municipality or other public authority (art.IV(5)); shares, stock, debentures or debenture stock in a company (art.IV(6)); an interest in a partnership (art.IV(7)); goodwill (art.IV(8)); ships and aircraft and shares in the same (art.IV(9)); patents, trademarks and designs (art.IV(10)); copyrights and rights or licences to use any copyright material, patent, trademark or design (art.IV(11)); rights or causes of action *ex delicto* (art.IV(12)); and "any other property" (art.IV(13)).

Taxing rights

33–75 As noted above, art.V of the Treaty limits the taxing rights of the state in which the deceased was not domiciled. In determining the rate of tax, that state may not take account of any property situated outside the state. If, for example, the deceased died with a Treaty domicile in Italy, the United Kingdom may only take account of property situated within the United Kingdom when determining the inheritance tax payable.

Article VI of the Treaty provides for tax credits. The state which imposes tax under its domicile right must give credit for the tax imposed by the other state on property situated in its territory. Note that this does not avoid all double taxation: if X dies domiciled in the United Kingdom for IHT purposes but Treaty domiciled in France and owns property in a third state which passes under a disposition or devolution regulated by some part of Great Britain both France and the United Kingdom will be able to impose tax and, since the property is not situated in either state, art.VI will not apply, so that no credit is available.

Under art.VI(2), the situs country must allow any "exemption, allowance or relief, or any remission or reduction of duty" which would have been applicable if the deceased had been domiciled in its territory.

Northern Ireland

33–76 The Treaty with Italy contains the same definitions and references to Northern Ireland as the Treaty with France (see para.33–52 above). The same curiosities will therefore arise in circumstances where the deceased dies domiciled in Northern Ireland but with property in Great Britain and in Italy or domiciled in Italy but with property in Northern Ireland.

IX. TREATY WITH THE NETHERLANDS

33–77 The Double Taxation Treaty between the United Kingdom and the Netherlands entered into force on June 16, 1980, at which time the existing Treaty between the United Kingdom and the Netherlands ceased to have effect. The transitional provisions in art.20(4) are no longer relevant. The Treaty was amended by a Protocol which came into force on June 3, 1996, in relation to tax charges arising on or after March 18, 1996.[43]

The taxes which are the subject of the Treaty are CTT and IHT (which is specifically **33–78** added by the Protocol) and, in the Netherlands:

(1) Succession duty *(het recht van successie)*;
(2) Gift duty *(het recht van schenking)*; and
(3) Transfer duty *(het recht van overgang)*.

In the Treaty these are referred to collectively as "Netherlands tax". The Treaty will also apply to any identical or substantially similar taxes imposed by either state in the future, and may be extended to any territory for whose international relations the United Kingdom is responsible, as well as to the Netherlands Antilles and Aruba, if the territory or country concerned imposes taxes substantially similar to those to which the Treaty applies. For the purposes of the Treaty, "The Netherlands" includes that part of the Netherlands situated in Europe, and "gift" means a lifetime transfer of value, the term "donor" being construed accordingly. The stated purpose of the Treaty is twofold: to avoid double taxation, and to prevent fiscal evasion.

The Treaty applies: **33–79**

(1) to estates of, and gifts made by, persons domiciled in either or both the United Kingdom and the Netherlands at the time of the gift or their death, as the case may be; and
(2) to property comprised in settlements made by persons domiciled in either the United Kingdom or the Netherlands at the time the settlement was made.

Avoidance of double taxation

Of the estate and gift tax treaties to which the United Kingdom is a party, that with **33–80** the Netherlands mirrors most closely the OECD Model.[44] The basic approach of the Treaty is to avoid double taxation in two ways. First, the general rule, established in art.8, is that property is taxable only in the state in which the deceased/donor was domiciled for Treaty purposes at the time of the death/gift in question. A number of qualifications are then carved out of this rule, as a result of which, in certain circumstances, tax may be charged by both states in respect of the same property. Such double taxation as this might otherwise occasion is avoided through a system of tax credits.

The general rule and fiscal domicile

As mentioned, under art.8, the general rule is that only the state in which the **33–81** deceased/donor was domiciled for Treaty purposes at the time of the death/gift in question is entitled to charge tax in respect of that death/gift. It may well be, of course, that each state would regard the individual as being one of its domiciliaries, be it on the

---

[43] Double Taxation Relief (Taxes on the Estates of Deceased Persons and Inheritances on Gifts) (Netherlands) Order (SI 1996/730).
[44] See para.33–03.

basis of the domicile (UK law) or of the residence (Netherlands Law) of the individual in question. The Treaty accordingly provides rules for determining in which state an individual is domiciled for Treaty purposes. First, by art.4(1) a person is domiciled for Treaty purposes:

(1) in the United Kingdom, if he is a UK domiciliary as a matter of general UK law or under the IHT deemed domicile provisions; or

(2) in the Netherlands, if he is resident there or treated as resident there for purposes of Netherlands tax. (For the purposes of inheritance tax and gift tax, nationals of the Netherlands are treated as resident for 10 years after leaving the Netherlands and other individuals are treated, for the purposes of gift tax, as resident for one year after leaving the Netherlands.)

33–82   This rule, of course, may result in an individual being regarded as domiciled for Treaty purposes in both states. Article 4(3) accordingly provides a number of tests, the first of which might be called the "nationality test". Under this test, an individual who at the time in question was a national of only one state (say, the United Kingdom), and who was resident in the other state (the Netherlands), but who had been resident there for less than seven out of the immediately preceding 10 years and who did not intend definitely to remain there is deemed to be domiciled in the state of which he was a national (the United Kingdom). For this purpose, the question of whether a person was resident in the United Kingdom is determined as for income tax purposes, "years" being taken to mean years of assessment ending with the year in which the death/gift occurs. This is subject to the important qualification that, in applying the income tax rules, no regard is had to the availability to the individual in question of any dwelling-house.[45]

33–83   In the event that the nationality test is insufficient to establish a single domicile, recourse is had under art.4(2) to the usual "tie-breaker" rules.[46]

Dual charge to tax/tax credits

33–84   As mentioned above, the general rule that only one state is entitled to charge tax is subject to certain qualifications. The effect of this is that in certain cases both states may charge tax if they are entitled to do so under their own law.

Where such a dual charge arises, art.8 makes provision for one state to give a tax credit so as to avoid double taxation. In such a case, the state required to give credit must allow as a credit against so much of its tax as is attributable to the property in question so much of the tax paid in the other state as is attributable to that property. For this purpose, tax charged on the death of a person by reason of a gift made within seven years of his death is brought into account, and in determining what tax is attributable to a gift only that tax remaining after any credit given in respect of any tax charged by a territory other than the United Kingdom or the Netherlands is brought into account.

33–85   The qualifications to the general rule, which fall into four categories, and the system of tax credits are as follows:

[45] The "available accommodation rule" that gave rise to the need for this exclusion in the Treaty provisions (and the provisions of other treaties, e.g. that with South Africa) has been largely abolished since the Treaty was negotiated. See *British Tax Review* (1993), pp.286–288.

[46] See, e.g. para.33–64.

(1) *Specified property.* Articles 5, 6 and 7 specify certain property which may be taxed on a basis. This property falls into four classifications:

    (a) Ships and aircraft: art.7 allows ships and aircraft and associated movable property to be taxed in the state where the effective management of the enterprise is situated, but extends the standard article to boats engaged in inland waterways transport, and associated equipment.

    (b) Immovable property: by art.5, immovable property (as rather widely defined)[47] may be taxed in the state in which the property is situated.

    (c) Permanent establishments: by art.6(1), assets (other than assets falling within the two categories mentioned above) which form part of the business property of a permanent establishment (as defined) of an enterprise may be taxed in the state in which that establishment is situated.[48]

    (d) Independent personal services: by art.6(5), assets other than assets falling within the "ships and aircraft" category pertaining to a fixed base used for the performance of independent personal services may be taxed in the state where that base is situated.[49]

When a dual charge arises in respect of property falling into one of the above categories, the state which does not tax on a situs basis under arts 5, 6 or 7 must give credit.

(2) *Nationality.* By art.11(1), if the deceased/donor had a Treaty domicile in one of the states (say, the Netherlands) at the time of the death/gift and was at that time a national of the other state (the United Kingdom) and had been domiciled within the meaning of the Treaty in the other state (the United Kingdom) at any time within the preceding 10 years, that other state (the United Kingdom) may impose tax according to its domestic law. In such a case by art.13(2), the state (the United Kingdom) in which the individual did not have a Treaty domicile must give credit.

(3) *Settled property.* By art.11(2), the United Kingdom may impose tax by reference to property comprised in a settlement unless when he made the settlement the settlor had a Treaty domicile in the Netherlands and was not a United Kingdom national who, for Treaty purposes, had been domiciled in the United Kingdom at any time within the immediately preceding 10 years. In such a case, by art.13(2), the United Kingdom must give credit.

(4) *Unpaid tax.* By art.11(3), if under the general rule property would only be taxable in the Netherlands and the deceased/donor is either:

    (a) a national of the United Kingdom (but not of the Netherlands); or

    (b) treated for the purposes of Netherlands tax as a Netherlands resident under its unilateral 10-year rule,

the United Kingdom may also impose tax by reference to that property under its law if notified by the Netherlands that the Netherlands tax chargeable on that property has not been paid.

Exemptions

It may be that property, other than "community property",[50] passes from a deceased **33–86** person who had a Treaty domicile in one state (say, the Netherlands) to his or her

---

[47] To include, livestock.

[48] By art.6(7), art.6(1) applies to an interest in a partnership if the partnership carries on any enterprise or performs independent personal services.

[49] By art.6(7), art.6(1) applies to an interest in a partnership if the partnership carries on any enterprise or performs independent personal services.

[50] For an explanation of community property, generally, see Ch.33.

spouse, that that property is taxable in the other state (the United Kingdom) solely by reason of arts 5, 6 or 7, and that the transferee's spouse was not domiciled in the other state (the United Kingdom) under the law of that state. In such a case the position depends on whether the deceased died domiciled in the Netherlands or the United Kingdom. By art.12(1), if he had a Treaty domicile in the Netherlands, then if the transfer would have been wholly exempt had the transferee's spouse been domiciled in the United Kingdom, not less than half of the value transferred is exempt from UK tax.[51] Thus, at the least, the limited spouse exemption is available, and it may be dramatically increased. Assume that Albert, a UK domiciliary who has become a national of, and resident in, the Netherlands, and who has a Netherlands domicile for Treaty purposes, dies, leaving his estate to his Dutch wife. If some of his estate consists of, say, land in the United Kingdom worth £200,000, half of so much of the value transferred on his death as is attributable to that land,[52] i.e. £100,000, not just £55,000 is exempt from UK tax.[53]

33–87   By art.12(2), if the deceased had a Treaty domicile in the United Kingdom, half of the value of the property taxable in the Netherlands under arts 5, 6 or 7 is exempt from Netherlands tax to the extent that it exceeds the amount of the personal exemption given under Netherlands law to a surviving spouse. This is subject to two qualifications. First, if the deceased was a Netherlands resident under Netherlands domestic law the exemption applies only to the extent that it is shown that the tax to which the exemption is given is not less than the tax that would have been due had the deceased been domiciled for Treaty purposes in the Netherlands. Secondly, the exemption is not available if UK law changes so that, at the time of the death, the United Kingdom, under its domestic law, taxes property passing from a deceased person with the same domicile as his spouse to that spouse to the extent of more than 50 per cent of its value.

Deductions

33–88   Article 10 provides in the usual way that in determining the amount on which tax is to be computed deductions shall be allowed in accordance with the law of the state in which the tax is imposed.

Time limits

33–89   Article 14 provides that any claim (or a credit or repayment based on the Treaty) must be made within six years from the date of the event giving rise to a liability to tax

---

[51] Art.12(1) provides that this is calculated "as a value on which no tax is payable"—so that no grossing-up is necessary—and "after taking account of all exemptions except those for transfers between spouses"—so that, e.g. the annual exemption must be ignored. It is hard to see how either of these qualifications is relevant since art.12(1) appears to apply only in relation to gifts made on death, and no grossing-up is required in respect of such gifts, nor is the annual exemption, etc. available to gifts made on death.

[52] Property not within arts 5–7 does not qualify for this treatment and may be taxed in the United Kingdom because of art.11.

[53] See paras 3–35 and following.

or, where later, within one year from the last date on which tax for which credit is given is due.

Prevention of fiscal evasion

Article 17 makes provision for the United Kingdom and the Netherlands to exchange such information as is necessary for carrying out: **33–90**

(1) the provisions of the Treaty; and
(2) the domestic laws of the states concerning taxes covered by the Treaty in so far as the taxation thereunder is not contrary to the Treaty.

Any information so exchanged is treated as secret and may be disclosed only to persons or authorities (including courts and administrative bodies) involved in the assessment or collection of, the enforcement or prosecution in respect of, or the determination of appeals in relation to, taxes covered by the Treaty.

Such persons or authorities may disclose the information in public court proceedings or in judicial decisions. The foregoing is subject to the qualification that in no case is art.17 to be construed as imposing on one of the states the obligation:

(a) to carry out administrative measures at variance with the laws and administrative practice of that or of the other state;
(b) to supply information which is not obtainable under the laws or the normal course of the administration of that or of the other state; and
(c) to supply information which would disclose any trade, business, industrial, commercial or professional secret or trade processes or the disclosure of which would be contrary to public policy.

X. TREATY WITH PAKISTAN

The Double Taxation Treaty with Pakistan was concluded in relation to estate duty. Estate duty in Pakistan was abolished with effect from June 28, 1979. The Treaty with Pakistan nevertheless still applies in relation to IHT, its continuing significance lying in the disapplication of the IHT deemed domicile rules.[54] **33–91**

The Treaty is relevant when considering whether IHT is payable on death, including in relation to a qualifying interest in possession or in respect of property subject to a reservation. It does apply in relation to lifetime transfers (including failed PETs).

Under art.V(2), where a person dies domiciled in some part of Pakistan, but not in some part of Great Britain, Great Britain can impose IHT at the time of his death only on property situated in Great Britain or which passes under a disposition or devolution regulated by the law of some part of Great Britain. The position of someone in this case is clear—the deemed domicile rules do not apply in determining whether he was domiciled in Great Britain—England, Wales and Scotland. See para 33–28 and following for further commentary on these issues.

Great Britain does not include Northern Ireland, but art.X provides that the treaty applies in relation to the estate duty imposed in Northern Ireland as it applies in relation

---

[54] See IHTA 1984 ss.267(2) and 158(6).

to the estate duty imposed in Great Britain see also the treatment of Northern Ireland and the treaty with France, discussed above.

XI. TREATY WITH SOUTH AFRICA

33–92   The Double Taxation Treaty between the United Kingdom and South Africa came into effect as from January 1, 1978. By art.18(4) where, on a death after December 31, 1977, and before the entry into force of the Treaty any provision of the 1946 Estate Duty Treaty (as amended by the 1954 Protocol), would have afforded any greater relief than the new Treaty, the provision in the old Treaty continues to have effect with respect to that death. By art.18(5), where on a death after entry into force of the Treaty and before March 27, 1981, any provision of the old Treaty (as amended by the 1954 Protocol) would have afforded any greater relief than the new Treaty in respect of either:

(1) any gift inter vivos made by the deceased before March 27, 1974; or
(2) any settled property in which the deceased had a beneficial interest in possession before March 27, 1974, but not at any time thereafter,

the provision in the old Treaty continues to have effect in the United Kingdom in relation to that gift or settled property, as the case may be.

33–93   The taxes which are the subject of the new Treaty are CTT, and, in South Africa, estate duty and donations tax. The Treaty also applies to any identical or substantially similar taxes which may be imposed by either state in the future, so IHT is included. For purposes of the Treaty, the term "transfer" includes, in the case of South Africa, a donation, and the term "transferor" is construed accordingly. The Treaty applies to any person who is within the scope of the above taxes. The stated purpose of the Treaty is twofold: to avoid double taxation, and to prevent fiscal evasion.

Avoidance of double taxation

33–94   The Treaty seeks to avoid double taxation in two ways. First, it establishes general taxing rights, under which one state has exclusive taxing rights. Secondly, in the event that a double charge is not avoided by the imposition of exclusive taxing rights, provision is made to give a tax credit. Each of these methods will be considered in turn.

Exclusive taxing rights

33–95   The general rule is found in art.5(1) which provides that if the deceased or the transferor was domiciled under the Treaty (see below) in one state at the time of the death/transfer but not in the other state, the state in which he was domiciled has exclusive taxing rights. This general rule is subject to a number of qualifications, which are discussed below. Before considering these qualifications, it will be helpful, given the fact that under the general rule a person's domicile for purposes of the Treaty may be critical, to consider the rules governing fiscal domicile.

Fiscal domicile

The rules governing a taxpayer's domicile for the purposes of the Treaty are **33–96** complicated by the fact that South Africa charges tax by reference to ordinary residence rather than domicile. Article 4(1) lays down the general test, which is that for the purposes of the Treaty an individual is domiciled in the United Kingdom at the time in question if he is domiciled here as a matter of general law or as a result of the deemed domicile provisions. An individual is domiciled in South Africa at the time in question, on the other hand, if he is ordinarily resident there. Obviously, this could result in an individual being domiciled both in the United Kingdom and in South Africa, and the Treaty accordingly provides further tests.

By art.4(2), if an individual is domiciled in both contracting states, he is deemed to be domiciled in the United Kingdom if:

(1) he was a national of the United Kingdom but not of South Africa; and
(2) he had not been resident or ordinarily resident in South Africa in seven or more of the 10 income tax years of assessment immediately preceding the time in question.

Conversely, by art.4(3), an individual is deemed to be domiciled in South Africa if at the time in question he was domiciled in both states, and:

(1) he was a national of South Africa but not of the United Kingdom; and
(2) he had not been resident or ordinarily resident in the United Kingdom in seven or more of the 10 income tax years of assessment ending with the year of assessment in which that time falls. For these purposes, the question of his residence or ordinary residence in the United Kingdom is determined as for the purposes of UK income tax, but without regard to any dwelling-house available in the United Kingdom for his use.[55]

It will be noted that the effect of art.4(2) is that a visitor to South Africa from the United Kingdom can live in South Africa for at least six years, so long as he retains his UK nationality, without being subject to South African gift or death duties on other than designated property which South Africa can tax on the basis of situs under arts 6–9.

Although art.4(2) and (3) are reciprocal, art.4(3) is less likely to be of assistance to individuals who have come to the United Kingdom from South Africa, since such an individual is unlikely both to remain ordinarily resident in South Africa and to become a UK domiciliary. Article 4(2) and (3) do not operate to render a person a domiciliary of a state if under the general law of that state he had ceased to be domiciled in that state more than three years before the time in question: see art.4(4). This provision was

---

[55] As from April 6, 1993, available accommodation is not a determinant factor for UK residence purposes.

apparently included in the Treaty at the request of South Africa in case the United Kingdom extended the IHT three-year deemed domicile period.

Tie-breaker provisions

33–97   It follows from the provisions in art.4(2) and (3), that the time may come, particularly under art.4(2), when a person becomes domiciled in both the United Kingdom and South Africa for purposes of the Treaty. This is most likely to happen in the case of a UK domiciliary who has gone to live in South Africa; after seven years, assuming he retains his UK domicile, he will be domiciled in the United Kingdom as a matter of general UK law, and in South Africa on the basis of his ordinary residence.

33–98   In such a case, recourse is had to the tie-breaker provisions in art.4(5), as follows:

(1) *Permanent home*. He is deemed to be domiciled in the state in which he had a permanent home available to him.
(2) *Centre of vital interests*. If he had a permanent home available to him in both states, his domicile is deemed to be in the state with which his personal and economic relations were closer, that state being regarded as the "centre of his vital interests".
(3) *Habitual abode*. If the state in which he had his centre of vital interests cannot be determined, or if he did not have a permanent home available to him in either state, his domicile is deemed to be in the contracting state in which he had an habitual abode.
(4) *Nationality*. If he had an habitual abode in both or neither of the states, his domicile is deemed to be in the state of which he was a national.

Normally, the first of the "tie-breaker" tests, the availability of a permanent home will be decisive, with the result that where the taxpayer has gone to South Africa, South Africa will have the exclusive right to tax him on a worldwide basis. This will be subject to the qualifications mentioned below at para.33–99. In particular, the United Kingdom will also be able to tax him on a worldwide basis if he was domiciled in the United Kingdom under art.4 during the previous 10 years, and will also be able to tax designated property under arts 6–9. In the event of a double charge, the taxpayer will be entitled to a credit for South African tax against his UK liability.[56]

The position where a UK domiciliary emigrates to South Africa and becomes domiciled there as a matter of UK law depends largely on whether or not the taxpayer retains his UK nationality. In any event, he will remain a UK domiciliary for three years under the deemed domicile provisions. If he retains his UK nationality, he will, under art.4(2), be domiciled only in the United Kingdom during those three years, with the result that South Africa would have the right to tax him only on designated property under arts 6–9. On the expiry of the three years, he would cease to be domiciled in the United Kingdom, and South Africa would have exclusive taxing rights, except that the United Kingdom would have the right to tax designated property under arts 6–9. At first glance, it would appear that the United Kingdom would retain secondary taxing rights on the basis that the taxpayer had been domiciled in the United Kingdom within the previous 10 years, but these secondary taxing rights are limited to any property situated

---

[56] See para.33–101.

in the United Kingdom not covered by arts 6–9[57] (e.g. an insurance policy). This is because a double taxation treaty cannot create a right to charge, except on the basis of situs as under arts 6–9, where one would not otherwise exist. If the emigre becomes a South African national, art.4(2) will not apply, so that during the first three years recourse must be had to the tie-breaker provisions.

Qualifications to exclusive taxing rights

The general rule that the state in which the deceased/transferor was domiciled at the time of the death/transfer in question has exclusive taxing rights is subject to four qualifications, as follows: **33–99**

(1) *Previous domicile*. The first qualification is that a state in which the taxpayer had been domiciled within 10 years preceding the death or transfer in question retains the right to tax property in the other state, even though the taxpayer is domiciled in that other state for the purposes of the Treaty at the time of the death or transfer in question. As already mentioned, this qualification should not be construed as giving a state a taxing right which it would not have under its own general law. Rather, it preserves a taxing right which a state would otherwise lose under the general rule. Assume, for example, that Drake emigrates to South Africa, takes up South African nationality and dies within two years. Article 4(2) will not apply, with the result that the tie-breaker provisions in art.4(5) must he applied. Assuming Drake had cut his ties with the United Kingdom, the only permanent home available to him would be in South Africa, with the result that for the purposes of the Treaty he would be domiciled in South Africa. That being the case, under the general rule South Africa would have exclusive taxing rights, subject, of course to arts 6–9. Under the 10 year qualification, however, the United Kingdom will also, on the basis of Drake's deemed UK domicile, be entitled to tax Drake on a worldwide basis: a credit will be given, of course, for South African tax.[58]

(2) *Designated property*. The second qualification to the general rule is that a state is entitled to tax certain designated property notwithstanding the fact that the taxpayer is not domiciled in that state. This follows from arts 6–9, which contain the following provisions:

    (a) under art.6, immovable property (as rather widely defined)[59] may be taxed in the state in which the property is situated;

    (b) under art.8, ships and aircraft operated in international traffic, and movable property pertaining to the operation of such ships and aircraft, may be taxed in the state in which the place of effective management of the enterprise is situated;

    (c) under art.9, shares, stock, debentures and debenture stock issued by companies incorporated in one of the states, and rights of unit holders in a unit trust scheme with a register of unit holders kept in one of the states may be taxed by that slate;

    (d) under art.7, assets (other than assets referred to in arts 6(1), 8 and 9) which form part of the business property of a permanent establishment (as defined) of an enterprise may be taxed in the state in which the permanent

[57] If the property is covered by arts 6–9, the United Kingdom will have primary taxing rights.
[58] See art.12(2), discussed below.
[59] To include, e.g. livestock.

establishment is situated (e.g. assets of the South African branch of a UK manufacturing partnership). The definition of "permanent establishment" is a wide one, incorporating elements of the definition used in the OECD model income tax and capital gains treaty; and

(e) under art.7(3), except for assets described in art.6, assets pertaining to a fixed base used for the performance of independent personal services may be taxed in the state in which the fixed base is situated (e.g. assets at the South African branch of a UK architect).

(3) *United Kingdom settlements.* The third qualification concerns settled property. In this respect, art.5(2) provides two things. First, if the property comes within the above-mentioned five categories, arts 6–9 apply, and the state in which the property is situated may tax the property. Secondly, settled property not coming within arts 6–9 is not taxable in the United Kingdom if at the time when the settlement was made the settlor was domiciled in South Africa and had not been domiciled in the United Kingdom within the immediately preceding 10 years. "Domicile" here means domicile for the purposes of the Treaty, with the result that a South African who has come to the United Kingdom will be able to make a settlement in respect of which no IHT will be chargeable so long as at the time he made the settlement:

(a) he was a national of South Africa but not of the United Kingdom;

(b) he had not been resident or ordinarily resident in the United Kingdom in the last seven tax years;

(c) he did not have a United Kingdom treaty domicile within the last 10 years; and

(d) he was still ordinarily resident in South Africa.

(4) *Saving clause.* Finally, by art.5(3), if under the general rule property would be taxable only in one state and tax, though chargeable, is not paid (otherwise than as a result of a specific exemption, deduction credit or allowance) in that state, tax may be imposed by reference to that property in the other state.

Deductions. allowances, etc.

33–100 Article 11 provides that in determining the amount on which tax is to be computed permitted deductions are to be allowed in accordance with the law in force in the territory in which the tax is imposed. Nothing contained in the Treaty is to be construed as obliging either state to grant to individuals not domiciled in that state, or to the estates of such individuals, any of the personal allowances, reliefs, and reductions for tax purposes which are granted to individuals so domiciled, or to their estates.

Tax credit

33–101 As was mentioned above, the second way in which the Treaty avoids double taxation is by providing for a system of tax credits. First, under art.12(1) where one state imposes tax in connection with any event by reference to any property which the other state may tax under arts 6–9, the first state must allow against so much of the tax it charges (before any Treaty relief) as is attributable to the property in question a credit equal to so much of the tax imposed by the other state in connection with the same event as is attributable to such property. The credit given by the first state for the tax charged by the second state cannot exceed the tax chargeable by the first state in respect of the property in question. Secondly, under art.12(2), in any other case where a state imposes tax by reference to any property and the deceased/transferor was domiciled in the other state at the time of the death/transfer the first state must allow against so much of the tax it charges (before any Treaty relief) as is attributable to such property a credit equal to so much of the tax imposed in the other state as is attributable to the property in question. Again, the credit is restricted as under art.12(1). Special provision is made to deal with the situation where the UK imposes tax on property not coming within arts 6–9 which is comprised in a settlement in which an interest subsists where at the time of the event giving rise to the liability to tax the individual entitled to the interest was domiciled in South Africa. In that case, under art.12(3) the United Kingdom must allow against so much of its tax (before Treaty relief) as is attributable to the settled property a credit equal to so much of the tax imposed in South Africa in connection with the same event as is attributable to such property subject to the usual credit restriction.

Time limits

Article 13 provides that any claim for a credit or for a repayment of tax must be **33–102** made within six years from the date of the event giving rise to the charge to tax, or, where later, within one year from the last date on which tax for which credit is given is due. The competent authority of the state may, in appropriate circumstances, extend this time limit where the final determination or payment of tax in the other state is delayed.

Prevention of fiscal evasion

Article 14 makes provision for the states to exchange information similar to that **33–103** found in the Treaty with Ireland.

Other provisions

The Treaty also contains provisions dealing with mutual agreement, non-discrimina- **33–104** tion and persons with diplomatic privileges.

XII. TREATY WITH SWEDEN

The Double Taxation Treaty between the United Kingdom and Sweden entered into **33–105** force on June 19, 1981 and was amended by a Protocol[60] following the introduction of IHT which is applicable in relation to charges to tax arising after March 17, 1986. This is subject to transitional provisions where the unamended treaty would benefit a taxpayer, until which time the existing Treaty between the United Kingdom and Sweden ceased to have effect. Under art.17(4), where on a death before March 27, 1981, any provision of that Treaty would have afforded a greater relief than the new Treaty in respect of (a) any gift inter vivos made by the deceased before March 27,

[60] SI 1989/986.

1974, or (b) any settled property in which the deceased had a beneficial interest in possession before March 27, 1974, but not at any time thereafter, that provision continues to have effect in the United Kingdom in relation to that gift or that settled property, as the case may be.

33–106   The taxes which are the subject of the Treaty, as amended by the Protocol are CTT and IHT, and, in Sweden, the inheritance tax and the gift tax. (The Treaty applies to any person who is within the scope of the tax which is the subject of the Treaty.) The Treaty will also apply to any identical or substantially similar tax as imposed by either state in the future in addition to, or in place of, these taxes. The stated purpose of the Treaty is twofold; to avoid double taxation, and to prevent fiscal evasion.

Avoidance of double taxation

33–107   The basic approach is to avoid double taxation in two ways. First, a general rule is established that property is taxable only in the state in which the deceased/transferor was domiciled for Treaty purposes at the time of the death/gift in question. A number of qualifications are then carved out of this rule, as a result of which in certain circumstances tax may be charged by both states in respect of the same property. Such double taxation as this might otherwise occasion is then avoided through the system of tax credits.

Exclusive taxing rights

33–108   The general rule is found in art.5(1), which provides that only the state in which the deceased/transferor was domiciled for Treaty purposes at the time of the death/transfer in question is entitled to charge tax in respect of that death/transfer, unless the deceased/transferor:

(1) was a national of the other state at the time of the death/transfer; and
(2) had been domiciled in that state within the 10 years immediately preceding the death/transfer.

This general rule is subject to a number of qualifications, which are discussed below. Before considering these qualifications it will be helpful to consider the rules governing fiscal domicile.

Fiscal domicile

33–109   The rules governing fiscal domicile are found in art.4. The basic rule is set out in art.4(1) and states that a person is domiciled:

(1) in the United Kingdom if he is domiciled there for IHT purposes;
(2) in Sweden if he is resident there for the purposes of Swedish inheritance tax or gift tax or is a Swedish national.

33–110   It may well be, of course, that this results in an individual being regarded as domiciled in both states. Article 4(2), following the OECD Model guidelines, accordingly provides a number of "tie-breaker" tests, as follows:

(1) *Permanent home.* He is deemed to be domiciled in the state in which he had a permanent home available to him.

(2) *Centre of vital interests.* If he had a permanent home available to him in both states, his domicile is deemed to be in the state with which his personal and economic relations were closer, that state being regarded as the "centre of his vital interests".

(3) *Habitual abode.* If the state in which he had his centre of vital interests cannot be determined, or if he did not have a permanent home available to him in either state, his domicile is deemed to be in the contracting state in which he had an habitual abode.

(4) *Nationality.* If he had an habitual abode in both or neither of the states, his domicile is deemed to be in the state of which he was a national.

(5) *Mutual agreement.* If he was a national of both or neither of the states, the question is to be settled by mutual agreement between the authorities.

Qualifications to exclusive taxing rights

There are five qualifications to the general rule that the state in which the individual **33–111** was domiciled for Treaty purposes at the time of the death/transfer may have exclusive taxing rights, as follows:

(1) *Designated property.* Under arts 6, 7 and 8, certain property may be taxed in the state with which it has a close connection notwithstanding the fact that the deceased/transferor is not domiciled in that state. Article 6 is concerned with immovable property, which is the subject of a special definition in art.6(2) (which extends, e.g., to livestock). Article 6 also applies to immovable property of an enterprise and to immovable property used for the performance of independent personal services. Article 7 deals with assets (other than those covered by art.6 or art.8) which form part of the business property of a permanent establishment (as defined) of an enterprise. Assets pertaining to a fixed base used for the performance of independent personal services may, under art.7, also be taxed in the state in which the fixed base is situated. The provisions of art.7 apply to an interest in a partnership if the business of an enterprise is carried on, or independent personal services are performed, by the partnership. Under art.8, ships and aircraft operated in international traffic and boats engaged in inland waterways transport, and movable property pertaining to the operation of such ships, aircraft and boats, may be taxed in the state in which the place of effective management of the enterprise is situated.

It may be that a conflict arises as to whether or not property is designated property. In such a case, art.9 provides that if the deceased/transferor was domiciled in one state (say, the United Kingdom) at the time of the death/transfer and by the law of that state any right or interest is regarded as not being designated property, but by the law of the other state (Sweden) that right or interest is regarded as designated property, then the law of the state in which the deceased/transferor was not a Treaty domiciliary (in this case, Sweden) determines the issue. Exceptionally, circumstances may arise in which the deceased/transferor was not domiciled in either state, and each state regards the property as situated in its territory with the result that tax will be imposed by each state. In this event, the competent authorities must determine the situs of the property by mutual agreement.

(2) *Visitors to Sweden.* By art.5(2), property (other than designated property) is not taxable in Sweden on a death/transfer even though the deceased/transferor was then domiciled in Sweden if at that time he:

(a) had not been domiciled in Sweden in accordance with Swedish law in seven or more of the 10 years immediately preceding that time;

(b) was a United Kingdom but not a Swedish national; and

(c) was an actual or a deemed United Kingdom domiciliary for IHT purposes.

(3) *Settled property.* By art.5(4), settled property (other than designated property) is not taxable in the United Kingdom if at the time the settlement was made the settlor was domiciled for Treaty purposes in Sweden. This is subject to the qualification that settled property does not come within this category if at the time he made the settlement the settlor was at that time a United Kingdom national and had been domiciled for Treaty purposes in the United Kingdom within the immediately preceding 10 years. For the planning implications of this see para.33–99, para.3.

(4) *Recent arrivals in the United Kingdom.* By art.5(3), property (other than designated property and settled property) is not taxable in the United Kingdom even though at the time of the death/transfer the deceased/transferor was then domiciled in the United Kingdom if at that time he:

(a) had not been resident in the United Kingdom in seven or more of the 10 years of assessment ending with that in which the taxable event falls (residence being determined as for income tax, but without regard to the availability of any dwelling-house);

(b) was a Swedish but not a UK national; and

(c) had been a Swedish domiciliary for Treaty purposes within the immediately preceding 10 years.

(5) *Saving clause*: Article 5(5) contains the usual saving clause.

Spouse exemption

33–112   The Treaty contains special provisions governing transfers on death to a spouse. It may be that property passes from a deceased person who has a Treaty, but not a UK general law, domicile in Sweden or is a national of Sweden to his or her Spouse, and that that property is taxable in the United Kingdom, e.g. because art.5(1) does not rule out a double charge, or by reason of arts 6, 7 or 8 above. If circumstances are such that the surviving spouse also has a Treaty domicile outside the United Kingdom, the limited IHT spouse exemption only would be available, with the result that some IHT might be payable. Fortunately, art.11(1) provides that in such circumstances half of the value transferred is exempt from UK tax (after taking account of any other available exemptions) provided that:

(1) the transfer would have been wholly exempt had the recipient spouse been a UK domiciliary; and

(2) a greater exemption for transfers between spouses would not have been given under UK law apart from the Treaty.

Thus, in the circumstances posited, at least half of the value transferred will be exempt from United Kingdom tax, unless, applying the limited IHT spouse exemption, a greater portion of the value transferred would be exempt, in which case that exemption prevails. This can produce substantial savings: see para.33–86.

Article 11(2) provides, in turn, that where property passes to a spouse from a deceased person who was a UK Treaty domiciliary or a UK national and the property rights of the spouse are not regulated by Swedish general law regarding matrimonial property, then, if the surviving spouse so requests, Swedish tax on that property is assessed as if the provisions of such Swedish law were applicable to the property.

Deductions

Article 10 provides in the usual way that in determining the amount on which tax is to be computed deductions shall be allowed in accordance with the law of the state in which the tax is imposed.　　**33–113**

Tax credits

The rules governing tax credits are found in art.12, and may be summarised as follows:　　**33–114**

(1) *Designated property*. Where tax is imposed by one state on the basis of domicile and by the other state because the property by reference to which the charge arises is designated property, the state charging on the basis of domicile must give credit for the tax paid in the country in which the designated property is situated.

(2) *Settled property*. The United Kingdom must give credit for any tax paid in Sweden on settled property if at the time the settlement was made the settlor was a Swedish domiciliary and a UK national.

(3) *Other property*. It may be that one state (say, the United Kingdom) imposes tax by reference to property (other than designated property or settled property as mentioned above) in circumstances in which the deceased/transferor was domiciled in that state at the time of the death/transfer but a national of the other state (Sweden). In such circumstances, the state of which he was a national (Sweden) must allow a credit for the tax paid in the other state.

Time limits

Article 13 provides that any claim for a credit or for a refund of tax based on a Treaty must be made within six years from the date of the event giving rise to a liability to tax or, where later, within one year from the last date on which tax for which the credit is given is due. In appropriate circumstances, one state may extend this limit where the final determination on the payment of tax in the other state is delayed.　　**33–115**

Mutual agreement procedure

If an individual considers that the actions of one or both of the contracting states result in him being taxed beyond the scope of the Treaty, under art.14, he may present his case to the competent authority in either state who will attempt to resolve the case　　**33–116** by mutual agreement with the competent authority in the other state. This includes the resolution of doubts regarding the interpretation or application of the Treaty.

Prevention of fiscal evasion

33–117   Article 15 makes provision for the United Kingdom and Sweden to exchange such information as is necessary for carrying out the provisions of the Treaty or for the prevention of fraud or the administration of statutory provisions against legal avoidance in relation to taxes which are subject to the Treaty. The usual rules apply to the treatment of this information and to the obligations of the states.

Termination

33–118   Article 18 provides that the Treaty shall remain in force until terminated by either state. This can be done any time after five years from the date on which the original treaty came into force, subject to a six months notice period. It will continue to apply in respect of the estate of a person dying before the end of that period or any other event giving rise to a tax liability in either state. The termination of the Treaty does not have the effect of reviving any previous treaty or arrangement.

XIII. TREATY WITH SWITZERLAND

33–119   The Double Taxation Treaty between the United Kingdom and Switzerland came into force in respect of deaths or other events occurring after March 5, 1995, replacing the estate duty treaty made in 1956. The Treaty has since been supplemented by a Protocol of December 17, 1993.

Scope of the Treaty

33–120   Since Swiss succession tax is imposed only on death the Treaty applies only to the following taxes:

(1) to UK IHT insofar as it applies to the estate of a deceased person. It does not, however, apply to lifetime gifts and, in particular, it does not apply to failed PETs. See below as to settlements;

(2) to Swiss cantonal and communal taxes imposed on estates and inheritances; and

(3) to any identical or substantially identical taxes imposed in the future by either state.[61]

---

[61] See fn.8 above as to proposals to introduce a federal gift and estate tax in Switzerland.

The preamble states that the Treaty's purpose is to avoid double taxation: there is no reference to the prevention of fiscal evasion.

The Treaty applies:

(a) to estates and inheritances where the deceased was domiciled at the time of his death in either or both of the states; and

(b) to property comprised in a settlement made by a person who was domiciled in either or both of the states when he made the settlement.

So far as settled property is concerned, it is clear that for IHT purposes the Treaty will apply on the death of an individual with a qualifying interest in possession but not to charges imposed on trusts subject to the relevant property regime. The explanatory memorandum issued by the Swiss Government seems to confirm that Switzerland is likely to take the same approach.

The IHT position is not entirely clear in one respect, i.e. whether the Treaty will apply to property held on trusts subject to the relevant property regime and clawed back into a person's estate on his death by the IHT reservation of benefit provisions. There seems to be no reason why it should not do so, either on the basis that it is settled property or that it is part of the individual's estate on the basis that an individual is treated as beneficially entitled to such property which, unless it is excluded property, forms part of his IHT estate.[62]

Swiss taxation

A detailed explanation of how succession tax is imposed in Switzerland is outside the scope of this chapter, but it will be helpful to outline the basic position. Estate tax is imposed by all but one (Schwyz) of the 26 cantons, each of which has its own system, not by the federal government.[63] Swiss cantons usually tax Swiss residents on a worldwide basis, without giving any unilateral relief for foreign taxes, though immovables situated outside Switzerland are usually exempt from Swiss tax. Conversely, non-residents are normally taxed only on real property situated in Switzerland, though some cantons levy succession tax on other assets as well, e.g. the Italian-speaking canton of Ticino taxes property belonging to a permanent establishment situated there, Geneva taxes household assets, art collections and works of art situated there, and various cantons, including Geneva, Vaud, Zug and Zurich, have a more extensive tax base.

Very few cantons now impose succession taxes on transfers between spouses and to close relatives, including the deceased's issue although, in some cases (e.g. Geneva and Jura) the exemption does not extend to individuals who benefit from a lump sum—or *forfait*—agreement).

While it must be stressed that regard must always be had to the particular system of the canton in question, the basic position is that Swiss tax is charged on a situs basis.

The framers of the Treaty thus faced a fundamental problem, namely how to resolve the conflict between the UK's domiciled based IHT and the situs-based approach in the various cantons. It is therefore not surprising that the Treaty took 15 years to negotiate.

---

[62] FA 1986 s.102(3) and IHTA 1984 s.5(1): see Ch.7 for a full commentary.

[63] See fn.8 above as to proposals to introduce a federal gift and estate tax in Switzerland.

The result is a complicated Treaty with some novel features, notably the recourse to situs to resolve disputes arising from dual domicile.

Avoidance of double taxation

33–123   The Swiss treaty adopts an unusual approach to avoiding double taxation by assigning to the two states rights which are sometimes exclusive and sometimes overlapping in rather complicated ways. The Treaty basically avoids double taxation in two ways:

  (1) *Exclusive taxing rights*: in two cases, it assigns exclusive taxing rights to one state, subject to special United Kingdom taxing rights discussed below.
  (2) *Dual taxing rights with tax credits and exemptions*: aside from the two cases just mentioned, where the taxpayer is Treaty domiciled in one state and the asset is situated in the other state the state in which the taxpayer is domiciled has a domicile taxing right and the situs state retains a taxing right. Double taxation is then avoided by tax credit or exemption.

Fiscal domicile

33–124   The practical effect of the Treaty and the 1993 Protocol is as follows:

  (1) *Basic rules*: art.4(1) provides basic rules for determining whether a person died domiciled in the United Kingdom or Switzerland. For this purpose, a person died domiciled in the United Kingdom if he was domiciled there for IHT purposes, taking into account the deemed domicile rules and in Switzerland if he was:
    (a) domiciled or resident in Switzerland in accordance with the law of Switzerland; or
    (b) a Swiss national and Swiss civil law requires his succession to be ruled in Switzerland. The Protocol provides that for this purpose the reference to civil law concerns Ch.6 of the *loi federale sur le droit international prive* of December 18, 1987.
  (2) *Deemed non-domicile*: two rules provide that a person is not deemed to be domiciled in a state:
    (a) situs override: the closing words of art.4 provide that notwithstanding the basic rules mentioned above, a deceased person shall be deemed not to be domiciled in one of the states if that state imposes tax only by reference to property situated in that State;
    (b) temporary employment: the 1993 Protocol provides a let-out for, in effect, nationals of one state who go to the other state just to work. Under the protocol an individual who was a national of one state but not of the other and who immediately before coming to the other state was domiciled in the first state shall not be domiciled in the other state if:
      (i) he was temporarily present in that other state by reason only of his employment (or was a spouse or other dependant of a person temporarily in that other state for such purpose);

(ii) that individual had retained the domicile of the state of which he was a national; and

(iii) that individual had no intention of becoming a permanent resident of the other state.

Thus, a Swiss national and domiciliary who satisfies these requirements will not be caught by the IHT deemed domicile rules. Nor will a UK national and domiciliary who satisfies these requirements become domiciled in Switzerland under the various Swiss rules discussed above.

(3) Tie-breaker rules: where, after applying the above tests an individual is domiciled in both states, the usual tie-breaker rules (see, e.g. the rules in the United Kingdom-Sweden Treaty discussed at para.33–110).

Classification of property: designated property and residual property

The Treaty effectively divides property into two basic categories which we shall call **33–125** "designated property" and "residual property", the latter being comprised of all property which is not designated property. Designated property consists of:

(1) immovable property (art.5);
(2) movable business property of an enterprise (art.6(1));
(3) movable property used for the performance of professional services (art.6(6));
(4) ships and aircraft operating in international traffic (art.7); and
(5) shares in UK companies (art.8(2)).

These kinds of designated property are discussed in more detail at paras 33–130 and following.

Exclusive taxing rights

Exclusive taxing rights exist in two cases. These rights are framed by reference: **33–126**

(a) in the first case, to property which is subject to a domicile-based charge in one state and not to a situs charge in the other state, in which case domicile determines the position; and

(b) in the second case, to property in one state which is subject to a charge in both states, in which case situs determines the position.

Domicile determinative on "foreign" property

The effect of arts 8(1)(b) and art.8(4) is that, subject to one qualification, where the **33–127** deceased died domiciled in both states only the state in which the taxpayer is Treaty domiciled can tax an asset where the asset is situated in that state or in a third state. The qualification is that, per art.8(4), the United Kingdom retains its domicile taxing right in respect of property situated in a third state if:

(a) the taxpayer was domiciled for IHT purposes in the United Kingdom when he died; or

(b) was a UK national but not a Swiss national who had been domiciled in the United Kingdom at any time within the five preceding years.

So, if the taxpayer has a Treaty domicile in Switzerland, Swiss tax can be imposed on property in, e.g. Italy, but so can IHT if the X satisfies either (a) or (b) above. But if X has a treaty domicile in the United Kingdom, only the United Kingdom can impose tax on the property.

Situs determinative on residual property

33–128   The effect of arts 8(1)(a) and art.8(3) is that, subject to one qualification, where the taxpayer was domiciled in each state under their respective domestic laws, e.g. as would be the case where an English domiciliary was resident in Switzerland, only the state in which the residual property is situated can tax the property. The only qualification is that, per art.8(3), the United Kingdom retains its taxing right in respect of the residual property situated in Switzerland if:

(a) the taxpayer was Treaty domiciled in the United Kingdom; when he died; or

(b) was a UK national but not a Swiss national who had been domiciled in the United Kingdom at any time within the five preceding years.

So, in a dual domicile case, if the property is situated in Switzerland, Swiss tax can be imposed but so can IHT if the deceased satisfies either (a) or (b) above. But if the property is situated in the United Kingdom, only the United Kingdom can impose tax on the property.

Determination of situs

33–129   The Protocol provides that the situs of any property dealt with in art.8 is to be determined by the law of the United Kingdom in effect on the date when the Treaty came into force.

Dual taxing rights

33–130   Save as discussed at para.33–128 where a situs right is an exclusive taxing right, where the taxpayer is treaty domiciled in one state and the asset is situated in the other

1208

state, the state in which the taxpayer is domiciled retains its taxing rights and in some cases the situs state retains its situs taxing right.

Situs taxing rights

A state in which a designated asset is situated retains its right to tax that asset as set out below. **33–131**

Immovable property

Under art.5, the state in which immovable property (as rather widely defined) is situated retains its right to tax that property. **33–132**

Ships and aircraft

Under art.7, the state in which is situated the management of ships and aircraft operating internationally retains its right to tax those ships and aircraft. **33–133**

Shares in UK companies

Under art.8(2) the United Kingdom retains the right to tax shares in UK companies. **33–134**

Enterprise with fixed place of business

Under art.6(1) a state retains the right to tax movable property (except for assets referred in arts 5, 7 and 8(2) which are already covered as discussed above) of an enterprise which forms part of the estate of a person domiciled in the other state which is the business property of a permanent establishment (as defined) situated in that first state. By art.6(7), this applies to an interest in a partnership if an enterprise is carried on by the partnership. **33–135**

Professional services

Under art.6(6), a state retains the right to tax movable property (except for assets referred in arts 5, 7 and 8(2) which are already covered as discussed above) used for the performance of professional services or other activities of an independent character and pertaining to a fixed base. By art.6(7), this applies to an interest in a partnership if **33–136** professional services or other activities of an independent character are performed by the partnership.

Residual property

33–137   The treatment of this property was discussed at para.33–128.

Spouse exemption

33–138   Circumstances may arise in which property passes to the spouse of a deceased person who was domiciled in or a national of Switzerland which is subject to IHT but does not qualify for the full spouse exemption. In that case, if the transfer would have been wholly exempt if the transferee spouse had been domiciled in the United Kingdom half the value transferred, before any grossing-up, and after taking account of all exemptions except those for transfers between spouses, is exempt. This can produce substantial tax savings.

Elimination of double taxation

33–139   Article 9 provides two methods of eliminating such double taxation as would arise from the allocation of taxing rights:

(1) the United Kingdom gives credit for Swiss tax charged under any exclusive taxing right or under arts 5, 6 or 7; and
(2) where the deceased died domiciled in Switzerland, Switzerland exempts from tax any designated property which may be taxed in the United Kingdom. Such an exemption does not prevent that property from being taken into account in computing the tax on other property or in determining the rate of such tax.

Non-discrimination

33–140   Article 11 contains various provisions concerning non-discrimination.

Mutual agreement procedure

33–141   Article 12 provides for the usual mutual agreement procedure for resolving disputes.

XIV. TREATY WITH THE UNITED STATES

33–142   The Double Taxation Treaty between the United Kingdom and the United States entered into force on November 11, 1979, at which time the existing Treaty between the United Kingdom and the United States ceased to have effect.[64]

The taxes which are the subject of the Treaty are CTT, and, in the United States, the **33–143** Federal gift tax and the Federal estate tax, including the tax on generation-skipping transfers. The Treaty will also apply to any identical or substantially similar taxes imposed by either state in the future, so IHT is also included. The Treaty does not extend to any taxes which may be imposed by the individual states of the United States. The United States for this purpose means the United States of America, but does not include Puerto Rico, the Virgin Islands, Guam or any other US possession or territory. The Treaty applies to any person who is within the scope of the tax which is the subject of the Treaty. The stated purpose of the Treaty is twofold; to avoid double taxation, and to prevent fiscal evasion.

Avoidance of double taxation

The Treaty avoids double taxation in two ways. First, it provides that in certain **33–144** circumstances one state is to have exclusive taxing rights. Secondly, in the event that both states are entitled to charge tax, double taxation is avoided through a system of tax credits. Each of these methods will be examined in turn.

Exclusive taxing rights

The general rule is found in art.5(1) which provides that if the decedent or transferor **33–145** was domiciled in one state at the time of the death/transfer but not in the other state the state in which he was domiciled has exclusive taxing rights. This general rule is subject to a number of qualifications, which are discussed below. Before considering these qualifications, it will be helpful, given the fact that under the general rule a person's domicile for purposes of the Treaty may be critical, to consider the rules governing fiscal domicile.

Fiscal domicile

The rules concerning fiscal domicile are found in art.4. The general rule is that an **33–146** individual is domiciled in the United Kingdom if he is domiciled in the United Kingdom for IHT purposes, while he is domiciled in the United States if he is a resident (domiciliary) thereof or if he is a national thereof and has been a resident (domiciliary)[65] thereof at any time during the preceding three years. It follows from these definitions that an individual may be domiciled in both states at the same time. Articles 4(2) and 4(3) contain provisions similar to those found in art.4(2) and (3) of the Treaty with South Africa, and the comments made in relation to those articles will apply

---

[64] For the position under the old treaty see "Deemed domicile doesn't apply to Americans" in *British Tax Review* (1975), p.325.

[65] In US statutes the term "residence" is used synonymously with the term "domicile". Strictly speaking, there is no such thing as a domicile in the United States. An individual will have as his residence (domicile) one of the individual states of the United States.

here.[66] There is nothing in the Treaty with the United States that is equivalent to art.4(4) in the Treaty with South Africa. In the event that after applying art.4(2) or (3) the individual is still domiciled for purposes of the Treaty in both states, art.4(4) provides the usual[67] "tie-breaker" test to determine fiscal domicile.

33–147   For the above purposes, art.3(1)(b) provides that the term "national" means, in relation to the United States, US citizens, and, in relation to the United Kingdom, any citizen of the United Kingdom and the Colonies, or any British subject not possessing that citizenship or the citizenship of any other commonwealth country or territory, provided that in either case he had a right of abode in the United Kingdom at the time of the death/transfer. By art.4(5), an individual who is a resident (domiciliary) of a United States possession solely by reason of:

(1) his being a citizen of such possession; or
(2) his birth or residence within such a possession,

is considered to be neither domiciled in nor a national of the United States.

33–148   A subject which can cause confusion is the domicile of a US national who married a UK domiciled husband before January 1, 1974. This is because such a woman can be domiciled in the United States under the Income Tax/CGT Treaty, but in the United Kingdom under the IHT Treaty. Advisers must accordingly be wary when planning for IHT of relying on correspondence from HMRC confirming that such a lady is domiciled outside the United Kingdom for, e.g. income tax purposes. The source of the discrepancy is art.4(4) of the Income Tax/CGT Treaty, which provides that a United States national who married a UK domiciliary before January 1, 1974, is deemed to have entered into that marriage on that date for the purpose of determining her domicile under that Treaty. Such a woman can thus claim that she has retained her domicile of origin in one of the United States (in the same way as can an American who married after that date, though it must be noted that HMRC may well contend that a woman who has lived in the United Kingdom for a substantial period has acquired a UK domicile of choice). Article 4(4), however, applies only for the purposes of the Income Tax/CGT Treaty, and not for purposes of the IHT Treaty. Assume, for example, that Nancy, a US national, married Frank in London in June 1968, at which time she accordingly acquired, under UK general law, a UK domicile of dependence which was in due course converted by the Domicile and Matrimonial Proceedings Act 1973 into a UK domicile of choice on January 1, 1974. Although Nancy may be domiciled in the United States under the Income Tax/CGT Treaty, she continues to be domiciled in the United Kingdom as a matter of UK general law and is thus domiciled in the United Kingdom under the IHT Treaty. Her position became even worse after April 5, 1985, when she acquired a deemed UK domicile under the 17-year rule.

Qualifications to exclusive taxing rights

33–149   There are six qualifications to the general rule that the state in which the individual was domiciled at the time of the death/transfer has exclusive taxing rights. These qualifications are as follows:

[66] See para.33–98.
[67] This is subject to the qualification that the "centre of vital interests" test applies even if the tax payer does not have a permanent home in either state.

(1) *Designated property.* Under arts 6 and 7, certain property may be taxed in the state in which that property is situated notwithstanding the fact that the decedent/transferor is not domiciled in that state. Article 6 is concerned with immovable property (real property); this is the subject of a special definition[68] in art.6(2). Article 6 also applies to immovable property of an enterprise, and to immovable property used for the performance of independent personal services. Article 7 deals with assets (other than those covered by art.6) which form part of the business property of a permanent establishment (as defined) of an enterprise. Assets pertaining to a fixed base used for the performance of independent personal services may, under art.7, also be taxed in the state in which the fixed base is situated.[69] Article 7 does not refer specifically to partnership interests but HMRC is understood to treat such interests as within the scope of the article.

(2) *Nationality.* By art.5(1)(b), neither the general rule nor the above-mentioned "designated property" qualification applies if at the time of the death/transfer the decedent/transferor was a national of the state in which he was not domiciled. This preserves the US' ability to tax on the basis of nationality.[70] It also means that a UK national will be liable to IHT on a worldwide basis if he is a UK national and a United Kingdom domiciliary for IHT purposes even though he is not a United Kingdom domiciliary for the purposes of the Treaty. By art.5(2) if, at the time of the death/transfer, the decedent/transferor was not domiciled in either state but was a national of one state (but not of both states), property which is taxable in the state of which he was a national is not taxable in the other state, unless it is taxable under arts 6 or 7. Thus, if a US citizen domiciled in the Bahamas dies owning property situated in the United Kingdom, the United Kingdom will treat him in the same way as a US domiciliary, and will not charge IHT on the UK property unless it is "designated property" under arts 6 or 7, since the United States is taxing the property, the United Kingdom gives up its right to do so.

(3) *Generation-skipping.* By art.5(3), neither the general rule nor the "nationality" qualification applies in the United States to property held in a generation-skipping trust or trust equivalent on the occasion of a generation-skipping transfer. Instead, except in relation to designated property under arts 6 and 7, tax is not imposed in the United States on such property if at the time when the transfer was made the deemed transferor was domiciled in the United Kingdom and was not a US national.

(4) *Settled property.* By art.5(4), neither the general rule nor the "nationality" qualification applies in the United Kingdom to property comprised in a settlement. Instead, except in relation to designated property under arts 6 and 7, tax is not imposed in the United Kingdom on such property if at the time when the settlement was made the settlor was domiciled (under the Treaty) in the United States and was not a UK national. This means that a US citizen who is not a UK national can make a settlement (of other than designated property) which is effectively outside the scope of IHT notwithstanding the fact that he is deemed to be a UK domiciliary for IHT purposes. HMRC is understood to agree that art.5(4) is sufficiently wide to prevent exit and periodic charges

---

[68] Which extends, e.g., to livestock.

[69] It will be noted that, unlike the treaty with South Africa (see para.33–99), shares, etc. issued by companies incorporated in one of the states is not designated property.

[70] Unlike the United Kingdom, where the charge to IHT is determined solely by reference to the decedent's/transferor's domicile status, the US taxes as much by reference to nationality as residence (domicile).

being imposed on relevant property comprised in settlements subject to the relevant property regime.

(5) *Saving clause.* Under art.5(5), if by reason of either the general rule or the above qualifications thereto any property would be taxable only in one state and tax, though chargeable, is not paid (otherwise than as the result of a specific exemption, deduction, exclusion, credit or allowance) in that state, tax may be imposed by reference to that property in the other state notwithstanding art.5(1)–(4).

The main purpose of this article is to deal with the case where the country of domicile or nationality cannot enforce its claim, typically because the individuals responsible for payment of the tax are not residing in the jurisdiction and the property on which the tax is assessed is not situated there. In practice, however, the operation of the article can have a more general impact.

Take, e.g., the administration of the estate of a US national, deemed domiciled in the United Kingdom for IHT purposes but with a fiscal domicile (under the Treaty) in the United States. As a result of the Treaty, the charge to IHT on the death will be limited to arts 5 and 6 designated property situated in the United Kingdom. HMRC, however, will continue to impose tax according to UK domestic law until evidence has been provided that the US tax has been paid or a specific exemption or allowance has been accepted in the United States. Given the mismatch between the due dates for payment of estate taxes in the United States and the United Kingdom[71] this can result in an unwelcome tax charge (and cash flow and funding issues) for such a deceased's personal representatives on their application for a grant of representation in the United Kingdom—although it is understood that HMRC may in certain circumstances, be persuaded to limit their initial assessment to UK situs assets only.

(6) *Situs disputes.* By art.5(6), if at the time of the death/transfer the decedent/transferor was not domiciled in either state,[72] and each state would regard any property as situated in its territory with the result that tax would be imposed in both states, the situs of the property is to be determined by the competent authorities of the states by mutual agreement. Where the property in respect of which the charge to tax arises is shares recourse is most likely to be had to art.5(6). US law distinguishes between shares in American companies and shares in foreign companies. Shares in American companies are always situated in the United States, while shares in foreign companies are situated where the share certificates are physically held. UK law, on the other hand, draws no such distinction; instead, the distinction is between bearer shares and other shares, bearer shares normally being situated where the share certificates are physically situated, while all other shares are regarded as being situated where the company's register is situated.[73]

Deductions, exemptions, etc.

33–150   Article 8 provides three kinds of exemption,[74] as follows:

[71] Federal estate tax assessable on a death does not fall due for payment until nine months after the date of death. The charge to IHT, by contrast, is payable, generally, on the earlier of the application for representation to the UK estate or six months after the end of the month of death.

[72] Art.5(2) (see qualification (2) above) might prevent one state from charging tax where the decedent/transferor was a national of the other state.

[73] See para.32–66.

[74] See also art.8(2) as to the availability of the US marital deduction.

(1) *Permitted deductions.* By art.8(1), in determining the amount on which tax is to be computed, permitted deductions are allowed in accordance with the law in force in the state in which tax is imposed.

(2) *Limitation.* By art.8(5), where property may be taxed in the United States on the death of a UK national who was neither a US domiciliary nor a US national, the tax imposed in the United States (provided a claim is made) is limited to the amount of tax which would have been imposed on such of the property as would have been taxable had the decedent become domiciled in the United States immediately before he died. The reason for this provision is that US tax is charged on non-domiciliaries at higher rates than on domiciliaries; art.8(5) gives non-domiciliaries the benefit of the lower rates.

(3) *Spouse exemption.* There are a number of provisions concerning transfers between spouses. First, where certain conditions are satisfied, art.8(3) overrides the £55,000 limit[75] which applies to transfers from a UK domiciliary to his foreign-domiciled spouse. The conditions are that the decedent/transferor was for Treaty purposes a US domiciliary or a US national, and his spouse was not for Treaty purposes a UK domiciliary. In such a case, 50 per cent of the value transferred, before any grossing-up, and after taking account of any other exemptions, the annual exemption, is exempt from US tax. By art.8(4)(a), this 50 per cent exemption is also available, if certain conditions are satisfied, in respect of property which on the death of a decedent domiciled in the United Kingdom for Treaty purposes became comprised in a settlement. The conditions are that:

(a) the personal representatives and the trustees of every settlement in which the decedent had an interest in possession immediately before his death so elect;

(b) under the settlement the spouse of the decedent is entitled to an immediate interest in possession;

(c) the spouse is for Treaty purposes a US domiciliary or a US national; and

(d) the transfer would have been wholly exempt if the spouse was for Treaty purposes a UK domiciliary.

By art.8(4)(b), if the spouse of the decedent subsequently becomes absolutely and indefeasibly entitled to any of the settled property, the 50 per cent exemption is lost retrospectively. It is to be noted that the conditions which must be satisfied under art.8(3) for "absolute entitlement relief" differ from those that must be satisfied under art.8(4) for "interest in possession" relief. In both cases, the decedent/transferor will be domiciled in the United Kingdom under UK law (otherwise the spouse exemption would not be limited to begin with), but absolute entitlement relief is available only where the decedent/transferor was for Treaty purposes a US domiciliary or a US national, while interest in possession relief is available only if he was for Treaty purposes a UK domiciliary. The Treaty therefore applies where the wife has a US domicile; or is a US national domiciled anywhere except in the United Kingdom. A US wife who has not taken her husband's domicile is likely to qualify under both these headings.

The wife must be given an immediate interest in possession in the husband's estate. A six months' survivorship period which is deemed by s.92 to have effect from the date of death probably satisfies this condition even if the income is to be accumulated, because of the reference in art.3(2) of the Treaty to undefined expressions having the

---

[75] Proposals were announced in the March 2012 Budget to increase the £55,000 limit to an amount equivalent to the nil rate band.

meaning under internal law. On the other hand, it may be safer to have an immediate interest in possession without any conditions.

If one complies with the above, the spouse relief is extended to 50 per cent of the value transferred, if this gives greater relief than the £55,000.

33–151   The cost of obtaining this relief is that one will have created a settlement with a UK domiciled settlor and therefore, on the wife's death, normal IHT will be payable. The Treaty deals with the obvious loophole that such liability might be avoided if the property were advanced to the wife absolutely. If this occurs, the Treaty exemption is deemed never to have been made and the tax on the husband's death is recalculated with the maximum spouse relief of £55,000.[76] This is why claiming relief under the Treaty requires the consent of the personal representatives and the trustees of every settlement in which the husband had an interest in possession at his death. The personal representatives and the trustees are therefore at risk during the wife's lifetime to pay additional tax and they will clearly require an indemnity.

Tax credits

33–152   Article 9 lays down certain rules governing tax credits. These rules are necessary since, as was seen above, in certain circumstances both the United Kingdom and the United States may be entitled to tax the same property. Three rules prevent double taxation where such a dual charge is imposed, as follows:

(1) *Worldwide basis*. In certain circumstances both states may charge tax on a worldwide basis where a taxpayer is domiciled for Treaty purposes in one state but a national of the other state. In such a case, the state of which he was a national gives credit for the tax paid in the state in which he was domiciled.

(2) *Designated property*. It may be that one state charges tax on a worldwide basis, while the other state charges tax under arts 6 or 7. In such a case, credit is given by the country taxing on the worldwide basis for the tax paid in the state charging under arts 6 or 7.

(3) *Settled property*. By art.9(3), where both states impose tax on the same event with respect to property which under UK law is settled property and which under US law would be regarded as property held in a trust or trust equivalent, double taxation is avoided in a somewhat complicated fashion. First, where one state imposes tax on property on the basis that the property is designated property under arts 6 or 7, the other state gives credit for this tax. Secondly, where the US imposes tax on property which is not designated property, then, under art.9(3), the United Kingdom must give credit for the US tax if:

(a) the event giving rise to the liability to tax was a generation-skipping transfer and the deemed transferor was a US domiciliary for Treaty purposes at the time of the event;

(b) the event giving rise to the liability to tax was the exercise or lapse of a power of appointment and the holder of the power was a US domiciliary for Treaty purposes at the time of the event; or

(c) neither (a) nor (b) applies, and the settlor or grantor was a US domiciliary for Treaty purposes at the time when the tax was imposed.

Thirdly, where the US imposes tax on property which is not designated property and art.9(3)(b) does not apply, the United States gives credit for the

---

[76] See fn.75 above.

1216

UK tax. In the relatively rare case where only one country regards the property as settled, e.g. where the United Kingdom regards it as comprised in a settlement but the United States does not regard it as held in a trust or trust equivalent, the rules at (1) (worldwide basis) and (2) (designated property) above will apply.

The rules determining the amount of credit that can be claimed are set down in art.9(4), the provisions of which are similar to those in the Treaties with South Africa and Ireland. Credit can be claimed for net tax only, i.e. no account is to be taken of tax not levied by reason of a credit otherwise allowed in another country—typically this would be in the form of a relief under another double tax treaty. As credits are matched on an asset by asset basis no credit is allowed in excess of the tax payable on the relevant asset in the country claiming the credit. Similarly, interest charges levied on the tax paid in the country with the primary taxing rights are disregarded. **33–153**

Time limits

By art.9(5), any claim for a credit or a refund under the Treaty must be made within six years from the date of the event giving rise to the liability to tax, or, where later, within one year from the last date on which the tax for which credit is given is due. As a claim for credit will not be considered until the tax for which it is allowable has been paid an eye needs to be kept firmly on the six year deadline. The competent authority may, however, in appropriate circumstances extend this time limit where the final determination or payment of tax in the other state is delayed. **33–154**

Prevention of fiscal evasion

Article 12 makes provision for the states to exchange information similar to that found in the Treaty with Ireland.[77] **33–155**

[77] See para.33–68.

Chapter 34

ASPECTS OF INTERNATIONAL ESTATE PLANNING

I. INTRODUCTION

34–01   As discussed in Chapter 32, IHT is a worldwide tax affecting, broadly speaking, all individuals domiciled in the United Kingdom for IHT purposes and any property situated in the United Kingdom owned by individuals, regardless of their domicile. Increasingly, the demands of internationally mobile individuals have to be taken into account when planning for IHT. In this chapter, we will consider:

(1) the impact of different succession regimes on IHT planning;

(2) the treatment, for IHT purposes, of entities that do not fall easily within concepts recognised by UK law; and

(3) how to minimise problems in aligning the IHT regime with the treatment of transfers for the purposes of non-UK estate/gift taxes.

We provide examples of how some of these issues can be dealt with successfully in practice by reference to particular problems encountered in relation to specific regimes, giving emphasis to those situations (and jurisdictions) we think UK practitioners are most likely to encounter in practice. This is an area on which there has been an increasing emphasis in recent years.

It is also to be hoped that, although the discussion in this chapter takes place within the overarching context of UK IHT, planners from other jurisdictions may find it helpful in identifying issues of general importance in international estate planning and may be able to adapt some of the specific IHT planning points to the rules relevant to their own jurisdictions.

Except where indicated, all references in this chapter to the domicile of individuals are references to domicile as determined for IHT purposes.[1]

In certain circumstances, the IHT s.18 exemption for transfers between spouses and civil partners is limited to £55,000[2] (unless enlarged by any relevant double tax treaty).[3] Unless stated otherwise, the discussion in this chapter assumes that the IHT s.18 exemption is available without limit; in practice, this will need to be checked in each case.

Impact of foreign taxes on IHT planning

In the context of IHT planning it is difficult to overestimate the importance of determining whether an individual is affected by foreign succession rules and/or foreign estate/gift taxes. The position is not made any easier by the fact that an individual may not be aware of his exposure to foreign tax, e.g. many US nationals or "green card" holders living outside the United States may be unaware of their continuing exposure to US tax by reason of their nationality or green card status.[4] **34–02**

Sometimes the impact of these issues (particularly those associated with pure succession rather than, immediately, with tax—the *renvoi* doctrine is an obvious example) only makes itself felt once the planning has been implemented—often on the individual's death. Where possible, however, these factors should be considered at the planning stage. By way of example: **34–03**

A is a national of Dubai who is deemed domiciled in the United Kingdom. He is married and has two children by his English wife. His solicitor advises him that one effective way to save, or at least postpone, IHT would be for the client to leave everything to his wife.

From an IHT point of view the advice given by the practitioner is sensible. However, whether the client can leave his property to his wife in this way depends on the law which governs the succession to his various assets. Under the common law of England and Wales there are no restrictions on the freedom of disposition (cf. however, the

---

[1] See paras 32–03 and following.

[2] According to announcements made in the March 2012 Budget, and the accompanying Policy Costings document, Finance Act 2013 will include provisions to increase the limited spouse exemption from £55,000 to a value equal to the nil rate band (presently £325,000); measures will also be included to allow non domiciled spouses and civil partners of UK domiciliaries to elect to be treated as domiciled in the UK for the purposes of IHT.

[3] See paras 3–35 and 33–36.

[4] Indeed many individuals are unaware that they are US citizens (e.g. by virtue of having been born in the United States). Similarly, many green card holders are unaware that they should formally relinquish their green card when they no longer live and work in the United States.

Inheritance (Provision for Family and Dependants) Act 1975, which applies to individuals domiciled in England and Wales as a matter of general law). Under Dubai law, on the other hand, two thirds of the estate of a Muslim is reserved to his Qu'ranic heirs who, in the example, would be the wife and the children (assuming the wife and children are themselves Muslim) of the testator. In addition, a non-Muslim cannot inherit from a Muslim. So, if Dubai law applied and the client is a Muslim, a will which left everything to the client's wife (who may not herself be a Muslim) might be wholly or partly inoperative and the IHT s.18 exemption would either not be available at all or would be restricted.

Will drafting

34–04   A will may purport to deal with property in a jurisdiction outside the United Kingdom or be drafted for a testator whose personal status (nationality, residence, domicile or religion) may mean that the laws of another jurisdiction may impact on his estate; in this context the impact of Brussels IV (see para.34–10, below) will need to be considered carefully, whether or not the testator is resident in a jurisdiction that has opted into its provisions.[5] A discussion on the international recognition of wills is outside the scope of this book. However, the form of will, or the circumstances in which it is drawn up, may be relevant in the context of foreign law issues. Wills executed during the final illness of the testator may not be recognised under *Shari'a* law, for instance, and provisions in the will not concerned with the disposition of property may affect questions as to whether the will itself is recognised at all.[6]

Importance of considering private international law

34–05   Because of the different approaches taken by various countries in relation to the choice of "connecting factors" (i.e. factors connecting an individual to a particular jurisdiction) and to the doctrine of *renvoi*,[7] clients are often advised to deal with their estate on a jurisdiction by jurisdiction basis, according to the location of their assets. Whilst this approach is sensible in devolution terms, as it guarantees that assets pass in accordance with the testator's wishes, in tax terms the question arises as to how HMRC will treat a transfer of property which is incompatible with the private international law of this country. Again, an example is helpful:

---

[5] Article 17 of Brussels IV will allow a testator to choose that the law of his nationality shall apply to succession under his will. Note that certain jurisdictions (including Italy and Switzerland) already allow for such a choice of law in certain circumstances. Under English law as it stands it is not open to a testator to choose the law governing the substance of his will. However, under the Recognition of Trusts Act 1987 and art.6 of the Hague Trusts Convention he is able to choose the law governing a trust—in *Re Barton (Deceased)* [2002] EWHC 264 (Ch), a testator died domiciled in Texas, leaving a will creating a trust of movables. He declared however that "this my will shall take effect in accordance with English law". Lawrence Collins J. held that the declaration could not provide effectively "that questions of succession should be governed by a law other than that of the domicile" but that the declaration could take effect as a choice of law to govern the part of the will setting up a trust.

[6] See the defendant's argument in *Al-Bassam v Al-Bassam* [2004] EWCA Civ 857 that a provision providing for cremation of the testator's body cast doubt on the general validity of the will as the provision was offensive to fundamental Islamic tenets.

[7] The application of the doctrine of *renvoi* will be restricted in most EU member states once Brussels IV (see para.34–10) comes into force on August 17, 2015.

A was an Italian citizen and domiciliary. He lived in the United Kingdom for 20 years so that he was deemed domiciled here for IHT purposes. He and his wife then moved to Switzerland together with their only child. A year later he met B with whom he commenced a relationship and he died shortly thereafter. Amongst A's property there was a bank account in Switzerland. In his English law will, A declared that his spouse and child should receive what was reserved to them by law and that the rest should pass to B. From an English perspective, the devolution of the bank account would be governed by Italian law according to A's domicile under which the surviving spouse has a statutory right to one-third of the estate. However, Switzerland will apply Swiss law by virtue of A's residence and, as a result, A's widow will be entitled to one-quarter of the estate. Will HMRC grant the IHT s.18 exemption in relation to one-quarter or to one-third of the estate? In practice, the s.18 exemption is likely to be applied to such part of the estate as the widow actually receives.

Where an individual deals with his assets in a foreign jurisdiction by having a will drawn up under local law, care must be taken to ensure that that will is limited to the property concerned and that the will does not unintentionally revoke an existing will in another jurisdiction.[8]

In theory, it may be arguable that a transfer of property which is incompatible with the country's private international law violates the UK's sovereignty and that, in exercising its taxing rights, HMRC should have regard solely to UK domestic rules, subject to the constraints of any international conventions. Quoting a French writer: **34–06**

> "By virtue of their sovereignty, States have the right to levy taxes according to principles which they regard as fair, opportune and practical without having regard to the measures taken by their neighbours".[9]

This stance appears to have been adopted in Finland, as it is understood that the Finnish tax authorities will consider charging tax on an heir in respect of a statutory share which the heir should have received under Finnish law, even though the foreign *lex successionis* does not provide for statutory shares.[10]

This is an area with very little precedent but it would seem that HMRC, in levying **34–07** IHT, has regard to the reality, rather than to the theoretical position. This is consistent with the wording of the legislation see, e.g. s.18(1), which provides that:

> "A transfer of value is an exempt transfer to the extent that the value transferred is attributable to property which becomes comprised in the estate of the transferor's spouse or civil partner or, so far as the value transferred is not so attributable, to the extent that that estate is increased."

The use of the words "becomes comprised" and "is increased" as opposed to "should become comprised" and "should be increased" indicates clearly that what counts is the

---

[8] See, for example, *Perdoni v Curati* [2011] EWHC 3442 (Ch) where the Court considered whether an Italian will that did not include specific revocation language revoked an earlier English will. In the event, it was held that the English will was not revoked as the law of the testator's domicile (England) had a presumption against implied revocation.

[9] "En vertu de leur souveraineté les Etats ont le droit de lever des impôts conformément aux principes qu'ils jugent équitables, opportuns et pratiques sans se préoccuper des mesures prises par leurs voisins", Oualid in: *Revue de Science et de Législations Financière*, 23 (1927) 5 here quoted from F.A. Mann, *The Doctrine of Jurisdiction in International Law* (1964); see also A.H. Qureshi, "The Freedom of a State to Legislate in Fiscal Matters under General International Law", in *IBFD Bulletin*, 1987/I, p.14ss.

[10] It is understood that this is a result of the method used by the Finnish tax authorities to calculate the tax. See also Prof. G.O. Zacharias Sundström, *European Succession Laws*, edited by Hayton (2002).

fact that the surviving spouse or civil partner has become the owner of assets comprised in the estate, regardless of how the surviving spouse or civil partner became the owner.

Other taxes

34–08   While this chapter looks at international estate planning from the perspective, and within the context, of IHT planning, regard needs to be had not just to the various legal systems that may be relevant, but also to all the relevant taxes. IHT cannot be considered in isolation from other UK taxes, particularly CGT, income tax and stamp duty land tax, nor can UK taxes be considered in isolation from relevant foreign taxes. Similar considerations apply in relation to the impact of foreign non-gift/estate taxes.

II. FOREIGN LAW CONCEPTS IN IHT PLANNING

34–09   IHT exists, of course, against the common law background of laws relating to succession and legal and beneficial ownership in England and Wales and the (rather different) laws of Northern Ireland (Scotland, of course, has its own system for which the IHT legislation makes specific provision—see paras 34–16 and 34–23, below). Most notably, IHT exists in the context of (relative) freedom of disposition. Under the common law of England and Wales there are no restrictions on the freedom of disposition, but this rule is tempered by the Inheritance (Provision for Family and Dependants) Act 1975 which allows certain family members (including spouses, civil partners and children) and dependants of a deceased who was domiciled under the general law in England and Wales to claim against the deceased's estate in certain circumstances.[11]

Where a practitioner becomes involved in international tax planning, it is essential to be aware of the different regimes that exist elsewhere in the world and, if only in general terms, of how these impact on IHT planning. No estate planning designed to be tax efficient will achieve its goal if it is ineffective under the relevant foreign civil law. In addition, any tax planning using foreign law regimes is unlikely to work if those regimes do not satisfy the requirements for the particular IHT treatment (e.g. the availability of the s.18 exemption) upon which the planning itself is based.

Brussels IV

34–10   On July 4, 2012 the European Parliament and Council formally adopted Regulation (EU) 650/2012 (known as "Brussels IV") which will apply to all EU Member States apart from the United Kingdom, Ireland and Denmark[12] as from August 17, 2015.[13] Brussels IV is aimed at simplifying problematical areas of cross-border succession in the EU area. It provides for a single criterion for determining both the jurisdiction and

[11] And, of course, the eventual disposition of the deceased's estate as the result of a claim can affect the amount of IHT payable, e.g. where an estate that passed under the deceased's will entirely to a surviving spouse is partly redirected to a non-exempt beneficiary.
[12] The United Kingdom and Ireland (but not Denmark) can opt into Brussels IV in the future.
[13] That is, Brussels IV will apply to deaths on or after that date.

the law applicable in cross-border cases (in the absence of an election to the contrary this will be the deceased's "habitual place of residence" as at the date of his death) and for a European "Certificate of Succession" to reduce the formalities and procedures required for beneficiaries and personal representatives. Although the United Kingdom has decided not to opt into Brussels IV, it will still be necessary for UK practitioners to be aware of its terms and its impact on estates with connections to an EU Member State.

HMRC's approach to foreign law regimes

The IHTM gives scant guidance in relation to the IHT consequences of foreign law **34–11** regimes, apart from containing general statements and health warnings, such as the one contained at IHTM11042:

> "*Special points to look out for [October 2007]*
> You will need to be on the lookout for, and carefully consider situations where spouse or civil partner (. . .) exemption is claimed on (. . .)
> * foreign property . . . or foreign domicile . . . The provisions of a person's UK will, or UK rules of intestacy, may not apply to foreign immovable property . . . There may be a foreign will, or the law of the country in which the property is situated or where the person was domiciled may apply. In some countries the surviving spouse or civil partner and children are entitled to specific parts or portions of the estate notwithstanding the terms of a person's will.
> * Property passing under the law of Scotland. Under Scots law certain rights of a deceased person are conferred on the surviving spouse or civil partner and the issue of that person . . . "

With regards to spouses, the old *CTO Advanced Instruction Manual* (now replaced by the IHTM) did contain a brief reference to matrimonial property regimes (Ch.S, Foreign Element at 39):

> "In foreign community of property cases you need to consider carefully the precise terms of any contract that limits, defines or modifies the rights the spouses would otherwise have in the community property. Difficult questions may arise regarding . . . whether the community property is subject to a 'settlement' as defined in IHTA 1984, s 43(2). The French community provisions include systems which spouses can elect at their option and which empower spouses to change the system under which they were married, even in cases where there was an ante-nuptial contract. It is especially important in French cases therefore to look carefully into the rights of the parties under any ante-nuptial contract and/or the French legal code and also into any changes in those rights that may have taken place."

The Notes for completing IHT400 adopt the approach of seeking information rather than providing guidance on matrimonial property and similar issues, for example:

> "The way in which assets may be owned jointly in the UK does not usually apply in other countries . . . You should use the questions on page 2 of Schedule IHT404 as a guide to the information we need."

To a certain extent, the similarities between Scottish law and the legal system of many continental European countries may be helpful, especially where the Act contains special provisions to deal with Scottish law (see, e.g., s.147(4) dealing with *legitim*). On the other hand, the direct limitation of the scope of such provisions to Scottish law indicates that Parliament did not envisage their application in an analogous or corresponding sense to other laws.

34–12   The position is different where the Act attaches legal consequences to a transaction that need not be governed by English law (such as a transfer of value) or where it expressly requires a functional approach based on the *effects* of a transaction, rather than its *legal nature*. This is the case for the definition of settled property under s.43(2). Once again, however, the IHTM fails to give any substantive guidance:

> "*16042 The statutory definition [of settlement]*
> Even if property does not come within the categories above there are circumstances where a settlement is deemed to have been created:
> 1.   . . .
> 2.   if the property would have come within the categories above had the disposition been regulated by any part of the law of the UK or, even if not, if the property is governed under foreign law by provisions which are the foreign equivalent of those that would apply".

Again the old *CTO Advanced Instruction Manual* (Ch.E.10) appeared to be more on the point, not in terms of providing substantive guidance but at least in defining the problem:

> "The test [under s.43(2)] is whether, if similar beneficial interests or rights subsisted under the law of any part of the United Kingdom, the disposition conferring them would constitute a 'settlement' as defined. This test is likely to be particularly difficult to apply in cases where no precisely similar interests or rights are known to English or Scottish law—for example Community of Property cases (see Ch.S, Foreign Element at S. 39)."

Forced heirship and community property

34–13   The most significant foreign law regimes likely to be encountered by the practitioner are (i) forced heirship rules, and (ii) community property regimes. Before embarking on substantial tax planning involving another jurisdiction it is important to check whether any form of forced heirship or community property regime applies. Practitioners need to be aware both of the potential impact on estate planning proposals of any applicable regime and of the practical impact on, for example, assets that the clients may consider to be subject to any such regime.

For an example of a transaction that took property outside a community property regime see *Slutsker v Haron Investments*.[14] In that case, relying on art.33 of the Family Code of the Russian Federation which provides for a community property regime between spouses, Mr Slutsker sought to establish a claim to an interest in a UK house that was held in a trust made by his former wife during their marriage and from which he had been excluded. On the basis of expert evidence the Court concluded that, for Russian law purposes, the property would not be recognised as subject to the matrimonial property regime as it was held in the name of a third party (the corporate trustee); Russian law has no concept of trusts and, given its formalistic approach, it would refuse to recognise the existence of the beneficial interest Mr Slutsker claimed he had, which was of a kind unparalleled in Russian law itself. The matter therefore fell to be concluded under English law under which, on the facts, Mr Slutsker could not establish a claim. Underhill J. noted that Mr Slutsker had "acquiesced in a sophisticated

---

[14] *Slutsker v Haron Investments* [2012] EWCH 2539 (Ch).

transaction under a foreign system of law, using mechanisms unknown under Russian law" and he had no legitimate complaint if Russian law afforded him no remedy in those circumstances.

Most practitioners will be aware that many countries in continental Europe have forced heirship rules and/or community property regimes. There is also an increasing awareness of the forced heirship rules that affect Islamic clients. There may be less awareness of the application of these regimes in other jurisdictions (certain of the United States for example).

Practitioners need to be aware, also, that the impact of foreign forced heirship rules cannot be appreciated fully without an understanding of the implications of community property regimes; see paras 34–24 and following.

Forced heirship regimes

Broadly, forced heirship regimes confer on a deceased's close relatives—typically, the surviving spouse and children—rights to claim a portion of the deceased's estate. The size of the share of each forced heir varies from regime to regime, as does the nature of their share. Some shares, for instance, can be renounced by the forced heirs, while others cannot. Normally the rights of the forced heirs do not extend to the entirety of the estate, the deceased retaining the ability to leave a portion of his estate to whomever he chooses. **34–14**

The application of a forced heirship regime can have fundamental estate planning implications. Assume a testator subject to a forced heirship regime who is married and has children. From an IHT standpoint, he might be advised to leave his estate to his wife with a view to taking advantage of the IHT spouse exemption, so as to prevent any charge to IHT arising on his death. His ability to adopt such an approach, however, depends on whether, under the forced heirship regime in question, his widow can receive the disposable portion of his estate and whether the couple's children can renounce in her favour the portions of the estate to which they are entitled.

Forced heirship in continental Europe

In most continental European countries (and in Guernsey and Jersey), forced heir- **34–15** ship rules do not limit the testator's legal ability to dispose of all his property in the way he prefers, but any disposition which exceeds the so-called disposable share may be challenged in certain circumstances. Usually, such a gift may be "reduced"; the term "reduction" has a different meaning in different countries. In some, it means that the donor's heirs may set the gift aside, either wholly or partially (specific performance or *actio in rem*—see e.g. art.924–2 of Luxembourg's civil code: "Les libéralités faites à des non-successibles qui excèdent la quotité disponible sont soumises à la réduction en nature". See also art.929: "Les droits réels créés par le donataire s'éteindront par l'effet de la réduction". See also the national report to the EU Commission on the harmonisation of the private international law rules in the field of successions, at p.569: "La réserve légale ou héréditaire constitue une partie déterminée de la succession et ne représente donc pas seulement une créance en argent contre cette même succession (cf. article 745 du C.C.). L'héritier réservataire a la saisine, c'est-à-dire qu'il est saisi de plein droit de sa part dans la succession de son père ou de sa mère.") but this is rather the exception. More commonly, a claim for reduction merely confers a right on the donor's heirs to receive monetary compensation from the donee (*actio in personam*);

this is the position, e.g., in Switzerland (see Federal Court decision 110 II 228 dated June 7, 1984). This is now also the position in France. Under French law, possession of the estate is automatically vested in the "forced" heirs ("*saisine*"), and the legatee has to request delivery of possession. Until relatively recently, the "forced" heir was entitled to refuse delivery of possession—thus, in practice, achieving a "reduction" in specie of the legacy. However, the 2007 reform of the French civil code increased the scope of testamentary freedom; one of the effects is that gifts/legacies are now given full effect subject to a claim for monetary compensation (art.924 of the French civil code (as amended, 2007):

> "Lorsque la libéralité excède la quotité disponible, le gratifié, successible ou non successible, doit indemniser les héritier réservataires à concurrence de la portion excessive de la libéralité, quel que soit cet excédent."

So, in many countries, "forced" heirship rules do not restrict an individual's capacity to dispose of his property, but simply confer more or less robust remedies on the deceased's heirs if he gives away "too much".

In some countries, the personal, claim-type, nature of "forced" heirship rights is strengthened by the existence of limitation periods which are designed to strike a fair balance between family cohesion and testamentary freedom. In Switzerland, for example, an action for reduction must be commenced no later than one year from the moment the heir became aware that the gift violates his rights and at the latest 10 years from the death of the donor (Swiss Civil Code art.533). In Italy, the period of limitation is 10 years (art.561cc and Cass. November 25, 1997 n.11809) and in France, five years or, in the case of a reserved heir, two years from the date he became aware of the violation of his rights and at the latest 10 years after the donor's death.[15]

34–16   The legal nature of the forced heir's rights has important implications for the IHT treatment of European estates. To the extent that a reserved heir only has a chose in action against the estate or the legatee who has taken "too much" under the estate (e.g. the deceased's spouse), the correct analysis would be to charge IHT by reference to the legacy contained in the will, subject to a subsequent adjustment if (and only if) a claim is made. In practice, this would enable a testator to leave the whole of his estate to his spouse or civil partner in the hope that his children will refrain from challenging the Will because of the potential IHT liability. As mentioned in para.34–11 above, the IHTM does not contain any useful guidance in this respect and s.147 (which applies to Scottish wills that contain an excessive disposition in favour of the testator's spouse) effectively enables the executors to choose whether to deduct the amount of any *legitim* or legal rights in their IHT calculations. If they do, and the *legitim*/legal rights remain unclaimed and unrenounced, tax will be repaid to the estate (as the s.18 exemption will "bite" on the whole of the legacy)—s.147(2). If they do not, and the deceased's children subsequently claim their *legitim*/legal rights within the limits mentioned in s.147(6), IHT will become payable on that part of the transfer to the spouse that has been defeated. This approach is sensible as it enables executors to take into account the family circumstances, namely the likelihood that the deceased's children will challenge the legacy in favour of the deceased's surviving spouse or civil partner. Section 147 offers a pragmatic solution to claim-based "forced" heirship rights, at least where they are subject to limitation periods under the applicable succession law. The problem with s.147 is that it only applies to Scottish *legitim* and legal rights. Accordingly, the IHT

---

[15] In France, the limitation period was previously 30 years.

treatment of continental European (and other) "forced" heirship rights has to be based on a legal analysis of the nature of the claim.

Clawback rules

In some countries, forced heirship rules also apply to inter vivos gifts which means that the recipient may have to give back the whole gift or part of it, whether in specie or by reference to its value ("clawback" rules). One of the main reasons why the United Kingdom decided against opting into Brussels IV was that, under its terms, the United Kingdom would have been obliged to apply the clawback provisions of the law of other EU Member States and this was regarded as causing an unacceptable degree of uncertainty in relation to lifetime gifts. Clawback rules certainly affect the marketability of gifted assets (because of the uncertainties relating to title). Accordingly, various legal systems provide for cut-off periods which effectively provide that "old" gifts are not taken into account for the purposes of calculating the size of the reserved portion. In Switzerland, an inter vivos gift may not be questioned if the donor survives five years from the date of the gift (Swiss Civil Code art.527(3)). In Germany, this period is 10 years (BGB s.2325), whilst Italy has a 20-year limit for transfers of land (CC art.563).

34–17

Planning

In practice, it may be possible to avoid or minimise the impact of forced heirship rights: see paras 34–37 and following.

34–18

Forced heirship in the Islamic world

In the same way as there is no "European succession law", so there is no unified Islamic succession law. Although the common primary source of Islamic civil laws (known as *Shari'a*) is the Qur'an, as supplemented by the "*sunna*" (i.e. transmitted eyewitness accounts of the prophet Muhammad's sayings and practices) and pre-Islamic customary law, the cultural diversity of a world that stretches from Pakistan to Nigeria (Turkey is a case of its own),[16] combined with an exposure to Ottoman, British and French influences, have produced various interpretations ("schools") of the *Shari'a*. Whilst the major contraposition is between Shia'h Muslims and Sunni Muslims, within each group different schools of jurisprudence have developed, each with its own peculiarities.[17] As a result, the basic principles of succession law (see below) are common to all, but there are substantive differences between various schools. To complicate matters further, the twentieth century has seen the emergence of eclecticism

34–19

---

[16] Turkey is the only country in the Muslim world to have abolished entirely the Shari'a and replaced it with codes based on European models. The civil code and the Code of Obligations (1926) are based on Swiss law. Major modifications were made to the Turkish civil code in 2001 to reflect fundamental social changes, e.g. the recognition of equal inheritance rights for illegitimate children and the introduction of a default community property regime.

[17] The main Shia'h school is the Jafari school, whilst the main Sunni schools of law are the Hanafi, Shafi'i, Maliki and Hanbali.

in the selection of sources in some countries, e.g. the succession law of Egypt, traditionally a Sunni country, contains a mix of Sunni and Shia'h provisions.[18]

The basic principle governing Islamic succession (which is contained in the Qur'an)[19] is that after payments of debts, funeral expenses, taxes and testamentary administration charges, at least two thirds of a deceased Muslim's estate (the "net estate") must be distributed according to a fixed and compulsory set of rules amongst surviving relatives. In the common case of a married person with children, the surviving spouse has a right to one-eighth (if a widow) or one-quarter (if a widower) of the net estate, with the balance of the net estate to be split between the person's daughters and sons in the proportion of 1:2, i.e. each son receives a share which is double that received by each daughter. Religious differences are very important: it is understood that most schools exclude non-Muslim heirs of a Muslim individual from any entitlement in the estate, although they may receive the disposable one-third share.

There are substantive differences between the various schools on important issues such as the possibility of leaving the one-third disposable share to a forced heir, or the option for a forced heir to renounce his or her reserved share during the life of the testator. In practice, these differences may have a huge impact on the testator's IHT planning.

Forced heirship in the United States

34–20   It is understood that Louisiana is the only state in the United States that provides for indefeasible forced heirship ("*legitime*") for children. However, the portion of one's estate that is subject to the forced portion has been continually decreased from the early 1980s and currently benefits only children who have not attained the age of 24 and incapacitated children ("forced heirs"). Under the present rules, donations inter vivos and *mortis causa* may not exceed three-fourths of the property of the donor if he leaves, at his death, one forced heir, and one-half if he leaves two or more forced heirs.[20]

In most states, the surviving spouse has a right of election between the property left in the will (if any) and a statutory share set by state law (usually one-third or one-half of the estate, though there are many variations).[21] By contrast, Louisiana provides that

---

[18] For an introduction to Islamic succession law, see among others J. Brugman, *Essays on Oriental Laws of Succession*, eds Leiden, E. J. Brill (1969); David Pearl, *A Textbook on Muslim Personal Law*, 2nd edn, (Croom Helm, 1987).

[19] See Sura (Ch.4), verses 7–12 and 4:19 of the Qur'an.

[20] The rules are in arts 1493–1495 of the Louisiana Civil Code. The provision for a so-called "*legitime*" in the code is a reminder of the US' complex history of French, Spanish and British influence. Today's Louisiana was part of the French province of Louisiana (a huge area of some 800,000 square miles stretching from New Orleans to the border with Canada), which the United States bought from Napoleon in the famous Louisiana Purchase of 1803, the largest area of territory ever to be added to the United States at one time. Whilst most United States states which emerged from the province of Louisiana (Arkansas, Missouri, Iowa, Minnesota, North and South Dakota, Nebraska, Oklahoma, Kansas, Montana, Wyoming and Colorado) adopted the English form of common law system, Louisiana maintained some very distinct French law features.

[21] One-third: e.g. New York (Estates, Powers and Trust Law §5–1.1 and §5–1.1A); one-half: e.g. Indiana (IC 29–1–3) and Connecticut (life estate of one-third). In California, the surviving spouse is generally entitled to the testator's one-half of the community property, though this may be excluded in the will (see Cal. Probate Code s.21610), whilst in Connecticut, the surviving spouse is entitled to a life estate of one-third in value of all the property passing under the will, legally or equitably owned by the deceased spouse at the time of his death, after payment of all debts and charges against the estate (Conn. Gen. Stat §45a–436(a) (2003)).

the surviving spouse is entitled to an additional "marital portion" if the deceased died "rich in comparison with the surviving spouse".[22] Note that in a community property state the surviving spouse is already entitled to a share (usually one half) of the community property at the death of the other spouse; see paras 34–25 and following.

California also provides for a statutory share for children who have been omitted **34–21** from the will, but this does not reflect an absolute entitlement but rather a presumptive entitlement, i.e. there is a presumption that the testator did not intend to cut out his children completely. The presumption can be displaced by an express provision in the will or if it can be established that the testator left substantially all the estate to the other parent or provided financially for the omitted child by transfers outside the estate with the intention that the transfer be in lieu of a testamentary provision.[23]

Forced heirship in the United Kingdom

Before leaving this very brief survey of forced heirship, it is worth noting that the **34–22** United Kingdom is itself no stranger to the concept.

The net moveable estate of a Scottish domiciliary is subject to the fixed rights of a **34–23** surviving spouse and issue. A surviving spouse is entitled to a third of the estate if the deceased left issue and a half if there are no surviving issue. Surviving issue are entitled to one-third of the estate where the deceased left a surviving spouse and one-half where there is no surviving spouse. The remaining part of the estate may be disposed of by will.

The effect for IHT purposes of the rights of the deceased's issue ("*legitim*") is dealt with specifically by s.147 where the deceased leaves a surviving spouse and a person under 18 entitled to claim *legitim*. Where a will leaves a surviving spouse a greater share of the estate than they would be entitled to taking account of *legitim*, IHT is charged initially as if the *legitim* took effect—i.e. if the will purports to give the whole estate to the spouse, one third will still be treated as passing to the issue and will be taxed to IHT accordingly. If the issue subsequently renounce their rights on, or within two years after, attaining 18,[24] the tax paid can be reclaimed. Alternatively, the deceased's executors can elect for IHT to be charged on the basis that the provisions of the will take effect.[25] If the issue do not renounce their claims, IHT is then charged at the rates in force at the death; such tax is chargeable against the issue and the persons in whom the property is vested.[26]

South of the Border, England and Wales do not have "forced" heirship rights. However, the Inheritance (Provision for Family and Dependants) Act 1975 seeks to

---

[22] Art.2434 of the Louisiana Civil Code provides that "the marital portion is one-fourth of the succession in ownership if the deceased died without children, the same fraction in usufruct for life if he is survived by three or fewer children, and a child's share in such usufruct if he is survived by more than three children. In no event, however, shall the amount of the marital portion exceed one million dollars".

[23] California Probate Code ss.21620–21621.

[24] Or such longer period as HMRC allows; IHTA 1984 s.147(6).

[25] IHTA 1984 s.147(3), (4) and (5).

[26] IHTA 1984 s.209.

restrict dispositions designed to defeat the powers of the court to award discretionary shares in an estate to dependants or to divorced spouses.

Matrimonial property regimes

34-24   In many countries, marriage is viewed as a partnership, as a result of which spouses acquire a joint interest in property, either in the form of joint ownership or in the form of a right to a share of the value of property upon dissolution of the marriage. Matrimonial property regimes are meant to combat the unfairness that can occur when one spouse amasses wealth during the marriage while the other devotes his or her time to unpaid work at home (the common scenario in traditional society) or pursues a less lucrative activity (a frequent scenario in today's society). Thus, these countries view marriage as a marital partnership or "community" under which spouses contribute equally (though differently) to the acquisition of property during the marriage so that they should both benefit from it, regardless of who actually acquired it.

Whilst the concept of matrimonial property is usually associated with civil law countries, the concepts behind it may be seen as not dissimilar to the approach of the English Family Courts in some recent divorce settlements. As matrimonial property regimes do not necessarily rest on co-ownership, the significant difference between the civil law system and the English system may be viewed as resting in the discretionary nature of the powers of the English courts as opposed to the formulaic approach applied in most civil law countries.

Other important differences relate to the IHT treatment of matrimonial property and its interrelationship with "forced" heirship. In the UK transfers to spouses are dealt with under s.18 without any distinction between matrimonial property and non-matrimonial property. By contrast, the distinction is of crucial importance in many civil law countries, as property that passes to the surviving spouse under the heading of matrimonial property is usually outside the scope of inheritance tax. Similarly, property that passes to the surviving spouse under the heading of matrimonial property is usually treated as being outside the estate (which means that it is not subject to any "forced" heirship claims). Contrast, the approach of the Inheritance (Provision for Family and Dependants) Act 1975 which makes little distinction between matrimonial property and non-matrimonial property.

34-25   The term "matrimonial property" has different meanings in different countries but, broadly, it defines a situation of shared financial benefit between spouses in relation to property acquired during marriage. Typically, the principle of shared benefit is achieved either by a community of title (co-ownership) or by the acquisition, by both spouses, of a notional interest in the value of property acquired during the marriage by either spouse or both which is to be converted into cash upon the dissolution of the marriage. The rules vary from country to country but it is important to understand that the principle underlying the concept of matrimonial property does not necessarily rest on co-ownership. The main function of matrimonial property regimes is to provide for fair division of the assets upon the dissolution of the marriage. Whilst co-ownership is probably the easiest way to achieve this goal, it also has adverse implications (e.g. in relation to the administration of assets and the relationship with third parties), which is why other countries have opted for a system based on separation of property coupled with financial compensation and reallocation of assets upon dissolution of the marriage.

The matrimonial property regimes of various countries operate to divide property between spouses, not only in the case of divorce, but also when the marriage has been dissolved by the death of one spouse.

The significance of matrimonial property regimes in IHT planning lies in their role in defining the size of the disposable estate; on death, if matrimonial property principles apply, the estate will be the balance of the deceased spouse's property after allowing for the portion of that property which is allocated to the surviving spouse in accordance with matrimonial property rules. In other words, matrimonial property comes first and succession comes second.[27]

Most community property countries allow the spouses to: **34–26**

(1) contract out of the ordinary system of community property/deferred community in favour of a system of complete separation of property; and

(2) modify the default regime, typically to include assets in, or exclude assets from, the community, or to modify the spouses' shares upon break-up of the marriage. Different community property countries have adopted different models and some law systems even provide for a co-existence of different models, as is the case in Switzerland where the parties who wish to be subject to a form of community property may choose between a *"communauté de biens"* (community of title) and the default *"régime ordinaire de la participation aux acquêts"* (broadly community of value). In addition, many countries allow the spouses to modify the model within certain limits by way of marital contracts.

It may even be possible for the spouses to agree that the *whole* property which is comprised in the community should pass to the surviving spouse. In some countries, e.g. Switzerland and France, it may be possible to use this technique effectively to bypass the testator's children's forced heirship rights (although there are some important limitations) thereby maximising the extent of s.18 exemption available.

Matrimonial property regimes in continental Europe

In some countries, including France and Italy, marriage has the effect of vesting   **34–27**
property acquired during the marriage in both spouses jointly, i.e. there is a community of title.[28] Usually, this community is a community of acquisitions, i.e. it extends only to assets and income acquired by a couple during marriage (including income from community property), but excluding inheritances, specific gifts to one of the spouses and property and profits clearly traceable to property owned before the marriage, all of which is separate property (though some countries, including France and Italy, treat income from separate property as community property). In consequence, the consent of both spouses is required for most acts of disposition relating to assets which fall into the community (Italy requires the consent of both spouses for *"atti di straordinaria amministrazione"*[29] generally, whilst the French civil code contains a comprehensive

---

[27] See *De Nicols v Curlier* [1900] A.C. 21 and *Re de Nicols* [1900] 2 Ch. 410 where the fact that a couple, married subject to French community of property laws, had subsequently become domiciled in England did not affect the enforceability of the community of property regime (as to both movable and immovable property) in favour of the wife following the husband's death, and despite the husband's having made an English will. See also, however, *Welch v Tennant* [1891] A.C. 639 which held that the law of the country in which the immovable property is situate would prevail as regards that property—the case is of persuasive authority only in England as it was an appeal from a Scottish court.

[28] For Italy, see Massimo Bianca, *Diritto Civile*, 3rd edn (Giuffre, 2000), Vol.II, p.87.

[29] Art.180 of the Italian Civil Code.

list of acts which require the spouses' "*cogestion*", including donations of assets and the disposition of immovables which form part of the community).

A second group of countries, which includes Finland, Germany and Switzerland, has adopted the model of "deferred community" or "participation of value", which is a system of separation of property combined with the right of each spouse to receive a specified share of their combined assets or the increase in value in those assets during the marriage ("*Zugewinngemeinschaft*" in Germany and "*Errungenschaftsbeteiligung*" in Switzerland).[30]

Community property regimes in the Islamic world

34–28   There is no such thing as community property under Islamic law. The Qur'an Sura 4:32 (Yusuf Ali translation) states: "to men is allotted what they earn, and to women what they earn". In addition, a woman is entitled to receive a dowry which will remain hers in the event of divorce (Suras 4:4 and 4:20).

It is understood that only Turkey (which abolished *Shari'a* in 1926) recognises community property (the previous separate property regime was replaced with a regime of participation in acquired property as part of the first major reform of the 1926 Civil Code in 2001).

Community property regimes in the United States

34–29   In the United States, property of married persons is either community property or separate property. A detailed analysis of the US community property laws is outside the scope of this book, but generally, community property comprises any assets and income acquired by a couple during marriage (including income from community property), with the exception of inheritances, specific gifts to one of the spouses and property and profits clearly traceable to property owned before the marriage, all of which is separate property (though Idaho, Louisiana, Texas and Wisconsin treat income from most separate property as community property).[31] In some states, e.g. California,[32] it is possible for the spouses to opt assets into or out of community property ("transmutation of property").

Community property laws differ from state to state within the United States. For example, California not only has rules governing the treatment of community property and separate property, but also has yet another set of rules governing the unique concept of quasi-community property.

California

Community Property

34–30   California Family Code s.760 provides that community property is that property which is purchased or acquired during marriage. That fact that property was acquired

[30] For Switzerland, see Bernhard Schnyder, Peter Tuor and Tuor-Schnyder-Schmid-Rumo-Jungo, *das Schweizerische Zivilgesetzbuch*, 12th edn (2002), pp.296 and following.
[31] See United States Internal Revenue Service Publication 555.
[32] Californian Family Code s.850.

during marriage is not an ironclad pronouncement of the property's ultimate character, but the timing of purchase during marriage provides a strong presumption that the property is properly classified as community property. In general, under community property, husband and wife are considered to each own a respective 50 per cent interest in the community estate. The community estate can be divided by aggregate value or by item. As such, each person can direct under the terms of his or her estate planning documents how his or her respective 50 per cent share will be devised upon death. There is no requirement that a person leave his or her community property interest to heirs. However, if either husband or wife should die intestate, pursuant to California Probate Code s.6401, the surviving spouse takes the decedent's 50 per cent share of the community property so that a total of 100 per cent of the community property is then vested with the surviving spouse. If the surviving spouse is not living then these assets pass to the lineal heirs.

Separate Property

In addition a person in California may have acquired separate property. This is **34–31** property acquired either before the marriage, received as a gift before or during marriage, or received as a bequest either before or during marriage. These assets will retain their separate property character unless the person who acquired the assets expressly "transmutes" his or her interest to give the other spouse an interest in the property. If a spouse wishes to change the character of property from either community to separate property or from separate to community property, this transfer has to be done by an expressed "transmutation." California Family Code s.852 requires that in order for there to be a valid transmutation of property it must be made in writing by express declaration joined in and consented to or accepted by the spouse whose interest in the property is adversely affected. A person can devise his or her separate property in total by will or trust to whomever he or she wishes. There is no requirement that a person leave his or her estate to heirs.

California Quasi-Community Property

Quasi-community property has similar features to community property. Quasi- **34–32** community property, as provided under the California Family Code s.125, means all real and personal property acquired, wherever situated, by either spouse while dom-iciled elsewhere which would have been community property if the spouse who acquired the property (the "acquiring spouse") had been domiciled in California at the time of its acquisition, even though that property was originally the acquiring spouse's separate property under the law of the state where the acquiring spouse was previously domiciled. When the couple move to California this property essentially shifted into a suspended state, until a triggering event determines its character.

The death of either spouse is such a triggering event (as is divorce), and depending on who dies first, this ordering will determine succession. In practice, the combination of California's community property regime coupled with the State's statutory intestacy rules can render vastly different results depending on whether the deceased died testate or intestate.

If the acquiring spouse dies first then quasi-community property is treated like community property: each spouse is considered to own a respective 50 per cent interest in the quasi-community estate and each spouse can devise by will or trust how his or her respective 50 per cent share will go. However, if the non-acquiring spouse dies first then this quasi-community property reverts to being entirely the separate property of the acquiring spouse and any provisions in the non-acquiring spouse's will or trust related to it are essentially rendered inapplicable to that property.

If the acquiring spouse dies intestate, then pursuant to California Probate Code s.6401, and similar to the rules of community property, the deceased spouse's 50 per cent share of the quasi-community property passes to the surviving spouse for a total of 100 per cent vested with the surviving spouse. However, as, if the non-acquiring spouse dies first, he or she has no rights over the quasi-community property which reverts to the surviving acquiring spouse, the non-acquiring spouse's heirs have no right to quasi-community property, except to the extent they are also the heirs of the surviving acquiring spouse. The surviving spouse can then devise as to 100 per cent of the property as he or she decides.

34–33   In general in the United States, where community property regimes apply, they do so if and while the spouses are domiciled in a community property state. Upon the death of a spouse, the community property regime terminates and the surviving spouse is usually entitled to one-half of the net community property, subject to any claim for reimbursement.

Nine states have adopted systems of community property as a result of past Spanish and French influences. In addition to Louisiana and California, Arizona, Idaho, Nevada, New Mexico, Texas, Washington and Wisconsin all have community property regimes.[33] Moreover, in 1998 Alaska introduced a law which allows couples to decide to enter into a written "community property agreement" or to establish a "community property trust".[34]

34–34   Although there have been attempts to introduce matrimonial community across the United States and to harmonise the existing laws, notably with the promulgation of a Uniform Marital Property Act in 1983 "to encourage sharing by spouses of property acquired during marriage, by creating a class of property in which husband and wife have an equal interest" by the National Conference of Commissioners on Uniform State Laws (NCCUSL),[35] only Wisconsin (a community property state) has so far adopted it.[36]

Matrimonial property in the United Kingdom

34–35   Scottish law provides for the concept of "matrimonial property",[37] being all the property belonging to the parties at the "relevant date" (the earlier of either the date of separation or the date of service of the summons for divorce). Matrimonial property includes property acquired before the marriage if it was for use as a family home or furniture as well as property acquired during the marriage but before the relevant date; other property acquired before the marriage, property acquired as a gift or inheritance and property acquired after separation is not matrimonial property. In general, Scots

[33] See United States Internal Revenue Service Publication 555.

[34] Alaska Community Property Act, a.k.a. Ch.75 of Title 34 of the Alaska Statutes.

[35] The NCCUSL is a non-governmental body formed in 1892 upon the recommendation of the American Bar Association for the purpose of promoting "uniformity in state laws on all subjects where uniformity is deemed desirable and practical". Its "Acts" are not binding but constitute legislative proposals addressed to the state legislatures.

[36] See Ch.766 of the Wisconsin Statutes & Annotations (WSA).

[37] Family Law (Scotland) Act 1985 s.10, as amended by the Family Law (Scotland) Act 2006.

law applies a rule of separation of property; under s.24 of the Family Law (Scotland) Act 1985, marriage does not, per se, affect the respective rights of the parties to the marriage in relation to their property (save in relation to the law of succession). In the event of a divorce or dissolution of civil partnership, the court may make any or all orders for capital provision, transfer of property, order for periodical allowance and for any "incidental order" as are reasonable, applying the principles set out in s.9 of the 1985 Act (fair division of the net value of matrimonial property; taking account of economic advantage derived by one party from contributions by the other, loss of financial support, etc.). Rather than imposing equal division of matrimonial property, the 1985 Act confers power on the court to order equal division, or division in such other proportions as are justified by special circumstances. The division of property on the death of either spouse or civil partner is dealt with exclusively under the succession law rules ("legal rights" (which apply both where there is a will and on an intestacy) or "prior rights" (which apply in cases of intestacy (or partial intestacy) only).

The word "matrimonial property" does not appear anywhere in the English statutes. **34–36** In England and Wales, the division of property upon divorce is dealt with by the Matrimonial Causes Act 1973, which confers broad discretionary powers on the court. The position is similar to that which exists in Scotland, in that the court has to take into account various factors (mentioned in s.25 of the Matrimonial Causes Act 1973) with a view to achieving a fair solution in light of the circumstances. However, whilst the traditional approach focused almost exclusively on meeting the recipient spouse's "reasonable requirements", in the landmark decision of *White v White* the House of Lords held that it was no longer acceptable to discriminate between husbands and wives and their traditional roles in family life and that judges should check their view of what would be fair in any given circumstances against a "yardstick of equality" and should only depart from equality if there is good reason for doing so. The presumption of equal division laid the basis for a discussion of the difference between matrimonial property and non-matrimonial property in the House of Lords decisions in *Miller v Miller* and *McFarlane v McFarlane*, Lord Nicholls of Birkenhead, at paras [21] and [22], summed up the main differences between the English approach and that of traditional matrimonial property countries as follows:

> "In some countries the law requires a sharp distinction between assets acquired during a marriage and other assets. In Scotland, for instance, one of the statutorily prescribed principles is that the parties should share the value of the 'matrimonial property' equally or in such proportions as special circumstances may justify . . . In England and Wales the Matrimonial Causes Act 1973 draws no such distinction. By section 25(2)(a) the court is bidden to have regard, quite generally, to the property and financial resources each of the parties to the marriage has or is likely to have in the foreseeable future. [22] This does not mean that, when exercising his discretion, a judge in this country must treat all property in the same way. The statute requires the court to have regard to all the circumstances. One of the circumstances is that there is a real difference, a difference of source, between (1) property acquired during the marriage otherwise than by inheritance or gift, sometimes called the marital acquest but more usually the matrimonial property, and (2) other property".

Thus, it is incorrect to say that the concept of matrimonial property is foreign to English law. The fact that each spouse has title to his/her property during the course of the marriage is not incompatible with the idea of matrimonial property regimes, as many countries adopt a similar approach of separation of property during marriage coupled with redistribution or financial compensation upon dissolution of the marriage (see paras 34–27 and following). Instead, the main difference between the English system and the many variations that one encounters on the continent is the discretionary approach to division on dissolution of the marriage. The other differences consist in the relevance (on the continent) and the irrelevance (in England and Wales) of matrimonial property for the purposes of calculating death duties and the inter-relationship between matrimonial property and "forced" heirship claims, as outlined in para.34–26.

Mitigating the effect of forced heirship and community property regimes

34–37   The following are some ideas which may help to mitigate the effects of forced heirship and community property regimes whilst maximising the IHT benefits and, in particular, the spouse exemption.

Using usufructs

34–38   A *usufruct* is the functional equivalent of an interest in possession in a trust under common law and can be defined as a right in rem which entitles the *usufructuary* to enjoy the subject-matter of the *usufruct* and to receive any natural or legal fruits which it may produce. In certain countries it is possible in certain circumstances to defer the forced heirship rights of children by conferring an *usufruct* on the surviving spouse. The treatment of *usufructs* for IHT purposes is discussed in more detail at para.34–65.

Opting out

34–39   It may be possible to opt out of a forced heirship or a matrimonial regime by using a contract:

(1) In some countries, the testator and his heirs can alter or even oust forced heirship rights by way of a testamentary contract.
(2) In some countries where there exists a community property regime it is possible to oust forced heirship rights by stipulating in a matrimonial contract that, in the event of either spouse's death, all the deceased spouse's property should pass to the surviving spouse as a matter of community property law. Since, under the law of most community property countries, an individual's estate is the balance of his property at the time of death, after allowing for the portion of that property which is allocated to the surviving spouse in accordance with community property rules, the contractual allocation of all the property to the surviving spouse effectively reduces the estate to nil. This technique also maximises the benefit of the spouse exemption.

Making lifetime gifts

34–40   The succession laws of many civil law countries (but not *Shari'a*) contain clawback rules, which are designed to bring inter vivos gifts back into the deceased's estate. These are anti-avoidance rules aimed at preventing an individual from reducing his or her death estate by lifetime planning. Although there is no case law on the issue in

England as yet, most commentators think the English courts would not enforce clawback rules in relation to inter vivos gifts. In Scotland, the rights of the surviving spouse and issue apply only to the estate owned by the deceased at death; therefore lifetime gifts, whether outright or in trust, can be used to avoid the rules.[38]

Using life assurance

Some jurisdictions do not consider an insurance policy to be part of the estate (unless **34–41** the estate is designated as beneficiary). Therefore the policyholder may distribute the proceeds of an insurance policy based on the owner's wishes. Be aware, however, that traditional life assurance is not an acceptable form of investment for many Islamic clients.

Converting personalty into realty and vice versa

Consideration should be given to converting personalty into realty[39] and vice **34–42** versa:

(1) As realty is usually governed by the *lex situs*, it might be possible to avoid forced heirship rules which affect the movable estate of an individual (e.g. by virtue of his domicile, nationality or residence) by converting movables into immovables situated in a country which does not have, or does not enforce, forced heirship rights. Such a conversion involves, of course, re-investment of the relevant assets.

(2) Conversely, it might be possible to convert immovable property situated in a country which applies forced heirship rules in relation to realty into movable property governed by the law of the country which governs the testator's personalty. This can be achieved by the use of a company as owner of the property, so that the company's shares and not the underlying realty will be comprised in the individual's estate. A typical example is the use of a *société civile immobilière* (or "SCI") to hold French property. Whilst a conversion of immovables (governed by the *lex situs*) into movables (governed by the law of the testator's domicile, residence or nationality) is always worth considering, account needs to be taken of other possibly adverse tax consequences. Moreover, the French *Caron* case[40] indicates that manipulation of a conflict of law rule solely to deny heirs their legally reserved share under the *lex situs* may be treated as an *abus de droit,* in which case it will be disregarded by the courts of the country where the property is situated.

Relying on a period of limitation

In most civil law countries, forced heirship rights do not limit the testator's right to **34–43** dispose of his property, but simply confer a claim on the heirs. In some countries, e.g.

---

[38] See *Agnew v Agnew* (1775) Mor 8210.

[39] Note that Brussels IV (see para.34–10 above) provides for no distinction to be made between movables and immovables in applying the applicable law of succession.

[40] *Caron v Odell*, Tribunal de grande instance of Aix, decision of March 9, 1982, and Cass. Civ, 1ère, decision of March 20, 1985.

Switzerland, Germany, Italy and, to some extent, France, such a claim must be made within a certain period after death or else the claim becomes time barred.

Counter attacks by forced heirs

34–44   In considering the possibility of mitigating the effect of a forced heirship regime, bear in mind that forced heirs may make strenuous efforts to assert their rights. Particular difficulties may arise where the property is held in a forced heirship jurisdiction—say, Arcadia—other than the deceased's home jurisdiction. Even though the property is not subject to Arcadian law, proceedings may be brought by the forced heirs in Arcadia and under Arcadian law, on the basis that the Arcadian courts may be inclined to allowing the forced heirs to enforce their rights.

Mismatched legal treatment

34–45   Finally, while considering foreign law concepts with no obvious equivalent in England, it is also worth bearing in mind that forms of ownership that may appear to be familiar may not have the same effect in succession and fiscal terms, e.g. a joint bank account held between husband and wife in the Netherlands will not, in the absence of a specific stipulation, pass automatically by survivorship on the first death but will fall to be divided between the surviving spouse (and joint account holder) and the other heirs.

III. FOUNDATIONS AND OTHER NON-UK ENTITIES

34–46   One of the problems facing the international estate planner is applying to a legal entity of one jurisdiction the tax regime of another jurisdiction whose legal system itself contains no such entity. In the following discussion this problem is approached by way of illustration from the standpoint of a UK based planner coming to grips with certain entities in other legal systems. It is not uncommon to find that assets in respect of which there is a potential exposure to IHT are held, or are proposed to be held, via legal entities that do not precisely mirror entities which exist under UK law and which may be difficult to classify under UK law, e.g. a Liechtenstein foundation. Alternatively, legal entities may be used which, although they do not cause problems of classification, may be treated differently for tax purposes in another jurisdiction, e.g. a US limited liability corporation which, although a company, may be treated as fiscally transparent for United States—but not United Kingdom—tax purposes.[41]

34–47   Where an individual uses an entity with no precise equivalent under English law he must appreciate that from a tax standpoint that use carries a degree of considerable

---

[41] See the list of classifications of foreign entities in the HMRC International Manual at INTM1800000. As noted below, the treatment of an entity for UK tax purposes may vary depending upon the tax concerned.

uncertainty, for two reasons. First, it will be necessary to determine how that entity is to be treated for UK tax purposes and this may be far from easy. Secondly, in some cases, and just to complicate matters, the treatment may vary according to the UK tax in question (this commentary makes no attempt to cover the considerations which can apply for taxes other than IHT).

Correct characterisation for IHT of foreign entities is essential. Furthermore, it is not **34–48** sufficient to identify an entity as having a functional UK equivalent, e.g. a family foundation may be said to be functionally equivalent to a settlement. In practice, one must go further and understand how the foreign entity works under foreign law and be able to explain this to HMRC together with one's reasons for contending that the entity should be treated for IHT purposes in a particular way. There is already authority for the proposition that, where an entity is not constituted under English law, its tax liability should be determined by reference to the entity's legal characteristics under its own governing law[42] (by way of contrast to this approach see the Irish Finance Act 2012's extension of the meaning of discretionary trust,[43] designed to encompass foundations although likely, in practice, to have a wider application). It should be borne in mind in this connection that, while the characteristics under foreign law of the foreign entity have to be analysed and expert evidence adduced as necessary, it is the law of the forum, where IHT is concerned, UK law, that decides how the foreign entity should be treated for IHT purposes. This is made particularly clear in the s.43(2) definition of "settlement" which provides:

> "'Settlement' means any disposition or dispositions of property ... whereby the property is for the time being ... *held in trust* ... *or would be so held* ... if the disposition or dispositions were regulated by the law of any part of the United Kingdom; or whereby, under the law of any other country, the administration of the property is for the time being *governed by provisions equivalent in effect to those which would apply if the property were so held*" (authors' italics).

The virtue of s.43(2) is that it contains an express extension to foreign law and at the same time acknowledges the existence of foreign law concepts which do not translate literally into trusts but which are functionally equivalent to trusts, and makes express provision for a comparative approach.

At least in theory, a difficult issue arises where a foreign law institution in a **34–49** particular case cannot be characterised or classified (e.g. as a "settlement" under s.43(2)) but is functionally similar to some other institution under the laws of any part of the United Kingdom. As UK statutes are construed literally (although there are some special rules which apply to tax statutes), it may be very difficult to assume that the ordinary meaning of the relevant term or terms used in the IHT legislation applies also to the foreign law institution. This is because the IHT legislation is couched in the conventional UK legislative idiom, which has been designed to avoid any uncertainties and ambiguities. This high degree of detail in relation to the language used makes the IHT legislation very inflexible and particularly unsuitable to deal with foreign law

---

[42] *Major v Brodie* [1998] S.T.C. 491.

[43] Irish Finance Act 2012 s.111 specifically provides for the definition of a discretionary trust in the Capital Acquisitions Tax Consolidation Act 2003 to be extended to encompass "any entity which is similar in its effect to a discretionary trust ... irrespective of how it is described in the place where it is established". Compare the wording of s.43(2) of the Act quoted on this page.

institutions. In these instances, it is submitted that weight should be given also to the purpose of the relevant sections of the 1984 Act and to comparative considerations.

34–50   It is interesting to note that the English courts have adopted this purposive approach in relation to the interpretation of double taxation treaties.[44] But not too much should be made of this; such treaties are based on a less detailed style of drafting because, by their nature, they are designed to deal with concepts which, while rooted in different legal traditions, are functionally similar. Article 3(2) of the OECD Model Convention provides that:

> "As regards the application of the Convention by a Contracting State, any term not defined therein shall, unless the context otherwise requires, have the meaning which it has under the law of that State concerning the taxes to which the Convention applies."

It is suggested that when a foreign law institution cannot be translated into an exact equivalent under the law of any part of the United Kingdom, the approach adopted by the OECD Model Convention might be followed when interpreting the 1984 Act, i.e. the foreign law institution should be interpreted according to its "context" in the light of the purpose of the relevant section or sections of the 1984 Act and taking into account comparative considerations.

34–51   Some of the problems to be encountered in dealing with non-UK type entities encountered in international tax planning (and an example of the effect of analysing those entities by reference to the principles mentioned above) may be illustrated by reference to:

      (1) foundations;
      (2) establishments;
      (3) usufructs; and
      (4) United States limited liability companies.

Foundations

34–52   A foundation may be described as a legal entity which is created when a person ("founder") "dedicates" assets to a specific purpose observing certain formalities. In some jurisdictions, a foundation only acquires legal personality upon registration with a specified authority, whilst in others it is sufficient for the founder to execute a document (typically known in civil law countries as the foundation "document," "instrument", "act" or "declaration"—a popular English translation is "charter") in accordance with certain formalities. In some jurisdictions, a foundation may also be created by will.

Traditionally, foundations—and in particular family foundations—were identified with Liechtenstein. However, foundations are known in most continental European jurisdictions although in many cases they can only be used for charitable purposes (a notable exception is Austria). In addition, a growing number of offshore jurisdictions (including Jersey,[45] Anguilla, the Bahamas, Cyprus, Malta, Panama, Saint Kitts and the Isle of Man) have also introduced foundations laws. The main reason for introducing

---

[44] See e.g. *IRC v Exxon Corp* [1982] S.T.C. 356 at 369; *IRC v Commerzbank AG* [1990] S.T.C. 285 at 297f–298h; *Union Texas Petroleum Corp v Critchley* [1988] S.T.C. 691. See also *British Tax Review* (1997), p.194 at 195.

[45] Guernsey is also expected to have its own foundations law by the end of 2012.

foundations is that they are seen as a more palatable alternative to trusts by many civilian clients; this is in spite of the fact that foundations are functionally very similar to trusts. With the increase in the number of jurisdictions with a foundations law, it is important to consider the specific characteristics of each foundation.

A settlement or a company?

Foundations[46] have certain characteristics in common with settlements and other **34–53** characteristics in common with companies as follows:

(1) A foundation is established by the "founder" who provides the funds and stipulates the terms for the ongoing administration of the foundation and the control of its assets. In this respect the founder resembles the settlor of a settlement.
(2) A foundation is a separate legal entity which owns its assets both legally and beneficially. Although trustees are legal persons, a settlement is not a legal entity, and trustees only own the settled assets legally, not beneficially.
(3) A foundation has a Council (sometimes referred to as a Board) which administers the foundation and which is more akin to a board of directors than to trustees.
(4) A foundation has "beneficiaries", not shareholders, but it is not clear whether those beneficiaries have the equivalent of an equitable interest in the foundation's assets, even if to the extent only that the beneficiary of a discretionary settlement enjoys certain rights. It is equally unclear what rights the beneficiaries have against the Council.

The foundation as a settlement

Like trusts, foundations enable the creation of a segregated pot of assets which cease **34–54** to be comprised in the estate of the person who created the structure (settlor/founder); nor do those assets form part of the estate of the person (trustee/foundation council) who is called to administer the funds in accordance with the terms of the constitutional documents (trust deed, foundation charter) and the law. In both cases, most laws provide that the creator of the structure may retain a right of revocation as well as certain intervention rights (including the right to change the constitutional documents and the right to act as trustee/foundation councillor). Obviously there are also fundamental differences between trusts and foundations; these differences stem from the fact that a foundation has legal personality, whilst a trust usually does not.[47] This means that title to the assets subject to a trust vests in the trustees, whilst the assets/liabilities of a foundation are owned/entered into by the foundation itself (acting through its administrators) rather than by its administrators personally. This makes a foundation easier to run in the case of a change of guard, as any assets and liabilities remain with the foundation (so that a chain of indemnity is unnecessary).

---

[46] The specific characteristics of a foundation will depend upon the law of the jurisdiction in which it is established.

[47] There are exceptions—see, e.g., Massachusetts business trusts.

On the other hand, the fact that the foundation represents a new (legal) person means that once established it becomes separate from its founder, in the same way as a child become separate from his parents. This being the case, traditional civil law jurisdictions have taken a cautious approach with regards to the reservation of powers by the founder, notably in relation to the change of the foundation's purpose(s), as this is contrary to the idea of there being two separate (legal) persons. However, this has been perceived as a hindrance to the use of foundations and various traditional jurisdictions, including Austria and Switzerland, have somewhat relaxed their rules in this respect.

Another traditional difference between trusts and foundations relates to their duration. However, the increasing abolition of the perpetuity principle and the principle against the remoteness of vesting in the offshore trust world means that this difference is becoming less relevant in practice.

At least in relation to Liechtenstein foundations, some indication of HMRC's approach may be found in the Second Joint Declaration[48] relating to the Liechtenstein Disclosure Facility. The Declaration includes guidance on the characterisation, recognition and treatment of certain Liechtenstein entities (in order "to assist taxpayers and financial intermediaries in meeting their obligations for the purposes of the [Memorandum of Understanding]").[49] According to this guidance, Liechtenstein trusts ("*Treuhandschaften*") and foundations ("*Stiftungen*") are to be "characterised, recognised and treated as trusts for UK tax purposes" as is any establishment ("*Anstalt*") that is not permitted under its articles to undertake a business activity and which carries no founder's rights.[50] Although the guidance is qualified, it at least provides a helpful starting point.

The foundation as a company

34–55   If a foundation is treated as a company for IHT purposes it will itself have no exposure to IHT, but if the company is a "close company", i.e. broadly speaking a company controlled by a small number of individual "participators", the amount of any value transferred by the company, including distributions to beneficiaries of the foundation, will be apportioned among the participators according to their respective rights and interests in the company.[51] For this purpose the members of the Council may be participators, as may the founder and, depending upon the foundation's terms, the beneficiaries.[52] Whether or not such an apportionment would be made and whether

---

[48] Second Joint Declaration by the Government of the Principality of Liechtenstein and Her Majesty's Revenue and Customs concerning the Memorandum of Understanding Relating to Taxes, September/October 2010.

[49] The guidance was stated to be "based on Liechtenstein and UK laws as of 1 January 2010" and to be subject to review and revision. It was also stated not "to affect the ability of affected persons to rely on UK law or practice permitting alternative characterisation, recognition and treatment. The parties further recognise that the ultimate UK taxation consequences for UK taxpayers will depend on the particular facts relating to specific entities or fiduciary relationships".

[50] By contrast an *Anstalt* that is permitted to undertake a business activity or has founder's rights or shares is to be treated as a company. See below.

[51] See paras 2–73 and following.

[52] As "any person who possesses or is entitled to acquire a right to receive or participate in 'distributions of the company' or 'any person who is entitled to secure that income or assets (whether present or future) of the company will be applied directly or indirectly for his benefit'". See Corporation Tax Act 2010 s.454.

such an apportionment would have adverse IHT consequences would depend on the personal circumstances of the participators.

The foundation as a settlement and as a company: hybrids

As a worst case scenario, it is possible that a foundation could be treated as a **34–56** settlement for some purposes (so that assets held directly by the foundation which are situated in the United Kingdom will not be excluded property, for instance) and as a corporate entity for others, and exposed to IHT in both respects.

The foundation as neither a settlement nor a company: escape artists and nominees

This possibility arises in two ways. First, it may be the case that a foundation simply **34–57** does not fit into the scheme of IHT as a settlement or as a company, but this is an argument HMRC are unlikely to accept. Most cases involve the parties to a dispute arguing for an alternative that best suits them in the circumstances. Secondly, the founder's rights may be so extensive or the administration of the foundation such, that, quite apart from the legal position, the foundation is, on the facts, acting as the founder's nominee.

Establishments

A Liechtenstein establishment (*Anstalt*) is a separate legal entity and may be set up **34–58** for business purposes, family functions, abstract purpose functions or a mixture of these. An establishment more nearly resembles a company than a trust (and is characterised by HMRC as "opaque")[53] although it can take different forms and, in those instances where the founder of the establishment gives control to a board of directors and where the beneficiaries include persons other than the founder himself, would appear to be very similar to a trust and may fall within the s.43(2) definition of settlement mentioned at para.34–48 above.

These different ways of characterising an *Anstalt* are demonstrated in the guidance included the Second Joint Declaration[54] relating to the Liechtenstein Disclosure Facility; an *Anstalt* that is not permitted under its articles to undertake a business activity and which carries no founder's rights is to be regarded as a trust for UK tax purposes but an *Anstalt* that is permitted to undertake a business activity or includes founder's rights or shares is to be treated as a company.[55]

The establishment operates on the basis that a "supreme authority" holds the **34–59** "founder's rights" (which may include, for instance, determining the beneficiaries, appointing and removing the Board of Directors, amending the establishment's articles and bye-laws and terminating the establishment). The beneficiaries are the persons who

[53] See the list of classifications of foreign entities in the HMRC International Manual at INTM1800000.
[54] Second Joint Declaration by the Government of the Principality of Liechtenstein and Her Majesty's Revenue and Customs concerning the Memorandum of Understanding Relating to Taxes, September/October 2010. See para.34–54 above.
[55] As is a trust enterprise ("*Treuunternehmen*").

derive economic benefit from the establishment. The bye-laws are generally used to nominate beneficiaries and the nature and extent of the beneficial interests. The Board of Directors is primarily responsible for the conduct of the establishment's affairs, the members of the board being elected by the supreme authority.

34–60   Although an establishment can have issued shares this is a relatively uncommon arrangement. In most establishments the capital is undivided so there are no members, participants or shareholders. The fact that the establishment has no shares would not of itself prevent it being characterised as a company, of course (cf. English companies limited by guarantee).

34–61   The founder's rights, which do not expire with the founder's death, may be assigned, transferred or inherited—but not pledged or encumbered (because they are not regarded as property rights). However, if the founder's rights are regarded as a contractual arrangement between the supreme authority and the establishment itself, it is arguable that those rights of themselves constitute a separate asset (i.e. a chose in action) in the estate of the beneficial holder of those rights. If the rights effectively give the holder the ability to call for the establishment's assets, such a chose in action could of itself form a valuable item of property in the holder's estate, irrespective of the IHT treatment of the establishment. The contrary argument would be that the rights are more in the nature of a general power of appointment and therefore not an asset of the holder—but, in that case, the establishment itself would have to be regarded as a settlement.

34–62   It is not uncommon for the founder's rights to be held by a third party as nominee for the founder. Where the founder's rights are owned by one or more persons the exercise of the rights generally requires the unanimous approval of all holders.

34–63   In practice, although the establishment is a very flexible entity, that flexibility can give rise to problems as the characterisation of an establishment causes difficulties in civil, as well as common, law jurisdictions.

34–64   As with foundations, the retention by the establishment's founder of extensive powers over the establishment may, in practice, lead to the establishment being treated as a nominee.

Usufructs

34–65   As was noted at para.34–38, a *usufruct* can be defined as a *right in rem* which entitles the *usufructuary* to enjoy the subject-matter of the usufruct and to receive any natural or legal fruits which it may produce. The precise nature of the *usufruct* varies from jurisdiction to jurisdiction. Depending upon the jurisdiction in question, a *usufruct* may be for IHT purposes the functional equivalent of an indefeasible life interest in a settlement, or arguably, more akin to an annuity arrangement.[56] The characterisation could make a significant difference for IHT purposes since an individual with a qualifying life interest (or any lesser qualifying interest in possession in settled property) is treated as owning the property in which his interest subsists.[57]

---

[56] For a more detailed discussion on the nature of usufructs and their IHT treatment, including consideration of characterising a usufruct as a lease for life, see Beth Norton and Emilie Totic, "Usufructs: Part 2: Inheritance tax" in *Private Client Business* (2011).
[57] IHTA 1984 s.49(1).

In practice, despite the difference among the rules of the various jurisdictions and arguments concerning the value of the *usufructuary*'s interest, Revenue practice is to treat a *usufruct* (and its equivalent, such as the German *Niessbrauchsrecht*) as the equivalent to a life interest in a settlement.[58]

Following the changes made to the IHT treatment of settlements in 2006, great care needs to be taken where a UK domiciliary is considering creating a usufruct as this will now be a chargeable transfer and will trigger an immediate charge to IHT to the extent the value transferred exceeds the available nil rate band. The usufruct will also be subject to continuing IHT charges under the relevant property regime and may also give rise to reservation of benefit issues.

US limited liability companies ("LLCs")

LLCs are most commonly encountered as entities established in the United States, **34–66** although LLCs exist in other jurisdictions also—the Cayman Islands and the Isle of Man, for example. The prevalence of US LLCs (and their popularity amongst non-US individuals to shelter assets from US estate tax) has partly arisen from the introduction by the United States Internal Revenue Service (in the face of numerous requests for rulings on tax status) of regulations allowing eligible entities to elect (the "check the box" election) to determine whether the entity is to be treated as (a) a company, or (b) a partnership (and therefore tax transparent); accordingly, although a US LLC is created as a company and resembles a company in its structure, its tax treatment in the United States (assuming the relevant election is made) will be that of a partnership. Such an election will not affect the UK treatment of an LLC but it may result in the same entity being treated very differently for United States and UK tax purposes.

LLCs come in a variety of forms. In some cases they might for certain purposes be **34–67** characterised as resembling more closely a type of unincorporated association than a corporate body, but even then they are distinguished by their ability to hold property as a separate legal entity.

For UK tax purposes an entity will, very broadly speaking, be classified as a **34–68** company if it meets the following criteria:

(1) it has a separate legal personality, distinct from its members or management; and

(2) its profits accrue to the entity itself, rather than to its members,

but as a partnership if it is legally a partnership, and taxed accordingly. For IHT purposes an LLC is likely to be treated as a company[59] and, normally, as a close company.

IV. CO-ORDINATING FOREIGN SUCCESSION TAXES AND IHT

Where there is exposure to estate taxation in more than one country a great deal of **34–69** care may be required to co-ordinate planning to limit the impact of succession taxes in

---

[58] The treatment of *usufructs* may also be seen as resembling that of proper liferents in Scotland where the interest of the liferenter is to the right to the liferent (and which was, prior to 1975, treated as having no value on the death of the proper liferenter); property subject to a liferent is now deemed for IHT purposes to be held on trust for the liferenter—see IHTA 1984 ss.43 and 47.

[59] See the list of classifications of foreign entities in the HMRC International Manual at INTM1800000. See also the income tax case of *Revenue and Customs Commissioners v Anson* [2012] UKUT 59 (TCC).

the countries concerned, so as to minimise the overall exposure to tax; it may therefore be insufficient simply to minimise IHT. In some instances, for instance, it may be advantageous in the longer term to accelerate a charge to tax in one jurisdiction so that it coincides with a taxable event in relation to the same property in another jurisdiction; the possibility of offsetting the tax in one jurisdiction against that payable in another may otherwise be lost.

34–70   In seeking to co-ordinate IHT and foreign succession taxes it is important to have an understanding of how those foreign taxes are charged. A comprehensive guide is clearly beyond the scope of this chapter but some of the relevant considerations are set out below.

Charge to tax in foreign jurisdiction

34–71   Will a particular transfer of property give rise to a foreign tax charge in circumstances where there is no charge (or at least no immediate charge) to IHT? For instance, a transfer which qualifies as a PET in the United Kingdom may give rise to an immediate tax charge in another jurisdiction. Exemptions which apply in certain circumstances (e.g. to gifts to spouses, civil partners and charities) may be affected by the foreign element. Similarly, the generous exemptions available in respect of business and agricultural property for IHT purposes may prevent any charge to IHT but may have no equivalent in a relevant foreign jurisdiction.

One increasingly relevant area is the question of whether a foreign jurisdiction has any equivalent to the United Kingdom Civil Partnership Act 2004 and, if it does, how far a similar exemption to that in s.18 may apply in the foreign jurisdiction.

Liability to taxation

34–72   The UK taxes on the basis of domicile but this is no guide to potential tax liability in other jurisdictions where liability to tax may depend on residence (e.g. Ireland) or nationality or citizenship (e.g. the United States).

34–73   Certain jurisdictions (e.g. Japan which effectively characterises an inheritance as a form of income) also exercise primary taxing rights against the recipients of gifts/inheritances rather than by reference to the donor (or his representatives). The Netherlands also seeks to tax the recipient, although the tax is by reference to the donor's status. In considering gifts during lifetime and on death it is therefore important to appreciate the personal fiscal circumstances of the recipients as well as those of the testator or donor.

Settled property

34–74   Each of the major common law jurisdictions—the United Kingdom, the United States, Canada, Australia and New Zealand—recognises trusts and has a sophisticated regime regulating the taxation of trusts. However, these regimes can diverge from each other in any number of ways. Consider the different treatment in the United Kingdom and the United States of a will trust conferring a pre-March 22, 2006 defeasible life interest or a post-March 21, 2006 defeasible IPDI; the United Kingdom would treat the trust property as comprised in the estate of the life tenant for IHT purposes while the United States would not regard the trust property as includible in the life tenant's estate for estate tax purposes. On the other hand, the United States may regard the trust property as includible in the estate of a person acting as trustee if that person is a beneficiary or a person with an "obligation of support" in relation to a beneficiary.

Looking at the civil law world, trusts are currently recognised as such by Italy, Liechtenstein, Luxembourg, the Netherlands, San Marino, Switzerland and Monaco, all of whom have ratified the Hague Convention on the Law Applicable to Trusts and on their Recognition concluded on July 1, 1985. In addition, Belgium has introduced private international law rules largely modelled on the Hague Trust Convention. The position in other countries is less straightforward.

France has not ratified the Hague Trust Convention (although there are over 20 judgments in the French courts (including appellate decisions) spanning a period from the 1880s to the present day).[60] Well-advised clients usually avoid using trusts to directly hold French assets, particularly following the changes to the French tax treatment of "foreign" trusts, their settlors and beneficiaries introduced in 2011.[61] Those changes imposed French gift and succession taxes on French situs assets held in trust and on assets (whatever their situs) held in trust where the settlor or beneficiaries are resident in France.[62] As part of the new tax regime France for the first time introduced a definition of a "trust" into the *Code général des impôts*[63]; a trust is now defined in the Code as all the legal relationships created under the law of a State other than France by a settlor, during lifetime or on death, that places property or legal obligations under the control of an administrator for the benefit of one or more beneficiaries or for the purpose of achieving a specific objective:

> *"Pour l'application du présent code, on entend par trust l'ensemble des relations juridiques créées dans le droit d'un Etat autre que la France par une personne qui a la qualité de constituant, par acte entre vifs ou à cause de mort, en vue d'y placer des biens ou droits, sous le contrôle d'un administrateur, dans l'intérêt d'un ou de plusieurs bénéficiaires ou pour la réalisation d'un objectif déterminé".*

The approach taken under the new provisions nevertheless demonstrates a very different approach to trusts to that taken by traditional trust jurisdictions.

Within the last few years, the Spanish Supreme Court has refused to give effect to a US will trust, although whether this can be seen to reflect a general approach by the Spanish Courts is difficult to gauge from the judgment: Having accepted that US law applied to the estate by virtue of the deceased's nationality, and having referred briefly to the difference between legal and equitable ownership as well as to the principles of the Hague Trust Convention, the Supreme Court moved on swiftly to strike out the claim on the basis that the appellant allegedly failed to provide sufficient evidence as to the content of that law. Reading the judgment it is not possible to see whether the Supreme Court's conclusions were based on a real deficiency of the claim or rather on reasons of convenience (see *Tribunal Supremo*, judgment n.338/2008 dated April 30, 2008).

Interestingly, of the civil law countries that formally recognise trusts, only Italy, Switzerland and San Marino have issued guidelines or enacted statutory provisions to

---

[60] See Béraudo & Tirard, *Les Trusts Anglo-Saxons et Les Pays de Droit Civil*, Academy & Finance, 2006.

[61] Law n° 2011–900 of July 29, 2011, *de finances rectificative pour 2011* (LFR 2011) passed by the French Parliament on July 6, 2011. The Law came into force with effect from July 31, 2011.

[62] The changes introduced are not limited to gift and succession taxes.

[63] See art.792–0 *bis*.-I.-1.

deal with their tax treatment of trusts. Both Switzerland and San Marino are offshore jurisdictions anxious that trusts administered by local professionals be subject to little or no taxation. In the absence of express statutory provisions, it was unclear in Switzerland whether trusts should be treated as flow-thorough entities or akin to companies for tax purposes. In order to reassure the local trust industry, on August 22, 2007 the Swiss tax authorities issued (non-binding) guidelines confirming that trusts administered out of Switzerland should be treated akin to companies. On the other hand, the Swiss authorities were concerned that Swiss residents might use trusts to avoid Swiss tax. Accordingly, the Swiss tax guidelines effectively provide that (with one exception) any income and/or gains realised by the trustees of a trust that was established by a Swiss settlor should be attributed to the settlor.

By contrast, Italy is an onshore jurisdiction that has fully embraced the trust concept. Case law has confirmed the general validity of so-called "internal trusts", i.e. trusts all the elements of which (with the exception of the proper law) are connected to Italy. In order to clarify the tax consequences of the establishment of trusts by Italians, the Italian Finance Act 2007 introduced express statutory rules to deal with this issue. In addition, in August 2007 and January 2008, the Italian tax authorities issued (non-binding) guidelines to clarify various interpretative issues. A detailed discussion of the Italian tax guidelines is outside the scope of this commentary. Suffice to say that trusts are treated akin to companies. Interesting issues and planning opportunities remain in connection with the establishment of trusts and the receipt of trust distributions.

Furthermore, civil law jurisdictions which do not recognise trusts may not include in a person's estate property held in trust which would be included in that person's estate for IHT purposes. For example, although an individual entitled to a qualifying interest in possession in settled property may be treated as owning that property for IHT purposes,[64] the taxing authorities in a civil law regime may or may not adopt a similar stance depending on, e.g. whether that individual is the settlor of the settlement, other rights which that individual may have in relation to the settlement and the nature and frequency of payments made to him. Certain jurisdictions will regard the trust property as being in the beneficial ownership of the trustees and seek to apply succession laws and to tax the property accordingly (and see para.34–78 below).

Jointly owned properties

34–75   Different jurisdictions can adopt quite different fiscal stances in relation to jointly owned property. For example, for US gift and estate tax purposes the respective contributions of the owners to the purchase price of a jointly-held asset may determine the extent to which that asset is treated as comprised in the estate of one co-owner rather than another, irrespective of whether the asset is in their joint legal ownership.

Powers of appointment and revocation

34–76   The different approach of jurisdictions to what is includible in an individual's estate may lead to unexpected taxation consequences for heirs. This can be illustrated by *Kempe v IRC*; in that case the UK deceased was entitled under the terms of a policy of life assurance funded by his US employer to appoint anyone he wished to receive the

---

[64] See paras 12–02 and following.

sum assured when he died, failing which it passed to his estate. The deceased had completed a standard form of nomination in favour of his sisters who assumed that the proceeds fell outside the deceased's estate and would not be subject to IHT. The proceeds would not have been subject to US estate tax. However, the Special Commissioner held that the deceased's powers over the policy amounted to a general power and the policy was accordingly taxable to IHT.

The retention of rights may also result, of course, in assets believed to be held outside an individual's estate being brought back within it. The retention by a settlor of a power to revoke a trust (provided it is not exercised) will not, of itself, undermine the integrity of a trust structure[65]; care should, however, be taken that the retention of such powers will not be seen as tantamount to ownership (as they were in the receivership case of *Tasarruf Mevduati Sigorta Fonu v Merrill Lynch Bank and Trust Co (Cayman) Ltd*[66]) or as themselves constituting property rights includible in the settlor's estate on death, as may be the case, for example under art.1112 of the Russian Civil Code.

Valuation

Two kinds of valuation issues can cause problems. First, different tax regimes have different rules for valuing property. For IHT purposes, for example, the value of certain property not owned by a person may be taken into account in valuing assets comprised in his estate while reliefs may operate to allow the value of property comprised in his estate on death to be revalued after his death to take account of posthumous changes in that value.[67] It may well be that these rules are not mirrored in a relevant foreign tax regime. Conversely, special foreign tax rules may have no IHT counterpart. Secondly, different rules may exist for valuing the tax effect of a gift. IHT is charged, inter alia, on the fall in value of a person's estate occasioned by the dispositions he makes during his lifetime. It follows that what matters is the amount by which the value of the donor's estate is diminished by a lifetime gift, not the value of that which he gives away nor, if it is different, the value to the donee of that which he receives. This is not necessarily the case with foreign equivalent taxes. Where those taxes value transfers on other principles, standard estate-planning techniques are likely to include gifts of partial or minority interests in assets. Where IHT is relevant, the UK's loss to donor principle may well mean that a substantial liability to IHT may be triggered.

34–77

Legal formalities and probate procedures

When dealing with assets in foreign jurisdictions, care should always be taken to ensure that local legal formalities are complied with and that the individuals concerned understand the practical effects of the steps taken. This is a particular concern where dealings with real property are concerned. In Italy, for example, the capacity of a person holding land as a trustee can be acknowledged as part of the formal land

34–78

---

[65] The integrity of the trust structure may, of course, be brought into question if the settlor retains other powers, or if a power to revoke is combined with wide-ranging restrictions on the trustees' powers. See, for example, *The AQ Revocable Trust* (2010) 13 I.T.E.L.R. 260.

[66] *Tasarruf Mevduati Sigorta Fonu v Merrill Lynch Bank and Trust Co (Cayman) Ltd* [2011] UKPC 17.

[67] See the rules governing qualifying interests in possession (para.12–02), related property (paras 25–65 and following) and revaluation reliefs (paras 25–109 and following.).

registration process; if it is not it will be assumed that the registered owner holds the land in his personal capacity. A failure to ensure the registration process is dealt with appropriately can lead to both to difficulties in passing title (on the death of the trustee, for example) and to an increase in the Italian tax and duties payable.

Be aware, also, of the difficulty that English wills and probate/administration procedures can cause in foreign jurisdictions which do not recognise the role of personal representatives in transferring the property to beneficiaries. The personal representatives may be regarded as beneficially entitled to the property and death taxes imposed accordingly. This may greatly increase the liability to foreign taxes where tax rates are determined by the proximity of the relationship between the deceased and those who take the property on his death if the personal representatives are unrelated third parties.

Corporate nominees

34–79   In some jurisdictions the use of a corporate nominee may avoid succession laws and estate taxes, if the local law treats the nominee as the absolute owner of the assets and consequently does not have regard to any change in the underlying beneficial ownership caused by, e.g. death. But one should not be too hasty to adopt such a tactic because any transfer by the nominee company to a new beneficial owner may itself give rise to a charge to tax and, if the rates of tax depend upon the proximity of the relationship between the transferor and transferee, the highest rates will again apply.

Nominees of UK situs *assets*

34–80   It is not uncommon to come across the position where a non-UK domiciled individual seeks to rely on the fact that UK property (e.g. shares) is held through a nominee arrangement as a basis for protection from IHT. Of course, it is no such thing. Holding assets through a nominee may (depending upon the terms of the nomineeship), avoid the need to apply for probate but it will not take the assets so held out of the scope of IHT nor avoid the obligation to submit an account of the assets for IHT purposes because the nomineeship will not affect the beneficial ownership of the asset.

V. CO-ORDINATING PLANNING

34–81   Having reviewed some of the main factors relevant to international estate planning this part of the chapter highlights, by way of example, some instances where those factors are of practical relevance with regard to particular jurisdictions.

Overlapping jurisdictions

34–82   Whereas IHT, although imposed on a worldwide basis, offers some relief by taxing non-UK domiciliaries only on their UK assets, other jurisdictions adopt a different approach. A number of jurisdictions impose estate and gift taxes by reference to residence (for instance, France and Ireland) while most jurisdictions that impose estate or gift tax will retain a right to tax land and, often, business enterprises, situated or carried on within the jurisdiction.

The US taxes on a worldwide basis both US nationals and individuals domiciled in **34–83** the United States for federal tax purposes (which generally includes permanent residents or "green card" holders) wherever they may be resident; it therefore continues to tax its own nationals even after they have ceased to have any connection with the United States, other than their nationality. Moreover, as discussed at para.33–149 the United Kingdom/United States double tax treaty includes a "savings" provision which enables the United States to tax its citizens without regard to the treaty saving provisions.

Double tax treaties

The liability of the foreign individual or his estate to IHT may be relieved or **34–84** modified under any available double tax treaty between the United Kingdom and his country of residence/domicile. Double tax treaties are therefore relevant in co-ordinated planning, but usually only as part of a comprehensive solution. In particular, many treaties apply only in a situation where, but for the treaty, there would be double taxation by reference to the same event.

Treaties—unpleasant surprises

Unfortunately, finding a solution for IHT problems may produce a mismatch **34–85** between taxing systems such that, although taxation is imposed in both countries by reference to the same property, the charge to tax arises on different occasions and no treaty relief is available. Thus, double tax treaties can sometimes fail to provide relief which one might have assumed to be available.

Spouses

Special care needs to be taken to ensure that charges imposed on the transfer of **34–86** property from one spouse to another dovetail in such a way that treaty relief is available. The interaction of IHT and United States gift and estate taxes demonstrates the difficulties involved and what can be done to overcome them; see para.34–92.

Treaties—pleasant surprises

The specific terms of each double tax treaty are always worth examining—treaties **34–87** can contain some pleasant surprises.

Enlarged spouse exemption

The treaties with the Netherlands, Switzerland, Sweden and the United States **34–88** contain a provision designed, in effect, to "split the difference" between the unlimited spouse exemptions in those jurisdictions and the IHT limited s.18 exemption where the transferor spouse is domiciled in the United Kingdom for IHT purposes and the transferee spouse is not. These treaties provide that where the transferor spouse had a treaty domicile in the foreign jurisdiction, e.g. the Netherlands, then if the transfer would have been wholly exempt had the transferee's spouse been domiciled in the United Kingdom not less than half of the value transferred is exempt from IHT. This can produce very substantial savings. Assume A, a UK domiciliary with a treaty domicile in the Netherlands, leaves his estate, worth £800,000, to his spouse. Without the treaty only £55,000[68] qualifies for the spouse exemption. With the treaty, on the other hand, £400,000 qualifies for the spouse exemption.

Overcoming the deemed domicile rules

34–89   Another pleasant surprise is that a double tax treaty may override the deemed domicile rules. This can happen in two ways.

First, a treaty may override those rules. Assume that A is a non-British national,[69] a Swiss national, who came here otherwise than for employment, has lived in the United Kingdom for many years and has become deemed domiciled in the United Kingdom because of his long residence here. He returns to Switzerland where he has always been domiciled as a matter of general UK law. For IHT purposes he will remain liable to IHT on his worldwide estate for a further three tax years.[70] Under the Swiss treaty, however, so long as he has a treaty domicile in Switzerland he will not be liable to IHT on his death in relation to any property situated outside the United Kingdom.

34–90   Secondly, a treaty may disapply the deemed domicile rules. This occurs under some of the estate duty treaties which still apply for IHT purposes.[71] Assume X, a wealthy Indian who has for twenty years lived in London, but who remains domiciled in India under both Indian and UK law, dies leaving valuable property situated outside the United Kingdom, both in India and elsewhere. Although he is deemed domiciled in the United Kingdom, he will not be liable to IHT on his non-UK assets[72] and this is so notwithstanding the fact that India abolished estate duty in 1985; see para.33–53.

Spouse exemptions

34–91   It is common for a tax regime to protect its tax base by imposing a charge where assets subject to the regime cease to be so subject. For IHT purposes, for instance, foreign property owned by a foreign domiciliary is effectively outside the scope of IHT. If the exemption for transfers between spouses was not limited, it would be a simple matter for a wife domiciled in the United Kingdom with a husband not so domiciled to avoid IHT by, e.g. leaving all her property (wherever situated) to her husband, who could then invest in foreign property which would, in his hands, be outside the scope of IHT. As explained above, the IHT legislation accordingly limits the s.18 exemption

---

[68] See fn.2 above for the changes announced in 2012 to the limited spouse exemption for non-UK domiciled spouses/civil partners.

[69] It is important to note that this type of tax planning may not work for British citizens, because of the secondary taxing right maintained by the United Kingdom; see para.33–127.

[70] That is, in order to fall outside the 17 year rule; see para.32–16 and following.

[71] See Ch.33 for details of the treaties that may override the deemed domiciled rules.

[72] Provided those assets do not pass under a will written under "British" law.

for transfers between a spouse domiciled in the United Kingdom to a spouse not so domiciled to £55,000.[73] Other foreign tax systems may impose similar restrictions: e.g. in the United States a spouse who is a United States national can leave property to a spouse who is not such a national only if certain stringent conditions designed to ensure that there is a charge on the death of the transferee "foreign" spouse (or earlier infringement of the conditions) are observed. Overcoming such restrictions so as to produce the best result in the jurisdictions concerned can be particularly interesting; see paras 34–96 and following. These territorial restrictions can give rise to the kind of problems which are perhaps at their most acute in the context of Anglo-American marriages.

Asymmetrical exemptions

34–92 Both IHT and the US gift tax and estate tax confer exemption from taxation on certain transfers between spouses but territorial restrictions mean that the exemptions are asymmetrical.

The IHT exemption

34–93 The IHT s.18 exemption is available where inter alia the transferor leaves property to their spouse either outright or under a settlement under which he or she is entitled to a qualifying interest in possession, e.g. an IPDI, unless the transferor is domiciled in the United Kingdom but the transferee spouse is not. The fact that the interest is defeasible because, e.g. the trustees can exercise a wide overriding power of appointment to appoint new trusts does not prevent the exemption from being available. No tax is charged on such a transfer but when the surviving spouse dies IHT will be charged (assuming the spouse has not remarried and left the property to his or her surviving spouse).

The US exemption

34–94 There is a US equivalent to the IHT spouse exemption. Called "the marital deduction" it also provides for total exemption for outright transfers to a spouse and for certain types of transfer into trust for the benefit of the spouse, but its availability is severely restricted where the transferee spouse is not a US national or "green card" holder.

The mismatched exemption

34–95 Problems can arise where insufficient care is taken to match up these exemptions. In the absence of planning to the contrary the above rules can produce two charges to tax even though it is intended under each system of taxation that there should be only one

---

[73] See fn.2 above for the changes announced in 2012 to the limited spouse exemption for non-UK domiciled spouses/civil partners.

charge. Assume a husband and wife, both of whom are domiciled in the United Kingdom for IHT purposes; the husband is a US national but his wife is not, nor does she hold a "green card". He predeceases his wife, leaving his entire estate to her. On his death there will be a charge to US estate tax, but no charge to IHT. On her death there will be a charge to IHT, but no charge to United States estate tax. No credit will be given under the double tax treaty between the countries because the charges will not have occurred on the same occasion.

QDOT to the rescue

34–96   It is possible to overcome this problem. The US restrictions will not apply if the gift to the spouse is in the form of a "qualifying domestic trust" (QDOT), in which case the marital deduction is available in full, with tax being deferred until the death of the spouse. The charge to tax in each jurisdiction will then occur by reference to the same event—the death of the surviving spouses—with the result that a tax credit will be available under the treaty. Two charges will have been effectively replaced by one.

Jointly owned property

34–97   Different jurisdictions can adopt quite different fiscal stances in relation to jointly owned property.[74] Assume a married couple, who are at all times domiciled outside the United Kingdom. The wife, who is a US national, out of her own funds purchases property in London in the joint names of herself and her husband, who is not a US national. For US gift and estate tax purposes she will be regarded as the sole owner of the property and thus as not having made a gift to her husband at the time of the purchase. For IHT purposes she will have given her husband half the house, but the IHT s.18 exemption will be available. If she predeceases him the property will pass to him by survivorship, at which time she will be regarded for IHT purposes as having given him the remaining half of the property and the IHT s.18 exemption will again be available. For US estate tax purposes, on the other hand, she will be regarded as having given him the whole of the property and it will be too late to use a QDOT. Moreover, splitting a joint tenancy during the lives of the joint tenants could trigger an immediate charge to United States gift tax if the value of the non US spouse's resulting tenant in common interest in the property (or its proceeds of sale) exceeds his contributions.[75]

Charities

34–98   Gifts to foreign charities raise two issues. First, is the gift itself charitable? Secondly, if it is, does it qualify for favoured tax treatment?

The answer to the first question depends on whether there is a mismatch between the UK law and the relevant foreign law concerning what is charitable. The answer to the

---

[74] See also IHTM15050 as to jointly-held property in Scotland.
[75] Complex tracing rules would apply to determining each spouse's contribution.

second question will depend upon where the foreign charity is established[76]; for gifts to charities that are established outside the United Kingdom, the European Union and certain specified territories[77] no favoured treatment will be available because the basic UK position is that only gifts to charities established in those jurisdictions qualify for favoured tax treatment.

Gifts to many foreign charities will therefore not enable the donor to deduct the gift from his taxable income or gains and will also be chargeable for IHT purposes.

34–99

One solution is for the taxpayer to make a gift to an umbrella UK charity, such as the Charities Aid Foundation, which then makes disbursements to foreign charities in a way that gives effect to the donor's intentions. Alternatively in some jurisdictions it may be possible to reach some sort of arrangement with a local charity with similar objects or which is willing to act as a conduit for a legacy to another overseas charity that would not normally attract relief.

The United States—the donor's dilemma

The charity laws in the United Kingdom and the United States have a common legal background, both being based upon the Charitable Uses Act 1601. This has the result that most objects recognised as charitable in the United Kingdom will also be regarded as charitable in the United States. But the United States jealously guards the favoured tax treatment given to gifts to charities with the result that gifts to a UK charity will not, in the absence of special arrangements, normally qualify for favoured US tax treatment. The only exception to this is where a an individual who is solely a US taxpayer leaves a legacy to a UK charity, in which case, provided the appropriate steps are taken, there will be no charge to US estate tax in respect of that legacy. Individuals minded to make gifts to charities and exposed to taxation in both jurisdictions face a dilemma. Assume X is a US national domiciled in the United Kingdom. If he makes a gift to a UK charity he qualifies for favoured UK tax treatment, but will obtain no US relief and may face a charge to US gift tax. If, on the other hand, he makes a gift to a US charity, he qualifies for favoured US treatment, but will obtain no UK tax relief and may face a charge to IHT.

34–100

The best of both worlds

Fortunately, there is a way out of this impasse, namely, that a US charitable corporation establishes a UK charitable company and elects for that company to be a disregarded entity for US tax purposes. The gift is regarded for US purposes as having been made directly to the US corporation and qualifies for favoured US treatment

34–101

---

[76] The United Kingdom used to restrict favoured tax treatment to gifts to charities established in the United Kingdom. However, this position changed following the decisions of the European Court of Justice in *Centro di Musicologia Walter Stauffer v Finanzant München für Körperschaften* (C-386/04) and *Hein Persche v Finanzant Lüdenscheid* (C-318/07) which determined that the practice of restricting charity tax reliefs to domestic organisations was discriminatory and breached the EU law principles of the free movement of capital and freedom of establishment.

[77] Iceland and Norway are specified territories for this purpose. IHTM11112 notes that a list of EU and other specified countries will be available on the HMRC Charities website in due course.

accordingly. The company is not disregarded for UK tax purposes, so the gift also qualifies for favoured UK treatment accordingly.[78]

Deeds of variation

34–102   An important IHT planning tool is the ability to rewrite a deceased's will[79] by varying, by an instrument in writing (commonly called "a deed of variation"), the dispositions of the will and to elect[80] that those dispositions shall for IHT purposes be treated as having been made by the deceased. Great care is needed where the estate in question is affected by foreign succession and tax considerations. Equally, the practitioner must be aware of the personal circumstances affecting all those involved.

34–103   Foreign tax systems generally do not contain equivalents to IHT deeds of variation and confusion sometimes arises as to the effect of such a deed under foreign law and foreign tax. Where the deceased is subject to forced heirship, advisers may fear that the deed must not infringe the forced heirship rules that applied in relation to the deceased. That fear is misplaced because it is only for IHT purposes that the deed is read back into the deceased's will; as a matter of general law the deed is a fresh disposition by the persons entering into it. This does not mean, however, that forced heirship is irrelevant. If a person making the fresh disposition is himself subject to forced heirship in respect of the assets inherited from the deceased, the forced heirship rules to which he is subject will have to be taken into account in relation to that fresh disposition. So far as foreign tax is concerned, the position is the same, the deed is a fresh disposition by the persons entering into it. As such, it will have no bearing on the tax position of the deceased but it may have tax consequences for those entering into it.

Assume H, a UK domiciliary, dies leaving the bulk of his estate to his second wife, W (also a UK domiciliary) but giving a substantial legacy to his son, S, by his first marriage to D, who is a Swiss national and also a US citizen. The advisers to the executors suggest that the IHT liability can be sheltered by S re-routing his legacy via a deed of variation. Under that deed the legacy is held on trusts under which his stepmother, W, has a qualifying interest in possession in respect of which the trustees have overriding powers of appointment which they may in due course exercise for S's benefit. An election can be made that the variation be treated for IHT purposes as having been effected by H, so that the IHT s.18 exemption is retrospectively accessed. S obtains advice that the relevant Swiss forced heirship rules do not prevent him from entering into the deed and that he would incur no charge to Swiss tax on doing so, and he proceeds with the plan but without taking US advice. The plan saves IHT but at a price—US federal gift tax on S's transfer to the trust for his stepmother.

Foreigners investing in the United Kingdom

34–104   Foreign domiciliaries investing[81] in the United Kingdom understandably have as their priority making what they regard as a good investment. Although they will

---

[78] A gift to the dual-qualified charity operated by the Charities Aid Foundation is one way in which gifts can benefit from this favourable US/UK tax treatment: details can be obtained from the Foundation itself.

[79] Or to vary the devolution of property under an intestacy or by virtue of co-ownership; see generally, paras 8–114 and following.

[80] An election can be made only in respect of a variation entered into within two years of the deceased's death.

[81] The investment by a foreign domiciliary in UK accommodation, e.g. a house in London in which he intends to reside when he is in the United Kingdom, gives rise to particular tax planning problems; see paras 7–198 and following.

normally be sensitive to the SDLT, income tax, CGT and, where appropriate, corporation tax implications of the investment, it is not uncommon for the IHT consequences of such an investment to be overlooked, often because those advising are commercially orientated and not mindful of estate planning issues.

From an estate planning standpoint, if the foreign domiciliary acquires the investment directly he will have effectively converted foreign assets which, by reason of his domicile, are not within the scope of IHT, into a UK asset which is within the scope of IHT. It may be, of course, that this is not a matter of concern because, e.g. the investment qualifies for 100 per cent business relief or 100 per cent agricultural relief,[82] or because a double tax treaty prevents the investment from having an overall adverse tax effect on his estate.

A double tax treaty is cold comfort

The fact that a double tax treaty applies is not, of course, the end of the matter. **34–105** Regard must be had to the nature of the protection afforded by the treaty. Most treaties operate by providing that both the jurisdiction in which the asset is situated and the jurisdiction in which the investor has his primary personal connection can impose tax, but that the jurisdiction with which he has his primary personal connection must allow a credit for the tax imposed in the other jurisdiction. The net result is that the investment suffers tax at the higher of the effective rates in the two jurisdictions.

Indirect investment

The normal course is therefore to invest indirectly via an offshore vehicle, an **34–106** offshore company, so that the relevant asset for IHT purposes is the holding of shares in the company, which is outside the scope of IHT. Careful consideration will have to be given to all the tax[83] and succession implications of using the vehicle in question. Although offshore companies have been the traditional vehicle of choice, in recent years partnerships have been used in a variety of situations.

UK domiciliaries holding non-UK assets

At the most basic level, the first decision for the UK domiciliary wishing to invest **34–107** abroad is the manner in which the investment is to be made and how it is to be retained subsequently, i.e. in the individual's own name, jointly with another (possibly the individual's spouse) or by means of some other structure.

The choice of ownership will depend on the nature of the asset itself (usually its **34–108** classification as movable or immovable property) and the individual's long term intentions with regard to it, e.g. an asset purchased for short to mid-term investment purposes may require different treatment from an asset purchased for the long term enjoyment of the family. Where the property is to be purchased jointly by spouses,

---

[82] See para.7–198.

[83] Significant changes to the SDLT and CGT treatment of high value UK residential properties held by companies and other "non-natural persons" were announced in the Budget of March 2012.

consideration will also need to be given to local community property regimes as these may, in certain cases, provide a greater degree of protection to the surviving spouse and avoid a charge to tax on the first death.

Investment products

34–109   The benefit of indirect ownership can be seen at its simplest in UK investment products such as unit trusts or unit-linked life policies which invest in overseas assets. These can provide a valuable means whereby the UK domiciliary can gain exposure to overseas markets without being subjected to the burden and expense of local administrative provisions, tax laws and possible succession rules.

Real property

34–110   It is now relatively common for individuals domiciled in the United Kingdom to own land abroad, often in the form of a holiday home. Planning traditionally involved owning the property through an offshore company, for three reasons. First, to avoid local transfer tax on a sale of the property, any sale being of the shares in the company rather than of the land. Secondly, to avoid local estate taxes. Thirdly, to avoid the succession issues involved in relation to property situated in a foreign jurisdiction, although sometimes the perceived problem with local succession laws may not be a problem in practice—in Spain, although joint tenancies and trusts will not be recognized, the *Lowenthal*[84] case has established that the law of the owner's domicile will be applied rather than local Spanish law. In France, while the normal method of joint outright purchase as a matter of French law is "*en division*" (the equivalent of a tenancy in common) it may also be possible for purchasing married couples to "opt in" to the French community property regime in so far as concerns French real property, provided the agreement to do so is reached before the purchase. The advantage is that the interest of the first spouse to die will pass free of tax to the survivor and, in addition, the deferral of any "forced" heirship rights of the couple's common children. Whilst the tax advantage has disappeared as a result of the introduction of spouse exemption in 2007 (so that transfers to spouses are generally treated alike in the United Kingdom and France, unless the limited IHT spouse exemption for non-domiciled spouses applies), the election of full community of property remains a valid planning tool to defer the "forced" heirship rights of the couple's children. This option is not, however, possible for unmarried joint purchasers although here it would be possible to purchase "*en tontine*" (the equivalent of a joint tenancy, although without the ability unilaterally to sever the tenancy); if property is held *en tontine* by two persons one half of the value of the property held *en tontine* will be included for French estate duty purposes in the estate of the first to die and the co-owner will be liable for that tax.

34–111   The provisions of any applicable tax treaty will need to be reviewed, as they may well assist in overriding domestic tax provisions in these circumstances. This is arguably the effect of the rules in the UK's treaty with France, e.g. where land in

---

[84] Spanish Supreme Court (Civil Division) judgment no.887/1996. See also *Denney v Denney (Royde-Smith)*, judgment no.436/1999.

France is held by a foreign company. Interposing a corporate structure in this way will not, of course, take the asset, even in its re-characterised form, out of the IHT net.

The holding of land through a corporate entity raises, of course, questions as to other taxes (particularly the possibility of increased capital gains) and, in relation to the UK's own anti-avoidance legislation, the possibility of such ownership arrangements resulting in charges to income tax under the shadow directorship provisions or pre-owned asset rules. Fortunately, s.100A of the IT(EP)A 2003 has clarified that the shadow director tax liability does not apply to foreign property held through corporate structures provided certain requirements are met. Where s.100A cannot be relied upon the shadow director tax liability[85] may be eliminated if corporate ownership of the property is in the form of a nomineeship such that HMRC accept that the property is being held by the company only as a nominee for the beneficial owner. In these circumstances the property would be considered as a personal asset rather than the asset of the company from which a taxable benefit is being derived. Regard also needs to be had, of course, to the foreign tax implications of using a nominee; see para.34–79. **34–112**

Some jurisdictions have introduced legislation designed to discourage the avoidance of local transfer taxes by effectively imposing tax fines on land owning offshore companies incorporated in tax havens.[86] In addition, both France and Spain levy an annual 3 per cent on the market value of properties held through certain offshore entities. **34–113**

VI. IHT AND EU LAW

The United Kingdom and the other EU Member States must ensure that their laws are applied in accordance with EU rules and that those laws do not discriminate on the grounds of nationality, or apply unjustified restrictions on the exercise of those freedoms guaranteed by the EU such as freedom of movement of persons and capital within the EU.[87] In the 2002 case of *Barbier* (relating to Netherlands inheritance tax) the ECJ made it clear that those principles of freedom of movement applied to inheritance taxes. Further cases have addressed concerns of discriminatory treatment by Member States relating to, for example, availability of reliefs/exemptions to non-residents,[88] the application of favourable valuation principles to assets with a situs within the taxing state[89] and the different treatment for inheritance tax purposes of deductibility of liabilities for residents and non-residents.[90] **34–114**

Recognising that the imposition of inheritance taxes within the EU was a matter of concern to an increasing number of EU persons, on December 15, 2011 the European Commission issued a Communication on "Tackling cross-border inheritance tax obstacles within the EU",[91] which sought to summarise the potential difficulties. The definition of "inheritance taxes" adopted in the Communication is a wide one, designed

[85] See IT(EP)A 2003 ss.103 and following.
[86] One example is Portugal which in 2003 introduced a greatly increased municipal tax where the company is in a "blacklisted" jurisdiction (the blacklist extending to most tax havens); as a result many companies holding Portuguese property re-domiciled to (non-blacklisted) Malta.
[87] *Barbier's Heirs v Inspecteur van de Belastingdienst Particulieren/Ondernemingen Buitenland te Heerlen* (C-364/01) [2003] E.C.R. I-15013.
[88] *Geurts v Administratie van de BTW, Registratie en Domeinen* (C-464/05) [2007] E.C.R. I-9325.
[89] *Jager v Finanzamt Kusel-Landstuhl* (C-256/06) [2008] E.C.R. I-123.
[90] *Eckelkamp v Belgium* (C-11/07) [2008] E.C.R. I-6845.
[91] The Communication and associated documents can be accessed at: *http://ec.europa.eu/taxation_customs/taxation/personal_tax/inheritance/index_en.htm* [Accessed November 13, 2012].

to encompass all taxes levied on the death of an individual whether or not the tax is identified by the State imposing it as an "inheritance" tax as such. In the recommendations accompanying the Communication, the Commission acknowledged that harmonisation of inheritance tax rules amongst all Member States was unrealistic. Instead, the Commission sought to draw attention to ways in which States themselves could act to reduce the main difficulties identified in the Communication.[92]

The two major concerns identified by the Commission States in cross-border situations which hinder the free movement of capital within the EU are:

(1) a lack of full relief against double taxation as between EU Member States; and

(2) instances of discrimination contrary to the principles of the EU Treaty.

It is therefore appropriate to consider the problems identified in the Communication in the context of IHT.

Double taxation

34–115   In the Communication, the Commission noted that (as discussed earlier in this chapter) double taxation may occur because different jurisdictions tax on different bases, including domicile, residence, nationality and situs, while different rules may apply to, for instance, movable and immovable property. Moreover, within the EU, there are relatively few double tax treaties covering inheritance taxes—only 33 treaties in total; the United Kingdom has treaties covering inheritance tax with only five other EU Member States (France, Italy, Ireland, the Netherlands and Sweden[93]). However, concerns relating to the availability and application of reliefs against double taxation are likely to have a limited impact on the United Kingdom and IHT, at least in the immediate future. For one thing, double taxation is not in itself contrary to EU law.[94] For another, the current IHT rules for the granting of unilateral relief, where bilateral relief may not be available, while imperfect, already provides a mechanism for dealing with a number of the situations identified by the Commission as potentially problematical.

Discriminatory issues in the context of IHT

34–116   The United Kingdom has already made changes to IHT in response to EU requests and press releases identifying specific discriminatory elements in relation to IHT. As noted earlier in this chapter, the United Kingdom has extended IHT relief in respect of gifts to charities to EU charitable organisations. Similarly, the ambit of agricultural property relief was extended to property within the European Economic Area following a Press Release[95] issued by the European Commission stating that the relief was discriminatory because:

[92] In the consultation responses to the Communication, the United Kingdom, Spain, Belgium and Germany were the four EU Member States whose tax laws were raised most frequently.
[93] For further details on the treaties, see Ch.33.
[94] See *Block v Finanzamt Kaufbeuren* (C-67/08) [2009] E.C.R. I-883.
[95] "Direct taxation: The European Commission requests the United Kingdom to end discriminatory provisions in the area of inheritance tax", IP/09/170, January 29, 2009.

"The limited scope of the relief may dissuade taxpayers from investing in agricultural and forestry property outside the UK. Consequently, the Commission considers that the United Kingdom's legislation, in its current state, is not compatible with the free movement of capital provided by Article 56 EC Treaty and Article 40 of the EEA Agreement."

More recently, in October 2012, the Commission published a "reasoned opinion" (the second step of the EU infringement procedure) that the restriction of the IHT spouse exemption on transfers to non-UK domiciled spouses/civil partners is of a discriminatory nature.[96] However, as already noted, the UK Government has already announced proposals to at least extend the current limited spouse exemption available to non-UK domiciled spouses and to allow for such spouses to "elect" into a UK domicile. Details of the proposed legislation are not available at the time of writing, but it will be interesting to see how far those proposals are seen to address the Commission's expressed concerns.

There may, of course, be other areas where IHT may be regarded as operating in a manner that infringes EU law. However, where the discriminatory issue is the availability of a relief or exemption, this is not to say that the UK Government's response may necessarily be to extend the existing relief/exemption to the whole of the EU. Issues of affordability mean that a relief/exemption might instead be withdrawn, or subjected to tighter conditions.[97]

VII. ENFORCEABILITY OF IHT

The position in relation to the cross-border enforceability of IHT and similar foreign **34–117** taxes has altered significantly over recent years.

In January 2008 the Convention on Mutual Administrative Assistance in Tax Matters of 1988 was ratified by the United Kingdom[98] and came into force on May 1, 2008; the Convention displaces the historic position whereby there was no concept in the UK of the enforceability of foreign revenue laws. The application of that historic concept (most famously illustrated in *Government of India v Taylor*[99] had already been undermined by developments in cross-border co-operation on money laundering issues and, within the EU, the introduction of measures designed to increase the enforceability of revenue debts. The Convention is significant in extending mutual enforceability to estate, inheritance and gift taxes.

In addition, the *Recovery of Taxes—The MARD Regulations 2011*[100] which implements in the United Kingdom the EU *Mutual Assistance in Recovery Directive* (2010/24/EU) came into force on January 1, 2012. The Regulations deal with the exchange of information, enforcement of claims, requests for notification and recovery, disputes, limitation, and disclosure between revenue authorities in EU Member States.

---

[96] Ref: IN/2010/2111.

[97] See, for example, the position in relation to tax on Furnished Holiday Lettings where the United Kingdom's initial reaction to the EU's findings of discrimination was to announce that the relief would be withdrawn; after consultation, the relief was retained and now extends to the EU but subject to more stringent conditions than previously applied.

[98] The Convention has also been ratified by Azerbaijan, Belgium, Denmark, Finland, France, Georgia, Iceland, Italy, the Netherlands, Norway, Poland, Slovenia, Spain, Sweden, Ukraine and the United States.

[99] *Government of India v Taylor* [1955] A.C. 49.

[100] SI 2011/2931.

Finally, the terms of the Agreement[101] on tax co-operation signed between the United Kingdom and Switzerland in October 2011 demonstrate a further development in IHT enforcement in providing for an IHT withholding arrangement. As well as providing for enhanced exchange of tax information between the United Kingdom and Switzerland, the Agreement (which is likely to come into force with effect from January 1, 2013) also provides for inheritance tax (at 40 per cent) to be levied on assets held by Swiss banks or other Swiss paying agents in which UK residents are beneficially interested.[102] The levy will not apply if the deceased's personal representatives authorise the Swiss bank to disclose the account details to HMRC or if it is certified that the deceased was neither domiciled nor deemed domiciled in the United Kingdom.

---

[101] Agreement between the Swiss Confederation and the United Kingdom of Great Britain and Northern Ireland on co-operation in the area of taxation, October 6, 2011 (as amended by the protocol dated March 20 and the mutual agreement of April 18, 2012). See also s.218 Finance Act 2012.

[102] Reference should be made to the terms of the Agreement itself for details.

INDEX

LEGAL TAXONOMY
FROM SWEET & MAXWELL

This index has been prepared using Sweet & Maxwell's Legal Taxonomy. Main index entries conform to keywords provided by the Legal Taxonomy except where references to specific documents or non-standard terms (denoted by quotation marks) have been included. These keywords provide a means of identifying similar concepts in other Sweet & Maxwell publications and online services to which keywords from the Legal Taxonomy have been applied. Readers may find some minor differences between terms used in the text and those which appear in the index. Suggestions to *sweet&maxwell.taxonomy@thomson.com*.

(All references are to paragraph number)

1302

1307